P9-DHP-787

THE NEW AMERICAN
ROGET'S
COLLEGE
THESAURUS
IN DICTIONARY FORM

GROSSET & DUNLAP

PUBLISHERS   NEW YORK

© 1958 BY ALBERT H. MOREHEAD

Prepared and edited by

The National Lexicographic Board

ALBERT H. MOREHEAD, *Chairman and General Editor*
LOY C. MOREHEAD, *President;* LOYD F. GEHRES, DONALD D. WOLF,
WALDEMAR VON ZEDTWITZ, *Vice-Presidents;* GEOFFREY MOTT-SMITH,
WILLIAM C. CAMPBELL, SALVATORE RAMONDINO

Staff for *The New American Roget's College Thesaurus*

JACK LUZZATTO *and* LOY MOREHEAD, *Editors*
WILLIAM C. CAMPBELL, WILLIAM T. ATWOOD, BETTY BRINKERHOFF,
ELIZABETH MACLEAN, *Associate Editors.*

ISBN: 0-448-01622-2 Indexed
ISBN: 0-448-01605-2 Trade

BY ARRANGEMENT WITH THE NEW AMERICAN LIBRARY

1981 PRINTING

PRINTED IN THE UNITED STATES OF AMERICA

CONTENTS

HOW TO USE THIS THESAURUS

PETER MARK ROGET WAS AN ENGLISH PHYSICIAN who was born in 1779 and died in 1869. As a hobby he liked to make lists of words and group them together when they were related to one another. Some were related because they were synonyms, such as *illegal* and *unlawful;* some because they were antonyms, such as *peaceful* and *warlike;* some because they were reminders of one another, such as *father* and *mother.* Altogether Mr. Roget made a thousand different groups, or *categories,* of related words. Every word he knew or could find in the dictionaries that he had was classified in one or more of these categories.

In 1852 Mr. Roget's list of words was published. He called the book a *thesaurus,* or treasury, of words. There were not many words in the first ROGET'S THESAURUS, compared to the number in a volume like this, but his book was the first collection of synonyms, antonyms, and other related words. Not only writers but many others found it invaluable. Dozens of editors, beginning with Mr. Roget's son, have revised the original Thesaurus, added to it, and brought it up to date (for many of the words in the original Roget list are now obsolete and many common words of today were unknown in his time); but every edition is still called ROGET'S THESAURUS in honor of the man who first had the idea.

This edition of ROGET'S THESAURUS is both a dictionary of synonyms and antonyms and a thesaurus or "treasury" of related words. To use it, simply look up the word for which you wish to have a synonym, an antonym, or a word related in some other way.

When a word is printed in SMALL CAPITALS, it means that if you look up that word, in its proper alphabetical order, you will find additional synonyms or other related words applying to the word you were looking up. Often you will also find other words of related meaning but different parts of speech; for example, when you are looking up a noun you will be referred to related verbs, adjectives, etc.

A word or phrase in parentheses shows how the preceding word is to be used in a sentence. A word or phrase in brackets is explanatory in some cases, and in other cases indicates that the bracketed word or phrase may or may not be used with the adjoining word, depending on the preference of the writer.

This is not a dictionary. It does not define words, except to the extent that they are defined in their synonyms. A word that has no natural synonyms is not entered merely to define it. The publishers of this Thesaurus also publish a companion volume, THE GROSSET WEBSTER DICTIONARY, in which may be found definitions of the words in this book.

Antonyms formed by simply adding *un-, in-, dis-,* etc., are not given, nor are words listed when they are simple negatives of other words. For ex-

1

ample, such a word as *unloved* is not entered, since one may merely look up the positive term, but *unbearable* is entered because the positive term has various dissimilar meanings.

Synonyms are often labeled *colloq.* (colloquial, informal, conversational); *slang, dial.* (dialectal), etc. This is a warning that either the entry word or the synonym in this sense is substandard. The reader may consult the dictionary for further information.

Familiar dictionary abbreviations are used for parts of speech: *n.*, noun; *v.*, verb; *v.i.*, intransitive verb; *v.t.*, transitive verb; *adj.*, adjective; *adv.*, adverb; *pron.*, pronoun; *prep.*, preposition; *conj.*, conjunction; *interj.*, interjection.

FOREIGN PHRASES. This Thesaurus includes foreign words and phrases related to English words and phrases; but foreign words and phrases that are not wholly anglicized are not listed in regular alphabetical order. They are collected on the final pages of this book, with definitions and with reference to the entries or categories in which their synonyms and related English phrases may be found.

THE NEW AMERICAN
ROGET'S COLLEGE THESAURUS

A

abaft, *adv.* aft, astern, behind. See REAR, NAVIGATION. *Ant.,* FRONT.

abandon, *v.t.* relinquish, resign, give up, forgo, surrender, discontinue, waive, abdicate; leave, quit, evacuate, withdraw (from); desert, forsake, maroon, discard, drop. *Colloq.,* let go, throw up, pull out of, have done with, turn one's back on, wash one's hands of. *Slang,* pull out on; rat on. *Ant.,* see PURSUIT.

abandon, *n.* RASHNESS, recklessness, imprudence, impetuosity, impulsiveness, audacity. *Ant.,* CARE.

abandoned, *adj.* dissipated, immoral, shameless, corrupt, unprincipled, depraved; lost, incorrigible, reprobate, unbridled. See IMPURITY. *Ant.,* see VIRTUE. (See also ABANDON, *v.*)

abash, *v.t.* humiliate, humble, shame; embarrass, disconcert, discountenance, awe. *Colloq.,* mortify, crush, take down a peg, put one's nose out of joint. See MODESTY. *Ant.,* see VANITY.

abate, *v.* DECREASE, lessen, moderate, diminish, subside; allay, slake, slacken, subdue; curtail, remit. *Colloq.,* let down (on), take off the edge (of). *Ant.,* INCREASE.

abbey, *n.* convent, monastery, nunnery, priory, cloister(s). See TEMPLE.

abbreviate, *v.* abridge, condense, contract, shorten, curtail, digest, clip, truncate, prune. See SHORTNESS, CONTRACTION. *Ant.,* see LENGTH.

abdicate, *v.* relinquish, resign, renounce, abandon, quit, surrender.

abdomen, *n.* belly, paunch, epigastrium, venter; midriff (*inexact*). *Colloq.,* corporation (*jocular*), solar plexus, guts (*now vulgar*). See INTERIOR.

abdominal, *adj.* celiac, coeliac, ventral, visceral.

abduct, *v.t.* kidnap, carry off, steal, transport, spirit away. *Colloq.,* shanghai. *Slang,* snatch. See STEALING.

aberration, *n.* DEVIATION, variation, distortion, disorientation; aberrance, INSANITY; ERROR. *Colloq.,* brainstorm. *Ant.,* TRUTH, SANITY.

abet, *v.t.* AID, assist, support; encourage, incite, instigate. *Ant.,* see HINDRANCE.

abeyance, *n.* suspension, suppression. See CESSATION.

abhor, *v.t.* HATE, dislike, detest, loathe, despise; abominate, execrate. *Colloq.,* can't stand. *Slang,* get a pain [in the neck] from. *Ant.,* LOVE.

abide, *v.* dwell, reside, live, stay; accept, endure, submit (to). See ABODE.

ability, *n.* POWER, SKILL, competency, capacity, efficiency, capability, aptitude, faculty, talent. *Colloq.,* knowhow. *Slang,* what it takes. *Ant.,* UNSKILLFULNESS, IMPOTENCE.

abject, *adj.* servile, degraded, contemptible; miserable, wretched; base. *Colloq.,* hangdog. See SERVILITY. *Ant.,* see INSOLENCE.

abjure, *v.* forswear, recant, renounce. See RELINQUISHMENT.

able, *adj.* capable, competent, skillful, efficient. See POWER, SKILL. *Ant.,* see IMPOTENCE, UNSKILLFULNESS.

abnormal, *adj.* aberrant, eccentric, irregular, anomalous; INSANE; monstrous. See UNCONFORMITY. *Ant.,* see SANITY, CONFORMITY.

ABODE [189]

Nouns—**1,** abode, dwelling, residence, domicile, address, habitation, berth, seat, lodging *or* lodgings, lodging place, quarters, headquarters, housing, place. *Colloq.,* diggings. *Slang,* dump, joint.

2, home, homeplace, homestead, hearth, hearthstone, fireside, inglenook, ingleside, household, ménage, housing, roof; ancestral halls, fatherland, native land, native soil, country.

3, retreat, asylum, cloister, hermitage, hideaway, hiding-place, sanctuary, *sanctum sanctorum*, cave, nest, den, cell, hive, hole, lair, haunt. *Slang,* hangout, hideout, stamping ground.

4, camp, barrack *or* barracks, bivouac, encampment, quarters, tent, casemate, motel, tourist camp, trailer camp.

5, house, dwelling, building, place, hall; casa, mansion, palace, villa, lodge, hermitage, castle, cottage, chalet, bungalow, manor-house; brownstone [house], flat, apartment [house], two-(etc.) family house, farmhouse, ranch house, split-level, town house, penthouse, tenement, hotel, ark, temple, skyscraper, trailer. *Slang,* diggings, digs.

6, hut, adobe, booth, bunkhouse, hogan, cabin, cottage, dugout, hutch, hovel, igloo, tupek, lean-to, log cabin, Quonset hut, rancho, shack, shanty, tepee, wickiup, wigwam, kiosk. *Slang,* dump, flophouse, [hobo] jungle.

7, inn, caravansary, club, hospice, hostel, hostelry, hotel, motel, rooming house, tavern; public house, barroom, alehouse, saloon; coffee house, canteen, café, restaurant. *Slang,* dive, dump, flophouse, gin mill, pub, honkytonk.

8, barn, cow barn, cowshed, doghouse, kennel, pound, henhouse, hutch, warren, pen, pigsty, shed, stable, stall, storehouse, booth, coop, dovecote, aviary, birdcage, birdhouse, perch, roost.

9, auditorium, armory, assembly hall, assembly room, study hall, audience hall, concert hall, theater, gymnasium; meeting house, chapel, church, TEMPLE. *Slang,* gym.

10, estate, hacienda, ranch, farm.

11, village, hamlet, town, pueblo, township, municipality, metropolis, city, capital, county seat, suburb, county, parish, state, province, country; ghetto, quarter; provinces, hinterlands. *Colloq.,* burg, one-horse town, Main Street. *Slang,* jerkwater [town], hick town, jumping-off place.

12, street, place, terrace, road, avenue, boulevard, row, alley, court, quadrangle, close, yard, passage, mews; square, mall, piazza, arcade, gardens, marketplace, block, commons.

13, anchorage, dock, basin, wharf, quay, port, harbor.

14, sanatorium, sanitarium, hospital, asylum, health resort, rest home, spa, watering place.

Verbs—see LOCATION, PRESENCE.

Adjectives—urban, suburban, rural, rustic, provincial; metropolitan, cosmopolitan; domestic, foreign.

---

abolish, *v.t.* annul, cancel, nullify, abrogate; exterminate. *Colloq.,* wipe out. See DESTRUCTION. *Ant.,* see PRODUCTION.

abominate, *v.t.* See ABHOR, HATE. *Ant.,* LOVE.

abortion, *n.* miscarriage, premature delivery [birth]; illegal operation; failure, fiasco; monstrosity, freak. See FAILURE.

abound, *v.i.* teem, swarm, be plentiful. See SUFFICIENCY. *Ant.,* see ABSENCE.

about, *adv. & prep.* —*adv.* around, round, on all sides; approximately; nearly, almost. See RELATION, NEARNESS. *Ant.,* see DIFFERENCE, DISTANCE. —*prep.* concerning, regarding, anent, respecting.

above, *adv. & prep.* —*adv.* aloft, overhead, up; earlier, before. See HEIGHT. *Ant.,* see LOWNESS. —*prep.* over, beyond; surpassing; more than, exceeding.

abrade, *v.t.* rub, wear (away), grind, grate. See FRICTION. *Ant., see* SMOOTHNESS.

abridge, *v.* abbreviate, shorten, condense, reduce, compress, contract, summarize, epitomize. See SHORTNESS. *Ant.,* see LENGTH.

abroad, *adv.* overseas, away, outside; roaming, wandering, at large. See ABSENCE. *Ant.,* see PRESENCE.

abrupt, *adj.* sudden, hasty, precipitate, short, curt; steep, precipitous, sheer, sudden *or* sharp [turn, etc.]. *Colloq.,* jerky. See SHARPNESS, INSTANTANEITY. *Ant.,* see BLUNT.

abscond, *v.i.* decamp, bolt, run away, flee, fly, depart. *Colloq.,* take off, take French leave. *Slang,* breeze, blow, scram, take a powder. See AVOIDANCE. *Ant.,* see PURSUIT.

ABSENCE [187]

Nouns—**1,** absence, withdrawal; nonexistence; nonresidence, noninhabitance, nonpresence, nonattendance, absenteeism, truancy; DISAPPEARANCE, DISPERSION. *Colloq.,* hooky, cut, French leave.

2, emptiness, void, vacuum, vacuity, vacancy; depletion, exhaustion; exemption; blank, clean slate.

3, absentee, truant.

4, nobody, nobody present, nobody on earth, not a soul, nary a soul, nobody under the sun, nary one, no one, no man, never a one.

Verbs—be absent, absent oneself, go away, stay away, keep away, keep out of the way, play truant, play hooky, take French leave, absent oneself without leave, slip away, slip off, slip out, keep aloof, hold aloof, withdraw, vacate. *Colloq.*, not show up, make oneself scarce, take French leave, cut. *Slang*, go A.W.O.L., jump, skip.

Adjectives—**1,** absent, non-attendant, not present, away, non-resident, missing, missing in action, lost, wanting, omitted, nowhere to be found, out of sight, gone, lacking, away from home, truant, absent without [official] leave, A.W.O.L., abroad, oversea, on vacation. *Colloq.*, minus.

2, empty, vacant, void, vacuous, untenanted, unoccupied, uninhabited, tenantless, deserted, abandoned, devoid, forsaken, bare, hollow, blank, clear, dry, free from, drained. *Colloq.*, Godforsaken.

Adverbs—nowhere; elsewhere; neither here nor there; somewhere else, not here. *Dial.*, nowheres.

Prepositions—without, wanting, lacking, less, minus, *sans*.

Antonym, see PRESENCE.

---

absolute, *adj.* complete, perfect, thorough, entire, total, essential, sheer, positive; unrestricted, unbounded, full, plenary; despotic, autocratic, supreme. See COMPLETION, GREATNESS. *Ant.*, see INSUFFICIENCY, LITTLENESS.

absolution, *n.* cleansing, exoneration, FORGIVENESS, shrift, dispensation, discharge. *Ant.*, RETALIATION.

absolve, *v.t.* forgive, cleanse, shrive, discharge, pardon. See FORGIVENESS. *Ant.*, see RETALIATION.

absorb, *v.* assimilate, take in, suck up; incorporate, integrate; engross, preoccupy, obsess. See THOUGHT.

abstain, *v.i.* forbear, refrain, desist, withhold. See AVOIDANCE, MODERATION. *Ant.*, see PURSUIT.

abstemious, *adj.* abstaining, abstinent, temperate, sober. See MODERATION. *Ant.*, see DRUNKENNESS.

abstract, *adj.* theoretical, metaphysical; abstruse, recondite. See IMAGINATION. *Ant.*, concrete.

abstract, *v. & n.* —*v.* withdraw, excerpt (from), remove. See STEALING. —*n.* compendium, summary, epitome, précis, abridgment.

abstruse, *adj.* profound, recondite, esoteric, subtle, deep, obscure, enigmatical. See KNOWLEDGE, SECRET.

ABSURDITY [497]

Nouns—**1,** absurdity, absurdness, imbecility, nonsense; paradox, inconsistency; inanity, fatuity, stupidity, asininity; ludicrousness, ridiculousness, ridiculosity, comicality.

2, blunder, muddle, bull, Irish bull; sophism, bathos; anticlimax, letdown; travesty, parody, caricature, lampoonery; foolery, buffoonery, mummery. *Colloq.*, monkey trick, monkey shine, moonshine.

3, jargon, doubletalk, twaddle, gibberish, fustian, empty talk. *Colloq.*, poppycock, stuff, stuff and nonsense. *Slang*, bull.

4, FOLLY; nonsense; RASHNESS; irrationality; paradox (see CONCEALMENT).

Verbs—**1,** play the fool, talk nonsense, talk through one's hat, be absurd, go from sublime to the ridiculous.

2, make a fool of, make absurd, burlesque, caricature, lampoon, ridicule.

Adjectives—**1,** absurd, nonsensical, preposterous, senseless, inconsistent, incongruous, ridiculous, extravagant, quibbling, foolish, fantastic, silly, unmeaning, without rhyme or reason, farcical, ludicrous, asinine, inane, stupid. *Slang*, screwy.

2, unintelligible, confused, MEANINGLESS, senseless.

Antonym, see MEANING.

abundance, *n.* plenty, copiousness, SUFFICIENCY, profusion, luxuriance, fullness; affluence, opulence, wealth. *Ant.,* see INSUFFICIENCY.

abuse, *v. & n.* —*v.t.* mistreat, injure, damage; malign, scold, berate, vilify, curse; flay. —*n.* injury, desecration; insult. See DISAPPROBATION. *Ant.,* see APPROBATION.

abut, *v.* join, touch, border (on). See NEARNESS.

abyss, *n.* abysm, deep, DEPTH(s), gulf, chasm, pit, bottomless pit, chaos.

academic, *adj.* scholastic, collegiate; educational; scholarly, erudite; theoretical. See TEACHING.

academy, *n.* SCHOOL, college, preparatory school, finishing school; society, learned society. See TEACHING.

accede, *v.i.* agree, ASSENT, CONSENT, acquiesce, concede, concur, yield, comply. *Ant.,* see DISSENT.

accelerate, *v.* hasten, expedite, anticipate, speed (up), quicken. See EARLINESS, HASTE. *Ant.,* see LATENESS, SLOWNESS.

accent, *v. & n.* —*v.* accentuate, emphasize, stress; pronounce. —*n.* emphasis, stress, tone; diacritical mark; pronunciation. See LANGUAGE, SPEECH, SOUND.

accept, *v.* ASSENT; take; adopt, believe, honor, admit, approve. See RECEIVING. *Ant.,* see DISSENT, GIVING.

access, *n.* APPROACH, avenue, way; admittance, entrée. *Colloq.,* [an] in; a line (to). *Ant.,* see REGRESSION.

accession, *n.* acceding, consent, ASSENT; increase, ADDITION, ACQUISITION; attainment. *Ant.,* DISSENT, LOSS.

accessory, *adj. & n.* —*adj.* contributory, helping; AUXILIARY, incident (to). —*n.* accomplice, assistant, confederate. See ADDITION.

accident, *n.* mishap, injury, casualty; CHANCE, contingency, fortuity. See ADVERSITY. *Ant.,* design, INTENTION.

acclimate, acclimatize, *v.t.* accustom, inure, habituate. See HABIT.

acclivity, *n.* ASCENT, rise, incline, pitch, slope, grade. *Ant.,* see DESCENT.

accommodate, *v.* adapt, adjust, conform, fit, suit; oblige, help out; lend money (to); put up (give lodging to). See AID, AGREEMENT. *Ant.,* see HINDRANCE, DISAGREEMENT.

ACCOMPANIMENT [88]

Nouns—**1,** accompaniment, adjunct, attribute; concomitance, company, association, companionship, partnership, copartnership, fellowship, coefficiency.

2, concomitant, accessory, coefficient; companion, attendant, fellow, associate, consort, spouse, colleague, comrade; accompanist; partner, copartner; satellite, hanger-on, shadow; escort, bodyguard, chaperon, retainer, duenna, convoy; cavalier, squire. *Colloq.,* chum, flunky, pal. *Slang,* pard.

Verbs—accompany, attend, hang on, wait on, go hand in hand with, keep company, row in the same boat, associate with, consort with, take up with; escort, chaperon, convoy. *Colloq.,* tote, squire. *Slang,* drag.

Adjectives—accompanying, attendant, concomitant, fellow, associated with, coupled with, accessory.

Adverbs—with, together with, along with, in company with, hand-in-hand, arm-in-arm, side-by-side, cheek-to-cheek, together.

Antonym, see DISJUNCTION.

accomplice, *n.* accessory, abettor, confederate, crony; partner, colleague. *Slang,* sidekick. See AUXILIARY.

accomplish, *v.t.* do, complete, fulfill, perform, effect, execute, achieve, consummate. See COMPLETION. *Ant.,* see FAILURE.

accomplished, *adj.* proficient, versed; talented. See SKILL. *Ant.,* see UNSKILLFULNESS.

accord, *v. & n.* —*v.i.* harmonize, conform, agree, accede: see AGREEMENT, ASSENT. —*v.t.* grant, bestow: see GIVING. —*n.* AGREEMENT, harmony, correspondence, conformity.

accordingly, *adv.* hence, so, therefore, thus; correspondingly, consistently, agreeably. See CIRCUMSTANCE, AGREEMENT.

accost, *v.t.* greet, hail, address. See SPEECH. *Ant.,* ignore.

account, *v. & n.* —*v.i.* report, relate, narrate: see DESCRIPTION. —*v.t.* attribute: see CAUSE. —*n.* report, recital, narrative, DESCRIPTION, story, tale, history, chronicle, statement.

ACCOUNTING [811]

Nouns—**1,** accounting, accountancy, bookkeeping, audit, calculation, reckoning, [commercial, business] arithmetic.
2, accountant, bookkeeper, calculator, actuary, Certified Public Accountant, C.P.A., chartered accountant (*Brit.*), auditor, [bank] examiner, clerk.
3, accounts, statistics, finance, budget, money matters.
4, ledger, journal, day book, cash book, petty cash book, bank book, pass book, balance sheet, profit and loss statement, accounts payable ledger, accounts receivable ledger, sales ledger.
5, asset, liability, expenditure, bill, invoice, balance, account, credit, debit.
Verbs—**1,** keep accounts, enter, post, book, credit, debit, carry over, balance, balance accounts, balance the books; bill, invoice, compute, settle accounts; take stock, take inventory; audit, examine the books.
2, falsify accounts, doctor accounts.

accredit, *v.* authorize, license, certificate, sanction. See REPUTE. *Ant.*, DISREPUTE.
accretion, *n.* See INCREASE.
accrue, *v.* accumulate, grow, inure. See ACQUISITION. *Ant.*, see LOSS.
accumulate, *v.* amass, gather; aggregate, collect, hoard. See ACQUISITION. *Ant.*, see LOSS.
accurate, *adj.* correct, exact, precise, truthful. See TRUTH. *Ant.*, see DEVIATION, ERROR.

ACCUSATION [938]

Nouns—**1,** accusation, charge, indictment, incrimination, inculpation; condemnation, denunciation, censure, invective, jeremiad; implication, imputation, slur; complaint, blame, reproach, recrimination, reproof; retort, reply in kind. See DISAPPROBATION.
2, LAWSUIT, litigation; plaint, complaint, citation, allegation; indictment, arraignment, impeachment, true bill; libel, slander.
3, accuser, critic, ENEMY; plaintiff, complainant; prosecutor, district attorney, attorney general. *Colloq.,* D.A.
4, accused, defendant, respondent, co-respondent, libelee.
Verbs—**1,** accuse, charge, tax (with), incriminate; inculpate, blame, complain against *or* of, reproach, reprove; indict, arraign, impeach, implicate, cite, summon.
2, denounce, inform (against), challenge, take to task, call to account. *Colloq.,* tell on, tattle (on), pin (something) on. *Slang,* put the finger on, rat (on); frame, trump up a charge.
Adjectives—accusing, accusatory; incriminatory, recriminatory, reproachful; imputative.
        Antonyms, see APPROBATION, VINDICATION.

accustom, *v.* habituate, familiarize, inure, addict. See HABIT.
ache, *n. & v.* —*n.* PAIN. —*v.i.* hurt, smart, throb, PAIN. *Ant.*, see PLEASURE.
achieve, *v.t.* accomplish, attain, reach. See COMPLETION. *Ant.*, see FAILURE, NEGLECT.
acknowledge, *v.* admit, confess, own; ANSWER, receipt. See ASSENT, DISCLOSURE. *Ant.*, see DISSENT, CONCEALMENT.
acquaint, *v.t.* inform, notify, tell; familiarize, teach. See INFORMATION.
acquiesce, *v.i.* agree, accede, ASSENT, concur, CONSENT. *Ant.*, see DISSENT.

ACQUISITION [775]

Nouns—**1,** acquisition, acquirement, obtainment, procurement; collection, accumulation, amassing, gathering, reaping, gleaning, picking (up).
2, receipt, profit, proceeds, produce, benefit; earning, pay, wages, emolument, salary, income, remuneration, REWARD; inheritance, legacy, bequest, patrimony, birthright, heritage; see RECEIVING.

3, seizure, confiscation, commandeering, expropriation; conquest, annexation; patronage, unearned increment; snatching, STEALING, theft, robbery, fraud, graft, bribery; spoils, plunder, loot, BOOTY, pay-off. *Colloq.,* the take, gravy, split, pickings, velvet.

4, acquirer, obtainer, *etc.;* buyer, purchaser, vendee; inheritor, legatee; good bargainer *or* trader; winner, captor, thief. *Colloq.,* horse-trader.

5, acquisitiveness, desire to acquire; ambition, hunger, avidity (for possessions); covetousness, avarice; greed, voracity.

Verbs—**1,** acquire, get, gain, obtain, secure, derive; win, earn, realize, receive, take; collect, amass, reap, scrape together; inherit; PURCHASE. *Colloq.,* come in for, step into; get hold of. *Slang,* clean up, line one's pockets.

2, profit, benefit, gain; make money by, turn to advantage, gain an advantage.

3, accrue (to), benefit, be profitable (to), fall to.

Adjectives—**1,** acquisitive; avaricious, greedy, grasping, covetous. *Slang,* on the make.

2, profitable, remunerative, gainful, paying, advantageous, productive. See MONEY.

Antonym, see LOSS.

acquit, *v.* exculpate, exonerate, excuse, clear, absolve, discharge, release, whitewash, liberate, pardon; perform, behave, CONDUCT. See VINDICATION, FORGIVENESS. *Ant.,* see ACCUSATION.

acquittal, *n.* exculpation, VINDICATION, exoneration; discharge, release, deliverance; FORGIVENESS, clearance, absolution, pardon, reprieve. *Ant.,* see ACCUSATION.

acrid, *adj.* pungent, biting, acid; corrosive, caustic. See TASTE.

acrimony, *n.* bitterness, rancor, acerbity, asperity, RESENTMENT.

across, *adv. & prep.* —*adv.* crosswise, athwart. —*prep.* on, over, athwart.

act, *n. & v.* See ACTION, DRAMA, CONDUCT.

ACTION [680]

Nouns—**1,** action, performance, operation, execution, PRODUCTION: process, procedure, transaction; affair, effort, job, deed, business, work, handiwork; CONDUCT, COMPLETION, EXERTION.

2, proceeding, LAWSUIT; battle, WARFARE.

3, doer; see AGENCY.

Verbs—**1,** act, do, perform, function, officiate, serve; operate, work, practice, exercise, commit; progress, advance, accomplish, cover ground; labor, toil, drudge, ply.

2, see DRAMA, AGENCY.

Adjectives—active, operative, in operation, in action, at work, on duty; functional, effective, efficient; see ACTIVITY.

Adverbs—in the act, conspicuously, flagrantly, *in flagrante delicto,* red-handed.

Antonym, see INACTIVITY, NEGLECT.

ACTIVITY [682]

Nouns—**1,** activity, action, activeness, ENERGY, animation; briskness, quickness, alertness, sharpness; readiness, alacrity, zeal, eagerness, vivacity, vigor, spirit; EXERTION.

2, movement, bustle, stir, fuss, ado; restlessness, wakefulness, sleeplessness, insomnia.

3, industry, diligence, assiduity, assiduousness, vigilance, sedulity; perseverance, persistence, patience.

4, interference, intrigue, tampering, meddling, dabbling, supererogation.

5, zealot, fanatic, enthusiast, devotee. *Colloq.,* busybody; hustler, go-getter. *Slang,* live wire.

Verbs—**1,** act, do, accomplish, bestir oneself; be active, busy, etc.

2, haste, make haste, bustle, fuss, push. *Colloq.,* pitch in, look sharp, be sharp, make the dust fly; put one's best foot forward; spread oneself thin, bite off more than one can chew.

3, plod, drudge, persist; buckle down, stick to, take pains.
4, meddle, interfere, tamper, intrude, obtrude. *Colloq.*, butt in, horn in, put in one's oar, poke one's nose in, be nosy.
*Adjectives—***1,** active, brisk, alert, spry, sharp, smart, quick, enterprising; ENERGETIC, eager, sedulous; lively, alive, vivacious, wideawake, keen, eager; frisky, forward, spirited; strenuous, zealous. *Colloq.*, up and doing, quick on the trigger, on the jump, on the go, on the job, on one's toes. *Slang,* on the beam, snappy.
2, working, on duty, at work; industrious, diligent, sedulous, painstaking, businesslike. *Colloq.*, in harness.
*Adverbs—*actively, etc. See HASTE.

Antonyms, see INACTIVITY, REPOSE.

actual, *adj.* real, veritable, true, genuine; concrete, factual. See EXISTENCE. *Ant.*, see NONEXISTENCE.
actuate, *v.* move, induce, compel, persuade; start, get under way.
acumen, *n.* acuteness, discernment, shrewdness, penetration; INTELLIGENCE.
acute, *adj.* shrewd, discerning, quick, astute; sharp, poignant, keen, pointed, severe. *Colloq.*, smart. See INTELLIGENCE.
adage, *n.* proverb, saw, saying, aphorism, motto. See KNOWLEDGE.
adapt, *v.* suit, conform, regulate, fit; ADJUST, convert, reconcile, harmonize, make suitable. See AGREEMENT, CONFORMITY.
add, *v.* increase; reckon, sum up, total; join. See ADDITION.
addict, *n.* devotee, fan, enthusiast; habitual user, slave (to). See HABIT.

ADDITION [37]

*Nouns—***1,** addition, increase, expansion, introduction, annexation, accession; corollary, concomitant, ACCOMPANIMENT.
2, adjunct; affix, prefix, suffix; appendix, insertion, interpolation, postscript, subscript, addendum, supplement, appendage; extension, annex, wing; rider, codicil, tab.
*Verbs—***1,** add, affix, annex, superimpose, append, join, subjoin; tack on to, saddle with; amplify, enlarge.
2, enumerate, total, compute, figure, calculate, reckon.
*Adjectives—*added, etc.; additive, accessory, supplementary, additional.
*Adverbs—*in addition, more, plus, extra, besides, also. *Colloq.*, to boot, into the bargain, over and above, and so forth or on.

Antonym, see DECREASE.

address, *v.t. & n.* —*v.t.* direct; court, woo; accost, greet, approach, speak to. —*n.* street and number; residence, home; speech, discourse, oration; cleverness, dexterity. See DIRECTION, SPEECH.
adduce, *v.t.* present, bring forward, cite, mention. See EVIDENCE.
adept, *adj. & n.* —*adj.* skillful, dexterous, apt; practiced, expert, proficient. —*n.* expert, master, connoisseur. See EXPERT. *Ant.*, see UNSKILLFULNESS.
adequate, *adj.* enough, sufficient, serviceable, satisfactory, ample. See SUFFICIENCY.
adjacent, *adj.* near, close by, next to; touching, bordering, contiguous, neighboring. See NEARNESS.
adjoin, *v.* touch, abut, border, meet, neighbor. See NEARNESS.
adjourn, *v.* defer, postpone; discontinue; END.
adjunct, *n.* ADDITION, appendix, appendage, annex; augmentation, part, accessory, reinforcement, extension; complement, postscript, insertion.
adjure, *v.t.* charge, bind or command by oath, appeal to, entreat. See REQUEST.
adjust, *v.t.* fix, ADAPT, true, regulate, straighten; settle, compensate, harmonize; equalize, rate. See ARRANGEMENT.
administer, *v.t.* govern, rule, control; give, dose, treat with, dispense. See AUTHORITY, GIVING.
admire, *v.t.* love, esteem, idolize, venerate, RESPECT; regard; WONDER, marvel. *Ant.*, HATE.
admission, *n.* concession, confession; DISCLOSURE; entry, admittance, ingress; CONSENT.

admit, *v.t.*   let in; induct, matriculate; concede, acknowledge; receive, allow. See DISCLOSURE, RECEIVING.

admonition, *n.*   caution, WARNING.

adolescence, *n.*   YOUTH, minority, juvenility; teens, teen-age, nonage; puberty. *Ant.,* see AGE.

adopt, *v.t.*   embrace, take to oneself, borrow, assume; foster, give a home to, accept as one's own. See CHOICE. *Ant.,* see REJECT.

adore, *v.t.*   LOVE, worship, admire, idolize. *Ant.,* HATE.

adorn, *v.t.*   decorate, ORNAMENT, embellish, deck, garnish, beautify.

adulterate, *v.t.*   mix, water down, weaken, dilute; corrupt. See DETERIORATION.

adultery, *n.*   infidelity, fornication, licentiousness. See IMPURITY.

advance, *v. & n.*   —*v.* progress, go forward, proceed; further, abet, second. —*n.* progress, rise; success, gain; prepayment. See PROGRESSION.

advantage, *n.*   SUPERIORITY, upper hand, leverage, the better (of); gain, odds, profit, advancement, favor. See INCREASE. *Ant.,* disadvantage.

adventure, *n.*   enterprise, undertaking; happening, EVENT; risk, hazard, venture.

adventurer, *n.*   voyager, traveler, wanderer, roamer; gambler, fortune-hunter; free-lance, soldier of fortune. See TRAVEL, CHANCE.

ADVERSITY [735]

Nouns—**1,** adversity, affliction; bad, ill, adverse *or* hard luck *or* fortune; evil lot; frowns of fortune; evil star *or* genius; ups and downs of life; hard case *or* lines; peck of troubles, hell upon earth; slough of despond. See EVIL, FAILURE, PAIN.

2, trouble, hardship, curse, blight, blast, load, pressure, POVERTY, tough sledding.

3, evil day; time out of joint; hard times; rainy day; gathering clouds, ill wind; visitation, infliction, affliction; bitter pill; care, trial, ordeal.

4, mishap, mischance, misadventure, misfortune; disaster, calamity, catastrophe; accident, casualty, cross, reverse, check, *contretemps,* rub; losing game; fall, downfall, ruination, undoing; DESTRUCTION.

Verbs—be badly off; go hard *or* ill with; fall on evil days; go downhill; go to rack and ruin; go to the dogs; fall from high estate; decay, sink, decline, go down in the world; have seen better days; come to grief; be all over *or* up with; bring a hornet's nest about one's ears. *Slang,* draw a blank; lose one's shirt.

Adjectives—**1,** unfortunate, unblest, unhappy, unlucky; unprosperous; luckless, hapless; out of luck; in trouble, in a bad way; in an evil plight; under a cloud; clouded; ill *or* badly off; in adverse circumstances; poor, down in the world, down at heel, down and out, undone; on the road to ruin, on one's last legs, on the rocks; born under an evil star; ill-fated, ill-starred, ill-omened. *Slang,* on the ropes.

2, adverse, untoward; disastrous, calamitous, ruinous, dire. *Slang,* up the spout.

Adverbs—if the worst come to the worst; from bad to worse; out of the frying pan into the fire.

Antonym, see PROSPERITY.

advertisement, *n.*   announcement, public notice, notice, bill; commercial, ad, want ad; publicity. See PUBLICATION.

ADVICE [695]

Nouns—**1,** advice, counsel, suggestion, recommendation; advocacy, exhortation, PERSUASION, expostulation, DISSUASION, admonition, WARNING; guidance, DIRECTION, instruction; charge, injunction.

2, adviser, prompter, counselor; monitor, mentor, Nestor, teacher (see TEACHING).

3, guide, manual, chart, reference, consultation, conference, INFORMATION.

Verbs—**1,** advise, counsel, suggest, prompt, admonish, recommend, prescribe, advocate, exhort, persuade; enjoin, charge, instruct, dictate; expostulate, dissuade, warn.

2, advise with; consult together; compare notes; hold a council, deliberate, be closeted with, confer, consult.
Adjectives—**1,** advisory, consultative, consultant; recommendatory, hortative, persuasive, dissuasive, admonitory, WARNING.
2, advisable, expedient, desirable, commendable; fitting, proper, suitable, meet.

---

advocate, *v. & n.* —*v.* favor, plead; recommend, suggest. See SUPPORT.
—*n.* patron, supporter, scholar; lawyer. *Ant.,* OPPONENT.
aeronaut, aeronautics, see AVIATION.
affable, *adj.* friendly, sociable, gracious, approachable. See COURTESY.
affair, *n.* occasion, occurrence, EVENT, happening; business; party, festivity; amour, love affair, liaison. *Colloq.,* to-do, fuss, shindig, blowout.
affect, *v.t.* influence, touch; concern, relate to; move, stir. See RELATION.

AFFECTATION [855]

Nouns—**1,** affectation, affectedness, artificiality, insincerity, histrionics, OSTENTATION; charlatanism, quackery; pose, pretension, airs; pedantry, euphuism; preciosity, preciousness; mannerism, conceit, foppery, dandyism, coxcombry. See ORNAMENT. *Slang,* side.
2, stiffness, formality; prudery, demureness, coquetry.
3, fop, faker, sham, pedant, bluestocking, prig; charlatan, DECEIVER.
Verbs—affect, act, put on *or* give oneself airs, feign, sham, simper, mince, attitudinize, pose, strike an attitude.
Adjectives—affected, pretentious, artificial, insincere, pedantic, stilted, stagy, theatrical, sham, mock, histrionic; unnatural, self-conscious, stiff, starchy, formal, prim, smug, demure, prudish, priggish, conceited, foppish, dandified; finical, finicky; mincing, simpering, namby-pamby.
Antonym, see SIMPLENESS, MODESTY.

---

affection, *n.* LOVE, regard, esteem, liking. *Ant.,* indifference.
affiliate, *v. & n.* —*v.i.* join, unite. —*n.* subsidiary, partner. See COÖPERATION, COMPACT.

AFFIRMATION [535]

Nouns—**1,** affirmation, statement, allegation, assertion, predication, declaration, averment.
2, asseveration, adjuration, swearing, oath, affidavit, deposition; avouchment, avowal, assurance; protestation, profession, word; acknowledgment, ASSENT. See RECORD, CHOICE.
3, remark, observation, expression, position, proposition; saying, dictum, sentence. See CERTAINTY.
4, PROMISE, pledge, vow; AGREEMENT.
Verbs—**1,** assert, say, affirm, predicate, declare, state; protest, profess; have one's say, declare oneself, speak up, give voice *or* utterance (to).
2, put forth, put forward; advance, allege, propose, propound, enunciate, broach, set forth, hold out, maintain, contend, claim; announce, pronounce, pretend.
3, depose, depone, aver, avow, avouch, asseverate, swear, attest (to); take one's oath; make an affidavit; kiss the book, vow, swear till one is black in the face; cross one's heart; be sworn, call Heaven to witness; vouch, warrant, certify, assure; swear by bell, book and candle.
4, insist, take one's stand upon; emphasize, lay stress on; lay down the law; raise one's voice; dogmatize; have the last word; rap out; repeat. See BELIEF.
5, PROMISE, commit oneself, assure, warrant, covenant.
Adjectives—declaratory, predicatory, pronunciative, affirmative; positive, CERTAIN; express, explicit, PATENT; absolute, emphatic, flat, broad, round, pointed, marked, distinct, decided, confident, trenchant, dogmatic, definitive, formal, solemn, categorical, peremptory; unretracted; predicable.
Adverbs—affirmatively, in the affirmative, *etc.;* with emphasis, *ex cathedra,* without fear of contradiction.
Antonym, see NEGATION.

afflict, *v.t.* beset, trouble, grieve, hurt, burden (with). See PAIN.
afford, *v.t.* manage, bear (expense); supply, yield, produce; make available, furnish. See GIVING.
afraid, *adj.* scared, frightened, alarmed, panicky, terror-stricken, fearful, apprehensive, cowardly, timorous, mousy. See FEAR. *Ant.,* see COURAGE.
after, *prep., adj. & adv.* —*prep.* past, beyond, behind. —*adj.* later, subsequent, following. —*ad'.* subsequently, afterward, not now, later.
again, *adv.* once more, afresh, anew, repeatedly, twice; encore. See REPETITION.

AGE [128]

Nouns—1, age, OLDNESS; old age, advanced age; senility, senescence; years, anility, gray hairs, climacteric, menopause; declining years, decrepitude, superannuation; second childhood, dotage; vale of years, decline of life, three-score years and ten; ripe age; longevity; gerontology, geriatrics; era, period (see CHRONOMETRY).
2, adultness, manhood, virility, maturity; prime of life; years of discretion, majority; adult. *Colloq.,* no chicken.
3, seniority, eldership; elder; VETERAN; primogeniture; firstling; *doyen,* father.
Verbs—1, be aged, grow old; age; decline, wane.
2, come of age, come to man's estate, attain majority, have cut one's eye-teeth, have sown one's wild oats.
Adjectives—1, aged, old, elderly, senile; matronly, anile; in years; ripe, mellow, run to seed, declining, waning, past one's prime; grayheaded, hoary, venerable, timeworn, antiquated, *passé,* effete, decrepit, superannuated; advanced in life *or* years; past one's prime, stricken in years; wrinkled; having one foot in the grave.
2, of full age; out of one's teens, grown up, mature, full grown, in one's prime, middle-aged, manly, virile, adult; womanly, matronly; marriageable, nubile; of a certain age, no chicken, old as Methuselah; patriarchal, ANCIENT.
Antonym, see YOUTH.

AGENCY [170]

Nouns—agency,·operation; force, working, power, function; office, maintenance, exercise, work, play; interworking, interaction; causality, causation (see CAUSE); INSTRUMENTALITY, INFLUENCE, ACTION; METHOD, *modus operandi.* See AGENT, SUBSTITUTION.
Verbs—1, operate, work; act, act upon; perform, play, support, sustain, maintain; take effect, quicken, strike.
2, come *or* bring into operation *or* play; have free play *or* rein; bring to bear upon.
Adjectives—operative, efficient, efficacious, practical, effectual; at work, on foot; acting, doing; in operation, in force, in action, in play; acted upon.

agent, *n.* doer, actor, AGENCY, representative; operator, performer, worker; salesman, deputy, factor, broker, go-between; CAUSE, POWER, active element.
aggravate, *v.* worsen, heighten, intensify, INCREASE; provoke, irritate, annoy, exasperate, exacerbate. See IRASCIBILITY. *Ant.,* see PACIFICATION, DECREASE.
aggravation, *n.* See EXAGGERATION, INCREASE, IRASCIBILITY, EXCITEMENT.
aggregate, *n.* total, amount, sum; combination, whole, all. See ASSEMBLAGE.
aggression, *n.* offense, ATTACK, war, invasion; belligerence. *Ant.,* see DEFENSE.
agile, *adj.* nimble, active, spry, limber, lithe; brisk, quick, acrobatic, athletic. See ACTIVITY. *Ant.,* see INACTIVITY.

AGITATION [315]

Nouns—1, agitation, stir, tremor, shake, ripple, jog, jolt, jar, jerk, shock; trepidation, quiver, quaver, dance; twitter, flicker, flutter.
2, perturbation, commotion, turmoil, turbulence, tumult, hubbub, rout,

bustle, fuss, racket, EXCITEMENT, flurry; DEMONSTRATION.

3, spasm, throe, throb, twinge, pang, palpitation, convulsion, paroxysm, disturbance, DISORDER, restlessness, CHANGEABLENESS; frenzy. *Slang*, heebie-jeebies.

4, ferment, fermentation; ebullition, effervescence, hurly-burly; tempest, storm, ground swell, heavy sea, whirlpool, vortex; maelstrom, whirlwind (see WIND).

Verbs—**1,** shake, tremble, quiver, quaver, quake, shiver, twitter, writhe, toss, shuffle, tumble, stagger, bob, reel, sway; wag, wiggle, waggle; wriggle [like an eel]; dance, stumble, shamble, flounder, totter, flounce, flop, prance; throb, pulsate, beat, palpitate, go pit-a-pat; flutter, flitter, flicker, bustle.

2, ferment, effervesce, foam; seethe, boil (over); bubble (up); toss about; shake like an aspen leaf; shake to its foundations; reel to and fro [like a drunken man].

3, agitate, shake, convulse, toss, tumble, bandy, wield, brandish, flap, flourish, whisk, jerk, hitch, jolt; jog, jiggle, joggle, jostle, buffet, hustle; disturb, stir, shake up, churn, jounce, wallop, whip, vellicate.

Adjectives—shaking, agitated, tremulous; giddy; convulsive, unquiet, restless, all atwitter. *Colloq.*, nervous. *Slang*, jittery.

Adverbs—by fits and starts; hop, skip and jump; in convulsions *or* fits.

Antonym, see REPOSE.

---

agnostic, *n.* unbeliever, skeptic, doubter. See DOUBT.

agony, *n.* PAIN, torture, excruciation; anxiety, anguish.

AGREEMENT [23]

Nouns—**1,** agreement, accord, accordance; unison, harmony, CONCORD, concordance, concert; CONFORMITY, conformance; UNIFORMITY, consonance; consistency, congruity, keeping; congeniality; correspondence, parallelism, apposition, union.

2, fitness, aptness, appropriateness, relevancy, pertinency; case in point; aptitude, coaptation, propriety, applicability, admissibility, commensurability, compatibility; cognation, RELATION; right man in the right place; very thing; just the thing.

3, adaptation, adjustment, accommodation, reconciliation, assimilation; consent, ASSENT, concurrence, COÖPERATION.

4, compact, contract, pact, meeting of minds.

5, negotiation, bargaining, diplomacy, mediation; ratification.

Verbs—**1,** agree, accord, harmonize, get along, get on; consent, ASSENT, acquiesce; correspond, tally, respond; meet, suit, fit, befit, do, adapt (to); fall in with, chime in with, square with, comport with; dovetail, assimilate; fit like a glove; match, become one. See SIMILARITY.

2, fit, suit, adapt, accommodate, adjust; dress, regulate, readjust; accord, harmonize, reconcile; dovetail, square. See EQUALITY.

3, contract, covenant, engage, promise; stipulate; make *or* come to terms; close, close with, conclude, settle, compromise; strike a bargain, come to an understanding; confirm, ratify; sign, seal.

Adjectives—**1,** agreeing, suiting, in accord, accordant, concordant, consonant, congruous, correspondent, congenial; becoming; harmonious, reconcilable, conformable; in accordance, in harmony *or* keeping with; at one with, of one mind, of a piece; consistent, compatible, proportionate; commensurate. *Slang*, in whack.

2, apt, apposite, pertinent, pat; to the point *or* purpose; happy, felicitous, germane, applicable, relevant, admissible; fit, adapted, apropos, appropriate, seasonable, suitable, deft; meet, EXPEDIENT; at home, in one's proper element.

3, confirmed, ratified; signed, sealed and delivered.

Antonym, see DISAGREEMENT.

AGRICULTURE [371]

Nouns—**1,** agriculture, cultivation, husbandry, farming, tillage, agronomy, gardening; horticulture, arboriculture, floriculture, vintage; landscape gardening; georgics, geoponics.

2, husbandman, horticulturist, gardener, florist; agriculturist; yeoman, farmer, cultivator, tiller of the soil; plowman, reaper, sower; rustic. *Colloq.*, hayseed, hick, rube, peasant.

3, farm, field, meadow, garden; nursery, greenhouse, hothouse, conservatory; bed, border, seed-plot; lawn, park, *parterre;* plantation, ranch, homestead; arboretum, orchard, vineyard, vinery. See ABODE.

Verbs—cultivate, till the soil, farm, garden; sow, plant, reap, mow, cut, dress the ground; dig, delve, dibble, hoe, plow, harrow, rake, weed.

Adjectives—agricultural; arable; praedial, rural, rustic, country, georgic; horticultural.

---

ahead, *adv.* before, in advance (of), leading, winning. See TIME, SUPERIORITY.

AID [707]

Nouns—**1,** aid, assistance, help, succor, relief, rescue; support, lift, advance, furtherance, promotion, operation; patronage, championship, countenance, favor, interest, advocacy; ministration; subministration; accommodation.

2, supplies, reinforcements; SUPPORT, ADJUNCT, AUXILIARY.

3, helper, assistant, aid, aide; accessory, confederate; AGENT; ally, colleague.

Verbs—**1,** aid, assist, help, succor, lend one's aid; come to the aid of; contribute, subscribe to; give *or* lend a hand, give one a lift, take in tow.

2, relieve, rescue, set on one's legs; pull through; give new life to, be the making of; reinforce; push forward; give a lift to; give a leg up; promote, further, forward, advance; speed, expedite, quicken, hasten; support, sustain, uphold, prop, hold up, bolster.

3, cradle, nourish, nurture, nurse, suckle, foster, cherish, foment; feed *or* fan the flames; serve; do service to, tender to, pander to, administer to; care for, tend, attend, wait on, take care of, squire.

4, oblige, accommodate, humor, encourage.

5, second, stand by, stick by, stick up for; back up; abet, take up the cudgels for; espouse (the cause of), advocate, give moral support to, keep in countenance, patronize; smile upon, favor, befriend, take in hand, side with; be of use to, benefit.

Adjectives—aiding, auxiliary, adjuvant, helpful, coadjuvant; ministrant, ancillary, accessory, subsidiary; at one's beck; friendly, amicable, favorable, propitious, well-disposed, neighborly, obliging.

Adverbs—with *or* by the aid of; on *or* in behalf of; on account of; for the sake of; on the part of.

Antonym, see HINDRANCE.

---

ail, *v.i.* fall ill, be sick suffer, fail (in health). See DISEASE.

aim, *n. & v.* —*n.* purpose, goal, end, course. —*v.* point, direct, aspire to, try for. See DIRECTION.

AIR [338]

Nouns—**1,** air, atmosphere, ether, ozone; ventilation, fresh *or* open air; sky, welkin; blue sky. See VAPOR.

2, troposphere, tropopause, layer, ozone layer, stratosphere, [Kennelly-] Heaviside layer, ionosphere, exosphere.

3, weather, climate, rise and fall of the barometer, isobar, weather map; aerology, meteorology, climatology; aneroid barometer, baroscope.

4, aeronautics, AVIATION.

5, aria, tune, see MUSIC.

6, APPEARANCE.

Verbs—**1,** air, ventilate, fan; aerate; see WIND.

2, publicize; see PUBLICATION.

Adjectives—**1,** containing air, flatulent, effervescent; windy.

2, atmospheric, airy, aerial, aeriform; meteorological.

Adverbs—outdoors, *al fresco.*

Antonym, see SUFFOCATE.

air-pipe, *n.* air shaft, airway; funnel, vent, tube, flue, chimney, ventilator; nostril, nozzle, blowhole; windpipe, spiracle, larynx, throat; pipe.

akin, *adj.* related, allied, kindred, like. See RELATION.

alacrity, *n.* promptness, responsiveness, speed, quickness. See ACTIVITY.

alarm, *n.* & *v.* —*n.* alarum, WARNING; tocsin; S.O.S., siren, danger signal, red light, red flag; condition red; bugbear, bogey, bugaboo. —*v.* frighten, panic, scare; shock, horrify; make uneasy; sound the alarm, bell, or tocsin; alert, warn; cry wolf. See FEAR. *Ant.*, see SAFETY.

alas, *interj.* too bad! See LAMENTATION.

alcoholic, *adj.* beery, winy, spirituous; convivial. See DRUNKENNESS.

alert, *adj.* watchful, on guard, wary; quick, ready, prepared, careful. See CARE.

alien, *adj.* & *n.* —*adj.* foreign, strange. —*n.* foreigner, stranger, immigrant.

alienate, *v.t.* estrange, turn against, make hostile. See HATE. *Ant.*, LOVE.

alienist, *n.* psychiatrist. *Slang,* headshrinker. See INSANITY.

alight, *v.* & *adj.* —*v.i.* descend, get off, land; dismount; arrive, disembark. See ARRIVAL, DESCENT. *Ant.*, DEPARTURE, ASCENT. —*adj.* glowing, lighted; on fire; burning. See LIGHT. *Ant.*, see DARKNESS.

alike, *adj.* analogous, resembling, like; akin; same, identical. See SIMILARITY. *Ant.*, see DIFFERENCE.

alive, *adj.* living, animate, quick, breathing; quick-witted, alert, brisk, spry. See LIFE, INTELLIGENCE, ACTIVITY. *Ant.*, see DEATH.

all, *n.* sum, total, aggregate, entirety. See WHOLE. *Ant.*, PART.

allay, *v.t.* lessen; soothe, mitigate, ease; calm. See MODERATION. *Ant.*, see VIOLENCE, INCREASE.

allegiance, *n.* loyalty, DUTY, devotion, homage. See OBEDIENCE. *Ant.*, see DISOBEDIENCE.

alleviation, *n.* lessening, mitigation; relief. See MODERATION. *Ant.*, VIOLENCE, INCREASE.

alley, *n.* passage, narrow street, lane, walk. See OPENING. *Ant.*, CLOSURE.

alliance, *n.* association, federation, league; treaty, accord; connection. See COÖPERATION, RELATION. *Ant.*, OPPOSITION.

allot, *v.* grant, assign, share, distribute. See APPORTIONMENT.

allow, *v.* grant, permit, concede; tolerate, suffer, let. See DISCLOSURE, PERMISSION. *Ant.*, see RESTRAINT.

alloy, *n.* & *v.* —*n.* compound, MIXTURE; admixture. See COMPOSITION. —*v.* adulterate, mix, combine. See MIXTURE.

allude, *v.* suggest, imply, connote. See CAUSE, INTERPRETATION.

allure, *n.* & *v.* —*n.* attraction, charm. —*v.* tempt, ATTRACT, CHARM, entice. See DESIRE.

ally, *n.* friend, co-worker, helper, supporter. See AID. *Ant.*, ENEMY.

almanac, *n.* calendar, ephemeris. See CHRONOMETRY.

almighty, *adj.* great, all-powerful, omnipotent. *Colloq.*, extreme. See DEITY.

almost, *adv.* nearly, not quite, all but, approximately. See NEARNESS. *Ant.*, see DISTANCE.

alms, *n.* charity, dole, gratuity. See GIVING.

aloft, *adv.* on high, overhead, above, up; in the air. See HEIGHT. *Ant.*, see LOWNESS.

alone, *adj.* & *adv.* —*adj.* apart, solitary. —*adv.* individually. See UNITY. *Ant.*, see ACCOMPANIMENT.

aloof, *adj.* distant, unneighborly, reserved, remote. See SECLUSION, DISTANCE. *Ant.*, see SOCIALITY, NEARNESS.

aloud, *adv.* audibly, vociferously, loudly. See LOUDNESS. *Ant.*, see SILENCE.

already, *adv.* by now, previously. See TIME, INSTANTANEITY.

also, *adv.* too, furthermore, besides, likewise. See ADDITION.

alter, *v.* CHANGE, modify, rearrange, vary, qualify. *Ant.*, see STABILITY.

alternate, *n.* & *v.* —*n.* substitute. —*v.* take turns, change, vacillate. See DISJUNCTION, OSCILLATION. *Ant.*, see CONTINUITY.

alternative, *n.* preference, choice of two, option. See CHOICE. *Ant.*, see REFUSAL.

although, *conj.* albeit, notwithstanding, though. See COMPENSATION. *Ant.*, see AGREEMENT.

altitude, *n.* HEIGHT, loftiness, tallness; elevation, perpendicular distance. *Ant.,* LOWNESS.

altogether, *adv.* entirely, all, collectively, totally. *Colloq.,* nude. See WHOLE. *Ant.,* PART.

altruism, *n.* BENEVOLENCE; selflessness; generosity, liberality, philanthropy. *Ant.,* MALEVOLENCE.

always, *adv.* at all times, invariably, continually, ever. See UNIFORMITY. *Ant.,* never.

amateur, *n.* nonprofessional, beginner, novice, tyro; dilettante; volunteer.

amative, amatory, *adj.* loving, affectionate; amorous, ardent; erotic. See LOVE. *Ant.,* see HATE.

ambiguous, *adi.* vague, undecided, uncertain; not specific; obscure, undefined. See DOUBT. *Ant.,* see CERTAINTY.

ambition, *n.* purpose, wish, hope, desire, INTENTION; aspiration, goal, end; resolve; zeal. See DESIRE, OSTENTATION. *Ant.,* see INDIFFERENCE.

ambush, *n. & v.* —*n.* ambuscade; hiding-place, cover, threat; disguise, camouflage; pitfall, trap, blind; bushwhacking. —*v.t.* lie in wait for; attack unexpectedly; bushwhack. See CONCEALMENT.

amenable, *adj.* agreeable; pliant, yielding, submissive. See DUTY, ASSENT. *Ant.,* see REFUSAL, NEGLECT.

amend, *v.* change; correct, rectify; improve; enlarge. See IMPROVEMENT. *Ant.,* see DETERIORATION.

amiable, *adj.* friendly, agreeable, kindly, pleasant; likeable. See COURTESY. *Ant.,* see DISCOURTESY.

amidst, *prep.* amid, AMONG, midst, mid (*poetic*). See MIXTURE.

amiss, *adv.* wrong, ill, badly, improperly. See EVIL. *Ant.,* see GOOD.

ammunition, *n.* bullets, shot, powder, bombs. See ARMS.

amnesia, *n.* forgetfulness, loss of MEMORY.

amnesty, *n.* pardon, remission, moratorium. See OBLIVION.

among, *prep.* midst, in the middle, included in, with. See MIXTURE.

amorous, *adj.* loving, passionate, AMATIVE. See LOVE. *Ant.,* see HATE.

amount, *n.* QUANTITY, sum, total, aggregate.

ample, *adj.* adequate, sufficient, plenty; large, expansive, roomy, spacious. See GREATNESS, SPACE. *Ant.,* see LITTLENESS.

amputate, *v.* sever, cut off. See DECREASE.

amulet, *n.* charm, token, talisman, good-luck piece. See PREDICTION.

AMUSEMENT [840]

Nouns—**1,** amusement, entertainment; diversion, divertisement, *divertissement*, distraction; recreation, hobby, avocation, relaxation, pastime, sport; labor of love, PLEASURE.

2, fun, frolic, merriment, jollity, joviality, laughter, REJOICING, jocosity, drollery, tomfoolery, mummery; pleasantry, WIT, quip, quirk.

3, play, game, gambol, romp, prank, antic, lark, escapade, spree, skylarking; vagary, monkeyshine, monkey trick, practical joke, RIDICULE.

4, dance, hop, ball, masquerade; reel, rigadoon, saraband, hornpipe, bolero, fandango, cancan, minuet, waltz, polka, galop, jig, fling, *allemande*, gavotte, mazurka, kozotzky, morisco, morris dance, quadrille, country dance, cotillion, *cotillon;* one-step, two-step, fox trot, turkey trot, Charleston, jitterbugging, bunnyhop, black bottom, cakewalk, tango, cha-cha, mambo, samba; tap dance, soft shoe. *Colloq.,* drag, hop, prom.

5, festivity, merrymaking, party (see SOCIALITY); fete, festival, gala, revel, revelry, carnival, Mardi Gras, brawl, saturnalia, high jinks; feast, banquet, wassail, carouse, carousal; jollification, junket, wake, picnic, field-day; treat; round of pleasures, dissipation, a short life and a merry one; jubilee, CELEBRATION, holiday; red letter day; May Day.

6, place of amusement, theater, ballroom, music hall; park, arbor, bowling green *or* alley, rink, casino, fun fair, amusement park, resort, watering place; midway, boardwalk.

7, game, sports, gymnastics, athletics, Olympic games, rodeo, racing; billiards, bowls; cards, chess, checkers, draughts, backgammon, dominoes, solitaire; gambling, CHANCE; fishing, hunting, safari; aquatics, swimming, water sports.

8, toy, plaything, bauble; doll, PUPPET, teetotum, knickknack.
Verbs—**1,** amuse, entertain, divert, enliven; tickle the fancy; titillate, raise a
smile, put in good humor; convulse with laughter; bring down the house,
be the death of one; recreate, solace, cheer, please, interest, treat, regale.
2, amuse oneself; play (a game, pranks, tricks, *etc.*); sport, disport, toy,
wanton, revel, junket, feast, carouse, make merry; drown care; drive dull
care away; frolic, gambol, frisk, romp, caper; sow one's wild oats, have
one's fling, take one's pleasure; make holiday; go a-Maying; while away
the time; kill time; dally. *Colloq.*, step out, have fun, cut a caper, carry on.
Slang, cut loose, whoop it up, make a night of it, go to town.
Adjectives—**1,** amusing, entertaining, diverting, recreative, pleasant, pleasing; laughable, ludicrous, witty; festive, jovial, jolly, jocund, roguish,
rompish, playful (as a kitten), sportive.
2, amused, pleased, tickled.
Antonym, see WEARINESS, PAIN.

anachronism, *n.* misdate, prolepsis, anticipation; metachronism, parachron-
ism, prochronism.
anaemia, *n.* bloodlessness, lack of blood. See DISEASE, IMPOTENCE. *Ant.,*
see POWER.
analogous, *adj.* like, parallel; related; corresponding, similar, resembling.
See SIMILARITY. *Ant.,* see OBLIQUITY, DIFFERENCE.
analysis, *n.* breakdown, separation, disintegration; investigation, study.
See INQUIRY, DECOMPOSITION. *Ant.,* synthesis, COMBINATION.
anarchy, *n.* lawlessness, terrorism, chaos, confusion, disorganization; nihilism. See DISORDER. *Ant.,* see AUTHORITY.
anatomy, *n.* body structure, framework; zoötomy; analysis. See REMEDY,
INQUIRY.

ANCESTRY [166]

Nouns—**1,** ancestry, paternity, maternity, parentage, RELATION; house,
stem, trunk, branch, tree, stock, stirps, pedigree, lineage, blood, kin, line,
family, tribe, sept, race, clan; family tree, genealogy, descent, extraction,
birth; forefathers, patriarchs.
2, parent, father, sire, dad, papa; paterfamilias; genitor, progenitor, pro-
creator; ancestor; grandsire, grandfather, forebears; motherhood, maternity; mother, dam, ma, mama, materfamilias, grandmother, granddam.
Adjectives—parental, paternal, maternal; family, ancestral, linear, patriarchal; direct, lineal, collateral.
Antonym, see DESCENT.

anchor, *n. & v.* —*n.* grapnel, kedge; mainstay, safeguard. —*v.* fasten, bind,
attach; hold fast. See STABILITY.
ancient, *adj.* aged, venerable; antique, antiquated; archaic, hoary. See
OLDNESS. *Ant.,* see NEWNESS.
anecdote, *n.* sketch, story, tale, joke, narrative. See DESCRIPTION.

ANGEL [977]

Nouns—**1,** angel, archangel; celestial being, choir invisible, heavenly host;
seraph, cherub; ministering spirit, guardian angel.
2, angelology; seraphim, cherubim, thrones, dominations *or* dominions,
virtues, powers, principalities, archangels, angels.
Adjectives—angelic, seraphic, cherubic, celestial, divine, supernatural.
Antonym, see DEMON.

anger, *n. & v.* —*n.* RESENTMENT, irritation; rage, choler, fury; annoyance.
—*v.* inflame, irritate, annoy, provoke, pique, incense; enrage, infuriate.
angle, *n.* peak, corner, point; fork; OBLIQUITY; aspect, guise. *Slang*, approach. See ANGULARITY.

ANGULARITY [244]

Nouns—**1,** angularity, obliquity; angle, cusp, bend, FOLD, NOTCH, fork,
bifurcation; elbow, knee, knuckle, ankle, groin, crotch, crutch, crane,

fluke; scythe, sickle; zigzag; corner, coign, quoin, nook, recess, niche, oriel; salient, projection.

2, right, acute, obtuse *or* oblique angle.

3, angulation; angular measurement, elevation, distance, velocity; trigonometry, trig; goniometry, altimeter, clinometer, graphometer, goniometer; theodolite; sextant, quadrant.

4, triangle, trigon, wedge; rectangle, square, lozenge, diamond; rhomb, rhombus; quadrangle, quadrilateral; parallelogram; quadrature; polygon, pentagon, hexagon, heptagon, octagon, decagon; cube, rhomboid; tetrahedron, octahedron, dodecahedron, icosahedron; prism, pyramid; parallelepiped.

5, lankiness, boniness, ungainliness.

Verbs—bend, fork, bifurcate, crinkle.

Adjectives—angular, bent, crooked; aquiline, sharp; jagged, serrated; falciform, furcated, forked, bifurcate, zigzag; dovetailed; knockkneed, crinkled, akimbo, geniculated; oblique (see OBLIQUITY).

Antonyms, see DIRECTION, CIRCULARITY.

---

anile, *adj.* childish, foolish, simple; senile. See AGE, OLDNESS.

ANIMAL [366, 364]

Nouns—**1,** animal kingdom, animal life, fauna; beast, brute, creature, living thing, creeping thing, dumb animal; domestic animal, wild animal, game; flesh, flesh and blood, corporeality, carnality; animation, animality.

2, biology, zoölogy, mammalogy, ornithology, herpetology, ichthyology, entomology; biologist, *etc.*

3, vertebrate, invertebrate; quadruped, biped; mammal, marsupial, cetacean; reptile, snake, amphibian; fish, crustacean, shellfish, mollusk, worm; insect, zoöphyte, arachnid, protozoan, animalcule.

4, livestock; cattle, kine, bird, poultry, fowl, swine; beasts of the field.

Adjectives—**1,** animal, zoölogical; bestial, carnal, corporal, corporeal, physical, fleshly; sensual; human.

2, mammalian, cetaceous, avian, reptilian, vermicular, piscatory; piscine, molluscous; aquatic, terrestrial; domestic, wild; carnivorous, herbivorous, insectivorous, omnivorous; equine, bovine, canine, feline, *etc.*

---

animate, *v. & adj.* —*v.* liven, impel; cheer, enliven, enspirit, encourage, inspire. —*adj.* moving; living. See CHEERFULNESS, EXCITEMENT, ANIMAL. *Ant.*, see DEJECTION, INACTIVITY.

annalist, *n.* recorder, historian, compiler, chronicler. See RECORD.

annex, *v.* add, acquire, join, attach, affix. See ADDITION.

annihilate, *v.* demolish, destroy; eliminate, exterminate, end; wreck. See DESTRUCTION, NONEXISTENCE.

anniversary, *n.* CELEBRATION.

annotate, *v.* make notes on, gloss, explain. See INTERPRETATION.

announc·, *v.* tell, proclaim, publish, make known; broadcast, report. See INFORMATION, PREDICTION.

annoy, *v.* vex, tease, harass, disturb, molest, trouble, bother, irritate, PAIN. *Ant.*, see PLEASURE.

annul, *v.t.* cancel, repeal, rescind, recall, retract, revoke, nullify, quash; dissolve (a marriage); set aside, invalidate. See NULLIFICATION.

anoint, *v.* oil, salve; crown.

anonymous, *adj.* unknown, unnamed, nameless, incognito. See NOMENCLATURE.

another, *adj.* different, one more. See DIFFERENCE. *Ant.*, see IDENTITY.

ANSWER [462, 587]

Nouns—**1,** answer, response, reply; acknowledgment; riposte, rejoinder, return, retort; repartee; antiphon; password; echo, oracle. *Colloq.*, comeback.

2, discovery, DISCLOSURE, solution, explanation, clue, INDICATION.

Verbs—**1,** answer, respond, reply; rebut, retort, rejoin; give answer; acknowledge, echo; CONFUTE.

2, satisfy, set at rest; determine, solve.
Adjectives—answering, responsive, conclusive.
       Antonym, see INQUIRY.

antagonism, *n.* animosity, ill-will, antipathy; ENMITY, hostility, opposition.
Ant., AGREEMENT.
anteroom, *n.* waiting room, entrance; lobby, vestibule, foyer. See RE-
CEPTACLE.

ANTIBIOSIS [662]

Nouns—**1,** antibiosis (see REMEDY); antibody, antibiotic, counteragent.
2, antibiotics, wonder drugs, miracle drugs; toxin, antitoxin, penicillin,
gramicidin; bacitracin, chloromycetin, dihydrostreptomycin, erythromycin,
gumagillin, magnamycin, neomycin, polymyxin, streptomycin, terramycin.
3, sulfa, sulfonamide, sulfadiazine, sulfanilamide, sulfapyridine, sulfathia-
zole.
Adjectives—antibiotic, bactericidal, bacteriostatic.

anticipate, *v.* await, expect, hope for; precede; foresee. See PREPARATION.
antidote, *n.* emetic, counterirritant. See REMEDY.
antipathy, *n.* repugnance, hate, aversion, abhorrence; incompatibility. See
HATE. *Ant.*, liking.
antiquity, *n.* old times; the past, ancient history; yesterday. See PAST.
anxiety, *n.* concern; fear, mental anguish, apprehensiveness, worry. See
CARE, FEAR, PAIN.
anyhow, *adv.* anyway; at any rate; nevertheless. See NEGATION.
apart, *adv.* separately, alone, independently; away. See DISTANCE, DIS-
JUNCTION.
apathy, *n.* coldness, INSENSIBILITY, unconcern. *Ant.*, FEELING, INTEREST.
ape, *n. & v.* —*n.* monkey, gorilla, anthropoid, simian. —*v.* IMITATE, copy,
mimic. *Ant.*, originate.
apiece, *adv.* for each, for one.
apology, *n.* excuse, regret, amends, pardon. See ATONEMENT.
apostate, *n.* backslider, renegade, turncoat, deserter, recreant; double
dealer, opportunist. See CHANGEABLENESS, IMPIETY. *Ant.*, see STABILITY,
PIETY.
appall, appal, *v.i.* horrify, shock; disgust, revolt. See FEAR, PAIN. *Ant.*,
GRATIFY, PLEASE.
apparatus, *n.* machine, machinery; equipment, instruments.
apparent, *adj.* plain, obvious, visible; EVIDENT, manifest, perceptible. See
APPEARANCE, VISIBILITY. *Ant.*, HIDDEN, MYSTERIOUS.
apparition, *n.* phantom, ghost, specter; dream. See VISION.
appeal, *n.* entreaty, plea, begging, petition; ATTRACTION. See REQUEST.

APPEARANCE [448]

Nouns—**1,** appearance, phenomenon, sight, show, scene, view; outlook,
prospect, vista, perspective, bird's-eye view, scenery, landscape, picture,
tableau; display, exposure, setting, *mise en scène.*
2, pageant, spectacle; peep show; magic lantern, phantasmagoria, panorama, diorama; pageantry, OSTENTATION, INDICATION.
3, aspect, phase, seeming; shape, FORM, guise, look, complexion, color,
image, mien, air, cast, carriage, port, demeanor; presence, expression, first
blush; point of view, light.
4, lineament, feature; contour, face, countenance, physiognomy, visage,
phiz, cast of countenance, profile, cut of one's jib.
Verbs—appear, become visible; seem, look, show; have, take on *or* assume
the appearance *or* semblance of; look like; cut a figure, figure; present to
the view. See VISION.
Adjectives—apparent, seeming, ostensible; on view; evident, manifest.
Adverbs—apparently, ostensibly, seemingly, as it seems, on the face of it,
prima facie; at first blush, at first sight; in the eyes of; to the eye.
       Antonyms, see ABSENCE, VISIBILITY.

appease, *v.t.* mollify, pacify, moderate, soothe; satisfy, slake. See PLEASURE.
append, *v.t.* add, attach (to), affix. See ADDITION.
appetite, *n.* hunger, DESIRE; relish, gusto; craving.
applause, *n.* praise; cheers, acclaim, plaudits, clapping. See APPROBATION.
applicable, *adj.* fitting, suitable, appropriate, relevant, pertinent. See UTILITY.
application, *n.* diligence, assiduity; suitability, relevancy; form (to fill out). See REQUEST, RELATION, ATTENTION.
apply, *v.* put on, USE; ask, solicit; work, persevere. See REQUEST.
appoint, *v.* prescribe, assign, ordain; place (in a job), nominate; equip. See COMMISSION, APPORTIONMENT.

APPORTIONMENT [786]

Nouns—**1,** apportionment, allotment, consignment, assignment, appointment; appropriation; dispensation, distribution, division, partition, deal. **2,** dividend, portion, contingent, share, allotment, lot, measure, dose; dole, meed, pittance; quantum, ration; ratio, proportion, quota, modicum, allowance.
Verbs—apportion, divide; distribute, dispense; billet, allot, detail, cast, share, mete; portion, parcel *or* dole out; deal, carve, administer; partition, assign, appropriate, appoint. *Slang,* divvy (up). See COÖPERATION.
Adjectives—apportioning; respective; proportional, proportionate, commensurate; divisible.
Adverbs—respectively, *pro rata,* each to each, severally, individually.

---

appraise, *v.* estimate, JUDGE, evaluate, assess.
appreciate, *v.* prize, esteem, value; INCREASE (in value); comprehend, understand; realize worth. See APPROBATION, KNOWLEDGE. *Ant.,* see DECREASE.
apprehend, *v.* seize, arrest; grasp, see, understand, perceive. See KNOWLEDGE, LAWSUIT.
apprenticeship, *n.* training, probation. See LEARNING.
approach, *n. & v.* —*n.* nearing; advent, coming; approximation, TENDENCY, NEARNESS; access; address; convergence. —*v.* near, come to; arrive; draw near, close up, pursue, tread on the heels of; address, broach a subject; approximate. *Ant.,* see DEPARTURE, DISTANCE, REGRESSION.

APPROBATION [931]

Nouns—**1,** approbation, approval, sanction, advocacy; esteem, estimation, good opinion, favor, admiration; appreciation, regard, account, popularity, kudos, credit; REPUTE.
2, commendation, praise, laudation; good word; meed, tribute, encomium; eulogy, panegyric; homage, hero worship; benediction, blessing, benison. **3,** applause, plaudit, clapping (of hands); acclaim, acclamation, cheer; paean, hosanna; thumbs up.
Verbs—**1,** approve; think good, much, well, *or* highly of; esteem; value, prize; set great store by; do justice to, appreciate; honor, hold in esteem, look up to, admire; like, favor, wish God speed; hail. *Colloq.,* hand it to. **2,** stand *or* stick up for; clap *or* pat on the back; endorse, give credit, recommend; commend, praise, laud, compliment, pay a tribute, applaud, cheer, encore; panegyrize, eulogize, cry up, puff, extol, magnify, glorify, exalt, swell, make much of, FLATTER; bless, give a blessing to; have *or* say a good word for; speak well *or* highly of; sing, sound *or* resound the praises of. *Slang,* give a big hand. **3,** redound to the honor *or* credit of; do credit to; recommend itself; pass muster.
4, be praised; receive honorable mention; be in favor *or* high favor with; ring with the praises of, gain credit, stand well in the opinion of; bring down the house; stop the show.
Adjectives—**1,** approving, commendatory, complimentary, benedictory, laudatory, panegyrical, eulogistic, lavish of praise.
2, approved, praised, popular; in good odor; in high esteem; RESPECTED.
3, deserving, worthy, praiseworthy, commendable, meritorious, estimable, creditable, unimpeachable; beyond all praise. *Colloq.,* in one's good books.

Adverbs—with credit, well. See GOOD.
Interjections—hear, hear! bravo! bravissimo! olé! nice going, so far so good; viva! encore!

Antonym, see DISAPPROBATION.

---

appropriate, *adj.* proper, fit, timely, suitable. See AGREEMENT.
appropriate, *v.t.* take, seize, confiscate; allot, assign. See BORROW. *Ant.*, see RELINQUISHMENT.
approve, *v.t.* accept, like, support, recognize, ratify, endorse. *Colloq.*, O.K. See APPROBATION.
approximate, *adj.* near, close, roughly correct. See NEARNESS, SIMILARITY, RELATION.
apt, *adj.* suitable, appropriate, fitting; quick, clever, skillful. *Colloq.*, likely. See AGREEMENT, SKILL.
aquatic, *adj.* watery; oceanic, marine, fresh-water, salt-water. See NAVIGATION.
aquiline, *adj.* Roman-nosed, beaked, curved, hooked. See ANGULARITY.
arable, *adj.* tillable, farmable; fertile. See AGRICULTURE.
arbitrary, *adj.* despotic, dictatorial; unreasonable; discretionary, willful. See RESOLUTION.
arbitration, *n.* intervention, MEDIATION, settlement (of dispute).
arbor, *n.* bower, pergola. See ABODE, RECEPTACLE.
arch, *n.* curve, arc, vault. See CONVEXITY.
arch, *adj.* CUNNING, sly, roguish.
archaic, *adj.* old, ancient; historic; obsolete, outdated. See AGE, OLDNESS. *Ant.*, modern, up-to-date.
archer, *n.* bowman. See COMBATANT, ARMS.
archetype, *n.* model, ideal type. See PREPARATION.
architect, *n.* builder, planner, designer, creator. See AGENT, ARTIST.
archive, *n.* chronicle, annal, RECORD.
ardent, *adj.* warm, passionate, zealous; fervent, eager. See ACTIVITY, LOVE. *Ant.*, apathetic, cool.
ardor, *n.* fervor, passion, enthusiasm, elan, zeal, WARMTH. See FEELING, LOVE, VIGOR.
area, *n.* space, tract, territory, expanse. See REGION.
arena, *n.* field (of combat); platform, lists, hustings; stadium, ring, amphitheater, stage; battlefield, cockpit; scene of action. See WARFARE, CONTENTION.
argument, *n.* debate, dispute; evidence, case. See REASONING.
arise, *v.i.* get up, awake; originate, begin. See BEGINNING, ASCENT.
aristocracy, *n.* patricians, NOBILITY.
arm, *n.* limb, member; branch, wing; weapon, strength. See ARMS, PART, POWER.
armistice, *n.* truce, respite, lull (in fighting), peace. See PACIFICATION.
armor, armour, *n.* steel plate, mail, shielding. See DEFENSE.

ARMS [727]

Nouns—**1,** arms, weapon(s), firearms, armament, matériel; panoply, stand of arms, military establishment; armory, arsenal, STORE: armor (see DEFENSE). **2,** ammunition, munitions, explosive, charge; ball, bolt, shot, grape [shot], chain shot, bullet, dumdum bullet, cartridge, shell, fragmentation shell, shrapnel; missile, projectile, grenade, bomb, depth charge, ashcan, atomic bomb, A-bomb, fission bomb, hydrogen bomb, H-bomb, thermonuclear bomb, blockbuster, torpedo, bombsight, guided missile, Nike, I.C.B.M. (intercontinental ballistics missile), V1, V2; cap and ball, powder and shot, cap, fuse, proximity fuse, detonator; powder, gunpowder, smokeless powder, cordite, melinite, lyddite, guncotton, nitroglycerine, TNT (trinitrotoluene), nuclear *or* thermonuclear warhead. **3,** artillery, gun(s), gunnery, cannon, battery, ordnance, ballistics; piece, fieldpiece, rifle, howitzer, mortar, siege artillery, coast artillery, field artillery, Big Bertha, French 75, two-pounder, ten-pounder, 8-inch, 16-inch, etc.; carronade, culverin, basilisk, falconet, jingle, swivel, petard; antiaircraft, AA, ack-ack. See PROPULSION.

4, machine gun, submachine gun, pompom, Gatling gun, Maxim gun, Bren gun, Thompson *or* Tommy gun. *Slang*, chopper.
5, small arms; musket, musketry, carbine, rifle, shotgun, fowling piece, breachloader, muzzle-loader, chassepot, blunderbuss, harquebus, arquebus, matchlock, flint-and-steel; .22, .25, .32, .38, .44, .45, 30-30, 30-'06, etc.; 8-gauge, 12-gauge, 16-gauge, etc.; Kentucky long rifle, Springfield, Enfield, Winchester, Lee-Enfield, Garand, etc.; pistol, automatic, semi-automatic, derringer, repeater, revolver, hammerless (revolver), six-shooter, six-gun; Colt, Smith & Wesson, Luger, Beretta, etc. *Slang*, gat, rod, heater, zip gun.
6, armor, armored vehicle, tank, panzer division.
7, sword, saber, broadsword, cutlass, falchion, scimitar, bilbo, rapier, skean, claymore, creese, kris; dagger, dirk, hanger, poniard, stiletto, stylet, dudgeon, bayonet; foil, epée, blade, steel; ax, poleax, battleax, halberd, tomahawk; bowie knife, bolo, kukri, pigsticker, switchblade knife, yataghan; cold steel.
8, pike, lance, spear, spontoon, javelin, dart, djerrid, arrow, reed, shaft, bolt, boomerang, harpoon, gaff; fishing spear.
9, club, mace, truncheon, staff, bludgeon, cudgel, life-preserver, shillelah; quarterstaff; battering ram (see IMPULSE); bat, cane, stick, knuckle-duster, brass knuckles *or* knucks; blackjack, sap, billy, nightstick.
10, bow, crossbow, arbalest, catapult, sling; archery, archer, bowman.
11, warship, see SHIP.
12, gas, poison gas, see KILLING.

army, *n.* troops, soldiers, military force; host, crowd, throng. See COMBATANT, MULTITUDE.
around, *adv. & prep.* surrounding, about; near, neighboring. See NEARNESS.
arouse, *v.* rouse, awaken; stir, excite, stimulate, whet. See EXCITEMENT.
arraignment, *n.* indictment, charge, accusation; censure. See ACCUSATION, LAWSUIT.

ARRANGEMENT [60]

Nouns—**1,** arrangement; PLAN, PREPARATION, disposition, allocation, distribution, sorting; grouping; assortment, allotment, apportionment; taxonomy, organization, analysis, classification.
2, digest, synopsis, compendium; table, register, RECORD, resumé; file, index, card index.
3, ORDER, array, system; regularity, uniformity, symmetry.
4, standard, form, formula, principle, RULE.
Verbs—**1,** arrange, dispose, place, form; put, set *or* place in order; set out, collate, pack, marshal, range, size, rank, group, parcel out, allot, distribute, deal; dispose of, assign places to; assort, sort; put *or* set to rights, put in shape *or* in array, reduce to order. *Colloq.*, pigeonhole.
2, classify, divide, segregate, alphabetize, file, string together, register, RECORD, catalog, tabulate, index, graduate, digest; harmonize, methodize, regulate, systematize, coördinate, organize.
3, unravel, disentangle, disembroil.
Adjectives—arranged, methodical, orderly, tidy, neat, regular, systematic. *Colloq.*, to rights, cut and dried.
Adverbs—methodically, systematically, like clockwork, in apple-pie order.
Antonym, see DISORDER.

array, *n.* CLOTHING, apparel; army, host, MULTITUDE; ARRANGEMENT system.
arrears, *n.* DEBT, bill (overdue).
arrest, *v.* seize, apprehend, capture, stop, halt, retard, suspend. *Colloq.*, nab. See END, RESTRAINT, LAWSUIT.

ARRIVAL [292]

Nouns—**1,** arrival, advent, landing; debarkation, disembarkation; homecoming, return, rencounter; reception, welcome.
2, home, goal, landing-place, destination; harbor, haven, port; terminus; anchorage, REFUGE; attainment (see COMPLETION).

3, newcomer, visitor. *Colloq.*, newborn child.
4, introduction, entrance, admittance, admission, RECEPTION.
Verbs—**1,** arrive, get to, come to, reach, attain; come up with *or* to; overtake; join, rejoin.
2, light, alight, dismount; land, go ashore, debark, disembark; detrain, deplane; put in *or* into; visit, cast anchor, pitch one's tent; get to one's journey's end; come *or* get back *or* home; return; appear, put in an appearance, come in, drop in. *Slang*, check in.
Antonym, see DEPARTURE.

---

arrogance, *n.*   pride, haughtiness, self-importance; INSOLENCE, presumptuousness. *Ant.*, HUMILITY; see MODESTY.
arrogate, *v.*   usurp, claim, seize, take; assume, appropriate, TAKE.
arrow, *n.*   shaft, bolt; missile; pointer. See ARMS, DIRECTION.
arsenal, *n.*   armory, storehouse, supply (of weapons); resources. See ARMS.
art, *n.*   craft, skill, cunning; science, technics; fine arts; PAINTING, SCULPTURE. See REPRESENTATION.
article, *n.*   object, thing; story, piece, essay, report. See SUBSTANCE, WRITING.
artifice, *n.*   trick, stratagem, ruse; device; cunning. See DECEPTION.
artificial, *adj.*   manmade, handcrafted; false, substitute, synthetic; sham, fake, deceptive; affected, unnatural. See AFFECTATION, DECEPTION.
artillery, *n.*   guns, cannon, ordnance. See ARMS.
artisan, *n.*   mechanic, craftsman, workman. See EXERTION, SKILL.

ARTIST [559]

Nouns—**1,** artist, virtuoso, master, maestro, academician, craftsman.
2, painter, limner, drawer, sketcher; illustrator, protraitist, water-colorist, miniaturist, pointillist, surrealist, genre painter, landscapist, seascapist; engraver, designer, etcher; reëtcher, retoucher; cartoonist, caricaturist; copyist, draftsman.
3, sculptor, sculptress, carver, chaser, modelist.
4, author, writer, poet, dramatist, novelist; actor, actress, Thespian, performer, dancer, ballerina; musician, composer, arranger, orchestrator, soloist, pianist, etc.; architect, builder; photographer, cameraman, cinematographer; commercial artist, advertising artist, layout man.
Antonym, see UNSKILLFULNESS.

---

artistic, *adj.*   talented, accomplished, cultural; beautiful, esthetic; skillful, masterly. See BEAUTY, TASTE.
artless, *adj.*   simple; ingenuous, unsophisticated, naïve; guileless, innocent.
artlessness, *n.*   SIMPLENESS, simplicity, naiveté, INNOCENCE, unsophistication; straightforwardness, bluntness. *Ant.*, see DECEPTION.

ASCENT [305]

Nouns—ascent, ascension, ELEVATION, mounting, rising, rise, LEAP; upswing, upsurge; acclivity, hill; flight of steps *or* stairs, stairway, staircase; ladder, accommodation ladder, gangway, fire escape; elevator, lift, escalator. See OBLIQUITY.
Verbs—ascend, rise, mount; arise, uprise; spring *or* shoot up; aspire, climb, clamber, surmount, scale the heights; tower, soar, hover; LEAP.
Adjectives—rising, scandent, buoyant; in the ascendant.
Adverbs—up, uphill.
Antonym, see DESCENT.

---

ascertain, *v.t.*   find, discover, make sure of, LEARN. See KNOWLEDGE.

ASCETICISM [955]

Nouns—**1,** asceticism, puritanism, austerity; abstinence, abstemiousness; mortification, maceration, sackcloth and ashes, flagellation; penance, fasting. See ATONEMENT.
2, ascetic, anchoret, anchorite, hermit, RECLUSE; puritan, sabbatarian.
Adjectives—ascetic, austere, puritanical, anchoritic; abstinent, abstemious.
Antonym, see PLEASURE, GLUTTONY.

ascribe, *v.t.* refer, impute, accredit; assign.
ashamed, *adv.* abashed, mortified, embarrassed. See REGRET, MODESTY.
ashen, *adj.* pale, waxen, gray, bloodless, wan. See COLORLESSNESS.
ashore, *adj.* on land, on shore. See LAND.
ask, *v.* interrogate, question, inquire; REQUEST, demand; plead, beg, entreat, beseech, implore. See INQUIRY.
askew, *adj.* crooked, awry, lopsided, oblique. See DISTORTION. *Ant.,* STRAIGHT.
aspect, *n.* look, APPEARANCE, side, view; expression, mien, bearing; phase, stage.
aspire, *v.i.* seek, desire, aim, strive (for). See HOPE.
ass, *n.* donkey, jackass, burro; fool, simpleton. See CARRIER, FOOL.
assail, *v.t.* ATTACK, set upon, assault; criticize. See OPPOSITION.
assassin, *n.* killer, slayer, murderer, thug. See KILLING.

ASSEMBLAGE [72]

Nouns—**1,** assemblage, assembly, gathering, forgathering, convocation, congregation, council, caucus, conclave, congress, convention, concourse, conflux, convergence; muster, levy, mobilization, posse, *posse comitatus,* roundup; caravan, convoy. See SOCIALITY.
2, compilation, collection, miscellany, store, compendium; symposium, panel; library, museum, menagerie; treasury, anthology.
3, crowd, throng; flood, rush, deluge; rabble, mob, press, crush, horde, body, tribe; crew, gang, knot, squad, band, party; swarm, shoal, school, covey, flock, herd, drove; array, bevy, galaxy; clique, coterie, faction, set, fraternity, sorority; corps, company, troop, army, host, MULTITUDE; clan, brotherhood, fellowship, association, PARTY.
4, volley, shower, storm, cloud; group, cluster, clump, set, batch, lot, pack; budget, assortment, bunch, bundle, fascine, bale; shock, rick, fardel, stack, sheaf, haycock.
5, accumulation, congeries, heap, lump, pile, agglomeration, conglomeration, aggregation, concentration, congestion, quantity.
Verbs—**1,** be *or* come together, assemble, collect, muster; meet, unite, join, rejoin; cluster, flock, swarm, surge, stream, herd, crowd, throng, associate; congregate, conglomerate, concentrate; rendezvous, resort; come, flock *or* get together; forgather; huddle.
2, get *or* bring together, assemble, muster, collect, collocate, call up, gather, convene, convoke, convocate; rake up, dredge; heap, mass, pile, pack, put up, cram; agglomerate, aggregate; compile; group, concentrate, unite, amass, accumulate; scare up.
Adjectives—assembled, closely packed, massed, dense, serried, crowded, teeming, swarming, populous; cumulative.
Antonym, see DISJUNCTION.

ASSENT [488]

Nouns—**1,** assent, acquiescence, admission; nod; accord, accordance, concord, concordance; AGREEMENT, AFFIRMATION; recognition, acknowledgment, avowal; confession (of faith).
2, unanimity, common consent, acclamation, chorus; *vox populi,* public opinion; CONCURRENCE, COÖPERATION, consensus.
3, ratification, confirmation, corroboration, substantiation; approval, acceptance, indorsement, CONSENT; compliance, willingness.
4, alacrity, readiness, eagerness, DESIRE; docility, pliability.
Verbs—**1,** assent, nod, acquiesce, agree; receive, accept, accede, accord, concur, lend oneself to, CONSENT: coincide, reciprocate, go with, be at one with, go along (with), chime in, echo, be in tune with, recognize; subscribe (to), conform (to), defer to; say yes, ditto, amen *or* aye (to), O.K.
2, acknowledge, own, admit, allow, avow, confess, concede, come (a)round to, abide by; confirm, affirm; ratify, approve, indorse, O.K., countersign; corroborate.
3, come to an understanding, come to terms; swim with the stream; be in the fashion, join in the chorus; be in every mouth; catch on (become fashionable).

Adjectives—**1,** assenting; of one accord *or* mind; of the same mind, at one with; agreed, acquiescent, content, willing.

2, uncontradicted, unchallenged, unquestioned, uncontroverted; carried, agreed; unanimous, agreed on all hands, carried by acclamation, affirmative.

Adverbs—**1,** yes, yea, ay, aye; true, good, well, very well, well and good; granted; even so, just so, to be sure; truly, exactly, precisely, that's just it, indeed, certainly, of course, indubitably, unquestionably, surely, sure, assuredly, no doubt, doubtless, and no mistake!; be it so, so be it, amen; willingly. *Slang,* yes sirree, yes sirree Bob!, you said a mouthful, you said it!

2, affirmatively, in the affirmative; with one voice, with one accord, unanimously, by common consent, in chorus, to a man, without a dissentient voice; as one man, one and all, on all hands.

3, willingly, fain, freely; heart and soul; with pleasure, nothing loath, graciously, without reluctance, of one's own accord.

Antonym, see DISSENT.

---

assert, *v.t.*   avow, declare, say, claim, affirm, state. See AFFIRMATION. *Ant.,* see NEGATION.

assess, *v.t.*   value, price, appraise, estimate; charge, tax. See JUDGE.

assets, *n.*   possessions, PROPERTY, goods, capital. *Ant.,* see LIABILITY.

assign, *v.*   give to, hand over; allot, distribute; delegate, commission. See APPORTIONMENT, GIVING.

assimilate, *v.t.*   digest, absorb; incorporate, merge (with). See JUNCTION, CHANGE.

assist, *v.t.*   AID, help, second, support.

associate, *v. & n.*   —*v.* join, fraternize, ally, combine (with), unite, connect, relate, link. See JUNCTION, RELATION. —*n.* friend, comrade; colleague, co-worker, partner.

assort, *v.t.*   arrange, classify; mix. See ARRANGEMENT.

assume, *v.t.*   suppose, take for granted; put on, affect, appropriate. See SUPPOSITION, ACQUISITION.

assure, *v.t.*   certify, make sure; insure, pledge, PROMISE. See CERTAINTY.

astern, *adv.*   aft, to the rear, abaft. See REAR.

astir, *adv.*   afoot; moving; up and about. See ACTIVITY.

astonish, *v.t.*   surprise, amaze, astound. See WONDER.

astray, *adv.*   lost, wandering; wrong, amiss, in error. See DOUBT.

astringent, *adj.*   sour, tart; binding, styptic. See CONTRACTION.

astrology, *n.*   stargazing, soothsaying, forecasting. See PREDICTION.

astronomy, *n.*   cosmology, cosmogony, astrochemistry, astrophysics. See UNIVERSE.

astute, *adj.*   clever, shrewd, quick, acute. See INTELLIGENCE. *Ant.,* STUPID.

asylum, *n.*   retreat, REFUGE, sanctuary, shelter; home, orphanage, sanitarium, sanatorium; mental hospital, psychopathic ward.

atheist, *n.*   heretic, unbeliever. See IRRELIGION. *Ant.,* see BELIEF.

athletic, *adi.*   sporting, gymnastic, acrobatic; agile, powerful, strong. See POWER, AMUSEMENT.

atom, *n.*   particle, iota, speck. See LITTLENESS, POWER.

atomize, *v.t.*   spray, vaporize, pulverize. See VAPOR.

ATONEMENT [952]

Nouns—**1,** atonement, reparation; COMPENSATION, quittance, quits; expiation, redemption, reclamation, conciliation, propitiation. See PENITENCE.

2, amends, apology, *amende honorable,* satisfaction, COMPENSATION; peace offering, burnt offering; scapegoat, sacrifice, sacrificial lamb.

3, penance, fasting, maceration, sackcloth and ashes, white sheet, shrift, flagellation, lustration; purgation, purgatory.

Verbs—**1,** atone (for); expiate; propitiate; make amends, pay for, make good; reclaim, redeem, redress, repair; ransom, absolve, purge, shrive; do penance, repent (in sackcloth and ashes); set one's house in order; wipe off old scores; make matters up; pay the penalty; recant. *Colloq.,* take back, eat one's words, eat humble pie, eat crow.

2, apologize, beg pardon, ask forgiveness, give satisfaction; fall on one's knees.

Adjectives—propitiatory, conciliatory, expiatory; sacrificial, piacular; apologetic.

Antonyms, see RESOLUTION, IMPIETY.

---

atrocity, *n.* outrage, enormity, brutality; barbarism. See MALEVOLENCE.

attach, *v.t.* connect, fasten; join, add on, affix. See ADDITION, JUNCTION.

ATTACK [716]

Nouns—**1,** attack; assault (and battery); onset, onslaught, charge; aggression, offense; WARFARE; incursion, inroad, invasion; irruption, outbreak; sally, sortie, raid, foray; boarding, *escalade;* siege, investment, besiegement, beleaguerment; storming, bombing, air attack, air raid, blitz, blitzkrieg, bombardment, cannonade.

2, fire, volley, fusillade, broadside; raking, crossfire; cut, thrust, lunge, pass; kick, punch; devastation, DESTRUCTION. See IMPULSE.

3, assailant, aggressor, offender, invader; pusher, go-getter.

Verbs—**1,** attack, assault, assail; set *or* fall upon; make *or* go to war (on *or* against); charge, impugn; break a lance with, enter the lists; aggress; assume *or* take the offensive; strike the first blow; throw the first stone; lift a hand *or* draw the sword (against); take up the cudgels; march (against); march upon, invade, harry; show fight.

2, strike (at), thrust at, hit, kick, slap, cut, shy (a stone), pelt; deal a blow (at); fetch one a blow; fling oneself at *or* upon, lunge at, pounce upon; lace into, light into, tear into, pitch into, launch out against; bait, slap on the face; make a pass at; bear down upon; close with, come to grips with, come to close quarters, bring to bay; ride full tilt against; let fly at, rush at, run at, fly at, have at; attack tooth and nail; press one hard; run down, strike at the root of; lay about one, run amuck. *Slang,* lay into; gang up on. See PUNISHMENT, IMPULSE.

3, fire, shoot at; open fire, pepper, bombard, shell, pour a broadside into, fire a volley; beset, besiege, beleaguer; lay siege to, invest; sap, mine; storm, board, scale the walls; cut and thrust, bayonet, butt, batter; bomb, strafe, dive-bomb, blitz.

Adjectives—attacking; aggressive, offensive; up in arms, on the warpath; forceful, belligerent, combative, warlike; competitive, pushing.

Adverb—on the offensive.

Antonym, see DEFENSE.

---

attain, *v.t.* win, gain, achieve; reach, succeed. See ARRIVAL, SUCCESS.

attempt, *n.* trial, effort, try, endeavor, ESSAY.

attend, *v.* accompany, escort; be present; heed, listen. See ACCOMPANIMENT, ATTENTION.

ATTENTION [457]

Nouns—**1,** attention, mindfulness, intentness, intentiveness, THOUGHT, thoughtfulness, advertence; observance, observation, consideration, reflection, heed, notice, note, regard; circumspection, study, scrutiny, inspection.

2, diligence, application, minuteness, attention to detail, absorption (of mind), preoccupation (with).

3, indication, calling *or* drawing attention to.

Verbs—**1,** attend (to), observe, look, see, view, remark, notice, regard, take notice, mark; give *or* pay attention, heed, be attentive, listen, hear, lend an ear to; trouble one's head about; give a thought to; occupy oneself with; contemplate; look into; see to; turn the mind to, apply oneself to, have an eye to; bear in mind, take into account *or* consideration; keep in sight *or* view; have regard to; take cognizance of, entertain, recognize; make *or* take note of; note.

2, glance at *or* over; cast the eye over; run over, dip into, scan, skim (through), examine cursorily. *Slang,* give the once-over.

3, examine closely *or* intently; scan, scrutinize, consider; pore over, inspect,

review, take stock of; fix, rivet *or* devote the mind *or* thoughts on *or* to; go over with a fine-toothed comb.
4, watch, hearken, listen (to); prick up the ears; keep the eyes open *or* peeled; be all ears, hang on one's words; have an ear to the ground.
5, catch *or* strike the eye; attract attention *or* notice; awaken *or* invite interest; be arresting *or* absorbing; intrigue; be uppermost in one's mind.
6, indicate; bring under one's notice; point out; lay the finger on, direct, call *or* draw attention to; show.
Adjectives—**1,** attentive, mindful, observant, regardful; alive *or* awake to; observing; occupied with; engrossed, wrapped up in; absorbed, rapt; breathless; intent on, open-eyed, on the watch.
2, absorbing, engrossing, eye-catching.
Interjections—see! look! mark! lo! behold! hark! mind! observe! lo and behold! attention! *nota bene;* N.B.; this is to give notice.
Antonym, see NEGLECT.

---

attenuate, *v.* weaken; thin out, rarefy. See DECREASE, NARROWNESS.
attic, *n.* upper room, loft, garret. See RECEPTACLE, HEIGHT.
attire, *n.* dress, CLOTHING, garb, array.
attitude, *n.* stand, pose, posture, position. See LOCATION.
attorney, *n.* LAWYER, solicitor, advocate, barrister, AGENT.
attract, *v.* allure, interest, CHARM, captivate, fascinate; draw (see ATTRACTION). See DESIRE, ATTRACTIVE.

ATTRACTION [288]

Nouns—attraction, attractiveness; drawing to, pulling towards, adduction, magnetism, gravity, gravitation; lodestone, lodestar; magnet, siderite.
Verbs—attract; draw *or* pull towards; adduce.
Adjectives—attracting, attrahent, attractive, adducent, adductive; magnetic.
Antonym, see REFUSAL.

---

attractive, *adj.* charming, alluring; engaging, interesting, winning, prepossessing; captivating, fascinating; seductive. *Colloq.,* cute.
attribute, *v.t. & n.* —*v.t.* impute, ascribe, assign, refer; charge to; blame *or* connect with, derive from. —*n.* trait, characteristic, quality, property; adjunct, symbol. See CAUSE, INTERPRETATION.
attribution, *n.* ascription; theory; reference to; etiology; accounting for; imputation, derivation from; affiliation, connection with. See CAUSE, INTERPRETATION.
audacity, *n.* boldness, COURAGE, nerve, temerity, daring, brass, gall; impudence; confidence, RASHNESS, insolence.
audience, *n.* hearing, interview; onlookers, hearers; assembly. See DRAMA, SPEECH.
auditorium, *n.* hall, meeting place; theater. See DRAMA.
august, *adj.* grand, noble, exalted, majestic, venerable. See GREATNESS.
auspicious, *adj.* favorable, promising, propitious; fortunate. See HOPE, PREDICTION, PROSPERITY. *Ant.,* UNFORTUNATE, UNTIMELY.
austere, *adj.* harsh, stern, severe, rigorous; ascetic, abstemious. See SEVERITY, ASCETICISM. *Ant.,* LUXURIOUS.
authentic, *adj.* genuine, real, authoritative, trustworthy. See TRUTH, CERTAINTY. *Ant.,* sham, false; see FALSEHOOD.
author, *n.* creator, originator; writer, inventor. See BOOK, WRITING, PRODUCTION.

AUTHORITY [737]

Nouns—**1,** authority, power, right, jurisdiction, title, prerogative; influence, prestige, patronage; command, control, rule, sway; dominion, sovereignty, empire, supremacy; suzerainty, seigniory; the crown, the sovereign; the state, realm, administration, people, body politic, polity; divine right, dynasticism, dynasty, régime.
2, government, administration; autocracy, aristocracy, oligarchy, hierarchy, theocracy, patriarchy, plutocracy, democracy; monarchy, absolute monarchy, kingdom, chiefdom; caliphate, pashalik; proconsulship, consulship;

prefecture, magistracy; directory, triumvirate, *etc.;* absolutism, despotism, tyranny, imperialism, czarism, dictatorship, authoritarianism, Fascism, Nazism, monolithic government, *Führer prinzip,* boss rule; communism, Marxism, socialism, syndicalism, collectivism, People's Republic; anarchism, nihilism; bureaucracy, red tape, officialdom; feudalism, feodality; gynarchy, gynocracy, matriarchy, petticoat government; autonomy, home rule, representative government; constitutional government, constitutional *or* limited monarchy.

3, mastery, hold, grasp, grip; octopus, fangs, clutches, talons; rod of empire, scepter.

4, usurpation, assumption *or* arrogation of authority.

5, sovereign, ruler, emperor, empress, king, queen, prince, princess; czar, tsar, Kaiser; boss, dictator, Duce, Führer, despot, tyrant, Pharaoh, judge, autocrat; president, chairman, the chair, premier, prime *or* first minister; potentate, chief, caliph, sultan, pasha, emir, sheik; master, captain, skipper, commanding officer, person in authority.

6, accession, succession, installation, coronation.

7, master, lord, *padrone;* superior, director, head, leader, foreman; mayor, *major domo,* prefect, chancellor, provost, magistrate, alcalde, burgomaster, seneschal, warden.

Verbs—**1,** have *or* wield authority; head, lead, command; dominate, control, boss; dictate, dispose, command, rule, govern, administer; preside; wear the crown, ascend the throne; have the upper *or* whip hand; rule the roost; lord it over, bend to one's will, give the law to, lay down the law; have under one's thumb, hold in the hollow of one's hand.

2, be under, subject to, *or* in the power of.

Adjectives—**1,** ruling, regnant, at the head, dominant, paramount, supreme, predominant, preponderant, in the ascendant, influential; gubernatorial; imperious; authoritative, executive, administrative, clothed with authority, official, *ex officio;* imperative, peremptory, overruling, absolute; arbitrary.

2, regal, sovereign, royal, monarchical, kingly, imperial, princely.

3, at one's command; in one's power; under control.

Adverbs—at one's pleasure; by a stroke of the pen; *ex cathedra;* with a high hand.

Antonyms, see SUBJECTION, OBEDIENCE.

---

autocrat, *n.* dictator, czar, despot, monarch. See AUTHORITY.

autograph, *n.* signature. See WRITING, EVIDENCE.

automatic, *adj.* mechanical; self-operating; instinctive. See NECESSITY.

automobile, *adj. & n.* —*adj.* self-propelling. See POWER. —*n.* car, VEHICLE.

autonomy, *n.* independence; self-government. See FREEDOM.

autopsy, *n.* post-mortem, examination (of cadaver). See INTERMENT.

autumn, *n.* fall, harvest time. See TIME.

auxiliary, *n. & adj.* —*n.* recruit, AID, assistant, helper; ADJUNCT, adjutant, aide; partner, colleague, mate, ally, friend, accomplice, confederate; accessory; branch. —*adj.* helping, helpful, accessory; subsidiary, subservient. See ADDITION. *Ant.,* see HINDRANCE.

avail, *v.* serve, do, suffice; help, benefit; use. See SUCCESS, UTILITY.

available, *adj.* handy, ready, convenient; usable. See PREPARATION, UTILITY. *Ant.,* unavailable; see ABSENCE.

avalanche, *n.* landslide, snowslide; overwhelming victory. See DESCENT, SUCCESS.

avenge, *n.* retaliate, REVENGE.

average, *n. & adj.* —*n.* normal, mean, rule, standard. —*adj.* mean, normal, ordinary, passable, fair. See MIDDLE, UNIMPORTANCE.

averse, *adj.* loath, reluctant, against, opposed, unwilling. See OPPOSITION, DISAPPROBATION. *Ant.,* willing.

avert, *v.t.* keep off, turn aside, ward off; turn away; prevent. See HINDRANCE.

AVIATION [268]

Nouns—**1,** aviation, flight, flying; avigation, aerial navigation; aeronautics, aerodynamics, aerostatics; air power, air transportation, airline (scheduled *and* nonscheduled), air coach; airways, airport, airfield, airdrome, landing field, flying field, runway, control tower, windsock; ballooning, balloonery.

2, air warfare; Air Force, RAF, Luftwaffe; formation flying, echelon; bombing, dive-bombing, pursuit, dogfight; group, wing, flight, squadron.

3, aircraft, heavier-than-air, lighter-than-air; balloon, captive balloon, observation balloon, barrage balloon; airship, dirigible, Zeppelin, blimp; airplane, aeroplane, plane, monoplane, biplane, wedgewing, seaplane, amphibian, hydroplane, flying boat; airliner, transport, pursuit plane, interceptor, fighter, bomber; jet plane, turbojet, JATO; autogiro, helicopter, whirlybird, Sikorsky; kite, boxkite; glider, crate, box, ship, jenny; parachute.

4, fuselage, tail, rudder, fin, stabilizer; cockpit, gondola, nacelle; propeller, prop; reciprocating engine, radial engine, jet engine, rocket; airfoil, wing, aileron, elevator; stick, Joyce *or* joy stick; landing gear, pontoon, altimeter, artificial horizon, artificial pilot, tachometer, airspeed indicator, rate-of-climb indicator, turn and bank indicator, inclinometer; bomb bay.

5, takeoff, landing, three-point landing, pancake; zoom, loop, loop-the-loop, soar, climb, glide; Immelmann turn, barrel roll; dive, nose dive, spiral, spin, tailspin; buzz, hedgehopping; thrust, lift, drag; airstream, slipstream, backwash, sideslip, drift; flying circus, barnstorming, stunt flying; skywriting; point of no return; visibility, ceiling, ceiling zero; air pocket, headwind, tailwind.

6, aviator, aeronaut, airman, balloonist, pilot, co-pilot, navigatior, bombardier; Daedalus, Icarus, Darius Green; air marshal, flying officer; airborne troops, paratroops.

7, space travel, spaceship; launching site, Cape Canaveral; rocket, stage, drop-off, capsule; escape velocity, orbit, free fall, weightlessness; astronaut, cosmonaut, Abel, Baker, Leika; countdown, [number] for go.

Verbs—fly, aviate, pilot, go by air; zoom, climb, stall, yaw, pitch, roll, bank, dive, glide, taxi, take off, land; stunt, buzz, hedgehop; strafe, dive-bomb; crash, crack up, prang, conk out, bail out.

Adjectives—aeronautic; airworthy; air-minded; airsick; airborne.

---

avidity, *n.* eagerness, longing; avarice, greed, DESIRE.

avocation, *n.* hobby. See AMUSEMENT, BUSINESS.

AVOIDANCE [623]

Nouns—**1,** avoidance, evasion, elusion; abstention, abstinence, forbearance, refraining, INACTIVITY; neutrality, nonbelligerency; retreat, REGRESSION, DEPARTURE, ESCAPE; truancy, hooky, French leave (see ABSENCE); subterfuge, quibble, equivocation; circuit, DEVIATION. *Colloq.*, sidestep, dodge. *Slang,* the slip, the go-by, the runaround, the brush-off.

2, shirker, slacker, malingerer, deserter, absentee, dodger, quitter; truant, fugitive, runaway, absconder, refugee; abstainer, teetotaler, nonparticipant. *Slang,* welsher, goldbrick.

Verbs—**1,** avoid, shun, eschew, refrain (from), not do, let alone, steer clear of, fight shy of; abstain, keep aloof, keep one's distance; evade, elude, dodge; give a wide berth to, set one's face against; shy away from; make way for, give place to; take no part in, have no hand in.

2, decamp, fly, bolt, elope, abscond; depart, go away; show *or* take to one's heels, beat a retreat, make oneself scarce, run for it, cut and run, steal away, slip off, take off; walk out on, go back on. *Colloq.*, shake off. *Slang,* skedaddle, shove off, skiddoo, take it on the lam, vamoose.

Antonym, see PURSUIT.

---

await, *v.* expect, wait for, anticipate, look forward to; impend, approach. See EXPECTATION, FUTURITY, LATENESS.

awake, *adj.* alert, heedful, observant, attentive. See ATTENTION.

award, *n.* prize, medal; compensation; decision, adjudication. See GIVING, JUDGMENT.

aware, *adj.* knowing, cognizant, informed; alert (to). See KNOWLEDGE.

away, *adv.* absent, elsewhere, far-off, gone. See DISTANCE.

awe, *n.* reverence, respect; FEAR, dread.

awkward, *adj.* clumsy, ungraceful, ungainly; gauche; embarrassing. See UNSKILLFULNESS.

ax, axe, *n.* sharp tool, chopper, hatchet. See ARMS, SHARPNESS.
axiom, *n.* rule, proposition; aphorism, maxim, truism. See TEACHING.
axis, *n* shaft, pivot; combination, league. See ROTATION.
axle, *n.* axis, spindle, pivot. See MIDDLE.
azure, *adj.* BLUE, sky-blue, cerulean. See COLOR.

B

babble, *v.i.* chatter, prattle, gossip; rave, gibber; gurgle. See LOQUACITY, ABSURDITY.
baby, *n.* INFANT, babe, child, tot; nursling, suckling; offspring. *Colloq.,* kid. *Ant.,* VETERAN.
bachelor, *n.* unmarried man, Coelebs, celebate. See CELIBACY. *Ant.,* see MARRIAGE.
back, *n. & v.* —*n.* REAR; behind, posterior, reverse; stern, aft; derrière. *Ant.,* FRONT. —*v.t.* SUPPORT, AID, assist; promote, finance; stand behind, encourage. —*v.i.* move backward, reverse. *Ant.,* see HINDRANCE.
backward, *adj.* retarded, slow, underdeveloped; delayed, tardy; unwilling, loath. See DULL, REAR.
badge, *n.* emblem, identification, label, sign. See INDICATION.

BADNESS [649]

Nouns—**1,** badness, hurtfulness, virulence, perniciousness, malignancy, malignity; ill-treatment, annoyance, molestation, abuse, oppression, persecution, outrage, tyranny; atrocity, torture, brutality, cruelty; injury, damage; ill turn, bad turn; peccancy, abomination; painfulness, pestilence, DISEASE; guilt, depravity, vice, IMPURITY, wickedness. See MALEVOLENCE.
2, bane, plague-spot, insalubrity; evil star, ill wind; skeleton in the closet, thorn in the side, thorn in the flesh.
3, bad influence, evil genius; imprecation, malediction, anathema. *Colloq.,* hoodoo. *Slang,* Jonah, jinx. See EVIL, EVILDOER.
4, imperfection, defectiveness, poorness, inferiority, mediocrity, indifference, ERROR, wrong.
5, IMPROBITY, knavery, immorality, turpitude, depravity, corruption; debasement, degradation, pollution; profligacy; atrocity.
Verbs—**1,** hurt, harm, injure, PAIN, wound; maltreat, abuse, ill-treat; molest; buffet, bruise, scratch, maul; smite, SCOURGE, crucify, break on the wheel *or* rack; do violence, do harm, do a mischief (to); stab, pierce, outrage, violate. *Colloq.,* kick around.
2, wrong, aggrieve, oppress, persecute; trample upon, tread upon, put upon; overburden, weigh down, victimize.
3, be vicious, sin, err, transgress, go astray; misdo, misbehave; fall, lapse, slip; trespass, deviate, sow one's wild oats.
Adjectives—**1,** bad, ill, untoward, arrant, as bad as can be, dreadful; horrid, horrible; dire; rank, peccant, foul, fulsome; rotten, rotten at the core, decayed, decomposed, putrid, tainted. *Slang,* cheesy, punk, lousy.
2, hurtful, harmful, baneful, baleful; injurious, deleterious, UNHEALTHY, detrimental, pernicious, mischievous, full of mischief, mischief-making, malefic, malignant, noxious, nocuous, noisome; prejudicial; disserviceable; disadvantageous; unlucky, sinister; obnoxious; disastrous; inauspicious; oppressive, burdensome, onerous; malign, MALEVOLENT; corrupt, virulent, venomous, envenomed, corrosive; poisonous, toxic, septic, deadly, KILLING, pestilent; destructive.
3, mean, paltry; injured, deteriorated, unsatisfactory, exceptionable, indifferent; below par, INFERIOR, imperfect; ill-contrived, ill-conditioned; wretched, pathetic, sad, grievous, deplorable, lamentable; pitiable; woeful, painful, unfortunate.
4, evil, wrong; depraved, vile, base, villainous; shocking, flagrant, scandalous, nefarious; reprehensible, wicked, sinful; hateful; abominable, repugnant, abhorrent, revolting, repulsive, repellent, disgusting, odious, detest-

able, execrable, cursed, accursed, confounded; damned, damnable; infernal, diabolic, malevolent, devilish; vicious. *Colloq.*, beastly, ungodly.
Adverbs—badly, amiss, awry, wrong, ill; to one's cost; where the shoe pinches.

Antonym, see GOODNESS.

baffle, *v.* foil, frustrate, balk, block; puzzle, nonplus, bewilder. See HINDRANCE.

bag, *n. & v.* —*n.* RECEPTACLE, case, container, pouch, sack. —*v.* trap, capture, take, catch; sag, droop, hang; bulge, protrude, swell. See TAKING.

bail, *n.* SECURITY, bond, pledge; guarantee, surety.

bait, *n. & v.* —*n.* lure, temptation. —*v.t.* decoy, lure, tempt; plague, worry, badger, ruffle. See ATTRACTION, PAIN.

bake, *v.* roast, cook; harden, dry; fire. See HARDNESS, HEAT.

balance, *n. & v.* —*n.* equilibrium, steadiness, stability; surplus, excess, rest, remainder; scales. See EQUALITY. —*v.* offset, even, square; equalize, level, adjust; equal, match. See NUMBER, RELATION.

bald, *adj.* bare, unadorned; hairless; treeless; undisguised. See DIVESTMENT.

balk, *v.* rebel; stop, shy; disappoint, hinder, thwart, foil, frustrate. See HINDRANCE, FAILURE.

ball, *n.* dance, reception, party; shot, projectile; sphere, globe. See AMUSEMENT, ARMS, CIRCULARITY.

ballot, *n. & v.* —*n.* vote, CHOICE, poll; franchise, VOICE. —*v.* poll, vote.

balm, *n.* ointment, salve, analgesic; sedative, anodyne. See MODERATION, REMEDY.

ban, *n.* PROHIBITION, restriction, proscription, interdict. See RESTRAINT.

band, *n.* strip, tape; belt, strap; FILAMENT; group, crowd; orchestra, brass band, military band. See ASSEMBLAGE, MUSICAL INSTRUMENTS, COLOR.

bandit, *n.* THIEF, robber, highwayman; brigand; outlaw.

bane, *n.* curse, mischief; thorn in the side, scourge, PAIN, nuisance, pest; harm, injury, DESTRUCTION; trouble; bale; poison, venom. See PUNISHMENT, EVIL, MALEVOLENCE. *Ant.*, see REMEDY, BENEVOLENCE, GOODNESS.

banish, *v.t.* exile, dismiss. expel. See EJECTION, PUNISHMENT. *Ant.*, repatriate; see RECEIVING.

bank, *n. & v.* —*n.* slope, hillside; mound, heap, ridge; beach, shore. See OBLIQUITY, LAND. —*v.* tilt, angle, slope. See ANGULARITY, AVIATION.

bankrupt, *adj. & v.* —*adj.* insolvent, ruined; indigent, penniless, destitute. *Slang*, broke. —*v.* impoverish; pauperize. See DEBT, FAILURE, POVERTY. *Ant.*, see MONEY, SUCCESS.

banner, *n.* flag, pennant; symbol, badge. See INDICATION.

banter, *n.* jest, chaff, badinage. *Colloq.*, kid. See WIT.

baptize, *v.* sprinkle, immerse, dip; name, christen; cleanse. *Colloq.*, dunk. See NOMENCLATURE, RITE.

bar, *n. & v.* —*n.* barrier, obstacle; hurdle; legal profession, court, bench; rod, bolt, rail. See PRISON, LAWYER, LAWSUIT. —*v.* forbid; restrict, reject; lock, bolt, fasten. See RESTRAINT. *Ant.*, see PERMISSION.

barbarian, *n.* foreigner, outsider, alien, savage, ruffian; EVILDOER.

bare, *adj.* unclothed, nude; uncovered; empty, unfurnished; mere, simple. See DIVESTMENT, INSUFFICIENCY. *Ant.*, see CLOTHING, SUFFICIENCY.

bargain, *n. & v.* —*n.* deal, agreement, transaction; inexpensiveness. See CHEAPNESS, AGREEMENT. *Ant.*, see PAYMENT. —*v.* contract, negotiate, haggle, BARTER.

bark, *n. & v.* —*n.* COVERING, rind, skin, shell; yelp, yap, bag. —*v.* howl, yelp. See CRY.

barrage, *n.* ATTACK, bombardment, *Ant.*, see DEFENSE.

barren, *adj.* unfertile, unprofitable; sterile; stark, bare; UNPRODUCTIVE.

barrier, *n.* obstacle, impediment, HINDRANCE, See INCLOSURE, PRISON.

barter, *n. & v.* —*n.* deal, swapping, exchange, trading. —*v.* swap, exchange, trade; dicker, bargain; traffic in, deal in. See BUSINESS, SALE.

base, *n. & v.* —*n.* basis, foundation, groundwork, SUPPORT; basement, substructure; ground; root; footing, floor; pavement; bottom; bedrock. —*v.* found, establish; predicate; ground, rest upon, build upon. *Ant.*, see HEIGHT.

base, *adj.* debased, impure; counterfeit, spurious; low, vile, despicable. See DISREPUTE, IMPURITY. *Ant.*, see REPUTE, VIRTUE.

bashful, *adj.* shy, diffident, self-effacing, timid. See MODESTY. *Ant.*, see VANITY.

basin, *n.* bowl, vessel, sink; hollow, valley. See CONCAVITY, RECEPTACLE. *Ant.*, see CONVEXITY.

basis, *n.* base, groundwork, foundation. See SUPPORT. *Ant.*, see HEIGHT.

basket, *n.* hamper, crate, pannier. See RECEPTACLE.

bass, *adj.* low, deep-toned, deep. See SOUND.

bath, *n.* washing, wash; dip, plunge; shower, Turkish bath. See CLEANNESS, WATER.

batter, *v.* smash, dent, destroy; beat, bruise. See DESTRUCTION, IMPULSE. *Ant.*, see SAFETY.

battle, *n.* fight, struggle, engagement, combat; contest. See WARFARE.

bay, *n.* estuary, bayou, fiord, sound.

be, *v.* exist, breathe; occur, take place. See EXISTENCE. *Ant.*, see NON-EXISTENCE.

beak, *n.* nose, bill, neb. *Slang,* magistrate. See CONVEXITY.

beam, *v. & n.* —*v.* shine, glow. —*n.* ray, gleam; joist, timber. See LIGHT, MATERIALS, SUPPORT.

bear, *v.* endure, tolerate; suffer; render, yield, hold, sustain; carry, transport, convey. See FEELING, PRODUCTION, SUPPORT.

bearded, *adj.* hairy, whiskered, awned, hirsute. See ROUGHNESS.

bearing, *n.* course, trend; carriage, manner; MEANING, significance, import; RELATION, connection, association. See DIRECTION, FRONT, PRESENCE.

beast, *n.* brute, quadruped; horse; blackguard. See ANIMAL, CARRIER, DISCOURTESY.

beat, *n. & v.* —*n.* accent, rhythm; pulse; track, course. See POETRY, REGULARITY, WAY. —*v.* throb, pulsate; strike, batter, bruise; conquer, defeat. See OSCILLATION, IMPULSE, PUNISHMENT, SUPERIORITY.

beatify, *v.* sanctify, hallow, consecrate, bless. See PIETY.

BEAUTY [845]

Nouns—**1,** beauty, the beautiful, loveliness, attractiveness; form, elegance, grace, charm, beauty unadorned; symmetry; comeliness, fairness, pulchritude; polish, style, gloss; good looks.

2, bloom, brilliancy, radiance, splendor, gorgeousness, magnificence; grandeur, glory; delicacy, refinement, elegance.

3, Venus, Hebe, the Graces, peri, houri, goddess; witch, enchantress; charmer, reigning beauty, belle; Adonis, Narcissus. *Colloq.,* eyeful, picture, dream, stunner, peach, knockout, raving beauty, good-looker.

4, beautifying; make-up, cosmetics; decoration, adornment, embellishment, ORNAMENTATION.

Adjectives—**1,** beautiful, beauteous; handsome; pretty, lovely, graceful, elegant; delicate, dainty, refined; fair, personable, comely, seemly; bonny, good-looking; well-favored, well-made, well-formed, well-proportioned; proper, shapely; symmetrical, regular, harmonious, sightly. *Colloq.,* easy on the eyes, nifty, stunning, devastating.

2, brilliant, shining; splendid, resplendent, dazzling, glowing; glossy, sleek; rich, gorgeous, superb, magnificent, grand, fine, sublime.

3, artistic, aesthetic; picturesque, well-composed, well-grouped; enchanting, attractive, becoming, ornamental; undeformed, undefaced, unspotted; spotless, immaculate; PERFECT, flawless.

Antonym, see UGLINESS.

because, *adv. & conj.* —*adv.* by reason of, owing to. —*conj.* since, for, for the reason that, as. See CAUSE.

become, *v.t.* befit, accord with, behoove; turn into, change to. See DUTY, CHANGE.

beckon, *v.* signal, summon, call. See INDICATION.

bed, *n.* couch, cot, resting place; BASE, foundation; garden. See SUPPORT.

befit, *v.t.* suit, harmonize with, fit; become, behoove. See AGREEMENT, DUTY. *Ant.*, see NEGLECT, DISAGREEMENT.

before, *adv.* foremost, ahead; forward; sooner, previously, heretofore. See
FRONT, PRIORITY. *Ant.*, see REAR, SEQUENCE.

beg, *v.* implore, beseech, petition, ask; ask alms. See POVERTY, REQUEST.

beget, *v.t.* engender, procreate, reproduce, generate. See PRODUCTION.

BEGINNING [66]

Nouns—**1,** beginning, commencement, opening, outset, incipience, inception;
introduction; alpha, initial; installation, inauguration, debut; embarkation,
rising of the curtain, curtain raiser; outbreak, onset; initiative, move, first
move; thin end of the wedge; fresh start, new departure. *Colloq.*, kickoff,
take-off; coming-out.

2, origin, CAUSE; source, rise; bud, germ, egg, embryo, rudiment; genesis,
birth, nativity, cradle, infancy; start, starting point; dawn, morning.

3, title page; head, heading, caption, title; introduction, prelude, prologue,
preamble, preface, foreword; front, forefront, van, vanguard.

4, entrance, entry, INGRESS; inlet, orifice, mouth, lips; porch, portal, portico,
door; gate, gateway; postern, wicket, threshold, vestibule; outskirts, border,
EDGE, frontier.

5, rudiments, elements, outlines, grammar, primer, alphabet, ABC, first
principles. See PREPARATION.

Verbs—**1,** begin, commence, rise, arise, originate, conceive, initiate, introduce, inaugurate; open, dawn, set in, enter upon; set out, DEPART; embark
in; make one's debut; set about, get under way, set to work, make a beginning *or* start; take the first step; break ground, break the ice, break cover;
cross the Rubicon; open fire; undertake. *Colloq.*, get going.

3, usher in; lead off, lead the way, take the lead, start from scratch, take the
initiative; inaugurate, head; lay the foundations, prepare, found, CAUSE,
set up, set on foot, start the ball rolling; launch, broach; open the door to.

Adjectives—**1,** initial, initiatory, initiative; primary, pristine; inceptive, introductory, incipient; inaugural; embryonic, rudimentary; primeval, primordial, primitive, aboriginal; natal.

2, first, foremost, leading; maiden.

Adverbs—at the beginning, in the beginning; first, in the first place, *imprimis*,
first and foremost; in the bud, in its infancy; from the beginning, from its
birth; *ab initio;* formerly, heretofore. *Colloq.*, from the word go, at the
drop of a hat.

Antonym, END.

---

behalf, *n.* interest, benefit, advantage. See SUBSTITUTION.

behave, *v.i.* act, bear oneself, conduct oneself. See ACTION, CONDUCT.

behead, *v.t.* decapitate, decollate. See KILLING, PUNISHMENT.

behind, *adv. & prep.* —*adv.* rearward, aft, backward; after, subsequently.
—*prep.* in back of, following. See REAR.

being, *n.* life, EXISTENCE, subsistence; person, creature. See SUBSTANCE.
Ant., see NONEXISTENCE.

BELIEF [484]

Nouns—**1,** belief; credence; credit; assurance; faith, trust, troth, confidence,
presumption, dependence on, reliance on. *Colloq.*, store. *Slang*, stock.

2, persuasion, conviction, CERTAINTY; opinion, mind, view; conception,
thinking; impression, IDEA; surmise, conclusion, JUDGMENT.

3, tenet, dogma, principle, precept, article of faith; ASSENT; system of opin-
ions, school doctrine, articles, canons; declaration *or* profession of faith;
tenets, creed, orthodoxy; catechism, TEACHING, cult, ism; PROPAGANDA.

4, credibility, believability, plausibility; PROBABILITY.

Verbs—**1,** believe, credit; give credence to; see, realize; assume, receive; take
for; take it; consider, esteem, presume; count on, depend on, pin one's
faith on, rely on, swear by; take on trust *or* credit; take for granted *or* gospel.
Colloq., set store by, bet on, bank on, bet one's bottom dollar on. *Slang*,
take stock in.

2, know, know for certain; have no doubt; rest assured; persuade *or* satisfy
oneself; make up one's mind.

3, confide in, believe in, put one's trust in; take one's word for, take at one's word.
4, think, hold; opine, be of opinion, conceive, fancy, apprehend; have, hold, entertain, hazard *or* cherish a belief *or* an opinion.
5, satisfy, persuade, assure; convince, convict, convert; wean, bring round; bring *or* win over; indoctrinate, TEACH; carry conviction; bring home to.
Adjectives—certain, sure, assured, positive, cocksure, satisfied, confident, unhesitating, convinced, secure; indubitable, undeniable, indisputable, incontrovertible; credible, reliable, trustworthy, infallible, to be depended on; satisfactory; probable; persuasive, impressive. See CREDULITY.

Antonym, see DOUBT.

---

belittle, *v.t.* run down, disparage, depreciate, dwarf, slight. See DETRACTION. *Ant.*, see APPROBATION.
bell, *n.* alarm, signal, call; chime; ring. See INDICATION.
belligerent, *adj.* warlike, pugnacious, quarrelsome. See CONTENTION. *Ant.*, see PACIFICATION.
bellow, *v.i.* roar, shout, bawl. See CRY.
belong, *v.i.* merge, form part of; be someone's; relate to. See JUNCTION, POSSESSION, RELATION.
below, *adv. & prep.* —*adv.* subordinate, lower, underneath. —*prep.* under, beneath. See INFERIORITY, LOWNESS. *Ant.*, ABOVE.
belt, *n. & v.* —*n.* girdle, band; strip; zone; circuit. —*v.t.* bind, encircle. *Colloq.*, whip. See CIRCULARITY.
bench, *n.* seat, settee; court, bar; board. See SUPPORT, LAWSUIT.
bend, *n. & v.* —*n.* curve, turn; angle, fork. See ANGULARITY, CURVATURE. *Ant.*, see DIRECTION. —*v.i.* give, yield; curve, bend. —*v.t.* control; shape. See SOFTNESS.
beneath, *adv. & prep.* —*adv.* underfoot, under, below. —*prep.* under; unworthy of. See LOWNESS. *Ant.*, ABOVE.
benefactor, *n.* good *or* guardian angel; friend, helper, patron; altruist, philanthropist, good Samaritan, savior, sponsor, friend-in-need. See AID, GIVING, BENEVOLENCE. *Ant.*, see EVILDOER.
beneficial, *adj.* useful, helpful, salutary, advantageous. See GOODNESS, USE. *Ant.*, see EVIL, WASTE.
benefit, *n. & v.* —*n.* profit, advantage, gain, GOOD, avail. See USE. —*v.* help, serve, assist; improve. See BENEVOLENCE, UTILITY. *Ant.*, MALEVOLENCE, EVIL.

BENEVOLENCE [906]

Nouns—**1,** benevolence, Christian charity; God's grace; good will; altruism, PHILANTHROPY, unselfishness; good nature, kindness, kindliness, loving-kindness, benignity, brotherly love, charity, humanity, fellow-feeling, sympathy; goodness of heart; *bonhomie;* kindheartedness; amiability, milk of human kindness, tenderness; LOVE; FRIENDSHIP; tolerance, consideration, generosity; mercy, PITY.
2, charitableness, bounty, almsgiving; good works, beneficence, act of kindness, good turn; good offices, labor of love; public service, social science, sociology.
3, philanthropist, good Samaritan, sympathizer, altruist, humanitarian. See BENEFACTOR, GIVING, GOODNESS.
Verbs—bear good will; mean well by; wish well; take an interest in, sympathize with, feel for; have one's heart in the right place; do as you would be done by; meet halfway; treat well; give comfort, do a good turn; benefit, render a service, be of use; AID, philanthropize; heap coals of fire on [a person's] head.
Adjectives—**1,** benevolent, benign; kindly, well-meaning; amiable, cordial, obliging, accommodating, indulgent, gracious, complacent, good-humored; unselfish, magnanimous; warmhearted, kindhearted; merciful, charitable, beneficent, altruistic, humane, bounteous, bountiful; public-spirited.
2, good-natured; sympathetic; complaisant, courteous; well-meant, well-intentioned; LIBERAL, generous, gracious.
3, fatherly, motherly, brotherly, sisterly; paternal, maternal, fraternal.

Adverbs—benevolently, charitably, with good intentions, with the best intentions; with all one's heart; liberally, generously.

Antonym, see MALEVOLENCE.

---

bequest, *n.* legacy, inheritance; patrimony; heritage. See GIVING.

bereft, *adj.* bereaved, deprived of, denuded. See LOSS. *Ant.*, see ACQUISITION.

berth, *n.* bunk, compartment; position, office; lodging. See BUSINESS, SUPPORT.

beside, *prep.* by, near, alongside, abreast. See NEARNESS. *Ant.*, see DISTANCE.

besides, *adv.* also, further, moreover. See ADDITION.

besiege, *v.t.* surround, beleaguer, storm; plague, pester. See ATTACK. *Ant.*, see DEFENSE.

best, *adj.* choice, precious, unequalled, unparalleled. See GOODNESS, PERFECTION. *Ant.*, see EVIL, IMPERFECTION.

bestow, *v.t.* donate, present, confer, give, bequeath. See GIVING. *Ant.*, see RECEIVING.

bet, *v.* wager, stake, gamble, play. See CHANCE.

betray, *v.* play false, trick; divulge, reveal. See DECEPTION, DISCLOSURE.

betrothal, *n.* engagement, espousal. See MARRIAGE.

better, *v.t.* mend, correct, relieve; defeat. See IMPROVEMENT. *Ant.*, see DETERIORATION.

BETWEEN [228]

Nouns—**1,** interjacence, intervenience, interlocation, interpenetration; permeation; interjection, interpolation, interlineation, interspersion, intercalation; interlocution, aside; parenthesis; episode; fly-leaf; embolism; intervention, interference, interposition, intrusion, obtrusion; insinuation; INSERTION, dovetailing; infiltration; partition, septum, diaphragm, midriff; party-wall, panel; half-way house.

2, intermediary; go-between, middleman, medium; intruder, interloper, trespasser, meddler. *Slang*, buttinsky, chiseler, gate-crasher.

Verbs—**1,** intervene, slide in, interpenetrate, permeate; pervade.

2, put between, introduce, import; interpose, interject, intercalate, interpolate, interline, interleave, intersperse, interweave, interlard; INSERT; sandwich, let in, wedge in, worm in, run in, work in, dovetail, splice, mortise; insinuate, smuggle; infiltrate, ingrain; interfere, put an oar in, thrust one's nose in; intrude, obtrude; have a finger in the pie. *Slang*, butt in, horn in, barge in, muscle in.

Adjectives—interjacent, intervenient, intervening, intermediate, intermediary, intercalary, interstitial; embolismal; parenthetical; episodic, mediterranean; intrusive; interfering; merged.

Adverbs & Prepositions—between, betwixt; among, amongst; amid, amidst; in the thick of; betwixt and between; parenthetically, *obiter dictum.*

Antonym, see EXTERIOR.

---

beverage, *n.* liquor, drink, potable. See FOOD.

beware, *v.* take care, be on guard; avoid, shun. See WARNING.

bewilder, *v.t.* puzzle, confuse, perplex; daze, stagger. See DOUBT, SECRET, WONDER.

beyond, *adv. & prep.* —*adv.* farther, yonder. —*prep.* over; past. See DISTANCE, SUPERIORITY. *Ant.*, see NEARNESS, INFERIORITY.

bias, *n. & v.* —*n.* prejudice, unfairness, partiality; bent, inclination; slope, diagonal. —*v.t.* influence, sway, prejudice. See DISTORTION, OBLIQUITY, TENDENCY. *Ant.*, see JUSTICE, DIRECTION.

bid, *n. & v.* —*n.* OFFER; invitation. —*v.* COMMAND, REQUEST; invite, enjoin. *Ant.*, see REFUSAL.

bier, *n.* litter, catafalque. See INTERMENT.

big, *adj.* large, bulky, huge; mountainous, enormous; massive, impressive; important, weighty. See GREATNESS, SIZE. *Ant.*, see LITTLENESS.

bigot, *n.* fanatic, dogmatist, zealot, formalist. See CERTAINTY.

bill, *n.* score, reckoning; invoice, statement, dun; account, charges; note, banknote, greenback; BEAK. See ACCOUNTING, MONEY.

billow, *v. & n.* —*v.i.* surge, swell. —*n.* undulation, wave. See WATER.

bind, *v.t.* restrain, secure, fasten; obligate. See COMPULSION, RESTRAINT, JUNCTION. *Ant.,* see DISJUNCTION.

bird, *n.* fowl, songbird, warbler; cock, hen; nestling, fledgling. See ANIMAL.

birth, *n.* origin, creation; genesis, inception; childbirth, parturition, delivery. See BEGINNING, PRODUCTION. *Ant.,* END, DESTRUCTION.

biscuit, *n.* cracker, hardtack, cookie; roll, bun; cake. See FOOD.

bisect, *v.* divide, bifurcate, halve, split, cleave, separate.

bit, *n.* scrap, mite; slice, piece; tool, drill; curb. See PART, LITTLENESS. *Ant.,* WHOLE.

bite, *n. & v.* —*n.* morsel, scrap; wound; itch. —*v.* cut; SNAP, nip. See FOOD.

bitter, *adj.* stinging, cutting; malignant, spiteful; rigorous; acrid, unpalatable. See MALEVOLENCE, SEVERITY. *Ant.,* see BENEVOLENCE, MODERATION.

black, *n. & v.* —*n.* darkness, midnight, Stygian hue, Negro. See COLOR. —*v.t.* shine, polish (shoes).

bladder, *n.* sac, vesicle, blister. See RECEPTACLE.

blade, *n.* cutter, edge; sword; knife; leaf (of grass); dandy, sport. See SHARPNESS, VEGETABLE.

blame, *n. & v.* —*n.* criticism, censure; culpability, GUILT. —*v.t.* charge, reproach, condemn. See ATTRIBUTION, DISAPPROBATION. *Ant.,* see APPROBATION.

bland, *adj.* affable, gracious; mild, unflavored. See COURTESY. *Ant.,* see DISCOURTESY, PUNGENCY.

blank, *adj.* empty, unfilled; vacant, vacuous, expressionless; unloaded. See NONEXISTENCE, INSUBSTANTIALITY.

blanket, *n. & v.* —*n.* COVERING. —*v.t.* cover; conceal.

blare, *n.* blast, peal, fanfare. See LOUDNESS.

blasphemy, *n.* irreverence, profanity; heresy. See IMPIETY. *Ant.,* see PIETY.

blast, *n. & v.* —*n.* explosion; discharge; gust; invective, ATTACK. —*v.t.* destroy, shatter, ruin; explode. See VIOLENCE, DESTRUCTION. *Ant.,* see PRODUCTION.

blaze, *n.* fire, flame; mark, spot. See HEAT, INDICATION.

bleach, *v.t.* whiten, blanch, lighten, dye. See COLORLESSNESS.

bleak, *adj.* raw, desolate, unsheltered; discouraging, unauspicious. See COLD, ADVERSITY.

bleed, *v.* flow, hemorrhage; let blood; overcharge, fleece; suffer. *Colloq.,* soak, skin. See PAIN, PAYMENT.

blemish, *n. & v.* —*n.* flaw, defect, disfigurement, IMPERFECTION; spot, taint, mark, stain, blot; wen, mole, pimple, scar; smear, smudge. —*v.* disfigure, mar, flaw, spoil; bruise, rot; stain; discolor, smear, spot, smudge; injure, harm, hurt; sully, disgrace, tarnish. *Ant.,* see CLEANNESS, PERFECTION.

blend, *n. & v.* —*n.* combination, MIXTURE, cross-breed. —*v.* merge, amalgamate; shade.

bless, *v.t.* hallow, glorify, consecrate; praise; thank. See DEITY.

blight, *n. & v.* —*n.* DETERIORATION, decay, rot; rust, smut. —*v.t.* stunt, rot, impair, corrupt; thwart, foil. See PAIN.

BLINDNESS [442]

*Nouns—***1,** blindness, sightlessness, anopsia; blind spot; amaurosis; cataract; DIMSIGHTEDNESS, benightedness; darkness.

2, Braille, Moon's type, New York point, American Braille; seeing-eye dog.

*Verbs—*be blind, not see; lose sight; grope in the dark; blind, darken, benight, obscure, eclipse, hide; put one's eyes out, gouge; blindfold, hoodwink, throw dust into one's eyes; screen, hide, dazzle. See CONCEALMENT.

*Adjectives—*blind; eyeless, sightless, unseeing; dark, stone-blind; undiscerning; unperceiving; dimsighted; blind as a bat, a mole *or* an owl.

*Adverbs—*blindly, sightlessly, gropingly; blindfold; darkly.

Antonym, see VISION.

---

blink, *v.* wink; flash, twinkle; disregard, ignore. See VISION, NEGLECT.

bliss, *n.* happiness, ecstasy, rapture, PLEASURE. *Ant.,* see PAIN.

blister, *n.* vesicle; bubble, sac. See RECEPTACLE.

blithe, *adj.* gay, lighthearted, merry. See CHEERFULNESS. *Ant.*, see DEJECTION.

blitz, blitzkrieg, *n.* ATTACK, bombing, raid; victory. See WARFARE.

blizzard, *n.* gale, storm, snowstorm, windstorm. See WIND.

bloat, *v.* distend, swell, puff up. See INCREASE. *Ant.*, see CONTRACTION.

blob, *n.* drop, mass; splash, splotch, blemish. See CONVEXITY.

block, *n. & v.* —*n.* HINDRANCE, obstruction; row, street; square (see ABODE); mass, lump; cube. —*v.t.* impede, check, stop, bar; thwart, foil.

blond, *adj.* light-colored, fair-skinned; light-haired, golden, yellow, flaxen, platinum. See COLORLESSNESS.

blood, *n.* serum, essence; gore; kindred, relationship, kinship; sap. See RELATION, FLUIDITY.

bloodletting, *n.* phlebotomy, venesection. See REMEDY.

bloodshed, *n.* KILLING; slaughter, shambles. See WARFARE.

bloodthirsty, *adj.* murderous, savage, inhuman. See KILLING, MALEVOLENCE. *Ant.*, see BENEVOLENCE.

bloom, *n. & v.* —*n.* blossom, flower; flowering. —*v.i.* blossom; mature; glow, flourish, thrive. See HEALTH, PROSPERITY, VEGETABLE.

blossom, *n.* flower, bud, bloom; develop, flourish. See VEGETABLE.

blot, *v. & n.* —*v.* stain, blemish, spot; sully. —*n.* spot, smear, blemish. See DISREPUTE, DESTRUCTION.

blow, *n. & v.* —*n.* knock, stroke, hit; DISAPPOINTMENT; blast, WIND, breeze, gale. See IMPULSE. —*v.* brag; gasp, pant, puff; sound; storm, breeze, whiff, waft. See SOUND, WIND.

blue, *adj.* azure, indigo; sapphire, turquoise, aquamarine, cobalt; Delft; (of laws) severe, Puritanical. *Colloq.*, sad, dejected, depressed, dispirited, downhearted. See COLOR, KNOWLEDGE, DEJECTION. *Ant.*, see CHEERFULNESS.

bluff, *n., adj. & v.* —*n.* cliff, bank, headland. —*adj.* rough, unceremonious, brusque, BLUNT. *Ant.*, see SHARPNESS. —*v.* mislead, brag, intimidate, hoax. See BOASTING, DECEPTION.

blunder, *n. & v.* —*n.* ERROR, mistake, slip; botch, mess; solecism. —*v.i.* botch, fail, err; mismanage, bungle, flounder. See FAILURE, UNSKILLFULNESS. *Ant.*, see SUCCESS.

blunt, *v. & adj.* —*v.t.* DULL, deaden, numb; callous, make insensitive; moderate. *Ant.*, see SHARPNESS. —*adj.* DULL; direct; brusque; undiplomatic, forthright. See DISCOURTESY.

blur, *v.* blot, smear; swim, be indistinct. See IMPERFECTION, VISION.

blush, *v.i.* COLOR, flush, glow, redden; embarrassment, MODESTY.

bluster, *n. & v.* —*n.* bravado; braggadocio, bullying, BOASTING, hectoring; FRONT. —*v.i.* swagger, play the bully, hector, vapor, gasconade; make a fuss, disturbance *or* uproar. *Ant.*, see MODESTY.

board, *n. & v.* —*n.* COUNCIL, cabinet, panel, committee, directorate; plank; cardboard; provisions, fare. —*v.* lodge, feed. See FOOD, LAYER.

BOASTING [884]

Nouns—**1,** boasting, boast, vaunting, vaunt; pretense, pretensions; puff; flourish, *fanfaronnade;* gasconade; braggadocio, bravado, flourish, swagger, bunkum; bounce; rodomontade, bombast, fine talk, tall talk, bombast, magniloquence, grandiloquence; heroics; chauvinism; EXAGGERATION; VANITY, much cry and little wool, highfalutin(g). *Slang,* dog, side, bunk, hot air, front.

2, boaster; braggart, Gascon, pretender, *soi-disant*; blusterer, bully, hectorer. *Slang,* blowhard, windbag, loudmouth.

Verbs—boast, make a boast of, brag; vaunt, puff, flourish, strut, swagger; preen *or* plume oneself; bluster, bluff; exult, crow over, neigh, chuckle, triumph; throw up one's cap. *Colloq.,* talk big, show off, blow one's own horn. *Slang,* give oneself airs, put on side *or* dog, put up a big front.

Adjectives—boastful, magniloquent, pretentious, *soi-disant*; vainglorious, conceited; bombastic, pompous, extravagant, high-flown, ostentatious, heroic, grandiose; jubilant, triumphant, exultant; in high feather; flushed with victory; cock-a-hoop; on stilts.

Adverbs—boastfully, bombastically, *etc.*

Antonym, see MODESTY.

boat, *n.* vessel, SHIP, craft; skiff, dory, dinghy, launch; liner, steamer; gondola, rowboat, canoe, outrigger; sailboat; bark. See NAVIGATION, CONCAVITY.

bob, *v. & n.* —*v.t.* dock, cut, curtail. —*v.i.* nod, bow, curtsy; jerk, LEAP, float. —*n.* haircut; shilling. See AGITATION, OSCILLATION, RESPECT.

body, *n.* anatomy; torso; structure, FORM; substance, SUBSTANTIALITY; ASSEMBLAGE, throng, aggregate; lump; person, figure, thing; WHOLE.

bog, *n.* swamp, morass, quagmire, MARSH, fen.

bogus, *adj.* false, fake; counterfeit, spurious. *Slang,* phony. See DECEPTION.

bogy, bogey, *n.* specter, spook, bugaboo; DEMON, hobgoblin, gremlin.

boil, *n. & v.* —*n.* sore, suppuration. —*v.* bubble, seethe; scald; cook; storm, fume, rage. See DISEASE, HEAT, VIOLENCE.

boisterous, *adj.* noisy, vociferous; unrestrained, rambunctious, riotous, stormy, uproarious; rough. See EXCITEMENT. *Ant.,* inexcitable.

bold, *adj.* daring, audacious, forward; intrepid, brave; impudent. See COURAGE, INSOLENCE. *Ant.,* see COWARDICE, SERVILITY.

bolt, *n. & v.* —*n.* lock, latch, bar; stroke, flash. See CLOSURE, LIGHTNING. —*v.* run, dash, run away; winnow, sift; gobble, gulp. See ESCAPE, GLUTTONY.

bombast, *n.* BOASTING, exaggeration, bluster, braggadocio, grandiloquence.

bond, *n.* union, connection, tie; accord, sympathy; guaranty, pledge; shackle. See JUNCTION, RELATION, SECURITY. *Ant.,* see DISJUNCTION.

bonus, *n.* reward, gift, premium, extra, dividend. See GIVING.

bony, *adj.* skeletal, stiff; osseous; lank, lean. See HARDNESS.

BOOK [593]

Nouns—**1,** book, writing, work, volume, folio, tome, opus; manuscript; treatise, dissertation; novel; tract, brochure; libretto; handbook, codex, manual, textbook, pamphlet, broadside, booklet, circular; PUBLICATION, edition, pocket edition, production; encyclopaedia; dictionary, lexicon, glossary, thesaurus; concordance, anthology, gazetteer, almanac, digest, compilation; part, issue, number, album, portfolio; periodical, review, serial, magazine; annual, journal.

2, writer, author, publisher, littérateur, essayist, novelist, short-story writer, playwright, dramatist, poet; editor; lexicographer, annotator, commentator; journalist, newspaperman, critic, reviewer, correspondent; hack, hackwriter, ghostwriter; librettist. *Colloq.,* potboiler, penny-a-liner, free lance, inkslinger.

3, ledger, account book (see ACCOUNTING); betting book (bookmaking).

bookkeeping, *n.* auditing, reckoning, ACCOUNTING.

bookworm, *n.* SCHOLAR, pedant; bibliophile. *Colloq.,* grind, longhair.

boom, *v. & n.* —*v.* push, boost, plug; flourish; thunder, drum, rumble (see LOUDNESS). —*n.* beam, spar, jib; prosperousness, SUCCESS. See IMPULSE, NAVIGATION, PROSPERITY.

boorish, *adj.* ill-mannered, vulgar, rude; rustic, clownish. See VULGARITY.

boost, *n. & v.* —*n.* AID, help, indorse; lift, hoist. —*v.i.* assist, promote, recommend; lift, hoist. See APPROBATION, ELEVATION. *Ant.,* see HINDRANCE, DISAPPROBATION.

booty, *n.* spoil, plunder, prize, loot, graft, swag, boodle, pork barrel, pickings, pillage, blackmail; prey. See ACQUISITION.

border, *n.* EDGE, LIMIT, margin, rim; frontier, boundary; trim (see ORNAMENT).

bore, *n. & v.* —*n.* diameter, caliber; nuisance, pest. See BREADTH, WEARINESS. *Ant.,* see NARROWNESS, AMUSEMENT. —*v.* drill, pierce; tire, weary, annoy. See OPENING.

borrow, *v.* take, receive (as a loan); appropriate, adopt, adapt, imitate, make use of; plagiarize, copy; pawn, pledge; pirate, steal, filch, pilfer. See DEBT.

bosh, *n.* nothing; nonsense. *Slang,* bunk. See SPEECH, ABSURDITY.

bosom, *n. & adj.* —*n.* breast, bust; heart, FEELING. See CONVEXITY. —*adj.* intimate, close, confidential. See FRIEND.

boss, *n.* knob, stud; manager, supervisor. See CONVEXITY, AUTHORITY.

botany, *n.* vegetable physiology, science of plant life, phytology; horticulture; vegetation, flora. See VEGETABLE.

botch, *v.* bungle, blunder; mar, spoil; mismanage. *Colloq.,* butcher. See UNSKILLFULNESS. *Ant.,* see SKILL.

bother, *n. & v.* —*n.* nuisance, annoyance; trouble; perplexity, worry. —*v.t.* irritate, pester, worry. See PAIN. *Ant.,* see PLEASURE.

bottle, *n.* flask, jug, carafe, decanter; flacon, phial; canteen. See RECEPTACLE.

bottom, *n.* BASE, foot, sole; foundation, support. *Ant.,* see HEIGHT.

bough, *n.* limb, branch, offshoot, arm. See PART, VEGETABLE.

bounce, *v.* rebound, spring; LEAP. *Slang,* eject.

bound, *v. & adj.* —*v.* LIMIT, confine, delimit, demarcate; LEAP, spring, vault. See CIRCUMSCRIPTION. —*adj.* see BIND.

boundary, *n.* LIMIT, border, confines, bounds. See CIRCUMSCRIPTION.

bounty, *n.* grant, subsidy; premium; generosity, munificence. See AID, BENEVOLENCE.

bouquet, *n.* FRAGRANCE, perfume, aroma; corsage, boutonniere, nosegay, garland. See ORNAMENT.

bourgeois, *adj.* middle-class; conservative. See MIDDLE.

bout, *n.* contest, match; prizefight. See CONTENTION.

bow, *n. & v.* —*n.* obeisance, curtsy, kowtow, salaam; FRONT, prow. —*v.i.* nod, incline, bend; yield, concede. See COURTESY, OBEDIENCE.

bow, *n.* curve, arc, crescent; bowknot; crossbow. See CURVATURE, ARMS.

bower, *n.* nook, arbor, grotto. See RECEPTACLE.

bowl, *n.* basin, vessel, dish, pan; cup, beaker; ARENA. See RECEPTACLE.

box, *n.* chest, case, carton, container; coffin. See RECEPTACLE.

boy, *n.* lad, YOUTH; servant (*now offensive*). See INFANT. *Ant.,* see AGE.

boycott, *v.t.* shun, blackball, ostracize. See REFUSAL.

brace, *v.t. & n.* —*v.t.* invigorate, refresh; SUPPORT, prop, strengthen. —*n.* bracket, stay, girder; pair. See NUMERATION, POWER. *Ant.,* see IMPOTENCE.

bracket, *n.* SUPPORT, shoulder; brace, group, class; parenthesis. See CONNECTION.

brag, *v.i.* boast, vaunt; swagger, bluster; bluff. See BOASTING.

braid, *n. & v.* —*n.* trim, ribbon. —*v.t.* intertwine, interweave, plait. See CROSSING, ORNAMENT.

brain, *n.* cerebrum, cerebellum; mentality, intelligence, mind; gray matter; INTELLECT.

brake, *v.* retard, check, curb; slow down, stop. See SLOWNESS.

branch, *n. & v.* —*n.* member, arm, bough, limb, ramification; descendant, shoot, offshoot; PART. See ANCESTRY, VEGETABLE. *Ant.,* see WHOLE. —*v.i.* fork, divide, bifurcate; radiate. See DEVIATION.

brand, *n.* kind, sort, stamp; stigma, stain; mark, identification, trademark; branding iron; torch. See DISREPUTE, HEAT.

bravado, *n.* bluster, braggadocio, BOASTING.

brave, *adj. & v.* —*adj.* courageous, fearless, valiant, bold. —*v.t.* defy, dare. See COURAGE. *Ant.,* see COWARDICE.

brawl, *n.* quarrel, fight, free-for-all, hubbub. See CONTENTION.

BREADTH [202]

Nouns—**1,** breadth, width, broadness, scope, extent, span; latitude, amplitude, spaciousness, expanse; diameter, bore, caliber, radius; thickness, bulk, corpulence, SIZE. See EXPANSION.

Verbs—broaden, widen, amplify, extend, enlarge, expand; thicken.

Adjectives—broad, wide, ample, extended; thick; outspread, outstretched; vast, spacious, immense, extensive, comprehensive.

Antonym, see NARROWNESS.

---

break, *n. & v.* —*n.* breach, interruption, disconnection, fracture, fissure, crack; boon, advantage. See DISJUNCTION. —*v.* crack, fracture, shatter; tame, subdue; violate, infringe. See BRITTLENESS, NEGLECT, DOMESTICATION.

breast, *n.* bosom, bust, mamma; spirit, affections. See CONVEXITY.

breath, *n.* respiration, inhalation, exhalation; breeze. See LIFE, WIND.

breeches, *n.* knickers, knickerbockers; small clothes; trousers, pantaloons. See CLOTHING.

breed, *v. & n.* —*v.* create, multiply, generate, produce. —*n.* strain, race, stock. See RELATION, PRODUCTION.

breeze, *n.* zephyr, gust, breath (of air). See WIND.

brevity, *n.* CONCISENESS, succinctness, briefness, SHORTNESS. *Ant.,* see LOQUACITY.

bribe, *n. & v.* —*n.* tribute, tip, perquisite, graft, bait. *Colloq.,* hush-money, grease. —*v.t.* tip, overtip; suborn, tempt, corrupt. *Colloq.,* grease. See BOOTY, GIVING.

bridal, *adj.* nuptial, connubial. See MARRIAGE.

bridge, *n. & v.* —*n.* span, trestle, viaduct, causeway; auction, contract. —*v.t.* connect, span, link, cross. See JUNCTION.

bridle, *v.* curb, check; harness; bristle. See RESTRAINT.

brief, *adj. & n. & v.* —*adj.* short, succinct, terse; quick, fleeting. —*n.* summary, argument. —*v.t.* instruct. See CONTRACTION, INFORMATION, LAWSUIT. *Ant.,* see LOQUACITY.

bright, *adj.* brilliant, shining, glistening; luminous; clever, intelligent; gay, flashing, sparkling. See COLOR, INTELLIGENCE, LIGHT. *Ant.,* see IGNORANCE, DARKNESS.

brilliant, *adj.* resplendent, radiant; luminous, sparkling, bright; (conspicuously) intelligent, clever, quick-witted. See BEAUTY, INTELLIGENCE, LIGHT. *Ant.,* DULL; see DARKNESS.

brim, *n.* EDGE, margin, border, rim, brink, bluff.

bring, *v.t.* fetch, carry, convey; command (a price); occasion. See CAUSE, TRANSFER. *Ant.,* SEND.

brisk, *adj.* alert, quick, lively, animated, sprightly; cool, sharp. See ACTIVITY, COLD. *Ant.,* see INACTIVITY.

bristle, *n. & v.* —*n.* hair, stubble, brush. See ROUGHNESS. *Ant.,* see SMOOTHNESS. —*v.i.* stand (erect), stick up; stiffen (as with anger). See SHARPNESS, RESENTMENT.

BRITTLENESS [328]

Nouns—brittleness, fragility, friability, frangibility, frailty; crispness, delicacy, crumbliness.

Verbs—break, crack, snap, split, shiver, splinter, crumble, shatter, fracture; bust, fly, give way; fall to pieces, break up, disintegrate, fragment, crumble into dust.

Adjectives—brittle, frangible, friable, fragile, breakable, frail, gimcrack, shivery, splintery; splitting; eggshell; crisp, crumbly, short, brittle as glass.

Antonym, see COHERENCE.

---

broach, *v.t.* launch, introduce; tap, open. See BEGINNING, OPENING.

broad, *adj.* wide; extensive; marked (as an accent); sweeping, comprehensive; liberal, tolerant. See BREADTH, MODERATION. *Ant.,* NARROW.

broadcast, *v. & n.* —*v.* scatter, distribute, disseminate; spread, transmit, publish. —*n.* program, show, telecast, hook-up. See PUBLICATION.

broil, *v. & n.* —*v.* cook, grill, roast, HEAT. —*n.* brawl, riot, disturbance, fracas. See CONTENTION.

broker, *n.* AGENT, jobber, middleman, factor, pawnbroker, stockbroker.

brood, *n. & v.* —*n.* hatch, progeny, breed. See DESCENT. —*v.i.* ponder, mope, meditate, ruminate. See THOUGHT.

brook, *n.* stream, creek, rivulet, run. See RIVER.

broom, *n.* brush, mop, besom, whisk. See CLEANNESS.

brother, *n.* friar; cadet, *frère, Frater*; kinsman, sibling; fellow, colleague, associate. See CLERGY, RELATION, FRIEND, SIMILARITY.

brow, *n.* forehead; SUMMIT, crest. See FRONT.

bruise, *n. & v.* —*n.* contusion, injury, black-and-blue spot, mouse, black eye. —*v.t.* batter, contuse, injure, crush. See PAIN, IMPULSE.

brunet, *adj.* dark, dark-haired, dark-complexioned; brown, swarthy. See COLOR.

brush, *n. & v.* —*n.* bristle; thicket, shrubbery; broom. —*v.* sweep; graze. See CLEANNESS, NEARNESS.

brusque, *adj.* gruff, curt, abrupt. See DISCOURTESY. *Ant.*, see COURTESY, SMOOTHNESS.

brute, *n.* beast, ANIMAL; ruffian, scoundrel. *Colloq.*, bull. See EVILDOER, MALEVOLENCE.

bubble, *n. & v.* —*n.* globule, blob. See CONVEXITY. —*v.i.* effervesce, boil, gurgle. See AGITATION.

bucket, *n.* pail, tub. *Slang,* growler. See RECEPTACLE.

buckle, *n. & v.* —*n.* clasp, fastening. —*v.* bend, twist; collapse. See CONNECTION, DISTORTION.

bud, *v.i.* sprout, shoot; germinate; burgeon. See EXPANSION.

buff, *adj. & v.* —*adj.* orange, yellow, tan. See COLOR. —*v.t.* polish, SMOOTH.

buffer, *n.* fender, bumper, polisher. See DEFENSE, SMOOTHNESS.

buffet, *v. & n.* —*v.t.* strike, slap, punch. —*n.* stroke, blow. See IMPULSE.

buffoon, *n.* FOOL, clown, jester; comedian, mountebank. See DRAMA.

bug, *n.* insect, anthropod, mite, nit, bedbug; vermin. See LITTLENESS.

build, *v.t.* construct, make, fashion; erect. See FORM, PRODUCTION.

bulb, *n.* knob, globe; tuber, corm; lamp. See CONVEXITY, VEGETABLE, LIGHT.

bulge, *v.* swell, protrude, project, bag. See CONVEXITY. *Ant.*, see CONCAVITY.

bulk, *n.* SIZE, QUANTITY, measure, amount, volume; mass, expanse; body; generality, majority.

bulletin, *n.* report, statement, INFORMATION. *Colloq.*, flash.

bullfighter, *n.* matador; picador, banderillo; toreador. See AMUSEMENT.

bully, *n. & v.* —*n.* BLUSTERER, swaggerer, brawler; plug-ugly; tyrant. —*v.t.* intimidate, browbeat, hector, bulldoze. See BOASTING, EVILDOER.

bump, *v.* collide, knock, strike, hit. See IMPULSE.

bunch, *n.* crowd, group; cluster, bundle. See CONVEXITY.

bundle, *n.* package, parcel, packet; bunch, bale. *Slang,* riches, WEALTH. See ASSEMBLAGE.

bung, *n.* stopper, cork, plug, CLOSURE.

bungle, *v.* spoil; botch; blunder. *Slang,* goof. See UNSKILLFULNESS.

buoy, *n.* float; marker; bellbuoy, lifebuoy. See NAVIGATION.

buoyant, *adj.* light, floating; resilient, springy; confident, sanguine. See ASCENT, HOPE.

burden, *n.* HINDRANCE, load, weight, encumbrance; charge. *Ant.*, see AID.

bureaucracy, *n.* officialism; officiousness; red tape. See AUTHORITY.

burglar, *n.* thief, housebreaker, robber, yegg, second-story man, cracksman. See STEALING.

burlesque, *n. & v.* —*n.* farce, parody; comedy, buffoonery. —*v.t.* satirize, parody, mimic, caricature. See IMITATION, RIDICULE.

burn, *v.* oxidize, consume; blaze, flame; fire; sear, char, scorch; destroy. See HEAT. *Ant.*, see COLD.

burrow, *n. & v.* —*n.* hole, tunnel, excavation, tube, foxhole. —*v.* dig, mine, penetrate. See CONCAVITY.

burst, *v.* rupture, break, rend; explode, shatter. *Slang,* bust. See VIOLENCE.

bury, *v.t.* inter, inhume, immure; cover, sink; relegate. See CIRCUMSCRIPTION, INTERMENT. *Ant.*, disinter.

bush, *n.* shrub, clump, thicket, hedge. See VEGETABLE.

BUSINESS [625]

Nouns—**1,** business, occupation, employment; PURSUIT; UNDERTAKING, venture; affair, concern, matter, case; task, work, job, chore, errand, commission, mission, charge, care, assignment. *Slang,* racket.

2, province, function, bailiwick, lookout, department, station, capacity, sphere, orb, field, line; walk, walk of life; beat, round, range, routine; race, career; vocation, calling, profession, cloth, faculty; art; craft, handicraft; trade, commerce, industry.

3, office, place, post, position, incumbency, living; situation, berth, employ; service; appointment, engagement; avocation. See ACTIVITY.

4, market, marketplace, mart, agora, fair, bazaar; STORE, shop, stall, booth, workshop; exchange, stock exchange, curb, bourse, rialto, pit, Wall Street, the street; bank.

5, businessman, MERCHANT, banker, broker, buyer, seller, bear, bull; financier, speculator; firm, concern, house, company, limited company, corporation, partnership.

Verbs—**1,** busy *or* occupy oneself with; undertake; contract, attempt; turn one's hand to; do business, keep a shop; ply one's trade.

2, officiate, preside, control; serve, act; do duty; discharge the duties of; hold office; hold a situation; be engaged in, have in hand; have on one's hands, bear the burden; have one's hands full. *Colloq.*, hold down a job.

Adjectives—businesslike, orderly, thorough, methodical, efficient, systematic; workaday; professional; vocational; official, functional; authoritative; busy, in hand, afoot; on foot, on the fire; going on; acting.

Antonyms, see INACTIVITY, REPOSE.

bustle, *n.* stir, rustle, fluster, flurry, ado. See ACTIVITY, AGITATION. *Ant.*, see INACTIVITY.

busy, *adj.* occupied, engaged, engrossed; employed; diligent; meddlesome. See ACTIVITY, BUSINESS. *Ant.*, idle; see INACTIVITY.

but, *conj. & prep.* —*conj.* still, yet, however. —*prep.* except, save, saving, excepting. See COMPENSATION.

butcher, *v.t.* slaughter, kill; bungle, spoil. See KILLING, UNSKILLFULNESS.

butt, *n.* target, goat, LAUGHINGSTOCK.

buttocks, *n.* rump, seat, hindquarters, breech. *Colloq.*, fanny, bottom. See REAR.

button, *n. & v.* —*n.* fastener; disk, boss; badge, emblem. —*v.* fasten, loop, close. See CLOSURE, JUNCTION, ORNAMENT. *Ant.*, see DISJUNCTION.

buy, *v. & n.* —*v.* PURCHASE, procure; draw, obtain; shop, market. —*n.* bargain (see CHEAPNESS). *Ant.*, see SALE.

by, *adv. & prep.* beside, alongside. See AGENCY, CAUSE, SIDE. *Ant.*, see OPPOSITION.

bygone, *adj.* former, PAST; antiquated, obsolete. *Ant.*, see FUTURITY.

bystander, *n.* witness, observer; SPECTATOR, onlooker. See PRESENCE.

C

cab, *n.* taxi, taxicab, hack, hackney, hansom. See VEHICLE.

cabinet, *n.* room, boudoir, chamber, closet; *étagère* (*Fr.*), case; repository; ministry, board, COUNCIL. See RECEPTACLE.

cage, *n. & v.* —*n.* prison, enclosure, bars; aviary, pen. —*v.t.* RESTRAIN, confine, imprison, incarcerate, pen. See RESTRAINT. *Ant.*, LIBERATE.

cajole, *v.t.* flatter, wheedle, inveigle; beguile, blandish; coax. *Colloq.*, jolly. See DECEPTION. *Ant.*, see SEVERITY.

cake, *v. & n.* —*v.i.* bake, harden; consolidate; thicken, congeal, condense. See COHERENCE. —*n.* mass, brick, block, floe. See DENSITY.

calamity, *n.* trouble, distress, misfortune, catastrophe, misery, affliction, disaster. See ADVERSITY. *Ant.*, see PROSPERITY.

calculate, *v.* compute, reckon; count, appraise; estimate. *Colloq.*, consider, deem, figure. See NUMERATION.

calefaction, *n.* see HEAT.

calendar, *n.* almanac; diary, journal; register, schedule; docket. See TIME.

calf, *n.* offspring, young. *Colloq.*, dogie. See ANIMAL.

caliber, *n.* gauge, bore; quality; ability, capability, capacity. See BREADTH, SIZE, SKILL.

calibrate, *v.t.* measure, graduate.

call, *v. & n.* —*v.* CRY, shout, yell; summon, bid; convoke, muster; choose, appoint, elect; name, designate; visit, interview. See CHOICE, ASSEMBLAGE, COMMAND, NOMENCLATURE, SOCIALITY. —*n.* summons, demand; shout, yell; signal; impulse, urge; visit.

calling, *n.* vocation, profession; occupation, trade, BUSINESS.

callous, *adj.* horny, tough; unfeeling, insensitive, insensible, hardened. See HARDNESS, INSENSIBILITY. *Ant.*, see SOFTNESS, SENSIBILITY.

calm, *adj. & v.* —*adj.* placid, serene, unruffled, cool, composed, undisturbed, unperturbed; phlegmatic, sedate; tranquil, still, motionless, halcyon; peaceful, pacific. —*v.t.* still, pacify. See REPOSE, SILENCE. *Ant.*, see EXCITEMENT.

camouflage, *v. & n.* —*v.t.* disguise, conceal, fake. —*n.* disguise, mask, simulation. See CONCEALMENT.

camp, *n.* encampment, bivouac, cantonment, shelter. See ABODE.

campaign, *n. & v.* —*n.* operations; plan. —*v.i.* canvass, electioneer; fight, war. See WARFARE, CHOICE. *Ant.*, see PACIFICATION.

can, *n. & v.* —*n.* tin, container. *Slang,* jail; toilet. See RECEPTACLE. —*v.t.* preserve, put up.

cancel, *v.t.* obliterate, efface, delete; postmark. See NULLIFICATION, DESTRUCTION. *Ant.*, see AFFIRMATION.

candid, *adj.* frank, straightforward; outspoken, blunt; impartial. See SIMPLENESS. *Ant.*, see DECEPTION.

candidate, *n.* nominee, office-seeker; applicant, aspirant; probationer. See REQUEST.

candle, *n.* taper, wax, wax candle, dip, *cierge* (*Fr.*). See LIGHT.

cannibal, *n.* man-eater, savage, anthropophagus. See EVILDOER.

canopy, *n.* covering, awning; tester; vault, sky; pavilion, cope; howdah. See COVERING.

cant, *n.* pretense, hypocrisy, insincerity; argot, lingo, SLANG, jargon.

canvass, *v.t.* examine, sift, discuss; solicit, campaign, poll, survey, seek; peddle, sell. See INQUIRY, REQUEST, SALE.

cap, *n. & v.* —*n.* headdress; skullcap; tam-o'-shanter, beret, beanie; kepi. —*v.* cover; match, outdo, excel. See CLOTHING, COVERING.

capable, *adj.* able, competent, proficient; susceptible. See SKILL. *Ant.*, see UNSKILLFULNESS.

capacity, *n.* content, colume, SIZE; aptitude, faculty; talent, skill, capability. See INTELLECT, POWER. *Ant.*, see LITTLENESS, IMPOTENCE.

caper, *v.i.* LEAP, jump, gambol, frisk, prance, skip, caracole, hop, spring.

capital, *adj. & n.* —*adj.* excellent, paramount, first-rate, first-class, unequaled, GOOD; IMPORTANT, primary, major, preëminent, principal; metropolitan. *Ant.*, see EVIL, UNIMPORTANCE. —*n.* metropolis, seat; funds, stock, assets, resources; opulence, riches, MONEY, WEALTH. See ABODE.

caprice, *n.* fancy, humor, idiosyncrasy, whim, crotchet, quirk; fad, vagary; whims(e)y, prank; escapade; vacillation, CHANGEABLENESS, eccentricity, capriciousness, fickleness, inconstancy. *Ant.*, see STABILITY.

captain, *n.* commander, MASTER, skipper; leader; chief, headman. See AUTHORITY. *Ant.*, see SERVANT.

captious, *adj.* caviling, carping, hairsplitting, faultfinding, hypercritical. See IRASCIBILITY.

captivate, *v.t.* CHARM, fascinate, infatuate, enchant, enamor; enthrall, enslave, bewitch. See DESIRE, PLEASURE. *Ant.*, see PAIN.

capture, *v.t.* seize, apprehend, arrest, TAKE; grab, nab, collar; bag, snare, trap. *Ant.*, see FREEDOM.

car, *n.* automobile, VEHICLE; bus, omnibus, trolley, coach, Pullman; cage; sedan, coupé, limousine, convertible. *Colloq.*, sleeper; jalopy.

CARE [459]

Nouns—**1,** care, solicitude, heed, heedfulness; scruple, conscientiousness, PROBITY; watchfulness, vigilance, surveillance, eyes of Argus, watch, vigil, lookout, watch and ward. See SAFETY.

2, alertness; ACTIVITY, ATTENTION; prudence, circumspection, CAUTION; forethought, precaution, FORESIGHT, PREPARATION.

3, tidiness, ORDER, CLEANNESS; accuracy, exactness; minuteness, attention to detail, meticulousness.

Verbs—**1,** be careful, take care, take pains, be cautious; take precautions; pay attention to; take care of; look *or* see to; look after; keep an eye on; keep watch, mount guard, watch; keep in sight *or* view; mind; mind one's business; keep tabs on.

2, look sharp; keep a sharp lookout; have all one's wits about one; watch for, expect; keep one's eyes open *or* peeled; sleep with one eye open; mind one's Ps and Qs; speak by the card; pick one's steps.

3, observe; do one's duty; make good; keep one's word *or* promise.
4, stop, look and listen; *timeo Danaos, festina lente, caveat emptor.*
Adjectives—**1,** careful, regardful, heedful; particular, painstaking, prudent, cautious; considerate, thoughtful; deliberative, provident, prepared; alert, guarded, on one's guard, on the *qui vive*, on the alert, on watch, on the lookout; awake, broad awake, vigilant; watchful, wakeful, Argus-eyed, wide-awake, expectant.
2, tidy, orderly, shipshape, clean; accurate, exact; scrupulous, conscientious.
Adverbs—carefully, *etc.;* with care, gingerly.

Antonym, see NEGLECT.

---

career, *n.* profession, calling, lifework; progress, success; history. See CONDUCT, BUSINESS.
careless, *adj.* carefree, nonchalant, unconcerned, free, casual, offhand; negligent, thoughtless, inconsiderate, inattentive, unobservant, unthinking; slack, slovenly; reckless, rash, indiscreet, imprudent. See NEGLECT.
caress, *v.t.* hug, kiss, clasp, embrace; fondle, pet, stroke, dandle. See ENDEARMENT.
cargo, *n.* freight, lading, shipment, load. See PASSAGE.
caricature, *n. & v.* —*n.* burlesque, parody, travesty. —*v.* satirize, exaggerate, take off, distort, MISREPRESENT. *Ant.,* see REPRESENTATION.
carnage, *n.* KILLING, massacre, bloodshed, slaughter; shambles, butchery.
carnal, *adj.* bodily, fleshly; worldly, sensual. See ANIMAL, IRRELIGION.
carol, *n.* song, lay, madrigal, noël. See MUSIC.
carom, *n.* cannon, rebound; shot. See RECOIL, IMPULSE.
carouse, *v.i.* feast, revel; debauch, drink. *Colloq.,* booze, go on a toot. See AMUSEMENT, DRUNKENNESS. *Ant.,* see WEARINESS, MODERATION.
carriage, *n.* bearing, presence, mien, behavior, conduct, front; wagon, cart, stage, stagecoach, coach, equipage. See APPEARANCE, VEHICLE.

CARRIER [271]

Nouns—**1,** carrier, porter, bearer; redcap, skycap; stevedore; conveyer, transporter; freighter, shipper; courier, messenger, runner; coolie; postman, mailman, letter carrier; engineer, conductor, motorman; teamster, trucker, truck driver, helper, expressman; chauffeur, driver, cabbie, hackie; coachman.
2, common carrier; railroad, railway, train; local, express, limited, freight (train); airline, airliner, transport; street car, trolley (car), tram, subway, tube, el, elevated line, interurban, rapid transit; omnibus, bus, coach, jitney, stage(coach), charabanc, taxi(cab), cab, hack; sledge, cart, dray, truck, trailer, semitrailer, VEHICLE.
3, beast of burden; horse, draft horse, packhorse, carthorse; ass, burro, jackass, hinny, jennet, donkey, mule; camel, dromedary, ox, llama, elephant; reindeer, dog, husky; carrier pigeon, passenger pigeon, homing pigeon.
4, basket, box, carton, tray, *etc.*

Antonym, see PASSAGE.

---

carry, *v.t.* uphold, SUPPORT; transport, bear, TRANSFER. *Colloq.,* lug, tote.
cart, *n.* wagon, carriage, tumbrel, tumbril; pushcart. See VEHICLE.
carve, *v.i.* cut, slice; mold, shape, fashion; chisel, engrave, sculpture. See DISJUNCTION, FORM.
case, *n.* instance, situation, plight; sheath, scabbard, holster; portfolio; suit, action, litigation; argument, proposition; box, container, carton, casket, cabinet; bag, suitcase, handbag, grip, valise. See BUSINESS, COVERING, LAWSUIT, RECEPTACLE, CIRCUMSTANCE.
cask, *n.* barrel, hogshead, keg, butt. See RECEPTACLE.
casket, *n.* coffin, reliquary; chest, box. See RECEPTACLE.
cast, *v. & n.* —*v.t.* throw, toss, heave, hurl, sling, fling; mold. See FORM, PROPULSION. —*n.* APPEARANCE, aspect, air; company, actors; casting, copy, mold, sculpture. See DRAMA, FORM.
caste, *n.* CLASS, rank, degree.
castrate, *v.t.* emasculate, unman; geld, spay. See IMPOTENCE.

casual, *adj.* accidental, adventitious, random, haphazard, cursory, happy-go-lucky; incidental, CHANCE, fortuitous, contingent, conditional.

casualty, *n.* chance, accident; disaster, calamity, misfortune. See ADVERSITY. *Ant.,* see PROSPERITY.

cat, *n.* feline, puss, pussy, tomcat, tabby, grimalkin, alley cat, mouser, kitten; lion, tiger, leopard. See ANIMAL.

catalogue, *n.* list, index, RECORD.

catastrophe, *n.* calamity, convulsion, débacle, disaster, upheaval, cataclysm, paroxysm; END. See ADVERSITY.

catch, *v.t.* take, seize; overtake; trawl, land, net, hook; surprise, detect; snare, trap; capture, arrest, apprehend; snatch. *Slang,* nab. See ACQUISITION. *Ant.,* see FREEDOM.

cathartic, *adj.* laxative, physic, purgative, aperient, purifying. See REMEDY.

catholic, *adj.* tolerant, liberal; universal, GENERAL. See BREADTH. *Ant.,* see NARROWNESS.

cattle, *n.* livestock; kine, cows, bulls, steers. See ANIMAL.

CAUSE [153]

Nouns—**1,** cause, origin, source, principle, element; leaven; groundwork, base, basis, foundation, SUPPORT; spring, fountain, fountainhead, headspring, head; genesis; descent, paternity, ANCESTRY; pivot, hinge, turning-point, lever; key; straw that breaks the camel's back.

2, causality, causation, origination; PRODUCTION; ground; reason (why); why and wherefore, *rationale,* occasion, derivation; undercurrents.

3, rudiment, fundamentals, egg, germ, embryo, bud, root, radix, radical, etymon, nucleus, seed, stem, stock, stirps, trunk, taproot; nest, cradle, nursery, womb, nidus, birthplace, hot-bed.

4, INFLUENCE, weight, sway, leverage; MOTIVE, impulse, consideration, motivation; temptation, enticement, inducement, allurement; inspiration, exhortation, persuasion, solicitation.

5, occasioner, prime mover, author, creator, producer, progenitor; mainspring, agent.

Verbs—**1,** be the cause of; originate; give rise to; cause, occasion, sow the seeds of, kindle; bring to pass, bring about; produce, create; give birth to, generate; set up, set afloat, set on foot; found, broach, institute, lay the foundation of; lie at the root of.

2, procure, induce; draw down, open the door to; evoke, entail, operate; elicit, provoke; conduce to, contribute; have a hand in, have a finger in the pie; determine, decide, turn the scale; have a common origin; derive from. See EFFECT.

3, move, prompt, motivate; weigh, tell, carry weight; sway, persuade, bear upon; inspire, inspirit, stimulate, rouse, arouse, animate, incite, instigate; impel, propel, enforce; hound, press, urge, exhort, spur, egg on.

Adjectives—caused, causal, original; primary, primitive, primordial; aboriginal; radical; embryonic, in embryo, *in ovo;* seminal, germinal; at the bottom of; connate, having a common origin.

Adverbs—because, by reason of, on account of; therefore.

Antonym, see EFFECT.

---

caustic, *adj.* corrosive, burning, mordant; sarcastic, satirical, biting, acrimonious; severe. See DISCOURTESY, RESENTMENT, DETRACTION. *Ant.,* see COURTESY, SERVILITY.

caution, *n.* cautiousness, deliberation; discretion, prudence, heed, needfulness, CARE, circumspection; vigilance. See WARNING, SAFETY. *Ant.,* see RASHNESS.

cave, *n.* recess, grotto, cavern; lair, burrow; den. See CONCAVITY, ABODE.

cavity, *n.* hole, excavation, hollow, pit; opening, depression, pocket, dent. See CONCAVITY. *Ant.,* CONVEXITY.

cease, *v.i.* stop, desist, discontinue; END, terminate; halt, pause. *Ant.,* see CONTINUITY.

cede, *v.t.* yield, grant, relinquish; assign, transfer; surrender, hand over. See RELINQUISHMENT. *Ant.,* see POSSESSION.

CELEBRATION [883]

Nouns—1, celebration, solemnization, jubilee, commemoration; ovation, pæan; triumph, jubilation; inauguration, installation, presentation; coronation ceremony, RITE.

2, bonfire, salute, salvo; flourish of trumpets, fanfare, colors flying, illuminations, fireworks; TROPHY, triumphal arch.

3, fête, festival, festivity, gala, gala occasion, holiday; harvest home; red-letter day; thanksgiving.

4, REJOICING, jubilation, jubilee, merrymaking.

Verbs—1, celebrate, keep, signalize, do honor to, commemorate, solemnize, hallow; inaugurate, install, crown.

2, pledge, drink to, toast; rejoice, make merry, kill the fatted calf, hold jubilee, jubilate. See REJOICING.

Adjectives—celebrated; famous; see REPUTE.

Antonym, see INDIFFERENCE.

---

celebrity, *n.* star, notable, name; eminence, fame, renown. See REPUTE.

celestial, *adj.* heavenly, angelic, divine, holy; unearthly, supernal, beatific; solar, astral, empyreal. See DEITY, HEAVEN. *Ant.*, see HELL.

CELIBACY [904]

Nouns—1, celibacy, singleness, single blessedness; bachelorhood, bachelorship, spinsterhood; misogamy, misogyny; virginity, *pucelage*; maidenhood; chastity.

2, unmarried man, bachelor, Cœlebs, agamist, misogamist, misogynist; monk; unmarried woman, spinster; maid, maiden, virgin; *femme sole*, old maid.

Adjectives—celibate, unmarried, unwedded, wifeless, spouseless; single; maiden, virgin, chaste.

Antonym, see MARRIAGE.

---

cell, *n.* protoplasm; cage, jail; compartment, room, vault. See RECEPTACLE, PRISON.

cement, *n.* mortar, plaster, concrete, putty, tar, solder; adhesive, glue, mucilage, paste. See CONNECTION.

cemetery, *n.* graveyard, churchyard, burial ground. *Slang*, Boot Hill. See INTERMENT.

censorious, *adj.* severe, critical, fault-finding, condemnatory. See SEVERITY.

censure, *v. & n.* —*v.t.* upbraid, chide, reprove, criticize, blame. *Slang*, hit, knock. —*n.* blame, criticism, disapproval. See DISAPPROBATION. *Ant.*, see APPROBATION.

census, *n.* poll, enumeration, count. See NUMERATION.

center, *n.* core, heart, MIDDLE, hub, nave; midpoint; focus, focal point, dead center; nucleus, pole, axis; spine.

central, *adj.* MIDDLE, mid, midmost; focal, nuclear, polar, pivotal.

centralization, *n.* centrality, centralness, focalization; concentration, convergence, convergency; cynosure; magnetism; center of attraction; focus; combination, merging, unity, oneness, federation.

ceremony, *n.* ritual, formality, punctilio, protocol; form, observance, RITE, sacrament, function. See OSTENTATION.

CERTAINTY [474]

Nouns—1, certainty; certitude, sureness, surety, assurance; dead *or* moral certainty; infallibility, reliability; NECESSITY.

2, positiveness, assuredness; dogmatism, dogmatist; doctrinaire, bigot, opinionist, Sir Oracle; *ipse dixit*.

3, fact, matter of fact; *fait accompli*; guarantee.

Verbs—1, be certain; stand to reason; admit of no doubt; render certain, insure, assure; clinch, make sure; determine, decide, settle, fix; set at rest, make assurance doubly sure.

2, dogmatize; lay down the law; bet one's bottom dollar; know like a book.

Adjectives—1, certain, sure, assured; solid, well-founded; unqualified, ab-

solute, positive, determinate, definite, clear, unequivocal, categorical, unmistakable, decisive, decided, ascertained, known, proven.
2, inevitable, unavoidable; sure as fate, sure as death and taxes; unerring, infallible; unchangeable; to be depended on; trustworthy, reliable; bound.
3, unimpeachable, undeniable, unquestionable; indisputable, incontestable, incontrovertible, indubitable; irrefutable, conclusive, without power of appeal; beyond a doubt, without a shadow of doubt; past dispute; beyond all question; undoubted, doubtless; clear as day.
4, authoritative, authentic, official, *ex cathedra.*
Adverbs—certainly, for certain, certes (Arch.), sure, no doubt, doubtless; and no mistake; sure enough; to be sure; of course, as a matter of course, at any rate, at all events; without fail; come what may *or* will; sink or swim; rain or shine; sight unseen; truly; no question; not a shadow of doubt.
Antonym, see DOUBT.

---

certificate, *n.* certification, warrant, diploma; policy, debenture, stock. See EVIDENCE, SECURITY.
cessation, *n.* stop, stoppage, ceasing; halt, arrestment; END, conclusion; desistance, discontinuance; pause, rest, lull, respite; period. See DEATH. *Ant.,* see CONTINUITY.
chafe, *v.t.* HEAT, warm; wear, rub; vex, anger, annoy, gall, eat. See RESENT-MENT, PAIN. *Ant.,* see PLEASURE.
chaff, *n.* husks, WASTE; banter, jesting, WIT, raillery.
chagrin, *n.* mortification, vexation. See PAIN. *Ant.,* see PLEASURE.
chain, *n.* series, progression, course, row, string; bond, fetter; concatenation. See CONTINUITY, CONNECTION.
chair, *n.* chairman, moderator, speaker, master of ceremonies, toastmaster; seat, stool, rocker, throne; professorship, judgeship, fellowship. *Colloq.,* M.C., emcee. See DIRECTOR, SUPPORT, TEACHING.
challenge, *v. & n.* —*v.* query, controvert, question, dispute; dare, defy. *Colloq.,* stump. See DOUBT. *Ant.,* see BELIEF, OBEDIENCE. —*n.* exception; invitation [to fight]. See CONTENTION.
chamber, *n.* room, apartment, salon; bedroom, cell; hall, exchange, bourse; legislature, assembly. See RECEPTACLE, LEGALITY.
champion, *v. & n.* —*n.* defender, protector, squire, knight; backer, supporter; conqueror, victor, winner. See AID, SUCCESS. *Ant.,* see FAILURE. — *v.t.* defend, protect.

CHANCE [156, 621]

Nouns—**1,** chance, accident, lot; fate, kismet, karma, DESTINY, luck, fortune; hap, hazard; casualty, contingency, adventure, fortuity; indetermination. See NECESSITY.
2, speculation, venture, UNCERTAINTY; random shot, guessing game, blind bargain, shot *or* leap in the dark, pig in a poke; fluke; potluck.
3, gambling, risk, gaming, lottery; betting, bet, stake, wager, dicing, game; wheel of Fortune, tossup, toss of the dice, roulette, Russian roulette, heads or tails, turn of the card(s) *or* wheel, raffle; casino, lottery, gambling house, policy *or* numbers racket, gambling hell, gaming table(s), bucket shop; race track, the turf, bookmaking, pari-mutuel [window(s)], Totalizator, handbook, bookmaker, bookie; gambler, gamester, dicer, adventurer, speculator, horseplayer, bettor, crapshooter, pokerface, *etc.*
4, probability, POSSIBILITY, contingency, expectancy; odds, odds-on, edge, advantage; theory of probabilities, law of averages.
Verbs—**1,** chance, befall, hap, turn up; fall to one's lot, be one's fate; happen upon, light upon, run into *or* across, stumble on.
2, chance (it), gamble, risk, venture, speculate; try one's luck, tempt fortune, take a chance, trust to chance; draw lots, toss a coin; shoot the works, go for broke; game, hazard, stake, bet, wager, play (for).
3, be possible or probable; have or stand a chance; bid fair; seem likely; expect, think likely, dare say, flatter oneself.
Adjectives—**1,** chance, random, accidental, adventitious, casual, fortuitous, contingent, causeless, indeterminate, uncontrollable; hit-or-miss, catch-as-catch-can.

2, unintentional, undirected, purposeless, undirected, haphazard, unpremeditated, unwitting.

3, PROBABLE, possible, likely, potential, conceivable, in the cards.

Adverbs—**1,** by chance, casually, at random, haphazard; incidentally, *en passant*, by the way; adrift.

2, possibly, probably, likely; perhaps, perchance, peradventure; maybe, mayhap, haply; God willing, *Deo volente, D.V.,* wind and weather permitting. *Colloq.,* like as not, dollars to doughnuts, on the off chance.

Antonym, see NECESSITY.

CHANGE [140]

Nouns—**1,** change, alteration, mutation, permutation, diversification, VARIATION, modification, SUBSTITUTION, modulation, mood, QUALIFICATION, innovation, metastasis, DEVIATION, turn; diversion; break.

2, transformation, transfiguration; metamorphosis; transmutation; transubstantiation; metagenesis, transanimation, transmigration, metempsychosis; avatar; alterative.

3, CONVERSION; REVOLUTION, overthrow; inversion, eversion, reversal; displacement; transposition; transference; CHANGEABLENESS, tergiversation. See DIFFERENCE.

Verbs—**1,** change, alter, vary, wax and wane; temper, modulate, diversify, qualify, tamper with; turn, shift, veer, tack, chop, shuffle, swerve, warp, deviate, turn aside, avert, evert, intervert; pass to, take a turn, turn the corner; work a change, modify, vamp, superinduce.

2, transform, translate, transfigure, transmute, transume; metamorphose; ring the changes; convert, reduce, resolve; innovate, introduce new blood, shuffle the cards; influence, turn the scale; shift the scene, turn over a new leaf; resume; recast, remodel, revamp; reverse, overturn, upset; invert, transpose; reform, reorganize; disturb.

3, be converted (into), turn into, become, come to; grow, mature, mellow, ripen; resolve (self) into; assume the form, *etc.,* of.

Adjectives—changed, altered; new-fangled, novel; CHANGEABLE, variable; transitional; modifiable; alterative.

Antonym, see STABILITY.

CHANGEABLENESS [149]

Nouns—**1,** changeableness, alterability; mutability; inconstancy, fickleness; versatility; mobility; instability, vacillation, indecision, IRRESOLUTION; fluctuation, fluidity, vicissitude; alternation, OSCILLATION; restlessness, fidgets, disquiet, disquietude, inquietude; unrest; AGITATION; iridescence.

2, moon, Proteus, Cheshire cat, chameleon, quicksilver, shifting sands, weathervane, kaleidoscope, harlequin, Cynthia of the minute, April showers; wheel of fortune; TRANSIENTNESS.

3, CAPRICE, whimsy, vagary, coquetry, fad; capriciousness.

Verbs—fluctuate, vary, waver, flounder, flicker, flitter, flit, flutter, shift, shuffle, shake, totter, tremble, vacillate, turn and turn about, ring the changes; sway *or* shift to and fro; change and change about; oscillate; vibrate; alternate; have as many phases as the moon. See CHANGE.

Adjectives—changeable, changeful; alterable; changing; mutable, variable, checkered; kaleidoscopic, ever-changing; protean; versatile; inconstant, unsteady, unstable, unfixed, unsettled; fluctuating; restless; agitated; erratic, fickle; irresolute, capricious; volatile, mercurial; touch-and-go; fitful, spasmodic; vibratory; vagrant, wayward; desultory; afloat; alternating; plastic, mobile; transient; iridescent; convertible, modifiable.

Adverbs—see-saw; off and on.

Antonym, see STABILITY.

---

changeling, *n.* child; Proteus; waverer, turncoat, renegade. See MYTHICAL DEITIES, CHANGEABLENESS. *Ant.,* see STABILITY.

channel, *n.* duct, conduit, PASSAGE; waterway, canal; pipe, tube, tunnel; aqueduct; wavelength, broadcasting channel; means of communication; way, road, route; artery, vein, blood vessel.

chant, *n.* song; plain song *or* chant, Gregorian chant; intonation; psalm, canticle, requiem. See MUSIC, HYMN.

chaos, *n.* DISORDER, shambles, confusion, jumble, disorganization; abyss, void. *Ant.*, see ORDER.

chapter, *n.* division, section; verse, canto, passage; branch, lodge, post, corps. See BOOK.

char, *v.t.* burn, singe, scorch, sear, carbonize. See HEAT.

character, *n.* type, manner, kind, CLASS; nature, disposition, temperament, personality; sign, brand, stamp; figure, LETTER, hieroglyphic, ideograph, pictograph; *Colloq.*, personage, eccentric, crank, original.

characteristic, *adj. & n.* —*adj.* distinctive, typical, peculiar. —*n.* quality, trait, mark, lineament, feature, peculiarity, attribute, distinction. See INDICATION, IDENTITY.

charge, *v. & n.* —*v.* command, exhort, instruct; assess, value, tax, burden; set a price; debit; strike, attack; fill, load, prepare; accuse, score. —*n.* ACCUSATION, allegation, impeachment, indictment; command, order, mandate, requirement; onset, onslaught, ATTACK; price, expense, tax, burden, liability, encumbrance, assessment, rate, debit; supervision, custody, ward, trust, CARE; load, blast. See ADVICE, COMPLETION, PAYMENT. *Ant.*, see DEFENSE.

charitable, *adj.* kind, generous, liberal, kindly, Christian, forgiving, big-hearted; altruistic, eleemosynary. See BENEVOLENCE, GIVING. *Ant.*, see MALEVOLENCE, RECEIVING.

charlatan, *n.* quack, pretender, fraud, mountebank, cheat. See DECEPTION.

charm, *v. & n.* —*v.t.* fascinate, hypnotize, enamor, bewitch, enchant, disarm, captivate, ATTRACT; soothe, calm, allay. —*n.* attractiveness, personality, captivation, fascination; amulet, talisman, good-luck piece, incantation, spell, magic. See DESIRE, LOVE, PLEASURE, SORCERY. *Ant.*, see HATE, PAIN.

chart, *n.* map, plan, graph. See INFORMATION.

chase, *v.t.* pursue, follow, hunt; dispel, put to flight, rout, repel. See PURSUIT. *Ant.*, see AVOIDANCE.

chasm, *n.* canyon, crevasse, rift, fissure, cleft; abyss. See GULF.

chaste, *adj.* virtuous, pure, undefiled, clean, innocent; SIMPLE, classic, severe. See INNOCENCE, SIMPLENESS. *Ant.*, see IMPURITY.

chatter, *n.* prattle, talk, gabble, gibberish. *Colloq.*, patter. See LOQUACITY. *Ant.*, see SILENCE.

CHEAPNESS [815]

Nouns—**1,** cheapness, inexpensiveness, cut rates, low price; good buy, loss leader, markdown, bargain; sale, discount, depreciation, drug on the market; irregulars, seconds; bargain basement, cutthroat competition. *Slang,* steal.
2, triviality, paltriness, insignificance; trashiness, worthlessness. See LOWNESS.
3, gratuity; gift (see GIVING); free seats, Annie Oakley, pass, free admission; nominal price; labor of love.

Verbs—be cheap, cost little; come down in price, be marked down; buy for a song; buy at a bargain, buy dirt cheap; get one's money's worth; beat down; depreciate, undervalue; cut (competitor's) throat. See ECONOMY, LOWNESS.

Adjectives—**1,** cheap; underpriced, low-priced; moderate, reasonable, inexpensive; worth the money; economical; cheap at the price; dirt-cheap; reduced, cutrate, half-price, marked down; depreciated, unsalable, a drug on the market.
2, gratuitous, gratis, free, for nothing; without charge, untaxed; scot-free; free of cost, complimentary; honorary. *Colloq.*, on the house, dime a dozen; five-and-ten.
3, trivial, paltry, insignificant; trashy, worthless.

Adverbs—cheaply, inexpensively; for a song; at cost price, at a reduction.

Antonyms, see PAYMENT, IMPORTANCE.

---

cheat, *v.i.* deceive, defraud, swindle, hoodwink, gull, dupe, delude, hoax, victimize. *Colloq.*, bilk, gouge, gyp, skin, take, fleece. See DECEPTION.

check, *v. & n.* —*v.t.* control, test, verify, tally, count; RESTRAIN, repress, halt, stop, arrest, impede, interrupt, curb; stunt. —*n.* draft, money order; interruption, rebuff; setback, reverse, stop, RESTRAINT; supervision, control, tab; drag, block, brake; pattern, design, plaid, tartan; ticket, token, bill, stub. See ADVERSITY, HINDRANCE, MONEY.

cheek, *n.* INSOLENCE, impertinence, sauce, impudence, effrontery; jowl. *Slang,* nerve, brass, gall, face, sass. See SIDE. *Ant.,* see COURTESY.

CHEERFULNESS [836]

*Nouns—***1,** cheerfulness; geniality, gaiety, sunniness; cheer, good humor, spirits, high spirits, animal spirits; glee, high glee, light heart; optimism (see HOPE). See LIGHTNESS, PLEASURE.
2, liveliness, life, alacrity, vivacity, animation.
3, mirth, merriment, hilarity, exhilaration; joviality, jollity; levity, jocularity, WIT; playfulness, fun, glee; laughter, merrymaking, AMUSEMENT.
4, contentment, contentedness; happiness, complacency, satisfaction, serenity, comfort, peace of mind, CONTENT.
*Verbs—***1,** be cheerful, have the mind at ease, smile, put a good face upon, keep up one's spirits; see the bright side; cheer up, brighten up, light up, bear up; chirp, take heart, cast away care, drive dull care away, perk up; rejoice, carol, chirrup; frisk, lilt. *Slang,* feel one's oats, kick up one's heels; keep a stiff upper lip.
2, cheer, enliven, elate, exhilarate, gladden, inspirit, animate, raise the spirits, inspire; invigorate, encourage, hearten, refresh; applaud. *Slang,* jazz up, give a shot in the arm.
*Adjectives—***1,** cheerful; genial, happy, cheery, of good cheer, smiling, sunny, blithe; in good spirits; high-spirited; happy as the day is long; gay as a lark; light, lightsome, lighthearted; buoyant, debonair, bright, free and easy, airy; saucy, jaunty.
2, lively, spry, sprightly, spirited, animated, vivacious; brisk, sparkling; sportive; full of play, full of spirit; all alive.
3, merry as a cricket *or* grig; joyful, joyous, jocund, jovial; jolly, blithesome, gleeful, hilarious, rattling; playful, playful as a kitten, tricksy, frisky, frolicsome; jocose, jocular, waggish; mirthloving, laughter-loving; mirthful, rollicking; elated, exultant, jubilant, flushed; rejoicing; cock-a-hoop; cheering, inspiriting, exhilarating; pleasing.
*Adverbs—*cheerfully, cheerily, with relish, with zest; in fine fettle, in high spirits *or* feather. *Slang,* sitting on top of the world, riding high.
Antonym, see DISCONTENT.

cherish, *v.t.* nurture, nourish, foster, protect, nurse; entertain, harbor, cling to; prize, treasure, hold dear, revere. See CARE, LOVE. *Ant.,* see NEGLECT, HATE.
chest, *n.* case, box, casket; coffer; cabinet, commode, locker, bureau; thorax, breast. See CONVEXITY, RECEPTACLE.
chew, *v.t. & i.* masticate, eat, gnaw, grind, champ. See FOOD.
chicken, *n.* fowl, cock, hen, pullet; fryer, broiler, capon. See ANIMAL, FOOD.
chief, *n.* leader, chieftain, president; captain, commander, general; superior, foreman, overseer; elder. See AUTHORITY. *Ant.,* see SERVANT.
child, *n.* tot, offspring, bairn, son, daughter. *Slang,* kid, brat. See YOUTH. *Ant.,* see OLDNESS, ANCESTRY.
childbirth, delivery, parturition, labor pains. See PRODUCTION.
childish, *adj.* infantile, puerile, juvenile, youthful, babyish; brattish; senile, simpleminded, weak, foolish, silly; credulous, naive, trustful. *Slang,* kiddish. See CREDULITY, SIMPLENESS. *Ant.,* see DOUBT, INTELLIGENCE.
chill, *n.* shivering, shakes, ague; COLDNESS, chilliness; frost. *Ant.,* see HEAT.
chimney, *n.* fissure, cleft; smokestack, spout, flue, pipe. See OPENING, GULF. *Ant.,* see CLOSURE.
china, *n.* chinaware, porcelain, crockery. *Colloq.,* dishes.
chip, *n.* piece, splinter, fragment, flake. See PART. *Ant.,* see WHOLE.
chivalrous, *adj.* knightly, gallant, noble, courteous, brave. See COURTESY.

CHOICE [609]

*Nouns—***1,** choice, option, selection, determination, discrimination, pick, preference; volition, predilection, DESIRE; adoption, decision, JUDGMENT; alternative; dilemma.

2, election, poll, ballot, vote, voice, suffrage; plebiscite; *vox populi;* electioneering; voting. *Colloq.,* ticket.

3, voter, balloter, elector; suffragist; electorate, constituency.

Verbs—**1,** choose, elect; fix upon, settle, decide; determine, make up one's mind (see RESOLUTION); exercise one's option; adopt, take up, embrace, espouse.

2, vote, poll, ballot; hold up one's hand; divide.

3, select; pick, pick and choose; pick over; pick out, single out; cull, glean, winnow; pick up, pitch upon; pick one's way; indulge one's fancy; set apart, mark out for; prefer; have rather, have as lief; fancy, DESIRE; take a decisive step; commit oneself to a course; cross the Rubicon; cast in one's lot with; take for better or for worse.

Adjectives—optional, elective; discretionary, voluntary, selective, preferential; chosen; CHOICE; GOOD; on approval; on the bandwagon.

Adverbs—optionally, at pleasure, at will, at one's discretion; at the option of; whether or not; once for all; for one's money; by choice, by preference; rather, before, sooner.

Antonym, see REFUSAL.

---

choke, *v.t. & i.* strangle, SUFFOCATE, garrotte, throttle; stifle; obstruct, clog, jam, plug. See CLOSURE, KILLING. *Ant.,* see OPENING.

choose, *v.* See CHOICE.

chop, *v.t. & i.* cut, mince, chip; cleave, lop, hack, hew; strike; lop. See DISJUNCTION.

chorus, *n.* choir, singers, choristers, dancers; refrain. See MUSICIAN, MUSIC.

Christmas, *n.* yule, Noël (Fr.). See RITE.

chronic, *adj.* continuing, persistent, constant; confirmed, settled, inveterate, rooted. See CONTINUITY.

chronicle, *n.* account, history, annals, RECORD.

CHRONOMETRY [114]

Nouns—**1,** chronometry, horometry, chronology, horology; date, epoch; style, era, times.

2, almanac, calendar, ephemeris; register, registry; chronicle, annals, journal, diary.

3, clock, watch; chronometer, chronoscope, chronograph; repeater; timekeeper, timepiece; dial, sundial, gnomon, pendulum, hourglass, clepsydra; time signal. See TIME.

Verbs—fix *or* mark the time; date, register, chronicle; measure, beat *or* mark time; bear date.

Adjectives—chronological, chronometrical, chronoscopic, chronographical.

---

church, *n.* worship, service; ministry, clergy; denomination; Christendom, Holy Church; chapel, cathedral, synagogue, shrine, altar, TEMPLE.

churchdom, *n.* priesthood; RELIGION, CLERGY; church. *Ant.,* see IRRELIGION.

cipher, *n.* naught, zero; nonentity; cryptogram, codes, cryptology; monogram, device. See CONCEALMENT.

circle, *v. & n.* —*v.t.* encircle, ring, girdle; circumnavigate; circumscribe; compass. —*n.* circumference; ring, circlet; sphere, orb, disk; set, clique. See PARTY, CIRCULARITY, CIRCUMSCRIPTION.

circuit, *n.* circumference, circle, compass; itinerary (of a circuit judge, *etc.*); detour, bypass, DEVIATION, circumnavigation; orbit. See TRAVEL, AVOIDANCE.

circuity, *n.* circuitousness, circling, coiling, turning; spiral, cycle, corkscrew; circumnavigating. See CIRCULARITY, CONVOLUTION.

CIRCULARITY [247]

Nouns—**1,** circularity, sphericity, roundness; rotundity.

2, circle, circlet, circumference, ring, areola, hoop, annulus, annulet, bracelet, armlet; ringlet; eye, grommet, loop; wheel, round, trolley; hub, nave; cycle, orb, ball, sphere, globe, orbit, zone, belt, cordon, band; sash, girdle, cestus, cincture, baldric, fillet, wreath, garland; crown, corona, halo;

coronet, chaplet, snood, necklace, collar; noose, lasso; meridian, equator, parallel, tropic.
3, ellipse, oval, ovoid, ellipsoid, spheroid, cycloid; epicycloid, epicycle; hemisphere, semicircle; quadrant, sextant, sector, segment.
Verbs—circle, surround; enclose, encompass; rotate, revolve.
Adjectives—circular, round, rounded, annular, ball-shaped, orbed, spherical, spheroidal, globular, cylindrical; oval, ovate; elliptical, egg-shaped; ROTUND.
Antonym, see ANGULARITY.

circulate, *v.t. & i.* pass, go about, change hands, mix, move; spread, publish, diffuse, disseminate, report, propagate; revolve, turn, circle. See MONEY, PASSAGE, PUBLICATION, ROTATION.
circumference, *n.* perimeter, boundary, compass. See OUTLINE.
circumlocution, *n.* periphrasis, verbiage, prolixity, garrulity, wordiness, indirection. See LOQUACITY. *Ant.*, see CONTRACTION.

CIRCUMSCRIPTION [229]

Nouns—circumscription, limitation, INCLOSURE; confinement, RESTRAINT; bound, LIMIT, boundary; envelope.
Verbs—circumscribe, LIMIT, bound, confine, enclose; surround, compass about; imprison, immure, incarcerate, restrict, restrain; wall in, fence in, hem in, hedge round; picket, pen, corral, enkraal; enfold, enclose, envelop, embrace, incase, wrap up; invest, clothe.
Adjectives—circumscribed, begirt, lapped; buried *or* immersed in; embosomed, in the bosom of, imbedded; hemmed in, pent in *or* up, mewed up; immured, imprisoned, encaged; landlocked; seagirt.
Antonym, see FREEDOM.

CIRCUMSTANCE [8]

Nouns—**1,** circumstance, situation, phase, position, posture, attitude, place, environment, point; terms; régime; footing, standing, status, STATE; OCCASION, eventuality, juncture, conjunction; contingency, event; quandary, dilemma, predicament; emergency; exigency, crisis, pinch, pass, impasse, push; turning point; bearings, how the land lies. *Colloq.*, pickle, fix, kettle of fish, hole.
2, OCCURRENCE, incident, fact, happening, phenomenon.
Verbs—OCCUR; meet with, encounter, undergo; fall to the lot of, be one's lot; suffer, endure; pass *or* go through.
Adjectives—circumstantial; given; conditional, provisional; critical, crucial; modal; contingent, incidental; adventitious, EXTRINSIC; occasional.
Adverbs—**1,** in the circumstances, under the circumstances; thus, in such wise; accordingly; therefore, consequently, that being the case, such being the case; that being so, since, seeing that; so, then; conditionally, provided, if, in case; if so, in the event of; in such a contingency *or* case; occasionally; provisionally, unless, except, without; according to circumstances, as the case may be, as the wind blows. *Colloq.*, thusly.
2, eventually; in the (natural) course (of things); as things go.
Antonym, see NONEXISTENCE.

circumvent, *v.t.* surround, entrap; frustrate, thwart, forestall, balk, foil. See DECEPTION, HINDRANCE. *Ant.*, see AID.
cite, *v.t.* illustrate, mention, bring forward, quote; arraign, summon. See EVIDENCE.
citizen, *n.* INHABITANT, resident, denizen; urbanite, cosmopolite; native.
city, *n.* town, municipality; capital, metropolis. *Colloq.*, burg, big town. See ABODE.
civil, *adj.* courteous, mannerly, polite, well-bred; civic, secular, lay. See COURTESY. *Ant.*, see DISCOURTESY, CLERGY.
civilize, *v.t.* educate, cultivate, refine; reclaim, enlighten. See IMPROVEMENT. *Ant.*, see DETERIORATION.
claim, *v. & n.* —*v.t.* ask, demand, requisition, require; lay claim to; contend, allege, assert. See AFFIRMATION, COMMAND, RIGHT. *Ant.*, see NEGATION. —*n.* demand, requisition, requirement, prerogative; lien, hold; plea,

counterclaim; title. See COMMAND, LAWSUIT, PROPERTY.

clamor, *n.* outcry, noise, hullabaloo, uproar, racket, tumult, din. See CRY, LOUDNESS. *Ant.,* see SILENCE.

clamp, *n.* grip, vise; fastener, clasp. See CONNECTION.

clan, *n.* family, blood, tribe, sept; brotherhood, association; breed, caste. See ASSEMBLAGE, RELATION.

clang, *v.i.* resound, peal, toll, ring. See LOUDNESS.

clap, *v.t. & i.* applaud, acclaim; strike, slap, bang, slam; impose, put. See APPROBATION, IMPULSE. *Ant.,* see DISAPPROBATION.

clash, *v. & n.* —*v.t.* collide, conflict; disagree, dispute, differ, contend. —*n.* collision, impact, concussion, brunt, noise, conflict, DISAGREEMENT. See IMPULSE, CONTENTION. *Ant.,* see AGREEMENT.

clasp, *v.t.* hug, embrace, enfold; fasten, hook, buckle; clutch, hold. See COHERENCE, ENDEARMENT, JUNCTION. *Ant.,* see DISJUNCTION.

class, *n.* CLASSIFICATION, division, category; order, family, genus, species, variety; race, tribe, caste, kind, sort, type, breed, clan; manner, description, character, stamp. *Slang,* quality. See SIMILARITY, PARTY, ARRANGEMENT.

classic, *adj.* standard; chaste, simple. See SIMPLENESS.

classification, *n.* grouping, category, allocation; ARRANGEMENT, systematization, taxonomy, order.

clatter, *n.* rattle, noise, racket, din. See LOUDNESS.

clause, *n.* article, paragraph, proviso, condition, stipulation, PART, section.

claw, *n.* talon, nail; pincer, nipper. *Slang,* hook.

clay, *n.* earth, potter's clay, kaolin; mud, loam; flesh. See LAND, MANKIND.

CLEANNESS [652]

Nouns—**1,** cleanness, cleanliness, PURITY, spotlessness; purification, circumcision; purgation, lustration, ablution; bath, shower, cleansing, wash, washing, lavation; dry-cleaning; sanitation, disinfection; fumigation; irrigation, lavage; drainage, sewerage, plumbing. See WATER.

2, bath, shower bath, lavatory, lavabo, bathhouse, public bath, swimming pool, Turkish *or* steam bath; laundry, washhouse.

3, brush, broom, besom; mop, hose, sponge, swab; carpet sweeper, dustpan, dust mop, vacuum cleaner; washing machine; duster; washcloth, washrag; towel, napkin; soap, detergent, scouring powder; disinfectant.

4, washerwoman, laundress; charwoman, maid, day-worker; houseman; cleaning man *or* woman, street-sweeper *or* cleaner. *Colloq.,* whitewing.

Verbs—**1,** clean, cleanse; rinse, wring, flush, wipe, mop, sponge, scour, rub, swab, scrub; dust, brush up; vacuum; wash, lave, launder; purify; expurgate; clarify, refine, filter, filtrate; drain, strain.

2, disinfect, purge, sterilize, fumigate, ventilate, deodorize; whitewash; sandblast.

3, sift, winnow, pick, weed, comb, rake, brush, sweep.

Adjectives—clean, cleanly; pure, chaste, immaculate; spotless, stainless; without a stain, unstained, unspotted, unsoiled, unsullied, untainted, unadulterated, uninfected; sweet; neat, spruce, tidy, trim; bright as a new penny; snowy, snow-white, white.

Antonym, see UNCLEANNESS.

---

clear, *adj.* plain, distinct, sharp, understandable, vivid; fair, unclouded, cloudless, fine; open, evident; lucid, pellucid, transparent, limpid; liquid, pure, silvery. See KNOWLEDGE, VISION. *Ant.,* see CONCEALMENT, DARKNESS.

cleave, *v.t. & i.* stick, hold fast, adhere, cling; sever, shear, split, rive, rend, divide. See COHERENCE, DISJUNCTION.

CLERGY [996]

Nouns—**1,** clergy, ministry, priesthood, presbytery, rabbinate, ulema, imamate; the cloth. See RELIGION.

2, clergyman, divine, ecclesiastic, churchman, priest, minister, preacher, pastor, leader of the flock, shepherd; father, father in Christ; padre, abbé, curé; patriarch; reverend; confessor.

3, Pope, pontiff, cardinal, eminence, reverence, primate, metropolitan, archbishop, bishop, prelate, diocesan, suffragan, priest, confessor; rabbi;

caliph, imam, muezzin; dean, subdean, archdeacon, prebendary, canon, rector, parson, vicar, chaplain, curate; deacon, preacher, reader, lecturer; missionary, propagandist, Salvationist, revivalist, gospel singer *or* preacher, evangelist; churchwarden, sidesman; almoner, verger, beadle, sexton, sacristan; acolyte, altar boy; chorister. *Slang,* sky pilot.

4, cenobite, conventual, abbot, prior, monk, friar, lay brother, pilgrim; Jesuits, Franciscans, Gray Friars, Friars minor, Minorites; Capuchins, Dominicans, Black Friars; Carmelites; Augustinians, Austin Friars; Carthusians, Benedictines, Cistercians, Trappists, Cluniacs, Maturines; Templars, Hospitallers; abbess, prioress, canoness; mother superior, nun, sister, novice, postulant.

5, holy orders, ordination, consecration, induction; clericalism, theocracy, hierarchy, ecclesiology; monasticism, monkhood, asceticism, cloistered life; papacy, pontificate; prelacy; consistory, synod, council, Sanhedrin.

Verbs—call, ordain, consecrate, induct; take orders, take the veil, take vows; beatify, canonize.

Adjectives—ordained, in holy orders, called to the ministry; clerical, priestly, ecclesiastical, pastoral, ministerial; episcopal, hierarchical.

Antonym, see LAITY, LAY.

---

clerk, *n.* salesman (or woman); registrar, scribe, secretary; copyist, writer. See CLERGY, SALE, WRITING.

clever, *adj.* adroit, skillful; talented, adept, gifted. *Colloq.,* smart, cute. See SKILL. *Ant.,* see UNSKILLFULNESS.

client, *n.* customer, buyer, patron. See SALE.

cliff, *n.* precipice, palisade, crag, bluff, steep.

climate, *n.* weather; temperature, rainfall, precipitation, *etc.*; region. See AIR.

climax, *n.* acme, zenith, SUMMIT, pinnacle; turning point, culmination.

climb, *v.t.* mount, scale, ascend, rise, go up; succeed; clamber, scramble. *Colloq.,* swarm, shinny, shin. See ASCENT. *Ant.,* see DESCENT.

clinch, *v.t.* confirm, conclude successfully; fasten, secure, rivet, clamp; clench, grapple; seize, grasp. See COMPLETION, JUNCTION, POSSESSION.

cling, *v.i.* stick, hold, cleave, adhere; grasp, hold on to, hug; persist. See COHERENCE, LOVE, RESOLUTION. *Ant.,* see RELINQUISHMENT.

clip, *v.t.* cut, snip, scissor, trim, shorten; prune, mow; dock. See SHORTNESS.

cloak, *n.* cape, wrap, mantle, robe, domino; shield, cover, disguise. See CLOTHING, DECEPTION.

clock, *n.* timepiece, chronometer (see CHRONOMETRY); Big Ben; electric clock, clock radio; [taxi] meter.

clog, *v.t.* obstruct, block, congest, choke; hamper, encumber, jam, impede, restrain. See HINDRANCE. *Ant.,* see AID, OPENING.

cloister, *n.* abbey, priory, convent, hermitage, monastery; quiet retreat, sanctuary. See ABODE, SECLUSION.

close, *adj.* compact, dense, firm; stifling, oppressive, muggy, stale, stuffy; stingy, tightfisted, frugal, niggardly; taut; confining, constrictive; near, intimate; secretive, reticent, reserved; approximate. See DENSITY, HEAT, JUNCTION, NEARNESS, PARSIMONY, SILENCE. *Ant.,* see RARITY, COLD, DISJUNCTION, DISTANCE, WASTE, LOQUACITY.

close, *v. & n.* See CLOSURE.

closet, *n.* cupboard, cabinet; locker, wardrobe, clothespress; room, cubbyhole. See RECEPTACLE, SPACE.

CLOSURE [261]

Nouns—closure, occlusion; blockade, obstruction, HINDRANCE; shutting up, CONTRACTION; constipation; embolism; blind alley, dead end, stone wall, *cul de sac*; imperforation, imperviousness, impermeability; stopper; cloture.

Verbs—close, occlude, plug; stop, shut *or* dam up; block, blockade; obstruct, hinder; fasten, bar, bolt, barricade, latch, lock, stop, seal, fence in, plumb; choke, strangle, throttle; ram down, tamp, dam, cram; trap, cage, hood, clinch; shut the door; confine, restrain (see RESTRAINT).

Adjectives—closed, shut, unopened; unpierced, imporous, imperforate, impervious, impermeable; impenetrable; impassable; untrodden; unventilated; airtight, watertight, waterproof; vacuum-packed, hermetically sealed; tight, snug.

Antonym, see OPENING.

CLOTHING [225]

Nouns—**1,** clothing, clothes, apparel, wear, dress, attire, array, raiment, garments, garb, costume, trousseau; millinery, footwear, underwear, outerwear; vestments.

2, suit, dress suit, evening clothes, tuxedo; coat, dinner coat *or* jacket, jacket, blazer; cutaway, frock coat, Prince Albert, overcoat, Mackinaw, mackintosh, lumberjack, lumberjacket, raincoat, slicker, Inverness, ulster, pea-jacket; sweater, cardigan, pullover, vest, blouse, tunic, waistcoat; trousers, pants, breeches, slacks, levis, overalls, dungarees, jeans; shirt, sportshirt; linen, undershirt, underpants, shorts, drawers, union suit, B.V.D.s; supporter, jockstrap, codpiece; dressing gown, smoking jacket; pajamas, pyjamas, nightshirt; shoe, boot, riding boot, Oxford, brogan, loafer, sneakers, moccasin; overshoes, galoshes, rubbers; spats, garters, chaps, leggings, puttees; hat, headgear, tophat, silk hat, opera hat, gibus, derby, Homburg, fedora, porkpie, felt hat, straw, panama, beaver, cap, nightcap, sailor, beret, beanie, skullcap, sombrero, shako, helmet, busby, kepi, overseas cap; tie, necktie, cravat, Ascot, bow tie, four-in-hand. *Colloq.*, tux. *Slang*, togs, duds, glad rags, soup and fish, tails; P.J.s; topper, stovepipe, kelly.

3, dress, gown, frock; suit, tailormade; blouse, bodice, middy blouse, sweater, shirtwaist, tunic; skirt, jumper, hoopskirt, crinoline; housedress, housecoat, smock, apron, negligée, robe, tea gown, kimono; coat, jacket, shortie; underwear, lingerie, slip, half-slip, petticoat, camisole, chemise, shift; corset, girdle, foundation, garter belt, stepins, brassière, bandeau; nightgown, pajamas; shoe, pump, Oxford, wedgie, casuals, sandal, slipper, mules, walking shoe; hat, bonnet, cloche, chapeau, hood, cowl, snood; hose, hosiery, stockings, nylons. See ORNAMENT, OSTENTATION. *Colloq.*, woolies, undies, panties; bra.

4, equipment, accouterments, trappings; harness, gear; uniform, dress uniform, fatigues; civilian clothes; cassock, robe, vestments. *Slang*, mufti, civvies.

Verbs—clothes, dress, attire, garb, costume, gown; invest; dress, don, put on, wear; accouter, equip, rig out, fit out, harness.

Adjectives—clothed, costumed, attired, dressed, clad.

Antonym, see DIVESTMENT.

CLOUDINESS [353]

Nouns—cloudiness, cloud, overcast; cumulus, altocumulus, cirrus, cirro-cumulus, stratus, cirro-stratus, nimbus; scud, raincloud, thunderhead; fog, mist, vapor, steam, haze, haziness, murk, murkiness. *Slang*, smog, soup, pea soup. See DARKNESS, DIMNESS.

Verbs—cloud, cloud over, shadow, obscure, overcast, threaten; SHADE.

Adjectives—cloudy, overcast, murky, misty, foggy, hazy, lowering, dirty, muggy; threatening; shady, umbrageous; obfuscated; opaque.

Antonym, see LIGHT.

---

clown, *n.* buffoon, comic, comedian, jester; boor; rustic, simpleton, clodhopper, oaf, bumpkin. *Colloq.*, duffer, lout, booby, nincompoop. See DRAMA, ABSURDITY. *Ant.*, see INTELLIGENCE.

cloy, *v.i.* glut, satiate, surfeit, sate; pall, bore.

club, *n.* cudgel, stick, bat, bludgeon; society, fraternity, sorority, association; nightclub, resort, rendezvous. See ARMS, ASSEMBLAGE.

clue, *n.* solution, suggestion, intimation, hint, key; guide. See ANSWER, INDICATION.

clump, *n.* cluster, bunch, patch, thicket, grove. See ASSEMBLAGE.

clumsy, *adj.* awkward, heavy, lumbering; bungling, stupid, bumbling, left-handed, incompetent; cumbersome, unwieldy. See UNSKILLFULNESS. *Ant.*, see SKILL.

clutch, *v.t.* hold fast, grip, keep, cling to, clench; snatch, seize, grasp, grab, collar; grip, clasp, squeeze, embrace. See ACQUISITION, POSSESSION. *Ant.,* see RELINQUISHMENT.

coach, *v. & n.* —*v.t.* teach, help, tutor. —*n.* trainer, director, teacher; stage, stagecoach, bus, omnibus, car, carriage, Pullman. See TEACHING, VEHICLE.

coagulate, *v.i.* clot, clabber, thicken, curdle; set, congeal. See DENSITY.

coal, *n.* ember, cinder; anthracite, bituminous *or* soft coal, charcoal, lignite, coke. See FUEL, HEAT.

coarse, *adj.* rough, harsh-textured, coarse-grained; uncouth, rude, crude, crass, low, vulgar, gross, common, unrefined; broad, bawdy, ribald. See ROUGHNESS, UGLINESS. *Ant.,* see BEAUTY, TASTE, SMOOTHNESS.

coast, *n.* shore, tideland, shoreline, waterfront, seacoast, beach. See LAND.

coat, *v. & n.* —*v.t.* cover, crust; plaster, paint, varnish, glaze; plate; protect. —*n.* jacket, overcoat, ulster, sack, cutaway, tunic; tegument, shell, envelope, skin, peel, rind, surface, cover. See CLOTHING, COVERING.

coax, *v.t.* cajole, inveigle, wheedle, persuade, urge. See CAUSE.

code, *n.* cipher, secret writing, cryptogram; law, canon, principle, codex, constitution, system, standard, rule. See LEGALITY, CONCEALMENT.

coerce, *v.t.* compel, drive, force, make. See COMPULSION.

coffin, *n.* casket, bier, pine box, sarcophagus. See INTERMENT.

cogent, *adj.* potent, forceful, convincing, persuasive, weighty, strong, compelling, trenchant. See POWER. *Ant.,* see IMPOTENCE.

cogitate, *v.i.* reflect, think, muse, ponder, mull, consider, meditate. See THOUGHT.

cognizant, *adj.* sensible (of), aware, knowing, conscious, observant. See SENSIBILITY. *Ant.,* see INSENSIBILITY.

COHERENCE [46]

Nouns—**1,** coherence, adherence, adhesion, adhesiveness; concretion, accretion; conglutination, coagulation, agglutination, agglomeration; aggregation; consolidation, set, gel, jell, jelly, cementation; sticking, soldering; tenacity, toughness; stickiness, viscosity; inseparability; conglomerate, concrete. See DENSITY.

2, gum, glue, mucilage, size; jelly, gelatine, starch, gluten, albumen; mire, mud, slush, ooze; syrup, molasses.

Verbs—**1,** cohere, adhere, stick, cling, cleave; hold, take hold of, hold fast, close with, clasp, hug; grow together, hang together; twine around; stick like a leech; stick close; cling like ivy, cling like a burr.

2, glue; agglutinate, conglutinate; cement, lute, paste, gum; solder, weld; cake, consolidate, solidify, agglomerate; gel, jell, jelly.

Adjectives—**1,** cohesive, adhesive, adhering, tenacious, tough; sticky; united, unseparated, sessile, inseparable, indivisible, inextricable, unbreakable, shatterproof, infrangible; compact, dense, solid.

2, mucilaginous, gelatinous, glutinous; viscid, viscous, semiliquid; mucid, mucous, tacky; deliquescent, emulsive, thick.

Antonym, see DISJUNCTION.

---

coil, *n.* spiral, curl, roll, winding, circle, CONVOLUTION.

coin, *v. & n.* —*v.t.* mint, strike, stamp; invent, originate, make. See FORM, PRODUCTION. —*n.* MONEY, specie, currency, change, piece; gold, silver, copper, nickel, dime, cent, *etc. Colloq.,* tin, brass.

coincidence, *n.* CONCURRENCE, conjunction, concomitance, correspondence, AGREEMENT.

COLD [383]

Nouns—**1,** cold, coldness, frigidity, severity, inclemency; iciness, winter, cold wave, cold snap; Siberia, Arctic, Antarctic; polar regions.

2, ice, snow, snowflake, snow flurry, snowfall, snowstorm, blizzard, snow-drift; sleet; hail, hailstone; rime, frost, hoarfrost; icicle, iceberg, ice floe, ice field, glacier.

3, chilliness, chill, coolness, shivering, goose flesh, rigor, horripilation, chattering of teeth, frostbite, chilblains.

4, REFRIGERATION; refrigerator, icebox, cooler; ice tray, ice cube, dry ice;

refrigerant, ammonia, freon; freezer, Deepfreeze, cold storage, locker.
Verbs—be cold, shiver, quake, shake, tremble, shudder, quiver; perish with
cold; chill, ice, freeze, quickfreeze. See REFRIGERATE.
Adjectives—cold, cool; chill, chilly; gelid, frigid, frozen, algid; fresh, keen,
bleak, raw, inclement; bitter, biting, cutting, nipping, piercing, pinching;
icy, glacial, frosty, freezing, wintry, boreal, arctic, Siberian, icebound,
snowbound; shivering, frostbitten, frost-nipped; stone cold, cold as marble,
cold as charity; cool as a cucumber; blue with cold; quickfrozen.
Adverbs—under refrigeration, on ice.
Antonym, see HEAT.

---

collapse, *v. & n.* —*v.i.* break down, fail; cave in. —*n.* prostration, dejection, exhaustion; downfall, ruin; cave-in. See FAILURE, IMPOTENCE. *Ant.*,
see SUCCESS, POWER.
colleague, *n.* associate, aide, partner, companion; co-worker, confrère.
See FRIEND. *Ant.*, see ENEMY.
collect, *v.t.* gather, collate, assemble, amass, compile; demand, ask payment,
exact; throng, congregate, flock; scrape up, round up, garner, accumulate,
save. See ASSEMBLAGE.
collide, *v.i.* bump, bunk, crash, clash, meet violently; interfere, impinge.
See IMPULSE.
collision, *n.* impact, concussion; smashup, crash; clash, opposition, interference; conflict, engagement, discord. See CONTENTION.
colonize, *v.t.* settle, pioneer, establish, found, populate; transport. See
LOCATION. *Ant.*, see DISPLACE.

COLOR [428]

Nouns—**1**, color, hue, tint, tinge, shade, dye, complexion, tincture, cast,
livery, coloration, glow, flush; tone, key; pure, primary, positive *or* complementary color; three primaries; spectrum, chromatic dispersion; secondary color, tertiary color; coloring, pigmentation, perspective, value;
brilliance, saturation; light, dark, medium.
2, chromatics; spectrum analysis; prism, spectroscope; VIBGYOR (the
spectrum: violet, indigo, blue, green, yellow, orange, red); rainbow, kaleidoscope.
3, pigment, coloring matter, paint, dye, wash, distemper, stain; medium;
mordant; oils, oil paint, watercolor, crayon, pastel, tempera, wash, PAINT-
ING.
4, black, jet, ink, ebony, coal, pitch, soot, crow, lampblack, blueblack,
India ink.
5, blue, ultramarine, cobalt, Prussian blue, indigo, lapis lazuli, sapphire,
turquoise.
6, brown, ocher, umber, sienna, sepia.
7, gray, neutral, silver, dun.
8, green, Paris green, emerald green, vert, celadon, verdancy.
9, orange, ocher, cadmium.
10, purple, amethyst, lilac, heliotrope.
11, red, scarlet, cinnabar, lake, cochineal, vermilion, red lead, madder,
rouge.
12, white, milkiness, snow, COLORLESSNESS.
13, yellow, gold, gamboge, yellow ocher, chrome yellow, banana, lemon.
14, variegation, iridescence, play of colors; chameleon.
Verbs—color, dye, tinge, stain, varnish, tint, paint, wash, ingrain, grain,
illuminate, emblazon, bedizen, imbue; paint.
Adjectives—**1**, colored, colorific, chromatic, prismatic; full-colored, high-
colored; double-dyed; polychromatic; bright, brilliant, vivid, intense,
deep; fresh, unfaded; rich, gorgeous, gay; gaudy, florid; garish; showy,
flaunting, flamboyant, flashy; raw, crude; glaring, flaring; discordant,
harsh, clashing, inharmonious; mellow, harmonious, pearly, sweet, delicate,
tender, refined.
2, black, sable, sloe-black, inky, coal-black, charcoal, jet-black, pitchy,
sooty.
3, blue, azure, cerulean, sky-blue, sea-blue, royal blue, copen.

4, brown, bay, tan, sorrel, auburn, chestnut, bronze, coppery, cinnamon, russet, chocolate, walnut, mahogany, khaki, cocoa, coffee, drab.
5, gray, steel-gray, French-gray, ashen, silvery, dove-gray, slaty.
6, green, emerald-green, pea-green, sea-green, bottle-green; olive.
7, orange, apricot, flame-colored, tangerine.
8, purple, violet, plum-colored, magenta, puce.
9, red, scarlet, crimson, pink, carmine, vermilion, cardinal, cerise, maroon, carnation, ruby-red, blood-red, beet-red, brick-red, Chinese red.
10, white, snowy, milky, chalky, creamy, pearly, ivory, off-white, oyster-white.
11, yellow, gold, saffron, lemon, cream-colored, amber, écru, buff, beige.
12, variegated, parti-colored, many-hued; iridescent, kaleidoscopic, opalescent; pied, paint, pinto, piebald, motley, mottled, marbled, dappled, pepper-and-salt, plaid, calico, brindled, tabby, grizzled, tortoiseshell, patchwork, crazy quilt.

Antonym, see COLORLESSNESS.

COLORLESSNESS [429]

Nouns—colorlessness, achromatism; decoloration, discoloration; pallor, pallidity; paleness, etiolation; neutral tint, monochrome, black-and-white.
Verbs—lose color, fade, become colorless, turn pale, pale; deprive of color, decolorize, bleach; tarnish, achromatize, blanch, etiolate, wash out, tone down.
Adjectives—uncolored, colorless, achromatic, aplanatic, hueless, pale, pallid; pale-faced; faint, dull, cold, muddy, leaden, dun, wan, sallow, dead, dingy, ashy, lurid, ghastly, deathly, ghostly, cadaverous, glassy, lackluster; blond, ash-blond, platinum-blond, fair; white; pale as death, pale as a ghost; white as a sheet.

Antonym, see COLOR.

---

colossus, *n.* giant, titan, monster, prodigy. See SIZE. *Ant.*, see LITTLENESS.
column, *n.* pillar, shaft; formation [of troops, ships, lines, figures]. See HEIGHT.

COMBATANT [726]

Nouns—**1,** combatant; disputant, litigant, belligerent; fighter, assailant; swashbuckler, fire-eater, duel(l)ist, bully; fighting-man, prizefighter, pugilist, boxer, bruiser, gladiator, wrestler; swordsman.
2, warrior, soldier, man-at-arms; campaigner, VETERAN; military man, G.I., doughboy, Tommy Atkins, *poilu*; armed force, troops, soldiery, forces, the army, standing army, regulars, militia, volunteers, auxiliaries, reserves, national guard, beefeater; guards, guardsman.
3, janizary; myrmidon; spahi, Cossack; irregular, mercenary; levy, draft; conscript, recruit, cadet, draftee, selectee, enlistee; guerrilla, partisan; commando.
4, private, rank and file, trooper, legionnaire, legionary, cannon fodder; officer, commander, subaltern, ensign, standard bearer; spearman, pikeman; halberdier, lancer; musketeer, rifleman, sharpshooter, sniper, skirmisher; grenadier, fusileer; archer, bowman.
5, horse *or* foot-soldier; infantry, infantryman, artillery, artilleryman, cavalry, cavalryman, horse; tanks, panzer, armor; paratrooper, paramarine; Uhlan, dragoon, hussar; cuirassier; gunner, cannoneer, bombardier; sapper, miner, engineer; light infantry, rifles, *chasseur*, zouave, camel corps, cameleers.
6, army, host; division, column, wing, detachment, garrison, brigade, regiment, corps, battalion, squadron, company, platoon, battery, squad; guard, legion, phalanx, cohort.
7, marine, navy, naval forces, fleet, flotilla, armada, squadron; man-of-war, ship of the line, ironclad, ship, warship, frigate, gunboat, flagship, cruiser; privateer; troopship, transport, corvette, torpedo boat, submarine, battleship, scout, dreadnaught, aircraft carrier, destroyer. *Slang*, gob, gyrene.
8, aviator, airman, pilot, bombardier, gun crew, tail gunner, belly gunner, navigator; dogfighter, ace; fighter, flying fortress, bomber, pursuit plane,

transport, jet, dive bomber; wing, flight, formation, escadrille, squadron, echelon; air force, air arm, Luftwaffe. *Slang*, fly boy, birdman.

combination, *n.* combine, merger; alliance, consolidation, union, amalgamation, coalition; conspiracy, cabal, league, junto; clique, set, coterie, faction; blend, alloy, MIXTURE, compound; pool, cartel, consolidation. See COÖPERATION, JUNCTION. *Ant.*, see DECOMPOSITION, DISJUNCTION.

combine, *v.* unite, mix, blend, merge; compound, compose; mix, intermix amalgamate, mingle; federate, incorporate, consolidate, coalesce; absorb, assimilate, take over, join; wed, marry, couple, pair, splice. See COÖPERATION, MIXTURE, JUNCTION. *Ant.*, see DECOMPOSITION, DISJUNCTION.

combustible, *adj.* inflammable, burnable. See FUEL.

come, *v.i.* arrive, reach; APPROACH, move toward, near; befall, happen, OCCUR. See ARRIVAL. *Ant.*, see DEPARTURE.

comfort, *n.* luxury; ease, coziness; enjoyment, satisfaction; solace, consolation; cheer, aid. See PLEASURE, RELIEF. *Ant.*, see PAIN, DISCONTENT.

comic, *adj.* funny, hilarious, laughable, sidesplitting, clownish, ludicrous, comical, droll, slapstick, farcical. See ABSURDITY.

COMMAND [741]

Nouns—**1,** command, commandment, order, ordinance, act, law, fiat, bidding, dictum, behest, call, beck, nod; despatch, dispatch, message; direction, injunction, charge, instructions; appointment, fixture. *Colloq.*, say-so. See AUTHORITY.

2, demand, exaction, imposition, requisition, claim, ultimatum, terms, REQUEST, REQUIREMENT.

3, dictation, dictate, mandate; caveat, decree, precept; writ, ordination, bull, edict, dispensation, prescription, brevet, ukase, warrant, passport, *mittimus, mandamus,* summons, subpoena, *nisi prius,* citation; word of command; bugle call, trumpet call; beat of drum, tattoo; order of the day.

Verbs—command, order, decree, enact, ordain, dictate, direct, give orders; prescribe, set, appoint, mark out; set *or* impose a task; set to work; bid, enjoin, charge, call upon, instruct; require, exact, impose, tax, task; demand, insist on, compel (see COMPULSION); claim, lay claim to, reclaim; cite, summon; call for, send for; subpoena; beckon; issue a command; make a requisition, decree, *or* order; give the word, give the signal; call to order; lay down the law; assume command (see AUTHORITY); remand.

Antonym, see OBEDIENCE.

commemorate, *v.t.* CELEBRATE, solemnize, observe, keep, memorialize. See RECORD. *Ant.*, see OBLIVION.

commence, *v.t.* See BEGINNING.

commend, *v.t.* praise, applaud, cite, acclaim, approve, compliment, recommend. See APPROBATION. *Ant.*, see DISAPPROBATION.

comment, *n.* observation, remark, note, reflection, criticism, annotation; aside, opinion. See INTERPRETATION.

commentator, *n.* reviewer, critic, editor, news analyst, newscaster. See INTERPRETATION.

commerce, *n.* BUSINESS, merchandising, trade, trading, BARTER.

COMMISSION [755]

Nouns—**1,** commission, delegation; consignment, assignment; procuration; deputation, legation, mission, embassy; agency, power of attorney; DEPUTY; proxy; task errand, charge, warrant, brevet, diploma; permit, PERMISSION, mandate, AUTHORITY.

2, appointment, nomination, charter; ordination; installation, inauguration, investiture; accession, coronation, enthronement.

3, fee, percentage, PAYMENT.

Verbs—commission, delegate, depute; consign, assign; charge; intrust, entrust; commit; authorize, empower, permit; put in commission, accredit; engage, hire, employ, bespeak, appoint, name, nominate, ordain; install, induct, inaugurate, invest, crown; enroll, enlist.

Adjectives—commissioned, delegated, assigned, *etc.*

Adverbs—for, instead of, in place of, in lieu of, as proxy for.
Antonym, see NULLIFICATION.

commit, *v.t.* perpetrate, perform, do; consign, entrust, deliver; confide, commend; take in custody, remand, condemn, imprison. See ACTION, COMMISSION; LAWSUIT.

commodity, *n.* goods, article, wares, product. See MERCHANDISE.

common, *adj.* ordinary, standard, usual, conventional; prevalent, general, universal, current, popular, customary, regular; vulgar, illbred, inferior, trivial, plebeian, coarse. See CONFORMITY, HABIT. *Ant.*, see UNCONFORMITY.

commonplace, *adj.* ordinary, usual, everyday; prosy, monotonous, stale, tedious, hackneyed, threadbare, trite, banal. See HABIT. *Ant.*, *see* WIT.

commonwealth, *n.* state, community, body politic, government. See AUTHORITY.

commotion, *n.* stir, fuss, ferment, hurlyburly, ado; turmoil, AGITATION, tumult, DISORDER, disturbance, EXCITEMENT, turbulence. *Ant.*, see ORDER.

COMMUNICATION [534]

Nouns—**1,** communication; messages, tidings, news (see INFORMATION).

2, communicator; messenger, envoy, emissary, legate; nuncio, ambassador; marshal, herald, crier, trumpeter, bellman, courier, runner; Mercury, Iris, Ariel; commissionaire; errand-boy; operator (radio, telephone, switchboard, *etc.*).

3, radio, television, cable, wireless, telephone, radiotelephony, telegraphy, *etc.*; newspapers, press; magazines, reviews, journals; switchboard.

4, bulletins; wire service, press service, syndicate service; mail, post, post office; letter-bag; telegram, cable, wire; carrier-pigeon; heliograph, wigwag, semaphore, signal; news flash, press release.

5, telepathy, thought transference, telekinesis, extrasensory perception.

6, intercourse; conversation, exchange of talk *or* ideas. See SPEECH, SOCIALITY.

7, newsman, reporter, newscaster, broadcaster, publisher, *etc.* (See PUBLICATION, INFORMATION).

Verbs—communicate, send messages, inform, tell, apprise, make aware; broadcast, newscast, publish, print, write, preach, disseminate news *or* information; radio, telegraph, wire, call, phone, telephone, cable; signal. See PUBLICATION.

Antonym, see CONCEALMENT.

communion, *n.* talk, conversation, intercourse, communication; concord, agreement, unity; sympathy; MASS, Lord's Supper, Sacrament, Eucharist. See RITE, SOCIALITY.

communist, *n.* socialist, anticapitalist, Marxist, communalist, leftist. *Colloq.*, Red; fellow-traveler, pink, parlor pink.

community, *n.* neighborhood, district, commonwealth; body, society, group; partnership, society. See PARTY, SOCIALITY.

compact, *n.* contract, covenant, AGREEMENT, bargain, bond, indenture; stipulation, COMPROMISE; pact, treaty; league, alliance; negotiation, bargaining, diplomacy, mediation; promise. *Colloq.*, deal.

compact, *adj.* CONCISE, succinct, terse, pithy, condensed; dense, thick, solid snug, tight. See DENSITY, CONTRACTION. *Ant.*, see RARITY, INCREASE.

companion, *n.* FRIEND, associate, colleague; pal, chum, comrade; shadow; escort; accomplice. See ACCOMPANIMENT. *Ant.*, see ENEMY.

company, *n.* companionship, fellowship; association, corporation, partnership; caste, troupe; group, assembly; troop, platoon, squad; society. *Colloq.*, crowd, gang, party. See ACCOMPANIMENT, ASSEMBLAGE, COMBATANT, DRAMA, BUSINESS, SOCIALITY.

compare, *v.* contrast; place side by side; collate, confront, parallel, relate, test. See RELATION, SIMILARITY.

comparison, *n.* comparing; contrast, collation, parallel; analogy, allegory; SIMILARITY. See RELATION.

compartment, *n.* division, partition, section, part; chamber, bin, cell. See SPACE, RECEPTACLE.

compass, *v. & n.* —*v.* bound, surround, define, encircle; beset, besiege; reach, accomplish, effect. —*n.* bounds, extent, scope, area, circumference, range; guide; gamut; needle (Naut.). See DIRECTION, LIMIT.

compassion, *n.* sympathy, tenderness, kindness, mercy, condolence; PITY, ruth, commiseration, heart. *Ant.*, see MALEVOLENCE.

compatible, *adj.* harmonious, well-matched, suitable, congruous. See AGREEMENT. *Ant.*, see DISAGREEMENT.

compel, *v.t.* See COMPULSION.

compendium, *n.* abstract, precis, epitome, summary, digest, synopsis, abridgment, condensation; compilation, anthology. See CONTRACTION, ASSEMBLAGE, SHORTNESS.

COMPENSATION [30]

Nouns—compensation, equation; commutation; satisfaction, indemnification, indemnity; COMPROMISE; neutralization; NULLIFICATION; counteraction, reaction; measure for measure; retaliation, equalization (see EQUALITY); robbing Peter to pay Paul; offset; counterpoise, counterbalance, ballast; equivalent, *quid pro quo;* bribe, hush money; recompense, PAYMENT; amends, ATONEMENT, redress, damages, balm.

Verbs—make compensation, compensate, indemnify; counteract, countervail, counterpoise; balance; outbalance, overbalance, counterbalance; set off; hedge, square, give and take; make up for, cover, fill up, neutralize, nullify; equalize; make good; recoup, square oneself, redeem, atone. *Colloq.*, lean over backwards.

Adjectives—compensating, compensatory; counteracting, countervailing, etc.; equivalent, equal.

Adverbs—in return, in consideration; but, however, yet, still, notwithstanding; nevertheless; although, though; albeit; at all events, at any rate; be that as it may, for all that, even so, on the other hand, at the same time, however that may be; after all, after all is said and done; taking one thing with another.

Antonym, see LOSS.

---

compete, *v.i.* vie, contend, strive, rival, cope with. See CONTENTION, OPPOSITION. *Ant.*, see PACIFICATION, COÖPERATION.

competence, *n.* capability, capacity, ability, efficiency, proficiency; means, resources, income, sufficiency. See SKILL, WEALTH. *Ant.*, see UNSKILLFULNESS, POVERTY.

compile, *v.t.* edit, write, make, compose; collect, arrange. See COMPENDIUM, COMPOSITION.

complain, *v.t.* lament, wail, repine; grumble, whine, fret, murmur; bewail. *Colloq.*, grouse. *Slang,* gripe. See LAMENTATION. *Ant.*, see REJOICING.

complaint, *n.* ACCUSATION, charge; DISEASE, ailment, sickness, indisposition, disorder; lament; grievance. See LAMENTATION. *Ant.*, see VINDICATION, HEALTH, REJOICING.

complete, *v. & adj.* —*v.t.* finish, END, conclude; mature, ripen; wind up; fill, charge, load, fulfill; make whole *or* entire; perfect. —*adj.* entire, total, whole; replete, full; mature, finished. See COMPLETION, PERFECTION. *Ant.*, see SHORTNESS, IMPERFECTION.

COMPLETION [729]

Nouns—**1,** completion; accomplishment, achievement, fulfillment; execution, performance; despatch, dispatch; consummation, culmination; finish, conclusion; close, END, terminus, ARRIVAL; wind-up; finale, dénouement; catastrophe, issue, outcome, upshot; result; final touch, crowning touch, finishing touch; *coup de grâce; ne plus ultra, fait accompli;* missing link; PERFECTION; elaboration; finality.

2, completeness, totality, wholeness, entirety; unity; all; solidity, solidarity; ideal, limit; SUFFICIENCY.

3, impletion; repletion, saturation, high water; fill, load, bumper, brimmer; bellyful. *Colloq.*, full house.

Verbs—**1,** complete, effect, effectuate; accomplish, achieve, compass, consummate; bring to maturity, bring to perfection; perfect, elaborate.

2, do, execute, make; go through, get through; work out, enact; bring about, bring to pass, bring to a head; despatch, dispatch; polish off; make short work of; dispose of, set at rest; perform, discharge, fulfill, realize; put in practice, carry out, make good, be as good as one's word; drive home; do thoroughly, not do by halves, go the whole hog; see out *or* through; round out, be in at the death, persevere, carry through, play out, exhaust. *Colloq.*, mop up, fill the bill, turn the trick, knock off, pull off, make a go of it, put through. *Slang*, do up brown, do to a turn, go all out.

3, finish, close, bring to a close, END, wind up, stamp, clinch, seal, set the seal on, put the seal to; give the final touch to; put the last hand to; crown, cap, cap the climax.

4, ripen, mature, culminate; come to a head, come to a crisis; come to its end; die a natural death, die of old age; run its course, run one's race; reach the goal; reach, arrive; get in the harvest.

5, fill, charge, load; replenish, piece out, eke out; fulfill, fill up, saturate. *Colloq.*, go the whole hog, go the limit.

Adjectives—complete, entire; WHOLE, perfect; full, good, absolute, thorough, plenary; solid, undivided; with all its parts; exhaustive, concluding, conclusive, crowning, final; radical, sweeping, thoroughgoing; dead; consummate, unmitigated, sheer, unqualified; unconditional, free; abundant, sufficient (see SUFFICIENCY); brimming, brimful, chock-ful; saturated, crammed; replete, redundant, fraught, laden, heavy laden; completing, supplemental, supplementary, complementary.

Adverbs—completely, altogether, outright, wholly, totally, *in toto*, quite; thoroughly, conclusively, finally; effectually, for good and all, nicely, fully, in all respects, in every respect; out and out, leaving no stone unturned, to all intents and purposes; utterly, to the utmost, all out, all hollow, stark; heart and soul, root and branch; down to the ground; lock, stock and barrel; bag and baggage; to the top of one's bent, to the limit, as far as possible; throughout; from first to last, from beginning to end, from end to end, from one end to the other, from head to foot, from top to toe, from top to bottom; fore and aft; every whit, every inch; *cap-à-pie*, up to the brim, up to the ears; with a vengeance. *Colloq.*, to the nines, to a fare-you-well; from the word go. *Slang*, for fair, from hell to breakfast, from soup to nuts; till Hell freezes over.

Antonyms, see INSUFFICIENCY, NEGLECT.

---

complex, *adj.* intricate, manifold, complicated, involved, knotty. See DISORDER. *Ant.*, see SIMPLENESS.

complexion, *n.* hue, color, tinge, tint; skin texture; aspect, APPEARANCE. See COLOR.

complicate, *v.t.* involve, embarrass, confuse; perplex; compound. See AGITATION. *Ant.*, see ARRANGEMENT.

complicity, *n.* guilt, association; collusion, participation, connivance, conspiracy. See COÖPERATION. *Ant.*, see OPPOSITION.

compliment, *v.t.* praise, flatter, commend, congratulate. See APPROBATION. *Ant.*, see DISAPPROBATION.

comply, *v.t.* CONSENT, conform, yield, submit, obey. See OBEDIENCE. *Ant.*, see REFUSAL, DISOBEDIENCE.

component, *n.* integral part; part, element, factor, constituent, ingredient; link, feature, member. *Colloq.*, makings, fixings.

COMPOSITION [54]

Nouns—**1**, composition, constitution, formation; COMBINATION, INCLUSION, admission, comprehension, reception. *Colloq.*, getup, setup.

2, composition, typography, make-up, typesetting. See PRINTING.

3, composition, musical work, authorship. See MUSIC, WRITING.

Verbs—be composed of, be made of, be formed of; consist of, be resolved into; include, hold, comprehend, take in, admit, embrace, embody; involve; implicate, drag into; compose, COMPOUND, constitute, form, make, put together, make up; enter into the composition of, be a component.

Adjectives—composing, containing, constituting, *etc.*

Antonym, see DECOMPOSITION, INSUBSTANTIALITY.

composure, *n.* placidity, serenity, self-possession, calmness. See MODERA-TION, REPOSE. *Ant.,* see EXCITEMENT.

compound, *v.t.* combine, compose, concoct, amalgamate, mix; join, unite. See MIXTURE.

comprehend, *v.t.* comprise, embrace, INCLUDE; grasp, apprehend, conceive, understand, see, know. See KNOWLEDGE. *Ant.,* see EXCLUDE, IGNORANCE.

compress, *v.t.* reduce, digest, abridge, consolidate, condense; crowd, squeeze, contract. See DENSITY. *Ant.,* see INCREASE, RARITY.

comprise, *v.t.* consist, involve, embrace, cover, embody; INCLUDE, comprehend, contain. See NUMBER.

COMPROMISE [774]

Nouns—compromise, commutation, MEDIATION; settlement, concession, middle term, COMPENSATION.

Verbs—**1,** compromise, commute, compound; take the mean, split the difference, strike a balance, meet one halfway, give and take; come to terms, CONTRACT; submit to arbitration; patch up, bridge over, arrange; adjust differences; agree; make the best of, make a virtue of necessity; take the will for the deed. *Slang,* go fifty-fifty.

2, mediate, arbitrate, reconcile, intercede, intervene.

Adjectives—conciliatory, diplomatic, give-and-take; mediatory, mediating, intermediary, intercessory.

Antonym, see OBSTINACY, RESOLUTION.

COMPULSION [744]

Nouns—compulsion, coercion, coaction, constraint, duress, obligation; enforcement, pressure, conscription; force, brute force, main force, physical force; the sword, martial law; draft, conscription; RESTRAINT, NECESSITY, *force majeure;* Hobson's choice. *Colloq.,* strong arm.

Verbs—compel, force, make, drive, coerce, constrain, enforce, necessitate, oblige; force upon, press; cram, thrust *or* force down the throat; make a point of, insist upon, take no denial; put down, dragoon; extort, wring from; drag into; bind over; pin *or* tie down; require, tax, put in force, put teeth in; restrain; hold down; commandeer, draft, conscript, impress.

Adjectives—compulsory, compelling; coercive, coactive; inexorable; obligatory, stringent, contingent, peremptory; forcible, not to be trifled with; irresistible.

Adverbs—compulsorily, by force, by force of arms; on *or* under compulsion, perforce; at sword's point, forcibly; under protest, in spite of; against one's will; under press of; *de rigueur,* willy-nilly.

Antonym, see FREEDOM.

---

compute, *v.t. & i.* figure, calculate, reckon; count, enumerate, number, tally. See NUMERATION.

comrade, *n.* FRIEND, companion, mate, fellow, chum, playmate, roommate, associate. *Ant.,* see ENEMY.

CONCAVITY [252]

Nouns—**1,** concavity, depression, dip; hollow, hollowness; indentation, intaglio, cavity, hole, dent, dint, dimple, follicle, pit, *sinus alveolus,* lacuna; excavation, crater; trough, furrow; honeycomb; cup, basin, bowl; cell, RECEPTACLE; socket.

2, valley, vale, dale, dell, dingle, bottom, glade, grove, glen, gully, cave, cavern, cove; grot, grotto; alcove, *cul-de-sac;* arch, arcade, curve; bay, gulf.

3, excavator, sapper, miner, digger.

Verbs—be concave; cave in; render concave, depress, hollow; scoop, scoop out; gouge, dent, dint; dig, delve, excavate, mine, sap, undermine, burrow, tunnel; stave in.

Adjectives—concave, depressed, hollow, stove in; retiring; retreating, cavernous; cellular, porous; spongy, honeycombed, alveolar; infundibular, funnel-shaped, cupular, bell-shaped; campaniform, capsular, vaulted, arched.

Antonym, see CONVEXITY.

CONCEALMENT [528]

Nouns—**1,** concealment; hiding; screen, smoke screen, AMBUSH, camouflage, trench, foxhole; disguise, masquerade, cloak, veil; incognito; cryptography, steganography, code.

2, stealth, stealthiness; slyness, CUNNING; SECLUSION, privacy, secrecy, secretness.

3, reticence; reserve; mental reservation; silence, taciturnity; *arrière pensée,* suppression, circumlocution, evasion, white lie, fib, misprision; underhand dealing; closeness, secretiveness, mystery; latency; stowaway. *Slang,* gobbledygook, doubletalk.

4, detective, operative, sleuth, private investigator, federal agent; secret agent, spy. *Colloq.,* plainclothesman, G-man. *Slang,* dick, flatfoot, bull; gumshoe.

Verbs—**1,** conceal, hide, secrete, put out of sight; lock up, bottle up; cover, screen, cloak, veil, shroud; draw the veil *or* curtain; curtain, shade, eclipse, becloud, mask, camouflage, disguise; ensconce, muffle, smother; whisper. *Slang,* stash, plant.

2, keep from, keep to oneself; keep dark, bury; sink, suppress; keep out of sight; keep in the background; stifle, hush up, smother, withhold, reserve; keep a secret, keep one's own counsel; hold one's tongue; not let the right hand know what the left is doing; hide one's light under a bushel.

3, keep *or* leave in the dark, blind, blindfold, hoodwink, deceive, mystify; puzzle, bamboozle, deceive (see DECEPTION), nonplus.

4, be concealed, hide oneself; lie in ambush, lie low, lurk, sneak, skulk, slink, prowl; play hide and seek; hide in holes and corners.

Adjectives—**1,** concealed, hidden; secret, recondite, arcane, esoteric, Masonic, mystic, cabalistic, occult, dark; cryptic, private, privy, clandestine, close, inviolate.

2, under cover, in ambush, in hiding, in disguise; in the dark; clouded, invisible; buried, underground, *perdu;* secluded (see SECLUSION); undisclosed, untold; covert, mysterious, unintelligible; inviolable; confidential, classified; unsuspected, LATENT.

3, furtive, stealthy, feline; skulking, surreptitious, underhand, hole and corner; sly, CUNNING; secretive, evasive; reserved, reticent, uncommunicative, buttoned up, taciturn.

Adverbs—secretly, in secret, privately, in private; in the dark; behind closed doors, hugger-mugger, under the rose, under the counter, under the table; *sub rosa,* in the background, aside, on the sly, with bated breath, *sotto voce,* in a whisper; in confidence, in strict confidence; confidentially; off the record, between ourselves, between you and me; *entre nous, in camera;* underhand, by stealth, like a thief in the night; stealthily, behind the scenes, behind one's back; incognito.

Antonym, see DISCLOSURE.

---

concede, *v.t.* CONSENT, yield, give in, assent, allow; accede; grant, admit, acknowledge, confess; RELINQUISH, cede, give up, surrender. See DISCLOSURE, GIVING. *Ant.,* see REFUSAL.

conceit, *n.* VANITY, pride, egotism, superciliousness, self-esteem; epigram, *bon mot* (Fr.), quip; whim, IMAGINATION, fantasy, fancy, caprice, notion, quirk. See WIT. *Ant.,* see MODESTY.

conceive, *v.t.* devise, frame, imagine, visualize, fancy; grasp, realize, take in, understand; form, become pregnant. See IMAGINATION, KNOWLEDGE, PRODUCTION. *Ant.,* see IGNORANCE.

concentrate, *v.t.* strengthen, distill, intensify, condense, consolidate; fix, aim, focus; converge, center, localize; collect, assemble, gather. See ASSEMBLAGE, MIDDLE, DENSITY. *Ant.,* DISPERSE; see RARITY.

concern, *v. & n.* —*v.t.* regard, affect, relate, refer to, pertain to, have to do with, bear upon, belong to; treat of; interest. —*n.* matter, affair; CARE, anxiety, worry, solicitude, regard; significance, IMPORT, interest. See RELATION. Ant., see NEGLECT, UNIMPORTANCE.

concerning, *prep.* regarding, pertaining to, respecting; re, *in re;* about, anent. See RELATION.

concert, *n.* recital, program, serenade, musicale; COÖPERATION, AGREEMENT, harmony, accord; conspiracy. See MUSIC. *Ant.*, see DISAGREEMENT, OPPOSITION.

concise, *adj.* succinct, short, brief, pithy, pointed, terse, laconic, epigrammatic, summary, compact. See CONTRACTION. *Ant.*, see LOQUACITY.

conclude, *v.t.* end, close, finish, windup, terminate; infer, deduce; arrange, settle; resolve, judge, determine. See COMPLETION, RESOLUTION.

concoct, *v.t.* prepare, invent, devise, contrive; brew; mix, cook; plan, make up, hatch. See PREPARATION.

concord, *n.* accord, harmony; AGREEMENT; sympathy, rapport, congruousness, congruence; concurrence; union, unity; PEACE, ASSENT; alliance, league, compact; entente; understanding. *Ant.*, see DISAGREEMENT, CONTENTION.

concrete, *adj.* actual, real, tangible; solid, hard; specific, definite, exact, particular. See SUBSTANCE, DENSITY. *Ant.*, see INSUBSTANTIALITY.

concur, *v.i.* agree, ASSENT, CONSENT, harmonize; see eye to eye with, pull together, parallel; unite; acquiesce. *Colloq.*, jibe. *Ant.*, see DISAGREEMENT.

concurrence, *n.* See COÖPERATION, AGREEMENT, CONVERGENCE.

condemn, *v.t.* sentence, doom; find guilty; damn, denounce, censure, blame, disapprove of, proscribe, forbid (use of), frown upon, reprove. See DISAPPROBATION, ACCUSATION. *Ant.*, see APPROBATION, VINDICATION.

condemnation, *n.* proscription; DISAPPROBATION; damnation; censure, disapproval, attainder; death warrant, judgment; verdict of guilt; conviction. See ACCUSATION. *Ant.*, see VINDICATION.

condense, *v.t. & i.* abridge, digest, curtail, abbreviate, shorten, cut, epitomize; thicken, concentrate, distill, solidify. See DENSITY, SHORTNESS. *Ant.*, see RARITY, LENGTH.

condescend, *v.i.* stoop, deign, descend, vouchsafe. See MODESTY, VANITY.

condiment, *n.* seasoning, sauce, spice, relish, herb; salt, pepper, cayenne, mustard, curry, onion, garlic, pickle, catsup, vinegar, mayonnaise, olive oil, salad dressing. See TASTE.

condition, *n.* fitness; STATE, birth, rank, place, estate, station, class; demand, QUALIFICATION, proviso; plight, situation, status, position, pass, case, circumstances. See REPUTE. *Ant.*, see DISREPUTE.

condolence, *n.* LAMENTATION, sympathy, pity, consolement, consolation, compassion, commiseration.

conduce, *v.i.* lead, tend, contribute, redound, advance. See TENDENCY.

CONDUCT [692]

Nouns—**1,** conduct, dealing, transaction, ACTION, BUSINESS; tactics, game, expedient, policy, polity; generalship, statesmanship, seamanship; strategy, strategics; PLAN, program, execution, manipulation, treatment, campaign, career, life, course, walk, race; husbandry; housekeeping, housewifery; stewardship; *ménage;* régime; economy, economics; political economy; management; government, DIRECTION.

2, conduct, behavior, deportment, comportment; carriage, demeanor, guise, mien, bearing, manner, OBSERVANCE; course of conduct, line of conduct, course of action; rôle, process, ways, practice, procedure, *modus operandi;* method.

Verbs—**1,** conduct, transact, execute, administer; deal with, have to do with; treat, handle, take steps, take measures; despatch, dispatch; proceed with, discharge; carry on, carry through, carry out, carry into effect; work out; go through, get through; enact; put into practice; officiate.

2, conduct oneself, behave oneself, comport oneself, demean oneself, carry oneself, acquit oneself; act one's age, give a good account of oneself; run a race, lead a life, play a game; take *or* adopt a course; steer *or* shape one's course; play one's part *or* cards; shift for oneself; paddle one's own canoe.

Adjectives—conducting, *etc.*, strategical, tactical, businesslike, practical, executive.

---

conductor, *n.* guide, escort, director; manager, operator, supervisor; guard; drum major, leader, choirmaster; transmitter, conveyor. See CARRIER, DIRECTOR, MUSICIAN.

confederacy, *n.* league, federation, union, alliance; compact, combine. See COMBINATION, PARTY.

confederate, *n.* AID, ally; accomplice; companion, associate.

confer, *v.i.* CONVERSE, discuss; consult, debate, deliberate; talk, parley, palaver; GIVE, grant, bestow. See ADVICE.

confess, *v.t.* acknowledge, avow, own, admit; disclose, tell, reveal, unbosom, unburden, divulge. See DISCLOSURE, PENITENCE.

confidant, *n.* confidante (*fem.*), FRIEND, intimate. *Ant.,* see ENEMY.

confide, *v.t. & i.* trust, believe in, rely on; entrust; commit; tell, divulge, unbosom, unburden. See BELIEF, DISCLOSURE. *Ant.,* see CONCEALMENT.

confidence, *n.* assurance, certainty, positiveness; spirit, boldness, self-reliance; communication, privacy, secret; faith, trust. See BELIEF, COURAGE, HOPE. *Ant.,* see DOUBT.

confine, *v.t.* imprison, incarcerate, immure, jail, detain; cage, pen; restrict, bound, limit. See CIRCUMSCRIPTION. *Ant.,* see FREEDOM.

confinement, *n.* childbirth, childbed; RESTRAINT, imprisonment, incarceration, captivity, custody, detention; CIRCUMSCRIPTION, limitation, restriction. See PRISON. *Ant.,* see FREEDOM.

confirm, *v.t.* establish, fix, strengthen; ratify, sanction, validate, approve, indorse; verify, substantiate, prove, uphold, corroborate. See ASSENT, EVIDENCE, STABILITY. *Ant.,* see DISSENT, REFUSAL.

confiscate, *v.t.* take, seize, commandeer, appropriate; CONDEMN, sequester. See ACQUISITION. *Ant.,* see RESTITUTION.

conflict, *n.* battle, combat, strife, fight, encounter, clash, collision, struggle; discord, antagonism, dissension, hostility. See CONTENTION, DISAGREEMENT, OPPOSITION, WARFARE. *Ant.,* see PACIFICATION, COÖPERATION.

CONFORMITY [82]

Nouns—**1,** conformity, conformance; OBSERVANCE, symmetry; adaptation, adjustment; conventionality, custom; AGREEMENT, compliance; UNIFORMITY, orthodoxy.

2, object lesson, example, instance, specimen, sample, quotation; exemplification, illustration, case in point; pattern, PROTOTYPE.

3, conformist, conventionalist, formalist; stickler.

Verbs—**1,** conform, accommodate, adapt, adapt oneself to; be regular; follow, go by *or* observe the rules; comply with, tally with, chime in with, fall in with; be guided by; follow the fashion *or* crowd; lend oneself to; pass muster, do as others do; in Rome do as the Romans do; go *or* swim with the stream *or* current. *Colloq.,* keep in step, toe the mark, come up to scratch.

2, exemplify, illustrate, cite, quote, give a case; produce an instance.

Adjectives—conformable, conforming, adaptable; regular (see REGULARITY), according to rule, well regulated, orderly; conventional, customary, ordinary, common, habitual, usual; typical, normal, formal; canonical, orthodox, sound, strict, rigid, positive, uncompromising; shipshape; exemplary, illustrative, in point.

Adverbs—conformably, by rule; aggreeably to; in conformity with, in accordance with, in keeping with; according to; consistent with; as usual; in order; of course, as a matter of course; *pro forma,* for form's sake, by the book, according to Hoyle; invariably, uniformly; for example, for instance; *exempli gratia; e.g.*

Antonym, see UNCONFORMITY.

---

confound, *v.t.* confuse, bewilder, perplex, nonplus, dum(b)found, dismay, mix up, puzzle; rout, overcome, overthrow. See DISORDER, DOUBT. *Ant.,* see CERTAINTY.

confront, *v.t.* face, oppose; resist, defy, brave. See OPPOSITION.

confuse, *v.t.* perplex, confound, distract, disconcert, flurry, addle, fluster, bewilder; disorder, mix, embroil, muddle, disarrange, misplace; abash; embarrass. See DISORDER. *Ant.,* see ARRANGEMENT.

confusion, *n.* abashment, embarrassment, discomfiture; perplexity, distraction, bewilderment; mix-up, chaos, disarrangement; turmoil, tumult. See DISORDER. *Ant.,* see ARRANGEMENT, ORDER.

confute, *v.t.* refute, rebut; ANSWER; silence; disprove, show up, confound, explode, invalidate. *Colloq.,* squash, squelch. *Ant.,* see AFFIRMATION, EVIDENCE.

congeal, *v.t. & i.* solidify, harden, fix, gel, jell, set, coagulate, stiffen, thicken; freeze; condense. See DENSITY, REFRIGERATE. *Ant.,* see RARITY.

congenial, *adj.* compatible, agreeable, sympathetic, kindred, harmonious. See AGREEMENT. *Ant.,* see DISAGREEMENT.

congratulate, *v.t.* felicitate; rejoice with; compliment; with many happy returns.

congratulation, *n.* congratulations; felicitation(s); gratulation; compliment(s).

congregation, *n.* ASSEMBLAGE, assembly, gathering, collection, meeting, aggregation; church, parish, flock, fold, brethren.

congress, *n.* COUNCIL, assembly, legislature, parliament; meeting, convention; intercourse. See ASSEMBLAGE.

conjecture, *n.* SUPPOSITION, hypothesis, extrapolation, speculation, guess; inference, surmise. See THOUGHT.

CONNECTION [45]

Nouns—**1,** connection, bond, tie, link; connective, interconnection; nexus; neck, isthmus; bridge, tunnel, causeway.

2, ligature, ligament; sinew, tendon, umbilical cord; cable, wire, strap, bridle, halter, lines, reins; thong, lasso, lariat; rope, cord, twine, string.

3, fastening, clamp, clasp, buckle, button, snap, hook, hook and eye, zipper; lace, lacing, latch, bolt, lock, padlock; anchor, buoy, moorings, guy rope, hawser, grappling iron, cable, painter; leash; belt, suspenders, braces, girdle, sash, cummerbund.

4, knot, slipknot, running knot, bowknot, surgeon's knot, square knot, *etc.,* noose.

5, nail, brad, finishing nail, spike, screw, toggle bolt, staple, tack, thumbtack, rivet.

6, cement, glue, paste, mucilage, gum; mortar, stucco, putty, lime, plaster, solder.

Verbs—connect, link, join (see JUNCTION), combine, attach, fasten; associate, relate (see RELATION).

Antonym, see DISJUNCTION.

---

connivance, *n.* COÖPERATION, collusion, CONSENT, complicity; PERMISSION, toleration, allowance, sufferance. *Ant.,* see OPPOSITION.

connoisseur, *n.* EXPERT, virtuoso; critic, JUDGE, epicure, adept. See TASTE. *Ant.,* see VULGARITY, IGNORANCE.

conquer, *v.t.* prevail, overcome, overthrow, vanquish, subdue, subjugate; win, triumph. See SUCCESS. *Ant.,* see FAILURE.

consanguinity, *n.* kin, kinship, kinfolk, kinsman, kinswoman, relation(s); relationship, blood, blood tie, family, ilk, breed; stock, strain; lineage, line; kidney; root, branch, tree; brotherhood, sisterhood; parentage, paternity, maternity; tribe, clan; generation; offspring, children, progeny; house, household; kith and kin; cousins, *etc.* See RELATION.

conscientious, *adj.* faithful, honorable, incorruptible, upright, trusty; scrupulous, just; religious; strict, thorough, particular, careful, painstaking. See CARE, PROBITY. *Ant.,* see NEGLECT, IMPROBITY.

conscious, *adj.* sensible, cognizant, percipient, understanding, keen; awake, aware, sentient. See INTELLIGENCE, KNOWLEDGE. *Ant.,* see IGNORANCE.

conscription, *n.* enlistment, draft, impressment. See COMPULSION.

consecrate, *v.t.* bless, sanctify, hallow; seal, dedicate, devote. See PIETY. *Ant.,* see IMPIETY.

consecutive, *adj.* See CONTINUITY.

consent, *n. & v.* —*n.* ASSENT, AGREEMENT, acquiescence, compliance; concurrence, harmony, concord; concession, acceptance; yielding; approval; confirmation, ratification. *Colloq.,* O.K., okay. —*v.i.* agree, concur, say yes; comply, yield, accede, acquiesce; permit, give one's consent. *Ant.,* see REFUSAL, DISSENT, DISAGREEMENT.

consequence, *n.* EFFECT, END, result, sequel, outcome, product, fruit; IM-

PORT, account, concern, interest, significance, matter, moment; notability, esteem, greatness, value, prominence; self-importance, arrogance, pomposity. See IMPORTANCE. *Ant.*, see UNIMPORTANCE.

consequential, *adj.* necessary, consequent, sequential; inferable, deducible; indirect, resultant; supercilious, pompous, arrogant, vainglorious, self-important. See EFFECT, VANITY. *Ant.*, see MODESTY.

conservation, *n.* maintenance, protection, keeping, preservation. See STORE. *Ant.*, see DESTRUCTION, WASTE.

conservative, *adj.* unprogressive; unchanging, stable; reactionary, diehard, Tory. *Slang,* mossback. See STABILITY. *Ant.*, see CHANGE.

conserve, *v.t.* See STORE.

consider, *v.t.* deliberate, ponder, brood, contemplate, meditate, ruminate, reflect; speculate, turn, revolve, weigh, muse; believe, JUDGE, deem; regard, heed, mark, notice, mind; entertain; review, esteem. See ATTENTION, THOUGHT. *Ant.*, see RASHNESS.

considerable, *adj.* large, sizable, substantial, important, big; tolerable, fair, respectable; material, noteworthy, weighty; intense, extraordinary. See GREATNESS, IMPORTANCE, SIZE. *Ant.*, see UNIMPORTANCE, LITTLENESS.

considerate, *adj.* THOUGHTFUL, kind, solicitous, humane, sympathetic. See FEELING. *Ant.*, see NEGLECT, DISRESPECT.

consign, *v.t.* deliver, commit, assign, delegate; remit, remand; send, dispatch, ship; condemn, devote. See TRANSFER, PASSAGE.

consist, *v.i.* lie, reside, inhere; include, comprise. See EXISTENCE, COMPOSITION. *Ant.*, see NONEXISTENCE, DECOMPOSITION.

consistent, *adj.* accordant, coherent, uniform, congruous, conformable, compatible, consonant, harmonious; reconcilable; homogeneous, regular. See AGREEMENT. *Ant.*, see DISAGREEMENT.

consolation, *n.* CONDOLENCE, solace, sympathy; assuagement, sop; encouragement. See RELIEF.

consolidate, *v.t.* unite, join, combine, affiliate, federate, syndicate, merge, pool, fuse, incorporate; compress; solidify. See JUNCTION, DENSITY. *Ant.*, see RARITY.

consonance, *n.* AGREEMENT, HARMONY; SIMILARITY; accordance, concord. *Ant.*, see DISAGREEMENT, DISCORD.

conspicuous, *adj.* prominent, notable, eminent, outstanding; signal, striking, salient, noticeable, obvious, marked; glaring, obtrusive, notorious, flagrant. See REPUTE, VISION. *Ant.*, see DISREPUTE, CONCEALMENT.

conspire, *v.i.* plot, intrigue, collude, scheme; concur, combine. See PLAN.

constant, *adj.* sta(u)nch, loyal, steadfast; fast, firm, unwavering, unchanging, unswerving, unflagging; PERMANENT, abiding, enduring; steady, stable; regular, even; continual, incessant. See PROBITY, STABILITY. *Ant.*, see CHANGE.

constitute, *v.i.* form, be, make, frame, compose; total; set up, establish, found; appoint, EFFECT. See CAUSE, COMPOSITION.

constitution, *n.* nature, make-up, temperament, physique, disposition; structure, construction; state, condition; law, edict, code, charter; designation, settlement; creation, foundation. See COMPOSITION, HABIT, LEGALITY.

constraint, *n.* pressure, force, stress; RESTRAINT, confinement, repression; reserve, embarrassment, stiffness; COMPULSION, obligation, coercion, necessity, duress. *Ant.*, see FREEDOM, WILL.

constrict, *v.t.* hamper, limit, CONTRACT, bind, cramp, squeeze, compress; choke, strangle, strangulate. *Ant.*, see EXPAND.

construction, *n.* building, fabrication, composition; formation, structure, erection; conformation; creation; translation, explanation. See FORM, INTERPRETATION, PRODUCTION. *Ant.*, see DESTRUCTION.

consult, *v.i.* advise, confer, counsel, discuss, consider. See ADVICE, THOUGHT.

consume, *v.t.* destroy, demolish, annihilate; burn, decompose, corrode; devour, swallow, eat, drink; exhaust, drain, use up, expend. See DESTRUCTION, USE, WASTE. *Ant.*, see PRESERVATION.

consummate, *adj. & v.* —*adj.* COMPLETE, perfect, finished, absolute; sheer, unmitigated; profound, intense. —*v.t.* COMPLETE, achieve, accomplish; PERFECT. See COMPLETION.

consumption, *n.* destruction; use; burning; tuberculosis. See DISEASE, WASTE. *Ant.,* see ECONOMY, STORE.

contact, *n. & v.* —*n.* TOUCH, contiguity, touching; tangential point, tangency; union, liaison, connection, JUNCTION; juxtaposition, proximity; abutment, adjacency; COÖPERATION. —*v.* TOUCH; meet, join; abut, adjoin; neighbor, border. See NEARNESS, COHERENCE. *Ant.,* see DISJUNCTION, DISTANCE.

contagion, *n.* communicability, infection, epidemic, pestilence, virus; DISEASE, transmission; poison, toxicity. See PASSAGE.

contain, *v.t.* receive, carry, accommodate; INCLUDE, comprise, involve, incorporate, embrace, embody, comprehend, hold; restrain, check. See COMPOSITION.

container, *n.* RECEPTACLE, utensil, jar, bottle, vase, vessel; box, carton, package, crate, bag, sack, can, case.

contaminate, *v.t.* corrupt, infect, taint, polute, soil; defile, sully, befoul, stain, dirty; debauch, deprave, degrade. See DETERIORATION, UNCLEANNESS. *Ant.,* see IMPROVEMENT, CLEANNESS.

contemplate, *v.t.* consider, meditate, ponder, muse, reflect; propose, purpose, PLAN, mean, aim, intend, design; view, behold. See THOUGHT, VISION. *Ant.,* see CHANCE, BLINDNESS.

contemporary, *adj.* simultaneous; coexistent, contemporaneous, coeval, synchronous, coincident, concomitant. See TIME.

CONTEMPT [930]

Nouns—contempt, contemptuousness, disdain, scorn, despisal, contumely; slight, sneer, disparagement, DETRACTION, DISAPPROBATION; derision, DISRESPECT; arrogance, insolence; ridicule, mockery; hoot, catcall. *Colloq.,* slam, dig, cut, cold shoulder.

Verbs—**1,** be contemptuous of, despise, contemn, scorn, disdain, feel contempt for, disregard, slight, not mind; pass by, NEGLECT; look down upon, hold cheap, hold in contempt; think nothing of, think small beer of; UNDERESTIMATE; take no account of, care nothing for; set no store by; not care a straw (see UNIMPORTANCE); set at naught.

2, laugh up one's sleeve, snap one's fingers at, shrug one's shoulders, snub, turn up one's nose at, pooh-pooh, damn with faint praise; sneeze at, sneer at; curl one's lip, toss one's head, look down one's nose at; draw oneself up; laugh at *or* off: be disrespectful; point the finger of scorn, hold up to scorn, laugh to scorn; scout, hoot, flout, hiss, scoff at, jeer, mock, revile, taunt; turn one's back, turn a cold shoulder; trample upon, trample under foot; spurn, kick; fling to the winds. *Colloq.,* cut, leave in the lurch *or* out in the cold, steer clear of, have no truck with, draw the color line. *Slang,* cut dead, pass up, give the go-by, brush off.

Adjectives—**1,** contemptuous; disdainful, scornful; withering, contumelious, supercilious, cynical, haughty, bumptious, cavalier; derisive.

2, contemptible, despicable; pitiable, pitiful; unimportant, despised, downtrodden; unenvied.

Adverbs—contemptuously, arrogantly, insolently, *etc.*

Interjections—bah! pooh! pshaw! tut! fiddle-de-dee! away with! *Slang,* in your hat! come off it!

Antonym, see APPROBATION, RESPECT.

---

contend, *v.i.* engage, contest, battle, struggle, strive, vie, compete; maintain, assert, argue, hold, allege; dispute, debate. See AFFIRMATION, CONTENTION, REASONING.

content, *v.t.* make contented; satisfy, appease, tranquillize, gratify, please, soothe, assuage, mollify, make happy, comfort. See PLEASURE, CHEERFULNESS. *Ant.,* see DISCONTENT.

CONTENTION [720]

Nouns—**1,** contention, strife; contest, contestation, altercation; struggle; belligerency, pugnacity, combativeness; competition, rivalry; litigation (see LAWSUIT); OPPOSITION.

2, controversy, polemics; debate; argument, discussion, war of words;

logomachy; paper war; high words, quarrel; bone of contention; discord, friction, incompatibility, misunderstanding, wrangling; dispute, squabble, tiff; disunion, breach; WARFARE.

3, conflict, skirmish, dogfight; encounter; *rencontre*, rencounter; collision, affair, brush, fight; battle royal, pitched battle; combat, action, engagement, joust, tournament; tilt, tilting, tourney, list; death struggle, Armageddon; shindy; fracas, clash of arms; tussle, scuffle, brawl, fray; mêlée, scrimmage, bush-fighting; naval engagement, sea fight. *Colloq.,* set-to, mix-up, free-for-all. *Slang,* scrap, run-in, hassle, rhubarb.

4, duel, single combat, monomachy; feud, vendetta; satisfaction, passage of arms, affair of honor.

5, wrestling, pugilism, boxing, fisticuffs; spar, mill, round, bout, game, event; prize-fighting; jujitsu, gymnastics; athletics; sports, games of skill, gymkhana.

6, match, race, relay race, foot race, dash, hurdles, automobile race, bicycle race, boat race, regatta; horse-racing, heat, steeplechase, handicap, claiming race, stake race, sweepstakes, trot, pace, Derby, sport of kings; field day; turf, sporting, bull-fight.

Verbs—**1,** contend, contest, oppose, strive, struggle, fight, combat, battle, engage, skirmish; contend with, grapple with, close with; try conclusions with, have a brush with, join issue, come to blows, be at loggerheads, set to, come to scratch, meet hand to hand; wrangle, quarrel.

2, scramble, wrestle, spar, exchange blows, exchange fisticuffs, tussle, tilt, box, stave, fence, encounter, fall foul of, measure swords; take up the cudgels *or* glove *or* gauntlet; enter the lists, couch one's lance; give satisfaction; lay about one, break the peace, lift one's hand against. *Colloq.,* square off, pitch into. *Slang,* scrap, put up a scrap, take on, lay into, light into; pull a gun.

3, compete with, cope with, vie with, race with; emulate; contend for, run a race.

Adjectives—contending; at loggerheads, at war, at issue; competitive, rival; belligerent; contentious, combative, bellicose, unpeaceful; warlike (see WARFARE); quarrelsome, pugnacious; pugilistic.

Antonym, see PACIFICATION.

---

contents, *n.* dimensions (of a container); capacity, volume; cargo, freight, load, loading; burden; cupful, basketful, bottleful, *etc.;* stuffing, packing, filling, wadding. See RECEPTACLE, COMPOSITION.

contest, *v.t.* See CONTENTION.

contingency, *n.* CHANCE, POSSIBILITY, likelihood, accident, casualty, prospect; situation, predicament, case. See CIRCUMSTANCE.

contingent, *adj.* possible; provisional, conditional, provisory, dependent; incidental, accidental, casual. See CHANCE, LIABILITY. *Ant.,* see INTENTION.

continual, *adj.* invariable, steady, regular, persistent, repeated, incessant; constant, unceasing. See FREQUENCY, CONTINUITY.

continuance, *n.* continuation, CONTINUITY, SEQUENCE, succession; persistence, perseverance, endurance; extension; prolongation; maintenance, perpetuation, permanence, unceasingness, ceaselessness; run, series, REPETITION. See FREQUENCY. *Ant.,* see END, SHORTNESS.

continue, *v.* persist; keep, go, carry, run *or* hold on; maintain, keep up; sustain, uphold; prolong, remain, last, endure, withstand; protract, prolong, persevere; be permanent; stay, stick. See CONTINUITY, SEQUENCE. *Ant.,* see END, SHORTNESS.

CONTINUITY [69]

Nouns—continuity; consecutiveness; succession, round, suite, progression, series, train, chain; CONTINUANCE, continuation, perpetuity; concatenation, scale; gradation, course; procession, column; retinue, caravan, cortège, cavalcade, rank and file, line of battle, array; running fire; pedigree, genealogy, lineage, race; rank, file, line, row, range, tier, string, thread, team; suit; colonnade.

Verbs—follow in a series, form a series; fall in; arrange in a series, string together, thread, graduate; tabulate, list, file.

Adjectives—continuous, continued; consecutive; progressive, gradual; serial, successive; immediate, unbroken, entire; linear; in a line, in a row; uninterrupted, unintermitting, unremitting; ceaseless; perennial, evergreen; constant, chronic, continual, repeated, persistent, repeating, persisting.

Adverbs—continuously, *etc.; seriatim;* in a line, in succession, in series, in turn; running, gradually, step by step, at a stretch; in file, in column, in single file, in Indian file.

Antonym, see DISJUNCTION.

---

contortion, *n.* DISTORTION, twist, dislocation, deformity; grimace.

contour, *n.* outline, profile, shape, form, conformation, figure. See APPEARANCE.

contraband, *adj.* forbidden, illegal, illicit, prohibited, smuggled. See RESTRAINT.

contract, *n.* compact, AGREEMENT, promise, bargain, covenant, stipulation, convention. *Ant.,* see DISAGREEMENT.

CONTRACTION [195]

Nouns—**1,** contraction, reduction, diminution; DECREASE; defalcation, decrement; lessening, shrinking, astringency; emaciation, attenuation, tabefaction, consumption; atrophy.

2, condensation, compression, compactness; COMPENDIUM, squeezing; strangulation; corrugation; contractility, compressibility; coarctation.

Verbs—**1,** contract, become small, become smaller; lessen, decrease, dwindle, shrink, narrow, shrivel, collapse, wither, lose flesh, reduce, wizen, fall away, waste, wane, ebb; decay, deteriorate (see DETERIORATION).

2, contract, render smaller, lessen, diminish, draw in, narrow, coarctate; constrict, constringe; condense, compress, squeeze, cramp, corrugate, crush, crumple up, warp, purse up, pack, stow; pinch, tighten, strangle; cramp; stunt, dwarf; pare, reduce, attenuate, rub down, scrape, file, grind, chip, shave, shear; shorten; circumscribe; restrain. See SHORTNESS, CIRCUMSCRIPTION, RESTRAINT.

Adjectives—contracting, contractive; astringent; shrunk, strangulated, wizened, stunted; waning, neap; compact.

Antonym, see INCREASE.

---

contradict, *v.t.* gainsay, deny, belie, controvert, refute, disprove, overthrow; dispute, dissent. See CONTENTION. *Ant.,* see IDENTITY, EVIDENCE.

contrariness, *n.* contrariety, OPPOSITION, obstinacy; antagonism, DISAGREEMENT, DISOBEDIENCE. *Ant.,* see AGREEMENT, OBEDIENCE.

contrary, *adj.* opposed, opposite, counter, contradictory; unfavorable, adverse; captious, willful, perverse; hostile, antagonistic. See OPPOSITION. *Ant.,* see AGREEMENT, COÖPERATION.

contrast, *n.* DIFFERENCE, opposition, antithesis, foil, dissimilarity, unlikeness, disparity; converse, counterpoint, obverse, contrary. See OPPOSITION. *Ant.,* see IDENTITY, SIMILARITY.

contribute, *v.t. & i.* give, subscribe, donate; help, aid, assist; conduce, advance, tend, serve, redound, go. See GIVING, CAUSE. *Ant.,* see RECEIVING.

contrivance, *n.* device, invention, construction, machine, apparatus, gear; PLAN, scheme, trick, stratagem. *Colloq.,* contraption. See INSTRUMENT.

control, *v. & n.* —*v.t.* command, dominate, govern, rule, regulate, direct, master; restrain, subdue, modify, check; test, verify. *Ant.,* see FREEDOM. —*n.* COMMAND, mastery, domination, sway, upper hand, power, regimentation, government, direction, management, dominion; RESTRAINT, ceiling, regulation. *Ant.,* see FREEDOM.

controversy, *n.* CONTENTION, dispute, argument, discussion, debate, quarrel, wrangle, altercation. *Ant.,* see AGREEMENT.

controvert, *v.t.* deny, contradict, contravene, traverse [legal], impugn, refute, confute, oppose, dispute, counter. See DEFENSE, NEGATION. *Ant.,* see AFFIRMATION.

convalesce, *v.i.* recover, recuperate, rally, revive, improve. See HEALTH.

convene, *v.i.* ASSEMBLE, gather, collect, congregate, meet; convoke. *Ant.,* DISPERSE.

convenience, *n.* accessibility, handiness, availability, suitability; advantage, accommodation, comfort, opportunity, ease. See USE. *Ant.*, see USELESSNESS.

convent, *n.* cloister, nunnery, abbey, priory. See TEMPLE.

convention, *n.* ASSEMBLAGE, gathering, congregation, congress, meeting, caucus, council; convocation; RULE, custom, usage, formality, practice; propriety, conventionality. See FASHION.

conventional, *adj.* customary, accepted, orthodox, approved, habitual, usual; formal. See CONFORMITY. *Ant.*, see UNCONFORMITY.

convergence, *n.* approach; ASSEMBLAGE, conjunction; meeting, confluence; focalization; JUNCTION; concurrence, concourse; concentration. *Ant.*, see DISJUNCTION.

conversation, *n.* talk, SPEECH, parley, colloquy, palaver; discussion, discourse, interview, dialogue; conference, chat. *Colloq.*, powwow, gab. *Slang*, huddle, confab, talkfest.

converse, *v. & n.* —*v.* talk, exchange talk; parley, speak, communicate with; chat, gossip, prattle; discuss, discourse, confer. —*n.* the opposite, reverse.

conversion, *n.* reduction, transformation; CHANGE, retooling, changeover, adaption; transmutation, transmogrification; alchemy; RESOLUTION, assimilation; change of religion; reformation, metamorphosis, metempsychosis. See DIFFERENCE, REVOLUTION.

convert, *v. & n.* —*v.t.* CHANGE, change *or* make over; retool, adapt; reorganize, remodel, regenerate; change (the religion of); reduce; transmute, transform, transmogrify; render; apply. See CHANGEABLENESS. —*n.* neophyte, disciple; renegade, apostate.

CONVEXITY [250]

Nouns—**1**, convexity, prominence, projection, swelling, bulge, protuberance, protrusion, growth.

2, excrescence, intumescence, outgrowth, tumor, tubercle, tuberosity; hump, hunch, bunch; tooth, knob, elbow; bulb, node, nodule; tongue; pimple, wen, weal, pustule, growth, sarcoma, carbuncle, corn, wart, furuncle, polyp, fungus, blister, boil (see DISEASE); papilla; breast, bosom, nipple, teat, mammilla; nose, probiscis, beak, snout; belly; withers, back, shoulder, lip. *Colloq.*, corporation, pot.

3, hill, HEIGHT, cape, promontory, headland; peninsula, neck, isthmus, point of land; reef; mole, jetty; ledge, spur.

4, cupola, dome, arch, balcony, eaves; pilaster; relief, bas relief, cameo.

Verbs—be convex; project, bulge, protrude, pout, bunch; jut out, stand out, stick out, poke out; stick up, bristle, start up, shoot up; swell, hand over, bend over; beetle; render prominent; raise, emboss, chase.

Adjectives—convex, prominent, protuberant; projecting; bossed; nodular, bunchy; clavate; mammiform; papulous; hemispheric, bulbous; bowed, arched; bold; bellied; tuberous, tuberculous; tumorous; cornute, odontoid; lentiform, lenticular; salient, in relief, raised, repoussé; bloated.

Antonym, see CONCAVITY.

---

convey, *v.t.* bear, carry, transport, transmit; impart, communicate; TRANSFER, grant, cede, will. See INFORMATION.

conveyance, *n.* VEHICLE, wagon, van, bus, car; TRANSFER, assignment, sale, legacy, disposal; transmission, communication. See PASSAGE.

convict, *v. & n.* —*v.t.* condemn, find guilty, doom, sentence. See JUSTICE, LAWSUIT, DISAPPROBATION. *Ant.*, see VINDICATION. —*n.* criminal, felon, jailbird, prisoner, captive. See EVILDOER, PRISON.

conviction, *n.* BELIEF, persuasion, faith, opinion, view; CONDEMNATION, sentence, penalty. *Ant.*, doubt, ACQUITTAL.

convince, *v.t.* persuade, satisfy, assure. See BELIEF. *Ant.*, see DOUBT.

convoke, *v.t.* convene, assemble, summon, call, collect, gather. See ASSEMBLAGE. *Ant.*, DISPERSE.

CONVOLUTION [248]

Nouns—**1**, convolution, winding; involution, circumvolution; wave, undulation, tortuosity, anfractuosity; sinuosity, sinuation; meandering, circuit; twist, twirl, windings and turnings; ambages; torsion; inosculation; reticulation, CROSSING.

2, coil, roll, curl, curlicue, buckle, spiral, helix, corkscrew, worm, volute, rundle; tendril; scallop, escalop; serpent, eel, maze, labyrinth.

Verbs—convolve, be convoluted, wind, twine, turn and twist, twirl; wave, undulate, meander; inosculate; entwine, intwine; twist, coil, roll; wrinkle, curl, crisp, twill; frizz, frizzle; crimp, crape, indent, scallop; wring, intort; contort; wreathe.

Adjectives—convoluted; winding, twisting, tortile, tortuous; wavy; undulatory; circling, snaky, snakelike, serpentine; anguilliform, vermiform; vermicular; mazy, sinuous, flexuous, sigmoidal; spiral, coiled, helical, turbinated; involved, intricate, complicated, perplexed; labyrinthine; peristaltic.

Adverbs—convolutely, in and out, round and round.

Antonym, see DIRECTION.

---

convoy, *v.t.* accompany, escort, conduct; watch, protect, guard, support. See ACCOMPANIMENT.

convulse, *v.t.* agitate, shake, disturb, trouble, excite, stir; rend, wring, hurt. See AGITATION, PAIN.

cook, *v.t.* prepare, concoct, fix, make; roast, broil, boil, fry, *etc. Colloq.* doctor. *Slang,* ruin, spoil. See HEAT.

cool, *v. & adj.* —*v.t.* chill, REFRIGERATE, ice, freeze, harden; calm, allay. See COLD, MODERATION. *Ant.,* see HEAT. —*adj.* COLD, chilly, frigid; bold, impudent; INEXCITABLE, self-controlled, calm, deliberate, composed, indifferent, unemotional, self-possessed; easygoing, placid; unfriendly, distant, lukewarm. *Ant.,* see FRIEND, EXCITEMENT. HEAT.

COÖPERATION [709]

Nouns—**1,** coöperation; coadjuvancy, coadjutancy; coagency, coefficiency; concert, concurrence, participation, collaboration; union, UNITY, combination, collusion, complicity, conspiracy.

2, association, alliance, colleagueship, copartnership; confederation, coalition, fusion; union; logrolling, fraternity, fellowship, freemasonry; unanimity, ASSENT; esprit de corps, party spirit; clanship, partisanship; concord, AGREEMENT. See PARTY.

Verbs—**1,** coöperate, concur; conduce, combine; fraternize; conspire, collude, connive, concert, lay heads together; confederate, be in league with; unite one's efforts; keep together, pull together, club together, hang together, hold together, league together, band together; be banded together; stand shoulder to shoulder; act in concert, join forces; understand one another, play into the hands of, hunt in couples. *Colloq.,* play ball.

2, side with, go along with, go hand in hand with, join hands with, make common cause with, unite with, join with, mix oneself up with, take part with, cast in one's lot with; join with, enter into partnership with; rally round, follow the lead of; come to, pass over to, come into the views of; be in the same boat. *Colloq.,* throw in with, line up with.

3, be a party to, lend oneself to; participate; have a hand in, have a finger in the pie; take part in; second, AID, take the part of, play the game of; espouse a cause, espouse a quarrel. *Colloq.,* sit in, chip in.

Adjectives—coöperating, in coöperation *or* league; coadjuvant, coadjutant; participatory, partaking; favorable to; unopposed. *Slang,* in cahoots with.

Adverbs—coöperatively; as one man; together; unanimously; shoulder to shoulder; side by side; hand in hand; in common; share and share alike; pro rata.

Antonym, see OPPOSITION.

---

coördinate, *v.t.* equalize, adapt, harmonize, synchronize, adjust; organize. See ARRANGEMENT. *Ant.,* see DISORDER.

copious, *adj.* adequate, abundant, plentiful, ample, rich, full, overflowing; wordy, profuse, diffuse, prolix. See SUFFICIENCY. *Ant.,* see INSUFFICIENCY.

copy, *v. & n.* —*v.* duplicate, imitate, reproduce, transcribe; parody, burlesque, mimic, travesty; forge, counterfeit; echo; reprint. *Colloq.,* fake.

—*n.* transcript; IMITATION, reproduction, model, likeness, image; duplication, tracing, ditto; replica, facsimile; reprint, REPETITION; counterfeit, sham; echo, double, twin, shadow; reflection, counterpart, effigy; written material, manuscript. *Slang*, spittin' image, dead ringer, takeoff.

cord, *n.* string, rope, band, bond, twine, tie. See FILAMENT, CONNECTION.

cordial, *adj.* sincere, heartfelt; hearty, genial, friendly, amicable, kindly, warm. See COURTESY. *Ant.*, see DISCOURTESY.

core, *n.* center, interim, heart, nucleus, kernel; pith, nut, nub, substance, gist. See MIDDLE, IMPORTANCE. *Ant.*, see EDGE.

corner, *n.* angle; nook, niche; control, monopoly; predicament. See ANGULARITY, POSSESSION, DIFFICULTY. *Ant.*, see CURVATURE.

corporation, *n.* association, syndicate, company, society, partnership, merger, trust. See PARTY, BUSINESS.

corpse, *n.* body, cadaver, carcass; remains, skeleton, bones. *Slang*, stiff. See DEATH. *Ant.*, see LIFE.

corpulence, *n.* fatness, fleshiness, obesity, plumpness, portliness, bulk. See SIZE. *Ant.*, see NARROWNESS, LITTLENESS.

correct, *v. & adj.* —*v.t.* improve, rectify, right, repair, remedy, amend, set right, reform, better; reprove, punish, chastise, discipline; counteract, neutralize. See IMPROVEMENT, DISAPPROBATION. —*adj.* RIGHT, regular, true, strict, accurate, exact, precise, perfect. *Ant.*, see WRONG.

correlation, *n.* correlativity; reciprocalness, reciprocation, reciprocity; mutuality, mutualness; interrelation, correspondence; analogy; likeness, SIMILARITY, INTERCHANGE. See RELATION.

correspond, *v.i.* match, tally, suit, correlate, agree, fit, harmonize; be analogous, homologous, like *or* similar; confirm, accord, complement; ANSWER, write (letters), intercommunicate, communicate. See SIMILARITY, AGREEMENT, COMMUNICATION. *Ant.*, see DIFFERENCE, DISAGREEMENT.

correspondence, *n.* correlation, likeness, SIMILARITY; analogy; homology; concurrence, AGREEMENT; intercourse, communication, congress; congruity, CONFORMITY; relation, accordance, harmony; letters, letter-writing, mail. *Ant.*, see DIFFERENCE, DISAGREEMENT.

correspondent, *n. & adj.* —*n.* writer, reporter, contributor. See WRITING, COMMUNICATIONS. —*adj.* corresponding; see CORRESPONDENCE, AGREEMENT. *Ant.*, see DISAGREEMENT.

corrigible, *adj.* amendable, rectifiable; amenable, tractable, docile. See IMPROVEMENT, WILL. *Ant.*, see DETERIORATION, REFUSAL.

corrode, *v.t.* consume, gnaw, bite, rust, decay, wear; eat, etch. See DETERIORATION. *Ant.*, see IMPROVEMENT.

corrugate, *v.t.* FURROW, wrinkle, groove. See ROUGHNESS. *Ant.*, see SMOOTHNESS.

corrupt, *v. & adj.* —*v.t.* demoralize, vitiate, deprave, defile, degrade, debase, debauch; bribe, pervert; contaminate, spoil, taint. —*adj.* wicked, demoralized, immoral, impure, dissolute, depraved, profligate, base; vicious; rotten, infected, tainted, spoiled. See IMPROBITY, UNCLEANNESS, EVIL. *Ant.*, see PROBITY, INNOCENCE.

cosmic, *adj.* universal, galactic, heavenly; vast, grandiose; harmonious, orderly. See UNIVERSE.

cost, *n.* price, charge, expense, expenditure, outlay, disbursement, PAYMENT.

costume, *n.* CLOTHING, clothes, dress, garb, attire, apparel; uniform. *Colloq.*, outfit, rig.

couch, *n.* bed, cot, pallet; lounge, divan, settee, convertible, davenport, chaise longue. See SUPPORT.

council, *n.* committee; cabinet, ministry; chamber, board, bench, staff, directory; congress, convention, conclave, caucus; ASSEMBLAGE, assembly.

count, *v.t.* compute, enumerate, tell, score, figure, account, matter, reckon; esteem, call, make, consider, estimate. See JUDGE, NUMERATION.

countenance, *n.* face, features, visage, physiognomy; approval, sanction, acceptance, favor, patronage; expression, complexion, aspect. *Slang*, mug. See APPEARANCE, APPROBATION, FRONT.

counter, *adj.* opposing, opposite, contrary, counterclockwise, cross, against. See OPPOSITION. *Ant.*, see IDENTITY.

counteract, *v.* check, defeat, fight; thwart, nullify, negate, frustrate; counter-

balance; overthrow; neutralize, render harmless. See OPPOSITION, NULLIFI-
CATION. *Ant.*, see AID.

counterevidence, *n.* rebuttal, disproof, refutation, NULLIFICATION, VINDI-
CATION, confutation, contradiction. *Ant.*, see EVIDENCE.

counterfeit, *adj. & n.* —*adj.* IMITATION, false, sham, forged, bogus, bastard,
spurious. *Slang*, fake, phony. —*n.* forgery, slug, sham, brummagem,
dummy, pretense. *Slang*, fake, phony. See DECEPTION, FALSEHOOD. *Ant.*,
see TRUTH.

counterpart, *n.* COPY, duplicate, double, facsimile, replica; likeness, image,
similitude, match, parallel, twin, mate; complement. See IDENTITY, SIMI-
LARITY. *Ant.*, see DIFFERENCE.

countersign, *n.* signal, sign, seal; password, shibboleth, watchword, identification. See INDICATION.

countless, *adj.* innumerable, myriad, infinite, numberless, uncountable, in-
calculable, illimitable. See MULTITUDE. *Ant.*, see RARITY.

country, *n.* LAND, REGION, tract, district, territory; countryside, plain, fields;
state, people, fatherland, home, nation, power. *Slang*, the sticks. See
AUTHORITY, SPACE.

couple, *v.t.* join, tie, link; yoke, unite, pair; marry. See JUNCTION, DUPLI-
CATION, MARRIAGE. *Ant.*, see DISJUNCTION.

COURAGE [861]

Nouns—**1,** courage, bravery, valor; resoluteness, boldness; spirit, daring,
gallantry, heroism, intrepidity; contempt of danger, defiance of danger;
audacity, RASHNESS, dash; DEFIANCE; confidence, self-reliance; chivalry,
prowess, derring-do; resolution, determination.

2, manliness, manhood; nerve, pluck, mettle, game; heart, heart of grace;
face, virtue, hardihood, fortitude; firmness, STABILITY; heart of oak; PERSE-
VERANCE. *Colloq.*, backbone, spunk. *Slang*, sand, guts.

3, exploit, feat, enterprise, achievement; deed, heroic deed, heroic act;
bold stroke.

4, man of courage, man of mettle; hero, heroine, demigod, demigoddess;
lion, tiger, panther, bulldog; gamecock, fighting-cock; bully, fire-eater.

Verbs—**1,** be courageous; dare, venture, make bold; brave, beard, defy; face,
confront, brave, defy, despise *or* mock danger; not turn a hair; look in the
face; face up to; face; meet; put a bold face upon, show fight; go through
fire and water, run the gantlet; bell the cat, take the bull by the horns,
beard the lion in his den.

2, take, muster, summon up *or* pluck up courage; nerve oneself, take heart;
hold up one's head, screw one's courage to the sticking place; come up to
scratch; stand to one's guns; stand against; bear up, bear up against; hold
out; persevere. *Colloq.*, keep a stiff upper lip. *Slang*, stand the gaff.

3, give courage, inspire courage; reassure, encourage, embolden, inspirit,
cheer, nerve, put upon one's mettle, rally, raise a rallying cry; pat on the
back, make a man of, keep in countenance.

Adjectives—**1,** courageous, brave; valiant, valorous; gallant, intrepid;
spirited, spiritful; high-spirited, high-mettled; mettlesome, plucky; manly,
manful; resolute, stout, stouthearted; iron-hearted, lion-hearted; enterprising; adventurous; venturous, venturesome; dashing, chivalrous; soldierly, warlike, heroic; strong-minded, hardy, doughty; firm, determined,
dogged, indomitable, persevering. *Colloq.*, gritty, bold as brass.

2, bold, bold-spirited; daring, audacious; fearless, dauntless, undaunted,
unappalled, undismayed, unawed, unabashed, unalarmed, unflinching, un-
shrinking, unblenching, unapprehensive; confident, self-reliant; bold as a
lion; fierce, savage; pugnacious, bellicose.

Antonym, see COWARDICE.

course, *n. & v.* —*n.* passage of time; lapse, flow, flight *or* process of time;
due course; race, career, circuit; way, path, route, road; DIRECTION, progress; orbit, itinerary; order, succession, bearing, comportment, CONDUCT;
series, system, ARRANGEMENT. —*v.* hunt, pursue, chase; run; TRAVEL; race.
See TIME, PASSAGE.

court, *v. & n.* —*v.t.* solicit, invite; curry favor, cultivate, cajole, praise;

woo, sue, make love. *Colloq.*, spark. —*n.* inclosure, yard, courtyard, quadrangle, patio; tribunal, bench, bar, jurisdiction, session; addresses, attention; palace, hall; retinue, following, train. See ENDEARMENT, COURTESY, REQUEST, LAWSUIT, SERVANT.

COURTESY [894]

Nouns—1, courtesy; courteousness; RESPECT, good manners, good behavior, good breeding; manners; politeness, urbanity, comity, gentility, breeding, cultivation, polish, presence; civility, civilization; amenity, suavity; good temper, good humor, amiability, easy temper, complacency, soft tongue, condescension, HUMILITY, affability, complaisance, amiability, gallantry.
2, compliment; fair words, soft words, sweet words; honeyed phrases; ceremonial; salutation, reception, presentation, introduction, mark of recognition, nod, recognition; welcome, respects, devoir; valediction, farewell, goodbye; regards, remembrances; kind regards, kind remembrances; love, best love, duty; CONDOLENCE.
3, obeisance, reverence, bow, courtesy, curtsy, scrape, salaam, kowtow, bowing and scraping; kneeling; genuflection (see WORSHIP); obsequiousness; salute, hand-shake, grip of the hand, embrace, hug, squeeze; accolade; loving cup; love token, kiss, buss (see ENDEARMENT).
Verbs—1, be courteous, show courtesy; receive, do the honors, usher, greet, hail, bid welcome; welcome, welcome with open arms; shake hands; hold out, press *or* squeeze the hand; bid Godspeed; speed the parting guest; cheer; serenade.
2, salute; embrace, kiss (see ENDEARMENT); kiss hands; drink to, pledge, hob and nob; move to, nod to; smile upon; uncover, cap; touch *or* take off the hat; doff the cap; present arms; make way for; bow; make one's bow; scrape, curtsy, courtesy; bob a curtsy, kneel; bow, bend the knee, prostrate oneself (see WORSHIP).
3, visit, wait upon, present oneself, pay one's respects, pay a visit (see SOCIALITY); dance attendance on (see SERVILITY); pay attentions to; do homage to (see RESPECT).
4, mind one's Ps and Qs, behave oneself, be all things to all men, conciliate, speak one fair, take in good part; look as if butter would not melt in one's mouth; mend one's manners.
5, render polite; polish, cultivate, civilize, humanize.
Adjectives—courteous, polite, civil, mannerly, urbane; well-behaved, well-mannered, well-bred, well-brought up; good-mannered, polished, civilized, cultivated; refined (see TASTE); gentlemanly; gallant; fine-spoken, fair-spoken, soft-spoken; honey-mouthed, honey-tongued; oily, bland; obliging, conciliatory, complaisant, complacent; obsequious; on one's good behavior; ingratiating, winning; gentle, mild; good-humored, cordial, gracious, affable, familiar; neighborly.
Adverbs—courteously; with a good grace; with open *or* outstretched arms; in good humor.

Antonym, see DISCOURTESY.

cove, *n.* inlet, creek, bay, lagoon; nook.
covenant, *v. & n.* —*v.i.* contract, agree, undertake, stipulate, engage, bargain. —*n.* agreement, contract, bargain, pact. See AGREEMENT.

COVERING [223]

Nouns—1, covering, cover; superposition, superimposition; canopy, awning, tent, pavilion, marquee; umbrella, parasol, sunshade; veil, SHADE; shield, DEFENSE; CLOTHING; (see CONCEALMENT).
2, roof, ceiling, thatch, tile; tiling, slates, slating, leads; shed, ABODE.
3, coverlet, counterpane, sheet, quilt, blanket, bedclothes, bedding; rug, carpet, linoleum; tapestry, drugget; housing.
4, peel, crust, bark, rind, cortex, husk, shell, coat; capsule; sheath, sheathing; pod, casing, case; wrapper, wrapping; envelope, vesicle.
5, veneer, facing; pavement; scale, LAYER; coating, paint; varnish; incrustation, ground, enamel; whitewash, plaster, stucco, compo; lining; cerement; ointment, grease.

6, integument; skin, pellicle, fleece, fell, fur, leather, hide; pelt, peltry; cuticle; epidermis.
Verbs—cover; superpose, superimpose; overlay, overspread; wrap, incase; face, case, veneer, pave, paper; tip, cap, bind; coat, paint, varnish, pay, incrust, stucco, dab, plaster, tar; wash; besmear, smear; bedaub, daub; anoint, do over; gild, plate, japan, lacquer, enamel, whitewash; overlie, overarch, overlap, overhang; CONCEAL.
Adjectives—covering, cutaneous, dermal, epidermal, cortical, cuticular, tegumentary, skinlike, skinny, scaly, squamous; covered, imbricated, armor-plated, ironclad; under cover.
Antonym, see DIVESTMENT.

covet, *v.t.* DESIRE, long for, crave, grudge, want, envy, wish.
cow, *n.* bovine, calf, heifer; kine, cattle. See ANIMAL.

COWARDICE [862]

Nouns—cowardice, cowardliness, pusillanimity; timidity, effeminacy; poltroonery, baseness; dastardness, dastardy; abject fear, funk; Dutch courage; FEAR, white feather, faint heart, cold feet.
2, coward, poltroon, dastard, sneak, craven, recreant; milksop, white-liver, sissy; alarmist, terrorist, pessimist; runagate, runaway, fugitive. *Colloq.*, rabbit, baby. *Slang*, fraidy-cat.
Verbs—be cowardly, be a coward; cower, skulk, sneak; quail, flinch, shy, fight shy, slink, turn tail; run away (see AVOID); show the white feather.
Adjectives—coward, cowardly; fearful, shy; timid, timorous; skittish; poor-spirited, spiritless, soft, effeminate; weak-minded, weak-hearted, faint-hearted, chicken-hearted, lily-hearted, pigeon-hearted; lily-livered, white-livered; milksop; unable to say "Boo" to a goose; dastard, dastardly; base, craven, sneaking, recreant; unwarlike, unsoldierlike, shy, shrinking, unmanned; frightened, afraid (see FEAR).
Antonym, see COURAGE.

coy, *adj.* bashful, reserved; chary; shrinking, shy, demure, retiring; coquettish. See MODESTY. *Ant.*, see VANITY.
crabbed, *adj.* ill-tempered, irascible, surly, growly, cross, peevish; difficult, complex; illegible, squeezed, irregular. See IRASCIBILITY, DISTORTION.
crack, *v. & n.* —*v.t.* SNAP, pop, rend, explode, bang; crackle; break, split, burst, cleave, fracture, crush. *Slang*, fail, bust, break down. See DISJUNCTION. *Ant.*, see JUNCTION. —*n.* SNAP, break, fracture; crevice, crackle, craze, chink, flaw, cleft, rift, rent, fissure; slit, rut, groove, seam; pop, crash, clap. *Ant.*, see COHERENCE.
craft, *n.* SKILL, expertness; art, handicraft; trade; vessel, SHIP, boat, CUNNING, artifice, artfulness, deceit, trickery. See BUSINESS. *Ant.*, see SIMPLENESS, NAVIGATION, UNSKILLFULNESS.
cram, *v.t.* crowd, stuff, press, force, drive, jam, pack, choke; satiate, surfeit, gormandize, gorge, guzzle; teach, study. See CLOSURE, GLUTTONY, TEACHING.
cramp, *v.t.* restrict, restrain, compress, hamper, handicap; fasten; cripple, paralyze, incapacitate. See HINDRANCE, IMPOTENCE. *Ant.*, AID, POWER.
crash, *n.* collision, shock, smash, shattering; failure, collapse, downfall; burst, blast. See DESTRUCTION, IMPULSE, LOUDNESS.
crass, *adv.* coarse, crude, gross, unrefined, raw; dense, stupid. See DENSITY, VULGARITY. *Ant.*, see RARITY, TASTE.
crave, *v.t.* DESIRE, long for, yearn for; ask, beg, seek, solicit, REQUEST, supplicate, beseech, pray, petition; need, require. See NECESSITY.
crawl, *v.i.* creep, lag, drag; cringe, fawn, cower, grovel. See SERVILITY, SLOWNESS. *Ant.*, see INSOLENCE, VELOCITY.
crazy, *adj.* INSANE, demented, distracted, mad, lunatic, crack-brained; cracked, unsound; shaky, rickety. See INSANITY. *Ant.*, see SANITY.
creak, *v.i.* squeak, grind, grate, rasp, stridulate. See LOUDNESS, SOUND.
cream, *n.* *crème* (Fr.), top milk, rich milk; best, flower, pick, élite; gist, kernel; cosmetic. See GOODNESS, FOOD, IMPORTANCE. *Ant.*, see POPULACE, UNIMPORTANCE.

create, *v.t.* CAUSE, make, form, bring into being, fashion, originate, occasion, constitute; PRODUCE, procreate, raise, rear, propagate, breed; devise, design, conceive, invent, construct, build; bring to pass; IMAGINE, visualize, envisage. See PRODUCTION. *Ant.*, see DESTRUCTION.

creator, *n.* DEITY, God, Supreme Being; author, maker, fashioner, originator, producer, inventor, designer. See CAUSE, PRODUCTION.

creature, *n.* ANIMAL, BEAST; creation, being, thing; human being, individual, mortal; SERVANT, instrument, slave, tool, dependent.

credence, *n.* BELIEF, assurance, reliance, credit, trust; recognition, acceptance, acknowledgment. *Ant.*, see DOUBT.

credible, *adj.* probable, likely; believable, trustworthy, reliable; conceivable, thinkable. See BELIEF. *Ant.*, see DOUBT.

credit, *n. & v.* —*n.* BELIEF, trust; recognition, acknowledgment; faith, reliance, confidence; honor, merit; asset; reputation, financial standing. —*v.t.* believe, accept; trust; have *or* put faith in; enter *or* apply (on the credit side); honor. See MONEY, BUSINESS, REPUTE, APPROBATION. *Ant.*, see DEBT.

CREDULITY [486]

Nouns—**1,** credulity, credulousness, gullibility; infatuation; self-delusion, self-deception; superstition; one's blind side; blind faith; bigotry, obstinacy. See BELIEF.

2, credulous person, DUPE.

Verbs—**1,** be credulous; swallow, gulp down; take on trust *or* faith; take for granted, take for gospel; run away with a notion *or* idea; jump to a conclusion, rush to a conclusion; take the shadow for the substance; catch at straws. *Colloq.*, swallow whole. *Slang*, swallow hook, line and sinker; bite; take the bait; fall for.

2, impose upon, deceive (see DECEPTION), dupe, delude, gull.

Adjectives—credulous, gullible; easily deceived, unsuspecting, simple, green, soft, childish, silly, stupid; overcredulous, overconfident; infatuated; superstitious.

Antonym, see DOUBT.

---

creed, *n.* BELIEF, tenet, doctrine, persuasion, credo, dogma, faith, formula.

creep, *v.i.* crawl, worm, swarm; grovel. See SLOWNESS. *Ant.*, see VELOCITY.

cremation, *n.* burning, incineration, suttee. See HEAT, INTERMENT.

crest, *n.* crown, tuft, topknot, comb, plume; summit, peak, ridge, tip, height, top; seal, device; culmination, climax. See CONVEXITY, HEIGHT. *Ant.*, see SUPPORT.

crew, *n.* force, gang, band, set, throng, mob, squad; ASSEMBLAGE, company; sailors. See NAVIGATION.

crib, *n.* manger, trough, box, stall, bin; cot, bed, cradle; hut, hovel; translation, key; plagiarism. *Slang*, pony, trot. See ABODE, RECEPTACLE, SUPPORT.

crime, *n.* offense, misdemeanor, felony, outrage; transgression, sin, evil, wrongdoing; illegality, lawbreaking. See GUILT. *Ant.*, see INNOCENCE.

criminal, *n.* offender, malefactor, felon, sinner, culprit, convict, EVILDOER.

cringe, *v.i.* cower, stoop, flinch, wince, crouch, shrink; fawn, truckle, crawl, grovel; sneak. See AVOIDANCE, SERVILITY. *Ant.*, see INSOLENCE.

cripple, *v.t.* disable, incapacitate, unfit; lame, paralyze, maim; hurt, enfeeble, cramp. See IMPOTENCE, HINDRANCE, DISTORTION. *Ant.*, see POWER.

crisis, *n.* turning point; juncture; exigency, emergency, extremity, pinch, trial, crux. See CIRCUMSTANCE, DIFFICULTY.

crisp, *adj.* brittle, curly, blunt, friable; sharp, definite, lively, clean-cut, clear; cold, stiff; SHORT, crunchy, crumbly; firm, fresh; bracing. See FEELING, FOOD. *Ant.*, see SOFTNESS.

criterion, *n.* standard, model, rule, test, measure, norm, touchstone.

critic, *n.* judge, connoisseur, expert, reviewer, commentator; censor, censurer. See DETRACTION, TASTE.

criticize, *v.t.* JUDGE, censure, excoriate, blame, reprove, flay; examine, dissect, analyze, review. *Slang*, roast. See DISAPPROBATION. *Ant.*, PRAISE.

crooked, *adj.* bent, curved, angular, sinuous, winding, askew, zigzag, twisted, warped; false, dishonest, fraudulent, deceptive, sneaking; oblique, aslant, distorted, awry. See IMPROBITY, DISTORTION. *Ant.*, see FORM.

crop, *n.* craw, gorge; whip; harvest, yield, fruit, product. See PRODUCTION.

cross, *n:, v. & adj.* —*n.* rood, crucifix; (Cap.) Christianity, the Church, Gospel; crosspiece, cross mark, X, ex; gibbet; burden, trial, trouble, affliction; hybrid, MIXTURE, crossbreed; half-caste, halfbreed. —*v.* crossbreed, cross-pollinate, mix; traverse, go across, ford; mark out, cancel, strike out; pass over; lie across *or* athwart; bar, line, crosshatch; intersect, bisect, cut across; circumvent, thwart, frustrate, foil, oppose, hinder, obstruct. See CONTENTION, NULLIFICATION, OPPOSITION, TRAVEL, DIRECTION. —*adj.* opposite, converse; peevish, touchy, snappish, testy, perverse; out of sorts *or* humor; sulky, sullen; ill-tempered. *Colloq.*, grouchy, crabby, cranky. See IRASCIBILITY. *Ant.*, see AGREEMENT, PLEASURE.

crossing, *n.* crossroad(s), intersection; decussation; underpass, bridge, tunnel; passage; traverse; latticework, grating, grid, gridiron, grille; crosshatching; thwarting, circumvention, frustration. See PASSAGE, TRAVEL, CONTENTION.

crouch, *v.i.* bend, squat, stoop, bow; cower, cringe, fawn. See DEPRESSION, SERVILITY. *Ant.*, see ELEVATION, INSOLENCE.

crowd, *n.* ASSEMBLAGE, gathering, concourse, horde, press, mass, gang, mob, multitude; host, herd, swarm, rout, crush, throng; set, coterie, clique; populace, rabble, hoi polloi (Gr.). See POPULACE.

crown, *v. & n.* —*v.t.* coronate, wreathe, enthrone, adorn, invest, install; top, cap, head, crest; COMPLETE, perfect, round out, finish. —*n.* chaplet, circlet, diadem, coronet, aureole; laurel, wreath, garland, reward, prize; pate, crest, top.

crucial, *adj.* decisive, determining, final; urgent, critical, supreme; trying, severe; cruciform. See IMPORTANCE. *Ant.*, see UNIMPORTANCE.

crude, *adj.* ROUGH, raw, unfinished, unwrought, unrefined, incomplete; unprepared, sketchy; coarse, crass, imperfect, plain, rude, tasteless, gross, immature, vulgar, uncouth. See IMPERFECTION, VULGARITY. *Ant.*, see COMPLETION, ELEGANCE.

cruelty, *n.* cold-bloodedness, harshness, barbarity, savagery, brutality, persecution, sadism, torture. See MALEVOLENCE. *Ant.*, see BENEVOLENCE.

crumble, *v.i.* disintegrate, break up, fall to pieces; decay, degenerate. See DESTRUCTION, DETERIORATION.

crush, *v.t.* press, mash, squash, squeeze, bruise; overcome, conquer, vanquish, subdue, quell, overwhelm, suppress, blot out; shame, disconcert. See CONTRACTION, DESTRUCTION. *Ant.*, see PRODUCTION, EXPAND.

crust, *n.* cake, coating, rind, shell, hull, incrustation. See COVERING. *Ant.*, see INTERIOR.

CRY [411]

Nouns—cry, shout, call; vociferation, exclamation, outcry, hullaballoo, chorus, clamor, hue and cry; plaint; lungs; stentor (see LOUDNESS); bark, ululation.

Verbs—cry, roar, shout, bawl, bellow, halloo, halloa, whoop, yell, howl, scream, screech, shriek, squeak, squeal, squall, whine, pule, pipe; call, bark, bray, mew, ululate; weep (see LAMENTATION); cheer; hoot; grumble, moan, groan, shrill; snore, snort; grunt; vociferate; raise *or* lift up the voice; call out, sing out, cry out; exclaim; rend the air; thunder; shout at the top of one's voice *or* lungs; strain the throat *or* voice *or* lungs; give a cry.

Adjectives—crying, clamant, clamorous; vociferous; stentorian (see LOUDNESS); open-mouthed, loudmouthed.

Antonym, see SILENCE.

crystal, *adj.* TRANSPARENT, lucid, pellucid, crystalline, clear.

cub, *n.* offspring, whelp, youngster, pup, puppy; novice. See ANIMAL, YOUTH. *Ant.*, see OLDNESS.

cudgel, *n.* club, bludgeon, staff, shillelagh, stick. See ARMS.

cue, *n.* hint, clue, intimation; catchword, signal, password. See INDICATION, INFORMATION.

culprit, *n.* offender, malefactor, wrongdoer, criminal, felon, convict. See EVILDOER. *Ant.*, see GOODNESS, INNOCENCE.

cultivate, *v.t.* farm, till, work, grow, develop; civilize, refine; pursue, court; foster, advance, cherish. See AGRICULTURE, IMPROVEMENT. *Ant.*, see DETERIORATION.

culture, *n.* cultivation, tillage; development, education, learning; enlightenment; refinement, breeding, polish; civilization. See AGRICULTURE, COURTESY, IMPROVEMENT, KNOWLEDGE. *Ant.*, see IGNORANCE.

cumbersome, *adj.* unwieldy, clumsy, burdensome, ponderous, cumbrous, oppressive. See HINDRANCE, UNSKILLFULNESS. *Ant.*, see CONVENIENT, SKILL.

cunning, *n. & adj.* —*n.* shrewdness, craft, foxiness; craftiness, wile, wiliness, guile, guilefulness, slyness, artfulness; DECEPTION; ingenuity, SKILL, dexterity, strategy. —*adj.* crafty, wily, guileful, sly, subtle, tricky, smart, foxy, shrewd; inventive, ingenuous, deft, skillful, adroit. *Colloq.*, cute, attractive. See CONCEALMENT. *Ant.*, see SIMPLENESS, UNSKILLFULNESS.

cup, *n.* mug, tankard, chalice, glass, goblet; excavation, hollow, crater. See CONCAVITY, RECEPTACLE.

cupboard, *n.* closet, storeroom; buffet, locker, press; pantry. See RECEPTACLE.

curb, *v. & n.* —*v.t.* RESTRAIN, subdue, control, check, repress; guide, manage; slacken, retard. See SLOWNESS. *Ant.*, VELOCITY. —*n.* restraint, check, control; curb market; brim, margin. See HINDRANCE, EDGE, SALE.

cure, *v.t.* heal, restore, relieve; preserve, dry, smoke, tan, pickle. See REMEDY, PRESERVATION.

CURIOSITY [455]

Nouns—**1**, curiosity, curiousness; interest, thirst for knowledge; inquiring mind; inquisitiveness; meddling. *Colloq.*, nosiness.
2, curious person; sightseer; questioner; newsmonger, gossip, busybody, peeping Tom, Paul Pry; eavesdropper. *Slang*, nosy Parker, snooper, rubberneck.
Verbs—be curious, take an interest in, stare, gape; prick up the ears, see sights; pry, peep; meddle. *Slang*, snoop, rubberneck.
Adjectives—curious, inquisitive, burning with curiosity, overcurious, curious as a cat; inquiring (see INQUIRY); prying; inquisitorial.
Antonym, see INDIFFERENCE.

---

curl, *v.t.* roll, wave, ripple, spiral, twist, coil. See CONVOLUTION.

currency, *n.* MONEY, coin, bill, cash, specie; publicity, circulation; topicality, timeliness. See PUBLICATION.

curse, *v. & n.* —*v.t.* execrate, damn, swear, denounce; blaspheme. —*n.* malediction, IMPRECATION, execration, anathema; bane, plague. *Ant.*, see APPROBATION.

curt, *adj.* SHORT, CONCISE, brief, succinct; snappish, tart, brusque, rude, bluff, BLUNT, abrupt. *Ant.*, see LOQUACITY, LENGTH.

curtail, *v.t.* shorten, clip, cut, abbreviate; abate, diminish, reduce, lessen, abridge; deprive. See SHORTNESS, DECREASE. *Ant.*, see LENGTH, INCREASE.

curtain, *n.* screen, veil, valance, drapery, portière, hanging, blind, SHADE. See AMBUSH, CONCEALMENT. *Ant.*, see DISCLOSURE.

CURVATURE [245]

Nouns—**1**, curvature, curving, curvity, curvation; incurvity, incurvation; bend; flexure, flexion; conflexure; crook, hook, bending; deflexion, inflexion; arcuation, devexity, turn; deviation, detour, sweep; curl, curling; bough; recurvity, recurvation; rotundity; sinuosity (see CONVOLUTION). See CIRCULARITY, ROTUNDITY.
2, curve, arc, arch, arcade, vault, bow, crescent, halfmoon, horseshoe, loop, crane-neck, parabola, hyperbola; catenary, festoon; conchoi, cardioid; caustic; tracery.
Verbs—**1**, be curved, sweep, swag, sag; deviate (see DEVIATION); turn; reenter.
2, render curved, curve, bend, incurvate; deflect, inflect; crook; turn, round, arch, arcuate, arch over, concamerate; bow, curl, recurve, frizzle.
Adjectives—curved, curviform, curvilineal, curvilinear; devious; recurved, recurvous; bowed, vaulted, hooked; falciform, falcated; semicircular, crescentic; luniform, lunilar; semilunar; conchoidal; cordiform, cordated;

cardioid; heart-shaped, bell-shaped, pear-shaped, fig-shaped; hook-shaped; kidney-shaped, reniform; lens-shaped, lentiform, lenticular; bowlegged (see DISTORTION); oblique (see OBLIQUITY); annular, circular (see CIRCULARITY).
Antonym, see DIRECTION.

custody, *n.* care, safekeeping, charge, protection, keeping; imprisonment, bondage. See RESTRAINT, SAFETY. *Ant.*, see FREEDOM.
custom, *n.* practice, use, usage, wont, fashion, precedent, rule; HABIT, mores (Lat.), convention; patronage, support, trade.
cut, *v.t.* incise, carve, dissect, slice, shave, trim, shape; separate, divide, split, sever; abridge, shorten, diminish, reduce, curtail; hurt, sting, wound, snub, ignore; reap, gather. See DISJUNCTION, SHORTNESS. *Ant.*, see IN-CREASE, JUNCTION, LENGTH.
cycle, *n.* period, age, epoch; circle, round; bicycle, velocipede, tricycle. *Slang*, bike. See TIME, VEHICLE, CIRCULARITY.
cylinder, *n.* barrel, tube, roller. See CIRCULARITY.
cynic, *n.* MISANTHROPE, pessimist; philosopher. See THOUGHT. *Ant.*, see SIMPLENESS.

D

dab, *n. & v.t.* —*n.* spot, pinch, small quantity. See LITTLENESS. —*v.t.* hit lightly. See IMPULSE.
dabble, *v.* splash, spatter; patter, trifle, fritter away. See INACTIVITY, WATER.
dagger, *n.* dirk, stiletto, poniard, knife, bodkin. See ARMS.
dainty, *adj.* delicate, exquisite, pretty; fastidious; delicious. See BEAUTY, TASTE. *Ant.*, see UGLINESS.
dally, *v.i.* trifle, delay, prolong, idle; flirt, philander. See AMUSEMENT, LATE-NESS. *Ant.*, see ACTIVITY.
damage, *v.t. & n.* —*v.* harm, injure, mar, impair. —*n.* DETERIORATION; injury. *Ant.*, see IMPROVEMENT.
damp, *adj. & v.t.* —*adj.* dank, humid. See MOISTURE, WATER. —*v.t.* muffle, subdue.
dance, *n. & v.i.* —*n.* party, ball. *Colloq.*, hop, prom. See AMUSEMENT. —*v.i.* glide, jig, flutter. See AGITATION.

DANGER [665]

Nouns—**1,** danger, peril, jeopardy, risk, hazard, insecurity, precariousness, slipperiness, instability; defenselessness.
2, exposure, LIABILITY; vulnerability; vulnerable point, heel of Achilles; forlorn hope.
3, dangerous course, leap in the dark, RASHNESS; road to ruin; hairbreadth escape; cause for alarm; source of danger; breakers ahead; storm brewing; clouds gathering; apprehension, WARNING.
4, trap, snare, pitfall, lure, whirlpool, maelstrom, ambush.
Verbs—**1,** be in danger; be exposed to danger, run into danger, encounter danger; run a risk; lay oneself open to (see LIABILITY); lean on a broken reed; feel the ground sliding from under one; have to run for it; have the odds against one; hang by a thread, totter; sleep *or* stand on a volcano; sit on a barrel of gunpowder, live in a glass house.
2, endanger, bring in danger, place in danger, put in danger; expose to danger, imperil; jeopardize; compromise.
3, adventure, venture, risk, hazard, stake, set at hazard; beard the lion in his den, play with fire, skate on thin ice, risk one's neck; run the gantlet; dare (see COURAGE); engage in a forlorn hope; sail too near the wind (see RASHNESS).
Adjectives—**1,** dangerous, hazardous, perilous, parlous; at stake, in question; precarious, ticklish; slippery; fraught with danger; untrustworthy; built upon sand, tottering, unstable, unsteady; shaky, topheavy, tumbledown,

ramshackle, crumbling; hanging *or* trembling in the balance; threatening (see WARNING), ominous, ill-omened; alarming (see FEAR); explosive.
2, in danger, endangered; unsafe, unprotected, insecure; defenseless, unshielded, vulnerable, exposed; open (to), LIABLE (to); at bay, on the rocks; hanging by a thread, between Scylla and Charybdis, between two fires; on the edge, brink *or* verge of a precipice, in the lion's den, on slippery ground, under fire, not out of the woods; with one's back to the wall; unprepared, off one's guard; helpless, in a bad way, in the last extremity. *Colloq.,* out on a limb; on thin ice. *Slang,* on the spot.
Antonym, see SAFETY.

dangle, *v.i.* hang, suspended; swing. See PEND, OSCILLATION.
dare, *v.t.* face, defy, challenge, brave; venture upon *or* into. See DEFIANCE, COURAGE. *Ant.,* see COWARDICE.

DARKNESS [421]

Nouns—**1,** darkness, dark; blackness (see COLOR); obscurity, gloom, murk; dusk, DIMNESS; SHADE, shadow, umbra, penumbra; skiagraphy; shading; distribution of shade; chiaroscuro.
2, Cimmerian darkness, Stygian darkness; night; midnight; dead of night; witching hour.
3, obscuration; adumbration; obfuscation; extinction, extinguishment, eclipse, total eclipse; gathering of the clouds; blackout, dim-out.
Verbs—be dark; darken, obscure, shade; dim; tone down, lower; overcast, overshadow; eclipse; obfuscate; adumbrate; cast into the shade; cloud, becloud; dim, bedim; darken, bedarken; cast, throw *or* spread a shadow; extinguish; put, blow *or* snuff out; doubt.
Adjectives—dark, darksome, darkling, darkened; obscure, tenebrous, somber, pitch dark, pitchy; black (see COLOR); sunless, moonless, lightless (see LIGHT); dusky; unilluminated; nocturnal; dingy, lurid, gloomy; murky; shady, umbrageous; overcast, dim (see DIMNESS); cloudy, opaque; dark as pitch, dark as a pit.
Adverbs—darkly, in the dark, in the shade.
Antonym, see LIGHT.

dart, *v. & n.* —*v.* hurl, cast, throw; spring, rush. See VELOCITY, PROPULSION. —*n.* javelin, spear, arrow. See ARMS.
dash, *v.t. & n.* —*v.* shatter, smash; frustrate, dishearten; hurl, cast. See DEPRESSION, DEJECTION, PROPULSION. —*n.* élan, spirit; spurt, *soupçon,* trace, slight addition. See ACTIVITY, VELOCITY, LITTLENESS.
daunt, *v.t.* intimidate, cow, dismay. See FEAR.
dawn, *n.* BEGINNING, origin, inception; early stage. *Ant.,* see END.
daze, *v.t.* confuse, dazzle, bewilder, awe; stun, shock, stupefy. See WONDER, SURPRISE, RESPECT, LIGHT.
dazzle, *v.t.* blind; impress, overpower; dum(b)found, bewilder. See RESPECT, WONDER.
dead, *adj.* deceased, perished, defunct; lifeless, inanimate; obsolete, extinct. See DEATH, NONEXISTENCE. *Ant.,* see LIFE, EXISTENCE.
deaden, *v.t.* benumb; muffle; damp. See INSENSIBILITY, IMPOTENCE, SILENCE. *Ant.,* SENSIBILITY.
deaf, *adj.* hard of hearing; inattentive; unhearing; earless, stone-deaf, tone deaf; oblivious of; deafened. *Ant.,* see HEARING.
deal, *v.t.* apportion, allocate, allot, distribute; BARTER; inflict; give, bestow, dole. See APPORTIONMENT, GIVING.
dear, *adj. & n.* —*adj.* expensive, costly, priceless, exorbitant, extortionate; precious, beloved, cherished, darling. —*n.* darling, beloved, love. *Colloq.,* honey, dearie, sweetheart. *Slang,* baby, babe, toots, tootsie, sugar. See PAYMENT, LOVE, ENDEARMENT. *Ant.,* see CHEAPNESS, HATE.

DEATH [360]

Nouns—**1,** death; expiration; decease, demise; END, cessation; loss of life, extinction of life, ebb of life; dissolution, departure, passing away, obit, release, eternal rest, rest, quietus, fall; loss, bereavement.

2, death warrant, death watch, death rattle, deathbed; stroke of death, agonies of death, shades of death, valley of the shadow of death, jaws of death, hand of death; last breath, last gasp, last agonies; dying day, dying breath; swan song; *rigor mortis;* Stygian shore. *Slang,* curtains, last roundup.

3, Death, King of terrors, King of Death; Grim Reaper, angel of death, Azrael; mortality; doom.

4, natural death, sudden death, violent death, untimely end, drowning, watery grave; suffocation, asphyxia; fatal disease (see DISEASE); death blow (see KILLING); euthanasia; genocide, extermination, mass murder; suicide.

5, necrology, bills of mortality, obituary; death-song (see LAMENTATION).

6, see CORPSE.

Verbs—**1,** die, expire, perish; drown, smother, suffocate; meet one's death, meet one's end; pass away, be taken; yield *or* resign one's breath; resign one's being *or* life; end one's days *or* life; breathe one's last; cease to live *or* breathe; depart this life; be no more; lose one's life, lay down one's life, relinquish *or* surrender one's life; sink into the grave; close one's eyes; fall dead, drop dead, drop down dead; break one's neck, give up the ghost, yield up the ghost; die in harness; die a violent death (see KILLING). *Slang,* kick off, kick the bucket, cash in, cash in one's chips; check out, croak, pop off; take a ride, be put on the spot, sign off.

2, pay the debt to nature, shuffle off this mortal coil, take one's last sleep; go the way of all flesh; come, turn *or* return to dust; cross the Styx; go to one's long account, go to one's last home, go west, go to Davy Jones' locker; cross the bar; receive one's death warrant, make one's will, die a natural death, go out like a candle; come to an untimely end; catch one's death.

Adjectives—**1,** dead, lifeless; deceased, demised, departed, defunct; late, gone, no more; exanimate, inanimate; out of the world, taken off, released; departed this life; dead and gone; launched into eternity, gathered to one's fathers, numbered with the dead; stillborn, extinct; lethal, fatal, deadly; dying, moribund. *Colloq.,* dead as a doornail; stiff; stone dead.

2, dying, moribund, *in extremis;* in the jaws of death; going, going off; on one's deathbed; at the point of death, at death's door, at the last gasp; with one foot in the grave. *Colloq.,* done for, on one's last legs; on the spot.

Antonym, see LIFE.

---

debasement, *n.* abasement, debauchery, corruption, degradation, DISREPUTE; adulteration, impairment, IMPURITY, MIXTURE. *Ant.,* see REPUTE, PROBITY.

debris, *n.* rubbish, rubble, detritus, wreckage, trash.

DEBT [806]

Nouns—**1,** debt, indebtedness, obligation, LIABILITY, indebtment, debit, score; charge, charge account; arrears, deferred payment, deficit, default; insolvency, nonpayment, bankruptcy, bad debt; interest, premium, usury; floating debt, floating capital.

2, debtor, debitor; mortgagor; defaulter; borrower. *Slang,* deadbeat.

3, lending, loan, advance, accommodation; financing, mortgage; borrowing, raising money, pledging, hypothecation, pawning.

4, lender, banker, mortgagee, pawnbroker, pawnshop.

Verbs—**1,** be in debt, owe; incur *or* contract a debt; run up a bill, run up a score, run up an account; borrow; run into debt, get into debt; outrun the constable; answer for, go bail for. *Slang,* run a tab, go on tick.

2, lend, advance, finance, accommodate (with), loan; mortgage, hypothecate, pledge, pawn, hock; borrow from Peter to pay Paul. *Slang,* touch.

3, repudiate, stop payment, dishonor. *Slang,* go broke.

Adjectives—indebted; liable, chargeable, answerable for, in debt, in embarrassed circumstances; in difficulties; encumbered, involved; involved in debt, plunged in debt; deep in debt; deeply involved; up against it; in the red; fast tied up; insolvent; minus, out of pocket; unpaid; unrequited, unrewarded; owing, due, in arrears, outstanding. *Slang,* in hock, on the cuff.

Antonym, see PAYMENT.

decay, *n. & v.i.* —*n.* DECOMPOSITION, DETERIORATION, disintegration, dilapidation, putrefaction, rot, caries. —*v.i.* rot, putrefy, mortify; disintegrate. *Ant.*, see IMPROVEMENT.

deceive, *v.* See DECEPTION.

deceiver, *n.* trickster, sharper, swindler, liar; humbug, charlatan, quack, mountebank; impostor, fraud, faker, sham, hoaxer, hoax, cheat; pretender, hypocrite; hoodwinker; Judas. *Slang*, con man, four-flusher, ringer.

decent, *adj.* decorous, chaste, pure in heart; acceptable, reasonable, tolerable. See PROBITY, GOODNESS. *Ant.*, see IMPURITY, BADNESS.

DECEPTION [545]

Nouns—**1**, deception, deceptiveness; falseness, untruth; imposition, imposture; fraud, fraudulence, deceit, deceitfulness, guile, bluff; knavery; CUNNING; FALSEHOOD.

2, delusion, illusion, gullery; juggling, jugglery; sleight of hand, legerdemain; prestidigitation; magic (see SORCERY); conjuring, conjuration; hocus pocus; trickery, chicanery; cozenage, circumvention, connivance, collusion; treachery, dishonesty (see IMPROBITY); practical joke; trick, cheat, wile, blind, feint, plant, bubble, fetch, catch, juggle, reach, hocus, thimble-rig, card-sharping, artful dodge, swindle; tricks upon travelers; stratagem, artifice; theft. *Colloq.*, hokey-pokey, sell, fake, hanky-panky. *Slang*, con game, racket, shell game, gyp; blarney, spoof.

3, snare, trap, pitfall, springe, decoy, gin; noose, hook; bait, decoy duck, baited trap; mousetrap, beartrap, steel trap, mantrap; cobweb, net, meshes, toils; AMBUSH; trapdoor, sliding panel, false bottom; spring-net, spring-gun, masked battery; mine, booby trap.

4, mockery, IMITATION, copy; counterfeit, sham, make-believe, forgery, fraud; lie; hollow mockery; whited sepulcher; tinsel, paste, false jewelry; man of straw; ormolu; jerrybuilding; illusion (see ERROR); mirage; German silver; Britannia metal; gerrymander. *Colloq.*, gold brick. *Slang*, phony.

5, DECEIVER; wolf in sheep's clothing, cheat, fraud; magician, conjuror; dodger, swindler, *etc.*

Verbs—**1**, deceive, take in; defraud, cheat, jockey, cozen, nab, play one false, bilk, bite, pluck, swindle, victimize, gull, hoax, dupe; abuse; mystify, blind one's eyes; blindfold, hoodwink; throw dust into the eyes; impose upon, practice upon, play upon, put upon, palm upon, foist upon; snatch a verdict; palm off; circumvent, overreach; outreach, outwit, outmaneuver; get around; steal a march upon, give the go-by, leave in the lurch. *Colloq.*, gouge, slip one over on. *Slang*, give the runaround, diddle, do, take for, get away with.

2, set a trap, lay a trap, lay a snare for; bait the hook, spread the toils, decoy, waylay, lure, beguile, delude, inveigle; hook, trick, entrap, ensnare; nick, springe; catch in a trap; entangle, hocus, practice on one's credulity, fool, befool, pull the wool over one's eyes; humbug; stuff up, sell; play a trick upon; play a practical joke upon; balk, trip up, send on a fool's errand; make game of, make a fool of, make an April fool of, make an ass of; trifle with, cajole, flatter; come over; dissemble, lie (see FALSEHOOD); misinform; mislead (see ERROR); betray (see IMPROBITY). *Colloq.*, bamboozle, fourflush, flimflam, bilk, put over.

3, load the dice, stack the cards *or* deck; live by one's wits, play at hide and seek; obtain money under false pretenses (see STEALING); conjure, juggle, practice chicanery; brace, touch, soak; swipe, pinch, lift (see STEALING); pass off, palm off, foist off, fob off.

Adjectives—deceived, deceiving, guileful, CUNNING, deceptive, deceitful; delusive, delusory; illusive, illusory; elusive, insidious; untrue (see FALSEHOOD); mock, sham, make-believe, counterfeit, pseudo, spurious, so-called, pretended, feigned, trumped up, bogus, fraudulent, tricky, factitious, artificial, bastard; surreptitious, illegitimate, contraband, adulterated, sophisticated; unsound, rotten at the core; disguised; meretricious; tinsel, pinchbeck; catchpenny; brummagem; simulated, plated. *Colloq.*, fake, doctored. *Slang*, phony.

Adverbs—deceptively, *etc.*; under false colors, under cover of; behind one's back, cunningly; slyly; on the sly.

decide, *v.t.* determine, elect; settle, fix; arbitrate. See RESOLUTION, CHOICE, CERTAINTY.

decipher, *v.t.* make out, decode; translate, interpret. See DISCLOSURE.

decision, *n.* firmness, RESOLUTION, JUDGMENT, determination; verdict, finding. See LAWSUIT.

declaim, *v.i.* recite, harangue, rant. See SPEECH.

declaration, *n.* AFFIRMATION, proclamation, statement, avowal. See PUBLICATION, SPEECH, EVIDENCE. *Ant.*, SILENCE.

decline, *n. & v.* —*n.* retrogression, decadence, wasting, DISEASE, AGE, DETERIORATION. *Ant.*, see HEALTH, YOUTH, IMPROVEMENT. —*v.* worsen, slump; refuse, turn down (an offer). See DETERIORATION, OLDNESS, AGE, REFUSAL. *Ant.*, see IMPROVEMENT, NEWNESS, YOUTH.

DECOMPOSITION [49]

Nouns—decomposition, disintegration, decay, corruption, UNCLEANNESS; analysis, dissection, RESOLUTION, catalysis, dissolution; dispersion; DISJUNCTION.

Verbs—decompose, decompound; disintegrate; corrupt; analyze, disembody, dissolve; resolve into its elements, separate into its elements; catalyze, electrolyze; dissect, decentralize, break up; disperse; unravel, unroll; crumble into dust.

Adjectives—decomposed, corrupt, decayed; catalytic, analytical.

Antonym, see COMPOSITION.

---

decoration, *n.* ORNAMENT, garnishment, trimming; trophy.

decoy, *v.t.* entice, lure, entrap. See ATTRACTION, DECEPTION.

DECREASE [36]

Nouns—**1,** decrease, diminution; lessening, subtraction, reduction, abatement, declension; shrinking, CONTRACTION, coarctation; abridgment, shortening, extenuation; DEDUCTION, DISCOUNT.

2, subsidence, wane, ebb, decline; DESCENT, decrement, reflux, depreciation; DETERIORATION, mitigation, MODERATION.

Verbs—**1,** decrease, diminish, lessen; abridge, shorten, shrink, contract, drop, fall *or* tail off; fall away, waste, wear; wane, ebb, decline; descend, subside; melt, die *or* fade away; retire into the shade, fall to a low ebb; run low, out, dry *or* short; dwindle, slacken, peter out.

2, bate, abate, discount; depreciate; lower, weaken, attenuate, fritter away; mitigate, moderate, dwarf, throw into the shade; reduce, subtract.

Adjectives—unincreased, decreased, decreasing, short, diminishing, waning, wasting away, wearing out, reduced, lessening, ebbing, dwindling, petering out, fading, disappearing, vanishing, falling off; dwarfish.

Adverbs—on the wane, on the decrease, smaller and smaller, less and less.

Antonym, see INCREASE.

---

decree, *n.* COMMAND, JUDGMENT, edict, ordinance, law, fiat. See LEGALITY. *Ant.*, see MISJUDGMENT, ILLEGALITY.

dedicate, *v.t.* give, devote, consecrate. See USE, REPUTE.

deduce, *v.* infer, conclude, gather, derive; reason, reckon, suppose, assume, presume, deem, opine, think, believe. See THOUGHT, REASONING.

deduct, *v.t.* subtract, take (away from), cut (out *or* away), remove, withdraw, delete, take out; decrease by. See DECREASE. *Ant.*, see ADDITION.

deduction, *n.* removal, subtraction, withdrawal; rebate, discount, minus, reduction, allowance; conclusion, inference, corollary; diminishment, curtailment, DECREASE. *Ant.*, see ADDITION.

deed, *n.* act, ACTION, feat, achievement, exploit; legal document, transfer. *Ant.*, see INACTIVITY.

deep, *adj. & n.* —*adj.* abysmal, bottomless; profound, abstruse, obscure; low-toned, bass; deeply felt; wise, cunning. See DEPTH, SOUND, FEELING, INTELLIGENCE. —*n.* ocean; depth; profundity.

deface, *v.t.* mar, disfigure, tarnish, mutilate, blemish; maim, mangle, scar. See DISTORTION, DETERIORATION, IMPERFECTION. *Ant.*, see IMPROVEMENT.

defame, *v.t.* traduce, vilify, revile, calumniate, asperse, abuse, malign. See DISREPUTE, DETRACTION. *Ant.,* see REPUTE.

defeat, *v.t. & n.* —*v.t.* thwart, frustrate, foil, outwit; rout, conquer, overcome, vanquish, subdue. *Slang,* lick. See HINDRANCE, FAILURE. *Ant.,* see AID, SUCCESS. —*n.* frustration, rout, vanquishment.

defect, *n.* decrement, BLEMISH, fault, flaw; IMPERFECTION; deficiency, lack, incompleteness. *Ant.,* see WHOLE, PERFECTION.

DEFENSE [717]

Nouns—**1,** defense, protection, guard, ward; shielding, PRESERVATION, guardianship; self-defense, self-preservation; RESISTANCE; safeguard (see SAFETY).
2, shelter, CONCEALMENT; fortification; munition, munitionment; bulwark, foss(e), moat, ditch, intrenchment; dike, parapet, embankment, mound, mole, bank; earthwork; fieldwork; fence, wall, dead wall; paling, sunk fence, haha, palisade, INCLOSURE; barrier, barricade; boom; portcullis, *chevaux de frise;* abatis; battlement, rampart, scarp; glacis, casemate, buttress, abutment; breastwork, curtain, bastion, redan, ravelin; redoubt; lines, loophole, machicolation; barrage balloon, radar screen, DEW line (Distant Early Warning line).
3, hold, stronghold, fastness; asylum, sanctuary, REFUGE; keep, dungeon, fortress, citadel, capitol, castle; tower, tower of strength; fort, blockhouse; shelter, air-raid shelter.
4, armor, shield, buckler, aegis, breastplate, cuirass, habergeon, mail, coat of mail, hauberk, lorication, helmet, steel helmet, siege cap, casque, cask, shako, bearskin; weapon, ARMS; antiaircraft battery.
5, defender, protector, guardian, guard, bodyguard, champion, knight-errant; garrison, patrol, national guard (see COMBATANT); sentinel, sentry, lookout; KEEPER, watchman; watchdog.
Verbs—defend, forfend, fend; shield, screen, shroud; fence round (see CIRCUMSCRIPTION); fence, intrench; guard (see SAFETY); guard against; take care of; bear harmless; keep off, ward off, fight off, beat off; parry, repel, repulse, put to flight; hold at bay, keep at bay, keep at arm's length; stand on the defensive, act on the defensive; man the barricades, hold the fort; show fight; maintain *or* stand one's ground; stand by; hold one's own; bear the brunt; fall back upon, hold. *Colloq.,* dig in.
Adjectives—defending, defensive; protective, preservative; mural, fortified, armored, armed, armed at all points, armed to the teeth; panoplied; iron-plated, ironclad; loopholed, castellated, machicolated, casemated; defended, invulnerable, proof against.
Adverbs—defensively; on the defense, on the defensive; in defense; at bay.
Antonym, see ATTACK.

---

defer, *v.* delay, suspend, postpone, stay, procrastinate; submit, yield, give in, abide by, RESPECT. See ASSENT, LATENESS, OBEDIENCE. *Ant.,* see INSOLENCE.

defiance, *n.* OPPOSITION; dare, challenge; threat; provocation; revolt, rebellion, mutiny, insurrection; INSOLENCE; DISOBEDIENCE, insubordination, insurgency; contempt; daring. See COURAGE, RASHNESS. *Ant.,* see OBEDIENCE, FEAR.

deficient, *adj.* lacking, wanting, inadequate, insufficient, imperfect, incomplete. See INFERIORITY, FAILURE, IMPERFECTION.

define, *v.t.* explain, interpret; circumscribe, LIMIT, demarcate. See INTERPRETATION, NOMENCLATURE, CIRCUMSCRIPTION.

definite, *adj.* exact, explicit, plain, limited, precise, unequivocal. See SPECIALITY, LIMIT, CERTAINTY, TRUTH, EVIDENCE.

deflate, *v.t.* exhaust, empty; reduce, humble.

deformity, *n.* malformation, disfigurement, monstrosity, DISTORTION, UGLINESS, IMPERFECTION.

defy, *v.t.* challenge, dare; scorn, disobey, oppose, FRONT. See COURAGE.

degeneracy, *n.* DETERIORATION, demoralization; viciousness, depravity, turpitude, VICE.

degradation, *n.* DETERIORATION, DISREPUTE, humiliation, shame, abasement; degeneracy, VICE.

degree, *n.* rank, station, grade, CLASSIFICATION, status; class, order; caliber; calibration; mark, INDICATION, line (on a thermometer, *etc.*); gradation, graduation; shade, intensity, STRENGTH; division, interval; range, scope, reach, extent; step, stage, phase, point; standard; pitch, HEIGHT. *Ant.*, see DISORDER.

DEITY [976]

Nouns—**1,** Deity, Divinity; Godhead, Godship; Omnipotence, Providence.
2, God, Lord; Jehovah, Yahweh, Jah, JHVH, Tetragrammaton; Supreme Being, First Cause; Author *or* Creator of all things; the Infinite, Eternal; the All-powerful, -wise, -merciful, *or* -holy.
3, [*attributes, perfections and functions*] infinite power, infinite wisdom, goodness, justice, truth, mercy; omnipotence, omniscience, omnipresence; unity, immutability, holiness, glory, majesty, sovereignty, infinity, eternity; the Trinity, Holy Trinity, Trinity in Unity; God the Father, Maker, Creator, *or* Preserver; creation, preservation, divine government; theocracy, thearchy; Providence, ways *or* dispensation of Providence; God the Son, Jesus, Christ, the Messiah, Anointed, Saviour, Redeemer; the Son of God, Man, *or* David; the Lamb of God, the Word; Emmanuel, Immanuel; the King of Kings and King of Glory, Prince of Peace, Good Shepherd, Light of the World, the Incarnation; salvation, redemption, atonement. propitiation, mediation, intercession, judgment, God the Holy Ghost, the Holy Spirit, Paraclete; inspiration, unction, regeneration, sanctification, consolation; special providence, *Deus ex machina;* avatar.
4, Allah; God of Abraham, *etc.;* Lord of Hosts, the Lord God.
Verbs—create, uphold, preserve, govern, atone, redeem, save, propitiate, predestinate, elect, call, ordain, bless, justify, sanctify, glorify.
Adjectives—almighty, holy, hallowed, sacred, divine, heavenly, celestial, sacrosanct, superhuman, supernatural; ghostly, spiritual, hyperphysical, unearthly; theistic, theocratic; anointed.
Adverbs—divinely, by divine right; with the help of God.
Antonym, see MANKIND.

DEJECTION [837]

Nouns—**1,** dejection, dejectedness; depression; lowness *or* depression of spirits; weight on the spirits, damp on the spirits; low spirits, bad spirits, drooping spirits, depressed spirits; heart sinking; heaviness of heart; heaviness, gloom; WEARINESS, disgust of life; homesickness; DISCONTENT; melancholy; sadness, melancholia, doldrums, vapors, megrims, spleen, horrors, hypochondria, pessimism; despondency, slough of despond; disconsolateness, discontent; hope deferred, blank despondency.
2, grief, sorrow, heartache, prostration; broken heart; despair; gravity, solemnity; long face, grave face, death's-head at the feast. *Colloq.*, blues, dumps, blue devils.
3, hypochondriac, pessimist; mope. *Colloq.*, wet blanket. *Slang*, sourpuss, killjoy.
Verbs—**1,** be dejected, grieve; mourn, lament; take on, give way, lose heart, despond, droop, sink; lower, look downcast, frown, pout; hang down the head; pull *or* make a long face; laugh on the wrong side of the mouth; grin a ghastly smile; look blue; lay *or* take to heart; mope, brood over; fret, sulk; pine, yearn, repine, REGRET; despair.
2, refrain from laughter, keep one's countenance, keep a straight face; be grave, look grave; repress a smile.
3, depress, discourage, dishearten; dispirit; damp, dull, lower, sink, dash, knock down, unman, prostrate, break one's heart; frown upon; cast a gloom *or* shade on; sadden; damp one's hopes, dash one's hopes, wither one's hopes; weigh on the mind, lie heavy on the mind; prey on the mind; depress the spirits.
Adjectives—dejected, cheerless, joyless, spiritless; uncheerful, unlively; unhappy, sad, triste, melancholy, dismal, somber, dark, gloomy, clouded, murky, lowering, frowning, lugubrious, funereal, mournful, lamentable, dreadful; dreary, flat, dull, dull as ditchwater *or* dishwater; depressing; oppressed with, or a prey to melancholy; downcast, downhearted;

down in the mouth, down on one's luck; heavyhearted; in the dumps, in the sulks, in the doldrums; in bad humor, sullen, mumpish, dumpish; mopish, moping; moody, glum; sulky, discontented, out of sorts, out of humor, out of spirits; ill at ease, low-spirited, in low spirits; weary, discouraged, disheartened; desponding; chopfallen, crestfallen.

2, sad, pensive, tristful; doleful, woebegone, tearful, lachrymose, in tears, melancholic, hypochondriacal, bilious, jaundiced, atrabilious, saturnine, splenetic; lackadaisical; serious, sedate, staid; grave, grave as a judge, sober, solemn, demure; grim, grimfaced, grim-visaged, rueful, wan, long-faced.

3, disconsolate; unconsolable, inconsolable; forlorn, comfortless, desolate, sick at heart; soul-sick, heart-sick; in despair, lost; overcome, broken down, borne down, bowed down; heart-stricken; cut up, dashed, sunk; unnerved, unmanned; downfallen, downtrodden; brokenhearted; careworn.

Adjectives—dejectedly, with a long face, with tears in one's eyes; sadly, *etc.*
Antonym, see CHEERFULNESS.

delay, *v. & n.* —*v.* put off, retard, postpone; linger, dally, loiter, procrastinate. See LATENESS, SLOWNESS, HINDRANCE. —*n.* postponement, procrastination. See DURABILITY.

delegate, *n. & v.t.* —*n.* DEPUTY, envoy, agent. —*v.t.* COMMISSION, entrust, depute, empower. See SUBSTITUTION.

delete, *v.t.* erase, cancel, expunge, take out, cross out, excise.

deliberate, *adj. & v.i.* —*adj.* intentional, studied; cool, careful, thoughtful, unhurried. See MEASUREMENT, SLOWNESS. —*v.i.* ponder, consider, think, weight. See THOUGHT, ADVICE.

delicacy, *n.* sensitiveness, tact, nicety; frailty, daintiness, exactness; tidbit, luxury; discrimination, TASTE, fastidiousness. See PURITY, IMPOTENCE, BEAUTY, FOOD.

delicious, *adj.* delectable, luscious, toothsome, palatable, savory. See TASTE.

delightful, *adj.* pleasing, enjoyable, charming, attractive, alluring. See PLEASURE.

delinquent, *adj. & n.* —*adj.* neglectful, defaulting, undutiful; culpable; negligent. —*n.* defaulter; transgressor, troublemaker, lawbreaker. See DEBT, EVILDOER. *Ant.*, see GOODNESS.

delirious, *adj.* mad, raving, wandering, unbalanced, frenzied. See INSANITY, FEELING, EXCITEMENT. *Ant.*, see SANITY.

deliver, *v.* discharge, give forth, emit, deal; free, liberate, release, emancipate; convey, carry to; save, rescue, redeem; rid; grant, cede, surrender; pronounce, speak, utter. *Colloq.*, make good (deliver the goods); bring home the bacon. See GIVING, FREEDOM, SPEECH.

delivery, *n.* surrender; conveyance; RELINQUISHMENT; childbirth, parturition; rescue, ESCAPE, salvation, redemption (see FREEDOM); address (see SPEECH). *Ant.*, see DANGER, RESTRAINT.

deluge, *n.* stream, flood, inundation; downpour, spate; plethora.

delusion, *n.* DECEPTION, SORCERY; illusion, fantasy, misconception, hallucination. See VISION, ERROR, INSANITY.

demand, *v.t. & n.* —*v.t.* require, charge; levy, exact, order, requisition. See COMMAND, PAYMENT. —*n.* REQUIREMENT, requisition; ultimatum; market, PRICE; COMMAND, SALE.

democratic, *adj.* unassuming, nonsnobbish; popular.

demolish, *v.t.* raze, level, ruin, wreck, destroy, wipe out. See DESTRUCTION. *Ant.*, see PRODUCTION.

DEMON [980]

Nouns—**1,** demon, demonry, demonology; evil genius, fiend, familiar, devil; bad spirit, unclean spirit; cacodemon, incubus, succubus; Frankenstein's monster; SATAN; Mephistopheles, Asmodeus, Belial, Ahriman; fury, harpy.

2, vampire, ghoul; ogre, ogress; gnome, affreet, genie, imp, bogie, kobold, fairy, brownie, pixy, elf, gremlin, dwarf, urchin, Puck, leprechaun, troll, sprite, bad fairy, nix, will-o'-the-wisp, poltergeist.

3, ghost, specter, apparition, spirit, shade, shadow, vision, hobgoblin; bugaboo, bogey; wraith, spook, banshee; evil eye.

4, merman, mermaid, merfolk; siren; satyr, faun; changeling, elf-child.
Adjectives—demonic, demoniacal; supernatural, weird, uncanny, unearthly, spectral; ghostly, ghostlike; elfin, elflike; fiendish, fiendlike; impish, haunted; satanic, diabolic(al), devilish; infernal, hellish, Plutonic.
Antonym, see ANGEL.

demonstrate, *v.t.* show, prove, establish, EVIDENCE; explain; expound; give an example; show how (something works); exhibit; manifest, sustain. See INTERPRETATION.
demonstration, *n.* substantiation, proof, EVIDENCE, testimony; exhibition, display; explanation, showing how; riot, tumult, turmoil, scene. See AGITATION, INTERPRETATION.
demoralize, *v.t.* disconcert, disorganize, confuse; corrupt, deprave. See IMPOTENCE, EVIL.
demur, *v.i. & n.* —*v.i.* hesitate, object, scruple. See DOUBT, DISSENT. —*n.* objection, irresolution, delay. See DISSENT, LATENESS.
demure, *adj.* modest, sedate, staid; diffident; prim, coy. See MODESTY.
den, *n.* lair, haunt, cavern; sanctum, study; dive, hangout. See ABODE, RECEPTACLE.
denote, *v.t.* signify, indicate, express, mean, specify. See EVIDENCE, MEANING, INDICATION.
denounce, *v.t.* decry, censure, arraign, charge, accuse; curse, rail at. See DISAPPROBATION, ACCUSATION.

DENSITY [321]

Nouns—**1,** density, denseness, solidity; solidness; impenetrability, impermeability; incompressibility; imporosity; cohesion (see COHERENCE); constipation, consistence, spissitude; specific gravity.
2, condensation; solidification; consolidation; concretion, coagulation; petrifaction, HARDNESS; crystallization, precipitation; deposit, thickening; indivisibility, indissolubility, infrangibility.
3, solid body, mass, block, knot, lump; concretion, concrete, conglomerate; precipitate; cake, clot, stone, curd; bone, gristle, cartilage.
Verbs—be dense, become solid, render solid; solidify, concrete, set, take a set, consolidate, congeal, coagulate; curd, curdle; fix, clot, cake, precipitate, deposit; cohere, crystallize; petrify, harden; condense, thicken, inspissate; compress, squeeze, ram down, constipate. *Colloq.*, jell.
Adjectives—dense. solid; solidified; coherent, cohesive (see COHERENCE); compact, close, serried, thickset; substantial, massive, lumpish; impenetrable, impermeable, imporous; incompressible; constipated; concrete, knotted, knotty; gnarled; crystalline; thick, stuffy; undissolved, unmelted, unliquefied, unthawed; indivisible, infrangible, indissolvable, indissoluble, infusible.
Antonyms, see RARITY, VAPOR.

deny, *v.t.* contradict, negate; refuse, withhold; doubt, reject; oppose, protest. See NEGATION, REFUSAL, RESTRAINT. *Ant.*, see BELIEF, AGREEMENT.

DEPARTURE [293]

Nouns—**1,** departure, leaving, decampment; retreat, embarkation; outset, start; removal; exit, EGRESS, exodus, hejira, evacuation, flight.
2, leave-taking, valediction, adieu, farewell, goodbye; stirrup-cup. *Colloq.*, send-off.
3, starting point, starting post; point *or* place of departure *or* embarkation; port of embarkation.
Verbs—**1,** depart; go, go away; take one's departure, set out; set off, march off, put off, start off, be off, move off, get off, pack off, go off, take oneself off; start, issue, march out, debouch; go forth, sally forth; sally, set forward; be gone, shake the dust off one's feet.
2, leave a place, quit, vacate, evacuate, abandon; go off the stage, make one's exit; retire, withdraw, remove; go one's way, go along, go from home; take flight, take wing; spring, fly, flit, wing one's way; fly away; embark; go on board, go aboard, set sail; put to sea, go to sea; sail, take ship; get

under way, weigh anchor, strike tents, decamp; take leave; see off, say goodbye, bid goodbye; DISAPPEAR, take French leave; abscond, avoid, (see AVOIDANCE). *Colloq.*, clear out, push off. *Slang*, toddle along, mosey along, check out, beat it, blow, lam, take the air, light out.

Adjectives—departing, leaving; valedictory; outward bound.

Adverbs—whence, hence, thence; with a foot in the stirrup; on the wing, on the move.

Interjections—farewell! adieu! goodbye! goodday! au revoir! fare you well! God bless you! God speed! *Colloq.*, byebye! *Slang*, so long!

Antonym, see ARRIVAL.

---

depend, *v.i.* rely, trust; dangle, be pendent; be contingent, rest. See BELIEF, CERTAINTY.

depict, *v.t.* delineate, picture, limn, portray. See REPRESENTATION.

deplorable, *adj.* lamentable, sad, regrettable, disastrous. See BADNESS, PAIN, ADVERSITY, DISREPUTE. *Ant.*, see APPROBATION.

deport, *v.t.* send away. banish, exile, expatriate. See EJECTION.

depose, *v.* swear, affirm, testify; dethrone, uncrown, unseat, oust, disbar. See NULLIFICATION.

deposit, *n.* precipitate, sediment, dregs, lees; pledge, PAYMENT, SECURITY. See REMAINDER.

deposition, *n.* affidavit, testimony, AFFIRMATION, dethronement, deposal. See EVIDENCE, NULLIFICATION.

depository, *n.* storehouse, warehouse, vault, TREASURY. See STORE.

depravity, *n.* degeneracy, corruption, turpitude, degradation, vileness. See BADNESS, EVIL, DETERIORATION.

deprecate, *v.t.* protest; regret; disfavor, disapprove; expostulate, inveigh *or* remonstrate (against). See DISAPPROBATION. *Ant.*, see APPROBATION.

depreciate, *v.* disparage, derogate, discredit, belittle. *Colloq.*, run down. *Slang*, knock; cheapen, slump, fall. See DETRACTION, CHEAPNESS. *Ant.*, APPROBATION.

DEPRESSION [308]

Nouns—1, depression, lowering; dip (see CONCAVITY); abasement, debasement; reduction.

2, overthrow, overset, overturn; upset; prostration, subversion, precipitation; bow; curtsy; genuflection, kowtow, obeisance. See RESPECT.

Verbs—1, depress, lower; let down, take down, take down a peg; cast; let drop, let fall; sink, debase, bring low, abase, reduce, pitch, precipitate; dent (see CONCAVITY).

2, overthrow, overturn, overset; upset, subvert, prostrate, level, fell; cast down, take down, throw down, fling down, dash down, pull down, cut down, knock down; raze, raze to the ground; trample in the dust; pull about one's ears.

3, sit, sit down; couch, crouch, squat, stoop, bend, bow; courtesy, curtsey; bob, duck, dip, kneel; bend, bow the head, bend the knee; bow down; cower.

Adjectives—depressed; at a low ebb; prostrate, overthrown; downcast.

Antonym, see ELEVATION.

---

deprive, *v.t.* dispossess, divest, despoil, usurp. *Ant.*, see GIVING.

depth, *n.* deepness, profundity; intensity; extent, completeness, thoroughness; bottom, pit, abyss; LOWNESS. *Ant.*, see HEIGHT.

deputy, *n.* agent, representative, delegate; substitute, proxy; envoy; factor; deputy sheriff. See SUBSTITUTION.

derangement, *n.* craziness, madness, lunacy, mania, aberration, dementia; disturbance, upset, imbalance; confusion, turmoil, DISORDER; disconcertment, discomfiture, discomposure. See AGITATION, INSANITY. *Ant.*, see ARRANGEMENT, SANITY.

derelict, *n. & adj.* —*n.* wreck, hull; abandoned property *or* person; drifter, beachcomber, castaway. —*adj.* castaway, wrecked, stranded, abandoned, deserted, forsaken; delinquent, negligent, neglectful, remiss. See NEGLECT, RELINQUISHMENT. *Ant.*, see DUTY.

dereliction, *n.* abandonment; NEGLECT; RELINQUISHMENT, desertion; negligence, failure in duty, delinquency. *Ant.*, see DUTY.

derisive, *adj.* mocking, sarcastic, contemptuous, supercilious, disdainful. See RIDICULE, DISRESPECT, CONTEMPT, DETRACTION.

derive, *v.* get, obtain, deduce; originate, arise. See ACQUISITION, RECEIVING, CAUSE.

derogatory, *adj.* discreditable, depreciative, disparaging, defamatory, humiliating. See DISREPUTE, DETRACTION. *Ant.*, see APPROBATION.

DESCENT [306]

Nouns—descent, descension, declension, declination, inclination, fall; falling, drop, cadence; subsidence, lapse; comedown, downfall, tumble, slip, tilt, trip, lurch; cropper, stumble; declivity, dip, hill; avalanche, debacle, landslip, landslide.

Verbs—**1,** descend; go down, drop down, come down; fall, gravitate, drop, slip, slide, settle; decline, set, sink, droop, come down a peg.

2, dismount, alight, light, get down; swoop; stoop; fall prostrate, precipitate oneself; let fall (see DEPRESSION); tumble, trip, stumble, lurch, pitch, topple; topple down, tumble down, tumble over; tilt, sprawl, plump down. *Colloq.*, come a cropper, take a spill *or* header.

Adjectives—descending, descendent; decurrent, decursive; deciduous; nodding to its fall.

Adverbs—down, downhill, downward, downstream, downstairs.

Antonym, see ASCENT.

DESCRIPTION [594]

Nouns—**1,** description, account, statement, report; exposé, DISCLOSURE; specification, particulars; summary, brief, abstract, *précis*, resumé; return, RECORD, catalogue, list; guidebook, INFORMATION; delineation, REPRESENTATION, sketch; monograph; minute account, detailed account, circumstantial account, graphic account; narration, recital, rehearsal, relation.

2, history; biography, autobiography; necrology, obituary; narrative, memoir, memorials; annals, chronicle, tradition, legend, story, tale, historiette; personal narrative, journal, life, adventures, fortunes, experiences, confessions; work of fiction, novel, novella, romance, love story, detective story; fairy tale, nursery tale; fable, parable, apologue. *Slang*, thriller, whodunit.

3, narrator, relator, historian, recorder, biographer, fabulist, novelist; raconteur, anecdotist, story-teller.

Verbs—describe, narrate, relate, recite, recount; set forth, draw a picture, limn; picture; portray, represent, characterize, particularize; sum up, run over, recapitulate, rehearse, fight one's battles over again; unfold, tell; give an account of, render an account of; report, make a report, draw up a statement; enter into details *or* particulars.

Adjectives—descriptive, graphic, narrative, well-drawn; historical, epic, suggestive, traditional; legendary; anecdotal, expository, storied; biographical, autobiographical.

Antonym, see DISTORTION.

desert, *n.* waste, barren, wilderness, solitude. See USELESSNESS, SPACE; reward, due, merit. See GOODNESS, JUSTICE.

desert, *v.* leave, forsake, abandon; secede, run away; leave in the lurch, be faithless. *Colloq.*, ditch. See AVOIDANCE.

deserve, *v.t.* merit, be worthy of. See JUSTICE.

design, *n. & v.t.* —*n.* PLAN, INTENTION, scheme, project; REPRESENTATION, drawing, diagram, pattern; decoration. See MEANING. —*v.t.* PLAN, intend; draw, sketch.

designate, *v.t.* name, specify, indicate; appoint. See NOMENCLATURE, ATTENTION, CHOICE.

DESIRE [865]

Nouns—**1,** desire, wish, fancy, fantasy; want, need, exigency.

2, mind, inclination, leaning, bent, animus, partiality, penchant, predilection; propensity, weakness, proclivity, WILLINGNESS; liking, LOVE, fondness, relish. *Slang*, yen.

3, longing, hankering, longing eye, wistful eye; solicitude, anxiety; yearning, coveting; aspiration, ambition, vaulting ambition; eagerness; zeal, ardor; impatience, overanxiety; impetuosity.

4, appetite, sharp appetite, keenness, hunger, torment of Tantalus, ravenousness, voracity, GLUTTONY; thirst, thirstiness; drought, mouthwatering; itch, itching. *Colloq.*, sweet tooth.

5, avidity, avarice, greed, greediness, itching palm, covetousness, grasping, craving, rapacity, passion, rage, furor, mania, dipsomania, kleptomania; prurience, cacoëthes, cupidity, lust, concupiscence (see GLUTTONY).

6, desirer, lover (see LOVE), amateur, enthusiast, votary, devotee, aspirant, solicitant, candidate. *Slang*, fan.

7, desideratum; want, REQUIREMENT; consummation devoutly to be wished; attraction, magnet, allurement, fancy, temptation, seduction, fascination, prestige, height of one's ambition, idol; whim, whimsy; hobby, hobbyhorse.

Verbs—**1,** desire, wish, wish for; be desirous, have a longing; HOPE; care for, affect, like, list; take to, take kindly to, cling to, take a fancy to; fancy; prefer, choose (see CHOICE); have an eye to, have a mind to; find it in one's heart, be willing, have a fancy for, have one's eyes upon; take into one's head, have at heart, be bent upon; set one's cap for, set one's heart upon, set one's mind upon; covet; want, miss, need, feel the want of; would fain have, would fain do; would be glad of;

2, be hungry, have a good appetite; hunger after, thirst after, crave after, lust after, itch after, hanker after; die for; burn to; fingers itch to; desiderate; sigh for, cry for, gasp for, pine for, pant for, languish for, yearn for, long for, be on thorns for hope for; aspire after; catch at, grasp at, jump at; woo, court, solicit; fish for, whistle for; ogle. *Colloq.*, make a play for.

3, cause desire, create desire, excite desire, provoke desire; whet the appetite; appetize, titillate, allure, attract, take one's fancy, tempt; hold out temptation, tantalize, make one's mouth water.

Adjectives—**1,** desirous; desiring, inclined, willing; partial (to), fain, wishful, optative; anxious, wistful, curious; at a loss for, sedulous, solicitous.

2, craving, hungry, sharp-set, peckish, ravening, with an empty stomach, thirsty, athirst, parched with thirst, dry, pinched with hunger, famished, hungry as a hunter, horse, *or* churchmouse; greedy, greedy as a hog, piggish; overeager; voracious, omnivorous, ravenous, open-mouthed, covetous, avaricious, rapacious, grasping, extortionate, exacting, sordid, insatiable, insatiate; unquenchable, quenchless; unsatisfied, unsated, unslaked.

3, eager, avid, keen; burning, fervent, ardent; agog; all agog; breathless, impatient, impetuous, bent on, intent on, set on, mad after, rabid, dying for, bad off for, devoured by desire; aspiring, ambitious, vaulting, skyaspiring.

4, desirable; desired, in demand; pleasing (see PLEASURE); appetizing, tantalizing.

Adverbs—desirously, wistfully, fain; solicitously, yearningly, fondly, ambitiously, *etc.*

Antonym, see HATE, SUFFICIENCY.

---

desist, *v.i.* stop, cease, abstain, quit, forbear. See END. *Ant.*, see CONTINUITY.

desk, *n.* *escritoire*, secretary, lectern.

desolate, *adj. & v.t.* —*adj.* bleak, barren, inhospitable, unpeopled; lonely, abandoned, forlorn; comfortless, miserable. See ABSENCE, SECLUSION, DEJECTION. *Ant.*, see ABODE, SOCIALITY. —*v.t.* waste, depopulate, devastate. See DESTRUCTION, DETERIORATION.

despair, *n.* hopelessness, sadness, DEJECTION, despondency, discouragement. *Ant.*, see HOPE, CHEERFULNESS.

desperate, *adj.* hopeless, incurable; reckless, rash, foolhardy; furious, heroic. See DEJECTION, RASHNESS.

despise, *v.t.* scorn, disdain, hold in contempt, DISLIKE. *Ant.*, see RESPECT.

despotism, *n.* dictatorship, autocracy, tyranny, oppression. See SEVERITY, AUTHORITY.

destination, *n.* goal, terminus, port; DESTINY, END, objective. *Ant.*, see BEGINNING, DEPARTURE.

DESTINY [152]

Nouns—**1,** destiny, future existence; imminence, future state, next world, world to come, afterlife; futurity.

2, destiny, fate, kismet, God's will, act of God, the will of God *or* Allah; Karma; doom, determinism, fatalism, predestination, predetermination, NECESSITY, inevitability; luck, star, lot, fortune, destination; a cross to bear, a row to hoe; wheel of fortune, spin *or* turn of the wheel, fall of the dice, *or* cards; the mills of the gods; hour of destiny.

Verbs—impend; hang *or* lie over; threaten, loom, await, come on, approach, stare one in the face; ordain, foreordain, preordain; predestine, doom, have in store for.

Adjectives—destined, impending, about to be, about to happen, coming, in store, to come, instant, at hand, near; near *or* close at hand; overhanging, hanging over one's head, imminent; brewing, preparing, forthcoming; in the wind, in the cards, in the offing, in reserve; in prospect, expected (see EXPECTATION), looming in the distance *or* future, *or* on the horizon.

Adverbs—**1,** in time, in the long run; all in good time; eventually, whatever may happen, as chance *or* luck would have it.

2, fatally, fatalistically, imminently, *etc.;* in the hands of fate, in the lap of the gods, in God's hands; out of luck, in luck; by chance.
Antonym, see CHANCE, NECESSITY.

destitute, *adj.* wanting, lacking; stripped, bereft, penniless, poverty-stricken. See INSUFFICIENCY, POVERTY. *Slang,* down and out.

destroy, *v.t.* demolish, ruin, devastate, raze; erase, blot out; kill. See DESTRUCTION. *Ant.*, see PRODUCTION.

DESTRUCTION [162]

Nouns—**1,** destruction; waste, dissolution, breaking up; disruption; consumption; disorganization.

2, fall, downfall, ruin, perdition, crash, smash, havoc, debacle; breakdown, breakup; prostration; desolation, bouleversement, wreck, shipwreck, catastrophe, cataclysm; extinction, annihilation; destruction of life (see KILLING); OBLITERATION; knock-down blow; doom, crack of doom.

3, destroying, demolition, demolishment; overthrow, subversion, REVOLUTION, sabotage; suppression; abolition, abrogation (see NULLIFICATION); sacrifice, ravage, devastation, incendiarism, extirpation, extermination, eradication; EXTRACTION; road to ruin; dilapidation, DETERIORATION.

4, destroyer, exterminator; nihilist; blight, moth; executioner.

Verbs—**1,** be destroyed, perish, fall, fall to the ground; tumble, topple; go *or* fall to pieces: break up; crumble to dust; go to the dogs, go to the wall, go to smash, go to wreck, go to pot, go to wrack and ruin; go by the board, go all to smash; be all over with, be all up with; totter to its fall.

2, destroy, do *or* make away with; exterminate; nullify, annul, OBLITERATE, wipe out; sacrifice, demolish, dismantle (see USELESSNESS); tear up; overturn, overthrow, overwhelm; upset, subvert, put an end to; seal the doom of; break up, cut up; break down, cut down, pull down, mow down, beat down; suppress, quash, put down; cut short, take off, blot out; dispel, dissipate, dissolve; consume; disorganize. *Colloq.*, do for, wipe out, cook one's goose. *Slang,* cook, lay out, K.O., knock into a cocked hat.

3, smash, quell, squash, squelch, crumple up, shatter, shiver; batter; tear to pieces, crush to pieces, cut to pieces, pull to pieces, pick to pieces; nip; ruin; strike out; throw down, knock down; fell, sink, swamp, scuttle, wreck, shipwreck, engulf, submerge; lay in ashes, lay in ruins; sweep away, eradicate, erase, expunge; raze, level.

4, deal destruction. lay waste, ravage, gut; swallow up, devour, desolate, devastate, sap, mine, blast, confound; exterminate, extinguish, quench, annihilate; snuff out, put out, stamp out; prostrate; trample under foot;

make short work of, make a clean sweep of, make mincemeat of; cut up root and branch; fling *or* scatter to the winds; throw overboard; strike at the root of, sap the foundations of, spring a mine, blow up.
Adjectives—destroyed, disrupted, perishing, trembling, nodding *or* tottering to its fall; in course of destruction; extinct; destructive, subversive, ruinous, incendiary, deletory; destroying; suicidal; deadly (see KILLING).

Antonym, see PRODUCTION.

---

detach, *v.t.* separate, disconnect, remove, sever, unfix, unfasten. See DISJUNCTION. *Ant.*, see JUNCTION.

detail, *n. & v.t.* —*n.* PART, unite, item; minute, particular, trifle. See SPECIALITY, UNIMPORTANCE. —*v.t.* particularize, itemize; appoint, assign. See SPECIALITY, CHOICE, APPORTIONMENT.

detain, *v.t.* delay, check, hold back; keep, retain. See LATENESS, HINDRANCE.

detect, *v.t.* discover, find out, perceive, espy, ferret out. See DISCLOSURE. *Ant.*, see CONCEALMENT.

deter, *v.t.* restrain, hinder, discourage, give pause, disincline. See RESTRAINT, HINDRANCE, FEAR. *Ant.*, see HOPE.

DETERIORATION [659]

Nouns—**1,** deterioration, debasement; wane, ebb; decline, declension; relapse, backsliding (see REGRESSION); recession, retrogradation, DECREASE.
2, degeneracy, degeneration, degenerateness, degradation; depravation, depravement; depravity, perversion, prostitution; demoralization, retrogression; decadence.
3, impairment, injury, damage, loss, detriment, outrage, havoc, inroad, ravage; scathe; vitiation; discoloration, oxidation; poisoning, leaven; pollution, contamination; canker; adulteration, alloy.
4, decay, DECOMPOSITION, disintegration, dilapidation, ravages of time, wear and tear; corrosion, erosion; mouldiness, rottenness; moth and rust, dry rot, blight; atrophy, collapse; disorganization, devastation, DESTRUCTION.
Verbs—**1,** deteriorate, be deteriorated, become deteriorated, degenerate; have seen better days, have seen better days, have seen better days, fall off; wane (see DECREASE); ebb; retrograde (see REGRESSION); decline, droop; go down, sink, go downhill, go from bad to worse; jump out of the frying pan into the fire; run to seed, lapse, be the worse for; break down, break; spring a leak, crack, start; shrivel (see CONTRACTION); fade, go off, wither, molder, rot, decay, go bad; rust, crumble, shake; totter, totter to its fall; perish (see DEATH). *Colloq.*, go to pot.
2, deteriorate; weaken (see IMPOTENCE); put back; taint, infect, contaminate, poison, envenom, canker, corrupt, exulcerate, pollute, vitiate, debase; denaturalize, leaven; deflower, debauch, defile, deprave, degrade; pervert, prostitute, demoralize, brutalize; render vicious; stain; discolor, alloy, adulterate, tamper with, prejudice; blight, rot, corrode, erode; wear away, wear out; gnaw, gnaw at the root of; sap, mine, undermine, shake, sap the foundations of, break up, disorganize, dismantle, dismast; destroy (see DESTRUCTION).
3, injure, impair, damage, harm, hurt, scathe, spoil, mar, despoil, dilapidate, waste; overrun; ravage; pillage (see STEALING); wound, stab, pierce, maim, lame, cripple, hamstring, mangle, mutilate, disfigure, blemish, deface, warp. *Colloq.*, play the devil with, play hell with, crack up.
Adjectives—**1,** deteriorated, altered, altered for the worse; injured, sprung; withering, spoiling, on the wane, on the decline; degenerate, effete; depraved; worse; the worse for; out of repair *or* tune; imperfect (see IMPERFECTION); the worse for wear; battered; weathered, weatherbeaten; stale, passé, shaken, dilapidated, frayed, faded, wilted, shabby, secondhand, threadbare; worn, worn to a thread, worn to a shadow, worn to rags; reduced to a skeleton; at a low ebb, in a bad way, on one's last legs; undermined; deciduous; tottering; past cure, hopeless, deleterious (see BADNESS). *Colloq.*, seedy, tacky; done for, out of commission. *Slang*, out of whack.
2, decayed, motheaten, wormeaten; mildewed, rusty, mouldy, spotted, time-worn, moss-grown; discolored; wasted, crumbling, mouldering, rotten,

cankered, blighted, tainted; decrepit; broken down; done for, done up; worn out, used up.
Antonym, see IMPROVEMENT.

determination, *n.* RESOLUTION, WILL, firmness; JUDGMENT.
determine, *v.t.* decide, resolve; END, settle; delimit, define, bound; specify, find out, restrict, differentiate; INFLUENCE, affect. See RESOLUTION, CIRCUMSCRIPTION, CAUSE. *Ant.*, see DOUBT.
detest, *v.t.* HATE, abhor, despise, abominate, DISLIKE. *Ant.*, see APPROBATION.
detour, *n.* DEVIATION, digression, excursion; byway, bypass. See AVOIDANCE.

DETRACTION [934]

Nouns—**1,** detraction, derogation, disparagement, depreciation, vilification, obloquy, scurrility, scandal, defamation, aspersion, traducement, slander, calumny, evil-speaking, backbiting; underestimation; libel, lampoon, skit; sarcasm, cynicism, derision, RIDICULE; criticism, invective (see DISAPPROBATION).
2, detractor, derogator, defamer, backbiter, slanderer; lampooner, satirist, traducer, libeler, calumniator, reviler, vituperator, castigator; shrew; reprover, censurer; cynic, critic, caviler, carper. *Colloq.*, knocker.
Verbs—detract, derogate, decry, depreciate, disparage; run down, cry down, sneer at (see CONTEMPT); deride, RIDICULE; criticize, pull to pieces, asperse, cast aspersions, blow upon, bespatter, blacken; vilify, revile, give a dog a bad name, brand, malign, backbite, libel, lampoon, traduce, slander, defame, calumniate, bear false witness against; speak ill of; anathematize, dip the pen in gall, view in a bad light. *Colloq.*, run down, take down a peg.
Adjectives—detracting, detractory, derogatory, defamatory, disparaging, libelous; scurrilous; abusive; slanderous, calumnious, calumniatory; sarcastic, sardonic, satirical, cynical.
Antonym, see APPROBATION.

devastate, *v.t.* waste, ravage, desolate, pillage; ruin, raze, destroy, demolish. See DESTRUCTION, DETERIORATION. *Ant.*, PRODUCTION.
develop, *v.* evolve, unfold, mature, grow; CAUSE, bring about, cultivate, produce, amplify. See INCREASE, TEACHING, IMPROVEMENT.

DEVIATION [279]

Nouns—deviation; swerving, obliquation, warp, refraction; flection, sweep; deflection, deflexure; declination; diversion, divergence, digression, departure from, aberration; zigzag; detour, bypass, byroad, circuit; wandering, vagrancy, evagation; oblique motion, sidling, knight's move.
Verbs—**1,** deviate, alter one's course, depart from, turn, trend; bend, curve (see CURVATURE); swerve, heel, bear off; deflect; divert, divert from its course; put on a new scent, shift, shunt, wear, draw aside, crook, warp.
2, stray, straggle; sidle, diverge, part, separate; digress, wander, wind, twist, meander, veer, tack; turn aside, turn a corner, turn away from; wheel, steer clear of; ramble, rove, drift; go astray, go adrift; yaw, dodge; step aside, ease off, make way for, shy; fly off at a tangent; glance off; wheel about, face about; turn to the right about; go out of one's way, lose one's way *or* bearings.
Adjectives—deviating, deviative, aberrant, errant; excursive, discursive; devious, desultory, loose; rambling; stray, erratic, vagrant, undirected; divergent, radial, forked, centrifugal; circuitous, indirect, zigzag; crablike; off one's beat, off the beaten track.
Adverbs—astray from, round about, wide of the mark; to the right about, all manner of ways; circuitously; obliquely, sidling.
Antonym, see DIRECTION.

device, *n.* scheme, trick, stratagem, ruse, expedient; badge, emblem, motto; mechanism, contrivance, INSTRUMENT, invention, gadget. See DECEPTION.
devil, *n.* satan, DEMON, fiend; wretch, unfortunate.

devise, *v.t.* bequeath, will; produce, invent, fashion, concoct. See GIVING, PRODUCTION, IMAGINATION.

devoid, *adj.* lacking, without, destitute, empty. See ABSENCE, INSUFFICIENCY. *Ant.*, see SUFFICIENCY, COMPLETION.

devote, *v.t.* give (oneself) to, employ (oneself) at; destine, dedicate, consecrate; attend, study. See UNDERTAKING, BUSINESS, NECESSITY, ATTENTION. *Ant.*, see AVOIDANCE.

devotee, *n.* enthusiast, zealot, fanatic, votary, follower, disciple. See AMUSEMENT, DESIRE, PIETY. *Slang*, fan, addict.

devour, *v.t.* eat; wolf; consume, destroy. See FOOD, GLUTTONY, DESTRUCTION, USE.

devout, *adj.* pious, reverent, religious, godly, worshiping, fervent, sincere. See PIETY, FEELING. *Ant.*, see IRRELIGION.

dexterous, *adj.* skillful, adroit, deft, clever. See SKILL. *Ant.*, see UNSKILLFULNESS.

diabolic, *adj.* devilish, demoniac, wicked, impious, malevolent. See DEMON, BADNESS, MALEVOLENCE.

diagram, *n. & v.t.* —*n.* PLAN, sketch, chart, blueprint, map. —*v.t.* draw, OUTLINE, layout.

dialect, *n.* language, diction, tongue; vernacular, idiom, argot, patois, jargon, cant; barbarism, colloquialism.

diameter, *n.* BREADTH, THICKNESS, width, caliber, bore. See SIZE.

dictate, *v.t.* enjoin, COMMAND, draw up, say for transcription; domineer, browbeat. See ADVICE, ARROGANCE.

dictatorial, *adj.* dogmatic, opinionated, despotic, arbitrary. See CERTAINTY, SEVERITY, ARROGANCE.

dictionary, *n.* wordbook, lexicon, vocabulary. See BOOK.

dictum, (*pl.* **dicta**), *n.* saying, maxim; decision, judgment; pronouncement.

die, *v.i.* expire, perish, pass away; demise, cease; fade out. See DEATH, END. *Slang*, go west, croak, kick the bucket.

die, *n.* mold, matrix, punch, thread-cutter, prototype, perforator.

diet, *n.* parliament, congress; food, aliment, edibles, intake, victuals; regimen. *Slang*, grub, chow. See FOOD, REMEDY, ASSEMBLAGE.

DIFFERENCE [15]

Nouns—difference; variance, variation, variety; diversity, dissimilarity; DISAGREEMENT, odds, incompatibility; DEVIATION; disparity, inequality, distinction, contradistinction; nice distinction, fine distinction, delicate distinction, subtle distinction, subtlety; incongruence, shade of difference, nuance; discordance, dissonance; discrimination; antithesis, contrariness; modification; moods and tenses; different thing, horse of another color. *Colloq.*, different story, something else again; no such thing.

Verbs—be different, differ, vary, mismatch, contrast; divaricate, diverge, deviate, disagree with; differentiate, specialize; vary, modify, CHANGE; discriminate, distinguish.

Adjectives—differing, different, diverse, heterogeneous; distinguishable, varied, modified; diversified, various, divers, all manner of; variform, daedal; incongruous, incompatible; distinctive, characteristic; discriminative; other, another, not the same; unequal, unmatched; widely apart, DISSIMILAR.

Adverbs—differently; otherwise.

Antonym, see IDENTITY.

differentiate, *v.t.* discriminate, distinguish, compare, contrast, isolate, particularize. See DIFFERENCE. *Ant.*, see SIMILARITY.

DIFFICULTY [704]

Nouns—**1,** difficulty, difficultness; hardness; impracticability, impossibility; hard work, uphill work; hard task, Herculean task; task of Sisyphus, Sisyphean labor; tough job. *Colloq.*, large order, hard row to hoe.

2, dilemma, horns of a dilemma; embarrassment; perplexity, uncertainty; intricacy; entanglement; crossfire; awkwardness, delicacy, Gordian knot, net, mesh, maze; coil (see CONVOLUTION); nice point, delicate point; vexed question, poser, puzzle, riddle, paradox; hard nut to crack; bone to pick.

3, quandary, strait, pass, pinch, pretty pass, stress, plight, brunt; critical situation, crisis; trial, rub, crux, emergency, exigency; scramble; quagmire, hot water, hornet's nest; sea of troubles; pretty kettle of fish; pickle, stew, imbroglio, mess, ado, impasse, deadlock; fix, *cul de sac;* hitch; stumbling block, HINDRANCE. *Colloq.,* scrape, jam, hole.

Verbs—**1,** be difficult, go against the grain, try one's patience, put one out; put to one's wit's end; go hard with; try one; pose, perplex; bother, non-plus, bring to a deadlock; be impossible.

2, meet with difficulties, labor under difficulties, get into difficulties; labor under a disadvantage; be in difficulty; fish in troubled waters, buffet the waves, swim against the stream *or* tide; have much ado with, have a hard time of it; bear the brunt; grope in the dark, lose one's way.

3, get into difficulties, get into a scrape; bring a hornet's nest about one's ears; flounder, boggle, struggle; not know which way to turn (see DOUBT); stick at, stick in the mud, stick fast; come to a standstill. *Colloq.,* put one's foot in it, get all balled up. *Slang,* take it on the chin.

4, render difficult; encumber, embarrass, nonplus, ravel, entangle, involve; put a spoke in the wheel, hinder (see HINDRANCE). *Colloq.,* stump, tree.

Adjectives—**1,** difficult, not easy, hard, tough; troublesome, toilsome, irk-some; laborious, onerous, arduous, Herculean, formidable; sooner *or* more easily said than done; difficult *or* hard to deal with; ill-conditioned.

2, awkward, unwieldy, unmanageable; intractable, stubborn, obstinate (see RESOLUTION); perverse, refractory, plaguy, trying, thorny, rugged; knotted, knotty; pathless, trackless, labyrinthine, convoluted (see CONVOLUTION); intricate, complicated, tangled; impracticable, impossible, not feasible; desperate, hopeless; embarrassing, perplexing, uncertain (see DOUBT); at the end of one's rope *or* tether, at one's wits' end, at a standstill; nonplused; stranded, aground, stuck fast; up a tree, at bay, driven into a corner, driven from pillar to post, driven to extremity, driven to the wall; out of one's depth, thrown out. *Colloq.,* in a pickle, floored. *Slang,* behind the eight-ball, in the soup, in a spot, in Dutch.

Adverbs—with difficulty, with much ado; hardly, uphill; against the stream, against the grain; in the teeth of, in a pinch; at long odds.

Antonym, see FACILITY.

---

diffuseness, *n.* circulation, dissemination; expansion, diffusion, scattering, broadcasting, strewing; LOQUACITY, verbosity, looseness, redundance, repe-tition, prolixity, verbiage, tautology.

dig, *v.* shovel, spade, excavate, grub, delve; labor, speed. See CONCAVITY.

digest, *v.t. & n.* —*v.t.* prepare, transform; absorb, assimilate; ruminate, ponder, weigh; shorten, abridge, condense. See THOUGHT, CHANGE, AR-RANGEMENT, IMPROVEMENT. —*n.* list, catalog; abstract, condensation, com-pendium. *Ant.,* see WHOLE.

dignity, *n.* REPUTE; nobility, eminence; PRIDE, stateliness, decorum; GREAT-NESS, station, honor.

digress, *v.i.* diverge, ramble, deviate. See DEVIATION, LOQUACITY.

dike, *n.* embankment, levee; ditch. See INCLOSURE.

dilapidated, *adj.* decayed, disintegrating, crumbling, tumbledown, ram-shackle. See DETERIORATION. *Ant.,* see NEWNESS.

dilate, *v.* expatiate, descant; stretch, distend, enlarge. See INCREASE. *Ant.,* see LITTLENESS, CONTRACTION.

dilemma, *n.* predicament, perplexity, quandary. See DOUBT, DIFFICULTY.

diligence, *n.* application, industry, assiduity, ACTIVITY.

diluted, *adj.* thin, weak, watery. See IMPOTENCE, WATER.

dimension, *n.* amplitude, area, extent, measurement, SIZE.

diminish, *v.* lessen, reduce, shrink, abridge; wane, dwindle, peter out. See LITTLENESS, CONTRACTION. *Ant.,* see EXPAND, INCREASE.

diminutive, *adj.* small, little, tiny, wee. See LITTLENESS. *Ant.,* see GREAT-NESS, HEIGHT, SIZE.

DIMNESS [422]

Nouns—dimness, obscurity, shadow, shade, gloom; DARKNESS, OPACITY, partial darkness, partial shadow, eclipse; partial eclipse; dusk, gloaming, twilight, evening, shades of evening; moonlight, moonbeam, moonshine, starlight, candlelight, firelight; paleness, half-light, faintness, nebulosity, glimmer, glimmering, aurora, daybreak, dawn.

Verbs—be dim, grow dim; flicker, twinkle, glimmer; loom, lower; fade, pale, gutter (out), dim, bedim, obscure, blur, cloud, mist; fog, befog; shadow, overshadow.

Adjectives—dim, dull, lackluster, dingy, darkish, dark; obscure, indistinct, faint, shadowed, glassy; cloudy, misty, opaque; muggy, nebulous, nebular; overcast, muddy, lurid, leaden, dun, dirty; looming; pale, colorless.

Antonym, see LIGHT.

dimsighted, *adj.* nearsighted, short-sighted, myopic, astigmatic; purblind; night-blind; bleary, red-eyed, peering, squinting; strabismic, blurry; cross-eyed. *Colloq.*, cockeyed, blind as a bat. See OBSCURITY, DARKNESS. *Ant.*, see VISION.

dingy, *adj.* discolored, grimy, dirty. See DIMNESS. *Ant.*, see LIGHT, COLOR.

dip, *n. & v.t.* —*n.* plunge, dive; declivity, slope; swim. See OBLIQUITY. —*v.t.* immerse, plunge.

diplomatist, *n.* tactful person, adroit person; diplomat, envoy, ambassador.

dire, *adj.* appalling, calamitous, fateful, dreadful, ominous; deplorable. See FEAR, ADVERSITY.

direct, *v. & adj.* —*v.t.* guide, lead; regulate, govern, CONDUCT, head, manage, supervise, boss, rule; aim, point; order, COMMAND, prescribe, bid, instruct, teach, coach, prompt; show, lead the way; address. —*adj.* straight, undeviating (see DIRECTION); BLUNT.

DIRECTION [278, 693]

Nouns—**1,** direction, bearing, course, set, drift, tenor, orientation, TENDENCY; incidence; bending, trending, dip, tack, aim; collimation; steering, steerage. **2,** point of the compass, cardinal points; north, east, south, west; orient, sunrise; occident, sunset; rhumb, azimuth, line of collimation. **3,** line, path, road, range, quarter, line of march; alignment. **4,** direction, management, government, CONDUCT, legislation, regulation, guidance; reins, reins of government; supervision, superintendence; surveillance, oversight; control, charge; COUNCIL, command, AUTHORITY; helm, rudder, needle, compass; guiding star, loadstar, lodestar, polestar; cynosure. **5,** directorship, presidency, premiership, senatorship, director; chair, portfolio; statesmanship, statecraft, kingcraft; ministry, ministration; administration; stewardship, proctorship; jurisdiction, AGENCY, regime.

Verbs—**1,** direct, bend, trend, tend, verge, incline, dip, determine; point toward; aim at, level at; go toward, steer toward; keep *or* hold a course; be bound for; bend one's steps toward; direct, steer, bend *or* shape one's course; go straight, go straight to the point. **2,** ascertain one's direction, orient, get one's bearings, see which way the wind blows; box the compass; follow one's nose. **3,** direct, manage, govern, CONDUCT; ORDER, prescribe, cut out work for; head, lead, lead *or* show the way; take the lead, lead on; regulate, guide, steer, pilot; take the helm; have the reins, handle the reins, hold the reins, take the reins; drive; tackle. *Colloq.*, run. **4,** superintend, supervise; overlook, control, keep in order, look after, see to, legislate for; administer, ministrate; have care of, have charge of; have *or* take the direction; take over; pull the strings *or* wires; RULE, COMMAND. hold office; preside, take, occupy *or* be in the chair; pull the stroke oar; *Colloq.*, boss.

Adjectives—**1,** direct, straight, undeviating, unswerving, straightforward; directed toward; pointing toward; bound for. **2,** directing, managing, governing, *etc.*; hegemonic, dictatorial; governmental, presidential, gubernatorial, mayoral, *etc.*

Adverbs—**1,** directly, directionally, straight, northward, northerly, *etc.*; hither, thither, whither; straight as an arrow; pointblank; in a line with; full tilt at; as the crow flies; before the wind; windward, leeward, in all directions, in all manner of ways. *Colloq.*, every which way. **3,** in charge, at the helm of, at the head of; on the throne, in the hands of.

Colloq., in the saddle, on top, in the driver's seat.
Prepositions—through, via, by way of; toward.
Antonym, see DEVIATION.

---

directly, *adv.* straightway, immediately, instantly, promptly; bluntly, flatly, unequivocally; expressly; straight. See INSTANTANEITY, DIRECTION.
director, *n.* manager, conductor, head, superintendent. See AUTHORITY.
dirge, *n.* requiem, threnody, funeral hymn, elegy. See LAMENTATION.
dirty, *adj.* unclean, filthy, soiled, foul; murky, miry, stormy; vile, sordid, mean; dishonest. See UNCLEANNESS, DIMNESS, IMPROBITY. *Ant.*, see CLEANNESS.
disabled, *v.t.* incapacitate, cripple, damage, unfit, maim. See IMPOTENCE.
disadvantage, *n.* drawback, check, HINDRANCE, See EVIL.

DISAGREEMENT [24]

Nouns—**1,** disagreement; discord, discordance; dissonance, dissidence, discrepancy; UNCONFORMITY, incongruity, incongruence; discongruity, misalliance; jarring; DISSENT, dissension, conflict, OPPOSITION; intrusion, interference; disunity.
2, disparity, mismatch, misjoining, disproportion, disproportionateness, variance, DIVERGENCE; repugnance.
3, unfitness, inaptitude, impropriety; inapplicability; inconsistency, irrelevancy, irrelation.
Verbs—disagree; clash, jar, dispute, quarrel, contend (see CONTENTION); interfere, intrude, come amiss; not concern, mismatch.
Adjectives—**1,** disagreeing, discordant, discrepant, incongruous; hostile, repugnant, incompatible, irreconcilable, inconsistent with; unconformable, exceptional; intrusive; disproportionate, unharmonious; unconsonant; divergent.
2, inapt, unapt, inappropriate, improper; unsuited, unsuitable; inapplicable; unfit, unfitting, unbefitting; unbecoming; ill-timed, unseasonable, *mal apropos*, inadmissible; inapposite, irrelevant; uncongenial; ill-assorted, mismatched, misjoined, misplaced; unaccommodating, irreducible, uncommensurable; out of character, out of keeping, out of proportion, out of joint, out of tune, out of place, out of season, out of its element; at odds with, at variance with.
Adverbs—in disagreement, in defiance, in contempt, in spite of; discordantly.
Antonym, see AGREEMENT.

---

disappear, *v.i.* vanish, drop from sight *or* view; dissolve, fade *or* melt away. *Colloq.*, withdraw, go away. *Slang*, beat it!, vamoose; get lost; take a powder. See ABSENCE, DEPARTURE. *Ant.*, see ARRIVAL, PRESENCE.
disappearance, *n.* vanishing; dissolution; fading, dissolving; DEPARTURE, evanescence, eclipse; sudden absence. *Ant.*, see APPEARANCE, PRESENCE, ARRIVAL.
disappointment, *n.* FAILURE, nonsuccess; DISCONTENT, chagrin; disillusion; bafflement, unfulfillment, a falling short (of one's hopes); fool's paradise, frustration. *Colloq.*, letdown. *Ant.*, see SUCCESS, HOPE.

DISAPPROBATION [932]

Nouns—**1,** disapprobation, disapproval; improbation; disesteem, disvaluation; odium, DISLIKE.
2, dispraise, discommendation; blame, obloquy; DETRACTION, disparagement, depreciation; denunciation; CONDEMNATION; ostracism, boycott. *Colloq.*, blacklist, blackball.
3, animadversion, reflection, stricture, objection, exception, criticism; hypercriticism, picking, quibbling; sardonic grin, sardonic laugh; sarcasm, insinuation, innuendo; lefthanded compliment; satire; sneer, derision, CONTEMPT; taunt, DISRESPECT. *Colloq.*, knock, slam.
4, cavil, carping, censure, censoriousness; reprehension, remonstrance, expostulation, reproof, reprobation, admonition, reproach; chiding, upbraiding, rebuke, reprimand, castigation, lecture, scolding, trimming; correction, setdown, rap on the knuckles, rebuff; slap, home thrust, hit;

frown, scowl, black look; diatribe; jeremiad, tirade, philippic. *Colloq.*, tongue-lashing, blowup, dressing down, rating, talking to. *Slang*, bawling out, what-for, calling down.

5, abuse, vituperation, invective, objurgation, contumely; hard words, cutting words, bitter words; clamor, outcry, hue and cry; hiss, hissing; sibilation, cat-call; execration.

Verbs—**1,** disapprove; DISLIKE; lament (see LAMENTATION); object to, take exception to; be scandalized at, think ill of; view with disfavor, view with jaundiced eyes; disvalue, improbate.

2, frown upon, look grave; knit the brows; shake the head at, shrug the shoulders; turn up the nose (see CONTEMPT); look askance, make a wry face at; set one's face against.

3, dispraise, discommend, disparage; deprecate, speak ill of, not speak well of; condemn; blame; lay blame upon; censure, reproach, pass censure on, reprobate; impugn; remonstrate, expostulate, recriminate; reprehend, chide, admonish; bring to account, call to account, call to order; take to task, reprove, lecture, bring to book; rebuke, correct; reprimand, chastise, castigate, lash, trounce, trim. *Colloq.*, knock, tonguelash, lace into, pick at, jump on, dress down, rip into, jump down one's throat, tell off, roast, haul over the coals, score, lay out. *Slang*, rap, call down, give what-for, jaw, lay into, light into.

4, accuse (see ACCUSATION); impeach, denounce; expose, brand, stigmatize; show up; raise a hue and cry against.

5, execrate, exprobate, look daggers, vituperate; abuse, scold, rate, objurgate, upbraid, fall foul of; jaw; rail, rail at; bark at; anathematize, call names; revile, vilify, vilipend; bespatter; backbite; rave against, fulminate against, exclaim against, protest against, inveigh against, declaim against, cry out against, raise one's voice against; decry; run down; clamor, hiss, hoot, mob, boycott, ostracize; draw up *or* sign a round robin; animadvert upon, reflect upon; look askance at; cast reflection upon, cast a slur upon; insinuate, damn with faint praise.

6, scoff at, point at; twit, taunt (see DISRESPECT); sneer at (see CONTEMPT); satirize, lampoon; defame (see DETRACTION); depreciate, find fault with, criticize, cut up; pull *or* pick to pieces; take exception; cavil, carp at; be censorious, pick holes, make a fuss about, kick against.

7, take down, set down; snub, snap one up, snap a person's head off; give a rap on the knuckles; throw a stone at; have words with.

8, incur disapprobation, incur blame, scandalize, shock, revolt; get a bad name, forfeit one's good name, be under a cloud, bring a hornet's nest about one's ears; be in one's bad books; take blame, stand corrected; have to answer for.

Adjectives—disapprobatory, disapproving, scandalized; disparaging, condemnatory, damnatory, denunciatory, reproachful, abusive, objurgatory, clamorous, vituperative; defamatory (see DETRACTION); satirical, sarcastic, sardonic, cynical, dry, sharp, cutting, biting, severe, withering, trenchant, hard upon; censorious, critical, captious, carping, hypercritical; sparing of praise, grudging of praise; disapproved, in bad odor, unapproved; unblest; at a discount, exploded; weighed in the balance and found wanting; blameworthy, reprehensible, to blame, worthy of blame; answerable, uncommendable, exceptionable, not to be thought of; bad, vicious (see IMPROBITY). *Colloq.*, in bad, in the doghouse.

Adverbs—with a wry face; reproachfully, *etc.*

Interjections—thumbs down! it won't do! it will never do! God forbid! Heaven forbid! away with! shame! for shame!

Antonym, see APPROBATION.

---

disaster, *n.* calamity, cataclysm, misfortune, catastrophe, tragedy. See ADVERSITY, EVIL.

discard, *v.t.* reject, abandon, eliminate, repudiate, throw aside. See REFUSAL, NEGLECT, NULLIFICATION.

discern, *v.t.* espy; discover, perceive, distinguish, detect. See VISION.

discharge, *v.t.* dismiss, retire; expel, shoot, fire; perform, do; settle, pay; free, acquit. See FREEDOM, VIOLENCE, CONDUCT, PAYMENT, ACQUITTAL.

disciple, *n.* follower, devotee, adherent, pupil.
discipline, *n.* training, drill, practice; RESTRAINT, control, repression; PUN-ISHMENT, correction. See TEACHING.
disclaim, *v.t.* disavow, deny, repudiate; disown, renounce. See NULLIFICA-TION, NEGATION.

DISCLOSURE [529]

Nouns—**1,** disclosure, divulgence, unveiling, revealing, revealment, revela-tion; exposition, exposure, exposé; whole truth; telling (see INFORMATION); acknowledgment, admission, concession; avowal; confession, confessional, shrift; dénouement, manifestation, PUBLICATION; clue, hint.
2, DISCOVERY, detection, realization, ascertainment, find, finding, unearth-ing; explanation, answer; first sight *or* glimpse; new method, *etc.*
Verbs—**1,** disclose, uncover, discover, unmask, dismask, draw, draw aside, lift *or* raise the veil *or* curtain; unveil, unfold, unseal, break the seal; lay open, lay bare; bring to light; let into the secret; tell, inform (see INFORMA-TION) breathe, utter, blab, let out, let fall, let drop, let slip; betray; bruit abroad, broadcast; tell tales, tell tales out of school; come out with; give vent to, give utterance to; open the lips, blurt out, vent, hint, intimate, whisper about; speak out, make manifest, make public; disabuse, set right, correct, open the eyes of. *Colloq.*, let on, let the cat out of the bag. *Slang*, spill the beans, peach.
2, acknowledge, allow, concede, grant, admit, own, confess, avow; turn inside out, make a clean breast; declare oneself, show one's hand *or* cards; unburden oneself *or* one's mind; open one's mind, lay bare one's mind; unbosom oneself; say *or* speak the truth; turn King's, Queen's *or* state's evidence. *Colloq.*, let one's hair down, get off one's chest. *Slang*, shoot off one's mouth, come clean, sing.
3, be disclosed, transpire, come to light; come in sight (see APPEARANCE); become known, escape the lips; come, leak *or* crop out; show its face *or* colors; break through the clouds, flash on the mind. *Slang*, come out in the wash.
4, DISCOVER; solve, unravel, smell out. *Colloq.*, spot, dope out.
Adjectives—disclosed, expository, revelatory, *etc.*
Antonym, see CONCEALMENT.

---

discomfort, *n.* uneasiness, distress, annoyance, embarrassment; PAIN, sore-ness. *Ant.*, see RELIEF.
disconcert, *v.t.* upset, discompose, embarrass; perplex, confuse; frustrate, thwart. See AGITATION, HINDRANCE.
disconsolate, *adj.* inconsolable, comfortless, hopeless; melancholy, forlorn, sad. See DEJECTION. *Ant.*, see HOPE, PLEASURE.

DISCONTENT [832]

Nouns—**1,** discontent, discontentment; dissatisfaction; inquietude, vexation, soreness, mortification, heartburning, querulousness, LAMENTATION; hyper-criticism. *Slang*, gripe.
2, malcontent, grumbler, growler, croaker. *Colloq.*, grouch. *Slang*, griper, grouser, fussbudget, crab.
3, disappointment, frustration; blighted hope; blow; nonfulfillment; vain expectation, disillusionment; mirage, fool's paradise; REGRET.
Verbs—**1,** be discontented, be dissatisfied; quarrel with one's bread and but-ter; repine; REGRET; take on, take to heart; shrug the shoulders; make a wry face, pull a long face; knit one's brows; look blue, look black, look blank, look glum, cut off one's nose to spite one's face; take in bad part, take ill; fret, chafe, grumble, croak; lament (see LAMENTATION). *Colloq.*, put out, cut up. *Slang*, grouse, gripe.
2, cause discontent, dissatisfy, vex, disappoint, mortify, disconcert, dis-hearten.
Adjectives—discontented, dissatisfied, unsatisfied, ungratified; dissident; dissenting, malcontent, exigent, exacting, hypercritical; repining, regretful; down in the mouth, morose, dejected (see DEJECTION); in high dudgeon, in the dumps, in bad humor; glum, sulky, sullen; sour, soured, out of humor,

out of temper; disappointing; unsatisfactory. *Colloq.*, grumpy, grouchy, sore.

Antonyms, see CHEERFULNESS, PLEASURE.

discontinuance, *n.* discontinuity, discontinuation; interruption, break, stop, stoppage, CESSATION, cease, suspension, END, intermittence. *Ant.*, see STABILITY, CONTINUITY.

discontinue, *v.* stop, cease; interrupt, break off *or* into; cut off, curtail, suspend, quit, lay off, desist, END.

discord, *n.* disharmony, cacophony, noise; DISAGREEMENT; harshness; CONTENTION, strife, conflict; quarreling, dissension, DIFFERENCE; dissonance, atonality; jangling, rasping *or* grating sound; incongruity, clash, clashing. *Ant.*, see AGREEMENT.

discount, *v. & n.* —*v.t.* rebate, allow, reduce; deduct, lessen, diminish; mark down, lower (the price); disregard, ignore; belittle. —*n.* allowance, qualification; markdown, rebate, refund, deduction; percentage. *Colloq.*, rakeoff, kickback. See DECREASE, CHEAPNESS. *Ant.*, see INCREASE.

discourage, *v.t.* depress, dishearten, dismay; dissuade, deter. See DEJECTION, DISSUASION, FEAR.

discourse, *v.i.* talk, discuss; declaim, hold forth, dissertate. See CONVERSATION, SPEECH.

DISCOURTESY [895]

Nouns—**1,** discourtesy, discourteousness; ill-breeding; rudeness, ill manners, bad manners; uncourteousness, inurbanity; illiberality, incivility; DISRESPECT, insult, INSOLENCE, impudence; barbarism, barbarity, brutality, misbehavior, blackguardism, conduct unbecoming a gentleman, VULGARITY; churlishness, perversity; moroseness, sullenness; sternness, austerity; moodiness, captiousness, IRASCIBILITY; cynicism, tartness, acrimony, acerbity, virulence, asperity.

2, scowl, black look, frown; short answer, rebuff; hard words, contumely; unparliamentary language.

3, bear, brute, boor, churl, blackguard, beast; frump. *Colloq.*, crosspatch, saucebox.

Verbs—be discourteous, be rude; insult (see INSOLENCE); treat with discourtesy; take a name in vain; make bold with, make free with; take a liberty; stare out of countenance, ogle, point at, put to the blush; cut; turn one's back upon, turn on one's heel; give the cold shoulder; keep at a distance, keep at arm's length; look coldly upon; show the door to; answer back, send away with a flea in the ear, add insult to injury; lose one's temper; sulk; frown, scowl, glower, pout; snap, snarl, growl.

Adjectives—**1,** discourteous, uncourteous; uncourtly; ill-bred, ill-mannered, disrespectful, ill-behaved, unmannerly, impolite; unpolished, uncivilized, ungentlemanly; unladylike; blackguard; vulgar (see VULGARITY); indecorous; foul-mouthed, abusive; uncivil, ungracious, unceremonious; cool; pert, forward, obtrusive, impudent, rude, saucy, precocious. *Colloq.*, fresh, sassy.

2, repulsive, unaccommodating, unneighborly, ungentle, ungainly; rough, ragged, bluff, blunt, gruff, churlish, boorish, bearish; brutal, brusque, stern, harsh, austere, cavalier; tart, sour, crabbed, sharp, short, trenchant, sarcastic, biting, caustic, virulent, bitter, acrimonious, venomous, contumelious; snarling; curly; perverse; sullen, peevish, irascible (see IRASCIBILITY).

Adverbs—discourteously; with discourtesy, with bad grace.

Antonym, see COURTESY.

discover, *v.t.* uncover, reveal, disclose, manifest; find, discern, espy, descry; see (for the first time); detect, unearth; realize. See DISCLOSURE, LOCATION, INTERPRETATION.

discovery, *n.* revelation, DISCLOSURE; detection, first sight *or* glimpse; unearthing; find, finding; invention, innovation. See LOCATION, NEWNESS. *Ant.*, see CONCEALMENT.

discredit, *v.t.* disparage, stigmatize, shame; doubt, disbelieve, impeach. See DISREPUTE, DOUBT. *Ant.*, see APPROBATION, BELIEF.

discreet, *adj.* prudent, judicious, careful, wary, cautious. See CAUTION, CARE. *Ant.,* see RASHNESS.

discretion, *n.* JUDGMENT; tact, taste, finesse. See SENSIBILITY, INTELLIGENCE, TASTE.

discrimination, *n.* differentation, DIFFERENCE, distinction; TASTE, judgment, insight, critical perception, discernment; bias, prejudice, exclusion. *Ant.,* see INDIFFERENCE.

discuss, *v.t.* talk over, debate, canvass, argue, analyze. See AGITATION, REASONING.

disdain, *n.* scorn, CONTEMPT, ARROGANCE, INSOLENCE, hauteur. *Ant.,* see RESPECT.

DISEASE [655, 657]

Nouns—**1,** disease, illness, sickness; ailing; morbidity, infirmity, ailment, indisposition; complaint, DISORDER, malady; distemper; breakdown, debility, INSANITY; visitation, attack, seizure, stroke, fit, convulsion; decay, DETERIORATION.
2, delicacy, loss of health, invalidation, invalidism, cachexia, atrophy, marasmus; indigestion, dyspepsia; autointoxication; tuberculosis, consumption, palsy, epilepsy, paralysis, infantile paralysis, poliomyelitis, muscular dystrophy; paresis; prostration; fever, malaria, typhoid, typhus, scarlet fever. *Colloq.,* galloping consumption, T.B.
3, sore, ulcer, abscess, boil; pimple, swelling, carbuncle, rot, canker, cancer, carcinoma, caries, mortification, corruption, gangrene, leprosy, eruption, rash, breaking out; inflammation.
4, invalid, patient, case; cripple, leper, consumptive, paralytic.
5, pathology, etiology, therapeutics, diagnosis.
6, insalubrity, insalubriousness, unhealthiness; taint, pollution, infection, contagion, septicity, toxicity, epidemic, endemic; plague, pestilence, virus, pox.
Verbs—be ill, ail, suffer, labor under, be affected with, be afflicted with; complain of; droop, flag, languish, halt; sicken, peak, pine; gasp; keep one's bed; feign sickness, malinger (see FALSEHOOD); disease, derange, affect, attack.
Adjectives—**1,** diseased; ailing, ill, ill of, taken ill, seized with; indisposed, unwell, sick, squeamish, poorly, seedy; laid up, confined, bedridden, invalided, in the hospital, on the sick list, in sick bay (Naut.); out of health, out of sorts; valetudinary. *Slang,* off one's feed, under the weather.
2, unsound, unhealthy; sickly, morose, infirm, drooping, flagging, lame, crippled, halting; withered; palsied, paralytic, dyspeptic, weak (see IMPOTENCE); decrepit; decayed, deteriorated; incurable, hopeless; in declining health; cranky; in a bad way, in danger, prostrate; moribund (see DEATH).
3, insalubrious, unhealthful, morbid, tainted, vitiated, contaminated, poisoned, poisonous; noxious, toxic, septic, virulent; harmful, insanitary.
Antonym, see HEALTH.

---

disfigure, *v.t.* deface, mar, mutilate, deform, BLEMISH.

disgrace, *v.t.* degrade, abase, dishonor, humiliate. See DISREPUTE. *Ant.,* see REPUTE.

disguise, *n.* camouflage, make-up, dissimulation, CONCEALMENT, mask, pretense. See DECEPTION.

disgust, *v.t. & n.* —*v.t.* nauseate, sicken, revolt, repel. —*n.* aversion, nausea, loathing, abhorrence. See HATE, PAIN.

dish, *n.* tableware, plate, saucer, *etc.;* serving; specific food, recipe. See RECEPTACLE.

dishonest, *adj.* untrue, untrustworthy, deceitful, false, cheating, fraudulent, crooked. See FALSEHOOD, IMPROBITY. *Ant.,* PROBITY.

disinfect, *v.t.* sterilize, sanitize, purify, fumigate, cleanse. See CLEANNESS.

disinherit, *v.t.* disown, deprive, cut off.

disintegrate, *v.* break up, separate, decompose; decay, decompose, crumble, dissolve, fall apart. See DISJUNCTION, DECOMPOSITION. *Ant.,* see WHOLE, PROBITY.

disinterestedness, *n.* UNSELFISHNESS; nonpartisanship; fairness, justness, EQUALITY; unbiased attitude, impartiality, evenhandedness. *Ant.,* see SELFISHNESS, IMPROBITY.

DISJUNCTION [44]

Nouns—**1,** disjunction, disconnection, disunity, disunion, disassociation, disengagement; abstraction, abstractedness; isolation; insularity, insulation; oasis; separateness, severalty; DISPERSION, APPORTIONMENT.
2, separation; parting, detachment, segregation; DIVORCE; elision; *cæsura,* divison, subdivision, break, fracture, rupture; compartition; dismemberment, disintegration, dislocation; luxation; severance, disseverance; scission, rescission, abscission; laceration; disruption; avulsion, divulsion; section, resection, cleavage; dissection; DECOMPOSITION.
3, fissure, breach, rent, split, rift, crack, slit, incision, fission.
4, discontinuity; interruption, break, gap, interval, fracture; parenthesis, intermission, cesura; alternation.
5, displacement, dislocation, transposition, dislodgement, removal, EJECTION; displaced person, D.P., refugee, exile; fish out of water.
Verbs—**1,** be disjoined, come off, fall off, fall to pieces; peel off; get loose.
2, disjoin, disconnect, disengage, disunite, dissociate, DIVORCE, part, detach, separate, cut off, rescind, segregate; set apart, keep apart; insulate, isolate; cut adrift; loose(n), unloose, undo, unbind, unchain, unlock, unpack, unravel; disentangle; set free, liberate.
3, sunder, divide, subdivide, sever, dissever, abscind; cut; incise; saw, chop, cleave, rive, rend, split, splinter, chip, crack, snap, break, tear, burst; rend asunder, wrench, rupture, shatter, shiver; hack, hew, slash; whittle. *Colloq.,* smash to smithereens.
4, cut up, carve, dissect, anatomize; take to pieces, pull to pieces, pick to pieces; disintegrate, dismember, disbranch, disband, disperse, displace, dislocate, disjoint; break up; mince; comminute, pulverize; apportion (see APPORTIONMENT).
Adjectives—disjoined, discontinuous, multipartite, abstract; disjunctive; isolated, insular, separate, disparate, discrete, apart, asunder, far between, loose, free; unattached, unannexed, unassociated; distinct; adrift; straggling; unconnected; scissile, divisible.
Adverbs—disjunctively, separately; one by one, severally, apart; adrift, asunder, in twain; in the abstract, abstractedly.
Antonym, see JUNCTION.

dislike, *n. & v.* —*n.* DISAPPROBATION; disgust, aversion, repugnance, repulsion, displeasure, disrelish, antipathy, distaste, disinclination. —*v.t.* disapprove, feel averse to; recoil from; feel distaste, disrelish *or* disgust for. See DISAPPROBATION, HATE. *Ant.,* see APPROBATION.
dislocate, *v.t.* displace, disarrange; disjoin, disarticulate. See DISJUNCTION. *Ant.,* see ARRANGEMENT, LOCATION.
dislodge, *v.t.* displace, topple; expel, evict, drive out. See EJECTION. *Ant.,* see LOCATION, RECEIVING.
dismal, *adj.* cheerless, depressing, gloomy; somber, funereal. See DARKNESS, DEJECTION. *Ant.,* see LIGHT, HOPE.
dismantle, *v.t.* take apart; raze, demolish; disrobe, undress. See DESTRUCTION, DIVESTMENT. *Ant.,* see PRODUCTION.
dismay, *n. & v.t.* —*n.* consternation, terror; discouragement. See FEAR, DEJECTION. —*v.t.* appall; discourage. *Ant.,* see HOPE, CHEERFULNESS.
dismiss, *v.t.* send away; discharge, liberate, disband; cancel (law). See NULLIFICATION, EJECTION, FREEDOM. *Ant.,* see RECEIVING.

DISOBEDIENCE [742]

Nouns—**1,** disobedience, insubordination, contumacy; infraction, infringement; naughtiness; violation, noncompliance; nonobservance.
2, revolt, rebellion, outbreak, rising, uprising, insurrection, riot, tumult, DISORDER; strike, resistance; barring out; defiance; mutiny, mutinousness, mutineering; sedition, treason; *lèse majesté;* violation of law (see ILLEGALITY); defection; secession.

3, insurgent, mutineer, rebel, revolter, rioter, traitor, communist, anarchist, demagogue; seceder, runagate, brawler.

Verbs—disobey, violate, infringe; shirk (see NEGLECT); defy; riot, run riot, run amuck, fly in the face of; take the law into one's own hands; kick over the traces; strike, resist (see OPPOSITION); secede; mutiny, rebel; turn restive; champ at the bit, strain at the leash.

Adjectives—disobedient; uncomplying, uncompliant; unsubmissive, naughty, unruly, ungovernable; insubordinate, refractory, contumacious; recalcitrant; resisting (see OPPOSITION); lawless, mutinous, seditious, insurgent, riotous, rebellious, defiant.

Antonym, see OBEDIENCE.

DISORDER [59]

Nouns—**1,** disorder, DERANGEMENT; irregularity; anomaly, UNCONFORMITY, anarchy, anarchism; untidiness, disunion; DISCORD; confusion, confusedness; disarray, jumble, huddle, litter, lumber; mess, mash, mishmash, muddle, hash, hodgepodge; dishevelment; laxity; imbroglio, chaos, medley.

2, complexity; complexness, complication, implication; intricacy, intrication; perplexity; network, maze, labyrinth; wilderness, jungle, involution, entanglement; coil, CONVOLUTION, tangled skein, knot, Gordian knot, wheels within wheels.

3, turmoil, ferment, AGITATION, to-do, trouble, row, disturbance, convulsion, tumult, uproar, riot, rumpus, scramble, fracas, embroilment, mélée, rough and tumble; whirlwind; Babel, Saturnalia, Donnybrook Fair; confusion twice confounded.

Verbs—be disorderly; put out of order; derange; ravel, ruffle, rumple, mess, muss, dishevel.

Adjectives—**1,** disorderly, orderless; out of order, out of place, irregular, desultory; anomalous, straggling; unmethodical; unsymmetric, unsystematic; untidy, slovenly; dislocated; promiscuous, indiscriminate; chaotic, anarchical; unarranged, disarranged; confused; deranged; topsy-turvy, shapeless; disjointed, out of joint.

2, complex, confused, intricate, complicated, perplexed, involved, labyrinthine, entangled, knotted, tangled, inextricable; tumultuous, riotous, violent (see VIOLENCE). *Colloq.,* out of kilter *or* whack; helter-skelter, mussy, messy, sloppy. *Slang,* balled *or* fouled up.

Adverbs—irregularly, *etc.*, by fits and starts; pell-mell; in a ferment; at sixes and sevens, at cross purposes; upside down. *Colloq.,* higgledy-piggledy; harum-scarum, willy-nilly, every which way.

Antonym, see ORDER.

---

disparage, *v.t.* depreciate, belittle, decry, run down; asperse, traduce. See DISAPPROBATION, DISRESPECT. *Ant.,* see APPROBATION.

dispatch, *v.t. & n.* —*v.t.* send; expedite; kill; accomplish. See VELOCITY, KILLING. —*n.* message, telegram; promptness, expedition; haste, speed; consummation, killing. See INFORMATION, ACTIVITY, HASTE, COMPLETION. *Ant.,* see SLOWNESS.

dispel, *v.t.* scatter, dissipate, disperse, dissolve. See DESTRUCTION, DISJUNCTION. *Ant.,* see ASSEMBLAGE.

dispense, *v.t.* distribute, apportion, sell, administer. See GIVING, APPORTIONMENT. *Ant.,* see ASSEMBLAGE.

disperse, *v.* diffuse, spread, disseminate; scatter, dissipate, strew; break up, separate, vanish, fade, dissolve. See DISJUNCTION, ABSENCE, DEPARTURE.

dispersion, *n.* dispersal, displacement, scattering, sowing broadcast; the Diaspora; diffusion; breakup, dissolution. See ABSENCE. *Ant.,* see ARRIVAL, PRESENCE.

displace, *v.t.* remove, eject, dismiss, discharge; depose, dethrone, unseat; shift, move, dislocate, dispossess, push aside. See CHANGE, EJECTION.

displaced person, refugee, evacuee; homeless *or* stateless person; D.P.; Ishmael, outcast; émigré, exile. See EXCLUSION.

displacement, *n.* dispossession, eviction, removal, ousting, EJECTION; replacement, dislocation; shift, move, dislodgement; expulsion; uprooting; migration, emigration; DISJUNCTION, evacuation; (ship's) tonnage.

display, *n. & v.t.* —*n.* show, exhibition, pomp, OSTENTATION. —*v.t.* show, manifest, exhibit, disclose; flaunt, show off. See EVIDENCE. *Ant.,* see CONCEALMENT.

disposition, *n.* ARRANGEMENT, classification, disposal, distribution, state; temperament, temper, nature, spirit; inclination, TENDENCY, propensity.

disprove, *v.t.* refute, confute, explode, defeat, negative. See NEGATION. *Ant.,* see EVIDENCE.

dispute, *v. & n.* —*v.t.* contradict, controvert, DOUBT, contest, question; argue, debate, quarrel, bicker. See NEGATION, REASONING, DISAGREEMENT, CONTENTION. —*n.* debate, argument, DISAGREEMENT. *Ant.,* see AGREEMENT.

disregard, *v.t.* ignore, neglect, overlook; disobey, defy; underestimate. See DISRESPECT, NEGLECT. *Ant.,* see RESPECT, ATTENTION.

DISREPUTE [874]

Nouns—**1,** disrepute, disreputableness, discredit, ill repute, bad name, bad odor, ill favor; DISAPPROBATION; ingloriousness, derogation, abasement, debasement; abjectness; degradation, odium, obloquy, opprobrium, ignominy; dishonor, disgrace; shame, humiliation; scandal, baseness, vileness, turpitude, IMPROBITY, infamy.

2, tarnish, taint, defilement, pollution, stigma, stain, blot, spot, brand, reproach, imputation, slur; badge of infamy, blot on one's escutcheon; bend *or* bar sinister.

Verbs—**1,** be in disrepute, be discredited, incur disgrace, have a bad name; disgrace oneself; stoop, foul one's own nest; look foolish, cut a sorry figure; slink away.

2, shame, disgrace, put to shame, dishonor, reflect dishonor upon; be a reproach to, derogate from; stigmatize, tarnish, stain, blot, sully, taint; discredit; degrade, debase, defile; expel (see PUNISHMENT); impute shame to, brand, post, vilify, defame, slur, give a bad name; disbar, unfrock, excommunicate.

Adjectives—**1,** disreputable, shameful; disgraceful, discreditable, despicable, heinous, questionable; unbecoming, unworthy; derogatory, degrading, humiliating, ignoble, *infra dignitatem,* undecorous; scandalous, infamous, too bad, deplorable, unmentionable; ribald, opprobrious; arrant, shocking, outrageous, notorious; odious, execrable; ignominious, scrubby, dirty, abject, vile, beggarly, pitiful, low, mean, knavish, shabby, base, dishonorable (see IMPROBITY).

2, in disrepute, at a discount, under a cloud, out of favor, down in the world, down at heel; stigmatized, discredited, disgraced; inglorious, nameless, obscure, unnoticed, unhonored, unglorified.

Adverbs—disreputably, shamefully, discreditably, *etc.,* to one's shame.

Antonym, see REPUTE.

DISRESPECT [929]

Nouns—**1,** disrespect, disesteem, disestimation, disfavor, DISREPUTE, disparagement, DISAPPROBATION; DETRACTION; irreverence; slight, NEGLECT; superciliousness, CONTEMPT, contumely, affront, dishonor, insult, indignity, outrage, DISCOURTESY; practical joking, left-handed compliment, scurrility, scoffing, derision; mockery, irony, RIDICULE, sarcasm.

2, hiss, hoot, gibe, flout, jeer, taunt, sneer, quip, slap in the face. *Slang,* razzberry.

Verbs—**1,** hold in disrespect, despise (see CONTEMPT); disregard, slight, trifle with, set at naught, pass by, push aside, overlook, turn one's back upon, laugh up one's sleeve; spurn, scorn.

2, be disrespectful, be discourteous, treat with disrespect, set down, browbeat; dishonor, desecrate; insult, affront, outrage; speak slightingly of; disparage (see DISAPPROBATION); call names, drag through the mud, point at, indulge in personalities; bite the thumb.

3, deride, scoff, sneer, laugh at, snigger, RIDICULE, gibe, mock, jeer, taunt, twit, roast, burlesque, laugh to scorn (see CONTEMPT); make game of, make a fool of; play a practical joke; lead one a dance; scout, hiss, hoot, mob. *Slang,* razz, give the razz(berry).

Adjectives—disrespectful; irreverent; disparaging (see DISAPPROBATION); in-

sulting, supercilious (see CONTEMPT); rude, derisive, sarcastic; scurrilous, contumelious; unrespected, unenvied, unsaluted; unregarded, disregarded.
Antonym, see RESPECT.

dissatisfy, *v.t.* DISCONTENT, displease, disappoint; vex, annoy, anger. *Ant.*, see PLEASURE.
dissect, *v.t.* cut up, anatomize; examine, analyze. See DISJUNCTION, INQUIRY.

DISSENT [489]

Nouns—**1,** dissent, dissension, dissidence, DISCORD, discordance, DISAGREE-MENT, nonagreement; difference *or* diversity of opinion; UNCONFORMITY; protestantism, recusancy, schism; disaffection; secession (see RELINQUISH-MENT), apostasy, recantation (see CHANGEABLENESS); DISCONTENT, caviling; protest, objection, expostulation, demur, exception, drawback; contradiction (see NEGATION); noncompliance (see REFUSAL).
2, dissentient, dissenter; recusant, schismatic, nonconformist; protestant, sectarian.
Verbs—dissent, demur; call in question, DOUBT; differ, beg to differ, disagree, contradict (see NEGATION); say no, refuse assent, refuse to admit; cavil, object, quibble, protest, raise one's voice against, take issue; repudiate; scruple; shake the head, shrug the shoulders; look askance; secede (see RELINQUISHMENT); recant (see CHANGEABLENESS). *Colloq.*, kick.
Adjectives—dissenting, dissident, dissentient; discordant, negative (see NE-GATION), unconsenting, refusing (see REFUSAL); noncontent, protestant, recusant; unconvinced, unconverted; sectarian, denominational, schismatic; unavowed, unacknowledged; out of the question; discontented (see DIS-CONTENT); unwilling.
Adverbs—dissentingly, at variance, at issue with; under protest.
Interjections—God forbid! not for the world! by no means! pardon me! *Colloq.*, not on your life! no sir(r)ee! not by a long shot!
Antonym, see ASSENT.

dissertation, *n.* lecture, sermon, tract; discussion, disquisition; treatise, discourse; exposition, study; critique, criticism; ESSAY, theme, thesis; comment, commentary; explanation. See REASONING, INTERPRETATION, INQUIRY.
dissimilar, *adj.* unlike, different, opposite; divergent, varying, various, variant; at variance, at odds; distinct, diverse. See DIFFERENCE.
dissimilarity, *n.* DIFFERENCE, differentness; unlikeness, unequality, variance, divergence, dissimilitude; uniqueness, novelty, originality; no comparison. *Ant.*, see SIMILARITY, COMPARISON.
dissipate, *v.t.* scatter, dispel, diffuse; WASTE, squander. *Ant.*, see PRESERVA-TION.
dissolute, *adj.* vicious, dissipated. *Ant.*, see PROBITY, GOODNESS.
dissolve, *v.* destroy, liquefy, break up, end; melt, vanish, evaporate, fade, disintegrate. See DECOMPOSITION.
dissuade, *v.t.* indispose to; turn one against; discourage, dishearten, give pause, deter; chill, cool off, dampen; shake. See RESTRAINT, HINDRANCE. *Ant.*, see BELIEF, CAUSE.
dissuasion, *n.* discouragement, damper; RESTRAINT, disinclination; HIN-DRANCE, determent. *Ant.*, see BELIEF, CAUSE.

DISTANCE [196]

Nouns—distance; SPACE, remoteness, farness; elongation; offing, background; removedness; perspective; parallax; reach, span, stride; MEASUREMENT; outpost, outskirt; horizon; aphelion; foreign parts, *ultima Thule, ne plus ultra,* antipodes, interstellar space; long range, giant's stride. *Colloq.,* jumping-off place.
Verbs—be distant; extend to, stretch to, reach to, spread to; range; remain at a distance; keep away, stand away, keep off, stand aloof, stand clear of.
Adjectives—distant, remote, telescopic; far off, faraway; wide of; stretching to; yon, yonder; ulterior, transmarine, transpontine, transatlantic, transpacific, transalpine; tramontane; ultramontane, ultramundane; hyper-

distend

borean, antipodean; inaccessible, out of the way; unapproached, unapproachable; incontiguous. *Colloq.*, God-forsaken; to hell and gone; back of beyond.

Adverbs—far off, far away; afar, off, away, a long way off; aloof; wide of, clear of; out of the way, out of reach; abroad, yonder, farther, further, beyond; far and wide, over the hills and far away; from pole to pole, to the ends of the earth, out of this world; out of hearing, nobody knows where; wide of the mark, a far cry to; apart, asunder; wide apart, wide asunder; at arm's length.

Antonym, see NEARNESS.

---

distend, *v.t.* stretch, expand, dilate, inflate, swell. See INCREASE. *Ant.*, see CONTRACTION.

distill, *v.* extract, express, concentrate; drip, trickle, evaporate.

distinct, *adj.* separate, unattached, discrete; definite, explicit; sharp, clear, well defined. See DISJUNCTION, VISION. *Ant.*, see DIMNESS.

distinction, *n.* DIFFERENCE, separateness, variation; DISCRIMINATION; dignity, refinement, ELEGANCE; eminence, importance, REPUTE. *Ant.*, see SIMILARITY.

distinguish, *v.t.* differentiate, characterize; separate, discriminate; discern, pick out. See DIFFERENCE, TASTE, VISION.

DISTORTION [243]

Nouns—**1,** distortion, detortion, contortion; twist, torque, torsion; crookedness, OBLIQUITY; grimace; deformity, malformation, malconformation; monstrosity, misproportion, asymmetry (see FORM), anamorphosis; UGLINESS; mutilation, disfigurement; talipes, clubfoot.

2, perversion, misinterpretation, misconstruction.

3, misinterpretation, misrepresentation, FALSEHOOD, EXAGGERATION, perversion.

Verbs—**1,** distort, contort, twist, warp, wrest, writhe, deform, misshape, mutilate, disfigure.

2, pervert, misinterpret, misconstrue.

Adjectives—distorted, contorted, out of shape, irregular, unsymmetrical, awry, wry, askew, crooked; not true, not straight; on one side, deformed, misshapen, misbegotten, misproportioned, ill-proportioned; ill-made; monstrous, grotesque; humpbacked, hunchbacked; bandy, bandylegged, bowlegged; knockkneed; taliped, splay-footed, clubfooted; round-shouldered; snub-nosed; stumpy, short (see SHORTNESS); gaunt, thin; bloated.

Adverbs—distortedly, crookedly, *etc.;* all manner of ways.

Antonym, see FORM.

---

distract, *v.t.* divert, turn aside; confuse, madden; entertain, amuse. See DEVIATION, AMUSEMENT.

distress, *n. & v.t.* —*n.* discomfort, trouble, DANGER, PAIN, affliction, trial, privation, harassment, grief, anxiety. See POVERTY, ADVERSITY. *Ant.*, see COMFORT, SAFETY. —*v.t.* trouble, harrow, PAIN, worry, grieve; hurt.

distribute, *v.t.* allot, parcel, apportion; disperse, scatter; divide, classify. See APPORTIONMENT, ARRANGEMENT. *Ant.*, see ASSEMBLAGE.

district, *n.* REGION, province, ward, quarter, section, tract, bailiwick.

distrust, *n. & v.t.* —*n.* DOUBT, suspicion, disbelief. —*v.t.* suspect, disbelieve, mistrust. See DOUBT, FEAR.

disturb, *v.t.* worry, agitate, trouble; disarrange, confuse; interrupt, unsettle. See AGITATION, DISJUNCTION.

DISUSE [614, 678]

Nouns—**1,** disuse, forbearance, abstinence; obsoleteness, obsolescence; RELINQUISHMENT, discontinuance, cessation.

2, desuetude, disusage, want of habit, want of practice, unaccustomedness, newness to; nonprevalence.

Verbs—**1,** not use; do without, dispense with, let alone, not touch, forbear, abstain, spare, waive, neglect; keep back, reserve.

2, lay up, lay by, lay on the shelf; shelve; set aside, put aside, lay aside; obsolesce, supersede.

3, discard (see EJECTION); abandon, dismiss, give warning; throw aside, relinquish; make away with, destroy (see DESTRUCTION); cast overboard; cast to the winds; jettison, dismantle (see USELESSNESS).

4, be unaccustomed to, break a habit, wean oneself of a habit.

Adjectives—**1,** disused, not used, unemployed, unapplied, undisposed of, unspent, unexercised, untouched, untrodden, unessayed, ungathered, unculled; uncalled for, not required; run down, obsolete, obsolescent.

2, unaccustomed, unused, unwonted, unseasoned, unhabituated, untrained, new, green, unskilled (see UNSKILLFULNESS); unhackneyed; unusual (see UNCONFORMITY); nonobservant.

Antonym, see USE.

---

ditch, *n.*   channel, trench, gully, canal, moat, watercourse.

dive, *n.*   plunge, dip, swoop; nose dive, power dive.

diverge, *v.i.*   separate, branch off, fork; sunder; divaricate, deviate; differ, vary, disagree; veer, swerve; detach; go off at a tangent; radiate. See DIFFERENCE, DEVIATION. *Ant.,* see AGREEMENT.

divergence, *n.*   DIFFERENCE; DEVIATION; dispersion; fork, forking, branching off; ramification, variation; DISAGREEMENT; divergency. *Ant.,* see AGREEMENT.

diversity, *n.*   DIFFERENCE, dissimilarity, VARIATION, variety. *Ant.,* see CONFORMITY.

divert, *v.t.*   amuse, beguile, entertain; distract, turn aside. See AMUSEMENT, DEVIATION.

DIVESTMENT [226]

Nouns—divestment, divestiture; taking off, undressing; nudity; bareness, undress, dishabille; nudation, denudation; decortication, depilation, excoriation, desquamation; mo(u)lting; exfoliation; ecdysis. *Colloq.,* the altogether, the raw.

Verbs—**1,** divest; uncover, denude, bare, strip; undress, disrobe (see CLOTHING); uncoif; dismantle; put off, take off, cast off; doff; slough off.

2, peel, pare, decorticate, excoriate, skin, scalp, flay; expose, lay open; exfoliate, mo(u)lt; cast the skin.

Adjectives—divested, denuded, bare, naked, shorn, nude; undressed, undraped; exposed, ecdysiastic, in dishabille; threadbare, ragged; in a state of nature, in one's birthday suit, with nothing on, stark naked; bald, baldheaded, bald as an egg; bare as the back of one's hand; out at elbows; barefoot; leafless, napless, hairless, beardless, cleanshaven. *Colloq.,* in the buff, in the altogether. *Slang,* raw, in the raw.

Antonym, see CLOTHING.

---

divide, *v.*   separate; partition, allot, assign; separate, split, part. *Colloq.,* split up. See APPORTIONMENT, DISJUNCTION.

divine, *adj.*   godlike, superhuman, celestial, holy, spiritual; religious. See DEITY, RELIGION.

DIVORCE [905]

Nouns—**1,** divorce, divorcement, separation, annulment.

2, divorcé, divorcée, grass widow, grass widower.

Verbs—divorce, get a divorce; separate, break up. *Colloq.,* split up; go to Reno.

Antonym, see MARRIAGE.

---

divulge, *v.t.*   disclose, reveal, let slip, tell. *Slang,* spill the beans, let the cat out of the bag. See DISCLOSURE. *Ant.,* see SECRET.

dizzy, *adj.*   giddy, lightheaded. See INSANITY. *Slang,* silly, mixed-up, flighty.

do, *v.t.*   perform, achieve, contrive, manage; solve, finish, work out; serve, render. See ACTION, COMPLETION, PRODUCTION. *Colloq.,* swindle, defraud.

docile, *adj.*   gentle, tractable, teachable, submissive. See ASSENT. *Ant.,* see UNCONFORMITY.

doctor, *n.*   physician, surgeon; learned man, sage. See REMEDY.

doctrine, *n.* creed, theory, dogma, tenet, principle. See BELIEF.
document, *n.* INSTRUMENT, writing, record, manuscript.
dodge, *v.* elude, evade, escape, avoid; duck, serve. See DEVIATION, AVOIDANCE.
dog, *n.* canine, cur, whelp; puppy, pup, tyke, bitch, slut. See ANIMAL. *Slang,* pooch, mutt.
dogma, *n.* doctrine, tenet, BELIEF.
dole, *n.* alms, pittance. See INSUFFICIENCY. *Slang,* handout.
dollar, *n.* *Slang,* buck, bean, iron man, simoleon, cartwheel. See MONEY.
domain, *n.* REGION, realm, dominion, territory, LAND, sphere of action; estate.
domestic, *adj.* household, homely; family, home, internal; native, home-grown, home-bred; tame. See ABODE, SECLUSION, DOMESTICATION.

DOMESTICATION [370]

Nouns—**1,** domestication, taming; animal husbandry; cattle-raising, dairy farming, ranching, stock breeding, horse training; veterinarianism, veterinary medicine.
2, menagerie, zoo, aquarium; stable, barn, sty, kennel, corral, ranch, hen-house, fishpond, hatchery; aviary, apiary.
3, husbandman, breeder, keeper, dairy farmer, groom, stableman; cowboy, cowpuncher, herdsman, shepherd, sheepherder, rancher, swineherd; apiarist, beekeeper; veterinary. *Colloq.,* vet, cowpoke.
Verbs—domesticate, tame, breed, train, break; groom, feed, water, milk, shear; round up, corral.
Adjectives—domesticated, domestic, tame, broken.

dominate, *v.t.* govern, control; domineer, overbear, tyrannize; predominate, stand out. See AUTHORITY, POSSESSION.
domineer, *v.i.* tyrannize, overbear, bully. See INSOLENCE, SEVERITY.
don, *v.t.* assume, put on. See CLOTHING.
donation, *n.* contribution, gift, present, benefaction, grant. See GIVING. *Ant.,* see ACQUISITION.
donkey, *n.* ass, jackass, burro; blockhead, FOOL.
doom, *n.* DESTINY, lot, fate, fortune; judgment, damnation, CONDEMNATION, DESTRUCTION, death.
door, *n.* gate, portal, entrance; barrier; inlet, outlet, path. See OPENING, INGRESS, EGRESS.
dot, *n.* spot, speck, point; jot, whit, iota. See LITTLENESS.
double, *adj., v.t. & n.* —*adj.* twofold, duplicate, duplex, dual. See DUPLICATION. —*v.t.* duplicate, increase, twofold. —*n.* twin, counterpart; understudy, stand-in.

DOUBT [485]

Nouns—**1,** doubt, dubiousness, dubiety; unbelief, skepticism, disbelief; agnosticism, IRRELIGION; incredulity, discredit.
2, jealousy, suspicion, distrust, anxiety, concern; green-eyed monster.
3, uncertainty, hesitation, hesitancy, perplexity; irresolution, indecision; demur, scruple, qualm, misgiving; dilemma, quandary; bewilderment, vacillation, CHANGEABLENESS.
4, doubter; unbeliever, doubting Thomas, man from Missouri; waverer, chameleon, flibbertygibbet.
Verbs—**1,** doubt, be doubtful, disbelieve, discredit; misbelieve; refuse to admit, DISSENT; refuse to believe; doubt the truth of; be skeptical or sceptical, distrust, mistrust; suspect, have doubts, harbor suspicions; have one's doubts; take with a grain of salt.
2, demur, stick at, pause, hesitate, falter, object, cavil, scruple. *Colloq.,* smell a rat.
3, cast doubt upon, raise a question; bring *or* call in question; question, challenge; dispute, deny (see NEGATION); cavil; cause *or* raise a doubt *or* suspicion.
4, be unbelievable, fill with doubt, startle, stagger; shake *or* stagger one's faith *or* belief.

5, be uncertain; wonder whether; shilly-shally, compromise; vacillate, waver; hem and haw, sit on the fence.

Adjectives—**1,** doubting, unbelieving; incredulous, skeptical, sceptical; distrustful of, shy of, suspicious of; heretical, faithless; dubious, scrupulous.
2, doubtful, uncertain, irresolute; disputable, unworthy *or* undeserving of belief (see BELIEF); questionable; suspect, suspicious; open to suspicion, open to doubt; staggering, hard to believe, incredible, not to be believed, inconceivable; fallible; undemonstrable; controvertible.

Adverbs—with a grain of salt, with reservations.

Antonym, see BELIEF.

---

dower, *n.* dowry, dot; inheritance. See PROPERTY.

down, *adv.* downward; under, beneath, below. See LOWNESS. *Ant.,* see HEIGHT.

downfall, *n.* drop, comedown, disgrace, demotion; overthrow; collapse, crash. See DESCENT, FAILURE, DESTRUCTION. *Ant.,* see SUCCESS.

downy, *adj.* fluffy, feathery, fleecy, flocculent, soft. See SMOOTHNESS. *Ant.,* see ROUGHNESS.

drab, *adj.* grayish, brownish, dun; monotonous, DULL, humdrum, uninteresting. *Ant.,* see COLOR.

draft, *n. & v.t.* —*n.* sketch, OUTLINE; breeze, air current, WIND; drink, dram; conscription, levy, load, pull, displacement; bill of exchange, demand note. See FOOD, COMPULSION, MONEY. —*v.t.* outline; draw, sketch, formulate; conscript, enlist, impress. See COMPULSION.

drag, *v.* draw, pull, tow, tug, haul; protract, draw out; lag, dawdle, inch along. See SLOWNESS.

drain, *v. & n.* —*v.* draw off, empty, exhaust, deprive; leak, drip, dry up. See EGRESS, WASTE. —*n.* outlet, spout, sewer, ditch, gutter.

dram, *n.* draft, drink. See FOOD.

DRAMA [599]

Nouns—**1,** drama, the drama, the stage, the theater, play; showbusiness, theatricals, theatrics; dramaturgy, stagecraft; histrionics; sock and buskin; Muse of Tragedy, Melpomene; Muse of Comedy, Thalia; Thespis; puppetry, Punch and Judy.
2, play, drama, stage play, piece, vehicle; tragedy, comedy, tragicomedy; opera, operetta, musical comedy, review, vaudeville, burlesque, farce, divertissement, extravaganza, harlequinade, pantomime, burlesque, *opéra bouffe*, ballet, spectacle, masque, melodrama; monolog(ue), duolog(ue), dialog(ue); trilogy; charade, mystery, morality play, miracle play; puppet show. *Slang,* legit.
3, act, scene, tableau; introduction; prologue, epilogue; turn, number; *entr'acte*, intermission, intermezzo, interlude, afterpiece; curtain; curtain call, encore.
4, performance, REPRESENTATION, *mise en scène*, stagery, stagecraft acting; impersonation; stage business, slapstick, buffoonery; part, role, character, cast, *dramatis personae*, road company, repertory, repertoire, summer theatre, amateur theatricals, stock. *Slang,* ham acting; gag.
5, motion picture, moving picture, film, cinema, talking picture. *Colloq.,* movie, movie show, talkie, the films, flickers, silverscreen.
6, theater, legitimate theater, playhouse, opera house; house; music hall; amphitheater, circus, hippodrome; puppet *or* marionette show. *Colloq.,* movie theater, off-Broadway theater.
7, auditorium, front of the house, stalls, boxes, pit, orchestra, balcony, loges, gallery; greenroom; stage, proscenium; scene, the boards; trap; mezzanine floor; flies; floats, lights, spotlight, footlights; orchestra; dressing rooms; flat, drop, wing, screen, side-scene; transformation scene, curtain; theatrical costume; make-up, greasepaint; properties. *Colloq.,* props. *Slang,* peanut gallery.
8, actor, player; stage player; performer; trouper, protagonist, leading man *or* woman; supporting cast; comedian, tragedian, villain, ingenue, understudy, foil, vaudevillian, Thespian, star; pantomimist, clown, harlequin, buffo, buffoon, farceur, Pantaloon, Columbine; Punch, Punchinello;

super, supernumerary, spear carrier, mummer, masker; mountebank; tumbler, juggler, acrobat; contortionist; librettist, scenario-writer, dramatic author; playwriter, playwright; dramatist. *Slang*, ham, ham actor, heavy, matinee idol, stooge, straight man, bit player.

Verbs—act, play, perform; put on the stage; personate (see REPRESENTATION); mimic, IMITATE, enact; play a part, act a part; rehearse; rant; tread the boards; star.

Adjectives—dramatic, theatrical, scenic, histrionic, comic, tragic, farcical, tragicomic, melodramatic, operatic; stagy.

Adverbs—on the stage, on the boards; before the footlights.

draw, *v.t.* haul, drag, pull, tug, extract; attract, allure; depict, sketch, draft; win, receive; displace; inhale; elicit, get; eviscerate. See ATTRACTION, COMPOSITION, PAINTING.

drawback, *n.* HINDRANCE, handicap, clog, encumbrance, restraint; objection, disadvantage. *Ant.*, see SUPERIORITY.

dreadful, *adj.* fearful, dire, frightful, shocking, horrible, awful. See FEAR.

dream, *n.* vision, fantasy, reverie, fancy; daydream, chimera, nightmare; delusion, hallucination. See IMAGINATION, INSUBSTANTIALITY.

dreary, *adj.* cheerless, gloomy, somber; depressing, lonely, wearisome. See DEJECTION, WEARINESS. *Ant.*, see CHEERFULNESS, HOPE.

dregs, *n.* refuse, sediment, silt, lees, grounds, heeltaps; scum, riffraff, off-scourings. See REMAINDER, POPULACE.

drench, *v.t.* douse, souse, soak, wet, saturate. See WATER. *Ant.*, see DRYNESS.

dress, *v.t. & n.* —*v.t.* clothe, attire, array; scold, reprove, berate. whip; adorn, garnish, decorate; align, equalize; prepare, bandage. See CLOTHING, DISAPPROBATION, ORNAMENT, REMEDY. *Ant.*, see DIVESTMENT. —*n.* CLOTHING, costume, vesture, garb, raiment, apparel, habit; frock, gown.

drift, *n. & v.i.* —*n.* pile, heap, deposit; movement, DEVIATION; tendency, meaning; mine passage. See ASSEMBLAGE, DIRECTION, MEANING. —*v.i.* procede aimlessly; pile up; approach, MOTION. *Ant.*, see STABILITY.

drill, *v.t. & i.* pierce, bore; train, exercise, practice. See OPENING, TEACHING.

drink, *v. & n.* —*v.* consume, swallow, imbibe; toss off, drain, guzzle; toast. *Slang*, lap up, swig, sop up; consume, swallow, tipple. —*n.* draft, potation; beverage, liquor. *Slang*, booze, hooch, moonshine. See FOOD, DRUNKENNESS. *Ant.*, see MODERATION.

drip, *v.i.* drop, dribble, trickle; leak, percolate. See WATER.

drive, *v.t.* propel, impel; urge forward, pursue; steer, control; conduct, carry out; ram, hammer, thrust; urge, force, compel, coerce. See COMPULSION, DIRECTION, TRAVEL, PROPULSION.

drivel, *n. & v.i.* —*n.* drool, slaver, slobber; nonsense, babble. —*v.i.* drool, slobber, babble, talk nonsense, dote. See ABSURDITY.

droop, *v.i.* bend, loll, slouch, sag; sink, languish, waste; wilt. See DEJECTION, DISEASE.

drop, *v. & n.* —*v.* let fall; give up, abandon; fall, plunge; faint, collapse; cease, terminate, END; drip. See DESCENT, RELINQUISHMENT, IMPOTENCE. —*n.* globule, bead; minim; bit, mite. See LITTLENESS.

drought, *n.* aridity, DRYNESS, thirst; lack, want, need, scarcity. See INSUFFICIENCY.

drown, *v.* suffocate (in liquid); submerge, inundate; muffle, overpower. See WATER, KILLING, SILENCE, DEATH.

drudge, *v.i.* toil, slave, grub, plod, hack, grind, plug. See EXERTION.

druggist, *n.* apothecary, pharmacist, chemist. See REMEDY.

DRUNKENNESS [959]

Nouns—**1,** drunkenness, intoxication; intemperance; drinking, inebriety, inebriation; ebriety, ebriosity; insobriety; wine-bibbing; bacchanals, bacchanalia, libations; alcoholism, dipsomania, oenomania; delirium tremens. *Colloq.*, D.T.s. *Slang*, hangover, pink elephants, binge, tear, bust, bat, bender, toot, jag.

2, liquor, hard liquor, drink, alcoholic drink, spirits, grog, the bottle, little brown jug; brandy, cognac, applejack, hard cider, gin, rum, whiskey,

liqueur, cordial; the grape, wine, white wine, red wine, cocktail, mixed
drink, toddy. *Colloq.*, moonshine, nightcap, pick-me-up, hair of the dog;
booze, hooch.
3, drunkard, alcoholic, dipsomaniac, sot, toper, tippler, bibber, wine-
bibber; hard drinker; soaker, sponge, tosspot; thirsty soul, revel(l)er,
carouser; Bacchanal, Bacchanalian; Bacchante; devotee of Bacchus.
Colloq., boozer, guzzler, souse, drunk. *Slang*, lush, tank, rumhound,
barfly, wino, dipso.
Verbs—**1,** get drunk, be drunk; see double; take a drop, take a drop too
much; imbibe, drink, tipple, guzzle, swizzle, soak, sot, carouse; take to
drink; drink up, drink hard, drink like a fish; drain the cup, take a hair of
the dog that bit one; wet one's whistle, crack a bottle, pass the bottle;
toss off. *Colloq.*, tope, booze, swig, swill. *Slang*, liquor up, lush, get high,
hit the bottle, paint the town red, have a jag on, pass out.
2, make one drunk, inebriate, fuddle, befuddle, besot, go to one's head.
Slang, pollute, plaster.
Adjectives—drunk, tipsy; intoxicated; inebrious, inebriate, inebriated; in
one's cups; in a state of intoxication; mellow, cut, fresh, high, merry,
elevated; flush, flushed; flustered, disguised; topheavy; overcome; maudlin,
crapulous, dead *or* roaring drunk. *Colloq.*, drunk as a lord, drunk as an
owl; boozy, out. *Slang*, boiled, soused, shellacked, fried, polluted, tanked,
cockeyed, spifflicated, squiffed, stinko, tight, three sheets to the wind, out
cold, stiff.

Antonym, see MODERATION.

DRYNESS [340]

Nouns—**1,** dryness, aridity, aridness, drought, ebb tide, low water; desicca-
tion; thirst; siccation; dehydration, anhydration; drainage; mummification.
2, dullness; see SLOWNESS.
Verbs—be dry, render dry, dry, dry up, soak up, sponge, swab, sipe; evaporate, desiccate; drain, parch, sear, wither; dehydrate.
Adjectives—dry, anhydrous, dehydrated, arid; dried, undamped; juiceless,
sapless; sear; thirsty, husky; rainless, without rain; *sec*, fine; dry as a bone,
bone-dry, dry-as-dust, dry as a stick, dry as a mummy, dry as a biscuit;
waterproof, watertight; desertlike, unirrigated, waterless, parched.

Antonym, see MOISTURE.

dual, *adj.* duplex, twofold, double, duplicate, twin, binary. See NUMERA-
TION.
dubious, *adj.* doubtful, uncertain; questionable, unreliable. See DOUBT.
Ant., see CERTAINTY.
duct, *n.* channel, canal, tube, pipe, flue.
ductile, *adj.* tractile, malleable; yielding, pliant; compliant, docile, obedient. See SOFTNESS, OBEDIENCE.
duel, *n.* single combat, contest, competition, rivalry; affair of honor. See
CONTENTION.
dull, *adj. & v.* —*adj.* unsharp, BLUNT; stupid, dense, slow, obtuse, thick;
deadened, numb; spiritless, vapid, vacuous; boring, wearisome, tedious;
dead, lifeless; sluggish, listless, lethargic; prosaic, prosy, dry, uninteresting;
lackluster, dim, cloudy, obscure, stale, jaded; humdrum, drab, monotonous;
commonplace, uninspired. See SLOWNESS. *Ant.*, see LIGHT, SHARPNESS,
WIT, INTELLIGENCE.
dumbness, *n.* aphonia, muteness, aphony, mutism; deaf-mutism, voicelessness; silence, taciturnity, inarticulateness. *Colloq.*, stupidity.
dupe, *n. & v.* —*n.* gull, victim, cully, cat's-paw; fool; puppet, tool; butt,
laughingstock, April fool. *Slang*, easy mark, sucker, chump, soft touch,
pushover, pigeon. —*v.t.* cheat, defraud, swindle; hoodwink, deceive, delude. See CREDULITY, DECEPTION.

DUPLICATION [90]

Nouns—duplication; doubling; gemination, ingemination, reproduction,
replica, reduplication; iteration, REPETITION; renewal; counterpart.

Verbs—duplicate, double; redouble, reduplicate; geminate, copy, repeat (see REPETITION); renew (see RESTORATION).

Adjectives—duplicate, duplicative, double, doubled, bifold, biform, bilateral, twofold, two-sided, duplex; double-faced; twin, ingeminate; second. *Colloq.*, ditto. *Slang*, dupe.

Adverbs—twice, once more; over again, as much again, twofold; secondly, in the second place, again.

Antonym, see DIFFERENCE, UNCONFORMITY.

---

duplicity, *n.* duality; double dealing, two-facedness, treachery, deceitfulness, fraud, guile. See NUMERATION, FALSEHOOD, IMPROBITY. *Ant.*, see TRUTH.

DURABILITY [110]

Nouns—**1,** durability, durableness, persistence, lastingness, CONTINUANCE, standing; permanence, STABILITY, survival, survivance; longevity, AGE; distance of time; protraction of time, prolongation of time; delay (see LATENESS).

2, diuturnity; AGE, century, eternity; SLOWNESS, perpetuity, PERMANENCE. *Colloq.*, blue moon, dog's age, month of Sundays, coon's age.

Verbs—**1,** endure, last, stand, remain, abide, continue; tarry, be late, drag on, protract, prolong; spin out, eke out, draw out; temporize, gain time, make time, talk against time; outlast, outlive, survive; live to fight again.

2, perpetuate, immortalize; maintain.

Adjectives—durable, lasting; of long duration, of long standing; permanent, chronic, long-standing; intransient, intransitive; intransmutable, persistent, lifelong, livelong; everlasting, immortal; longeval, long-lived; diuturnal, evergreen, perennial; never-ending, unremitting; perpetual, interminable, eternal; unfailing; lingering, protracted, prolonged, spun out, long-pending, long-winded; slow.

Adverbs—**1,** durably, long; for a long time, for an age, for ages, for ever so long; for many a long day; long ago; all day long, all year round, the livelong day, as the day is long; morning, noon and night; hour after hour, day after day; for good; permanently.

2, always, ever, evermore, forever, for aye, world without end, perpetually. *Colloq.*, for keeps, for good, till Hell freezes over, till the cows come home.

Antonym, see TRANSIENTNESS.

---

duration, *n.* continuance, persistence; term, time, period. See TIME, LENGTH.

during, *prep.* pending, through, in the time of, until. See TIME.

dusk, *n.* twilight, gloaming; semidarkness; gloom, half-light. See DIMNESS.

dust, *n.* powder; earth, soil, pounce; dirt, lint, ash, soot, flue. See POWDERINESS, UNCLEANNESS.

DUTY [926]

Nouns—**1,** duty, moral obligation, accountableness, accountability, liability, onus, responsibility; bounden duty; call of duty; allegiance, fealty, tie; engagement, PROMISE; part; function, calling, BUSINESS.

2, morality, morals, ethics; Ten Commandments; conscientiousness, PROBITY; conscience, inward monitor, still small voice; sense of duty.

3, propriety, fitness, seemliness, decorum, the thing, the proper thing.

4, OBSERVANCE, fulfillment, discharge, performance, acquittal, satisfaction, redemption; good behavior.

Verbs—**1,** be the duty of, be incumbent on, be responsible, behoove, become, befit, beseem; belong to, pertain to; fall to one's lot; devolve on; lie upon, lie on one's head, lie at one's door; rest on, rest on the shoulders of.

2, take upon oneself, PROMISE, be bound to, be sponsor for; incur a responsibility; be under obligation, stand under obligation; have to answer for, owe it to oneself.

3, impose a duty, enjoin, require, exact; bind, bind over; saddle with, prescribe, assign, call upon, look to, oblige.

4, enter upon, perform, observe, fulfill, discharge, satisfy *or* acquit oneself of a duty *or* an obligation; act one's part, redeem one's pledge, do justice to, be at one's post; do one's duty (see VIRTUE); be on good behavior, mind one's Ps and Qs.

Adjectives—obligatory, binding, imperative, peremptory; stringent, severe, behooving, incumbent on; obligated, under obligation; obliged by, bound by, tied by; saddled with; due to, beholden to, bound to, indebted to; tied down; compromised; duty bound; amenable, liable, accountable, responsible, answerable; right, meet, due, moral, ethical, casuistical, conscientious, ethological.

Adverbs—dutifully, in duty bound, on one's own responsibility, at one's own risk.

Antonym, see NEGLECT.

---

dwarf, *n.* midget, pygmy, Lilliputian. See LITTLENESS. *Colloq.*, runt. *Slang*, shrimp. *Ant.*, see SIZE.
dwell, *v.i.* live, reside, abide. *Slang*, hang out; harp, iterate. See PRESENCE, REPETITION, ABODE.
dwindle, *v.i.* diminish, shrink, lessen, run low, wash away. See DECREASE. *Ant.*, see INCREASE.
dye, *v.t.* COLOR, tint, stain. *Ant.*, see COLORLESSNESS.
dynamic, *adj.* forceful, vigorous, impelling; propulsive. See POWER, IMPULSE. *Ant.*, see IMPOTENCE.

E

each, *adv.* every, apiece, severally, seriatim, respectively.
eager, *adj.* desirous, keen, fervent, fervid, hot-headed, earnest, intent; zealous, ardent, agog; avid, anxious, athirst. See ACTIVITY. *Ant.*, see INACTIVITY.
eagle, *n.* erne, ringtail, eaglet, bald eagle, golden eagle, harpy, sea eagle. See ANIMAL.
ear, *n.* head, spike; auricle, concha; handle, knob; heed, observance. See EFFECT, ATTENTION, HEARING.

EARLINESS [132]

Nouns—**1,** earliness, punctuality, promptitude, despatch, dispatch, expedition, readiness.
2, HASTE, speed, celerity, swiftness, rapidity, acceleration; suddenness, abruptness.
3, prematurity, precocity, precipitation, anticipation; a stitch in time.
Verbs—**1,** be early, be beforehand, take time by the forelock, anticipate, forestall; have the start; steal a march upon; gain time, preëmpt, bespeak. *Slang*, jump the gun, get *or* have the jump on.
2, accelerate, expedite, hasten, quicken; make haste, hurry, speed, scamper, run, race, rush.
Adjectives—**1,** early, prime, timely, seasonal, punctual, forward; prompt, instant, ready; summary.
2, premature, precipitate, precocious; prevenient, anticipatory, ahead of time; forward, advanced.
3, sudden, instantaneous, instant, abrupt; unexpected; near, near at hand, immediate.
Adverbs—**1,** early, soon, anon, betimes, ere long, before long, punctually, promptly, to the minute, in time, in good time, in good season, in due time, time enough.
2, beforehand, prematurely, precipitately, hastily, too soon, before its time; in anticipation; unexpectedly.
3, suddenly, instantaneously, at short notice, *extempore*, on the spur of the moment, in short order, right away *or* off, at once, on the spot, on the instant, at sight, offhand, out of hand, straightway; forthwith, incontinently, summarily, immediately, briefly, shortly, quickly, speedily, apace, presently, at the first opportunity, by and by, in a while, directly.
Antonym, see LATENESS.

earnest, *adj.* intent, intense, serious, grave, solemn, sober, weighty, purposeful, determined; eager, impassioned, animated, cordial, zealous, fervent, ardent. See FEELING, IMPORTANCE, RESOLUTION.

earth, *n.* planet, globe, world; ground, LAND, dirt, soil, mold. See UNIVERSE.

ease, *n.* comfort, luxury; rest, repose; CONTENT, enjoyment, complacency; FREEDOM, relief; leisure, convenience; FACILITY, readiness, expertness; unconstraint, naturalness. See PLEASURE. *Ant.,* see DISCONTENT, DIFFICULTY, PAIN.

eastern, *adj.* east, oriental. See SIDE.

easy, *adj.* comfortable, restful, indolent, unconcerned, untroubled; free, unembarrassed, careless, smooth, unconstrained, natural, graceful; effortless, ready, facile, simple; moderate, MILD, gentle, indulgent; tractable, compliant; light, unexacting. See FACILITY. *Ant.,* see DIFFICULTY, SEVERITY.

eat, *v.t. & i.* consume, devour, feed, fare; erode, corrode, wear, rust. See FOOD, DETERIORATION. *Ant.,* see IMPROVEMENT.

ebb, *v.i.* recede, fall back, outflow, withdraw; decline; waste, decay. See DECREASE, REGRESSION. *Ant.,* see INCREASE.

eccentric, *adj.* elliptic, parabolic, hyperbolic; irregular, deviating; peculiar, queer, odd, strange, bizarre, singular; erratic, cranky, abnormal. See INSANITY, UNCONFORMITY. *Ant.,* see SANITY, CONFORMITY.

echo, *v. & n.* —*v.i.* reverberate, resound, reply, ring; repeat, reproduce. See IMITATION, REPETITION. —*n.* reverberation, REPETITION, response, repercussion.

eclipse, *n.* obscure, darken, cloud, hide, conceal; outshine, surpass, overshadow. See DARKNESS, REPUTE. *Ant.,* see LIGHT, DISREPUTE.

ECONOMY [817]

Nouns—**1,** economy, thriftiness, frugality, thrift, CARE, husbandry, good housewifery, good management *or* administration, retrenchment.

2, savings, reserves; parsimony, cheeseparing, stinginess, scrimping.

Verbs—be economical, frugal, thrifty, saving, *or* sparing; economize, save; retrench; cut corners, skimp, make both ends meet, meet one's expenses, pay one's way; husband, save money, lay by *or* away, put by, lay aside, store up; hoard, accumulate, amass, salt away; provide for a rainy day; feather one's nest.

Adjectives—economical, frugal, careful, thrifty, saving, chary, sparing, parsimonious, miserly, stingy, scrimping.

Adverbs—sparingly, frugally, thriftily, economically, carefully, parsimoniously.

Antonym, see WASTE.

---

ecstasy, *n.* rapture, joy, transport, bliss, exaltation; gladness, intoxication, enthusiasm; trance, frenzy, inspiration. See PLEASURE. *Ant.,* see PAIN.

eddy, *n.* countercurrent, whirlpool.

EDGE [231]

Nouns—**1,** edge, verge, brink, brow, brim, margin, confine, LIMIT, boundary, border, skirt, rim, flange, SIDE; mouth, jaws, lip.

2, threshold, door; portal, entrance, gate, gateway; coast, shore.

3, frame, fringe, flounce, frill, trimming, edging, skirting, hem, welt, furbelow, valance, selvage.

Verbs—edge, verge, border, bound, skirt, rim, fringe; sidle or inch along.

Adjectives—border, bordering, rimming, fringing, marginal, skirting; labial, labiated, marginated.

Adverbs—edgewise, edgeways, sidewise, sideways.

Antonym, see INTERIOR.

---

edict, *n.* decree, bull, law, rule, order, fiat, proclamation. See COMMAND.

edifice, *n.* building, structure; palace, church. See PRODUCTION. *Ant.,* see DESTRUCTION.

edit, *v.t.* redact, revise, arrange, digest, correct, prepare; select, adapt, compose, compile; issue, publish. See IMPROVEMENT, PUBLICATION. *Ant.,* see DETERIORATION.

edition, *n.* redaction; issue, impression, printing. See PUBLICATION.

educate, *v.t.* TEACH, train, instruct, enlighten, edify, school; develop, cultivate; discipline, form.

educe, *v.t.* draw forth, bring out, develop, elicit, evolve; deduce, infer, evoke.

efface, *v.t.* OBLITERATE, erase, expunge, excise, delete, dele, strike, cancel, wipe out, blot. *Ant.*, see RECORD.

EFFECT [154]

Nouns—**1**, effect, consequence, result, upshot, issue, outcome, consummation, SEQUEL, END, conclusion, dénouement; development, outgrowth, aftermath, aftereffect. *Slang*, payoff.
2, PRODUCTION, produce, product, output, work, handiwork, performance; creature, creation; offspring, offshoot, fruit, first-fruits, crop, harvest; effectiveness.
Verbs—**1**, effect, CAUSE, produce, bring about, give rise to.
2, be the effect of; be due or owing to; originate in or from; rise, arise, spring, proceed, emanate, come, grow, issue, *or* result from; come out of; depend, hang, *or* hinge upon.
Adjectives—**1**, owing to, resulting from, due to, attributable to, caused by, dependent upon, derived from, evolved from; derivative, hereditary.
2, consequent; resultant, contingent, eventual.
Adverbs—of course, it follows that, therefore, naturally, consequently, as a consequence, in consequence, through, necessarily, eventually.
Antonym, see CAUSE.

---

effeminate, *adj.* womanish, unmanly, WEAK, SOFT.

effervesce, *v.i.* bubble, hiss, foam, fizz, ferment. See AGITATION.

efficient, *n.* effective, effectual, efficacious, operative; skillful, capable, productive, competent. See POWER, SKILL. *Ant.*, see IMPOTENCE, UNSKILLFULNESS.

effort, *n.* EXERTION, endeavor; strain, stress, attempt, venture, struggle, trial, labor, work, achievement, production. *Colloq.*, push. *Ant.*, see REPOSE.

ego, *n.* self, personality, I. See INSUBSTANTIALITY, INTELLECT. *Ant.*, see SUBSTANCE.

EGRESS [295]

Nouns—**1**, egress, exit, issue, emergence, outbreak, outburst, eruption, emanation, evacuation, exudation, leakage, oozing, gush, outpouring, effluence, effusion, drain, drainage, outflow, outcome, output, discharge, EXCRETION.
2, export, expatriation, deportation, emigration, exodus, DEPARTURE; emigrant, migrant, colonist, outcast.
3, outlet, vent, spout, tap, sluice, floodgate; exit, way out, mouth, window, gate, gateway, porthole, door, OPENING, path, conduit.
Verbs—**1**, emerge, emanate, issue, pass off, evacuate, exit, exeunt, depart, escape.
2, leak, run out, percolate, exude, strain, drain, ooze, filter, filtrate, dribble, gush, spout, flow, well out, pour, trickle; effuse, debouch, come forth, break *or* burst out.
Adjectives—emergent, emerging, outgoing, emanative, effluent, eruptive, leaky.
Antonym, see INGRESS.

EJECTION [297]

Nouns—**1**, ejection, emission, effusion, rejection, expulsion, eviction, extrusion, trajection, discharge.
2, egestion, evacuation, vomiting, eructation, bloodletting, removal, phlebotomy, tapping, drainage, clearance, EXCRETION.
3, deportation, banishment, exile, ostracism, coventry; excommunication, interdict; deposition, relegation, extradition, dislodgment, DISPLACEMENT; discharge, dismissal, ouster. *Slang*, the gate, the sack, the air, the bum's rush.
Verbs—**1**, give vent to, let out, send out, exhale, excrete, shed, void, evacuate, emit, extrude, effuse, spend, expend, pour forth; squirt, spurt, spill, slop,

perspire, exude, tap, draw off, bail out, broach.

2, eject, reject, expel, discard; throw *or* push out, off, away, *or* aside; shovel *or* sweep out; brush off, cast adrift, turn *or* bundle out; throw overboard, send packing, turn out, pack off; bow out, show the door to; boycott; discharge, read out of, send flying, kick upstairs. *Slang*, give the gate, the sack, *or* the bum's rush to; fire; give *or* get the air.

3, evict, oust, dislodge, relegate, deport, banish, exile, empty; drain, clear off *or* out, suck, draw off, clean out, make a clean sweep of, purge; displace.

4, unpack, unlade, unload, unship.

Adjectives—emitting, emissive, ejective, expulsive, eliminative.

Interjections—begone! get you gone! get away! go away! off with you! go about your business! be off! avaunt! *Slang*, take off! get lost! beat it! scram!

Antonym, see RECEIVING.

elaborate, *v. & adj.* —*v.t.* work out, develop, devise, labor, perfect, embellish, execute, refine. See COMPLETION, IMPROVEMENT. —*adj.* labored, studied, complicated, detailed, painstaking, finished, perfected. See COMPLETION, PREPARATION.

elapse, *v.i.* slip away, pass, expire, intervene, glide. See PASSAGE.

elasticity, *n.* resilience, resiliency, spring, springiness; adaptability; ductility; flexibility, RECOIL; buoyancy; stretchableness; rubberiness, extensibility. *Ant.*, see HARDNESS.

elate, *v.t.* EXCITE, enliven, exhilarate, exalt, animate, lift up, flush, elevate; please, gladden, delight. See CHEERFULNESS. *Ant.*, see DEJECTION, DEPRESSION.

elder, *adj. & n.* —*adj.* older, earlier, superior, senior. See AGE. —*n.* ancestor, senior. See AGE.

elect, *v.t.* choose, select, decide on, fix upon; call, ordain. See CHOICE. *Ant.*, see REFUSAL.

electric, *adj.* voltaic, magnetic, galvanic; thrilling, exciting, stimulating. See FEELING, POWER. *Ant.*, see INSENSIBILITY, IMPOTENCE.

ELEGANCE [578]

Nouns—**1,** elegance, refinement, clarity, PURITY, ease, grace, gracefulness, polish, finish, propriety, appropriateness, good taste, harmonious simplicity, rhythm, harmony, symmetry.

2, (good) style, euphony, classicism, purism; purist, classicist, stylist.

Verbs—show elegance *or* refinement; discriminate; round a period.

Adjectives—**1,** elegant, polished, classical, correct, artistic, chaste, pure, appropriate, refined, in good taste, harmonious.

2, easy, fluent, mellifluous, balanced, euphonious; neatly put, well expressed.

Antonym, see VULGARITY.

element, *n.* COMPONENT, part, substance, constituent, ingredient; factor, principle, germ, rudiment, fundamental, origin. See CAUSE. *Ant.*, see EFFECT.

elementary, *adj.* rudimentary, incipient, primary, fundamental, basic; introductory; SIMPLE, uncompounded.

ELEVATION [307]

Nouns—**1,** elevation; raising, lifting, erection; sublimation, exaltation; prominence, eminence; advancement, promotion, preferment; uplift, IMPROVEMENT; HEIGHT, hill, mount, mountain.

2, lever, crane, derrick, windlass, capstan, winch, crowbar, jimmy, pulley, crank, jack, dredge, elevator, lift, dumbwaiter, hoist, Escalator, moving stairway.

Verbs—**1,** heighten, elevate, raise, lift, erect, set up, stick up, heave, buoy, weigh.

2, exalt, sublimate, place on a pedestal, promote, advance, improve.

3, take up, fish up; dredge.

4, stand up, spring to one's feet; hold one's head up, rise up, get up, jump up.

Adjectives—**1,** elevated, raised, lifted up; erect; eminent, lofty; stilted. **2,** ennobled, exalted, uplifted.

Antonym, see DEPRESSION.

---

elf, *n.* sprite, fairy, imp, puck, pixy; gnome, goblin. See MYTHICAL DEITIES.
elicit, *v.t.* draw forth, EXTRACT, evoke, educe, extort. *Ant.*, instill.
eligible, *adj.* qualified, fitted, suitable, desirable.
eliminate, *v.t.* expel, excrete, remove, get rid of, exclude, set aside, drop, cast out, eradicate; omit, ignore, leave out, neglect, pass over; suppress, EXTRACT; refine, simplify, clarify.
eloquence, *n.* oratory, rhetoric, power; fluency, persuasiveness, volubility. See LOQUACITY, SPEECH, POWER. *Ant.*, see SILENCE, IMPOTENCE.
elude, *v.t.* ESCAPE, evade, avoid; dodge, foil, baffle.
emanate, *v.t. & i.* emit, effuse, exhale, radiate; flow, proceed, issue, come, spring, arise. See EGRESS. *Ant.*, see INGRESS.
emancipate, *v.t.* LIBERATE, free, release, deliver, manumit, set free, enfranchise. See FREEDOM. *Ant.*, see RESTRAINT.
embark, *v.t.* ship, board, set sail, sail; begin, engage, elist, invest. See DEPARTURE, UNDERTAKING. *Ant.*, ARRIVAL.
embarrass, *v.t.* discomfort, demoralize, disconcert, discomfit, nonplus, bother, abash, encumber, trouble, hamper, complicate, perplex. See DIFFICULTY. *Ant.*, see FACILITY.
embellish, *v.t.* ORNAMENT, decorate, adorn, beautify, deck, bedeck, enrich.
embezzle, *v.t. & i.* steal, misappropriate, misapply, peculate, defalcate.
embitter, *v.t.* SOUR, envenom, poison, exasperate, anger, irritate. See AGGRAVATION, DETERIORATION. *Ant.*, see RELIEF, IMPROVEMENT, SWEETNESS.
emblem, *n.* symbol, token, sign, mark, device. See INDICATION.
embody, *v.t.* incorporate, join, unite, organize, impersonate, personify, incarnate; comprise, contain, include; express, voice.
embrace, *v.t.* clasp, clutch, hold, fold, hug, cherish, love, caress; include, comprehend, take in, comprise, involve, embody; encircle, enclose, surround; receive, welcome; take up, adopt, espouse. See CHOICE, COMPOSITION, ENDEARMENT. *Ant.*, see REFUSAL.
emerge, *v.i.* issue, appear; arise, come forth. See EGRESS. *Ant.*, see INGRESS.
emergency, *n.* juncture, crisis; exigency, necessity, pinch, extremity. See CIRCUMSTANCE.
emigration, *n.* migration, departure, exodus. See EGRESS. *Ant.*, see INGRESS.
eminence, *n.* height, altitude, elevation; distinction, rank, importance. See GREATNESS, REPUTE. *Ant.*, see DISREPUTE, LOWNESS.
emit, *v.t.* discharge, emanate, radiate, breathe, exhale, send forth, throw off, issue; deliver; voice. See EJECTION, SPEECH. *Ant.*, see RECEIVING.
emotion, *n.* FEELING, sentiment, passion, sensibility, sensation.
emphasize, *v.t.* accentuate, stress, mark, underline, underscore. See AFFIRMATION, IMPORTANCE. *Ant.*, see NEGATION, UNIMPORTANCE.
employ, *v.t.* USE, occupy, make use of, devote, utilize; hire, engage.
empower, *v.t.* enable, make able, endow, invest; authorize, commission. See PERMISSION, POWER. *Ant.*, see RESTRAINT, IMPOTENCE.
empty, *v. & adj.* —*v.t.* void, deplete, exhaust, evacuate, drain, deflate, discharge, unload. See CONTRACTION, EJECTION. *Ant.*, see INCREASE. —*adj.* hollow, vacant, exhausted, depleted, untenanted, devoid; prolix, verbose, long-winded, garrulous; hungry; vain, unsubstantial, useless, foolish, trivial, unfeeling, fruitless, inane. See ABSENCE. *Ant.*, see PRESENCE, SUBSTANCE.
emulate, *v.t.* rival, vie, compete, strive, contend. See OPPOSITION, REPUTE. *Ant.*, see COÖPERATION, DISREPUTE.
enable, *v.t.* empower, invest, endow; authorize. See POWER. *Ant.*, see IMPOTENCE.
enact, *v.t.* decree, make, pass, order, ordain; play; execute, perform, do. See ACTION, COMMAND, PASSAGE. *Ant.*, see INACTIVITY.
enchant, *v.t.* bewitch, conjure; captivate, please, charm, delight, fascinate. See PLEASURE, SORCERY. *Ant.*, see PAIN.
encircle, *v.t.* ENVIRON, surround, embrace, encompass, inclose; span, ring, loop, girdle.

enclosure, *n.* See INCLOSURE.

encounter, *v. & n.* —*v.t.* meet, come across; engage, struggle, contend. See ARRIVAL, OPPOSITION, CONTENTION. *Ant.,* see DEPARTURE, COÖPERATION. —*n.* meeting, interview; collision; combat, battle, skirmish, brush, engagement. See CONTENTION, IMPULSE. *Ant.,* see PACIFICATION.

encourage, *v.t.* animate, strengthen, hearten, fortify, inspirit, cheer, inspire, reassure, rally, comfort; abet, embolden, incite, urge, instigate; help, foster, promote, advance, advocate. See HOPE, CAUSE. *Ant.,* see DEJECTION.

encroach, *v.i.* advance, infringe, usurp, invade, trespass, intrude, overstep, violate. See INJUSTICE. *Ant.,* see JUSTICE.

encumber, *v.t.* burden, hamper, load, clog, oppress; obstruct, hinder, impede, embarrass, retard, check, handicap. See HINDRANCE. *Ant.,* see AID.

END [67]

Nouns—**1,** end, close, termination, conclusion, finis, finish, finale, period, terminus, stopping (point); CESSATION, stop, expiration, halt.
2, extreme, extremity; acme, peak; tip, nib, point; tail, tail end, fag end, bitter end, verge, peroration.
3, consummation, dénouement, finish, COMPLETION, doomsday, crack of doom, day of Judgment, final curtain, last stages, expiration, DEATH, end of all things, quietus, finality. *Slang,* payoff, curtains.
4, finishing stroke, death blow, knockout, K.O., *coup de grâce.*
5, goal, destination, object, purpose.
Verbs—**1,** end, close, finish, terminate, conclude, be all over, expire, die (see DEATH); come to a close, run its course, run out, pass away, be through.
2, bring to an end, put an end to, make an end of, determine; complete; stop, shut up shop, ring down the curtain; call a halt.
3, CEASE, halt, expire, lapse, stop; curtail, cut short.
Adjectives—**1,** ending, final, terminal, definitive, crowning, completing, last, ultimate, conclusive.
2, end, at an end, settled, decided, over, played out.
Adverbs—finally, definitely, conclusively; at the last; once and for all, to the bitter end.

Antonym, see BEGINNING.

ENDEARMENT [902]

Nouns—**1,** endearment, caress; blandishment; fondling, billing and cooing, dalliance, embrace, salute, kiss, buss, smack, osculation.
2, courtship, affections, wooing, suit, addresses, *amour,* lovemaking, LOVE, flirting, flirtation, gallantry; coquetry. *Slang,* necking, spooning, petting, smooching.
3, lover's knot, love token, love letter; *billet-doux,* valentine.
4, engagement, betrothal, marriage, honeymoon.
5, flirt, coquette; philanderer, lover; paramour. *Slang,* vamp, gold digger, *femme fatale;* wolf, Don Juan, Casanova, loverboy, sheik.
6, dear, darling, sweetheart, precious, LOVE, honey, honeybunch.
Verbs—**1,** caress, fondle, pet; coax, wheedle, cosset, coddle, make much of; cherish, foster; clasp, hug, cuddle, fold in one's arms, nestle; embrace, kiss, buss, smack, salute.
2, make love, bill and coo; toy, dally, flirt, coquet, philander; court, woo, pay addresses; set one's cap for, be sweet on; ogle, cast sheep's eyes on. *Slang,* spoon, pet, neck; make a pass at, pitch woo, smooch, spark.
3, fall in love with; propose, pop the question; plight one's troth.
Adjectives—**1,** endearing, winsome, lovable, kissable, affectionate, caressing.
2, lovesick, lovelorn. *Slang,* spoony.

Antonyms, see DETRACTION, HATE.

---

endeavor, *v. & n.* —*v.i.* try, attempt, seek, struggle, strive, ESSAY, labor, aim, OFFER. *Ant.,* see REFUSAL. —*n.* trial, try, attempt, effort, struggle, exertion, OFFER. *Ant.,* see REFUSAL.

endless, *adj.* interminable, incessant, uninterrupted, unceasing, continuous, PERPETUAL; never-ending, unending, everlasting, continual, undying, eternal, imperishable; boundless, indefinite, illimitable, unlimited, immeasurable. See CONTINUITY. *Ant.*, see DISCONTINUITY, INSTANTANEITY.

endow, *v.t.* dower, settle upon, bequeath, bestow, enrich, endue; furnish, invest, clothe. See GIVING. *Ant.*, see RECEIVING.

endue, *v.t.* clothe, furnish. See POWER. *Ant.*, see IMPOTENCE.

endure, *v.t. & i.* continue, remain, wear, last; abide, bear, suffer, bear up, sustain, undergo; tolerate, put up with, stand, brook, permit. See FEELING, DURABILITY, SUPPORT. *Ant.*, see CHANGE.

enemy, *n.* foe, OPPONENT, adversary, antagonist, foeman; Fate, Fury, *bete noir*, archenemy, Nemesis, evil *or* malignant spirit; antipathy, aversion; inimical person *or* power. See HATE, OPPOSITION. *Ant.*, FRIEND.

energetic, *adj.* brisk, forceful; active; strong, vibrant, powerful, vigorous; driving; animated, mettlesome; enthusiastic; potent, powerful; hearty, healthy. See POWER, ACTIVITY.

energy, *n.* POWER, strength, vigor; potency, capacity, drive; zeal, enthusiasm, spirit, mettlesomeness, vitality; ACTIVITY; verve, dash, élan, spiritedness; work; efficacy, efficiency. *Colloq.*, get-up-and-go, ginger, vim, pep, push. *Ant.*, see INACTIVITY, IMPOTENCE.

enervate, *v.t.* weaken, devitalize, unnerve, paralyze, soften, emasculate, unman, debilitate, enfeeble, effeminate. See IMPOTENCE, SOFTNESS.

enforce, *v.t.* compel, force, oblige; urge, lash, goad; strengthen; execute, sanction, put in force. See COMPULSION, CAUSE.

enfranchise, *v.t.* LIBERATE, set free, release; naturalize; empower, license, qualify. See PERMISSION. *Ant.*, see RESTRAINT.

engage, *v.t.* bind, obligate, pledge, PROMISE, betroth; hire, enlist, employ, book, retain, brief; reserve, secure; occupy, interest, engross, attract, entangle, involve, interlock; set about, take up; fight, contend. See COMMISSION, UNDERTAKING, USE, WARFARE. *Ant.*, see NULLIFICATION, WASTE.

engagement, *n.* betrothal, obligation, PROMISE, agreement, pledge; appointment, interview; occupation, employment; battle, action, skirmish, brush, encounter. See BUSINESS, CONTENTION, SOCIALITY. *Ant.*, see PACIFICATION.

ENGRAVING [558]

Nouns—**1,** engraving, chalcography; line, mezzotint, stipple engraving; drypoint, etching, copperplate, steel, wood engraving; xylography, glyptography, cerography, lithography, photolithography, glyphography; gravure, photogravure, rotogravure; photoengraving.

2, impression, print, engraving, plate, etching, lithotint, cut, linoleum cut, woodcut; mezzotint, aquatint. *See* PRINTING.

3, graver, burin, etching-point, style; plate, stone, wood-block, negative, die, punch, stamp.

Verbs—engrave, grave, stipple, etch, bute, lithograph.

Adjectives—sculptured, engraved, graven; carved, carven, chiseled.

engross, *v.t.* copy, write, transcribe; absorb; monopolize, control; occupy, engage, fill. See DEPTH, ATTENTION.

enhance, *v.t.* intensify; exaggerate; advance, augment, INCREASE, elevate. *Ant.*, see DECREASE.

enigma, *n.* question, riddle, mystery, puzzle, problem, conundrum, SECRET.

enjoin, *v.t.* COMMAND, bid, direct, order, instruct, charge; counsel, admonish; PROHIBIT, forbid, restrain; exact, require. See ADVICE, DUTY. *Ant.*, see NEGLECT, PERMISSION.

enjoy, *v.t.* like, relish, love, gloat over, delight in; experience; hold, possess. See PLEASURE, POSSESSION. *Ant.*, see PAIN.

enlarge, *v.t.* increase, extend, widen, broaden; aggrandize, amplify, magnify, augment, expand, elaborate, expatiate; dilate, distend, swell. See INCREASE, GREATNESS. *Ant.*, see CONTRACTION, LITTLENESS.

enlighten, *v.t.* brighten, illuminate; educate, civilize, instruct, INFORM, teach, edify.

enliven, *v.t.* animate, exhilarate, inspirit, quicken, fire, brighten, stimulate, rouse, invigorate; cheer, elate, encourage. See CHEERFULNESS. *Ant.*, see DEJECTION.

enmity, *n.* hostility, unfriendliness, antagonism, HATE, ill-will; grudge, rancor, anger, spite, animus, animosity, dislike, antipathy; feud, vendetta. *Ant.*, see FRIEND.

enormity, *n.* wickedness, offense, atrocity, outrage; immensity, enormousness, GREATNESS. See GUILT. *Ant.*, see LITTLENESS, INNOCENCE.

enormous, *adj.* monstrous, excessive; large, titanic, tremendous, huge, immense, colossal, gigantic, vast, prodigious, stupendous. See SIZE.

enough, *adj.* adequate, sufficient, equal; ample, abundant, plenteous. See SUFFICIENCY.

enrage, *v.t.* anger, exasperate, provoke, incense, irritate; madden, inflame, infuriate. See RESENTMENT.

enrich, *v.t.* endow, aggrandize, make wealthy; embellish, ORNAMENT, adorn, beautify; fertilize; cultivate, develop. See IMPROVEMENT, MONEY. *Ant.*, see DETERIORATION, POVERTY.

enroll, *v.t.* LIST, record, enter, register; enlist, serve. *Ant.*, see EJECTION.

ensue, *v.t. & i.* follow, succeed, supervene, happen, result; pursue, seek after. See EFFECT. *Ant.*, see CAUSE.

entangle, *v.t.* tangle, ravel, mesh, entrap, mat, ensnare, inveigle, twist, snarl; perplex, involve, embroil, embarrass. See DECEPTION, DIFFICULTY, DISORDER. *Ant.*, see FACILITY, ARRANGEMENT.

enter, *v.t.* penetrate, pierce; go in, come in; trespass, invade, board; begin, start, take up; LIST, record, inscribe, enroll, register, file; join. See COMPOSITION, INGRESS. *Ant.*, see EGRESS.

enterprise, *n.* project, scheme, venture, adventure, attempt, UNDERTAKING, essay; business; energy. *Colloq.*, push, go-ahead. See ACTIVITY. *Ant.*, see INACTIVITY.

entertain, *v.t.* receive, welcome; amuse, divert, regale; harbor, shelter, cherish; maintain, keep up; consider, dwell upon, heed. See ATTENTION, SOCIALITY, THOUGHT. *Ant.*, see NEGLECT, SECLUSION.

enthusiasm, *n.* ecstasy, frenzy, fanaticism; fire, spirit, force; ardor, zeal, fervor, vehemence, eagerness; optimism, assurance. See ACTIVITY, FEELING, HOPE, POWER. *Ant.*, see INACTIVITY, DEJECTION, IMPOTENCE.

entire, *adj.* COMPLETE, absolute, unqualified; total, gross, all; WHOLE, intact, undiminished, unimpaired, perfect, unbroken; undivided, unalloyed.

entitle, *v.t.* qualify, fit, capacitate, authorize; name, call, designate, dub, style. See NOMENCLATURE, JUSTICE. *Ant.*, see INJUSTICE.

entrance, *n.* entry, INGRESS, entree, incoming, ingoing; debut, induction; admission, access, admittance, approach; entry, aperture, door, lobby, gate, portal, way; BEGINNING, start, commencement, introduction; invasion, penetration. See RECEIVING. *Ant.*, see END, EGRESS, EJECTION.

entreat, *v.t.* REQUEST, ask, beg, crave, pray, beseech, implore, supplicate, plead, solicit, coax.

enumerate, *v.t.* compute, count, tell off, number, name over; mention, recount, rehearse, recapitulate, detail, specify. See NUMERATION.

enunciate, *v.t.* announce, state, proclaim, declare; pronounce, articulate. See AFFIRMATION, VOICE. *Ant.*, see NEGATION.

envelop, *v.t.* COVER, wrap, enshroud, enfold, surround, inclose, hide.

environment, *n.* environs; neighborhood, surroundings, LOCATION; home; vicinity, vicinage; background, scene, locale, setting; atmosphere, influences; outskirts, suburbs, purlieus; *milieu.* *Colloq.*, stamping ground, hangout.

envy, *n. & v.* —*n.* enviousness, jealousy; covetousness, cupidity, spite; ill-will, malice; greenness. —*v.* begrudge; DESIRE, crave, covet, hanker, turn green. *Ant.*, see BENEVOLENCE.

epicure, *n.* epicurean, bon vivant (Fr.), gourmet (Fr.). See TASTE.

episode, *n.* digression, excursus; OCCURRENCE, incident, happening, action.

epistle, *n.* LETTER, communication, missive.

epitome, *n.* compendium, abridgment, abstract, synopsis, summary, brief.

epoch, *n.* date; period, era, age. See TIME.

EQUALITY [27]

Nouns—**1,** equality, parity, coextension; symmetry, balance, poise, evenness, monotony, level, equivalence; equipoise, equilibrium, ponderance; par, quits; IDENTITY, likeness, SIMILARITY, equalizer, equalization, equation, coördination, adjustment.

2, tie, draw, dead heat. *Colloq.*, photo finish.

3, match, peer, compeer, equal, mate, fellow, brother, equivalent, parallel; tit for tat; a Roland for an Oliver.

Verbs—**1,** be equal, equal, match, keep pace with, come up to, be on a level with, balance; measure up to.

2, make equal, equalize, level, balance, equate, trim, adjust, poise, fit, strike a balance, restore equilibrium, readjust; handicap; share and share alike.

Adjectives—**1,** equal, even, level, monotonous, coequal, symmetrical, coördinate; on a par with; up to the mark.

2, equivalent, tantamount; quits; homologous; synonymous, analogous, similar, as broad as it is long, much the same, the same; equalized, drawn, neck-and-neck; half-and-half. *Slang*, fifty-fifty.

Adverbs—equally, to all intents and purposes, nip and tuck; on even footing. *Colloq.*, from scratch.

Antonym, see DIFFERENCE.

equanimity, *n.* evenness, composure, repose, poise; calmness, serenity, tranquillity, self-possession, self-control, inexcitability. *Ant.*, see EXCITEMENT.

equip, *v.t.* furnish, outfit, provide; accouter, appoint, dress, accommodate, array, attire; arm, gird. See CLOTHING, PREPARATION.

equivalent, *adj. & n.* —*adj.* EQUAL, alike, identical, same, tantamount, synonymous; analogous, correspondent, interchangeable; convertible, reciprocal. See RELATION, INTERPRETATION. —*n.* equal; price, worth; analogue. See COMPENSATION, SUBSTITUTION.

equivocation, *n.* equivocalness; quibble, quibbling; evasion, shiftiness; ambiguity, double meaning, *double-entendre*; DECEPTION, prevarication, white lie; DISTORTION, half-truth, sophistry, casuistry; dodge, subterfuge. *Colloq.*, smoke screen, red herring. See CONCEALMENT, FALSEHOOD. *Ant.*, see TRUTH, DISCLOSURE.

era, *n.* See TIME.

eradicate, *v.t.* abolish; blot out, erase, extirpate, exterminate, weed out, eliminate, uproot. See DESTRUCTION, EJECTION. *Ant.*, see PRODUCTION.

erase, *v.t.* efface, rub out, expunge, cancel, obliterate, blot out. See DESTRUCTION. *Ant.*, see PRODUCTION.

erect, *v. & adj.* —*v.t.* raise, exalt; rear; build, construct; establish, set up, institute; create. See ELEVATION, PRODUCTION. *Ant.*, see DEPRESSION, DESTRUCTION. —*adj.* upright, straight, vertical, perpendicular; uplifted. See DIRECTION. *Ant.*, see CURVATURE.

erosion, *n.* eating away, wearing away, disintegration. See DETERIORATION. *Ant.*, see IMPROVEMENT.

err, *v.i.* mistake, misjudge; nod, slip, trip, blunder; sin, transgress; fall, wander, stray. See ERROR, BADNESS. *Ant.*, see TRUTH, VIRTUE.

errand, *n.* business, COMMISSION, mission, charge, task, trip, message.

erratic, *adj.* abnormal, IRREGULAR, eccentric, odd, CAPRICIOUS, queer, peculiar; wandering, uncertain, changeable. See CHANGEABLENESS.

ERROR [495]

Nouns—**1,** error, fallacy; falsity (see FALSEHOOD), untruth; misconception, misapprehension, misunderstanding; inexactness, inaccuracy; LAXITY, misconstruction, misinterpretation, miscomputation, MISJUDGMENT, misstatement.

2, mistake, miss, fault, blunder; oversight; misprint, erratum; slip, blot, flaw, trip, stumble; slip of the tongue, *lapsus linguae*, slip of the pen, lapse; solecism; typographical *or* clerical error; malapropism; bull, break. *Slang*, boner, howler, typo.

3, delusion, illusion, false impression, self-deception; bias; heresy; hallucination, optical illusion, dream, fancy, fable, fantasy, phantom, mirage.

Verbs—**1,** mislead, misguide, lead astray, lead into error, beguile, misinform, delude, give a false impression, falsify, misstate; deceive, lie; dupe.

2, err, be in error, be mistaken; mistake, receive a false impression, be in the

wrong; take for; blunder, misapprehend, misconceive, misinterpret, misunderstand, miscalculate, misjudge; be at cross purposes, slip up, slip a cog.
3, trip, stumble, lose oneself, go astray.
Adjectives—**1**, erroneous, untrue, false, fallacious; apocryphal, unreal, ungrounded; groundless, unsubstantial; heretical, unsound, illogical, untrustworthy, unauthenticated; exploded, refuted.
2, inexact, inaccurate, incorrect, ungrammatical, faulty.
3, illusive, illusory, delusive; mock, imaginary, spurious, fancied, deceptive, deceitful, perverted.
4, in error, mistaken, aberrant, wide of the mark, astray, at fault, on a false scent, at cross purposes.
Antonym, see TRUTH.

eruption, *n.* efflorescence, rash; outbreak, commition; discharge, expulsion. See DISEASE, EJECTION, VIOLENCE. *Ant.,* see HEALTH, RECEIVING, MODERATION.

ESCAPE [671]

Nouns—**1**, escape, elopement, flight; evasion, avoidance, retreat; narrow escape *or* squeak, close call, hairbreadth escape; impunity, reprieve, deliverance, liberation, manumission, rescue; jailbreak, freedom. *Slang,* close shave, getaway, lam.
2, outlet, loophole, OPENING, EGRESS; puncture, aperture; safety-valve, fire escape, ladder, life net, lifeboat, parachute; refuge, sanctuary, asylum; ACQUITTAL.
3, refugee, fugitive, escapee, runaway, runagate, deserter.
Verbs—escape, get off, get well out of, save one's bacon, weather the storm; elude, make off, give one the slip, slip through the fingers, wriggle out of; break out *or* loose, make a getaway, find a loophole. *Slang,* get away with murder, fly the coop, take it on the lam, lam out.
Adjectives—escaping, escaped, fled, free, scotfree, at large, well out of.
Adverbs—on the run. *Slang,* on the lam, over the hill.
Antonym, see RESTRAINT.

escort, *v. & n.* —*v.t.* accompany, conduct, convoy, guard, walk, attend, usher. See SAFETY. *Ant.,* see DANGER. —*n.* attendant, companion, conductor, convoy, bodyguard.
essay, *n. & v.* —*n.* COMPOSITION, article, DISSERTATION, discourse, paper, monograph; trial, effort, attempt, EXPERIMENT. —*v.t.* try, attempt, endeavor, strive; test, venture, speculate.
essence, *n.* being, substance, element, entity, reality, nature, life; extract, distillation; perfume; principle, inwardness; sense, gist, core, kernel, pith, quintessence, heart, purport. See BELIEF, FORM, REQUIREMENT, SUBSTANCE. *Ant.,* see DOUBT, INSUBSTANTIALITY.
establish, *v.t.* confirm, fix, settle, secure, set, stabilize; sustain, install, root, ensconce; appoint, enact, ordain; found, institute, constitute, create, organize, build, set up; verify, prove, substantiate; determine, decide. See EVIDENCE, PRODUCTION, STABILITY. *Ant.,* see DESTRUCTION, CHANGEABLENESS.
estate, *n.* state, rank, condition, station, DEGREE; PROPERTY, fortune, possessions, effects, interest, land, holdings.
esteem, *n.* RESPECT, regard, favor, admiration, estimation, honor; reverence, worship. See APPROBATION. *Ant.,* see DISAPPROBATION, DISRESPECT.
estimate, *v. & n.* —*v.t.* consider, gauge, JUDGE; value, appraise, evaluate, rate, assess, measure; compute, reckon, calculate. See NUMERATION. —*n.* JUDGMENT, opinion, appraisal, report, criticism; calculation. See NUMERATION. *Ant.,* see MISJUDGMENT.
estrange, *v.t.* alienate, separate, withdraw; fall out, be unfriendly; disunite, part, wean; transfer. See DISJUNCTION. *Ant.,* see JUNCTION, FRIEND.
eternal, *adj.* perpetual, endless, everlasting, continual, ceaseless; timeless, infinite, unending; constant; immortal, imperishable, deathless. See DURABILITY. *Ant.,* see INSTANTANEITY.

ethereal, *adj.* airy, delicate, light, tenuous, fragile, fairy; HEAVENLY, celestial, empyreal. See INSUBSTANTIALITY. *Ant.*, see HELL, SUBSTANCE.

ethics, *n.* morals, morality, rules of conduct. See DUTY. *Ant.*, see NEGLECT.

etiquette, *n.* manners, decorum, custom, formality, good form. See FASHION.

eulogize, *v.t.* praise, compliment, celebrate, glorify, laud, panegyrize, extol. See CELEBRATION. *Ant.*, see DETRACTION.

evacuate, *v.t.* empty, clear, eject, expel, purge, scour; discharge, defecate, void, emit; leave, quit, vacate, abandon. See DEPARTURE. *Ant.*, see ARRIVAL, RECEIVING.

evade, *v.t.* avoid, elude; dodge, shun; baffle, foil, parry; escape, slip away; ignore, violate, neglect; equivocate, prevaricate, quibble. See AVOIDANCE.

evaporate, *v.t. & i.* emanate, pass off, escape; vaporize, distill; condense, solidify, dehydrate; dessicate; vanish, disappear. See DRYNESS, INSUBSTANTIALITY. *Ant.*, see MOISTURE, SUBSTANCE.

even, *adj.* level, EQUAL, smooth, flat, flush, UNIFORM, regular, unvaried, PARALLEL; equable, even-tempered, unruffled, placid; equitable, fair, impartial, just; straightforward, plain, direct; abreast, alongside; true, plumb, STRAIGHT. *See* HORIZONTAL. *Ant.*, see INJUSTICE, OBLIQUITY, CURVATURE, UNCONFORMITY.

evening, *n.* dusk, nightfall, eventide, close of day; gloaming, twilight; sundown, sunset; curfew; eve, even (poetic); decline, old age, sunset years.

event, *n.* occasion, occurrence, happening; affair, episode, incident; gala affair *or* occasion, holiday; experience; CIRCUMSTANCE, issue, outcome, result.

eventual, *adj.* final, ultimate, coming; contingent. See FUTURITY, CHANCE. *Ant.*, see PAST.

ever, *adv.* always, eternally, perpetually, incessantly, continually, constantly, forever; once, at any time; in any case, at all. See DURABILITY. *Ant.*, see INSTANTANEITY.

every, *adj.* each, all; complete, entire.

everyone, *n.* everybody, *tout le monde* (Fr.).

evict, *v.t.* eject, oust, remove, expel, put out, dispossess. See EJECTION. *Ant.*, see RECEIVING.

EVIDENCE [467]

Nouns—**1,** evidence, facts, premises, data, grounds, INDICATION, DEMONSTRATION, confirmation, corroboration, SUPPORT, ratification, proof; state's, king's, queen's, oral, documentary, hearsay, external, extrinsic, internal, intrinsic, circumstantial, *ex parte*, presumptive, collateral *or* constructive evidence.

2, testimony, attestation, deposition, affirmation; examination; exhibit.

3, citation, reference, AUTHORITY, warrant, credential, testimonial; diploma, voucher, certificate, docket, RECORD, document, deed, warranty; signature, seal, identification.

4, witness, indicator, eyewitness, deponent, sponsor, bystander, testifier, attestor.

Verbs—**1,** be evidence, evince, evidence, manifest, show; betoken, tell of, indicate, denote, imply, involve, argue, bespeak; have *or* carry weight, tell, speak volumes, speak for itself.

2, rest *or* depend upon; bear witness, give evidence, testify, depose, witness, vouch for; sign, seal, set one's hand and seal, certify, attest, acknowledge.

3, confirm, ratify, support, bear out, uphold, warrant, establish, authenticate, substantiate, verify, DEMONSTRATE.

4, adduce, attest, cite, quote, refer, bring into court; allege, plead; produce witnesses; collect evidence, make out a case. *Colloq.*, have *or* get the goods on one.

Adjectives—evidential, documentary; indicative, indicatory, deducible; grounded on, founded on, based on, corroborative, confirmatory; supportive, authentic, conclusive; circumstantial, by inference, according to, *a fortiori.*

Antonym, see NEGATION.

evident, *adj.* apparent, plain, obvious, distinct; broad, unmistakable, palpable, patent, open, MANIFEST, clear; downright, overt, indubitable. See APPEARANCE, CERTAINTY. *Ant.,* see DOUBT.

EVIL [619]

Nouns—**1,** evil, ill, harm, hurt; mischief, nuisance; disadvantage, drawback; disaster, accident, casualty, mishap, misfortune, calamity, catastrophe, tragedy, ruin, DESTRUCTION, ADVERSITY, mental anguish *or* suffering; BANE, curse, SCOURGE. *Slang,* jinx, Jonah, hoodoo, hex.
2, blow, buffet, stroke, scratch, bruise, wound, gash, mutilation; damage, LOSS, DETERIORATION.
3, BADNESS, wickedness, sin, depravity, VICE, iniquity, IMPIETY, immorality, corruption.
4, outrage, WRONG, injury, foul play; bad *or* ill turn; disservice, spoliation, grievance, crying evil.
Verbs—harm, hurt, injury, wrong, wound, ruin, outrage, dishonor, victimize.
Adjectives—**1,** evil, bad, ill, sinful, wicked, wrong, depraved, vicious, immoral, corrupt.
2, harmful, hurtful, injurious, malignant, malevolent, prejudicial, virulent, disastrous, ruinous.
Adverbs—badly, amiss, wrong, ill, to one's cost.
Antonym, see GOODNESS.

EVILDOER [913]

Nouns—**1,** evildoer; sinner, transgressor, profligate, LIBERTINE; oppressor, despot, tyrant; incendiary, anarchist, destroyer, vandal, iconoclast, terrorist.
2, savage, brute, ruffian, barbarian, caitiff, desperado; bully, rough, hooligan, hoodlum, tough, plugugly, hellion; fraud, swindler, confidence man, THIEF; murderer, killer (see KILLING), cutthroat, butcher, villain; rascal, knave, scalawag, rogue, badman, scapegrace, rowdy, scamp, Apache; pimp, procurer, whoremaster, white slaver; criminal, felon, convict, jailbird, delinquent, troublemaker, forger; black sheep, blackguard, prodigal son, fallen angel, ne'er-do-well. *Slang,* torpedo, trigger man, gorilla, hood.
3, hag, beldam(e), Jezebel, jade, nag, shrew, fishwife; murderess; ogress, harpy, Fury, maenad; adulteress, paramour, mistress; prostitute, whore, harlot, strumpet, trull, trollop, wanton, loose woman, courtesan; madam(e), procuress, bawd, hussy, streetwalker, drab, white slave; dragon, harridan, vixen, virago; witch, siren, Circe, Delilah, Medusa, Gorgon; enchantress, sorceress. *Slang,* roundheels.
4, monster, fiend, DEMON, devil, devil incarnate, fiend in human shape; Frankenstein's monster; cannibal, bloodsucker, vampire, ghoul, vulture, ogre.
5, culprit, offender, malefactor; recidivist; traitor, betrayer, Judas (Iscariot), Benedict Arnold, Quisling; conspirator, snake in the grass; turncoat, renegade, apostate; informer. *Slang,* rat, squealer. See IMPROBITY.
Antonym, see GOODNESS.

---

evince, *v.t.* exhibit, display, show, manifest, EVIDENCE, demonstrate, disclose, indicate, prove. *Ant.,* see NEGATION.
evolution, *n.* evolvement, unfolding, growth, expansion, development, elaboration; Darwinism, natural selection; mutation. See PRODUCTION, PROGRESSION, CHANGE. *Ant.,* see REGRESSION.
exact, *v. & adj.* —*v.t.* ask, require, claim, demand; extort, take, wring, wrest, force, impose. See COMMAND. —*adj.* strict, rigorous; accurate, precise, delicate, nice, fine, correct, literal, verbatim; faithful, lifelike, close; definite, absolute, direct. See MEANING, SIMILARITY, TRUTH. *Ant.,* see DIFFERENCE, ERROR.

EXAGGERATION [49]

Nouns—exaggeration, EXPANSION, magnification, overstatement, hyperbole, stretch, strain, coloring, high coloring, false coloring, caricature, extravagance; Baron Munchausen; fringe, embroidery, traveler's tale, yarn, tall story *or* tale, overestimation, tempest in a teapot; much ado about nothing; puffery, boasting, rant; figure of speech, stretch of the imagination; flight of fancy.

Verbs—exaggerate, magnify, pile up, aggravate; amplify, expand, OVER-ESTIMATE, hyperbolize; overstate, overdraw, overpraise, overshoot the mark, strain, stretch, strain *or* stretch a point, spin a long yarn; draw the longbow, run riot, heighten, overcolor, embroider, misrepresent, puff, boast.

Adjectives—exaggerated, overwrought; bombastic, florid, flowery, magniloquent, high-flown, hyperbolical; fabulous, extravagant, preposterous; egregious, outré; high-flying, tall, steep.

Antonym, see TRUTH.

exalt, *v.t.* elevate, raise, advance, lift up, dignify, promote, honor; praise, glorify, magnify, extol, aggrandize, elate, uplift; intensify, heighten. See APPROBATION, ELEVATION, INCREASE. *Ant.,* see DISAPPROBATION, DEPRESSION, DECREASE.

examine, *v.t.* investigate, inspect, survey, probe, canvass, search; scrutinize, peruse, dissect, scan; test, interrogate, try, question; audit, review. See ATTENTION, INQUIRY. *Ant.,* see NEGLECT, ANSWER.

example, *n.* sample, specimen, piece; instance, case, illustration; pattern, type, standard, copy, model, ideal; precedent; warning; problem, exercise. See CONFORMITY, TEACHING. *Ant.,* see UNCONFORMITY.

exasperate, *v.t.* anger, enrage, infuriate; irritate, vex, nettle, provoke, roil, peeve, annoy. See RESENTMENT.

excavation, *n.* cavity, hole, pit, mine, shaft, quarry, opening. See CONCAVITY. *Ant.,* see CONVEXITY.

exceed, *v.t.* transcend, surpass, excel, outdo, outstrip, beat; overstep, pass, overdo, go beyond. See SUPERIORITY. *Ant.,* see INFERIORITY.

excel, *v.t.* exceed, surpass, eclipse, outdo, outstrip. See SUPERIORITY. *Ant.,* see INFERIORITY.

except, *prep.* unless, saving, save, but, excepting, barring. See UNCONFORMITY. *Ant.,* see CONFORMITY.

excerpt, *n.* extract, quote, citation, selection; sentence, verse, section, PASSAGE.

excess, *n.* immoderation, INTEMPERANCE, dissipation, indulgence; superabundance, superfluity, extravagance, exorbitance; REDUNDANCE, remainder. *Ant.,* see MODERATION.

exchange, *n.* reciprocity, substitution; trade, BARTER, commerce; conversion, INTERCHANGE; market.

excitability, *n.* impetuosity, VIOLENCE, vehemence, passion, rage; impatience; AGITATION, fury, storminess, IRASCIBILITY; restlessness, nervousness, perturbation, disquietude; tizzy; tempestuousness, fit, outburst, seizure, paroxysm; ferment; desperation, distraction; immoderation; frenzy, mania; fuming, ferocity, fierceness; touchiness, temper, irritability, peevishness, jumpiness, skittishness. See EXCITEMENT. *Ant.,* see MODERATION.

EXCITEMENT [824]

Nouns—**1,** excitement, excitation; stimulation, piquancy, provocation; animation, AGITATION, perturbation; fascination, intoxication, enravishment, entrancement, high pressure; passion, thrill.

2, disturbance, tumult, turmoil, commotion, hubbub, fluster, fuss, bustle, hurly-burly, hullabaloo, pandemonium, furor(e).

3, excitability, impetuosity, turbulence; impatience, IRASCIBILITY; effervescence, ebullition; fanaticism.

Verbs—**1,** excite, affect, TOUCH, move; impress, strike, interest, animate, inspire, impassion, stir *or* warm the blood; awaken, evoke, provoke; raise, arouse, stir; fire, kindle, enkindle, set on fire, inflame, fan the flames, foster, heat, warm, foment, raise to fever heat.

2, stimulate, inspirit, stir up, work up, sharpen, whet, incite, give a fillip, put on one's mettle; stir or play on the feelings; touch a chord, go to one's heart, touch to the quick.

3, absorb, rivet the attention, prey on the mind, intoxicate; overwhelm, overpower, upset; turn one's head, carry *or* sweep off one's feet, fascinate, enrapture.

4, agitate, perturb, ruffle, fluster, shake, disturb, startle, shock, stagger; give one a turn; stun, irritate, sting; cut to the quick, try one's temper, pique, infuriate, madden, make one's blood boil, lash into fury, get on one's nerves.
5, be excited, flare up; work oneself up; seethe, boil, simmer, foam, fume, rage, rave; run amuck *or* mad, lose one's head. *Colloq.*, burst a blood vessel, have a fit.

Adjectives—**1,** excited, wrought up, on the *qui vive*, in a quiver, in a fever, in hysterics; black in the face, overwrought; hot, flushed, feverish; all atwitter; flaming, boiling, boiling over, seething, foaming (at the mouth), fuming, raging; wild, frantic, mad, distracted, beside oneself, out of one's mind *or* wits, ready to burst, stung to the quick.
2, exciting, warm, glowing, fervid, swelling, heart-stirring, thrilling; soul-stirring, agonizing, sensational, hysterical; overpowering, overwhelming, piquant, spicy, provocative, tantalizing.
3, excitable, irritable, irascible, impatient; feverish, hysterical; mettlesome, skittish; jumpy, nervous, jittery; tempestuous, impulsive, impetuous, ungovernable; demonstrative, fiery, hotheaded, enthusiastic, impassioned, fanatical, rabid.

Adverbs—excitedly, excitingly; with bated breath. *Colloq.*, in a dither, all agog.

Antonym, see INDIFFERENCE.

exclaim, *v.i.* cry out, shout, ejaculate, clamor, vociferate. See CRY.
exclude, *v.t.* bar, prohibit, preclude; reject; displace; keep *or* shut out; except; omit, leave out; eliminate; restrain, hinder, prevent; withhold; blackball, ostracize, boycott, excommunicate. See EJECTION.
exclusion, *n.* omission, rejection, debarring; exception; repudiation, ostracism, exile, banishment; dismissal, displacement, segregation, isolation; PROHIBITION; EJECTION. *Ant.*, see INCLUSION.
exclusive, *adj.* cliquish, clannish; closed; sole, unique; one and only, barring all others; excluding, exclusory, prohibitive; select, restrictive. See SECLUSION. *Ant.*, see SOCIALITY.

EXCRETION [299]

Nouns—**1,** excretion, discharge, emanation, exhalation, exudation, extrusion, secretion, effusion, extravasation, evacuation, dejection, defecation, EJECTION.
2, perspiration, sweat, saliva, spittle, rheum, sputum, spit, salivation, catarrh, diarrhea, *ejecta, excreta*, urine, feces, excrement; hemorrhage, bleeding, flux.
Verbs—excrete, eject, discharge, emit, evacuate, defecate; emanate, exhale, exude, perspire, sweat; cast off, shed.
Adjectives—excretive, excretory, ejective, eliminative; fecal, urinary; sweaty.

excruciating, *adj.* torturing, painful, agonizing, racking, acute. *Ant.*, see PLEASURE.
excursion, *n.* expedition, trip, sally, tour, outing, JOURNEY, jaunt; digression. See DEVIATION.
excuse, *v.t.* pardon, remit, overlook, condone, forgive, extenuate, justify; exonerate, absolve, acquit, exempt, free, apologize. See VINDICATION. *Ant.*, see RETALIATION, ACCUSATION.
execrable, *adj.* abominable, bad, detestable; poor, inferior, wretched. *Ant.*, see GOODNESS.
execute, *v.t.* perform, do, accomplish, make, administer, enforce, effect; finish, complete, fulfill; kill, put to death, behead, lynch, hang, gas, electrocute; seal, sign. See COMPLETION, PUNISHMENT.
executive, *n.* director, manager, official, administrator. *Colloq.*, boss. *Slang*, brass.
exemplify, *v.t.* typify; illustrate, explain, quote. See CONFORMITY. *Ant.*, see UNCONFORMITY.

EXEMPTION [927]

Nouns—exemption, FREEDOM, irresponsibility, immunity, liberty, license, release, exoneration, excuse, dispensation, exception, absolution, discharge, exculpation; RELEASE.

Verbs—exempt, release, acquit, discharge, remit; liberate, free, set at liberty, let off, pass over, spare, excuse, dispense with, give dispensation, license; stretch a point, absolve, forgive, exonerate.

Adjectives—1, exempt, free, at liberty, scot-free, released, unbound, unencumbered, irresponsible, unaccountable, not answerable, immune, privileged, excusable, allowable.

2, not having, devoid of, destitute of, without, unpossessed of, unblest with, exempt from, off one's hands; tax-free, untaxed, untaxable.

Antonym, see LIABILITY, DUTY.

EXERTION [686]

Nouns—1, exertion, ENERGY, effort, strain, tug, pull, stretch, struggle, bout, spurt, trouble, pains, endeavor.

2, gymnastics, exercise, athletics, calisthenics, acrobatics; training, sport, play, drill; ado.

3, labor, work, toil, task, travail, manual labor, sweat of one's brow, elbow grease, wear and tear, toil and trouble, yeoman work, uphill work, drudgery, slavery, heavy duty.

4, laborer, worker, toiler, drudge, slave; workhorse, packhorse, galley slave, Trojan.

Verbs—1, exert oneself, strive, strain, pull, tug, ply, struggle, try.

2, labor, work; toil, moil, sweat, plug, plod, drudge, slave; buckle down, dig in, bear down, wade into, come to grips; set one's shoulder to the wheel; work like a horse; burn the candle at both ends; keep one's nose to the grindstone; persevere, take pains, do one's best, strain every nerve, spare no pains, move heaven and earth, burn oneself out. *Slang*, sweat blood.

Adjectives—laboring; laborious; strained, toilsome, troublesome, wearisome, uphill, Herculean; hardworking, painstaking, strenuous, energetic.

Adverbs—laboriously, lustily; with might and main, with all one's might, tooth and nail, hammer and tongs, heart and soul; by the sweat of one's brow; energetically. *Colloq.*, like mad.

Antonym, see REPOSE.

exhale, *v.t.* breathe, expel, emanate, emit, expire, transpire, respire, blow. See EXCRETION, WIND.

exhaust, *v.t.* drain, empty. let out, deflate; weaken, deplete, overtire, prostrate, fag, FATIGUE; spend, impoverish, consume, use, expend; develop, finish, end. See COMPLETION, EJECTION. *Ant.*, see RECEIVING, RESTORATION.

exhibit, *v.t.* show, present, display, produce, demonstrate, stage, expose, evince; reveal; flaunt. See EVIDENCE, OSTENTATION, PRODUCTION. *Ant.*, see DESTRUCTION.

exhilarate, *v.t.* elate, exalt, inspirit; enliven, animate, cheer, make merry, invigorate, gladden. *Ant.*, see DEJECTION.

exile, *v.t.* expel, remove, banish, expatriate.

EXISTENCE [1]

Nouns—1, existence, LIFE, being, entity, *ens, esse*, subsistence, coëxistence, PRESENCE.

2, reality, actuality; positiveness, fact, matter of fact, stubborn fact, not a dream, no joke, sober reality, TRUTH, verity, actual existence.

Verbs—exist, be; have being, subsist, live, breathe; stand, obtain, be the case; occur, consist in, lie in, have place, prevail, endure, find oneself, vegetate, come or bring into existence; arise, begin; come forth, appear, become, be converted.

Adjectives—1, existing, existent, extant; in existence, current, prevalent.

2, real, actual, positive, absolute, authentic, true; substantial, substantive, enduring, well-founded.

Adverbs—actually, really, truly, positively, in fact, in point of fact, in reality, indeed, *de facto, ipso facto*.

Antonym, see NONEXISTENCE.

exit, *n.* departure; withdrawal; DEATH. See EGRESS. *Ant.,* see LIFE, INGRESS.
exorbitant, *adj.* excessive, immoderate, unreasonable; extravagant, expensive, DEAR. See GREATNESS. *Ant.,* see CHEAPNESS, LITTLENESS.
expand, *v.* widen, enlarge, extend, grow, INCREASE, swell, fill out; dilate, stretch, spread; aggrandize, distend, develop, amplify, spread out, magnify, inflate, stuff, pad, cram, exaggerate; fatten; blow up. *Ant.,* see DECREASE, CONTRACTION.
expanse, *n.* area, stretch, spread, reach, extent, breadth. See SPACE.
expansion, *n.* growth, spread, enlargement, inflation, extension; INCREASE, amplification; swelling. See SIZE. *Ant.,* see DECREASE.
expatiate, *v.i.* enlarge, descant, dilate, expand; rant. See LOQUACITY. *Ant.,* see CONTRACTION.

EXPECTATION [507]

Nouns—**1,** expectation, expectancy, anticipation, reckoning, calculation, foresight, PREDICTION, imminence, contingency; contemplation, lookout, prospect, perspective, horizon.
2, suspense, waiting, anxiety, apprehension, curiosity; HOPE, BELIEF, faith.
Verbs—expect, look for, look out for, look forward to; hope for, anticipate; have in prospect, keep in view, wait *or* watch for, keep a sharp lookout for, await; bide one's time; foresee, prepare for, predict, forestall, count upon, believe in, think likely.
Adjectives—**1,** expectant, expecting; open-mouthed, agape, all agog, on tenterhooks; ready, curious, eager, anxious, apprehensive.
2, expected, foreseen, in prospect, prospective in view, impending, imminent. *Colloq.,* on deck.
Adverbs—expectantly, on the watch, with bated breath, with ears pricked up, on edge.
Interjections—no wonder! of course!
Antonym, see DOUBT.

---

expedience, *n.* expediency, desirableness, desirability, advisability; eligibility, seemliness, fitness, utility, propriety, opportunism, opportunity. See USE.
expedition, *n.* haste, dispatch, promptness, speed, alacrity; JOURNEY, quest, tour, trip, jaunt, excursion; crusade, campaign. See ACTIVITY, WARFARE. *Ant.,* see INACTIVITY.
expel, *v.t.* eject, extrude, excrete, discharge, dispel, eliminate; exclude, remove, evict, dislodge, dispossess, oust; excommunicate; banish, exile, deport, expatriate. *Slang,* bounce. *Ant.,* see RECEIVING.
expend, *v.t.* spend, lay out, pay, pay out, disburse; USE, consume; exhaust; give; WASTE, use up. See PAYMENT. *Ant.,* see RECEIVING.
expenditure, *n.* expense(s), outlay, spending, PAYMENT, cost(s); disbursement, outgo, overhead; price; purchase(s). See USE, WASTE. *Ant.,* see RECEIVING.
experience, *v.t.* have, know, see, meet, encounter; undergo, suffer, brave, sustain; enjoy, realize, apprehend, understand. See OCCASION, FEELING, KNOWLEDGE, TASTE. *Ant.,* see IGNORANCE.
experiment, *n. & v.* —*n.* experimentation; essay, attempt; analysis; investigation; trial, test, check, assay, ordeal; empiricism, trial and error, feeler; trial balloon, test flight, speculation, random shot, leap *or* shot in the dark. *Colloq.,* dry run, milk run. —*v.i.* essay, try; prove, verify, test; grope, fumble, throw out a feeler, fish for, cast about for, explore, inquire. See INQUIRY, UNDERTAKING.
expert, *n. & adj.* —*n.* adept, connoisseur, virtuoso, master; master hand, top sawyer, prima donna, first fiddle, old hand; practiced eye, marksman, crack; conjuror; veteran, champion, ace; old stager *or* campaigner; genius, mastermind, tactician, strategist. *Slang,* sharp, shark, wizard, whiz. —*adj.* proficient, adept, apt, skilled, crack. *Ant.,* see UNSKILLFULNESS.
expire, *v.i.* exhale, breathe out, emit; die, perish; END, cease, terminate, stop. See DEATH, WIND. *Ant.,* see LIFE, BEGINNING.
explain, *v.t.* expound, solve, elucidate, resolve, fathom, account for; dem-

onstrate, construe, INTERPRET, define, describe, develop, detail, criticize, comment. See ANSWER. *Ant.*, see INQUIRY.

explicit, *adj.* express, written, unreserved, outspoken, plain, positive, clear, unambiguous, open, definite. See INFORMATION, EVIDENCE.

explode, *v.t.* destroy; burst, detonate, fire, discharge; reject; refute, expose, disprove. See NEGATION, VIOLENCE. *Ant.*, see EVIDENCE, MODERATION.

exploit, *v. & n.* —*v.t.* utilize, profit by; abuse, misapply. *Colloq.*, milk, work. See USE. —*n.* deed, act, feat, achievement. See COURAGE.

explore, *v.t.* seek, search, fathom, prospect, penetrate, range, examine, investigate, inquire into. See INQUIRY. *Ant.*, see ANSWER.

export, *n.* commodity, exportation. See EGRESS. *Ant.*, see INGRESS.

expose, *v.t.* disclose, reveal, divulge; unearth; unmask, denude, bare, uncover; exhibit, display; offer, submit; subject to, risk, weather, lay open, endanger, imperil; turn out, cast out, abandon; denounce, brand. See DANGER, DISAPPROBATION, DISCLOSURE, DIVESTMENT, EVIDENCE. *Ant.*, see SAFETY, APPROBATION, CONCEALMENT, CLOTHING.

exposition, *n.* explanation, exegesis, elucidation, commentary; show, exhibition; fair; statement, discourse; exposure, abandonment. See DISCLOSURE, INTERPRETATION, EVIDENCE, BUSINESS. *Ant.*, see CONCEALMENT.

expostulate, *v.i.* remonstrate, reason, dissuade; object, protest, rebuke. See ADVICE, DISAPPROBATION.

expound, *v.t.* state, express, set forth; explain, interpret, elucidate. See TEACHING.

express, *v.t.* squeeze, press out; extort; exude; represent, symbolize, show, demonstrate, reveal, denote, signify, delineate, exhibit, depict; state, tell, frame, enunciate, broach, expound, couch, utter, voice, communicate, speak; ship. See EVIDENCE, MEANING, SPEECH.

expurgate, *v.t.* bowdlerize; purge, purify, cleanse; emasculate, castrate, See CLEANNESS. *Ant.*, see UNCLEANNESS.

exquisite, *adj.* accurate, exact; fastidious, appreciative, discriminating; choice, selected, refined, rare; accomplished, perfected; intense, keen, SHARP, excellent, delicate, beautiful, matchless, dainty, charming, delightful. See BEAUTY, TASTE, GOODNESS, PLEASURE. *Ant.*, see UGLINESS, EVIL, PAIN.

extant, *adj.* surviving, existent. See EXISTENCE. *Ant.*, see NONEXISTENCE.

extemporaneous, *adj.* unpremeditated, spontaneous, extempore, improvised, impromptu, offhand, unprepared. See IMPULSE. *Ant.*, see PREPARATION.

extend, *v.t.* continue, lengthen, elongate, widen, enlarge, stretch, draw out, prolong, protract, expand, spread, broaden; increase; hold out, proffer. See INCREASE, LENGTH. *Ant.*, see CONTRACTION, SHORTNESS.

extenuate, *v.t.* excuse, forgive, pardon, mitigate, palliate; attenuate; diminish, weaken. See VINDICATION. *Ant.*, see RETALIATION, ACCUSATION, POWER.

EXTERIOR [220]

Nouns—**1,** exterior, exteriority, outwardness, externality, extraneousness, eccentricity, circumjacence.

2, outside, surface, superficies; skin (see COVERING), superstratum, facet, SIDE.

Verbs—be exterior, be outside, lie around, surround, encompass, environ, enclose, encircle, loop, gird, hem in.

Adjectives—**1,** exterior, external, outer, outmost, outermost, outward, round about, superficial, skin deep, eccentric, EXTRINSIC.

Adverbs—externally, outwardly, out, outer, without, outward(s); out-of-doors, in the open air, *al fresco.*

Antonym, see INTERIOR.

---

exterminate, *v.t.* abolish, destroy, annihilate; extirpate, eradicate, root out. See DESTRUCTION. *Ant.*, see PRODUCTION.

external, *adj.* EXTERIOR, outward, outer, outside, extraneous; foreign; perceptible, visible, physical, extraneous, superficial. *Ant.*, see INTERIOR.

extinct, *adj.* extinguished, quenched; exterminated, nonexistent, obsolete; died out, passed away, dead, gone. *Ant.*, see EXISTENCE.

extol, *v.t.* praise, applaud, commend, glorify; celebrate, exalt. See APPRO-
BATION. *Ant.,* see DISAPPROBATION.
extort, *v.t.* elicit, extract, draw, exact; wring, wrench, force; squeeze. See
ACQUISITION, STEALING. *Ant.,* see RESTORATION.
extra, *adj.* additional, accessory, spare, supplementary, redundant.

EXTRACTION [301]

Nouns—**1,** extraction, removal; elimination, extrication, eradication, evul-
sion; wrench, expression, squeezing; extirpation, extermination, EJECTION,
suction.
2, EVOLUTION, derivation, origin, ANCESTRY, DESCENT.
3, extractor, corkscrew, forceps, pliers; pump, pulmotor, vacuum cleaner.
Verbs—**1,** extract; draw, pull, tear *or* pluck out; wring from, wrench, extort,
root out, rout out, dig out; grub up, rake out, uproot, pull up; extirpate,
eradicate, eliminate, remove; express, squeeze out.
2, educe, elicit, evolve, extract, derive, bring forth. *Colloq.,* milk, pump.
Antonym, see ADDITION, INSERTION.

extraneous, *adj.* foreign, alien; ulterior, exterior, external, outlandish;
excluded, inadmissible, exceptional. *Ant.,* see RELATION.
extraordinary, *adj.* unusual, singular, uncommon, remarkable, phenom-
enal, abnormal; eminent, rare, notable. See GREATNESS, UNCONFORMITY.
Ant., see LITTLENESS, CONFORMITY.
extravagant, *adj.* profuse, PRODIGAL, lavish, excessive, extreme; wasteful,
profligate, rampant, wild; bombastic, fantastic; high, exorbitant, unreasonable; unreal, flighty, visionary; absurd, fanciful, grotesque. See GREAT-
NESS, IMAGINATION, ABSURDITY. *Ant.,* see CHEAPNESS, LITTLENESS.
extreme, *adj.* remote, utmost, farthest, last, final, ultra, radical, drastic;
excessive, inordinate, deep, intense, desperate, outrageous, immoderate,
greatest. See END, GREATNESS, REVOLUTION. *Ant.,* see BEGINNING, LITTLE-
NESS.
extricate, *v.t.* free, disentangle, loose, liberate, relieve, disengage. See
FREEDOM. *Ant.,* see RESTRAINT.
extrinsic, *adj.* extrinsical, objective, extraneous, foreign, adventitious, incidental, accidental, nonessential, subsidiary, contingent, outward, external.
Ant., INTRINSIC.
exude, *v.t. & i.* emit, discharge, ooze, leak, trickle, drain. See EGRESS.
Ant., see INGRESS.
exult, *v.i.* rejoice, vaunt, jubilate, gloat, triumph, glory. *Colloq.,* crow.
See BOASTING, REJOICING. *Ant.,* see LAMENTATION.
eye, *n. & v.* —*v.t.* watch, ogle, stare, view, observe, scrutinize, inspect. See
VISION. *Ant.,* see BLINDNESS. —*n.* orb, visual, organ; optic; eyesight, perception; VISION. *Ant.,* see BLINDNESS.

F

fable, *n.* parable, allegory, moral tale, apologue; myth, fiction, story. See
DESCRIPTION, FALSEHOOD. *Ant.,* TRUTH.
fabric, *n.* cloth, textile, material, tissue; structure, framework. See PRO-
DUCTION, FORM.
fabricate, *v.t.* build, construct, manufacture; invent, make up, trump up,
concoct. See PRODUCTION, IMAGINATION, FALSEHOOD, DECEPTION.
face, *n. & v.* —*n.* countenance, visage, physiognomy, lineaments, features;
FRONT, façade, facet, obverse; van, first line. *Slang,* mug, map, phiz, puss.
See APPEARANCE. —*v.t.* encounter, confront, veneer, plate, sheathe. See
OPPOSITION, COVERING.

FACILITY [705]

Nouns—facility, ease; easiness; capability; feasibility, practicability (see
CHANCE); flexibility, pliancy (see SOFTNESS); SMOOTHNESS; dexterity, SKILL;

plain sailing, smooth sailing; smooth water, fair wind; clear coast, clear stage; sinecure, child's play; full *or* free play (see FREEDOM); disencumbrance, disentanglement; LUBRICATION; PERMISSION. *Slang*, snap, soft snap, cinch, breeze, picnic.

Verbs—**1,** be easy, be feasible; go smoothly, run smoothly; have full *or* free play (see FREEDOM); work well; flow *or* swim with the stream; drift *or* go with the tide; see one's way; have it all one's own way; have the game in one's own hands; walk over the course; win in a walk, win hands down; take in one's stride; make light of, make nothing of; be at home in.

2, render easy, facilitate, smooth, ease; popularize; lighten, lighten the labor; free, clear; disencumber, disembarrass, disentangle, disengage; disobstruct, unclog, extricate, unravel; untie *or* cut the knot; disburden, unload, exonerate, emancipate, free from; humor; lubricate; relieve (see RELIEF); leave the matter open; give the reins to; make way for; open the door to; prepare the ground *or* way; smooth *or* clear the ground, way, path *or* road; pave the way, bridge over; permit (see PERMISSION); leave a loophole. *Colloq.*, grease the ways.

Adjectives—**1,** facile, simple, easy; feasible, practicable; easily managed *or* accomplished; within reach, accessible, easy of access, open to.

2, manageable, wieldy; tractable; submissive; yielding, ductile; pliant, soft; glib, slippery; smooth (see SMOOTHNESS); unburdened, disburdened, disencumbered, unembarrassed; exonerated; unloaded, unobstructed, in the clear, untrammeled; unrestrained, free; at ease, light; at home; in one's element. *Colloq.*, soft, nothing to it, easy as falling off a log, like water off a duck's back. *Slang*, easy as pie.

Adverbs—facilely, easily; readily, smoothly, swimmingly, on easy terms, without a hitch; single-handed; without striking a blow.

Antonym, see DIFFICULTY.

---

fact, *n.* reality, actuality, certainty; OCCURRENCE, event, phenomenon. See EXISTENCE. *Ant.*, FALSEHOOD.

faction, *n.* clique, combination, cabal, splinter party; sect, denomination; DISCORD, dissidence, dissension. See PARTY.

factor, *n.* COMPONENT, element, part, constituent, condition; AGENT.

factory, *n.* manufactory, mill, shop, works, WORKSHOP.

faculty, *n.* ability, aptitude, power, talent, knack; professorate, teaching staff.

fad, *n.* craze, rage, vogue; fancy, hobby. See CHANGEABLENESS.

fade, *v.i.* pale, dim, bleach, whiten; vanish, disappear; languish, wither, shrivel. See DIMNESS, COLORLESSNESS, NONEXISTENCE, DETERIORATION.

FAILURE [732]

Nouns—**1,** failure, unsuccessfulness, nonsuccess, nonfulfillment; dead failure, abortion, miscarriage; labor in vain; no go; inefficacy; vain attempt, abortive attempt, slip 'twixt cup and lip.

2, blunder, mistake, ERROR; fault, omission, miss, oversight, slip, trip, stumble, false *or* wrong step; *faux pas;* botch (see UNSKILLFULNESS); scrape, mess, fiasco, breakdown; mishap, misfortune, ADVERSITY; collapse, smash, blow, explosion; fall, downfall, ruin, perdition; wreck (see DESTRUCTION); deathblow; bankruptcy (see DEBT); wild-goose chase; losing game. *Slang*, flop, dud, washout, has-been.

3, repulse, rebuff, defeat, rout, overthrow, discomfiture; beating, drubbing; quietus; nonsuit; subjugation; checkmate, stalemate.

4, failure, also-ran, flash in the pan; victim; bankrupt. *Slang*, flop, goner.

Verbs—**1,** fail, be unsuccessful, not succeed; labor *or* toil in vain; lose one's labor; bring to naught, make nothing of; roll the stone of Sisyphus (see USELESSNESS); do by halves; lose ground (see REGRESSION); fall short of. *Slang*, flop, peter out, not get to first base.

2, miss, miss one's aim, miss the boat *or* bus, miss the mark; make a slip, blunder (see ERROR); make a mess of; miscarry; abort; go up like a rocket and come down like the stick; reckon without one's host, back the wrong horse.

3, limp, halt, hobble, slip, trip, stumble, miss one's footing; fall, tumble;

lose one's balance; overreach oneself; flounder, falter, stick in the mud, run aground; tilt at windmills; come up against a stone wall; burn one's fingers; break one's back; break down, sink, drown, founder, have the ground cut from under one; get into trouble, get into a mess *or* scrape; come to grief (see ADVERSITY); go to the wall, go under, go to the dogs, go to pot; bite the dust; be defeated; have the worst of it, lose the day; come off second best, throw in the sponge *or* towel, lose; succumb; not have a leg to stand on. *Colloq.*, flunk, flunk out, go to smash; cut one another's throats, have two strikes against one. *Slang*, fall down on, lay an egg, fold up.

4, come to nothing, end in smoke; fall through, fall flat; slip through one's fingers; hang *or* miss fire; collapse; topple down (see DESCENT); go to wrack and ruin (see DESTRUCTION); go amiss, go wrong, go hard with, go on a wrong tack; take a wrong turn; explode; dash one's hopes (see FAILURE); sow the wind and reap the whirlwind; jump out of the frying pan into the fire. *Slang*, the jig is up.

Adjectives—**1,** unsuccessful, failing; tripping, at fault; unfortunate (see ADVERSITY); abortive, stillborn; fruitless, bootless; ineffectual, ineffective; inefficient, impotent (see IMPOTENCE); inefficacious; lame, hobbling, insufficient (see INSUFFICIENCY); unavailing, useless (see USELESSNESS).

2, aground, grounded, swamped, stranded, cast away, wrecked, foundered, capsized, shipwrecked; nonsuited; foiled; defeated, vanquished, conquered; struck down, borne down, broken down, downtrodden; overborne, overwhelmed; all up with; lost, undone, ruined, broken, bankrupt (see DEBT); played out; done up, done for; dead beat, knocked on the head; destroyed (see DESTRUCTION); frustrated, crossed, unhinged, disconcerted, dashed; thrown off one's balance; unhorsed; in a sorry plight; hard hit; left in the lurch; stultified, befooled, dished, hoist by one's own petard; victimized, sacrificed; wide of the mark (see ERROR); thrown away (see WASTE); unattained; uncompleted. *Colloq.*, whipped, licked, out of the running. *Slang*, washed out.

Adverbs—unsuccessfully; to little or no purpose, in vain.

Antonym, see SUCCESS.

---

faint, *v. & adj.* —*v.i.* swoon; lose heart *or* courage; fail, fade, weaken. *Colloq.*, pass out. —*adj.* see WEARINESS, COLORLESSNESS, IMPOTENCE.

faintness, *n.* WEAKNESS; giddiness, dizziness; shakiness; DIMNESS (of color *or* light); LOWNESS (of sound), inaudibility; feebleness. *Ant.*, see LOUDNESS, POWER.

fair, *adj.* beautiful, handsome, goodlooking, pretty, comely; blond, light; unsullied, unblemished; pleasant, fine; impartial, equitable, just; moderate, passable; sunny, cloudless. See BEAUTY, COLORLESSNESS, DRYNESS, JUSTICE. *Ant.*, DARKNESS, UGLINESS, INJUSTICE.

fairy, *n.* fay, sprite, pixy, elf, brownie, gnome, leprechaun. See MYTHICAL DEITIES.

faith, *n.* trust, reliance, confidence, EXPECTATION; BELIEF, creed.

faithful, *adj.* loyal, devoted; conscientious, trustworthy; exact, lifelike. See PROBITY, OBEDIENCE. *Ant.*, FALSEHOOD, IMPROBITY.

fake, *n.* counterfeit, imposture, make-believe; impostor. See DECEPTION.

fall, *v.i. & n.* —*v.i.* plunge, drop, sink, tumble, topple; perish, be deposed; come to grief; happen, occur, take place; sin, misbehave, lapse. See DESCENT, DESTRUCTION, DETERIORATION. *Ant.*, SUCCESS. —*n.* slope, declivity; downfall, defeat, comedown; drop, slump; plunge, tumble, header; autumn.

fallacy, *n.* ERROR, untruth, misconception; false meaning. *Ant.*, TRUTH.

fallible, *adj.* unreliable, untrustworthy, dubious. See DOUBT.

fallow, *adj.* uncultivated, untilled, unsown. See NEGLECT.

FALSEHOOD [544]

Nouns—**1,** falsehood, falseness; falsity, falsification; DECEPTION, untruth; guile; lying, misrepresentation; mendacity, perjury, forgery, invention, fabrication.

2, perversion of truth, suppression of truth; perversion, distortion, false coloring; EXAGGERATION, prevarication, equivocation, shuffling, fencing, evasion, fraud; mystification, CONCEALMENT, simulation, IMITATION, dissimulation, dissembling; DECEPTION, deceit; sham, pretense, pretending, malingering. *Colloq.*, make-believe, play-acting, bunk.

3, lip service; hollowness; duplicity, double-dealing, insincerity, hypocrisy, cant, humbug; pharisaism; Machiavellianism; crocodile tears, mealy-mouthedness, quackery; charlatanism, charlatanry; cajolery, flattery; Judas kiss; perfidy, bad faith, unfairness (see IMPROBITY); artfulness (see SKILL); misstatement (see ERROR). *Colloq.*, front. *Slang*, four-flushing.

4, half-truth, white lie, pious fraud; irony.

5, liar, fibber, prevaricator, falsifier, perjurer; Ananias, Baron Munchausen.

Verbs—**1,** be false, speak falsely, tell a lie, lie, fib; lie like a trooper; forswear, perjure oneself, bear false witness; misstate, misquote, miscite, misreport, misrepresent; belie, falsify, pervert, distort; put a false construction upon, misinterpret; misinform, mislead; prevaricate, equivocate, quibble; fence, mince the truth, beat about the bush, blow hot and cold, play fast and loose; garble, gloss over, disguise, color, varnish, dress up, embroider; exaggerate. *Slang*, throw the bull.

2, invent, fabricate; trump up, get up; forge, hatch, concoct; romance, imagine (see IMAGINATION); cry "wolf!"; dissemble, dissimulate; feign, assume, put on, pretend, make believe; play false, play a double game; act a part; play a part; affect; simulate; palm off, pass off for; counterfeit, sham, make a show of; malinger; cant, play the hypocrite, deceive (see DECEPTION). *Colloq.*, let on, play-act, play possum, put on a front. *Slang*, four-flush, go through the motions.

Adjectives—false, deceitful, mendacious, unveracious, fraudulent, dishonest; faithless, truthless, trothless; unfair, uncandid, evasive; uningenuous, disingenuous; hollow, insincere, forsworn; canting; hypocritical, pharisaical; Machiavellian, two-faced, double-dealing; Janus-faced; smooth-faced, smooth-spoken, smooth-tongued, tongue in check; plausible; mealy-mouthed; affected; collusive, collusory, artful, CUNNING; perfidious (see IMPROBITY); spurious, deceptive (see DECEPTION); untrue, falsified.

Adverbs—falsely; slily, slyly, crookedly, *etc.*

Antonym, see TRUTH.

---

falter, *v.i.* hesitate, waver, hang back, vacillate; shuffle, stumble, totter; stammer. See DOUBT, SLOWNESS, SPEECH.

fame, *n.* REPUTE, renown, prestige, celebrity; honor, distinction, glory, eminence; notoriety. See IMPORTANCE. *Ant.*, DISREPUTE.

familiarity, *n.* intimacy, acquaintance, fellowship; KNOWLEDGE; informality, unconstraint; forwardness, impudence. See FRIEND, SOCIALITY, FREEDOM.

family, *n.* household; forefathers, children, descendants, lineage; clan, tribe, kindred; group, association, classification. See RELATION, ANCESTRY.

famine, *n.* starvation, hunger, scarcity. See INSUFFICIENCY. *Ant.*, SUFFICIENCY.

fan, *n. & v.t.* —*n.* fanner, blower, winnower, flabellum; ventilator. See WIND. —*v.t.* blow, winnow, cool, refresh, ventilate, stir up. See AIR, COLD. *Slang*, strike out.

fan, *n.* devotee, follower, enthusiast, supporter. See AMUSEMENT. *Slang*, rooter, addict.

fanatic, *n.* zealot, enthusiast, dogmatist.

fancy, *n., v.t. & adj.* —*n.* IMAGINATION; idea, CAPRICE, whim, preference; reverie, daydream. See DESIRE. —*v.t.* imagine; believe; like, DESIRE, take to. See BELIEF, SUPPOSITION, IMAGINATION. —*adj.* ornate, showy; superior, extravagant. See ORNAMENT, OSTENTATION.

fantastic, *adj.* bizarre, grotesque; imaginative, fanciful; extravagant, irrational, absurd. See IMAGINATION, ABSURDITY.

far, *adv. & adj.* —*adv.* remotely, distantly, widely, afar. —*adj.* remote, distant. See DISTANCE. *Ant.*, NEARNESS.

farce, *n.* buffoonery, ABSURDITY, burlesque; broad comedy, travesty.

farewell, *interj. & n.* —*interj.* good-by(e)! *vale!* aloha! *auf Wiedersehen! a rivederci! adieu! au revoir!.* *Slang*, so long. —*n.* parting, leave-taking, DEPARTURE, Godspeed, valedictory. *Ant.*, ARRIVAL.

farm, *n. & v.t.* —*n.* ranch, rancho, plantation, farmstead, grange. —*v.t.* cultivate, till. See AGRICULTURE.

farsighted, *adj.* hypermetropic, eagle-eyed; foresighted, longheaded, prudent, provident. See PREDICTION, VISION, PREPARATION.

farther, *adj. & adv.* —*adj.* more distant, further, additional. —*adv.* beyond, in addition, moreover.

fascination, *n.* charm, ATTRACTION, allurement, captivation, enamorment; bewilderment; enchantment, SPELL; obsession. See LOVE.

FASHION [852]

Nouns—**1,** fashion, style, *ton, bon ton,* society; good society, polite society; drawing room, civilized life, civilization; town; *haut monde, beau monde,* high life, court; world; *haute couture;* fashionable world; Vanity Fair; show, OSTENTATION.

2, manners, breeding, politeness, COURTESY; AIR, demeanor, APPEARANCE; *savoir faire;* gentlemanliness, gentility; decorum, propriety, convention, conventionality, punctilio; form, formality; etiquette, social usage, custom, HABIT; mode, vogue, go, rage, TASTE, distinction; dress (see CLOTHING). *Slang,* the last word, *le dernier cri.*

3, man *or* woman of fashion, man *or* woman of the world; height of fashion, leader of fashion; arbiter; upper ten thousand (see NOBILITY); élite. *Colloq.,* upper crust, the four hundred; socialite. *Slang,* café society.

4, See METHOD, PRODUCTION.

Verbs—be fashionable, be the rage; follow the fashion, conform to the fashion; go with the stream (see CONFORMITY); keep up appearances, behave oneself; set the style *or* fashion; bring into style *or* fashion. *Colloq.,* be in the swim.

Adjectives—fashionable, in fashion, modish, stylish, recherché; newfangled, *à la mode, comme il faut;* presentable; conventional, customary, genteel; well-bred, well-mannered, well-behaved, well-spoken; gentlemanly, ladylike; civil, polite, courteous (see COURTESY); polished, refined, thoroughbred, courtly; *distingué; dégagé,* suave, jaunty; dashing, fast.

Antonym, see VULGARITY.

---

fast, *v.i & adj.* —*v.i.* starve, diet, abstain. —*adj.* swift, speedy, fleet, quick, rapid; secure, firm, permanent, profound); wild, rakish. See VELOCITY, JUNCTION, CLOSURE, IMPURITY. *Ant.,* SLOWNESS.

fastening, *n.* lock, catch, clasp, latch; tether, bolt, chain. See RESTRAINT.

fastidious, *adj.* finicky, finical, per(s)nickety, squeamish; nice, overnice; particular, fussy, crotchety; delicate, meticulous, precise, exact, precious; clean, dainty, well-groomed; punctilious; thin-skinned, queasy; prudish, straitlaced; effeminate; namby-pamby; critical, discriminating, choosy; astute, keen. *Colloq.,* picky. See CLEANNESS, CARE. *Ant.,* see UNCLEANNESS, NEGLECT, DISORDER.

fasting, *n.* fast, abstention from food; voluntary hunger; rigid dieting; starvation, hunger, famishment; hunger strike; total abstinence (from food). *Ant.,* see FOOD, GLUTTONY.

fat, *adj.* plump, stout, corpulent, obese, portly, chubby; fertile, profitable, rich; greasy, unctuous. See SIZE. *Ant.,* LITTLENESS.

fatal, *adj.* deadly, lethal, mortal; fateful, critical. See KILLING.

fate, *n.* DESTINY, lot, fortune, doom, predestination, chance. See NECESSITY.

fates, *n.pl.* Moirai, Parcae, Norns. See NECESSITY, DESTINY.

father, *n.* sire, forefather, male parent; founder, patriarch; priest, pastor. See ANCESTRY, CLERGY. *Eccl.* The Father, God.

fatherland, *n.* homeland, native country, home. See ABODE.

fatigue, *v. & n.* —*v.* weary, tire, exhaust; jade, fag; bore, irk, wear; weaken, debilitate, overstrain, overtax, overwork. —*n.* tiredness, WEARINESS, exhaustion, lassitude, feebleness; exertion, strain; faintness, labor, work, toil, drudgery; jadedness, ennui, boredom. *Ant.,* see RESTORATION.

fault, *n.* failing, shortcoming, peccadillo; flaw, blemish, defect, imperfection; ERROR, slip, inadvertency; sin, venial sin, vice, minor vice. See GUILT, IMPERFECTION. *Ant.,* TRUTH.

favor, *n.* good will, esteem, APPROBATION, approval; partiality, bias, interest;

patronage, backing; concession, dispensation; kindness, service, good turn; token, badge. See AID, PERMISSION, GIVING.

favorite, *n. & adj.* —*n.* darling, pet; idol, hero, jewel, apple of one's eye; CHOICE, preference; spoiled child *or* darling; sweetheart, darling, dear one. *Colloq.*, teacher's pet, white-haired boy. See LOVE. *Ant.*, see HATE, RE-FUSAL.

fawn, *v.i.* cringe, grovel, toady, truckle, cower, ingratiate, curry favor, flatter. See SERVILITY.

FEAR [860]

Nouns—**1,** fear, fearfulness, timidity, timorousness, diffidence, want of confidence; solicitude, anxiety, worry, care, apprehension, apprehensiveness, misgiving; mistrust, DOUBT, suspicion, qualm; hesitation, irresolution; fright, alarm, dread, awe, terror, horror, dismay, consternation, panic, scare, stampede.
2, nervousness, restlessness, inquietude, disquietude; flutter, trepidation, fear and trembling, perturbation, tremor, quivering, shaking, trembling, palpitation, cold sweat; abject fear (see COWARDICE); funk, heartsinking, despondency, DESPAIR. *Colloq.*, buck fever, creeps, shivers, gooseflesh. *Slang,* jitters, heebie-jeebies.
3, intimidation, terrorism, reign of terror, THREAT, menace.
4, bugbear, bugaboo; scarecrow; hobgoblin, DEMON; nightmare, Gorgon, ogre; *bête noire.*
Verbs—**1,** fear, stand in awe of; be afraid; have qualms; be apprehensive, distrust, DOUBT; hesitate; falter, funk, cower, crouch; skulk (see COWARD-ICE); take fright, take alarm, panic, stampede.
2, start, wince, flinch, shy, shrink; fly, flee (see AVOIDANCE); tremble, shake; shiver, shiver in one's boots *or* shoes; shudder, flutter; tremble like a leaf *or* an aspen leaf, quake, quaver, quiver, quail; grow *or* turn pale; blench, stand aghast.
3, inspire *or* excite fear *or* awe; raise apprehensions; alarm, startle, scare, cry "wolf," disquiet, dismay; fright, frighten; affright, terrify; astound; frighten out of one's wits; awe; strike terror; appal(l), unman, petrify, horrify; make one's flesh creep, make one's hair stand on end, make one's blood run cold, make one's teeth chatter; take away one's breath; make one tremble; haunt; prey *or* weigh on the mind.
4, put in fear, terrorize, intimidate, cow, daunt, overawe, abash, deter, discourage; browbeat, bully; threaten (see WARNING), menace.
Adjectives—**1,** fearing, frightened, in fear, in a fright, afraid, fearful; timid, timorous, chicken-hearted; nervous, diffident, coy, faint-hearted, tremulous, shaky, afraid of one's shadow, apprehensive, restless, fidgety.
2, aghast; awestricken, horror-stricken, terror-stricken, panic-stricken; frightened to death, white as a sheet; pale as death, pale as ashes, pale as a ghost; breathless, in hysterics. *Colloq.*, yellow. *Slang,* chicken.
3, inspiring fear, alarming; formidable, redoubtable; perilous (see DANGER); portentous, ominous; fearful, dreadful, fell; dire, direful; shocking, terrible, terrifying, terrific; tremendous; horrid, horrible, horrific; ghastly; awful, awe-inspiring.
Adverbs—in fear, fearfully, with fear and trembling, with the tail between the legs.

Antonyms, see HOPE, COURAGE.

---

fearless, *adj.* bold, brave, courageous, dauntless, gallant, daring, valorous, valiant, intrepid. See COURAGE. *Ant.*, CARE, COWARDICE.
feasible, *adj.* practicable, possible, workable. See CHANCE. *Ant.*, see DIF-FICULTY.
feast, *n.* banquet, spread, repast; holiday, holyday, festival. See FOOD, RITE, SUFFICIENCY. *Ant.*, INSUFFICIENCY.
feat, *n.* deed, gest, accomplishment, exploit; stunt. See ACTIVITY, COURAGE, DIFFICULTY.
feather, *n.* plume, plumage, down, aigrette; kind, sort, variety. See COVER-ING.

feature, *n.* lineament, aspect; trait, peculiarity, property; something note-worthy, outstanding characteristic; presentation, film, story. See FORM, INDICATION, IMPORTANCE.

federation, *n.* league, union, confederacy, association, alliance. See COÖP-ERATION, PARTY.

fee, *n.* PAYMENT, pay; COMPENSATION, emolument; assessment, dues, tax; gratuity, tip.

feeble, *adj.* weak, strengthless, nerveless; enervated, weakened, debilitated, anemic; infirm, sickly; languid, drooping; frail, faint; flimsy; puny; tot-tering, doddering; dim, indistinct, poor; spiritless, lifeless, flat, tame, watery; irresolute, uncertain, weak-willed, indecisive; unenthusiastic, apa-thetic; indefinite, blurred. See IMPOTENCE, DIMNESS. *Ant.,* see POWER, HEALTH.

feed, *v.* eat, dine, consume; graze, devour; nourish, nurture, bait, graze; supply, provide, furnish. See FOOD.

FEELING [821]

Nouns—**1,** feeling, sensation, sentience, emotion, SENSIBILITY, sensitivity; endurance, tolerance, sufferance, experience, response; PITY, pathos, sympathy, LOVE; impression, inspiration, affection, tenderness; warmth, glow, unction, gusto, vehemence; fervor, fervency; heartiness, cordiality; earnestness, eagerness; ardor, élan, zeal, passion, enthusiasm, verve, furor(e), fanaticism; EXCITEMENT; excitability, ecstasy; PLEASURE.

2, blush, suffusion, flush; tingling, thrill; turn, shock; AGITATION; quiver, heaving, flutter, flurry, fluster, twitter, tremor; throb, throbbing; lump in the throat; pulsation, palpitation, panting; trepidation, perturbation; pother, stew, ferment.

3, TOUCH, tangibility, contact, manipulation.

Verbs—**1,** feel, receive an impression; be impressed with; entertain, harbor *or* cherish feeling; respond; catch fire, catch infection; enter the spirit of.

2, bear, suffer, support, sustain, endure, abide, experience, TASTE, prove; labor *or* smart under; bear the brunt of, brave, stand.

3, swell, glow, warm, flush, blush, change color, mantle; turn color, turn pale, turn black in the face; tingle, thrill, heave, pant, throb, palpitate, go pit-a-pat, tremble, quiver, flutter, twitter; shake, be agitated, be excited, look blue, look black; wince, draw a deep breath. *Colloq.,* blow off steam.

4, TOUCH; handle, finger, paw; fumble, grope.

Adjectives—**1,** feeling, sentient, sensuous; sensorial, sensory; emotive, emotional; tactile, tactual, tangible, palpable.

2, warm, quick, lively, smart, strong, sharp, acute, cutting, piercing, in-cisive; keen, razor-sharp; trenchant, pungent, racy, piquant, poignant, caustic.

3, impressive, deep, profound, indelible; pervading, penetrating, absorbing; deep-felt; heartfelt; swelling, soul-stirring, electric, thrilling, rapturous, ecstatic.

4, earnest, wistful, eager, breathless; fervent, fervid; gushing, passionate, warmhearted, hearty, cordial, sincere, zealous, enthusiastic, flowing, ardent, burning, consumed with, red-hot, fiery, flaming; seething, boiling, boiling over; rabid, raving, feverish, fanatical, hysterical; impetuous, excitable.

5, impressed by, moved by, touched, affected, seized by, imbued with; de-voured by; wrought up, excited, struck all of a heap; rapt, in a quiver, enraptured.

Adverbs—feelingly, with feeling, heart and soul, from the bottom of one's heart, at heart, *con amore, con brio,* heartily, devoutly, head over heels.

Antonym, see INSENSIBILITY.

---

feign, *v.t.* simulate, pretend, counterfeit, sham. See FALSEHOOD, AFFECTA-TION.

felicitous, *adj.* happy, well-chosen, pertinent, apt, pat, neat. See AGREE-MENT, ELEGANCE.

fell, *v.t.* bring down, cut down, chop down, drop.

fellow, *n.* person, man, boy; comrade, associate, colleague; compeer, equal; SCHOLAR. *Colloq.,* chap, guy. See MANKIND, FRIEND, EQUALITY, SOCIALITY.

FEMALE [374]

Nouns—**1,** female, womankind, womanhood, femininity, muliebrity; fair sex, weaker sex. *Slang*, femme, frail, dame, skirt, broad, sister, tomato.

2, madam, madame, mistress, Mrs., lady, donna, belle, matron, dowager, goody, gammer; good woman, goodwife; squaw; wife (see MARRIAGE); matronhood; miss, mademoiselle; girl (see YOUTH).

3, hen, bitch, sow, doe, roe, mare, she-goat, nanny-goat, ewe, cow; lioness, tigress; vixen.

Adjectives—female, feminine, womanly, ladylike, matronly, maidenly; womanish, effeminate, unmanly.

Antonym, see MALE.

feminist, *n.* -suffragist, suffragette. See FEMALE.

fence, *n.* barrier, barricade, wall, stockage, paling, hedge, railing. *Slang*, receiver (of stolen goods). See INCLOSURE, EVILDOER.

ferment, *n. & v.i.* —*n.* yeast, leaven; uproar, turmoil, agitation. See ACTIVITY. —*v.i.* effervesce, work, raise, seethe.

ferocity, *adj.* fierceness, savagery, brutality, cruelty. See MALEVOLENCE. *Ant.*, see MODERATION.

fertile, *adj.* prolific, productive, fruitful, rich; creative, inventive. See PRODUCTION, IMAGINATION.

fertilizer, *n.* manure, compost, guano; soil enricher.

fervor, *n.* intenseness, enthusiasm, ardor, passion, zeal. See ACTIVITY, FEELING.

festivity, *n.* CELEBRATION, merrymaking; gayety, jollity. See AMUSEMENT.

fetch, *v.t.* retrieve, bring, carry; heave, deal, yield.

fever, *n.* pyrexia, frenzy, delirium. See DISEASE, INSANITY.

few, *adj.* not many, little; scant, scanty, meager, scarce, rare; INFREQUENT; several, two *or* three, hardly any. See LITTLENESS, RARITY.

fiber, *n.* filament, thread, strand; shred; TEXTURE, structure.

fickleness, *n.* capriciousness, instability, inconstancy. See CHANGEABLENESS. *Ant.*, see PROBITY, DURABILITY.

fiction, *n.* fabrication, falsehood; romance, myth, hypothesis. See FALSEHOOD, DESCRIPTION. *Ant.*, see TRUTH.

fidelity, *n.* faithfulness, reliability, loyalty; exactness. See TRUTH, PROBITY. *Ant.*, see IMPROBITY.

fidget, *v.i.* be restless, be impatient, toss, twitch, twiddle. See AGITATION.

field, *n.* clearing, grassland; expanse, range, plot; playground, links, court, airport, aerodrome, ARENA; scope, sphere, realm. See REGION, AMUSEMENT, BUSINESS.

fiendish, *adj.* diabolical, devilish, inhuman, cruel. See DEMON, MALEVOLENCE.

fierce, *adj.* ferocious, truculent; tigerish, savage; intense, violent; aggressive, bellicose; vehement. See VIOLENCE, WARFARE, EXCITEMENT. *Ant.*, see MODERATION.

fiery, *adj.* impetuous, hot-tempered, fervid; irritable; blazing, glowing; inflamed. See HEAT, EXCITEMENT, IRASCIBILITY.

fight, *n.* battle, affray, brawl, quarrel; contest, struggle; pugnacity. See CONTENTION. *Slang*, scrap, mill.

FIGURATIVE [521]

Nouns—figurativeness, figure of speech; metaphor; way of speaking, colloquialism; phrase; figure, trope, metonymy, enallage, catachresis, synecdoche, autonomasia; irony; image, imagery; metalepsis, type, anagoge, simile, personification, allegory, apologue, parable, fable; allusion, adumbration; application; hyperbole, EXAGGERATION.

Verbs—speak figuratively, employ figures of speech, employ metaphor; personify, allegorize, adumbrate; apply, allude to.

Adjectives—figurative, metaphorical, catachrestic, typical, parabolic, symbolic, allegorical, allusive, anagogical; ironical; colloquial.

Adverbs—figuratively, metaphorically; so to speak, so to say; as it were; in a manner of speaking.

Antonym, see MEANING, LITERAL.

figure 142

figure, *n. & v.* —*n.* FORM, shape, configuration, outline; body; REPRESENT-ATION, image, effigy; APPEARANCE; pattern, diagram; figure of speech (see FIGURATIVE); emblem, symbol, NUMBER, digit; figurehead; cast, bust, statue. —*v.* ornament, decorate; symbolize, represent, signify, delineate, embody; imagine, conceive, picture; draw, outline; compute, calculate, do sums; appear, perform, act; cut a figure, matter; stand out.

FILAMENT [205]

Nouns—**1,** filament, line; fiber, fibril; funicle, vein, hair, capillament, capillary, cilium, tendril, gossamer; hairline.
2, string, thread, cotton, sewing silk, twine, twist; whipcord, tape, ribbon, cord, rope, yarn, hemp, oakum, jute.
3, strip, shred, slip, spill, list, band, fillet, ribbon; roll, lath, splinter, shiver, shaving; cable, wire, cord, line.
Adjectives—filamentous, filaceous, filar, filiform; fibrous, fibrilous; threadlike, wiry, stringy, ropy; capillary, capilliform; funicular, wire-drawn; anguilliform; flagelliform; hairy, ciliate.

file, *n. & v.t.* —*n.* ARRANGEMENT, classification; LIST, dossier, record, catalogue, inventory. —*v.t.* classify, arrange, store; catalogue, record; submit, deliver. See STORE.
filial, *adj.* dutiful; sonlike, daughterly. See DESCENT.
fill, *v.t.* make complete, load, pervade, permeate; plug, cork; occupy, serve well, satisfy. See COMPLETION, SUFFICIENCY, PRESENCE, CLOSURE, BUSINESS.
film, *n.* coating, membrane; haze, blur, scum. See COVERING.
filth, *n.* dirt, ordure; obscenity. See UNCLEANNESS, IMPURITY. *Ant.,* see CLEANNESS.
final, *adj.* last, terminal, ultimate; decisive. See END, COMMAND.
find, *v.t.* discover, detect, espy; acquire, get, gain, obtain; learn, ascertain, perceive; provide; decide. See ACQUISITION, DISCLOSURE. *Ant.,* see LOSS.
fine, *n., v.t. & adj.* —*n.* PENALTY, forfeit, amercement. —*v.t.* amerce, mulct, penalize. —*adj.* pure, superior; admirable, excellent; small, tiny, slender; flimsy, delicate; worthy, estimable; skilled, accomplished; refined, polished; subtle, nice; keen, sharp; fair, pleasant. See GOODNESS, BEAUTY, LITTLE-NESS, NARROWNESS.
finger, *n. & v.t.* —*n.* digit; pointer. See FEELING, DIRECTION. —*v.t.* TOUCH, toy with; thumb, feel.
finish, *v.t. & n.* —*v.t.* END, terminate, complete, conclude; perfect, polish. See COMPLETION. —*n.* COMPLETION, conclusion; SKILL, polish, surface, patina.
fire, *n. & v.t.* —*n.* flame, blaze, conflagration, holocaust; enthusiasm, verve. See HEAT, FEELING. —*v.t.* kindle, ignite; shoot, detonate; inspire, arouse. *Slang,* dismiss, discharge. See HEAT, PROPULSION, POWER.
firm, *adj. & n.* —*adj.* immovable, secure; unalterable, steadfast; solid, hard; steady, vigorous; resolute, determined. See STABILITY, PROBITY, DENSITY, RESOLUTION. *Ant.,* see CHANGEABLENESS, SOFTNESS. —*n.* partnership, company, business house. See PARTY.
first, *adj. & adv.* —*adj.* earliest, original, prime; leading, chief, fundamental. See BEGINNING, FRONT. *Ant.,* END. —*adv.* firstly, originally, at first; before, ahead; sooner, rather. See BEGINNING, PRIORITY, CHOICE.
fish, *v. & n.* —*v.* angle; pull out, dredge, seek, solicit. See PURSUIT, DESIRE. —*n.* See ANIMAL.
fissure, *n.* cleft, chink, OPENING, crack, rift, breach.
fit, *n., v. & adj.* —*n.* CAPRICE, whim, fancy, notion; paroxysm, convulsion, seizure. See AGITATION. —*v.* equip, furnish, outfit; adapt; grace, beautify; accommodate; clothe; suit, meet, conform. See AGREEMENT, EQUALITY, PREPARATION, BEAUTY, CLOTHING. —*adj.* appropriate, suitable, fitting, proper; expedient, advantageous; vigorous, well, sound. See AGREEMENT, OCCASION, HEALTH. *Ant.,* see DISAGREEMENT.
fix, *v.t.* stabilize, establish; repair, adjust, mend; settle, decide; place. See STABILITY, RESTORATION, AGREEMENT, LOCATION. *Ant.,* see DISJUNCTION.
flabby, *adj.* limp, soft, flaccid. See SOFTNESS. *Ant.,* see HARDNESS.
flag, *n. & v.i.* —*n.* banner, pennant, ensign, standard; iris; flagstone. See

INDICATION. —*v.i.* droop, pine, languish. See INACTIVITY, DISCONTINUITY.

flagrant, *adj.* glaring; notorious; outrageous, shocking. See EVIDENCE, EVIL.

flame, *n.* blaze, fire; excitement, passion, zeal. See HEAT, EXCITEMENT. *Ant.*, see COLD.

flank, *n. & v.t.* —*n.* SIDE, wing (of an army). —*v.t.* be beside, go around a side. *Ant.*, see OPPOSITION.

flap, *n. & v.i.* —*n.* tab, fly, lap, tag. —*v.i.* swing, sway, flop, beat; wave. See MOTION.

flash, *v.i.* flare, blaze; burst, streak; gleam, scintillate; retort. See LIGHT, WIT

flat, *adj. & n.* —*adj.* plane, level, even, flush, HORIZONTAL; flat as a flounder *or* pancake. —*n.* plain, prairie. *Colloq.*, puncture, blowout. See SMOOTHNESS.

flatness, *n.* horizontality, levelness; level; SMOOTHNESS, evenness; plane surface; LOWNESS; dullness, SLOWNESS, lifelessness, tameness, tastelessness; monotony, staleness, vapidity, deadness; absoluteness, bluntness, forthrightness, positiveness, directness. *Ant.*, see CONCAVITY, CONVEXITY, HEIGHT, ROUGHNESS.

flatter, *v.t.* praise, compliment, adulate, blandish; cajole, beguile. See FLATTERY, DECEPTION. *Slang*, jolly. *Colloq.*, butter up, softsoap. *Ant.*, see DETRACTION.

flattery, *n.* sycophancy, toadyism; adulation; cajolery, wheedling; coaxing; blandishment, fawning, obsequiousness, SERVILITY. *Colloq.*, buncombe, soft soap, oil, buttering up, blarney, baloney. See DECEPTION. *Ant.*, see DETRACTION.

flaunt, *v.t.* parade, display; brandish. See OSTENTATION.

flavor, *n.* TASTE, seasoning, savor. *Ant.*, FLATNESS.

flaw, *n.* IMPERFECTION, defect, fault, mar, crack; ERROR, mistake; gust, squall, flurry. See WIND. *Ant.*, see PERFECTION.

flee, *v.i.* decamp, run away, fly, abscond. See AVOIDANCE.

fleece, *v.t.* swindle, despoil, rob, strip. See STEALING, DECEPTION.

fleet, *n. & adj.* —*n.* navy; flotilla, squadron, argosy, armada. See SHIP, COMBATANT. —*adj.* swift, speedy, nimble; transient, brief. See VELOCITY, TRANSIENTNESS. *Ant.*, see SLOWNESS.

flesh, *n.* animal tissue, meat, pulp; MANKIND, materiality, carnality; blood relative. See FOOD, RELATION.

flexible, *adj.* pliant, limber, lithe, supple, adaptable. See SOFTNESS. *Ant.*, see HARDNESS.

flicker, *v.i.* waver, flutter, quiver, blink. See CHANGEABLENESS, LIGHT.

flight, *n.* decampment, hegira, ESCAPE, elopement; course, onrush; covey, flock, shower, volley; wing, squadron. See AVOIDANCE, MOTION, ASSEMBLAGE.

flimsy, *adj.* sleazy, gossamer, fragile; tenuous, unsubstantial; feeble, weak. See IMPOTENCE, RARITY. *Ant.*, see DENSITY, POWER.

flinch, *v.i.* wince, shrink, RECOIL. See AVOIDANCE, COWARDICE.

fling, *v.t.* throw, cast, hurl, sling. See PROPULSION.

flippant, *adj.* pert, impertinent, disrespectful; thoughtless, frivolous. *Slang*, fresh. *Colloq.*, flip.

flirt, *n. & v.i.* —*n.* coquette, philanderer. See INSOLENCE, ENDEARMENT. *Slang*, vamp. —*v.i.* coquet, philander, dally; jerk, fling, throw, toss.

flit, *v.i.* fly, dart, decamp, dash off, take wing, hurry away. See DEPARTURE, MOTION.

float, *v.* glide, drift, be wafted, hover, soar, be buoyed up; ferry, ship, raft; launch. See TRAVEL, STABILITY.

flock, *n.* drove, herd; covey, flight, bevy; congregation. See MULTITUDE.

flood, *n.* deluge, inundation; torrent, freshet; cloudburst, spate; superabundance. See SUFFICIENCY, WATER.

floor, *n.* flooring, deck, pavement; story, level; rostrum. See SUPPORT, RECEPTACLE.

flounder, *v.i.* wallow, welter, struggle, stagger, fumble, grope. See DOUBT, UNSKILLFULNESS.

flourish, *v. & n.* —*v.* wave, wield, flaunt, brandish; grow, prosper, thrive.

See VEGETABLE, PROSPERITY, AGITATION. —*n.* ornamental stroke; fanfare; bold gesture.

flow, *v.i.* run, glide, trickle, stream, sweep along; issue. See MOTION, WATER.

flower, *n.* bloom, blossom, posy; élite, elect, best, pick; ORNAMENT. See VEGETABLE, GOODNESS.

flowing, *adj.* running, gliding; fluent, graceful, smooth; loose, billowy. See WATER, ELEGANCE.

fluctuate, *v.i.* alternate, wave, vacillate, vary, shift. See CHANGEABLENESS. *Ant.,* see STABILITY.

fluent, *adj.* flowing, graceful, voluble. See ELEGANCE, LOQUACITY.

fluid, *n. & adj.* liquid; gas, vapor; juice, sap, lymph; plasma, blood, gore; ichor; solution, decoction, brew. —*adj.* fluent; flowing, liquid; plastic; sappy, succulent, juicy; watery, serous; mobile. See WATER. *Ant.,* SOLID.

fluidity, *n.* liquidity; fluence; CHANGEABLENESS, mobility; plasticity. See MOTION, SOFTNESS. *Ant.,* see DENSITY, STABILITY.

flurry, *n. & v.t.* —*n.* squall, gust, scud, blast; hubbub, ferment. See WIND, ACTIVITY. —*v.t.* ruffle, excite, fluster. See AGITATION.

flush, *v. & n.* —*v.* blush, redden; rinse; start, rouse. See COLOR, CLEANNESS. —*n.* blush, redness; elation, thrill; gush, rush. See HEAT, FEELING, WATER.

flutter, *v.* flicker, tremble, flap, shake, whip; bustle, fidget, twitter, quiver; agitate, ruffle. See AGITATION, HASTE, EXCITEMENT.

fly, *v.i.* soar, wing, aviate; float, wave; speed, bolt, dart; flee, decamp, vamoose, disperse, scatter. See AVIATION, VELOCITY, AVOIDANCE, ESCAPE.

foam, *n. & v.i.* —*n.* froth, suds, lather, spume. —*v.i.* froth, spume. See CLOUDINESS.

focus, *n. & v.* —*n.* point; focal *or* central point; concentration, convergence; center, hub; core, heart, nucleus; sharpness (*Photog.*). See MIDDLE, VISION. —*v.* concentrate, converge; centralize, contract; rally, gather, meet.

foe, *n.* ENEMY, adversary, antagonist, opponent. *Ant.,* see FRIEND.

fog, *n.* mist, smog, vapor, haze, cloud; uncertainty, obscurity. See CLOUDINESS.

foil, *v.t. & n.* —*v.t.* frustrate, baffle, balk, circumvent. See DISAPPOINTMENT. *Ant.,* see AID. —*n.* contrast, setoff; leaf, sheet (of metal); dueling sword. See OPPOSITION, LAYER, ARMS.

fold, *n. & v.* —*n.* crease; bend, lapping, plait; wrapping, wrap; wrinkle, corrugation; flap, lapel, turnover; gather, pleat, ruffle, flounce; crow's-feet; furrow; pen, kraal, corral (see INCLOSURE). —*v.* double (over); crease, bend; swathe, swaddle, wrap; wrinkle, furrow; gather, pleat; hug, clasp, embrace; envelop; enfold. See ROUGHNESS. *Ant.,* see SMOOTHNESS.

foliage, *n.* leafage, verdure. See VEGETABLE.

folk, *n.* people, commonalty, race; kin. See MANKIND, POPULACE.

follow, *v.* go *or* come after; succeed; tread on the heels of; come *or* be next; pursue (see PURSUIT); attend, associate with, go with, accompany; adhere to, SUPPORT; obey, heed; copy, imitate, use as a model; practice; ensue, result, be the outcome of. See SEQUENCE. *Ant.,* see PRIORITY.

following, *n.* followers, supporters, adherents; attendance, train, retinue. See ACCOMPANIMENT, AID. *Ant.,* see OPPOSITION.

folly, *n.* See ABSURDITY, FOOL, RASHNESS. *Ant.,* see KNOWLEDGE.

fond, *adj.* affectionate, loving tender; foolish, doting. See LOVE.

FOOD [298]

Nouns—**1,** food, aliment, nourishment, nutriment; sustenance, nurture, subsistence, provender, fodder, provision, ration, keep, commons, board; fare, cheer; diet, regimen; bread, staff of life; prey; forage, pasture, pasturage; comestibles, eatables, victuals, edibles; meat, viands; delicacy, dainty; fleshpots; festive board; ambrosia; good cheer; hearty meal. *Slang,* grub, chow.

2, meal, repast, feed, spread; mess; dish, plate, course; refreshment, entertainment; refection, collation, picnic; feast, banquet; breakfast; *déjeuner,* lunch, luncheon; dinner, supper, snack, dessert; potluck, *table d'hôte;* table, cuisine, bill of fare, menu. *Colloq.,* brunch.

3, meat, joint, roast, *pièce de résistance, entrée, hors d'œuvre;* hash, stew, ragout, fricassee; pottage, potage, broth, soup, consommé, purée; pie,

pasty, *vol-au-vent;* pudding, omelet; pastry; sweets; CONDIMENT.
4, drink, beverage, liquor, nectar, broth, soup; potion, dram, draught; nip, sip, sup, gulp. *Colloq.*, swig, pull, soft drink. *Slang*, swill.
5, wine, spirits, liquor, liqueur, cocktail, beer, ale; grog, toddy, flip, punch, negus, cup, wassail; gin, whisk(e)y (see DRUNKENNESS); coffee, chocolate, cocoa, tea. *Slang*, hair of the dog (that bit one).
6, eating, ingestion, mastication, manducation, rumination; GLUTTONY; mouth, jaws, mandible, chops; drinking, potation, draught, libation; carousal (see AMUSEMENT); DRUNKENNESS.
Verbs—**1,** eat, feed, fare, devour, swallow, take; gulp, bolt, snap; fall to; despatch, dispatch; take down, get down, gulp down; lay in, tuck in; lick, pick, peck; gormandize (see GLUTTONY); bite, champ, munch, crunch, chew, masticate, nibble, gnaw; live on; feed on, batten on, fatten on, feast upon; browse, graze, crop; regale, carouse; eat heartily, do justice to; banquet; break bread, break one's fast; breakfast, lunch, dine, take tea, sup. *Colloq.*, put away; drink like a fish; come and get it! soup's on!
2, drink, drink in, drink up, drink one's fill; quaff, sip, sup; lap; wash down; tipple (see DRUNKENNESS).
Adjectives—eatable, edible, esculent, comestible, alimentary; cereal; dietetic; culinary; nutritive, nutritious; succulent; potable, bibulous; omnivorous, carnivorous, herbivorous, graminivorous.

---

fool, *n. & v.* —*n.* buffoon, jester, clown, harlequin, zany, merry-andrew; idiot, nitwit, halfwit, booby, num(b)skull, oaf, goose, blunderer, ninny, nincompoop, blockhead, dunce, simpleton; sucker, dupe, butt. *Slang*, sap, chump, bonehead, fathead, meathead, marblehead, knucklehead, jackass, jerk, ass, boob, dope. —*v.* delude, cheat, dupe, gull, deceive; see DECEPTION. *Slang*, horse around.
foolhardy, *adj.* daring, brash, reckless, venturesome. See RASHNESS. *Ant.* see CARE.
foolish, *adj.* silly, fatuous; unwise, ill-considered; ridiculous, nonsensical, absurd. See ABSURDITY.
foot, *n.* BASE, bottom, footing; hoof, paw; foot soldiers, infantry. See SUPPORT, COMBATANT.
fop, *n.* dandy, dude, swell, buck, blade, gay blade, coxcomb, macaroni; exquisite. *Slang*, toff, snappy dresser, Dapper Dan, Beau Brummell, clotheshorse. See AFFECTATION, OSTENTATION. *Ant.* see DISORDER.
forbid, *v.t.* prohibit, inhibit, interdict, ban, taboo. See RESTRAINT.
force, *n.* COMPULSION, coercion; STRENGTH, brawn, might; MEANING, effect; troops, soldiery, army. See COMBATANT.
fore, *adj.* foremost; former, prior, previous. See FRONT, PRIORITY.
foreboding, *n.* portent; presentiment, premonition, apprehension. See PREDICTION.
forecast, *v.t.* predict, divine, prognosticate; foretell, presage, portend. See PREDICTION.
forefathers, *n.* ancestors, forebears, sires, progenitors. See ANCESTRY.
foregoing, *adj.* preceding, previous, former, aforesaid. See PRIORITY. *Ant.*, see SEQUENCE.
foreign, *adj.* alien, strange, exotic; extraneous, unrelated. *Ant.*, see INHABITANT.
foremost, *adj.* leading, first, precedent; chief, best, principal. See BEGINNING.
forerunner, *n.* precursor, predecessor; harbinger; herald, announcer, John the Baptist; leader, vanguard, scout, picket. See PRIORITY.
foresight, *n.* providence, forethought, prudence, PREPARATION; foreknowledge, prescience; anticipation; clairvoyance, second sight; prevision; foreboding, premonition, presentiment; foretaste, preview; foreshadowing, foretelling, forecasting, prophecy, prophetic vision. See EXPECTATION, FUTURITY.
forest, *n.* wood, woods, tall timber, timberland, woodland; grove, copse, thicket, coppice. See VEGETABLE.
foretell, *v.t.* presage, portend; forecast, prognosticate, predict. See PREDICTION.

forethought, *n.* prudence, providence; premeditation, anticipation. See
PREPARATION.

forever, *adv.* always, ever, eternally; incessantly, unceasingly. See DURA-
BILITY.

forfeit, *n.* PENALTY, fine. See LOSS.

forge, *v.t.* make, fabricate; invent, counterfeit. See PRODUCTION, FALSE-
HOOD.

forget, *v.t.* disregard, overlook, dismiss, omit; disremember. See NEGLECT,
OBLIVION. *Ant.*, see MEMORY.

FORGIVENESS [918]

Nouns—forgiveness, pardon, condonation, grace, remission, absolution,
amnesty, oblivion; indulgence; reprieve; excuse, exoneration, quittance,
release, indemnity; bill, act, covenant *or* deed of indemnity; exculpation,
ACQUITTAL; conciliation; reconciliation, PACIFICATION; propitiation; longa-
nimity, placability.

Verbs—**1,** forgive, pardon, condone, think no more of, let bygones be bygones, shake hands, forget an injury, forgive and forget; excuse, pass over,
overlook; wink at (see NEGLECT); bear with; allow for, make allowances for;
let one down easily, not be too hard upon, bury the hatchet; let off, remit,
absolve, give absolution, reprieve; acquit (see ACQUITTAL).

2, beg, ask *or* implore pardon; conciliate, propitiate, placate; make one's
peace with, make up a quarrel (see PACIFICATION).

Adjectives—forgiving, placable, conciliatory, indulgent; forgiven, unre-
sented, unavenged, unrevenged.

Antonym, see RETALIATION.

---

fork, *v.i.* bifurcate, diverge, separate, branch off. See DISJUNCTION.

forlorn, *adj.* abandoned, deserted, forsaken; hopeless, wretched, miserable.
See SECLUSION, HOPELESSNESS. *Ant.*, see SOCIALITY, CHEERFULNESS.

FORM [240]

Nouns—**1,** form, formation, forming, figure, shape; conformation, configuration; make, frame, construction, cut, set, build, trim, cut of one's jib;
stamp, type, cast, mo(u)ld; FASHION; contour, OUTLINE; architecture, structure; sculpture. See FORM.

2, feature, lineament, anatomy, profile; turn; phase, aspect, APPEARANCE;
posture, attitude, pose.

3, morphology, histology, structural botany; isomorphism.

Verbs—form, shape, figure, FASHION, carve, cut, chisel, hew, cast; rough-hew;
rough-cast; sketch; block out, hammer out; trim; lick into shape, put into
shape; model, knead, work up into, set, mo(u)ld, sculpture; cast, stamp;
build, construct.

Adjectives—formed, formative; plastic, fictile; isomorphous.

Antonym, see DISORDER.

---

former, *adj.* erstwhile, whilom, sometime, quondam; foregoing, preceding.
See PAST, PRIORITY.

formidable, *adj.* appalling, tremendous; arduous, Herculean. See FEAR,
DIFFICULTY.

formulate, *v.t.* frame, devise, concoct, formularize. See PRODUCTION.

forsake, *v.t.* desert, abandon; quit, forswear. See RELINQUISHMENT.

fort, *n.* stronghold, fortress, fortification. See DEFENSE.

fortify, *v.t.* strength, buttress, barricade; uphold, sustain. See POWER,
EVIDENCE.

fortitude, *n.* COURAGE, patience, endurance.

fortune, *n.* fate, lot; CHANCE, luck; WEALTH, possessions, property. See
NECESSITY, DESTINY. *Ant.*, see POVERTY.

forward, *adj. & v.t.* —*adj.* FRONT, anterior, foremost; precocious; ready;
prompt; enterprising, aggressive; intrusive, officious; pert, saucy, flip;
future, coming. See EARLINESS, ACTIVITY, INSOLENCE. —*v.t.* advance,
impel, dispatch, deliver.

fossil, *n.* relic, petrifaction; fogy. See OLDNESS, VETERAN.

foster, *v.t.* nourish, nurture, cherish; encourage, support. See AID. *Ant.,* see NEGLECT.
foul, *adj.* dirty, soiled, disgusting; stormy, unpleasant; obscene, indecent; unfair, underhand. See UNCLEANNESS, IMPURITY, IMPROBITY. *Ant.,* see CLEANNESS.
found, *v.t.* establish, institute, originate. See PRODUCTION.
foundation, *n.* base; basis; endowment; institution. See LOCATION, SUPPORT.
founder, *n.* & *v.i.* —*n.* producer, establisher, originator. —*v.i.* sink, be swamped; collapse, crash; go lame. See NAVIGATION, FAILURE.
fountain, *n.* spring, well, jet, spray; source. See CAUSE, WATER, STORE.
fowl, *n.* bird; hen, stewing chicken. See ANIMAL, FOOD.
fox, *n.* reynard; slyboots, crafty person. See ANIMAL, DECEPTION. *Slang,* slicker.
fraction, *n.* part; half, quarter, eighth, *etc.*; portion, piece, bit; section, segment; scrap, fragment; very small part. *Ant.,* see WHOLE.
fracture, *n.* break, split, crack, cleft. See DISJUNCTION.
fragile, *adj.* delicate, frail, breakable; tenuous, gossamer. See IMPOTENCE, BRITTLENESS. *Ant.,* see POWER, COHERENCE.
fragment, *n.* bit, part, portion, scrap. See PART. *Ant.,* see WHOLE.

FRAGRANCE [400]

Nouns—**1,** fragrance, aroma, redolence, spice, spiciness, perfume, perfumery, bouquet; ODOR, essence.
2, incense; frankincense, myrrh; pastil, pastille; perfumes of Arabia; attar; bergamot, balm, civet, musk, potpourri; nosegay; scent, scentbag; sachet, smelling salts, vinaigrette; cologne, eau de Cologne.
Verbs—be fragrant, have a perfume; smell sweet; scent, perfume, embalm.
Adjectives—fragrant, aromatic, redolent, spicy, balmy, scented; sweet-smelling, sweet-scented; perfumed; fragrant as a rose; muscadine, ambrosial.

Antonym, see MALODOROUSNESS.

frail, *adj.* fragile, brittle, delicate; weak, infirm, weak-willed. See IMPOTENCE, DOUBT. *Ant.,* see POWER.
frame, *v.t.* & *n.* —*v.t.* construct, fashion, fabricate, formulate, enclose; incriminate falsely, trump up. See PRODUCTION, ARRANGEMENT, ACCUSATION. —*n.* framework, skeleton; EDGE, boundary, confines; temper, humor; form; shape; plot, conspiracy. See SUPPORT.
franchise, *n.* privilege, right, prerogative. See FREEDOM.
frank, *adj.* ingenuous, candid, straightforward, forthright, sincere, open. See TRUTH, SIMPLENESS. *Ant.,* see DECEPTION, CONCEALMENT.
frantic, *adj.* distraught, distracted, frenzied, wild. See INSANITY, EXCITEMENT.
fraternity, *n.* brotherhood; fellowship; secret society. See CONSANGUINITY, PARTY.
fraternize, *v.i.* associate, band together; consort with, mingle with. See SOCIALITY.
fraud, *n.* deception, swindle; imposture, artifice; imposter, humbug. *Slang,* confidence game, bunco. See DECEPTION. *Ant.,* see TRUTH.
freak, *n.* abnormality, fluke, monstrosity; CAPRICE, sport, whim. See UNCONFORMITY.

FREEDOM [748]

Nouns—**1,** freedom, liberty, independence; license, PERMISSION; FACILITY; immunity, EXEMPTION; release, parole, probation, discharge.
2, scope, range, latitude, play; free play, full play, full scope; swing, full swing, elbow room, margin, rope, wide berth, liberty hall.
3, franchise, emancipation, liberation, enfranchisement; autonomy, self-government, self-determination; liberalism, free trade; nonintervention, noninterference, Monroe Doctrine; free speech, freedom of speech *or* of the press.
4, freeman, freedman, citizen.

5, free land, freehold; allodium; mortmain.

Verbs—1, be free, have scope, have the run of, have one's own way, have a will of one's own, have one's fling; do what one likes, wishes, pleases *or* chooses; go at large, feel at home; fend for oneself; paddle one's own canoe; stand on one's rights; be one's own man; shift for oneself; take a liberty; make free with, make oneself at home; take leave, take French leave.

2, set free, LIBERATE, release, let go; permit (see PERMISSION); allow *or* give scope to; give a horse his head; make free of; give the freedom of; give the franchise; enfranchise; *laisser faire;* live and let live; leave to oneself, leave alone, let alone. *Colloq.*, give one leeway, give one enough rope.

3, unfetter, untie, loose, unchain, unshackle, unbind; disengage, disentangle, clear, extricate, unloose.

Adjectives—1, free, free as air; independent, at large, loose, scot free; left alone, left to oneself; free and easy; at one's ease; *dégagé*, quite at home; wanton, rampant, irrepressible, unvanquished; freed, liberated; freeborn; autonomous, freehold, allodial. *Colloq.*, on one's own.

2, in full swing, uncaught, unconstrained, unbuttoned, unconfined, unrestrained, unchecked, unprevented, unhindered, unobstructed, unbound, uncontrolled, untrammeled, unsubject, ungoverned, unenslaved, unenthralled, unchained, unshackled, unfettered, unreined, unbridled, uncurbed, unmuzzled; unrestricted, unlimited, unconditional; absolute; discretionary, optional (see CHOICE); exempt; unassailed, unforced, uncompelled; impartial, unbiased, spontaneous.

Adverbs—*ad libitum*, at will, freely, *etc.*

Antonym, see SUBJECTION.

---

freeze, *v.* congeal, turn to ice, make ice; harden; die; immobilize; chill, ice, frost, refrigerate; kill. See COLD, INACTIVITY.

freight, *n.* cargo, load, shipment; burden. See TRAVEL.

frenzy, *n.* fury, agitation; excitement, enthusiasm; delirium, furor. See VIOLENCE, EXCITEMENT.

FREQUENCY [136]

Nouns—frequency, oftenness; REPETITION, RECURRENCE, persistence; PERSEVERANCE; prevalence; CONTINUANCE.

Verbs—do frequently; do nothing but, keep on, continue (see CONTINUITY); persist; recur.

Adjectives—frequent, many times, not rare, incessant, perpetual, continual, constant, steadfast, unceasing; everyday, repeated (see REPETITION); habitual (see HABIT).

Adverbs—often, oft, ofttimes, oftentimes; frequently; repeatedly (see REPETITION); not unfrequently; in rapid succession; many at time, daily, hourly, every day; perpetually, continually, constantly, incessantly, without ceasing, at all times, night and day, day after day; morning, noon and night; ever and anon; most often; commonly, habitually (see HABIT); sometimes, occasionally, between times, at times, now and then, once in a while, from time to time, often enough, again and again. *Colloq.*, every so often.

Antonym, see RARITY.

---

fresh, *adj.* novel, recent; new, unfaded, unjaded, unhackneyed, unused; healthy, vigorous, unfatigued; unsalted; cool, refreshing, keen; inexperienced. See ADDITION, NEWNESS, COLD, HEALTH. *Slang*, impertinent. *Ant.*, see OLDNESS, WEARINESS.

fret, *v.* agitate, irritate, vex; worry, chafe, fume, complain. See PAIN, AGITATION.

friar, *n.* monk, brother; fra. See CLERGY.

FRICTION [331]

Nouns—friction, attrition, rubbing; frication, confrication, abrasion, sanding, sandpapering, erosion, limation, rub; massage.

Verbs—rub, scratch, abrade, file, rasp, scrape, scrub, fray, graze, curry, buff, scour, polish, rub up; gnaw; file, sand, sandpaper, grind (see POWDERINESS); massage, knead.

Adjectives—frictional, abrasive, attritive.
Antonym, see SMOOTHNESS.

FRIEND [890]

Nouns—**1,** friend, acquaintance, neighbor, well-wisher; alter ego; bosom friend, fast friend; partner; fidus Achates; *persona grata;* associate, compeer, comrade, mate, companion, confrère, intimate, confidant(e).
2, patron, Maecenas; tutelary saint, good genius, advocate, partisan, sympathizer; ally; friend in need; associate.
3, crony, chum, pal; playfellow, playmate; schoolfellow, schoolmate; shopmate, shipmate, messmate; fellow, boon companion. *Slang*, sidekick.
4, Pylades and Orestes, Castor and Pollux, Nisus and Euryalus, Damon and Pythias, David and Jonathan, Three Musketeers.
5, friendship, friendliness, amity, brotherhood; harmony, concord, peace; cordiality, fraternization; fellowship, familiarity, intimacy, comradeship. See SOCIALITY.
Verbs—be friendly; make friends with, receive with open arms; fraternize; befriend. *Colloq.*, hit it off, take to, stand in with.
Adjectives—friendly, amicable, cordial; hospitable, neighborly, brotherly, sisterly; hearty, warmhearted, familiar; on good terms, friends with.
Antonym, ENEMY.

---

fright, *n.* dread, dismay, terror, panic, alarm, consternation. See FEAR.
frigid, *adj.* COLD, icy, freezing; passionless, cold-blooded, formal. See INSENSIBILITY. *Ant.*, see HEAT.
fringe, *n.* EDGE, border, outskirts; edging; perimeter.
frivolity, *n.* LEVITY, flightiness, giddiness, FOLLY. See UNIMPORTANCE.
frolic, *v.i.* play, gambol, caper, romp, disport. See AMUSEMENT.

FRONT [234]

Nouns—**1,** front, forefront, fore, forepart; foreground; face, disk, frontage, façade, proscenium, frontispiece; anteriority; priority; obverse; pioneer, forerunner; BEGINNING.
2, front rank, front lines; van, vanguard; advanced guard; outpost.
3, face, brow, forehead, visage, physiognomy, countenance, features; rostrum; beak; bow, stem, prow, jib. *Slang*, mug, puss, kisser.
Verbs—be in front, stand in front; front, face, confront, brave, defy; bend forward; come to the front, come to the fore.
Adjectives—front, fore, frontal, anterior.
Adverbs—frontward, in front; before, in the van, ahead, right ahead; foremost, headmost; in the foreground, in the lee; before one's face, before one's eyes; face to face, vis-à-vis.
Antonym, see REAR.

---

frontier, *n.* borderland, outskirts; wilderness; new land. See EDGE, LIMIT.
frown, *v.i. & n.* —*v.i.* scowl, lower, glower; look with disfavor (upon). See IRASCIBILITY, DISAPPROBATION. —*n.* scowl, disapproving look. *Ant.*, see APPROBATION.
frugal, *adj.* prudent, saving, provident, thrifty; sparing, stinting. See ECONOMY, MODERATION. *Ant.*, see WASTE.
fruit, *n.* product, yield, harvest; offspring, result, outgrowth. See PRODUCTION, EFFECT.
frustrate, *v.t.* defeat, thwart, circumvent, cross, baffle, nullify. See HINDRANCE. *Ant.*, see AID, SUCCESS.
fuel, *n.* tinder, firing, combustible(s); coal, OIL, gas, gasoline, kerosene, *etc.*; wood, paper; inflammables; firewood, kindling; matches; powder keg, tinderbox; materials for burning. See HEAT.
fugitive, *adj. & n.* —*adj.* transient, ephemeral, evanescent, fleeting. —*n.* runaway, eloper, absconder; refugee, escapee. See AVOIDANCE, ESCAPE.
fulfill, *v.t.* satisfy, realize, gratify; execute, discharge; effect, carry out. See COMPLETION. *Ant.*, see FAILURE.
full, *adj.* filled, sated, satiated, glutted, gorged; replete; whole, complete,

entire; loose, baggy; sonorous; plump, rounded; brimming. See COM-
PLETION, SUFFICIENCY. *Ant.*, see INSUFFICIENCY.

fumble, *v.* grope, search; paw; fluff, flubb, muff, bungle. See UNSKILLFUL-
NESS.

fume, *v.i.* chafe, fret, rage; smoke, reek. See PAIN, RESENTMENT, HEAT.

fun, *n.* sport, diversion, amusement, jollity. See AMUSEMENT.

function, *n. & v.i.* —*n.* faculty, office, duty, role, province; observance,
economy. See AGENCY, BUSINESS, RITE. —*v.i.* operate, act, serve. See
ACTIVITY.

fundamental, *adj.* basic, essential, underlying, original, clemency, intrinsic;
rudimentary.

funeral, *n.* obsequies; burial, INTERMENT, entombment.

funereal, *adj.* mournful, sad, solemn, somber, lugubrious; black, dark.
See DARKNESS, DEJECTION. *Ant.*, see CHEERFULNESS.

funny, *adj.* amusing, droll, comic; absurd, laughable, mirth-provoking,
ludicrous. See WIT, ABSURDITY.

furies, *n.* avengers, Erinyes, Eumenides, Dirae. See DEMON.

furious, *adj.* raging, violent, fierce, storming, turbulent, unrestrained.
Colloq., mad, angry. See RESENTMENT, VIOLENCE.

furnace, *n.* See HEAT.

furnish, *v.t.* equip, outfit; provide, yield, supply. See SUBSTITUTION, PRO-
DUCTION. *Ant.*, see DIVESTMENT.

furrow, *n. & v.* —*n.* trench, groove, rut, score, cut, channel, seam, ditch,
track; line, wrinkle, crease; pucker, corrugation; fluting; hollow; chamfer.
—*v.* score, cut, seam, channel, wrinkle, *etc.* See ROUGHNESS. *Ant.*, see
SMOOTHNESS.

further, *adj. & v.t.* —*adj.* farther, more remote, more, additional. See AD-
DITION. —*v.t.* AID, advance, promote, expedite.

furtive, *adj.* stealthy, sly, surreptitous, sneaking, skulking, covert. See
CONCEALMENT. *Ant.*, see DISCLOSURE.

fury, *n.* rage, frenzy; VIOLENCE, turbulence. See INSANITY.

fuse, *v.* merge, unite, combine, amalgamate; melt, dissolve. See JUNCTION,
MIXTURE, HEAT.

fuss, *n.* ado, bustle, hubbub, confusion, AGITATION; fret, fidget.

futile, *adj.* ineffectual, vain, idle, useless. See IMPOTENCE, USELESSNESS.
Ant., see UTILITY.

FUTURITY [121]

Nouns—futurity, future, hereafter, time to come; approaching *or* coming
years *or* ages; millenium, doomsday, day of judgment, crack of doom;
remote future; approach of time, advent, time drawing on, womb of time;
DESTINY, POSTERITY, eventuality; prospect (see EXPECTATION); foresight.

Verbs—look forward, anticipate, expect (see EXPECTATION), foresight; forestall (see EARLINESS); come on, draw on; draw near; approach, await;
threaten, impend (see DESTINY).

Adjectives—future, to come, coming, impending (see DESTINY); next, near;
near at hand, close at hand; eventual, ulterior, in prospect (see EXPECTATION).

Adverbs—in (the) future, prospectively, hereafter, tomorrow, the day after
tomorrow; in course of time, in process of time, in the fullness of time;
eventually, ultimately, sooner or later, in the long run; one of these days;
after a while, after a time; from this time, henceforth, thence; thenceforth,
whereupon, upon which; soon, on the eve of, on the point of, on the brink
of; about to; close upon.

Antonym, see PRIORITY.

G

gabble, *v.* chatter, prattle; gibber. See LOQUACITY, ABSURDITY, SPEECH. *Ant.*, see SILENCE.

gadfly, *n.* horsefly; goad, spur; irritant. See CAUSE.

gaff, *n. & v.* spear, hook. *Colloq.*, punishing ordeal, rough going; pace. See ARMS.

gag, *v.* muffle, silence; choke, strangle. See SILENCE. *Ant.*, see SPEECH.

gain, *n. & v.* —*n.* ACQUISITION, INCREASE, profit; amplification. —*v.* earn, win; reach, attain; persuade. See ADDITION. *Ant.*, see LOSS, DECREASE.

gait, *n.* step, pace, stride; trot, gallop, walk; shuffle, saunter. See MOTION.

gale, *n.* WIND, storm, tempest.

gall, *n. & v.* —*n.* bitterness. —*v.* irritate, chafe; annoy, exasperate; vex. See PAIN. *Ant.*, see PLEASURE.

gallant, *n. & adj.* —*n.* gigolo; squire of dames, escort. —*adj.* chivalrous, polite; brave, courageous. See COURAGE, COURTESY. *Ant.*, see COWARDICE, DISCOURTESY.

gallery, *n.* balcony, corridor; loft; salon. See DRAMA, PAINTING, SCULPTURE.

gallop, *n. & v.* run, canter. See MOTION. *Ant.*, see INACTIVITY.

gamble, *n. & v.* —*n.* CHANCE, wager, risk. —*v.* speculate, risk, bet.

gambol, *v.* leap, frolic, cavort, romp; play.

game, *n. & adj.* —*n.* AMUSEMENT, diversion, sport, play; contest, match; plan, purpose; CHANCE. —*adj.* sporting; gritty, plucky.

gang, *n.* group, band; set, clique; association; mob, horde. See MULTITUDE, PARTY.

gangrenous, *adj.* mortified, necrose. See DISEASE. *Ant.*, see HEALTH.

gap, *n.* DISCONTINUITY; INTERVAL; OPENING; vacancy; break, lacuna, hiatus. *Ant.*, see CONTINUITY, NEARNESS, CLOSURE.

gape, *v.* open, spread, yawn; stare, gaze. See OPENING, WONDER. *Ant.*, see CLOSURE.

garble, *v.* deface, distort, misreport. See DISTORTION. *Ant.*, see TRUTH.

garden, *n.* herbary, nursery; flowerbeds. See AGRICULTURE.

garland, *n.* ORNAMENT, festoon, wreath, lei.

garment, *n.* CLOTHING, robe, dress, vestment(s), habiliment.

garner, *v.* harvest, collect, accumulate. See STORE.

garnish, *v.* ORNAMENT, trim, decorate, embellish; season, flavor.

garret, *n.* crawl space, loft, attic.

gas, *n.* aëriform *or* elastic fluid; vapor, fume, reek; AIR, ether; fuel; helium, neon, hydrogen, nitrogen, oxygen, *etc.*, (*chemical gases*); firedamp, chokedamp, methane, ethane, marsh gas; carbonation (soda water, *etc.*); flatulence; illuminating gas, natural gas, laughing gas (nitrous oxide), tear gas, poison gas (lewisite, carbon monoxide, mustard gas, chlorine, phosgene, *etc.*); gas attack. *Colloq.*, gasoline, petrol. *Slang*, hot air, bombast, empty talk. *Ant.*, see DENSITY.

gaseous, *adj.* gassy, gaslike; flatulent; volatile, evaporable; gasiform, aëriform; carbonated; reeky, reeking, fumy, smelly. See GAS, ODOR.

gash, *n. & v.* slash, gouge, slit; cut; scratch, score. See DISJUNCTION. *Ant.*, see JUNCTION.

gasp, *v.* pant, labor, choke; puff; exclaim. See WEARINESS.

gate, *n.* OPENING, gateway, entry, portal; sluice, floodgate. See INCLOSURE. *Ant.*, see CLOSURE.

gather, *v.* infer, conclude; congregate, group, amass; shirr, pucker; collect, harvest, glean; cluster, huddle, herd; fester, suppurate. See INCREASE, DISEASE. *Ant.*, see DECREASE, DISJUNCTION.

gaudy, *adj.* garish; showy; cheap, blatant, tawdry; flashy. See CHEAPNESS, COLOR. *Ant.*, see SIMPLENESS, COLORLESSNESS.

gauge, *n. & v.* —*n.* measure, templet, template; caliber, SIZE. —*v.* measure, estimate, JUDGE, evaluate. See MEASUREMENT.

gaunt, *adj.* haggard, bony, lean, emaciated; repellant. *Ant.*, see BREADTH.

gay, *adj.* lively, vivacious, blithe; convivial, festive. See CHEERFULNESS, COLOR. *Ant.*, see DEJECTION, COLORLESSNESS.

gaze, *v.* stare, ogle, pore, look, watch. See VISION.

gear, *n.* CLOTHING, dress; cogwheel; equipment, tools, apparatus. See INSTRUMENT.

gem, *n.* jewel, stone; prize; work of art. See ORNAMENT, GOODNESS.

general, *adj.* prevalent, rife, widespread; universal, sweeping, extensive; wide; common, popular, catholic; comprehensive; prevailing; habitual; usual, ordinary; vague, indefinite; generic. See CONFORMITY, HABIT. *Ant.*, see UNCONFORMITY.

generality, *n.* universality; rifeness, prevalence; extent; catholicity; vague statement, vagueness; comprehensiveness; looseness; ruck, mass, masses, common run, majority; most people, everybody, the bulk, collective mass. See CONFORMITY, DOUBT. *Ant.*, see UNCONFORMITY.

generate, *v.* make, produce; proliferate, procreate, breed, impregnate; engender. See POWER, PRODUCTION. *Ant.*, see IMPOTENCE, DESTRUCTION.

generosity, *n.* BENEVOLENCE, philanthropy, liberality, munificence, prodigality; altruism, magnanimity. See GIVING. *Ant.*, see ECONOMY.

genial, *adj.* affable, cordial, jovial, friendly, hearty, pleasant. See CHEERFULNESS. *Ant.*, see DEJECTION.

genius, *n.* spirit, pixy; brilliance, INTELLIGENCE; talent, bent, gift, ability. See SKILL, INTELLECT.

gentle, *adj.* mild, calm; soothing, kindly, tolerant; considerate, courteous; well-bred, high-born; tame, docile. See COURTESY, MODERATION, NOBILITY, DOMESTICATION. *Ant.*, see DISCOURTESY, VIOLENCE.

gentleness, *n.* MODERATION, mildness; kindness, amenity, lenience. *Ant.*, see VIOLENCE.

genuine, *adj.* true, right, real, authentic; sincere, unaffected; honest, valid. See GOODNESS, PURITY. *Ant.*, see BADNESS, IMPURITY.

germ, *n.* microörganism; seed, embryo; microbe, bacterium; BEGINNING, rudiment. See CAUSE. *Ant.*, see END, EFFECT.

gesture, *n. & v.* —*n.* motion, signal, gesticulation. —*v.* wave, signal, nod, beckon. See INDICATION.

get, *v.* secure, obtain, procure, take, acquire; win, earn, attain; understand, comprehend; see ACQUISITION. *Ant.*, see LOSS.

gewgaw, *n.* trinket, knickknack, bauble. See ORNAMENT.

ghastly, *adj.* pale, deathly, ashen, livid; horrible, terrible, fearsome, hideous. See UGLINESS, COLORLESSNESS. *Ant.*, see BEAUTY, COLOR.

ghost, *n.* apparition, phantom, spirit, SHADE, specter.

ghostly, *adj.* ghostlike, spectral, phantasmal. See DEATH.

giant, *n.* jumbo, monster, titan, colossus. See SIZE. *Ant.*, see LITTLENESS.

gibe, *n.* sneer, taunt, jeer, ridicule. See DISRESPECT. *Ant.*, see RESPECT.

giddy, *adj.* frivolous, irresponsible; dizzy, flighty, capricious. See INSANITY, CHANGEABLENESS.

gift, *n.* present, donation, favor, bounty; contribution, gratuity, tip; largess(e); talent, aptitude, ability. See GIVING, POWER. *Ant.*, see RECEIVING, IMPOTENCE.

gigantic, *adj.* monstrous, elephantine, titanic, huge, enormous, colossal, immense. See SIZE. *Ant.*, see LITTLENESS.

giggle, *v.* laugh, chuckle, titter. See AMUSEMENT.

gird, *v.* bind, strap, secure; encircle, surround; support, fortify. See POWER, CIRCULARITY.

girdle, *n.* band, belt, girth; corset, cummerbund. See CLOTHING, CIRCULARITY.

girl, *n.* lass, maid, damsel; SERVANT, clerk. See FEMALE.

girth, *n.* OUTLINE; circumference, belt, girdle, band.

gist, *n.* MEANING, essence, significance, point.

GIVING [784]

Nouns—**1,** giving, bestowal, donation; presentation, presentment; accordance; cession, concession; delivery, consignment; dispensation; communication; endowment; investment, investiture; award; almsgiving, charity, liberality, generosity, philanthropy (see BENEVOLENCE).

2, gift, donation, present, *cadeau* (*Fr.*), boon, favor; benefaction, grant; offering, oblation, sacrifice, immolation; bonus, bonanza.

3, allowance, contribution, subscription, subsidy, tribute; alimony. pension; fee, recompense (see PAYMENT); consideration; bribe, bait; peace-offering.

4, bequest, legacy, devise, will; dot, appanage; voluntary settlement, voluntary conveyance, transfer; amortization.

5, alms, charity, largess(e), bounty, dole; oblation, offertory; honorarium, gratuity, Christmas box, Easter offering; tip, drink money, *pourboire*, lagniappe, premium. *Slang*, handout.

6, giver, grantor; donor, testator, testatrix; feoffer, settlor.

7, godsend, manna, windfall, blessing.

8, liberality, generosity, munificence, lavishness, magnanimity, bountifulness.

Verbs—**1,** give, donate, bestow, confer, grant, accord, award, assign; present, give away, dispense, dispose of, deal out, dole out, mete out, pay out, squeeze out; make a present, allow, contribute, subscribe; invest, endow, settle upon, bequeath, will, leave, devise; deliver, hand, pass, make over, turn over; entrust, consign, vest in; concede, cede, yield, part with, spend; pay (see PAYMENT).

2, furnish, supply, make available, help; administer to, minister to; afford, spare; accommodate with, favor with; shower down upon; lavish, pour on, thrust upon; bribe; cross, tickle *or* grease the palm; offer, sacrifice, immolate. *Colloq.*, chip in. *Slang*, kick in, tip, fork over, cough up.

Adjectives—giving, given; allowed, allowable; donative, concessional; communicable; charitable, eleemosynary; LIBERAL.

Antonyms, see RECEIVING, ACQUISITION.

---

glad, *adj.* happy, content, joyful; blithe, beatific; pleased; blissful. See PLEASURE. *Ant.*, see PAIN.

gladden, *v.* please, gratify, elate, uplift, exhilarate, delight. See CHEERFULNESS, PLEASURE. *Ant.*, see PAIN.

glamour, *n.* charm, romance, enchantment, bewitchment, captivation, allure; sex appeal. See SORCERY.

glance, *n. & v.* —*n.* glimpse; ray, beam, look; ricochet, skim, stroke. —*v.* peek, glimpse, look; graze, brush, strike. See VISION.

glare, *n. & v.* —*n.* scowl, frown, glower; stare. —*v.* flare, shine, glitter; blinding light. See LIGHT, VISION. *Ant.*, see DARKNESS, BLINDNESS.

glass, *n.* crystal; mirror, lens, slide; beaker, tumbler, goblet, snifter; pane; (*pl.*) spectacles, eyeglasses. See OPTICAL INSTRUMENTS, RECEPTACLE.

glaze, *n.* luster, shine; coating; ice; glass, glassiness.

gleam, *n. & v.* —*n.* light, beam, flash, glimmer, ray. —*v.* shine, glow, glitter, glimmer. See LIGHT. *Ant.*, see DARKNESS.

glee, *n.* CHEERFULNESS, delight, joy, merriment, gaiety, mirth. *Ant.*, see DEJECTION.

glib, *adj.* smooth, facile, fluent, voluble, ready. See LOQUACITY. *Ant.*, see CONTRACTION, SILENCE.

glide, *v.* float, flow, skim; slip, slide, coast; pass, elapse; skate, swim, ski. See MOTION, AVIATION.

glimmer, *n. & v.* —*n.* glance, appearance, view, flash, slight. —*v.* peep, glance, see, peek. See VISION.

glitter, *v. & n.* shine, flash, gleam, twinkle, glow, glisten, glint, sparkle, beam. See LIGHT. *Ant.*, see DARKNESS.

gloat, *v.* boast, exult, rejoice; stare, gape; revel, glory, delight. See BOASTING, PLEASURE. *Ant.*, see PAIN.

globe, *n.* ball, sphere; earth; orb. See ROTUNDITY.

gloom, *n.* DEJECTION, sadness, dolefulness, melancholy; shadow, shade, dimness, obscurity; pessimisim. See DARKNESS. *Ant.*, see LIGHT, CHEERFULNESS.

glorify, *v.* exalt, magnify, revere; exaggerate; praise, honor; transform; flatter. See ELEVATION, REPUTE. *Ant.*, see DEPRESSION, DISREPUTE.

glory, *n.* aureole, halo, nimbus; radiance, brilliance; fame, dignity; effulgence; honor, kudos, renown. See BEAUTY, LIGHT, REPUTE. *Ant.*, see UGLINESS, DARKNESS, DISREPUTE.

gloss **154**

gloss, *n.* luster, sheen, shine, finish, polish; glaze, veneer; DECEPTION, speciousness. See LIGHT, SMOOTHNESS. *Ant.*, see DARKNESS, ROUGHNESS.
glove, *n.* mitten, gauntlet. See CLOTHING.
glow, *n. & v.* —*n.* flush, sheen, light, radiance, warmth. —*v.* shine, gleam, flush, burn, blaze, flame. See HEAT, LIGHT, FEELING.
glower, *n.* scowl, frown, glare. See RESENTMENT.
glue, *n. & v.* —*n.* mucilage, paste, cement, adhesive. —*v.* stick, attach; adhere, cement.
glum, *adj.* morose, dismal, sullen, moody, gloomy, surly, low, unhappy. See DEJECTION. *Ant.*, see CHEERFULNESS.

GLUTTONY [957]

Nouns—**1,** gluttony, gluttonousness, hoggishness; greed, greediness; voracity, rapacity, edacity, crapulence; epicurism; good living, high living; guzzling; good cheer, blow out; feast; gastronomy.
2, epicure, bon vivant, gourmand, gourmandizer, gourmet; glutton, cormorant; gastronome. *Colloq.*, pig, hog.
Verbs—be gluttonous, gormandize, gorge; overgorge, overeat; engorge, eat one's fill, indulge one's appetite; cram, stuff; guzzle; bolt, raven, wolf, devour, gobble up; gulp; eat out of house and home; have a tapeworm inside. *Colloq.*, eat like a horse.
Adjectives—gluttonous, greedy, hungry, voracious, rapacious, edacious, omnivorous, crapulent, swinish; gorged, overfed; insatiable.
Antonym, see ASCETICISM.

gnaw, *v.* chew, masticate, crunch; rankle, irritate, distress. See FOOD, PAIN. *Ant.*, see PLEASURE.
go, *v.* leave, depart, withdraw, retire, exit; vanish, disappear, evaporate, evanesce; operate, work, run, function, succeed; proceed, pass; wend, stir; extend, reach; elapse, pass; wither, fade, die; burst, explode. See DEPARTURE, PASSAGE.
goal, *n.* object, end, aim, ambition; (in games) finish line, home, cage, goalposts, end zone, basket, field goal, foul; point, tally, marker. See DESIRE.
god, *n.* deity, idol, divinity; Olympian. See MYTHICAL DEITIES.
godly, *adj.* divine; pious, reverent, religious, devout, righteous. See PIETY. *Ant.*, see IMPIETY.
gold, *n.* MONEY, wealth; bullion, *aurum*; gilding, gilt, goldplate. *Ant.*, see POVERTY.

GOOD, GOODNESS [648]

Nouns—**1,** goodness, good; excellence, merit; VIRTUE, value, worth, price; welfare, benefit; BENEVOLENCE. See PROBITY.
2, SUPERIORITY, PERFECTION, masterpiece, *chef d'oeuvre*, prime, flower, cream, pride, élite, pick, nonesuch, nonpareil, *crème de la crème*, flower of the flock, salt of the earth; champion; all wool and a yard wide.
3, gem, gem of the first water; bijou, precious stone, jewel, pearl, diamond, ruby, brilliant, treasure; good thing; *rara avis*, one in a million.
4, good man, model, prince, paragon, angel, saint; BENEFACTOR, philanthropist, altruist.
Verbs—**1,** produce *or* do good, be beneficial, profit (see UTILITY); serve, help, avail, benefit; confer a benefit; be the making of, do a world of good, make a man of; produce a good effect; do a good turn, improve (see IMPROVEMENT).
2, be good, excel, transcend, be superior (see SUPERIORITY); stand the test; pass muster; challenge comparison, vie, emulate, rival.
Adjectives—**1,** good, beneficial, valuable, of value, excellent, superior (see SUPERIORITY); serviceable, useful (see UTILITY); advantageous, profitable, edifying, salutary, healthful (see HEALTH); genuine (see TRUTH); moderately good, tolerable (see IMPERFECTION); best, first-class, first-rate, capital, prime; harmless, unobnoxious, innocuous, innocent, inoffensive. *Colloq.*, above par, tiptop, topnotch, top-drawer, A-1, gilt-edge(d). *Slang,* bang-up, grand, great, swell.

2, VIRTUOUS, moral, creditable, laudable, exemplary.
Adverbs—to the good, beneficially, in one's favor *or* interests. *Colloq.*, out of this world; not half bad.
Antonym, see BADNESS.

---

goods, *n.pl.* belongings, wares, merchandise, stock, effects; commodities. See PROPERTY.

gorge, *n. & v.* —*n.* gully, ravine, canyon, pass. —*v.* overeat, gormandize, stuff, bolt, gulp. See GLUTTONY.

gorgeous, *adj.* beautiful, superb, breathtaking, magnificent, splendid. See BEAUTY. *Ant.*, see UGLINESS.

gossip, *n. & v.* —*n.* busybody, talebearer, chatterer; reports, rumors. —*v.* talk, speculate, report, tattle, whisper. See CURIOSITY, INFORMATION, SPEECH.

government, *n.* régime, administration; control, rule, regulation; state, economy; kingship, regency; protectorate, democracy, republic, autocracy, dictatorship, totalitarian state. See AUTHORITY, DIRECTION.

gown, *n.* peignoir, negligée, nightgown; dress, garment, evening gown, robe; vestment(s), cassock; frock, smock; slip. See CLOTHING.

grab, *v.* take, snatch, seize, capture; clutch; annex. See ACQUISITION. *Ant.*, see RESTORATION.

grace, *n. & v.* —*n.* delicacy, tact, culture; graciousness, courtesy; attractiveness, charm; compassion, mercy; saintliness, PIETY, sinlessness. —*v.* honor, decorate; improve. See BEAUTY, TASTE.

graceless, *adj.* ungracious, tactless; inept, awkward, clumsy; inelegant; sinful, corrupt. See UGLINESS, EVIL. *Ant.*, see BEAUTY, VIRTUE.

gracious, *adj.* gentle, courteous, tactful; kind, thoughtful, benign; affable, obliging. See BENEVOLENCE, COURTESY. *Ant.*, see DISCOURTESY.

grade, *n.* level, quality, class; rank, standing; gradation, slope, tilt, slant. See OBLIQUITY.

graduate, *n. & v.* —*n.* measure, beaker. —*v.* raise, adjust, modify; measure, classify, grade. See AGREEMENT, ARRANGEMENT.

graft, *v. & n.* —*v.* inoculate, bud, transplant, implant, join. —*n.* transplanted shoot *or* part; corruption, porkbarrel politics, political swindling.

grain, *n.* fruit, cereal, seed, grist, kernel; TEXTURE, temper, TENDENCY, DIRECTION; mite, speck, bit. See LITTLENESS.

GRAMMAR [567]

Nouns—**1,** grammar; accidence, syntax, analysis, synopsis, praxis, punctuation, syllabication, syllabification; parts of speech; participle; noun, substantive, pronoun, verb, adjective, adverb, preposition, interjection, conjunction; inflection, inflexion, case, declension, conjugation.
2, tense; present, past, preterit(e), future; imperfect, perfect, past perfect, pluperfect; progressive, *etc.*
3, mood, mode; infinitive, indicative, subjunctive, imperative.
4, STYLE; philology, LANGUAGE; PHRASE, phraseology.
Verbs—parse, analyze; punctuate; conjugate, decline, inflect.
Antonym, see ERROR.

---

grand, *adj.* large, impressive, magnificent, stately, majestic; pretentious, ostentatious. See GREATNESS, NOBILITY, OSTENTATION.

grant, *n. & v.* —*n.* gift, allotment, contribution. —*v.* bestow, give, yield; agree, concede; permit; contribute, consent. See GIVING, PERMISSION.

granular, *adj.* grainy, mealy, gritty, granulated, sandy. See POWDERINESS.

graphic, *adj.* pictorial, descriptive; vivid; diagrammatic; delineative; picturesque; forcible, powerful. See PAINTING, SCULPTURE, MEANING, POWER.

grapple, *v.* seize, grasp, clutch, struggle, contend. See OPPOSITION, CONTENTION.

grasp, *v.* hold, clasp, seize; comprehend, understand. See MEANING, ACQUISITION, TAKING.

grass, *n.* lawn, greenery, turf, sod, verdure. See VEGETABLE.

grate, *v.* scrape, grind, rasp, abrade, scratch, rasp. See FRICTION.

grateful, *adj.* appreciative, thankful; welcome, agreeable, refreshing. See GRATITUDE, PLEASURE. *Ant.*, see INGRATITUDE.

gratification, *n.* satisfaction; entertainment; fulfillment; diversion, feast; ease, comfort; indulgence, consummation. See PLEASURE. *Ant.*, see PAIN.

grating, *n.* lattice, openwork, grillwork, grid.

GRATITUDE [916]

Nouns—gratitude, gratefulness, thankfulness; indebtedness; acknowledgment, recognition, thanksgiving; thanks, praise, benediction; paean; *Te Deum*, WORSHIP, grace; thank-offering; requital.

Verbs—be grateful, thank; give, render, return, offer *or* tender thanks; acknowledge, requite; thank *or* bless one's stars.

Adjectives—grateful, thankful, appreciative, obliged, beholden, indebted to, under obligation.

Interjections—thanks! much obliged! thank you! thank Heaven! Heaven be praised! thanks a million! *gracias! merci!*.

Antonym, see INGRATITUDE.

---

grave, *n. & adj.* —*n.* burial place, sepulcher, tomb, mausoleum. See INTERMENT. —*adj.* important, weighty, serious; sedate, dignified; momentous, solemn; dull, somber. See COLOR, DEJECTION, IMPORTANCE. *Ant.*, see UNIMPORTANCE.

GRAVITY [319]

Nouns—**1,** gravity, gravitation; weight, weighing; heaviness; ponderosity, pressure, burden; ballast, counterpoise; lump, mass, load, lading, freight; lead, millstone. *Colloq.*, heft.

2, weight; avoirdupois, troy, apothecaries' weight; grain, scruple, dram, ounce, pound, load, stone, hundredweight, ton, carat, pennyweight.

3, balance, scales, steelyard, beam, weighbridge, spring balance.

4, gravity, seriousness, solemnity, SOBRIETY; IMPORTANCE, weight, moment, momentousness.

Verbs—be heavy; gravitate, weigh, press, cumber, load; weight, weigh down; outweigh, overbalance.

Adjectives—**1,** gravitational, weighty; weighing; heavy, ponderous, ponderable; lumpish, lumpy; cumbersome, burdensome; cumbrous, unwieldy, massive. *Colloq.*, hefty.

2, grave, sober, solemn, serious; important, critical; momentous.

Antonym, see LEVITY.

---

graze, *v.* TOUCH, brush; scratch, abrade, rub; pasture, browse, feed, crop. See FOOD, FRICTION.

grease, *n. & v.* —*n.* OIL, fat; graphite; suet, lard, tallow. —*v.* lubricate; anoint. See SMOOTHNESS.

GREATNESS [31]

Nouns—**1,** greatness, magnitude; amount, SIZE, dimensions; MULTITUDE, number; immensity, enormity; INFINITE; might, strength, POWER, intensity, fullness.

2, IMPORTANCE, eminence, prominence, grandeur, distinction, fame, REPUTE, notability.

3, great quantity, quantity, deal, volume, world; bulk, mass (see WHOLE); stock (see STORE); bushel, load, cargo; cartload, vanload, truckload, shipload; flood, spring tide; abundance, SUFFICIENCY; majority, plurality, predominance. *Colloq.*, plenty, sight, pot, scads, oodles, slew, heap.

Verbs—run high, soar, tower, transcend; rise to a great height; know no bounds; enlarge, INCREASE; expand.

Adjectives—**1,** great; greater (see SUPERIORITY); large, considerable, fair, above par; big, huge (see SIZE); ample; abundant, enough (see SUFFICIENCY); full, intense, strong; passing, heavy, plenary, deep, high; signal, at its height, in the zenith; worldwide, widespread, extensive; wholesale; many (see MULTITUDE).

2, goodly, noble; mighty; arch; profound, intense, consummate; extraordinary; important (see IMPORTANCE); unsurpassed (see SUPERIORITY); complete (see COMPLETION).

3, vast, immense, enormous, extreme; exaggerated (see EXAGGERATION); marvelous (see WONDER); unlimited, infinite. *Colloq.,* whopping, fearful, terrific.

4, absolute, positive, stark; perfect, finished; remarkable, noteworthy.

*Adverbs—***1,** absolutely, completely, entirely (see COMPLETION); abundantly (see SUFFICIENCY); greatly, much, in a great measure, richly; to a large *or* great extent; on a large scale; wholesale; mightily, powerfully; intensely. *Colloq.,* no end, plenty, real, mighty.

2, supremely, preëminently, superlatively (see SUPERIORITY); immeasurably, infinitely; immoderately, monstrously (see EXAGGERATION); remarkably, notably, exceptionally, marvelously (see WONDER). *Colloq.,* terribly, awfully.

Antonym, see LITTLENESS.

---

greed, *n.* DESIRE; cupidity, avidity, avarice; covetousness, rapacity; greediness.

greet, *v.* address, hail, salute; welcome, receive, entertain, admit. See COURTESY, RECEIVING. *Ant.,* see DISCOURTESY, GIVING.

grief, *n.* distress, bereavement, sorrow, dolor; affliction, trouble, tribulation. See PAIN. *Ant.,* see PLEASURE.

grievance, *n.* complaint, annoyance, irritation; injustice, wrong; tribulation, injury. *Slang,* gripe. See EVIL, PAIN. *Ant.,* see GOODNESS.

grill, *n.* & *v.* —*n.* grating, grid. —*v.* broil, roast, toast, sear, pan-fry, barbecue. See FOOD.

grim, *adj.* fearful, stern, fierce, forbidding; inflexible; ruthless; grisly, horrible. See RESOLUTION, UGLINESS. *Ant.,* see DOUBT, BEAUTY.

grimace, *n.* face, scowl, leer, expression, *moue* (Fr.). See DISTORTION, AFFECTATION.

grimy, *adj.* soiled, dirty, foul, filthy. See UNCLEANNESS. *Ant.,* see CLEANNESS.

grind, *v.* pulverize, crush; sharpen, whet, file, polish; masticate, crunch; rasp, grate; oppress, harass. See FRICTION, SEVERITY, POWDERINESS.

grip, *n.* & *v.* —*n.* handle; handclasp; hold, control; suitcase, bag, satchel. —*v.* seize, grasp, clutch, hold. See ACQUISITION, RECEPTACLE.

grit, *n.* sand, roughage, gravel; COURAGE, pluck, stamina, endurance. See RESOLUTION, POWDERINESS.

groan, *n.* & *v.* —*n.* CRY, LAMENTATION, moan. —*v.* grumble, lament, moan, whine, whimper.

groom, *n.* & *v.* —*n.* bridegroom, benedict. —*v.* dress, tend, polish, curry. See DOMESTICATION, CLOTHING.

groove, *n.* FURROW; HABIT, routine, rut; trench, channel, indentation.

grope, *v.* feel, essay, fumble; attempt; hunt, search. See FEELING.

gross, *adj.* bulky, large, fat, obese; coarse, crass; brutish, callous, unrefined, insensitive; vulgar, crude, sensual; obscene. See GREATNESS, VULGARITY. *Ant.,* see LITTLENESS, TASTE.

grotesque, *adj.* strange, unnatural, abnormal; bizarre, fantastic, odd; misshapen, startling. See ABSURDITY, UNCONFORMITY.

ground, *n.,* *v.* & *adj.* —*n.* earth, terra firma, soil; foundation, basis; cause, reason; viewpoint. —*v.* base, establish; settle, fix; instruct. —*adj.* pulverized, grated; whittled, sharpened, abraded. See LAND, SUPPORT, CAUSE.

group, *n.* & *v.* —*n.* ASSEMBLAGE, company, association; clique, set; collection, cluster, company. —*v.* collect, gather, classify, sort, combine; cluster. See ARRANGEMENT.

grove, *n.* thicket, coppice, copse, woodland. See VEGETABLE.

grovel, *v.* fawn, creep, cringe; wallow, humble (oneself). See SERVILITY.

grow, *v.* mature, become, develop; increase, extend, expand, enlarge; nurture, raise, cultivate; germinate, breed, sprout; flourish, thrive. See AGRICULTURE, INCREASE, VEGETABLE.

growl, *v.* mutter, grumble; snarl; complain, howl. See LAMENTATION.

grudge, *v.* stint, dole; begrudge, withhold. See PARSIMONY.

gruesome, *adj.* ghastly, fearful, grisly, hideous. See UGLINESS. *Ant.,* see BEAUTY.

gruff, *adj.* bluff, surly, rough, harsh, coarse. See DISCOURTESY, ROUGHNESS. *Ant.,* see COURTESY.

grumble, *v.* rumble, growl, complain, mutter. See LAMENTATION.

guarantee, *v.* vouch, undertake, warrant; pledge; promise, insure, secure. See SECURITY.

guard, *n. & v.* —*n.* safeguard, shield, baffle; cover, protection; pad, hood; catch; protector, sentinel, watchman, sentry; escort, patrol, convoy; warder, warden. —*v.* protect, defend, shield, watch, patrol. See DEFENSE, SAFETY, COVERING. *Ant.,* see ATTACK.

guess, *n. & v.* —*n.* surmise, supposition, assumption, conjecture, theory. —*v.* suppose, divine, predict, surmise, conjecture. See SUPPOSITION.

guest, *n.* visitor, company, caller, FRIEND. See TRANSIENTNESS.

guide, *n. & v.* —*n.* tracker, leader, instructor, pilot; map, instructions; guidebook, chart, manual. —*v.* lead, direct; regulate; train. See CONDUCT, DIRECTION, INFORMATION, TEACHING.

guild, *n.* COMBINATION, union, association, club, society.

guile, *n.* DECEPTION, deceitfulness; trickery, cunning, craftiness.

GUILT [947]

Nouns—guilt, guiltiness, culpability, chargeability, criminality, IMPROBITY, sinfulness (see BADNESS); misconduct, misbehavior, misdoing, misdeed; malpractice, fault, sin, ERROR, transgression, dereliction, delinquency; lapse, slip, trip, *faux pas,* peccadillo; flaw, blot, omission; failing, FAILURE; offense, trespass; misdemeanor, misfeasance, misprision; malefaction, malfeasance, crime, felony; enormity, atrocity, outrage; deadly sin; mortal sin.

Adjectives—guilty, to blame, culpable, sinful, criminal; derelict, at fault, censurable, reprehensible, blameworthy; exceptionable.

Adverbs—guiltily; *in flagrante delicto;* red-handed, in the act.

Antonym, INNOCENCE.

guise, *n.* APPEARANCE, aspect, pretense, semblance; costume, mien.

gulf, *n.* arm (of the sea), bay; chasm, canyon, abyss; OPENING; rift, gap, separation; void, crevasse, pit, abysm, deep.

gullible, *adj.* confiding, unsuspicious, believing, trustful. See CREDULITY.

gully, *n.* arroyo, gulch, trench, ditch, wadi, gorge, ravine.

gun, *n.* pistol, firearm, revolver, cannon, musket, rifle. See ARMS.

gunman, *n.* thug, ruffian, gangster. *Slang,* hood. See EVILDOER.

gush, *v.* pour, flow, jet, spurt; effuse, issue, emit, spout. See EGRESS.

gust, *n.* puff, burst, flurry, blow, breeze, blast. See EXCITEMENT, WIND.

gusto, *n.* PLEASURE, enthusiasm, enjoyment, relish, zest, delight. *Ant.,* see PAIN.

gymnastics, *n.pl.* athletics, acrobatics, exercises, calisthenics. See CONTENTION.

H

HABIT [613]

Nouns—**1,** habit, habitude, wont, way; prescription, custom, use, usage; practice; matter of course, prevalence, OBSERVANCE; conventionalism, conventionality; mode, FASHION, vogue; etiquette; CONFORMITY; rule, standing order, precedent, routine, red tape; rut, groove, beaten path; bad habit; addiction, quirk, trick; training, EDUCATION; seasoning, hardening, inurement; second nature, acclimatization.

2, habitué, addict, frequenter, drunkard (see DRUNKENNESS). *Colloq.,* dope fiend.

Verbs—**1,** be wont, fall into a custom, conform to (see CONFORMITY); follow the beaten path.

2, be habitual, prevail; come into use, take root; become second nature.

3, habituate, inure, harden, season, caseharden; accustom, familiarize;

naturalize, acclimatize; keep one's hand in; train, educate; domesticate; take to, get the knack of; learn; cling to, adhere to; repeat (see REPETITION).
Adjectives—**1,** habitual, customary; accustomed; of everyday occurrence; wonted, usual, general, ordinary, common, frequent, everyday; well-trodden, well-known; familiar, hackneyed, trite, commonplace, conventional, regular, set, stock, established, routine, stereotyped; prevailing, prevalent; current; fashionable (see FASHION); deep-rooted, inveterate, besetting; ingrained.
2, wont; used to, given to, addicted to, habituated to; in the habit of; seasoned, imbued with; devoted to, wedded to.
Adverbs—habitually; always (see CONFORMITY); as usual, as is one's wont, as a rule, for the most part; generally, of course, most often, frequently.
Antonyms, see DISUSE, IRREGULARITY.

---

habitat, *n.* habitation; environment, native heath; quarters. See ABODE.
hack, *v.* chop, hew, slash, cut. See DISJUNCTION.
hackneyed, *adj.* dull, trite, stale, used, banal, commonplace. See HABIT. *Ant.,* see IMAGINATION.
hag, *n.* harridan, vixen, termagant, shrew, witch, crone. See EVILDOER.
haggard, *adj.* thin, worn, drawn, gaunt; emaciated, cadaverous, skeletal. See WEARINESS, UGLINESS.
haggle, *v.* cavil; bargain, chaffer, dicker. See SALE.
hail, *n. & v.* —*n.* pellet, hailstone. —*v.* hail; salute, greet; call, summon; accost, address. See COURTESY, SPEECH. *Ant.,* see DISCOURTESY, SILENCE.
hair, *n.* filament, hirsuteness; thatch; crowning glory, tresses; beard, whisker(s); mop, locks, bristles; pile, nap. See ROUGHNESS. *Ant.,* see SMOOTHNESS.
hale, *adj.* healthy, robust, hearty, vigorous, sound. See HEALTH. *Ant.,* see DISEASE.
half, *n.* hemisphere; bisection; moiety. See NUMERATION.
half-breed, *n.* mestizo, *métis(se)*, mulatto; half-blood, half-caste; mule; hybrid, mongrel. See MIXTURE.
halfhearted, *adj.* INDIFFERENT, apathetic, listless, unenthusiastic; insincere; timid. *Ant.,* see DESIRE.
half-witted, *adj.* unintelligent, foolish, moronic; mentally retarded. See INSANITY. *Ant.,* see INTELLIGENCE.
hall, *n.* PASSAGE, corridor; auditorium, building; college; dormitory; edifice. See ABODE.
hallelujah! *interj.* praise the Lord!, alleluia, hosanna. See RELIGION.
hallow, *v.* bless, sanctify, consecrate, enshrine. See PIETY.
hallucination, *n.* phantasm, phantom, mirage; fancy, delusion, chimera, illusion; DECEPTION. See NONEXISTENCE, ERROR. *Ant.,* see TRUTH, EXISTENCE.
halo, *n.* corona, aura, nimbus, glory, aureole. See LIGHT. *Ant.,* see DARKNESS.
halt, *v., n. & adj.* —*v.* stop, check, arrest, pause, cease. —*n.* stop, interruption, immobility. —*adj.* crippled, disabled. See END. *Ant.,* see CONTINUITY.
hammer, *n. & v.* —*v.* strike, beat, drum, pound, ram. —*n.* mallet, gavel, sledge. See IMPULSE, REPETITION.
hamper, *v.* encumber, hinder, impede, trammel, obstruct, fetter, restrict. See HINDRANCE. *Ant.,* see AID.
hand, *n. & v.* —*n.* fist, extremity; helper, workman, employee, laborer; playing cards held; handwriting. *Colloq.,* applause; greeting. See AGENCY, INDICATION, WRITING. —*v.* pass, deliver, convey, give, transmit.. See GIVING. *Ant.,* see RECEIVING.
handbag, *n.* pocketbook, purse; valise, grip, portmanteau. See RECEPTACLE.
handbook, *n.* guide, instructions, manual. See INFORMATION.
handcuff, *n. & v.* —*n.* manacle(s). *Slang,* bracelet(s). —*v.* shackle, manacle, fetter. See RESTRAINT. *Ant.,* see FREEDOM.
handicap, *v.* penalize, encumber, inconvenience, burden, hamper. See HINDRANCE. *Ant.,* see AID.

handle, *n. & v.* —*n.* shaft, hilt, grip, knob. —*v.* manipulate, USE, wield; direct, control, manage; feel, paw, TOUCH; operate, direct, conduct. See DIRECTION, SERVANT.

handsome, *adj.* attractive, comely, good-looking, personable; fine; generous, ample; striking. See BEAUTY, BENEVOLENCE. *Ant.*, see UGLINESS, ECONOMY.

handwriting, *n.* calligraphy, penmanship, script, graphology, chirography. See WRITING.

handy, *adj.* convenient, near, available, ready; adept, dexterous, apt; competent, capable; expert. See SKILL, UTILITY. *Ant.*, see UNSKILLFULNESS, USELESSNESS.

hang, *v.* dangle, trail, drop, drape; pend; execute; lynch; suspend; put up (picture, *etc.*), fasten, place. See COHERENCE, PUNISHMENT.

hanker, *v.* desire, covet, crave, long for, yearn for.

haphazard, *adj.* CHANCE, casual, aimless, random; hit-or-miss.

happen, *v.* befall, eventuate, occur. See CHANCE.

happy, *adj.* fortunate, lucky; gay, contented, joyous, ecstatic; felicitous, apt; glad. See AGREEMENT, CHEERFULNESS, PLEASURE. *Ant.*, see DISAGREEMENT, DEJECTION, PAIN.

harangue, *n.* SPEECH; discourse; tirade, scolding, diatribe; address, declamation.

harass, *v.* distress, badger, trouble, vex, plague, torment, irritate, heckle, beset; worry; afflict, depress; sadden. *Slang,* needle. See PAIN. *Ant.*, see PLEASURE.

harbinger, *n.* OMEN, sign, forerunner, token, precursor.

harbor, *n. & v.* —*n.* REFUGE; port, retreat; haven, shelter; mole. —*v.* protect, shield, shelter; cherish, keep.

hardly, *adv.* scarcely, barely; improbably; rarely. See RARITY. *Ant.*, see FREQUENCY.

HARDNESS [323]

Nouns—1, hardness, rigidity, inflexibility, temper, callosity; SEVERITY; toughness; petrifaction; lapidification, lapidescence; vitrification, ossification; crystallization.

2, Mohs scale; flint, marble, rock, crystal, quartz, granite, adamant, diamond; iron, steel; nails; brick; concrete.

Verbs—harden, stiffen, petrify, temper, ossify, vitrify; callous; set, congeal.

Adjectives—hard, rigid, stubborn, stiff, firm; starch, starched; stark, unbending, unlimber, unyielding; inflexible, tense; proof; diamondlike, diamantine, adamantine, adamant; concrete, stony, granitic, vitreous; horny, calloused, corneous; bony, osseous.

Antonym, see SOFTNESS.

---

hardship, *n.* ADVERSITY, difficulties, trouble; calamity, affliction. *Ant.*, see PROSPERITY.

hardy, *adj.* sturdy, tough, vigorous; resolute, daring; durable. See COURAGE, DURABILITY. *Ant.*, see COWARDICE, IMPOTENCE, TRANSIENTNESS.

harem, *n.* seraglio.

hark, *v.* listen, harken; hear. See HEARING, ATTENTION.

harlot, *n.* bad woman, LIBERTINE, strumpet, prostitute; paramour, courtesan.

harm, *n. & v.* —*n.* DETERIORATION, EVIL, dishonor, injury. —*v.* TOUCH, damage, injure; desecrate, abuse, break; DETERIORATION; EVIL. *Ant.*, see IMPROVEMENT, GOODNESS.

harmony, *n.* AGREEMENT, concurrence, concord; (musical) accompaniment; order, symmetry; tunefulness, euphony; congruity; proportion; unison; peace, amity, friendship. See PACIFICATION, MUSIC, CONFORMITY. *Ant.*, see CONTENTION.

harness, *n. & v.* —*n.* bridle, traces, hackamore; gear. —*v.* control, utilize; curb, yoke. See DOMESTICATION, RESTRAINT.

harsh, *adj.* acrimonious, ungenial, severe, rough, ungracious; sharp, sour; discordant, hoarse, grating; brutal, heartless, cruel; austere, stern; rigorous, hard. See DISCOURTESY, ROUGHNESS, SEVERITY. *Ant.*, see COURTESY, SMOOTHNESS.

harvest, *n.* crop, yield, product, issue, outcome. See EFFECT, STORE, PRODUCTION.

HASTE [684]

Nouns—haste, urgency; despatch, dispatch; acceleration, spurt, forced march, rush, dash; VELOCITY; precipitancy, precipitation, precipitousness; impatience, impetuosity; brusquerie; hurry, drive, scramble, bustle.

Verbs—**1,** haste, hasten; make haste, hurry, rush, dart, dash, whip on, push on, press; scurry, scuttle along, bustle, scramble, plunge, bestir oneself (see ACTIVITY); lose no time, make short work of; work against time. *Colloq.,* hurry up, hustle, make tracks, step on it. *Slang,* shake a leg, make it snappy, get a move on.

2, speed, speed up, expedite; quicken, accelerate. *Slang,* step on the gas, give 'er the gun.

Adjectives—hasty, hurried, brusque; abrupt, cursory, precipitate, headlong, furious, boisterous, impulsive, impetuous, eager, impatient, hotheaded; feverish, breathless, pressed for time, hard-pressed, urgent.

Adverbs—hastily, precipitately, helter-skelter, slapdash, full-tilt, headlong; apace, amain; all at once (see INSTANTANEITY); at short notice, immediately (see EARLINESS); express, posthaste.

Antonym, see SLOWNESS.

hat, *n.* cap, headgear, bonnet; headdress; derby, bowler; turban, cloche. See CLOTHING.

hatch, *v.* invent, originate; incubate; concoct, devise. See DOMESTICATION, FALSEHOOD, IMAGINATION.

HATE [898]

Nouns—**1,** hate, hatred, abhorrence, loathing; disaffection, disfavor; alienation, estrangement, coolness; enmity, hostility, animosity, RESENTMENT; umbrage, pique, irritation, grudge; dudgeon, spleen, spite, despite, venom, venomousness, bitterness, bad blood; acrimony; malice, MALEVOLENCE, implacability, REVENGE; repugnance, DISLIKE, odium, unpopularity; detestation, antipathy.

2, object of hatred, abomination, aversion, *bête noire;* enemy.

Verbs—**1,** hate, detest, despise, abominate, abhor, loathe; shrink from, view with horror, hold in abomination, revolt against, execrate; DISLIKE.

2, excite *or* provoke hatred, be hateful; repel, envenom, incense, irritate, rile; horrify.

Adjectives—**1,** averse, set against, hostile; bitter, acrimonious (see DISCOURTESY); implacable, revengeful (see RETALIATION); invidious, spiteful, malicious (see MALEVOLENCE).

2, hated, despised, unloved, unbeloved, unlamented, unmourned, disliked; forsaken, rejected, lovelorn, jilted.

3, obnoxious, hateful, abhorrent, despicable, odious, abominable, repulsive, loathsome, offensive, shocking; disgusting, disagreeable.

4, be unfriendly, on bad terms, estranged, *etc.*

Antonym, see LOVE.

haughty, *adj.* overbearing, arrogant, supercilious, proud, lordly, superior. See HEIGHT, INSOLENCE. *Ant.,* see LOWNESS, SERVILITY.

haul, *v.* drag, pull, draw; transport, deliver; lug.

haunt, *n. & v.* —*n.* SHADE, ghost, spirit, spook; resort, rendezvous, retreat, den. *Slang,* hangout. —*v.* frequent, attend; obsess; visit. See FEAR, DEATH, ABODE.

have, *v.* own, hold; retain, possess; keep, maintain. See POSSESSION.

haven, *n.* REFUGE, sanctuary, asylum, shelter; harbor, port; snuggery; protection. See SAFETY.

hazard, *n. & v.* —*n.* DANGER, CHANCE, risk, gamble; accident, adventure, contingency. —*v.* risk, venture, gamble.

haze, *n.* film, opacity; mist, fog; dimness, obscurity. See CLOUDINESS. *Ant.,* see LIGHT.

head, *n. & v.* —*n.* pate, poll; (*slang*) noggin, bean; chief, DIRECTOR, manager, leader; title, heading, caption; talent, ability, JUDGMENT; CLASS, category, type, grouping. See BEGINNING, INTELLECT, HEIGHT. —*v.* lead, direct, precede; guide, RULE, control, manage. See DIRECTION, PRIORITY.

headlong, *adj.* hasty, hurried; rash, precipitate; heedless, reckless. *Ant.,* see SLOWNESS.

heal, *v.* mend, cure; repair, restore; ease. See REMEDY, RESTORATION.

HEALTH [654]

Nouns—**1,** health, healthiness; sanity; soundness; vim, vigor and vitality; strength, robustness; bloom, prime; *mens sana in corpore sano;* hygeia; clean bill of health; convalescence, recovery, cure.
2, salubrity, healthfulness; hygiene, sanitation.
Verbs—**1,** be healthy; bloom, flourish; be in *or* enjoy good health; convalesce, recuperate, recover (see RESTORATION); get better, improve (see IMPROVEMENT); take a new lease on life; cure, restore.
2, be salubrious, be healthful, agree with.
Adjectives—**1,** healthy, well, sound, hearty, hale, fresh, green, whole; florid, flush, hardy, stanch, brave, robust, vigorous; unscathed, uninjured, untainted; in the pink of condition; sound as a bell; fresh as a daisy, fresh as a rose, in one's prime. *Colloq.,* fine, in the pink, in fine feather *or* fettle, chipper, fit as a fiddle, peppy.
2, salubrious, healthful, wholesome, sanitary, prophylactic, benign, bracing, tonic, invigorating; good for; hygienic; innocuous, innocent, harmless, uninjurious, uninfectious, sanitary.

Antonym, see DISEASE.

HEARING [418]

Nouns—**1,** hearing, sense of hearing; audition; auscultation; eavesdropping; audibility; acute ear, *etc.*; ear for music.
2, ear, auricle, acoustic organ, auditory apparatus, eardrum, tympanum; hearing aid, ear trumpet, speaking trumpet; amplifier, amplification, bone conduction; otology; acoustics (see SOUND).
3, hearer, auditor, listener, eavesdropper; audience.
4, hearing, interview, audience; trial (see INQUIRY). *Colloq.,* audition.
Verbs—**1,** hear, overhear; hark, harken; listen, give an ear, lend an ear, bend an ear, heed, attend, prick up one's ears.
2, become audible, fall upon the ear, catch or reach the ear, be heard; ring, resound. *Colloq.,* be all ears, listen in, drink in.

Antonym, see DEAF.

hearsay, *n.* NEWS, gossip, rumor, talk, report.
heart, *n.* center, substance; kernel, pith, gist, core; breast; spirit, COURAGE; sympathy, affection, understanding; nature, soul. See TENDENCY, MIDDLE, CENTRALITY.
heartbroken, *adj.* miserable, unhappy, wretched, hurt, forlorn, disheartened, disconsolate, anguished. See PAIN, DEJECTION. *Ant.,* see PLEASURE.
hearten, *v.* cheer, encourage, brighten, reassure, comfort, rally. See COURAGE, CHEERFULNESS.
heartless, *adj.* unmerciful, cruel, cold, unfeeling, uncaring, unsympathetic, callous; unkind, inconsiderate, insensitive. *Ant.,* see BENEVOLENCE.
hearty, *n. & adj.* —*n.* comrade, sailor. —*adj.* sturdy, robust, strong, well, vigorous, healthy. See FEELING, HEALTH.

HEAT [382]

Nouns—**1,** heat, caloric; temperature, warmth, ardor, fervor, fervency; incalescence, incandescence; flush, glow; temperature, fever; white heat, blood heat, body heat, fever heat.
2, fire, spark, scintillation, flash, combustion, flame, blaze; bonfire; campfire, forest fire, wildfire, sheet of fire, lambent flame; devouring element; sun; fireworks, pyrotechnics.
3, torridity, hot weather, summer, midsummer, dogdays; heat wave, hot spell, sirocco, simoom; broiling sun; pyrology; thermology, thermotics, thermodynamics, THERMOMETER.

4, heater, stove, range; furnace; hot air, steam heat, hot water, radiator, register; blast furnace, electric furnace; kiln, oven; forge, crucible, alembic; Bunsen burner; torch, acetylene torch, electric welder; crematory, pyre; incinerator; fireplace, hearth, grate; brazier; bed warmer, electric blanket, heating pad; heat pump; heliostat.

Verbs—heat, warm; be hot, glow, flush, sweat, swelter, bask, smoke, reek, stew, simmer, seethe, boil, burn, broil, blaze, flame; smo(u)lder; parch, fume, pant; thaw.

Adjectives—**1,** hot, warm; mild, genial; tepid, lukewarm, unfrozen; thermal, thermic, calorific; fervent, fervid; ardent, aglow; red-hot, white-hot, piping-hot; like a furnace, like an oven; hot as fire, like the fires of Hell.
2, sunny, torrid, tropical, estival, canicular; close, sultry, stifling, stuffy, sweltering, suffocating, oppressive; reeking; baking.
3, fiery, incandescent, incalescent; candent, glowing, smoking; on fire; blazing, in flames, alight, afire, ablaze; smo(u)ldering, in a glow, feverish, in a sweat; blood-hot, warm as toast; volcanic, plutonic, igneous; isothermal, isothermic.

Antonym, see COLD.

heathen, *n. & adj.* —*n.* pagan, infidel, unbeliever. —*adj.* irreligious, idolatrous, pagan; unconverted; atheistic. See IRRELIGION. *Ant.*, see RELIGION, BELIEF.

heave, *v.* lift, hoist, raise; throw, pitch, toss; swell, expand; undulate. See ELEVATION.

HEAVEN [981]

Nouns—**1,** heaven, kingdom of heaven, kingdom of God, of God; future state, eternal blessedness, eternity; Paradise, Eden, abode *or* isle of the blessed; celestial bliss, glory. *Slang,* Kingdom come.
2, Olympus; Elysium, Elysian fields, garden of the Hesperides, Valhalla, Nirvana, the happy hunting grounds, seventh heaven.
3, sky, firmament, welkin, blue empyrean, the ether, heavens.
4, Golden Age, Utopia, never-never land, millennium, land of Canaan, promised land.

Adjectives—heavenly, celestial, supernal, unearthly, from on high, paradisiac(al), paradisaic(al), beatific, elysian, ethereal, Olympian.

Antonym, see HELL.

heavy, *adj.* weighty, weighted, ponderous; unwieldy; massive; grave; burdensome; oppressive, cumbersome; tedious, tiresome; dull, gloomy, overcast; strong, pressing, large; loaded, sagging; somber, dismal, dejected, sad, melancholy; slow, inert, sluggish; grievous, serious. See WEIGHT, DEJECTION. *Ant.*, see LIGHTNESS.

heckle, *v.t.* plague, taunt; challenge; interrupt; dispute. See DISAGREEMENT. *Ant.*, see AGREEMENT.

hector, *v.* bully, torment, plague, domineer, bluster. See INSOLENCE. *Ant.*, see SERVILITY.

hedge, *n. & v.* —*n.* shrubbery, hedgerow. —*v.* evade; protect, shelter; temporize; trim. See COMPROMISE.

heed, *n. & v.* —*n.* ATTENTION, notice, regard, consideration. —*v.* observe, CARE, notice, attend, regard; consider. See OBEDIENCE, COURTESY.

HEIGHT [206]

Nouns—**1,** height, altitude, elevation; eminence, pitch; loftiness, sublimity; tallness, stature, prominence (see CONVEXITY).
2, mount, mountain; hell, cape; headland, foreland; promontory, ridge, hogback; dune; vantage ground; down; moor, moorland; Alp; uplands, highlands; heights, SUMMIT; knoll, hummock, hill, hillock, barrow, mound, mole; steeps, bluff, cliff, crag, tor, peak, pike, escarpment, edge, ledge, brae, height.
3, tower, pillar, column, obelisk, monument, steeple, spire, minaret, campanile, turret, dome, cupola, pole, pikestaff, maypole, flagstaff; topmast, topgallantmast, moonraker; skyscraper; ceiling, COVERING.

4, colossus, giant (see SIZE).

Verbs—be high, tower, soar, command; hover, cap, culminate; mount, perch, surmount; cover (see COVERING); overtop (see SUPERIORITY); stand on tiptoe; grow, upgrow, rise (see ASCENT); heighten, elevate (see ELEVATION).

Adjectives—high, elevated, eminent, exalted, lofty; tall; gigantic, towering, soaring, elevated, upper; highest, top, topmost, uppermost; capital, paramount; upland, hilly, mountainous, alpine, aerial; sky-high, tall as a steeple. *Colloq.*, high as a kite.

Adverbs—on high, high up, aloft, up, above, aloof, overhead; upstairs, abovestairs; in the clouds; on tiptoe, on stilts.

Antonym, see LOWNESS.

---

heinous, *adj.* dreadful, abominable; terrible, awful; atrocious, hateful, monstrous. See BADNESS, EVIL.

heir, *n.* (*fem.* heiress) legatee, inheritor, beneficiary. See POSSESSION.

HELL [982]

Nouns—**1,** hell, Hades, bottomless pit, place of torment; Pandemonium, Tophet; hellfire, everlasting fire, fire and brimstone; underworld; purgatory, limbo, gehenna, abyss, bottomless pit; hell on earth.

2, Tartarus, Hades, Avernus, Styx, Stygian creek, pit of Acheron, Cocytus; infernal regions, inferno, realms of Pluto; Pluto, Rhadamanthus, Erebus; Charon; Satan (see DEMON).

Adjectives—hellish, infernal, Stygian, Plutonian.

Antonym, see HEAVEN.

---

helmet, *n.* headgear, skullcap, casque, headpiece; crest, morion. See CLOTHING.

help, *n. & v.* —*n.* servants, staff, employees; aid, assistance, succor; relief, REMEDY. —*v.* assist, serve, befriend; relieve, ameliorate, better. See AID, IMPROVEMENT. *Ant.*, see DETERIORATION, HINDRANCE.

helpless, *adj.* impotent, powerless; defenseless, vulnerable, resourceless; prostrate, crippled; dependent. See IMPOTENCE. *Ant.*, see POWER.

hence, *adv.* herefrom, away; so, therefore. See CAUSE, DEPARTURE.

herald, *n. & v.* —*n.* forerunner, precursor, announcer, messenger, harbinger. —*v.* proclaim, announce, declare; introduce; precede, warn, inform. See PREDICTION, PRIORITY.

herd, *n. & v.* —*n.* group, flock, drove; gathering; troop, pack, crowd. See MULTITUDE. —*v.* drive, tend, collect; gather, assemble; corral, group. See ASSEMBLAGE. *Ant.*, see DISJUNCTION.

here, *adv.* hereabouts, hither, hitherward. See ARRIVAL, LOCATION.

hereafter, *adv.* subsequently, henceforth, henceforward, eventually, ultimately. See FUTURITY. *Ant.*, see PAST.

hereditary, *adj.* inheritable, transmissible, heritable, ancestral, patrimonial. See ANCESTRY, DESCENT.

heresy, *n.* unbelief, dissent, heterodoxy. See IRRELIGION. *Ant.*, see RELIGION.

heritage, *n.* bequest, inheritance, legacy, hereditament, patrimony. See POSSESSION, PROPERTY.

hermit, *n.* anchorite, recluse, ascetic, solitary.

heroic, *adj.* courageous, intrepid, valiant, brave, mighty, fearless, gallant; great, huge, large. See COURAGE, SIZE. *Ant.*, see COWARDICE, LITTLENESS.

hesitate, *v.i.* falter, waiver, shrink, demur. See DOUBT. *Ant.*, see RESOLUTION, CERTAINTY.

heterodox, *adj.* unorthodox, recusant; heretical, uncanonical, apocryphal; pantheistic; pagan, heathen; agnostic, free-thinking, dogmatic, bigoted; sectarian; dissenting; unbelieving, infidel. See IRRELIGION. *Ant.*, see RELIGION.

hew, *v.t.* fell; chop, cut, hack; chip. See DISJUNCTION.

hidden, *adj.* concealed, secreted; covered, screened, obscured; suppressed; veiled, disguised, camouflaged; latent, unmanifested. See CONCEALMENT. *Ant.*, see DISCLOSURE, INFORMATION.

hide, *n. & v.* —*n.* skin, pelt, coat; leather. See COVERING. —*v.* cover, secrete, cloak, veil; dissemble, falsify; disguise, camouflage. See CONCEAL-MENT. *Ant.*, see DISCLOSURE, INFORMATION.

hidebound, *adj.* bigoted, prejudiced, narrow; illiberal; unyielding. See IMPIETY. *Ant.*, see PIETY.

hideous, *adj.* abominable, frightful, odious, dreadful, detestable, horrible, repulsive, unsightly, revolting. See UGLINESS. *Ant.*, see BEAUTY.

high, *adj.* elevated, lofty, tall; towering, eminent; acute, sharp, shrill; prominent, important, directorial; costly, dear, expensive; overripe, gamy. *Colloq.*, elated. *Slang*, drunk; advanced. See HEIGHT. *Ant.*, see LOWNESS.

highway, *n.* road, turnpike, highroad, thoroughfare. See TRAVEL.

hilarity, *n.* CHEERFULNESS, mirth, amusement, enjoyment, gaiety, laughter, glee.

hill, *n.* grade, slope; rise, ascent; elevation, mound. See HEIGHT. *Ant.*, see LOWNESS.

HINDRANCE [706]

Nouns—**1,** hindrance, prevention, preclusion, obstruction, stoppage; interruption, interception, impedition; retardment, retardation; embarrassment, coarctation, stricture, restriction; RESTRAINT; inhibition, PROHIBITION; blockade, CLOSURE, DIFFICULTY.

2, interference, interposition; obtrusion; discouragement, DISSUASION.

3, impediment, let, obstacle, obstruction, knot, check, hitch, contretemps; drawback, objection; stumbling block, ill wind; head wind, OPPOSITION; trammel, hobble, tether; counterpoise; bar, stile, turnstile, barrier; gate, portcullis; barricade (see DEFENSE); wall, breakwater; bulkhead, block, buffer, stopper, boom, dam, weir.

4, encumbrance; clog, drag, stay, stop; preventive, prophylactic; load, burden, onus, millstone, *impedimenta;* dead weight; lumber, pack; incubus, old man of the sea; remora; red herring, false trail.

5, damper, wet blanket, hinderer, marplot, killjoy, interloper; opponent (see OPPOSITION).

Verbs—**1,** hinder, impede, delay; embarrass; interpose, interfere, meddle; keep, fend, stave, *or* ward off; obviate; avert, turn aside, draw off, prevent, forfend, nip in the bud; retard, slacken, check, let; counteract, countercheck; preclude, debar, foreclose, estop, inhibit (see PROHIBITION); shackle, restrain (see RESTRAINT); restrict. *Colloq.*, drag one's feet.

2, obstruct, stop, stay, bar, block, block up; barricade; dam up, close (see CLOSURE); put on the brake, put a spoke in the wheel; put a stop to (see END); interrupt, intercept; oppose (see OPPOSITION); hedge in, cut off; cramp, hamper; clog, cumber, encumber; choke; saddle *or* load with; overload, trammel, tie one's hands; inconvenience, incommode, discommode. *Slang*, gum up, throw a monkey wrench in the works.

3, fall foul of; handicap; thwart, foil, frustrate, disconcert, balk, baffle, override, circumvent; spoil, mar, clip the wings of, cripple (see DETERIORATION); dishearten, DISSUADE, deter, discourage; discountenance, throw cold water on, throw a wet blanket on; cut the ground from under one, take the wind out of one's sails, undermine; be *or* stand in the way of; act as a drag; be a millstone around one's neck. *Colloq.*, cook one's goose, spike one's guns. *Slang*, cramp one's style.

Adjectives—hindering, preventive, deterrent; obstructive, impeditive, interceptive; in the way of, unfavorable; onerous, burdensome, cumbersome, cumbrous; binding, blocking, obtrusive; hindered, waterlogged, heavy-laden; hard-pressed.

Antonym, see AID.

---

hinge, *n.* joint, pivot, center, axis; basis, crisis; hook. See CAUSE, JUNCTION.

hint, *n. & v.i.* —*n.* intimation, suggestion, allusion, reference, implication; tip; trace; reminder; insinuation. See INFORMATION, MEMORY. —*v.i.* suggest, allude, imply, intimate. See INFORMATION.

hire, *n. & v.* —*n.* rental, employment; fee, remuneration. —*v.* rent, lease; employ, engage.

hiss, *n. & v.* —*n.* sibilation, fizz, sizzle; spit. —*v.* sibilate, fizz, sizzle; CONDEMN.

history, *n.* RECORD, chronicle, annals, biography; story, narrative; memoirs, autobiography; tale, anecdote. See DESCRIPTION.

hit, *n. & v.* —*n.* *Colloq.*, success, smash; favorite; popularity. —*v.* strike, club, batter; touch, contact, reach, find; knock, smite. See ARRIVAL, CHANCE, IMPULSE.

hitch, *n. & v.* —*n.* HINDRANCE, knot; obstruction, obstacle, inconvenience, impediment; interruption, pause, stop; tug, jerk, pull; limp, hobble; accident, mischance. See AGITATION, SLOWNESS, END. —*v.* hobble, shuffle, limp; tie, knot, fasten, yoke; attach. See JUNCTION, SLOWNESS. *Ant.*, see DISJUNCTION.

hoard, *n. & v.* —*n.* collection, store, reserve, stock, supply, savings. —*v.* save, preserve, retain, store, amass; treasure; hide; accumulate, collect.

hoarse, *adj.* threaty, raucous, harsh, husky, thick, grating, rasping; croaking, STRIDENT.

hoary, *adj.* old, aged, venerable, ancient; frosty, white; gray, grayed. See AGE. *Ant.*, see YOUTH.

hoax, *n. & v.t.* —*n.* DECEPTION, trick; deceit, fraud, fakery, humbug, canard. —*v.t.* dupe, deceive, trick, fool, swindle; (*slang*) sell. See SALE.

hobble, *n. & v.* —*n.* shackle, bond, binding. —*v.* limp, stagger; halt, bind, shackle, handicap, limit. See RESTRAINT, SLOWNESS.

hobby, *n.* avocation, AMUSEMENT, fad, recreation, relaxation, whim. See BUSINESS.

hodgepodge, *n.* MIXTURE, medley, conglomeration; stew, hash, jumble.

hog, *n.* pig, swine, boar, sow; beast, glutton. See ANIMAL.

hoist, *n. & v.t.* —*n.* elevator, lift, derrick, crane. —*v.t.* lift, raise, jack, rear. See ELEVATION.

hold, *n. & v.* —*n.* grasp, clutch, grip; tenure, POSSESSION; control, INFLUENCE, domination; ownership, keeping; anchor, rein. —*v.* have, occupy, retain, own, possess; restrain, repress, control, pinion, curb; check, stop, interrupt, pause; clutch, grasp, grip, seize; pin, clip, fasten; believe, declare, opine, state, think; insist, persist; last, endure, continue; cling, cleave, stick, adhere; keep, defend, protect, guard. See BELIEF, COHERENCE, DEFENSE, DURABILITY, RECEIVING, RESTRAINT, RETENTION, STORE, SUPPORT, RESOLUTION.

holding, *n.* PROPERTY, POSSESSION, tenure; claim, interest.

hole, *n.* OPENING, aperture, gap, cavity; excavation, hollow; slot, puncture; cave; space. See CONCAVITY.

holiday, *n.* vacation; festival, celebration, recreation. See AMUSEMENT.

hollow, *n. & adj.* —*n.* CONCAVITY, depression, dent; cavity, hole; valley, gully, basin; channel, groove; FURROW. *Ant.*, see CONVEXITY. —*adj.* thin, unresonant; sepulchral, deep, empty, void, unfilled, vacant; unsound, weak, uncertain, unconvincing; specious, false, unsubstantiated, inadequate.

holy, *adj.* consecrated, saintly; blessed, sacred, godly. See PIETY, DEITY. *Ant.*, see IMPIETY.

homage, *n.* RESPECT, tribute, honor; deference, allegiance, devotion; veneration; submission; reverence. See OBEDIENCE.

home, *n.* domicile, residence, ABODE. dwelling; shelter, refuge, asylum, sanctuary; habitat, habitation, environment; native land, fatherland, country, homeland.

homely, *adj.* plain, simple; unbeautiful; homelike; homespun; rustic; unpretentious, down-to-earth. See SIMPLENESS, UGLINESS. *Ant.*, see BEAUTY, ORNAMENT.

honesty, *n.* candor, frankness; sincerity; trustworthiness, uprightness; truthfulness, veracity, PROBITY. *Ant.*, see IMPROBITY, DECEPTION.

honor, *n. & v.t.* —*n.* PROBITY, integrity; REPUTE, glory, title, distinction, award; WORSHIP, RESPECT, deference. —*v.t.* revere, reward; elevate; recognize; respect; accept (as payable). *Ant.*, see DISREPUTE.

honorary, *adj.* nominal, in name only; titular; gratuitous; emeritus. See CHEAPNESS, NOMENCLATURE.

hood, *n. & v.t.* —*n.* COVERING; cape, cowl, coif. *Slang,* gangster, hoodlum. See CLOTHING, EVILDOER. —*v.t.* shield, cover, protect; camouflage; blindfold. See CONCEALMENT.

hoodoo, *n.* Jonah, bad luck, jinx; witchcraft, voodoo, obeah; SORCERY, SPELL.

hoodwink, *v.t.* delude, deceive, fool, hoax; blind. See DECEPTION, BLIND-NESS, CONCEALMENT.

hoof, *n.* foot, ungula; dewclaw.

hook, *n. & v.t.* —*n.* CURVATURE, crook, bend; gaff. —*v.t.* catch, fasten; curve, bend; link, join. See JUNCTION. *Ant.*, see DISJUNCTION.

hop, *n. & v.i.* —*n. Colloq.*: dance; leap, spring. —*v.i.* jump, leap, bounce, spring, bound, dance.

HOPE [858]

Nouns—**1,** hope, hopes, DESIRE; trust, confidence, reliance, faith, BELIEF; assurance, secureness, security; reassurance.

2, good omen, good auspices, promise; good, fair, *or* bright prospect; clear sky; ray of hope, cheer; silver lining; Pandora's box, balm in Gilead. *Slang,* pie in the sky.

3, assumption, presumption; anticipation, EXPECTATION; hopefulness, buoyancy, optimism, enthusiasm, aspiration.

4, castles in the air *or* in Spain, pot of gold at the end of the rainbow; Utopia, millennium, hope of Heaven (see HEAVEN); daydream, airy hopes, fool's paradise; mirage.

Verbs—**1,** hope, trust, confide, rely on, lean upon; pin one's hopes upon (see BELIEF); feel *or* rest assured, feel confident.

2, DESIRE, wish, anticipate; look on the bright side of, see the sunny side, make the best of it, hope for the best; put a good face upon; keep one's spirits up; take heart, be of good cheer; flatter oneself.

3, hope against hope, clutch at straws, count one's chickens before they are hatched.

4, encourage, cheer, assure, reassure, buoy up, embolden; promise, bid fair, augur well, look up.

Adjectives—**1,** hoping, in hopes, hopeful, confident; secure, certain (see BELIEF); sanguine, in good heart, buoyed up, buoyant, elated, flushed, exultant, enthusiastic; fearless, undespairing, self-reliant.

2, within sight of; promising, propitious; of good omen; auspicious, encouraging, cheering, bright, roseate, rose-colored.

Antonym, see DEJECTION.

---

hopelessness, *n.* futility, despair, desperation; despondency, DEJECTION; pessimism; DISAPPOINTMENT. *Ant.*, see HOPE, EXPECTATION, CHEERFULNESS.

horde, *n.* mass, group, throng, mob, gang, crowd, pack. See MULTITUDE, ASSEMBLAGE.

horizontal, *adj.* level, flat, plane; prone, supine, recumbent; flush. See LAYER.

horrible, *adj.* alarming, dreadful, horrifying, appalling, frightful, horrendous, hideous, abominable, revolting, execrable, dire. See FEAR, PAIN.

horror, *n.* terror; loathing, disgust, revulsion; detestation, abhorrence; dread, aversion. See HATE, FEAR.

horse, *n.* equine; stallion, mare, colt, filly, foal, gelding; steed, mount; trotter, pacer, hackney; nag, hack, pony, charger; cavalry; sawhorse; broncho, mustang, cayuse; Arab. See ANIMAL, CARRIER, COMBATANT.

hospital, *n.* sanitarium, sanatorium; clinic; pesthouse; infirmary. See REMEDY.

hospitality, *n.* SOCIALITY, cordiality; welcome, entertainment.

host, *n.* MULTITUDE, throng, mass, horde, army, legion, array; element; entertainer, innkeeper, hostess. See COMBATANT, FRIEND.

hostage, *n.* SECURITY, pledge, guarantee, bond.

hostile, *adj.* antagonistic, opposed, warlike, unfriendly, belligerent. See HATE. *Ant.*, see FRIEND.

hot, *adj.* heated, roasted, burning, torrid, fervid, incandescent, flaming, fiery, ardent, boiling; peppery, biting. See HEAT, SHARPNESS.

hotel, *n.* inn, hostelry, tavern. See ABODE.

hound, *n. & v.t.* —*n.* dog; beagle, basset, bloodhound, dachshund, greyhound, foxhound, *etc.*; cur, wretch. See ANIMAL, EVILDOER. *Ant.*, see GOODNESS. —*v.t.* plague, worry, pursue, harass, bait, persecute; hunt; drive, incite. See MALEVOLENCE. *Ant.*, see BENEVOLENCE.

house, *n. & v.t.* —*n.* ABODE, residence, dwelling, habitation; cottage, bungalow, mansion; shanty, hut, shack; legislature; firm, organization, company; family, ancestry, lineage. —*v.t.* shelter, protect; cover, contain, harbor. See CONTINUITY, ABODE, PARTY, SAFETY.

hovel, *n.* shanty, hut, cabin, shack, den, shed. See ABODE.

hover, *v.i.* fly; poise, hang, linger; waver, vacillate. See AIR, DOUBT, NEARNESS.

how, *adv.* whereby, wherewith, why, however.

howl, *n. & v.i.* —*n.* bellow, shriek, yowl, bay, keen. —*v.i.* wail, complain, ululate, bawl, yowl. See CRY, LAMENTATION, WIND.

huddle, *v.i.* crowd, group, gather, bunch, lump, collect. See ASSEMBLAGE.

hue, *n.* COLOR, tint, shade; tone, complexion, tinge. *Ant.,* see COLORLESSNESS.

hug, *v.t.* caress, embrace, enfold, clasp; cherish; press, fit. See LOVE, NEARNESS.

huge, *adj.* tremendous, gargantuan, enormous, gigantic, vast, immense. See SIZE.

hum, *n. & v.i.* —*n.* buzz, murmur, drone, bumble. —*v.i.* thrum, drone, buzz, murmur, croon, burr; sing. *Ant.,* see LOUDNESS.

human, *adj. & n.* —*adj.* mortal; earthly; humane, civilized. —*n.* man, woman, child, girl, boy; earthling. See MANKIND.

humane, *adj.* kind, merciful, tender, sympathetic; civilized. See BENEVOLENCE. *Ant.,* see MALEVOLENCE.

humble, *adj. & v.t.* —*adj.* lowly, unassuming, modest; meek, submissive; poor, obscure, paltry, mean. —*v.t.* abase, shame, humiliate. See MODESTY, INFERIORITY, LOWNESS, OBSCURITY, SIMPLENESS.

humbug, *n.* DECEIVER, imposter, pretender; deception, hoax, fraud; charlatanry.

humdrum, *adj.* DULL, routine, monotonous, prosaic, tiresome; ordinary, unremarkable, unexciting.

humid, *adj.* moist, damp, wet, dank. See MOISTURE. *Ant.,* see DRYNESS.

humiliate, *v.* shame, abash, abase; degrade, debase, demean, humble, degrade, disgrace, mortify; cause to eat humble pie *or* crow; cause to lose face; take down a peg. *Colloq.,* squelch. *Ant.,* see VANITY.

humility, *n.* humbleness, lowliness, meekness; abasement; submissiveness, shame, confusion, abashment, mortification; unassumingness, MODESTY. *Ant.,* see VANITY.

humor, *n. & v.t.* —*n.* disposition, mood, temper; CAPRICE, drollery, WIT; fun; jest; choler, melancholy, depression, anger; facetiousness. —*v.t.* indulge, favor, grant, oblige, gratify. See PERMISSION.

humorist, *n.* joker, jester, wag, wit; comedian, comic, clown, buffoon; funmaker; merry-andrew, fool; practical joker; punster. *Colloq.,* gagman, wisecracker.

hunger, *n. & v.i.* —*n.* DESIRE, craving; famine, hungriness, emptiness; GLUTTONY, appetite, voracity, greed. —*v.i.* desire, crave, yearn; famish, starve.

hunt, *n. & v.* —*n.* chase, drag; PURSUIT, search. —*v.t.* chase, stalk, follow, trace, pursue, run, trail, hound. —*v.i.* shoot, poach, trap, snare, hawk, ferret. See INQUIRY.

hurl, *v.t.* throw, project, pitch, toss, fling, cast; dart. See PROPULSION.

hurricane, *n.* storm, tempest; VIOLENCE, furor(e); cyclone, typhoon, whirlwind. See WIND.

hurry, *v.* press, rush, drive, force; hasten, speed, accelerate, quicken, facilitate, scurry. See HASTE.

hurt, *n. & v.* —*n.* damage, PAIN, ache, injury, wound, bruise, offense; loss, harm; distress, grief. —*v.* ache, PAIN, throb; injure, wound; damage, harm; offend, distress; grieve; bruise. See BADNESS, DETERIORATION, EVIL. *Ant.,* see GOODNESS, IMPROVEMENT, PLEASURE.

husband, *n.* mate, spouse; benedict, bridegroom; man. See MARRIAGE.

husbandry, See AGRICULTURE.

hush, *n. & v.t.* —*n.* silence, quiet, stillness, calm. —*v.t.* calm, stifle, muffle; soothe, allay, still; hide, suppress. See CONCEALMENT, MODERATION, SILENCE.

husk, *n.* shell, integument, rind, skin. See COVERING.

husky, *adj.* strong, sturdy, powerful, robust, healthy; harsh, throaty, hoarse.
hut, *n.* shack, shanty, hovel, shelter, cabin. See ABODE.
hybrid, *n. & adj.* —*n.* MIXTURE, crossbreed, cross. mongrel; mestizo, mulatto, quadroon, octroon, half-caste, half-breed, Creole. —*adj.* mixed, crossbred; mongrel; graded, half-blooded. See UNCONFORMITY. *Ant.,* see CONFORMITY.
hygienic, *adj.* cleanly, sanitary, uncontaminated; wholesome, salutary; clean. See HEALTH, CLEANNESS.
hymn, *n.* song of praise; hallelujah, hosanna; canticle, sacred song, spiritual; psalm, paean, song of devotion; psalmody; chant, plainsong; anthem; response; evensong, vespers, matins; noël, nowell, Christmas carol. See RELIGION, MUSIC.
hypnotic, *adj.* mesmeric, fascinating, magnetic; soporific, narcotic, quieting, lethargic; irresistible.
hypochondriac, *n.* worrier, self-tormenter, pessimist; morbid person. See DEJECTION. *Ant.,* see CHEERFULNESS.
hypocrisy, *n.* deceit, dissembling, pretense, falsity, DECEPTION, insincerity; sanctimony, cant, Phariseeism. See FALSEHOOD, IMPIETY. *Ant.,* see TRUTH, PIETY.
hypothesis, *n.* condition; SUPPOSITION, theory, postulate, assumption.
hysterical, *adj.* uncontrolled, wild, emotional; convulsive; frenzied, frenetic. See FEELING.

I

ice, *n. & v.* —*n.* frost, rime, frozen water; glacier, iceberg, floe; icicle. *Slang,* diamonds. —*v.* freeze, chill. See COLD.
icy, *adj.* freezing, COLD, frosty, frigid, gelid, rimed, frozen; Arctic, polar. *Ant.,* see HEAT.
idea, *n.* THOUGHT, concept, notion; opinion, conceit, BELIEF, impression; principle; invention, IMAGINATION. See SUPPOSITION, APPEARANCE, PREPARATION.
ideal, *n. & adj.* —*n.* model, paragon; idol, hero; perfect example. See PERFECTION. —*adj.* visionary; unattainable, Platonic, abstract, Utopian, perfect; impracticable. See IMAGINATION. *Ant.,* see IMPERFECTION.

IDENTITY [13]

Nouns—identity, identicalness, oneness, sameness; coincidence, coalescence; convertibility; EQUALITY; selfness, self, oneself, individuality; identification; monotony, synonymity; tautology (see REPETITION); facsimile, COPY; *alter ego* (see SIMILARITY); same; selfsame, very same, one and the same; very thing, actual thing; no other.
2, selfness, self, individuality, SPECIALITY; very thing; no other; personality; I, ego, myself, himself, *etc.*
Verbs—be identical, coincide, coalesce; diagnose; treat as the same, treat as identical; render the same, render identical; identify; recognize the identity of.
Adjectives—identical; the same, selfsame; coincident, coalescent, coalescing; indistinguishable; one; synonymous, analogous, equivalent (see EQUALITY); much the same, much of a muchness; unaltered; tantamount.
Adverbs—specially, in particular; each, apiece, one by one, in detail; identically.
Adverbs—identically, *etc.*

Antonym, see DIFFERENCE.

idiocy, *n.* imbecility, VACUITY, cretinism, feeblemindedness; foolishness, vapidity, senselessness. *Ant.,* see INTELLECT.
idle, *adj. & v.i.* —*adj.* vain, useless, futile, fruitless, pointless, aimless; out of work, unemployed, inactive; at rest; vacant, empty. See USELESSNESS, INACTIVITY, VANITY. *Ant.,* see ACTIVITY, USE, UTILITY. —*v.i.* rest; loaf, dawdle, trifle, dillydally. *Ant.,* see USE, ACTIVITY.

IDOLATRY [991]

Nouns—**1**, idolatry, idolism; demonism, demonolatry; idol worship, demon worship, devil worship, fire worship, sun worship; zoölatry, fetishism; bibliolatry; deification, apotheosis, canonization; hero worship; animism.
2, sacrifice, hecatomb, holocaust; human sacrifice, immolation, infanticide, self-immolation, suttee.
3, idolater, idol worshiper, devil worshiper, *etc.*
4, idol, golden calf, graven image, fetish, avatar, *lares et penates*, household gods.
Verbs—idolatrize, idolize, worship (idols, pictures, relics); deify; canonize, make sacrifice.
Adjectives—idolatrous, pagan; hero-worshiping.
Antonym, see RELIGION.

if, *conj.* supposing, in case that, provided; whether. See SUPPOSITION.
ignoble, *adj.* vile, base; knavish; detestable; low, common. See VULGARITY, POPULACE. *Ant.*, see NOBILITY.
ignominious, *adj.* shameful, disgraceful; degrading, humiliating. See DISREPUTE. *Ant.*, see REPUTE.
ignoramus, *n.* dunce, dolt, know-nothing; greenhorn; novice. *Slang,* lowbrow, dumbbell, dope, stupe, stupid. See FOOL, IGNORANCE. *Ant.*, see KNOWLEDGE.

IGNORANCE [491]

Nouns—**1**, ignorance, nescience; illiteracy; DARKNESS, blindness; incomprehension, inexperience, simplicity, SIMPLENESS; unawareness.
2, unknown quantities, sealed book, *terra incognita*, virgin soil, unexplored ground; dark ages.
3, smattering, glimmering; dilettantism, superficiality; bewilderment (see DOUBT); incapacity; blind spot.
Verbs—be ignorant, not know, have no idea, have no notion, have no conception; not have the remotest idea; not know from Adam; ignore, be blind to; keep in the dark *or* in ignorance (see CONCEALMENT); see through a glass darkly; not know what to make of.
Adjectives—**1**, ignorant; unknowing; unaware, unacquainted, unapprised, unwitting, witless; a stranger to; unconversant; uninformed, uncultivated, unversed, uninstructed, untaught, uninitiated, untutored, unschooled, unguided, unenlightened; behind the times; in the dark, benighted; hoodwinked, misinformed; at sea (see DOUBT).
2, shallow, superficial, green, rude, empty, half-learned, illiterate.
Adverbs—ignorantly, unawares; for anything one knows; not that one knows.
Antonym, see KNOWLEDGE.

ignore, *v.t.* overlook, pass by, disregard; slight, omit, NEGLECT; snub. See IGNORANCE.
ill, *adj. & adv.* —*adj.* unwell, sick indisposed; nauseous. See DISEASE. *Ant.*, see HEALTH. —*adv.* poorly, badly; wrongly, improperly; clumsily. See UNSKILLFULNESS, BADNESS.

ILLEGALITY [964]

Nouns—**1**, illegality, lawlessness, unlawfulness, unconstitutionality; illegitimacy, bar sinister, bastardy; criminality; outlawry; extralegality; DISOBEDIENCE, UNCONFORMITY.
2, violence, brute force; tyranny, despotism; mob law, lynch law, martial law, drumhead law, kangaroo court; rebellion, *coup d'état*, *Putsch*, usurpation.
3, offense, crime, transgression, infringement, felony, violation *or* breach (of law), delinquency. See EVILDOER.
4, racketeering, confidence *or* bunco game, swindling, *etc.*
5, undueness, invalidity, impropriety, absence of right, usurpation, encroachment.

Verbs—offend against *or* violate the law; break *or* flout the law; take the law into one's own hands; smuggle, run, poach.
Adjectives—illegal, prohibited, UNDUE, unsanctioned, not allowed, unlawful, outlaw(ed), illegitimate, illicit, contraband, actionable, criminal; unchartered, unconstitutional; unwarranted, unwarrantable; unauthorized; informal, unofficial, injudicial, extrajudicial; lawless, arbitrary, licentious; despotic, summary, irresponsible; unanswerable, unaccountable; null and void.
Adverbs—illegally; with a high hand; in violation; outside *or* beyond the law.
Antonym, see LEGALITY.

illegitimate, *adj.* bastard; unlawful, illicit, crooked; illogical. See ILLEGALITY. *Ant.*, see RIGHT, LEGALITY.
illicit, *adj.* illegal, unlawful, unsanctioned. See ILLEGALITY. *Ant.*, see LEGALITY, RIGHT.
illogical, *adj.* unreasoned, faulty, fallacious, specious, implausible, absurd; ridiculous. *Ant.*, see REASONING.
ill-treatment, *n.* abuse, cruelty, mistreatment, maltreatment; manhandling; carelessness. See NEGLECT, BADNESS.
illuminate, *v.t.* LIGHT, illumine; clarify, elucidate, explain; decorate (with gold). *Ant.*, see DARKNESS.
illustrate, *v.t.* design, pictures for, decorate (with pictures); give as an example, exemplify; explain, clarify. See ORNAMENT, INTERPRETATION.
illustrious, *adj.* renowned, eminent, distinguished, famous, celebrated. See REPUTE. *Ant.*, see DISREPUTE.
image, *n.* picture; reflection; double, counterpart, likeness; portrait, statue, figure; IDEA, concept. See SIMILARITY, APPEARANCE, REPRESENTATION.

IMAGINATION [515]

Nouns—**1,** imagination, imaginativeness; originality; invention; fancy; creativeness, inspiration; verve, improvisation.
2, ideality, idealism; romanticism, utopianism, castle-building; dreaming; ecstasy; reverie, trance; somnambulism.
3, conception, concept, excogitation; cloudland, wonderland, dreamland; flight of fancy; brain child; imagery; conceit, figment, figment of the imagination; myth, dream, VISION, shadow, chimera; phantasm, unreality, illusion, hallucination, mirage, fantasy; whim, whims(e)y; vagary, rhapsody, romance, extravaganza; bugbear, nightmare; castles in the air, castles in Spain; Utopia, Atlantis, happy valley, millennium; fairyland; fabrication; creation; FICTION; stretch of the imagination (see EXAGGERATION). *Colloq.*, pipedream.
4, imaginer, idealist, romanticist, visionary; romancer, dreamer; enthusiast; rainbow-chaser; tilter at windmills.
Verbs—imagine, fancy, conceive; idealize, realize; dream, dream of; create, originate, devise, invent, coin, fabricate; improvise; set one's wits to work; strain one's imagination; rack, ransack *or* cudgel one's brains; excogitate; give play to the imagination, indulge in reverie; conjure up a vision; suggest itself (see THOUGHT).
Adjectives—imagined, imaginary; imagining, imaginative; original, inventive, creative, fertile; fabulous, legendary, mythological; chimerical, visionary; notional; fancy, fanciful, fantastic(al); whimsical; fairy, fairylike; romantic, high-flown, flighty, extravagant, fanatic, enthusiastic, Utopian, quixotic; ideal, unreal; in the clouds, unsubstantial (see INSUBSTANTIALITY); illusory (see ERROR).
Antonym, see SIMPLENESS.

imbecility, *n.* See INSANITY. *Ant.*, see SANITY, KNOWLEDGE.
imbue, *v.t.* saturate; tinge, COLOR, suffuse; instill, inspire, INFLUENCE. See MIXTURE.

IMITATION [19]

Nouns—**1,** imitation; copying, transcription; REPETITION, DUPLICATION, reduplication, quotation; paraphrase, takeoff, parody, travesty, burlesque;

COPY, plagiarism, counterfeiting, forgery (see FALSEHOOD); reflection; REPRODUCTION; mockery, mimicry; simulation, pretense, sham, impersonation, imposture; facsimile, REPRESENTATION; semblance; assimilation.

2, imitator, mimic, echo, cuckoo, parrot, ape, monkey, mockingbird; forger, plagiarist, counterfeiter. *Colloq.,* copycat.

Verbs—imitate, copy, mirror, reflect, reproduce, repeat; echo, reëcho, catch; transcribe; match, parallel; mock, take off, mimic, ape, simulate, personate, impersonate; act (see DRAMA); represent (see REPRESENTATION); counterfeit, parody, travesty, caricature, burlesque; feign, dissemble (see FALSEHOOD); follow, pattern after; follow suit; take after, model after; emulate.

Adjectives—imitated, imitating; mock, mimic; modeled after, molded on; quasi, pseudo; paraphrastic; literal; imitative; secondhand; imitable; unoriginal.

Adverbs—imitatively; literally, to the letter, *verbatim, literarium; sic;* word for word.

Antonyms, see IDENTITY, TRUTH.

immaculate, *adj.* clean, spotless, unsullied; chaste, pure, virgin, untouched. See CLEANNESS, PURITY. *Ant.,* see GUILT, UNCLEANNESS.

immanent, *adj.* INTRINSIC, innate, inherent; universal (as God).

immaterial, *adj.* unsubstantial, incorporeal, disembodied; irrelevant, impertinent; impalpable, intangible; trivial, unimportant, inconsequential. See INSUBSTANTIALITY, UNIMPORTANCE. *Ant.,* see SUBSTANCE, RELATION, IMPORTANCE.

immaturity, *adj.* greenness, unripeness, unreadiness; YOUTH. *Ant.,* see OLDNESS, PREPARATION.

immediate, *adj.* prompt, instant, present; next; first. See EARLINESS.

immemorial, *adj.* prehistoric, ancient; beyond recollection. See OLDNESS.

immense, *adj.* vast, great, tremendous, huge; infinite; overwhelming. See SIZE.

immerse, *v.* bathe, dip, baptize; duck, plunge; submerge.

immigrant, *n.* newcomer, settler, colonist; *Colloq.,* greenhorn. See INGRESS. *Ant.,* see EGRESS.

imminent, *adj.* impending, close at hand, about to occur; near, threatening. See EARLINESS.

immoderate, *adj.* excessive, overdone; extreme; unreasonable, extravagant. See GREATNESS. *Ant.,* see MODERATION.

immoral, *adj.* WRONG, EVIL; corrupt, lewd, bawdy; dissolute, licentious, loose, indecent, adulterous; vicious, dishonest. See BADNESS, EVIL. *Ant.,* see RIGHT, VIRTUE.

immortal, *adj. & n.* —*adj.* everlasting; divine, godlike; deathless, imperishable; famous, glorious. *Ant.,* see INSTANTANEITY, DEATH. —*n.* god, demigod; great man. See DEITY, GREATNESS.

immovable, *adj.* immobile, fixed, unbudging; firm, steadfast, rocklike; stubborn, obdurate. See RESOLUTION, STABILITY. *Ant.,* see MOTION.

immunity, *n.* EXEMPTION, freedom (from); privilege. *Ant.,* see SENSIBILITY, TENDENCY.

impact, *n.* brunt, shock; percussion; collision; contact, TOUCH, bump, slam. See IMPULSE. *Ant.,* see RECOIL, AVOIDANCE.

impair, *v.t.* damage, weaken, wear (out), spoil, mar; vitiate, reduce. See DETERIORATION. *Ant.,* see IMPROVEMENT, RESTORATION.

impart, *v.t.* share, give, lend; tell, disclose, divulge, reveal, communicate. See GIVING, INFORMATION. *Ant.,* see SECRET.

impartial, *adj.* nonpartisan; unprejudiced, unbiased, fair; dispassionate, disinterested, equitable. See PROBITY, EQUALITY. *Ant.,* see MISJUDGMENT.

impasse, *n.* deadlock; blind alley, stone wall, dead end; standstill. See END.

impassioned, *adj.* ardent, fervent; heated; passionate, hot; frenzied, frantic; stirred, excited. See EXCITEMENT. *Ant.,* see COLD.

impassive, *adj.* stolid, phlegmatic; stoical, calm; undemonstrative, unimpressible, immobile, immovable; unsusceptible. See INSENSIBILITY. *Ant.,* see EXCITEMENT, SENSIBILITY.

impediment, *n.* HINDRANCE, obstacle, block, obstruction.

impel, *v.t.* drive, push, urge, move forward; force, constrain; incite, compel, induce. See IMPULSE, MOTION.

impend, *v.i.* threaten, be about to occur, hang over; loom. See DESTINY.

impenetrable, *adj.* solid, dense; impermeable, impassable; -proof; abstruse, mysterious, esoteric; unintelligible; incomprehensible, unfathomable. See DENSITY.

impenitence, *n.* unrepentance, obduracy, incorrigibility, relentlessness, recusancy; lack of contriteness, remorse *or* regret; consciencelessness. See HARDNESS, MALEVOLENCE. *Ant.*, see PENITENCE, ATONEMENT, PITY.

imperative, *adj. & n.* —*adj.* urgent, essential, necessary, compulsory; unavoidable. See COMMAND, REQUIREMENT. *Ant.*, see USELESSNESS. —*n.* COMMAND; *Colloq.*, a must; (*Gram.*) word of command; imperative mood.

IMPERFECTION [651]

Nouns—**1,** imperfection; imperfectness, incompleteness, faultiness; deficiency; inadequacy, INSUFFICIENCY, peccancy, BADNESS; immaturity, mediocrity, shortcoming.

2, fault, defect, weak point; mar, blemish; flaw, snag, DISTORTION; taint, attainder; bar sinister; WEAKNESS; half-blood; drawback. *Colloq.*, no great shakes; not much to boast of; catch; screw loose; a fly in the ointment.

3, BLEMISH, deformity, disfigurement, mar, injury; eyesore.

Verbs—be imperfect, not pass muster, fall short. *Colloq.*, get by.

Adjectives—**1,** imperfect, deficient, defective; faulty, unsound, tainted; out of order, out of tune; cracked, leaky; sprung; warped (see DISTORTION); lame; injured, (see DETERIORATION); peccant, bad (see BADNESS); frail, WEAK, lame, infirm; inadequate, insufficient; found wanting; below par; shorthanded; below *or* under its full strength *or* complement. *Colloq.*, not up to scratch. *Slang*, on the blink; fouled (up), snafu.

2, indifferent, middling, ordinary, mediocre; average, MEAN; so-so; tolerable, fair, passable; pretty well, pretty good; good enough, well enough; decent; not bad, not amiss; bearable, better than nothing; secondary, inferior, run of the mine *or* mill, secondrate, second-best. *Colloq.*, fair to middling.

3, blemished, pitted, discolored, impaired, marred, deformed.

Adverbs—imperfectly, almost; to a limited extent, rather (see LITTLENESS); pretty, moderately; only; considering, all things considered, enough.

Antonym, see PERFECTION.

---

imperil, *v.t.* endanger, jeopardize, risk. See DANGER. *Ant.*, see SAFETY, ESCAPE.

impersonate, *v.t.* pose (as); imitate, take off (*Colloq.*), mimic; personify; play the impostor. See REPRESENTATION.

impertinent, *adj.* insolent, saucy, fresh (*Colloq.*), cheeky, impudent; irrelevant, inapt, inapposite. See INSOLENCE. *Ant.*, see COURTESY, RELATION.

impetuous, *adj.* impulsive, rash, headlong; rushing, unrestrainable. See IMPULSE, VIOLENCE. *Ant.*, see RESTRAINT.

IMPIETY [988]

Nouns—**1,** impiety, impiousness; sin; irreverence; profaneness, profanity, profanation; blasphemy, desecration, sacrilege; scoffing; hardening, fall from grace; backsliding, declension, perversion, reprobation, IRRELIGION.

2, assumed piety, hypocrisy (see FALSEHOOD); pietism, cant, pious fraud; lip service; misdevotion, formalism, austerity; sanctimony, sanctimoniousness; pharisaism, precisianism; sabbatism, sabbatarianism; sacerdotalism; bigotry (see NARROWNESS).

3, sinner, EVILDOER; scoffer, blasphemer, profaner, sacrilegist; worldling; hypocrite; backslider; bigot; Pharisee, ranter, fanatic; sons of Belial, children of darkness.

Verbs—profane, desecrate, blaspheme, revile, scoff; swear (see IMPRECATION); commit sacrilege; fall from grace, backslide.

Adjectives—impious; irreligious; desecrating, profane, irreverent, sacrilegious, blasphemous; unhallowed, unsanctified, unregenerate; hardened, perverted, reprobate; hypocritical, canting, sanctimonious, unctuous, pharisaical, overrighteous; bigoted, fanatical.

Adverbs—impiously; under the mask, cloak, pretence, form *or* guise of religion.

Antonym, see PIETY.

implant, *v.t.* plant, embed, fix, set in; inculcate, instill; graft, engraft.

implement, *n. & v.* —*n.* tool, utensil, INSTRUMENT. —*v.* equip; effect; fulfill. See POWER, USE. *Ant.*, see HINDRANCE, NULLIFICATION.

implicate, *v.t.* involve, entangle, embroil; incriminate; connect, associate. See ACCUSATION. *Ant.*, see DISJUNCTION.

implication, *n.* involvement; allusion, inference; innuendo, suggestion. See MEANING.

implore, *v.t.* beg, beseech, entreat, plead. See REQUEST.

imply, *v.t.* hint, suggest, infer, intimate; involve. See EVIDENCE, INFORMATION.

impolite, *adj.* rude, inconsiderate, uncivil, ill-mannered, ill-bred. See DISCOURTESY. *Ant.*, see COURTESY.

import, *n. & v* —*n.* MEANING, significance, IMPORTANCE; trend, drift, purport. See INGRESS. —*v.* bring in; introduce; imply, indicate. See MEANING.

IMPORTANCE [642]

Nouns—**1,** importance, import, consequence, moment, prominence, consideration, mark, materialness, primacy; significance, concern; emphasis, interest; distinction, prestige, grandeur, majesty; GREATNESS, SUPERIORITY, notability, REPUTE; weight, value, GOODNESS; usefulness (see UTILITY).

2, GRAVITY, seriousness, solemnity; no joke, no laughing matter; pressure, urgency, stress; matter of life and death; exigency.

3, memorabilia, notabilia, great doings; red-letter day, milestone, turning point.

4, substance, gist, essence; main chance, be all and end all, cardinal point; sum and substance, *sine qua non*; breath of life; cream, salt, core, kernel, heart, nucleus; key, keynote, keystone; cornerstone; trump card; salient points; essentials, fundamentals.

5, personage, notable, figure, prima donna, chief. *Slang*, big gun, VIP.

Verbs—**1,** import, signify, matter, boot, be somebody, carry weight; cut a figure (see REPUTE); overshadow; count for; lie at the root of.

2, attach importance to, value, care for; set store by; mark (see INDICATION); underline; put in italics *or* capitals, capitalize, italicize; accentuate, emphasize, stress, lay stress on; make a fuss *or* stir about, make much of.

Adjectives—**1,** important; of importance, momentous, material; not to be overlooked, not to be despised, not to be sneezed at; egregious; weighty, influential; of note (see REPUTE); notable, prominent, salient, signal; memorable, remarkable; worthy of remark, worthy of notice; never to be forgotten; stirring, eventful, significant, telling, trenchant, emphatic, pregnant.

2, grave, serious; urgent, pressing, critical, instant.

3, paramount, essential, vital, all-absorbing; cardinal, chief, main, prime, primary, principal, leading, capital, foremost, overriding; in the front rank, firstrate; superior (see SUPERIORITY); considerable (see GREATNESS); marked; rare (see RARITY).

Adverbs—importantly, materially, in the main; above all, *par excellence*.

Antonym, see UNIMPORTANCE.

impose, *v.t.* burden (with), inflict; force (upon); levy, tax; delude, take advantage (of), palm off, foist; obtrude. See DECEPTION.

imposing, *adj.* dignified, awe-inspiring; impressive; grand, stately, commanding. See REPUTE.

impossible, *adj.* not possible; absurd, contrary to reason; unreasonable, incredible, inconceivable, improbable, prodigious, unimaginable; impracticable, unachievable; insuperable; infeasible; insurmountable; unattainable, unobtainable; out of reach, out of the question; desperate, hopeless. *Ant.*, see CHANCE.

imposture, *n.* masquerade, pretense; fraud, DECEPTION; impersonation.

IMPOTENCE [158]

Nouns—**1,** impotence; inability; disability; disablement, impuissance, incapacity, incapability; inaptness, ineptitude, inefficiency, incompetence; disqualification.

2, inefficacy (see USELESSNESS); FAILURE; helplessness, prostration, exhaustion, enervation; emasculation, castration.

3, eunuch; cripple; blank cartridge, flash in the pan, dummy. *Slang*, washout, dud.

Verbs—**1,** be impotent; collapse, faint, swoon, drop.

2, render powerless; unman, unnerve, enervate; emasculate, castrate, geld; disable, disarm, incapacitate, disqualify, unfit, invalidate, deaden, cramp, exhaust, weaken, debilitate; muzzle, cripple, maim, lame, hamstring, draw the teeth of; throttle, strangle, garrote, silence; break the back; unhinge, unfit. *Colloq.*, hog-tie.

Adjectives—**1,** impotent, powerless, unable, incapable, incompetent; inefficient, ineffective; inept; unfit, unfitted; unqualified, disqualified; unendowed; crippled, disabled; paralytic, paralyzed; emasculate(d); waterlogged, rudderless; on one's back; done up, dead beat, exhausted, shattered, demoralized; without a leg to stand on, *hors de combat*, out of commission.

2, harmless, unarmed; defenseless, unfortified, indefensible, vincible, pregnable, untenable; null and void, nugatory, inoperative, good for nothing; ineffectual (see FAILURE); inadequate (see INSUFFICIENCY); inefficacious (See USELESSNESS).

Antonym, see POWER.

---

impoverish, *v.t.* pauperize, make poor; exhaust, drain; reduce, deplete; rob; weaken. See POVERTY, INSUFFICIENCY. *Ant.*, see IMPROVEMENT, MONEY.

impracticable, *adj.* unworkable, inexpedient, not feasible; idealistic, visionary; unrealistic.

IMPRECATION [908]

Nouns—imprecation, malediction, malison, curse, denunciation, execration; anathema, ban, proscription, excommunication, commination, fulmination; calumny, calumniation, contumely, invective, diatribe, jeremiad, tirade, vituperation, disparagement, obloquy; abuse, billingsgate, sauce; cursing, profanity, swearing, oath; THREAT.

Verbs—imprecate, curse, damn, swear (at); execrate, beshrew, scold; anathematize (see DISAPPROBATION); vilify, denounce, proscribe, excommunicate, fulminate, thunder against; threaten; defame (see DETRACTION).

Adjectives—imprecatory, denunciatory, proscribed, abusive, cursing, cursed, accursed.

Interjections—woe to! woe betide! damn! confound! blast! curse! devil take! hang! out with! a plague upon! out upon!

Antonym, see APPROBATION.

---

impress, *v.t.* stamp, mark, print, imprint, engrave; dint, dent; inspire, affect strongly, overawe; interest; strike; draft, compel (service); *Colloq.*, crimp, shanghai. See EXCITEMENT, PRINTING, RESTRAINT, INDICATION.

impressive, *adj.* imposing, effective; awesome, majestic, stately, moving, stirring, weighty, large, considerable. See FEELING, GREATNESS, EFFECT. *Ant.*, see UNIMPORTANCE.

IMPROBITY [940]

Nouns—**1,** improbity; dishonesty, dishonor; disgrace, DISREPUTE; fraud, DECEPTION; lying, FALSEHOOD; bad faith; infidelity; inconstancy, faithlessness, Judas kiss, betrayal; breach of promise, trust, *or* faith; renegation, renegadism, disloyalty, treason, high treason; apostasy (see CHANGEABLENESS, GUILT); IMPURITY. See EVILDOER.

2, villainy, baseness, abjection, debasement, turpitude, moral turpitude, laxity; perfidy, perfidiousness, treachery, duplicity, double-dealing; unfairness, knavery, roguery, rascality, foul play; trickery, venality, nepotism; corruption; simony, barratry, graft, malfeasance.

3, VICE, depravity, infamy, looseness, profligacy. See LIBERTINE.

Verbs—**1,** be dishonest, play false; forswear, break one's word, faith *or* promise; jilt, betray; sell out; lie (see FALSEHOOD); live by one's wits; misrepresent; steal (see STEALING); hit below the belt. *Colloq.*, go back on.
2, be vicious, sin, fall, lapse, slip, trip, offend, trespass, deviate, misdo, misbehave; go to the devil, go wrong.
Adjectives—**1,** dishonest, dishonorable, unscrupulous; fraudulent (see DECEPTION); knavish, disgraceful, disreputable (see DISREPUTE); wicked, sinful, VICIOUS, criminal.
2, false-hearted, unfair; two-faced; crooked, insidious, Machiavellian, dark, slippery; perfidious, treacherous, perjured; infamous, arrant, foul, base, vile, ignominious, blackguard; corrupt, venal; recreant, inglorious, discreditable, improper; faithless, false, unfaithful, disloyal; treacherous, renegade; untrustworthy, unreliable, undependable, trustless; lost to shame, dead to honor.
Adverbs—dishonestly, like a thief in the night, underhandedly, by fair means or foul.

Antonym, see PROBITY.

improper, *adj.* indecent, bawdy, lewd, *risqué*, indelicate, immodest; WRONG, inapt, unsuitable, mistaken, unfitting, incorrect, inexcusable, erroneous, out of place. See DISCOURTESY, IMPURITY. *Ant.*, see RIGHT, PURITY.

IMPROVEMENT [658]

Nouns—**1,** improvement, uplift; melioration, amelioration, betterment; mend, amendment, emendation; advancement, advance, progress, PROGRESSION; ASCENT; promotion, preferment; ELEVATION, INCREASE; cultivation, civilization; culture. *Colloq.*, crusade, crusading.
2, reform, reformation, revision; correction, refinement, enhancement, elaboration, PERFECTION, purification (see CLEANNESS); repair, RESTORATION; recovery.
3, reformer, radical, progressive. *Colloq.*, do-gooder, crusader.
Verbs—**1,** improve; better, mend, amend; turn to good account, profit by, reap the benefit of; make good use of, make capital of; advance (see PROGRESSION); ascend (see ASCENT); INCREASE; fructify, ripen, mature; pick up, come about, rally, take a turn for the better; turn over a new leaf, turn the corner; recover (see RESTORATION). *Colloq.*, look up, snap out of it.
2, meliorate, ameliorate; palliate, mitigate; turn the tide; correct, rectify; enrich, mellow, elaborate, fatten; promote, cultivate, advance, forward, enhance; bring forward, bring on; foster (see AID); invigorate, strengthen.
3, touch up, brush up, refurbish, renovate, polish, make the most of, set off to advantage; prune; repair, restore (see RESTORATION); put in order.
4, revise, edit, correct; doctor, REMEDY; purify; relieve, refresh, infuse new blood into; reform, remodel, reorganize.
Adjectives—improving, improved; progressive; better, better off, better for; reformatory, emendatory; reparatory, restorative, remedial; corrigible, improvable.
Adverbs—*Colloq.*, over the hump, out of the woods.

Antonym, see DETERIORATION.

improvise, *v.* invent, devise (at the moment), extemporize; *Colloq.*, ad lib. See IMPULSE. *Ant.*, see PREPARATION.
impudence, *n.* INSOLENCE; gall, cheek, effrontery, boldness; *Colloq.*, nerve, freshness. See DISCOURTESY. *Ant.*, see COURTESY, FEAR, CARE.

IMPULSE [276]

Nouns—**1,** impulse, impulsion, impetus; momentum; push, thrust, shove, jog, jolt, brunt, throw; explosion (see VIOLENCE); PROPULSION; percussion, concussion, collision, clash, encounter, cannon, shock, crash, bump; impact; charge, ATTACK; beating, PUNISHMENT; dynamics, mechanics.
2, blow, dint, stroke, knock, tap, rap, slap, smack, pat, dab; fillip; slam, bang; hit, whack, cuff, swap, punch, thump, pelt, kick; cut, thrust, lunge. *Colloq.*, bat, clout, lick, clip. *Slang*, belt, sock, wallop.
3, hammer, sledgehammer, maul, mallet, flail; ram, battering ram, pile-

driver, punch, bat; cudgel, weapon; ax(e) (see SHARPNESS).

4, sudden thought; impromptu, improvisation; inspiration, flash, spurt.

Verbs—**1,** give impetus; impel, push; start, set going; drive, urge; thrust, prod; elbow, shoulder, jostle, hustle, shove, job, jolt, bump; impinge.

2, strike, knock, hit, tap, rap, slap, pat, thump, beat, bang, slam, dash; punch, whack; hit hard, strike hard; batter; pelt, buffet, belabor; fetch one a blow; poke at, pink, lunge; kick, butt; make a pass at, strike at, ATTACK; whip (see PUNISHMENT). *Colloq.*, belt, lambaste, clip, swat, larrup, wallop. *Slang*, knock galley-west.

3, collide; fall *or*, run foul of; throw (see PROPULSION).

Adjectives—**1,** impelling, impellent; dynamic, impelled.

2, impulsive, extemporaneous, impromptu, offhand, improvised, unmeditated, unpremeditated; natural, unguarded; spontaneous, voluntary (see WILL).

Adverbs—**1,** impulsively, explosively, *etc.*

2, impulsively, extempore, extemporaneously; offhand, impromptu, improviso; on the spur of the moment.

        Antonym, see THOUGHT, RECEIVING.

---

impunity, *n.* freedom (from reprisal), EXEMPTION, immunity (to laws). See ACQUITTAL.

IMPURITY [961]

Nouns—**1,** impurity; UNCLEANNESS; immodesty; grossness, indelicacy, indecency; pornography, obscenity, ribaldry, smut, bawdy, *double entendre*.

2, concupiscence, lust, carnality, flesh, salacity; pruriency, lechery, lasciviousness, lewdness, lubricity; incontinence, unchastity; debauchery, license, immorality, libertinism, fornication, liaison; wenching, venery, dissipation; incest; perversion, sodomy, pederasty, homosexuality, Lesbianism; sadism, masochism; seduction, defloration, defilement, abuse, violation, rape, (criminal) assault *(euphemisms);* harlotry, whoredom, concubinage; cuckoldry, adultery, infidelity.

3, immorality, laxity, looseness of morals, iniquity, turpitude, depravity, pollution, profligacy, shame, vice.

4, brothel, bagnio, bawdyhouse, whorehouse, house of ill fame, bordello, red-light district.

Verbs—debauch; defile; deflower, rape, ravish, seduce; prostitute; abuse, violate; commit adultery.

Adjectives—**1,** impure; unclean; immodest, shameless; indecorous, indelicate, indecent; loose, coarse, gross, broad, promiscuous; smutty, ribald, obscene, bawdy, pornographic, risqué; concupiscent, prurient, lustful; lewd, lascivious, lecherous, libidinous, ruttish, salacious; unfaithful, adulterous; incestuous; unchaste, incontinent; light, wanton, licentious, rakish, debauched, dissipated, dissolute; loose, meretricious, of easy virtue, on the streets; gay.

2, vicious, immoral, dissolute, profligate, sinful, iniquitous.

        Antonym, see PURITY.

---

inability, *n.* IMPOTENCE, incapacity, powerlessness; UNSKILLFULNESS, incompetence, inefficiency. *Ant.*, see POWER, SKILL.

inaccurate, *adj.* erroneous, fallacious, incorrect, WRONG; mistaken; inexact, unprecise; misleading. See ERROR. *Ant.*, see TRUTH, CARE.

INACTIVITY [683, 681]

Nouns—**1,** inactivity; inaction; inertness; obstinacy; lull, cessation, REPOSE, rest, quiescence; rustiness; idleness, sloth, NEGLECT, laziness, indolence; unemployment, dilatoriness, dawdling; malingering; passiveness, passivity, dormancy; stagnation; procrastination; time on one's hands; *laissez faire*, noninterference; *dolce far niente*, lotusland.

2, dullness, languor; sluggishness, SLOWNESS, delay (see LATENESS); torpor, torpidity, torpescence; stupor, stupefaction, INSENSIBILITY; drowsiness, nodding; mesmerism, hypnotism, lethargy; heaviness, FATIGUE, weariness.

3, sleep, slumber, somnolence, sound *or* heavy sleep; Morpheus; coma, swoon, trance; catalepsy; dream; hibernation, estivation; nap, catnap, doze, siesta. *Colloq.,* forty winks, snooze. *Slang,* shuteye.

4, sedative, tranquil(l)izer, sleeping draft *or* pill, soporific, opiate (see REMEDY). *Slang,* knockout drops.

5, idler, drone, do-little, dummy, silent partner; fifth wheel; truant (see AVOIDANCE); lounger, loafer; lubber, slowpoke (see SLOWNESS); opium eater, lotus-eater; slug; laggard, sluggard; clock-watcher, good-for-nothing; slumberer, sleepyhead, dormouse.

6, halt, standstill, full stop; stalemate, impasse, block, check, checkmate; red light.

Verbs—**1,** be inactive, let the grass grow under one's feet; take one's time, dawdle, lag, hang back, slouch, loll, lounge, loaf, laze, loiter; sleep at one's post *or* at the switch, flag, languish.

2, relax, take it easy; vegetate, lie fallow; waste, consume, kill, *or* lose time; twiddle one's thumbs; not lift a finger *or* hand; idle, trifle, fritter, *or* fool away time; piddle, potter, putter, dabble, fiddle-faddle, dally, shilly-shally, dilly-dally; ride at anchor, rest on one's oars, rest on one's laurels; hang fire, postpone. *Colloq.,* cool one's heels.

3, sleep, slumber; hibernate; oversleep; sleep like a top *or* log; doze, drowse, snooze, nap; dream; snore; nod, yawn; go to bed, turn in; REPOSE. *Colloq.,* drop off. *Slang,* hit the hay, hit the sack, pound the ear.

Adjectives—**1,** inactive; motionless, quiescent, stationary; unoccupied, idle; indolent, lazy, slothful, idle, remiss, slack, torpid, sluggish, languid, supine, heavy, dull, leaden, lumpish; inert, inanimate; listless; dilatory, laggard; lagging, slow; rusty, flagging, lackadaisical, pottering, irresolute.

2, sleeping, asleep; dormant, comatose, dead to the world, in the arms of Morpheus; sleepy, drowsy, somnolent; torpid, lethargic, heavy; napping; tranquil(l)izing, soporific, hypnotic; balmy, dreamy; sedative. *Slang,* dop(e)y; out of this world.

Antonym, see ACTIVITY.

---

inadequate, *adj.* scanty, wanting, short, below par; incomplete, partial, deficient, lacking. See INSUFFICIENCY. *Ant.,* see SUFFICIENCY.

inadvertent, *adj.* unintentional, adventitious, accidental, CHANCE; heedless, inattentive, careless, regardless, thoughtless. *Ant.,* see ATTENTION.

inadvisable, *adj.* inexpedient, not recommended; impracticable; ill-advised, unwise, imprudent; risky.

inane, *adj.* pointless, senseless; empty, vacuous; idiotic, foolish. See ABSURDITY. *Ant.,* see MEANING, KNOWLEDGE.

inarticulate, *adj.* voiceless, speechless, mute, stammering; unexpressed, unspoken, indistinct; unjointed. See SILENCE, DISJUNCTION. *Ant.,* see VOICE, JUNCTION.

inattention, *n.* inattentiveness; abstraction, absence of mind, preoccupation, distraction, reverie, woolgathering, daydreaming, brown study; oversight, inadvertence, disregard, heedlessness, NEGLECT; insouciance, INDIFFERENCE; coldness, neutrality; apathy; INSENSIBILITY; RASHNESS, carelessness, nonchalance, unconcern. *Ant.,* see ATTENTION, CARE.

inaudible, *adj.* unhearable; faint, muffled. *Ant.,* see SOUND, LOUDNESS.

inaugurate, *v.t.* install (in office), induct, invest; start, launch, initiate, institute, open. See BEGINNING.

inauspicious, *adj.* unpropitious, ill-omened, unfavorable, unlucky. See PREDICTION, ADVERSITY. *Ant.,* see PROSPERITY.

incapable, *adj.* powerless, unable; inefficient, incompetent; unqualified, unfitted, untrained. See INSUFFICIENCY. *Ant.,* see SUFFICIENCY.

incapacity, *n.* DISABILITY, IMPOTENCE, incompetence; inability, lack, deficiency. *Ant.,* see POWER.

incarnate, *v.t.* shape, form, embody; animate, quicken (with life). See SUBSTANCE. *Ant.,* see INSUBSTANTIALITY.

incendiary, *n.* pyromaniac, firebug; arsonist. See HEAT.

incentive, *n.* stimulus, goad, spur; MOTIVE, reason; provocation.

incessant, *adj.* endless, continual, unceasing; uninterrupted. See FREQUENCY, CONTINUITY. *Ant.,* see END, DISJUNCTION.

incident, *n.* occasion; EVENT, episode, happening; minor adventure.

incidental, *adj.* secondary, minor, subordinate; casual, CHANCE, accidental; current.

incite, *v.t.* stir, urge, impel; actuate, provoke, instigate; encourage, stimulate; spur, goad. See IMPULSE, CAUSE.

inclement, *adj.* unlenient, harsh, severe, merciless; foul (of weather), cold, windy, bitter. See SEVERITY. *Ant.,* see PITY.

inclination, *n.* propensity, leaning, bent, predisposition; slope, slant, ramp; fondness, liking; predilection. See TENDENCY, OBLIQUITY, DESIRE.

INCLOSURE [232]

*Nouns—***1,** inclosure, enclosure, envelope, case, RECEPTACLE, wrapper, girdle.
2, pen, fold; sheepfold, paddock, pound, coop, sty, pigsty, stall, kennel, corral, net, kraal, compound.
3, wall; hedge, fence, pale, paling, balustrade, rail, railing, dike, ditch, fosse, moat, levee.
4, barrier, barricade, parapet, rampart, stockade; jail (see PRISON).
*Verbs—*enclose, inclose, confine, surround, circumscribe, envelope, pen in, hem in, impen.

Antonym, see EXTERIOR.

---

include, *v.t.* comprise, comprehend, contain, admit, embrace, receive; enclose, circumscribe, compose, incorporate, encompass; reckon *or* number among, count in; refer to, place under, take into account. *Ant.,* EXCLUDE.

inclusion, *n.* admission; comprehension; acceptance, reception; incorporation. *Ant.,* see EXCLUSION.

incoherence, *n.* unintelligibility, irrationality, inconsistency; incongruity; maundering, raving; nonadhesion; immiscibility; looseness, FREEDOM. See DISJUNCTION. *Ant.,* see COHERENCE.

incombustible, *adj.* noninflammable, flameproof, fireproof, unburnable. See COLD. *Ant.,* see HEAT.

income, *n.* revenue; dividends, interest; receipt(s), emoluments, fees, earnings. See ACQUISITION. *Ant.,* see PAYMENT.

incompatible, *adj.* inharmonious, inconsistent, antipathetic, incongruous, uncongenial; clashing, discordant, disagreeing. See DISAGREEMENT. *Ant.,* see AGREEMENT.

incompetence, *n.* disqualification; inability, inefficiency; IMPOTENCE; unfitness, incapability, incapacity, UNSKILLFULNESS. See INSANITY.

incompleteness, *n.* incompletion; deficiency, shortness, want, lack; IMPERFECTION, INSUFFICIENCY, inadequacy, SHORTNESS; lack of wholeness. *Ant.,* see WHOLE, PERFECTION, COMPLETION, SUFFICIENCY.

incomprehensible, *adj.* unintelligible; unfathomable, abstruse, inscrutable. *Ant.,* see MEANING.

inconceivable, *adj.* unimaginable; unthinkable; incredible.

incongruity, *n.* disharmony; inconsistency, incompatibility, ABSURDITY. *Ant.,* see AGREEMENT, COHERENCE.

inconsiderate, *adj.* careless, heedless, thoughtless; tactless; neglectful. See NEGLECT. *Ant.,* see THOUGHT, CARE.

inconsistency, *n.* CHANGEABLENESS, fickleness; incompatibility; CONTRARINESS, contradiction. *Ant.,* see AGREEMENT.

inconvenient, *adj.* awkward, embarrassing, troublesome; inopportune, untimely, unseasonable; unsuitable.

incorporate, *v.* embody; federate, merge, consolidate; unite, blend, join. See JUNCTION.

incorrect, *adj.* WRONG, erroneous, fallacious; mistaken, false, untrue; inaccurate, unprecise. See ERROR, FALSEHOOD. *Ant.,* see TRUTH, RIGHT.

incorrigible, *adj.* irreclaimable, abandoned, beyond redemption; intractable, hopelessly delinquent. See EVILDOER. *Ant.,* see VIRTUE.

INCREASE [35]

*Nouns—*increase, augmentation, enlargement, extension; dilation, EXPANSION; advance, appreciation; gain, profit, increment, accretion; accession, ADDITION; development, growth; aggrandizement, AGGRAVATION; intensification, magnification, multiplication; rise, ASCENT; EXAGGERATION, exacerbation; bonus; spread, dispersion; flood tide.

Verbs—**1,** increase, augment, add to, enlarge, extend; dilate, sprout, EXPAND, swell, burgeon, bud; grow, wax, get ahead, gain strength; advance; develop, grow, run up, shoot up; rise; ascend (see ASCENT); enhance, amplify; raise, give a bonus. *Slang,* step up, jack up, hike.

2, aggrandize; raise, exalt; deepen; heighten; strengthen; intensify, enhance, magnify, redouble; aggravate, exaggerate; exasperate, exacerbate; add fuel to the flames, spread, disperse.

Adjectives—increased, increasing, multiplying, enlarged, on the increase, undiminished; additional, extra, added (see ADDITION); swollen, turgid, bloated, distended; larger, bigger, exaggerated.

Adverbs—increasingly, *etc.;* crescendo.

Antonym, see DECREASE.

---

incredibility, *n.* unbelievableness, inconceivableness; absurdity, preposterousness. See DOUBT. *Ant.,* see BELIEF.

incredulity, *n.* See DOUBT. *Ant.,* see CREDULITY, BELIEF.

incredulous, *adj.* skeptical, doubting, doubtful, dubious; unbelieving, distrusting; suspicious; unconvinced. See DOUBT. *Ant.,* see CREDULITY, BELIEF.

incur, *v.t.* acquire; become liable to risk; bring about. *Ant.,* see AVOIDANCE.

incurable, *adj.* hopeless, doomed; irremediable, irreparable; unhealable. See DISEASE. *Ant.,* see REMEDY.

incursion, *n.* encroachment; inroad, invasion; attack, foray, raid. See DESCENT.

indecent, *adj.* immoral, obscene, improper; salacious, lewd, lascivious, bawdy; immodest. See IMPURITY, UNCLEANNESS. *Ant.,* see PURITY, CLEANNESS.

indecision, *n.* irresolution, hesitation, uncertainty, vacillation, shilly-shally. *Ant.,* see RESOLUTION, CERTAINTY.

indefinite, *adj.* unclear, undefined, blurred; vague, uncertain, unspecified; indeterminate; equivocal. See DOUBT. *Ant.,* see CERTAINTY.

indent, *v.t.* impress, hollow, dent, dint; NOTCH; knock in; set in; incise, cut; pit, dimple. See CONCAVITY.

independence, *n.* FREEDOM, liberty; self-reliance; self-government, autonomy; self-sufficiency; (enough) money. See FREEDOM, MONEY.

INDICATION [550]

Nouns—**1,** indication; symbolism, symbolization; denotation, connotation, signification; specification, designation; sign, symbol; index, indicator; point, pointer; exponent, note, token, symptom; MANIFESTATION; type, figure, emblem, cipher, device; REPRESENTATION; epigraph, motto; lineament, feature, trait, characteristic, earmark, peculiarity, PROPERTY; diagnosis; footprint, fingerprint; means of recognition.

2, gesture, gesticulation; pantomime; wink, glance, leer; nod, shrug, beck; touch, nudge; dactylology, sign language; cue, implication, suggestion, hint (see INFORMATION), clue, key; scent, track, spoor.

3, signal, rocket, blue light, watchfire, watchtower; telegraph, semaphore, flagstaff; cresset, fiery cross; calumet, white flag.

4, mark, line, stroke, dash, score, stripe, scratch, tick, dot, point, NOTCH, nick; asterisk, star, dagger; punctuation; period, comma, colon, semicolon, interrogation point, question mark, exclamation point, quotation marks, dash, parentheses, brace, brackets; red letter, italics, sublineation, underlining, underscoring; accent, diacritical mark, acute, grave, circumflex, macron, dieresis, tilde.

5, identification, badge, caste mark; criterion; countercheck, countermark, countersign, counterfoil; tally, label, ticket, billet, letter, counter, card, bill; stamp; trademark, brand, hallmark; signature; autograph; credentials (see EVIDENCE); attestation; cipher; seal, signet; superscription, endorsement; title, heading, docket; shibboleth, watchword, catchword, password; open sesame; cachet; insignia, ensign; banner, flag, colors, streamer, standard, eagle, oriflamme, tricolor, Stars and Stripes; pennon, pennant, jack, ancient, gonfalon, union jack; bunting; heraldry; crest; arms, coat of arms; armorial bearings, hatchment, scutcheon, escutcheon; shield, supporters.

6, beacon, cairn, post, staff, flagstaff, hand, pointer, vane, cock, weathervane, guidepost, signpost; landmark, lighthouse; polestar, lodestar; address, direction, name; sign, signboard, milestone; traffic signal, traffic light, stoplight.

7, call, bugle, trumpet, bell, alarum, cry.

Verbs—**1,** indicate, denote, betoken, imply, argue, testify (see EVIDENCE); connote, designate, specify, manifest, reveal, disclose, exhibit; represent, stand for; typify, symbolize.

2, signal; warn, wigwag, semaphore, flag; beck, beckon; nod; wink, glance, leer, nudge, shrug, gesticulate.

3, wave; unfurl, hoist, *or* hang out a banner; wave the hand; give a cue, show one's colors; give *or* sound an alarm; sound the tocsin, beat the drum; raise a (hue and) cry.

4, note, mark, stamp, earmark; label, ticket, docket; dot, spot, score, dash, trace, chalk; print.

Adjectives—indicating, indicative, indicatory; denotative; connotative; diacritical, representative, representational, significant, suggestive; typical, symbolic, symptomatic, characteristic, demonstrative, diagnostic, exponential, emblematic.

Adverbs—indicatively; in token of; symbolically.

Antonym, see CONCEALMENT.

---

indict, *v.i.* accuse, charge, formally; arraign. See ACCUSATION.

INDIFFERENCE [866]

Nouns—**1,** indifference, neutrality; coldness, frigidity; unconcern, insouciance, nonchalance; inattention, lack of interest, anorexia, apathy, INSENSIBILITY; supineness (see INACTIVITY); disdain (see CONTEMPT); recklessness, RASHNESS; carelessness, NEGLECT.

2, sameness, equivalence, EQUALITY.

Verbs—be indifferent, be neutral; take no interest in, have no desire for, have no taste for, have no relish for; not care for; care nothing for, care nothing about; not care a straw (see UNIMPORTANCE); not mind; set at naught, make light of; spurn, disdain (see CONTEMPT).

Adjectives—indifferent, neutral, cold, frigid, lukewarm; cool, cool as a cucumber; unconcerned, insouciant, phlegmatic, dispassionate, easygoing, devil-may-care, careless, listless, lackadaisical; half-hearted; unambitious, unaspiring, undesirous, unsolicitous, unattracted; unattractive, unalluring, undesired, undesirable, uncared for, unwished, unvalued; all one (to); insipid; vain.

Adverbs—indifferently; for aught one cares.

Interjections—never mind! who cares!

Antonym, see ATTENTION, DESIRE.

---

indigenous, *adj.* native; innate, inborn; inherent, natural (to).

indignation, *n.* RESENTMENT, ire, wrath, anger; displeasure, vexation.

indirect, *adj.* oblique; roundabout, circuitous; not straight; underhand, crooked, furtive; hinted, implied, inferential. See DEVIATION. *Ant.,* see DIRECTION.

indiscretion, *n.* carelessness, recklessness; blunder, *faux pas*, lapse, slip. See GUILT. *Ant.,* see CARE.

indispensable, *adj.* vital, needful, necessary; essential, required. See NECESSITY. *Ant.,* see USELESSNESS.

indistinct, *adj.* inaudible; imperceptible, unclear, foggy, blurry, shadowy; vague, obscure, dim; faint. *Ant.,* see VISION.

individuality, *n.* UNCONFORMITY, differentness; distinctness; oneness, uniqueness; personality; peculiarity, originality; character. *Ant.,* see CONFORMITY.

indolence, *n.* ease; sloth, idleness, sluggishness, laziness; INACTIVITY. *Ant.,* see ACTIVITY.

indorse, *v.t.* approve, support, second; recommend; subscribe (to); sign. See APPROBATION, AGREEMENT. *Ant.,* see DISAPPROBATION.

induce, *v.t.* CAUSE, bring about; urge, persuade, impel influence; EFFECT. *Ant.,* see RESTRAINT.

induction, *n.* inauguration, installation (in office); inference, REASONING, conclusion; generalization.

indulge, *v.t.* pamper, spoil, favor, humor; gratify; take pleasure (in); revel. See PLEASURE. *Ant.,* see SEVERITY.

industrious, *adj.* active, busy, hard-working; diligent, assiduous, sedulous. See ACTIVITY.

industry, *n.* labor, work; occupation, trade, BUSINESS, ACTIVITY; diligence.

inelastic, *adj.* unstretchable; inflexible, inductile; flabby, lax, limp, soft, flaccid; unresilient, rigid, unyielding. See HARDNESS, SOFTNESS. *Ant.,* see ELASTICITY.

inelegant, *adj.* graceless, ungraceful; vulgar, common, unrefined; harsh, abrupt; dry; stiff; cramped, formal, forced, labored; artificial, mannered, ponderous; turgid, affected, euphuistic; barbarous, barbaric, uncouth, vulgar, gross, grotesque, rude, crude. See AFFECTATION, VULGARITY. *Ant.,* see ELEGANCE.

inequality, *n.* disparity; odds; DIFFERENCE; unevenness; imbalance, partiality; shortcoming; makeweight. See SUPERIORITY, INFERIORITY. *Ant.,* see EQUALITY.

inertness, *n.* inertia, INACTIVITY, stillness, movelessness; laziness, sluggishness, torpor, lethargy, sloth, indolence; dullness, lifelessness, dispiritedness; passiveness, passivity. *Ant.,* see ACTIVITY.

inevitable, *adj.* inescapable, unavoidable, sure. See CERTAINTY. *Ant.,* see DOUBT.

inexcitable, *adj.* unexcitable; imperturbable; unsusceptible, insensible, dispassionate; coldblooded, unirritable; enduring, stoical, Platonic, philosophic; staid, grave; sober, easygoing, peaceful, placid, calm; quiet, meek, tame, patient, mild, tranquil, serene; cool, undemonstrative, temperate, moderate; composed, collected, meek, tolerant, patient, patient as Job; submissive; tame, content, resigned, chastened, subdued, gentle; mild, mild as milk; clement, bearing with, longsuffering. *Ant.,* see EXCITEMENT.

inexcusable, *adj.* unpardonable, unforgivable, unjustifiable. See ACCUSATION.

inexhaustible, *adj.* limitless, endless; unfailing. See SUFFICIENCY. *Ant.,* see INSUFFICIENCY.

inexpedient, *adj.* undesirable; inadvisable, inappropriate; improper, objectionable; unapt, inconvenient, embarrassing, disadvantageous; unfit, inconstant; ill-contrived, ill-occasioned, unsatisfactory; unprofitable, useless, inopportune, untimely, unseasonable; out of place, improper, unseemly, injudicious; clumsy, awkward; cumbrous, cumbersome; impracticable; unnecessary. See HINDRANCE. *Ant.,* see EXPEDIENCE, RELATION.

inexperienced, *adj.* green, raw, untrained, fresh; naïve. See UNSKILLFULNESS. *Ant.,* see SKILL.

inexpressible, *adj.* unutterable, ineffable, beyond words, indescribable. See GREATNESS.

infallibility, *adj.* reliable, dependable, RIGHT; unfailing, unerring, unerrable, certain. See CERTAINTY. *Ant.,* see DOUBT, ERROR.

infamous, *adj.* shameful, abominable, disgraceful, unspeakable, contemptible; heinous, atrocious, base, discreditable. See IMPROBITY. *Ant.,* see PROBITY.

infancy, *n.* babyhood, childhood; BEGINNING, cradle, genesis. See YOUTH. *Ant.,* see AGE, OLDNESS.

infant, *n.* baby, babe, suckling, nursling, child; boy, girl; bairn, *enfant,* papoose; offspring, young; brat, tot, toddler. *Colloq.,* kid, kiddy, chick, *bambino;* pup, whelp, kitten, cub, foal, colt, lamb; big baby, thumbsucker, crybaby. *Slang,* mama's boy. See YOUTH. *Ant.,* see AGE.

infatuation, *n.* enamorment, fascination (by); passion; folly; gullibility; dotingness. See LOVE, CREDULITY.

infection, *n.* epidemic, contagion, plague, contamination; ILLNESS; taint, toxicity, gangrene, poisoning. See DISEASE.

infer, *v.t.* gather, reason, deduce, conclude; presume; construe. See REASONING.

INFERIORITY [34]

Nouns—**1,** inferiority, minority, subordinacy; SHORTCOMING, inadequacy, deficiency; minimum; smallness; IMPERFECTION; poorness, meanness; subservience.

2, inferior, subordinate, junior, underling; second fiddle. *Slang,* second-stringer, long shot.

Verbs—fall short of, not pass, not measure up to. *Colloq.,* take a back seat. See DECREASE.

Adjectives—inferior, smaller (see LITTLENESS); minor, junior, less, lesser, deficient, minus, lower, subordinate, secondary; secondrate, imperfect; short, inadequate, out of depth; subaltern; weighed in the balance and found wanting; not fit to hold a candle to. *Colloq.,* out of the picture.

Adverbs—below par; at the bottom of the scale; at a low ebb. *Colloq.,* not up to snuff.

Antonym, see SUPERIORITY.

infernal, *adj.* hellish, Plutonian, Stygian; fiendish, diabolical, demoniac(al). See EVIL. *Ant.,* see VIRTUE.

infidelity, *n.* betrayal, treachery; faithlessness, fickleness; adultery; skepticism, unbelief. See IMPROBITY, IRRELIGION.

infinite, *adj.* limitless, boundless, unbounded; eternal, timeless, endless; measureless, unlimited, illimitable; interminable, inexhaustible, bottomless; vast, huge, great, immense, enormous; countless, numberless. See SPACE, MULTITUDE, TIME. *Ant.,* see END, LIMIT, CIRCUMSCRIPTION.

infinity, *n.* boundlessness, endlessness, *etc.* (see INFINITE); infinitude, immensity; eternity, perpetuity, immortality. See SPACE.

infirmity, *n.* fault; feebleness; illness. See IMPOTENCE, DISEASE.

inflame, *v.* anger, excite, arouse; incite, animate, kindle; HEAT, blaze up; provoke, irritate; redden, flush. See VIOLENCE.

inflammable, *adj.* burnable, combustible. See HEAT.

inflate, *v.t.* puff *or* blow up, aerate; expand, dilate, distend; exaggerate. See WIND, INCREASE, VANITY. *Ant.,* see CONTRACTION.

inflect, *v.* bend, turn, curve; modulate, vary; (*Gram.*) conjugate, decline. See CURVATURE, CHANGE, GRAMMAR. *Ant.,* see DIRECTION.

inflexible, *adj.* unbending, rigid, unyielding; firm, rocklike, steadfast; grim, stern. See HARDNESS, RESOLUTION. *Ant.,* see SOFTNESS, DOUBT.

inflict, *v.t.* burden *or* trouble with; impose, put upon; do (to); give (punishment, *etc.*). See SEVERITY.

infliction, *n.* SCOURGE, affliction; trouble; adversity; curse, disgrace; imposition; administering (to).

influence, *n. & v.* —*n.* influentialness; IMPORTANCE, POWER, mastery, sway, dominance, AUTHORITY, control, ascendancy, persuasiveness, ability to affect; reputation, weight; magnetism, spell; conduciveness; pressure. *Slang,* drag, pull. —*v.t.* affect; move, induce, persuade; sway, control, lead, actuate; modify; arouse, incite; prevail upon, impel; set the pace, pull the strings; tell, weigh. *Ant.,* see IMPOTENCE.

informal, *adj.* casual, free, easy, irregular; unofficial; unconventional, unceremonious. See UNCONFORMITY. *Ant.,* see CONFORMITY.

INFORMATION [527]

Nouns—**1,** information, enlightenment, acquaintance, KNOWLEDGE; publicity (see PUBLICATION); COMMUNICATION, intimation; notice, notification; enunciation, annunciation; WORD, advice(s), announcement; REPRESENTATION, presentment; case, estimate, specification, report, advice, monition; release, communiqué, dispatch; tidings, bulletin, news, intelligence; flash (news), spot news; scoop, beat, exclusive (story), inside story *or* information; returns, RECORD; account, DESCRIPTION; statement, AFFIRMATION. *Slang,* info, dope, lowdown, inside story.

2, mention, acquainting; instruction, TEACHING; outpouring; intercommunication, communicativeness; hint, suggestion, innuendo, implication, allusion, inkling, whisper, passing word, word in the ear, subaudition, cue, byplay; gesture (see INDICATION); gentle *or* broad hint; word to the wise; insinuation. *Slang,* hot tip.

3, informant, authority, teller, spokesman, intelligencer, publisher, broadcaster, newscaster, reporter, exponent, mouthpiece; informer, talebearer, scandalmonger, eavesdropper, detective; spy, newsmonger, messenger (see COMMUNICATION); *amicus curiae;* Sherlock Holmes; pilot, guide. *Colloq.,* squealer, stool pigeon, tipster, tattletale. *Slang,* snitcher, tout.

4, guidebook, handbook; manual; map, plan, chart, gazetteer; itinerary (see TRAVEL).

5, rumor, gossip, hearsay; scandal, titbit, canard; item, topic, talk of the town, common currency, byword, household word.

Verbs—**1,** inform, tell, acquaint, impart, make acquainted with, apprize, advise, enlighten, awaken; give a piece of one's mind, tell one plainly, speak volumes, open up; let fall, mention, express, intimate, represent, communicate, make known; publish (see PUBLICATION); notify, signify, specify, disclose (see DISCLOSURE); explain (see INTERPRETATION); undeceive, correct, disabuse, open the eyes of; let one know; give one to understand; give notice; point out; instruct, teach; direct the attention to (see ATTENTION). *Colloq.,* fill one in on, put wise.

2, announce, annunciate, report; bring, send, leave, *or* give word; retail, render *or* give an account (see DESCRIPTION); state, affirm (see AFFIRMATION).

3, hint, give an inkling of, imply, insinuate, intimate; allude to, suggest, prompt, give the cue, breathe; get to; whisper; inform on, betray, turn state's evidence. *Colloq.,* tip off; put a flea in one's ear; tell on, squeal, tattle, rat, doublecross; let in on, spill, spill the beans, let the cat out of the bag.

4, be informed, know (see KNOWLEDGE); learn, receive news, get wind *or* scent of; gather (from); awaken to, open one's eyes to; become alive *or* awake to; hear, overhear, find out, understand; come to one's ears, come to one's knowledge, reach one's ears. *Colloq.,* catch on. *Slang,* get wise to, wise up.

Adjectives—informative, informed, informational, reported, published; expressive, explicit, open, clear, plainspoken; declaratory, expository; enunciative, communicative, communicatory; knowledgeable.

Antonym, see CONCEALMENT.

---

infrequency, *n.* rareness, rarity; fewness; seldomness, uncommonness, unusualness; scarceness, oddness. *Ant.,* see FREQUENCY.

infringement, *n.* trespass, encroachment; infraction, breach; plagiarism, violation (of copyright, patent, *etc.*). See ILLEGALITY. *Ant.,* see LEGALITY.

infuse, *v.t.* steep, soak; introduce, implant, instill; tinge, imbue; pour into, mix in. See MIXTURE.

ingenuity, *n.* SKILL; cleverness; inventiveness; originality. See IMAGINATION.

ingenuous, *adj.* artless, naïve, simple; candid, frank, open; trusting, unsuspecting. See SIMPLENESS.

ingratiating, *adj.* charming, winsome, winning, captivating; pleasing, attractive. See COURTESY.

INGRATITUDE [917]

Nouns—**1,** ingratitude, ungratefulness, thanklessness.

2, ingrate, a serpent in one's bosom.

Verbs—look a gift horse in the mouth; bite the hand that feeds one.

Adjectives—ungrateful, unmindful, unthankful; thankless, ingrate, wanting in gratitude; forgotten, unacknowledged, unthanked, unrequited, unrewarded; ill-requited.

Antonym, see GRATITUDE.

---

ingredient, *n.* COMPONENT, PART, element, constituent.

INGRESS [294]

Nouns—**1,** ingress; entrance, entry, entrée; introgression; influx; intrusion, inroad, incursion, invasion; irruption; penetration, interpenetration; import, infiltration; immigration; access, admission, admittance, reception;

insinuation (see BETWEEN); INSERTION; inlet; way in; mouth, door, OPENING, path, way; conduit, channel; immigration.

2, incomer, immigrant, colonist; entrant; newcomer; fifth column.

Verbs—enter; go in, come in, pour in, flow in, creep in, slip in, pop in, break in, burst in; gain entrée; set foot on; burst *or* break in upon; invade, intrude; insinuate itself; penetrate, interpenetrate; infiltrate; find one's way into, wriggle into, worm oneself into; trespass; give entrance to, receive, insert; bore from within.

Adjectives—ingressive; incoming, ingoing, inward; entrant.

Antonym, see EGRESS.

INHABITANT [188]

Nouns—**1,** inhabitant, habitant; resident, dweller, indweller; occupier, occupant; householder, boarder, renter, lodger, tenant; inmate; incumbent, sojourner, *locum tenens*, settler, colonist, squatter, nester; backwoodsman, islander; denizen, citizen; burgher, townsman, burgess; villager, cottager; aborigine; compatriot, fellow citizen. *Slang*, city slicker, sooner; hick, hayseed, rube.

2, native, indigene, aborigine, newcomer.

3, population, POPULACE, public, people (see MANKIND); colony, settlement, household; garrison, crew.

Verbs—inhabit, be present (see PRESENCE); dwell, reside, sojourn, occupy, lodge; settle; squat; colonize; billet.

Adjectives—indigenous; native, natal; aboriginal, primitive; domestic, domiciled, naturalized, vernacular, domesticated; domiciliary.

Antonym, see RELATION.

---

inhale, *v.* breathe; breathe in. See WIND.

inherent, *adj.* native, innate; INTRINSIC, essential.

inherit, *v.t.* succeed (to); get, acquire, receive; possess. See ACQUISITION.

inheritance, *n.* bequest, bequeathment, legacy; heritage; patrimony. See PROPERTY.

inhibit, *v.* circumscribe, restrain; hamper, check, cramp; repress, suppress. See RESTRAINT. *Ant.*, see FREEDOM.

inhuman, *adj.* cruel, barbarous, bestial, brutal, sadistic, savage. See MALEVOLENCE, EVIL. *Ant.*, see BENEVOLENCE.

iniquity, *n.* vice, immorality; sin, wickedness, transgression, crime, wrongdoing; INJUSTICE.

initial, *adj. & n.* —*adj.* first, BEGINNING, introductory, primary. *Ant.*, see END. —*n.* letter, monogram.

initiate, *v.t.* admit, introduce, take in (a member); start, commence, inaugurate, institute. See BEGINNING. *Ant.*, see END.

inject, *v.t.* insert, introduce; wedge in, force in; inoculate; intersperse, interject. See BETWEEN.

injunction, *n.* COMMAND, order, admonition; direction; REQUIREMENT.

injure, *v.t.* wound, hurt; damage, abuse, deface, mar, impair; WRONG, disgrace, dishonor; insult; mistreat; maltreat. See DETERIORATION, EVIL, MALEVOLENCE. *Ant.*, see IMPROVEMENT.

INJUSTICE [925]

Nouns—injustice, unjustness, unfairness, bias, partiality, prejudice, inequity, inequitableness; favoritism, nepotism, partisanship. See IMPROBITY, ILLEGALITY.

Verbs—**1,** be unjust, do injustice to, be unfair, be inequitable, favor, show partiality.

2, lynch, railroad, frame.

Adjectives—unjust, unfair, partial, prejudiced, inequitable, partisan, nepotistic, biased, one-sided.

Antonym, see JUSTICE.

---

inkling, *n.* clue, suggestion, hint; whisper; surmise. See INFORMATION.

inlet, *n.* creek, cove; entrance, INGRESS; channel. *Ant.*, see EGRESS.

inn, *n.* hotel, hostelry; tavern, bar and grill. See ABODE.

innate, *adj.* natural, inborn; inherent; congenital.
inner, *adj.* inward, internal, INTERIOR, inside. *Ant.,* see EXTERIOR.

INNOCENCE [946]

Nouns—**1,** innocence, guiltlessness, blamelessness, incorruption, impeccability; PURITY, VIRTUE, virginity, chastity; artlessness, naïveté, SIMPLENESS; immaculacy, CLEANNESS.
2, innocent, child, lamb, dove, saint, newborn babe; virgin, maid.
Verbs—be innocent, have a clear conscience; exonerate, acquit (see ACQUITTAL); exculpate (see VINDICATION.) *Colloq.,* whitewash.
Adjectives—innocent, not guilty; unguilty; guiltless, faultless, sinless, stainless, bloodless, spotless, *sans peur et sans reproche;* clean, immaculate; unspotted, unblemished, unerring; unsullied, undefiled (see PROBITY); unravished, virginal, pure, white as snow, virtuous; unhardened, Saturnian; Arcadian, artless, naïve, simple, unsophisticated; inculpable, unculpable; unblamed, unblamable, blameless, above suspicion; irreproachable, irreprovable, irreprehensible; unexceptionable, unobjectionable, unimpeachable; salvable; venial; harmless, inoffensive, innocuous; dovelike, lamblike; innocent as a lamb, saint, child, babe unborn, *etc.;* more sinned against than sinning, unreproved, unimpeached. *Colloq.,* in the clear.
Adverbs—innocently, *etc.;* with clean hands; with a clear conscience.
Antonym, see GUILT.

---

innocuous, *adj.* harmless, mild, inoffensive; innocent. See HEALTH. *Ant.,* see DETERIORATION.
innovation, *n.* CHANGE, alteration; NEWNESS, novelty; variation; departure.
innumerable, *adj.* countless, uncountable; myriad, numberless. See INFINITE. *Ant.,* see LIMIT.

INQUIRY [461]

Nouns—**1,** inquiry, enquiry; question, REQUEST; search, research, quest; PURSUIT; examination, test, intelligence test; review, scrutiny, investigation, inspection, probe; trial, hearing; inquest, inquisition; exploration, exploitation, ventilation; sifting, calculation, analysis, dissection; resolution; induction; Baconian method; autopsy, *post mortem;* strict inquiry, close inquiry, searching inquiry, exhaustive inquiry; narrow search, strict search; study, CONSIDERATION. *Colloq.,* exam.
2, questioning, interrogation, interrogatory; interpellation; challenge, examination, cross-examination, catechism; feeler, Socratic method, leading question; discussion (see REASONING); reconnoitering, reconnaissance; prying, espionage. *Colloq.,* grilling, third degree.
3, question, query, problem, proposition, *desideratum,* point to be solved, subject of inquiry, field of inquiry, subject of controversy; point *or* matter in dispute; moot point; issue, question at issue; bone of contention (see DISCORD); fair question, open question; questionnaire; enigma (see SECRET); knotty point (see DIFFICULTY).
4, inquirer, investigator, inquisitor, inspector, querist, examiner, prober, cross-examiner; spy; detective, operative; catechist; analyst; quidnunc (see CURIOSITY). *Colloq.,* private eye, op. *Slang,* shamus.
Verbs—**1,** inquire, seek, search; look for, look about for, look out for; scan, reconnoiter, explore, sound, rummage, ransack, pry, peer, look round; look *or* go through *or* over; spy; peer *or* pry into every hole and corner; trace; ferret out; unearth; leave no stone unturned; seek a clue, hunt, track, trail, hound; follow the trail *or* scent; pursue (see PURSUIT); thresh out; fish for; feel *or* grope for.
2, investigate; follow up; look at, look into; preexamine; discuss, canvass, agitate; examine, study, consider, calculate; delve into, probe, sound, fathom; scrutinize, analyze, anatomize, dissect, sift, winnow; audit, review; take into consideration (see THOUGHT); take counsel (see ADVICE). *Colloq.,* kick around.
3, ask, question, demand; ventilate; grapple with *or* go into a question; interrogate, catechize, pump, cross-question, cross-examine; pick the brains of; feel out.

Adjectives—inquiring, inquisitive, curious; catechetical, inquisitorial, analytic; in search of, in quest of; on the lookout for, interrogative; in question, in dispute, in issue, under discussion, under consideration, under investigation; *sub judice*, moot, proposed; doubtful (see DOUBT).
Adverbs—what? why? wherefore? whence? whither? where? how goes it? how is it? what is the reason? what's the matter? what's in the wind? what on earth? when? who? *Colloq.*, how come? what's up? what's new?
Antonym, see ANSWER.

inquisition, *n.* examination, questioning; tribunal (Spanish Inquisition); cross-examination; probe, investigation; INQUIRY. *Colloq.*, third degree, brainwashing. See SEVERITY, MALEVOLENCE.
inquisitive, *adj.* questioning; curious, prying, meddlesome, busybodyish. See CURIOSITY.

INSANITY [503]

Nouns—**1,** insanity, lunacy, derangement, craziness, feeblemindedness; psychosis, psychopathy, schizophrenia, split personality, paranoia, *dementia praecox*, neurosis; madness, mental illness, abnormality, aberration; dementia, frenzy, raving, delirium, hallucination; lycanthropy; rabies, hydrophobia; disordered reason *or* intellect; diseased, unsound, *or* abnormal mind; anility, senility, dotage.
2, vertigo, dizziness, swimming; sunstroke, moon-madness.
3, fanaticism, infatuation, craze; oddity, idiosyncrasy; eccentricity, twist, quirk.
4, mania; monomania, megalomania, nymphomania, bibliomania, pyromania, logomania, Theomania, kleptomania, dipsomania, Anglomania; delirium tremens; hypochondriasis (see DEJECTION); melancholia, hysteria; phobia (see FEAR).
5, madman, idiot, imbecile, cretin, moron, lunatic. *Slang*, nut, loon.
6, insane asylum, sanitarium, sanatorium, mental hospital *or* institution, bedlam, madhouse. *Slang*, nuthouse, booby hatch, bughouse, loony bin.
Verbs—**1,** be insane, be out of one's mind; lose one's senses *or* reason; lose one's faculties *or* wits; go mad, run mad *or* amuck, rave, rant, dote, ramble, wander; drivel; take leave of one's senses; lose one's head. *Slang*, have a screw loose, have bats in the belfry, not have all one's marbles *or* buttons; go off one's nut *or* rocker; see things; flip (one's lid).
2, render insane, drive mad *or* crazy, madden, dement, addle the wits of, derange; infatuate, obsess, turn the brain, turn one's head.
Adjectives—**1,** insane, mad, lunatic; crazy, crazed, *non compos mentis;* unhinged, unbalanced, psychopathic, psychotic, psychoneurotic, manic-depressive; not right, cracked, touched; bereft of reason; unhinged, unsettled in one's mind; insensate, reasonless, beside oneself, demented, daft; frenzied, frenetic; possessed, possessed of a devil; far gone, maddened, moonstruck; scatterbrained, crackbrained, off one's head; maniacal; delirious, irrational, lightheaded, incoherent, rambling, doting, wandering; amuck, frantic, raving, stark mad, staring mad. *Slang*, crazy as a bedbug, loco, dotty, psycho, nutty, screwy, wacky; tetched, pixilated, bughouse; mental (*Brit.*).
2, rabid, giddy, vertiginous, wild; mazed, flighty; distracted, distraught; mad as a hatter *or* March hare; of unsound mind; touched (in one's head), not in one's right mind; out of one's mind, senses, *or* wits; on the ragged edge. *Slang*, off one's nut.
3, fanatical, obsessed, infatuated, odd, eccentric; hipped; hypochondriac; imbecile, silly.
4, monomaniacal, kleptomaniacal, *etc.*
Adverbs—insanely; like one possessed; maniacally, *etc.*
Antonym, see SANITY.

insatiable, *adj.* greedy, voracious; unappeasable, quenchless, unquenchable. See DESIRE. *Ant.*, see SUFFICIENCY.
inscribe, *v.t.* write; mark, engrave; enter, enroll, LIST. See WRITING.
insect, *n.* bug; fly, moth, butterfly, beetle, ant, *etc.* See ANIMAL.

INSENSIBILITY [823, 376, 381]

Nouns—**1,** insensibility, insensibleness; moral insensibility; inertness, inertia, impassibility, impassibleness, impassivity; inappetency, apathy, phlegm, dullness, hebetude, supineness, lukewarmness.

2, coldness, cold fit, cold blood, cold heart; frigidity, *sangfroid;* stoicism, imperturbability, inexcitability; nonchalance, unconcern, dry eyes; insouciance, indifference; recklessness, RASHNESS, callousness; heart of stone, marble, deadness; thickness of skin.

3, torpor, torpidity, lethargy, coma, trance; SLEEP, vegetation, suspended animation; stupor, stupefaction; paralysis, palsy.

4, numbness; unfeeling, anesthesia, analgesia, narcosis.

5, anesthetic, ether, chloroform, nitrous oxide, opium; refrigeration.

Verbs—**1,** be insensible, become insensible, black out, draw a blank; have a rhinoceros hide; show insensibility, not mind, not care, not be affected by; have no desire for, have, feel, *or* take no interest in; not care a straw (see UNIMPORTANCE); disregard (see NEGLECT); set at naught; turn a deaf ear to; vegetate.

2, render insensible *or* callous; blunt, obtund, numb, benumb, paralyze, chloroform, deaden, hebetate, stun, stupefy; inure, harden, harden the heart; steel, caseharden, sear.

Adjectives—**1,** insensible, unconscious; impassive, impassible; dispassionate; blind to, deaf to, dead to; unsusceptible, insusceptible; unimpressionable, passionless, spiritless, heartless, soulless; unfeeling, indifferent, lukewarm, careless, regardless; inattentive, neglectful.

2, callous, thickskinned, pachydermatous, impervious; hard, hardened inured, casehardened; steeled against; proof against; imperturbable, inexcitable, unfelt; unconcerned, nonchalant, insouciant, *sans souci.*

3, unambitious; unaffected, unruffled, unimpressed, uninspired, unexcited, unmoved, unstirred, untouched, unshocked, unstruck; unblushing, shameless; unanimated, vegetative; apathetic, phlegmatic; dull, frigid; cold, coldblooded, coldhearted; cold as charity; flat, obtuse, inert, supine, languid, half-hearted; numb, numbed; comatose; anesthetic, stupefied, chloroformed; dead, deadened; narcotic.

Adverbs—insensibly, *etc.;* in cold blood; with dry eyes.

Antonym, see SENSIBILITY.

---

insertion, *n.* inset, inlay; injection, inoculation; introduction, insinuation, impregnation, implantation; intervention, infusion, installation; INTERMENT; submersion, submergence, immersion. See ADDITION, BETWEEN. *Ant.,* see EXTRACTION.

insight, *n.* discernment, perceptiveness, perception; INTUITION; penetration, understanding. See KNOWLEDGE.

insignia, *n.pl.* badges (of office), emblems. See INDICATION.

insignificance, *n.* meaninglessness; inconsequentiality, UNIMPORTANCE, triviality, smallness, worthlessness. See CHEAPNESS. *Ant.,* see IMPORTANCE, MEANING.

insincere, *adj.* false, deceptive; hypocritical, two-faced; half-hearted; untrue; affected. See DECEPTION, AFFECTATION. *Ant.,* see TRUTH, FEELING.

insinuate, *v.t.* hint, suggest, intimate; ingratiate (oneself), curry favor; insert, instill, introduce (stealthily). See INFORMATION, STEALING.

insipidity, *n.* tastelessness; wishy-washiness; dullness, tameness; flatness, unsavoriness; weakness; vapidity; wateriness. *Ant.,* see TASTE.

insist, *v.i.* state (firmly, repeatedly), maintain, hold to; persist; urge, press; demand (strongly). See AFFIRMATION, COMPULSION.

insnare, ensnare, *v.t.* trap, entrap; capture, catch; entangle, ensnarl, entoil; bait, decoy. See DECEPTION.

INSOLENCE [885]

Nouns—**1,** insolence, arrogance; haughtiness, airs; overbearance; presumption, pomposity, snobbery; domineering, tyranny, terrorism (see SEVERITY); DEFIANCE.

2, impertinence; sauciness, flippancy, petulance, bluster; swagger, swaggering, bounce; impudence, assurance, audacity; hardihood, front, shamelessness, effrontery, PRIDE, VANITY. *Colloq.*, brass, cheek, face, nerve, sauce, sass; smart aleck. *Slang*, gall, crust, lip; wise guy.

Verbs—**1,** be insolent, bluster, vapor, swagger, swell, give oneself airs, snap one's fingers; swear (see AFFIRMATION); roister; arrogate; assume, presume; make bold, make free; take a liberty, patronize. *Slang*, have a nerve.

2, domineer, bully, dictate, hector; lord it over; exact; snub, huff, beard, fly in the face of; bear down, beat down; browbeat, intimidate; trample down *or* under foot; dragoon, ride roughshod over.

3, outface, outlook, outstare, outbrazen, outbrave; stare out of countenance; brazen out; lay down the law; talk big, act big; talk back, get on a high horse; toss the head, carry with a high hand; overreach.

Adjectives—**1,** insolent, haughty, arrogant, imperious, dictatorial, arbitrary; highhanded, high and mighty; contumelious, supercilious, snobbish, overbearing, intolerant, domineering, overweening, high-flown. *Colloq.*, stuck-up; cocky, uppity. *Slang*, high-hat, fresh, nervy, flip.

2, flippant, pert, cavalier, saucy, sassy, forward, impertinent, malapert; precocious, assuming, would-be, bumptious; bluff; brazen, shameless, aweless, unblushing, unabashed; boldfaced, barefaced, brazenfaced; impudent, audacious, presumptuous, free and easy; roistering, blustering, hectoring, swaggering, vaporing.

Adverbs—insolently, *etc.;* with a high hand; where angels fear to tread.

Antonym, see SERVILITY.

---

insolvency, *n.* FAILURE, bankruptcy; lack of funds. See DEBT. *Ant.*, see PAYMENT, MONEY.

insomnia, *n.* sleeplessness; chronic wakefulness. *Ant.*, see REPOSE.

inspect, *v.t.* examine, scrutinize; check, check up; oversee; investigate, look into. See ATTENTION, VISION.

inspire, *v.* breathe, breathe in; stimulate, animate, liven, enliven; spur, give an incentive. See EXCITEMENT.

instability, *n.* CHANGEABLENESS, unsteadiness; unsoundness; inconstancy, undependableness. *Ant.*, see STABILITY, PROBITY, FREQUENCY.

install, *v.t.* put in, set up; induct, inaugurate, invest. See LOCATION, CELEBRATION.

installment, *n.* down payment, time payment; episode, PART (of a series); installation, setting up *or* putting in. See LOCATION.

instance, *n.* example, illustration, demonstration. See CONFORMITY.

instant, *adj. & n.* —*adj.* prepared instantly; sudden, immediate, direct, instantaneous; lightninglike. See INSTANTANEITY. —*n.* second, moment; minute; twinkling, jiffy.

INSTANTANEITY [113]

Nouns—**1,** instantaneity, instantaneousness, immediacy, precipitancy, suddenness, abruptness; moment, instant, second, minute; twinkling, trice, flash, breath, crack, burst, flash of lightning.

2, epoch, time; time of day *or* night; hour, minute; very minute, very time, very hour; present time, right, true, exact, *or* correct time. *Colloq.*, jiffy. *Slang*, half a shake, sec.

Adjectives—instantaneous, momentary, sudden, instant, abrupt; extemporaneous; precipitate, immediate, hasty; quick as thought, quick as lightning.

Adverbs—instantaneously, instantly, immediately, now, right now, in less than no time; presto, *subito,* instanter, suddenly, at a stroke, at a word, at the drop of a hat; in a moment, in the twinkling of an eye, at one jump, in the same breath, at once, all at once; plump, slap; at one fell swoop; at the same instant; immediately, *ex tempore,* on the spot, on the spur of the moment; just then; slapdash. *Colloq.,* in a jiffy, like a shot, yesterday, in nothing flat, in two shakes. *Slang*, like a bat out of hell.

Antonym, see LATENESS.

---

instead, *adv.* in place, in lieu (of); substituting for. See SUBSTITUTION.

instigate, *v.t.* incite, provoke; initiate; stimulate, urge, promote. See CAUSE.

instill, *v.t.*   inculcate; implant, impart; pour in, mix in, infuse.

instinct, *n.*   TENDENCY; knack, IMPULSE, prompting, discernment; INTUITION.

institute, *v.t. & n.*   —*v.t.* found, inaugurate; organize, start, begin, commence; originate, organize. See BEGINNING. —*n.* institution; SCHOOL, college; foundation; society; museum; hospital, *etc.*

instruction, *n.*   TEACHING, tutelage, education; training, coaching; COMMAND, ORDER, direction, directive; ADVICE.

instrument, *n.*   utensil, implement, tool, device, contrivance; hammer, saw, lever, key, knife, *etc.*; MEANS, AGENCY; appliance, apparatus; representative; MUSICAL INSTRUMENT; machine, mechanism, motor, engine; document, deed, paper, RECORD, charter; speedometer, thermometer; controls, gauges (of a plane *or* vehicle), *etc.*

instrumentality, *n.*   instrument, AID; subservience, subserviency; intervention, medium, vehicle, hand; AGENCY; expedient, MEANS, agent, go-between; robot, cat's-paw; stepping stone; key; open sesame; passport, tool, device, implement, appliance. See USE, UTILITY.

INSUBSTANTIALITY [4]

Nouns—**1,** insubstantiality, unsubstantiality; nothingness, nihility; nothing, naught, nil, nullity, zero, cipher, no one, nobody; never a one; no such thing, none in the world; nothing whatever, nothing at all, nothing on earth; not a particle (see LITTLENESS); all talk, moonshine, stuff and nonsense; shadow; phantom; dream (see IMAGINATION); *ignis fatuus*; air, thin air; bubble; mockery; hollowness, blank; void (see ABSENCE); inanity, fool's paradise.

2, nobody, puppet, dummy, man of straw, John Doe and Richard Roe; cipher, nonentity; flash in the pan.

3, immateriality, immaterialness; incorporeality, disembodiment; spirit, soul, ego; spiritualism, spirituality.

Verbs—be insubstantial; vanish, evaporate, fade, dissolve, melt away; disappear, vanish; immaterialize, dematerialize; disembody, spiritualize.

Adjectives—insubstantial, unsubstantial; baseless, groundless; unfounded, ungrounded; bodiless, incorporeal, spiritual, immaterial, unearthly; psychical, supernatural; visionary, imaginary (see IMAGINATION); dreamy; shadowy, ethereal, airy, spectral; vacant, vacuous; empty (see ABSENCE); blank, hollow; nominal; null; inane.

Antonym, see SUBSTANCE.

---

insufferable, *adj.*   abominable, unspeakable, incorrigible; unendurable, unbearable, insupportable; agonizing, excruciating. See PAIN.

INSUFFICIENCY [640]

Nouns—**1,** insufficiency; inadequacy, inadequateness; incompetence, IMPOTENCE; deficiency, incompleteness, IMPERFECTION, SHORTCOMING, emptiness, poorness, depletion, vacancy, flaccidity; ebb tide; low water; bankruptcy, insolvency (see DEBT).

2, paucity, stint; scantiness, smallness; none to spare; bare necessities; scarcity, dearth; want, need, deprivation, lack, POVERTY, destitution, indigence, exigency; inanition, starvation, famine, drought; dole, pittance; short allowance *or* rations, half-rations.

Verbs—**1,** be insufficient, not suffice, fall short of (see FAILURE); run dry; want, lack, need, require; be in want, live from hand to mouth.

2, render insufficient, exhaust, deplete, drain of resources; impoverish (see WASTE); stint, begrudge (see PARSIMONY); cut back, retrench; bleed white.

Adjectives—**1,** insufficient, inadequate; too little (see LITTLENESS); not enough; unequal to; incompetent, impotent (see IMPOTENCE); weighed in the balance and found wanting; perfunctory (see NEGLECT); deficient; wanting, imperfect; ill-furnished, ill-provided, ill-stored, badly off.

2, slack, at a low ebb; empty, vacant, bare; short (of), out of, destitute (of), devoid (of), denuded (of); dry, drained; not to be had for love or money, not to be had at any price; empty-handed.

3, meager, poor, thin, sparing, spare, stinted; starved, half-starved, famine-stricken, famished; jejune; scant, small, scarce; scurvy, stingy; at the end

of one's tether; without resources (see MEANS); in want, poor (see POVERTY); in debt (see DEBT). *Colloq.*, skimpy. *Slang*, shy of, fresh out of.
Adverbs—insufficiently, *etc.*; in default, for want of; failing.
Antonym, see SUFFICIENCY.

insular, *adj.* isolated; islanded, insulated; aloof; narrow, limited, illiberal; isolationist. See NARROWNESS.
insulate, *v.t.* cover, protect, shield; set apart, isolate, detach. See COVERING, DISJUNCTION. *Ant.*, see JUNCTION.
insult, *n. & v.* —*v.* slap, abuse, affront, offend. See DISCOURTESY. *Ant.*, see COURTESY. —*n.* outrage; slap, affront, sauce, cheek, impudence.
insurance, *n.* guarantee, guaranty, warranty, coverage, protection; insurance policy (fire, life, auto, burglary, *etc.*); assurance, SECURITY.
insurgent, *adj. & n.* —*adj.* rebellious, insubordinate, mutinous, in revolt, uprising. See DISOBEDIENCE. *Ant.*, see OBEDIENCE. —*n.* rebel, insubordinate, mutineer, revolutionist, insurrectionist. See OPPOSITION.
intact, *adj.* whole, unimpaired, uninjured; untouched. See COMPLETION. *Ant.*, see DETERIORATION.
intangible, *adj.* immaterial, vague, impalpable; untouchable; unspecific; not concrete, abstract. See INSUBSTANTIALITY.
integrity, *n.* honor, PROBITY, uprightness; wholeness, completeness, oneness. See WHOLE. *Ant.*, see IMPROBITY.

INTELLECT [450]

Nouns—**1,** intellect, intellectuality, mentality, brain, brains, mind, understanding, reason (see REASONING), rationality; faculties, senses, consciousness, observation, percipience, perception, apperception, perspicuity, grasp, intelligence, INTUITION, association of ideas, instinct, conception, JUDGMENT, wits, mental capacity, genius; WIT, ability, SKILL, WISDOM; logic, THOUGHT, meditation.
2, soul, spirit, ghost, inner man, heart, breast, bosom; seat of thought; sensory, brain; head, cerebrum, cranium; gray matter. *Slang*, upper story, noodle.
3, psychology, psychopathology, psychotherapy, psychiatry, psychoanalysis, psychometry; ideology; philosophy; phrenology, craniology, cranioscopy; ideality, idealism; transcendentalism, spiritualism, immateriality; THOUGHT.
4, psychologist, psychopathologist, alienist, psychiatrist, psychometrist, psychotherapist, psychoanalyst, analyst.
Verbs—intellectualize (see THOUGHT); note, notice, mark; take notice, take cognizance; be aware, be conscious; realize; appreciate; ruminate (see THOUGHT); fancy, imagine (see IMAGINATION).
Adjectives—intellectual, mental, rational, subjective, metaphysical, spiritual, ghostly; psychical, psychological; cerebral; percipient, aware, conscious; subconscious; immaterial; logical, reasoning, reasonable; thoughtful, thinking, meditative, contemplative.
Antonym, see INSANITY.

INTELLIGENCE [498]

Nouns—intelligence, capacity, comprehension, apprehension, understanding; INTELLECT; parts, sagacity, mother wit, wit, *esprit*, intelligence quotient, I.Q., acuteness, shrewdness; acumen, subtlety, penetration; perspicacy, perspicuity, perspicacity, percipience; discernment, good judgment; levelheadedness, DISCRIMINATION; CUNNING; refinement (see TASTE); KNOWLEDGE; head, brains, mind; eagle eye; genius, inspiration, soul; talent, aptitude (see SKILL).
Verbs—be intelligent; have all one's wits about one; understand; grasp an idea; comprehend; take a hint; see through, see at a glance, see with half an eye; penetrate; discern (see VISION); foresee.
Adjectives—intelligent, quick, keen, acute, alive, awake, bright, sharp; nimble- *or* quick-witted; wide awake; canny, shrewd, astute; clear-headed; far-sighted; discerning, perspicacious, penetrating, piercing; alive to, aware

of (see KNOWLEDGE); clever (see SKILL); arch (see DECEPTION). *Colloq.,*
brainy, not so dumb. *Slang,* have all one's marbles, not born yesterday,
Antonyms, see IGNORANCE, INSANITY.

intelligibility, *n.* clearness, clarity, explicitness; comprehensibility; lucidity,
perspicuity; legibility, plain speaking, precision; obviousness; realization,
recognition. See MEANING, INTERPRETATION. *Ant.,* see UNINTELLIGIBILITY.
intemperance, *n.* indulgence, overindulgence; self-indulgence; DRUNKEN-
NESS, GLUTTONY, dissipation; licentiousness. *Ant.,* see MODERATION.
intend, *v.* MEAN, purpose; design, plan; have in mind; aim, contemplate.
intense, *adj.* violent, sharp, strong; passionate, vivid; deep, dark; poignant,
keen, acute; extreme. See FEELING, DEPTH, HEIGHT, POWER.
intensity, *n.* DEPTH; FEELING; POWER, force, STRENGTH, vigor; darkness
(shade), brilliance; extremity.
intention, *n.* intent, intentionality; MEANING, purpose; project, motive, plan,
UNDERTAKING; predetermination; design, ambition; contemplation, mind,
animus, view, purview, proposal; study, lookout; decision, determination,
resolve, RESOLUTION; wish, DESIRE. *Ant.,* see CHANCE.
inter, *v.t.* bury, entomb, inearth. See INTERMENT.
intercede, *v.i.* mediate, arbitrate; intervene, interpose. See COMPROMISE.
intercept, *v.t.* stop, interrupt, check, hinder; catch, nab, seize; cut off. See
HINDRANCE.

INTERCHANGE [148]

Nouns—interchange, EXCHANGE, interchangeableness, interchangeability;
commutation, permutation, intermutation; reciprocation, reciprocity, transposition, shuffling; alternation; hocus-pocus; barter; a Roland for an
Oliver, tit for tat, an eye for an eye, RETALIATION; crossfire, battledore and
shuttlecock; *quid pro quo,* musical chairs.
Verbs—interchange, exchange, counterchange, transpose, bandy, shuffle,
change hands, change partners, swap, permute, reciprocate, commute;
give and take, put and take, pay back, requite, return the compliment;
play at puss in the corner, retaliate.
Adjectives—interchanged, interchanging, interchangeable, reciprocal, mutual,
communicative, intercurrent.
Adverbs—in exchange, *vice versa,* backward(s) and forward(s), by turns,
turn and turn about.
Antonym, see SUBSTITUTION.

intercourse, *n.* communication; CONVERSATION, converse, communion;
coitus, congress; SOCIALITY; fellowship, association; commerce, dealings,
BUSINESS, trade.
interest, *v. & n.* —*v.* concern; TOUCH, affect; fascinate, engross, intrigue;
hold (the attention), engage, absorb. See EXCITEMENT. —*n.* concern;
welfare, benefit; PAYMENT (of a percentage), sum, advantage, profit; PART,
share, holding; claim, title. See DEBT, IMPORTANCE, RIGHT, PROPERTY.
interfere, *v.i.* butt in, meddle, interpose; hinder, hamper; clash, obstruct,
collide, oppose. See HINDRANCE, BETWEEN.

INTERIOR [221]

Nouns—interior, interiority; intrinsicality; inside, insides, subsoil, substratum; CONTENTS; substance, pity, marrow; backbone; heart, bosom,
breast; vitals, viscera, entrails, bowels, belly, intestines, guts; womb; lap;
recesses, innermost recesses; cave (see CONCAVITY).
Verbs—be inside, be within; place within, keep within; enclose, circumscribe
(see CIRCUMSCRIPTION); intern(e); imbed, insert; imprison (see RESTRAINT).
Adjectives—interior, internal; inner, inside, inward, inmost, innermost;
deep-seated; intestinal; inland; subcutaneous; interstitial (see BETWEEN);
inwrought; enclosed; intramural; domestic, indoor, vernacular; endemic.
Adverbs—internally, inwardly, inward(s), inly; herein, therein, wherein;
indoors, within doors; at home, in the bosom of one's family.
Prepositions—in, inside, within.
Antonym, see EXTERIOR.

interloper, *n.* intruder, trespasser; uninvited guest; meddler, interferer, intermeddler. See BETWEEN.

interlude, *n.* intermission, intermezzo, *entr'acte;* pause, interval; episode; gap, space. See TIME.

intermediary *n.* go-between, mediator; arbiter, arbitrator, umpire, referee; middleman. See BETWEEN, COMPROMISE.

intermediate, *adj.* BETWEEN; MIDDLE, intervening; half-way. See MEAN.

INTERMENT [363]

Nouns—**1,** interment, burial, sepulture; inhumation.

2, obsequies, funeral (rites), last rites, extreme unction; wake; pyre, funeral pile, cremation, immolation; knell, passing bell, tolling; dirge (see LAMENTATION); dead march, muffled drum; elegy, panegyric, funeral oration; epitaph; obit, obituary, death notice.

3, grave clothes, shroud, winding sheet, cerement; coffin, casket, shell, sarcophagus, urn, pall, bier, hearse, catafalque, cinerary urn.

4, grave, pit, sepulcher, tomb, vault, crypt, catacomb, mausoleum, golgotha, house of death, narrow house; cemetery, necropolis; burial place, burial ground; graveyard, churchyard; God's acre; cromlech, barrow, cairn; bonehouse, charnel house, morgue, mortuary; monument, marker, cenotaph, shrine; stele, gravestone, slab, tombstone; memorial. *Slang,* boneyard.

5, undertaker, embalmer, mortician, sexton, gravedigger.

Verbs—inter, bury; lay in the grave, consign to the grave *or* tomb; entomb, intomb, inhume; lay out; perform a funeral; cremate, immolate; embalm, mummify.

Adjectives—funereal, funebrial; mortuary, sepulchral, cinerary; elegiac; necroscopic.

Adverbs—in memoriam; post-obit, *post-mortem;* beneath the sod.

Interjections—rest in peace! *requiescat in pace;* R.I.P.

intermittent, *adj.* fitful, off-and-on, recurrent; periodic, discontinuous, interrupted, broken; flickering. *Ant.,* see REGULARITY.

intern, interne, *v.t. & n.* —*v.t.* detain, hold; shut up *or* in, confine. See INTERIOR. —*n.* internee; prisoner; student doctor, resident doctor.

internal, *adj.* inner, inside, INTERIOR; innate, inherent; domestic (not foreign), inland.

interpose, *v.i.* step in *or* between; interfere, meddle; mediate, arbitrate; intervene, interrupt. See HINDRANCE, COMPROMISE, BETWEEN.

INTERPRETATION [522]

Nouns—**1,** interpretation, definition; explanation, explication; solution, ANSWER; *rationale;* strict interpretation; DEMONSTRATION; MEANING; acception, acceptation, acceptance; LIGHT, reading, lection, construction, version; semantics.

2, translation, rendering, rendition; literal translation, free translation; secret; clue (see INDICATION); DISSERTATION; ATTRIBUTION.

3, exegesis; expounding, exposition; comment, commentary; inference, deduction (see REASONING); illustration, exemplification; glossary, annotation, scholium, note; elucidation; symptomatology; reading of signs, semeiology; diagnosis, prognosis; metoposcopy; paleography, philology (see WORD); equivalent, synonym; polyglot.

4, decipherment, decodement; cryptography, cryptanalysis; key, solution, ANSWER.

5, interpreter, explainer, translator; expositor, exponent, expounder; demonstrator, definer, simplifier, popularizer; oracle, teacher; commentator, annotator; decoder, cryptographer, cryptanalyst.

Verbs—interpret, explain, define, construe, translate, render; do into, turn into; paraphrase, restate; read; spell out, make out; decipher, unravel, disentangle; find the key of, enucleate, resolve, solve; read between the lines; account for; find *or* tell the cause of; throw *or* shed light; clear up, elucidate; illustrate, exemplify; unfold, expound, comment upon, annotate;

key; popularize; understand by, put a construction on, be given to understand. *Colloq.*, get across.

Adjectives—interpretive, interpretative; definitive; inferential, deductive, explanatory, expository; explicative, explicatory; exegetical, illustrative; polyglot; literal; paraphrastic, metaphrastic; cosignificative, synonymous; equivalent (see EQUALITY).

Adverbs—interpretively, interpretatively, in explanation; that is to say, *id est*, *videlicet*, to wit, namely, in short, in other words; literally, strictly speaking, in plain words *or* English; more simply.

Antonym, see ABSURDITY.

---

interrogation, *n.* INQUIRY, inquisition, questioning; probe, investigation, examination; cross-examination.

interruption, *n.* break, interference, stoppage, obstruction. See END, HINDRANCE.

intersect, *v.i.* cut; bisect; interrupt; meet, cross.

interval, *n.* interspace; separation, DISJUNCTION; break, fracture, gap, hole, OPENING; chasm, hiatus, caesura; interruption, interregnum; interstice, lacuna, cleft, mesh, crevice, chink, cranny, crack, chap, slit, fissure, scissure, rift, flaw, breach, rent, gash, cut, incision, leak; dike; gorge, defile, ravine, gulf, canyon, crevasse, abyss, abysm; inlet, strait; gulch, gully; pass. See BETWEEN. *Ant.*, see NEARNESS, CONTINUITY.

intervene, *v.i.* interfere, interrupt, interpose; come between; mediate, arbitrate; intercede; occur, happen, take place. See BETWEEN, COMPROMISE, OCCASION.

interview, *v.t. & n.* —*v.t.* converse with; question (for information *or* opinion). —*n.* questioning; consultation; meeting. See SPEECH.

intimate, *adj., n. & v.t.* —*adj.* close, friendly, familiar; private, personal. —*v.t.* hint, suggest; announce, impart. —*n.* FRIEND, crony, boon *or* bosom companion. See NEARNESS, DISCLOSURE.

intimidate, *v.t.* bully, cow, scare, subdue, frighten; overawe, terrify. See FEAR.

intolerable, *adj.* beyond endurance, unbearable, insupportable, insufferable. See PAIN. *Ant.*, see PLEASURE.

intolerance, *n.* bigotry, bias, prejudice; dogmatism, NARROWNESS.

intoxicate, *v.* make drunk, inebriate; fuddle, befuddle; excite, exalt, elate, overjoy. See DRUNKENNESS, EXCITEMENT. *Ant.*, see MODERATION.

intractable, *adj.* unmanageable, ungovernable; obstinate, perverse; refractory, rebellious. See UNCONFORMITY. *Ant.*, see CONFORMITY.

intricate, *adj.* complicated, complex; involved, devious, CUNNING. See DISORDER.

intrigue, *n. & v.* —*n.* plot, conspiracy, skullduggery; spying, espionage, scheming; love affair, amour. See LOVE. —*v.* fascinate, interest; plot, plan, scheme; spy.

intrinsic, *adj.* intrinsical; subjective; fundamental, normal; implanted, inherent, essential, natural; innate, inborn, inbred, ingrained, incarnate; hereditary, inherited, immanent; congenital, indigenous; inward, internal, virtual; characteristic. *Ant.*, EXTRINSIC.

introduction, *n.* preface, foreword, prelude; presentation; (new) acquaintanceship; INSERTION, BEGINNING. See COURTESY, RECEIVING.

intrude, *v.i.* interlope, intervene, interfere; butt in, trespass, encroach; overstep, obtrude.

intrust, entrust, *v.t.* confide, trust, consign; charge; show faith *or* reliance in. See COMMISSION.

intuition, *n.* intuitiveness, insight, perceptivity, instinct, association, apprehension; premonition, presentiment; clairvoyance, sixth sense, extrasensory perception, second sight. *Colloq.*, hunch. See INTELLECT, INTELLIGENCE. *Ant.*, see REASONING.

intuitive, *adj.* instinctive, impulsive; natural, innate.

inure, *v.t.* toughen, accustom, familiarize, harden, habituate. See HARDNESS.

invade, *v.t.* enter, encroach, violate, trespass; ATTACK, assail, harry; encroach. See INGRESS.

invalid, *adj.* void, null, worthless, useless; valueless, unusable; sickly, ill, unhealthy, unwell, weak. See IMPOTENCE. *Ant.*, see POWER.

invaluable, *adj.* inestimable, priceless, pressing, invaluable, impayable. See GOODNESS, USE. *Ant.*, see EVIL, USELESSNESS.

inveigle, *v.i.* lure, attract, ensnare, cajole, entangle, persuade, decoy, allure. See DECEPTION.

invent, *v.t.* devise, conceive, contrive, originate; imagine, fabricate, improvise; create; spin; forge, design; feign. See IMAGINATION.

INVERSION [218]

Nouns—inversion, eversion, subversion, reversion, retroversion, introversion; contraposition, OPPOSITION; contrariety, contrariness; reversal; turn of the tide; overturn; somersault, somerset; revulsion; transposition, anastrophy, metastasis, anastrophe, tmesis, parenthesis; metathesis; palindrome; pronation and supination.

Verbs—be inverted; turn, go, *or* wheel around *or* about; turn, *or* topple over; capsize; invert, subvert, retrovert; introvert; reverse; overturn, upset, turn topsy-turvy; transpose, put the cart before the horse, turn the tables, turn turtle, keel over.

Adjectives—inverted, wrong side out; inside out, upside down; bottom upwards; supine, on one's head, topsy turvy; inverse; reverse, opposite (see OPPOSITION); topheavy.

Adverbs—inversely, heels over head, head over heels, *vice versa*.

Antonym, see DIRECTION.

invest, *v.i.* endue, endow, clothe, array; surround, besiege, beleaguer; install, induct; dress, adorn; confer. See CELEBRATION, CLOTHING, POWER.

investigate, *v.t.* inquire, examine, question; search, probe. See INQUIRY.

invigorate, *v.i.* strengthen, liven, refresh, enliven, restore, energize, animate. See POWER. *Ant.*, see IMPOTENCE.

invincible, *adj.* inconquerable, powerful, indefatigable, unyielding, indomitable, uncompromising. See OPPOSITION, POWER. *Ant.*, see IMPOTENCE.

invisible, *adj.* imperceptible; undiscernible, indiscernible; unapparent, nonapparent; out of sight, not in sight; behind the scenes, unseen, covert, latent; eclipsed, dim, faint, mysterious, dark, obscure; confused; indistinct, indistinguishable; shadowy, indefinite. *Ant.*, visible; see APPEARANCE.

invite, *v.t.* summon, ask; tempt, attract, lure; bid; solicit; challenge; court. See REQUEST.

invoice, *n.* LIST, bill, summation.

invoke, *v.i.* beseech, plead, beg; call, summon; wish, conjure; attest. See REQUEST.

involuntary, *adj.* spontaneous, instinctive, automatic, reflex. See NECESSITY.

involve, *v.t.* imply, include; complicate, entangle, inculpate, incriminate, commit; mean. See COMPOSITION.

involved, *adj.* complicated, complex; incomprehensible, tangled, conglomerate, intricate, mazy; incriminated, embarrassed, inculpated. See CONVOLUTION.

inward, *adj.* inside, private; in, interior, incoming; mental, spiritual, hidden. See INTERIOR.

IRASCIBILITY [901]

Nouns—**1,** irascibility, temper; crossness; susceptibility; petulance, irritability, tartness, acerbity, pugnacity, contentiousness (see CONTENTION); excitability; bad, hot, fiery, *or* quick temper; hot blood; ill humor, surliness, SULLENNESS; asperity, acrimony, churlishness, DISCOURTESY; fury, huff, miff, anger, RESENTMENT; MALEVOLENCE. *Colloq.*, crankiness.

2, hothead, blusterer; shrew, vixen, virago, termagant, scold, Xant(h)ippe; spitfire. *Colloq.*, fire-eater, crank, grouch, crosspatch. *Slang*, ugly customer, sourpuss, sorehead.

Verbs—be irascible, have a temper, have a devil in one; fire up, be angry (see RESENTMENT); sulk, mope, fret, frown, glower. *Colloq.*, be *or* get sore.

Adjectives—irascible; bad-tempered, ill-tempered; irritable, susceptible; ex-

citable (see EXCITEMENT); thin-skinned, sensitive (see SENSIBILITY); fretful, fidgety; hasty, overhasty, quick, warm, hot, testy, touchy, huffy; pettish, petulant; waspish, snappish, peppery, fiery, passionate, choleric, shrewish; querulous, captious, moody, moodish; quarrelsome, contentious, disputatious; pugnacious, bellicose (see CONTENTION); cantankerous, churlish, discourteous (see DISCOURTESY); fractious, peevish; in a bad temper; sulky; angry (see RESENTMENT); resentful, vindictive (see RETALIATION). *Colloq.* grouchy, ugly, sore, cranky, cross as two sticks, cross as a bear.
Antonym, see COURTESY.

iridescent, *adj.* opalescent, prismatic; colorful, glowing. See COLOR.
irksome, *adj.* troublesome, irritating, tiresome, tedious, wearisome. See DIFFICULTY.
irony, *n.* RIDICULE, satire, sarcasm.
irrational, *adj.* unreasonable, insensible; brainless, brutish, reasonless, absurd. See ABSURDITY.
irregularity, *n.* variability, DEVIATION, caprice, uncertainty; tardiness, unpunctuality; intermittence, fitfulness, inconstancy. See STABILITY. *Ant.*, REGULARITY.
irrelevant, *adj.* inappropriate, unfitting, unrelated, inconsistent, inapplicable.

IRRELIGION [989]

Nouns—1, irreligion, irreligiousness, ungodliness, IMPIETY.
2, scepticism, DOUBT; unbelief, disbelief; incredulity, incredulousness; want of faith; pyrrhonism; agnosticism, iconoclasm, atheism; materialism; positivism; nihilism, infidelity, freethinking, antichristianity, rationalism, heathenism, paganism.
3, atheist, skeptic, sceptic, doubting Thomas; apostate, renegade; unbeliever, infidel, pyrrhonist; heathen, alien, gentile; freethinker, iconoclast, latitudinarian, rationalist; materialist, positivist, nihilist, agnostic; heretic; heathen, pagan.
Verbs—disbelieve, lack faith; DOUBT, question; scoff.
Adjectives—irreligious, undevout; godless, godforsaken, graceless, ungodly, unholy, unsanctified, unhallowed; atheistic, agnostic; sceptical, freethinking; unbelieving, unconverted; incredulous, doubting, faithless, unchristian, gentile, antichristian; worldly, mundane, earthly, carnal.
Antonym, see RELIGION.

irresistible, *adj.* overpowering, killing, overwhelming, stunning, puissant. See POWER. *Ant.*, see IMPOTENCE.
irresolute, *adj.* infirm of purpose, of two minds, half-hearted; dubious, undecided, unresolved, undetermined; hesitating, on the fence; at a loss; vacillating, unsteady, CHANGEABLE, unsteadfast, fickle, capricious, volatile; WEAK, timid, cowardly. See DOUBT, FEAR, COWARDICE. *Ant.*, see COURAGE, RESOLUTION.
irritable, *adj.* fretful, petulant, peevish, touchy, sensitive. See IRASCIBILITY.
irritate, *v.t.* annoy, provoke, bother, trouble; irk, exasperate, nettle, ruffle.
island, *n.* isle, ait; cay, key; atoll, (coral) reef, ledge.
isolate, *v.t.* segregate; insulate, separate, quarantine. See DISJUNCTION.
isolation, *n.* separation, quarantine; loneliness, solitude, segregation. See SECLUSION. *Ant.*, see SOCIALITY.
issue, *n. & v.* —*n.* product; offspring; progeny; result; discharge; outcome, result; question, dispute. See EFFECT, EGRESS, INQUIRY, POSTERITY. —*v.i.* leave, depart, debouch, emerge; circulate, despatch, send, publish; emit, discharge, exude; eliminate; spout, spurt; flow, spring. See DEPARTURE, EFFECT, ESCAPE, MONEY, PUBLICATION.
itch, *n. & v.* —*n.* itching; desire to scratch; tickling; prickly sensation; mange, manginess; DESIRE, craving, hankering; cacoethes, cacoethes scribendi (writer's itch); the itch, scabies, psora; itchiness; burning, tingling. —*v.i.* tingle, prickle, burn; crave, long for, yearn, hanker.
item, *n.* piece, detail, particular; entry, article; term, paragraph.

itinerant, *adj.* wandering, nomadic, wayfaring; peripatetic; traveling. See TRAVEL.

itinerary, *n.* JOURNEY, route, circuit, course; guidebook.

J

jab, *n. & v.* punch, blow; poke. See IMPULSE.

jabber, *n. & v.i.* —*n.* gibberish, babble, blather, nonsense, jabberwocky; prattle, talk, gossip, chatter. —*v.i.* talk, rattle on, prattle, chatter, gibber, gabble. See SPEECH, ABSURDITY.

jack, *n. & v.t.* —*n.* MAN, fellow; KNAVE, bower; lifting device, lever; sailor, hand; jack-of-all-trades; ass, mule, donkey, rabbit; connection (electrical). *Slang,* money; applejack. See AGENCY. —*v.t.* lift, raise.

jackal, *n.* See ANIMAL; henchman, hireling. *Slang,* dogrobber.

jacket, *n.* coat, sack *or* suit coat, dinner *or* smoking jacket, tuxedo, sport coat; windbreaker, pea jacket *or* coat; COVERING; peel, rind, skin. See CLOTHING.

jackpot, *n.* prize, highest *or* all stakes. See CHANCE.

jaded, *adj.* weary; surfeited; blasé, dulled. See WEARINESS.

jagged, *adj.* sharp, rough, snaggy, notched, pointed, zigzag. See ROUGH-NESS. *Ant.,* see SMOOTHNESS, FLATNESS.

jail, *n.* See PRISON.

jangle, *n. & v.* —*n.* harsh noise, DISCORD, clangor; ringing, jingle; bickering, dispute. —*v.* clash, clang, rattle, ring, jingle; upset (nerves). See SOUND.

jam, *n. & v.* —*n.* crowd, press, crush; blockage, impasse; jelly, fruit preserve. See FOOD. —*v.* crowd, press, crush; wedge, shove, push, cram; block.

jar, *n. & v.* —*n.* vessel, Mason jar, container, jug. —*v.* shock, jolt; jounce, shake, rattle; clash. See DISAGREEMENT, IMPULSE, RECEPTACLE.

jargon, *n.* lingo, shoptalk, patois, cant, argot; *Slang,* jive, doubletalk; gibberish. See SPEECH, ABSURDITY.

jaw, *n. & v.i.* —*n.* mandible, jawbone. —*v.i.* chatter, talk, jabber.

jealous, *adj.* jaundiced, yellow; green-eyed, grudging, covetous, envious; suspicious; anxious, concerned. See DOUBT. *Ant.,* see BELIEF.

jealousy, *n.* jealousness, envy, covetousness, distrust, mistrust, suspicion, DOUBT; anxiety, concern; jaundiced eye, green-eyed monster. *Ant.,* see BELIEF, BENEVOLENCE.

jeer, *v. & n.* —*v.* sneer, scoff, taunt, gibe, mock; RIDICULE, make fun of, belittle. —*n.* taunt, gibe, mockery; hoot, catcall, hissing. *Ant.,* see APPROBATION.

jelly, *n.* jam, preserve; gelatin; mush. See FOOD.

jeopardy, *n.* DANGER, risk, peril, hazard. *Ant.,* see SAFETY.

jerk, *v. & n.* —*v.* twist, tweak, pull, SNAP; start, twitch, jitter, jump. —*n.* start, jump, twitch; spasm; pull, SNAP. *Slang,* nitwit, FOOL; nobody. See IMPULSE.

jest, *n. & v.i.* —*n.* joke, jape; WIT, humor, clowning; practical joke; jocularity, pun, gag, wisecrack, witticism, *bon mot*; sport, fun; make-believe, fooling. —*v.i.* FOOL, joke; crack wise, gag; play the fool.

jester, *n.* WIT, HUMORIST, joker, gagman, comedian; FOOL, clown, buffoon.

jet, *v., n. & adj.* —*v.* STREAM, spurt, gush, shoot, spout, pour, rush, squirt. —*n.* STREAM, fountain; outgush, spurt; jet plane. See WATER, AVIATION. —*adj.* black, pitch, pitchy, ebony, ebon; dark, raven. See COLOR.

jewel, *n.* stone, gem; diamond, ruby, sapphire, emerald, *etc.*

jewelry, *n.* gems, beads, trinkets, stones; bracelets, bangles, necklaces, *etc.* See ORNAMENT.

jilt, *v.t.* reject or cast off (a lover); leave in the lurch. See REFUSAL.

jingle, *n. & v.* —*n.* clink, tinkle; ring; jangle. See SOUND.

jitter, *v.i. & n.* —*v.* twitch, fidget, jerk, jump, vibrate. See IMPULSE. —*n.* vibration. —*n.pl.* heebie-jeebies, shakes, nervousness. *Ant.,* see STABILITY.

job, *n.* work, occupation, calling; piece of work, stint; position, situation, duty. See BUSINESS.

jocularity, *n.* humor; mirth, laughter; sportiveness, jesting, joshing, kidding, facetiousness; WIT.

jog, *v.* jiggle, push, shake, jostle. See IMPULSE.

join, *v.* unite, link, connect, tie, bind; federate, associate, affiliate; become a member; marry. See JUNCTION, PARTY.

joint, *n. & adj.* —*n.* connection, link, juncture; articulation (of bones). *Slang*, dive, den, haunt, hangout. See JUNCTION, ABODE. —*adj.* combined, shared, common to both parties. See JUNCTION, PARTY.

joke, *n. & v.i.* —*n.* funny story, jest, gag, pun; wisecrack, witticism, WIT, *bon mot*; fooling, kidding, joshing, lack of earnestness. —*v.i.* josh, jest, gag. *Slang*, horse around.

jostle, *v.t.* push, bump; elbow, shoulder; collide with. See IMPULSE. *Ant.,* see AVOIDANCE, RECOIL.

journal, *n.* diary, daybook, record; newspaper, magazine, periodical. See PUBLICATION, CHRONOMETRY.

journalist, *n.* newsman, newspaperman, reporter; writer, editor, copyreader. See RECORD, BOOK.

journey, *n. & v.* —*n.* trip, tour; voyage, cruise, crossing; expedition; tramp, hike; pilgrimage, hadj; caravan; trek. —*v.* travel; voyage, sail, cross; tour, roam, range, venture, explore; ride, drive, motor. See TRAVEL.

jovial, *adj.* genial, cordial; gay, merry; jolly, convivial. See CHEERFULNESS. *Ant.,* see DEJECTION.

joy, *n.* REJOICING; PLEASURE, happiness, delight, mirth, gayety; *joie de vivre*. *Colloq.,* fun. *Ant.,* see DEJECTION.

jubilant, *adj.* joyful; triumphant, exultant; elated, REJOICING, in high spirits. *Ant.,* see DEJECTION.

jubilee, *n.* CELEBRATION; anniversary; REJOICING.

judge, *n. & v.* —*n.* jurist, justice, (the) court; chancellor; judge of assize, recorder, justice of the peace, J.P., magistrate; his worship, his honor, his Lordship, Lord Chancellor, Chief Justice; archon, tribune, praetor; mufti, cadi, mullah; judge advocate; arbiter, arbitrator, mediator, umpire, referee; censor; connoisseur; tribunal. *Slang*, beak. —*v.* adjudge, adjudicate; arbitrate, try, try a case, sit in judgment, sentence, condemn; deem, conclude, consider, appraise. See JUSTICE, TASTE.

judgment, *n.* discretion; TASTE, discernment, insight; adjudication, arbitration; decision, finding, verdict, sentence, decree; estimation, valuation, appreciation; assessment; opinion, CHOICE; award, estimate; review, criticism. *Ant.,* see MISJUDGMENT.

judicial, *adj.* judiciary, juridical, legal, judicious; judging, judgelike; censorious. See JUSTICE.

juggle, *v.* manipulate; perform tricks with objects; handle many things at once.

juicy, *adj.* moist, sappy, not dry, succulent; rich, tasty, tempting. See TASTE. *Ant.,* see DRYNESS.

jumble, *n. & v.* —*n.* mixup, confusion, DISORDER; pi. —*v.* mix up, disarrange, muddle, mess. *Ant.,* see ARRANGEMENT.

jump, *n. & v.* hop, LEAP, bound, spring, vault; start, twitch, jerk.

JUNCTION [43]

Nouns—**1,** junction, connection, conjunction, COHERENCE, joining, joinder, union, annex, annexation, attachment; ligation, accouplement; MARRIAGE, knot, wedlock; confluence; hookup, network, communication, concatenation; fusion, blend, merger; meeting, reunion, ASSEMBLAGE.

2, joint, joining, juncture, pivot, hinge, articulation, seam, suture, stitch; chain, link; miter, mortise, tenon, dovetail; closeness, tightness.

3, combination, unification, incorporation, merger, amalgamation, coalescence, MIXTURE.

Verbs—**1,** join, unite, knot, knit, conjoin, connect, associate, put together, hold together, piece together, roll into one, combine, compound, incorporate.

2, attach, affix, fasten, bind, secure; blend, merge, fuse; tie, sew, stitch, tack, knit, button, hitch, knot, lash, truss, bandage, braid, splice, gird, tether, moor, picket, harness, chain; fetter, lock, latch, leash, couple, link, yoke, bracket, span, marry, wed.

3, pin, nail, bolt, clasp, clamp, screw, rivet, solder, weld, mortise, miter, dovetail, graft, entwine; interlace, entangle, intertwine.

Adjectives—**1,** joined, joint; conjoint, conjunct, conjunctive, corporate, compact, hand in hand.

2, firm, fast, tight, taut, secure, set, inseparable, indissoluble.

3, blent, blended, wedded, married, merged, fused. See MIXTURE.

Adverbs—jointly, in conjunction with, fast, firmly, intimately.

Antonym, see DISJUNCTION.

juncture, *n.* joint, point, connection; contingency, emergency. See JUNCTION.

junior, *n. & adj.* younger, lesser, subordinate. See INFERIORITY, AGE.

junk, *n. & v.* —*n.* rubbish, WASTE, refuse, trash, discard, castoffs; scrap, salvage, wreck, wreckage; stuff, miscellany, claptrap. See SHIP. —*v.t.* scrap, wreck, tear down, dismember; salvage; discard, cast off, jettison. See DESTRUCTION. *Ant.,* see PRESERVATION.

jurisdiction, *n.* judicature; administration; province, dominion, control; magistracy, AUTHORITY; tribunal; municipality, corporation, bailiwick.

jurist, *n.* JUDGE; legal expert.

juror, *n.* juryman; panelist, JUDGE.

jury, *n.* trial jury, grand jury; panel; board of judges.

just, *adj. & adv.* —*adj.* fair, RIGHT; impartial, nonpartisan; lawful, legal; exact, accurate, precise. See PROBITY. —*adv.* precisely, exactly; almost, nearly, within an ace of.

JUSTICE [924]

Nouns—**1,** justice, justness, fairness, fair treatment, impartiality, equity, equitableness; poetic justice, rough justice; nemesis; scales of justice; fair trial, trial by jury. See LAWSUIT, LEGALITY, PROBITY. *Colloq.,* square deal, straight shooting, a square shake.

2, due, dueness, rightfulness, RIGHT, VINDICATION. See JUDGMENT.

Verbs—**1,** do justice to, be fair, treat fairly, deal fairly, be impartial, see justice done, play fair, give the devil his due. *Colloq.,* give a square deal, play the game, give a sporting chance.

2, be just, right, *or* due; have right, title *or* claim to; be entitled to; have a claim upon, belong to, deserve, merit, be worthy of.

3, demand, claim, call upon for, reclaim, exact, insist on, take one's stand, make a point of, require, lay claim to; substantiate, vindicate (see VINDICATION).

Adjectives—**1,** just, fair, impartial, equal, equable, fair and square, dispassionate, disinterested, unbiased, evenhanded.

2, just, RIGHT, equitable, due, square, fit, fitting, correct, proper, meet, becoming, seemly; decorous, creditable; allowable, lawful, legal, legitimate, licit.

3, having a right to, entitled to, deserving, meriting, worthy of; deserved, merited.

Adverbs—justly, rightfully, duly, by right, by divine right, fairly, in justice, as is just *or* fitting. *Colloq.,* on the level, aboveboard, on the square.

Antonym, see INJUSTICE.

justification, *n.* excuse; DEFENSE; VINDICATION, exoneration; adjustment. See ARRANGEMENT. *Ant.,* see WRONG.

justify, *v.* exonerate, excuse, warrant, vindicate, acquit, absolve; prove right, free from blame; make to fit, set properly. See VINDICATION, ARRANGEMENT.

jut, *v.i.* protrude, project, beetle, stand out, overhang. See CONVEXITY.

juvenile, *n. & adj.* —*n.* youngster, minor, adolescent; boy, girl. *Colloq.,* kin. —*adj.* puerile, young, undeveloped, immature; childish. See YOUTH. *Ant.,* see AGE.

K

kaleidoscopic, *adj.* variegated, varying; forming many patterns; colorful. See COLOR.

kaput, *adj.* ruined, done for, destroyed. See FAILURE, DESTRUCTION.

keel, *v. & n.* —*v.* provide with a keel; turn (over); fall down (with over), drop like a log. See DESCENT. —*n.* main timber of a ship's bottom.

keen, *adj.* piercing, stinging, nippy; sharp, edged, cutting, razorlike; eager, enthusiastic, ardent; acute, clever, shrewd, quick. See DESIRE, SHARPNESS, FEELING, INTELLIGENCE.

keep, *v. & n.* —*v.* retain; hold; have, possess; receive, preserve; celebrate (holidays), maintain; sustain, continue; hold back, save, cling to, detain. See POSSESSION, PRESERVATION. *Ant.,* see RELINQUISHMENT. —*n.* donjon, dungeon; PRISON, prison tower, cell, jail.

keeper, *n.* custodian; jailer, warden, watchman, watchdog; gamekeeper, ranger; doorman, tiler; curator; protector, guardian; observer (of rites); celebrator; preserver; supporter, maintainer. See SAFETY, PRISON. *Ant.,* see NEGLECT, RELINQUISHMENT.

keepsake, *n.* memento, souvenir, reminder, token. See MEMORY.

keg, *n.* barrel, cask. See RECEPTACLE.

ken, *n.* KNOWLEDGE; scope.

kernel, *n.* nub, gist, core, pith, point, center, essence; grain, nut, seed, nucleus. See CENTRALITY, MEANING, IMPORTANCE.

key, *n.* answer, solution, code book, decipherment; pitch, tonality, register. See INTERPRETATION, MUSIC.

keynote, *n.* tonic (note of scale); basic principle.

kick, *v. & n.* —*v.* strike with the shoe, punt; spurn; stamp. *Colloq.,* complain, gripe, bellyache, grumble. —*n.* RECOIL; thrill, excitement, fun. *Colloq.,* complaint, grievance, gripe. See IMPULSE, OPPOSITION.

kidnap, *v.* carry away (a person), abduct. See STEALING.

KILLING [361]

Nouns—**1,** killing, homicide, manslaughter, murder, assassination; bloodshed, slaughter, carnage, butchery, decimation, pogrom, massacre, war, WARFARE.

2, death blow, finishing stroke, *coup de grâce*, quietus, gassing, electrocution, defenestration, execution; martyrdom; suffocation, poisoning, strangulation, garrot(t)e, hanging, decapitation, guillotine, violent death; traffic death, fatal accident, casualty, fatality.

3, butcher, slayer, murderer, Cain, assassin, cutthroat, garrotter, bravo, thug, executioner; regicide, matricide, parricide, fratricide, infanticide; suicide, suttee, hara-kiri, immolation; germicide, insecticide.

4, hunting, coursing, shooting; sportsman, huntsman, fisherman, hunter, Nimrod; slaughterhouse, shambles, abattoir; charnel house.

Verbs—**1,** kill, put to death, slay, shed blood; murder, assassinate, butcher, slaughter, immolate, massacre, do away with, put an end to; run over; dispatch, do for. *Colloq.,* liquidate. *Slang,* bump off, take for a ride.

2, strangle, garrot(t)e, hang, throttle, poison, choke, stifle, gas, electrocute, suffocate, smother, asphyxiate, drown, execute, behead; put to the sword, stone, deal a death blow, wade knee-deep in blood; blow out one's brains, commit suicide.

Adjectives—**1,** killing, murderous, sanguinary, bloodstained, bloodthirsty, homicidal, redhanded; bloody, ensanguined, gory.

2, mortal, fatal, lethal, deadly, internecine, suicidal.

Antonym, see LIFE.

kind, *n. & adj.* —*n.* sort, species, CLASS, type, ilk, breed, character, nature. —*adj.* gentle, tender; sympathetic; mild; friendly, obliging, benign; solicitous; lenient; helpful.

kindle, *v.* ignite, start (fire), fire, set ablaze; stir, excite, rouse, provoke. See HEAT, EXCITEMENT.

kindling, *n.* tinder, FUEL, firewood, combustibles.

kindness, *n.* GOOD, friendliness, sympathy, mildness, BENEVOLENCE; favor, AID, SERVICE; graciousness, tenderness, gentleness; leniency, mercy. *Ant.,* see MALEVOLENCE.

kindred, *n.* relatives, kinfolk(s), kinsmen; clan, tribe; brothers, sisters, cousins, parents, *etc.*; kindred spirits, congenial people; SIMILARITY. See RELATION.

king, *n.* ruler, monarch, emperor, sovereign; royalty; master.

kingdom, *n.* domain, empire, realm; LAND; country. See REGION.

kingly, *adj.* royal, majestic, regal, imperial; noble, magnificent. See AUTHORITY.

kinsman, *n.* relative, blood relation; clansman. See RELATION.

kiss, *n. & v.* —*n.* smack, osculation, caress; merest touch. See ENDEARMENT. —*v.* caress, osculate; brush lightly, TOUCH, graze.

knack, *n.* adeptness, ability, dexterity, handiness, trick, SKILL. *Ant.,* see UNSKILLFULNESS.

knave, *n.* rogue, rascal, villain, scamp, scapegrace, blackguard, reprobate, miscreant; jack, bower (*cards*); churl, menial, SERVANT. See EVILDOER. *Ant.,* see GOODNESS.

kneel, *v.* bend (to pray), genuflect. See DEPRESSION.

knickknack, *n.* bric-à-brac, trifle, trinket, gewgaw. See ORNAMENT, UNIMPORTANCE.

knight, *n.* cavalier, chevalier; paladin, champion, Galahad; Templar; noble. See LOVE, DEFENSE, NOBILITY, CLERGY.

knit, *v.* weave, work with wool, interlace (yarn); draw together, contract. FURROW, wrinkle. See JUNCTION.

knob, *n.* knot, lump, node, protuberance, boss; door handle. See CONVEXITY.

knock, *n. & v.* —*v.* pound, strike, hit, rap, tap; tamp; bump, collide. *Colloq.,* belittle, depreciate. See IMPULSE, DISAPPROBATION. —*n.* stroke, bump; rap, rapping, noise. *Colloq.,* slur, aspersion.

knoll, *n.* hill, hillock, rise (of ground), mound, hummock. See HEIGHT.

knot, *n. & v.* —*n.* snarl, tangle; puzzle, problem; cluster, group; lump node; measure (*Naut.*). —*v.* tangle, snarl; tie, bind, fasten. See ASSEMBLAGE, CONVEXITY, DIFFICULTY.

KNOWLEDGE [490]

Nouns—**1,** knowledge, cognizance, cognition, acquaintance, ken, privity, familiarity, comprehension, apprehension, recognition, appreciation; INTUITION, conscience, consciousness, awareness, perception, precognition; light, enlightenment; glimpse, insight, inkling, glimmer, suspicion, impression.

2, science, philosophy, theory, doctrine, encyclopedia; erudition, learning, lore, scholarship, reading, letters, literature, book-learning, bookishness, INFORMATION, store of knowledge, education, culture; attainments, accomplishments, proficiency, SKILL, wisdom, omniscience. *Colloq.,* knowhow.

3, study, instruction; reading, inquiry; apprenticeship. See SCHOOL, TEACHING.

4, SCHOLAR, SAGE, savant, pundit, academician.

Verbs—**1,** know, ken, wot; be aware of; ween, trow; possess; apprehend, conceive, comprehend, realize, understand, appreciate, fathom, make out; recognize, discern, perceive, see, experience.

2, know full well; have in one's head, have at one's fingertips, know by heart, be master of, know what's what; see one's way, discover, LEARN, study, ascertain.

Adjectives—**1,** knowing, cognitive, conscious, cognizant, aware, perceptive.

2, aware of, cognizant of, conscious of, apprised of, told, acquainted with, privy to, no stranger to, up to, alive to; proficient in, versed in, at home in; conversant with, familiar with. *Slang,* hip, hep, wise, wised up.

3, erudite, scholarly, instructed, learned, lettered, educated, well-informed, well-read, well-grounded, well-educated, enlightened, shrewd, bookish, scholastic, solid, profound, accomplished, omniscient; sage, wise, intellectual; emeritus.

4, known, ascertained, well-known, recognized, noted, proverbial, familiar, hackneyed, trite, commonplace.

5, knowable, cognizable, ascertainable, perceptible, discernible, comprehensible.

Antonym, see IGNORANCE.

L

labor, *n.* work, toil; effort; task; travail; proletariat. See EXERTION. *Ant.,* idleness, leisure; capital; see INACTIVITY.

laborer, *n.* worker, workman, workingman, toiler.

laborious, *adj.* hard, arduous, tiresome, irksome. See EXERTION. *Ant.,* easy; see FACILITY.

labor-saving, *adj.* helpful, automatic, mechanical.

labyrinth, *n.* maze, tangle, meander; complexity, intricacy. See DISORDER.

lace, *n. & v.* —*n.* cord, lacing; braid; openwork, network. See CONNECTION, ORNAMENT. —*v.t.* weave, twine; interlace; bind, tie; flavor, mix, spoke. See JUNCTION, MIXTURE. *Colloq.,* whip, lash.

lacerate, *v.t.* tear, mangle; harrow, distress. See PAIN.

lack, *n. & v.* —*n.* want, deficiency, shortage, need. —*v.t.* need, require. See INSUFFICIENCY. *Ant.,* see SUFFICIENCY.

lad, *n.* boy, youth, stripling. See YOUTH.

ladle, *n.* spoon, dipper; metal pot. See RECEPTACLE.

ladylove, *n.* sweetheart, darling. See LOVE. *Colloq.,* best girl. *Slang,* girl friend.

lag, *v.i.* linger, drag, fall behind, hang back. See SLOWNESS.

lair, *n.* den, covert, burrow, form, cave. See ABODE.

laity, *n.* flock, fold, congregation; assembly; churchgoers; parishioners; parish, brethren, people; laymen, laywomen, laic; secular. See LAY. *Ant.,* see CLERGY.

lake, *n.* loch, lough; pond, pool, tarn, lakelet, mere. See WATER.

lame, *adj.* crippled, halt; weak, ineffectual. See DISEASE, FAILURE.

LAMENTATION [839]

Nouns—**1,** lamentation, lament, wail, complaint, plaint, murmur, mutter, grumble, groan, moan, whine, whimper, sob, sigh, cry, outcry, scream, howl, frown, scowl. *Slang,* gripe, beef, bellyaching.

2, tears, weeping, lachrymation, languishment; condolence, sympathy, compassion, pity, consolation, commiseration.

3, mourning weeds, crape, sackcloth and ashes; knell, dirge, coronach, keen, requiem, elegy, monody, threnody, jeremiad.

4, lamenter, mourner, grumbler, Niobe, Jeremiah, Rachel.

Verbs—**1,** lament, mourn, deplore, grieve, weep over, bewail; REGRET; condole with, commiserate; fret, wear mourning, wear sackcloth and ashes.

2, sigh, heave a sigh; wail, cry, weep, sob, greet, blubber, snivel, whimper, pule, shed tears; burst into tears, cry one's eyes out; scream, mew, growl, groan, moan, roar, bellow; frown, scowl, make a wry face, gnash one's teeth, wring one's hands, tear one's hair, beat one's breast.

3, complain, murmur, mutter, whine, grumble, clamor, make a fuss about. *Slang,* gripe, bellyache.

Adjectives—lamenting, in mourning, in sackcloth and ashes, sorrowful, sorrowing, unhappy, mournful, tearful, lachrymose, plaintive, querulous, in tears, with tears in one's eyes; elegiac(al).

Interjections—alas! alack! O dear! too bad! sorry! woe is me! alas the day! alackaday! waly waly! what a pity! *O tempora, O mores!*

Antonym, see CELEBRATION.

lamina, *n.* LAYER, stratum, sheet, plate, scale. See COVERING.
laminate, *v.t.* stratify, plate, veneer, overlay. See LAYER.

LAND [342]

Nouns—**1,** land, earth, ground, dry land, *terra firma.*
2, continent, mainland, peninsula, delta; neck of land, isthmus, ISLAND; oasis, desert; promontory, highland; real estate, property, acres.
3, coast, shore, strand, beach, bank, lea, seaside, seacoast, rock-bound coast, alluvium.
4, soil, glebe, clay, loam, marl, mold, topsoil, subsoil, clod, rock, shale, chalk, gravel, dust, sand.
Verbs—land, light, alight, ground; disembark, come *or* go ashore.
Adjectives—earthly, terrestrial; continental, midland, littoral, riparian, alluvial, landed, territorial; earthy.
Adverbs—ashore, on shore, land, *etc.;* aground, on solid ground.
Antonym, see WATER.

landholder, *n.* landowner, occupant; landlord. See POSSESSION.
landlord, *n.* proprietor, owner; host, innkeeper, boniface. See POSSESSION, FRIEND. *Ant.,* tenant, guest.
landlubber, *n.* landsman, raw seaman. See NAVIGATION.
lane, *n.* path, byway, passageway; route, corridor, track.
language, *n.* SPEECH, tongue, lingo, vernacular, mother tongue; idiom, parlance, phraseology; dialect, patois, cant, jargon, slang, argot; pig *or* dog Latin, pidgin English, *bêche de mer*; Esperanto, Ito, Basic English, lingua franca; dactylology, sign language; ancient *or* dead language. *Slang,* jive, doubletalk, gobbledygook. See MEANING, COMMUNICATION, WRITING.
languid, *adj.* weak, feeble, weary; listless, apathetic. See IMPOTENCE, INSENSIBILITY. *Ant.,* vigorous, energetic.
languish, *v.i.* weaken, fail, fade, decline; pine, droop. See IMPOTENCE, DISEASE, DEJECTION. *Ant.,* flourish.
languor, *n.* WEARINESS, lassitude, listlessness; indolence, inertia. See INACTIVITY.
lank, *adj.* lean, spare, gaunt, bony. See NARROWNESS. *Ant.,* stocky.
lapse, *n. & v.* —*n.* passage, interval; oversight, peccadillo. See END, CONVERSION, GUILT. —*v.i.* pass, glide away; err.
large, *adj.* big, great, huge, colossal, enormous, immense.ᐧ See SIZE. *Ant.,* small, tiny, minute; see LITTLENESS.
lascivious, *adj.* lustful, lewd, salacious, unchaste, wanton. See IMPURITY. *Ant.,* chaste, pure; see PURITY.
lash, *v.t.* beat, whip, flog, scourge; berate, rebuke, satirize. See PUNISHMENT, DISAPPROBATION.
last, *v.i.* endure, persist, continue, abide. See TIME, DURABILITY.
lasting, *adj.* durable, enduring, persisting, permanent. See DURABILITY. *Ant.,* see TRANSIENTNESS.
late, *adj.* tardy; belated, delayed; dilatory; new, recent; former, sometime. See LATENESS, NEWNESS, PAST. *Ant.,* see EARLINESS.
latency, *n.* latentness; passivity, passiveness, quiescence, dormancy; invisibility, SILENCE; CONCEALMENT, imperceptibility. See LATENT. *Ant.,* see EVIDENCE.

LATENESS [133]

Nouns—lateness, tardiness, SLOWNESS, unpunctuality; delay, procrastination, deferring, deferment, postponement, adjournment, prorogation, retardation, respite; protraction, prolongation; stop, stay, reprieve, moratorium.
Verbs—**1,** be late, tarry, wait, stay, bide, take time; dawdle, dilly-dally, linger, loiter, take one's time, gain time, bide one's time; hang fire, stand over, lie over.
2, put off, defer, delay, lay over, suspend, stave off, waive, retard, remand, postpone, adjourn, procrastinate, spin out, draw out, prorogue, hold *or* keep back, tide over, temporize, play for time, get under the wire, sleep on it.
3, lose an opportunity, be kept waiting, dance attendance; cool one's heels, wait, await. *Slang,* sweat it out.

Adjectives—late, tardy, slow, behindhand, belated, backward, unpunctual, dilatory, delayed, delaying, procrastinating, in abeyance; UNTIMELY.

Adverbs—late, backward; late in the day, at the eleventh hour, at length, at last, ultimately, behind time, too late, after hours, ex post facto; slowly, leisurely, deliberately, at one's leisure; in the nick of time.

Interjections—too late! now or never!

Antonym, see EARLINESS.

---

latent, *adj.* hidden, concealed, lurking; occult, secret; implied, dormant, unapparent, in the background, invisible, dark, unknown, unseen; impenetrable; covert, undiscovered, under cover; indirect, inferential, tacit, implicit, allusive, understood. See CONCEALMENT. *Ant.*, see EVIDENCE.

lateral, *adj.* sidelong. See SIDE.

latitude, *n.* range, extent, scope, FREEDOM.

latter, *adj.* later, last mentioned. See PAST. *Ant.*, former; see PRIORITY.

laud, *v.t.* praise, extol, eulogize. See APPROBATION. *Ant.*, belittle, disparage; see DISAPPROBATION.

laugh, *v.i.* guffaw, snicker, giggle, titter, chuckle. See REJOICING.

laughable, *adj.* ludicrous, amusing, comical; absurd; facetious, humorous. See ABSURDITY.

laughingstock, *n.* fool; target, butt, game, fair game, April fool; queer fish, odd fish; mockery; monkey, buffoon. *Slang*, fall guy. See RIDICULE. *Ant.*, see RESPECT.

laughter, *n.* laughing, guffaw, snicker, giggle, titter, chuckle. See REJOICING.

launch, *v.t.* float, start, get going; throw, cast, hurl. See BEGINNING, PROPULSION.

lavish, *adj. & v.* —*adj.* prodigal, profuse, bountiful, LIBERAL. *Ant.*, parsimonious. —*v.t.* give liberally; squander.

law, *n.* statute, ordinance, regulation, mandate; precept, axiom, jurisprudence. See RULE, MAXIM, PRECEPT, LEGALITY.

law-abiding, *adj.* obedient, upright. See OBEDIENCE, PROBITY. *Ant.*, lawless.

lawful, *adj.* legal, legitimate; permissible; valid. See LEGALITY, PERMISSION.

lawless, *adj.* disorderly, unruly, insubordinate, mutinous. See ILLEGALITY, DISOBEDIENCE. *Ant.*, law-abiding.

lawlessness, *n.* disorder, mutiny, mob rule, anarchy.

lawn, *n.* grass plot, green, greenyard. See AGRICULTURE, VEGETABLE.

LAWSUIT [969]

Nouns—**1**, lawsuit, suit, action, CAUSE, litigation, proceedings, dispute; hearing, trial; jurisdiction (see LEGALITY); verdict, JUDGMENT, award; recovery, damages.

2, citation, arraignment, prosecution, impeachment; accusation, true bill, indictment; apprehension, arrest; committal; imprisonment; writ, summons, subpoena, habeas corpus, pleadings, declaration, bill, claim, bill of right, affidavit, answer, replication, PLEA, demurrer, rejoinder, rebuttal, summation; appeal, motion, writ of error, case, decision, precedent, reports.

3, JUDGE, justice, magistrate, surrogate, referee, chancellor; judiciary, the bench; coroner, sheriff, constable, bailiff, officer, policeman, gendarme, suitor, litigant, plaintiff, defendant, appellant, claimant; LAWYER, bar.

4, court, tribunal, judicatory; court of law, equity, chancery, appeals; Supreme Court, woolsack, drumhead; court-martial. *Slang*, kangaroo court.

5, courtroom, chambers, dock, jury-box, witness-box *or* -stand.

Verbs—sue, litigate; bring to trial, put on trial, accuse, hale to court; prefer a claim, file; serve (with a writ), cite, apprehend, arraign, prosecute, bring an action against, indict, impeach, attach, distrain, commit, arrest, summon(s), give in charge; empanel a jury, implead, join issue, try; sit in judgment, judge, adjudicate; rule, award, affirm, deny.

Adjectives—litigious, litigant, contentious; judicial, legal, appellate.

---

lawyer, *n.* jurist; legal adviser; district *or* prosecuting attorney, attorney general, prosecutor; advocate, barrister, solicitor, counsel, counselor (-at-law); King's *or* Queen's counsel; attorney (-at-law); bencher; bar; pleader; Portia; a Daniel come to judgment; judge advocate; devil's advocate; pettifogger, shyster. *Colloq.*, D.A.; ambulance chaser; sea lawyer. *Slang*, mouthpiece, lip. See LAWSUIT.

lax, *adj.* loose, flaccid, limp, slack; remiss, careless, weak; relaxed, lawless, chaotic, disorderly; unbridled; anarchical, unauthorized. See SOFTNESS, MODERATION. *Ant.*, see AUTHORITY, HARDNESS.

laxity, *n.* laxness, looseness, slackness, flaccidity, limpness; toleration, lenity, FREEDOM, relaxation, remission, loosening, DISORDER, disorganization, chaos. *Ant.*, see AUTHORITY, HARDNESS.

lay, *adj. & v.* —*adj.* secular, noncleric, nonprofessional. —*v.t.* put, place, deposit; allay, suppress; impose; ascribe; present. See LOCATION, RELIEF, JUSTICE, CAUSE.

LAYER [204]

Nouns—**1,** layer, stratum, couch, bed, zone, substratum, floor, stage, story, tier, slab, fold, flap, ply, veneer, lap, table, tablet, board, plank, platter, course.
2, plate, lamina, sheet, flake, foil, wafer, scale, coat, peel, membrane, film, leaf, slice, rasher, shaving, integument.
3, stratification, shale, scaliness, squamosity, lamination.
Verbs—slice, shave, pare, peel, plate, coat, veneer, cover, laminate, stratify.
Adjectives—lamellar, lamellate, laminated, micaceous; schistous, scaly, squamous, filmy, membranous, flaky, foliated, foliaceous, stratified, stratiform, tabular, discoid.

---

layman, *n.* laic, secular.

lazy, *adj.* indolent, slothful; slow, sluggish. See INACTIVITY. *Ant.*, industrious; see ACTIVITY.

lead, *v.t.* conduct, direct; precede; open, start; bring; spend, pass. See AUTHORITY, DIRECTION, PRIORITY, BEGINNING.

leaden, *adj.* gray, somber; slow, heavy; gloomy, cheerless. See DIMNESS, INACTIVITY.

leader, *n.* guide, bellwether; director, conductor; head, commander, chief. See AUTHORITY, MUSICIAN.

leadership, *n.* superintendence, chieftainship, stewardship, guidance. See DIRECTION, AUTHORITY.

leaf, *n.* frond, blade; lamina, sheet, flake. See VEGETABLE, LAYER.

leafage, *n.* foliage, leaves, verdure. See VEGETABLE.

league, *v.i.* confederate, unite, join. See JUNCTION.

leak, *v.i.* seep, ooze, escape; become known. See EGRESS, DISCLOSURE.

lean, *v. & adj.* —*v.i.* slant, incline; depend, rely; tend. See SUPPORT, BELIEF, TENDENCY. —*adj.* spare, meager, lank, gaunt. See NARROWNESS.

LEAP [309]

Nouns—**1,** leap, jump, hop, spring, bound, vault; bounce (see RECOIL).
2, dance, caper; curvet, prance, skip, gambol, frolic, romp, buck.
3, leaper, jumper, kangaroo, jerboa, chamois, goat, frog, grasshopper, flea, hoptoad; jumping bean, jumping jack, pogo stick; spring.
4, high jump, broad jump, pole vault; lover's leap; springboard; leap frog, hopscotch.
Verbs—leap, jump, hop, spring, bound, vault, cut capers, trip, skip, dance, prance, gambol, frolic, romp, cavort, caper, curvet, foot it, bob, bounce, flounce, frisk.
Adjectives—leaping, bounding, springy, saltatory, frisky, lively, bouncy, frolicsome, skittish.
Phrases—a hop, skip, and a jump; leap in the dark; look before you leap; leap year; which way the cat jumps. *Colloq.*, get the jump on, jump the gun; jump in the lake.

---

learn, *v.t.* memorize, acquire; discover, detect; find out. See DISCLOSURE, INFORMATION.

learned, *adj.* erudite, scholarly, well-informed. See KNOWLEDGE. *Ant.* ignorant, unscholarly; see IGNORANCE.

learner, *n.* beginner, apprentice; student, pupil, scholar. See SCHOOL.

learning, *n.* acquisition of knowledge *or* skill; KNOWLEDGE, scholarship, erudition; study, self-instruction, reading, INQUIRY, education. See SCHOOL. *Ant.,* see TEACHING, IGNORANCE.

lease, *n. & v.* —*n.* leasehold; contract. See PROPERTY. —*v.t.* rent, let, demise; hire.

leash, *n.* leader, thong; hunting, trio.

least, *adj.* smallest, minimum, minutest. See INFERIORITY, LITTLENESS.

leathery, *adj.* tough, tanned, coriaceous.

leave, *v.* —*v.t.* abandon, surrender; quit, forsake; deliver; cease, desist, forego; bequeath; relinquish. See DEPARTURE, RELINQUISHMENT, GIVING, END. —*v.i.* go away, depart. See DEPARTURE. *Ant.,* see ARRIVAL.

leaven, *n.* yeast, ferment; CAUSE, generator.

leave-taking, *n.* withdrawal, valediction; adieu, Godspeed. See DEPARTURE.

lecture, *v.t.* address, discourse, expound; reprove, rebuke, scold. See TEACHING, DISAPPROBATION.

ledge, *n.* shelf, bench, berm, reek, lode. See HEIGHT, SUPPORT.

left, *n. & adj.* —*n.* sinistrality, sinistration; left hand, left side, near side; port, portside, larboard; verso; left wing, radicalism, Communism; Socialism. —*adj.* sinister, sinistral, sinistrous; left-hand, left-handed; awkward, near, portside; radical, pinkish, leftish, Communistic, Communist, red, pink. See RADICAL. *Ant.,* see RIGHT.

leg, *n.* limb, SUPPORT; course, tack, lap; side. See TRAVEL.

LEGALITY [963]

Nouns—**1,** legality, legitimacy, legitimateness, legalization, constitutionalism, constitutionality, lawfulness, legal process, due process of law.
2, legislation, legislature, law, code, codex, constitution, charter, enactment, statute, canon, precept, ordinance, regulation; bylaw; decree, order; sanction, AUTHORITY.
3, jurisprudence, codification, equity; common, civil, statute or constitutional law; ecclesiastical law; divine law, law of Moses, unwritten law; military law, maritime law; Uniform Code of Military Justice.
4, jurisdiction, administration, province, dominion, domain, bailiwick, magistracy, AUTHORITY, police power, eminent domain.
Verbs—**1,** legalize, legitimatize, legitimize, authorize, sanction; enact, ordain, decree, order, pass a law, legislate; codify, formulate, regulate.
2, administer, govern, rule; preside, judge, arbitrate.
Adjectives—**1,** legal, legitimate, according to law, vested, constitutional, chartered, legalized, lawful, permitted, statutory; official, *ex officio;* legislative. *Slang,* legit; kosher.
2, jurisdictional, judicatory, judiciary, judicial, juridical; judging, judicious.
Adverbs—legally, legitimately, by law, in the eye of the law. *Slang,* on the square, on the up and up, on the level.
Antonym, see ILLEGALITY.

---

legend, *n.* tradition, tale, saga; myth, edda; inscription, motto. See DESCRIPTION, RECORD.

leggings, *n.* gaiters, spats, puttees, chaps. See CLOTHING.

legible, *adj.* readable, decipherable, clear, plain. *Ant.,* illegible.

legislator, *n.* lawmaker, congressman, parliamentarian. See AUTHORITY, ASSEMBLAGE.

legislature, *n.* lawmaking body, congress, parliament. See ASSEMBLAGE.

legitimate, *adj.* lawful, legal; genuine, logical, justifiable. See LEGALITY, TRUTH, VINDICATION.

leisure, *n.* spare time; idle hours; time on one's hands; holiday, vacation; LOWNESS. deliberation; rest, ease, idleness, REPOSE. *Ant.,* see HASTE, ACTIVITY.

lend, *v.* advance, accommodate with, finance; loan; entrust, intrust; pawn; lend-lease; let, demise, lease, sublet. See DEBT. *Ant.,* BORROW.

LENGTH [200]

Nouns—**1,** length, lengthiness, longitude, span, extent, distance, range; footage, yardage, mileage.
2, line, bar, stripe, strip, string, row, streak, spoke, radius, diameter.
3, lengthening, prolongation, production, protraction, tension, extension, elongation.
4, line, nail, inch, hand, palm, foot, cubit, yard, ell, fathom, pole, rod, furlong, mile, league, chain; meter; centimeter, *etc.;* kilometer.
Verbs—**1,** stretch out, extend, sprawl, reach to, stretch to.
2, lengthen, render long, extend, elongate, stretch, prolong, produce, protract, let out, draw out, spin out.
3, enfilade, rake; look along; view in perspective.
Adjectives—**1,** long, lengthy, outstretched, lengthened, elongated, protracted, interminable, no end of, unshortened, over all.
2, linear, longitudinal, oblong, lineal.
Adverbs—lengthwise, at length, longitudinally, endwise, along, tandem, in a line, in perspective; from end to end, from stem to stern, from head to foot, from top to bottom, from head to toe; cap-a-pie; from dawn to dusk; fore and aft.

Antonym, see SHORTNESS.

---

leniency, *n.* lenience, lenity; MODERATION; tolerance, toleration; mildness, gentleness; favor; SOFTNESS; indulgence, clemency, mercy, forbearance, quarter, compassion, ruth, PITY. See FORGIVENESS. *Ant.,* see SEVERITY.
lenient, *adj.* gentle, indulgent, merciful.
lens, *n.* refractor, eyeglass, magnifying glass, reading glass. See OPTICAL INSTRUMENTS.
less, *adj. & adv.* —*adj.* inferior, not so much, minor. —*adv.* under, short of. See INFERIORITY.
lessen, *v.t.* reduce, diminish, mitigate, abate, shorten. See DECREASE, MODERATION. *Ant.,* see INCREASE, EXAGGERATION.
lesson, *n.* instruction, task, exercise, example; admonition, reprimand. See TEACHING.
let, *v.t.* allow, permit, lease, rent. See PERMISSION.
lethargy, *n.* lassitude, indifference, apathy, stupor. See INACTIVITY, INSENSIBILITY. *Ant.,* alertness, energy.
letter, *n.* character, symbol; cuneiform, hieroglyphic; capital, majuscule; small letter, minuscule; alphabet, ABC; consonant, vowel, digraph, diphthong. See WRITING.
level, *adj. & v.* —*adj.* horizontal, flat; even; aligned; cool, well-balanced. See HORIZONTAL, SMOOTHNESS, EQUALITY. —*v.t.* raze; flatten; equalize. See DESTRUCTION, SMOOTHNESS. *Ant.,* build, restore.
lever, *n.* crowbar, pry, prize, jimmy. See ELEVATION.
leverage, *n.* advantage; purchase, hold. See INFLUENCE.
levity, *n.* lightness; imponderability, buoyancy, weightlessness; volatility; frivolity, flippancy, jocularity; flightiness, giddiness; triviality, want of seriousness. See LIGHT, CHANGEABLENESS, UNIMPORTANCE. *Ant.,* see GRAVITY, IMPORTANCE, WEIGHT.
levy, *n.* assessment, tax; draft, conscription. See ASSEMBLAGE, PRICE.
lewd, *adj.* obscene, salacious, indecent, unchaste. See IMPURITY. *Ant.,* pure, chaste.
liable, *adj.* subject; in danger; open, exposed, responsible, accountable; incurring, contingent, incidental, possible; apt, likely. See DEBT, DUTY. *Ant.,* see EXEMPTION, FREEDOM.
liability, *n.* liableness, responsibility; POSSIBILITY, probability, contingency, susceptibility. See DEBT, DUTY. *Ant.,* see EXEMPTION, FREEDOM.
liar, *n.* prevaricator, equivocator, falsifier, fibber, deceiver; see DECEPTION, FALSEHOOD.
libel, *n.* defamation, calumniation, slander, aspersion. See DETRACTION.
liberal, *adj.* free, generous; charitable; hospitable; lavish, bounteous, unsparing, ungrudging, openhanded, freehanded, large-hearted; munificent, princely, prodigal; easy come, easy go; progressive, politically unconserva-

tive. See GIVING, BENEVOLENCE, MODERATION. *Ant.*, see ECONOMY, PARSI-MONY.

liberate, *v.t.* free, set free, set at liberty; give one's freedom; emancipate, release; enfranchise, manumit; discharge, dismiss, let go, let loose, let out; deliver; absolve, acquit; unfetter, untie, loose, loosen, unbind, unchain, unshackle. See FREEDOM. *Ant.*, see RESTRAINT.

liberation, *n.* disengagement, release, emancipation; enfranchisement; manumission; discharge, dismissal; deliverance, redemption; extrication; absolution, acquittal, ESCAPE, FREEDOM, liberty. *Ant.*, see RESTRAINT.

libertine, *n.* voluptuary, rake, roué, debauchee, rip, profligate; lecher, satyr; pimp, pander, Don Juan, Casanova; courtesan, doxy, prostitute, strumpet, harlot, bawd, procuress, whore, wanton, *fille de joie,* streetwalker, tart, chippy, wench, trollop, light o' love; nymphomaniac. See IMPURITY, EVIL-DOER. *Ant.*, see GOODNESS.

liberty, *n.* freedom, independence, emancipation; right, license, privilege. See FREEDOM, PERMISSION. *Ant.*, slavery, dependence, suppression.

library, *n.* athenaeum, bookroom. See BOOK.

license, *n.* PERMISSION, authority; FREEDOM; licentiousness.

lie, *v.i.* prevaricate, falsify, deceive. See FALSEHOOD.

lie, *v.i.* recline; rest, be situated; extend. See LOCATION, PRESENCE.

LIFE [359]

Nouns—**1,** life, vitality, existence, being, living, animation, vital spark, vital flame, respiration, breath, breath of life, lifeblood, life force, vital force, yivification, revivification, resurgence.

2, physiology, biology, embryology, biochemistry.

Verbs—**1,** live, be alive, be, breathe, respire, subsist, exist, walk the earth.

2, see the light, be born, come into the world, draw breath, quicken, revive, come to, come to life.

3, give birth to, bring to life, put life into, vitalize, vivify, reanimate, animate, keep alive, keep body and soul together, keep the wolf from the door, support life.

Adjectives—living, alive, vital, existing, extant, in the flesh, in the land of the living, breathing, quick, animated, lively, alive and kicking, tenacious of life.

Antonym, see DEATH.

---

lifeless, *adj.* inanimate, inert, sluggish, spiritless. See DEATH. *Ant.*, living, lively.

lifelike, *adj.* realistic, natural, accurate. See SIMILARITY, DESCRIPTION.

lift, *v.t.* raise, elevate, exalt; uplift. See ELEVATION, IMPROVEMENT. *Ant.*, see DEPRESSION.

ligature, *n.* bond, tie, slur, surgical thread. See PRINTING, CONNECTION.

light, *adj.* airy, feathery, fluffy, puffy, vapory, zephyry; foamy, yeasty; subtle; weightless, ethereal, sublimated, volatile; buoyant, floating; portable; frivolous, jesting, jocular, lightsome; giddy, dizzy, flighty; flippant, pert, insouciant; humorous; trivial. See LIGHTNESS. *Ant.*, HEAVY.

LIGHT [420]

Nouns—**1,** light, ray, beam, stream, gleam, streak, pencil; sunbeam, moonbeam, aurora, day, sunshine, light of day, sun, sunlight, moonlight, starlight, daylight, daybreak, noonday.

2, glow, glimmering, glimmer; glitter, shimmer, flicker, glint; spark, scintilla, sparkle, scintillation, flash, blaze, coruscation, flame, fire, lightning bolt.

3, luster, sheen, shimmer, gloss; tinsel, spangle; brightness, brilliancy, splendor, effulgence, dazzle, resplendence, dazzlement, phosphorescence, incandescence, luminousness, luminosity, lucidity, radiation, irradiation, radiance, illumination, reflection, refraction.

4, photology, photometry, photics, optics, catoptrics, photography, heliography, radioscopy.

5, luminary, illuminant; electric, fluorescent, neon, gas, *etc.* light; candlelight, lamplight, firelight; candle, taper, lamp, torch, brand, flambeau, lantern, searchlight, flashlight; bulb, globe, mantle, jet; chandelier, candelabrum, sconce, candlestick; limelight, footlights, spotlight; rocket, flare, beacon; fireworks, pyrotechnics; halo, aureole, nimbus, gloriole, aura, glory.

Verbs—**1**, shine, glow, glitter, glister, glisten, flicker, twinkle, gleam, flare, glare, beam, shimmer, glimmer, flicker, sparkle, scintillate, coruscate, flash, blaze, be bright, reflect light, dazzle, radiate, shoot out beams.

2, lighten, enlighten; light, light up, clear up, brighten, irradiate, shine, give *or* shed light; throw light upon, illume, illumine, illuminate, strike a light, kindle.

Adjectives—**1**, shining, luminous, luminescent, lucid, lucent, luciferous, light, lightsome, bright, vivid, resplendent, lustrous, shiny, beamy, scintillant, radiant, lambent; glossy, sunny, cloudless, clear, unclouded; glinting, gleaming, beaming, effulgent, splendid, resplendent, glorious, blazing, ablaze, meteoric, phosphorescent, glowing; lighted, lit, ablaze, on.

3, actinic, photographic, heliographic, optic, optical.

Antonym, see DARKNESS.

---

lightness, *n.* buoyancy; LEVITY, flightiness; gaiety, volatility; nimbleness, grace; paleness. See ACTIVITY. *Ant.*, heaviness, somberness, clumsiness.

lightning, *n.* thunderbolt, levin, firebolt. See LIGHT.

like, *adj. & v.* —*adj.* similar, resembling, characteristic. See SIMILARITY. *Ant.*, unlike, dissimilar. —*v.t.* enjoy, desire, fancy. See PLEASURE, LOVE.

likeness, *n.* portrait, effigy, counterpart; similarity, resemblance. See SIMILARITY, REPRESENTATION.

liking, *n.* fondness, inclination, preference. See DESIRE, LOVE.

limb, *n.* branch; arm, leg, member.

LIMIT [233]

Nouns—limit, boundary, bounds, confines; enclave; curbstone, term; bourn(e), verge, pale; termination, terminus, END, terminal, stint, frontier, precinct, border, marches, boundary line, landmark, line of demarcation, point of no return, Rubicon, turning point. See RESTRAINT.

Adjectives—definite, determinate, terminal, frontier, limited, circumscribed, restricted, confined.

Verbs—limit, restrict, bound, confine, define, circumscribe, restrain, qualify.

Adverbs—thus far, so far and no further, just so far; within bounds.

Antonyms, see FREEDOM, INFINITY.

---

limp, *adj. & v.* —*adj.* limber, flabby, soft. See SOFTNESS. —*v.t.* hobble, hitch; drag. See TRAVEL.

line, *v. & n.* —*v.t.* interline, face. —*n.* mark; cord, string; crease, wrinkle; verse, note; route, system; vocation, calling; lineage; row, file. See INDICATION, FILAMENT, POETRY, BUSINESS, ANCESTRY, CONTINUITY.

lineage, *n.* ANCESTRY, family, pedigree.

lineal, *adj.* linear; hereditary, ancestral. See ANCESTRY.

lineament, *n.* feature, characteristic, singularity.

linear, *adj.* aligned, straight; lineal. See CONTINUITY, DIRECTION.

linger, *v.i.* delay, dally, loiter, poke; remain, persist. See LATENESS, DURABILITY

linguist, *n.* polyglot, philologist, etymologist. See SPEECH.

lining, *n.* inner coating, inner covering, interlining; filling, stuffing; wainscot, wainscoting; gasket, washer; facing, sheathing, bushing; ceiling. See COVERING, INTERIOR.

link, *n. & v.* —*n.* tie, BOND; component, liaison. See BETWEEN. —*v.t.* join, unite, couple. See JUNCTION.

lion, *n.* cat; hero, celebrity. See ANIMAL, REPUTE.

lip, *n.* EDGE, verge; labium; flange. *Slang*, impertinence.

liquefaction, *n.* liquescence, liquescency; liquidization, fluidization, melting, thaw, deliquation; dissolution; solution, infusion; flux; decoction, mixture; solvent, menstruum, dissolvent. *Ant.*, see DENSITY.

liquefy, *v.* run, melt, thaw; dissolve; liquidize, fluidize. See LIQUEFACTION.

liquid, *adj.* fluid, smooth, flowing. See SOUND. *Ant.*, solid.

liquidate, *v.t.* pay, settle, wind up. See PAYMENT. *Slang*, kill.

liquor, *n.* liquid, fluid, broth, stock, juice, essence; spirits, whiskey, *Schnapps,* vodka, aquavit, rum, gin, brandy, applejack; corn, rye, Scotch, Irish, Bourbon, Canadian, *etc.*; alcohol, John Barleycorn; draft, dram, shot, snort. *Slang,* booze, moonshine, white mule. See FOOD, DRUNKENNESS.

list, *n. & v.* —*n.* catalog(ue); calendar; inventory; schedule, register; RECORD, tally, file; tabulation, index, table; glossary, vocabulary; program, directory; menu, roll, roster; bill of lading, invoice. —*v.t.* catalog(ue), register, RECORD, *etc.*

listen, *v.i.* harken, attend; hear; grant; heed. See HEARING, ATTENTION.

listless, *adj.* languid, spiritless, apathetic, lethargic. See INACTIVITY. *Ant.,* spirited, keen; see ACTIVITY.

literal, *adj.* verbatim, word-for-word, exact, prosaic. See MEANING.

literary, *adj.* bookish, scholarly. *Slang,* long-haired. See KNOWLEDGE.

literate, *adj.* lettered, educated. See KNOWLEDGE. *Ant.,* illiterate.

literature, *n.* books, belles-lettres, letters. See BOOK, SPEECH.

litigant, *n.* suitor, party. See LAWSUIT.

litigate, *v.t.* contest, dispute, sue, prosecute. See LAWSUIT.

litigious, *adj.* actionable; contentious, disputatious. See LAWSUIT.

litter, *n.* disorder, scraps; bedding; stretcher, palanquin; offspring. See VEHICLE, DESCENT. *Ant.,* order, neatness; see ARRANGEMENT.

LITTLENESS [193]

Nouns—**1,** littleness, smallness, minuteness, diminutiveness, thinness, shortness, NARROWNESS, exiguity; epitome, abstract, brief; microcosm; rudiment; vanishing point.

2, dwarf, pygmy, pigmy, Lilliputian, chit, midget, peanut, urchin, elf, doll, puppet, Tom Thumb, manikin; homunculus.

3, animalcule, monad, mite, insect, fly, midge, gnat, shrimp, peewee, minnow, worm, maggot, entozoön, am(o)eba, microbe, germ, bacterium, grub, tomtit, runt, mouse, small fry, mustardseed, peppercorn, pebble, grain of sand, molehill.

4, point; atom, molecule, ion, electron, neutron; fragment, particle, crumb, powder; pinpoint, dot, speck, mote, jot; decimal, fraction; modicum, minimim; *minutiae;* trifle; *soupçon,* shade, scintilla; grain, scruple, granule, minim; sip, dab, drop, droplet, dash, driblet, sprinkling, tinge; scrap, tag, splinter, chip, sliver, morsel, crumb; snick, snack; thimbleful; nutshell. *Colloq.,* smidgen.

5, micrography, microscopy, micrology, microphotography; microscope, micrometer, vernier.

Verbs—belittle, become small, decrease, contract.

Adjectives—**1,** little, SMALL, minute, diminutive, microscopic, inconsiderable, exiguous, puny, wee, tiny, petty; minikin, knee-high, miniature, pygmy, pigmy, undersized, dwarf, dwarfed, dwarfish, stunted, limited, cramped, Lilliputian; pocket, portable, short; thin, weazened, scant, scrubby, granular, powdery, shrunken.

2, impalpable, intangible, evanescent, imperceptible, invisible, inappreciable, infinitesimal, atomic, molecular, rudimentary, embryonic.

Adverbs—little, slightly, in a small compass, on a shoestring, in a nutshell, on a small scale; partly, partially; some, rather, somewhat; scarcely, hardly, barely.

Antonym, see SIZE.

---

live, *v.i.* exist, be alive; abide; subsist; survive. See LIFE, DURABILITY, PRESENCE. *Ant.,* die, perish; see DEATH.

liveliness, *n.* animation, vivacity, sprightliness. See ACTIVITY. *Slang,* pep. *Ant.,* languid, dull; see INACTIVITY.

living, *adj.* alive, quick, existing. See LIFE. *Ant.,* dead; see DEATH.

lizard, *n.* lacerta; gecko, chameleon.

load, *n.* burden; cargo, lading, shipment; charge. See GRAVITY, TRAVEL.

loadstone, *n.* magnet; allurement. See ATTRACTION.

loafer, *n.* idler, lounger, dawdler, vagrant. See INACTIVITY. *Slang,* bum.

loathe, *v.t.* detest, abhor, abominate. See HATE.

local, *adj.* restricted, narrow, provincial; native, endemic. See REGION.

LOCATION [184]

Nouns—**1,** location, localization, lodgment, stowage, collocation, packing, establishment, settlement, installation, fixation, placement, insertion. See ABODE.

2, place, situation, locality, locale, site, position, post, stand, neighborhood, environment, whereabouts; bearings, orientation; spot.

3, anchorage, mooring, encampment; plantation, colony, settlement, cantonment.

4, colonization, domestication, habitation, naturalization, acclimatization.

Verbs—**1,** place, situate, locate, localize, make a place for, put, lay, set, seat, station, lodge, quarter, post, park, install, house, stow, establish; fix, pin, root, graft, plant, lay down, deposit; cradle; moor, anchor, tether, picket; pack, tuck in; vest, replace, put back; billet on, quarter upon, saddle with, load, freight, put up.

2, inhabit, domesticate, colonize, naturalize, take root, sit down, settle down, settle, take up one's abode, establish oneself, squat, perch, bivouac, encamp, pitch one's tent, put up at, keep house.

Adjectives—located, placed, situate(d), ensconced, embedded, rooted, domesticated, vested in, moored, at anchor.

Adverbs—here, there, here and there; hereabout(s), thereabout(s), whereabout(s); in place.

Antonym, see DISJUNCTION.

---

lock, *v.t.* fasten, secure, make fast. See CLOSURE, JUNCTION.
lodestone, see LOADSTONE.
lodge, *v.i.* dwell, sojourn; settle; file, be flattened. See LOCATION, PRESENCE.
lofty, *adj.* towering, high; haughty, patronizing; distinguished, noble; sublime. See HEIGHT, REPUTE, INSOLENCE.
logical, *adj.* rational, reasonable, sane. See REASONING.
loincloth, *n.* breechclout, breechcloth. See CLOTHING.
loiter, *v.i.* linger, poke, dawdle. See SLOWNESS. *Ant.,* hasten, bustle.
lone, *adj.* solitary, lonely; single.
lonely, *adj.* solitary, lone, lonesome, desolate, alone.
long, *adj. & adv.* —*adj.* lengthy, elongated; tedious; extended, protracted. See LENGTH. —*adv.* in great degree, for a time, during. See DURABILITY.
longing, *n.* yearning, craving, hankering, hunger. See DESIRE.
look, *v. & n.* —*v.i.* behold; perceive, discern; inspect, scan; stare; seem, appear. See VISION, APPEARANCE, ATTENTION. —*n.* glance, view; APPEARANCE, aspect. See VISION.
lookout, *n.* vigilance; observatory; watch, sentinel; prospect, vista. See VISION, APPEARANCE, WARNING. *Colloq.,* concern.
loop, *n.* ring, circle, noose, eyelet, ambit. See CIRCULARITY.
loose, *adj. & v.* —*adj.* free, detached; flowing, unbound; vague, incoherent; unrestrained; dissipated. See DISJUNCTION, DIRECTION, BADNESS. —*v.t.* free; unbind, undo; relax. See FREEDOM.
loosen, *v.t.* relax, slacken.
loot, *n.* booty, spoil, plunder.

LOQUACITY [584]

Nouns—**1,** loquacity, loquaciousness, talkativeness, volubility, verbosity, garrulity, multiloquence, prolixity, flow of words, gift of gab, eloquence, fluency.

2, DIFFUSENESS, expatiation, dilation; REPETITION, prolixity.

3, jaw, gab, jabber, chatter, prattle, gossip, cackle, twaddle, blabber, blather, blarney, small talk. *Slang,* gas, hot air.

4, talker, chatterer, chatterbox, babbler, ranter, driveler, gossip, windbag, magpie, jay, parrot.

Verbs—be loquacious, run on, descant, expatiate, dilate; protract, spin out, dwell on, harp on; talk glibly, patter, prate, palaver, chatter, prattle, jabber, jaw, babble, gabble, talk oneself hoarse; digress, perorate, maunder, ramble; gossip. *Slang,* shoot the breeze, shoot off one's mouth.

Adjectives—loquacious, talkative, wordy, garrulous, prolix, verbose; profuse,

copious, voluble, fluent, gossipy; diffuse, pleonastic, maundering, periphrastic, roundabout, digressive, rambling; glib, effusive, gushy, eloquent, chattering, chatty, open-mouthed; long-winded, long-drawn-out, discursive.
Adverbs—at length; *in extenso; ad nauseam.*
Antonym, see SILENCE.

lordly, *adj.* noble, imposing; imperious, arrogant, dictatorial. See REPUTE, INSOLENCE.

lore, *n.* erudition, scholarship, learning. See KNOWLEDGE.

LOSS [776]

Nouns—loss; perdition; forfeiture, lapse, privation, bereavement, deprivation, dispossession, riddance, WASTE, dissipation, expenditure, leakage; DESTRUCTION.
Verbs—lose, incur *or* meet with a loss; miss, mislay, let slip, allow to slip through the fingers; forfeit, get rid of, WASTE, dissipate, squander.
Adjectives—**1,** losing, not having, shorn of, deprived of, denuded, bereaved, bereft, minus, cut off, dispossessed, rid of, quit of, out of pocket.
2, lost, long-lost; dissipated, wasted, forfeited, missing, gone, irretrievable, destroyed, off one's hands.
Antonym, see ACQUISITION.

lot, *n.* fate, DESTINY, fortune; batch, sum.

LOUDNESS [404]

Nouns—**1,** loudness, noisiness, vociference, sonorousness, vehemency, intensity, power; stridency, raucousness, cacophony.
2, resonance, reverberation, echo, ringing, tintinnabulation; roll, rumble, drumming, tattoo, rat-a-tat, rub-a-dub.
3, din, clamor, clang, clangor, rattle, clatter, noise, roar, uproar, racket, pandemonium, hubbub, shrillness, hullaballoo; charivari; trumpet blast, fanfare, ring, peal, toll, alarum, blast, boom, thunder, thunderclap; boiler factory.
4, flashiness (see OSTENTATION).
Verbs—be loud, peal, ring, swell, clang, boom, thunder, fulminate, roar, resound, reverberate; shout, vociferate, bellow, rend the air, fill the air, ring in the ear, pierce the ears, deafen, stun, make the rafters ring. *Slang,* raise the roof.
Adjectives—loud; sonorous; highsounding, big-sounding, deep, full, powerful, noisy, clangorous, thunderous, thundering, dinning, deafening, earsplitting, obstreperous, rackety, uproarious, shrill, clamorous, vociferous, stentorian, enough to wake the dead; flashy (see OSTENTATION).
Adverbs—loudly, noisily, aloud, at the top of one's voice, lustily, in full cry.
Antonym, see SILENCE.

LOVE [897]

Nouns—**1,** love, fondness, liking; inclination, DESIRE; regard, admiration, affection, tenderness, heart, attachment, yearning; gallantry; PASSION, flame, devotion, infatuation, adoration, idolatry.
2, benevolence, sympathy, fellowship, friendship, humanity, brotherly love, mother *or* maternal love, parental affection.
3, Cupid, Venus, Eros; true lover's knot, engagement ring, love token; love affair, *amour, liaison,* romance, love story, plighted troth, courtship.
4, attractiveness, popularity, charm, fascination.
5, lover, suitor, follower, admirer, adorer, wooer, beau, honey, sweetheart, inamorato, swain, young man, boy friend, flame, love, truelove; Lothario, Romeo, Casanova, Don Juan, gallant, paramour, *amoroso,* fiancé. *Slang,* wolf, lover boy.
6, inamorata, ladylove; idol, darling, duck, angel, goddess, true love, girl, sweetheart, beloved; betrothed, affianced, fiancée. *Colloq.,* steady, girl friend, honeybunch, date, sweetie.
Verbs—**1,** love, like, fancy, care for, favor, become enamored, fall *or* be in love with; revere, take to, make much of, hold dear, prize, hug, cling to,

cherish, pet; adore, idolize, love to distraction, dote on, desire; throw oneself at, lose *or* give one's heart. *Slang,* go for, fall for, shine up to, be sweet on, be nuts about, carry a torch for; go steady; pitch woo, spoon, spark.

2, excite, love; win, gain *or* engage the love, affections, *or* heart; take the fancy of; attract, endear, charm, fascinate, captivate, bewitch, seduce, enamor, enrapture, turn the head.

3, get into favor; ingratiate oneself, pay court to, set one's cap for; flirt; keep company.

Adjectives—**1,** loving, fond of; taken with, smitten, attached to, enamored, charmed, in love, lovesick, affectionate, tender, sweet on, amorous, amatory, amative, erotic, uxorious, ardent, passionate, romantic, rapturous, devoted. *Slang,* going steady.

2, loved, beloved, well beloved, dearly beloved, dear, dear one, precious, darling, pet, favorite.

3, lovable, adorable, lovely, sweet, attractive, seductive, winning, charming, engaging, enchanting, captivating, fascinating, bewitching.

Antonym, see HATE.

lovelorn, *adj.* lovesick; jilted. See LOVE, HATE.
lovely, *adj.* beautiful, comely, exquisite, captivating. See PLEASURE, BEAUTY.
lover, *n.* suitor, wooer, sweetheart. See LOVE. *Colloq.,* beau. *Slang,* boyfriend.
lovesick, *adj.* languishing, lovelorn. See LOVE.
lowborn, *adj.* humble, plebeian, common. See POPULACE.

LOWNESS [207]

Nouns—**1,** lowness, shortness, FLATNESS, deepness, depth; debasement, depression, prostration, HUMILITY, degradation.

2, lowlands; basement, cellar, dungeon, ground floor, hold; low water; low tide, ebb tide, neap tide, bottom floor, bedrock.

Verbs—**1,** below, lie low, lie flat, underlie, crouch, slouch, flatten, wallow, grovel, crawl.

2, lower, depress, let *or* take down, debase, reduce, drop, sink, humble, HUMILIATE.

Adjectives—low, neap, debased, nether, nethermost, sunken, fallen, flat, level with the ground, lying low, crouched, squat, prostrate, depressed, deep.

Adverbs—under, beneath, underneath, below, down, downward(s), at the foot of, underfoot, underground, downstairs, belowstairs, at a low ebb, below par.

Antonym, see HEIGHT.

loyal, *adj.* faithful, true, devoted. See PROBITY. *Ant.,* disloyal, treacherous.
lubricate, *v.* oil, grease; anoint; lather, soap; wax; slick, slick up.
lubrication, *n.* greasing, oiling; oiliness; anointing, anointment, unction, unctuousness. See SMOOTHNESS. *Ant.,* see FRICTION.
lucid, *adj.* clear, limpid, transparent, understandable, rational. *Ant.,* cloudy, confused.
luck, *n.* CHANCE, fortune; good fortune. See PROSPERITY.
lucky, *adj.* fortunate, opportune, auspicious. See OCCASION.
lull, *n.* calm, intermission. See END.
luminary, *n.* see LIGHT. *Ant.,* see DARKNESS.
luminous, *adj.* luminary, lighted, glowing; incandescent, radiant, lit, alight, self-luminous; phosphorescent, luminescent. See LIGHT. *Ant.,* see DARKNESS.
lump, *n.* PROTUBERANCE, swelling, chunk, mass; consolidation, aggregation. See SIZE, CONVEXITY, ASSEMBLAGE.
lunatic, *n.* MADMAN, bedlamite, maniac, psychopath.
lung, *n.* lights, bellow. See WIND.
lurch, *v.i.* sway, pitch, stagger, stumble. See NAVIGATION, DESCENT.
lure, *v.t.* entice, decoy, tempt, coax, reduce. See REQUEST, ATTRACTION.
lurid, *adj.* pallid, ghastly; glaring, eerie; sinister, sensational. See DARKNESS.
lurk, *v.i.* skulk, sneak, prowl. See CONCEALMENT.

luscious, *adj.* sweet, delicious, ambrosial. See TASTE, SWEETNESS.

luster, *n.* gloss, sheen, brightness, splendor; brilliance, fame. See LIGHT, BEAUTY, REPUTE.

lusty, *adj.* robust, vigorous, hearty, sturdy. See HEALTH, SIZE.

luxuriant, *adj.* lush, abundant, profuse; fertile, rich. See PRODUCTION, VEGETABLE.

luxurious, *adj.* sumptuous, elegant; voluptuous, self-indulgent. See PLEASURE. *Ant.,* simple.

luxury, *n.* self-indulgence, prodigality; dainty; elegance, sumptuousness, extravagance. See PLEASURE. *Ant.,* simplicity.

lyric, *n.* poem, song. See POETRY.

M

machine, *n.* apparatus, contrivance, mechanism, device; motor, engine; airplane, car, bicycle; organization, cabal. See VEHICLE, PARTY.

mad, *adj.* crazy, insane; rabid; frantic, foolish, turbulent. See INSANITY, VIOLENCE. *Colloq.,* angry. *Ant.,* see SANITY.

magazine, *n.* storehouse, arsenal, reservoir; periodical. See STORE, BOOK.

magic, *n. & adj.* —*n.* SORCERY; witchery, glamour, spell; legerdemain. —*adj.* mystic, occult; enchanting.

magician, *n.* witch, wizard, sorcerer; prestidigitator. See SORCERY.

magesterial, *adj.* arbitrary, dictatorial; arrogant, pompous.

magnanimous, *adj.* generous, high-minded, great-souled. See PROBITY.

magnetism, *n.* ATTRACTION, magnetic force. See POWER.

magnificent, *adj.* grand, splendid; awe-inspiring; noble, superb. See REPUTE.

magnify, *v.t.* enlarge, augment; laud, glorify. See INCREASE, APPROBATION. *Ant.,* see CONTRACTION.

magnitude, *n.* SIZE, bulk; extent; hugeness, immensity. See GREATNESS.

maid, *n.* girl, lass, maiden, miss; virgin, spinster; SERVANT, domestic. See YOUTH, CELIBACY.

maidenly, *adj.* modest; gentle; girlish. See YOUTH.

mail, *n. & v.t.* —*n.* post, letters, CORRESPONDENCE. —*v.t.* post, send, forward. See COMMUNICATION.

maim, *v.t.* cripple, disfigure, mutilate, lame. See DETERIORATION.

main, *n. & adj.* —*n.* conduit, pipe; strength, power; sea, OCEAN. —*adj.* chief, principal; sheer. See SUPERIORITY.

mainstay, *n.* SUPPORT, supporter, dependence.

maintain, *v.t.* SUPPORT, carry; preserve, keep; possess, have; uphold; allege, affirm. See PRESERVATION, VINDICATION.

maintenance, *n.* SUPPORT, subsistence; PRESERVATION, conservation; AID, defense.

majestic, *adj.* noble, august, stately, imposing. See GREATNESS.

major, *adj.* principal, chief; greater. See SUPERIORITY. *Ant.,* see INFERIORITY.

majority, *n.* adulthood; preponderance, excess, SUPERIORITY. See YOUTH. *Ant.,* see INFERIORITY.

make, *v.t.* create, produce; prepare; obtain, get; cause, compel; amount to. See PRODUCTION, ACTION, COMPULSION.

makeshift, *n.* expedient, substitute, stopgap. See SUBSTITUTION.

make–up, *n.* COMPOSITION, personality; placement; cosmetics, beautification.

malady, *n.* DISEASE, sickness, illness, infirmity.

malcontent, *n.* grumbler, faultfinder; insurgent, rebel; *Colloq.,* griper. See DISCONTENT, OPPOSITION.

MALE [373]

Nouns—**1,** male, man, he, *homo,* gentleman, sir, MASTER, yeoman, wight, swain, fellow, blade, chap, gaffer, husband, bachelor, Mr., mister, boy, stripling, youth, lad; *homme; hombre.* *Slang,* guy, bloke, bimbo, bozo, geezer, *etc.*

2, cock, drake, gander, dog, boar, stag, hart, buck, horse, stallion, tomcat, ram, billygoat, bull, rooster, cob, capon, ox, gelding, steer.

3, mankind, human beings, human race, man; manhood, male sex, virility, manliness, maleness, masculinity.

Adjectives—male, masculine, manly, virile, gentlemanly, boyish; adult; man-like; android, anthropoid.

Antonym, see FEMALE.

---

malediction, *n.* IMPRECATION, curse, anathema, execration. *Ant.,* see AP-PROBATION.

malefactor, *n.* EVILDOER, wrongdoer, criminal, felon. *Ant.,* see GOODNESS.

MALEVOLENCE [907]

Nouns—**1,** malevolence; evil *or* bad intent; misanthropy, ill-nature; ENMITY, HATE; malignity, malice, malice aforethought, maliciousness, spite, resentment, venom, rancor; virulence, mordacity, acerbity, churlishness, hardness of heart, obduracy; cruelty, cruelness, brutality, savagery, ferocity, barbarity, inhumanity; truculence, ruffianism; heart of stone, evil eye, cloven foot *or* hoof, poison pen.

2, ill turn, bad turn, affront, insult, indignity, outrage, abuse, atrocity, ill usage, intolerance, persecution.

3, misanthrope, man-hater, misogynist, woman-hater, cynic.

Verbs—**1,** be malevolent, bear *or* harbor a grudge, bear malice.

2, hurt, injure, harm, wrong, do harm, outrage, disoblige, malign, molest, worry, harass, annoy, harry, bait, tease, play the devil with, wreak havoc, do mischief, hunt down, hound, persecute, oppress, grind, maltreat, bedevil, illtreat, ill use, do one's worst, show *or* have no mercy. *Colloq.,* have it in for. *Slang,* do one dirt, rub it in.

Adjectives—**1,** malevolent, ill-disposed, ill-intentioned, evilminded, misanthropic, malicious, malign, malignant, rancorous, spiteful, caustic, bitter, acrimonious, virulent, malefic, maleficent, venomous, invidious.

2, harsh, disobliging, unkind, unfriendly, antisocial; churlish, surly, sullen; coldblooded, coldhearted, hardhearted, stony-hearted, selfish, unnatural, ruthless, relentless.

3, cruel, brutal, savage, ferocious, inhuman, barbarous, fell, truculent, bloodthirsty, murderous, atrocious, fiendish, demoniacal, diabolical, devilish, infernal, hellish, Satanic.

Antonym, see BENEVOLENCE.

---

malformation, *n.* DISTORTION, deformity. *Ant.,* see FORM.

malice, *n.* MALEVOLENCE, spite, ill will, animosity. *Ant.,* see GOODNESS, BENEVOLENCE.

malign, *v.t.* libel, slander; calumniate, asperse, traduce, besmirch, MISREPRESENT; backbite. See DETRACTION.

mallet, *n.* hammer, club, maul. See ARMS.

MALODOROUSNESS [401]

Nouns—**1,** malodorousness, malodor, fetor, fetidness, bad smell, smelliness, bad odor, stench, stink, foul odor, rankness, goatishness, goatiness, mephitis, mustiness, rancidness, rancidity, foulness; opprobrium; bad breath, halitosis.

2, polecat, skunk, stoat, rotten egg, asafoetida, skunk cabbage, stinkpot, stinker, stink bomb; stinkweed.

Verbs—be malodourous, have a bad smell, stink, stink in the nostrils, stink like a polecat, smell offensively.

Adjectives—malodorous, fetid, smelling, stinking, stinky, smelly, high, bad, foul, strong, offensive, noisome, gassy, rank, rancid, gamy, tainted, fusty, musty, putrid, suffocating, mephitic, goaty, goatish.

Antonym, see FRAGRANCE.

malpractice, *n.* improper treatment, illegal treatment; misconduct. See BADNESS.

maltreat, *v.t.* abuse, ill-treat, misuse. See BADNESS.

mammoth, *adj. & n.* —*adj.* huge, giant, gigantic, tremendous, prodigious, colossal, enormous. See GREATNESS, SIZE. *Ant.,* see LITTLENESS. —*n.* elephant, behemoth.

man, *n. & v.* —*n.* see MALE, MANKIND. —*v.* run, operate; supply a crew *or* men for; staff. See DEFENSE. *Ant.,* see FEMALE.

manage, *v.t.* administer, conduct; control; contrive; manipulate. See DIRECTION.

manageable, *adj.* tractable, docile, obedient; wieldy, governable. See FACILITY. *Ant.,* see UNCONFORMITY.

management, *n.* DIRECTION, control, administration; directorate, administrating body.

manager, *n.* executive, superintendent, supervisor, director; *Colloq.,* boss.

mandate, *n.* COMMAND, edict, statute, ordinance; COMMISSION.

maneuver, *n.* artifice, stratagem, tactic. See DECEPTION.

manger, *n.* trough, bin, crib, feed box. See RECEPTACLE.

mangle, *v.t.* break, crush, mutilate; press, iron. See DETERIORATION, SMOOTHNESS.

manhood, *n.* adulthood, maturity; VIRILITY, COURAGE, manliness.

mania, *n.* madness, frenzy, lunacy; obsession, craze; INSANITY.

manicure, *v.t.* trim, clip, cut, pare, file; polish, buff, lacquer.

manifest, *v. & adj.* —*v.t.* bring forward, show, display, evidence, trot out, bring to light; demonstrate; proclaim, publish, disclose. —*adj.* apparent, obvious, evident; salient, striking, prominent; flagrant; pronounced; definite, distinct; conspicuous, unmistakable, plain, clear; open, overt; patent. See EVIDENCE. *Ant.,* see CONCEALMENT.

manifestation, *n.* plainness, visibility; demonstration; exhibition; display, show, showing, showing off; indication, publicity, DISCLOSURE, revelation, openness, prominence, conspicuousness. See EVIDENCE. *Ant.,* see CONCEALMENT.

manipulate, *v.t.* operate, control, manage; juggle, falsify. See USE, DECEPTION.

MANKIND [372]

Nouns—**1,** mankind, man, humanity, human race, human species, *homo sapiens* (*sapiens*), humankind; human nature, mortality, flesh, generation.
2, anthropology, anthropography, ethnography, ethnology, sociology.
3, human being; person, individual, creature, fellow creature; mortal; somebody, one; soul, living soul; earthling; party; MALE, man, FEMALE, woman.
4, people; persons, folk; public, society, world, community, general public, nation, nationality, STATE, realm, commonweal, commonwealth, republic, body politic, population, POPULACE.
Adjectives—human; anthropoid; ethnic, racial; mortal, personal, individual; national, civil, public, social; cosmopolitan, universal.

---

manly, *adj.* masculine; straightforward, courageous, honorable. See COURAGE. *Ant.,* see FEMALE.

manner, *n.* kind, sort; style, mode; CONDUCT, behavior; way, method.

mannerism, *n.* eccentricity, peculiarity, idiosyncrasy; AFFECTATION.

manners, *n.* CONDUCT, behavior, deportment; COURTESY, politeness.

manor, *n.* mansion, hall, hacienda; estate, territory, demesne. See ABODE.

mansion, *n.* house, manor, hall, villa. See ABODE.

mantle, *n.* COVERING; cloak, cape, robe. See CLOTHING.

manual, *adj. & n.* —*adj.* nonautomatic, by hand. —*n.* guide, handbook, text; keyboard, control, dial; system, exercise, regimen. See INFORMATION, MUSICAL INSTRUMENTS.

manufacture, *v.t.* make, produce, fabricate. See PRODUCTION.

manure, *n.* fertilizer, compost, dung. See AGRICULTURE.

manuscript, *n.* script, handwriting, author's original. See WRITING.

many, *adj.* numerous, multitudinous, manifold. See MULTITUDE.

many-sided, *adj.* versatile; multilateral, polyhedral. See CHANGEABLENESS, SIDE.

map, *n.* PLAN, chart, projection; diagram. *Slang,* face.

mar, *v.t.* disfigure, deface, blemish, scratch, impair. See DETERIORATION.

marauder, *n.* raider, plunderer, freebooter, pillager. See STEALING.

marble, *adj.* hard, vitreous, unyielding; lifeless, insensible, cold; white, pale, colorless; variegated, particolored, pied, striated, mottled. See COLOR, HARDNESS, INSENSIBILITY.

march, *v.i.* tramp, pace, parade, file, advance. See TRAVEL.

margin, *n.* EDGE, border, rim, brink, verge, limit; leeway. See SPACE.

marginal, *adj.* bordering, coastal, littoral. See EDGE.

marine, *adj.* nautical, naval; pelagic, maritime. See NAVIGATION.

mariner, *n.* sailor, seaman, crewman. See NAVIGATION. *Colloq.,* tar, salt.

mark, *n. & v.t.* —*n.* goal; imprint, stain; label, badge; token, symptom; symbol; standard, demarcation. See INDICATION. —*v.t.* inscribe, stain; note; check, indicate; delimit. See ATTENTION.

marked, *adj.* noticeable, conspicuous; watched, followed. See INDICATION, SUPERIORITY.

market, *n.* marketplace, mart; agora; fair, bazaar; STORE, shop, stall, booth, counter; farmers' market, flea market, supermarket; chain store; exchange, stock exchange, change, curb, bourse, rialto, pit, Wall Street, the street; black market. See BUSINESS, SALE.

marksman, *n.* sharpshooter, dead shot, crackshot. See PROPULSION.

MARRIAGE [903]

Nouns—**1,** marriage, matrimony, wedlock, union; intermarriage, nuptial tie, married state, bed and board, cohabitation, wedded bliss; engagement (see PREDICTION).

2, wedding, nuptials, Hymen, espousal; leading to the altar; epithalamium; temple of Hymen; honeymoon; sea of matrimony.

3, engagement, betrothal, understanding; proposal, fiancé(e), betrothed.

4, bride, bridegroom, groom; bridesmaid, maid of honor, matron of honor, best man, usher.

5, married man, Benedict, partner, spouse, mate, husband, man, good provider, consort, old man, squaw-man; married woman, bride, wife, partner, concubine, old woman, frau, goodwife, spouse, mate, helpmate, helpmeet, rib, better half, squaw, lady, matron. *Slang,* ball and chain.

6, (married) couple, pair, man and wife, bride and groom, newlyweds; Darby and Joan, Mr. and Mrs., lovebirds, loving couple.

7, monogamy, bigamy, polygamy, polygyny, polyandry, Mormonism; morganatic marriage, common-law marriage, concubinage.

Verbs—**1,** marry, wive, take a wife; be married, be spliced; wed, espouse. *Slang,* get hitched, walk down the aisle, tie the knot.

2, marry, join, couple, unite, make one, tie the nuptial knot; give in marriage.

3, propose; betroth, affiance, plight troth; bespeak; pin; publish banns.

Adjectives—matrimonial, marital, conjugal, connubial; wedded, nuptial, hymeneal, spousal, bridal; engaged, betrothed, affianced; marriageable, nubile.

Antonym, see CELIBACY, DIVORCE.

---

marsh, *n.* marshland, swamp, swampland, morass, moss, fen, bog, peat bog; mire, quagmire, quicksand; slough; sump; wash, bottoms, mud, slush. See WATER, MOISTURE.

marshal, *v. & n.* —*v.t.* array, dispose, order, arrange; mobilize, activate, assemble, collect, utilize. See ARRANGEMENT. —*n.* officer, authority, sheriff. See AUTHORITY.

mart, *n.* see MARKET.

martial, *adj.* military, warlike, soldierly. See WARFARE. *Ant.,* see PACIFICATION.

martyr, *n.* victim, sacrifice, scapegoat; symbol, example; sufferer; saint. See RELIGION.

marvel, *n.* WONDER, PRODIGY.

marvelous, *adj.* wonderful, prodigious, surprising, extraordinary. See WONDER.

masculine, *adj.* manly, strong, virile.

mash, *v.t.* crush, smash, squeeze, compress, bruise, batter. See IMPULSE.

mask, *n. & v.t.* —*n.* false face, disguise, CONCEALMENT; effigy; shield, COVERING. —*v.t.* screen, conceal, hide.

masquerader, *n.* masker, domino, mummer; impostor. See CONCEALMENT, DECEPTION.

Mass, *n.* Divine Service, Eucharist, Communion. See RITE.

mass, *n.* bulk, SIZE; lump, wad, accumulation. See ASSEMBLAGE.

massacre, *n.* KILLING, slaughter, butchery, carnage.

massage, *v.t.* rub, rub down; knead, stroke; manipulate. See FRICTION.

massive, *adj.* bulky, ponderous, solid, imposing. See SIZE. *Ant.*, see LITTLE-NESS.

mast, *n.* pole, timber, upright, column, spar. See SHIP.

master, *n.* padrone; lord; commandant, commander, captain; chief, chieftan, sachem, ataman, hetman; head, headman; governor, leader, superior, director, foreman, boss; potentate, liege, suzerain, sovereign, ruler, monarch; autocrat, dictator, despot, tyrant, oligarch; crowned head, emperor, czar, king, *etc.*; expert, ARTIST, adept. See AUTHORITY, SKILL. *Ant.*, see SERVANT, UNSKILLFULNESS.

masterpiece, *n.* masterwork, *chef d'oeuvre.* See SKILL.

mastery, *n.* rule, victory; ascendency, supremacy; SKILL. See AUTHORITY.

mat, *n. & v.* —*n.* pad, rug, runner, doormat, doily. See COVERING. —*v.* tangle, snarl; plait, braid, weaven, entwine. See JUNCTION. *Ant.*, disentangle, unweave.

match, *n.* lucifer, vesta; linstock, fuse; complement, peer; contest, bout; union, matrimony. See EQUALITY, CONTENTION, MARRIAGE.

matchless, *adj.* unequaled, peerless, unrivaled. See SUPERIORITY.

mate, *n.* companion, chum, comrade; consort, spouse; husband, wife. See ACCOMPANIMENT, FRIEND, MARRIAGE.

material, *adj. & n.* —*adj.* bodily, corporeal, corporal, physical; somatic, sensible, tangible, ponderable, palpable, substantial; embodied, real; venal, mercenary; materialistic. —*n.* cloth, fabric; matter, SUBSTANCE; written matter. See MATERIALS. *Ant.*, see INSUBSTANTIALITY.

materiality, *n.* see SUBSTANCE.

MATERIALS [635]

Nouns—**1,** materials, raw material, substances, stuff; stock, staples; FUEL; grist; stores, provisions, MEANS; baggage, personal property.

2, metal, stone, clay, brick, bricks and mortar, crockery, composition; putty; concrete, cement; wood, lumber, timber; ore; iron, copper, *etc.*; steel; paper; goods, fabric, cloth, material, textiles.

3, plastic(s); synthetic resin; nitrocellulose, cellulose nitrate, Celluloid; acetate cellulose, ethyl cellulose, Cellophane; vinyl, Vinylite, polyvinyl acetate; polystyrene, styrene; phenol-formaldehyde, Bakelite; hard rubber, Neolite, Velon, Nylon, Orlon, Dacron; synthetic rubber, butyl, Butadiene; rayon, fiber, viscose, Celanese; urea, casein, lignite, lignin, wood flour.

4, resin, rosin, gum, lac; bitumen, pitch, tar, asphalt, gilsonite.

maternal, *adj.* motherly, motherlike. See ANCESTRY.

mathematician, *n.* arithmetician, calculator, statistician. See NUMERATION.

mathematics, *n.* computation, calculation, reckoning, arithmetic. See NUMERATION.

matrimonial, *adj.* nuptial, connubial, conjugal, marital. See MARRIAGE.

matrimony, *n.* MARRIAGE, espousal; nuptials. See RITE.

matron *n.* married woman, wife, mother, widow; housekeeper, DIRECTOR. See MARRIAGE.

matter, *n. & v.i.* —*n.* substance, material; subject, TOPIC; BUSINESS; affair; cause, ground; predicament, DIFFICULTY. See SUBSTANCE. —*v.i.* signify, import; count. See IMPORTANCE.

matter-of-fact, *adj.* practical, prosaic, unimaginative, formal. See SIMPLENESS.

mature, *adj. & v.i.* —*adj.* ripe, developed, full-grown, adult. *Ant.*, see YOUTH. —*v.i.* ripen, develop, grow up. See YOUTH, PREPARATION.

maturity, *n.* ripeness, completeness, adulthood. See PREPARATION, OLDNESS. *Ant.*, see YOUTH.

maxim, *n.* aphorism, apothegm, dictum, saying, adage, saw, proverb, precept, rule, sentence, motto, word, moral, byword, household word, bromide, cliché; wise, trite *or* hackneyed saying, platitude; axiom, theorem, truism. See TEACHING.

maximum, *adj. & n.* —*adj.* supreme, utmost; greatest, highest. —*n.* most, utmost; greatest possible (number, degree, *etc.*). See SUPERIORITY. *Ant.*, see LITTLENESS.

may, *v.* can; might; be allowed, permitted, *etc.* See PERMISSION.

maybe, *adv.* perhaps, mayhap, perchance; possibly, conceivably, feasibly. See DOUBT.

mayor, *n.* administrator, president; burgomaster, magistrate, major domo; city manager. See AUTHORITY.

maze, *n.* labyrinth, network; bewilderment, perplexity. See DISORDER.

meadow, *n.* mead, lea, pasture, mowing. See VEGETABLE, PLAIN.

meager, *adj.* spare, scanty, sparse, poor; lean, gaunt. See INSUFFICIENCY, NARROWNESS. *Ant.*, see SUFFICIENCY.

meal, *n.* repast, refection; breakfast, dinner, lunch, *etc.* See FOOD. *Slang*, feed, eats.

mean, *adj.* humble; ignoble; insignificant; sordid, niggardly.

MEAN [29]

Nouns—mean, medium; average, normal, rule, balance; mediocrity, generality; golden mean, middle course, middle compromise, neutrality, MODERATION, middle of the road. *Colloq.*, fence-sitting.

Verbs—split the difference, reduce to a mean, strike a balance, pair off; average, divide; take a middle course.

Adjectives—mean, intermediate, middle, medial, medium, average, mediocre, middle-class, commonplace, normal; median.

Adverbs—on the average, in the long run, taking all things together, in round numbers.

MEANING [516]

Nouns—**1,** meaning, significance, signification; sense, expression; import, purport, implication, drift, tenor, spirit, bearing; scope, purpose, aim, intent, INTENTION, object; allusion, suggestion, synonym, INTERPRETATION, connotation.

2, matter, subject, subject matter, argument, text, sum and substance, gist.

Verbs—mean, signify, express, import, purpose, convey, imply, connote, infer, indicate, tell of, speak of; touch on; point to, allude to, drive at, have in mind, intend, aim at, declare; understand by, interpret.

Adjectives—meaning, meaningful, expressive, suggestive, allusive, significant, eloquent, pithy, full of meaning, pregnant with meaning; declaratory, intelligible, literal; synonymous, tantamount, equivalent; implied, explicit, express, implicit.

Adverbs—meaningly, significantly, *etc.*; to that effect, that is to say, to all intents and purposes.

Antonym, see ABSURDITY.

meaningless, *adj.* senseless, pointless; trivial, insignificant; nonsensical. See ABSURDITY. *Ant.*, see MEANING.

MEANS [632]

Nouns—means, resources, POWER, SUPPORT, wherewithal, MONEY, MATERIALS, WEALTH, ways and means, capital, backing, stock in trade, PROVISION, STORE, appliances, conveniences, cards to play, expedients, measures, two strings to one's bow, AID, INFLUENCE, medium, INSTRUMENT, INSTRUMENTALITY. *Colloq.*, ace in the hole; enough rope.

Verbs—have means, have the power; enable, empower; back, finance, underwrite.

Adverbs—by means of, with, by all means; wherewith, herewith, therewith, wherewithal, how, in what manner, through, by the instrumentality of, with the aid of, by the agency of, with the help of.

Antonym, see IMPOTENCE.

mean-spirited, *adj.* abject, groveling; contemptible, petty.
measure, *n.* QUANTITY, extent; gauge; standard; amount, allotment; legislative bill; step, course. See MEASUREMENT, APPORTIONMENT.

MEASUREMENT [466]

Nouns—**1,** measurement, measure, admeasurement, mensuration, survey, valuation, appraisement, appraisal, metage, assessment, assize, estimate, estimation; dead reckoning, reckoning, gauging; extent, SIZE, LENGTH, DISTANCE, quantity, amount.
2, measure, standard, rule, foot-rule, yardstick, balance, sextant, quadrant, compass, calipers, gauge, meter, gas meter, line, rod, check; level, plumb line, lead, log, tape, square, T square, index, scale, Beaufort scale (wind velocity measure), engineer's chain, Gunter's chain (surveyor's), graduated scale, vernier, anemometer, dynamometer, THERMOMETER, barometer, bathometer, galvanometer, goniometer, speedometer, micrometer, hydrometer, tachometer, altimeter, hygrometer, ammeter, voltimeter; pedometer; radiometer, potentiometer, sphygmomanometer, *etc.*
3, coördinates, ordinate and *abscissa*, polar coördinates, latitude and longitude, declination and right ascension, altitude and azimuth.
4, geometry, *etc.*; stereometry, chronometry, barometry, thermometry, hypometry; surveying, geodesy, geodetics, orthometry, topography, micrometry, altimetry, anthropometry, electrometry, craniometry.
5, measurer, surveyor, geometer, geodetist, topographer.
Verbs—measure, meter, value, assess, rate, appraise, estimate, set a value on, appreciate, size up, span, pace, step; gauge, plumb, weigh, probe, sound, fathom; heave the lead; survey, graduate, calibrate.
Adjectives—measuring, metric, metrical, measurable; geodetic(al); barometric(al); latitudinal, *etc.*

meat, *n.* pith, essence, SUBSTANCE, core. See FOOD.
mechanical, *adj.* machinelike, automatic, powerdriven, powered; involuntary, unreasoning. See POWER, COMPULSION.
meddle, *v.i.* tamper; interfere, intrude. See ACTIVITY, BETWEEN.
meddlesome, *adj.* officious, obtrusive, interfering. See ACTIVITY, BETWEEN.
meddlesomeness, *n.* officiousness; interference, intrusion. See ACTIVITY, BETWEEN.
mediate, *v.* intercede, step in, meet halfway, arbitrate, reconcile, interpose, interfere, intervene. See PACIFICATION, COMPROMISE.
mediation, *n.* intermediation, intercession, intervention; interference; parley, negotiation, arbitration; intercession; COMPROMISE. See PACIFICATION.
medicine, *n.* REMEDY, drugs; therapy, physic; medical profession.
medieval, *adj.* feudal, knightly, courtly; antiquated, old-fashioned, outdated, quaint. See OLDNESS.
mediocre, *adj.* ordinary, commonplace; middling; normal; indifferent, tolerable, passable, fair, run of the mine *or* mill. *Colloq.*, no great shakes, so-so. See MIDDLE. *Ant.*, see SUPERIORITY.
meditate, *v.* muse, ponder, cogitate; contemplate, purpose. See THOUGHT.
medium, *n.* MEAN; surrounding; go-between, agent; AGENCY, instrumentality, means. See BETWEEN, COMPROMISE.
medley, *n.* jumble, miscellany, variety, MIXTURE. See DISORDER.
meek, *adj.* subdued, humble, patient, submissive. See MODESTY.
meet, *v.* encounter; intersect; oppose; greet, welcome; satisfy; refute; assemble, gather; contend. See ARRIVAL, AGREEMENT, OPPOSITION, ASSEMBLAGE.
meeting, *n.* encounter; assembly; JUNCTION; duel; tangency. See ARRIVAL, ASSEMBLAGE.
melancholy, *adj.* dejected, dispirited, sad, depressed. See DARKNESS, DEJECTION. *Colloq.*, blue.

mellow, *adj.* soft, rich, ripe; mellifluous; subdued, delicate. See SOFTNESS, SOUND, PREPARATION. *Ant.*, see HARDNESS.

melody, *n.* tune, theme, song, aria. See MUSIC.

melon, *n.* fruit, cantaloupe, honeydew, Persian melon, watermelon, *etc.* *Slang*, pot, boodle, graft. See VEGETABLE, MONEY.

melt, *v.* thaw, dissolve, disappear, vanish; fuse, thaw, dissolve, soften. See PITY, TRANSIENTNESS.

member, *n.* unit, constituent, element, PART; fellow, adherent, partner, *etc.* See MANKIND, SOCIALITY.

membrane, *n.* film, lamina, sheet, sheath, layer. See NARROWNESS.

memoir, *n.* RECORD; reminiscence, autobiography. See DESCRIPTION.

memorable, *adj.* noteworthy, signal, outstanding; unforgettable. See IMPORTANCE, MEMORY.

memorial, *adj. & n.* —*adj.* commemorative. See MEMORY. —*n.* monument, shrine, tablet; anniversary. See RECORD.

MEMORY [505]

Nouns—**1,** memory, remembrance, retention, retentiveness, tenacity, reminiscence, recognition, recurrence, recollection, retrospect, retrospection, afterthought.

2, reminder, suggestion, prompting, hint; token, memento, souvenir, keepsake, relic, memorandum, memo, memoir; memorial, commemoration, Memorial *or* Decoration Day, monument; memorabilia; flashback.

3, art of memory; artificial memory, mnemonics, mnemotechnics, mnemotechny, mnemonics, Mnemosyne; retentive, photographic memory; rote, repetition.

Verbs—**1,** remember, remind, retain the memory of; keep in view, bear in mind, hold in mind, remain in one's memory, mind, *or* head.

2, recur to the mind, flash across the memory; haunt, run in the head.

3, recognize, recollect, bethink oneself, recall, call up, retrace, look back, think back upon, review, call to mind, carry one's thoughts back, reminisce.

4, suggest, prompt, put *or* keep in mind, remind, call *or* summon up; renew; tax, jog, refresh, *or* awaken the memory.

5, memorize; have, learn, know, *or* say by heart, *or* rote; repeat, have at the tip of one's tongue; commit to memory; con, fix, make a note of.

6, keep the memory alive, keep in memory, commemorate, memorialize, honor the memory of.

Adjectives—remembering, remembered, mindful, reminiscent, retentive, retained in the memory, fresh, alive, green, unforgotten, within one's memory, indelible; uppermost in one's thoughts; memorable, memorial, commemorative.

Adverbs—by heart *or* rote, without prompting, word for word; in memory of, in memoriam.

Antonym, see OBLIVION.

---

menace, *n. & v.* —*n.* threat, danger, hazard, peril. —*v.t.* threaten, intimidate, bully; impend, loom. See WARNING. *Ant.*, see SAFETY.

mend, *v.t.* repair, restore, correct, improve. See IMPROVEMENT, RESTORATION.

mendicancy, *n.* beggary, mendicity. *Colloq.*, panhandling. See POVERTY.

menial, *n. & adj.* —*n.* SERVANT, slavery, flunky. —*adj.* humble; servile; degrading, mean. *Ant.*, see AUTHORITY.

mental, *adj.* intellectual, cognitive, rational, psychologic. See INTELLECT.

mentality, *n.* INTELLECT, intelligence, mind, understanding.

mention, *v.t.* communicate, designate, let fall; cite, speak of. See INFORMATION.

menu, *n.* bill of fare, fare, diet, LIST, carte. See FOOD.

mercenary, *adj.* calculating, selfish, sordid, venal, grasping. See PARSIMONY.

merchandise, *n. & v.* —*n.* wares, commodities; effects; goods, articles; stock, stock in trade; produce; supplies, stores, cargo. —*v.* buy, sell; market, vend; trade, barter, traffic, deal; retail, wholesale; peddle, hawk; distribute. See SALE, BUSINESS.

merchant, *n.* trader, dealer, tradesman, merchandiser; shopkeeper, store-keeper; businessman; retailer, wholesaler, middleman, jobber; salesman, seller, vendor, vender, monger, huckster, hawker, peddler; sutler, coster-monger, fishmonger; canvasser, agent, door-to-door salesman. See SALE, BUSINESS.

merciful, *adj.* compassionate, lenient, forbearing, humane. See PITY. *Ant.*, see SEVERITY.

merciless, *adj.* cruel, hardhearted, pitiless, relentless. See SEVERITY. *Ant.*, see PITY.

mercy, *n.* PITY, LENIENCY, forbearance, compassion. *Ant.*, see SEVERITY.

mere, *adj.* nothing but, plain, bare, simple. See LITTLENESS.

merely, *adv.* barely, simply, only, purely. See LITTLENESS.

merge, *v.t.* unite, blend, coalesce, absorb. See MIXTURE, JUNCTION.

merit, *n.* desert(s), reward, due; worth, excellence; VIRTUE. See GOODNESS.

merited, *adj.* deserved, earned; due. See JUSTICE.

merry, *adj.* jovial, gay, blithe, vivacious. See CHEERFULNESS. *Ant.*, see DEJECTION.

mesmerism, *n.* hypnotism, animal magnetism.

mesmerize, *v.t.* hypnotize; fascinate, captivate.

mess, *n.* DIFFICULTY; predicament; DISORDER, litter, jumble; botch. See UNSKILLFULNESS.

message, *n.* COMMUNICATION, dispatch; note. See INFORMATION.

messenger, *n.* emissary, envoy, apostle, missionary; courier, carrier, bearer, errand boy, runner. See COMMUNICATION.

metal, *n.* MINERAL, MATERIAL, element, alloy, ore.

metaphorical, *adj.* allegorical, FIGURATIVE.

metaphysical, *adj.* abstruse, speculative, esoteric, transcendental.

meter, *n.* rhythm, cadence, lilt; gauge, measuring device. See POETRY, MEASUREMENT.

method, *n.* way, manner, wise; style, form, mode, FASHION; guise; *modus operandi*, procedure, routine, regimen, line of conduct; order, oderliness; system, plan, scheme; path, route, course. See PREPARATION. *Ant.*, see DISORDER.

methodical, *adj.* orderly, systematic, precise. See ARRANGEMENT.

methodize, *v.t.* systematize, arrange, organize. See ORDER, ARRANGEMENT.

mettle, *n.* spirit, COURAGE, disposition.

mettlesome, *adj.* high-strung, courageous, plucky. See COURAGE, EXCITE-MENT.

microbe, *n.* bacterium, germ. See LITTLENESS.

microscopic, *adj.* minute, tiny, infinitesimal. See LITTLENESS.

MIDDLE [68]

Nouns—**1,** middle, midst, MEAN, medium, middle term; center, core, hub, kernel; umbilicus; halfway house; nave, navel, nucleus; heart, axis, bull's-eye; marrow, pith; equidistance, bisection, half distance, equator; diaphragm, midriff; interjacence.
2, focus, focal point, convergence, concentration, centralization, corradiation.

Verbs—center on, focus, concentrate, meet, unite, converge.

Adjectives—middle, medial, median, mean, mid; midmost, intermediate, equidistant, central, focal, axial, equatorial, concentric, convergent.

Adverbs—in the middle, midway, halfway or midships, *in medias res*.

Antonym, see EXTERIOR.

middle age, middle life, maturity, prime.

middle–aged, *adj.* mature, in (one's) prime.

middleman, *n.* go-between, intermediary, AGENT. See COMPROMISE.

midmost, *adj.* central; MIDDLE, mean. See CENTRALITY.

midway, *adj.* halfway, MIDDLE.

mien, *n.* APPEARANCE, AIR, demeanor, bearing. See CONDUCT.

might, *n.* POWER, force, STRENGTH. *Ant.*, IMPOTENCE.

migrate, *v.i.* journey, TRAVEL; emigrate, immigrate.

mild, *adj.* gentle, easy, bland, soft, harmless; lenient, tolerant, merciful, humane, generous, forbearing; weak, neutral; placid, tranquil, temperate, moderate; comfortable. clement (of weather, temperature); meek, submissive, conciliatory. See MODERATION.

mildew, *n.* mold, decay, rot, must. See DETERIORATION.

military, *adj.* martial, soldierly. See WARFARE. *Ant.*, see PACIFICATION.

milky, *adj.* lacteal; white, pale, chalky; spiritless, timorous. See COLOR.

mill, *n.* grinder, millstone, millrace; factory, plant, works, shop, (*pl.*) industry. See BUSINESS.

mimic, *v.t.* imitate, impersonate; ape, copy; mock. See IMITATION.

mind, *n. & v.t.* —*n.* consciousness, understanding; INTELLECT; purpose, intention, opinion. See INTELLIGENCE, REASONING. —*v.t.* heed, obey; notice, tend; object to. See ATTENTION, CARE.

mine, *n.* lode, vein, deposit; pit, open pit, burrow, excavation; explosive, bomb; source, treasure trove. See RECEPTACLE.

MINERAL [358]

Nouns—**1,** mineral, mineral world *or* kingdom, inorganic matter, unorganized *or* inanimate matter, inorganization; lithification, petrification, petrifaction; stone, metal (see MATERIALS).

2, mineralogy, geology, geognosy, geoscopy, metallurgy, lithology, petrology.

Verbs—mineralize, petrify, lithify; turn to dust.

Adjectives—mineral, inorganic, inorganized, inanimate, azoic.

mingle, *v.t.* blend, mix, merge, intermingle, conjoin. See MIXTURE.

minimum, *n.* modicum; least amount, least quantity. See LITTLENESS.

minister, *n.* legate, envoy, ambassador; cabinet officer; clergyman, pastor, *etc.* See DEPUTY, CLERGY.

ministry, *n.* state officers (*Brit.*); diplomatic service; priesthood, CLERGY.

minor, *adj.* lesser, inferior, secondary. See INFERIORITY. *Ant.*, see SUPERIORITY.

minority, *n.* few, handful; smaller group; nonage, childhood. See RARITY, YOUTH. *Ant.*, see MULTITUDE, SUPERIORITY.

minstrel, *n.* poet, troubadour, bard. See POETRY, MUSICIAN.

minus, *adj.* less, lacking; negative. See LOSS, ABSENCE. *Ant.*, see ADDITION.

minute, *adj.* small, tiny; exact, precise. See LITTLENESS. *Ant.*, see SIZE.

minuteness, *n.* SMALLNESS, meticulousness, precision, exactitude. See ATTENTION, UNIMPORTANCE. *Ant.*, see SIZE, IMPORTANCE.

minutiae, *n.pl.* details, trivia. See UNIMPORTANCE.

miraculous, *adj.* preternatural, supernatural, prodigious, wondrous. See WONDER.

mire, *n.* mud, muck, dirt; quagmire, MARSH. See UNCLEANNESS.

mirror, *n.* looking glass, glass, reflector; cheval *or* pier glass, *etc.* See DESCRIPTION, SMOOTHNESS.

mirth, *n.* hilarity, jollity, merriment, glee. See CHEERFULNESS. *Ant.*, see DEJECTION, MODERATION.

misanthrope, *n.* man-hater, antisocial person, cynic, egotist; woman-hater, misogynist. See MALEVOLENCE. *Ant.*, see BENEVOLENCE.

misanthropic, *adj.* antisocial, *etc.*; morose, sour, crabbed, sullen. See MALEVOLENCE. *Ant.*, see BENEVOLENCE.

misapprehend, *v.t.* misunderstand, mistake, misinterpret. *Ant.*, see KNOWLEDGE.

miscalculate, *v.t.* misjudge, err, misreckon. See MISJUDGMENT.

miscarry, *v.i.* fail, go wrong, fall through; abort. See FAILURE. *Ant.*, see SUCCESS.

miscellaneous, *adj.* heterogeneous, indiscriminate, mixed, many-sided. See MIXTURE.

miscellany, *n.* anthology, analecta; medley, MIXTURE. See BOOK.

mischief, *n.* harm, injury; prank. See BADNESS, MALEVOLENCE.

misconception, *n.* delusion, mistake, misunderstanding. See ERROR.

misconduct, *n.* impropriety, misdemeanor, misbehavior, mismanagement. See BADNESS.

misdeed, *n.* offense, WRONG, malefaction. See GUILT.

miser, *n.* hoarder, niggard, moneygrubber, skinflint. See PARSIMONY. *Slang,* penny pincher, tightwad.
miserable, *adj.* wretched, forlorn, doleful; mean, paltry. See PAIN, UNIMPORTANCE. *Ant.,* see PLEASURE.
misery, *n.* wretchedness, privation; distress, anguish. See PAIN. *Ant.,* see PLEASURE.
misfortune, *n.* bad luck; mishap, disaster, calamity, catastrophe; ADVERSITY. *Ant.,* see CHANCE, WEALTH.
misgiving, *n.* DOUBT, apprehension, premonition, anxiety; qualm. See FEAR.
mishap, *n.* accident, mischance, misfortune. See ADVERSITY, CHANCE.
misinformation, *n.* misintelligence; misteaching, misguidance, misdirection; misinstruction, misleading, perversion; sophistry. See FALSEHOOD. *Ant.,* see TRUTH, INFORMATION.
misinterpretation, *n.* misapprehension, misunderstanding, misconstruction, misapplication; misconception, mistake; misrepresentation, perversion, EXAGGERATION, false construction, falsification. See DISTORTION, FALSEHOOD. *Ant.,* see TRUTH, INTERPRETATION.

MISJUDGMENT [481]

Nouns—**1,** misjudgment, miscalculation, misconception, miscomputation, ERROR, hasty conclusion, misinterpretation.
2, prejudgment, prejudication, foregone conclusion, preconception, predilection, presumption, presentiment, preconceived idea, *idée fixe.*
3, partisanship; clannishness, provincialism; bias, warp, twist, prejudice; hobby, fad, quirk, crotchet; partiality, infatuation, blind side *or* spot, mote in the eye; onesided views, narrow conception, superficial ideas, narrowmindedness, bigotry, pedantry, hypercriticalness.
Verbs—**1,** misjudge, misestimate, misconceive, misreckon, miscompute, miscalculate, overestimate, underestimate.
2, forejudge, prejudge, presuppose, prejudicate, dogmatize; have a bias, have only one idea, jump *or* rush to conclusions, view with a jaundiced eye, not see beyond one's nose; bias, warp, twist, prejudice.
Adjectives—misjudging, wrongheaded, prejudiced, jaundiced, short-sighted, purblind, one-sided, superficial, narrowminded, illiberal, intolerant, hypercritical, besotted, infatuated, fanatical, dogmatic, opinionated, self-opinionated, bigoted, crotchety, impracticable, unreasoning.
Antonym, see JUSTICE, INTERPRETATION.

mislay, *v.t.* misplace, lose. See LOSS.
mislead, *v.t.* deceive, delude, lead astray. See ERROR, DECEPTION.
mismanage, *v.t.* botch, mishandle; misconduct, maladminister. See UNSKILLFULNESS.
misnomer, *n.* misnaming; malapropism; nickname, so(u)briquet, pet name, assumed name, alias; pen name, *nom de plume,* stage name, pseudonym. See NOMENCLATURE.
misplace, *v.t.* derange; mislocate, displace, mislay. See LOSS.
mispronounce, *v.t.* misspeak, missay; garble. See SPEECH.
misrepresentation, *n.* misstatement, DISTORTION, EXAGGERATION, perversion, falsification; bad likeness; caricature, burlesque, travesty; mimicry, mockery, parody, takeoff, IMITATION. *Ant.,* see REPRESENTATION, TRUTH.
misrule, *n.* mismanagement, misgovernment; confusion, tumult, DISORDER. See UNSKILLFULNESS.
miss, *v.* fail; omit, skip, overlook; avoid; escape; lose. See FAILURE, NEGLECT.
misshapen, *adj.* deformed, malformed, distorted, grotesque. See DISTORTION. *Ant.,* see FORM, BEAUTY.
missile, *n.* projectile, trajectile; guided missile. See ARMS.
missing, *adj.* omitted; gone, absent; lacking. See ABSENCE.
mission, *n.* errand, task, assignment; calling; deputation. See BUSINESS, COMMISSION.
misstatement, *n.* ERROR, mistake; MISREPRESENTATION, perversion, FALSEHOOD.
mist, *n.* fog, haze, vapor, drizzle. See CLOUDINESS.

mistake, *v.t. & n.* —*v.t.* misunderstand, err, misidentify. See MISJUDGMENT. —*n.* ERROR, blunder, misunderstanding, slip.

mistress, *n.* possessor, employer; matron, head, TEACHER; paramour, sweetheart. See LIBERTINE.

misunderstanding, *n.* misapprehension; quarrel, disagreement, falling-out. See CONTENTION, ERROR.

misuse, *n. & v.* —*n.* misusage, misemployment; misapplication; misappropriation; abuse, profanation, perversion, prostitution, ill-use; desecration; WASTE. —*v.t.* misemploy, misapply, misappropriate; ill-use. *Ant.,* see USE.

mite, *n.* louse, insect, chigoe, chigger, *etc.;* coin, penny, sou. See LITTLENESS.

mitigate, *v.t.* lessen, moderate, ameliorate, palliate, allay, relieve. See RELIEF, MODERATION.

MIXTURE [41]

Nouns—**1,** mixture, admixture, commixture, intermixture, alloyage; matrimony, JUNCTION, COMBINATION, union, amalgamation; permeation, imbuement, impregnation, fusion, infusion, suffusion, transfusion, infiltration; seasoning, sprinkling, interlarding, interpolation, adulteration; assortment, variety; miscegenation, interbreeding, intermarriage, mixed marriage; hybridization, crossing, crossbreeding.

2, tinge, tincture, TOUCH, dash, smack, sprinkling, spice, seasoning, infusion, soupçon.

3, alloy, amalgam, compound, blend, mixture, mélange, miscellany, medley, olio, mess, hodgepodge, patchwork, odds and ends, jumble; salad, sauce; hash, mash; gallimaufry, salmagundi, potpourri, mosaic; crazy quilt, mishmash; pi.

4, half-breed, half-caste, half-blood, mulatto; quadroon, octoroon; cross, hybrid, mongrel; ladino, mestizo; Eurasian; mestee, *métis, métisse.*

Verbs—mix, join, combine, commix, intermix, mix up with, mingle, commingle, intermingle, stir up, knead, brew, impregnate with, interlard, intertwine, interweave, associate with; instil(l), imbue, transfuse, infuse, suffuse, infiltrate, tinge, tincture, season, sprinkle, blend, cross, allow, amalgamate, compound, adulterate, contaminate, infect.

Adjectives—mixed, composite, half-and-half; hybrid, mongrel; combined, united; amalgamated, alloyed; impregnated (with), ingrained; heterogeneous, motley, variegated, miscellaneous, promiscuous, indiscriminate, miscible.

Prepositions—among, amongst, amid, amidst, with, in the midst of.

moan, *v.* wail, sigh, groan, bewail, lament. See LAMENTATION.

mob, *n.* rabble, riffraff; *hoi polloi;* common herd, *canaille;* crowd, POPULACE. See ASSEMBLAGE.

mobile, *adj.* movable, loose, free; animate. See MOTION. *Ant.,* stationary, fixed.

mock, *v.t. & adj.* —*v.t.* RIDICULE, mimic, tantalize, jeer at; disappoint. See IMITATION. —*adj.* false, IMITATION, sham, pseudo. See DECEPTION. *Ant.,* see TRUTH.

mode, *n.* STATE, manner, method, custom; FASHION, style.

model, *n.* PROTOTYPE, pattern, mock-up; COPY, miniature, replica; style, type; mannequin, lay figure; exemplar, paragon. See REPRESENTATION, GOODNESS.

MODERATION [174]

Nouns—**1,** moderation, moderateness, temperance, temperateness, gentleness, SOBRIETY; quiet; tranquillity, inexcitability, relaxation, abatement, remission, mitigation, tranquilization, assuagement, pacification; *juste milieu,* golden mean (see MIDDLE).

2, sedative, palliative, lenitive, balm, opiate, anodyne; lullaby; moderator, temperer.

3, LENIENCY, lenity, tolerance, toleration, clemency, PITY.

4, abstainer, nondrinker, teetotaler, dry, prohibitionist; W.C.T.U. (Women's Christian Temperance Union), Anti-Saloon League, Alcoholics Anonymous.

Verbs—**1,** be moderate, keep within bounds, sober up, settle down, **keep the** peace, relent; abstain, be temperate, take the pledge.
2, moderate, soften, mitigate, temper, mollify, dull, blunt, subdue, chasten, tone down, lessen, check, palliate; tranquilize, assuage, appease, lull, soothe, still, calm, cool, quiet, hush, quell, sober, pacify, tame, allay, slacken, smooth, alleviate, deaden, smother; cool off, tone down, taper off.
3, tolerate, bear with; indulge, spare the rod; spare; give quarter; PITY. *Slang*, pull one's punches; let one down easy.
Adjectives—moderate, lenient, gentle, mild, soft, tolerant, easy-going, forbearing; sober, temperate; reasonable, tempered; tame, lulling, hypnotic, sedative, palliative. *Colloq.*, on the (water) wagon.
Adverbs—moderately, gingerly, within bounds or reason.
Antonym, see VIOLENCE.

modern, *n.* contemporary; late, recent; up-to-date. See NEWNESS.
modernism, *n.* modernity, height of fashion; surrealism, *etc.;* liberalism See NEWNESS, FASHION, PAINTING. *Ant.*, see OLDNESS.

MODESTY [881]

Nouns—modesty; HUMILITY; diffidence, timidity, bashfulness; shyness, un obtrusiveness; shame; reserve, constraint; demureness.
Verbs—**1,** be modest, retire, give way to, draw in one's horns, retire into one's shell, keep in the background, keep one's distance, hide one's light under a bushel.
2, be humble; deign, condescend; demean oneself, stop, submit; hide one's face, hang one's head, eat humble pie; blush, redden, change color; feel small. *Colloq.*, eat crow, draw in one's horns.
Adjectives—modest, diffident, humble, timid, timorous, bashful, shy, nervous; coy; sheepish, shamefaced, blushing; overmodest, unpretentious, unobtrusive, unassuming, unaspiring, reserved, demure. *Colloq.*, decent.
Adverbs—modestly, humbly, meekly; quietly, privately; without ceremony; with downcast eyes, on bended knee.
Antonym, see VANITY.

modicum, *n.* little, pittance, bit. See LITTLENESS, APPORTIONMENT.
modification, *n.* CHANGE, alteration, mutation; limitation, QUALIFICATION; modulation. See SOUND.
modify, *v.t.* CHANGE, vary, alter; limit, reduce; temper, soften.
modulation, *n.* regulation, abatement, inflection, modification. See CHANGE, SOUND.
Mohammedan, *n. & adj.* —*n.* Mussulman, Moslem, Islamite. —*adj.* Moslem, Islamic. See RELIGION.

MOISTURE [339]

Nouns—moisture, moistness, humidity, dampness, damp, dew, fog, mist, marsh; hygrometry; dankness, clamminess; wet, wetness. See WATER.
Verbs—moisten, wet, sponge, sprinkle, damp, dampen, bedew, saturate, soak, drench, water.
Adjectives—moist, damp, watery, humid, wet, dank, muggy, dewy, juicy; wringing wet, wet through, wet to the skin, saturated; soggy, reeking, dripping, soaking, soft, sodden, sloppy, muddy, swampy, marshy.
Antonym, see DRYNESS.

mold, *n. & v.t.* —*n.* matrix, die; FORM, shape, figure; stamp, cast. —*v.t.* frame, shape, model, cast; knead, work. See SCULPTURE.
moldy, *adj.* musty, mildewed, fusty; stale, antiquated. See UNCLEANNESS, OLDNESS.
molecule, *n.* particle, atom, mite, micron. See LITTLENESS.
molest, *v.t.* disturb, annoy, vex, pester, harass. See PAIN.
mollify, *v.t.* placate, pacify, soothe, appease, calm. See RELIEF.
mollycoddle, *n.* milksop, sissy. *Slang*, pantywaist. See SOFTNESS, IMPOTENCE.
molt, *v.t.* shed; cast *or* slough off. See DIVESTMENT.

molten, *adj.* melted, fused, liquefied. See HEAT.

moment, *n.* IMPORTANCE, consequence, significance; momentum, IMPULSE; instant, trice, flash. See INSTANTANEITY.

momentous, *adj.* important, consequential, great, notable, signal; serious, solemn, memorable; influential. See IMPORTANCE.

momentum, *n.* impetus, moment. See IMPULSE.

monarch, *n.* sovereign, ruler, potentate, king. See AUTHORITY.

monarchy, *n.* kingdom, princedom, principality. See AUTHORITY.

monastery, *n.* cloister, lamasery, abbey, convent, priory. See TEMPLE.

monasticism, *n.* monkhood, monachism, friarhood. See CLERGY, RELIGION.

MONEY [800]

Nouns—**1,** money, finance, funds, treasure, capital, assets; ways and means, wherewithal, almighty dollar; money matters, resources, backing.

2, sum, amount; balance, balance sheet; proceeds, accounts, lump sum, round sum.

3, gold, silver, copper, nickel; bullion, ingot, nugget, gold brick; currency, circulating medium, specie, coin, cash, hard cash, dollar, sterling; money in hand, ready money; lucre, pelf. *Slang*, dough, jack, brass, spondulix, boodle, gelt, folding money, lettuce, cabbage, kale, mazuma, moolah, long green, shekels, simoleons, beans, chips, berries, bucks; the needful; pony, quid, bob, tenner, grand, century, sawbuck, two bits; bill, yard, G note, C note; red cent.

4, WEALTH, opulence, affluence, riches, fortune; competence, solvency; prosperity; substance; property; mint, gold mine, Golconda, El Dorado, purse of Fortunatus.

5, petty cash, pocket money, pin money, mad money, change, small coin, stiver, mite, farthing, sou, penny, shilling, groat, guinea; wampum; paper money, money order, note, bank note, promissory note, I.O.U., bond, bill, bill of exchange; draft, check, cheque, traveler's check; order, warrant, coupon, debenture, assignat, greenback. *Slang*, blue chips.

6, counterfeit, false or bad money, stage money; base coin, flash note. *Colloq.*, slug.

7, dearness, costliness (see DEAR); overcharge, extravagance, exorbitance, pretty penny; inflation. See EXPENDITURE. *Slang*, highway robbery.

8, rich man, capitalist, financier, millionaire, multimillionaire, billionaire; nabob, Croesus, Dives, Maecenas, Midas, Barmecide; plutocrat, tycoon; heir, heiress. *Slang*, moneybags.

9, numismatics, science of coins, coin-collecting.

Verbs—**1,** monetize, issue, utter; circulate; coin, mint, enrich; counterfeit, forge; amount to, come to, total.

2, have money, roll in money, wallow in wealth, make a fortune, feather one's nest, strike it rich. *Colloq.*, have money to burn, hit the jackpot, make a killing.

Adjectives—**1,** monetary, pecuniary, fiscal, financial, numismatical.

2, wealthy, rich, affluent, opulent, well-to-do, well off. *Colloq.*, flush. *Slang*, in the chips; filthy rich; loaded.

3, DEAR, expensive, costly; precious, extravagant, at a premium.

Antonym, see POVERTY.

monk, *n.* friar, brother, cleric; pilgrim, palmer, mendicant; ascetic, hermit, anchorite, cenobite, eremite, recluse, solitary; abbot, prior, father, abbé. See RELIGION.

monkey, *n.* simian, primate, ape; imitator, mimic. See ANIMAL, IMITATION.

monopolize, *v.t.* engross, absorb, appropriate, corner. See POSSESSION.

monopoly, *n.* trust, cartel, syndicate, pool; corner. See PARTY, RESTRAINT.

monotonous, *adj.* wearisome, humdrum, tedious; unvaried, repetitious. See REPETITION. *Ant.*, see CHANGE.

monster, *n.* monstrosity, freak; prodigy; giant; DEMON, brute. See UNCONFORMITY, SIZE, UGLINESS.

monstrous, *adj.* huge, enormous; hideous, terrifying, revolting; fiendish, heinous; abnormal, freakish. See SIZE, UGLINESS, EVIL, UNCONFORMITY.

monument, *n.* memorial, cenotaph, tombstone; outstanding work. See INTERMENT, RECORD.

mood, *n.* temper, humor, disposition, inclination. See TENDENCY.

moody, *adj.* capricious, variable; gloomy, pensive, sad; peevish, testy; sullen, glum. See TENDENCY.

moon, *n.* satellite; month; lunation. See UNIVERSE.

moor, *n.* heath, moorland, down, brae.

mop, *n. & v.* swob, wipe; floor mop, dry mop; brush, broom; tuft. See CLEANNESS.

mope, *v.i.* brood, fret, sulk, pout. See DEJECTION, IRASCIBILITY.

moral, *adj.* ethical; righteous, just, virtuous; logical, probable. See PROBITY, VIRTUE. *Ant.,* see EVIL, IMPROBITY.

morality, *n.* VIRTUE, righteousness, uprightness, rectitude, ethics. See DUTY *Ant.,* see EVIL, IMPROBITY.

morbid, *adj.* unhealthy, diseased; gloomy, unwholesome. See DISEASE, DEJECTION.

more, *adj. & adv.* additional, in addition, added, beside, besides, to boot, over and above, further. See ADDITION.

morning, *n.* morn, morningtide, forenoon, ante meridian, a.m., A.M., dawn, crack of dawn, daybreak, break of day; aurora; sunrise, sunup, cockcrow. See TIME. *Ant.,* see EVENING.

morose, *adj.* sulky, sullen, gloomy, crabbed, glum, dour. See IRASCIBILITY. *Ant.,* see CHEERFULNESS.

morsel, *n.* mouthful, bite, crumb, scrap, bit. See LITTLENESS, FOOD.

mortal, *adj.* human, ephemeral; fatal, deadly; dire; implacable. See MANKIND, TRANSIENTNESS, KILLING.

mortification, *n.* humiliation, vexation, embarrassment, chagrin. See PAIN.

mortuary, *n. & adj.* —*n.* morgue, funeral home. —*adj.* funerary, funereal. See INTERMENT.

most, *adj.* greatest, most numerous; the majority of, nearly or almost all. See NUMERATION.

mother, *n.* parent, mamma; abbess, prioress; matron, matriarch. See ANCESTRY, CLERGY.

motif, *n.* musical theme; subject, TOPIC, concept. See MUSIC.

MOTION [264]

Nouns—**1,** motion, movement, move, mobility, movableness; APPROACH; motive power; mobilization; evolution, CHANGEABLENESS, restlessness, unrest; kinematics, kinetics.
2, progress, locomotion; journey, voyage, transit, TRAVEL; speed, VELOCITY, rate, clip.
3, stream, flow, flux, run, course, flight, drift, DIRECTION.
4, step, pace, tread, stride, gait, footfall, carriage.
Verbs—**1,** be in motion, move, go; hie; budge, stir; pass, flit, hover round; shift, slide, glide; roll on, flow, stream, run, drift, sweep along; wander, walk; dodge; keep moving, pull up stakes.
2, put *or* set in motion, move, impel, propel, mobilize, motivate.
3, motion, signal, gesture, direct, guide.
Adjectives—moving, in motion, transitional, motory, motive, shifting, movable, mobile; mercurial, restless, changeable, nomadic, erratic; kinetic; impending, imminent.
Adverbs—under way, on the move, on the wing, on the march.
Antonyms, see INACTIVITY, REPOSE.

---

motionless, *adj.* still, immobile, stationary, inert, fixed. See REPOSE, INACTIVITY.

motivate, *v.* induce, move; draw on, give an impulse to, inspire, prompt, stimulate, inspirit, rouse, arouse, animate, incite, provoke, instigate, INFLUENCE, bias, sway; tempt, seduce; bribe, suborn; enforce, impel, propel, whip, lash, goad. See IMPULSE, ACTIVITY. *Ant.,* see INACTIVITY.

motive, *n.* motivation, reason, ground, CAUSE; OCCASION; principle, mainspring, keystone; intention; inducement, consideration, ATTRACTION; temptation, enticement; bewitchment, spell, fascination; INFLUENCE, IMPULSE, incitement, instigation; inspiration, encouragement; ADVICE, incentive, stimulus, spur, goad, bribe, bait; sop.

motor, *n.* engine; see POWER.

mottled, *adj.* spotted, blotched, dappled; motley. See COLOR.

motto, *n.* MAXIM, adage, precept, device.

mound, *n.* heap, hillock, knoll, hill, tumulus. See HEIGHT. *Ant.,* see SMOOTHNESS.

mount, *v.t.* ascend, rise, soar, go up, climb; set, place. See ASCENT, ELEVATION.

mountain, *n.* hill, peak, elevation, alp, mount. See HEIGHT.

mountaineer, *n.* highlander, mountain climber. *Slang,* hillbilly. See HEIGHT.

mourn, *v.* lament, sorrow, grieve; bewail, bemoan, deplore. See LAMENTATION.

mourner, *n.* lamenter, griever; mute, pallbearer. See INTERMENT, LAMENTATION.

mourning, *n.* LAMENTATION, grief; weeds, crepe, sackcloth.

mouth, *n.* oral cavity, lips; muzzle; entrance, exit, INLET. See OPENING. *Slang,* kisser, trap.

movable, *adj.* portable, mobile; changeable. See CHANGEABLENESS.

move, *v.* transport, impel, actuate, incite, arouse, influence, propose; stir, act; remove. See IMPULSE, ACTION.

movement, *n.* MOTION, gesture; maneuver; progress; crusade, drive. See ACTION.

movie, *n.* motion picture, moving picture, movies, pictures, film, cinema; photoplay, show, the screen, screenplay, silver screen. *Colloq.,* talkie, flicker. *Slang,* the flicks. See DRAMA.

moving, *adj.* motile; stirring; touching, affecting; impressive, exciting. See MOTION.

mow, *v.t.* cut, clip, reap, scythe. See DECREASE.

much, *n. & adj.* —*n.* abundance, ample, plenty, a lot, a great deal, a volume; wealth, SUFFICIENCY. —*adj.* many; abundant, ample, copious, plentiful, profuse. *Ant.,* see INSUFFICIENCY.

mud, *n.* mire, muck, ooze, gumbo.

muddle, *n.* confusion, mess, DISORDER, befuddlement.

muffle, *v.t.* deaden, stifle, mute, dampen; wrap up, swathe, envelop. See SILENCE, CLOTHING.

muffled, *adj.* muted, dampened; enwrapped, swathed. See SILENCE.

muffler, *n.* scarf, comforter; silencer, deadener. See CLOTHING, SILENCE.

muggy, *adj.* humid, dank; oppressive; sultry, sticky. See MOISTURE.

mule, *n.* hinny, crossbreed; intransigent, pighead.

mull, *v.i.* think, reflect, consider, ruminate, ponder. See THOUGHT.

multiformity, *n.* variety, diversity; multifariousness, diversification. See NUMBER.

multiplication, *n.* procreation, reproduction; INCREASE, productiveness. See PRODUCTION, NUMERATION.

MULTITUDE [102]

Nouns—**1,** multitude, numerousness, multiplicity, profusion.
2, legion, host, crowd, great numbers, numbers, array, army, sea, galaxy, scores, peck, bushel, swarm, bevy, cloud, flock, herd, drove, flight, covey, hive, brood, litter, farrow. *Colloq.,* lots, stacks, heaps, scads, oodles, barrels, rafts, piles, millions.
3, greater number, majority; multiplication.
Verbs—be numerous, swarm, teem, crowd, swarm; outnumber, multiply, swarm like locusts.
Adjectives—many, several, sundry, divers, various, not a few; ever so many, numerous, endless, countless, numberless, myriad, legion, profuse, manifold, multiplied, multitudinous, multiple, teeming, swarming, pullulating, populous, crowded, thick, studded; a world of, no end of, thick as fleas, infinite, *Slang,* lousy with.
Adverbs—galore; countlessly, numberlessly, infinitely, *etc.*
Antonym, see RARITY.

mumble, *v.t.* mutter, murmur, mouth. See SPEECH.

mundane, *adj.* worldly, earthly; temporal, carnal. See IRRELIGION. *Ant.,* see DEITY, HEAVEN.

munificent, *adj.* generous, liberal, lavish, bounteous, bountiful, freehanded, openhanded; benevolent, philanthropic, charitable, altruistic; unsparing, princely, profuse. See BENEVOLENCE.

munitions, *see* ARMS.

murder, *n.* homicide, manslaughter. See KILLING.

murderer, *n.* assassin, manslayer, cutthroat; killer, butcher. See KILLING.

murderous, *adj.* bloodthirsty, sanguinary, deadly, brutal. See KILLING.

murk, *n.* gloom, dusk, dark, blackness, obscurity. See DIMNESS.

murmur, *v.i.* mumble, mutter, grumble; rustle, purl, ripple; whisper, breathe. See LAMENTATION.

muscular, *adj.* strong, brawny, sinewy, vigorous. See POWER. *Ant.,* see IMPOTENCE.

muse, *v.i.* ponder, meditate, dream, ruminate. See THOUGHT.

museum, *n.* gallery, repository, archives, exhibition. See STORE.

Muses, *n.* the Nine; inspiration. See MUSICIAN.

MUSIC [415]

Nouns—**1,** music, melody, strain, tune, air, sonata; rondo, rondeau, pastorale, concerto, concert, musicale, overture, symphony, cadenza; cadence; fugue, toccata, round, canon; serenade; opera, light *or* comic opera, operetta; oratorio, composition, opus, arrangement, movement; full score; minstrelsy, band, concert piece; score; musical score (screen music).
2, vocal music, chant; psalm, psalmody, Gregorian chant, plain song, hymn, anthem, song, canticle, cantata, lay, ballad, ditty, carol, pastoral, recitative, aria; sea chantey, work song, folk song, popular song, ballade, jingle.
3, slow music, adagio, minuet; lullaby; dirge, pibroch; martial music, march; instrumental music, band music, symphonic music, concert music, light music, dinner music, *etc.*
4, dance music, syncopation, ragtime, jazz; bolero, fandango, tango, mazurka, gavotte, minuet, polka, waltz, two-step, fox trot, reel, jog, hornpipe, conga, rumba, samba, cha-cha. *Slang,* swing, jive; blues, progressive jazz, bop, bebop, stomp, yodeling, hillbilly *or* country music, crooning.
5, solo, duet, duo, trio, quartet, part song, descant, glee, madrigal, catch, round, chorus, antiphony, accompaniment, second; bass, basso profundo, alto, contralto, tenor, soprano, mezzo-soprano, baritone, barytone, coloratura; dramatic *or* lyric soprano, *etc.*
6, staff, key, bar, space, clef, signature, note, tone, rest, slur, pitch.
Verbs—compose, arrange, adapt, transpose, melodize, harmonize, orchestrate; perform, play, sing.
Adjectives—musical, instrumental, vocal, choral, singing, lyric, operatic; harmonious, melodious, tuneful, symphonic, orchestral.
Adverbs—*adagio, largo, andante, a cappella; moderato, allegro, spiritoso, vivace; presto, sforzando, scherzo, rallentando, staccato, crescendo, diminuendo, obbligato, pizzicato; forte, fortissimo, piano, pianissimo, etc.*

MUSICAL INSTRUMENTS [417]

Nouns—**1,** musical instruments; band; orchestra; trio, quartet, quintet, *etc.*
2, harp, lyre, lute, dulcimer, mandolin, guitar, gittern, cithern, rebec, cither, zither, ukulele, banjo; violin, fiddle, cello, viol, viola, viola da gamba; Cremona, Stradivarius, Amati, Guarnerius; violoncello, bass; bass viol, theorbo, psaltery, recorder.
3, piano, pianoforte, grand piano, grand, baby grand, harpsichord, clavichord, spinet, virginal, hurdy-gurdy, (A)eolian harp, calliope.
4, organ, pipe organ, harmonium, barrel organ; sirene; pipe, pitchpipe, flute, fife, piccolo, flageolet, clarinet, cornet; oboe, hautboy, bassoon, serpent, horn, bugle, French horn, saxhorn, sackbut, trumpet, trombone, saxophone; accordion, concertina; bagpipes; whistle; ocarina; althorn, tuba; harmonica, mouth organ, kazoo. *Slang,* squawk box (harmonium), squeeze box (accordion), ax(e) (saxophone), 88s *or* eighty-eights (piano), licorice stick (clarinet), *etc.*

5, cymbal, bell, gong, tambour, tambourine, tympanum, snare *or* trap drum, drum, bass drum, bongo, tomtom; kettledrum; timbal, timbrel; castanets; musical glasses, sounding board, rattle, bones, steel drums.
6, tuning fork; triangle, Jew's harp; xylophone, marimba, glockenspiel, reed, celeste.
7, baton, wand, stick; drumsticks; music stand; metronome.
8, strings, brass, winds, drums, percussion, wood-winds, reeds, horns.

MUSICIAN [416]

Nouns—**1,** musician, artist(e), performer, player, minstrel; bard, instrumentalist, organist, pianist, violinist, flutist, flautist, harper, harpist, cellist, fiddler, bugler, fifer, trumpeter, piper, oboist, drummer, saxophonist, trombonist, clarinetist, accordionist, *etc.*
2, band, orchestra, string orchestra, brass band, jazz band, combo, ensemble; choir, chorus.
3, vocalist, melodist, singer, warbler, *minnesinger*, chanter, chantress, songstress, caroler, chorister; crooner, blues singer, folk singer, yodeler, calypso singer, scat singer, patter singer.
4, songbird, nightingale, philomel, thrush, mocking bird.
5, Orpheus, Apollo, the Muses, Euterpe, Terpsichore; siren, Lorelei.
6, conductor, lead, bandmaster, choirmaster, concertmaster; composer, arranger; first violin.
7, performance, execution, TOUCH, expression, solmization, fingering.
Verbs—**1,** play, pipe, strike up, fiddle, beat the drum; blow *or* sound the horn; twang, plunk, pluck, pick, thrum, strum.
2, execute, perform; accompany; compose, set to music, arrange.
3, sing, chant, hum, warble, carol, chirp, chirrup, trill, twitter, whistle, intone, lilt.

---

muss, *n.* DISORDER, tangle, confusion, mix-up, mess, muddle.
must, *v.* ought, should, have (got) to, need, needs must, have no choice (but to); be required, obliged, bound, compelled, doomed, destined, *etc.* See NECESSITY.
muster, *v.t.* assemble, collect, gather, mobilize; poll. See ASSEMBLAGE.
mute, *v. & adj.* —*v.* SILENCE; speak softly, whisper; still, muzzle, muffle, suppress, smother, gag, strike dumb. *Colloq.*, squelch. —*adj.* dumb, mum, tongue-tied, tongueless, voiceless, speechless; aphonic; tacit; silent, gagged, muzzled; inarticulate. *Ant.*, see SOUND.
mutilate, *v.t.* maim, destroy, cripple; disfigure, deface, mar. See DISTORTION, DETERIORATION.
mutilated, *adj.* mangled, butchered, garbled, defaced, marred. See IMPERFECTION, DETERIORATION.
mutiny, *n.* rebellion, revolt, uprising, insurrection, insurgence. See DISOBEDIENCE, REVOLUTION.
mutter, *v.* murmur, grumble, mumble, growl. See SPEECH, LAMENTATION.
mutual, *adj.* reciprocal, common, joint, correlative. See INTERCHANGE.
muzzle, *v.t.* restrain, bridle, gag, silence, throttle. See RESTRAINT, SILENCE.
mysterious, *adj.* mystic, baffling, dark, cryptic, occult, inscrutable, obscure, enigmatic. See CONCEALMENT, SECRET.
mystery, *n.* SECRET, enigma, puzzle, cabala; RITE, sacrament. See CONCEALMENT.
mystic, *adj.* hidden, secret; mysterious; esoteric, occult. See SECRET, CONCEALMENT.
mystify, *v.t.* puzzle, perplex, bewilder, obscure, confound, baffle. See CONCEALMENT. *Ant.*, see MEANING.
myth, *n.* legend, tradition; phantasy, fiction. See IMAGINATION, FALSEHOOD, MYTHICAL DEITIES.
mythical, *adj.* unreal; fabulous, fictitious, mythological. See IMAGINATION, FALSEHOOD.

MYTHICAL DEITIES [979]

Nouns—**1,** mythical deities, heathen gods and goddesses; god, goddess, deity, divinity, demigod; pantheon, mythology, folklore.

2, *Greek:* Zeus, Apollo, Ares, Hephaestus, Hermes, Poseidon, Hades, Eros, Dionysus; Hera, Athena, Artemis, Aphrodite; Titans: Uranus, Gaea, Cronos, Oceanus, Coeus, Crius, Hyperion, Rhea, Mnemosyne, Themis, Phoebe, Dione, Cyclops.

3, *Roman:* Jupiter, Jove, Apollo, Mars, Vulcan, Mercury, Neptune, Pluto, Cupid, Bacchus; Juno, Minerva, Diana, Venus.

4, *Norse:* Woden, Odin, Thor, Balder, Loki, Bragi; Freya; Sigurd, Brynhild, Gudrun, Fafnir, the Valkyries.

5, *Hindu:* Vishnu, Siva, Shiva, Brahma, Indra, Buddha.

6, *Egyptian:* Ra, Osiris, Horus, Set, Anubis, Thoth; Isis.

7, *Babylonian & Semitic:* Baal, Bel, Astarte, Ashtoreth, Ishtar, Ashur.

8, nymph, dryad, hamadryad, naiad, nereid, oread; sylph; salamander, undine; Pan, faun, satyr; mermaid, merman.

9, fairy, fay, sprite, elf, brownie, pixie, pixy, Puck, Robin Goodfellow, dwarf, gnome, troll, kobold, peri, hobgoblin, leprechaun.

10, familiar spirit, familiar, genius, genie, jinni; demon, incubus, succubus, vampire, harpy, werewolf; ogre, ogress.

Adjectives—mythical, mythological, legendary; fairylike, nymphlike, elfin.

N

nag, *n. & v.* —*n.* horse; nagging person. —*v.* pester, badger, scold; fret, complain; irritate, annoy, plague. See CONTENTION.

nail, *n. & v.t.* —*n.* fingernail, toenail, ungula; talon, claw; tack, brad, spoke; hobnail, clout; pin, peg. —*v.t.* pin, fix. *Colloq.*, capture, catch. See RESTRAIN, JUNCTION.

naïve, *adj.* ingenuous, unsophisticated, unworldly, artless. See SIMPLENESS.

naked, *adj.* uncovered, bare, stripped; nude, unclothed, unclad, unappareled. See DIVESTMENT. *Ant.,* see CLOTHING.

name, *n. & v.t.* —*n.* nomen, praenomen, cognomen, surname; NOMENCLATURE, appellation; TITLE, term, denomination; alias, nickname, pen name, pseudonym; sobriquet, epithet; designation; reputation, fame, REPUTE. —*v.t.* TITLE, call, designate, christen, entitle; appoint, call, nominate; style; mention. See COMMISSION.

nameless, *adj.* anonymous, unnamed; obscure, unknown, unchristened, untitled; inglorious, unnamable, abominable, indescribable. See DISREPUTE. *Ant.,* see REPUTE, NOMENCLATURE.

namely, *conj. & adv.* to wit, as follows, specifically, *viz., videlicet,* that is, *i.e.*

nap, *n.* sleep; pile, surface, TEXTURE.

napkin, *n.* linen, serviette; towel, diaper, handkerchief; sanitary napkin. *Slang,* wipe.

narcotic, *n. & adj.* —*n.* soporific, anaesthetic; opiate, anodyne; dope, drug; sedative, tranquillizer. See REMEDY. —*adj.* stupefying, narcotizing, tranquillizing.

narrate, *v.t.* describe, tell, relate; recount, recite; inform, rehearse; RECORD, state, report, retail. See DESCRIPTION.

narrative, *n.* tale, statement, account, RECORD, story, report, recital, history; recitation. See DESCRIPTION.

narrator, *n.* raconteur, chronicler, storyteller; RECORDER. See DESCRIPTION.

NARROWNESS [203]

Nouns—**1,** narrowness, closeness, exiguity, LITTLENESS; THINNESS, tenuity, emaciation; narrowing; tapering, CONTRACTION; hair's-breadth, finger's-breadth, line; strip, streak, vein.

2, shaving, chip, filament, thread, hair; skeleton, shadow, spindleshanks, lantern jaws, skin and bone; neck, waist, isthmus, hourglass; pass; ravine, narrows, gap.

Verbs—be narrow, narrow, taper; slice, shave, pare, trim, thin, thin down *or* out, slim, reduce, attenuate.

Adjectives—**1,** narrow, close; slender, thin, fine; threadlike, finespun, slim;

wasp-waisted; scant, scanty; spare, delicate; contracted, unexpanded.
2, emaciated, lean, meager, gaunt, rawboned, lanky, weedy, skinny;
starved, attenuated, shriveled, worn to a shadow.
3, confined, limited; cramped, pinched, close, tight, constricted, prejudiced,
illiberal, insular, provincial, circumscribed, small. *Colloq.*, stiff-necked.
Antonym, see BREADTH.

nasty, *adj.* foul, filthy; distasteful, disgusting, horrid; dirty; nauseating,
loathsome; obscene; ill-tempered, disagreeable, dangerous. See IMPURITY,
PAIN. *Ant.*, see PURITY, PLEASURE.
nation, *n.* country, state, realm; republic, kingdom, empire; sovereignty,
AUTHORITY, polity, body politic; commonwealth, community; tribe, people.
native, *n. & adj.* —*n.* INHABITANT, aborigine, countryman. —*adj.* indigenous; innate, inherent; aboriginal; endemic, natal, natural.
natural, *adj.* unaffected, spontaneous, artless, unstudied; unsophisticated,
naïve, ingenuous; normal, ordinary, regular; unadorned, unadulterated;
inherent, innate, inborn. See SIMPLENESS, TRUTH. *Ant.*, see AFFECTATION,
DECEPTION.
naturalist, *n.* zoölogist, herpetologist, botanist, horticulturist, ichthyologist,
geologist, arborist, arboriculturist.
nature, *n.* character, type, sort, kind; essence, basis, essential; constitution,
quality; disposition, structure; temperament, bent, CLASS, FORM; heart;
creation, universe.
naughty, *adj.* disobedient, wayward, mischievous, troublesome, perverse.
See DISOBEDIENCE.
nausea, *n.* qualm, seasickness, queasiness; disgust, aversion, loathing; illness, sickness. See DISEASE. *Ant.*, see HEALTH.
nauseate, *v.t.* sicken, disgust, revolt.
nauseous, *adj.* sick, queasy, qualmish; emetic; offensive, loathsome, repulsive, sickening.

NAVIGATION [267, 269]

Nouns—**1,** navigation; boating, yachting, yacht-racing, seafaring, sailing,
cruising, voyaging; oarsmanship, rowing, sculling, canoeing, paddling;
racing.
2, voyage, sail, cruise, race, boat *or* yacht race; PASSAGE; circumnavigation;
headway, sternway, leeway; sideslip; seaway; dead reckoning.
3, oar, paddle, scull, screw, sail, gaff, canvas, fish's tail; paddle wheel, side
wheel, stern wheel; rudder, leeboards, rigging, sail, sheet, line, rope, main-
sheet; mast, boom, pole; beam; keep; bow, stern.
4, navigator, sailor, mariner, seaman, seafarer, tar, jack, old salt, able seaman, A.B.; bluejacket, marine, naval cadet, midshipman, middy; captain,
skipper, mate; ferryman, bargeman, longshoreman, bargee, gondolier;
rower, sculler, canoeist, paddler, oarsman; boatswain, coxswain, bosun,
steersman, leadsman, helmsman, pilot, crew; watch.
Verbs—**1,** navigate, sail, set sail, put to sea, take ship, weigh anchor, get
under way, spread sail, have sail; plow the deep, buffet the waves, ride the
storm; warp, luff, scud, float, drift, cruise, coast, steam, hug the shore,
circumnavigate.
2, row, paddle, pull, scull, punt, raft, float.
Adjectives—sailing, seafaring, nautical, maritime, naval, seagoing, coasting,
afloat, navigable.
Adverbs—under way, under sail, under canvas, under steam.

navy, *n.* fleet; ships, warships. See COMBATANT.
Nazi, *n. & adj.* fascist, Hitlerite, racist; National Socialist, NSDAP; reactionary, economic royalist; brownshirt, blackshirt; authoritarian, totalitarian. See AUTHORITY, RIGHT.

NEARNESS [197]

Nouns—**1,** nearness, closeness, proximity, propinquity, approximation, vicinity, neighborhood, adjacency, contiguity; APPROACH, convergence; likeness,
SIMILARITY.

2, short distance, step, *or* way; shortcut; earshot; close quarters, close range, stone's throw, hair's-breadth, span.

3, purlieus, neighborhood, vicinage, environs, suburbs, confines, border-land.

4, bystander, neighbor.

Verbs—**1,** adjoin, abut, hang about, touch on, border on, verge upon; stand by, approximate, tread on the heels of, cling to, clasp, hug; hover over.

2, near, draw near, come near, APPROACH, converge, crowd, press.

Adjectives—near, nigh, close at hand, near at hand; close, neighboring; adjacent, adjoining, proximate; impending, imminent, at hand, handy; near the mark, intimate.

Adverbs—**1,** near, nigh; hard, close, *or* fast by; close to, at the point of; next door to, within reach, within call, within earshot, within an ace of, but a step, not far from, at no great distance; on the verge *or* brink of; on the outskirts, in the neighborhood of, in the offing, around the corner, at one's fingertips, on the tip of one's tongue, under one's nose; within a stone's throw, in sight of, at close quarters; cheek by jowl; beside, alongside, side by side, tête-à-tête; in juxtaposition, at the threshold, bordering upon, in the way.

2, nearly, almost, about, thereabouts; roughly, in round numbers; approximately, as good as, well nigh.

Antonym, see DISTANCE.

---

nearsighted, *adj.* shortsighted, myopic. See VISION.

neat, *adj.* tidy, orderly; compact, trim, shapely; pure, unmixed; deft, skillful, adroit; pat, felicitous. See AGREEMENT, CLEANNESS, SIMPLENESS, SKILL. *Ant.*, see DISAGREEMENT, UNCLEANNESS, UNSKILLFULNES.

NECESSITY [601]

Nouns—**1,** necessity, necessitation, obligation, COMPULSION, subjection; dire necessity, inexorable fate; what must be.

2, requirement, need, want, requisite, demand; needfulness, essentiality, indispensability; urgency, exigency; *sine qua non*, matter of life and death; stress, pinch.

3, DESTINY, fatality, fate, kismet, doom, foredoom, predestination, foreordination, lot, fortune, inevitableness, fatalism.

4, Fates, Parcae, three Sisters, book of fate; God's will, will of heaven, will of Allah; wheel of fortune; Hobson's choice; last shift, last resort.

Verbs—**1,** lie under a necessity; be doomed, be destined, be in for, be under the necessity of, have no choice, have no alternative, have one's back to the wall, be driven into a corner.

2, necessitate, demand, REQUIRE; destine, doom, foredoom, predestine, preordain; compel, force, oblige, constrain.

Adjectives—**1,** necessary, needful, required, requisite, essential, imperative, indispensable; compulsory, uncontrollable, inevitable, unavoidable, irresistible, irrevocable, inexorable, ineluctable; urgent, exigent, pressing, crying; instant.

2, fated, destined, preordained, fateful, doomed.

3, involuntary, instinctive, automatic, blind, mechanical, unconscious, unwitting, unthinking, impulsive.

Adverbs—necessarily, of necessity, of course, needs must, perforce, willing or unwilling, willy-nilly, compulsorily; like it or not.

Antonym, see WILL.

---

neck, *v.* channel, isthmus, strait, pass; cervix; constriction, narrowing; scruff, nape. See NARROWNESS. *Ant.*, see BREADTH.

necklace, *n.* beads, chain, string, pearls; pendant, lavallere; collar, choker. See ORNAMENT.

necktie, *n.* tie, cravat, scarf; string, bow, four-in-hand, Ascot, Windsor, half-Windsor, black, white, *etc.* (tie). See CLOTHING.

necrology, *n.* obituary. See DEATH.

necromancy, *n.* SORCERY, enchantment, magic.

nectar, *n.* honey, honeydew; delicious beverage. See SWEETNESS.

need, *n. & v.t.* —*n.* NECESSITY, REQUIREMENT; DESIRE, want, privation, lack, POVERTY, destitution; USE. —*v.t.* require, crave, claim, demand, yearn; lack, want.
needless, *adj.* unnecessary, pointless, purposeless, superfluous, repetitious.
nefarious, *adj.* EVIL, unlawful; detestable, base, shameful; wicked, illegal.

NEGATION [536]

Nouns—negation, negativeness, abnegation, denial, disavowal, disclaimer, abjuration, contradiction, contravention, protest, QUALIFICATION, repudiation, retraction, refutation, rebuttal, disproof, confutation, REFUSAL, prohibition.
Verbs—negate, deny, contradict, contravene, controvert, gainsay, disown, disaffirm, disclaim, disavow, recant, revoke, abrogate, veto; dispute, impugn, traverse, call in question, doubt, give the lie to; repudiate, set aside, ignore, confute, rebut, refute, qualify, refuse.
Adjectives—negative, denying, denied, contradictory, contrary, recusant, dissenting.
Adverbs—no, nay, not, nowise, not a bit, not at all, not in the least, no such thing, nothing of the kind, quite the contrary, far from it, on no consideration, on no account, in no respect, by no means, for the life of me; negatively, never, not ever. *Dial.*, nohow. *Slang*, like fun; in a pig's eye; not on your life.

Antonym, see AFFIRMATION.

NEGLECT [460]

Nouns—1, neglect, neglectfulness, carelessness, heedlessness, thoughtlessness, DERELICTION; omission, oversight, laches, default, supineness; RASHNESS, imprudence, recklessness; procrastination; inexactness, inaccuracy (see ERROR).
2, LAXITY, laxness, slackness, looseness, slovenliness; unpreparedness, improvidence, unreadiness; disregard, nonobservance, evasion, nonperformance, FAILURE.
3, INATTENTION, absence of mind, preoccupation, woolgathering.
4, neglector, trifler, procrastinator, waster, wastrel, drifter, slacker; Micawber.
Verbs—1, be negligent, neglect, let slip, let go, lay aside, lose sight of, overlook, disregard, ignore; pass over, up, *or* by; let pass, wink at, connive at, gloss over, leave out in the cold; leave in the lurch.
2, be lax, loose, remiss, slack, unprepared, etc.; relax; ignore, *laisser faire;* hold a loose rein, give enough *or* too much rope, tolerate.
3, scamp, do by halves, cut, slight, skimp, trifle with, slur, slur *or* skip over, skim the surface; miss, skip, omit, postpone, procrastinate, put off, defer, shelve, pigeonhole, table, shut one's eyes to, turn a deaf ear to, forget, be caught napping, let the grass grow under one's feet.
Adjectives—1, neglectful, unmindful, negligent, LAX, slack, heedless, careless, thoughtless, forgetful, perfunctory, remiss, inconsiderate; unprepared, unready, off one's guard, unwary, unguarded, unwatchful; offhand, cursory; supine, asleep, indolent; inattentive, unobservant, unmindful, unheeding, thoughtless, inadvertent; indifferent, imprudent, slovenly, inexact, inaccurate, improvident, asleep at the switch.
2, neglected, unheeded, uncared for, unnoticed, unattended to, unmissed, shunted, shelved, abandoned, unweighed, unexplored, hid under a bushel, out in the cold.
Adverbs—neglectfully, negligently, anyhow, in an unguarded moment.
Antonym, see CARE.

negotiable, *adj.* conveyable, assignable, transferable. *Colloq.*, spendable.
negotiate, *v.* accomplish, arrange; bargain, dicker, contract, overcome, achieve, EFFECT. See AGREEMENT.
Negro, *n.* African, Ethiopian, Sudanese.
neighborhood, *n.* community, vicinity, district, REGION, environs, presence, venue. See NEARNESS.
neology, *n.* See SPEECH.

nerve, *n. & v.t.* —*n.* COURAGE, STRENGTH, vigor, vitality; grit, determination, RESOLUTION. —*v.t.* embolden, steel, strengthen, invigorate.

nervous, *adj.* jumpy, jittery, fidgety, uneasy; tense, fearful; sensitive, neurotic. See EXCITEMENT, AGITATION.

nest, *n.* aerie, hammock, lair, den; hotbed, coterie; nursery, cradle; resort, haunt, retreat. See ASSEMBLAGE, CAUSE, ABODE.

nestle, *v.i.* lodge, snuggle, lie, cuddle. See ENDEARMENT.

net, *n.* seine, web, snare, mesh; trap, catch. See DECEPTION.

nettle, *v.* trouble, irritate; prickle; ruffle, annoy, provoke; vex, offend. See PAIN. *Ant.*, see PLEASURE.

network, *n.* reticulation; net, netting, mesh, interlacing, openwork; hookup, web, interconnection.

neutral, *adj.* nonpartisan; indifferent, disinterested, unconcerned; undecided, irresolute, indeterminate; inert, inactive; impartial; neuter, asexual, sexless; barren, unfruitful, sterile. See MEAN. *Ant.*, see SIDE, WARFARE.

neutrality, *n.* indifference, nonpartisanship, aloofness, noninterference, unconcern, impartiality, indecision, indetermination. *Ant.*, see SIDE.

neutralize, *v.t.* nullify, cancel; offset, negate, counterbalance; destroy, defeat, overpower.

never, *adv.* ne'er, nevermore, not ever. See TIME.

NEWNESS [123]

Nouns—**1,** newness, recentness, freshness, greenness, novelty, immaturity, YOUTH; innovation, renovation.

2, modernism, modernity, latest fashion, latest thing, upstart, mushroom, *nouveau riche*, upstart, parvenu.

Verbs—renew, restore, modernize, renovate.

Adjectives—**1,** new, novel, recent, fresh, green, young, evergreen, raw, immature, virgin, untried, not dry behind the ears; untrodden, unbeaten.

2, late, modern, neoteric, new-fashioned, newfangled, just out, up to the minute, brand new, vernal, renovated, fresh as a daisy, up-to-date, abreast of the times.

Adverbs—newly, freshly, afresh, anew, lately, just now, only yesterday, latterly, of late, not long ago, a short time ago.

Antonym, see OLDNESS.

---

news, *n.* INFORMATION; intelligence, tidings, word, ADVICE; message, communication, dispatch, despatch; bulletin, communiqué, news flash; broadcast; telegram, cablegram, letter; report, rumor, hearsay, CRY; talk; gossip, scandal, tittle-tattle, canard, whisper; news channel. *Colloq.*, grapevine, pipeline. See COMMUNICATION, PUBLICATION.

newspaper, *n.* paper; daily, journal, weekly, gazette, sheet, tabloid. See PUBLICATION, RECORD.

New Testament, See SACRED WRITINGS.

next, *adv.* beside, nearest; adjacent, adjoining, bordering, contiguous; following, ensuing, succeeding, successive; after, later. See NEARNESS, SEQUENCE.

nice, *adj.* pleasing, agreeable, attractive, enjoyable; tasteful, proper, genteel; precise, accurate, exact, meticulous; delicate, fine, sensitive; appealing; overrefined, critical, squeamish. See PLEASURE, TRUTH.

niche, *n.* hollow, recess; corner, nook. See ANGULARITY.

nick, *n. & v.t.* —*n.* NOTCH, chip, gouge, dent, jag, indentation. —*v.t.* cut, chip, dent, jag, gouge.

nickname, *n.* pet name, diminutive, sobriquet; appellation. See NOMENCLATURE.

niggardly, *adj.* cheap, stingy, miserly, close, parsimonious, ungenerous; grudging; tight; mean. See CHEAPNESS, PARSIMONY.

night, *n.* DARKNESS, evening, nightfall, midnight, nighttime, eventide. *Ant.*, see LIGHT.

nimble, *adj.* spry, active, sprightly, supple, agile, lively, brisk, alert, quick. *Ant.*, see GRAVITY.

nine, *n.* See NUMERATION.

nip, *v.t.* nibble, bite; cut, snip, pinch, chip, shorten. See DISJUNCTION.

no, *adv.* none, not; NEGATION. *Ant.,* see AFFIRMATION.

NOBILITY [875]

Nouns—**1,** nobility, aristocracy, quality. gentility, rank, condition, distinction, blood, blue blood, birth, high birth, high degree; pedigree, lineage.
2, the nobility, aristocracy, peerage, upper classes, *haut monde*, élite, *noblesse*, gentry, fashionable world, *beau monde*, high society.
3, noble, nobleman, lord, peer, grandee, magnifico, hidalgo, don, aristocrat, gentleman, patrician. *Slang*, swell, nob, toff.
4, king, emperor, prince, crown prince, duke, marquis, marquess, earl, viscount, baron, baronet, knight, chevalier, squire, count, laird, thane, seignior, esquire, Kaiser, czar, margrave; emir, sheik, raja(h), maharajah, sultan.
5, queen, empress, princess, begum, rani, ranee, maharani, sultana, czarina; duchess, marchioness, countess; lady, dame.
6, personage, *crême de la crême*, notable, celebrity, bigwig, magnate. *Slang*, big shot, upper crust, four hundred.
Adjectives—noble, exalted, princely, titled, patrician, aristocratic, wellborn, highborn, of gentle blood, of family, genteel, blue-blooded.
Antonym, see POPULACE.

nobody, *n.* nonentity, cipher, upstart, jackanapes; *Slang*, jerk, twirp. See UNIMPORTANCE. *Ant.,* see IMPORTANCE.
nod, *n. & v.* —*n.* salute, greeting, recognition; sign, signal; permission, agreement. —*v.t.* dip, incline, bob. —*v.i.* greet, signal, sign; sleep, nap, doze. See COURTESY, INACTIVITY, INDICATION.
noise, *n.* uproar, hubbub, din, racket, clamor, pandemonium; crash, rattle, clatter. See LOUDNESS. *Ant.,* see SILENCE.
noiseless, *adj.* soundless, quiet, silenced, muted, hushed, still. See SILENCE. *Ant.,* see SOUND.
noisy, *adj.* clamorous; rackety, clattery; boisterous, blatant, uproarious, loud, strident, deafening. See LOUDNESS.
nomad, *n.* wanderer, gypsy, rover. See TRAVEL.

NOMENCLATURE [564]

Nouns—**1,** nomenclature; naming, nomination, terminology, glossology, baptism, christening.
2, name, appellation, appellative, designation, TITLE, head, heading, nomination, byname, epithet; proper name, Christian name, first name, cognomen, patronymic, surname, nickname, alias, synonym, antonym; honorific, title; pseudonym, pen name, *nom de plume* (SEE MISNOMER). *Slang*, moniker, handle.
3, term, expression, noun, WORD, byword, technical term, cant.
Verbs—name, call, term, denominate, designate, style, entitle, dub, christen, baptize, characterize, specify, label; misname, nickname.
Adjectives—named, called, so-called, hight, yclept; known as, alias, cognominal, titular, nominal; pseudonymous, *soi-disant*, so-called, self-styled; nameless, anonymous.
Antonym, see MISNOMER.

nominate, *v.t.* propose, name; suggest, propound; appoint. See BEGINNING.
nonalcoholic, *adj.* abstemious, teetotal; nonintoxicating; unfermented. See MODERATION. *Ant.,* see DRUNKENNESS.
nonchalance, *n.* INDIFFERENCE, insouciance, unconcern; casualness, carelessness.
nonconformist, *n.* dissenter, separatist; rebel; heretic. *Ant.,* see CONFORMITY.
nonconformity, *n.* heterodoxy, individuality, rebellion; originality. See UNCONFORMITY. *Ant.,* see CONFORMITY.
nondescript, *adj.* indefinable, unclassifiable, indescribable, random; odd; casual, undistinguished. See UNCONFORMITY. *Ant.,* see CONFORMITY.
nonentity, *n.* nothing, negation; nobody; nullity. See NONEXISTENCE. *Ant.,* see EXISTENCE.

nonessential, *adj.* unimportant, irrelevant, unnecessary, incidental, accidental. See UNIMPORTANCE. *Ant.*, see IMPORTANCE.

NONEXISTENCE [2]

Nouns—**1,** nonexistence, inexistence, nonentity, nonsubsistence, negativeness, nullity, nihility, blank, nothingness, ABSENCE, no such thing, void, vacuum, OBLIVION.

2, annihilation, extinction, obliteration, nullification, destruction.

Verbs—**1,** not exist, be null and void, cease to exist, pass away, perish, become extinct, die out, disappear, melt away, dissolve, leave no trace, go, be no more, die.

2, annihilate, render null, nullify, abrogate, destroy, obliterate, extinguish, remove. See DESTRUCTION, KILLING.

Adjectives—**1,** nonexistent, null and void, negative, blank, missing, omitted, absent.

2, unreal, baseless, unsubstantial, imaginary, visionary, ideal, fabulous, legendary, chimerical, supposititious, vain.

3, unborn, uncreated, unbegotten, unconceived, unproduced, unmade.

4, annihilated, extinct, exhausted, perished, gone, lost, departed, defunct, dead.

Antonym, see EXISTENCE.

---

nonexpectation, *n.* See SURPRISE.

nonpayment, *n.* default, defalcation; insolvency, bankruptcy; unprofitableness; repudiation; reneging. *Slang,* welshing. See DEBT. *Ant.*, see PAYMENT.

nonpreparation, *n.* See NEGLECT. *Ant.*, see PREPARATION.

nonsense, *n.* absurdity, senselessness, silliness, trash, foolishness. See ABSURDITY.

nook, *n.* retreat, corner, cover, niche, recess. See ANGULARITY.

noon, *n.* noontime, midday, noonday, lunchtime. See MORNING.

noose, *n.* hitch, catch; loop, halter, ring, lariat, lasso. See CONNECTION.

normal, *adj.* ordinary, regular, average, usual, typical. See CONFORMITY. *Ant.*, see UNCONFORMITY.

north, *adj. & n.* northerly, northern, northward; arctic, polar.

nose, *n.* proboscis, snout, muzzle, beak; nasal organ, olfactory organ; nostrils. See ANIMAL.

nosegay, *n.* posy, bouquet, corsage. See FRAGRANCE.

notability, *n.* worthiness, achievement, position; celebrity, lion, dignitary. See NOBILITY.

notable, *adj.* celebrated, noteworthy, distinguished, renowned, famous, remarkable. See REPUTE.

notch, *n. & v.* —*n.* nick, cut, gash, score; groove, rut, pit, pock; cleft, dent, dint, indentation; dimple; defile, pass, gap, OPENING; hole, belt hole; saw, serra, tooth; crenel, scallop; embrasure, battlement, machicolation, castellation; tally, mark, degree, calibration, step, peg. —*v.t.* nick, cut, gash, score, dent, indent, jag; scarify; crimp, scallop; crenelate; tally, calibrate, mark (in degrees), peg.

note, *n. & v.* —*n.* letter, epistle, missive; acknowledgment, comment, reminder; observation, memo(randum), excerpt, notation; explanation, remark, annotation, abstract; distinction, fame; tone, sound, pitch. See ATTENTION, WRITING, INDICATION, INTERPRETATION, MUSIC, RECORD, REPUTE. —*v.t.* observe, notice, remark, attend, need, jot. See INTELLECT, MEMORY, WRITING.

noted, *adj.* famous, notable, eminent, distinguished, celebrated. See REPUTE. *Ant.*, see DISREPUTE.

noteworthy, *adj.* extraordinary, notable, remarkable, considerable, exceptional. See GREATNESS. *Ant.*, see LITTLENESS.

nothing, *n.* zero, cipher, nought, blank; nothingness; nonentity, bagatelle, trifle. See UNIMPORTANCE, INSUBSTANTIALITY. *Ant.*, see IMPORTANCE, SUBSTANCE.

notice, *n. & v.t.* —*n.* ATTENTION, observation, recognition, perception; circular, poster, bulletin; placard, announcement; warning, sign; considera-

tion. See PUBLICATION, INFORMATION, RESPECT. —*v.t.* see, observe, perceive, regard, heed, detect, recognize, note. See ATTENTION, CARE.

noticeable, *adj.* striking, conspicuous, perceptible, prominent, observable. See GREATNESS. *Ant.*, see LITTLENESS.

notify, *v.* inform, warn, apprise, advise, tell, acquaint. See ADVICE, INFORMATION.

notion, *n.* IDEA, THOUGHT, opinion; fancy, caprice, inclination; BELIEF, conception.

notoriety, *n.* flagrancy, blatancy, notoriousness, DISREPUTE.

notwithstanding, *adv. & prep.* —*adv.* nevertheless, although, however, yet. See COMPENSATION. —*prep.* despite, even.

nourish, *v.t.* nurture, sustain, feed, foster, support. See AID, FOOD.

nourishment, *n.* FOOD, nutrient, nutriment; sustenance.

novel, *n. & adj.* —*n.* story, book, romance, epic. See DESCRIPTION. —*adj.* new, unusual, different, remarkable, surprising, unique, unexpected. See NEWNESS.

novice, *n.* beginner, LEARNER, student, amateur, probationer, neophyte, apprentice; tyro, greenhorn. See BEGINNING, IGNORANCE. *Ant.*, see END, KNOWLEDGE.

now, *adv.* immediately, here, presently, today, yet.

noxious, *adj.* noisome, harmful, poisonous, injurious, deleterious, pernicious. See BADNESS. *Ant.*, see GOODNESS.

nozzle, *n.* spout, outlet, vent, valve, faucet, nose, OPENING.

nucleus, *n.* center, heart, core, kernel; basis, foundation. See CENTRALITY.

nude, *adj.* naked, stripped, bare, unclad, unclothed, exposed. *Colloq.*, raw. See DIVESTMENT. *Ant.*, see CLOTHING.

nudge, *n. & v.t.* —*n.* push, TOUCH, jolt, poke, contact. —*v.t.* poke, push, TOUCH, jog, remind. See INDICATION.

nugatory, *adj.* useless, ineffectual, worthless, futile; helpless. See IMPOTENCE, UNIMPORTANCE. *Ant.*, see POWER, IMPORTANCE.

nuisance, *n.* pest, annoyance, irritation, bore, bother. See PAIN. *Ant.*, see PLEASURE.

NULLIFICATION [756]

Nouns—nullification, abrogation, annulment, cancellation, revocation, repeal, rescission, defeasance, renege; dismissal, deposal, deposition, dethronement, disestablishment, disendowment, deconsecration; abolition, abolishment, dissolution; counterorder, countermand, denial, repudiation, recantation, retroaction; *nolle prosequi;* thumbs down, veto.

Verbs—**1,** abrogate, annul, cancel, destroy, abolish, revoke, repeal, reverse, retract, recall, overrule, override, set aside, dissolve, quash, nullify, invalidate, nol-pros, declare null and void, disestablish, disendow, deconsecrate.
2, disclaim, deny, ignore, repudiate, record, break off.
3, countermand, counterorder, do away with, throw overboard, throw to the dogs, scatter to the winds.
4, dismiss, discharge, discard, cast off, out, aside, away, *or* adrift; get rid of. *Slang*, fire, sack, bounce; send packing; give the gate *or* the boot *or* one's walking papers; give the pink slip.
5, depose, divest of office, cashier, displace, break, oust, unseat, unsaddle, dethrone, unfrock, ungown, disbar, disbench.
Antonym, see AFFIRMATION.

nullity, *n.* NEGATION, invalidation, annihilation, obliteration, blankness, nothingness. *Ant.*, see AFFIRMATION.

numb, *adj. & v.* —*adj.* unfeeling; deadened; frozen, benumbed; dazed, shocked; an(a)esthetized, narcotized, drugged, paralyzed; dull, torpid, insensitive; desensitized; lifeless. —*v.t.* deaden, benumb, freeze; narcotize, drug, desensitize; stupefy, paralyze. See INSENSIBILITY, COLD. *Ant.*, see SENSIBILITY, FEELING.

NUMBER [84]

Nouns—**1,** number, symbol, numeral, figure, cipher, digit, integer, counter, round number, formula, function, series.

2, total, amount, quantity, sum, DIFFERENCE, product, multiplier, multiplicand, coefficient, dividend, divisor, factor, quotient, subtrahend, FRACTION, mixed number, numerator, denominator, decimal, reciprocal; Arabic *and* Roman numbers *or* numerals.

3, ratio, proportion, PROGRESSION; arithmetical *or* geometrical progression, percentage.

4, power, root, exponent, index, logarithm, differential, integral.

Verbs—number, numerate, count. See NUMERATION.

Adjectives—numeral, numerable, divisible, reciprocal, whole, prime, fractional, decimal, proportional; Arabic, Roman; exponential, algebraic, logarithmic, differential, integral, positive, negative; rational, irrational; radical, real, imaginary, impossible; approximate, round; exact; perfect.

NUMERATION [85]

Nouns—**1,** numeration, numbering, counting, tally, enumeration, pagination, summation, reckoning, computation, calculation, cybernetics, MEASUREMENT; statistics, poll, census, roll call, recapitulation.

2, mathematics; arithmetic, algebra, trigonometry, (differential, integral) calculus; addition, subtraction, multiplication, division; equation; (square, cube) root; exponent, prime; reduction, approximation, differentiation, integration.

3, abacus, logometer, slide rule, table, Napier's rods, logarithm, log, antilogarithm; calculator, calculating machine, adder, adding machine, cash register; computer, electronic computer *or* brain, punch-card machine, Univac (*T.N.*). *Slang,* magic brain.

5, mathematician, arithmetician, calculator, abacist, algebraist, statistician.

6, UNITY; duality, dualism, biformity; triality, trinity; quaternity.

7, duplication, duplicate; triplication, triplicate; trebleness, trine; quadruplication, quadruplicate, *etc.*

8, bisection, bipartition, halving; trisection, tripartition; quadrisection, quadripartition, quartering, quarter; quinquesection; decimation.

9, one, single, unity, ace; two, deuce, couple, brace, pair, binomial, square; three, trey, triad, triplet, trio, trinomial, third power, cube; four, tetrad, quartet, quaternion; five, quintet; six, sextet, half-a-dozen; seven, septet; eight, octet; nine, ennead; ten, decade, decad; twelve, dozen; twenty, score; hundred, century, centenary; thousand, million, billion, trillion. See ZERO.

Verbs—**1,** number, count, tell, tally, enumerate, muster, poll, count noses, recapitulate; score, cipher, compute, calculate, sum up, total, add, subtract, multiply, divide.

2, check, prove, demonstrate, balance, audit, take stock.

3, double, couple, pair, yoke; triple, treble, triplicate, cube; quadruplicate.

4, bisect, halve, trisect, quarter, decimate.

Adjectives—**1,** numeral, numerical, arithmetical, analytic, algebraic, statistical, numerable, computable.

2, one, first, annual, single, unique; two, second, double, duplicate, twain, dual, biannual, biennial, binary, binomial, twin, duplex; three, third, triple, treble, triform, trinary, trinal, trinomial, tertiary, trine, triplicate, threefold; four, fourth, quadruple, quadruplicate, quarter, quaternary, quaternal, quadratic; five, fifth, quintuple, quinary; sixth, sextuple; eight, octuple; tenth, decimal, tenfold; twelfth, dozenth, duodenary; hundredth, centennial, centenary, centuplicate; thousandth, millennial.

3, bisected, bipartite, bifid; trisected, tripartite, trifid; quartered, quadripartite; quinquepartite, quinquefid; octifid; tenth, decimal, tithe; twelfth, duodecimal; sixtieth, sexagesimal; sexagenary; hundredth, centesimal; thousandth, millesimal.

Adverbs—twice, doubly; thrice, trebly, triply, thirdly; fourthly.

Prepositions—plus, minus, times.

---

numerous, *adj.* many, myriad, multitudinous, plentiful, numberless, various, thick. See MULTITUDE. *Ant.,* see RARITY.

nun, *n.* sister, ecclesiastic, *religieuse* (*Fr.*). See CLERGY.

nuptial, *adj. & n.* —*adj.* connubial, bridal. —*n.pl.* MARRIAGE, wedding.

nurse, *n. & v.t.* —*n.* attendant, nursemaid; *Colloq.,* nanny. —*v.t.* foster,

tend, serve, cherish; suckle; entertain, manage. See REMEDY.
nurture, *v.t.* sustain, support, feed, nourish; foster, cherish; educate, train, rear. See AID, PREPARATION.
nut, *n.* kernel, stone, nutmeat; seed, core. See FOOD.
nutritious, *adj.* nutritive, wholesome, digestible, nourishing. See FOOD, HEALTH.
nymph, *n.* dryad, naiad, houri, undine. See MYTHICAL DEITIES.

O

oaf, *n.* FOOL, dullard, dunce, blockhead, idiot. *Slang,* dope, jerk.
oath, *n.* curse, epithet, expletive, imprecation, profanity; pledge, bond. See AFFIRMATION, IMPRECATION.
obdurate, *adj.* flinty, adamant, unyielding, inflexible; stubborn, adamantine, hardened, unshakable, unfeeling; firm. See HARDNESS, RESOLUTION. *Ant.,* see SOFTNESS.

OBEDIENCE [743]

Nouns—**1,** obedience, compliance; SUBMISSION, submissiveness, SUBJECTION; nonresistance; passiveness, passivity, resignation, malleability, tractability, ductility; acquiescence, obsequiousness, SERVILITY.
2, allegiance, loyalty, fealty, homage, deference, devotion.
Verbs—obey, comply, SUBMIT; observe, respect, abide by, meet, fulfill, carry out; perform, satisfy, discharge; kneel or bow to, kowtow, salaam, make an obeisance; resign oneself, grin and bear it, make a virtue of necessity; be at the beck and call of, do one's bidding, do what one is told, serve (see SERVANT).
Adjectives—obedient, observant, acquiescent, complying, compliant; loyal, faithful, devoted; at one's call, at one's command, at one's orders, at one's beck and call; tame, tamed, under control; restrainable; resigned, passive; tractable, docile, submissive; henpecked; pliant, unresisting.
Adverbs—obediently, etc.; in compliance with, in obedience to; as you please, if you please.

Antonym, see DISOBEDIENCE.

obeisance, *n.* homage, deference, obedience; bow, salaam, kowtow, curts(e)y, genuflection; prostration. See COURTESY, OBEDIENCE.
obese, *n.* fat, overweight, stout, plump, fleshy, bulky; corpulent, ponderous, adipose, HEAVY.
object, *n. & v.i.* —*n.* thing, item; goal, aim, purpose, objective. —*v.i.* disapprove, demur, challenge, protest, resist, kick. *Slang,* beef, gripe. See OPPOSITION.
objection, *n.* remonstrance, protest; drawback, criticism; barrier, obstacle; exception, protestation. See DISAPPROBATION, HINDRANCE. *Ant.,* see APPROBATION, AID.
objectionable, *adj.* censurable, culpable; unpleasant, undesirable, obnoxious, offensive, harmful. See DISAPPROBATION.
objective, *adj. & n.* —*adj.* not subjective; unemotional, unprejudiced, unbiased, impersonal. See INDIFFERENCE. —*n.* object, goal, aim, ambition. See DESIRE.
obligation, *n.* DUTY, PROMISE; debt; AGREEMENT, bond, incumbency, responsibility, liability, indebtedness; contract, mortgage.
obligatory, *adj.* compulsory, imperative, necessary, unavoidable. See DUTY.
oblige, *v.* compel, force, constrain, bind, impel; accommodate, favor, assist, gratify, please. See AID, COMPULSION.
obliging, *adj.* accommodating, helpful, considerate, serviceable, kind, gracious. See COURTESY. *Ant.,* see DISCOURTESY.

OBLIQUITY [217]

Nouns—**1,** obliquity, obliqueness, DEVIATION, divergence; inclination, slope, slant; crookedness; leaning; bevel, tilt; bias, list, twist, swag, cant, DISTOR-

TION; bend (see CURVATURE); ANGULARITY; tower of Pisa; indirectness.

2, acclivity, rise, ascent, gradient, upgrade, rising ground, hill, bank; steepness, diagonality; cliff, precipice (see VERTICAL); escarpment, scarp; declivity, downhill, dip, fall, ascent, descent.

3, clinometer; sine, cosine, angle, hypotenuse; diagonal; zigzag; talus.

Verbs—**1,** be oblique, diverge, deviate; slope, slant, lean, incline, shelve, stoop; decline, descend; bend, heel, careen, sag, slough, cant, sidle.

2, render oblique; sway, bias; slope, slant; incline, bend, crook; cant, tilt; distort (see DISTORTION).

Adjectives—**1,** oblique, inclined; sloping, tilted, recumbent, clinal, askew, aslant, indirect, wry, awry, crooked; knockkneed, distorted (see DISTORTION); beveled, out of the perpendicular; diagonal; transverse, CROSSING, athwart, antiparallel; curved (see CURVATURE).

2, uphill, rising, ascending, acclivitous; downhill, falling, descending; declining, anticlinal; steep, sheer, abrupt, precipitous, breakneck; not straight, not true.

Adverbs—obliquely, diagonally; on one side; askew, askant, askance, edgewise; out of plumb; at an angle; sidelong, sideways; slopewise, slantwise; by a side wind; out of kilter.

Antonym, see PARALLEL, STRAIGHT, DIRECTION.

---

obliterate, *v.t.* efface, erase, expunge, cancel; blot out, take out, rub, sponge *or* scratch out; dele, delete, strike out, wipe out, wash out; wipe *or* rub off; wipe away; deface, render illegible; leave no trace. See DESTRUCTION, OBLIVION, ABSENCE. *Ant.,* see RECORD, PRESENCE.

OBLIVION [506]

Nouns—oblivion, obliviousness, forgetfulness, obliteration (of the past); INSENSIBILITY; amnesia, failure *or* lapse of memory; waters of Lethe, waters of oblivion, nepenthe; limbo.

Verbs—forget, be forgetful, fall, sink *or* fade into oblivion; have on the tip of one's tongue; come in at one ear and go out the other; misremember; unlearn, efface, obliterate; think no more of; put behind one; let the dead bury the dead; let bygones be bygones (see FORGIVENESS); slip *or* escape the memory; fade; lose, lose sight of. *Colloq.,* file and forget.

Adjectives—oblivious, forgetful, mindless, nepenthean, Lethean; forgotten, unremembered, past recollection, bygone, buried *or* sunk in oblivion; clean forgotten; gone out of one's head.

Adverbs—in limbo; out of sight, out of mind.

Antonym, see MEMORY.

---

obnoxious, *adj.* repulsive, loathsome, hateful, offensive, odious. See HATE. *Ant.,* see PLEASURE.

obscene, *adj.* foul, lewd, dirty, indecent, coarse, smutty. See IMPURITY. *Ant.,* see PURITY.

obscurity, *n.* dimness, DARKNESS, gloom, CLOUDINESS, obscureness, obscuration; ambiguity, abstruseness, mysteriousness; indefiniteness, inexactness; unintelligibility, vagueness, unclearness; humbleness, lowliness; namelessness, privacy, retirement, SECLUSION; remoteness. See SECRET, CONCEALMENT. *Ant.,* see LIGHT, EVIDENCE, REPUTE.

obsequies, *n.pl.* funeral, burial. See INTERMENT.

obsequious, *adj.* abject, fawning, sycophantic, cringing, subservient, truckling, compliant. See SERVILITY. *Ant.,* see INSOLENCE.

observance, *n.* performance, compliance; OBEDIENCE; fulfillment, satisfaction, discharge; acquittance, acquittal; adhesion; acknowledgment; fidelity; orthodoxy, ceremony, RITE, punctilio, protocol. See CELEBRATION, CARE. *Ant.,* see NEGLECT, IRRELIGION.

observation, *n.* notice, perception, regard; comment, consideration, remark. See AFFIRMATION, ATTENTION. *Ant.,* see NEGATION, NEGLECT.

observe, *v.* see (see VISION); comply with, RESPECT, acknowledge, abide by; obey, cling to, adhere to, be faithful to, meet, fulfil(l); carry out, carry into execution; execute, perform, keep, satisfy, discharge, do one's duty; perform, fulfil(l) *or* discharge an obligation; acquit oneself; perform an office; keep one's word *or* promise; keep faith with; officiate. See CELE-BRATION, CARE. *Ant.*, see NEGLECT.

obsess, *v.t.* haunt, beset, besiege. See FEAR.

obsolescence, *n.* disuse, disappearance; antiquity. See OLDNESS. *Ant.*, see NEWNESS.

obsolete, *adj.* past, extinct, outworn, disused, discarded, antiquated, dead. See OLDNESS. *Ant.*, see NEWNESS.

obstacle, *n.* HINDRANCE, DIFFICULTY, OPPOSITION, barrier, obstruction, snag, impediment; barrage; baffle. *Ant.*, see AID, FACILITY, COÖPERATION.

obstinacy, *n.* obstinateness, tenacity; stubbornness; perseverance; doggedness; immovability; inflexibility, HARDNESS; obduracy, obduration, insistence, RESOLUTION, selfwill, will of iron; contumacy, pigheadedness, perversity; wil(l)fulness, intractability; bigotry, intolerance, dogmatism; bias, fixed idea, fanaticism, zealotry, monomania. *Colloq.*, cussedness. *Ant.*, see DOUBT, SOFTNESS, MODERATION.

obstreperous, *adj.* noisy, troublesome, clamorous, recalcitrant, riotous, vociferous. See VIOLENCE. *Ant.*, see MODERATION.

obstruct, *v.t.* block, stop, impede, choke, retard, clog; occlude, shut; dam, foul; barricade, blockade; check, hedge; overgrow; encumber. See HINDRANCE. *Ant.*, see AID.

obtain, *v.t.* acquire, get, procure, gain, secure, attain. See ACQUISITION, SECURITY. *Ant.*, see LOSS.

obtainable, *adj.* attainable, procurable, accessible. See CHANCE, ACQUISITION.

obtrude, *v.* intrude, thrust, interfere.

obvious, *adj.* manifest, patent, clear, evident, plain; undisguised, unconcealed. See EVIDENCE. *Ant.*, see CONCEALMENT.

OCCASION [134]

Nouns—occasion, opportunity, OPENING, room; CIRCUMSTANCE, EVENT; opportuneness; crisis, turn, juncture, psychological moment, conjuncture; turning point; given time; nick of time; chance of a lifetime; golden opportunity; clear field; spare time; LEISURE.

Verbs—seize an opportunity; suit the occasion; strike while the iron is hot; make hay while the sun shines, take time by the forelock; take the bull by the horns. *Slang*, get the jump on, jump the gun.

Adjectives—opportune, timely, well-timed, seasonable; providential, lucky, fortunate, happy, favorable, propitious, auspicious, critical; apropos, suitable (see AGREEMENT).

Adverbs—opportunely, *etc.*; in proper time, in due time, course *or* season; for the nonce; in the nick of time, in the fullness of time; just in time, at the eleventh hour; now or never; by the way, by the by; *en passant, à propos;* parenthetically, while on the subject; *ex tempore;* on the spur of the moment; on the spot (see EARLINESS); when the coast is clear.

Antonym, see LATENESS.

occult, *adj.* mystic, mysterious, supernatural, SECRET, hidden.

occupant, *n.* possessor, tenant, lodger, transient, occupier, INHABITANT, roomer, holder.

occupation, *n.* tenure, occupancy, holding, tenancy; habitation; work, trade, BUSINESS, employment, calling, profession, pursuit. See POSSESSION.

occupy, *v.t.* hold, inhabit, keep, fill, tenant, have; take, beset, garrison; interest, engage, engross, busy; employ. See BUSINESS.

occur, *v.* happen; take place, take effect; come, become of; come off, come about, come to pass, pass, present itself; fall; fall out, turn out; hap, befall, betide, bechance; prove, eventuate, turn up, crop up; arrive, ensue, arise, start, take its course; meet with; come to mind; experience. See CIRCUMSTANCE.

occurrence, *n.* eventuality; event, incident, happening; affair, episode; transaction, proceeding, fact; matter of fact; phenomenon; advent; BUSINESS, concern; CIRCUMSTANCE, particular, casualty, accident, adventure, PASSAGE, crisis, pass, emergency, contingency, consequence. *Colloq.*, happenstance, goings-on.

ocean, *n.* sea, great sea, high seas; salt water, deep water, blue water; the [bounding] main, the [briny] deep; the Seven Seas; the big pond, the ditch; the big sea water; the South Seas, the frozen seas; the billow, wave, tide *or* flood; the deep blue sea, wine-dark sea; Father Neptune, Poseidon; the watery waste. See WATER. *Ant.*, see LAND.

ocular, *adj.* optic, visual; retinal, conjunctival; perceptible, visible. See VISION.

odd, *adj.* strange, unusual, unnatural; curious, quaint, queer, bizarre, droll; singular, single; unmatched, unpaired, lone; extra, left. See REMAINDER, ABSURDITY.

oddity, *n.* curiosity, freak; singularity, strangeness, peculiarity; quaintness, eccentricity, oddness; crank, eccentric. See INSANITY, UNCONFORMITY. *Ant.*, see SANITY, CONFORMITY.

odds, *n.* DIFFERENCE, PROBABILITY, advantage; disparity. See CHANCE. *Ant.*, see EQUALITY.

odious, *adj.* disgusting, repulsive, detestable, offensive, loathsome, hateful. See PAIN. *Ant.*, see PLEASURE.

ODOR [398]

Nouns—odor, odorousness, smell, scent, effluvium; emanation, exhalation; fume, essence, trail, redolence; pungency, FRAGRANCE; sense of smell, olfaction; act of smelling. See MALODOROUSNESS.

Verbs—**1,** have an odor, smell of, smell, exhale; give out a smell; scent, reek, stink.

2, smell, scent; snuff, snuff up; sniff; nose, inhale; get wind of.

Adjectives—odorous, odoriferous; smelling, strong-smelling; strong-scented; redolent, aromatic, fragrant, pungent; reeking; olfactory.

---

offense, *n.* insult, affront, DISCOURTESY; aggression, ATTACK; transgression, fault, crime, sin, WRONG, EVIL.

offer, *n. & v.* —*n.* proffer; presentation; tender, bid; overture; proposal, proposition; MOTION; invitation; candidacy, offering. —*v.* proffer, present, tender; bid; propose, move; make a motion; make an offer, make advances; invite; put forward; offer for sale; press; lay at one's feet; offer *or* present oneself; volunteer, come forward; stand for; bid for; seek; bribe. See GIVING, SALE. *Ant.*, see REQUEST.

offering, *n.* bid, proposal, proposition; offertory, gift, sacrifice; overture, advance. See GIVING. *Ant.*, see RECEIVING, REFUSAL.

offhand, *adv. & adj.* —*adv.* casually, impromptu, extemporaneously; abruptly, carelessly. —*adj.* casual, abrupt, extemporaneous, careless; unpremeditated, unplanned. See IMPULSE.

office, *n.* headquarters, department, bureau, room, branch; position, status, rank, function; post, job, duty, service. See AGENCY, BUSINESS.

officer, *n.* policeman; functionary, official, bureaucrat; president, vice-president, secretary, treasurer; registrar; mayor, governor. See AUTHORITY, BUSINESS.

official, *n. & adj.* —*n.* officer, functionary, dignitary. *Ant.*, see SERVANT. —*adj.* authoritative, functional, authentic, authorized. See AUTHORITY.

officialism, *n.* AUTHORITY, officiality, bureaucracy; red tape.

officiate, *v.* preside, serve, supervise, direct, function. See BUSINESS, RITE.

officious, *adj.* interfering, meddlesome, obtrusive, pushing, presumptuous; bossy. See ACTIVITY. *Ant.*, see INACTIVITY.

officiousness, *n.* interference, presumption, meddlesomeness, inquisitiveness, prying, meddling. See ACTIVITY. *Ant.*, see INACTIVITY.

offset, *v.t.* neutralize, balance, counteract, cancel, counterbalance, counterpoise.

offshoot, *n.* ramification, incidental, result; branch, shoot, sprout; scion. See ADDITION.

offspring, *n.* child, children, young, sons, daughters, progeny, descendants. See POSTERITY. *Ant.*, see ANCESTRY.

often, *adv.* ofttime(s), oftentimes, frequently, repeatedly, recurrently, oft. See FREQUENCY. *Ant.*, see RARITY.

oil, *n. & v.* —*n.* petroleum; olein(e); fat, grease; ointment; lubricant;

unguent; olive, cooking, corn, salad, peanut *or* cottonseed oil; butter, oleomargarine, margarine; fish oil, cod liver oil, castor oil; lard, tallow, suet, blubber; petrol, gas, gasoline, kerosene, fuel oil, coal oil, diesel oil, *etc.;* oil paint; oil painting; volatile oils, fixed oils; lotion, suntan oil; flattery, blandishment, unctuousness, unction; slickness, SMOOTHNESS; bribery. *Slang,* soft soap, banana oil. —*v.* LUBRICATE, grease; anele, anoint; butter, smear. *Colloq.,* bribe, tip, grease the palm; flatter, butter up, softsoap. *Ant.,* see FRICTION, ROUGHNESS.

oiliness, *n.* greasiness, fattiness; unctuousness. *Ant.,* see ROUGHNESS.

oily, *adj.* smooth, unctuous, plausible; fatty, oleose, greasy, oleaginous.

ointment, *n.* unguent, balm, pomade, salve, cream. See REMEDY.

OLDNESS [124]

Nouns—**1,** oldness, AGE, antiquity; maturity; decline, decay, senility; seniority, eldership; primogeniture.

2, archaism; relic (of the past); antiquities, fossils, prehistoric animal; antiquarianism.

3, tradition, prescription, custom, immemorial usage, common law.

Verbs—be old; have had *or* seen its day; whiten; turn gray *or* white; become old, AGE, fade, obsolesce, senesce.

Adjectives—**1,** old, older, oldest, eldest, ancient, antique; of long standing, time-honored, venerable, hoary; senior, elder, eldest; first-born.

2, prime; primitive, primeval, primordial, primordinate; aboriginal (see BEGINNING); diluvian, antediluvian; prehistoric, patriarchal, preadamite; fossil, paleozoic, preglacial, antemundane.

3, archaic, classic, medieval, pre-Raphaelite; immemorial, traditional, prescriptive, customary; inveterate, rooted; antiquated, obsolete, of other times, of the old school, out of date, out of fashion; stale, old-fashioned, dated, superannuated, behind the times; exploded; gone out, gone by; passé, run out; senile (see AGE); timeworn; crumbling (see DETERIORATION); extinct; secondhand; old as the hills, old as Methuselah, old as history. *Colloq.,* back-number, hasbeen; old-fangled, corny.

Antonym, see NEWNESS.

Old Testament, see SACRED WRITINGS.

omen, *n.* WARNING, foreboding; sign, significance, portent; PREDICTION, straw in the wind; INDICATION, harbinger, token, foretoken; prognostication, soothsaying, augury, prophecy, foreshadowing; presage; evil omen, good omen.

ominous, *adj.* foreboding, inauspicious; prophetic; significant, bodeful, doomful, fateful; unlucky, ill-omened, ill-fated; WARNING, prognosticating; unpropitious, unfavorable. See PREDICTION, NECESSITY. *Ant.,* see HOPE.

omission, *n.* EXCLUSION, exception, elimination, cut; FAILURE, NEGLECT, DERELICTION; apostrophe, ellipsis; deficit, shortage; evasion. *Ant.,* see COMPLETION.

omit, *v.t.* NEGLECT, skip, spare, overlook; delete, remove, reject; evade, except, exclude, miss, drop; pass, forget. *Ant.,* see CARE.

omnipotence, *n.* almightiness, infinite power. See DEITY, POWER.

omniscient, *adj.* all-seeing, all-knowing. See KNOWLEDGE.

omnivorous, *adj.* devouring, all-consuming, gluttonous, eating everything. See FOOD.

on, *adv. & prep.* —*adv.* forward, onward, ahead. See PROGRESSION. —*prep.* upon, at.

once, *adv.* formerly, previously, latterly. See TIME.

one, *adj.* individual, sole, only, solitary, single. See NUMERATION.

onerous, *adj.* difficult, troublesome, burdensome, wearing, oppressive; discouraging.

one-sided, *adj.* unfair, biased, partial; prejudiced; unbalanced, lopsided, asymmetric, awry; unilateral. See DISTORTION, MISJUDGMENT, SIDE.

onlooker, *n.* SPECTATOR, observer, watcher, viewer, witness, bystander; nonparticipant.

only, *adv. & adj.* —*adv.* solely, singly, exclusively, merely, but. —*adj.* sole, solitary, apart, alone, unique. See NUMERATION.

ooze, *v.* seep, leak, filter; drip, percolate. See EGRESS.

opacity, *n.* opaqueness, nontransparency, DIMNESS, filminess, CLOUDINESS. See DARKNESS. *Ant.*, see TRANSPARENT, VISION.

opaque, *adj.* nontransparent, adiaphanous, dim; filmy, cloudy; obscure, unintelligible, obtuse. See DIMNESS, CLOUDINESS. *Ant.*, TRANSPARENT.

OPENING [260]

Nouns—**1**, opening, hole, foramen; aperture, hiatus, yawning, oscitancy, dehiscence, pandiculation; chasm (see INTERVAL).

2, puncture, perforation, interstice, terebration; pinhole, keyhole, loophole, porthole, peephole, pigeonhole; eye, eyelet, slot, oriel; porousness, porosity.

3, outlet, inlet; vent, vomitory; embouchure; crater, orifice, mouth, sucker, muzzle, throat, gullet; pore; nozzle.

4, door, doorway, entrance, entry, portal, porch, gate, ostiary, postern, wicket, trapdoor, hatch; arcade; gateway, hatchway, gangway; embrasure, window, casement, LIGHT; skylight, fanlight; lattice.

5, way, path, thoroughfare; CHANNEL, PASSAGE, tube, pipe; vessel, tubule, canal, gutter, fistula; chimney, flue, tap, funnel, gully, tunnel, main; mine, pit, adit, shaft; gallery, alley, aisle, glade, vista, bay window, bow window; dormer, lantern; bore, caliber.

6, sieve, screen, colander; honeycomb; NOTCH, cleft, embrasure.

7, opener, key, skeleton key, passkey, master key; passe-partout; latch; passport, password, pass; can opener; punch.

Verbs—**1**, open, gape, gap, yawn, bilge; fly open; ope (*Poet.*).

2, perforate, pierce, tap, bore, drill; mine; tunnel; transfix; enfilade, impale, spike, spear, gore, spit, stab, pink, puncture, lance, stick, prick, riddle, punch; stave in; cut a passage through, make way for, make room for, open up *or* out; cut, expose, lay open, break open, breach, broach.

Adjectives—open; perforate(d), wide open, ajar; unclosed, unstopped; ope (*Poet.*), oscitant, gaping, yawning, patent; tubular, cannular, fistulous; pervious, permeable; foraminous; vesicular, vascular; porous, follicular, honeycombed; notched, nicked, crenate; infundibular, riddled; tubulous, tubulated; opening; aperient.

Antonym, see CLOSURE.

operate, *v.* CONDUCT, manage, direct, go, run, work, function, act. See ACTION, AGENCY.

operative, *adj.* effective; operating, acting, working, functioning, effectual. See AGENCY.

opiate, *n.* narcotic, palliative, drug, sedative, tranquillizer, analgesic. See MODERATION, REMEDY.

opinion, *n.* IDEA, THOUGHT, BELIEF, conviction; theory, JUDGMENT, view; MOTION, mind, tenet, dogma; verdict; speculation, apprehension; public opinion, poll, survey.

opinionated, *adj.* convinced; unconvincible, bigoted, dogmatic, prejudiced, hidebound, positive. See RESOLUTION, MISJUDGMENT. *Ant.*, see FREEDOM.

opponent, *n.* antagonist, adversary; OPPOSITION; enemy, foe, assailant, oppositionist, disputant, rival, competitor. *Ant.*, see AID.

opportune, *adj.* fortuitous, timely, seasonable, felicitous, suitable, apt, apropos. See OCCASION. *Ant.*, see EARLINESS, LATENESS.

opportunity, *n.* OPENING; OCCURRENCE; CHANCE, OCCASION; SPACE, scope, PLACE; leisure.

oppose, *v.t.* contrast, confront; combat, counter, resist, hinder; contradict, refute, cross; repel, withstand; obstruct; contravene. See OPPOSITION. *Ant.*, see AID.

OPPOSITION [708]

Nouns—**1**, opposition, antagonism, antipathy; ENMITY, dislike, HATE; oppugnancy, oppugnation; impugnation; contravention, contradiction; counteraction; counterplot; crossfire, undercurrent, riptide, undertow, headwind; clashing, collision, conflict, cross-talk; competition, rivalry, emulation, race; RESISTANCE, RESTRAINT, HINDRANCE, CONTRARINESS.

2, opposition, contraposition, polarity; INVERSION; opposite side, reverse, inverse; counterpart; antipodes; opposite poles; north and south; heads or tails; anode and cathode.

3, insurrection, rebellion, riot; strike, lockout, walkout; boycott.

Verbs—**1,** oppose, counteract, run counter to, withstand, resist, counter, restrain (see RESTRAINT); hinder (see HINDRANCE); antagonize, oppugn, fly in the face of, kick against, fall foul of; set against, pit against; DEFY, face, confront, cope with; make a stand, make a stand against; protest against, vote against, raise one's voice against; disfavor, turn one's back upon; set at naught, slap in the face, slam the door in one's face; freeze out; be at cross purposes, play at cross purposes; thwart.

2, stem, breast, encounter; stem *or* breast the tide, current *or* flood; beat up against; grapple with; contend (see CONTENTION); do battle (see WARFARE); contradict, contravene; belie; run against, beat against; militate against; come in conflict with; emulate, compete, rival, vie with.

3, be opposite, oppose, juxtapose, contrapose; subtend.

Adjectives—**1,** opposing, opposed; adverse, antagonistic; contrary; at variance (see DISAGREEMENT); at issue, at war with; unfavorable, unfriendly; hostile, inimical, cross, unpropitious; up in arms; resistant; competitive, emulous.

2, opposite; reverse, inverse; antipodal, fronting, facing, diametrically opposite.

Adverbs—contrarily, conversely; *vice versa;* at cross purposes; against the grain; against the current, stream, wind *or* tide; with a head wind; in spite, in despite, in defiance; in the way of, in the teeth of, in the face of; across; athwart.

Prepositions—over, against; over *or* up against; face to face, *vis-à-vis:* counter to, in conflict with; *versus, contra.*

Antonyms, see COÖPERATION, SIDE.

---

oppress, *v.t.* persecute, burden, crush, afflict, grieve, load, depress; overbear, compress, overtax, overburden; tyrannize. See GRAVITY, MALEVOLENCE. *Ant.,* see BENEVOLENCE.

oppressive, *adj.* tyrannical, cruel, burdensome, onerous, hard, grinding, grievous. See GRAVITY, SEVERITY. *Ant.,* see LIGHT.

opprobrious, *adj.* abusive, insulting, offensive, slanderous, derogatory, contemptuous, malicious. See DETRACTION, ATTACK, DISCOURTESY.

OPTICAL INSTRUMENTS [445]

Nouns—**1,** optical instruments, lens; spectacles, glasses, bifocals, pince nez, eyeglass, monocle, lorgnette, goggles; Polaroid lenses, contact lenses; sunglasses; spyglass, magnifying glass; opera glass, fieldglass, binoculars; glass eye; telescope, periscope, spectroscope, microscope; optics, optometry. *Slang,* specs, cheaters.

2, mirror, looking glass, pierglass, cheval glass; reflection.

3, camera, camera lucida, camera obscura; motion-picture camera; kinescope, television camera; stereoscope, stereopticon, viewer, magic lantern, kaleidoscope; projector.

4, optometrist; lens grinder; oculist, optician; microscopist, *etc.*

5, electric eye, photoelectric cell.

---

optimism, *n.* hopefulness, CHEERFULNESS, encouragement, brightness, enthusiasm; confidence, assurance. *Ant.,* PESSIMISM.

optional, *adj.* discretionary, voluntary, elective, nonobligatory. See CHOICE. *Ant.,* see REFUSAL.

oracle, *n.* prophet, seer, soothsayer, augur, fortune-teller, witch; sibyl; Delphic oracle; Sphinx, Cassandra, sorcerer, interpreter. See PREDICTION.

oral, *adj.* verbal, vocal, spoken, unwritten. See SPEECH.

orally, *adv.* aloud, vocally. See SPEECH.

orange, see COLOR.

oration, *n.* SPEECH, declamation, oration, discourse, address.

oratory, *n.* SPEECH, elocution, declamation, eloquence, expression.

orchestra, *n.* See MUSICAL INSTRUMENTS.

ordain, *v.* install, appoint, invest; decree, predestine, destine; frock. See CLERGY, COMMISSION. *Ant.*, see MANKIND.

ordeal, *n.* trial, strain, cross, tribulation, test.

order, *n.* orderliness; regularity; uniformity, symmetry; harmony; subordination; course, even tenor, routine; method; disposition; ARRANGEMENT, array; precision, system; ECONOMY, discipline; gradation, PROGRESSION; CONTINUITY; rank, PLACE. —*v.t.* make *or* restore order; make orderly, arrange, range, array; give an order, COMMAND, REQUEST; organize, regulate, regularize, systematize; classify; alphabetize, list. *Ant.*, see DISORDER.

orderly, *adj. & n.* —*adj.* regular; in order, in trim, in its proper place; neat, tidy, trig, spruce, well-regulated; correct, methodical; shipshape, businesslike, systematic. —*n.* aide, assistant, attendant; hospital *or* military assistant. See ARRANGEMENT, AID. *Ant.*, see DISORDER.

ordinance, *n.* law, regulation, ORDER, decree; appointment, DESTINY; rule, enactment. See COMMAND.

ordinary, *adj.* usual, medium, average, unremarkable, commonplace, regular, common; inferior, low; middling, second-rate; undistinguished. See CONFORMITY. *Ant.*, see UNCONFORMITY.

ordnance, *n.* guns, cannon, artillery. See ARMS.

organization, *n.* systematization, coördination, ARRANGEMENT, regimentation, classification, formation, structure, creation, set-up, PLAN, PRODUCTION. *Ant.*, see DISJUNCTION, destruction.

orgy, *n.* debauch, carouse, dissipation; rite; revelry, carousal. See DRUNKENNESS.

origin, *n.* BEGINNING, CAUSE, commencement; descent, source, fountainhead, derivation, rise.

original, *adj.* novel, unique; primary, initial; creative; earliest, primal, aboriginal; inventive. See BEGINNING, IMAGINATION, UNCONFORMITY. See END, CONFORMITY.

originate, *v.* start, invent, begin, inaugurate, initiate, CAUSE, proceed, spring. See BEGINNING, DESCENT, IMAGINATION.

ORNAMENT [577, 847]

Nouns—**1,** ornament, ornamentation, ornateness; adornment, decoration, embellishment.

2, garnish, polish, varnish, gilding, lacquer, enamel; cosmetics; ormolu.

3, pattern, diaper, powdering, paneling, lining, graining; detail, texture, richness; tracery, moulding, filet, flourish, fleur-de-lis, arabesque, fret, astragal, zigzag, acanthus, pilaster.

4, pargeting, embroidery; brocade, trocatelle, lace, fringe, trapping, border, edging, trimming; hanging, tapestry, arras.

5, wreath, festoon, garland, chaplet, flower, nosegay, bouquet, posy, lei; tassel, shoulderknot, epaulet, aiguillette, frog; star, rosette, bow; feather, plume, plumage, panache, aigrette, fine feathers.

6, jewelry, bijoutry; bijou, trinket, locket, necklace, bracelet, anklet, earring, carcanet, chain, chatelaine, brooch, pin, torque; slave bracelet, costume jewelry; gem, precious stone; diamond, brilliant, beryl, emerald, chalcedony, agate, heliotrope; girasol(e); onyx, sardonyx; garnet, lapis-lazuli, opal, peridot, chrysolite, sapphire, ruby; spinel, topaz; turquoise; zircon, jacinth, hyacinth, carbuncle, rhinestone, amethyst; pearl, coral.

7, finery, frippery, gewgaw, gimcrack, tinsel, spangle, clinquant, brummagem, pinchbeck, paste; gaudiness, VULGARITY.

8, illustration, illumination, vignette; headpiece, tailpiece, scroll, flowers, rhetoric, work of art.

Verbs—**1,** ornament, embellish, decorate, adorn, beautify, smarten; furbish, polish; gild, varnish, whitewash, enamel, japan, lacquer, paint, grain, enrich, silver, chrome.

2, garnish, trim, dizen, bedizen, prink, prank; trip out; deck, bedeck, dight, bedight, array; dress up, spangle, bespangle, powder, embroider, work; chase, emboss, fret; emblazon, illuminate; illustrate.

Adjectives—**1,** ornamented, beautified (see BEAUTY); ornate, rich, gilt, gilded; tasselated, festooned, ornamental, decorative, becoming, smart, gay, flowery, glittering; spangled.

2, pranked out, bedight, well-groomed, fresh as a daisy; in full dress *or* fashion, *en grande toilette;* in best bib and tucker, in Sunday best, showy, flashy; gaudy, garish; gorgeous. *Slang,* sporty, sharp; snazzy, Sunday-go-to-meeting; in glad rags, dressed to kill, all dressed up like a Christmas tree.

Antonym, see SIMPLENESS.

orthodoxy, *n.* See RELIGION.

OSCILLATION [314]

Nouns—oscillation; vibration, libration, pendulation, motion of a pendulum, nutation, undulation; pulsation, pulse; fluctuation; vacillation, wavering; irresolution, indecision, UNCERTAINTY; wave, swing, beat, shake, wag, see-saw, dance; alternation, reciprocation; coming and going; ebb and flow, flux and reflux, ups and downs; CHANGEABLENESS.

Verbs—oscillate; vibrate, librate, reciprocate, alternate, undulate, wave; rock, swing; pulsate, beat; wag; tick; play; fluctuate, dance, curvet, reel, quake; quiver, quaver; shake, flicker; wriggle; roll, toss, pitch; flounder, stagger, totter; move up and down, bob up and down; pass and repass, ebb and flow, come and go; waver, teeter, seesaw, vacillate; hesitate, shilly-shally, hem and haw, blow hot and cold.

Adjectives—oscillating, oscillatory, undulatory, pulsatory, libratory; vibratory, pendulous; wavering, fluctuating, IRRESOLUTE.

Adverbs—to and fro, up and down, backward and forward, seesaw, zigzag, in and out, from side to side.

Antonym, see INACTIVITY, REPOSE.

ostensible, *adj.* apparent, outward; professed, pretended. See APPEARANCE.

OSTENTATION [882]

Nouns—**1,** ostentation, ostentatiousness, display, show, flourish, parade; pomp, array, STATE, solemnity, flourish; dash, splash, glitter, strut, bombast, pomposity; tinsel, tawdriness; pretense, pretension, pretentiousness; airs, showing off; veneer, façade, gloss; magnificence, splendor; AFFECTATION, VANITY, ORNAMENT, VULGARITY. *Colloq.,* dog, swank. *Slang,* side, front, ritz, ritziness.

2, pageant, pageantry, DEMONSTRATION, exhibition, flying colors, tomfoolery; flourish *or* fanfare of trumpets; spectacle, procession; fête, gala, field day, review, march, promenade. *Colloq.,* turnout.

3, dress; court dress, full dress, evening dress *or* gown, ball dress, fancy dress; full regalia, tailoring; millinery, frippery; foppery, equipage. *Slang,* glad rags, Sunday best.

4, ceremony, ceremonial; ritual; form, formality; etiquette; punctilio, punctiliousness; stateliness, RITE; protocol.

5, attitudinarian; fop, dude; posturer, poser, poseur, pretender, hypocrite (see DECEIVER). *Colloq.,* show-off. *Slang,* grandstander.

Verbs—be ostentatious; put oneself forward; court attention; star; figure; make a show *or* display; glitter; show off, parade; display, exhibit, put forward; sport, brandish, blazon forth; dangle, flaunt, emblazon, prink, primp; set off, mount, have framed; put a good face upon. *Colloq.,* cut a figure, cut a dash, cut a wide swath, make a splash, splurge, play to the gallery, trot out, put on the dog, show off. *Slang,* grandstand, put on a front, strut one's stuff.

Adjectives—ostentatious, showy, dashing, pretentious; jaunty; grand, pompous, palatial; high-sounding; turgid, garish; gaudy, gaudy as a peacock; conspicuous, flaunting, flashing, flaming, glittering; gay, splendid, magnificent, sumptuous; theatrical, dramatic, spectacular; ceremonial, ritual; solemn, stately, majestic, formal, stiff, ceremonious, punctilious, starched; in best bib and tucker, in Sunday best, on parade.

Adverbs—ostentatiously, pompously, *etc.;* with a flourish of trumpets, with flying colors.

Antonym, see PLAINNESS.

ostracize, *v.t.* exclude, banish, bar, blackball; outcast.
other, *adj.* different, separate, distinct; else, another, additional. See ADDITION, DIFFERENCE.
oust, *v.t.* depose, evict, remove, dismiss, dislodge. See EJECTION. *Ant.,* see RECEIVING.
out, *adv.* without, outside; outdoors. See EXTERIOR. *Ant.,* see INTERIOR.
outbreak, *n.* outburst, eruption; rebellion, uprising; revolt, insurrection; outburst, disturbance. See DISOBEDIENCE, VIOLENCE. *Ant.,* see OBEDIENCE.
outcast, *n.* pariah, derelict, exile; castaway, outsider, outlaw; leper. See UNCONFORMITY. *Ant.,* see CONFORMITY.
outcome, *n.* issue, END, termination, result, consequence, outgrowth, sequel, upshot. See EFFECT. *Ant.,* see CAUSE.
outcry, *n.* clamor, tumult, exclamation, shout, uproar, bellow. See CRY.
outdo, *v.t.* excel, exceed, overdo, surpass, outstrip, beat. See SUPERIORITY. *Ant.,* see INFERIORITY.
outer, *adj.* outside, outward, external, EXTERIOR. *Ant.,* see INTERIOR.
outfit, *n.* ensemble, garments, suit; group, unit; equipment, gear. See CLOTHING. *Ant.,* see DIVESTMENT.
outflow, *n.* effluence, efflux, outpouring, issue, effusion; ESCAPE. See EGRESS.
outgrowth, *n.* development, result, outcome, offshoot; excrescence. See EFFECT. *Ant.,* see CAUSE.
outing, *n.* excursion, junket, field day, picnic. See SOCIALITY.
outlandish, *adj.* bizarre, *outré,* eccentric, strange, odd, foreign, barbarous, grotesque, queer. See ABSURDITY.
outlast, *v.* outlive, survive, outwear. See DURABILITY.
outlaw, *n.* criminal, bandit, fugitive, outcast; desperado. See EVILDOER. *Ant.,* see GOODNESS.
outlet, *n.* loophole, port; sluice, floodgate; faucet, tap, spout, conduit; exit, vent, opening. See EGRESS, ESCAPE.
outline, *n. & v.* —*n.* profile, silhouette, contour; lines, features, lineaments; tracing, tracery; bounds, boundary; EDGE, circumference, perimeter; sketch, plan, blueprint, schematic, scheme, drawing, draft, rough sketch; synopsis, summary, résumé; diagram, skeleton, broad outline; chart, map. —*v.t.* sketch; diagram; silhouette, delineate; model, block in, plan; boil down, summarize, trace, draw, depict, delimit, design, picture, demonstrate. See APPEARANCE, DESCRIPTION, SHORTNESS.
outlive, *v.t.* survive, outlast. See DURABILITY. *Ant.,* see CHANGE.
outlook, *n.* APPEARANCE, prospect, probabilities, forecast; scene, view, vista. See FUTURITY.
outlying, *adj.* distant, suburban, remote; frontier. See EXTERIOR.
output, *n.* produce, yield, harvest, product, PRODUCTION.
outrage, *n.* VIOLENCE, WRONG, affront, harm, damage, injury, abuse; transgression, infraction, violation. See EVIL.
outright, *adj.* complete, unqualified, unmitigated, consummate, out-and-out. See COMPLETION.
outrun, *v.t.* overtake, defeat, beat, surpass, outdistance, outstrip.
outset, *n.* BEGINNING, start, commencement, departure. *Ant.,* see END.
outshine, *v.t.* outdo, eclipse, excel, overshadow, outstrip. See DISREPUTE.
outside, *adj.* EXTERIOR, outer, external, outward. *Ant.,* see INTERIOR.
outskirts, *n.pl.* suburbs, environs, surroundings; border, EDGE; purlieus. See NEARNESS. *Ant.,* see CENTRALITY.
outspoken, *adj.* frank, bluff, unreserved, blunt, loud, plain-spoken. See SIMPLENESS. *Ant.,* see DECEPTION, CONCEALMENT.
outstanding, *adj.* prominent, exceptional, superior, conspicuous, remarkable, noticeable, eminent; unpaid, uncollected, owed, due, unsettled. See IMPORTANCE, DEBT. *Ant.,* see UNIMPORTANCE.
outstretched, *adj.* extended, reaching; proffered, offered; expanded, outspread. See BREADTH.
outstrip, *v.t.* outspace, outrun, excel, exceed, outdo, outdistance; eclipse, surpass. See SUPERIORITY. *Ant.,* see INFERIORITY.
outward, *adj.* EXTERIOR, outer, outside, out. *Ant.,* see INTERIOR.
outweigh, *v.t.* overweigh, outbalance, overbalance, exceed. See SUPERIORITY. *Ant.,* see INFERIORITY.

outwit, *v.t.* frustrate, circumvent, outsmart. See DECEPTION.

oval, *adj.* elliptical, ovoid, ovate. See CIRCULARITY.

over, *adv. & prep.* —*adv.* past, across, by; again; beyond; extra, above, more, remaining, left. —*prep.* on, above. See END, OPPOSITION, REPETITION, SUPERIORITY.

overawe, *v.t.* frighten, intimidate, daunt, abash, cow; impress. See FEAR.

overbalance, *v.t.* surpass, overweigh, outweigh, unbalance. See SUPERIORITY. *Ant.*, see INFERIORITY.

overbearing, *adj.* domineering; bullying; lordly, arrogant, dictatorial; overwhelming. See INSOLENCE. *Ant.*, see SERVILITY.

overcast, *adj.* cloudy, murky, shadowy, gloomy, dark, leaden. See CLOUDINESS.

overcautious, *adj.* timorous, fearful, overcareful, unenterprising. See CARE. *Ant.*, see RASHNESS.

overcharge, *v.* rook, fleece, do, cheat, extort. *Colloq.*, scalp, gyp. See PAYMENT. *Ant.*, see CHEAPNESS.

overcoat, *n.* greatcoat, duster, topcoat, ulster, raglan. See CLOTHING.

overcome, *v. & adj.* —*v.* conquer, subdue, defeat, overthrow, surmount. See SUCCESS. *Ant.*, see FAILURE. —*adj.* subdued, conquered, defeated, broken, crushed, downcast.

overestimation, *n.* EXAGGERATION; overvaluation, VANITY; megalomania; eulogy; optimism, pessimism, overenthusiasm; much ado about nothing; storm in a teacup, tempest in a teapot; overstatement. See MISJUDGMENT. *Ant.*, see MODERATION, UNDERESTIMATION.

overrunning, *n.* overstepping; trespass; inroad, encroachment, infringement; infraction; extravagation, transcendence; redundance, EXAGGERATION.

oversee, *v.t.* manage, superintend, direct, supervise, COMMAND; overlook. See DIRECTION.

overshoe, *n.* boot, arctic, galosh, rubber. See CLOTHING.

oversight, *n.* omission, ERROR, blunder, slip; management, directorship, supervision. See DIRECTION. *Ant.*, see COMMISSION.

overstate, *v.t.* exaggerate, overclaim, overdo, overdraw, overembellish. See EXAGGERATION. *Ant.*, see DETRACTION.

overstep, *v.i.* transgress, trespass, cross, encroach, exceed; intrude, infringe.

overtake, *v.t.* catch, pass, reach, overhaul. See ARRIVAL.

overthrow, *v.t.* overcome, defeat, upset, abolish, confute; overturn, demolish, ruin. See DEPRESSION, DESTRUCTION, SUCCESS.

overture, *n.* advance, approach, proposal, bid; prelude, preliminary, introduction. See OPENING.

overturn, *v.t.* invert, upset, reverse; overthrow, destroy. See REVOLUTION.

overwhelm, *v.t.* overpower, crush, submerge, defeat, conquer, overcome. See DESTRUCTION.

overwork, *v.* overdo, tire, weary, exhaust, overtax, overburden, overtask. See WEARINESS, WASTE.

ovum, *n.* cell, egg, seed.

owe, *v.i.* See DEBT. *Ant.*, see CREDIT.

own, *v.* admit, confess, concede, acknowledge; possess, have, hold. See DISCLOSURE, POSSESSION.

owner, *n.* holder, master, bearer, proprietor, proprietress, occupant. See POSSESSION.

ownership, *n.* proprietorship, PROPERTY, possessorship, dominion, title; holding. See POSSESSION.

P

pace, *n. & v.* —*n.* rate, speed, VELOCITY; step, measuring step; stride; gait, amble, rack, single-foot. —*v.* walk, step, stride; walk to-and-fro; measure; lead, set the pace. See MOTION.

pachyderm, *n.* thick-skinned animal; elephant, rhinoceros; insensitive person. See ANIMAL, INSENSIBILITY.

PACIFICATION [723]

Nouns—**1,** pacification, conciliation; reconciliation, reconcilement; propitiation, appeasement, mollification, mediation; shaking of hands, accommodation, ARRANGEMENT, adjustment; terms, COMPROMISE; amnesty; deed of release; fraternization.

2, peace offering; peace treaty; olive branch; truce, armistice; suspension of hostilities; breathing spell; convention; flag of truce, white flag.

Verbs—**1,** pacify, tranquilize, compose; allay (see MODERATION); reconcile, unite, reunite, propitiate, placate, conciliate, meet halfway, hold out the olive branch, accomodate, heal the breach, make peace, restore harmony, bring to terms, pour oil on troubled waters, handle with kid gloves.

2, settle differences, arrange matters; set straight; make up a quarrel, come to an understanding, come to terms; bridge over, hush up; make it up; make matters up; shake hands. *Colloq.*, bury the hatchet, smoke the peace-pipe.

3, raise a siege; sheathe the sword; lay down one's arms; beat swords into plowshares; come around.

Adjectives—pacific, peaceful, calm; peaceable, unwarlike, peaceful, peace-loving, peace-making; pacifying, soothing, mollifying; appeasing; pacificatory, propitiatory, conciliatory; pacified.

Antonyms, see CONTENTION, WARFARE.

---

pack, *n. & v.* —*n.* stow, bale, package, packet; load, burden, bundle; knapsack; crowd, mob, MULTITUDE; herd, flock, bevy, covey. See ASSEMBLAGE. —*v.* stow, bale, package; cram, tamp; cake, solidify; add to; stuff; load, burden.

package, *n.* parcel, package, pack, carton. See ASSEMBLAGE, RECEPTACLE.

pact, *n.* compact, covenant, treaty; bargain, AGREEMENT.

pad, *n. & v.* —*n.* cushion, mat, buffer; writing tablet. —*v.* walk softly; cushion, stuff, wad; enlarge (an expense account). See INCREASE.

pagan, *adj. & n.* —*adj.* heathen, ungodly; idolatrous. —*n.* heathen, idolater. See IRRELIGION, RELIGION.

page, *n. & v.* —*n.* servant; attendant; call boy, pageboy, bellboy; one side of a leaf (book paper or writing paper). —*v.* summon, call; number pages. See NUMBER.

pageant, *n.* exhibition, show, parade, display. See OSTENTATION.

pail, *n.* bucket, can, canister, pot, pan, kettle. See RECEPTACLE.

PAIN [828, 378]

Nouns—**1,** pain, suffering, sufferance; ache; aching, smart; twinge, twitch, gripe, headache; hurt, cut; sore, soreness, painfulness; discomfort, malaise; spasm, cramp; nightmare; crick, stitch, thrill, twinge, convulsion, throe; throb, throbbing, pang; sharp, piercing, throbbing, shooting, gnawing *or* burning pain; anguish, agony; excruciation, torment, torture; rack; crucifixion; martyrdom; vivisection.

2, mental suffering, pang, anguish, agony, torture, torment, purgatory (see HELL).

3, ADVERSITY; trial, ordeal, shock, blow, burden, load; concern, grief, sorrow, distress, affliction, woe, bitterness; lovesickness; heartache; unhappiness, infelicity, misery, tribulation, wretchedness, desolation; despair; extremity, prostration, depth of misery; hell on earth; reign of terror; slough of despond (see ADVERSITY); peck *or* sea of troubles; dog's life.

4, embarrassment, shame, DISCONTENT; DEJECTION; DISEASE.

Verbs—**1,** feel, experience, suffer, endure, *or* undergo pain; suffer, ache, smart, bleed; tingle, shoot; twinge, twitch, writhe, wince; make a wry face. *Colloq.*, see stars.

2, grieve; mourn, lament (see LAMENTATION); yearn, repine, pine, droop, languish, sink; despair; break one's heart; eat one's heart out.

3, give, cause *or* inflict pain; pain, hurt, wound, chafe, sting, bite, gnaw, gripe; pinch, tweak, grate, gall, fret, prick, pierce, wring, convulse; embarrass, shame; torment, torture; rack, agonize; crucify; excruciate; break on the wheel, put on the rack; spank, beat, thrash, flog (see PUNISHMENT).

4, sicken, disgust, revolt, nauseate, disenchant; repel, offend, shock, stink in the nostrils; turn the stomach; make one sick, set the teeth on edge; go against the grain, grate on the ear, stick in one's throat *or* craw; rankle, gnaw, corrode; horrify, appall, chill the blood; make the flesh creep, make the hair stand on end; make the blood curdle or run cold; make one shudder; raise one's hackles.

Adjectives—**1**, in pain, suffering, pained, afflicted, worried, displeased, aching, griped, sore; on the rack, in limbo; in hell; heavy-laden, stricken, crushed, victimized, ill-used; unfortunate, hapless; unhappy, heartbroken; lovesick, lovelorn, brokenhearted; in despair; agonized, tortured, crucified, racked, broken on the wheel.

2, causing pain, hurting, hurtful, painful; dolorous; cutting, corroding, consuming, racking, excruciating, searching, grinding, grating, agonizing; envenomed.

3, distressing, afflicting, afflictive; grievous, piteous; woeful, rueful, mournful, deplorable, pitiable, lamentable; sad, affecting, touching, pathetic; ruinous, disastrous, calamitous, tragical.

4, intolerable, insufferable, insupportable, unbearable, unendurable; more than flesh and blood can bear; enough to drive one mad.

Antonym, see PLEASURE.

painstaking, *adj.* careful, particular, meticulous, scrupulous; diligent. See EXERTION, CARE.

PAINTING [556]

Nouns—**1**, painting; depicting; drawing; design; chiaroscuro; composition; treatment, perspective, balance, technique; portrait, miniature, landscape, seascape, mural, still life, scene; prospect; panorama; cartoon.

2, school, style; the grand style, fine art, high art, commercial art, genre, portraiture; classicism, romanticism, impressionism, realism, pointillism, Dadaism, modernism, surrealism, cubism.

3, palette; easel; brush, paintbrush, pencil, charcoal, crayons, chalk, pastel; paint, water color, oils, oil paint; varnish, gouache, tempera, distemper, fresco, enamel; encaustic painting.

4, painting, picture, piece, tableau, canvas; oil painting; fresco, cartoon; drawing, pencil drawing, watercolor drawing; sketch, outline; study, sketch, scene, view; illustration.

5, picture gallery, art gallery, studio, atelier, museum, exhibition, show.

6, painter, ARTIST, portrait *or* landscape painter, *etc.;* realist, surrealist, impressionist, cubist, pointillist, postimpressionist, *etc.;* house painter, *etc.*

Verbs—paint, design, limn, draw, sketch, pencil, scratch, shade, stipple, hatch, crosshatch, hachure, dash off, block out, chalk out, square up; color, tint, dead-color, wash, varnish; paint in oils; stencil; depict, represent.

Adjectives—pictorial, graphic, picturesque; painted; classic, romantic, realistic, impressionistic, *etc.;* pencil, oil, pastel, tempera, water-color, *etc.*

pair, *n. & v.* —*n.* couple, duo, brace; mates; two of a kind. —*v.* match, mate, couple, suit, unite. See NUMERATION, SIMILARITY.

palatable, *adj.* tasty, savory; toothsome, appetizing; pleasant, agreeable; easy to take. See TASTE, PLEASURE.

pale, *adj., v.i. & n.* —*adj.* wan, waxen, ashy, ashen, colorless, bloodless; blond; faint, dim, vague; sickly. See COLORLESSNESS, DIMNESS, LIGHT. *Ant.,* see COLOR. —*v.i.* whiten, blanch, blench; fade, dim. —*n.* fence; border, boundary, LIMIT. See CIRCUMSCRIPTION.

pall, *v.i. & n.* —*v.i.* jade, weary; cloy, sicken, satiate. See SUFFICIENCY. —*n.* murk, smoke, smog, fog; gloomy atmosphere. See CLOUDINESS.

palliate, *v.t.* extenuate, excuse; mitigate, soften; relieve, ameliorate. See FORGIVENESS, VINDICATION, SOFTNESS, MODERATION.

pallor, *n.* paleness, bloodlessness, wanness, sallowness, whiteness, COLORLESSNESS. *Ant.,* see COLOR.

palpable, *adj.* evident, PLAIN, clear, manifest, obvious, apparent, unmistakable, definite, unquestionable, distinct. See EVIDENCE.

palpitate, *v.i.* beat, pulse, throb; vibrate; quake, shake. See AGITATION.

paltry, *adj.* trifling, trivial, inconsequential; mean, petty, worthless; contemptible, sorry, pitiable; insignificant. See UNIMPORTANCE, POVERTY, PITY.

pamper, *v.t.* humor, indulge, spoil, pet, coddle, gratify, overindulge. See PLEASURE. *Ant.,* see SEVERITY.

pan, *n.* pot, kettle, saucepan; skillet, spider, grill; dishpan; utensil, vessel. See RECEPTACLE.

panacea, *n.* universal remedy, REMEDY, cure-all, cure.

pander, *n. & v.* —*n.* cater to; encourage (in bad habits); pimp. —*n.* pimp; go-between. See EVIL, EVILDOER.

panegyric, *n.* praise; encomium, eulogy; APPROBATION, laudation.

panel, *n.* jury, board of judges; board, table.

pang, *n.* PAIN, twinge, shoot, throe, ache.

panic, *n. & v.* —*n.* terror, fright, FEAR, consternation, wild alarm; stampede; business disaster, widespread depression. See FAILURE. —*v.* alarm, frighten; stampede. *Colloq.,* bring down the house, wow (the audience).

pant, *v.* gasp, breathe heavily, puff, blow; crave, yearn for, long for. See WEARINESS, DESIRE.

pants, *n.pl.* trousers, breeches; slacks, flannels, jeans, Levis, dungarees; pantaloons, knickerbockers, knickers, plus-fours; shorts, pedal-pushers, chinos, jodhpurs; bloomers, briefs, panties. See CLOTHING.

papacy, *n.* papal system *or* office; the Vatican. See CLERGY.

papal, *adj.* of the Pope *or* the Vatican; pontifical. See CLERGY.

paper, *n.* writing paper; wallpaper; newsprint; rag paper, pulp paper, foolscap, *etc.;* free tickets; paper money, bill, banknote; *Colloq.,* folding money; certificate, deed, document; newspaper, journal; monograph, article, composition. See COVERING, WRITING, MONEY, PUBLICATION, RECORD.

par, *n.* EQUALITY, equal footing; par *or* face value; level; expert golf score.

parable, *n.* allegory, analogy; fable, moral tale; comparison, similitude. See FIGURATIVE, DESCRIPTION.

parade, *n. & v.* —*n.* show, display, pageant, pageantry; march, procession; OSTENTATION, pretension. See CONTINUITY. —*v.* show, display; march; air, vent; flaunt, show off.

paradise, *n.* Eden, HEAVEN, Promised Land, Canaan, land of milk and honey; Utopia, Arcadia; never-never land; bliss, happiness; Elysian fields, Elysium; Shangri-La. *Ant.,* see HELL.

paradox, *n.* apparent contradiction; inconsistency; illogical truth; ABSURDITY.

paragon, *n.* ideal, model, perfect example, pattern; nonesuch, nonpareil. See PERFECTION. *Ant.,* see IMPERFECTION.

parallel, *n. & adj.* —*n.* parallelism; coextension, parallel lines; analogy, comparison. —*adj.* coextensive, side by side. See SIMILARITY.

paralysis, *n.* stroke, disablement, complete halt (of activity); paraplegia, hemiplegia, malfunction. See DISEASE, IMPOTENCE.

paralyze, *v.* cripple; demoralize; disable; deaden; bring to a full stop. See IMPOTENCE.

paramount, *adj.* chief, first, supreme, all-important. See SUPERIORITY. *Ant.,* see INFERIORITY.

paramour, *n.* mistress, ladylove; lover. See LOVE.

parapet, *n.* wall, rampart, breastwork, embankment, DEFENSE; railing.

paraphernalia, *n.pl.* apparatus, gear, equipment; belongings; PROPERTY.

paraphrase, *n. & v.* —*n.* free translation, restatement. *Colloq.,* switch. —*v.* restate, alter, express differently, reword. See INTERPRETATION.

parasite, *n.* sycophant, flatterer, fawner, hanger-on; leech, bloodsucker; (*Biol.*) inquiline, commensal; symbion(t), symbiotic (inhabitant of host's body). *Colloq.,* free loader. See SERVILITY.

parcel, *n.* package, bundle, pack, packet; PART, portion, piece; LAND, lot, division, section. See ASSEMBLAGE.

parch, *v.* dry, dry up; roast, scorch; become thirsty. See DRYNESS.

parched, *adj.* dry, scorched, arid, waterless; thirsty; burned, crisped. See DRYNESS, DESIRE.

pardon, *v.t. & n.* —*v.t.* forgive, excuse; release (from penalty); overlook; tolerate. See FORGIVENESS. —*n.* excuse, release, FORGIVENESS; indulgence; remission; toleration.

pare, *v.t.* peel, trim, cut, shave, slice; reduce, shorten. See LAYER, DECREASE, CONTRACTION.

parental, *adj.* motherly, fatherly, maternal, paternal; protective, loving, tender. See ANCESTRY.

pariah, *n.* outcast, untouchable, outcaste. See DISREPUTE.

parity, *n.* EQUALITY, equal basis; SIMILARITY, equivalence; par. *Ant.,* see INEQUALITY.

park, *v.* leave standing (as a car); leave, deposit, place. See LOCATION, CIRCUMSCRIPTION.

park, *n.* parkway; playground; public gardens, botanical gardens, zoo; woodland, pleasance; grove; picnic grounds; village *or* bowling green, common; parking lot *or* space; amusement center, fair grounds, fun fair. See AMUSEMENT, LOCATION.

parley, *n. & v.i.* —*n.* conference, talk, discussion, CONVERSATION, COUNCIL; palaver. —*v.* talk, confer, palaver, converse.

parlor, *n.* living room, front room, drawing room. See RECEPTACLE.

parochial, *adj.* provincial, local; narrow, illiberal; of the parish; church-controlled (as schools, *etc.*). See REGION, MISJUDGMENT, SCHOOL.

parody, *n.* takeoff; IMITATION; travesty, burlesque. See COPY.

paroxysm, *n.* fit, seizure, spasm; convulsion, ATTACK; outburst, frenzy. See AGITATION, EXCITEMENT, VIOLENCE; PAIN.

parry, *v.* fend *or* ward off, avert, turn aside; evade; fence; deflect. See AVOIDANCE, NEGATION.

PARSIMONY [819]

Nouns—**1,** parsimony, parsimoniousness, stinginess, miserliness; stint; illiberality, avarice, greed, avidity, rapacity, extortion, venality, cupidity; SELFISHNESS. See also ECONOMY.
2, miser, niggard, churl, skinflint, scrimp, lickpenny, curmudgeon, harpy; extortioner, usurer. *Slang,* tightwad, pennypincher.
Verbs—be parsimonious, grudge, begrudge, stint, pinch, gripe, dole out, hold back, withhold, starve, famish, live on nothing; drive a hard bargain; cheapen, beat down; have an itching palm, grasp, grab.
Adjectives—parsimonious, penurious, stingy, miserly, mean, shabby, piddling, scrubby, pennywise, near, niggardly, close; close-fisted, grasping, tight-fisted; tight, sparing, chary; grudging, griping; illiberal, ungenerous, hidebound, sordid, mercenary, venal, covetous, usurious, avaricious, greedy, extortionate, rapacious. *Colloq.,* skimping.
Antonym, see GIVING.

---

parson, *n.* clergyman; pastor, minister, preacher, rector. See CLERGY.

parsonage, *n.* parson's house; manse, rectory. See TEMPLE.

part, *n., adj. & v.* —*n.* portion; item, particular; section; clause, paragraph, passage, excerpt; sector, segment; fraction, fragment; parcel, component; piece, lump, bit; cut, cutting, chip, slice, scale; shard; small part; morsel, particle, instal(l)ment; dividend; share, allotment; member, limb, lobe, arm, wing, scion, branch, bough, joint, link, offshoot. *Colloq.,* hunk, chunk, smithereen. —*adj.* fractional, fragmentary, sectional; divided; broken, splintered, *etc.;* separated, individual; partial, incomplete. —*v.* divide; split, break; partition; part company, separate; sever, break up. See DISJUNCTION. *Ant.,* see WHOLE.

partake, *v.* share, share in; take (food *or* drink); receive (part of). See COÖPERATION.

partial, *adj.* incomplete, fractional, unfinished, PART; biased, partisan, one-sided, prejudiced; favoring. See MISJUDGMENT, SIDE.

partiality, *n.* preference, favoring; bias, prejudice, one-sidedness, liking, taste (for), penchant, predilection. See MISJUDGMENT, DESIRE. *Ant.,* see EQUALITY.

participate, *v.i.* partake; share, share in; come in for a share; prorate; go shares, go halves; share and share alike; have *or* own in common, possess *or* use jointly; join in; go in with, have a hand in; coöperate. *Colloq.,* go Dutch. *Slang,* kick in, feed the kitty. See SOCIALITY. *Ant.,* see SECLUSION.

participation, *n.* sharing, COÖPERATION, partaking; gregariousness, mixing, SOCIALITY; mutuality, common use of; joint stock, common stock, partnership; collectivism, communism, socialism; communion; community; mutual benefit, action *or* enjoyment; joint endeavor *or* enterprise. *Slang,* cahoots.

particle, *n.* speck, iota, jot, whit, bit; atom, molecule; (*Gram.*) suffix, prefix; conjunction, preposition, interjection. See LITTLENESS, GRAMMAR.

particular, *adj. & n.* —*adj.* demanding, painstaking, meticulous; definite, specific; fussy, finicky, per(s)nickety, overnice; special, outstanding; personal; precise, exact. See TASTE, IMPORTANCE. —*n.* fact, specification, datum, detail.

particularize, *v.* specify, itemize, mention particularly, detail. See DESCRIPTION.

parting, *n.* leavetaking, DEPARTURE; farewell, severance, separation; partition, division. See DISJUNCTION.

partisan, *adj. & n.* —*adj.* partial, one-sided, pro, favoring, interested. —*n.* supporter, ally, follower, adherent; aide; champion; guerrilla, underground fighter. See AID.

partisanship, *n.* party spirit, loyalty (to party); unfairness, bias, prejudice; clannishness, closeness (of relations); provincialism. See PARTY, INJUSTICE.

partition, *n.* wall, screen, diaphragm, barrier; separation, severance, cutting-off; section, portion; division. See DISJUNCTION, BETWEEN.

partly, *adv.* in part, not wholly; incompletely, partially, in a way, not quite.

partner, *n.* sharer, associate. *Colloq.,* sidekick, pal, pard, pardner; co-owner; spouse, mate. See ACCOMPANIMENT, MARRIAGE.

partnership, *n.* co-ownership, business association; COÖPERATION, alliance. See ACCOMPANIMENT.

PARTY [712]

Nouns—**1,** party, faction, side; denomination, communion; community, body, fellowship, fraternity; confraternity; brotherhood, sisterhood; sodality; family, clan (see ANCESTRY).

2, gang, crew, band, horde, posse, phalanx; clique, ring, set, circle, coterie, club. *Colloq.,* crowd, mob, bunch.

3, corporation, corporate body, company; guild; establishment, partnership, copartnership; firm, house; joint concern, joint stock company; syndicate, trust; joint account.

4, society, association; institute, institution; union, trade union; league, alliance, *Verein, Bund, Zollverein;* combination, trust, syndicate; coalition, federation; confederation, confederacy; junta, cabal; freemasonry. See COÖPERATION.

5, party, entertainment, affair; tea party, dinner party, birthday party, *etc.* See SOCIALITY.

Adjectives—in league, in partnership, in alliance; partisan, denominational; bonded together, banded together, linked together; confederated, federative; joint, mutual.

Antonym, see AGREEMENT, SECLUSION

---

pass, *n. & v.* —*n.* gap, gorge; way, OPENING, NOTCH, defile, PASSAGE; free ticket; crisis, predicament, condition, CIRCUMSTANCE. —*v.* go through *or* by, bypass; get a passing mark, make the grade, do (pass muster); cross; hand over; admit, allow, tolerate; while away *or* spend (the time); authorize, O.K., sanction; permit (see PERMISSION).

passable, *adj.* allowable, acceptable, tolerable; passing, fair, good enough. See IMPERFECTION.

PASSAGE [302]

Nouns—**1,** passage, transmission; permeation; penetration; interpenetration; transudation, infiltration; osmosis, endosmosis, exosmosis; intercurrence; access, ingress, egress; road, highway, thoroughfare, boulevard, avenue, street; byway, lane, pike, alley, trail; high road, the King's highway; roadway; turnpike, thruway, expressway, freeway, parkway, superhighway, limited-access highway.

2, CHANNEL, gate, OPENING; progress, flow, current, stream, flight; duration, COURSE.

3, transference, transportation, transit; conveyance, VEHICLE; portage, cartage, freight, shipment; shifting, transposition, transplantation, translation.

*Verbs—***1,** pass, pass through; perforate, penetrate, permeate, thread, enfilade; go through, go across; go over, pass by, bypass, pass over; cut across; ford, cross; work *or* make one's way through; thread *or* worm one's way through; force one's way; find a way; transmit, make way; clear the course *or* track; traverse, go over the ground.

2, TRANSFER, transport, convey, bear; conduct, convoy; ship, shift, send, dispatch, consign, post, mail, deliver, transfuse, draw, decant.

*Adjectives—*passing, elapsing, progressive; intercurrent; transient, portable, assignable, movable.

*Adverbs—*in passing, *en passant*, in transit, under way.

Antonym, see INERTNESS.

---

passion, *n.* LOVE; fervor, ardor; intensity, fever; infatuation, DESIRE; emotion; rage, anger, fury; EXCITEMENT. *Colloq.*, predilection, preference.

passive, *adj.* nonresistant; inactive, inert, quiet; unemotional, untouched, unstirred, indifferent. See INACTIVITY. *Ant.*, see ACTION, ACTIVITY, FEELING.

passiveness, *n.* inaction, INACTIVITY, inertness; nonresistance, passivity, QUIESCENCE; INDIFFERENCE; neutrality; sluggishness, SUBMISSION.

passport, *n.* official permit; pass; safe-conduct. See PERMISSION.

password, *n.* countersign, shibboleth, watchword. See INDICATION.

PAST [122]

*Nouns—***1,** past, past tense, preterition; PRIORITY; the past, yesterday; days of yore *or* of old; times past *or* gone by; bygone days; olden times, the good old days, yesteryear; auld lang syne, eld.

2, antiquity, antiqueness; time immemorial; remote past; archaism, antiquarianism, medievalism, pre-Raphaelitism; retrospection; looking back; MEMORY; ANCESTRY. *Colloq.*, ancient history.

3, paleontology, paleography, paleology, arch(a)eology.

*Verbs—*be past, have expired, have run its course, have had its day; pass; pass by, go by, go away, pass away, pass off; lapse, blow over; look back, trace back; exhume.

*Adjectives—*past, gone, bygone, foregone; elapsed, lapsed, expired, no more, run out, blown over, that has been, extinct, never to return, exploded, forgotten, irrecoverable; obsolete (see OLDNESS); once, former, pristine, quondam, *ci-devant*, late; ancestral; foregoing; last, latter; recent, overnight; past, perfect, preterite, past perfect, pluperfect; looking back; retrospective, retroactive; arch(a)eological, *etc. Colloq.*, ex-.

*Adverbs—*formerly; of old, of yore; erst, erstwhile, whilom, erewhile, time was, ago; over; in the olden time; anciently, long ago, long since; a long time ago; yesterday; last year, season, *or* month; *ultimo;* lately, retrospectively; before now; hitherto, heretofore; no longer; once, once upon a time; from time immemorial, in the memory of man; time out of mind; already, yet, up to this time; *ex post facto.*

Antonym, see TIME, FUTURITY.

---

pastime, *n.* AMUSEMENT, recreation, entertainment, play, diversion.

pastor, *n.* clergyman, minister, *etc.* See CLERGY.

pastry, *n.* cake, crust, shell; pie, tart, strudel. See FOOD.

pasture, *n.* field, meadow, grassland; paddock, pasturage, range.

pasty, *adj.* doughy, soft; pallid, pale; gluey, viscid, glutinous. See COLORLESSNESS.

pat, *n. & adj.* —*n.* caress, stroke; rap, tap; strike, beat, smack. —*adj.* apt, suitable, ready, appropriate, .fitting; timely, fortuitous. See AGREEMENT. *Ant.*, see DISAGREEMENT.

patch, *n. & v.t.* —*n.* piece, segment, spot; repair, mend; field, lot. —*v.t.* repair, reconstruct, rebuild, revamp, adjust. See COMPROMISE, RESTORATION.

patent, *adj.* obvious, plain, clear, evident, apparent; noticeable; open. See EVIDENCE.

paternity, *n.* fatherhood, fathership, parentage; see ANCESTRY.

path, *n.* trail, lane, road, footpath, route, way, course; lead, example. See DIRECTION.

pathetic, *adj.* piteous, pitiable, saddening, touching; distressing, heart-rending, sad; pitiful. See PAIN, PITY, FEELING. *Ant.*, see PLEASURE.

pathos, *n.* passion, warmth; sentiment, FEELING.

patience, *adj.* LENIENCY, tolerance; PERSEVERANCE, persistence; forbearance, long-suffering, SUBMISSION, endurance. *Ant.*, see EXCITEMENT, DISCONTENT.

patient, *adj.* tolerant, lenient, forbearing, long-suffering; gentle, kindly; unhurried, persistent, persevering, unremitting. *Ant.*, see EXCITEMENT.

patrician, *adj.* noble, well-born, aristocratic. See NOBILITY. *Ant.*, see POPULACE.

patron, *n.* customer; benefactor, supporter; saint, DEITY; defender, backer. See AID.

patronage, *n.* condescension, favor; custom, interest, SUPPORT, assistance; auspices. See AID.

patter, *v.i. & n.* —*v.i.* chatter, mumble, ramble, babble, jabber, mutter; tap, pitter-patter. —*n.* dialect, cant, chatter, babble. See LOQUACITY, SPEECH.

pattern, *n.* FORM, original; mold, example; PLAN, last; model, ideal. See PERFECTION. *Ant.*, see IMPERFECTION.

pauper, *n.* beggar, bankrupt, mendicant. See POVERTY. *Ant.*, see MONEY.

pause, *n. & v.i.* —*n.* CESSATION, REST, hesitation, INACTION; lull, stop, discontinuance, suspension. —*v.i.* desist, halt, stop, cease, break. *Ant.*, see CONTINUITY.

pawn, *v.t.* pledge. *Slang*, hock. See DEBT, SECURITY.

PAYMENT [807]

Nouns—**1**, payment, defrayment; discharge; acquittance, quittance; settlement, clearance, liquidation, satisfaction, reckoning, arrangement, repayment, reimbursement; retribution. See MONEY. *Colloq.*, a pound of flesh; an arm and a leg.

2, COMPENSATION, recompense, remuneration, REWARD, indemnity, EXPENDITURE.

3, salary, stipend, wages, pay, emolument, allowance; bonus, premium, fee, honorarium, tip, scot, tribute, hire; bribe, blackmail, hush money.

4, PRICE, charge, expense; dues, duty, tariff, toll; tax; sales, excise, income, poll, head tax; assessment, tithe, exaction; ransom, salvage, brokerage, *etc.*

Verbs—**1**, pay, defray, make payment; pay down, pay in advance; redeem; pay in kind; discharge, settle, quit, acquit oneself of; account with, reckon with, settle with, be even with, be quits with; strike a balance; settle *or* square accounts with; wipe off old scores; satisfy; pay in full; clear, liquidate; pay up.

2, pay one's way, pay the piper, pay the costs, do the needful; ante up; expend; lay down. *Colloq.*, foot the bill, chip in. *Slang*, tickle *or* grease the palm, cough up, kick in, fork over, shell out.

3, disgorge, make repayment; expend, disburse; repay, refund, reimburse, retribute; REWARD, make compensation. *Slang*, pay through the nose, pay cash on the barrel-head *or* on the line; pay cold cash.

Adjectives—paying, paid, owing nothing, out of debt, quits, square.

Adverbs—to the tune of; on the nail; money down.

Antonym, see NONPAYMENT.

---

peace, *n.* amity, friendship, harmony, concord; tranquility, REPOSE, quiescence; truce, PACIFICATION; neutrality. *Ant.*, see CONTENTION, WARFARE.

peacemaker, *n.* pacifier; mediator, intermediary, intercessor. See COMPROMISE, PACIFICATION. *Ant.*, see WARFARE, CONTENTION.

peak, *n.* SUMMIT, top, apex, pinnacle; point, crag; crest, HEIGHT; climax. See SHARPNESS. *Ant.*, see LOWNESS.

peaked, *adj.* wan, worn, pale, haggard, tired, weary, fatigued; ailing, unwell, unhealthy, ill, poorly, sickly; thin, gaunt, frail. See WEARINESS.

peal, *n. & v.i.* —*n.* reverberation, blast, ring, outburst, boom. —*v.i.* ring, toll, reverberate, SOUND. See LOUDNESS.

pearly, *adj.* nacreous, silvery, grayish, whitish. See COLOR.

peasant, *n.* countryman; peon, *paisano,* coolie, boor, muzhik, fellah; farmer, laborer, worker; rustic. See POPULACE, AGRICULTURE.

peck, *v.i.* nip, bite, pick, snip; tap, rap. See IMPULSE.

peculiar, *adj.* individual, indigenous, idiosyncratic; idiomatic; strange, odd, unusual, queer; particular, especial. See UNCONFORMITY. *Ant.,* see CONFORMITY.

pedagogic, *adj.* academic, educational, teacherly, professional, scholastic. See TEACHING.

pedant, *n.* SCHOLAR, theorist, academician, doctrinaire; prig, bluestocking. See AFFECTATION.

pedantic, *adj.* precise, formal, narrow; bookish, stilted; affected, sophomoric. See SCHOLAR, AFFECTATION.

peddle, *v.t.* sell; canvass, hawk, retail. See SALE.

peddler, pedlar, *n.* hawker, huckster, colporteur, sutler, vendor, trader, dealer. See SALE.

pedestrian, *n.* walker, ambler, stroller, peregrinator, hiker; itinerant.

pedigree, *n.* genealogy, lineage, ANCESTRY, DESCENT, family; background.

peek, *v.i.* peep, glance, look, watch; pry. See VISION.

peel, *v.t.* strip, divest, bare, uncover, skin, shell, husk, pare. See DIVESTMENT.

peep, *n. & v.i.* —*n.* chirp, cheep, chirrup; sly look. —*v.i.* peer, peek, look; spy, pry. See SOUND, VISION.

peer, *n. & v.i.* —*n.* equal; nobleman, lord; match. —*v.i.* squint, stare, peep, pry; gaze; scrutinize. See NOBILITY, EQUALITY, VISION. *Ant.,* see POPULACE.

peerless, *adj.* unequaled, matchless, unbeatable, supreme, unrivaled; indomitable. See SUPERIORITY. *Ant.,* see INFERIORITY.

peevish, *adj.* irascible, fretful, complaining, cranky, cross, irritable, touchy. See IRASCIBILITY. *Ant.,* see CHEERFULNESS.

peg, *n.* spike, dowel, pin, bolt; fastener. See CONNECTION.

pelf, *n.* money, loot, lucre. See ACQUISITION, MONEY. *Ant.,* see LOSS, POVERTY.

pellet, *n.* pill, tablet, capsule; missile, pebble, hailstone, bullet. See ARMS.

pelt, *n. & v.* —*n.* fur, hide, skin, peltry. —*v.* bombard, pepper, stone, strike; drive, beat; hurl, throw, pitch, fling. See IMPULSE, PROPULSION.

pen, *n. & v.t.* —*n.* stockade, INCLOSURE, fold, stall, coop, cage, pound, corral, paddock; stylus, quill. —*v.t.* confine, jail, impound, enclose, restrain, cage, coop; write, indite, inscribe. See RESTRAINT, WRITING.

penalize, *v.t.* punish; fine; imprison, chastise; handicap. See PUNISHMENT.

penalty, *n.* retribution, PUNISHMENT; PAIN, penance, ATONEMENT; the devil to pay; penalization; handicap, fine, amercement; forfeit, forfeiture, damages, confiscation.

penance, *n.* ATONEMENT, discipline, punishment; flagellation, fasting; PRICE, suffering, repayment. See RITE.

pend, *v.i.* hang, depend, swing, dangle; flap, trail, flow; overhang, impend; suspend; hang fire. See FUTURITY. *Ant.,* see SUPPORT, CERTAINTY.

pendency, *n.* dependency; uncertainty; absence of support; suspension, hanging; pendulousness, overhang, droop, sag, sagginess, sagging. *Ant.,* see SUPPORT.

penetrate, *v.t.* bore, burrow, pierce, enter, perforate, permeate; invade; cut; discern, perceive, understand; uncover. See INGRESS, INTELLIGENCE, PASSAGE.

penetrative, *adj.* astute, discerning, piercing; sharp, subtle, acute, penetrating. See FEELING, INTELLIGENCE.

PENITENCE [950]

Nouns—**1,** penitence, contrition, compunction, repentance, remorse, REGRET. **2,** self-reproach, self-reproof, self-accusation, self-condemnation, self-humiliation; pangs, qualms, prickings, twinge, *or* voice of conscience; awakened conscience.

3, acknowledgment, confession (see DISCLOSURE); apology, penance, ATONEMENT; recantation.

4, penitent, Magdalene, prodigal son, a sadder and a wiser man.

Verbs—**1,** repent, be penitent, be sorry for; rue; REGRET, think better of; recant; plead guilty; sing *miserere*, sing *de profundis;* confess oneself in the wrong; acknowledge, confess (see DISCLOSURE); humble oneself; beg pardon, apologize, do penance (see ATONEMENT).

Adjectives—penitent, regretful, regretting; regrettable, lamentable.

---

penitentiary, *n.* PRISON, jail, reformatory.

penmanship, *n.* chirography, handwriting. See WRITING.

pennant, *n.* banner, flag, streamer, pennon. See INDICATION.

penniless, *adj.* indigent, needy, bankrupt, impecunious, poor. *Slang,* broke. See POVERTY. *Ant.,* see MONEY.

pension, *n.* allowance, annuity, allotment, settlement.

pensive, *adj.* thoughtful, reflective, meditative, musing; melancholy, sad, dejected. See THOUGHT, DEJECTION. *Ant.,* see CHEERFULNESS.

penurious, *adj.* stingy, mean, miserly, parsimonious. See PARSIMONY.

penury, *n.* POVERTY, lack, indigence, destitution, pauperism. *Ant.,* see MONEY.

people, *n.* See MANKIND, POPULACE.

perceive, *v.t.* apprehend, appreciate, discern; observe, notice, see; comprehend, know. See FEELING, KNOWLEDGE.

percentage, *n.* COMPENSATION, COMMISSION, discount; fee; allowance.

perceptible, *adj.* appreciable, discernible, visible; tangible, observable, sensible; cognizable. See KNOWLEDGE.

perceptive, *adj.* knowledgeable, observant, understanding; aware, sympathetic; knowing, cognitive. See KNOWLEDGE.

perch, *n. & v.i.* —*n.* rest, roost, nest, seat. —*v.i.* poise, PLACE, roost, settle, alight, sit.

percolate, *v.i.* drip, trickle, permeate; ooze, filter.

perdition, *n.* DESTRUCTION, downfall, ruin, LOSS, fall. See FAILURE.

peremptory, *adj.* commanding, arbitrary, tyrannical, dogmatic; compulsory, binding; absolute, decisive, conclusive. See AUTHORITY, COMPULSION, SEVERITY.

perennial, *adj.* enduring, lasting, endless, persistent; successive, consecutive. See CONTINUITY. *Ant.,* see DISJUNCTION, END.

PERFECTION [650]

Nouns—**1,** perfection, perfectness, indefectibility; impeccancy, impeccability, faultlessness, excellence.

2, paragon; pink of perfection, acme of perfection; *ne plus ultra;* SUMMIT, model, standard, pattern, mirror; masterpiece; transcendence, transcendency, SUPERIORITY, quintessence.

3, see COMPLETION.

Verbs—be perfect, transcend; bring to perfection, perfect, ripen, mature, consummate, COMPLETE.

Adjectives—perfect, faultless; indefective, indeficient, indefectible; immaculate, spotless, impeccable; unblemished, sound, scatheless, intact; right as rain; consummate, finished, best, model, standard; inimitable, unparalleled, nonpareil; superhuman, divine; *sans peur et sans reproche.*

Adverbs—to perfection, to a fare-thee-well; perfectly, etc.

---

perforate, *v.t.* bore, drill, pierce, puncture, penetrate, prick; punch, riddle; tunnel. See OPENING.

perforator, *n.* piercer, borer, augur, gimlet, stylet, drill, awl, bradawl; corkscrew; dibble; trocar, trepan, probe; bodkin, needle, stiletto; reamer; can opener; warder; lancet; punch, gouge; spear. See OPENING.

perform, *v.t.* enact, play, execute; fulfill, achieve, discharge; act, do; operate, work, CONDUCT. See ACTION, AGENCY, COMPLETION, DRAMA, MUSIC, SUPPORT. *Ant.,* see INACTIVITY.

performance, *n.* ACTION, REPRESENTATION, achievement; rendition, execution, TOUCH. See EFFECT, DRAMA.

performer, *n.* actor, player, MUSICIAN, instrumentalist; doer, executor. See AGENCY, DRAMA.

perfume, *n.* FRAGRANCE, aroma; cologne, scent; sachet, attar, perfumery.

perfunctory, *adj.* formal, indifferent, careless; mechanical, crude. *Ant.,* see COMPLETION.

perhaps, *adv.* MAYBE, possibly, perchance, mayhap, conceivably.

peril, *n.* DANGER, hazard, risk, CHANCE, exposure. *Ant.,* see SAFETY.

period, *n.* second, minute, hour; day, week, month; quarter, year, decade; lifetime, generation, TIME; century, age, millennium, era, epoch; stop, full stop (see WRITING).

periodic, *adj.* recurrent, cyclic, intermittent, epochal; periodical, seasonal.

periodical, *n.* magazine, journal, quarterly, weekly, monthly. See BOOK.

periodicity, *n.* REGULARITY, reoccurrence, cycle. *Ant.,* see IRREGULARITY.

perish, *v.i.* expire, die, crumble. See DEATH, DESTRUCTION, NONEXISTENCE. *Ant.,* see LIFE.

perishable, *adj.* impermanent, destructible; temporal, mortal; unenduring. See TRANSIENTNESS. *Ant.,* see DURABILITY.

perjury, *n.* false swearing, FALSEHOOD, perversion, forswearing, fraud. *Ant.,* see TRUTH.

permanence, *n.* permanency, STABILITY, immutability, lastingness, OBSTINACY; persistence, endurance, fixedness; DURABILITY, constancy; standing, unchangingness, status quo; maintenance, preservation; conservation; conservatism. *Ant.,* see CHANGE.

permeate, *v.t.* pervade, saturate, overspread, infiltrate, penetrate. See PASSAGE, PRESENCE.

PERMISSION [760]

Nouns—**1,** permission, leave; allowance, sufferance; tolerance, toleration; FREEDOM, liberty, law, license, concession, grace; indulgence, lenity; favor, ASSENT, dispensation, EXEMPTION, release; connivance; vouchsafement; open door.

2, authorization, warranty, accordance, admission, permit, warrant, brevet, precept, sanction, authority, firman; free hand, pass, passport; furlough, license, *carte blanche,* ticket of leave; grant, charter, patent. *Colloq.,* green light, go-ahead signal, okay, O.K.

Verbs—**1,** permit; give permission, give power; let, allow, admit; suffer, bear with, tolerate, recognize; accord, vouchsafe, favor, humor, indulge, stretch a point; wink at, connive at; shut one's eyes to; gratify, give *carte blanche;* leave alone, leave to one's own device, leave the door open; open the door to, open the floodgates; give the reins to.

2, grant, empower, charter, enfranchise, confer a privilege, license, authorize, warrant; sanction; entrust, COMMISSION; sanctify, ordain, prescribe. *Colloq.,* okay, O.K., write one's own ticket.

Adjectives—permitting, permissive, indulgent; permitted, permissible, allowable, lawful (see LEGALITY); unconditional.

Adverbs—permissibly, by leave, with leave, on leave; under favor of; *ad libitum,* freely; with no holds barred.

Antonym, see RESTRAINT.

---

pernicious, *adj.* malign, ruinous, poisonous, detrimental, injurious, harmful; wicked. See BADNESS. *Ant.,* see GOODNESS.

perpendicular, *adj.* erect, upright; sheer, precipitous; VERTICAL, plumb.

perpetrate, *v.t.* commit, inflict; perform, do, practice. See ACTION.

perpetual, *adj.* eternal; everlasting, everliving, everflowing; continual, sempiternal; endless, neverending, unending; ceaseless, incessant, uninterrupted; unceasing; interminable, having no end; unfading, evergreen, amaranthine; deathless, immortal, undying, imperishable. See CONTINUITY. *Ant.,* see TRANSIENTNESS.

perpetuity, *n.* perpetualness; eternity, infinity; immortality, everlastingness, incessancy, CONTINUITY; perpetuation; endlessness. See DURABILITY. *Ant.,* see TRANSIENTNESS.

perplex, *v.* puzzle, bewilder, confuse, mystify, confound, nonplus; distract, disconcert. See DOUBT. *Ant.*, see CERTAINTY.

perplexity, *n.* UNCERTAINTY, bewilderment, confusion, quandary, puzzlement, embarrassment, predicament, hesitation. See DIFFICULTY. *Ant.*, see CERTAINTY.

perquisite, *n.* REWARD, bonus, gratuity, tip; bribe; due.

persecute, *v.t.* molest, oppress, maltreat, pursue, beset; abuse, injure; hound, annoy, trouble. See MALEVOLENCE, PAIN.

perseverance, *n.* continuance, permanence; firmness, STABILITY; constancy, steadiness; tenacity *or* singleness of purpose; persistence, plodding, patience; industry; pertinacity; gameness, pluck, stamina, backbone; indefatigability; bulldog courage, sand, grit; patience, determination. *Colloq.*, stick-to-itiveness. See RESOLUTION. *Ant.*, see CHANGEABLENESS, DOUBT.

persist, *v.i.* persevere, continue, remain, endure, stand, abide, plod. See CONTINUITY, DURABILITY. *Ant.*, see END.

persistent, *Adj.* durable, permanent, persevering, constant, steadfast, unfailing; enduring, unchanging. *Ant.*, see END.

person *n.* individual, body, somebody, anybody; man, woman, child; human, humanity. See MANKIND.

personage, *n.* dignitary, official, celebrity, notable, figure, somebody, bigwig. *Colloq.*, VIP, big wheel. See IMPORTANCE. *Ant.*, see UNIMPORTANCE.

personal, *adj.* private, individual, intimate, own, special, particular.

personality, *n.* character, individuality, self, ego; celebrity, notable. See MANKIND, REPUTE.

personify, *v.t.* embody, typify, symbolize, exemplify; represent, personate. See REPRESENTATION.

perspicacity, *n.* discernment, DISCRIMINATION, acuteness, keenness; shrewdness; penetration, insight, acumen. See INTELLIGENCE.

perspicuity, *n.* INTELLIGIBILITY; manifestation; definiteness, definition; exactness.

perspire, *v.t.* exude, sweat, exhale, excrete, swelter. See EXCRETION, HEAT.

persuade, *v.t.* induce, prevail upon, win; convince, satisfy, assure. See BELIEF, CAUSE.

persuasible, *adj.* docile, tractable, convincible; amenable, unresistant; persuadable. See ASSENT. *Ant.*, see REFUSAL.

persuasion, *n.* argument, PLEA, exhortation; conviction; INFLUENCE, insistence. See BELIEF, CAUSE.

persuasive, *adj.* inducive; cogent, convincing, logical; winning. See CAUSE.

pert, *adj.* impudent, saucy, flippant; forward, bold; perky. *Slang*, fresh, flip, sassy. See DISCOURTESY, INSOLENCE. *Ant.*, see COURTESY, SERVILITY, MODESTY.

pertain, *v.i.* apply, refer; belong, relate; appertain, concern; affect. See RELATION.

pertinacious, *adj.* persevering, persistent; obstinate, unyielding, constant, resolute, firm. See RESOLUTION.

pertinent, *adj.* relevant, apposite, applicable; apt. See RELATION.

perturbation, *n.* disturbance; disquiet, uneasiness, discomposure, apprehension, worry; trepidation, restlessness. See AGITATION, EXCITEMENT, FEAR.

peruse, *v.t.* read, con, study; examine.

pervade, *v.t.* fill, permeate, penetrate, imbue, overspread, impregnate, saturate; infiltrate. See PRESENCE.

pervasion, *n.* saturation, infiltration, permeation, penetration. See PRESENCE.

perverse, *adj.* contrary, stubborn, obstinate; reactionary, ungovernable, wayward; cross, petulant. See RESOLUTION, SULLENNESS.

perversion, *n.* DISTORTION, misuse, UNCONFORMITY, misrepresentation, misconstruction; corruption, debasement. See EVIL. *Ant.*, see CONFORMITY, VIRTUE.

perversity, *n.* OBSTINACY, obduracy, perverseness; waywardness, UNCONFORMITY, contumacy, wickedness; OBLIQUITY. *Slang*, mulishness, cussedness. See EVIL. *Ant.*, see VIRTUE, CONFORMITY.

pervert, *v.t.* apostatize, distort, twist, garble, debase, misrepresent, corrupt, mislead, misinterpret, misstate; equivocate. See DISTORTION, EVIL.

pessimism, *n.* despondency; gloom, depression, despair, DEJECTION, cynicism, morbidity. *Ant.,* see CHEERFULNESS, HOPE.

pessimist, *n.* alarmist, depreciator, cynic. *Ant.,* see HOPE, CHEERFULNESS.

pest, *n.* plague, pestilence, epidemic; parasite, infestation; nuisance, trouble; BANE, SCOURGE, curse. *Ant.,* see REMEDY.

pester, *v.t.* plague, annoy, trouble, vex, irritate, displease. See PAIN.

pestilence, *n.* DISEASE, plague, epidemic. *Ant.,* see HEALTH.

pet, *n. & v.t.* —*n.* FAVORITE, beloved, dearest, darling. —*v.t.* cherish, fondle, caress, embrace, stroke, cuddle. See ENDEARMENT, LOVE.

petition, *n. & v.t.* —*n.* PLEA, REQUEST, entreaty, supplication, prayer; asking, address. —*v.t.* ask, beg, entreat, REQUEST, plead, appeal, implore.

petitioner, *n.* solicitor; applicant, beggar. See REQUEST.

petrify, *v.t.* calcify, turn to stone, lapidify, fossilize; stun, astonish; stupefy, shock; stiffen, harden, paralyze. See DENSITY, HARDNESS, MINERAL, WONDER.

petty, *adj.* trivial, unimportant, small, mean, trifling; contemptible, spiteful; beggarly. See DISREPUTE, UNIMPORTANCE. *Ant.,* see IMPORTANCE, BENEVOLENCE.

petulant, *adj.* fretful, irritable, complaining, peevish, cross. See IRASCIBILITY.

phantom, *n.* unreality, VISION; spector, illusion, apparition, ghost, spirit, SHADE, shadow. See APPEARANCE. *Ant.,* see SUBSTANCE.

pharmacist, *n.* chemist, apothecary, druggist. See REMEDY.

phase, *n.* APPEARANCE, STATE, condition, situation, aspect; shape, FORM, angle. See CIRCUMSTANCE, SIDE.

phenomenon, *n.* PRODIGY; marvel, WONDER; happening, OCCURRENCE; event.

philanthropy, *n.* altruism, humanity, humanitarianism; BENEVOLENCE, good will to men, public welfare; generosity, openheartedness, openhandedness. See UNSELFISHNESS. *Ant.,* see MALEVOLENCE, SELFISHNESS.

philistine, *n.* vandal; bigot, uncultured person, yahoo, barbarian; mediocrity. See NARROWNESS.

philosophical, *adj.* contemplative, deliberative, thoughtful, speculative; imperturbable, calm; wise, rational; stoical, Platonic, Socratic. See REASONING, THOUGHT.

phlegmatic, *adj.* stolid, dull, apathetic; calm, imperturbable, languid, unemotional, inert, COLD. See INSENSIBILITY. *Ant.,* see SENSIBILITY.

phonetic, *adj.* phonic, phonal, phonetical, sonant; vocal, voiced, lingual, tonic, oral, spoken. See SOUND, SPEECH.

photograph, *n.* picture; photo, film, snapshot, reproduction; portrait. See REPRESENTATION.

phrase, *n. & v.* —*n.* expression; sentence, paragraph, clause; figure of speech, euphemism; idiom; locution; motto, maxim. —*v.t.* express, word, term, couch; voice. See FIGURATIVE, WRITING, INTERPRETATION.

physic, *n. & v.t.* —*n.* laxative, cathartic, purgative; drug, medicine; pill, dose. —*v.t.* purge, drench; treat, doctor. See REMEDY.

physical, *adj.* bodily, anatomical; material, substantial. See SUBSTANCE, *Ant.,* see INSUBSTANTIALITY, INTELLECT.

physician, *n.* doctor, medic, medico, surgeon, specialist; practitioner; consultant, adviser, healer. See ADVICE, REMEDY.

piazza, *n.* square, PLACE, street; porch, veranda, portico.

pick, *n. & v.t.* —*n.* best, cream, flower, élite, CHOICE; selection. —*v.t.* select, choose; pluck, garner, gather; cull. See ACQUISITION, GOODNESS. *Ant.,* see REFUSAL.

picket, *n. & v.t.* —*n.* post, pale, fence; sentry, guard, sentinel, patrol. See SHARPNESS, WARNING. —*v.t.* enclose, bar, fence; tether, restrain. See CIRCUMSCRIPTION, RESTRAINT, WARNING.

pickle, *v.t.* preserve, salt, corn, brine, marinate. See PRESERVATION.

pickpocket, *n.* THIEF, robber, cutpurse. *Slang,* dip. See STEALING.

picnic, *n.* excursion, junket, outing, festivity. See AMUSEMENT.

pictorial, *adj.* delineatory, graphic, depicting; illustrated. See PAINTING.

picture, *n.* image, likeness, counterpart; portrayal, REPRESENTATION, view, scene, tableau, setting; drawing, PAINTING, photograph, sketch, etching, canvas. See APPEARANCE, PAINTING.

picturesque, *adj.* artistic, graphic, attractive; vivid; quaint. See BEAUTY. *Ant.*, see UGLINESS.

piece, *n. & v.t.* —*n.* scrap, morsel, bit; section, fragment, PART. —*v.t.* unite, combine, patch, repair. See RESTORATION, JUNCTION. *Ant.*, see WHOLE.

pier, *n.* wharf, quay, mole, dock, breakwater; pillar, shaft, SUPPORT.

pierce, *v.t.* puncture, penetrate, perforate, bore, drill; stab, wound; affect; nip, chill. See SHARPNESS, OPENING, COLD.

piercing, *adj.* sharp, penetrating, keen, acute; discerning; cutting, biting; painful, affecting, chilling; high, shrill. See COLD, FEELING, SHARPNESS.

PIETY [987]

Nouns—**1,** piety, piousness, devoutness; RELIGION, theism, faith, BELIEF; religiousness, holiness, saintliness; reverence, worship, veneration, devotion; grace, unction, edification; sanctity, sanctitude; consecration; theopathy. **2,** beatification, canonization; sanctification; adoption, regeneration, conversion, justification, salvation, redemption; inspiration; bread of life; body and blood of Christ.

3, believer, convert, theist, Christian, devotee, pietist; the good, the righteous, the just, the believing, the elect; saint, Madonna; the children of God, the Kingdom, *or* light.

Verbs—**1,** be pious, have faith, believe, venerate, revere; be converted.

2, sanctify, beatify, canonize, inspire, consecrate, enshrine, keep holy; convert, edify, redeem, save, regenerate.

Adjectives—pious, religious, devout, devoted, reverent, godly, humble, pure, holy, spiritual, pietistic; saintly, saintlike; seraphic, sacred, solemn; believing, faithful, Christian, Catholic; elected, adopted, justified, sanctified, beatified, canonized, regenerated, inspired, consecrated, converted, unearthly.

Antonym, see IMPIETY.

---

pig, *n.* hog, sow, boar, swine; glutton; sloven, slob. See ANIMAL, GLUTTONY, UNCLEANNESS.

pigment, *n.* COLOR, stain, dye, tint, paint, SHADE. *Ant.*, see COLORLESSNESS.

pile, *n. & v.t.* —*n.* structure, building, edifice; heap, mass; quantity. See ASSEMBLAGE. —*v.t.* accumulate, load, amass, furnish.

pilfer, *v.* filch, rob, steal, plunder, thieve; shoplift. See STEALING.

pilgrim, *n.* wayfarer, traveler, migrant; settler, pioneer, newcomer; palmer, devotee. See PASSAGE.

pilgrimage, *n.* JOURNEY, crusade, mission, quest, expedition; LIFE, lifetime.

pillage, *n. & v.t.* —*n.* spoilation, plunder, vandalism, theft, depredation. —*v.t.* plunder, rape, thieve, rob, steal. See STEALING.

pillar, *n.* column, pedestal, SUPPORT, post, obelisk.

pillow, *n.* cushion, bolster, headrest, pad. See REPOSE.

pilot, *n.* helmsman, steersman, guide; counselor; aviator, airman. See AVIATION, DIRECTION, INFORMATION, NAVIGATION.

pin, *n. & v.t.* —*n.* peg, spoke, dowel; fastener, bolt, toggle; needle, bodkin, skewer, style; brooch, scarfpin, fraternity pin, tiepin; badge. —*v.t.* fasten, hold, bind, rivet, attach, secure. See ORNAMENT, JUNCTION.

pinch, *n. & v.* —*n.* stress, strain, pressure, emergency, DIFFICULTY, plight, predicament; pinching, nip. See CIRCUMSTANCE, PAIN. —*v.* nip, compress, tighten, squeeze; chill, bite, hurt. See CONTRACTION, PAIN.

pine, *v.i.* languish, long, crave; wither, droop. See DEJECTION, DESIRE. *Ant.*, see CHEERFULNESS.

pinnacle, *n.* SUMMIT, peak, top, acme, crown.

pioneer, *n.* forerunner, settler; originator; leader.

pious, *adj.* devout, religious, holy, dedicated. See PIETY. *Ant.*, see IMPIETY.

pipe, *n.* PASSAGE, tube, main; briar, corncob, meerschaum; flute, fife, bagpipe, flageolet. See MUSICAL INSTRUMENTS, OPENING, RECEPTACLE.

piquant, *adj.* pungent, flavorful, strong, sharp; tart; keen, stimulating. See FEELING, SHARPNESS.

pique, *v.t.* sting, cut, nettle, irritate, vex, offend; prick, jab; intrigue, stimulate, arouse interest. See EXCITEMENT, PAIN, ATTENTION.

pirate, *n. & v.t.* —*n.* buccaneer, marauder, corsair, freebooter, searobber, privateer. —*v.t.* plagiarize, steal; rob, plunder, picaroon, appropriate. See STEALING.

pistol, *n.* automatic, firearm, gun, derringer, revolver. *Colloq.,* shooting iron. *Slang,* gat, heater. See ARMS.

pit, *n.* hole, hollow, indentation, crater, excavation; abyss, HELL, Hades; mine, chasm; trap, snare. See CONCAVITY.

pitch, *n. & v.* —*n.* note, modulation, tone; ROLL, plunge, toss, dip, reel, lurch; slant, slope, drop; ascent, rise, grade, HEIGHT, range; resin, tar. —*v.t.* throw, toss; build, erect, set, establish; cast, heave. —*v.i.* ROLL, reel, plunge, toss; slope.

piteous, *adj.* grievous, sorrowful; pitiable, pathetic; wretched, miserable, deplorable. See PAIN, PITY.

pitfall, *n.* trap, snare, gin, pit; rocks, reefs, coral reef, sunken rocks, snags; sands, quicksands, slippery ground; breakers, shoals, shallows; precipice. See DANGER. *Ant.,* see SAFETY.

pith, *n.* pulp, core, heart; essence, kernel, substance, gist. See MEANING, CONTRACTION.

pithy, *adj.* concise; vigorous, forceful, powerful; meaningful; terse, brief, laconic. See CONTRACTION, MEANING. *Ant.,* see LOQUACITY.

pitiable, *adj.* miserable, paltry, wretched, deplorable; insignificant, woeful, pathetic. See BADNESS, PAIN, PITY.

pitiful, *adj.* compassionate, merciful, sympathetic, tender; deplorable, disreputable, pitiable, wretched; lamentable, piteous. See BADNESS, CONTEMPT, DISREPUTE.

pitilessness, *n.* inclemency; severity; MALEVOLENCE; mercilessness, cruelty, unfeelingness, ruthlessness. *Ant.,* see FEELING, PITY.

pittance, *n.* bit, mite, driblet; dole; pension, alms, allowance. See INSUFFICIENCY.

pitted, *adj.* blemished, variolate; honeycombed, favose, pocked, dented; cratered. See CONCAVITY. *Ant.,* see SMOOTHNESS.

PITY [914]

Nouns—pity, compassion, commiseration; lamentation, condolence; empathy, fellow-feeling, tenderness, yearning, forbearance, humanity, mercy, clemency; leniency, lenity, charity, ruth, quarter, grace.

Verbs—**1,** pity; have, give, show, *or* take pity; commiserate, condole, sympathize; feel for, be sorry for; weep, melt, thaw, forbear, relax, relent, give quarter; give the *coup de grâce,* put out of one's misery; have mercy; be charitable; be lenient.

2, excite pity, touch, affect, soften; melt, melt the heart; propitiate, disarm; deprecate, deplore.

Adjectives—pitying, piteous, pitiful; compassionate, sympathetic, affected, touched; merciful, clement, ruthful; humane; humanitarian, philanthropic, tenderhearted, softhearted, lenient, forbearing; melting, weak.

Antonym, see SEVERITY.

---

pivot, *n. & v.i.* —*n.* axis, turning point; gudgeon; joint, axle, hinge; focus; jewel. —*v.i.* swivel, turn, whirl; ROLL. See CAUSE, JUNCTION, ROTATION.

placard, *n.* notice, poster, billboard, advertisement, bill. See PUBLICATION.

place, *n.* lieu; spot, point; niche, nook, hole; pigeonhole, RECEPTACLE, compartment; premises, precinct, station; locality; somewhere, someplace, anyplace; situation.

placid, *adj.* serene, unruffled; calm, cool, collected; gentle, peaceful, quiet, undisturbed. *Ant.,* see EXCITEMENT, AGITATION.

plain, *adj.* simple; unornamented, unadorned, unvarnished; homely, homespun; neat; severe, chaste, pure; Anglo-Saxon; dry, unvaried, monotonous; earthy, down-to-earth; outspoken, blunt, direct, forthright, straight from the shoulder, down to brass tacks; in plain words, in plain English. See SIMPLENESS. *Ant.,* see ORNAMENT.

plain, *n.* prairie, tableland, steppe, savanna, tundra, heath, desert, pampas, mesa, llana; meadow, pasture, field. See LAND. *Ant.,* see HEIGHT.

plaintive, *adj.* mournful, wistful, sad, melancholy, sorrowful. See LAMEN-
TATION. *Ant.*, see REJOICING.
plan, *n. & v.* —*n.* scheme, design, project; proposal, proposition; schedule;
RESOLUTION, MOTION, provision, PREPARATION; system, order; organization,
ARRANGEMENT; CAUSE; sketch, skeleton, outline, layout; policy, CONDUCT;
strategy, stratagem, trick; device, makeshift, shift; measure, step; move,
plot, conspiracy, machination; counterplot. —*v.* scheme, design, contrive,
project, schedule; propose, sketch; devise, invent, lay out, map out; predetermine; concert, prepare, hatch, concoct; systematize, organize; arrange;
plot, counterplot, conspire, connive, intrigue. See IMAGINATION, ACTIVITY.
Ant., see CHANCE.
plane, *n. & v.t.* —*n.* level, stratum, grade, surface. —*v.t.* smooth, mill,
even, traverse, shave, level. See SMOOTHNESS.
plant, *n. & v.* —*n.* VEGETABLE, herb, organism, flower, seedling, shrub,
sprout, shoot; machinery, factory, equipment. *Slang*, hoax, trick, frameup.
See INSTRUMENT, DECEPTION. —*v.* implant, deposit, settle; colonize; sow
seed; engender. See AGRICULTURE, LOCATION.
plastic, *adj.* moldable, malleable, ductile, formable, pliant, impressionable,
formative. See FORM, SOFTNESS. *Ant.*, see HARDNESS.
plate, *n. & v.t.* —*n.* platter, dish, utensil, tray; slab, sheet, planch; coating,
veneer, coat. See LAYER, RECEPTACLE. —*v.t.* overlay, laminate; gild, silver,
platinize; veneer; electroplate. See COVERING.
plateau, *n.* PLAIN, mesa; platform; highland, tableland.
platform, *n.* stand, dais, rostrum, pulpit, stage; foundation, base, basis;
policy, PLAN. See SCHOOL, SUPPORT.
platitude, *n.* commonplace, cliché, truism, axiom, banality, proverb, trite-
ness.
platter, *n.* trencher, tray, waiter, dish, plate. See RECEPTACLE.
plaudit, *n.* acclaim, praise, applause, compliment, encomium, clapping.
See APPROBATION. *Ant.*, see DISAPPROBATION.
plausible, *adj.* suave, smooth, bland, credible, reasonable, believable;
specious, colored; justifiable, defensible. See CHANCE, INDICATION.
play, *n. & v.* —*n.* sport, frolic, fun, AMUSEMENT, game, recreation; DRAMA,
comedy, tragedy; scope, latitude, sweep, range. —*v.* operate, wield, ply;
act, perform; compete; pluck, bow, strike, beat; move, caper, gambol,
dally, idle, disport. See FREEDOM.
player, *n.* performer, actor, MUSICIAN, instrumentalist; participant, competitor. See DRAMA.
playful, *adj.* frolicsome, mischievous, sportive, frisky, roguish, prankish;
jolly, rollicking. See AMUSEMENT, CHEERFULNESS.
plaything, *n.* toy, doll, bauble; puzzle, kite, ball, top; bagatelle, trifle,
trinket. See AMUSEMENT, UNIMPORTANCE.
plea, .*n.* REQUEST; petition; assertion, allegation, advocation, advocacy;
pretext; excuse, VINDICATION; pretense, subterfuge, feint; blind.
plead, *v.* allege, assert, state; use as a plea; take one's stand upon; beg,
petition, urge, REQUEST. See VINDICATION.
pleasant, *adj.* see PLEASURE.
pleasantry, *n.* WIT, jest, banter, chaff, chit chat, persiflage.
please, *adv. & v.* —*adv.* if you please, pray, *s'il vous plait, bitte, por favor*;
kindly, do. See REQUEST, COURTESY. —*v.* gratify, satisfy, delight. See
PLEASURE, APPROBATION. *Ant.*, see DISAPPROBATION.

PLEASURE [377, 827]

Nouns—**1,** pleasure, enjoyment, gratification; voluptuousness, sensuality;
luxuriousness; GLUTTONY; titillation, appetite, gusto; creature comforts,
comfort, ease, luxury, lap of luxury; purple and fine linen; bed of down, bed
of roses, life of Riley; velvet, clover; treat; refreshment, feast; AMUSEMENT;
fleshpots, epicureanism, sybaritism, hedonism.
2, delectation; relish, zest; satisfaction, contentment, complacency; well-
being; good, snugness, comfort, cushion, *sans souci*, peace of mind.
3, joy, gladness, delight, glee, cheer, sunshine; CHEERFULNESS; happiness,
felicity, bliss; beatitude, beatification; enchantment, transport, rapture,

ravishment, ectasy; *summum bonum;* HEAVEN; unalloyed happiness. *Slang,*
bang, thrills, kicks, charge.
4, honeymoon, palmy days, halcyon days; golden age, golden time; Arcadia,
Eden, Utopia, happy valley, time of one's life; prime, heyday.
5, pleasurableness, pleasantness, agreeableness, delectability; attractiveness,
charm, fascination, enchantment, glamour, liveliness, BEAUTY; sunny side,
bright side.
Verbs—**1,** feel pleasure, be pleased, take pleasure in; revel in, delight in, rejoice in, like, LOVE; take to, take a fancy to; enjoy, relish, luxuriate in, riot
in, bask in, swim in, wallow in; thrive on. feast on; gloat over, smack the
lips; be in clover, live on the fat of the land, walk on air, live in comfort,
bask in the sunshine. *Colloq.,* live high off the hog; take the gravy train.
Slang, have a ball.
2, cause, give or afford pleasure; please, charm. delight; gladden, take,
captivate, enamor, fascinate; enchant, entrance, enrapture, transport, bewitch; ravish, enravish; bless, beatify; satisfy, gratify; slake, satiate, quench;
indulge, humor, flatter, tickle, tickle the palate, regale, refresh; enliven;
treat; amuse; strike *or* tickle one's fancy; tickle one pink; warm the cockles
of the heart; do one's heart good; attract, allure, stimulate, interest; thrill.
Colloq., hit the spot. *Slang,* send; give a kick, bang, *or* charge.
Adjectives—**1,** pleased, glad, gladsome; pleased as Punch; happy, blissful;
happy as a king, *or* as the day is long; thrice blest; in clover, in paradise, in raptures, on top of the world; ecstatic; overjoyed, entranced,
etc.; ecstatic, beatific; unalloyed, cloudless.
2, causing pleasure; pleasing, pleasant, pleasurable; agreeable; grateful,
gratifying, welcome, welcome as the flowers in May; to one's taste *or* liking;
cordial, genial; sweet, delectable, nice, dainty; delicate, delicious, dulcet;
luscious, palatable; cozy, snug; sumptuous, luxurious, voluptuous; attractive, inviting, prepossessing, engaging; winning, winsome, taking, fascinating, captivating; seductive, alluring, enticing; appetizing, entrancing, etc.;
empyrean, elysian, heavenly; palmy, halcyon. *Slang,* scrumptious, hunky-
dory.

Antonym, see PAIN.

plebeian, *adj.* unrefined, ill-bred, common, vulgar; lowborn, obscure, proletarian. See POPULACE. *Ant.,* see NOBILITY.
plebiscite, *n.* referendum, election, ballot, vote. See CHOICE.
pledge, *n. & v.t.* —*n.* PROMISE, SECURITY; gage, pawn, collateral, hostage,
deposit; WORD, troth, vow, guarantee; bond, oath. —*v.t.* deposit, wage,
pawn, hypothecate, mortgage; vow, undertake, engage, honor; toast.
Slang, hock. See PASSAGE, REPUTE, DEBT.
plentiful, *adj.* abundant, copious, ample, plenteous, enough, sufficient;
generous. See SUFFICIENCY. *Ant.,* see INSUFFICIENCY.
plenty, *n.* SUFFICIENCY, abundance, profusion, amplitude, copiousness;
wealth, luxury. *Ant.,* see INSUFFICIENCY.
pleonasm, *n.* REDUNDANCE, verbosity, diffuseness, tautology, superfluity,
circumlocution, wordiness.
pliable, *adj.* plastic, ductile, malleable; flexible, supple, limber, yielding;
docile, tractable, obedient, compliant, submissive. See SOFTNESS, OBEDIENCE.
pliant, *adj.* pliable, malleable, flexible, compliant, yielding. See SOFTNESS.
Ant., see HARDNESS.
plight, *n.* quandary, predicament, dilemma; trouble, DIFFICULTY, scrape,
crisis; situation, condition; betrothal, engagement. See CIRCUMSTANCE.
plod, *v.i.* persevere, persist; trudge, walk; labor, drudge, toil, work. See
ACTIVITY, RESOLUTION, SLOWNESS.
plot, *n. & v.* —*n.* diagram, PLAN, outline; field, enclosure, paddock, lot;
scheme, conspiracy, intrigue, collusion. See REGION, LAND. —*v.* conspire,
machinate, scheme, intrigue; chart, PLAN, lay out.
plow, plough, *v.t.* cultivate, dig, till, turn, break, FURROW. See AGRICUL-
TURE.
pluck, *n. & v.t.* —*n.* COURAGE, bravery, valor, stamina, endurance, grip,
determination, WILL. See RESOLUTION. *Ant.,* see COWARDICE. —*v.t.* pull,
jerk; pick, gather, garner.

plug, *n.* stopper, cork, dowel, plunger, tampon; quid, wad; wadding, padding, stopple, spigot.

plumage, *n.* feathers, down, feathering. See COVERING, ORNAMENT.

plumb, *adj. & v.t.* —*adj.* perpendicular, VERTICAL, erect; straight, true. *Colloq.*, downright; utterly. See DIRECTION. —*v.t.* sound (depths), fathom; do plumbing.

plume, *n.* quill, feather, egret, panache, plumage. See COVERING, ORNAMENT.

plummet, *n.* weight, plumb, bob, lead.

plump, *adj., adv. & v.* —*adj.* corpulent, fat, chubby, stout, fleshy, buxom, pudgy, rotund; blunt, direct, unqualified. —*adv.* suddenly, directly. —*v.* fatten, fill, distend; blurt; fall. *Colloq.*, plop (down); SUPPORT, root (for). See SIZE, IMPULSE.

plumpness, *n.* rotundity, obesity, corpulence, chubbiness, fatness. See SIZE.

plunder, *n. & v.* —*n.* pillage, loot, sack, spoil, booty; advantage, gain; spoliation, rapine. —*v.* devastate, harry, despoil, strip, rifle, loot, forage, pillage, ransack, maraud, rob, depredate. See STEALING.

plunge, *v. & n.* —*v.* dip, submerge; dive; sink, fall, drop; douse, go *or* put under water; gamble, bet heavily; fling, jump. *Colloq.*, go off the deep end. —*n.* dive, swim, dip; submersion; *Colloq.*, venture, a bold action.

plural, *adj.* not singular; more than one; at least two. See NUMBER.

plus, *adj., adv. & prep.* and; additional, extra, added (to). See ADDITION.

ply, *v.t.* exert, urge, ATTACK, apply; play, work; USE, exercise, manipulate, wield. See EXERTION.

pocket, *n. & v.t.* —*n.* pouch, bin, purse; hollow, placket. See CONCAVITY, RECEPTACLE. —*v.t.* appropriate, take, steal. See STEALING.

pocketbook, *n.* purse, wallet; bag, handbag; pouch, sporran. *Slang*, leather, kick. See RECEPTACLE.

POETRY [597]

Nouns—**1**, poetry, *ars poetica*, poesy; Muse, Calliope, Erato; versification, rhyming, prosody, orthometry; poem, ode, epode, idyl, lyric, blank verse, free verse, *vers libre;* eclogue, pastoral, bucolic, dithyramb, anacreontic; sonnet, ode, roundelay, rondeau, rondo, roundel, ballade, villanelle, triolet, pantoum, madrigal, canzonet, cento, monody, elegy; dramatic poetry, lyric poetry; opera, libretto; light verse, comic verse, *vers de société*.

2, song, ballad, lay; lullaby (see MUSIC); nursery rhymes; popular song.

3, doggerel, jingle, limerick, purple patches, macaronics.

4, canto, stanza, stich, verse, line; couplet, heroic couplets, triplet, quatrain; strophe, antistrophe.

5, rhyme, rime, assonance; meter, measure, foot, numbers, strain, rhythm; accentuation, stress, ictus; iamb(ic), dactyl, spondee, trochee, anapest; hexameter, pentameter, etc.

6, poet, poet laureate; bard, lyrist, skald, troubadour, trouvère, minstrel, minnesinger, meistersinger; versifier, poetaster.

Verbs—poetize, sing, versify, make verses; rhyme; scan.

---

poignant, *adj.* painful, pungent, intense, piercing, sharp, keen, biting. See PAIN, SHARPNESS.

point, *n.* object, MEANING, significance, intent, aim; speck, dot, spot; PLACE, LOCATION; pin, needle, prick, spike, prong, tip, END; PERIOD, LIMIT; goal, site. See IMPORTANCE, SHARPNESS, LITTLENESS.

pointed, *adj.* direct, concise, terse, pithy, brief; sharp, barbed, spiked. See CONTRACTION, SHARPNESS. *Ant.*, see LOQUACITY.

poise, *n.* equilibrium, balance, steadiness; self-possession, dignity, composure, imperturbability, coolness, nonchalance. See ORDER. *Ant.*, see AGITATION, EXCITEMENT.

poison, *n. & v.t.* —*n.* venom, toxicity, virus, bane. —*v.t.* corrupt, defile; intoxicate; drug, envenom; kill, murder. See DETERIORATION, KILLING.

poisonous, *adj.* venomous, toxic, deadly, virulent, noxious. See BADNESS.

poke, *v.* prod, nudge, stick, push; jab, punch. See IMPULSE.

pole, *v.t. & n.* —*v.t.* push, jab, prod, thrust, punch, nudge. See IMPULSE. —*n.* shaft, staff, post, stick, beam, mast; terminal, axis, hub, pivot; extremity, North *or* South Pole. See CENTRALITY, OPPOSITION.

polestar, *n.* lodestar, Polaris; guide; magnet, cynosure. See ATTRACTION, DIRECTION, UNIVERSE.

policeman, *n.* patrolman, officer; peace officer, traffic cop, motorcycle cop; constable, sheriff, deputy, state trooper; detective, plainclothesman; gendarme, bobby. *Slang,* cop, copper, flatfoot, bull, flic. See SAFETY.

policy, *n.* CONDUCT, administration, management; EXPEDIENCE, tactics, strategy; art, WISDOM; platform, PLAN.

polish, *n. & v.t.* —*n.* sheen, luster, shine, glaze, gloss; refinement, culture; COURTESY, tact, suavity, diplomacy; discernment, DISCRIMINATION. —*v.t.* shine, buff, burnish; scrub, scour, brighten; refine, perfect. See PERFECTION, SMOOTHNESS. *Ant.,* see DISCOURTESY, ROUGHNESS.

polite, *adj.* mannerly, civil, courteous, gracious; gallant, courtly, polished, refined. See COURTESY. *Ant.,* see DISCOURTESY.

politic, *adj.* discreet, expedient, artful, strategic; prudent, wise, judicious; wary, calculating. See CARE, KNOWLEDGE. *Ant.,* see RASHNESS.

poll, *n. & v.t.* —*n.* election, ballot; register; pate, head, skull. See CHOICE. —*v.t.* cut, crop, top; survey, canvass, tabulate.

pollute, *v.t.* contaminate; foul, desecrate; taint, soil, defile; corrupt, demoralize. See DETERIORATION, UNCLEANNESS. *Ant.,* see CLEANNESS.

poltroon, *n.* cad; dastard, craven, coward. See COWARDICE. *Ant.,* see COURAGE.

pommel, pummel, *v.t.* pound, beat, punch, maul, trounce, drub, flail, flog; sandbag, blackjack. See PUNISHMENT.

pomp, *n.* glory, grandeur, show, OSTENTATION, magnificence, display, STYLE, splendor. *Ant.,* see SIMPLENESS.

pompous, *adj.* boastful, self-important, ostentatious; high flown, bombastic, stilted; haughty, vain, grandiose, puffed up, arrogant. *Colloq.,* stuffy, snooty, stuffed-shirt. See OSTENTATION. *Ant.,* see SIMPLENESS.

pond, *n.* LAKE, pool, fishpond, mill pond, tarn.

ponder, *v.* think, muse, cogitate; reflect, meditate, weigh, deliberate, consider. See THOUGHT.

ponderous, *adj.* heavy, weighty, bulky, massive. See GRAVITY.

pool, *n. & v.t.* —*n.* association, amalgamation, fund; pond, puddle; reservoir, lake; swimming pool, natatorium. —*v.t.* combine, coöperate, share, contribute. See COÖPERATION.

poor, *adj.* indigent, penniless, impoverished, needy, beggarly, impecunious, insolvent, moneyless; inferior, faulty, unsatisfactory, imperfect, defective; humble; weak, flimsy. See BADNESS, INSUFFICIENCY, POVERTY. *Ant.,* see GOODNESS, SUFFICIENCY, MONEY.

poorness, *n.* lack, want, dearth, scarcity; inferiority, insignificance. See POVERTY. *Ant.,* see MONEY.

POPULACE [876]

Nouns—**1,** populace; the people, multitude, crowd, masses; bourgeoisie; commonalty; democracy; common people, lower classes, hoi polloi, rank and file, the ruck, proletariat, great unwashed.

2, mob, rabble, rout; horde, canaille; dregs; scum of society *or* the earth; riffraff; ragtag and bobtail; small fry.

3, commoner, man in the street, the average man, the little man, one of the people, democrat, plebeian, proletarian, republican, bourgeois; Mrs. Grundy, Philistine, Babbitt. *Slang,* Joe Blow, John Q. Public.

4, peasant, countryman, boor, churl, villein; serf; dockwalloper, longshoreman, navvy; swain, clown, clod, clodhopper; hobnail, yokel, bumpkin; plowman, rustic, tiller of the soil; white-collar man, girl, or worker; hewers of wood and drawers of water. *Slang,* hick, jay, hayseed, rube; goon.

5, beggar, mudlark, *sans culotte,* raff, tatterdemalion, hobbledehoy, caitiff, ragamuffin, pariah; guttersnipe, urchin, street urchin *or* arab; tramp, hobo, knight of the road, vagabond, vagrant, bum, weary Willie. *Slang,* bindlestiff.

Adjectives—plebeian, proletarian, common, democratic; homely, homespun; vulgar, lowborn, baseborn; unknown to fame, obscure, untitled; rustic, loutish, boorish, clownish, churlish; barbarous, barbarian, barbaric.

Antonym, see NOBILITY.

popular, *adj.* common, public, plebeian; acceptable, cheap; approved, like, praised; elect, chosen; desirable; admired, famous, celebrated, noted, See APPROBATION, CHOICE, DESIRE, REPUTE. *Ant.,* see DISAPPROBATION, REFUSAL, DISREPUTE.

population, *n.* inhabitants, people, race; residents; nation. See INHABITANT.

porch, *n.* veranda, portico, piazza; entrance, portal; stoa. See OPENING. RECEPTACLE.

porous, *adj.* open; absorbent; perforated, honeycombed; sandy; permeable, loose, pervious. See OPENING. *Ant.,* see SMOOTHNESS.

port, *n.* REFUGE, harbor, shelter, haven; OPENING, embrasure, porthole; APPEARANCE, bearing, deportment, demeanor; LEFT, larboard (*Naut.*).

portable, *adj.* transportable, movable, carriable.

portage, *n.* carrying (of boats); carrying. See TRAVEL.

portal, *n.* entrance, door, entry, doorway, gateway, portcullis. See OPENING.

portend, *v.t.* signify, presage, augur, forebode, foreshadow, omen, foretoken, mean. See PREDICTION, INDICATION.

portent, *n.* WONDER, marvel, phenomenon; sign, foreshadowing, foreboding, token; importance, MEANING. See INDICATION.

porter, *n.* doorman, *concierge* (*Fr.*), gatekeeper, guard, sentinel, warder; bearer; *Colloq.,* redcap. See CARRIER.

portfolio, *n.* briefcase, bag, portmanteau, attaché case; LIST (of stocks, *etc.*), catalog. See RECEPTACLE.

portico, *n.* colonnade, stoa, veranda, porch. See RECEPTACLE.

portion, *n. & v.t.* —*n.* share, allotment, due, ration; PART, serving, morsel, fragment; fate, lot, DESTINY; dividend; section. —*v.t.* dower, apportion, divide, endow. See APPORTIONMENT. *Ant.,* see WHOLE.

portly, *adj.* dignified, imposing, stately; fat, fleshy, stout, corpulent; bulky. See SIZE.

portmanteau, *n.* trunk, suitcase, valise; PORTFOLIO; combined word. See RECEPTACLE.

portrait, *n.* picture, likeness; depiction, DESCRIPTION; photograph, sketch. See PAINTING, REPRESENTATION.

portray, *v.t.* depict, delineate, describe, picture; represent, act; draw. See REPRESENTATION.

pose, *n. & v.i.* —*n.* attitude; AFFECTATION; position, posture; aspect, figure. —*v.i.* attitudinize, affect; propound; question, puzzle, quiz, inquire, nonplus. See AFFIRMATION, DOUBT.

position, *n.* SITUATION, placement, point, spot, PLACE, LOCATION, site; billet, berth, post, station office, rank, status; caste; LOCATION, site; incumbency; dignity, honor. See BUSINESS, CIRCUMSTANCE, REPUTE.

positive, *adj.* certain, decided, emphatic, unqualified, absolute; inescapable, peremptory, firm. See AFFIRMATION, CERTAINTY. *Ant.,* see DOUBT, NEGATION.

POSSESSION [777]

Nouns—**1,** possession, ownership (see PROPERTY); occupancy, occupation; hold, holding; tenure, tenancy, feudality, dependency; monopoly, corner, retention; heritage, inheritance, heirship, reversion; fee, seigniority; bird in hand; nine points of the law; vested interests.
2, possessor, holder; occupant, occupier; tenant, renter, lodger, lessee; owner; proprietor, proprietress; master, mistress, lord; landholder, landowner, landlord, landlady; lord of the manor, laird; legatee, devisee; heir, heiress, inheritress, inheritrix.

Verbs—**1,** possess, have, hold, occupy, enjoy; be possessed of, own, command; inherit, come to, come in for; acquire (see ACQUISITION); RETAIN.
2, belong to, appertain to, pertain to; be in one's possession; vest in.

Adjectives—**1,** possessing, having; worth; possessed of, seized of, master of, in possession of; in fee simple; outright; endowed with, blest with, fraught with; possessed; on hand, by one; in hand, in store, in stock; in one's hands, at one's command, to one's name, at one's disposal; one's own.
2, retentive, retaining, tenacious; reserved, entailed.
    Antonym, see POVERTY, DEBT.

possibility, *n.* potentiality, likelihood; what may be, what is possible; practicability, feasibility; contingency, CHANCE.

possible, *adj.* potential, conceivable, credible; practicable, feasible, performable, achievable, within reach, accessible, surmountable; attainable, obtainable; contingent. See POSSIBILITY. *Ant.,* IMPOSSIBLE.

post, *n. & v.* —*n.* station, position; incumbency, PLACE, office, mail; stake, picket, newel, pillar, pier. —*v.* mail; inform, publish, RECORD, enter, transfer; speed, hurry; move up and down (on horseback). See BUSINESS, LOCATION, VELOCITY.

poster, *n.* PUBLICATION, billboard, advertisement, placard, bill.

posterity, *n.* progeny; breed; issue, offspring, brood, litter; seed; farrow; spawn; family, grandchildren, heirs, child, son, daughter; scion; shoot, sprout, branch; offshoot, ramification; descendant; heir, heiress; heir apparent, heir presumptive; chip off the old block; rising *or* younger generation; heredity. See ANCESTRY, DESCENT.

posthaste, *adv.* speedily, hastily, at top speed, apace, expeditiously, swiftly. See RASHNESS, VELOCITY.

postpone, *v.t.* procrastinate, delay, defer; shelve, adjourn, table. See LATENESS, NEGLECT.

postscript, *n.* ADDITION, appendix, afterthought; P.S., P.P.S.

posture, *n.* pose, attitude; bearing, position, carriage; mood, condition. See FORM.

pot, *n.* crock, jug, tankard; kettle, pan, vessel; mug. See RECEPTACLE.

potent, *adj.* powerful, strong, mighty; intense, influential; effectual, effective, forceful; capable, able. See POWER. *Ant.,* see IMPOTENCE.

potentate, *n.* king, sovereign, ruler, monarch. See AUTHORITY.

potential, *adj.* dynamic, magnetic, charged; dormant, latent; unfulfilled, promising. See POWER.

pottery, *n.* earthenware, china, porcelain, crockery; dishes, utensils.

poultry, *n.* chickens, ducks, geese, turkeys; fowl(s), hens, broilers, fryers, roosters; pigeons, squab. See ANIMAL.

pounce, *v.i.* spring, leap, jump; snatch, grasp, seize; ambush. See SURPRISE.

pound, *v.t.* beat, thump, drum, bruise, tenderize; pulverize. See POWDERINESS, IMPULSE.

pour, *v.* flow, emerge; decant, fill; issue; rain, flood, shower. See EGRESS, WATER.

pout, *v.i.* sulk, grimace, moue. See DEJECTION.

POVERTY [804]

Nouns—**1,** poverty, inepecuniousness, indigence, penury, pauperism, destitution, want; need, neediness; lack, necessity, privation, distress, difficulties; bad, poor *or* needy circumstances; reduced *or* straitened circumstances; slender means, straits; hand-to-mouth existence; beggary; mendicancy, loss of fortune, bankruptcy, insolvency (see DEBT).

2, poor man, pauper, mendicant, beggar, starveling.

Verbs—**1,** be poor, want, lack, starve, live from hand to mouth, have seen better days, go down in the world, go to the dogs, go to wrack and ruin; not have a penny to one's name; beg one's bread; tighten one's belt. *Slang,* go broke.

2, render poor, impoverish, reduce to poverty; pauperize, fleece, ruin, strip.

Adjectives—poor, indigent; poverty-stricken; poor as a church mouse; poor as Job's turkey; penniless, impecunious; hard up; out at elbows *or* heels; seedy, shabby; beggarly, beggared; destitute, bereft, in want, needy, necessitous, distressed, pinched, straitened; unable to keep the wolf from the door, unable to make both ends meet; embarrassed, involved; insolvent, bankrupt, on one's uppers, on the rocks. *Colloq.,* in the hole, broke, stony, looking for a handout.

Antonym, see MONEY.

POWDERINESS [330]

Nouns—**1,** powderiness; grittiness, sandiness; efflorescence; friability.

2, powder, dust, sand, sawdust; grit; meal, bran, flour, farina; crumb, seed, grain; particle (see LITTLENESS); filings, débris, detritus, floc.

3, pulverization, grinding, comminution, attenuation, granulation, disintegration, subaction, trituration, levigation, abrasion, detrition, crystallization, limation; filing; erosion, corrosion (see DETERIORATION).

4, mill, grater, rasp, file, mortar and pestle, teeth, grinder, grindstone, quern; chopper.

Verbs—pulverize, comminute, crystallize, granulate, triturate, levigate; scrape, file, abrade, rub down, grind, grate, rasp, pound, contuse, beat, crush, crunch, crumble; rust, shatter, disintegrate.

Adverbs—powdery, pulverulent, granular, mealy, floury, farinaceous, branny, furfuraceous, flocculent, dusty, sandy; arenose, arenarious, arenaceous; gritty; efflorescent; friable, crumbly, shivery; attrite; in pieces, shards, flinders, *etc.*

Antonym, see COHERENCE.

POWER [157]

Nouns—**1,** power, potence, potency, potentiality; puissance, might, force; ENERGY; dint; right hand, right arm; ascendancy, ascendency, sway, control; prepotency; almightiness, omnipotence; AUTHORITY, STRENGTH. *Slang*, steam.

2, ability; ableness; competency; efficiency, efficacy; validity, cogency; enablement; vantage ground; INFLUENCE; capability, MEANS, capacity; faculty, quality, attribute, endowment, virtue, gift, property, qualification, susceptibility. *Slang*, the stuff, something on the ball, what it takes.

3, pressure, elasticity; gravity, electricity, magnetism, electromagnetism; ATTRACTION; force of inertia, dead force, living force; ENERGY, hydroelectric power, waterpower; atomic power, horsepower; FRICTION, suction; torque, thrust.

4, engine, motor, dynamo, generator; pump, mill, windmill; power plant; Diesel, gas, gasoline, internal combustion, steam engine; reciprocating, jet, rocket engine; turbine.

Verbs—**1,** be powerful; be able; can; sway, control; compel (see COMPULSION).

2, strengthen, fortify, harden; empower, enable, invest, endue, arm, reinforce.

3, invigorate, energize, stimulate, kindle, refresh, restore.

Adjectives—**1,** powerful, puissant; potent, potential; capable, able; equal to, up to; cogent, valid; effective, effectual; efficient, efficacious, adequate; competent; STRONG, omnipotent; all-powerful, almighty; electric, magnetic; attractive; energetic, forcible, forceful, incisive, trenchant, electrifying; influential (see IMPORTANCE); productive (see PRODUCTION).

2, resistless, irresistible; invincible, indomitable, invulnerable, impregnable, unconquerable; overpowering, overwhelming.

Adverbs—powerfully, strongly, irresistibly, etc.

Antonym, see IMPOTENCE.

powerlessness, *n.* IMPOTENCE; paralysis, incapacity, weakness, inability, disablement. *Ant.*, see POWER.

practicable, *adj.* possible, feasible; useful, practical; workable, achievable.

practical, *adj.* pragmatical, useful, operative; effective. See AGENCY, UTILITY. *Ant.*, see USELESSNESS.

practice, *n. & v.* —*n.* training, drill, exercise; custom, HABIT; manner, METHOD, procedure. —*v.* exercise, apply; perform, act, do; drill, rehearse. See ACTION, TEACHING, USE, CONDUCT.

prairie, *n.* PLAIN, grassland, mesa, steppe, llano, savanna.

praise, *n. & v.t.* —*n.* commendation, acclaim, approval, applause; eulogy; homage; benediction, thanksgiving, grace. —*v.t.* acclaim, approve, commend, extol, eulogize, applaud; glorify, laud. See APPROBATION. *Ant.*, see DISAPPROBATION.

praiseworthy, *adj.* commendable, good, laudable, meritorious, admirable. See APPROBATION. *Ant.*, see DISAPPROBATION.

prance, *v.i.* caper, cavort, spring, dance, slip.

prank, *n.* CAPRICE, frolic, caper, trick, jest, escapade.

prattle, *n. & v.t.* —*n.* chitchat, babbling, chatter. —*v.i.* murmur, chatter, babble, jabber. See LOQUACITY, SPEECH.

pray, *v.i.* implore, ask, beg, REQUEST, solicit, petition, entreat; WORSHIP.

prayer, *n.* worship; invocation, supplication; intercession; orison, matin; beseeching, petition, entreaty, REQUEST; collect; litany, liturgy; Lord's prayer, paternoster; hallelujah, hosanna, praise to the Lord; Mass; communication with God; devotion(s), praise, thanksgiving; Hail Mary, Ave Maria; the rosary; Psalm; Shema, Kol Nidre, Kaddish (*Jewish*); Allahu akbar, Fatihah, shahada, rak'ah (*Moslem*); Ram, Ram, Siva, Siva (*Hindu*). See RELIGION.

preach, *v.* exhort, evangelize, lecture, sermonize, moralize. See RITE, TEACHING.

preacher, *n.* moralizer; clergyman, *etc.* See CLERGY.

preamble, *n.* prologue, introduction, preface, prelude.

precarious, *adj.* dangerous, risky; critical; doubtful, uncertain, unsafe, insecure, unstable. See TRANSIENTNESS, DOUBT. *Ant.,* see SAFETY.

precaution, *n.* CARE, CAUTION, WARNING; safeguard, PROVISION, protection; anticipation, forethought. See PREPARATION, SAFETY. *Ant.,* see NEGLECT, RASHNESS.

precede, *v.* lead; come *or* go before, come first; introduce, usher in; prefix; premise, prelude, preface; forerun; go ahead, go in advance; herald, head, take the lead; lead the way, steal a march. *Colloq.,* get in on the ground floor. See PRIORITY.

precedence, *n.* PRIORITY; SUPERIORITY, IMPORTANCE; antecedence, antecedency, anteriority; precession. See FRONT. *Ant.,* see REAR.

precedent, *n.* HABIT, standard, model; PROTOTYPE; custom, practice, usage; decision, case. See LAWSUIT.

precept, *n.* instruction, charge; prescript, prescription; recipe, receipt; golden rule; MAXIM, rule, canon, law, code, act, statute, rubric, regulation; FORM, formula, formulary, order, COMMAND. See TEACHING.

precession,. *n* precedence, PRIORITY, forerunning, antecedence, going before; FRONT, van, lead; going *or* being first. *Ant.,* see SEQUENCE.

precinct, *n.* neighborhood, district, area; enclosure, boundary, LIMIT; environs. See REGION.

precious, *adj.* priceless, costly; precise, overnice; beloved, dear. See PAYMENT, LOVE. *Ant.,* see CHEAPNESS.

precipice, *n.* cliff, drop, bluff, declivity.

precipitate, *adj. & v.* —*adj.* rash, hasty, hurried, headlong, impetuous. See RASHNESS, HASTE. *Ant.,* see CARE, LEISURE. —*v.* CAUSE, foment; hasten, speed, expedite; separate (as a chemical solution); fall (as rain, snow, *etc.*).

precipitation, *n.* HASTE, impetuosity, rush; RASHNESS; deposit, silt; rain, snow, dew, hail; condensation. *Ant.,* see SLOWNESS.

precipitous, *adj.* steep, abrupt, clifflike, sheer. See OBLIQUITY.

precise, *adj.* exact, accurate, definite, punctilious; fastidious; unbending, rigid; prim, precious. See FORM, TRUTH. *Ant.,* see ERROR.

preclude, *v.t.* prevent, stop, prohibit, obviate, check; forestall. See HINDRANCE.

precocious, *adj.* advanced, overforward, premature. See EARLINESS. *Ant.,* see LATENESS.

preconception, *n.* anticipation, prejudgment; prejudice. See MISJUDGMENT.

precursor, *n.* See FORERUNNER.

predacious, *adj.* rapacious, predatory, raptorial, plundering, pillaging, ravening. See STEALING.

predatory, *adj.* robbing, ravening, predacious, plundering. See STEALING.

predecessor, *n.* FORERUNNER, precursor, harbinger, herald; ancestor, antecedent, progenitor. See ANCESTRY. *Ant.,* see SEQUENCE.

predestine, *v.* foredoom, predestinate, preordain, foreordain. See PREDICTION.

predetermine, *v.t.* premeditate, predestine, preresolve; preconcert; prearrange; foreordain, doom; plan. *Colloq.,* stack the cards. See NECESSITY, PREDICTION. *Ant.,* see IMPULSE, CHANCE.

predicament, *n.* condition, quandary, fix, corner, dilemma, mess, scrape, crisis, emergency. *Colloq.,* spot. See CIRCUMSTANCE, DIFFICULTY.

PREDICTION [511]

Nouns—**1,** prediction, announcement; premonition, WARNING; intuition, prophecy, prognosis, prognostication, premonstration; augury, auguration; foreboding, presentiment, premonition; ominousness; auspices, forecast; OMEN, horoscope, soothsaying; fortune-telling; divination; necromancy (see SORCERY); spiritualism, clairvoyance; extrasensory perception; psi; sixth sense; astrology, horoscopy; prefiguration, prefigurement; prototype, type.
2, FORESIGHT, precognition, prescience, prevision.
3, prophet, oracle, fortune-teller, soothsayer, crystal-gazer; Cassandra.
Verbs—**1,** predict, prognosticate, prophesy, divine, foretell, soothsay, augur, tell fortunes; cast a horoscope; advise, PROMISE; forewarn (see WARNING); presage, bode, forebode, foretoken, portend, foreshadow; typify, protypify; herald, announce; loom, impend.
2, bid fair; promise; lead one to expect; be the precursor *or* forerunner.
3, foresee, anticipate, foreknow, presurmise, expect.
Adjectives—**1,** predicting, predictive, prophetic, oracular, sibylline; ominous, portentous; auspicious; prescient; minatory, monitory, premonitory.
2, premeditated, predesigned, predetermined; psychokinetic.
Antonym, see CHANCE.

---

predilection, *n.* partiality, preference, prejudice, bias. See TENDENCY, MISJUDGMENT. *Ant.,* see HATE.
predominant, *adj.* prevalent, controlling, ascendant, ruling, supreme. See POWER. *Ant.,* see IMPOTENCE, INFERIORITY.
preëminent, *adj.* outstanding, conspicuous, notable, distinguished, renowned; foremost, paramount, superior, supreme. See REPUTE, SUPERIORITY. *Ant.,* see INFERIORITY.
preface, *n. & v.t.* —*n.* foreword, prologue, preamble, introduction, prelude, preliminary. —*v.t.* introduce, open, premise, precede. See PRIORITY.
prefer, *v.t.* select, fancy, choose, adopt; OFFER; promote, advance. See CHOICE, IMPROVEMENT.
pregnant, *adj.* significant, weighty, potential; gravid, parturient; impregnated, big (with child), *enceinte* (*Fr.*). See IMPORTANCE, PRODUCTION. *Ant.,* see UNIMPORTANCE.
prejudge, *v.t.* presuppose, assume, presume. See MISJUDGMENT.
prejudice, *n. & v.t.* —*n.* partiality, bias, opinion; predilection, prepossession; detriment, injury; intolerance. See MISJUDGMENT.
preliminary, *adj.* introductory, preparatory, prefatory. See BEGINNING, PREPARATION.
prelude, *n.* preface, foreword, prologue, introduction, precursor. See MUSIC, PRIORITY.
premature, *adj.* untimely, underripe, immature, precocious, unprepared, incomplete; forward. See EARLINESS.
premeditate, *v.t.* calculate, plan, predesign, resolve, prearrange.
premiere, *n.* opening, debut, first night, inauguration, bow. See DRAMA.
premises, *n.pl.* building, LAND, house, apartment, office, *etc.;* bases, data, testimony, facts. See EVIDENCE, PLACE, REASONING.
premium, *n.* REWARD, prize, PAYMENT, recompense, gift, bounty, fee, bonus. See RECEIVING.
premonition, *n.* foreboding, presentiment, portent, forewarning. See WARNING.
premonitory, *adj.* cautionary, ominous, portentous, betokening, minatory. See WARNING.
preoccupation, *n.* inattentiveness, prepossession, distraction, absorption, engrossment. *Colloq.,* brown, study. *Ant.,* see ATTENTION.

PREPARATION [673]

Nouns—**1,** preparation, preparing; providing; provision, providence, prearrangement, anticipation, FORESIGHT; precaution, predisposition; forecast, PLAN; rehearsal; training, education (see TEACHING); inurement, HABIT; novitiate.
2, ARRANGEMENT, clearance; adjustment (see AGREEMENT); tuning, equipment, outfit.

3, groundwork, keystone, cradle, steppingstone; foundation.

4, preparation of food, cuisine, cooking, cookery; culinary art; preparation of the soil, tilling, plowing, sowing, semination, cultivation; manufacture, PRODUCTION.

5, preparedness, readiness, ripeness, mellowness; maturity.

6, preparer, trainer, TEACHER; pioneer, pathfinder, trailblazer; FORERUNNER.

Verbs—**1,** prepare; get ready, make ready; make preparations, settle preliminaries, get up, predispose; set *or* put in order (see ARRANGEMENT); forecast, PLAN; lay the foundations, basis *or* groundwork; roughhew; nurture (see AID); hatch, cook, brew.

2, equip, arm, man; fit out, fit up; furnish, rig, dress; ready, set, prime, attune; adjust, put in working order, put in tune; pack; prepare for, train, teach, rehearse; make provision for; take steps, measures, *or* precautions; provide, provide against, set one's house in order; clear the decks for action.

3, prepare oneself; serve an apprenticeship; get into harness, gird up one's loins, buckle on one's armor; shoulder arms, get up steam; save for a rainy day; keep one's powder dry.

Adjectives—**1,** preparing, in preparation, in embryo, in hand; brewing, hatching, brooding; in store for, in reserve; precautionary, provident; preparative, preparatory; provisional; under revision; preliminary (see PRECEDENCE).

2, prepared, in readiness, ready, handy; planned, strategic, schematic; in working order; in practice; practised, skilled; in battle array, in war paint; armed to the teeth, sword in hand; booted and spurred; on the alert, vigilant, *semper paratus*. *Colloq.*, on the mark, all set, on tap, ready to roll.

Adverbs—in preparation, in anticipation of; against, for; under construction, afoot, afloat, under consideration, on foot. *Colloq.*, in the works, on the fire.

Antonym, see NEGLECT.

---

preponderance, *n.* prevalence, control, predominance, supremacy, ascendancy. See INFLUENCE, SUPERIORITY.

prepossessing, *adj.* appealing, attractive; charming, winning, winsome, engaging. See ATTRACTION, PLEASURE. *Ant.*, see UGLINESS.

preposterous, *adj.* ridiculous, absurd, nonsensical, idiotic; foolish, extravagant; improper, unsuitable. See ABSURDITY.

prerogative, *n.* franchise, RIGHT, privilege; birthright; l iberty, advantage.

prescribe, *v.t.* urge, suggest, advise; order, advocate, decree; appoint, institute; ordain. See ADVICE, COMMAND.

prescription, *n.* medicine; formula, recipe; mandate, decree, edict. See REMEDY, COMMAND.

PRESENCE [186]

Nouns—**1,** presence, attendance; ASSEMBLAGE; occupancy, occupation, habitation, inhabitancy, residence, ABODE; permeation, pervasion; diffusion, dissemination; occurrence; ubiety, ubiquity, omnipresence, EXISTENCE.

2, SPECTATOR, bystander, attender, patron, audience; beholder, observer, witness.

Verbs—**1,** be present; exist; look on, witness, watch; attend, remain; find oneself, present oneself; show one's face; occur; lie, stand. *Colloq.*, show up.

2, occupy, people, inhabit, dwell, reside, stay, sojourn, live, abide, lodge, nestle, roost, perch; take up one's abode (see LOCATION); frequent, haunt; tenant. *Slang*, hang out.

3, fill, pervade, permeate; be diffused, be disseminated; overspread, overrun; run across.

Adjectives—present; occupying, inhabiting; moored (see LOCATION); resident, residential; domiciled, domiciliary; ubiquitous, omnipresent; peopled, populated, inhabited.

Adverbs—here, there, where, everywhere, aboard, on board, at home, afield; on the spot; here, there and everywhere (see SPACE); in the presence of, before, in person; under the eyes of, under the nose of; in the face of. *Colloq.*, in the flesh; live (*Radio & T.V.*).

Antonym, see ABSENCE.

present, *n.* present time, moment, *or* day; the present, the times, this day and age; the time being; the nonce; time of life; now, the here and now. See TIME.

present, *n. & v.t.* —*n.* gift, favor, gratuity, offering, bonus, donation. See GIVING. *Ant.,* see RECEIVING. —*v.t.* award, endow, give, assign, deliver, proffer, tender, pass, bestow. See GIVING. *Ant.,* see RECEIVING, REFUSAL.

presentiment, *n.* PREDICTION, foreboding, anticipation, premonition, apprehension; foretaste, prescience, OMEN.

presently, *adv.* soon, shortly, immediately, eventually. See EARLINESS. *Ant.,* see LATENESS.

PRESERVATION [670]

Nouns—**1,** preservation; conservation; safekeeping (see STORE); maintenance, SUPPORT; conservation, ECONOMY; salvation, deliverance.

2, preserver, conserver, preservative; embalming; curing, pickling, salting, smoking, canning; dehydration; tanning; refrigeration, freezing, quick-freezing.

Verbs—**1,** preserve, maintain, keep, sustain, support; keep up, keep alive; bank up, nurse; save, rescue; make safe (see SAFETY); take care of, guard, defend (see DEFENSE).

2, conserve; dry, cure, salt, pickle, corn, smoke; dehydrate, quick-freeze; bottle, pot, tin can; tan; husband; embalm, mummify; immortalize.

Adjectives—preserving, preservative; hygienic; preserved, unimpaired, unsinged, unmarred, safe and sound; intact, unscathed, with a whole skin.

Antonyms, see WASTE, DETERIORATION.

---

preside, *v.i.* supervise, superintend, control, rule, direct, manage. See AUTHORITY.

president, *n.* head, chairman, dean, principal, chief, ruler. See AUTHORITY.

press, *n. & v.* —*n.* crush, throng, crowd; pressure, urgency; closet, wardrobe, repository; printing machinery; ASSEMBLAGE; newspapers. See IMPORTANCE, PRINTING, PUBLICATION, RECEPTACLE. —*v.* crush, push, force; iron, smooth; compel, force, urge, beg, persuade; hug, embrace; squeeze, wring; solicit, entreat, importune. See COMPULSION, ENDEARMENT, GRAVITY, SMOOTHNESS.

pressing, *adj.* critical, important, urgent; exacting, demanding; persistent.

pressure, *n.* strain, COMPULSION, NECESSITY, urgency, stress; persuasion, coercion, persuasiveness; affliction, trouble; distress; heaviness, compression. See ADVERSITY, GRAVITY, IMPORTANCE, CONTRACTION.

prestige, *n.* REPUTE, reputation, dignity, fame, note, importance.

presume, *v.i.* impose, venture; deduce, assume, infer, presuppose; infringe, take liberties. See FREEDOM, SUPPOSITION.

presumption, *n.* audacity, assurance, arrogance, haughtiness; impetuosity; deduction, conclusion, inference, guess, hypothesis. See INSOLENCE, RASHNESS.

presuppose, *v.t.* assume, presume, imply. See SUPPOSITION.

pretend, *v.i.* sham, feign, dissemble, simulate; counterfeit, lie, fake; claim, aver. See FALSEHOOD. *Ant.,* see TRUTH.

pretender, *n.* claimant; impostor; fraud, humbug, hypocrite; deceiver. See DECEPTION.

pretense, *n.* show, pretension, AFFECTATION, sham, IMITATION, OSTENTATION; UNTRUTH, makeshift, simulation, excuse, pretext, evasion.

pretension, *n.* OSTENTATION, pretense, AFFECTATION, profession, airs; claim. See VANITY. *Ant.,* see MODESTY, SIMPLENESS.

pretentious, *adj.* showy, gaudy; overdone, exaggerated; affected, unnatural; garish, ostentatious; conceited, vain. See AFFECTATION, OSTENTATION, VANITY. *Ant.,* see MODESTY, SIMPLENESS.

pretext, *n.* subterfuge, pretense, excuse, justification, VINDICATION; cover, cloak, blind, sham, evasion. See DECEPTION.

pretty, *adj. & adv.* —*adj.* attractive, comely, good-looking; delicate, precise. See BEAUTY. *Ant.,* see UGLINESS. —*adv.* rather; moderately.

prevail, *v.i.* preponderate, predominate, rule, obtain; exist, be; overcome;

succeed, induce, persuade. See EXISTENCE, HABIT, SUCCESS, CAUSE. *Ant.*, see FAILURE.

prevalence, *n.* dominance, prominence; ubiquitousness, commonness, universality, currency; reign, power, sway. See SUPERIORITY.

prevalent, *adj.* customary, current; predominant, prominent, prevailing, preponderant; general, rife, current. See HABIT.

prevaricate, *v.i.* quibble, cavil, equivocate, palter. See FALSEHOOD. *Ant.*, see TRUTH.

prevent, *v.t.* preclude, hinder, stop, check, impede, forestall, avert, restrain, prohibit. See HINDRANCE. *Ant.*, see AID.

prevention, *n.* HINDRANCE; preventive, preclusion, inhibition, RESTRAINT, interception, stoppage, restriction. *Ant.*, see AID.

preventive, *adj.* inhibitory, deterrent, preclusive; prophylactic; prohibitive. See HINDRANCE. *Ant.*, see AID.

previous, *adj.* antecedent, anterior; preceding, foregoing, former, prior. See PRIORITY.

prey, *n. & v.i.* —*n.* victim, quarry, game, kill; loot, prize, spoil. See KILLING. —*v.i.* plunder, pillage, ravage; haunt, wear. See STEALING.

price, *n. & v.* —*n.* amount, cost, expense, prime cost; charge, figure; demand; fare, duty, toll, tax, ransom; salvage, tariff; worth, costliness, expense, rate, value; current *or* market price, quotation. —*v.t.* fetch, sell for, cost, bring in, yield, afford. See PAYMENT.

priceless, *adj.* invaluable, precious; expensive, costly. *Ant.*, see CHEAPNESS.

prick, *v.t.* puncture, pierce, stick; sting, wound; prod, urge, incite, goad, spur. See SHARPNESS, PAIN.

prickly, *adj.* thorny, barbed, bristly, spiny, thistly, burry; stinging, tingling. See ROUGHNESS, SHARPNESS. *Ant.*, see SMOOTHNESS.

pride, *n.* self-respect, dignity, *noblesse oblige;* VANITY, haughtiness, hauteur, self-esteem.

priest, *n.* father, clergyman, *etc.* See CLERGY.

priggish, *adj.* pedantic, affected; fastidious, prim, precious; conceited, egotistic. See AFFECTATION.

prim, *adj.* precise, demure, formal, priggish; fussy, prudish. See AFFECTATION.

primary, *adj.* chief, original, initial, first, elementary; immediate; primitive, prime, principal. See BEGINNING, CAUSE, IMPORTANCE. *Ant.*, see END, EFFECT, UNIMPORTANCE.

prime, *adj.* original, first, initial; primitive, primeval; chief, leading, main; CHOICE, finest. See BEGINNING, IMPORTANCE, OLDNESS. *Ant.*, see END, UNIMPORTANCE, NEWNESS.

primitive, *adj.* aboriginal, primeval, crude, unpolished, unrefined; primal, primary; prime; old, original, antiquated. See OLDNESS. *Ant.*, see NEWNESS.

primness, *n.* prudery, prudishness, priggishness; formality; preciousness, stiffness. See AFFECTATION.

prince, *n.* monarch, ruler, sovereign; nobleman; chief. *Slang,* swell guy. See NOBILITY, AUTHORITY, SUPERIORITY.

princely, *adj.* regal, royal, titled, noble; magnanimous, generous, munificent. See NOBILITY. *Ant.*, see POPULACE, PARSIMONY.

principal, *n. & adj.* —*n.* chief, leader, head; constituent, client; buyer, seller; capital, *corpus.* See MONEY. —*adj.* foremost, chief, prime, greatest, main, leading. See IMPORTANCE. *Ant.*, see UNIMPORTANCE.

principle, *n.* tenet, code, doctrine, conviction; theory, premise; postulate; RULE, law, precept; equity, integrity, PROBITY, nature, origin, source, CAUSE. See BELIEF. *Ant.*, see IMPROBITY.

PRINTING [591]

Nouns—**1,** printing; typography, stereotype, electrotype; block printing; lithography, planography, collotype; offset, letterpress, gravure, rotogravure; intaglio; ENGRAVING; PUBLICATION; composition, typesetting; Linotype, Monotype, Intertype; imposition; mat, matrix; reproduction; graphic arts.

2, type, case, lower case, upper case, capital; font; typeface, roman, italic, lightface, boldface; stick, stone; shank, serif; Gothic, oldstyle *or* modern type, *etc.;* print.

3, impression, proof, galley, galley proof, page proof, repro(duction) proof, revise, run, rerun; plate, replate.

4, printing press, press, proof press; job press, flatbed press, cylinder press, rotary press.

5, printer, compositor, typographer, pressman, makeup man, proofreader, copyholder; stone hand; printer's devil, proof boy.

Verbs—print, imprint; compose, impose, set, make up; proofread, revise; makeready; go to press.

Adjectives—printed; in type; typographical; graphic; in black and white.

PRIORITY [116]

Nouns—priority, antecedence, anteriority, precedence, primogeniture; pre-existence; precession; precursor, forerunner; PAST; premises.

Verbs—**1,** be prior, precede, come *or* go before; lead; pre-exist; dawn; presage (SEE PREDICTION).

2, be beforehand, be early (SEE EARLINESS); steal a march upon, anticipate, forestall; have *or* gain a start; steal one's thunder, anticipate. *Slang,* beat out, scoop.

Adjectives—prior, previous; preceding, precedent; anterior, antecedent; fore-handed; pre-existing, pre-existent; former, foregoing; afore-mentioned, above-mentioned; aforesaid; said; introductory, precursory; preliminary, prefatory; preparatory.

Adverbs—before, formerly, prior to; earlier; previously, ere, heretofore, erstwhile, already, yet, beforehand; in advance, ahead; in the van *or* fore-front; in front, foremost; on the eve of; *ante bellum;* before Christ; B.C.; antediluvian, before the fact.

Antonym, see SEQUENCE.

PRISON [752]

Nouns—**1,** prison, penitentiary; jail, lockup, gaol, cage, coop, den, cell; cell block; stronghold, fortress, keep, dungeon, Bastille, oubliette; Sing Sing, Dartmoor, Alcatraz; Bridewell, house of correction, debtors' prison, prison farm, workhouse; guardroom, guardhouse; alimony jail; brig, hold; round-house, station house, station, police station; house of correction, reforma-tory, reform school, protectory; house of detention; pen, fold, corral, pound; INCLOSURE; penal colony *or* settlement; stocks, stone walls. *Slang,* jug, can, calaboose, calabozo, hoosegow, pen, big house, stir, clink, cooler, school, quad. See RESTRAINT.

2, prisoner, captive, felon; convict; trusty, parolee; ticket-of-leave man. *Colloq.,* jailbird. *Slang,* lag, con.

3, warden, KEEPER, jailer, gaoler, turnkey, guard, warder. *Slang,* screw.

Verbs, Adjectives—see RESTRAINT.

Antonym, see FREEDOM.

privacy, *n.* SECLUSION; intimacy; solitude; secrecy. *Ant.,* see SOCIALITY, ACCOMPANIMENT.

private, *adj.* personal; secluded; intimate; sequestered; privy, confidential, unofficial; individual, special. See SECLUSION. *Ant.,* see SOCIALITY.

privation, *n.* want, LOSS, POVERTY, indigence; deprivation, bereavement, dispossession. *Ant.,* see MONEY, SUFFICIENCY.

privilege, *n.* option, franchise; prerogative, RIGHT; favor, EXEMPTION, ex-ception, immunity, liberty. See FREEDOM. *Ant.,* see RESTRAINT.

prize, *n. & v.t.* —*n.* TROPHY, medal, award, decoration, laurel; premium, bonus, REWARD; advantage, privilege; pick, élite. —*v.t.* cherish, treasure, esteem, value. See APPROBATION, LOVE. *Ant.,* see DISAPPROBATION.

probable, *adj.* likely; hopeful; to be expected; in a fair way; plausible, ostensible, well-founded, reasonable, credible, believable, presumable, pre-sumptive, apparent, *prima facie;* in the cards. See CHANCE.

probation, *n.* trial, test, examination.

probe, *v.t.* prod, pierce, stab; sound, fathom; search, investigate, sift, explore; verify. See INQUIRY MEASUREMENT.

PROBITY [939]

Nouns—**1,** probity, integrity, rectitude; uprightness; honesty, faith; honor; good faith, *bona fides;* clean hands, PURITY; dignity, respectability; right, JUSTICE; INNOCENCE, VIRTUE.

2, constancy; faithfulness, fidelity, loyalty; incorruption, incorruptibility; allegiance, devotion; trustworthiness, TRUTH, candor, veracity, sincerity.

3, punctilio, delicacy, nicety, conscientiousness; scrupulosity, scrupulousness, scruple, point of honor; punctuality, honor system.

4, loftiness of purpose; unselfishness, disinterestedness, sublimity, chivalry.

5, gentleman, man of honor, honest man, man of his word, *fidus Achates;* truepenny. *Colloq.,* square-shooter, brick. *Slang,* trump, regular fellow, good egg, right guy.

Verbs—be honorable; deal honorably, squarely, impartially, *or* fairly; speak *or* tell the truth; do one's duty; keep one's promise *or* word; be as good as one's word; keep faith with; his word is his bond. *Colloq.,* be on the level; be on the up and up; level.

Adjectives—**1,** upright; honest; veracious, truthful; virtuous, honorable, law-abiding; fair, right, just, equitable, impartial, square; open and aboveboard; straightforward, frank, candid, openhearted. *Slang,* on the level, on the up and up, straight, square-shooting, legit.

2, constant, faithful, loyal, staunch; true, true-blue, true to the core; trusty, trustworthy; as good as one's word, reliable, dependable, to be depended on, steadfast, incorruptible, above suspicion.

3, conscientious; DISINTERESTED, right-minded; high-principled, high-minded; scrupulous, religious, strict; nice, punctilious, correct, punctual; respectable, reputable, gentlemanly.

4, inviolable, inviolate; innocent, pure; stainless, unstained, untarnished, unsullied, untainted; uncorrupt, incorruptible; chivalrous, *sans peur et sans reproche.*

Adverbs—honorably, bone fide; on one's honor, on the square, in good faith, honor bright, with clean hands.

Antonym, see IMPROBITY.

---

problem, *n.* question, proposition, exercise; perplexity, poser, puzzle, enigma, riddle; issue; query. *Ant.,* see ANSWER.

problematical, *adj.* questionable, unsettled, perplexing; uncertain, enigmatic. See DOUBT. *Ant.,* see CERTAINTY.

proboscis, *n.* trunk, snout, nose. See CONVEXITY.

procedure, *n.* process, METHOD, tactics, proceeding, way, course; practice, CONDUCT; policy, FORM. See AGENCY.

proceed, *v.i.* continue, progress, advance; move, arise; emanate, result; issue. See PROGRESSION, CONTINUITY. *Ant.,* see REGRESSION, DISJUNCTION, END.

proceeding, *n.* ACTION, progress, move, measure, step, procedure. *Ant.,* see INACTIVITY.

proceeds, *n.pl.* balance, profit, gain, yield, earnings, receipts, issue, outcome, results; income. See ACQUISITION, MONEY.

process, *n.* CONDUCT, METHOD, procedure, COURSE, practice; outgrowth, protuberance, appendage, projection. See CONVEXITY.

procession, *n.* cavalcade, parade, train, column, file; PROGRESSION, sequence, succession. See CONTINUITY, TRAVEL.

proclaim, *v.t.* announce, declare, broadcast, circulate, publish, herald. See PUBLICATION.

proclivity, *n.* inclination, TENDENCY, propensity, proneness. See IMPULSE.

procrastination, *n.* postponement, delay, dilatoriness; negligence, omission. See LATENESS, NEGLECT. *Ant.,* see EARLINESS, CARE.

procure, *v.t.* acquire, purchase, get, obtain; buy, hire; effect. See ACQUISITION, CAUSE. *Ant.,* see LOSS, SALE.

procurer, *n.* pander, bawd, pimp, procuress; obtainer. See EVILDOER.

prodigality, *n.* profligacy, unthriftiness, WASTE; profusion, profuseness; extravagance; squandering; excess, lavishness, liberality. *Ant.,* see PARSIMONY.

prodigious, *adj.* immense, enormous, vast, gargantuan, huge; remarkable, wonderful; monstrous; astonishing. See GREATNESS, WONDER. *Ant.*, see LITTLENESS.

prodigy, *n.* phenomenon; wonder, marvel, miracle; monster; curiosity, sight, spectacle; precocious child, child prodigy. *Slang*, boy wonder. See UNCONFORMITY.

produce, *n. & v.t.* —*n.* goods, yield, harvest; fruit, vegetables; stock, commodity, product. See ACQUISITION, SALE. —*v.t.* show, exhibit; create, originate, bear, breed, hatch; make, FASHION, manufacture.

producer, *n.* See PRODUCTION.

product, *n.* yield, output, produce; outcome, result. See ACQUISITION, EFFECT, PRODUCTION.

PRODUCTION [161]

Nouns—**1,** production, creation, construction, formation, fabrication, manufacture; building, architecture, erection, edification; coinage; organization; putting together, establishment; workmanship, performance, operation; achievement, COMPLETION.

2, bringing forth, parturition, birth, childbirth, delivery, confinement, travail, labor, midwifery, obstetrics; gestation, evolution, development, growth; genesis, generation, procreation, progeneration, propagation; fecundation, impregnation; spontaneous generation; biogenesis, abiogenesis, parthenogenesis; authorship, PUBLICATION, works.

3, product; edifice, building, structure, fabric, erection; invention, composition; WRITING, BOOK, PAINTING, MUSIC; flower, fruit, work, handiwork.

4, productiveness, fecundity, fertility, luxuriance; pregnancy, pullulation, fructification, multiplication; fertilization.

5, producer, creator, originator, inventor, author, founder, generator, mover, architect, maker.

6, manufacture, manufacturing, fabrication; mass production, assembly line; automation.

Verbs—**1,** produce, perform, operate, do, make, form, construct, fabricate, frame, contrive; mass produce, manufacture; weave, forge, coin, carve, chisel; build, raise, rear, erect, put together; set up, run up, establish, constitute, compose, organize, institute; achieve, accomplish, complete, perfect.

2, produce, flower, bear fruit, fructify; teem, ean, yean, farrow, drop, whelp, pup, kitten; bear, lay, bring forth, give birth to, lie in, be delivered of; evolve, pullulate, usher into the world.

3, make productive, create; beget, get, generate, fecundate, impregnate; reproduce, proliferate, procreate, progenerate, propagate; fertilize, spermatize, conceive; bud, bloom, blossom, burgeon; engender; bring into being, call into being, bring into existence; breed, hatch, develop, bring up; induce, superinduce; suscitate, CAUSE, acquire (see ACQUISITION).

Adjectives—produced, producing, productive, prolific, fertile, fecund, creative, procreative; formative; genetic, genital; pregnant; *enceinte*, big with, fraught with; teeming, parturient, puerperal. *Colloq.*, expectant, in the family way.

Antonym, see DESTRUCTION.

---

profane, *adj. & v.t.* —*adj.* vulgar; sacrilegious, impious, unhallowed. —*v.t.* debase,, desecrate, defile, pollute; abuse. See IMPIETY.

profess, *n.* pretend, feign; teach, instruct; affirm, declare, avow; own, admit. See AFFIRMATION, TEACHING. *Ant.*, see NEGATION.

profession, *n.* vocation, calling, occupation; sham, evasion, pretense; AFFECTATION, pretension; relief; acknowledgment, declaration, avowal. See AFFIRMATION, TEACHING. *Ant.*, see NEGATION.

proficient, *adj.* expert, dext(e)rous, adept, adroit; well-versed, practiced; masterly, skillful. See SKILL. *Ant.*, see UNSKILLFULNESS.

profile, *n.* OUTLINE, side, shape, contour.

profit, *n. & v.i.* —*n.* advantage, benefit, interest; gain, earnings, return. See ACQUISITION, INCREASE. *Ant.*, see LOSS, DECREASE.

profitable, *adj.* remunerative, lucrative, paying, gainful; advantageous, productive; serviceable, useful. See ACQUISITION, RECEIVING, USE. *Ant.*, see LOSS, DECREASE.

profound, *adj.* erudite, learned, abstruse; heavy, weighty, deep; heartfelt, intense; complete, thorough. See FEELING, GREATNESS, KNOWLEDGE. *Ant.*, see LITTLENESS, IGNORANCE.

profuse, *adj.* excessive, redundant; prodigal, wasteful, extravagant, lavish. *Ant.*, see INSUFFICIENCY.

profusion, *n.* abundance, multiplicity; excess, waste, superfluity, extravagance; plenty. See MULTITUDE, SUFFICIENCY. *Ant.*, see RARITY, INSUFFICIENCY.

progeny, *n.* children, offspring, descendants, family. See POSTERITY. *Ant.*, see ANCESTRY.

prognosticate, *v.t.* prophesy, foretell, augur, predict. See PREDICTION.

program, *n.* playbill, prospectus, syllabus; agenda; forecast, draft, outline.

PROGRESSION [282]

Nouns—progression, progress, progressiveness; MOTION; advance, advancing, advancement; ongoing; flood-tide, headway; march (see TRAVEL); rise; IMPROVEMENT.

Verbs—progress, advance, proceed; get on, get along, get underway; gain ground; go with the stream, current, *or* tide; hold *or* keep one's course; go, move, pass on, push *or* press on, forward, ahead; make one's way, work one's way; make progress *or* headway; make rapid strides; gain leeway. *Slang*, go great guns, get rolling, get cracking.

Adjectives—advancing, progressing, progressive, advanced.

Adverbs—progressively; forward, onward; forth, on, ahead; under way, en-route, on one's way, on the road, on the high road; in progress.

Antonym, see REGRESSION.

---

progressive, *adj.* enterprising, advanced, moving; improving, advancing; successive, continuing, continuous. See CONTINUITY, IMPROVEMENT, PROGRESSION. *Ant.*, see DISJUNCTION, REGRESSION.

prohibit, *v.* inhibit; forbid, veto, disallow; bar; debar, forfend, restrain, withhold, circumscribe, clip the wings of; restrict; interdict, taboo; padlock; ban; proscribe; exclude, shut out; discriminate; warn off; disbar, unfrock. See RESTRAINT. *Ant.*, see PERMISSION, FREEDOM.

prohibition, *n.* forbiddance; veto; interdiction; injunction; embargo, ban, taboo *or* tabu, proscription; restriction, RESTRAINT, HINDRANCE; forbidden fruit; Volstead Act, Eighteenth Amendment, dry law. See ILLEGALITY. *Ant.*, see PERMISSION, FREEDOM.

project, *n. & v.t.* —*n.* PLAN, purpose, enterprise; endeavor. —*v.t.* protrude, bulge, jut; throw, hurl, pitch; devise, PLAN, scheme, intend. See CONVEXITY. PROPULSION.

projectile, *n.* ball, pellet, bullet, missile, shell. See ARMS.

projection, *n.* extension, shelf; protuberance, protrusion; prominence, spur, eminence; transference, visualization. See CONVEXITY.

prolific, *adj.* fruitful, fecund, productive, fertile; lavish. See PRODUCTION.

prolix, *adj.* lengthy, wordy, long-winded, discursive, verbose, diffuse; tedious. See LOQUACITY, WEARINESS. *Ant.*, see CONTRACTION.

prologue, *n.* preface, introduction, proem, preamble, prelude. See BEGINNING.

prolong, *v.t.* extend, protract, hold; sustain, perpetuate, continue; lengthen. See CONTINUITY, LENGTH. *Ant.*, see END, SHORTNESS.

prominence, *n.* notability, IMPORTANCE, eminence, fame; swelling, protuberance, excrescence, bulge, mound. See CONVEXITY, RELIEF, REPUTE. *Ant.*, see DISREPUTE.

prominent, *adj.* notable, important, salient, memorable; convex, raised, protuberant, projecting; influential, distinguished, eminent; conspicuous, noticeable. See CONVEXITY, IMPORTANCE, REPUTE. *Ant.*, see UNIMPORTANCE, DISREPUTE.

promiscuous, *adj.* indiscriminate, mixed, miscellaneous, confused. See MIXTURE. *Ant.*, see TASTE.

PROMISE [768]

Nouns—promise, UNDERTAKING, word, troth, pledge, parole, word of honor, vow, avowal; oath (see AFFIDAVIT); profession, assurance, warranty, guarantee, insurance, obligation; covenant, contract, COMPACT; affidavit; engagement, affiance; betrothal, betrothment, troth, engagement, *etc.*

Verbs—**1,** promise; give *or* make a promise; undertake, engage; make *or* enter into an engagement; bind, pledge, *or* commit oneself; take upon oneself; vow; dedicate, swear (see AFFIRMATION); give, pledge, *or* plight one's word; plight one's troth; betroth, plight faith; assure, warrant, guarantee; covenant (see COMPACT); attest (see EVIDENCE); contract an obligation; become bound to, become sponsor for; answer for, be answerable for; secure; give security; underwrite.

2, extract a promise, adjure, administer an oath, put to one's oath, swear a witness, swear in.

Adjectives—promising, promissory; votive; under hand and seal, upon oath, under oath; promised, affianced, pledged, bound; committed, compromised; in for it.

---

promontory, *n.* spit, headland, cape. See HEIGHT.

promote, *v.t.* advance, further; AID; improve, dignify, elevate, raise; back, SUPPORT, encourage. See IMPROVEMENT. *Ant.,* see DETERIORATION.

promoter, *n.* founder, organizer, planner; backer, supporter, encourager. See PLAN.

promotion, *n.* elevation, advancement; preferment; AID; graduation. See IMPROVEMENT. *Ant.,* see HINDRANCE, DETERIORATION.

prompt, *v.t. & adj.* —*v.t.* incite, induce, motivate; actuate; remind, suggest, mention. See INFORMATION, MEMORY, CAUSE. —*adj.* immediate, ready, punctual, unretarded; alert, quick, active; instant, instantaneous; reasonable, early. See ACTIVITY, EARLINESS. *Ant.,* see LATENESS.

promulgate, *v.t.* publish, disseminate, proclaim, sponsor, advocate. See PUBLICATION.

prone, *adj.* inclined, disposed, likely, predisposed; recumbent, flat, prostrate, HORIZONTAL. *Ant.,* see VERTICAL.

pronounce, *v.t.* speak, say, utter, enunciate, articulate; deliver, JUDGE, conclude; affirm, assert. See AFFIRMATION, SPEECH, VOICE.

pronunciation, *n.* utterance, saying, voicing, articulation, enunciation, orthoëpy. See VOICE.

proof, *n.* EVIDENCE, substantiation, verification, confirmation; conclusiveness; corroboration, ratification; trial, test; sample, impression. *Ant.,* see NEGATION.

prop, *n. & v.t.* —*n.* SUPPORT, brace, stay, pillar, underpin, shore, column, block, base; foundation; mainstay, assistant, helper, staff; fulcrum; truss. —*v.t.* SUPPORT, uphold, brace, encourage, back; truss; shore, underpin, underset.

propaganda, *n.* publicity; persuasion, proselytization, movement. See TEACHING.

propagate, *v.t.* breed, generate, produce, disseminate; spread, broadcast, publish, increase; multiply. See PRODUCTION, PUBLICATION.

propel, *v.t.* push, force, impel, thrust, shove, activate, move, drive. See PROPULSION.

propensity, *n.* TENDENCY, aptitude, inclination, talent, bent, proclivity, disposition.

proper, *adj.* correct, fastidious; suitable, becoming; decorous, demure, chaste, delicate; individual, special, limited, own, appropriate, pertinent, apropos, meet; seemly, befitting; equitable, fair, RIGHT, just.

PROPERTY [780]

Nouns—**1,** property, POSSESSION, ownership, proprietorship, lordship; seigniority; empire, dominion (see AUTHORITY); interest, stake, estate, RIGHT, title, claim, demand, holding; tenure; vested, contingent, beneficial, *or* equitable interest; USE, trust, benefit; fee simple, fee tail.

2, dower, dowry, dot; jointure, appanage; inheritance, heritage, patrimony; alimony; legacy (see GIVING).

3, assets, belongings, MEANS, resources, circumstances; wealth, MONEY; credit; patent, copyright; landed property, real property, real estate, realty, land, lands; tenements; hereditaments; territory, state, kingdom, principality, realm, empire; dependence; protectorate, sphere of influence; manor, domain, demesne; farm, plantation, hacienda; freehold, leasehold; fixtures, plant; easement.

4, personal property *or* effects; personalty, chattels, goods, effects, movables; stock in trade; things, traps, gear, paraphernalia; equipage; parcels, appurtenances; impedimenta; luggage, dunnage, baggage; bag and baggage; pelf; cargo, lading, freight.

Verbs—possess (see POSSESSION); own; belong to, pertain to.

Adjectives—one's own; landed, manorial, allodial; freehold, leasehold; feudal.

Antonym, see POVERTY.

prophecy, *n.* PREDICTION, prognosis, forecast, prognostication, presage, augury, divination.

prophet, *n.* oracle, soothsayer, prognosticator, sibyl; predictor, seer, diviner.

prophylactic, *adj.* preventive; precautionary; preservative, protective. See HEALTH. *Ant.*, see DISEASE.

propinquity, *n.* NEARNESS, vicinity, proximity; adjacence; RELATION; juxtaposition. *Ant.*, see DISTANCE.

propitiate, *v.t.* pacify, conciliate, reconcile; intercede, calm, mediate; atone. See ATONEMENT, COMPROMISE, PACIFICATION. *Ant.*, see HATE, OPPOSITION.

propitiatory, *adj.* apologetic, conciliatory, expiatory; sacrificial, atoning. See ATONEMENT, PACIFICATION. *Ant.*, see HATE, OPPOSITION.

propitious, *adj.* encouraging, auspicious; gracious; fortunate, prosperous, favorable; timely, opportune; thriving. See HOPE, PROSPERITY. *Ant.*, see FEAR, ADVERSITY.

proportion, *n.* dimension, ratio, extent; share, PART, quota, distribution, allotment; adjustment, UNIFORMITY; magnitude. See APPORTIONMENT, RELATION, SIZE, FORM. *Ant.*, see LITTLENESS, DISTORTION.

proportional, *adj.* commensurable, measurable, proportionate. See NUMBER.

proportionate, *adj.* commensurate, proportionable, proportional, according. See AGREEMENT, EQUALITY, RELATION.

proposal, *n.* OFFER, statement, recommendation, proposition, MOTION, suggestion; REQUEST; overture, advance.

propose, *v.t.* propound, advance, present, state; recommend; suggest; court, woo; intend; proffer, nominate. See ENDEARMENT, MOTION, SUPPOSITION.

proposition, *n.* OFFER, PLAN, project, proposal, undertaking; axiom, hypothesis, theorem, postulate, problem, thesis, predication. See REASONING.

propound, *v.t.* propose, state, suggest. See SUPPOSITION.

proprietor, *n.* manager, owner; MASTER, lord. See POSSESSION.

propriety, *n.* decorum, conventionality, suitability; aptness, fitness; fastidiousness, becomingness, delicacy, seemliness; prudery. See AGREEMENT. *Ant.*, see DISAGREEMENT.

PROPULSION [284]

Nouns—**1,** propulsion, projection; push (see IMPULSE); ejaculation; EJECTION; throw, fling, toss, shot; see ARMS.

2, propeller, driver, turbine (see POWER); shooter, archer, bowman, rifleman, marksman, pitcher; good shot, crackshot; sharpshooter.

Verbs—propel, project, throw, fling, cast, pitch, chuck, toss, jerk, heave, shy, hurl; pitch; dart, lance, tilt; jet, squirt, spurt, ejaculate; fulminate, bolt, drive, sling, pitchfork; send; send off, let off, fire off; discharge, shoot; launch, catapult, send forth; let fly; dash; put *or* set in motion; set going, start; give a start, give an impulse to; impel, expel, put to flight, send flying.

Adjectives—propelled, propelling, propulsive, projectile.

Antonym, see HINDRANCE.

prosaic, *adj.* unimaginative, DULL, uninteresting, commonplace, prosy, plain, sober. *Ant.*, see WIT, ORNAMENT.

proscribe, *v.t.* outlaw, forbid, interdict, prohibit, condemn, excommunicate, exile, curse. See RESTRAINT. *Ant.*, see PERMISSION.

prosecute, *v.t.* urge, pursue, follow, continue, press; arraign, sue, indict, charge. See LAWSUIT, PURSUIT.

proselyte, *n.* convert, follower, neophyte. See CHANGE.

prospect, *n.* view, outlook, scene, landscape, vista, sight; PROMISE, probability, HOPE, EXPECTATION, foresight. See APPEARANCE, FUTURITY.

prospective, *adj.* probable, foreseen, expected; coming; imminent. See EXPECTATION, FUTURITY.

prospectus, *n.* presentation, brochure; description, sketch; design, scheme. See LIST, PLAN.

PROSPERITY [734]

Nouns—prosperity, welfare, well-being; affluence, WEALTH, SUCCESS; thrift; good fortune, blessings, luck; sunshine; fair weather, fair wind; fat years, palmy days, halcyon days; golden time, golden age; bed of roses; fat of the land, milk and honey, good times; godsend, windfall, manna from heaven. *Colloq.*, land-office business; lucky break, streak *or* run of luck, Lady Luck; boom; heyday.

Verbs—**1,** prosper, grow, multiply, thrive, flourish; be prosperous; go well, smoothly, *or* swimmingly; flower, blow, burgeon, blossom, bloom, fructify, bear fruit; fatten, batten.

2, rise, rise in the world, get on in the world; climb the ladder of success; make one's way or fortune; feather one's nest; bear a charmed life; bask in the sunshine; have a run of luck; have good fortune; take a favorable turn; live on the fat of the land, live in clover; win out, make a strike. *Slang*, make one's pile, make a hit, strike it rich.

Adjectives—prosperous; thriving; rich, wealthy; fortunate, lucky, in luck; auspicious, propitious, providential; palmy, halcyon.

Phrases—every dog has his day; sitting on top of the world, born with a silver spoon in one's mouth, be fruitful and multiply; have money to burn.

Antonym, see ADVERSITY.

---

prostrate, *adj. & v.t.* —*adj.* recumbent, prone, flat, supine; debased, abased, humbled; helpless, powerless, resigned. —*v.t.* debase, abase, flatten; bow, submit. See IMPOTENCE, OBEDIENCE.

prosy, *adj.* prosaic, DULL, stupid, commonplace; unpoetic, uninspired, pedestrian; jejune, tedious. See WEARINESS. *Ant.*, see WIT, AMUSEMENT.

protect, *v.t.* defend, guard, shelter, shield, screen; preserve, save, champion, secure. See SAFETY. *Ant.*, see ATTACK.

protection, *n.* safeguard, DEFENSE, shelter, screen; AID, SUPPORT, PRESERVATION; championship, custody, care, guard; foil. See INFLUENCE, RESTRAINT, SECURITY. *Ant.*, see ATTACK, FREEDOM.

protector, *n.* guard, warder, defender, champion; patron; chaperon; guardian, conservator, custodian. See DEFENSE, SAFETY. *Ant.*, see ATTACK, DANGER.

protest, *n. & v.t.* —*n.* objection, complaint, remonstrance, contradiction, disapproval, expostulation, protestation. See DISSENT, DISAPPROBATION. *Ant.*, see APPROBATION, ASSENT. —*v.t.* object, remonstrate, complain, contradict, repudiate, default. ` See DEBT.

prototype, *n.* original; model, pattern; precedent; standard, type; archetype; module, exemplary, example, paradigm; test, copy, design; keynote, die, mold; matrix, last.

protract, *v.t.* extend, lengthen; prolong, continue; postpone, defer, delay. See CONTINUITY, LATENESS, LENGTH. *Ant.*, see END, SHORTNESS.

protrude, *v.* jut, bulge, extend, project. See CONVEXITY. *Ant.*, see CONCAVITY.

protuberance, *n.* projection, bulge, jut, protuberancy, prominence, excrescence, lump, swelling. See CONVEXITY. *Ant.*, see SMOOTHNESS.

protuberant, *adj.* prominent, projecting, swollen, bulging, lumpy, hummocky. See CONVEXITY. *Ant.*, see SMOOTHNESS.

proud, *adj.* lordly, majestic, dignified, straight, stately; lofty, arrogant, haughty, supercilious, vainglorious; cavalier, uppish. See VANITY, REPUTE. *Ant.,* see MODESTY, DISREPUTE.

prove, *v.t.* confirm, verify, substantiate, show, demonstrate, document, check, try, test. See EVIDENCE. *Ant.,* see NEGATION,

proverb, *n.* MAXIM, axiom, adage, precept, saying.

provide, *v.* furnish, supply; make provision for, lay in, lay in a stock, lay away; find; arm; cater, provision, purvey; forage; stock, stock with; make good, replenish; fill, fill up; feed; take measures, prepare *or* plan for, have in store, have in reserve; keep, keep handy, keep at hand; have to fall back on; STORE, save for a rainy day. See ECONOMY, MEANS, AID, FOOD. *Ant.,* see WASTE.

provided, *adv.* if, supposing, though. See CIRCUMSTANCE.

providential, *adj.* fortunate, lucky, fortuitous, timely, opportune, reasonable, auspicious. See PROSPERITY, OCCASION. *Ant.,* see ADVERSITY.

provider, *n.* breadwinner; steward, caterer, vitualer, commissary. See STORE.

province, *n.* function, sphere; field, department, division, bailiwick, district; control; domain, jurisdiction. See BUSINESS, REGION.

provincial, *adj.* intolerant, illiberal; insular, narrow; local, rural, countrified; rustic. See NARROWNESS, MISJUDGMENT.

proviso, *n.* CONDITION(s), stipulation, clause, AGREEMENT; reservation, covenant.

provisory, *adj.* provisional, conditional, dependent, subject.

provocation, *n.* AGGRAVATION, irritation, vexation, annoyance, indignity, affront. See RESENTMENT. *Ant.,* see PACIFICATION.

provoke, *v.t.* annoy, irritate, exasperate, nettle; excite, anger, incite, evoke, elicit; vex. See AGGRAVATION, CAUSE, EXCITEMENT, RESENTMENT. *Ant.;* see PACIFICATION.

prowess, *n.* COURAGE, bravery, heroism; SKILL, competence. *Ant.,* see COWARDICE, UNSKILLFULNESS.

prowl, *v.i.* ramble, wander, roam; lurk, slink, sneak; rove. See CONCEALMENT, MOTION.

proximity, *n.* NEARNESS, vicinity, propinquity, neighborhood. See PRESENCE. *Ant.,* see DISTANCE, ABSENCE.

proxy, *n.* SUBSTITUTE, AGENT, delegate, representative; AGENCY; procurator. See COMMISSION.

prude, *n.* formalist, puritan, prig. See AFFECTATION, MODESTY. *Ant.,* see IMPURITY.

prudence, *n.* discretion, carefulness, caution, circumspection, tact; policy, foresight; CARE; thoughtfulness, judiciousness. See KNOWLEDGE, REASONING. *Ant.,* see RASHNESS.

prudent, *adj.* discreet, wary, circumspect, prudential, careful, heedful, chary, cautious; wise, politic. See CARE, KNOWLEDGE. *Ant.,* see RASHNESS.

prudery, *n.* propriety; prudishness, stiffness, coyness, primness, preciousness. See AFFECTATION, MODESTY. *Ant.,* see IMPURITY.

prudish, *adj.* prim, demure, precious, affected, precise. See AFFECTATION, MODESTY.

prune, *v.t.* trim, stop, abbreviate, thin, lop. See DECREASE, AGRICULTURE,

pry, *v.* examine, search, seek, peer, ransack, peek, reconnoiter; raise, force, prize, lever. See CURIOSITY, INQUIRY, VISION.

pseudo, *adj.* spurious, counterfeit, simulated, false, fake, mock. See IMITATION, SIMILARITY.

psychotherapy, *n.* psychotherapeutics, psychiatry.

public, *adj.* popular, common, general; civic, political, national; notorious, known, published; communal, free. See POPULACE, PUBLICATION. *Ant.,* see SECLUSION.

PUBLICATION [531]

*Nouns—***1,** publication; announcement; NEWS, intelligence, INFORMATION; promulgation, propagation, proclamation; circulation; bulletin, edition; hue and cry; banns; notification; divulgation, DISCLOSURE; publicity, notoriety, currency; *vox populi;* report; newscast, broadcast, telecast, simulcast, radio. *Colloq.*, spotlight, blurb; white glare of publicity. *Slang*, plug, write-up.

2, the press; newspaper, journal, gazette, paper; daily, weekly; BOOK, volume; magazine, review, periodical; monthly, bimonthly, *etc.*

3, advertisement; press *or* publicity release; placard, bill, broadside; poster; billboard, hoarding; circular, brochure, circular letter; manifesto; public notice, skywriting. *Colloq.*, ad, want ad, classified ad; commercial; spot announcement; hitchhiker, cowcatcher.

4, publisher, publicist, journalist, columnist, press agent; announcer, broadcaster, newscaster, commentator, analyst.

Verbs—**1,** publish; make public, make known, publicize, advertise, circularize; AIR; voice, broach, utter; circulate, promulgate; spread abroad; disseminate; edit, get out; issue; bandy about; bruit abroad; drag into the open; raise a hue and cry; spread the word *or* the Gospel; put on the wire; wash one's dirty linen in public; make a scene; wear one's heart on one's sleeve.

2, report; proclaim, herald, blazon; trumpet forth; announce; beat the drum; shout from the housetops; advertise, post; rumor, gossip, chatter, tattle.

Adjectives—published, public, current, newsy, new, in circulation; notorious; flagrant, arrant; open; encyclical, promulgatory; broadcast.

Adverbs—publicly; in print; in the air; on the air.

Antonym, see SILENCE, CONCEALMENT.

---

publicity, *n.* notoriety, limelight; utterance, outlet, vent. See AIR, PUBLICATION.

pucker, *n. & v.* —*n.* wrinkle, crease, crinkle, ruffle, shirring. —*v.* contract; corrugate, crinkle, wrinkle, shirr, ruffle.

puerile, *adj.* trivial, foolish, trifling, weak, nonsensical; childish, immature, boyish, juvenile. See YOUTH, UNIMPORTANCE. *Ant.*, see AGE, IMPORTANCE.

puff, *n. & v.* —*n.* swelling; blow, breath, cloud, wind, breeze; gesture, praise. —*v.* brag, boast, praise, commend; blow, pant, gasp; inflate. See APPROBATION, BOASTING, INCREASE, VANITY.

pugilism, *n.* boxing, fisticuffs. See CONTENTION.

pugnacious, *adj.* combative, quarrelsome, militant, belligerent, contentious, bellicose. See CONTENTION, IRASCIBILITY. *Ant.*, see PACIFICATION.

pull, *n. & v.* —*n.* POWER, sway; jerk, wrench, tug; magnetism, GRAVITY, ATTRACTION, influence. —*v.* tug, wrench, haul, drag, draw; extract; row, paddle; tow. See EXTRACTION.

pulpiness, *n.* pulp; paste, dough; curd; pap; jam, pudding; poultice; SOFTNESS; mush, mushiness, squashiness, fleshiness, pastiness. *Ant.*, see HARDNESS.

pulpit, *n.* platform, rostrum, desk; priesthood, ministry. See CLERGY, TEMPLE.

pulse, *v.i.* throb, beat, quiver, palpitate; thump; shudder, tremble; pulsate, vibrate. See OSCILLATION, AGITATION.

pulverizable, *adj.* friable, crushable, powderable, crumbly, pulverable. See POWDERINESS. *Ant.*, see HARDNESS.

pump, *v.t.* interrogate, question, catechize; inflate, puff up. See INQUIRY, WIND. *Ant.*, see CONTRACTION.

punch, *v.t.* strike, hit, poke, beat, knock; puncture, perforate, pierce. See IMPULSE.

punctilious, *adj.* conscientious, scrupulous; exact, precise; formal, ceremonious; severe, strict. See OSTENTATION, TRUTH. *Ant.*, see DISCOURTESY.

punctual, *adj.* prompt, regular, precise, punctilious; periodical; early; timely. See EARLINESS. *Ant.*, see LATENESS.

punctuate, *v.t.* point, interpoint, interpunctuate; accentuate; interrupt. See END, IMPORTANCE.

puncture, *n. & v.t.* —*n.* perforation, hole, pinprick, OPENING. —*v.t.* pierce, jab, perforate, prick.

pungency, *n.* piquancy; strong taste, tang, raciness; SHARPNESS, acrimony; astringency, acerbity; gaminess; tartness, SOURNESS. *Colloq.*, zip, punch, ginger. See TASTE. *Ant.*, see INSIPIDITY, FLATNESS.

PUNISHMENT [972]

Nouns—**1**, punishment; chastisement, chastening; corréction, castigation; discipline, infliction, trial; judgment, PENALTY; retribution; thunderbolt, Nemesis; requital, RETALIATION; penology.
2, capital punishment, execution, electrocution, hanging, gassing, firing squad, decapitation, crucifixion, lynching, stoning; imprisonment (see PRISON and RESTRAINT); torture, rack, thumbscrew, question; transportation, banishment, expulsion, exile; ostracism; Coventry; stocks, pillory; penal servitude, hard labor; solitary confinement; galleys; beating, hiding, rawhiding, flagellation, the lash, gauntlet, whipping post; rap on the knuckles, spanking, thrashing, box on the ear; blow (see IMPULSE); walking the plank, keelhauling; picket, picketing; martyrdom, *auto-da-fé:* hara kiri, tarring and feathering, riding on a rail. *Colloq.*, the chair. *Slang*, hot seat, rope necktie, necktie party, kangaroo court, Judge Lynch, Jack Ketch.
3, SCOURGE, whip, lash, etc.; drop, gallows, gibbet, scaffold, rope, noose, halter, block, ax; stake, cross; guillotine, electric chair, gas chamber.
Verbs—**1**, punish, chastise, chasten; castigate, correct, inflict punishment; retaliate, administer correction, deal out justice; visit upon; pay; make short work of, give short shrift, give a lesson to, serve one right, make an example of. *Colloq.*, give one his come-uppance; paddle; settle one's hash. *Slang*, give what for, give hell, make it hot for.
2, strike, hit, *etc.* (see IMPULSE).
3, execute, electrocute; behead, decapitate, guillotine; hang, gibbet, bowstring; shoot; decimate; burn at the stake; boil in oil; break on the wheel; crucify; impale; flay; lynch; torture, put on the rack, picket. *Colloq.*, string up. *Slang*, burn, fry.
4, banish, exile, transport, expel, ostracize; rusticate; drum out; dismiss, disbar, disbench; strike off the roll, unfrock; post.
5, suffer punishment; take one's medicine; pay the piper. *Slang*, take it.
Adjectives—punishing, penal, punitory, punitive; castigatory.
Antonym, see REWARD.

---

puny, *adj.* small, underdeveloped, undersized, tiny; stunted. See LITTLENESS, IMPOTENCE.
pupil, *n.* student, schoolchild, schoolgirl, schoolboy; learner, tyro, SCHOLAR. *Ant.*, see TEACHING.
puppet, *n.* marionette; manikin, doll; figure, tool, cats'-paw, hireling, henchman, vassal. See AID, REPRESENTATION. *Ant.*, see AUTHORITY.
purblind, *adj.* obtuse, dull, stupid; mole-eyed. *Ant.*, see INTELLIGENCE, VISION.
purchase, *n. & v.* —*n.* buying, purchasing, shopping; bargain; ACQUISITION, EXPENDITURE; preëmption, refusal; bribery, installment buying, buying on time, layaway plan; grip, hold, footing, [mechanical] advantage. —*v.t.* procure; rent, hire, buy in; bribe, buy off, suborn; pay for; shop, market, go shopping. See PAYMENT. *Ant.*, see SALE.
pure, *adj.* blameless, innocent; clean, spotless; chaste, virginal, virtuous; unadulterated; guiltless, stainless, unsullied; honest, uncorrupted, unviolated. See CLEANNESS, PROBITY, INNOCENCE. *Ant.*, see IMPURITY, IMPROBITY.
purge, *v.t.* cleanse, clarify, purify; flush, wash, clear; atone; pardon, absolve, acquit; expiate; evacuate, remove; liquidate, kill. See ATONEMENT, CLEANNESS. *Ant.*, see UNCLEANNESS, KILLING.
purify, *v.t.* purge, cleanse, chasten, clarify, clean; sterilize. See CLEANNESS. *Ant.*, see UNCLEANNESS.
puritanical, *adj.* strict, prudish, prim, severe, rigid. See AFFECTATION, SEVERITY.
purity, *n.* decency, decorum, delicacy; continence, chastity; honesty; VIRTUE, modesty, shame; pudicity, virginity. *Ant.*, see IMPURITY, IMPROBITY.
purlieus, *n.pl.* neighborhood, environs, surroundings, outskirts, limits, bounds, confines. See NEARNESS. *Ant.*, see DISTANCE.
purple, *adj.* See COLOR.
purport, *n.* MEANING, significance, import, sense. *Ant.*, see ABSURDITY.
purpose, *n.* INTENTION, determination, RESOLUTION, resolve; END, aim, view. See WILL. *Ant.*, see CHANCE.

purse, *n.* handbag, reticule, pocketbook, wallet, moneybag; money, exchequer, funds. See MONEY.

PURSUIT [622]

Nouns—**1,** pursuit; pursuing, prosecution; pursuance; enterprise, UNDERTAKING, BUSINESS; adventure, quest, INQUIRY; hue and cry; game, hobby.
2, chase, hunt, steeplechase, coursing; venery; foxhunt.
3, pursuer, hunter, huntsman, sportsman, Nimrod; hound, bloodhound.
Verbs—**1,** pursue, prosecute, follow; run, take, make, or chase after; gun for; carry on, engage in, undertake, set about; endeavor, court, REQUEST; seek, aim at, fish for; press on.
2, chase, give chase, course, dog, hunt, hound; track down; tread *or* follow on the heels of; run down; trail, shadow, dog. *Slang,* tail.
Adjectives—pursuing, in quest of, in pursuit, in full cry, in hot pursuit; on the trail *or* scent.
Adverbs—in pursuance of; after. *Colloq.,* on the prowl.
Antonym, see AVOIDANCE.

---

purvey, *v.t.* deliver, yield, hand, give; provide, furnish, cater, PROVISION.
pus, *n.* matter, suppuration, purulence. See UNCLEANNESS.
push, *n. & v.* —*n.* nudge, thrust, shove; pressure, exigency; crisis, pinch; endeavor, effort, drive, determination, PERSEVERANCE, persistence, aggressiveness. —*v.t.* drive, urge, force; propel, advance, impel; shove, encourage, hearten; prosecute. See IMPULSE, PROPULSION, PURSUIT, DIFFICULTY, EXERTION.
put, *v.t.* PLACE, locate, set, deposit, plant, fix, lay; cast, throw; thrust; impose, rest, stick. See LOCATION, PROPULSION.
putrefy, *v.i.* rot, decay, decompose. See DECOMPOSITION.
putrid, *adj.* decomposed, decayed, rank, foul, rotten, corrupt. See UNCLEANNESS. *Ant.,* see CLEANNESS.
puzzle, *n. & v.t.* —*n.* riddle, conundrum, poser, enigma; mystification, perplexity, complication; dilemma, bewilderment, confusion. See SECRET, DOUBT. *Ant.,* see CERTAINTY, ANSWER. —*v.t.* confound, perplex, bewilder, confuse, mystify.
pygmy, pigmy, *n.* dwarf, midget, atomy; Lilliputian. See LITTLENESS. *Ant.,* see GREATNESS.

Q

quack, *n.* charlatan, quacksalver, mountebank. See DECEPTION.
quackery, *n.* charlatanism, charlatanry. See FALSEHOOD.
quaff, *v.t.* drink; swill, guzzle. See FOOD.
quail, *v.i.* shrink, cower, recoil, flinch. See AVOIDANCE, FEAR.
quaint, *adj.* pleasingly odd, old-fashioned, picturesque. See UNCONFORMITY.
quake, *v.i.* tremble, quiver, shake, shudder. See AGITATION, EXCITEMENT.

QUALIFICATION [469]

Nouns—**1,** qualification, limitation, modification, restriction, coloring, leavening; allowance, consideration, extenuating circumstances; condition, proviso, PROVISION, exception; prerequisite, EXEMPTION; stipulation, specification, saving clause.
2, see ABILITY, REPUTE, SKILL.
Verbs—qualify, LIMIT, modify, leaven, allow for, make allowance for, discount.
Adjectives—qualifying, conditional, provisional; restrictive, contingent.
Adverbs—conditionally, admitting, admittedly, provided, if, unless, but, yet; according as; supposing; with the understanding, even, although, though, for all that, after all, at all events; with a grain of salt; wind and weather permitting; if possible; subject to; with this proviso.

quality, *n.* attribute, property; excellence; trait, characteristic; status, brand, grade; NOBILITY, gentility.

qualm, *n.* twinge, pang, throe; misgiving, uneasiness; remorse. See PAIN, FEAR, PENITENCE.

quandary, *n.* dilemma, plight, perplexity, bewilderment. See DOUBT.

quantity, *n.* magnitude; SIZE, dimensions, amplitude, mass, amount, quantum, measure, substance, strength, mathematics, amount, NUMBER; MULTITUDE; handful, mouthful, spoonful, *etc.*, batch, lot, dose.

quarrel, *n. & v.i.* —*n.* altercation, wrangle, squabble; dispute, controversy, feud; arrow; *Colloq.*, spat. See DISCORD, ARMS. —*v.i.* dispute, disagree, wrangle, squabble; find fault.

quarrelsome, *adj.* contentious, disputatious, pugnacious, combative. See IRASCIBILITY, CONTENTION.

quarter, *n. & v.i.* —*n.* one-fourth; three-month period; 25 cents; district, REGION, DIRECTION; lodging, billet; mercy. See NUMERATION, SIDE, PITY. —*v.t.* quadrisect; divide, cut up; billet, station. See LOCATION.

quarters, *n.* ABODE, lodgings, residence; billet, barracks.

quash, *v.t.* suppress, subdue, crush; set aside, nullify, annul, void. See NULLIFICATION.

quaver, *v.i.* quiver, shake, tremble; tremolo, warble, trill. See OSCILLATION, MUSIC.

quay, *n.* wharf, dock, pier, mole, levee. See EDGE.

queen, *n.* woman ruler, mistress; king's wife, king's widow; belle. See AUTHORITY, NOBILITY.

queer, *adj.* odd, singular, strange; giddy, faint. *Colloq.*, deranged. *Slang*, shady, counterfeit. See UNCONFORMITY.

quell, *v.t.* subdue, suppress, crush; quiet, allay. See REPOSE, SUBJECTION.

quench, *v.t.* put out, snuff out, extinguish; damp, chill; slake, sate, satisfy. See DESTRUCTION.

querulous, *adj.* whining, complaining, fretful, petulant, peevish; finicky. See LAMENTATION.

query, *n.* INQUIRY, question, DOUBT.

question, *n. & v.t.* —*n.* problem, subject; query, interrogation; DOUBT, dispute. See INQUIRY. —*v.t.* interrogate, examine, cross-examine, quiz, dispute, challenge, DOUBT.

questionable, *adj.* doubtful, dubious, debatable, controversial; suspicious. See DOUBT.

quibble, *n.* evasion, EQUIVOCATION, sophism, cavil.

quick, *adj.* rapid, swift, fleet; brief; prompt, alert; ready, unhesitating; hasty, irascible; sensitive, keen; alive, living, sentient. See VELOCITY, ACTIVITY, FEELING, IRASCIBILITY. *Ant.*, see SLOWNESS, INACTIVITY.

quicken, *v.t.* revive, refresh, arouse, animate; hasten, speed, accelerate. See VELOCITY, RESTORATION. *Ant.*, see SLOWNESS.

quickly, *adv.* speedily, promptly, readily; anon, instanter. See EARLINESS, VELOCITY. *Ant.*, see SLOWNESS.

quickness, *n.* VELOCITY, swiftness; alertness, alacrity, promptitude; agility; briskness. See ACTIVITY. *Ant.*, see SLOWNESS.

quiescent, *adj.* still; motionless, moveless; fixed; stationary; stagnant; becalmed, quiet; tranquil, unmoved, undisturbed, unruffled; calm, restful; sleeping, silent. See INACTIVITY. *Ant.*, see MOTION, ACTIVITY, AGITATION.

quiet, *adj. & n.* —*adj.* peaceful, tranquil, serene; hushed, silent; modest, restrained; gentle, calm; unostentatious. See MODERATION, SILENCE, REPOSE. —*n.* peacefulness, calm; SILENCE, hush. *Ant.*, see AGITATION, LOUDNESS.

quirk, *n.* flourish; quip, taunt, jibe; quibble, evasion; peculiarity, trick, eccentricity. See WIT, INSANITY.

quit, *v.* satisfy, requite; resign, abandon, relinquish; leave; cease, stop, desist. See PAYMENT, RELINQUISHMENT, END.

quite, *adv.* entirely, utterly, wholly; really, actually. See COMPLETION. *Colloq.*, rather, somewhat, very.

quitter, *n.* shirker, evader, avoider. See AVOIDANCE. *Slang*, slacker, welsher.

quiver, *v.i.* tremble, shudder, shiver, flutter, vibrate, shake, quaver. See AGITATION.

quiz, *v.t.* interrogate, question, examine; tease, banter. See INQUIRY.
quota, *n.* allotment, share, proportion, percentage. See APPORTIONMENT.
quotation, *n.* citation, excerpt, REPETITION; PRICE. See EVIDENCE.
quote, *v.t.* repeat, cite, instance, refer to, abstract. See EVIDENCE.

R

rabble, *n.* crowd, proletariat, POPULACE, common herd, *hoi polloi;* mob, *canaille,* riffraff, scum.
rabid, *adj.* mad, furious; fanatical, overzealous. See FEELING, EXCITEMENT.
race, *n. & v.* —*n.* onrush, advance; competition; sprint, dash, speed contest; STREAM; channel, millrace, tide, RIVER; career; family, clan, tribe; people, ethnic group. See RELATION, VELOCITY. —*v.* run swiftly, career; hasten; compete; speed, drive fast. See VELOCITY.
racial, *adj.* tribal, family; hereditary, ancestral. See RELATION, ANCESTRY.
rack, *v.t.* strain, exert; torture, distress, torment, agonize. See THOUGHT, PAIN.
racket, *n.* uproar, din, clatter, hubbub; frolic, carouse, rumpus. *Slang,* pursuit, activity, criminal activity. See LOUDNESS, DISORDER, BADNESS, EVIL.
racy, *adj.* spirited, lively; piquant; risqué, suggestive. See POWER, IMPURITY. *Ant.,* see PURITY.
radiance, *n.* LIGHT, luster, brightness; brilliance, splendor, glory. See BEAUTY.
radiant, *adj.* shining, sparkling, glowing; splendid, resplendent, glorious. See LIGHT, BEAUTY.
radiate, *v.* omit, scatter, diffuse, spread, dispense, shine, glare, beam, glow. See ABSENCE, LIGHT.
radiation, *n.* DISPERSION, DIFFUSION, emission, emanation; radiance, illumination. See LIGHT.
radical, *adj. & n.* —*adj.* fundamental, INTRINSIC; extreme, drastic, thorough; sweeping, revolutionary. —*n.* liberal, leftist, left-winger (see LEFT); reformer, rebel, revolutionary; anarchist, nihilist, Communist, Bolshevik, red, pink, parlor pink, fellow-traveler. *Slang,* Commie, pinko. See COMPLETION, REVOLUTION.
radio, *n.* wireless, radio telegraphy, radio telephony; radiogram. See COMMUNICATION.
raft, *n.* flatboat, barge, float, pontoon. See SHIP.
rafter, *n.* beam, timber, crosspiece, joist. See SUPPORT.
rage, *n. & v.i.* —*n.* fury, frenzy, wrath, violence; fashion, fad, craze. See INSANITY. —*v.i.* storm, rave, bluster. See EXCITEMENT.
ragged, *adj.* tattered, frayed, shabby, seedy, worn; in shreds; in patches; patched, torn, rough; tatterdemalion, ragamuffin; dogeared. See DETERIORATION. *Ant.,* see TASTE.
raid, *n. & v.t.* —*n.* ATTACK, invasion, onset, incursion; foray. See STEALING. —*v.t.* ATTACK, invade; pounce upon.
railing, *n.* fence, barrier, balustrade. See INCLOSURE.
raillery, *n.* banter, badinage, persiflage, quizzing. See RIDICULE. *Slang,* kidding, ribbing.
raiment, *n.* CLOTHING, apparel, attire, vesture, garb.
rain, *n. & v.* —*n.* shower, precipitation, rainstorm, downpour. —*v.* shower, pour, drizzle; bestow, lavish, shower upon. See GIVING, WATER.
raise, *v.t.* lift, elevate; rouse, arouse, stir up, incite; resurrect; erect, build, exalt, honor; INCREASE; cultivate, breed. See ELEVATION, DOMESTICATION, AGRICULTURE, EXCITEMENT, IMPROVEMENT.
rake, *v.t. &. n.* —*v.t.* gather, collect; comb, ransack, search, rummage; enfilade, spray with bullets. See ASSEMBLAGE, INQUIRY. —*n.* LIBERTINE, roué, rakehell.
rally, *v.t.* muster, marshal; call together; revive, restore, rouse, encourage; banter, chaff. See ARRANGEMENT, COURAGE.
ram, *v.t.* butt, batter, bump; pound, drive, tamp; cram, stuff. See DENSITY.

ramble, *v.i.* stroll, saunter, stray, wander; digress, maunder. See TRAVEL, LOQUACITY, DEVIATION.

ramification, *n.* divergence, division, branching; PART, offshoot, spur.

ranch, *n.* range, farm, grange. See LAND, ABODE.

rancid, *adj.* rank, stale, putrid, malodorous, frowzy. See DETERIORATION. *Ant.,* see SWEETNESS, NEWNESS.

rancor, *n.* spite, malice, bitterness, vengefulness, vindictiveness, MALEVO-LENCE, HATE, hatred. See IRASCIBILITY, RETALIATION.

random, *adj.* haphazard, casual, CHANCE, fortuitous, aimless.

range, *n.* row, series, chain; scope, extent; habitat; LIMIT, span, latitude; compass, register; DISTANCE. See CONTINUITY, SPACE.

rank, *adj. & n.* —*adj.* lush, luxuriant, vigorous; coarse; malodorous, fetid, rancid, offensive; arrant, extreme, gross. —*n.* row, line; position, caste, quality; status, grade, standing, footing. See REPUTE.

rankle, *v.i.* fester, irritate, gall, pain. See PAIN.

ransack, *v.t.* rummage, scour, search diligently; rifle, loot, pillage. See INQUIRY, STEALING.

ransom, *v. & n.* —*v.t.* redeem, liberate, rescue. —*n.* redemption, release, liberation, rescue. See FREEDOM. *Ant.,* kidnap, TAKE.

rant, *v.i.* rage, rave, scold, nag; harangue. See IRASCIBILITY.

rap, *v.t.* tap, knock, blow, cuff, box, clout. *Slang,* swat, sock, criticize. See IMPULSE, DISAPPROBATION.

rapacity, *n.* greed, cupidity, extortion, ravenousness, voracity. See DESIRE, GLUTTONY.

rape, *v.t.* seize, plunder; seduce, debauch, ravish. See IMPURITY.

rapid, *adj. & n.* —*adj.* swift, speedy, fleet, prompt, quick. See VELOCITY. *Ant.,* see SLOWNESS. —*n.pl.* swift current. See WATER.

rapt, *adj.* ecstatic, enraptured, transported; absorbed, engrossed. See PLEASURE, ATTENTION, THOUGHT.

rapture, *n.* ecstasy, transport, bliss, joy, delight. See PLEASURE.

rare, *adj.* scarce, unusual; tenuous (see RARITY); underdone, half-done, half-cooked, raw.

RARITY [322]

Nouns—**1,** rarity, tenuity, subtlety, thinness, lightness, compressibility; rare-faction, attenuation, dilatation, inflation.

2, rareness, scarcity, uncommonness, INFREQUENCY; collector's item.

Verbs—**1,** rarefy, expand, dilate, attenuate, thin out.

2, be scarce.

Adjectives—**1,** rare, subtle, thin, fine, tenuous, compressible, slight, light, ethereal; rarefied, unsubstantial.

2, scarce, unusual, infrequent, uncommon, few; odd, curious, singular.

Adverbs—rarely, infrequently, *etc.;* seldom, once in a great while.

Antonym, see DENSITY, FREQUENCY, MULTITUDE.

rascal, *n.* scoundrel, knave, rogue, reprobate, blackguard; imp, scamp. See EVILDOER. *Ant.,* see GOODNESS.

rascality, *n.* knavery, villainy, roguery, blackguardism. See IMPROBITY. *Ant.,* see PROBITY.

RASHNESS [863]

Nouns—**1,** rashness, temerity, incautiousness, imprudence, indiscretion, reck-lessness, overconfidence, audacity, precipitancy, precipitation, impetuosity, foolhardiness, heedlessness, thoughtlessness, desperation, Quixoticism; gaming, gambling, blind bargain, leap in the dark, fool's paradise.

2, desperado, hotspur, madcap, daredevil, fire-eater, bully, bravo, scape-grace, Don Quixote, adventurer; gambler, gamester; stunter, stuntman; speeder. *Slang,* speed demon.

Verbs—be rash, stick at nothing, play a desperate game, play with fire, walk on thin ice, go out of one's depth, take a leap in the dark, buy a pig in a poke, tempt Providence, clutch at straws, lean on a broken reed; run the ga(u)ntlet; dare, risk, hazard, gamble. *Slang,* take a flyer.

Adjectives—rash, daring, incautious, indiscreet, imprudent, improvident, temerarious, heedless, careless, reckless, giddy, wild, madcap, desperate, devil-may-care, hot-blooded, hotheaded, headlong, headstrong, breakneck; foolhardy, harebrained, precipitate, overconfident, adventurous, venturesome, Quixotic, free-and-easy; risky, hazardous.

Adverbs—rashly, recklessly, *etc.;* hotfoot, headlong, posthaste, head-over-heels, headforemost.

Antonym, see CARE, CAUTION, SAFETY.

rate, *n.* ratio, percent; DEGREE; proportion, rank, class; PRICE, value; VELOCITY.

rather, *adv.* somewhat, passably, preferably, more correctly, sooner. See LITTLENESS, CHOICE.

ratification, *n.* confirmation, validation, approval, sanction; indorsement, authentication, corroboration. See EVIDENCE, ASSENT. *Ant.,* see DISAPPROBATION.

ratify, *v.t.* approve, confirm, validate; indorse, verify. See EVIDENCE, ASSENT. *Slang,* O.K. *Ant.,* see DISAPPROBATION.

ratio, *n.* proportion, rate, percentage, relative value. See RELATION.

ration, *v.t.* apportion, allocate, allot, dole out; limit restrict, withhold. See APPORTIONMENT.

rational, *adj.* sound, sane, logical, sensible, reasonable. See REASONING, INTELLIGENCE.

rattle, *v.* clatter, chatter, clack; babble, prattle, gabble, jabber; fluster, befuddle, upset. See ABSURDITY.

raucous, *adj.* harsh, grating, rasping, hoarse, strident. See LOUDNESS.

ravage, *v.t.* lay waste, pillage, plunder, sack, devastate, destroy. See DESTRUCTION.

rave, *v.i.* bluster, storm, rant, tear; ramble, wander. See EXCITEMENT, INSANITY.

ravenous, *adj.* rapacious, hungry, greedy, voracious, gluttonous. See DESIRE, GLUTTONY.

ravine, *n.* gorge, gulf, canyon, cañon, gully, gap, notch.

ravish, *v.t.* CHARM, captivate, fascinate, enchant, enthrall; deflower, rape, violate. See VIOLENCE.

raw, *adj.* crude; unprepared, uncooked; undisciplined, unexperienced; skinned, scraped, abraded; bleak, piercing; unpolished, boorish. See COLD, UNSKILLFULNESS, VULGARITY.

ray, *n.* skate; beam, gleam, radiation. See ANIMAL, LIGHT.

raze, *v.t.* demolish, level, tear down, obliterate. See DESTRUCTION.

reach, *v. & n.* —*v.* TOUCH, attain, gain, get to, arrive at, pass, INFLUENCE; stretch, extend. See EQUALITY, DISTANCE, TRANSPORTATION. —*n.* stretch, span, range, expanse, scope. See DISTANCE, FREEDOM.

reaction, *n.* response, revulsion, reflex, RECOIL. See OPPOSITION.

reactionary, *n.* conservative, recalcitrant, Tory, stand-patter, diehard; fogy. See STABILITY.

read, *v.* peruse, con; interpret, decipher, predict; pronounce; study; teach, admonish. See INTERPRETATION.

reader, *n.* peruser; critic; elocutionist; proofreader; lecturer, prelector; textbook. See PRINTING, TEACHING, SPEECH, BOOK.

ready, *adj.* prepared, available, handy; prompt, quick; apt, ingenious; alert; ripe. See UTILITY, PREPARATION, ACTIVITY, SKILL.

real, *adj.* actual, veritable, true, genuine; certain, sure, authentic; fixed. See EXISTENCE, TRUTH. *Ant.,* see FALSEHOOD, IMAGINATION.

realism, *n.* actuality, naturalism, genre, verity. See TRUTH, PAINTING. *Ant.,* see FALSEHOOD.

realistic, *adj.* lifelike, faithful, graphic. See DESCRIPTION.

reality, *n.* TRUTH, actuality, verity, factuality, fact. See EXISTENCE.

realize, *v.t.* comprehend, appreciate, understand; objectify, imagine; gain, net; produce, bring in; fulfill, attain. See KNOWLEDGE, COMPLETION, ACQUISITION, SALE.

really, *adv.* surely, indeed, truly, honestly, certainly, positively, absolutely; very, emphatically; genuinely, actually. See AFFIRMATION.

realty, *n.* real estate, landed property. See PROPERTY.

reap, *v.t.* mow, cut, gather, harvest; acquire. See AGRICULTURE, ACQUISITION.

rear, *v.* erect, construct, establish; raise, elevate; foster, nurture, bring up; breed. See ELEVATION, DOMESTICATION, TEACHING.

REAR [235]

Nouns—**1,** rear, back, posteriority; rear guard; background, hinterland, back door; postern; rumble seat; reverse; END.

2, nape, chine, heels, tail, tail end, rump, croup, buttocks, posterior, backside; breech, loin, dorsal region, lumbar region, hindquarters; bottom, *derrière* (*Fr.*).

3, stern, poop, afterpart, heelpiece, crupper, tail; wake, train; straggler.

Verbs—be behind, fall astern, bend backwards, straggle, bring up the rear, follow, need; END, tail off; back, back up, reverse.

Adjectives—back, rear, hind, hindmost, hindermost, postern, dorsal, after, caudal, lumbar, posterior, aftermost, aft.

Adverbs—behind, in the rear, in the background, behind one's back, back to back, backward, rearward; after, aft, abaft, astern, aback.

Antonym, see FRONT.

reason, *n.* SANITY, INTELLECT, common sense, JUDGMENT, explanation; ground, CAUSE. See INTELLIGENCE. *Ant.*, see INSANITY.

reasonable, *adj.* sound, sensible; fair, moderate; rational, logical. See REASONING, INTELLIGENCE, KNOWLEDGE, CHEAPNESS. *Ant.*, see INSANITY.

REASONING [476]

Nouns—**1,** reasoning, ratiocination, rationalism, deduction, dialectics, induction, generalization, logic, synthesis, analysis, rationalization.

2, debate, polemics, CONTENTION; discussion, INQUIRY; dissertation, exposition, explanation.

3, argument, case, proposition, terms, premise, postulate, data, principle, inference, syllogism, hypothesis; induction, deduction.

4, reasoner, logician, dialectician, disputant, controversialist, wrangler, arguer, debater, polemicist, polemist, casuist, rationalist, rationalizer.

Verbs—reason, deduce, induce, infer; argue, discuss, debate, dispute, wrangle; philosophize, consider.

Adjectives—**1,** reasoning, thinking, sapient; rationalistic; argumentative, controversial, dialectic, polemical, discursive; disputatious.

2, logical, relevant, rational; inductive, deductive, syllogistic; *a priori, a posteriori.*

Adverbs—for, because, hence, seeing that, since, so, inasmuch as, whereas, in consideration of; therefore, consequently, ergo, accordingly, *a fortiori;* Q.E.D., *reductio ad absurdum.*

Antonym, see INTUITION.

rebate, *n.* DISCOUNT, refund, repayment, DEDUCTION.

rebel, *v.i.* revolt, resist, mutiny, rise up. See DISOBEDIENCE.

rebellion, *n.* revolt, uprising, insurrection, insurgence, mutiny, sedition, revolution. See DISOBEDIENCE.

rebellious, *adj.* insurgent, mutinous, seditious; uncontrollable, unmanageable; disobedient, defiant. See DISOBEDIENCE. *Ant.*, see OBEDIENCE.

rebound, *v.i.* bounce, ricochet, react, bound back, RECOIL.

rebuff, *n. & v.t.* —*n.* snub, slight, cut; repulse, rout, check. See CONTEMPT, FAILURE. —*v.t.* repel, repulse; snub, cut, slight. *Slang*, high-hat, coldshoulder.

rebuild, *v.t.* recreate, refashion, reform, restore. See RESTORATION.

rebuke, *n. & v.t.* —*n.* reproof, reprimand, admonition. See DISAPPROBATION. —*v.t.* reprove, reprimand, chide, admonish, upbraid. See DISAPPROBATION.

rebut, *v.t.* ANSWER, contradict, oppose, refute. See NEGATION.

recall, *v.t.* recollect, remember; revoke, annul, withdraw; retract; revive, restore. See MEMORY, NULLIFICATION, CHANGEABLENESS.

recant, *v.t.* withdraw, take back, renounce, retract, disavow, repudiate. See CHANGEABLENESS, NULLIFICATION.

recapitulate, *v.t.* summarize, restate, review, rehearse. *Colloq.*, recap. See REPETITION, DESCRIPTION.

recast, *v.t.* recompose, reconstruct, refashion; remold; recompute. See REVOLUTION.

recede, *v.i.* retrograde, retrogress, retrocede; go, retire, withdraw; shrink, ebb, wane; move away, drift away, move off, sheer off, fall back, depart, retreat, run away. See REGRESSION. *Ant.*, see PROGRESSION.

receipt, *n.* recipiency, reception, RECEIVING; share, receipts; income, revenue; proceeds, return, net profits, earnings; rent; remuneration, wages, stipend, salary, emolument, pay, fee, commission; pension, annuity, alimony, allowance; allotment. *Slang*, split, take, gate. See PAYMENT, ACQUISITION. *Ant.*, see GIVING.

RECEIVING [785]

Nouns—**1,** receiving, reception, receipt, recipiency, acquisition, acceptance, admission.

2, receiver, recipient, assignee, devisee, heir, legatee, grantee, donee, lessee, beneficiary, pensioner.

3, receipts, income, revenue, intake, proceeds, return, yield, earnings, dividends; salary, remuneration (see PAYMENT); rent; pension; alimony, allowance. *Slang*, spit, take, gate.

Verbs—**1,** receive, take, get, acquire, obtain, take in, catch, pocket, put into one's pocket; accept, admit, take off one's hands.

2, be received, come in, come to hand, go into one's pocket, fall to one's lot, accrue; yield, pay, return, bear.

Adjectives—receiving, recipient, receptive, pensionary.

Antonym, see GIVING.

---

recent, *adj.* late, new, fresh, modern. See NEWNESS. *Ant.*, see OLDNESS.
recently, *adv.* lately, newly, latterly. See NEWNESS.

RECEPTACLE [191]

Nouns—**1,** receptacle, recipient, receiver; compartment, cell, follicle, hole, corner, niche, recess, nook, crypt, booth, stall, pigeonhole, cubbyhole, cove.

2, capsule, vesicle, cyst, pod, calyx, utricle, arc.

3, stomach, paunch, ventricle, crop, craw, maw, gizzard, mouth, gullet.

4, pocket, pouch, fob, sheath, scabbard, socket, bag, sack, purse, wallet, scrip, poke, knapsack, haversack, briefcase, valise, suitcase, handbag, portmanteau, satchel, etui, reticule, quiver. *Slang*, kick.

5, chest, box, coffer, caddy, case, casket, caisson, trunk, bandbox, cage, manger, rack.

6, vessel, bushel, barrel, canister, basket, pannier, hopper, creel, crate, cradle, bassinet, hamper, tray, hod, scuttle, utensil, CARRIER.

7, vat, ca(u)ldron, tank, cistern; cask, puncheon, keg, tun, butt; firkin; carboy, amphora; bottle, jar, decanter, ewer, cruse, vase, carafe, crock, flagon, magnum, demijohn, flask, stoup, jigger, noggin; vial, phial, flacon; cruet; urn, tub, bucket, pail; pot, pan, tankard, jug, pitcher, mug; retort, alembic, test tube; tin, can, kettle, bowl, basin, punchbowl, cup, goblet, chalice, tumbler, glass; saucepan, skillet, tureen; vacuum bottle *or* jug.

8, plate, platter, dish, trencher, porringer, saucer, crucible.

9, shovel, trowel, spoon, spatula, ladle, dipper, scoop.

10, closet, commode, cupboard, cellaret, locker, chiffonier, bin, bunker, buffet, press, safe, sideboard, desk, bureau, secretary, till, bookcase, cabinet.

11, chamber, apartment, room, cabin, office, court, hall; suite, flat, salon, parlor; dining, living, waiting, sitting, *or* drawing room; antechamber; stateroom; gallery, pew, box; boudoir, sanctum, bedroom, dormitory, refectory, playroom, nursery, schoolroom, library, study, studio; bathroom, lavatory, smoking room, den, lounge; rumpus room.

12, attic, loft, garret; cellar, basement, vault, hold, cockpit; kitchen, pantry, scullery; storeroom; dairy; laundry, bathroom, lavatory, outhouse; penthouse; lean-to, garage, hangar, shed, toolhouse, roundhouse.

13, portico, porch, veranda, lobby, court, hall, vestibule, foyer, corridor, PASSAGE.
14, conservatory, greenhouse, summerhouse, hothouse, alcove, grotto, hermitage.

---

reception, *n.* admission, admittance, entrée, entrance; importation; introduction, taking; party, affair. See RECEIVING. *Ant.,* see EJECTION, EXCLUSION.
recess, *n.* alcove, niche, nook, bay; intermission, pause, interim, rest, break, breathing spell, coffee break. See END, RESTORATION, RECEPTACLE, CONCAVITY.
recession, *n.* retirement, withdrawal; REGRESSION, retreat, retrocession, retrogression; departure, flight; depression, hard times, temporary setback. *Ant.,* see PROGRESSION.
recipe, *n.* receipt, formula, instructions, directions, method, prescription, ingredients. See FOOD.
recipient, *n.* receiver, donee, beneficiary, devisee, legatee, heir, pensioner.
reciprocal, *adj.* mutual, complementary, interchangeable, alternative, correlative. See RELATION, OSCILLATION, INTERCHANGE.
reciprocation, *n.* repayment, INTERCHANGE, exchange, reciprocity, alternation. See RELATION, OSCILLATION.
reciprocity, *n.* reciprocation, INTERCHANGE, exchange; alternation. See RELATION.
recital, *n.* telling, narration, rehearsal; account, recapitulation; concert, musicale. See REPETITION, SPEECH, MUSIC.
recitation, *n.* declamation, elocution, recital, lesson. See SPEECH, TEACHING.
recite, *v.* rehearse, relate, repeat, declaim, detail, recapitulate. See NUMERATION, SPEECH, DESCRIPTION.
reckless, *adj.* careless, foolhardy, incautious, heedless, rash, devil-may-care. See RASHNESS, NEGLECT. *Ant.,* see CARE.
reckon, *v.* calculate, count, compute, estimate; esteem, consider, believe; think, suppose. See ADDITION, REASONING, BELIEF. *Colloq.,* guess.
reckoning, *n.* calculation, computation, count; accounting, settlement; bill, tally, score. See ADDITION, NUMBER, PAYMENT.
reclaim, *v.t.* redeem, restore, reform, recover, retrieve. See PENITENCE, RESTORATION.
recline, *v.i.* lie, rest, couch, repose, loll. See REPOSE.
recluse, *n.* hermit, anchorite, ascetic, eremite. See SECLUSION.
recognition, *n.* identification, perception, cognizance; acknowledgment, commendation, appreciation. See KNOWLEDGE, MEMORY, COURTESY.
recognize, *v.t.* acknowledge, concede, remember; perceive, realize, know, distinguish; salute, greet, appreciate. See VISION, DISCLOSURE, KNOWLEDGE.

RECOIL [277]

Nouns—recoil, reaction, retroaction, revulsion, rebound, ricochet, bounce, boomerang, kick, backlash, repercussion, reflex, return, repulse, reverberation, echo; reactionary, reactionist.
Verbs—**1,** recoil, react, rebound, reverberate, echo, spring back, fly back, kick, ricochet, reflect, boomerang, carom, bounce, shy.
2, cringe, cower, wince, flinch, quail, shrink; retreat, fall back, retire; falter, fail.
Adjectives—recoiling, refluent, repercussive, recalcitrant, reactionary; flinching, cowering, *etc.*

---

recollection, *n.* remembrance, reminiscence, MEMORY, retrospection, reflection.
recommend, *v.t.* commend, advise, suggest; commit, entrust; urge, advocate. See ADVICE, APPROBATION.
recommendation, *n.* testimonial; suggestion; ADVICE, council; advocacy. See APPROBATION.
recompense, *n. & v.t.* —*n.* REWARD, COMPENSATION, PAYMENT, requital. —*v.t.* requite, REWARD, repay, remunerate, indemnify, atone. See COMPENSATION, ATONEMENT.

reconcile, *v.t.* conciliate, propitiate, placate, appease; harmonize, accord; settle. See CONFORMITY, PACIFICATION.

recondite, *adj.* mysterious, obscure, SECRET, abstruse, profound, esoteric, cryptic. See CONCEALMENT.

recondition, *v.t.* repair, renew, overhaul, renovate, restore, regenerate, rejuvenate. See RESTORATION.

reconnoiter, *v.* investigate, survey, spy out, scout. See VISION. *Slang,* case.

RECORD [551]

Nouns—**1,** record, note, minute; register, roll, diptych, entry, memorandum, COPY, duplicate, docket; muniment, deed; document; testimony, deposition, affidavit, certificate; notebook, statistic; registry, registration, enrollment; tabulation, transcript, transcription, entry, booking, signature.

2, gazette, newspaper, magazine; almanac, calendar; diary, log, journal, daybook, ledger; archive, scroll, chronicle, annals; legend, history, biography.

3, monument, hatchment, slab, tablet, trophy, obelisk, pillar, column, monolith; memorial; memento, testimonial, medal; commemoration.

4, trace, vestige, relic, remains, scar, footstep, footprint, track, mark, wake, trail, spoor, scent.

5, phonograph record; recording, tape recording, transcription. *Colloq.,* disk, waxing, platter.

6, recorder, registrar, register, notary, prothonotary, clerk, amanuensis, secretary, stenographer, scribe, bookkeeper; editor, author, journalist; annalist, historian, chronicler, biographer, antiquary, antiquarian, archivist.

7, recording instrument, recorder, ticker, ticker tape; tracer; timer, dater, stopwatch, speedometer (see MEASUREMENT), log, turnstile; seismograph; phonograph, tape *or* wire recorder, adding machine, cash register.

Verbs—record, put on record, chronicle, hand down to posterity, commemorate, write, put in writing; jot down, note, make a note; enter, book; post, make an entry of, enroll, register; mark, sign, attest, file; wax, tape, transcribe.

Antonyms, see OBLIVION, OBLITERATE.

---

recount, *v.t.* tell, recite, repeat, rehearse, relate, narrate, enumerate; recapitulate. See NUMERATION, DESCRIPTION.

recoup, *v.t.* regain, retrieve, indemnify, reimburse. See RESTORATION.

recover, *v.* regain, get back, redeem, retrieve, reclaim, salvage; get well, recuperate. See RESTORATION, ACQUISITION.

recovery, *n.* restitution, reclamation, salvage, retrieval, recuperation. See RESTORATION, ACQUISITION.

recreant, *adj.* cowardly, craven, dastardly, disloyal, false, treacherous; apostate, renegade. See COWARDICE, CHANGEABLENESS.

recreation, *n.* diversion, sport, pastime, REFRESHMENT. See AMUSEMENT.

recruit, *v.t. & n.* —*v.t.* enlist, raise, furnish, supply, replenish; restore, renew. See STORE, RESTORATION. —*n.* conscript, draftee; newcomer, novice, tyro. See COMBATANT, LEARNER. *Slang,* rookie, boot. *Ant.,* see VETERAN.

rectangular, *adj.* orthogonal, oblong, foursquare, square. See LENGTH, ANGULARITY.

rectify, *v.t.* correct, improve, repair, purify, redress, amend. See IMPROVEMENT, RIGHT.

rectitude, *n.* uprightness, integrity, righteousness, goodness, VIRTUE, honesty. See PROBITY. *Ant.,* see IMPROBITY.

recumbent, *adj.* lying, reclining, leaning. See OBLIQUITY.

recuperation, *n.* recovery, IMPROVEMENT, convalescence. See RESTORATION.

recur, *v.* return, come back, reoccur, repeat, intermit, revert. See REPETITION.

recurrence, *n.* REPETITION, return, intermittence, iteration, periodicity.

redeem, *v.t.* ransom, recover, rescue, restore, liberate, deliver, convert, fulfill, perform. See RESTORATION, PENITENCE.

redress, *v.t. & n.* —*v.t.* RIGHT, correct, repair, reform, relieve, remedy. See RESTORATION, ATONEMENT. —*n.* amends, restitution, reparation, requital.

reduce, *v.t.* diminish, lessen, curtail, lower; allay, alleviate; set (a fracture);

demote, abase, subjugate, subdue; diet, slenderize. See DECREASE, CONTRACTION, NARROWNESS. *Ant.*, see INCREASE.

reduced, *adj.* lessened, marked down, cheapened; indigent, impoverished, diluted, watered down, impaired, deteriorated; defeated, vanquished. See CHEAPNESS, POVERTY, DETERIORATION, FAILURE.

reduction, *n.* lessening, abatement, attenuation, condensation; degradation, abasement; setting (a fracture); subjugation. See DECREASE, CONTRACTION.

redundance, *n.* redundancy; repetition, tautology; superabundance, superfluity, superfluence; profuseness, profusion, repletion, plethora; surfeit, oversupply, overflow, inundation, drug on the market, glut, excess, surplus, surplusage; coals to Newcastle. See SUFFICIENCY. *Ant.*, see INSUFFICIENCY.

reef, *n.* sandbar, shoal, bank, ledge.

reel, *v.i.* sway, stagger, waver, spin, wheel. See AGITATION.

reëstablish, *v.t.* restore, renew, revive, refound. See RESTORATION.

refashion, *v.t.* make over, remake, remodel, revolutionize. See REVOLUTION.

refer, *v.* submit, commit, send, direct, assign, ascribe, attribute. See CAUSE, EVIDENCE, ADVICE. —*v.i.* allude, advert, apply, concern, appeal. See RELATION.

referee, *n.* arbiter, arbitrator, umpire, mediator, moderator, JUDGE.

reference, *n.* citation, allusion; testimonial, credentials; bearing, concern, applicability. See RELATION, EVIDENCE.

reference book, encyclopedia, dictionary, yearbook, atlas, almanac, catalog(ue), concordance, thesaurus. See BOOK.

refine, *v.t.* purify, cleanse, educate, improve, cultivate, elaborate. See CLEANNESS, IMPROVEMENT.

refined, *adj.* well-bred, cultivated, polished; subtle. See ELEGANCE, COURTESY.

refinement, *n.* elegance, finish, culture, polish; delicacy, propriety, TASTE, DISCRIMINATION. See IMPROVEMENT, TRUTH, COURTESY.

reflect, *v.* throw back, cast back, mirror, COPY, imitate, reproduce, echo, meditate, ponder, muse, ruminate. See THOUGHT, IMITATION, SOUND.

reflection, *n.* refraction, image, echo, duplication, counterpart, COPY; meditation, rumination, retrospection; insinuation, innuendo. See LIGHT, SOUND, THOUGHT, DISAPPROBATION.

reflux, *n.* ebb, refluence, subsidence, backwater. See DECREASE, REGRESSION. *Ant.*, see INGRESS.

reform, *v.t. & n.* —*v.t.* better, reclaim, restore, improve, redeem, regenerate, convert. See CHANGE, PENITENCE. —*n.* IMPROVEMENT, amendment, regeneration, reformation; crusade.

reformation, *n.* reform, improvement, betterment, correction; regeneration. See IMPROVEMENT, PIETY. *Ant.*, see DETERIORATION.

reformer, *n.* altruist, crusader, zealot, missionary. See IMPROVEMENT. *Slang,* do-gooder.

refraction, *n.* bending, deflection, DISTORTION; distorted image. See DEVIATION, LIGHT, VISION.

refractory, *adj.* unruly, unmanageable, obstinate, stubborn, intractable. See RESOLUTION. *Ant.*, see OBEDIENCE.

refrain, *v.i. & n.* —*v.i.* abstain, cease, desist, forbear. —*n.* chorus, burden, repetend. See REPETITION. *Ant.*, see CONTINUITY.

refresh, *v.* brace, strengthen, reinvigorate; AIR, freshen up; recruit, repair, restore, revive; stimulate, animate; recuperate, get better, recover, revive, regain one's strength. *Colloq.*, perk up; buck up; give a new lease on life. See RESTORATION. *Ant.*, see WEARINESS.

refreshment, *n.* recovery, invigoration, RESTORATION; revival; repair; refection, renewal, renovation; repast, regalement; RELIEF, relaxation, stimulation. *Colloq.*, pick-me-up. *Ant.*, see WEARINESS.

refrigerate, *v.* cool, ice, freeze, congeal, infrigidate; benumb, chill, chill to the marrow; quickfreeze. See COLD. *Ant.*, see HEAT.

refrigerator, *n.* See COLD.

refuge, *n.* asylum, sanctuary; hideout, hideaway; safe harbor; any port in a storm; last resort; SUPPORT, SECLUSION; anchor, anchorage; home, hospital; retreat, den, lair. See SAFETY. *Ant.*, see DANGER.

refund, *v.t.* return, give back, pay back, repay, reimburse. See PAYMENT, RESTORATION.

REFUSAL [764]

Nouns—**1,** refusal; nonacceptance, denial, declining, declination; rejection, repudiation, exclusion; resistance; repulse, rebuff; disapproval; recusancy abnegation, protest, disclaimer; DISSENT, revocation, renunciation.
2, unwillingness, indisposition, disinclination, reluctance, aversion.
Verbs—refuse, REJECT, deny, decline; negate; grudge, begrudge, be deaf to; turn a deaf ear to; discountenance, not hear of, turn down, wash one's hands of, stand aloof. See RESISTANCE.
Adjectives—**1,** refusing, recusant; uncomplying, unaccommodating, unconsenting, deaf to; UNWILLING.
2, refused, rejected, ungranted, out of the question, not to be thought of, impossible.
Adverbs—no, on no account, not for the world; no, thank you; never. *Colloq.*, not a chance, not on your life.
Antonym, see OFFER.

---

refuse, *n.* trash, truck, rubbish, waste, leavings, garbage. See USELESSNESS.
refute, *v.t.* confute, controvert, disprove, deny, dispute. See NEGATION.
regain, *v.t.* recover, retrieve, get back, get back to. See ACQUISITION.
regal, *adj.* royal, splendid, stately, majestic; kingly, autocratic. See AUTHORITY, NOBILITY.
regalement, *n.* REFRESHMENT, feasting, entertainment. See PLEASURE.
regalia, *n.* emblems, decorations, insignia.
regard, *v.t. & n.* —*v.t.* consider, deem, observe, mark, note, RESPECT, esteem, concern. See INTELLECT. —*n.* reference, concern, gaze, ATTENTION, deference, esteem. See CARE, REPUTE.
regardful, *adj.* heedful, attentive, observant, considerate, respectful. See CARE. *Ant.,* see NEGLECT.
regardless, *adj.* heedless, careless, indifferent, negligent. See NEGLECT. *Ant.,* see CARE, ATTENTION.
regenerate, *adj. & v.t.* —*adj.* reformed, reborn, converted. See PIETY. —*v.t.* produce anew, make over; revivify; reform, convert. See RESTORATION, PIETY.
regeneration, *n.* renewal, regrowth, palingenesis; redemption, new birth. See RESTORATION, PIETY.
regent, *n.* viceroy, deputy, ruler, trustee. See AUTHORITY, COMMISSION.

REGION [181]

Nouns—**1,** region, sphere, ground soil, area, hemisphere, latitude, meridian, zone, clime, climate; quarter, district, beat, orb, circuit, circle; vicinity, neighborhood, precinct, pale, department, domain, bailiwick, dominion, section, tract, territory. See PLACE, LOCATION, SPACE.
2, country, canton, county, shire, province, arrondissement, parish, township, parish, hundred, riding, principality, duchy, realm, kingdom, empire.
3, arena, march; patch, plot, enclosure, enclave, field, court.
Adjectives—regional, sectional, territorial, local, parochial, vicinal, provincial, topographical.

---

register, *n. & v.t.* —*n.* RECORD, ROLL, LIST; registration, enrollment. —*v.i.* enroll, LIST; mark, RECORD; express, indicate. See INDICATION, DRAMA.
registrar, *n.* secretary, register. See RECORD.
registration, *n.* enrollment, booking, registry. See RECORD.

REGRESSION [283]

Nouns—**1,** regression, retrocession, retrogression, retrogradation, retroaction, retreat, withdrawal, retirement, return, REVERSION; RELAPSE, RECESSION, recess; recidivism, backsliding, fall, DETERIORATION.
2, reflux, refluence, backwater, regurgitation, ebb, resilience, reflection, RECOIL.
Verbs—regress, recede, return, revert, retreat, retire, retrograde; lapse, re-

lapse; back down *or* out, withdraw, rebound; recoil, turn back, fall back, put back; lose ground, fall astern, back water, put about, wheel, counter-march; ebb, regurgitate, balk, jib, shrink, shy; turn, turn tail, about-face, turn around, turn one's back upon; retrace one's steps, beat a retreat, go home. *Slang,* pull in one's horns.
Adjectives—**1,** regressive, receding; retrograde; retrogressive, refluent, reflex, recidivous, crablike; reactionary, recessive, receding.
2, relapsing, backsliding, recrudescent; reversionary, atavistic.
Adverbs—back, backward(s), reflexively, in retreat.
Antonym, see PROGRESSION.

regret, *n. & v.* —*n.* remorse, compunction; repining, homesickness, nostalgia; LAMENTATION, penitence; bitterness, heartache, heartburning, sorrow, grief, contrition, repentance; disappointment, DISCONTENT. See PENITENCE. —*v.* deplore, bewail, lament, repine, rue; rue the day; repent (of); feel sorry *or* contrite. *Ant.,* see REJOICING.
regular, *adj.* steady, punctual, constant; orderly, correct, methodical; periodic, serial, recurrent, recurring, cyclical, rhythmical, intermittent; routine. *Colloq.,* fine (a regular fellow). See STABILITY, TIME.
regularity, *n.* steadiness, punctuality; periodicity, recurrence; order, method; intermittence, beat, pulsation; rhythm, alternation; routine. See STABILITY, TIME.
regulate, *v.t.* ORDER, manage, legislate, rule, direct; adjust, rectify, fix, organize, systematize, tranquilize, moderate. See ARRANGEMENT.
regulation, *n.* adjustment, arrangement (see REGULATE); LAW, rule, order, ordinance.
rehabilitate, *v.t.* restore, reinstate, reëstablish. See RESTORATION.
rehearse, *v.t.* repeat, recite, enumerate; drill, practice, prepare. See REPETITION, PREPARATION.
reign, *v.i.* rule, govern, command, hold sway. See AUTHORITY.
reimburse, *v.t.* repay, compensate, indemnify. See PAYMENT, RESTORATION.
reinforce, *v.t.* strengthen, support, buttress, replenish. See POWER, RESTORATION.
reinforcements, *n.* replenishment, AID, recruits, auxiliaries. See STORE.
reins, *n.* lines, RESTRAINT, guidance.
reject, *v.t.* set aside, lay aside; give up, decline, refuse, exclude, except; repudiate, scout, cast to the winds, throw to the dogs, toss overboard, throw away; disclaim, deny, discard. See REFUSAL. *Ant.,* see CHOICE, ASSENT.
rejection, *n.* repudiation, exclusion; REFUSAL, rebuff. *Ant.,* see APPROBATION.

REJOICING [838]

Nouns—**1,** rejoicing, exultation, triumph, jubilation, joy, revelry, reveling, merrymaking, jubilee, CELEBRATION, paean, thanksgiving, congratulation.
2, smile, simper, smirk, gloat, grin; laughter, giggle, titter, snigger, snicker, crow, chuckle, horse laugh, guffaw; fit, shout, roar *or* peal of laughter; risibility.
3, cheer, hurrah, hooray, shout, yell, hallelujah.
Verbs—**1,** rejoice, thank one's stars, congratulate oneself, clap one's hands, fling up one's cap; dance, skip; sing, chirrup, hurrah; cry for joy, leap with joy, exult, glory, triumph, celebrate; be tickled.
2, make merry, smile, simper, smirk, grin, laugh, giggle, titter, snigger, crow, snicker, chortle, chuckle, cackle; cheer, hurrah, yell, shout, roar, split one's sides.
3, enjoy, revel in, delight in, be glad.
Adjectives—rejoicing, jubilant, exultant, triumphant, flushed, glad, gladsome, elated, laughing, risible, bursting with laughter, convulsed with laughter; laughable.
Interjections—hurrah! three cheers! hail! Heaven be praised! *Slang,* swell! great! oh, boy!
Antonym, see LAMENTATION.

rejoin, *v.t.* reply, retort, respond; reunite, reassemble, join again. See ANSWER, ASSEMBLAGE.

rejoinder, *n.* ANSWER, reply, retort, response.

rejuvenescence, *n.* rejuvenation, reinvigoration. See YOUTH.

relapse, *n. & v.* —*n.* recurrence (of illness *or* behavior); DETERIORATION, backsliding, REGRESSION. —*v.i.* lapse, fall back, backslide, fall ill again.

relate, *v.t.* TELL, recount, report, narrate. See INFORMATION, DESCRIPTION.

RELATION [9]

Nouns—relation, relationship, bearing, reference, CONNECTION, concern, dependence, cognation; CORRELATION, analogy, SIMILARITY, affinity, reference; alliance, homogeneity, association, approximation, affiliation, kinship, CONSANGUINITY, interest, relevancy; COMPARISON, ratio, proportion, link, tie, bond of union.

Verbs—1, be related, relate to, refer to, bear upon, regard, concern, touch, affect, have to do with; pertain to, belong to, interest; correspond.

2, relate, bring into relation with, bring to bear upon, connect, associate, draw a parallel, link, COMPARE; correlate, interrelate, reciprocate, alternate.

Adjectives—1, relative, correlative, cognate, relating, referable; belonging, appurtenant.

2, related, connected, implicated, associated, affiliated, allied to; akin, like, similar, relevant; reciprocal, mutual, common, correspondent, interchangeable, alternate.

3, approximating, proportionate, proportional, allusive, comparable.

Adverbs—relatively, pertinently, comparatively; *en rapport*, in touch with.

Prepositions—as to, as for, as regards, regarding, about, concerning, anent, relating to, with relation to, with reference to, with regard to, apropos of, on the score of; under the head of, in the matter of, in re, re.

Antonym, see DIFFERENCE.

---

relative, *n.* relation, kinsman; comparative, dependent. See RELATION.

relax, *v.t.* rest, relent, slacken, loosen, abate, relieve, ease, mitigate. See SOFTNESS, INACTIVITY, PITY. *Ant.*, see HARDNESS, EXCITEMENT.

relaxation, *n.* ease, REPOSE, diversion, recreation; abatement, loosening. See AMUSEMENT, MODERATION.

relaxed, *adj.* loose, slack; not tense, at ease. See REPOSE. *Ant.*, see ACTIVITY, AGITATION.

release, *v.t.* free, liberate, give out, relinquish. See RELINQUISHMENT.

relegate, *v.t.* consign, commit, assign, refer, banish. See EJECTION, GIVING.

relent, *v.i.* soften, yield, submit, PITY. See SOFTNESS.

relentless, *adj.* pitiless, merciless, implacable, remorseless; inexorable, indefatigable. See RESOLUTION, RETALIATION, SEVERITY. *Ant.*, see PITY.

relevant, *adj.* pertinent, fitting, apposite, apropos, germane, appropriate. See RELATION.

reliable, *adj.* trustworthy, dependable, trusty, responsible. See CERTAINTY, PROBITY. *Ant.*, see DOUBT, IMPROBITY.

reliance, *n.* dependence, trust, confidence, faith, credence. See BELIEF.

relic, *n.* memento, souvenir, keepsake, token, antique, remains. See MEMORY, RECORD.

RELIEF [834]

Nouns—1, relief, deliverance, amelioration, easement, softening, alleviation, mitigation, MODERATION, palliation, soothing, assuagement, slaking.

2, solace, consolation, comfort, encouragement.

3, lenitive, restorative, palliative, alleviative, cushion, anodyne, tranquilizer, painkiller, analgesic, anesthetic.

Verbs—1, relieve, ease, alleviate, mitigate, palliate, soothe, salve, soften, mollify, poultice; replace, take over, spell, substitute for; assuage, allay, disburden, lighten; quench, slake.

2, cheer, comfort, console, encourage, bear up, pat on the back, set at ease; remedy, cure, refresh.

3, be relieved, breathe more freely, take comfort.

Adjectives—relieving, consolatory, comforting, soothing, assuaging, assuasive, balmy, lenitive, palliative, remedial, curative.

Antonym, see AGGRAVATION, INCREASE.

RELIGION [983]

Nouns—**1,** religion, faith; theology, divinity, deism, theism, monotheism, polytheism; hagiology; truth, belief, creed, doctrine, dogma, canonicity; declaration, profession, *or* confession of faith; articles of faith; conformity, orthodoxy, strictness. See PIETY.

2, Christianity, Catholicism, Protestantism (Presbyterianism, Methodism, Lutheranism, Quakerism, Mormonism, Christian Science, *etc.*); Judaism; Mohammedanism, Moslemism, Islam; Buddhism, Shintoism, Confucianism, Hinduism, Brahmanism, Sikhism, Lamaism, *etc.;* the Church, Holy Church, Established Church; temple of the Holy Ghost, Universal Church, Apostolic Church, Roman Catholic Church, Greek Orthodox Church, Church of Christ, Scientist; Church of the New Jerusalem; Presbyterian, etc. Church; Society of Friends; Church of Jesus Christ of Latter-Day Saints; Church of Christ; true believer, Christendom, Christians; Islam; Jewry; Christian, Catholic, Protestant (Presbyterian, Christian Scientist, Swedenborgian, Moravian, *etc.*), Quaker, Friend, Mormon, Jew; Moslem; Buddhist; Brahman, Hindu, *etc.*

3, scriptures, canons, SACRED WRITINGS; catechism; Apostles Creed, Nicene Creed, Athanasian Creed.

4, WORSHIP; PRAYER; HYMN, hymnody, psalmody; sacrifice, oblation, incense, libation, offering, offertory; disciple, fasting, asceticism; RITE, divine service, office, duty, Mass, matins, evensong, vespers.

5, CLERGY, clergyman; theologian, theist, monotheist; congregation, flock, worshiper, communicant, celebrant; presbyter, elder, vestryman, usher.

Verbs—WORSHIP, adore, revere; pray, invoke, supplicate, say one's prayers, tell one's beads; return thanks, say grace; praise, glorify, magnify; bless, give benediction; attend services, attend Mass, go to church; communicate, take communion.

Adjectives—religious, pious, devout; Godfearing; reverential (see RESPECT); orthodox, sound, strict, canonical, authentic, faithful, catholic; theological; doctrinal, dogmatic, denominational, sectarian; Christian, Catholic, Protestant, Lutheran, Calvinistic, *etc.;* evangelical, scriptural; divine, true; Jewish, Judaic, Hebrew, Hindu, Mohammedan, *etc.*

Antonym, see IRRELIGION.

RELINQUISHMENT [782, 624]

Nouns—**1,** relinquishment, abandonment, renunciation, abjuration, abrogation, expropriation, dereliction; cession, surrender, dispensation; resignation, abdication, withdrawal, retirement; riddance.

2, desertion, defection, secession, withdrawal; discontinuance, DISUSE, desuetude.

3, derelict, foundling. outcast, castoff, castaway.

Verbs—**1,** relinquish, give up, surrender, yield, cede, let go, spare, drop, RESIGN, forgo, renounce, abandon, expropriate, give away, dispose of, part with, lay aside, lay on the shelf, discard, cast off, dismiss, get rid of, eject, divest oneself of, wash one's hands of, throw overboard, throw to the winds; sweep away, jettison, maroon.

2, desert, forsake, leave in the lurch, depart from, secede from, renege, withdraw from, back out of, leave, quit, vacate. *Slang*, ditch, give the gate.

3, break off, leave off, desist, stop, cease, give over, shut up shop, throw in the sponge, give up the argument, drop out.

Adjectives—**1,** relinquished, abandoned, cast off, derelict, unowned, unappropriated, left; dropped.

2, renunciatory, abjuratory, abdicant; relinquishing, *etc.*

Antonym, see POSSESSION.

---

relish, *n.* zest, gusto, flavor, spice, CONDIMENT, appetizer; liking, fondness. See PLEASURE, DESIRE.

reluctance, *n.* unwillingness, hesitation, aversion, disinclination. *Ant.*, see ASSENT.
rely, *v.i.* trust, depend, count. See BELIEF.

REMAINDER [40]

Nouns—**1,** remainder, residue, result, remains, remnant, vestige, rest, relic, leavings, heeltap, odds and ends, cheese parings, orts, residuum, dregs, lees, grounds, silt, sediment, slag, refuse, stubble, fag end, ruins, wreck, butt, skeleton, stump, alluvium; dross, cinder, ash, clinker.
2, surplus, overplus, excess, balance, superfluity, survival.
Verbs—remain, be left, be left over, exceed, survive.
Adjectives—remaining, left; left over, left behind, residual, residuary, over, odd, unconsumed, sedimentary, surviving; net, exceeding, over and above; superfluous.

remark, *v.t. & n.* —*v.t.* note, observe, animadvert, comment on, mention. See ATTENTION. —*n.* observation, statement, comment. See SPEECH.
remarkable, *adj.* noteworthy, notable, extraordinary, striking, unusual, singular, uncommon. See UNCONFORMITY, WONDER. *Ant.*, see CONFORMTY.

REMEDY [662]

Nouns—**1,** remedy, help, redress, RESTORATION; antidote, counterpoison, counterirritant, counteragent, antitoxin, antibody, prophylactic, antiseptic, corrective, restorative, sedative, palliative, febrifuge; germicide, specific, emetic, carminative, antibiotic (see ANTIBIOSIS).
2, physic, medicine, simples, drug, potion, draught, draft, dose, pill, tincture, medicament.
3, nostrum, receipt, recipe, prescription; panacea, sovereign remedy, cure, cure-all, elixir, *elixir vitae,* philosopher's stone, balm, balsam, cordial, ptisan, tisane, patent medicine.
4, salve, ointment, oil, lenitive, lotion, cosmetic, embrocation, liniment, depilatory; compress, bandage, poultice, plaster.
5, treatment, therapy, regimen; dietetics; bloodletting, bleeding, venesection, phlebotomy, cupping, leeches; surgery, operation, section.
6, pharmacy, pharmacology, pharmaceutics; therapeutics, pathology, neurology, homeopathy, allopathy, hydrotherapy, surgery, orthopedics, osteopathy, chiropractic, dentistry, midwifery, obstetrics, psychiatry.
7, hospital, infirmary, pesthouse, lazaretto, dispensary, clinic, sanatorium, spa, Red Cross.
8, doctor, physician; dentist; surgeon, general practitioner, neurologist, pathologist, psychiatrist, oculist, *etc.;* resident, interne; anesthetist; attendant; apothecary, pharmacist, druggist; leech; *accoucheur, accoucheuse,* midwife, oculist, dentist, aurist, nurse, sister.
Verbs—remedy, doctor, dose, physic, nurse, operate, minister to, treat, attend; dress the wounds, plaster; prevent, relieve, cure, palliate, restore; bleed.
Adjectives—remedial, restorative, corrective, curative, palliative, healing, sanatory, sanative; antitoxic, antiseptic, prophylactic, medical, medicinal, surgical, therapeutic, tonic, analeptic, balsamic, anodyne, hypnotic, neurotic, narcotic, sedative, lenitive, demulcent, emollient, detergent; disinfectant, febrifugal, laxative, dietetic, alimentary, nutritious, nutritive, peptic; curable.
Antonym, see DISEASE.

remember, *v.t.* keep *or* bear in mind, call to mind, recall, recollect. See MEMORY. *Ant.*, see OBLIVION.
remembrance, *n.* recollection, MEMORY, reminiscence, impression; memorial, memento, token, souvenir; fame, immortality. See RECORD.
remind, *v.t.* prompt, hint, suggest, jog. See MEMORY.
reminder, *n.* cue, hint, memo, memorandum, souvenir; remembrance, prompter. *Colloq.,* a string around a finger. See MEMORY.
reminiscent, *adj.* retrospective, suggestive, reminding. See MEMORY.
remiss, *adj.* lax, slack, careless, neglectful, dilatory, sluggish. See NEGLECT.

remission, *n.* annulment, cancellation; pardon, forgiveness; suspension, respite. See FORGIVENESS, NULLIFICATION, END.

remit, *v.t.* forgive, pardon, excuse, exempt, relax, slacken; pay, send. See FORGIVENESS, RESTORATION.

remnant, *n.* REMAINDER, residue, fragment, scrap, vestige.

remodel, *v.t.* rearrange, rebuild, modernize; renovate, rehabilitate, refurbish. See NEWNESS, RESTORATION.

remonstrance, *n.* protest, objection; reproof, expostulation. See DISSENT.

remorse, *n.* self-reproach, regret, compunction, contrition, PENITENCE.

remote, *adj.* distant, secluded, alien, irrelevant, slight. See DISTANCE, SECLUSION. *Ant.,* see NEARNESS.

removal, *n.* dismissal, discharge; withdrawal, transfer, DEPARTURE; EXTRACTION. See EJECTION.

remove, *v.* depart, go away, move; displace, shift, elminate, take off, discharge, evict. See DESTRUCTION, EJECTION, DEPARTURE.

remunerate, *v.t.* pay, reimburse, recompense, requite, REWARD.

remunerative, *adj.* profitable, paying, rewarding, compensatory, gainful, lucrative; worthwhile. See ACQUISITION, COMPENSATION, UTILITY.

renaissance, *n.* new birth, revival. See RESTORATION.

rend, *v.t.* tear, shred, rip, rive, split; harrow; cut, cleave. See DISJUNCTION.

render, *v.t.* give, pay, deliver, furnish, supply, yield, produce, perform; express, translate, interpret. See GIVING, INTERPRETATION.

rendezvous, *n.* tryst, appointment, date, meeting, assignation; ASSEMBLAGE.

renew, *v.t.* revive, restore, renovate; resume, continue; replace, renovate, replenish. See RESTORATION.

renewal, *n.* resumption, CONTINUANCE; renovation, RESTORATION; replacement, replenishment.

renounce, *v.t.* abjure, disclaim, disown, repudiate, reject, give up, abandon, surrender. See NEGATION, REJECTION, RELINQUISHMENT.

renovate, *v.t.* renew, restore, repair, freshen, purify. See RESTORATION.

renown, *n.* REPUTE, fame, reputation, glory, distinction, kudos.

renowned, *adj.* famous, well-known, distinguished, celebrated, noted. See REPUTE. *Ant.,* unknown, obscure.

rent, *n.* tear, slit, fissure; split, division, rupture, schism; payment, return, rental. *Colloq.,* tenement.

reorganize, *v.t.* resystematize, remodel, reform, rehabilitate, reëstablish. See CHANGE, RESTORATION.

repair, *v. & n.* —*v.i.* betake oneself, go. See TRAVEL. —*v.* mend, renovate, restore; amend, remedy. *Ant.,* see DETERIORATION. —*n.* RESTORATION, renovation, mending, redress.

reparation, *n.* amends, redress, RESTITUTION, indemnity. See PAYMENT, ATONEMENT.

reparative, *adj.* mending, restorative, remedial, corrective, compensatory. See COMPENSATION, RESTORATION.

repartee, *n.* witty retort, clever rejoinder, sally, persiflage, banter. See ANSWER, WIT. *Slang,* snappy comeback, wisecrack.

repay, *v.t.* reimburse, indemnify, refund; recompense, requite. See PAYMENT.

repayment, *n.* reimbursement, reparation, redress, amends. See PAYMENT.

repeal, *v.t.* revoke, annul, nullify, vacate, abrogate. See NULLIFICATION.

repeat, *v.t.* iterate, quote, recite; redo, duplicate. See REPETITION.

repeated, *adj.* repetitious, recurrent, frequent, incessant. See REPETITION.

repel, *v.t.* repulse, resist, reject, scatter, drive apart; disgust, revolt. See REFUSAL, PAIN. *Ant.,* see ATTRACTION.

repellent, *adj.* repulsive, resistant, forbidding, distasteful. See RESISTANCE, PAIN. *Ant.,* see ATTRACTION.

repent, *v.* rue, regret; be contrite, feel self-reproach, be penitent. See PENITENCE.

repentant, *adj.* penitent, regretful, sorry, contrite. See PENITENCE.

REPETITION [104]

Nouns—**1,** repetition, reiteration, harping; recurrence, renewal, reappearance; résumé, recapitulation, succession, run; tautology, monotony,

rhythm, periodicity, redundance, alliteration; diffuseness (see LOQUACITY).
2, echo, burden of a song, refrain, encore, rehearsal; reverberation, drumming, chimes; twice-told tale, old story, second edition; old wine in new bottles. *Slang,* chestnut.
Verbs—**1,** repeat, iterate, reiterate, reproduce, duplicate, renew, echo, re-echo, drum, harp upon, hammer, redouble.
2, recur, revert, return, reappear; redound, resume, rehearse, retell, go over the same ground, return to, recapitulate, reword; chew one's cabbage twice.
3, reproduction, DUPLICATION, reduplication; COPY; SIMILARITY.
Adjectives—repeated, repetitive, repetitious, recurrent, recurring, frequent, incessant; monotonous, harping, iterative, chiming, retold, aforesaid, abovementioned, habitual.
Adverbs—repeatedly, often, again, anew, over again, afresh, once more, ditto, encore, over and over, time after time, frequently.

Antonym, see END.

---

repine, *v.i.* fret, complain, mope, grieve, despond. See DISCONTENT, DEJECTION.
replace, *v.t.* put back; supplant, succeed, supersede; substitute; restore, return; move. See SUBSTITUTION, RESTORATION.
replenish, *v.t.* refill, restock, renew; stock up. See RESTORATION.
repletion, *n.* surfeit, SATIETY, overfullness, glut, engorgement. See SUFFICIENCY.
reply, *n.* ANSWER, response, retort, rejoinder; countermove.
report, *v.t. & n.* —*v.t.* state, review; rehearse, give tidings, announce, give notice of, proclaim. See INFORMATION, PUBLICATION. —*n.* RECORD, account, statement; news; rumor; hearsay; fame, REPUTE; bang, blast, detonation. See INFORMATION.
reporter, *n.* news gatherer, journalist, newspaperman. See BOOK. *Slang,* leg man, newshound, newshawk.

REPOSE [687]

Nouns—**1,** repose, rest, INACTIVITY, relaxation, breathing time *or* spell, halt, pause, respite; sleep, slumber.
2, LEISURE, spare time, idleness, ease.
3, quiescence, quiet, stillness, tranquillity, calm, peace, composure; stagnation, stagnancy, immobility.
4, day of rest, Sabbath, Sunday, Lord's day, holiday, vacation, recess; pause, lull.
Verbs—**1,** repose, rest, take one's ease, recline, lie down, go to bed, go to sleep, sleep.
2, relax, unbend, slacken, take breath, rest upon one's oars, pause; loaf, idle, while away the time, take a holiday, shut up shop. *Colloq.,* take it easy, take a breather, take time out, kill time.
Adjectives—reposing, resposed, reposeful, calm, quiet, restful, relaxed, unstrained; QUIESCENT, quiet; leisurely, slow, unhurried, calm.
Adverbs—at rest, at ease, calmly, peacefully; at a standstill; at leisure, unhurriedly.

Antonyms, see EXERTION, ACTIVITY.

---

repose, *v.t.* lay, place, entrust, deposit, put. See SUPPORT.
repository, *n.* vault, warehouse, museum, burial vault. See STORE, RECEPTACLE.
reprehensible, *adj.* blameworthy, hateful, censurable. See DISAPPROBATION.

REPRESENTATION [554]

Nouns—**1,** representation, IMITATION, illustration, delineation, depiction, depictment, imagery, portraiture, design, designing, art, fine arts, PAINTING, drawing, SCULPTURE, ENGRAVING, photography.
2, personation, personification, impersonation; drama, motion picture, movie, *etc.*
3, picture, drawing, sketch, draft, tracing, COPY, photograph, daguerreotype; image, likeness, ICON, portrait, effigy, facsimile.

4, figure, puppet, marionette, doll, figurine, manikin, model, waxwork, bust, statue, statuette, figurehead.

5, map, plan, chart, ground plan, blueprint, projection, elevation; diagram, cartography, atlas, outline, view.

6, ARTIST, designer, sculptor, draftsman, delineator.

Verbs—**1,** represent, delineate, depict, portray; photograph, figure, picture, describe, draw, sketch, trace, copy, mould, illustrate, symbolize, paint, carve, engrave.

2, personate, personify, impersonate, pose as, act, play, mimic, imitate.

Adjectives—representative, representing, depictive, illustrative, imitative, figurative, like, graphic, descriptive.

---

representative, *adj. & n.* —*adj.* typical, characteristic, illustrative, descriptive, exemplary; (of government) democratic, legislative, popular, republican. —*n.* delegate, nominee, agent, DEPUTY; Congressman, Assemblyman, legislator, Member of Congress *or* Parliament, M.P. See AGENCY, REPRESENTATION.

repress, *v.t.* suppress, restrain, check, curb, control, quell, stifle, smother. See RESTRAINT. *Ant.,* see FREEDOM.

reprieve, *n.* delay, stay, respite, suspension; pardon. See LATENESS, FORGIVENESS.

reprimand, *n.* reproof, rebuke, censure, admonition, reprehension. See DISAPPROBATION.

reprisal, *n.* RETALIATION, REVENGE, requital, indemnity.

reproach, *v.t. & n.* —*v.t.* blame, rebuke, upbraid, censure; stigmatize. See DISAPPROBATION, ACCUSATION. *Ant.,* see APPROBATION. —*n.* reproof, blame, disgrace, discredit, dishonor. See DISAPPROBATION, DISREPUTE, ACCUSATION.

reprobate, *n.* sinner, scoundrel; rogue, blackguard. See EVILDOER.

reproduction, *n.* renovation, RESTORATION, renewal; reprint, copy, duplicate, DUPLICATION; regeneration, generation, propagation; multiplication; REPRESENTATION.

reproof, *n.* admonition, criticism, censure, rebuke, chiding. See DISAPPROBATION.

reprove, *v.t.* admonish, censure, rebuke, chide, criticize. See DISAPPROBATION. *Ant.,* see APPROBATION.

reptile, *n.* saurian, crocodilian, serpent, lizard, *etc.;* toady, bootlicker. See ANIMAL, SERVILITY.

repudiate, *v.t.* renounce, disavow, disclaim, disown, divorce, deny; disclaim. See DISSENT, REFUSAL.

repugnance, *n.* DISLIKE, aversion, antipathy, disgust; inconsistency, contradictoriness; OPPOSITION. *Ant.,* see ATTRACTION.

repugnant, *adj.* distasteful, repulsive, incompatible, contrary, antagonistic. See DISAGREEMENT, HATE.

repulsion, *n.* driving from, repulse; rejection, rebuff; dislike, repugnance, disgust, loathing; antagonism, antipathy, aversion, hostility. See HATE, DEFENSE. *Ant.,* see ATTRACTION.

REPUTE [873]

Nouns—**1,** repute, reputation, distinction, mark, name, figure; note, notability, vogue, celebrity, fame, famousness, renown, popularity, credit, prestige, glory, honor; luster, illustriousness, account, regard, RESPECT, reputableness, respectability, good name, fair name.

2, dignity, stateliness, solemnity, grandeur, splendor, NOBILITY, majesty, sublimity; greatness, IMPORTANCE, eminence, pre-eminence.

3, rank, standing, station, place, status, precedence, position, place in society, degree, caste, condition.

4, elevation, ascent, exaltation, dignification, aggrandizement; dedication, consecration, enthronement, canonization, CELEBRATION, enshrinement, glorification.

5, hero, man of mark, celebrity; lion, notability, somebody, pillar of the church; chief, first fiddle, flower, pink, pearl, paragon, star. *Slang,* VIP, big wheel.

6, ornament, honor, feather in one's cap, halo, aureole, nimbus, blaze of glory, laurels.

7, memory, posthumous *or* lasting fame, immortality, immortal name.

Verbs—1, be distinguished, shine, shine forth, figure, cut a figure, splash; make a splash, live, flourish, glitter, gain honor, play first fiddle, take precedence, win laurels, win spurs, leave one's mark, star, come into vogue.

2, rival, surpass, outshine, outrival, outvie, emulate, eclipse, cast into the shade, overshadow.

3, enthrone, immortalize, deify, exalt; consecrate, dedicate, enshrine, lionize, crown with laurel; honor, confer honor, do honor to, accredit, dignify, glorify, look up to, aggrandize, elevate. *Slang*, build up.

Adjectives—1, reputable, creditable, honorable, respectable, in good order, in high favor.

2, distinguished, *distingué*, noted, of note, honored, popular; fashionable; remarkable, notable, celebrated, renowned, talked of, famous, famed, conspicuous, foremost, in the ascendant; illustrious, glorious, splendid, brilliant, radiant, bright.

3, eminent, prominent; peerless, superior, pre-eminent; great, dignified, proud, noble, worshipful, lordly, grand, stately, august, princely, imposing, solemn, transcendent, majestic, sacred, sublime, heroic.

4, imperishable, deathless, immortal, neverfading, time-honored, sacrosanct.

Antonym, see DISREPUTE.

REQUEST [765]

Nouns—1, request, requisition, petition, PLEA, suit, prayer; motion, overture, application, proposition, proposal, offer, canvass, address, appeal, apostrophe, orison, incantation.

2, mendicancy; asking, begging, postulation, solicitation, invitation, entreaty, importunity, beseechment, supplication, imploration, obtestation, invocation, interpellation; charity case.

3, requester, petitioner, beggar, solicitor, canvasser, door-to-door salesman; applicant, suppliant, suitor, demander, importuner; bidder, asker. *Slang*, moocher, cadger, sponge, free-loader, panhandler.

Verbs—1, request, ask, beg, crave; sue, pray, petition, solicit; invite, beg, beg leave, crave *or* ask a boon; apply to, call upon, call for, commandeer, enlist, requisition, ask a favor.

2, entreat, beseech, plead, supplicate, implore, adjure, cry to, kneel to, appeal to; invoke, ply, press, urge, beset, importune, dun, cry for help; hound. *Colloq.*, buttonhole.

3, beg from door to door, go a-begging, cadge, pass the hat. *Slang*, sponge, mooch, panhandle, free-load.

Adjectives—1, requesting, precatory, suppliant, supplicant, supplicatory.

2, importunate, clamorous, urgent, cap in hand, on bended knee.

Adverbs—prithee, do, please, pray, be so good as, be good enough, if you please.

Antonym, see DISOBEDIENCE.

requirement, *n.* want; NECESSITY; the necessary *or* requisite; requisition, demand; needfulness, essentiality, indispensability; urgency, exigency, *sine qua non*, matter of life and death. See COMPULSION. *Ant.*, see FREEDOM, CHANCE.

requisite, *adj.* necessary, required; imperative, essential, indispensable, urgent, pressing. See NECESSITY, COMPULSION.

requisition, *n.* demand, ORDER, claim, exaction, REQUEST. See COMMAND.

requital, *n.* retribution, RETALIATION; compensation, REWARD.

requite, *v.t.* retaliate, avenge; repay, indemnify, make amends, REWARD.

rescind, *v.t.* revoke, repeal, recall, annul. See NULLIFICATION.

rescue, *v.t.* liberate, set free, deliver, save; recover, reclaim. See FREEDOM.

research, *n.* INQUIRY, investigation, study, exploration.

resemblance, *n.* SIMILARITY, likeness, similitude; IMITATION, COPY.

resemble, *v.t.* simulate, imitate, approximate, be similar, look like. See SIMILARITY.

RESENTMENT [900]

Nouns—**1**, resentment, displeasure, animosity, anger, wrath, indignation, exasperation; pique, umbrage, huff, miff, soreness, dudgeon, acerbity, virulence, bitterness, acrimony, asperity, spleen, gall, rankling; ill-humor, bad humor, temper, irascibility, hate, irritation, bile, choler, ire, fume, dander, ferment, ebullition, pet, dudgeon, tiff, passion, fit, tantrums. See IRASCIBILITY, MALEVOLENCE.

2, sullenness, moroseness, sulks, black looks, scowl.

Verbs—**1**, resent, take amiss, take to heart, take offense, take in bad part, fly into a rage, bridle, bristle, flare up; sulk, pout, frown, scowl, lower, glower, snarl, growl, gnarl, gnash, snap, look daggers, grind one's teeth; chafe, fume, kindle, seethe, boil, boil with indignation, rage, storm, foam, vent one's spleen, lose one's temper, quiver with rage; burst with anger. *Colloq.*, take hard, blow one's top.

2, anger, affront, offend, give umbrage, hurt the feelings, insult, fret, ruffle, nettle, pique, irritate, sting to the quick, rile, provoke, chafe, wound, incense, inflame, enrage, aggravate, envenom, embitter, exasperate, infuriate, rankle, put out of humor, raise one's dander, make one's blood boil, drive one mad.

Adjectives—**1**, resentful, offended, SULLEN; wrought up, worked up, indignant, hurt. *Colloq.*, sore.

2, angry, irate; wrathful, wroth, cross, sulky, bitter, virulent; acrimonious, warm, burning; boiling, fuming, raging; foaming at the mouth; convulsed with rage; in a stew, fierce, wild, rageful, furious, mad with rage, fiery, rabid, savage; flushed with anger, in a huff, in a passion, up in arms, in high dudgeon.

Adverbs—resentfully, angrily, *etc.;* in the heat of passion, in the heat of the moment.

Antonym, see GRATITUDE.

---

reserve, *n.* restriction, QUALIFICATION; RESTRAINT, CAUTION, reticence, dignity; STORE, stock. See SILENCE, MODESTY.

reserved, *adj.* undemonstrative, diffident, distant, reticent; set aside. See MODESTY, SILENCE.

reservoir, *n.* cistern, reserve, source, supply. See WATER, STORE.

reside, *v.i.* live, dwell, abide, sojourn, lodge. See PRESENCE.

residence, *n.* ABODE, home, dwelling, habitation; sojourn. See PRESENCE.

residue, *n.* REMAINDER, rest, remnant, leavings.

resign, *v.* give *or* throw up; lay down; throw in the cards, wash one's hands of, abjure, renounce, forgo, disclaim, retract; deny, abrogate, get rid of, abdicate; vacate, retire; tender one's resignation, quit. See RELINQUISHMENT.

resignation, *n.* retirement, abdication, renunciation, abjuration, quitting, surrender. See RELINQUISHMENT.

resin, *n.* rosin; gum; lac; sealing wax; amber; bitumen, pitch, tar, asphalt, asphaltum; varnish, copal, mastic, megilp, lacquer, japan.

resist, *v.t.* defy, oppose, combat, withstand. —*v.i.* struggle, persevere, defend, fight. See OPPOSITION.

resistance, *n.* stand; OPPOSITION; renitence, repulse, rebuff, repulsion; insurrection, rebellion, riot; strike, lockout, walkout, tieup; boycott, passive resistance. See WARFARE, ATTACK, OBSTINACY. *Ant.*, see OBEDIENCE.

resistless, *adj.* powerless, unresisting; irresistible, ineluctable. See NECESSITY, ATTRACTION.

RESOLUTION [604]

Nouns—**1**, resolution, resoluteness, determination, WILL, decision, strength of mind, resolve, firmness, steadfastness, ENERGY, manliness, VIGOR, pluck, backbone, COURAGE, devotion, devotedness.

2, mastery over self, self-control, self-command, self-possession, self-reliance, self-restraint, self-denial, moral courage, PERSEVERANCE, tenacity, OBSTINACY, doggedness.

Verbs—**1**, resolve, determine, have determination, be resolved, make up one's mind, will, decide, form a resolve; conclude; devote oneself to, set one's teeth, put one's foot down, take one's stand; stand firm, steel oneself, stand no nonsense; put one's heart into, take the bull by the horns, go in for, insist upon, make a point of, set one's heart upon; stick at nothing, go the limit. *Colloq.*, go all out, go the whole hog.

2, PERSEVERE, persist; stick it out, die hard, fight, insist.

Adjectives—resolute, resolved, determined, strong-willed, self-possessed, decided, definitive, peremptory, unhesitating, unflinching, firm, indomitable, game, inexorable, relentless, unshakable, inflexible, OBSTINATE, steady, persevering.

Adverbs—resolutely, in earnest, seriously, earnestly, heart and soul, at any risk, at any price, cost what it may, all or nothing, rain or shine, sink or swim.

Antonym, see DOUBT.

resonance, *n.* vibration; reverberation, resounding, rebound; reflection, echo; ringing, tintinnabulation; ring, boom, rumble; deep note, bass note. See LOUDNESS.

resort, *v.i. & n.* —*v.i.* gather, flock, frequent; turn to; have recourse to. See TRAVEL, PRESENCE, USE. —*n.* haunt, meeting place; REFUGE, resource. See ABODE.

resound, *v.i.* echo, reëcho, ring, reverberate, peal. See LOUDNESS, SOUND.

resources, *n.* assets, WEALTH, prosperity; ingenuity, expedients. See MONEY, MEANS.

RESPECT [928]

Nouns—**1,** respect, regard, consideration, COURTESY, ATTENTION, deference, reverence, honor, esteem, estimation, veneration, admiration; approbation, devotion, homage.

2, homage, fealty, obeisance, genuflection, genuflexion, kneeling, prostration, obsequiousness, salaam, kowtow, bow, salute.

3, respects, regards, duty, devoirs.

Verbs—**1,** respect, regard, revere, reverence, hold in reverence, honor, venerate, esteem, think much of, look up to, defer to, pay attention to, do honor, hail, salute, pay tribute to, kneel to, bow to, bend the knee to, prostrate oneself, WORSHIP.

2, command *or* inspire respect; awe, overawe; dazzle; impress.

Adjectives—**1,** respectful, deferential, decorous; reverent, reverential, worshipful (see RELIGION); obsequious, ceremonious.

2, respected, estimable, in high esteem, time-honored, venerable, emeritus.

Adverbs—deferentially, *etc.;* with due respect, in honor (of), in homage (to).

Antonym, see DISRESPECT.

respectable, *adj.* worthy, reputable, estimable; moderate, fairly good. See REPUTE.

respective, *adj.* particular, individual, several.

respectively, *adv.* severally, one by one, each to each; in order. See APPORTIONMENT, SEQUENCE.

respire, *v.i.* breathe. See WIND.

respite, *n.* postponement, intermission, pause, reprieve, cessation, intermission. See LATENESS, REPOSE.

resplendent, *adj.* shining, lustrous, radiant, gleaming, gorgeous. See LIGHT, BEAUTY.

response, *n.* ANSWER, reply, rejoinder; responsory. See MUSIC.

responsible, *adj.* trustworthy, dependable; answerable, accountable, liable, chargeable; solvent. See ANSWER, DUTY, MONEY.

responsive, *adj.* sympathetic, sensitive, receptive, adaptable; antiphonal. See SOFTNESS, ANSWER.

rest, *n.* REMAINDER, remains, balance, residuum.

restaurant, *n.* café, eating house, coffee house, cafeteria, diner, automat, canteen. See FOOD.

restful, *adj.* soothing, quiet, reposeful, tranquil. See REPOSE.

restitution, *n.* RESTORATION, reparation, amends, *amende honorable;* ATONEMENT; remuneration; recovery, repossession; redemption; return, compen-

sation; making good; rehabilitation; indemnification; retrieval; repair. See
ACQUISITION.

restless, *adj.* nervous, restive, impatient; fidgety, skittish, jumpy, unquiet,
disturbed. See AGITATION, EXCITEMENT.

restlessness, *n.* AGITATION, disquiet, fidgets, jitters; wanderlust. See
CHANGEABLENESS. *Ant.,* see STABILITY.

RESTORATION [660]

Nouns—**1,** restoration, reinstatement, replacement, rehabilitation, re-estab-
lishment, reconstruction, REPRODUCTION, renovation, renewal, revival, RE-
FRESHMENT, resuscitation, reanimation, revivification, reorganization.

2, renaissance, renascence, second youth, rejuvenescence, resurrection, resurgence, rebirth, recrudescence, new birth; regeneration, regeneracy, re-
conversion.

3, recovery, convalescence, recuperation, cure, repair, reparation, reclamation, redress, retrieval, relief, healing, rectification, cicatrization.

4, restitution, return, rendition, redemption, reinvestment, atonement; redress, replevin, REVERSION; *status quo ante.*

Verbs—**1,** restore, put back, reinstate, rehabilitate, re-establish, reinstall; reconstruct, rebuild, reorganize, reconstitute, reconvert; renew, renovate, regenerate; make *or* do over.

2, recover, rally, revive, come to, come around, pull through, be oneself
again, get well, rise from the grave, survive, live again.

3, redeem, reclaim, recover, retrieve, rescue.

4, redress, cure, heal, REMEDY, doctor, physic, medicate; bring round, set
on one's legs; resuscitate, reanimate, revivify, reinvigorate, refresh, make
whole, recoup, make good, make all square, rectify, put to rights, set
straight, correct, put in order, refit, recruit, reinforce.

5, repair, mend, fix, retouch, vamp, tinker, patch up, darn, stop a gap,
staunch, caulk, splice, bind up wounds.

6, return, give back, bring back, render up, give up, let go, disgorge, reimburse, remit; get back, revert. *Slang,* cough up, kick back.

Adjectives—**1,** restored, renewed, convalescent, none the worse; refreshed.

2, restoring, restorative, recuperative, sanative, curative, remedial, sanatory,
salubrious (see HEALTH); refreshing, bracing.

3, restorable, recoverable, retrievable, curable.

Antonym, see DESTRUCTION.

RESTRAINT [751]

Nouns—**1,** restraint, HINDRANCE, coercion, constraint, COMPULSION, inhibition, deterrence, DISSUASION, repression, discipline, control, check, curb;
limitation, restriction; PROHIBITION; monopoly.

2, confinement, durance, duress; imprisonment, incarceration, solitary confinement; isolation ward; entombment; limbo; captivity; blockade, siege,
besiegement, beleaguerment.

3, arrest, custody, keep, CARE, charge, ward, protection. See KEEPER.

4, bond(s), irons, chains, pinions, gyves, fetters, shackles, manacles, hand-
cuffs (*slang,* bracelets); straitjacket; muzzle, gag, yoke, collar, halter, harness; bit, brake, curb, snaffle, bridle; seine; martingale, lead; tether, hobble,
picket, band, leash; bolt, bar, lock, latch; bars, PRISON.

Verbs—**1,** restrain, check, put under restraint, enthrall, enslave, restrict, debar, hinder, constrain, enjoin; coerce, curb, control, hold back, hold in,
hold in check, hold in leash; withhold, keep under, repress, suppress,
smother, pull in, rein in; prohibit, inhibit, DISSUADE.

2, enchain, fasten, fetter, shackle, trammel; bridle, gag, pinion, manacle,
handcuff, hobble, bind, pin down, tether, picket, tie up, tie down, secure;
moor, anchor, belay.

3, confine; shut up, lock up, box, bottle up, cork up, seal up, hem in, bolt
in, wall in, rail in; impound, pen, coop, enclose, cage.

4, imprison, immure, incarcerate, entomb, put in irons; arrest, take into
custody, capture, take prisoner, lead into captivity; send to prison; commit;
give in custody, subjugate.

Adjectives—**1,** restrained, constrained, imprisoned, pent up, jammed in,

wedged in, under lock and key, on parole; in custody, laid by the heels;
bound; icebound, snowbound.

3, prohibitive, prohibitory; proscriptive, restrictive; taboo, prohibited, forbidden, banned, illegal, not allowed, unauthorized; out of bounds, off
limits.

4, stiff, restringent, straitlaced, hidebound, reserved, binding.

Interjections—hands off! keep out! no trespassing; no thoroughfare.

Antonym, see FREEDOM.

---

restrict, *v.t.* check, LIMIT, confine, restrain, circumscribe, hinder, impede.
See CIRCUMSCRIPTION, HINDRANCE, RESTRAINT.

restriction, *n.* CIRCUMSCRIPTION, limitation, curb, RESTRAINT, embargo,
PROHIBITION.

restrictive, *adj.* prohibitory, prohibitive, hindering, restraining, limiting.
See RESTRAINT.

result, *n.* consequence, conclusion, outcome, upshot, fruit, EFFECT, product.
See PRODUCTION.

resume, *v.t.* recommence, reoccupy, retake, reassume; continue. See REPE-
TITION, ACQUISITION, CONTINUITY.

resurrect, *v.t.* restore, revive, rebuild, reëstablish, renew, rehabilitate. See
RESTORATION.

resuscitate, *v.t.* revive, restore, reanimate; refresh, revivify. See RESTORA-
TION, IMPROVEMENT.

retail, *v.t.* sell, dispense, vend, peddle, spread (gossip). See SALE, COM-
MUNICATION.

retain, *v.t.* keep, maintain; remember, engage, save, reserve. See MEMORY,
STORE.

retake, *v.t.* resume; recover, recapture, retrieve; refilm. See ACQUISITION.

RETALIATION [718]

Nouns—**1,** retaliation, reprisal, requital, counterstroke, retribution, COM-
PENSATION, reciprocation, reciprocity, retort, recrimination, ACCUSATION,
tit for tat, give and take, blow for blow, *quid pro quo*, measure for measure,
the biter bit.

2, revenge, vengeance, avengement; vendetta, feud; an eye for an eye.

3, vengefulness, vindictiveness, implacability, rancor, MALEVOLENCE, ruthlessness.

4, avenger, vindicator, Nemesis, Eumenides; retribution.

Verbs—**1,** retaliate, retort, requite, repay, turn upon, pay back, return in
kind, pay in the same coin, cap, reciprocate, turn the tables upon, return
the compliment, give as good as one gets, give and take, be quits, be even
with, pay off old scores; make it quits.

2, revenge, avenge, take one's revenge, wreak vengeance, have a bone to
pick, harbor a grudge, bear malice, rankle in the breast.

Adjectives—**1,** retaliative, retaliatory, recriminatory, retributive.

2, revengeful, vengeful, vindictive, rancorous, ruthless, unforgiving, implacable, relentless.

Antonym, see FORGIVENESS.

---

retard, *v.t.* delay, slow down, check, hinder, impede, postpone, hold up.
See SLOWNESS, HINDRANCE.

retardation, *n.* delay, slow down, HINDRANCE; obstacle. See SLOWNESS.
Ant., see PROGRESSION, VELOCITY.

retention, *n.* retaining, keeping; detention, custody; tenacity, retentiveness;
hold, grasp, grip. See POSSESSION, PRISON, MEMORY. *Ant.*, see OBLIVION,
RELINQUISHMENT.

reticence, *n.* reserve, TACITURNITY, secretiveness, muteness. See CONCEAL-
MENT. *Ant.*, see LOQUACITY, DISCLOSURE.

retinue, *n.* train, following, suite, cortège, attendants, retainers. See
ACCOMPANIMENT.

retire, *v.* withdraw, retreat, leave, resign, rusticate, lie low, keep aloof; put
out. See DEPARTURE. *Colloq.*, go to bed.

retirement, *n.* withdrawal, departure, SECLUSION, privacy, isolation, retreat, RESIGNATION.

retort, *n.* reply, rejoinder, witticism, sally; alembic. See ANSWER, WIT, HEAT. *Slang,* comeback.

retract, *v.t.* withdraw, recall, take back, recant, disavow, repudiate, revoke. See CHANGEABLENESS, NULLIFICATION.

retreat, *n. & v.i.* —*n.* withdrawal, retirement, SECLUSION; shelter, asylum; REFUGE, resort. See ABODE, REGRESSION. —*v.i.* withdraw, retire, fall back.

retribution, *n.* compensation, redress, separation, reprisal, reciprocation; nemesis; amends. See RETALIATION, PAYMENT.

retrieve, *v.t.* recover, regain, reclaim, repair, restore, make amends, fetch. See ACQUISITION.

retroactive, *adj.* retrospective, regressive, *ex post facto.* See PAST.

retrograde, *adj.* retreating, retrogressive, reversed, deteriorating, degenerate, decadent. See REGRESSION, DETERIORATION.

retrospect, *n.* reminiscence, remembrance, retrospection, review. See MEMORY.

retrospective, *adj.* looking backward, reminiscent; retroactive. See PAST.

return, *v. & n.* —*v.* restore, put back, bring back, echo, yield, render, reply, reciprocate; nominate, elect; come back, recur, reappear, revert. —*n.* ARRIVAL, homecoming, REVERSION, recurrence, reappearance, rebound, ANSWER, reply, recovery, RETALIATION, RESTITUTION, COMPENSATION. See REPETITION.

reunion, *n.* gathering, ASSEMBLAGE, assembling, convention; reconciliation. See SOCIALITY, RESTORATION.

reveal, *v.t.* disclose, show, divulge, announce, display, exhibit, expose, bare. See OPENING, DISCLOSURE.

revel, *v.i. & n.* —*v.i.* disport, gambol, romp, carouse; delight in, enjoy. See PLEASURE. —*n.* lark, spree, carouse. See AMUSEMENT.

revelation, *n.* disclosure, manifestation, exposition, revealment; Bible. See APPEARANCE, SACRED WRITINGS.

revelry, *n.* merrymaking, festivity, conviviality, jollification. See AMUSEMENT.

revenge, *n. & v.* —*n.* retaliation, reprisal; vengeance, vindictiveness, vengefulness; spite, rancor; feud, vendetta, grudge fight; requital; nemesis; tit-for-tat; retribution. —*v.* avenge, strike back, retaliate, requite, pay back, take an eye for an eye *or* a pound of flesh; spite; feud with; satisfy a grudge. See RETALIATION, MALEVOLENCE. *Ant.,* see FORGIVENESS, PITY.

revenue, *n.* income, receipts; earnings, profits, net, yield, dividends; taxes, tariff, customs, duties. See RECEIVING.

reverberate, *v.i.* reëcho, resound, be reflected. See SOUND.

reverberation, *n.* echo, repercussion, reflection, rebound. See SOUND.

revere, *v.t.* venerate, honor, RESPECT, esteem, admire; WORSHIP. See LOVE.

reverence, *n.* veneration, homage, honor, RESPECT; WORSHIP; obeisance. *Ant.,* see DISRESPECT.

reverie, *n.* daydream, musing, fancy, brown study, wool-gathering. See IMAGINATION.

reversal, *n.* setback; turnabout, tit-for-tat; inversion; repeal; change of decision; upset; abrogation. See CHANGE, DETERIORATION. *Ant.,* see STABILITY.

reverse, *n. & v.t.* —*n.* antithesis, converse, opposite; misfortune, setback, comedown, defeat; tail, back (of coin), about-face, rightabout. See OPPOSITION, ACTIVITY, CHANGEABLENESS. —*v.t.* transpose, invert, evert, turn around; back; revoke, annul, set aside. See NULLIFICATION.

reversion, *n.* reverting; return, returning; revulsion; RESTORATION; REGRESSION; inversion; recurrence; alternation; RECOIL; relapse; atavism; turning point, turn of the tide; escheat. *Ant.,* see PROGRESSION.

revert, *v.* return, turn back; recur, relapse; RECOIL, retreat; restore; undo; turn the tide *or* scale. *Ant.,* see PROGRESSION.

review, *v.t. & n.* —*v.t.* reëxamine, reconsider, revise, recall, rehearse, criticize, inspect. See INQUIRY, MEMORY. —*n.* retrospection, recollection; critique; criticism; inspection, parade; résumé, recapitulation, summary. See THOUGHT, DESCRIPTION.

revile, *v.t.* abuse, vilify, malign, asperse, calumniate, deride. See IMPRECA-
TION, CONTEMPT.
revise, *v.t.* alter, correct, reconsider, edit, rewrite. See IMPROVEMENT.
revival, *n.* resuscitation, revivification, reanimation; WORSHIP, camp meeting; reëstablishment, reintroduction. See RESTORATION.
revive, *v.t.* reanimate, revivify; refresh; bring back, reëstablish; rally, perk
up. See MEMORY, RESTORATION.
revocation, *n.* annulment, repeal, NULLIFICATION, abrogation.
revoke, *v.t.* recall, repeal, annul, rescind, withdraw, abrogate; recant,
repudiate, disavow. See NULLIFICATION, CHANGEABLENESS.
revolt, *n.* uprising, rebellion, insurgence, insurrection, mutiny, sedition.
See DISOBEDIENCE.
revolting, *adj.* disgusting, repellent, loathsome, repulsive. See UNCLEAN-
NESS.

REVOLUTION [146]

Nouns—**1,** revolution, radical *or* sweeping change, clean sweep, coup d'état,
uprising, counterrevolution, rebellion, breakup, upset, overthrow, reversal,
débâcle, cataclysm, convulsion.
2, ROTATION, turning, spinning, gyration, revolving; cycle.
Verbs—**1,** revolutionize, change radically, rebel, revolt, remodel, recast, reform, change the face of, break with the past.
2, revolve, rotate, turn, spin, whirl, twirl, gyrate, wheel, go (a)round.
Adjectives—**1,** revolutionary, rebellious, insurgent, radical, revulsionary,
cataclysmic.
2, rotating, turning, revolving, spinning, *etc.* See ROTATION.
Antonym, see INACTIVITY.

---

revolve, *v.* rotate, roll, circle, spin, recur. See ROTATION.
reward, *n. & v.* —*n.* recompense, remuneration, meed, prize, guerdon;
indemnity, indemnification; quittance; COMPENSATION, reparation, redress,
requital, amends, return, *quid pro quo;* salvage; perquisite; spoils; salary,
pay, PAYMENT, emolument; tribute, bonus, tip, premium, fee, honorarium.
Slang, jackpot, payoff. —*v.* recompense, repay, requite, remunerate, compensate; enrich, indemnify, satisfy; pay off. *Ant.,* see PUNISHMENT.
rhetoric, *n.* oratory, eloquence, elocution, declamation, floridity. See
SPEECH, ORNAMENT.
rhythm, *n.* meter, cadence, lilt, pulsation. See POETRY.
rhythmic, *adj.* metrical, pulsating, periodic, recurrent.
rich, *adj.* wealthy, affluent, opulent; fruitful, fertile, luxuriant; abundant,
bountiful; sumptuous; gorgeous; sonorous, mellow. See MONEY, PRODUC-
TION. *Ant.,* see POVERTY, INSUFFICIENCY.
riches, *n.* wealth, possessions, fortune, affluence, opulence.
rich man, Croesus, Midas, Dives, millionaire, capitalist, moneybags. See
MONEY. *Ant.,* see POVERTY.
rickety, *adj.* shaky, infirm, weak, ramshackle; rachitic. See IMPOTENCE.
Ant., see POWER, STABILITY.
rid, *v.t.* eliminate, abolish, clear, eject; free, disburden, disencumber; get
rid of. See EJECTION.
riddance, *n.* ridding, EJECTION, disposition, retirement, discharge; disen-
cumberment, *etc.;* (see RID); freedom, deliverance, release.
riddle, *n.* conundrum, enigma, puzzle; problem, poser. See SECRET.
ride, *v.i.* drive, tour, journey, travel; jog, gallop, trot, *etc.;* cycle, pedal.
—*v.t.* be borne (on, in, by); sit (a horse); mount, straddle. See PASSAGE.
rider, *n.* postscript, codicil, appended clause, ADDITION; horseman, cyclist,
passenger. See TRAVEL.
ridge, *n.* fold, welt, wrinkle, flange; arete, spine, esker. See CONNECTION,
HEIGHT.

RIDICULE [856]

Nouns—**1,** ridicule, derision, scoffing, mockery, quiz, banter, irony, persiflage, raillery, chaff, badinage; sarcasm; squib, lampoon, satire, skit, quip,
grin, leer.

2, parody, burlesque, travesty, farce, caricature; comedy, buffoonery, practical joke.

3, ridiculousness, etc.; ABSURDITY, anticlimax, laughingstock, FOOL, object of ridicule, fair game, April fool, jest, joke, queer fish, odd fish, mockery, monkey, buffoon.

Verbs—**1,** ridicule, deride, jeer; laugh, grin *or* smile at; snigger, snicker, scoff, banter, rally, chaff, joke, twit, poke fun at, play tricks upon, fool, show up; satirize, parody, caricature, lampoon, burlesque, travesty, make fun of, make game of, make a fool of.

2, be ridiculous, play the fool, make a fool of oneself, commit an absurdity, raise a laugh.

Adjectives—derisive, derisory, mock; sarcastic, ironical, quizzical, burlesque, satirical, scurrilous. See ABSURDITY.

Antonym, see RESPECT.

---

riding, *n.* horsemanship, motoring; district, bailiwick (*Eng.*). See TRAVEL, REGION.

rife, *adj.* prevalent, widespread, epidemic; abundant, plentiful, profuse, teeming. See MULTITUDE. *Ant.*, see INSUFFICIENCY.

riffraff, *n.* rabble, *canaille*, dregs of society. See POPULACE.

rift, *n.* crack, cleft, crevice, fissure; schism, breach. See CONTENTION.

right, *n. & adj.* —*n.* dextrality; dexter; starboard; off side; reactionism, conservatism, Toryism. —*adj.* dextral, dexter; off (side), starboard, recto; rightist, conservative, Tory, antileftist; reactionary. See SIDE. *Ant.*, see LEFT.

RIGHT, RIGHTNESS [922]

Nouns—**1,** rightness, right, what ought to be, what should be, fitness, propriety; JUSTICE, morality, PROBITY, honor, virtue, lawfulness.

2, privilege, prerogative, title, claim, grant, POWER, franchise, license.

3, rightness, correctness, accuracy, precision; exactness; TRUTH.

Verbs—**1,** be right, be just, stand to reason.

2, right, make right, correct, remedy, see justice done, play fair, do justice to, recompense, hold the scales even, give every one his due.

Adjectives—**1,** right, upright, good, just (see JUSTICE); reasonable, suitable, becoming.

2, right, correct, proper, precise, exact, accurate, true.

Adverbs—rightly, justly, fairly, correctly; in justice, in equity, in reason, without distinction of persons, on even terms.

Antonym, see WRONG.

---

righteous, *adj.* godly, upright, just, moral, good; puritanical. See VIRTUE, PIETY. *Ant.*, see IMPIETY.

rightful, *adj.* lawful, legal, equitable, just, true, fit, legitimate, entitled. See JUSTICE.

rigid, *adj.* stiff, inflexible, unyielding; set, firm, obdurate, strict; rigorous, cleancut. See HARDNESS, TRUTH, SEVERITY. *Ant.*, flexible, lax.

rigor, *n.* harshness, hardness, austerity, SEVERITY, stringency, rigorousness, strictness, rigidity, inflexibility, sternness. *Ant.*, see SOFTNESS.

rim, *n.* EDGE, border, margin, curb, brink.

rind, *n.* skin, peel, epicarp, integument. See COVERING.

ring, *v. & n.* —*v.* encircle, girdle, environ, encompass, hem in; toll, chime, clang; peal, toll, chime, tinkle; resound, reverberate. See SOUND. —*n.* circlet, circle, annulet, hoop, signet, girdle; machine, gang; ARENA; ringing, peal, chime. See CIRCULARITY.

riot, *n.* brawl, meeting, uprising; DISORDER, row, fracas, uproar, tumult. See DISOBEDIENCE.

riotous, *adj.* seditious, insurgent; boisterous, unruly, clamorous. See DISOBEDIENCE, VIOLENCE.

rip, *v.t.* TEAR, split, rend, slit, sever, part. See DISJUNCTION.

ripe, *adj.* matured, perfected, complete, mellow, consummate. See PREPARATION, COMPLETION.

ripen, *v.t.* mature, prepare, perfect, mellow, season, temper. See PERFEC-TION, PREPARATION.

ripple, *v.i. & n.* —*v.i.* gurgle, babble, purl. See RIVER. —*n.* riffle, wavelet.

rise, *v.i. & n.* —*v.i.* arise, ascend, soar, slope upward; loom, appear; increase, augment; originate, spring from; get up; prosper; revolt. See ASCENT, OBLIQUITY. BEGINNING. *Ant.,* DESCENT. —*n.* ASCENT; acclivity, slope; origin, source; appreciation, INCREASE; promotion, advancement; revolt. See CAUSE, IMPROVEMENT.

rising, *adj.* mounting, growing, advancing, ascending. See ASCENT.

risk, *v.t.* CHANCE, venture, hazard, gamble, jeopardize; invest. See DANGER.

risky, *adj.* dangerous, hazardous, perilous, uncertain; risqué, indelicate. See DANGER.

risqué, *adj.* suggestive, indelicate, off-color, racy, spicy, sexy, daring. See IMPURITY.

RITE [998]

Nouns—**1,** rite, ceremony, ceremonial, ordinance, observance, duty, form, function, solemnity, sacrament; service. See RELIGION.

2, ministration, preaching, sermon, homily, lecture, discourse, preachment.

3, seven sacraments; baptism, christening, immersion; confirmation, laying on of hands; Eucharist, Lord's supper, communion, consecration, transubstantiation, consubstantiation; Mass; penance, ATONEMENT, repentance, confession; extreme unction, last rites; holy orders, ordination; matrimony.

4, canonization, transfiguration, telling of beads, processional, purification, incense, holy water, aspersion, offertory, burial, excommunication.

5, relics, rosary, beads, reliquary, host, cross, crucifix, pax, pyx, *agnus Dei,* censer, rood.

6, ritual, rubric, canon, ordinal, liturgy, prayer book, Book of Common Prayer, litany, lectionary, missal, breviary, Mass book; psalter, hymn book, hymnal, psalmody.

7, ritualism, ceremonialism, Sabbatarianism; ritualist, Sabbatarian.

8, holyday, feast, fast, Sabbath, Passover, Pentecost, Advent, Christmas, Epiphany, Lent, Holy week, Easter, Whitsuntide, Michaelmas.

Verbs—perform service, minister, officiate, baptize, confirm, lay hands on, administer *or* receive the sacrament; administer *or* receive extreme unction, anoint, anele; preach, sermonize, lecture.

Adjectives—ritual, ritualistic, ceremonial, liturgical, baptismal, eucharistical, sacramental.

---

rival, *n. & v.t.* —*n.* competitor, contender, antagonist, emulator, OPPONENT. —*v.t.* vie with, cope with; exceed, excel. See CONTENTION, SUPERIORITY.

rivalry, *n.* CONTENTION, competition, OPPOSITION; emulation.

river, *n.* waterway, stream, creek, brook, watercourse, spring, fount, fountain, rill, rivulet, streamlet, runnel, tributary; torrent, rapids, flood, freshet; current, tide, race; waterfall, cascade; cataract; jet, spurt, squirt, spout, sluice; shower, downpour. See WATER.

road, *n.* way, path, track, PASSAGE, highway, roadway, thoroughfare, trail.

roam, *v.i.* wander, range, ramble, rove, stray, stroll. See DEVIATION.

roar, *v.i. & n.* —*v.i.* shout, bellow, howl, bawl; resound, ROLL, rumble, thunder; guffaw. See LAMENTATION. —*n.* uproar, vociferation; ROLL, rumble, boom, rote; guffaw. See LOUDNESS.

roast, *v.t.* grill, barbecue, broil; bake; toast, parch. See HEAT. *Slang,* ridicule.

rob, *v.t.* plunder, rifle, pillage, steal, purloin, burglarize; defraud. See STEALING.

robber, *n.* THIEF, burglar, bandit, brigand, pirate, poacher.

robbery, *n.* theft, thievery, burglary, holdup, pillage, plunder, brigandage, piracy, larceny. *Slang,* stick up.

robe, *n.* cloak, mantle, gown, vestment, robe of state; purple. See CLOTHING.

robot, *n.* automaton, mechanical man, golem.

robust, *adj.* vigorous, healthy, lusty, strong, sturdy, stalwart. See POWER, HEALTH.

rock, *v.i. & n.* —*v.i.* swing, sway, oscillate, teeter. See OSCILLATION. —*n.* crag, boulder, cliff; REFUGE, haven, SUPPORT, DEFENSE. See LAND. *Colloq.,* stone.

rocky, *adj.* rugged, stony,. hard; unfeeling. See ROUGHNESS, HARDNESS. *Slang,* dizzy, shaky.

rod, *n.* wand, pole, staff, switch, SCEPTER, caduceus. See SUPPORT. *Slang,* pistol, gat.

rogue, *n.* vagabond, scoundrel, cheat, scamp; imp, skeesicks.

roguish, *adj.* dishonest; mischievous, prankish, waggish. See AMUSEMENT.

role, *n.* PART, character, career, function, BUSINESS, CONDUCT, DRAMA.

roll, *n. & v.* —*n.* drumming, rumble, rattle, clatter, patter, toll; reverberation, echoing, thunder; tattoo, rat-a-tat, rub-a-dub, pitter-patter, dingdong, ticktock, charivari, quaver, peal of bells. —*v.* drum, rumble, thunder, rattle, clatter, patter, hum, trill, chime, peal, toll, tick, beat; reverberate, re-echo, resound. See RECORD.

romance, *n.* novel, love story; exaggeration, fiction, tall story; love affair, gest, fantasy. See FALSEHOOD, DESCRIPTION.

romantic, *adj.* sentimental, heroic, picturesque, idealistic; dreamy, poetic, fantastic, visionary, quixotic. See IMAGINATION, SENSIBILITY.

romp, *v.i.* frolic, caper, cavort, gambol, frisk. See AMUSEMENT.

roof, *n.* COVERING, housetop, rooftop, shelter, ceiling; home, rooftree; top, summit. See ABODE, HEIGHT.

room, *n.* chamber, hall, apartment; SPACE, capacity, elbow-room; lodging. See RECEPTACLE.

roomy, *adj.* spacious, commodious, capacious, ample. See SPACE.

root, *n. & v.* —*n.* rootlet, radicle, radicel, taproot; radical; base, origin, essence, source; etymon. See NUMBER, CAUSE, WORD. —*v.* plant, implant; eradicate, extirpate; take root; acclaim, cheer. See LOCATION, APPROBATION, EJECTION.

rope, *n.* cord, line; hawser, painter, lanyard; lasso, riata; hangman's noose, execution; string, twist. See FILAMENT.

roseate, *adj.* rosy, blooming; optimistic, promising, propitious. See COLOR, HOPE. *Ant.,* see DEJECTION.

rosy, *adj.* blushing, blooming, bright, promising, hopeful. See COLOR, HOPE.

rot, *v.i. & n.*—*v.i.* decay, decompose, putrefy; degenerate, waste. See DETERIORATION. —*n.* decay, decomposition, putrefaction. *Slang,* nonsense, piffle, twaddle, baloney.

ROTATION [312]

Nouns—**1,** rotation, REVOLUTION, gyration, turning, circulation, roll; circumrotation, circumvolution, circumgyration, turbination, convolution.

2, whir, whirl, turn, wheel, pirouette, eddy, vortex, whirlpool, cyclone, tornado; vertigo; maelstrom.

3, wheel, screw, whirligig, windmill, propeller, top, roller, flywheel; caster; axis, axle, spindle, pivot, pin, hinge, pole, swivel, bobbin, mandrel, reel.

Verbs—rotate, roll, revolve, spin, turn, turnaround, circulate, gyrate, wheel, whirl, twirl, eddy, trundle, bowl, roll up, furl, spin like a top; whirl like a dervish.

Adjectives—rotary, rotating, rotatory, rotational, rotative, whirling, circumrotatory, trochilic, dizzying, vertiginous, gyratory, vortical; centrifugal, centripetal.

Antonym, see DIRECTION, INACTIVITY.

---

rotten, *adj.* decomposed, putrefied, putrid; unsound, treacherous; corrupt, dishonest; offensive, disgusting. See UNCLEANNESS, DETERIORATION.

rotund, *adj.* round, circular; cylindric, cylindrical; spherical, globular, globous, globose; gibbous; campanulate, egg-shaped, ovoid, oviform, bulbous; chubby, buxom, fat, plump, obese, corpulent, well-padded, roly-poly, pudgy. See CIRCULARITY, CURVATURE.

rotundity, *n.* rotundness, rondure, roundness; cylindricity; sphericity; globosity; corpulence, pudginess, chubbiness, plumpness, WEIGHT, embonpoint, obesity, fatness; fullness, sonority, resonance; sphere, globe, ball; spheroid, ellipsoid; drop; globule. See CIRCULARITY, CURVATURE.

ROUGHNESS [256]

Nouns—**1**, roughness, unevenness, ruggedness, asperity, rugosity, corrugation, nodosity, nodulation, hairiness, arborescence, tooth, grain, texture, ripple.
2, brush, hair, beard, shag, mane, whiskers, mustache, imperial, toupée, goatee, tress, lock, curl, ringlet; plumage, plumosity, bristle, plume, crest, feather, tuft, fringe.
3, plush, corduroy, nap, pile, floss, fur, down, moss, bur.
Verbs—rough, roughen, ruffle, crisp, crumple, corrugate, make one's hackles stand up; rub the wrong way; rumple; go against the grain.
Adjectives—**1**, rough, uneven, scabrous, knotted, rugged, angular, irregular, crisp, gnarled, unpolished, unsmooth, roughhewn, craggy, cragged, scraggy; prickly, bristling, sharp; lumpy, bumpy, knobbed, ribbed, corduroy.
2, feathery, plumose, tufted, hairy, ciliated, filamentous, hirsute; bushy, leafy, whiskery, bearded, pilous, pilose, filar, shaggy, shagged, fringed, setaceous, bristly.
Antonym, see SMOOTHNESS.

---

round, *adj. & n.* —*adj.* circular, annular, spherical, globular, cylindrical; approximate. See CIRCULARITY, NUMBER. —*n.* REVOLUTION, cycle; CIRCUIT, ambit, course, itinerary, beat; series, catch, rondeau; routine, rut.
rouse, *v.* waken, arouse, animate, stir, stimulate, excite, incite, inflame. See POWER, VIOLENCE.
route, *v.t.* stampede, panic; discomfit, defeat, repulse. See SUCCESS.
route, *n.* path, road, way, course, PASSAGE, track, itinerary.
routine, *n.* practice, procedure, system, HABIT, round, rut.
rove, *v.i.* wander, ramble, meander.
roving, *adj.* vagrant, restless, inconsistent, vacillating. See CHANGEABLENESS.
row, *v.t. & n.* —*v.t.* paddle, scull. See NAVIGATION. —*n.* rank, file, tier, range. See CONTINUITY, ARRANGEMENT.
row, *n.* quarrel, brawl, rumpus, melee. See DISORDER, CONTENTION.
rowdy, *n.* ruffian, tough, hoodlum, bully, thug. See EVILDOER.
rowdyism, *n.* hoodlumism, ruffianism, delinquency. See VULGARITY.
rower, *n.* oarsman, oar, sculler, galley slave, waterman, gondolier. See NAVIGATION.
royal, *adj.* regal, imperial, princely, magnificent. See AUTHORITY, NOBILITY.
royalty, *n.* royal family, sovereignty; kindliness, NOBILITY; fee, share. See AUTHORITY.
rub, *v.t.* buff, abrade, scour, polish; chafe, massage, stroke; graze. See FRICTION, NEARNESS, SMOOTHNESS.
rubbish, *n.* trash, waste, debris, litter, junk. See USELESSNESS.
rude, *adj.* barbarous, crude, primitive, rustic; harsh, rugged; coarse, uncouth; discourteous, uncivil, insolent. See VULGARITY, NEGLECT, DISCOURTESY. *Ant.,* see COURTESY, COMPLETION.
rudiment, *n.* element, germ, embryo, root. See CAUSE.
rudimentary, *adj.* elementary, abecedarian; embryonic, undeveloped, imperfect, vestigial. See BEGINNING.
rudiments, *n.* elements, beginnings, principia. See BEGINNING.
rueful, *adj.* sorrowful, regretful, doleful; pitiable, deplorable, pathetic. See DEJECTION, PAIN. *Ant.,* see CHEERFULNESS.
ruffian, *n.* rowdy, bully, tough, thug. See EVILDOER.
ruffle, *v.t.* gather, shir(r), crinkle, corrugate, plait; agitate, ripple, tousle; rumple, disarrange; vex, irritate. See AGITATION, EXCITEMENT.
rug, *n.* mat, carpet; lap robe. See COVERING.
rugged, *adj.* craggy, shaggy, rough, unkempt; harsh, stern, austere; robust, hale. See ROUGHNESS, POWER. *Ant.,* see SMOOTHNESS, IMPOTENCE.
ruin, *n. & v.t.* —*n.* DESTRUCTION, downfall, perdition; wreck, remains, relic. See FAILURE, REMAINDER. —*v.t.* wreck, raze, demolish, impoverish, seduce. See POVERTY, IMPURITY.
ruinous, *adj.* dilapidated, rundown; disastrous, calamitous, desolating, tragic. See DETERIORATION, PAIN.

rule, *n. & v.* —*n.* canon, law, code, act, statute, regulation, DIRECTION, formula, FORM, maxim, standard, model, precedent, principle, regularity, uniformity, constancy, punctuality, routine, CONFORMITY. —*v.* govern, control, reign; master, curb; prevail, predominate; restrain. See ARRANGEMENT, AUTHORITY, LEGALITY, RESTRAINT.

ruler, *n.* MASTER, overlord, potentate, governor; straightedge, rule. See MEASUREMENT.

ruling, *adj.* governing, commanding, leading, predominant, prevalent. See AUTHORITY, SUPERIORITY.

rumble, *n.* roll, hollow roar, reverberation; back seat (of car). See SUPPORT.

rumor, *n.* report, hearsay, gossip, common talk. See INFORMATION.

rump, *n.* croup, buttocks; REMAINDER, fag, end; steak. See REAR, FOOD.

rumple, *v.t.* muss, dishevel, tousle, wrinkle, crumple. See ROUGHNESS.

run, *v. & n.* —*v.* scurry, hasten, travel, ply, flow, liquefy, act, function, extend, complete, pass into, continue, elapse; operate, thrust, compete, smuggle. See TIME, MOTION, VELOCITY, DIRECTION, STEALING. —*n.* swift pace; race; trip, flow; SEQUENCE; demand; yard; brook.

rung, *n.* rundle, round, spoke; step, degree. See SUPPORT.

runner, *n.* race horse, racer, sprinter; MESSENGER, courier, solicitor; blade, skid; rotor; rug, mat, scarf; operator; sarmentum; tackle.

runt, *n. & adj.* —*n.* dwarf; pigmy. —*adj.* stunted, underdeveloped, tiny, wee. See LITTLENESS.

rupture, *n.* DISCORD, schism, split, falling-out; break, rift, breach; hernia. See DISEASE.

rural, *adj.* rustic, provincial, countrified, bucolic, pastoral, arcadian, agrarian. See ABODE.

ruse, *n.* trick, stratagem, artifice, wile, subterfuge. See DECEPTION.

rush, *v. & n.* —*v.* hurry, scurry, dash, speed, gush, surge; hasten, hurry, expedite, precipitate, urge, drive; assault, attack; advance. See HASTE. —*n.*, HASTE, dash, precipitation; surge, gush, onrush; stampede. See VELOCITY.

rust, *v.* corrode, oxidize; deteriorate. See DETERIORATION.

rustic, *adj. & n.* —*adj.* rural, countrified, bucolic; artless, unsophisticated; unpolished, rude, backwoods. —*n.* peasant, farmer, bumpkin, boor. See POPULACE.

rustle, *v.i.* crackle, swish, whisk, whisper. *Colloq.*, steal (cattle).

rusty, *adj.* reddish-brown; timeworn, frowsy, antiquated; out of practice. See OLDNESS, INACTIVITY, DETERIORATION.

rut, *n.* groove, beaten path, track, FURROW; HABIT, routine.

ruthless, *adj.* relentless, merciless, inexorable, cruel. See SEVERITY.

S

Sabbath, *n.* day of rest, Lord's Day; Sunday, Saturday; First Day. See RITE.

sac, *n.* pouch, pocket; cyst; vesicle; sound, bladder. See RECEPTACLE.

sack, *n. & v.t.* —*n.* bag; DESTRUCTION, pillage; wine. —*v.t.* ravage, plunder, pillage, despoil.

sacrament, *n.* RITE, ceremony; host, consecrated bread *or* wine.

sacred, *adj.* hallowed, sanctified, sacrosanct, holy; consecrated, dedicated, inviolable. See DEITY, PIETY.

SACRED WRITINGS [985, 986]

Nouns—**1,** Scripture, the Scriptures, the Bible, the Book, the Good Book, Holy Writ, Holy Scriptures; inspired writings, Gospel; revelation, inspiration; text; King James Bible, Douay Bible, Vulgate; Talmud, Masorah, Torah; Haggadah, Halakah; exegesis.

2, Old Testament, Septuagint, Pentateuch; Octateuch; the Law, Jewish Law, the Prophets; major Prophets, minor Prophets; Hagiographa, Hagiology; Hierographa, Apocrypha.

3, New Testament; Gospels, Evangelists, Acts, Epistles, Apocalypse, Revelation.

4, Koran, Alcoran; the Eddas; Zend-Avesta; Veda, Upanishad, Bhagavad-Gita; Book of Mormon.

5, prophet (see ORACLE); evangelist, apostle, disciple, saint; the Apostolic Fathers; Holy Man.

6, Gautama Buddha; Zoroaster; Lao-tse; Mohammed; Confucius; Joseph Smith.

Adjectives—scriptural, biblical, sacred, prophetic; evangelical, evangelistic, apostolic, inspired, apocalyptic, ecclesiastical, canonical, textuary; exegetic, Masoretic, Talmudic; apocryphal.

Antonym, see IMPIETY.

---

sacrifice, *n. & v.* —*n.* oblation, offering, hecatomb, holocaust; immolation, self-denial. See RELIGION, WORSHIP. —*v.t.* renounce, give up; immolate. See GIVING.

sad, *adj.* sorrowful, downcast, dejected, unhappy, woeful, woebegone, depressed, disconsolate; melancholy, gloomy, cheerless, somber, dismal; heavy, heavy-hearted; regrettable, shameful. *Colloq.*, blue. See DEJECTION, PAIN, BADNESS. *Ant.*, see PLEASURE, CHEERFULNESS.

sadden, *v.t.* distress, grieve, discourage, make unhappy. See DEJECTION.

safeguard, *n.* DEFENSE, protection, safety device, shield, (a)egis; passport, safe-conduct, convoy. See SAFETY, PERMISSION.

safekeeping, *n.* CARE, custody, guardianship, protection. See SAFETY.

SAFETY [664]

Nouns—**1,** safety, safeness, security, surety, impregnability; invulnerability, invulnerableness; ESCAPE, means of escape, safety valve; safeguard, passport, safe conduct; confidence (see HOPE).

2, guardianship, wardship, wardenship; tutelage, custody, safekeeping; preservation, protection, auspices, aegis.

3, protector, guardian; KEEPER, warden, warder; preserver, custodian; duenna, chaperone; escort, convoy; guard, shield (see DEFENSE); guardian angel, tutelary saint; watchman, policeman; sentinel, sentry, scout (see WARNING); garrison; watchdog; Cerberus, doorman, doorkeeper.

4, REFUGE, asylum; precaution (see PREPARATION); quarantine, *cordon sanitaire*.

Verbs—**1,** be safe; save one's bacon; ride out *or* weather the storm; land upon one's feet; bear a charmed life; ESCAPE.

2, safeguard; protect; take care of (see CARE); preserve, cover, screen, shelter, shroud, flank, ward; guard (see DEFENSE); escort, convoy; garrison; watch, mount guard, patrol; take precautions (see PREPARATION); take shelter *or* REFUGE.

Adjectives—**1,** safe, secure; in safety, in security; on the safe side; under the shield *or* aegis of; under the wing of; under cover, under lock and key; out of danger, out of harm's way; on sure ground, at anchor, high and dry, above water; unthreatened, unmolested; protected.

2, snug, seaworthy; weatherproof, waterproof, fireproof, bulletproof, bombproof; defensible, tenable, proof against, invulnerable; unassailable, unattackable, impregnable, inexpugnable.

3, safe and sound; harmless; scatheless, unscathed; not dangerous; protecting, guardian, tutelary; preservative; trustworthy.

Adverbs—safely, with safety, with impunity, without risk; out of danger; in the clear.

Antonym, see DANGER.

---

sagacious, *adj.* penetrating, shrewd, astute, hardheaded. See SAGE.

sage, *n. & adj.* —*n.* wise man, magus, savant, philosopher, wise counselor, Nestor, Solon, pundit. —*adj.* wise, intelligent, sapient, astute, discerning; grave, serious; prudent, judicious; thoughtful. See KNOWLEDGE. *Ant.*, see IGNORANCE.

sail, *v.* cruise, voyage; navigate, traverse. See NAVIGATION.

sailor, *n.* seaman, mariner, seafarer, sea dog, salt, tar, bluejacket. *Slang,* windjammer, gob. See NAVIGATION.

salary, *n.* stipend, pay, remuneration, wage(s), hire, COMPENSATION, PAYMENT.

SALE [796]

Nouns—**1,** sale, selling, disposal; auction, market, custom, BARTER; BUSINESS; salesmanship; vendibility, vendibleness, salability.

2, seller, vendor, vender; MERCHANT; auctioneer, pedler, peddler, huckster, pitchman; salesman, saleswoman, *etc.*

3, clearance sale, end-of-month sale; bargain basement *or* counter; fire sale; black market, gray market.

4, MERCHANDISE, stock, produce, *etc.*

Verbs—sell, vend, dispose of, effect a sale; trade, merchandise, market, offer, barter, distribute, dispense, wholesale, retail; deal in; traffic (in); liquidate, turn into money, realize, auction (off); bring under the hammer; put up (at auction) *or* for sale; hawk, peddle, bring to market; undersell; make *or* drive a bargain.

Adjectives—salable, marketable, vendible; unsalable, unpurchased, unbought; cutrate, bargain-counter.

Adverbs—for sale, on the market, over the counter, under the counter; marked up, marked down, under the hammer, on the auction block; in *or* on the market.

Antonym, see PURCHASE.

salesman, *n.* MERCHANT, shopman, storekeeper, seller; solicitor, peddler, hawker, pitchman, huckster, drummer, traveling salesman; clerk, salesclerk, saleswoman (-girl, -lady, *etc.*).

salient, *adj.* outstanding, prominent, striking, conspicuous; notable, momentous, signal. See IMPORTANCE.

saliva, *n.* spit, spittle, sputum. See EXCRETION.

salivate, *v.i.* spit, expectorate; drool, slaver. See EJECTION.

sallow, *adj.* yellow, muddy, sickly, pallid, wan, jaundiced. See COLOR, COLORLESSNESS.

saloon, *n.* hall, dining room, main cabin; sedan, four-door; bar, tavern, taproom, bistro. *Slang,* oasis. See DRUNKENNESS, RECEPTACLE.

salty, *adj.* briny, brackish, saline; corned, salted; racy, pungent. See TASTE.

salubrity, *n.* healthfulness, wholesomeness. See HEALTH. *Ant.,* see DISEASE.

salute, *v.* welcome, greet, hail; uncover, bow, curtsy, present arms, dip colors. See INDICATION, SPEECH, COURTESY.

salvation, *n.* redemption, deliverance, reclamation, salvage. See RESTORATION, PRESERVATION.

salve, *n.* ointment, balm, unguent; REMEDY, lenitive, emollient; FLATTERY.

same, *adj.* identical, selfsame, interchangeable, alike, equal, equivalent; monotonous. See IDENTITY. *Ant.,* see DIFFERENCE.

sample, *n.* specimen, example, exemplar, pattern; prototype, archetype; trial, portion, taste, teaser. See CONFORMITY.

sanatorium, sanitarium, *n.* health resort, retreat, hospital, rest home. See REMEDY, INSANITY.

sanctify, *v.t.* consecrate, bless, hallow, purify, beatify; sanction, authorize. See DIETY, PIETY, PERMISSION.

sanction, *n.* PERMISSION, confirmation, ratification, approval, APPROBATION; interdiction, penalty, PUNISHMENT. See DISAPPROBATION.

sanctuary, *n.* sacred place, chancel; REFUGE, asylum, immunity.

sandy, *adj.* gritty, granular; arenaceous; yellowish, blondish. See POWDERINESS, COLOR.

sanguinary, *adj.* sanguineous, gory, bloody, bloodthirsty, murderous; savage, cruel. See KILLING.

sanitarium, see SANATORIUM.

SANITY [502]

Nouns—sanity, saneness, soundness, reason; rationality, normality, sobriety; lucidity; senses, sound mind, *mens sana.*

Verbs—be sane, keep one's senses *or* reason; come to one's senses, sober up; bring to one's senses.
Adjectives—sane, rational, reasonable, *compos mentis*, of sound mind; self-possessed; sober, in one's right mind; in possession of one's faculties.
Adverbs—sanely, reasonably, *etc.*; in reason, within reason.
Antonym, see INSANITY.

sap, *n. & v.* —*n.* plant juice, lifeblood; vigor, vitality; trench, FURROW. —*v.t.* undermine; tunnel; enfeeble, debilitate, devitalize. See CONCAVITY, IMPOTENCE. *Ant.*, see IMPROVEMENT.
sarcasm, *n.* irony, derision, CONTEMPT, RIDICULE, taunt, gibe.
sarcastic, *adj.* scornful, contemptuous, withering, cynical, satiric, ironical, sardonic. See RIDICULE, CONTEMPT.
Satan, *n.* the Devil, Lucifer, Mephistopheles, Belial; Beelzebub, Asmodeus, Apollyon; the tempter, EVIL, the evil one, the evil spirit, the Prince of Darkness, the cloven hoof; Pluto, god of the underworld; the foul fiend, the archfiend; the devil incarnate; the serpent, 666 (*Rev. or Apoc.* 13:18); DEMON. *Slang*, the deuce, the dickens, old Nick, old Scratch, old Harry. *Ant.*, see ANGEL.
satanic, *adj.* diabolic, demonic, demoniac, devilish; infernal, hell-born, hellish, fiendish, Plutonic; Mephistophelian. See DEMON. *Ant.*, see ANGEL.
satiate, *v.* sate, satisfy; cloy, jade, make blasé; quench, slake; pall; glut, gorge, surfeit; bore; spoil; have enough of, have one's fill, have too much of. See SUFFICIENCY. *Ant.*, see INSUFFICIENCY.
satire, *n.* RIDICULE, sarcasm, irony, mockery, travesty, burlesque. See CONTEMPT.
satirical, *adj.* cutting, bitter, sarcastic, wry, ironic, sardonic, lampooning, cynical. See CONTEMPT, DISAPPROBATION.
satisfaction, *n.* COMPENSATION, gratification, enjoyment, contentment; ATONEMENT, reparation, redress, amends; fulfillment. See PLEASURE, RESTORATION. *Ant.*, see DISCONTENT.
satisfy, *v.t.* CONTENT, set at ease; gratify, sate, appease; convince, assure; pay, liquidate, discharge; fulfill, meet; suffice, do, answer. See PLEASURE, BELIEF, PAYMENT, SUFFICIENCY. *Ant.*, see DISCONTENT, DOUBT, INSUFFICIENCY.
saturate, *v.t.* soak, fill, drench, impregnate, imbue. See MIXTURE, COMPLETION, WATER.
saucy, *adj.* pert, impertinent, impudent, bold; smart, chic, piquant. See INSOLENCE.
saunter, *v.i.* stroll, loiter, amble, meander, ramble. See TRAVEL.
savage, *adj.* wild, untamed, uncivilized, uncultivated, barbarous, ferocious; fierce, feral, cruel, rude; angry, enraged. See VIOLENCE, MALEVOLENCE. *Ant.*, see BENEVOLENCE.
save, *v. & prep.* —*v.t.* rescue, deliver, preserve, salvage, safeguard; STORE, lay up, keep, hoard; redeem, convert; spare, avoid; economize, conserve. See PRESERVATION, PIETY. —*prep.* saving, except, excepting, barring, but, excluding.
savings, *n.* backlog, reserves, nest egg, bank account. See STORE.
Saviour, Savior, *n.* Christ, Jesus [of Nazareth], Messiah, the [Lord's] Anointed; Redeemer, Son of God, [our] Lord. See DEITY.
savoriness, *n.* savor, palatability; relish, zest, gusto; tastiness, TASTE; delicacy, appetizingness; nidor. *Ant.*, see UNSAVORINESS.
savory, *adj.* zestful, to one's taste, good, palatable; nice, dainty, delectable; toothsome; gustful, appetizing, delicate, delicious, exquisite, rich, luscious, ambrosial; mouth-watering. *Colloq.*, tasty. *Slang*, scrumptious. See TASTE.
say, *v.t.* speak, tell, declare, state, aver, affirm, mention, allege, recite. See SPEECH, AFFIRMATION.
saying, *n.* saw, MAXIM, proverb, adage, byword, epigram, precept, apo(ph)-thegm; dictum, *ipse dixit.* See AFFIRMATION.
scab, *n.* crust, cicatrice, eschar, incrustation; nonunion worker, strike-breaker. *Slang*, fink. See COVERING, DETERIORATION.
scaffold, *n.* framework, scaffolding, platform; gallows, gibbet. See SUPPORT.

scale, *n. & v.* —*n.* weighing device, balance, steelyard; lamina, flake, incrustation, horny plate, squama, lamella, eschar; DEGREE, graduation, table, ratio, proportion; gamut. See MEASUREMENT, layer, COVERING, MUSIC. —*v.* weigh; peel, husk, exfoliate, flake; climb, surmount. See DIVESTMENT, ASCENT.

scamp, *n. & v.* —*n.* good-for-nothing, rogue, rascal, scalawag. See EVIL-DOER. —*v.t.* skimp, scrimp; slight, botch, work carelessly. See NEGLECT.

scandal, *n.* disgrace, infamy, shame, humiliation, stigma; defamation, slander, backbiting, calumny. See DISREPUTE.

scant, *adj.* limited, meager, inadequate, sparse; barely sufficient. See IN-SUFFICIENCY. *Ant.,* see SUFFICIENCY.

scarce, *adj.* rare, uncommon, deficient, scanty, few. See INSUFFICIENCY. *Ant.,* plentiful; see SUFFICIENCY.

scarlet, *adj.* bright red. See COLOR.

scatter, *v.t.* strew, DISPERSE, disseminate, dispel, dissipate. *Ant.,* see AS-SEMBLAGE.

scene, *n.* view, vista, landscape, panorama; site, LOCATION, setting; episode, event; outburst, tantrum; picture, tableau, pageant. See APPEARANCE, RE-SENTMENT.

scenery, *n.* prospect, landscape, view, scene; *mise en scène,* setting, backdrop, wings, borders, *etc.* See APPEARANCE, DRAMA.

scent, *v. & n.* —*v.t.* smell, detect; perfume. —*n.* ODOR, FRAGRANCE, aroma; sachet, perfume; track, trail, spoor..

scepter, sceptre *n.* staff, mace, rod, baton, wand; rod of empire; insignia of authority. See INDICATION, AUTHORITY.

scheme *n.* PLAN, plot, project, design, intrigue; diagram, tabulation, system, method.

scholar, *n.* savant, pundit, pandit, sage; professor; graduate, academician, academist; master, doctor; fellow, don; licentiate; philosopher; magus; mathematician, scientist; littérateur, intellectual; intelligentsia; bookworm; learned *or* literary man; man of learning, letters, *or* education; pedant, pedagogue; student. See KNOWLEDGE, SCHOOL. *Ant.,* see IGNORANCE.

scholarship, *n.* learning, erudition, KNOWLEDGE; scholastic, aid, fellowship. See REPUTE.

SCHOOL [542]

Nouns—**1,** school, academy, university, alma mater, college, seminary, lyceum; institute, institution, institution of learning; gymnasium; class, semester.

2, day, boarding, primary, elementary, grammar, grade, secondary, high, junior high, summer, [college] preparatory, *or* graduate school; parochial, denominational, public, *or* private school; kindergarten, nursery school; crèche; reformatory; law *and* medical school; teachers' college, dental college; normal school; correspondence school; vocational, trade, business, secretarial *and* music school; conservatory; art, dramatic, *and* dancing school; military school *or* academy. *Colloq.,* prep school; reform school.

3, curriculum, course; tuition; catalog; class, form, grade, seminar; classroom, lecture room; desk, blackboard; textbook, schoolbook; slate, chalk, eraser; three R's, ABC's.

4, learner, student, scholar, schoolboy, pupil; novice, neophyte, probationer; matriculation, graduation; undergraduate, freshman, sophomore, junior, senior, plebe, yearling, collegian, upperclassman; graduate, alumnus, alumna; faculty, professorship; chair, fellowship; master, proctor, teacher, instructor, lecturer, professor; provost, dean, bursar. See TEACHING.

Verbs—go to school, attend; matriculate, enroll, register; graduate, be graduated; TEACH, LEARN.

Adjectives—scholastic, academic, collegiate; educational, curricular, extra-curricular.

science, *n.* KNOWLEDGE, SKILL, efficiency, technology.

scientific, *adj.* systematic, accurate, exact, sound. See TRUTH.

scion, *n.* sprout, shoot, twig, cutting, graft; heir, descendant. See DESCENT.

scoff, *v.i.* jeer, be contemptuous *or* derisive, flout, laugh. See CONTEMPT.

scold, *v.* reprove, rebuke, rate, chide, berate, tongue-lash. *Slang,* bawl out. See DISAPPROBATION.

scope, *n.* extent, range, compass, capacity, SPACE, sphere, field. See BUSINESS.

scorch, *v.t.* char, singe, brown, blacken, toast, roast, parch, shrivel, wither; denounce, upbraid. See DRYNESS, HEAT. *Colloq.,* speed, burn up the road.

score, *n.* account, reckoning, tally, RECORD, reason; twenty; music, orchestration, arrangement. See ACCOUNTING, MUSIC.

scorn, *n. & v.t.* —*n.* CONTEMPT, disdain, superciliousness; derision, ridicule. —*v.t.* despise, disdain, contemn, spurn. *Ant.,* see APPROBATION.

scoundrel, *n.* knave, villain, rascal, rogue, blackguard. See EVILDOER.

scour, *v.t.* scrub, abrade, polish, cleanse. See FRICTION.

scourge, *n. & v.* —*n.* whip, strap, belt, lash, horsewhip; PUNISHMENT, curse, affliction, bane, nuisance, plague. —*v.t.* whip, lash, flay, beat; punish, afflict, plague.

scout, *n.* spy, observer, spotter, outrider, reconnoiterer, FORERUNNER. See CONCEALMENT.

scowl, *v.i.* frown; lower, glower. See IRASCIBILITY.

scramble, *v.i.* clamber, swarm, struggle, scrabble, tussle, scuffle. See ASCENT, CONTENTION.

scrap, *n.* bit, crumb, morsel; splinter, chip; whit, tittle, jot, speck; fight, bout, tussle. See LITTLENESS, CONTENTION.

scrape, *v. & n.* —*v.* graze, brush; scratch, rasp, abrade, grind, grate; rasp, grate; curtsy, bow. See NEARNESS, FRICTION. —*n.* abrasion, scratch; DIFFICULTY, plight, PREDICAMENT.

scratch, *v.* score, gash, scrape, rasp, wound, lacerate, deface; erase, withdraw, reject; scribble, scrawl; irritate, scrape; rasp, sputter; scribble. See DETERIORATION, FRICTION.

scrawl, *v.t.* scribble, scratch. See WRITING.

scream, *v.i.* shriek, screech, shrill, yell, CRY. See LOUDNESS.

screen, *n. & v.* —*n.* partition, curtain, shield, mask, protection, shelter; netting, mesh; sieve, sifter, bolter; cinema, movies. See COVERING, DARKNESS. —*v.t.* shelter, shield, protect, hide, conceal, veil, shroud; sift, sort. See DEFENSE, CONCEALMENT.

screw, *n.* spiral, helix, volute; twist; propeller, prop, jack; pressure, coercion; extortionist, niggard, skinflint. *Slang,* jailer, turnkey. See CONVOLUTION, ROTATION, PARSIMONY.

scribble, *v. & n.* —*v.t.* scrawl, scratch, write carelessly. —*n.* scrawl, hen tracks. See WRITING.

scribe, *n.* scrivener, secretary, amanuensis, clerk, copyist; writer, author. See WRITING, BOOK.

scrimmage, *n.* free-for-all, fracas, scuffle, tussle, brawl. See CONTENTION.

scriptural, *adj.* biblical, sacred; prophetic, evangelical, evangelistic, apostolic, inspired, apocalyptic, ecclessiastical. See SACRED WRITINGS.

Scriptures, *n.pl.* See SACRED WRITINGS.

scroll, *n.* ROLL, rolled manuscript, LIST, memorial; volute, flourish. See WRITING, ORNAMENT.

scrub, *v.t.* rub, scour, holystone, swab, mop. See FRICTION, CLEANNESS.

scruple, *n.* DOUBT, perplexity, misgiving, reluctance, unwillingness, qualm, conscience. See PROBITY.

scrupulous, *adj.* exact, careful; FASTIDIOUS, meticulous, punctilious; conscientious. See PROBITY. *Ant.,* see IMPROBITY.

scrutiny, *n.* examination, inspection, investigation, INQUIRY. See VISION.

sculptor, *n.* modeler, carver. See ARTIST, SCULPTURE, ENGRAVING.

SCULPTURE [557]

Nouns—**1,** sculpture, sculpting; carving; statuary, statue, statuette, bust, head (see REPRESENTATION); cast (see COPY); relief, relievo; high relief, low relief, bas relief; intaglio, cameo; anaglyph; medal, medallion.
2, marble, bronze, terra cotta, clay, alabaster; ceramics, ceramic ware, pottery, porcelain, china, earthenware.
Verbs—sculpture, carve, grave, cut, chisel, model, mould; cast.

Adjectives—sculptured; carven, graven; in relief; ceramic, marble, anaglyptic.

scum, *n.* froth, foam; slag, dross; mother (in fermentation); riffraff. See REMAINDER, POPULACE.
scurfy, *adj.* flaky, scabby, squamous, flocculent, furfuraceous. See LAYER, POWDERINESS.
scurrilous, *adj.* abusive, foul-mouthed, vituperative, insulting, coarse, vulgar, opprobrious. See IMPURITY.
sea, *n.* OCEAN, main, lake; wave, billow, swell; vast amount, profusion, MULTITUDE. See WATER, GREATNESS.
seacoast, *n.* seashore, seaside, seaboard. See LAND.
seal, *n. & v.* —*n.* die, stamp, signet; embossment, wafer, stamp; guarantee, confirmation; safeguard, stopper. See PROTOTYPE, ASSENT. —*v.t.* stamp, ratify, confirm; fasten, secure, occlude. See COMPLETION, ASSENT, CLOSURE.
seam, *n.* ridge, JUNCTION; scar, wrinkle, furrow; stratum, bed, LAYER.
seaman, *n.* mariner, sailor, salt, tar, seadog, seafarer. *Slang,* gob. See NAVIGATION.
search, *v. & n.* —*v.t.* hunt, seek, look for; explore, examine; probe; test. See INQUIRY. —*n.* quest, PURSUIT; INQUIRY, examination, scrutiny, exploration.
searching, *adj.* penetrating, keen, sharp; rigorous, unsparing. See SEVERITY.
season, *n. & v.* —*n.* period, TIME, spell, interval. —*v.t.* harden, acclimate, habituate, accustom; prepare, AGE, cure, ripen, dry out; spice, flavor. See HABIT, PREPARATION, PUNGENCY.
seat, *n.* chair, bench, *etc.* (see SUPPORT); site, LOCATION, ABODE; villa, estate; membership. *Colloq.,* buttocks, rump.
seaweed, *n.* algae, fucus, kelp, conferva. See VEGETABLE.
secede, *v.i.* withdraw, separate, bolt. See RELINQUISHMENT.

SECLUSION [893]

Nouns—**1,** seclusion, privacy; retirement; reclusion, recess; snugness; delitescence; rustication, *rus in urbe;* solitude; solitariness, isolation; loneness, withdrawal, hermitism, eremitism, anchoritism, voluntary exile, aloofness; inhospitality, inhospitableness; unsociability; domesticity.
2, cell, hermitage; cloister, convent; holy of holies, Most Holy Place, *sanctum sanctorum;* depopulation, desertion, desolation; desert, wilderness.
3, recluse, hermit, cenobite, eremite, anchoret, anchorite; St. Anthony; Simeon Stylites; Timon of Athens; solitaire, ruralist, cynic, Diogenes. *Colloq.,* lone wolf.
Verbs—be secluded, keep aloof, stand in the background; shut oneself up, creep into a corner, rusticate; retire; take the veil, take orders; abandon (see RELINQUISHMENT).
Adjectives—secluded, sequestered, retired, delitescent, private; conventual, cloistered, out of the world; out of the way; snug, domestic, stay-at-home; unsociable, unsocial, antisocial; inhospitable, cynical, solitary; lonely, lonesome; isolated, single; unfrequented, uninhabited, uninhabitable; tenantless; abandoned.
Antonym, see SOCIALITY.

second, *n.* moment, instant, trice, twinkling; interval, lower part, lower voice; backer, supporter, assistant. See INSTANTANEITY, MUSIC, AID.
secondary, *adj.* subordinate, minor, inferior, secondrate; resultant, consequent. See INFERIORITY. *Ant.,* primary; see IMPORTANCE.
secondhand, *adj.* used, hand-me-down; indirect, hearsay, unoriginal. See OLDNESS. *Ant.,* new, original; see NEWNESS.

SECRET [533]

Nouns—secret; dead secret, profound secret; mystery; sealed book; skeleton in the closet; confidence; problem, enigma, riddle, puzzle, crossword puzzle, acrostic, double acrostic, jigsaw puzzle, nut to crack, conundrum, charade, rebus, logograph (see DIFFICULTY); anagram; Sphinx, riddle of the

Sphinx; labyrinth; unintelligibility; *terra incognita; arcanum*, esotery, eso-
tericism, occult, occultism. See CONCEALMENT.
Verbs—secrete, hide, conceal, disguise; classify; keep to oneself, keep under
one's hat.
Adjectives—**1,** secret, concealed, patent, enigmatical, puzzling, labyrinthine,
veiled, hidden, problematical, paradoxical, inscrutable, unintelligible;
esoteric, occult, mystic.
2, classified; restricted, confidential, secret, top secret, most secret.
Antonyms, see DISCLOSURE, INFORMATION.

secretary, *n.* amanuensis, clerk; minister, administrator; desk, escritoire.
See WRITING, AGENCY, RECEPTACLE.
secrete, *v.t.* hide, conceal, mask; separate, prepare, excrete. See CONCEAL-
MENT, EJECTION, EXCRETION.
sect, *n.* denomination, faction, following, school, fellowship. See RELIGION.
sectarian, *adj.* denominational; nonconformist, unorthodox, heterodox,
heretical; dissident, schismatic, recusant, iconoclastic. See DISSENT, IR-
RELIGION.
secular, *adj.* LAY, temporal, profane, mundane, earthly. See IRRELIGION.

SECURITY [771]

Nouns—**1,** security, guaranty, guarantee; gage, warranty, bond, tie, pledge,
plight, mortgage, debenture, hypothecation, bill of sale, lien, pawn; stake,
deposit, earnest, collateral.
2, promissory note; bill, bill of exchange; I.O.U.; covenant, acceptance,
indorsement, signature; execution, stamp, seal; sponsor, sponsorship;
surety, bail; hostage; recognizance; indemnity; authentication, verification,
warrant, certificate, voucher, RECORD; probate, attested copy; receipt,
acquittance; discharge, release.
3, title deed, instrument; deed, deed poll; assurance, indenture; charter,
COMPACT; charter-poll; paper, parchment, settlement, will, testament, last
will and testament; codicil.
4, see SAFETY, justice.
Verbs—give security, give bail, go bail; put up, deposit, pawn, mortgage,
hypothecate; guarantee, warrant, assure; accept, indorse, underwrite, insure;
execute, stamp; sign, seal.
Antonym, see DANGER.

sedate, *adj.* staid, calm, INEXCITABLE, serious, dignified, serene, demure,
decorous. *Ant.,* frivolous, gay; see EXCITEMENT.
sediment, *n.* alluvium, silt, settlings, precipitate, lees, dregs, heel taps. See
REMAINDER.
sedition, *n.* AGITATION, incitement, insurgence, disloyalty. See DISOBEDI-
ENCE.
seduce, *v.t.* lead astray, lure, entice, corrupt, inveigle; debauch, betray.
See IMPURITY.
sedulous, *adj.* diligent, industrious, assiduous, persevering, persistent. See
ACTIVITY. *Ant.,* see NEGLECT, INACTIVITY.
see, *v.* view, descry, behold; discern, perceive, comprehend; observe, note;
know, experience; ascertain, make sure; meet; escort. See VISION, KNOWL-
EDGE.
seed, *n.* germ, ovule, semen, milt; CAUSE, origin; offspring, children, descendants; grain. See BEGINNING, DESCENT.
seek, *v.t.* search for, hunt, pursue; request, solicit; try, attempt. See
INQUIRY, PURSUIT.
seem, *v.i.* appear, look. See APPEARANCE.
seemly, *adj.* decorous, proper, becoming, decent, fitting. See OCCASION.
seer, *n.* prophet, crystal gazer, clairvoyant; soothsayer, ORACLE.
seesaw, *v.i.* teeter, teeter-totter; waver, vacillate, dilly-dally; crossruff. See
OSCILLATION.
seethe, *v.* boil, stew, simmer; steep, soak; fume, chafe. See HEAT, RESENT-
MENT.

seize, *v.t.* grasp, clutch; capture, arrest, appropriate, confiscate; comprehend, understand. See ACQUISITION, INTELLIGENCE.

seizure, *n.* confiscation, appropriation, arrest, capture; attack, fit, spell, stroke. See ACQUISITION, RESTRAINT, DISEASE.

seldom, *adv.* rarely, not often, infrequently. See RARITY.

select, *v.t.* choose, pick, prefer, elect, opt, specify, designate. See CHOICE.

self-denial, *n.* self-sacrifice, abnegation, renunciation, ASCETICISM.

self-esteem, *n.* PRIDE, self-respect; egotism, conceit, VANITY. *Ant.,* see MODESTY.

self-governing, *adj.* autonomous, independent, sovereign. See FREEDOM.

self-indulgent, *adj.* unrestrained, selfish, sensual, voluptuous, unbridled, sybaritic. See SELFISHNESS. *Ant.,* see MODERATION, RESTRAINT.

SELFISHNESS [943]

Nouns—**1,** selfishness, self-indulgence, self-interest; egotism, egoism; VANITY; nepotism; worldliness; egomania, megalomania; illiberality; meanness, PARSIMONY.

2, selfish person, self-seeker, fortune-hunter, worldling; egotist, egoist, monopolist, nepotist; dog in the manger; spoiled child *or* brat.

Verbs—be selfish; indulge oneself; look after one's own interests; feather one's nest; take care of number one; have an eye to the main chance; know on which side one's bread is buttered; give an inch and take an ell.

Adjectives—selfish, self-seeking, self-indulgent, self-interested, self-centered; egotistic, egotistical; mean, mercenary, venal; earthly, mundane; worldly, materialistic, worldly-wise.

Adverbs—selfishly, ungenerously.

Antonym, see GIVING.

sell, *v.* vend, market, dispense, peddle, transfer, offer for sale; betray, prostitute. *Slang,* persuade. See SALE.

semblance, *n.* likeness, resemblance, aspect; counterfeit, COPY, IMITATION; APPEARANCE, seeming, similitude, show, PRETEXT. See SIMILARITY. *Ant.,* see DIFFERENCE.

semiliquidity, *n.* stickiness, viscidity, viscosity; glutinosity; adhesiveness; inspissation, incrassation; thickening, gelatinousness; muddiness, miriness, slushiness. See COHERENCE.

seminary, *n.* SCHOOL, academy; theological school; seminar.

send, *v.t.* dispatch, forward, transmit, broadcast; impel, drive. See PASSAGE, PROPULSION. *Slang,* excite, move.

senility, *n.* dotage, second childhood, superannuation, old age, degeneration, decrepitude. See AGE, OLDNESS, INSANITY.

senior, *adj.* elder, older; superior, top ranking. See AGE. *Ant.,* see YOUTH.

sensation, *n.* FEELING, perception, consciousness, impression; furor. See SENSIBILITY.

sensational, *adj.* melodramatic, thrilling, startling; lurid, yellow. See EXCITEMENT.

sense, *n.* MEANING, import; perception, FEELING; JUDGMENT, appreciation; opinion, consensus. See SENSIBILITY, WISDOM.

senseless, *adj.* unconscious; foolish, stupid, dull; meaningless, unreasonable, absurd. See INSENSIBILITY, ABSURDITY. *Ant.,* sensible, wise; see MEANING.

SENSIBILITY [375, 380, 822]

Nouns—**1,** sensibility, sensitivity, sensitiveness; FEELING, perceptivity, esthetics; sensation, impression; consciousness (see KNOWLEDGE).

2, sensibleness, impressionableness, affectibility; susceptibleness, susceptibility, susceptivity; mobility; tenderness, SOFTNESS; sentimentality, sentimentalism.

3, sensation, tickle, tickling, titillation, itch, itchiness, itching; formication; aura; tingling, prickling; pins and needles.

Verbs—**1,** sensible of; feel, perceive; render sensible, sharpen, cultivate, tutor; cause sensation, impress; excite *or* produce an impression.

2, be sensitive, have a tender, warm *or* sensitive heart; take to, treasure; shrink; touch to the quick, touch the heart.

3, itch, tingle, creep, thrill, sting; prick, prickle; tickle, titillate.

Adjectives—sensible, sensitive, sensuous; esthetic, perceptive, sentient; conscious; acute, sharp, keen, vivid, lively, impressive, thin-skinned; impressionable; susceptible, susceptible; alive to; gushing; warmhearted, tenderhearted, softhearted; tender, soft, sentimental, romantic; enthusiastic, highflying, spirited, mettlesome, vivacious, lively, expressive, mobile, excitable; oversensitive, thin-skinned; fastidious; alert, aware.

Antonym, see INSENSIBILITY.

---

sensitive, *adj.* perceptive, conscious, impressionable, tender, susceptible, sentient; alert, aware; sentimental. See SENSIBILITY, FEELING.

sensual, *adj.* voluptuous, carnal; salacious. lewd; sybaritic, epicurean. See IMPURITY.

sensualist, *n.* voluptuary; epicure; LIBERTINE. *Ant.,* see ASCETICISM.

sensuous, *adj.* sensitive, aesthetic, hedonistic; emotional, pleasurable. See SENSIBILITY, PLEASURE.

sentence, *n.* statement, expression; JUDGMENT, decision, penalty. See SPEECH.

sententious, *adj.* terse, laconic, pithy, succinct, curt. See CONTRACTION. *Ant.,* see LOQUACITY.

sentient, *adj.* perceptive, sensitive, feeling, responsive, alive. See SENSIBILITY, FEELING.

sentiment, *n.* opinion, FEELING; sensitivity, delicacy, sympathy; motto, toast. See SENSIBILITY.

sentimental, *adj.* emotional, romantic, simpering, maudlin, mawkish. See SENSIBILITY. *Ant.,* see HARDNESS.

sentinel, *n.* watchman, sentry, guard, lookout, picket. See DEFENSE.

separate, *v. & adj.* —*v.t.* divide, disunite, disconnect, part, detach, sever, keep apart, isolate, segregate, sift, screen. —*adj.* disconnected, distinct, alone, isolate, unconnected, individual. See DISJUNCTION. *Ant.,* see JUNCTION.

sequel, *n.* upshot, outcome, following event; continuation; consequence; appendix, postscript; second part; epilogue, afterword. See SEQUENCE, ACCOMPANIMENT, REAR.

SEQUENCE [281, 63]

Nouns—**1,** sequence, coming after; going after, following, consecutiveness, succession, extension, continuation, order of succession, successiveness; CONTINUITY.

2, successor, SEQUEL, continuance; FUTURITY, posteriority.

Verbs—**1,** succeed; come after, come on, come next; follow, ensue, step into the shoes of; alternate; place after, suffix, append.

2, follow, pursue, go after, fly after; attend, beset, dance attendance on, dog; hang on the skirts of; tread on the heels of; lag, get behind.

Adjectives—**1,** succeeding, successive; sequent, subsequent, consequent; ensuing, proximate, next; consecutive, alternate; latter, POSTERIOR.

2, following, attendant, trailing.

Adverbs—after, subsequently; behind, in the rear of, in the wake of; successively; sequentially, consequentially, consequently.

Antonym, see PRIORITY.

---

serene, *adj.* calm, placid, tranquil, unperturbed; INEXCITABLE; clear, unclouded.

serf, *n.* bondman, esne, villein, vassal; peasant. See SERVANT.

series, *n.* sequence, set, succession, chain, progression, cycle. See CONTINUITY.

serious, *adj.* grave, momentous, solemn; earnest, resolute; important, weighty; alarming, critical. See IMPORTANCE, RESOLUTION.

sermon, *n.* homily, lecture, discourse, DISSERTATION, exhortation. See SPEECH.

SERVANT [746]

Nouns—**1,** servant, servitor, domestic, menial, help; retainer, follower, henchman, subject, liegeman; retinue, suite, cortège, staff, court; major domo, chamberlain.
2, attendant, squire, usher, page; waiter, butler, steward; livery servant, lackey, footman, flunky, bellboy, valet, *valet de chambre;* man; equerry, groom; jockey, hostler; orderly, messenger.
3, employee, staff, personnel, secretary; clerk; subsidiary; AGENT.
4, maid, maidservant; handmaid(en); lady's maid, nurse, *bonne,* ayah, wet nurse, nursemaid, housemaid, parlor maid, waitingmaid, chambermaid, kitchen maid, scullery maid; *femme de chambre, fille de chambre; chef de cuisine,* cook, scullion; maid of all work, hired hand, laundress, charwoman.
5, serf, vassal, slave, bondsman, bondswoman; bondslave; villein; pensioner, dependent; hanger-on, satellite; parasite (see SERVILITY); protégé, ward; hireling, underling, mercenary, puppet, creature, henchman, cat's-paw, myrmidon, errand boy, office boy; batman, dog robber.
Verbs—serve, work for, tend; wait on, attend (upon), squire.
Adjectives—serving, ministering, tending; in the train of, in one's pay, in one's employ, on the payroll; at one's call (see OBEDIENCE); in bondage.
Antonym, see AUTHORITY.

---

service, *n.* AID, help, duty; servitude, ministration, employment; public utility; worship, ritual, armed forces; wear, usefulness, USE; set, equipment, serving, helping. See BUSINESS, UTILITY, RITE, FOOD.

SERVILITY [886]

Nouns—**1,** servility, obsequiousness, subserviency; abasement; prostration, genuflection, WORSHIP; fawning, ingratiation; tuft-hunting, time-serving, flunkyism; sycophancy, FLATTERY; humility. *Slang,* apple-polishing.
2, sycophant, parasite; toady; tuft-hunter; snob, flunky, slavey, lapdog; hanger-on, leech, sponger; time-server, fortune-hunter; flatterer, lickspittle; henchman, hireling, tool, cat's-paw; courtier. See SERVANT. *Slang,* yesman, handshaker, baby-kisser, back-slapper.
Verbs—**1,** cringe, bow, stoop, kneel, bend the knee; sneak, crawl, crouch, cover; truckle to, curry favor with; grovel, fawn, lick the feet of, kiss the hem of one's garment.
2, pay court to; dance attendance on, hang on the sleeve of, fetch and carry, do the dirty work of.
3, flatter, adulate; wheedle, cajole; overpraise; humor, puff. *Colloq.,* soft-soap, butter up, lay it on thick.
Adjectives—servile, obsequious, abject; soapy, oily, unctuous; flattering, adulatory, mealy-mouthed, fulsome; pliant, cringing, fawning, slavish, groveling, sniveling, mealy-mouthed; beggarly, sycophantic, parasitical; base, mean, sneaking, skulking.
Adverbs—servilely, abjectly, *etc.;* with hat in hand; abased.
Antonym, see INSOLENCE.

---

session, *n.* sitting, meeting; period, term, semester; conference, hearing, convocation. See ASSEMBLAGE.
set, *v. & n.* —*v.* place, put, station; arrange, prepare; adjust, regulate; fix, assign, appoint; plant, set out; overthrow, unsettle; sink, go down, solidify, jell, harden; start out; tend; fit. See LOCATION, COMMAND, DESCENT, DENSITY. —*n.* clique, coterie, group; collection, series, outfit; TENDENCY, trend, drift; carriage, posture; agglutination, solidification. See COHERENCE, DIRECTION, PARTY.
settle, *v.* define, fix, confirm, appoint; agree upon; resolve, determine, decide, conclude; tranquilize, calm; reconcile, adjust, compose; discharge, square, pay, set at rest; place, establish; colonize; defeat, outwit; locate, settle down, take residence; sink, subside, sag, solidify; precipitate; alight; arrange, agree. See LOCATION, STABILITY, RESOLUTION, AGREEMENT, PAYMENT.

settler, *n.* colonist, pioneer, emigrant, homesteader. See INHABITANT.
sever, *v.t.* cut off, cleave, separate, sunder, part; disjoin, dissolve. See
DISJUNCTION. *Ant.*, see JUNCTION.
several, *adj.* individual, distinct, separate, particular; different, various;
few, sundry. See MULTITUDE.
severance, *n.* separation, division, partition; cleavage, scission; break. See
DISJUNCTION.

SEVERITY [739]

Nouns—**1,** severity; strictness, harshness, rigor, stringency, austerity; inclemency; pitilessness, arrogance.
2, arbitrary power, absolutism, despotism; dictatorship, autocracy, tyranny,
domineering, oppression; inquisition, reign of terror, martial law; iron heel
or hand; brute force *or* strength; coercion, COMPULSION; strong hand.
3, tyrant, dictator, disciplinarian, martinet, stickler, despot, taskmaster,
hard master, Draco, oppressor, inquisitor, extortioner, harpy, vulture,
Simon Legree, slavedriver, drillmaster.
Verbs—be severe, give no quarter, domineer, bully, tyrannize; rack, put the
screws on, be hard on; come down on; ill-treat; rule with a rod of iron;
oppress, override; trample (under foot); tread upon; crush under an iron
heel, ride roughshod over; keep a tight rein; work in a sweatshop.
Adjectives—severe, strict, hard, harsh, dour, rigid, stiff, stern, rigorous, uncompromising, exacting, exigent, inexorable, inflexible, obdurate, austere,
relentness, Draconian, Spartan, stringent, straitlaced, searching, unsparing,
ironhanded, peremptory, absolute, positive, imperative; coercive, tyrannical, extortionate, grinding, withering, oppressive, inquisitorial; inclement,
ruthless, cruel; haughty, arrogant.
Adverbs—severely, *etc.;* with a high hand, with a heavy hand; at sword's
point.

Antonym, see MODERATION.

sew, *v.t.* stitch, mend, baste, seam. See JUNCTION.
sex, *n.* gender; sexuality; MALE, FEMALE, masculine, feminine.
sexy, *adj.* voluptuous, seductive; lewd, lascivious; wanton, sensational,
bold. See IMPURITY.
shabby, *adj.* dilapidated, seedy, rundown, threadbare; mean, sorry, pitiful,
contemptible. See DETERIORATION, UNIMPORTANCE.
shack, *n.* hut, shanty, shed, hovel. See ABODE.
shackle, *n. & v.* —*n.* fetter, manacle, gyve, handcuff, bond; check, curb.
See PRISON, RESTRAINT. —*v.t.* bind, restrain; handcuff, manacle, chain.
shade, *n. & v.* —*n.* shadiness, shadow, umbrage, gloom, gloaming, DIM-
NESS, DARKNESS; obscurity; duskiness; shading, tone; curtain, veil, film,
haziness, haze, mist, mistiness, CLOUDINESS; COLOR, hue, tint; nuance;
DEGREE, slight difference; blind, curtain, shutter, Venetian blind; spirit,
ghost, phantom, specter, apparition, haunt. —*v.t.* hide, conceal; darken,
shadow; cover, veil; COLOR, tinge, tint; obscure, overshadow. *Colloq.,*
beat, outdo. *Ant.*, see LIGHT.
shadow, *n. & v.* —*n.* umbra, silhouette, SHADE; inseparable companion,
sleuth; reflection; shelter, protection; trace, suggestion; ghost. —*v.t.* overcast, darken, shade; foreshadow, adumbrate; trail, tail, dog. See DARK-
NESS, CLOUDINESS, SEQUENCE, PREDICTION.
shaft, *n.* arrow, spear; beam, ray; handle; bar, axle; thill; column, pillar;
well, pit. See ARMS, DEPTH, HEIGHT, SUPPORT.
shake, *v.* vibrate, agitate, shiver, brandish, flourish, rock, sway, wave,
rattle, jolt, worry, jar; unsettle, disillusion, impair, unnerve; tremble,
quiver, quaver, quake, shudder, flutter, vibrate. See AGITATION, EXCITE-
MENT.
shallow, *adj. & n.* —*adj.* not deep, shoal; superficial, slight, trivial, flimsy;
unprofound; flighty, inane, foolish. —*n.* shoal, sandbar, sandbank, shoal
water. See IGNORANCE, LOWNESS. *Ant.*, see DEPTH. KNOWLEDGE,
shallowness, *n.* emptiness, vacuity, lack of depth *or* profundity; flightiness,
triviality, inanity, superficiality. See IGNORANCE. *Ant.*, see DEPTH, KNOWL-
EDGE.

sham, *n. & adj.* —*n.* counterfeit, imitation, fake; pretense, dissimulation; humbug. —*adj.* make-believe, spurious, bogus, fake. See DECEPTION, FALSEHOOD.

shame, *n. & v.* —*n.* humiliation, mortification, abashment; ignominy, reproach, disgrace, dishonor. —*v.t.* humiliate, mortify, abash, disgrace. See DISREPUTE.

shameless, *adj.* brazen, barefaced, unblushing, graceless, wanton, immodest. See INSOLENCE, IMPURITY.

shape, *n.* FORM, figure, contour; pattern, mold; STATE, condition.

share, *n. & v.* —*n.* portion, PART, allotment, quota, dole. *Slang,* cut. —*v.t.* apportion, allot, assign, mete; participate. See APPORTIONMENT, COÖPERATION.

shark, *n.* dogfish, hammerhead, *etc.;* sharper, swindler. *Slang,* expert. See ANIMAL, THIEF.

SHARPNESS [253]

Nouns—**1,** sharpness, acuity, acumination; spinosity; PUNGENCY, acerbity.
2, point, spike, spine, spiculum; needle, pin; prick, prickle; spur, rowel; barb, barbwire; spit, cusp; horn, antler; snag, thorn, briar, bramble, thistle; bristle; nib, tooth, tusk, fang; spoke, cog, ratchet.
3, crag, crest, *arête,* cone, peak, sugarloaf, pike; spire, pyramid, steeple.
4, wedge, knife, cutting edge, blade, razor; scalpel, probe, lancet; plowshare; hatchet, ax(e), pickax(e), mattock, pick, adz(e), bill; billhook, cleaver, slicer, cutter; scythe, sickle; scissors, shears; sword (see ARMS); bodkin, PERFORATOR.
5, sharpener, hone, strop; grindstone, whetstone, steel; ABRASIVE.
Verbs—be sharp, have a point; bristle with; sharpen, point, aculeate, whet, barb, spiculate, set, strop, grind; cut (see DISJUNCTION).
Adjectives—**1,** sharp, keen; acute, acicular, aciform; aculeated, acuminated; pointed; tapering; conical, pyramidal; spiked, spiky, ensiform, peaked, salient; cusped, cuspidate; cornute; prickly, spiny, spinous; thorny; bristling; studded; thistly, briary; craggy, rough, snaggy; digitated, two-edged, fusiform; dentiform; toothed, odontoid; starlike, stellate; arrow-headed; arrowy, barbed, spurred; cutting; sharp-edged, knife-edged; sharpened.
2, PUNGENT, stinging, acrid, caustic, spicy, strong. See TASTE.
Antonym, see BLUNT.

---

shatter, *v.* splinter, shiver, smash, disintegrate; destroy; madden, craze; crash, shatter. See BRITTLENESS, DISJUNCTION, INSANITY.

shave, *v.t.* pare, plane, crop; skim, graze; cheapen, mark down, trim. See DECREASE, CHEAPNESS.

sheath, *n.* scabbard, case, envelope, casing; involucre, capsule, fascia, lorica. See COVERING.

shed, *n. & v.* —*n.* shelter, lean-to; shack, shanty, hangar, trainshed. See ABODE. —*v.t.* spill, pour out; drop, cast off; mo(u)lt, slough off; spread, diffuse, scatter. See DIVESTMENT, EJECTION.

sheep, *n.* ram, ewe, lamb; bighorn, karakul; mutton; congregation, parish; follower. See ANIMAL, MANKIND.

sheepish, *adj.* shamefaced, blushing, downcast, coy. See MODESTY.

sheer, *adj.* utter, absolute; mere, simple; thin, diaphanous; perpendicular, precipitate, VERTICAL, steep. See COMPLETION.

shelf, *n.* ledge, mantel, mantelpiece; sandbank, reef. See SUPPORT, HEIGHT.

shell, *v. & n.* —*v.t.* bomb, bombard, cannonade, strafe, pepper; shuck, strip, pod, hull. See ATTACK, DIVESTMENT. —*n.* case; carapace; husk; seashell; bomb, grenade, explosive, shrapnel, torpedo; boat, cockleshell, racing boat. See COVERING, ARMS.

shelter, *n.* REFUGE, retreat, sanctuary, asylum; cover, security, protection, SAFETY. See COVERING.

shepherd, *n.* herder, sheepherder, herdsman; pastor, clergyman; Good Shepherd. See DOMESTICATION, CLERGY, DEITY.

shield, *n.* armor, safeguard, screen; protection, protector, aegis, egis; ARMS, escutcheon. See DEFENSE, COVERING, INDICATION.

shift, *v. & n.* —*v.* veer, vary, CHANGE; equivocate; contrive, get along, transfer; substitute, vary. —*n.* CHANGE, SUBSTITUTION, DISLOCATION; expedient, subterfuge, trick; period *or* spell of work. See DEVIATION.

shiftless, *adj.* lazy, indolent, improvident, thriftless, negligent, happy-go-lucky. See NEGLECT, INACTIVITY. *Ant.,* see ACTIVITY, PREPARATION.

shifty, *adj.* unreliable, tricky; CUNNING; evasive, slippery; alert, resourceful.

shine, *v.* glow, gleam, scintillate; excel; polish, wax, burnish. See LIGHT, FRICTION, SKILL.

shingle, *n.* roof slate, wall slate; signboard; beach gravel; bob, short haircut. See COVERING.

shiny, *adj.* gleaming, glossy, lustrous, refulgent. See LIGHT. *Ant.,* DULL; see DARKNESS.

SHIP [273]

Nouns—**1,** ship, vessel, sail; craft, bottom; airship (see AVIATION).

2, navy, marine, fleet, flotilla; shipping, merchant marine.

3, warship, man-of-war, battleship, cruiser, destroyer, submarine, (aircraft) carrier, flattop; transport, tender, storeship; freighter, merchant ship, merchantman; packet; whaler, slaver, collier, coaster, lighter; fishing *or* pilot boat; dragger, trawler; hulk; yacht; liner; tanker, oiler.

4, bark, barque, brig, brigantine, barkantine; schooner; sloop, cutter, corvette, clipper, yawl, ketch, smack, lugger; barge, scow; cat, sailer, sailing vessel; steamer, steamboat, steamship; paddle steamer; tug; tugboat.

5, boat, pinnace, launch; lifeboat, longboat, jollyboat, bumboat, flyboat, cockboat, canalboat, ferryboat; shallop, gig, skiff, dinghy, scow, cockleshell, wherry, punt, outrigger; float, raft, rubber raft, pontoon; fireboat, motorboat; cabin cruiser, houseboat; class boat.

6, catamaran, coracle, gondola, carvel, caravel; felucca, caique; dugout, canoe; bireme, trireme; galley, hooker, argosy, carrack; galliass, galleon, galliot; junk, praam, proa, prahu, saic, sampan, xebec, dhow; dahabeah.

Verbs—sail, cruise, steam, drift, navigate. See NAVIGATION.

Adverbs—afloat, aboard, on board, aboardship, on shipboard, amidship(s).

shirk, *v.* evade, shun, NEGLECT; slack, soldier, malinger. *Slang,* goldbrick. See AVOIDANCE.

shiver, *v.i.* tremble, shudder, quiver, shake; shatter, splinter, burst. See AGITATION, BRITTLENESS.

shoal, *n.* SCHOOL, MULTITUDE, host, horde; shallow, sandbar. See ASSEMBLAGE, LOWNESS.

shock, *v. & n.* —*v.t.* shake, jar, jolt; startle, surprise, horrify, scandalize, disgust; paralyze, stun; galvanize, electrify. See SURPRISE, PAIN. —*n.* concussion, jar, impact; brunt, onset, assault; earthquake, temblor; prostration, stroke, paralysis, shellshock, apoplexy; ordeal, calamity; stack, stook; crop, thatch, mop (of hair). See VIOLENCE, AGITATION, DISEASE, ASSEMBLAGE, ROUGHNESS.

shocking, *adj.* distressing, horrible, abominable, odious, opprobrious, ghastly, indecent; dire, frightful, fearful, appalling, horrendous. See BADNESS, FEAR, DISREPUTE.

shoe, *n.* footwear; footgear; sandal, boot, loafer, casual, sneaker; runner, (tire) casing; brake lining. See CLOTHING.

shoemaker, *n.* cobbler, bootmaker, cordwainer. See CLOTHING.

shoot, *v.* rush, dart; sprout, burgeon, grow; fire, discharge; detonate, explode; kill, wound, hit; propel, drive, emit. See VELOCITY, VIOLENCE, INCREASE, KILLING, PROPULSION.

shop, *n.* mart, MARKET, store, bazaar, emporium; office, workshop, works, factory, mill. See BUSINESS.

shore, *n.* coast, beach, coastline; bank, strand, shingle, seaside. See LAND.

shortcoming, *n.* failing, foible, weakness, fault; deficiency, defect, default; delinquency, FAILURE, NEGLECT, remissness; inadequacy, INSUFFICIENCY, shortage, lack. See IMPERFECTION, ERROR. *Ant.,* see SUFFICIENCY, PERFECTION.

shorthand, *n.* stenography, phonography, stenotypy, stenology; Pitman, Gregg. See WRITING.

shorthanded, *adj.* understaffed, short (of help). See INSUFFICIENCY.

SHORTNESS [201]

Nouns—shortness, brevity, briefness; LITTLENESS; shortening, abbreviation, abridgement, retrenchment, curtailment; compression, digest, condensation, reduction, CONTRACTION; epitome, synopsis, compendium; conciseness.

Verbs—be short, shorten, curtail, abridge, digest, abbreviate, take in, reduce; compress, contract; epitomize; retrench, cut short, scrimp, cut, chop up, hack, hew; cut down; clip, dock, lop, prune; shear, shave; mow, reap, crop; snub; truncate, stunt, nip in the bud, check the growth of; foreshorten.

Adjectives—short, brief, curt, succinct, epitomized, compendious, compact, concise, summary; stubby, shorn, stubbed; stumpy, thickset, pug; squat, dumpy; dwarfed, dwarfish, little; oblate.

Adverbs—shortly, in short; concisely; abruptly.

Antonym, see LENGTH.

---

shortsighted, *adj.* myopic, nearsighted; improvident; unimaginative, lacking foresight. See VISION, DIMSIGHTED.

short-winded, *adj.* dyspn(o)eic, broken-winded, asthmatic, wheezy. See WEARINESS.

shot, *adj. & n.* —*adj.* propelled, struck (see SHOOT); interspersed, interwoven. See MIXTURE. —*n.* bullet, ball, pellet; discharge, stroke, attempt; injection, inoculation, hypodermic, hypo. See ARMS, REMEDY.

shout, *v. & n.* scream, call, bawl, bellow, yell; whoop, cheer, bawl, roar. See CRY, REJOICING.

show, *v. & n.* —*v.t.* exhibit, display; explain, teach; demonstrate, prove, guide, escort. See INDICATION, TEACHING, EVIDENCE, DISCLOSURE. *Ant.* see CONCEALMENT. —*n.* display, exhibition, play, entertainment, pageant, spectacle; pomp, OSTENTATION; semblance, APPEARANCE, PRETEXT. See DRAMA.

shower, *n.* rain, sprinkle, drizzle; spate; volley; fall; gift party. See WATER, ASSEMBLAGE, GIVING.

showy, *adj.* conspicuous, colorful; ornate, florid, flashy, gaudy, pretentious, ostentatious. See COLOR, VULGARITY, OSTENTATION.

shrew, *n.* termagant, scold, virago, vixen, fishwife, henpecker, beldame. See IRASCIBILITY.

shrewd, *adj.* clever, keen, farsighted, astute; CUNNING, wily, artful; sharp, acute, piercing. See SKILL. *Ant.,* DULL, fumbling.

shrewdness, *n.* keenness, acumen; craft, craftiness; astuteness, sagacity, discernment, CUNNING.

shriek, *v.i.* scream, screech, shrill, squeal. See LOUDNESS.

shrill, *adj.* sharp, piercing, STRIDENT, high-pitched, piping, penetrating, poignant. See LOUDNESS.

shrine, *n.* altar, TEMPLE; receptacle (for sacred objects); reliquary; tomb.

shrink, *v.* contract, shrivel, diminish, wizen; flinch, draw back, RECOIL, wince, quail, cower; compress, reduce, DECREASE. See CONTRACTION. *Ant.,* INCREASE.

shrivel, *v.* shrink, wrinkle, wizen, pucker; wither, sear. See CONTRACTION, DETERIORATION, DRYNESS.

shroud, *n.* winding sheet, graveclothes; pall; screen, cloak, veil; CONCEALMENT. See INTERMENT, COVERING.

shudder, *v.i.* tremble, quake, quiver, shiver, vibrate. See COLD, FEAR, OSCILLATION.

shuffle, *v.* rearrange, switch, shift, mix, intermingle, jumble; scuff, drag; fidget, shift; rearrange, mix; scuffle, shamble, slouch; equivocate, quibble, evade. See INTERCHANGE, MIXTURE, SLOWNESS, CHANGEABLENESS.

shun, *v.t.* avoid, elude, evade, eschew; cut, ignore; steer clear of. See AVOIDANCE, CONTEMPT. *Ant.,* see ACCOMPANIMENT, SOCIALITY.

shut, *v.t.* close, fold; imprison, confine; silence; cease operations, terminate; bar, exclude; blockade. See CLOSURE. *Ant.,* see OPENING.

shy, *adj.* bashful, reserved, retiring, demure; cautious, suspicious, wary; timid, skittish, fearful. See MODESTY, COWARDICE. *Slang,* short, lacking. *Ant.,* see INSOLENCE, COURAGE.

sibilant, *adj. & n.* hissing; whispering; whistling; (sound) like S.

sick, *adj.* ill, ailing, diseased; nauseated; disgusted; bored. *Slang,* fed-up. See DISEASE, WEARINESS. *Ant.,* see HEALTH.

sicken, *v.* ail, become ill; languish; droop, waste away; be nauseated; feel disgust; cloy, weary; make ill, afflict; nauseate, revolt. See DISEASE, PAIN, DISLIKE. *Ant.,* see REMEDY.

sickly, *adj.* invalid, ailing, unwell; debilitated, languid, peaked; wan, pale, washed out, faint; mawkish, nauseating. See DISEASE, COLORLESSNESS. *Ant.,* see HEALTH.

SIDE [236]

Nouns—**1,** side, flank, quarter, lee, leeward, weather, windward; skirt, EDGE, margin, border; hand; cheek, jowl; wing; profile; temple; loin, haunch, hip; laterality; gable, gable-end; broadside; outside, inside (see EXTERIOR, INTERIOR); east, west (see DIRECTION); orientation.

2, see RIGHT (side), LEFT (side), PARTY (partisanship).

Verbs—be on one side, flank, outflank; sidle; skirt, border.

Adjectives—side, lateral, sidelong; collateral; parietal, flanking, skirting; flanked; sidelong, bordering.

2, many-sided; multilateral, bilateral, trilateral, quadrilateral.

Adverbs—sideways, sidewise, sidelong; laterally; broadside on; on one side, abreast, alongside, beside, aside; by, by the side of; side by side; cheek by jowl; to windward, to leeward; right and left.

Antonym, see MIDDLE.

---

siege, *n.* investment, encirclement; besiegement, blockade, beleaguerment; PERIOD, long spell. See ATTACK.

siesta, *n.* nap, snooze, doze, rest. See INACTIVITY, REPOSE.

sieve, *n.* riddle, colander, sifter, screen, strainer, bolter. See OPENING.

sift, *v.t.* separate, bolt, screen, sort; examine, scrutinize, segregate, eliminate. See ARRANGEMENT, CHOICE.

sigh, *v.i.* breathe heavily, sadly, *or* wearily; suspire, sough, moan; long, yearn, grieve (with *for*). See WIND, DESIRE.

sight, *n.* VISION, eyesight; view, vista, scene; APPEARANCE, aspect, look; spectacle, display; visibility; aim, observation; eyesore (see UGLINESS). *Colloq.,* abundance, quantity. *Ant.,* see BLINDNESS.

sign, *n.* OMEN, portent; INDICATION, symptom, token, mark; symbol, emblem; gesture, signal; trace, vestige; signboard, shingle; guidepost. See RECORD.

signal, *n., adj. & v.* —*n.* sign, watchword, cue; alarm, WARNING, DIRECTION, order; traffic light, beacon, foghorn, wigwag; CAUSE; broadcast radio impulse. —*adj.* memorable, conspicuous, momentous. See IMPORTANCE. —*v.t.* speak, hail, call, beckon, gesticulate; semaphore, wigwag; radio, broadcast, beam. See NAVIGATION, INDICATION.

signature, *n.* autograph, hand, sign-manual; subscription; mark, endorsement; identifying theme, music, letters, *etc.;* identification; attestation. See INDICATION, NOMENCLATURE. *Slang,* fist, John Hancock.

significance, *n.* MEANING, import, expressiveness; IMPORTANCE, consequence. See REPUTE. *Ant.,* see UNIMPORTANCE.

signify, *v.t.* show; declare, portend; mean, denote, express, connote, indicate. See MEANING, IMPORTANCE, INDICATION.

SILENCE [403]

Nouns—**1,** silence; stillness, quiet, peace, hush, lull; inaudibility.

2, muteness, dumbness, aphony, voicelessness; taciturnity, reticence; deadness, dullness.

3, silencer, muffler, damper, MUTE.

Verbs—be silent, hold one's tongue, silence, render silent, quiet, still, hush; stifle, muffle, stop; smother, muzzle, mute, gag, put to silence.

Adjectives—**1,** silent; still, stilly; quiet, noiseless, soundless; hushed, soft, solemn, awful, tomblike, deathlike, silent as the tomb *or* grave; inaudible, FAINT; tacit.

2, MUTE, dumb, mum, tongue-tied, voiceless, speechless, muffled, gagged; TACITURN, reticent, uncommunicative.

Adverbs—silently, mutely, *etc.*

Interjections—hush! silence! shut up!

Antonym, see SOUND.

---

silly, *adj.* witless, foolish, stupid, childish; fatuous, inane; senseless, absurd, ridiculous. See ABSURDITY.

SIMILARITY [17]

Nouns—**1,** similarity, resemblance, likeness, similitude, semblance; affinity, approximation, parallelism; AGREEMENT; analogy; family likeness; alliteration, rhyme, pun.

2, REPETITION; sameness, IDENTITY, uniformity, EQUALITY; parallel; simile; image, REPRESENTATION; striking, speaking, *or* faithful likeness; double, twin, picture. *Slang,* ringer, spittin' image.

Verbs—**1,** be similar, look like, look alike, resemble; bear resemblance; smack of; approximate; parallel, match; take after; imitate; assimilate.

2, COMPARE, identify, parallel, relate.

Adjectives—similar; resembling, like, alike; twin, analogous, analogical; parallel, of a piece; so; much the same; near, close, something like; comparable; mock, pseudo, simulating, representing; exact, lifelike, faithful; true to nature, true to life, the very image, the very picture of; like two peas in a pod, cast in the same mold.

Adverbs—similarly, as if, so to speak, as it were, quasi, just as.

Antonym, see DIFFERENCE.

SIMPLENESS [42]

Nouns—**1,** simpleness, purity, homogeneity; CLEANNESS.

2, simplicity, ARTLESSNESS; plainness, homeliness; undress; chastity, SEVERITY.

Verbs—simplify; clear, purify, clean; disentangle (see DISJUNCTION).

Adjectives—**1,** simple, homogeneous, single, pure, clear, sheer, neat; unmixed, uncomplex; elementary; unadulterated, unsophisticated, unalloyed; pure and simple; free from, exempt from; exclusive.

2, PLAIN, homely, homespun; ordinary; bald, flat; dull, ARTLESS, ingenuous, unaffected, free from affectation *or* ornament; chaste, severe; unadorned, unornamented, ungarnished, unvarnished, unarranged, untrimmed.

Adverbs—simply, purely; solely, only; unadornedly; in plain terms, words, English, *etc.;* bluntly, pointblank.

Antonyms, see MIXTURE, ORNAMENT.

---

simpleton, *n.* dunce, blockhead, moron, ninny, nincompoop, innocent, FOOL. *Slang,* nitwit, dope, jerk.

simulate, *v.t.* imitate, resemble, mimic; feign, counterfeit, pretend. See FALSEHOOD, AFFECTATION, IMITATION.

simultaneous, *adj.* coincident, concurrent, contemporaneous, in concert, in unison, synchronous. See TIME, INSTANTANEITY.

sin, *n. & v.* —*n.* IMPIETY, sacrilege, transgression, wickedness, IMPURITY, iniquity, VICE; offense, crime, fault, ERROR, peccadillo. —*v.i.* transgress, err, offend. See GUILT. *Ant.,* see VIRTUE.

since, *adv. & conj.* —*adv.* ago, later, subsequently, afterwards. See SEQUENCE. —*conj.* because, inasmuch as, after. See CAUSE.

sincere, *adj.* honest, genuine; ingenuous, forthright, unreserved, candid; cordial, hearty, earnest. See TRUTH. *Ant.,* see FALSEHOOD.

sinecure, *n.* easy job. *Slang,* snap, pipe, cinch, gravy. See FACILITY.

sing, *v.* troll; chant, carol, intone, warble; laud, praise; vocalize; yodel; versify; hum, whistle. See MUSICIAN, POETRY.

singe, *v.t.* scorch, sear, burn slightly. See HEAT.

singer, *n.* vocalist, songster, cantor, precentor, troubadour, minstrel; *chanteur, chanteuse;* nightingale, thrush, crooner; chantyman, chanter; bard, poet. See MUSICIAN.

single, *adj.* one, separate, solitary, individual; unmarried; unique, sole; sincere, honest, unequivocal. See NUMBER, CELIBACY.

singular, *adj.* unique, individual; peculiar, unusual, odd, eccentric; exceptional, rare; extraordinary. See UNCONFORMITY, NUMBER.

sinister, *adj.* ominous, unlucky, portentous; LEFT; EVIL, bad; unpropitious, baleful, injurious; ill-starred. See BADNESS, ADVERSITY. *Ant.,* see GOODNESS, RIGHT.

sink, *v.* founder, drown, go down; ebb, wane, decline, lapse, settle, subside, precipitate; retrograde, go downhill; languish, droop, flag; despond; fail, deepen, dig, lower; debase, abase, bring low; submerge, immerse, bury; discourage, dampen; invest, risk, venture. See DEPTH, DESCENT, DEPRESSION, DETERIORATION, DEJECTION.

sinuous, *adj.* twisting, winding, serpentine, meandering, crooked, devious, tortuous. See CONVOLUTION. *Ant.,* see DIRECTION.

siren, *n.* water nymph; temptress, Circe, Lorelei, Delilah, Jezebel; alarm, WARNING, signal. *Slang,* vamp, vampire, gold digger.

sister, *n.* kinswoman; nun, sister of mercy, *religieuse;* woman associate, *soror,* sorority member, fellow membre; nurse; counterpart. See RELATION, CLERGY, SIMILARITY.

sit, *v.i.* sit down, perch; pose; hold session, convene; fit, suit; brood; be situated. See DEPRESSION, DOMESTICATION, LOCATION.

situate, *v.* place, locate; set, station, put; lie, be situated. See LOCATION.

situation, *n.* place, LOCATION; position, site; STATE, predicament, plight, case, circumstances; job, office, post, station, employment. See BUSINESS.

SIZE [192]

Nouns—**1,** size, magnitude, dimension, bulk, volume; largeness; GREATNESS, expanse, SPACE; extent, scope; amplitude; mass; proportions, MEASUREMENT; capacity, LIMIT, tonnage; caliber; corpulence, obesity; plumpness, fatness, *embonpoint,* avoirdupois, girth, corporation; hugeness, enormousness, immensity, monstrosity.

2, giant, titan, Brobdingnagian, Antaeus, Goliath, Anak, Gog and Magog, Gargantua, Cyclops; monster, mammoth, whale, porpoise, behemoth, leviathan, elephant, hippopotamus; colossus. *Colloq.,* whopper, bumper.

Verbs—be *or* become large, expand, enlarge; grade, assort, graduate.

Adjectives—**1,** large, big, great; considerable, bulky, voluminous, ample, massive, massy; capacious, comprehensive; spacious, mighty, towering, magnificent; huge, immense, enormous, mighty; vast, stupendous; monstrous, titanic, gigantic; giant, stupendous, colossal; Cyclopean, Brobdingnagian, Gargantuan.

2, corpulent, stout, fat, plump, full, lusty, strapping, bouncing; portly, burly, well-fed, full-grown; stalwart, brawny, fleshy; goodly; lumbering, unwieldy; whopping, thumping, thundering, hulking; overgrown, bloated; big as a house.

Antonym, see LITTLENESS.

---

skeleton, *n.* frame, framework; OUTLINE, diagram; bones, bony structure. See SUPPORT.

skeptic, *n.* doubter, agnostic, freethinker, doubting Thomas, questioner; infidel; unbeliever. See IRRELIGION, DOUBT. *Ant.,* see BELIEF.

sketch, *v.t.* draw, outline, block out, rough in; state briefly; draft, chart, map. See REPRESENTATION, PREPARATION.

SKILL [698]

Nouns—**1,** skill, skillfulness, address; dexterity, dexterousness; adroitness, expertness, proficiency, adequacy, competence, craft, finesse, facility, knack; mastery, mastership; excellence, ambidexterity, versatility; artistry, wizardry.

2, accomplishment, acquirement, attainment; art, science; technicality, technology; KNOWLEDGE, experience, SAGACITY; discretion, diplomacy; craftiness, cunning; management.

3, cleverness, talent, ability, ingenuity, capacity, parts, faculty, endowment, forte, turn, gift, genius; INTELLIGENCE, sharpness, readiness, IMAGINATION;

uptness, aptitude; capability, qualification. *Slang*, the goods, what it takes, know-how.

4, masterpiece, master stroke, *coup de maître, chef d'oeuvre, tour de force.*

5, EXPERT, master, virtuoso; strategist, diplomat; adept.

Verbs—be skillful, excel in, be master of; have a turn for, play one's cards well; hit the nail on the head; have all one's wits about one; have one's hand in. *Slang*, know one's stuff; have been around.

Adjectives—**1,** skillful, dext(e)rous; adroit, expert, apt, handy, quick, deft, ready, smart, proficient, good at, up to, at home in, master of, a good hand at; masterly, crack, accomplished, versed in, conversant (see KNOWLEDGE); experienced, practiced, skilled, up in, well up in; in practice; competent, efficient, qualified, capable fitted, fitted for, up to the mark, trained, initiateu, prepared, primed, finished.

2, clever, able, ingenious, felicitous, gifted, talented, endowed; inventive, shrewd, sharp, intelligent; ambidextrous, sure-footed; artistic, workmanlike, businesslike, statesmanlike.

Adverbs—skillfully, well, artistically; with skill.

Antonym, see UNSKILLFULNESS.

---

skin, *v. & n.* —*v.t.* flay, peel, decorticate. See DIVESTMENT. *Slang*, fleece, cheat. —*n.* integument, cuticle, dermis, epidermis; pelt, hide; rind; veneer, plating, lamina; parchment. See COVERING.

skip, *v.* caper, spring, LEAP, hop, trip, frisk, gambol, frolic; omit, pass over, stay away; ricochet. *Slang*, decamp, play truant. See NEGLECT, DEPARTURE.

skirmish, *n.* clash, brush, tilt, encounter, engagement. See CONTENTION.

skirt, *n.* overskirt, kilt, petticoat, coattail; purlieu, borderland, EDGE, margin, outskirts. See CLOTHING. *Slang*, woman, girl.

skulk, *v.i.* lurk, sneak, slink, steal, hide; cower. See CONCEALMENT, COWARDICE.

sky, *n.* firmament, heavens, HEAVEN, welkin.

slack, *adj.* careless, lax, negligent, remiss; loose, limp, flaccid, relaxed; sluggish, stagnant; dull, slow, not busy. See NEGLECT, INACTIVITY, SOFTNESS, INSUFFICIENCY. *Ant.*, see ACTIVITY, SEVERITY, HARDNESS.

slacken, *v.* retard, diminish, lessen; loosen, relax; abate; languish, decline; ease up, dwindle. See MODERATION, REPOSE, SLOWNESS.

slacker, *n.* shirker, quitter, evader. See AVOIDANCE.

slake, *v.t.* quench, satisfy, appease, allay, abate, sate. See SUFFICIENCY, MODERATION.

slander, *n.* scandal, aspersion, defamation, calumny, disparagement. See DETRACTION.

slang, *n.* argot, jargon, cant, lingo, patois, vernacular; dialect; colloquialism, neologism, vulgarism. See SPEECH.

slant, *n.* OBLIQUITY, slope, inclination, declination, tilt, pitch; bias, leaning.

slap, *v.t. & n.* hit, smack, swat, cuff; insult. See IMPULSE, DISCOURTESY, PUNISHMENT.

slate, *n.* LIST, ballot, ticket; blackboard; slab, rock, roof. See LAYER.

slattern, *n.* sloven; slut, trollop. See EVILDOER.

slaughter, *n.* butchering; butchery, massacre, carnage, murder. See KILLING.

slave, *n. & v.* —*n.* bondsman, bond servant, thrall, serf; drudge, peon, vassal, menial; addict, victim. See SERVANT. *Ant.*, see FREEDOM. —*v.i.* toil, drudge; overwork.

slavery, *n.* bondage; forced labor; servitude, chains, captivity; drudgery, toil; addiction, submission. See SUBJECTION.

slay, *v.i.* kill, slaughter, dispatch; murder, assassinate. See KILLING.

sled, *n.* sledge, sleigh; bobsled; dogsled; skid, cutter, pung. See VEHICLE.

sleep, *n. & v.* —*n.* slumber, somnolence, nap, doze, drowse, rest, REPOSE; coma; hypnosis. —*v.i.* slumber, repose, doze, nap; be dead *or* dormant. See INACTIVITY. *Ant.*, see ACTIVITY.

sleeping pill, barbiturate, opiate; tranquil(l)izer, sedative. *Slang*, goof ball.

sleepless, *adj.* wakeful, insomniac, restless; alert, vigilant. See ACTIVITY, CARE. *Ant.*, see REPOSE, INACTIVITY.

sleepwalker, *n.* somnambulist, noctambulist, nightwalker.

slender, *adj.* slim, thin, skinny, attenuated; tenuous, slight, meager. See NARROWNESS, INSUFFICIENCY. *Ant.,* see BREADTH.

sleuth, *n.* bloodhound; detective, Hawkshaw, gumshoe; plainclothesman; shadow, operative, (private) investigator. *Slang,* dick, private eye, shamus, op. See CONCEALMENT.

slice, *v.t.* cut, slash, carve, shave, skive. See DISJUNCTION, LAYER.

slide, *v.i.* glide, slip, coast, skim; steal, pass. See MOTION.

slight, *adj. v. & n.* —*adj.* slender, slim, frail, delicate; trivial; meager, scant. See NARROWNESS, UNIMPORTANCE. —*v.t.* ignore, cut, snob, rebuff; scamp, neglect. —*n.* snub, rebuff, cut. See CONTEMPT.

slim, *adj.* slender, thin, slight; frail, weak, meager. See NARROWNESS, IN-SUFFICIENCY. *Ant.,* see BREADTH, SIZE.

slime, *n.* ooze, mire, sludge, mud, muck; primordial slime; filth. See COHERENCE, UNCLEANNESS.

slip, *v. & n.* —*v.* glide, slide; misstep; steal; ESCAPE, elapse; blunder, err; don (with on). See FAILURE, ERROR. —*n.* misstep, slide; blunder, ERROR; scion, graft; *faux pas,* indiscretion; ESCAPE; undergarment; pillowcase; dock; strip, sheet; chit, girl; ceramic cement.

slippery, *adj.* slimy, greasy, slick, glassy, glare; shifty, elusive, unreliable. See SMOOTHNESS. *Ant.,* see ROUGHNESS.

slobber, *v.i.* slaver, drivel, dribble, drool, be sentimental. See EJECTION.

slope, *n.* slant, tilt, pitch, inclination; incline, grade, gradient, ramp, ascent, rise. See OBLIQUITY.

sloth, *n.* laziness, idleness, INACTIVITY, inertia; SLOWNESS, sluggishness. *Ant.,* see ACTIVITY.

sloven, *n.* slouch, slattern, slipshod person; slut. *Colloq.,* slob. See DISORDER.

SLOWNESS [275]

Nouns—**1,** slowness, languor, INACTIVITY; leisureliness; retardation; slackening; delay, LATENESS; walk, stroll, saunter, snail's pace, jog-trot, dog-trot; slow motion. *Colloq.,* slowdown, slowup.

2, dullness, flatness, monotony; boredom.

3, laggard, lingerer, loiterer, sluggard, tortoise, plodder; snail; dawdler. *Colloq.,* slowpoke.

Verbs—**1,** move slowly, creep, crawl, lag, linger, loiter, stroll, saunter, walk, plod, trudge, stump along, lumber; trail, drag; dawdle, worm one's way, steal along; toddle, waddle, slouch, shuffle, halt, hobble, limp, shamble; flag, falter, totter, stagger; take one's time; hang fire (see LATENESS). *Colloq.,* take one's own sweet time. *Slang,* get no place fast, mosey along.

2, slow, retard, relax; slacken, check, moderate, rein in, curb; reef; strike sail, shorten sail, take in sail; put on the drag, brake, apply the brake; clip the wings; reduce the speed; slacken speed, slacken one's pace; lose ground; slack off *or* down.

Adjectives—slow, slack; tardy; dilatory, inactive, gentle, easy, leisurely; deliberate, gradual; DULL, uninteresting; languid, sluggish, slow-paced, snail-like; creeping. *Colloq.,* slow as molasses.

Adverbs—slowly, leisurely; at half speed, under easy sail; at a snail's pace; in slow time; in slow motion; gradually, by degrees *or* inches, step by step, drop by drop, inch by inch, bit by bit, little by little.

Antonym, see VELOCITY.

---

sluggish, *adj.* inactive, stagnant, torpid, slow; lazy, slothful, dull, indolent; languid, apathetic, lethargic. See INACTIVITY. *Ant.,* see ACTIVITY.

slumber, *n.* sleep, nap, doze, quiescence. See INACTIVITY, REPOSE.

slur, *v.t.* slight, disparage, calumniate, traduce, asperse; skim, skip, gloss over; elide. See DETRACTION, NEGLECT. *Ant.,* see VINDICATION.

slush, *n.* slosh, sludge, slop; gush, effusiveness, sentimentality. See CO-HERENCE, LOQUACITY.

sly, *adj.* CUNNING, furtive, wily; crafty, deceitful, stealthy, underhand; roguish, mischievous. See CONCEALMENT.

small, *adj.* little, tiny, short, wee; dwarfish, undersized, stunted; minute, infinitesimal; dainty, petite; trivial, unimportant, petty; puny, slight, weak;

mean, paltry, unworthy; pygmy, Lilliputian, minikin. See LITTLENESS.
Ant., see SIZE, GREATNESS.

smart, *adj. & v.* —*adj.* chic, stylish, jaunty, dapper; severe, sharp, keen;
witty, pert, sparkling; brisk, energetic, fresh; shrewd, clever. See SKILL,
FASHION, FEELING, WIT. —*v.i.* sting, PAIN, rankle.

smash, *v.t.* shatter, crush; hit, strike; ruin, destroy, disintegrate. See DE-
STRUCTION.

smattering, *n.* superficiality, slight knowledge, sciolism. See IGNORANCE.

smear, *v.t.* daub, bedaub, besmirch, smudge; grease, anoint, defame;
slander. See UNCLEANNESS, DISREPUTE.

smell, *v.* scent; stink; sniff, snuff, inhale; detect, nose out. See ODOR,
MALODOROUSNESS, DISCLOSURE.

smile, *v.i.* grin, simper, smirk; beam, look with favor; sneer, RIDICULE. See
REJOICING.

smog, *n.* smoky fog. See CLOUDINESS.

smoke, *v.* reek, fume, smo(u)lder; steam; puff, inhale; smoke-dry, cure;
fumigate; begrime, pollute. See DRYNESS, UNCLEANNESS, HEAT.

smolder, smoulder, *v.i.* reek, fume, smoke; hang fire, be latent, lurk. See
HEAT, CLOUDINESS.

SMOOTHNESS [255]

Nouns—**1,** smoothness, polish, gloss, glaze; slickness, slipperiness; suavity;
blandness; evenness.
2, smooth surface, level, plane; velvet, silk, satin; glass, ice; FLATNESS.
3, lubrication, greasing, oiling; oiliness, unctuousness; lubricant, grease,
oil, fat, soap, emollient, ointment.
4, plane, roller, steamroller; sandpaper, ABRASIVE, buffer, burnisher, polisher; wax, varnish; iron, mangle.
Verbs—smooth, plane; file; mow, shave; level, roll; pave; polish, rub, shine,
buff, burnish, calender, glaze; varnish, wax; iron, press; LUBRICATE.
Adjectives—**1,** smooth; polished, even; level; plane, flat, HORIZONTAL; sleek,
glossy, silken, silky; downy, velvety; slippery, glassy; greasy, oily; soft,
unwrinkled; smooth as glass, silk, ice, *or* velvet; slippery as an eel; bald,
bald as an egg *or* billiard ball.
2, slippery, greasy, oily, slick, unctuous, lubricating.
Antonym, see ROUGHNESS.

---

smother, *v.t.* suffocate, stifle; suppress, repress; extinguish, deaden. See
KILLING, RESTRAINT.

smug, *adj.* sleek, trim, neat; self-satisfied, complacent; priggish, conceited.
See AFFECTATION.

smuggler, *n.* contrabandist, bootlegger, runner. See STEALING.

snake, *n.* serpent, reptile, ophidian; snake in the grass, deceiver, double-
dealer. See ANIMAL, DECEPTION.

snap, *n. & v.* —*n.* snap, crackle, rapping; pop, crack; report; clap, smack;
vigor; pep, verve, dash, élan; smartness, spruceness, crispness; *Colloq.*,
sinecure, cinch, soft job; spell (of weather). —*v.* break, crack, crackle;
knock, rap, tap; snarl, bark, scold; bite, nip. See DISJUNCTION, IMPULSE,
IRASCIBILITY.

snare, *n.* trap, springe, gin; artifice, pitfall, ambush. See DECEPTION.

snarl, *v.i.* growl, gnar; speak savagely, be surly; grumble. See DISCOURTESY.

snatch, *v.t.* grab, seize, grasp, clutch, jerk, twitch, pluck, wrench; steal.
Slang, kidnap. See STEALING.

sneak, *v. & n.* —*v.i.* slink, skulk, crawl, steal. —*n.* skulker, sneak thief;
coward. See COWARDICE; STEALING.

sneer, *v.* smile, jeer, taunt, scoff; flout, deride. See CONTEMPT.

snicker, *v.i.* snigger, titter, laugh, giggle, chuckle; RIDICULE.

sniff, *v.* sniffle; smell, scent; breathe, inhale, detect. See ODOR, WIND.

snob, *n.* sycophant, toady, fawner; bounder, upstart; parvenu, social
climber. See SERVILITY, VULGARITY, AFFECTATION.

snoop, *n. & v.* —*v.i.* pry; investigate, probe; meddle; play detective. —*n.*
snooper, pry, meddler, busybody. See ACTIVITY.

snooze, *n.* nap, doze, sleep, forty winks. See INACTIVITY.

snub, *v., n. & adj.* —*v.t.* cut, ignore, slight, rebuff, cold-shoulder; chech, curb, halt. —*n.* rebuff, slight, cut. —*adj.* turned-up, blunt, retroussé. See DISCOURTESY, HINDRANCE.

snuff, *v.t.* extinguish, put out; quench; sniff, inhale; smell, scent; snuffle, sniffle. See END, WIND, ODOR.

snug, *adj.* cozy, comfortable; sheltered, trim, compact, neat. See PLEASURE, CLOSURE.

snuggle, *v.i.* nestle, cuddle, lie snug. See ENDEARMENT.

soak, *v.t.* wet, drench, saturate, steep; absorb; permeate. *Slang,* strike, drink. See WATER. *Ant.,* see DRYNESS.

soap, *n.* cleanser, cleansing agent; lather; detergent; shampoo. *Slang,* softsoap; corniness, sentimentality. See CLEANNESS.

soar, *v.i.* fly, fly high; tower; glide. See AVIATION, HEIGHT.

sob, *v.i.* weep, cry; sigh; cough, moan. See LAMENTATION.

sober, *adj.* grave, quiet, sedate, staid, serious; abstemious, not drunk; drab, plain, severe, unadorned; calm, moderate; thoughtful; subdued; inconspicuous; demure; earnest; solemn, somber. See MODERATION. *Ant.,* see DRUNKENNESS, LOUDNESS, OSTENTATION.

sobriety, *n.* soberness, abstemiousness, MODERATION. See SOBER.

social, *adj. & n.* See SOCIALITY.

socialism, *n.* public ownership, communism, collectivism; communalism. See AUTHORITY, COÖPERATION.

SOCIALITY [892]

Nouns—**1,** sociality, sociability, sociableness, FRIENDSHIP; social intercourse, community; fellowship, companionship, camaraderie; familiarity, intimacy; brotherhood; gregariousness; congeniality, compatibility.

2, conviviality, good fellowship, joviality, jollity, *savoir vivre,* festivity, festive board, merrymaking. See REJOICING.

3, welcome, greeting; hearty *or* warm welcome *or* reception; urbanity (see COURTESY); familiarity; hospitality, heartiness, cheer.

4, social circle, sewing circle, family circle; coterie, society; club; social gathering, assembly (see ASSEMBLAGE); PARTY, entertainment, reception, levee, at home, *conversazione, soirée;* garden party; housewarming; reunion; debut, visit, visiting; call. *Colloq.,* get-together, hen party, stag party, coming-out party.

5, sociable person, good company, companion, crony. *Colloq.,* joiner; good mixer, back-slapper, hand-shaker, hail-fellow-well-met.

Verbs—**1,** be sociable, know; be acquainted, associate with, keep company with, club together, consort, bear one company, join; make acquaintance with; make advances, fraternize, hobnob, mix with, mingle with; embrace; be, feel, *or* make oneself at home with; make free with; be hospitable.

2, visit, pay a visit; call upon; drop in, look in; look one up; entertain, give a party, be at home, keep open house, do the honors, receive with open arms, welcome, bid one welcome, give a warm reception to; kill the fatted calf; see one's friends.

Adjectives—sociable, companionable, friendly; conversable, cozy, chatty, conversational; social, neighborly, gregarious, affable; convivial, festive, festal; jovial, jolly, hospitable; welcome; free and easy. *Colloq.,* clubby, chummy.

Adverbs—socially, companionably, intimately, *etc.*

Antonym, see SECLUSION.

---

society, *n.* MANKIND, humanity, folk; culture, civilization, group; companionship, fellowship; *bon ton,* élite, aristocracy; sodality, solidarity, association, league, union, alliance; parish, congregation. See SOCIALITY, PARTY. *Ant.,* see SECLUSION.

sod, *n.* turf, sward, glebe; clod, divot. See VEGETABLE, LAND.

sodden, *adj.* soaked, saturated, soggy, doughy; dull; drunken, befuddled. See MOISTURE, DRUNKENNESS.

sofa, *n.* couch, seat, lounge, divan, settee, love seat. See SUPPORT.

SOFTNESS [324]

Nouns—**1,** softness, pliableness, pliancy, pliability, flexibility; malleability; ductility, tractility; extendability, extensibility; plasticity; flaccidity, flabbiness, laxity; sensitivity, responsiveness, susceptibility.
2, clay, wax, butter, dough, pudding; cushion, pillow, featherbed, down, padding, wadding; foam rubber.
3, softening, mollification; mellowness, relaxation; MODERATION.
Verbs—soften, mollify, mellow, relax, temper; mash, knead, squash; melt, liquefy; bend, yield, relent, relax, give.
Adjectives—soft, tender, supple, pliant, pliable; flexible, flexile; sensitive, responsive, susceptible; lithe, lithesome, lissom, limber, plastic; ductile; tractile, tractable; malleable, extensile; yielding, flabby, limp, flimsy; flaccid, flocculent; downy, feathery, fleecy; spongy, doughy; mellow; velvety, silky, satiny.
Adverbs—soft as butter, soft as down, soft as silk; yielding as wax.
Antonym, see HARDNESS.

---

soggy, *adj.* saturated, soppy, soaked; sodden, doughy. See MOISTURE.
soil, *n. & v.* —*n.* loam, earth, sod, topsoil, dirt, mold, ground; stain, blotch, smudge, smear, filth. —*v.t.* besmear, dirty, daub, stain; defile, sully. See LAND, UNCLEANNESS.
sojourn, *v. & n.* —*v.i.* tarry, abide, stay, lodge. —*n.* temporary stay; stopover; visit; temporary dwelling. See PRESENCE.
solace, *n. & v.* —*n.* comfort, consolation, RELIEF. —*v.t.* soothe, calm, comfort; cheer, console; assuage, mitigate. See PITY.
soldier, *n.* warrior, fighting man. See COMBATANT.
soldierly, *adj.* military, martial; brave, courageous; gallant; snappy, spruce; erect. See WARFARE.
sole, *adj.* only, one, single, unique, exclusive, individual. See NUMBER, SIMPLENESS.
solecism, *n.* ERROR, lapse, slip, blunder; grammatical error; barbarism, *faux pas,* social error, impropriety; incongruity, mistake. See GRAMMAR, MISJUDGMENT.
solemn, *adj.* awesome, impressive; grave, serious, dignified; formal, ceremonious; reverent, ritualistic. See IMPORTANCE, DEJECTION, PIETY. *Ant.,* see CHEERFULNESS, UNIMPORTANCE.
solicit, *v.t.* REQUEST, invite, ask, entreat, importune, beg, canvass.
solicitous, *adj.* considerate; anxious, concerned; eager, careful. See CARE.
solicitude, *n.* CARE, concern, anxiety; consideration; uneasiness. See FEAR.
solid, *adj.* dense, compact, hard, firm, rigid; substantial; unbroken, undivided, whole, intact; sound, valid; stable, solvent; genuine, real. See DENSITY, STABILITY, SUBSTANCE, CERTAINTY, ASSENT, TRUTH. *Ant.,* FLUID, liquid; see INSUBSTANTIALITY.
soliloquy, *n.* monologue; apostrophe. *Colloq.,* aside. See SPEECH.
solitary, *adj.* alone, lonesome; single, individual, lone; deserted, remote, unfrequented; unsocial, retiring. See ASCETICISM, SECLUSION. *Ant.,* see SOCIALITY.
solitude, *n.* SECLUSION, privacy, isolation; remoteness; loneliness; wilderness. See SECLUSION. *Ant.,* see SOCIALITY.
solution, *n.* ANSWER, explanation, INTERPRETATION, key, clue; disintegration, dissolution; lixivium, decoction; LIQUEFACTION.
solve, *v.t.* explain, interpret; ANSWER; resolve, clear up; decipher, decode.
solvent, *adj. & n.* —*adj.* financially sound, moneyed; responsible, reliable; soluble, separative, dissolvent, diluent. —*n.* dissolvent, dissolver, liquefier. See WATER.
somber, *adj.* gloomy, dark, overcast; sad, dismal, leaden, depressing, funereal. See DARKNESS, CLOUDINESS, DEJECTION. *Ant.,* see LIGHT, CHEERFULNESS.
somebody, *n.* one, someone; person, individual; bigwig, person of importance, personage. See PARTY, IMPORTANCE. *Ant.,* see UNIMPORTANCE.
somehow, *adv.* some way, by some means. See CAUSE.
something, *n.* thing, object, anything; matter, part; affair, event. See SUBSTANCE.

sometimes, *adv.* occasionally, now and then. See OCCASION.
somewhere, *adv.* someplace; anywhere, somewhere about; approximately. See LOCATION.
somnolent, *adj.* sleepy, drowsy, slumb(e)rous; dozing; lethargic. See RE-POSE, INACTIVITY. *Ant.,* see ACTIVITY.
son, *n.* male child, boy, offspring; descendant, inheritor. See RELATION.
song, *n.* lyric, ballad, popular song; aria; carol, lilt, madrigal, glee, ditty; minstrelsy, poem, chanty, lay, birdsong, folksong, spiritual, *etc.* See MUSIC, POETRY.
sonorous, *adj.* resonant, deep-toned, rich, majestic; grandiloquent, high-flown. See LOUDNESS, ORNAMENT.
soon, *adv.* anon, presently; promptly, quickly; readily, willingly. See EARLINESS. *Ant.,* see LATENESS.
soothe, *v.t.* calm, quiet, tranquilize; relieve, assuage, mitigate; console, comfort. See MODERATION, RELIEF. *Ant.,* see AGITATION.
sophisticate, *n.* worldling; blasé person; cosmopolitan, man-about-town, man of the world. *Ant.,* see SIMPLENESS.
sophistication, *n.* pretentious wisdom; affectation; worldliness; worldly-wise attitude; blasé airs; superficial polish *or* culture; cosmopolitan veneer. *Ant.,* see SIMPLENESS.
sophistry, *n.* sophism; false *or* specious reasoning; casuistry; fallaciousness, paralogism; shift, subterfuge, equivocation; ABSURDITY, inconsistency; hair-splitting. See FALSEHOOD. *Ant.,* see REASONING, TRUTH.

SORCERY [992, 994]

Nouns—**1,** sorcery; the occult; magic, the black art, necromancy, theurgy, thaumaturgy; demonology, diablerie, bedevilment; voodoo, obeah, witch-craft, witchery; white magic, black magic; black Mass; fetishism, vam-pirism; conjuration; bewitchery, enchantment, mysticism, second sight, mesmerism, animal magnetism; od force, odylic force; clairvoyance; spiritualism, spirit-rapping, table-turning; divination (see PREDICTION); sortilege, hocus-pocus (see DECEPTION). See SECRET.
2, spell, charm, incantation, cabala, runes, abracadabra, open sesame, mumbo-jumbo, evil eye.
3, exorcism; countercharm; bell, book and candle; talisman, amulet, periapt, phylactery, philter; fetish, agnus Dei.
4, wand, caduceus, rod, divining rod, magic lamp *or* ring, wishing cap, Fortunatus' cap.
5, sorcerer, magician; thaumaturgist, theurgist; conjuror, voodooist, ne-cromancer, seer, wizard, witch; lamia, hag, warlock, charmer; medicine-man; shaman, medium, clairvoyant, mesmerist; *deus ex machina;* sooth-sayer, ORACLE; Cagliostro, Mesmer; Circe, siren, weird sisters. See also DEMON.
Verbs—practice sorcery, conjure, charm, enchant; bewitch, bedevil; en-trance, mesmerize, magnetize; fascinate; taboo; wave a wand; rub the ring *or* lamp; cast a spell; hold a seance, call up spirits, raise spirits from the dead. *Slang,* hoodoo, jinx.
Adjectives—magic, magical; occult; SECRET, mystic, weird, cabalistic, talis-manic, phylacteric, incantatory; charmed, bewitched; spellbound, haunted.
Antonym, see RELIGION.

---

sordid, *adj.* mean, base, ignoble; covetous, niggardly; mercenary, self-seeking; dirty, foul. See PARSIMONY.
sore, *adj. & n.* —*adj.* painful, tender; grieved, distressed; harsh, severe, intense, dire. *Slang,* aggrieved, resentful, disgruntled. See PAIN, DISCON-TENT. —*n.* wound, abrasion, ulcer, sore spot. See DISEASE.
sorrow, *n.* grief, sadness, distress; contrition, remorse, PENITENCE; afflic-tion, woe. See DEJECTION, ADVERSITY. *Ant.,* see PLEASURE, REJOICING.
sorry, *adj.* rueful, regretful, penitent; sympathetic, sorrowful; pitiful, shabby, paltry, wretched, mean. See PENITENCE, UNIMPORTANCE. *Ant.,* see REJOICING, PLEASURE.
sort, *n. & v.* —*n.* CLASS, kind, variety, group, category, DESCRIPTION. —*v.t.*

segregate, separate, isolate; size, grade, group, match; assort, arrange, classify: sift, screen. See SIZE, ARRANGEMENT.

soul, *n.* psyche, spirit, mind; vital principle; essence; person, mortal, individual; ego; heart, fire, élan; genius. See MANKIND, INTELLIGENCE.

sound, *adj., n. & v.* —*adj.* whole, undamaged; healthy, robust; logical, true, valid, reliable, trustworthy; solvent; strong, firm; thorough; unbroken. See PERFECTION, HEALTH, STABILITY, CERTAINTY, MONEY. —*n.* channel, bay, GULF. —*v.* fathom, plumb, measure; probe; investigate, examine. See DEPTH, INQUIRY.

SOUND [402]

Nouns—**1,** sound, noise, strain; accent, twang, intonation, tone; cadence; sonorousness, audibility (see HEARING); resonance, voice, LOUDNESS.

2, sound, tone, tonality, intonation, inflection, modulation; pitch, key, timbre, tone color.

3, acoustics, phonics, phonetics, phonology, phonography; diacoustics, diaphonics, telephonics, radiophony.

4, vociferation, roar, cry, utterance, voice; snap, crash, bang, boom, roll, clatter, detonation, explosion.

Verbs—**1,** sound, make a noise; give out *or* emit sound.

2, speak (see SPEECH), snap, roll, reverberate, detonate, *etc.* See LOUDNESS.

Adjectives—sounding; soniferous, sonorous, resonant, audible, distinct; sonant, sonic, stertorous; phonetic, audible; acoustic, phonic; phonetic.

Antonym, see SILENCE.

sour, *v. & adj.* —*v.* be sour, ferment; acidify, acidulate, curdle, turn. *Colloq.,* lose interest, taste for, *or* zest. —*adj.* acid, acidulous, acidulated; astringent, acerbic, tart; crabbed; acetous, acetose; vinegary, vinegarish, sourish; curdled; hard, rough; sour as a pickle *or* lemon. See TASTE. *Ant.,* see SWEETNESS.

source, *n.* CAUSE, origin, fountainhead, fount, derivation. See BEGINNING.

sourness, *n.* acid, acidity; surliness. See SOUR, TASTE, IRASCIBILITY.

southern, *adj.* southerly, austral. See DIRECTION.

souvenir, *n.* memento, keepsake, relic. See MEMORY.

sovereign, *n.* monarch, ruler; potentate; king, queen, emperor. See AUTHORITY.

sow, *v.t.* strew, scatter, disseminate, broadcast; plant, seed. See AGRICULTURE, DISCLOSURE.

SPACE [180]

Nouns—**1,** space, extension, extent, superficial extent, area, expanse; sphere, range, latitude, field, way, expansion, compass, sweep, play, swing, spread, capacity, stretch; open space, free space; void, emptiness, ABSENCE of space; waste, wild, wilderness; moor, prairie, campagna; abyss, unlimited space, INFINITY, universe, creation; heavens, sky; interplanetary space; world; length and breadth of the land.

2, room, scope, spare room, elbow room; margin; leeway, headway. *Slang,* room to swing a cat.

3, proportions, dimensions, acreage, acres, breadth, width; square inches, feet, yards, *etc.* See MEASUREMENT.

Adjectives—spacious, roomy, extensive, expansive, capacious, ample; widespread, vast, worldwide, uncircumscribed; unlimited, endless; infinite, universal; boundless, shoreless, trackless, pathless, bottomless.

Adverbs—extensively, wherever; everywhere; far and near, far and wide, right and left, all over, all the world over; throughout the world; under the sun, in every quarter, in all quarters, in all lands; here, there and everywhere; from pole to pole, from end to end; on the face of the earth, in the wide world, from all points of the compass; to the four winds, to the uttermost parts of the earth; infinitely, *ad infinitum.*

Antonym, see CIRCUMSCRIPTION.

spade, *n. & v.* —*n.* shovel, spud; card suit (*pl.*). —*v.* dig, delve, shovel, excavate. See CONCAVITY.

span, *v.t & n.* —*v.t.* measure; encircle; stretch over, bridge. —*n.* bridge; extent; period; lifetime; nine-inch spread; team, yoke. See MEASUREMENT, JUNCTION, AGE.

spank, *v.t.* slap, paddle, wallop; punish, chastise. See PUNISHMENT.

spanking, *adj. & n.* —*adj.* brisk, lively, fresh; moving swiftly. See VELOCITY. —*n.* PUNISHMENT, hiding, thrashing.

spar, *v. & n.* —*v.i.* box; stall; bandy words, argue, bicker. See CONTENTION. —*n.* mast, pole, gaff, boom, sprit, yard; varnish. See HEIGHT, COVERING.

spare, *v. & adj.* —*v.t.* be lenient; save; refrain, abstain, forbear, withhold; exempt; give up, surrender, forego, relinquish. See PRESERVATION, INACTIVITY, RELINQUISHMENT. —*adj.* lean, gaunt, bony; extra, reserve; frugal. See NARROWNESS, STORE. *Ant.,* see WASTE.

spark, *n.* flash; inspiration; iota, jot; beau, swain, gallant. See HEAT, LOVE.

sparkle, *v.i.* glisten, spark, twinkle, flash, glitter, scintillate; effervesce, bubble; be vivacious. See LIGHT.

sparse, *adj.* scattered, sporadic; thin, few, meager, scanty. See RARITY.

spasm, *n.* throe, paroxysm, convulsion, seizure; fit, furor, momentary enthusiasm. See DISEASE, AGITATION.

spatter, *v.t.* splash, sprinkle; besprinkle, bedraggle, bespatter; sully, soil. See WATER, UNCLEANNESS.

speak, *v.* talk, converse; lecture, discourse, orate; say, utter, pronounce; express, communicate. See SPEECH.

speaker, *n.* presiding officer, chairman, orator, spokesman; loudspeaker. See SPEECH, AUTHORITY.

spear, *n.* lance, pike, javelin; blade. See ARMS.

special, *adj.* particular, individual, specific; distinctive, distinct, unique; personal; original; private, respective, definite; especial, certain; different, peculiar; characteristic, exclusive; singular, exceptional, idiosyncratic. See IDENTITY, UNCONFORMITY.

specialize, *v.i.* specify, be specific, particularize, individualize, concentrate on one thing, work in one field; go into detail; work as a specialist.

speciality, *n.* trait, characteristic, personality, individuality; singularity, peculiarity, originality; main product, activity, *or* field. See TENDENCY, UNCONFORMITY. *Ant.,* GENERALITY.

species, *n.* variety, sort, CLASS, category.

specimen, *n.* sample, example, representative, instance, pattern, taster. See CONFORMITY.

specious, *adj.* plausible, ostensible, apparent, casuistic, insincere. See DECEPTION, APPEARANCE. *Ant.,* genuine, sincere.

speck, *n.* BLEMISH, speckle, spot, macula; particle, iota, mite, mote, dot. See LITTLENESS.

spectacle, *n.* sight; phenomenon; pageant, parade, show; exhibition, scene, display. See APPEARANCE, OSTENTATION, RIDICULE.

spectacles, *n.pl.* eyeglasses, glasses, goggles; contact lenses; lorgnette. *Slang,* specs, cheaters. See OPTICAL INSTRUMENTS.

spectator, *n.* beholder, observer, looker-on, onlooker, watcher, viewer, witness, eyewitness, bystander, passerby; sightseer, rubberneck, sidewalk superintendent; inspector; audience, house; the gallery, grandstand, *or* bleachers.

specter, spectre, *n.* ghost, spirit, apparition, vision, shadow, shade; wraith, phantom, phantasm, haunt, spook; aura, emanation, materialization, reincarnation, illusion, delusion, hallucination. See INSUBSTANTIALITY.

speculate, *v.i.* ponder, contemplate, meditate, conjecture, surmise; gamble, play the market. See THOUGHT, CHANCE, BUSINESS.

SPEECH [582]

Nouns—**1,** speech, talk, faculty of speech; locution, parlance, vernacular, oral communication, word of mouth, parole, palaver, prattle; effusion, discourse; SOLILOQUY; interlocution, CONVERSATION, LOQUACITY. *Colloq.,* gab, confab, powwow, corroboree.

2, formal speech, speechifying, oration, recitation, delivery, peroration, valedictory; oratory, elocution, eloquence; rhetoric, declamation; bombast, grandiloquence; burst of eloquence; fecundity; flow or command of language; power of speech, gift of gab, blarney. *Slang*, spiel, line, earful.

3, allocution, exhortation, appeal, harangue, lecture, sermon, tirade, diatribe, invocation.

4, LANGUAGE, linguistics, grammar, lexicography, etymology; semantics, general semantics, meaning, denotation, connotation; WRITING, literature, philology, classics, letters, *belles lettres*, humanities, Muses.

5, WORD, phone, phoneme, syllable, stem, root; PHRASE, sentence; syntax, idiom; utterance, remark, statement, pronouncement, observation, comment; question, INQUIRY; answer, reply; aside, apostrophe, rhetorical question.

6, vocalization, enunciation, articulation, delivery; vociferation, exclamation, ejaculation; clearness, distinctness; whisper, stage whisper.

7, speaker, spokesman; prolocutor, interlocutor; mouthpiece, orator; Demosthenes, Cicero; rhetorician; stump or platform orator; speechmaker, patterer, improvisator, monologist; gossip.

8, linguist, philologist; grammarian; semanticist, etymologist, lexicographer.

9, accent, accentuation; emphasis, stress; brogue, burr; pronunciation, euphony.

Verbs—**1,** speak, talk, speak of; say, utter, pronounce, deliver, comment, remark, recite, VOICE, give utterance to; breathe, let fall, come out with; rap out, blurt out; chatter, open one's mouth; lift or raise one's voice; speak one's mind; state, assert, declare. *Colloq.*, gab, shoot one's mouth off, shoot the breeze, talk a blue streak.

2, hold forth; make or deliver a speech, speechify, orate, declaim, stump, flourish, spout, rant, recite, discourse, have or say one's say; expatiate, be eloquent, have the gift of gab.

3, soliloquize, apostrophize, talk to oneself; tell, impart, inform (see INFORMATION); converse, speak to, talk together; communicate, divulge (see DISCLOSURE); express, phrase, put into words; translate, interpret.

4, allocute, exhort, appeal, harangue, lecture, preach, invoke, sermonize.

5, enunciate, pronounce, articulate; accentuate, aspirate; exclaim, ejaculate, cry; shout, yell, mouth.

Adjectives—**1,** speaking, spoken; vocal, oral, lingual, phonetic, outspoken; eloquent, elocutionary; oratorical, rhetorical; declamatory, bombastic, grandiloquent; talkative (see LOQUACITY).

2, lingual, linguistic; idiomatic, colloquial, dialectic, vernacular, provincial; polyglot; literary.

3, conversational, discursive, interlocutory; chatty, sociable.

Adverbs—orally; vocally; by word of mouth, *viva voce*, from the lips of; loudly, softly, *sotto voce*.

Antonym, see SILENCE.

---

speed, *v. & n.* —*v.i.* HASTE, hasten, hurry, accelerate. —*n.* VELOCITY, dispatch, expedition, swiftness. *Ant.*, see SLOWNESS.

spell, *n. & v.* —*n.* charm, trance; talisman; incantation, sorcery, magic; witchery, allure, glamour; enchantment; spellbinding. —*v.* give the letters of a word; relieve (in a work shift). See SORCERY, RELIEF, LETTER.

spell, *n.* term, period, interval; TIME; turn, stretch; breathing spell, respite.

spend, *v.t.* disburse, pay out, expend; consume, exhaust; pass. See PAYMENT, BUSINESS.

spendthrift, *n.* wastrel, prodigal, profligate, squanderer. See WASTE. *Ant.*, see PARSIMONY.

spent, *adj.* used up, exhausted, fatigued, dead-tired, fagged; effete, worn-out, impotent. See WEARINESS, DETERIORATION.

sperm, *n.* semen, seed, germ. See CAUSE.

sphere, *n.* orb, globe, ball; environment, province, status, field, range. See CIRCULARITY, CLASS.

spice, *v.t.* season, flavor; make piquant. See TASTE.

spill, *v.* overturn, upset; splash; brim over, slop, pour out. See EJECTION, DEPRESSION. *Slang*, tell, let slip. See DISCLOSURE.

spin, *v.* twirl, whirl, rotate; protract, draw out; gyrate, swirl, reel, eddy. See ROTATION, LOQUACITY.

spine, *n.* backbone; ridge, *arête;* thorn, prickle, spike, spiculum, quill, barb. See REAR, HEIGHT, SHARPNESS.

spinster, *n.* maid, maiden, old maid; spinner. See CELIBACY. *Ant.,* see MARRIAGE.

spiral, *adj.* coiled, winding, helical, turbinate, cochlear. See CONVOLUTION.

spirit, *n.* vitalness, essence; soul; ghost, fairy, angel, demon; disposition, temper, mood, humor; ENERGY, vivacity, élan, verve, intrepidity; enthusiasm, dash, gallantry, intent. See MEANING, ACTIVITY.

spirited, *adj.* animated, lively, mettlesome, bold, ardent; blithe, debonair, jaunty; sparkling, racy. See ACTIVITY, CHEERFULNESS.

spit, *v.* impale, transfix, pierce, stab; sprinkle, drizzle, discharge (bullets); sputter, utter explosively; expectorate, hiss. See OPENING, EJECTION.

spite, *n.* malice, ill-will, grudge, malignity, MALEVOLENCE. *Ant.,* see BENEVOLENCE.

splash, *v.* spatter, bespatter; dash, plop, spill; slop, splash, dabble, paddle. See EJECTION, WATER, UNCLEANNESS.

splendid, *adj.* gorgeous, magnificent; heroic, glorious; resplendent. See BEAUTY, REPUTE. *Colloq.,* excellent. *Ant.,* see UGLINESS.

splice, *v.t.* join, unite, interweave. *Slang,* marry. See JUNCTION.

split, *v.t.* rive, rend, cleave, splinter; divide, separate; apportion. See DISJUNCTION. *Ant.,* see JUNCTION.

spoil, *v. & n.* —*v.* damage, ruin, impair; overindulge, humor; despoil, plunder, sack, pillage, rob; decay, putrefy, rot, mold, ferment. See DETERIORATION. —*n.* plunder, loot, booty, spoils, spoliation. See ACQUISITION.

spoken, *adj.* oral, vocal; verbal. See SPEECH. *Ant.,* see WRITING.

sponsor, *n.* patron, backer; surety, guarantor; godparent; advertiser. See AID.

spontaneous, *adj.* instinctive, automatic, involuntary; extemporaneous, uninhibited, unforced, natural. See IMPULSE, WILL.

spool, *n.* spindle, bobbin, reel. See ROTATION.

sport, *n.* recreation, athletics, pastime, angling, hunting, chase; jesting, merriment; mockery, RIDICULE; freak, mutant; gamester, gambler. *Slang,* spender, flashy dresser. See AMUSEMENT.

sportsman, *n.* Nimrod, hunter, angler; athlete, ballplayer, golfer, *etc.;* honorable competitor. See PURSUIT, AMUSEMENT.

spot, *n.* place, locality, site; blotch, dapple, speckle, macula; smear, spatter, daub, blot; BLEMISH, flaw, stain, stigma. See LOCATION, UNCLEANNESS.

spotless, *adj.* clean, unsullied, immaculate; pure, unblemished, impeccable. See PERFECTION, CLEANNESS. *Ant.,* see UNCLEANNESS.

spouse, *n.* mate, husband, wife, consort. See MARRIAGE.

spout, *n.* tube, pipe, trough, nozzle, rainspout, gargoyle; jet, spurt, geyser, waterspout. See PASSAGE.

sprain, *v.t.* wrench, strain, twist. See DETERIORATION.

spray, *n. & v.* —*n.* spindrift, spume, scud; fusillade, barrage; sprinkler, atomizer; slender branch, sprig. —*v.t.* sprinkle, atomize; pepper, riddle (with bullets). See VAPOR, WATER, ATTACK.

spread, *v. & n.* —*v.* scatter, strew; disseminate, diffuse, circulate; cover; unfold, stretch; part, separate; show, display; expand, disperse, deploy. —*n.* diffusion, expansion; extent, expanse; bedspread, coverlet; meal, banquet, collation; layout; ranch. See SIZE, COVERING, FOOD, INCREASE, PUBLICATION, OPENING.

sprightly, *adj.* gay, brisk, vivacious, animated; scintillating, smart. See CHEERFULNESS, WIT. *Ant.,* DULL.

spring, *v. & n.* —*v.* LEAP, bound, dart, start; bounce, RECOIL, rebound; arise, rise; result from, derive from; release; detonate; reveal, disclose; bend, twist. *Slang,* release; bail. —*n.* LEAP, bound; elasticity, RECOIL; well, fount, origin, source; coil. See BEGINNING.

sprinkle, *v.* scatter, spread, SOW; spray, wet; speckle, mottle, powder; drizzle, shower. See DISCLOSURE, WATER.

sprinkler, *n.* spray, sprayer, atomizer, nozzle, watering can, watering cart; fire-extinguishing system. See WATER.

sprout, *v.i.* germinate, shoot, bud, burgeon. See INCREASE.

spruce, *adj.* trim, neat, tidy, shipshape; smart, dapper, chic. See ARRANGE-
MENT. *Ant.,* see DISORDER.

spur, *n.* spine; rowel; incentive, goad, stimulus; projection, headland,
siding. See SHARPNESS, CAUSE.

spurious, *adj.* false, counterfeit, sham, specious; bastard, illegitimate. See
DECEPTION, ILLEGALITY. *Ant.,* see LEGALITY, TRUTH.

spurn, *v.t.* flout, scout, reject, repudiate, repel, contemn, scorn, disdain.
See REFUSAL, CONTEMPT. *Ant.,* see RECEIVING.

spurt, *v. & n.* —*v.i.* gush, squirt, spout, jet; dash, speed, sprint. See EJEC-
TION. —*n.* jet, spout, squirt, spray, gush; burst. See WATER, VELOCITY.
Ant., see SLOWNESS.

spy, *n.* secret agent, scout, undercover man, informer, stool pigeon. See
INFORMATION, CONCEALMENT.

squalid, *adj.* filthy, dirty, foul, sordid, repulsive, wretched. See UNCLEAN-
NESS. *Ant.,* see CLEANNESS.

squall, *n. & v.* —*n.* gust, blow, blast; turmoil; scream, CRY. See WIND,
DISORDER. —*v.i.* blow, bluster; scream, bawl, wail.

squander, *v.t.* WASTE, lavish, dissipate. *Ant.,* see PARSIMONY.

square, *n. & v.* —*n.* tetragon, quadrilateral, equilateral rectangle; block;
quadrangle; plaza, court; T square. See NUMERATION, ABODE, MEASURE-
MENT. *Slang,* meal; misfit, booby. —*v.t.* quadrate; balance, settle, reconcile; set, adjust. See AGREEMENT.

squash, *v.t.* crush, mash, squeeze, flatten; squelch. See DESTRUCTION.

squat, *adj.* dumpy, stocky, pudgy. See SHORTNESS. *Ant.,* see HEIGHT.

squeeze, *v.t.* press, compress; express, extract; stuff, cram; exact, extort,
blackmail. See CONTRACTION, COMPULSION. *Ant.,* see INCREASE.

squelch, *v.t.* disconcert, discomfit, rout, crush; SILENCE, stifle, muffle.
See DESTRUCTION.

squint, *n.* cross-eye, strabismus; peek, peering, glance. See VISION.

stab, *v.t.* pierce, puncture, perforate, stick, prick, pink; distress, hurt. See
SHARPNESS, PAIN.

STABILITY [150]

Nouns—**1,** stability; immutability, unchangeableness, constancy, firmness,
equilibrium, immobility, soundness, vitality, stiffness, solidity aplomb;
establishment, fixture; permanence; obstinacy, RESOLUTION; inflexibility
(see HARDNESS).

2, rock, pillar, tower, foundation, leopard's spots; rock of Gibralter.

Verbs—**1,** be stable, be *or* stand firm; stick fast; weather the storm; settle
down, take root; entrench oneself.

2, establish, settle, ascertain, fix, set, retain, keep *or* take hold; make good,
make sure; perpetuate.

Adjectives—**1,** stable, fixed, steadfast, firm, fast, steady, balanced; confirmed,
valid, immovable, irremovable, riveted, rooted; settled, established, vested;
incontrovertible; tethered, anchored, moored; firm as a rock; firmly seated
or established; deep-rooted, ineradicable; inveterate; obstinate; stuck fast,
aground, high and dry, stranded.

2, unchangeable, immutable; unaltered, unalterable; constant, PERMANENT;
invariable, undeviating; durable, perennial; indefeasible, irrevocable, irre-
versible, inextinguishable, irreducible; indissoluble; indestructible, undying,
deathless, immortal, imperishable, indelible, indeciduous.

3, convervative, Tory, reactionary, diehard.

Adverbs—*in statu quo;* at a standstill.

Antonym, see CHANGEABLENESS.

---

stable, *n.* barn, stall, mews. See DOMESTICATION.

staff, *n.* walking stick, cane, cudgel; scepter, wand, baton, truncheon,
crosier; flagpole; assistants, crew, aides, associates, personnel, force. See
SUPPORT, SERVANT.

stage, *n.* platform, rostrum, scaffold; DRAMA, theater; ARENA, field, scene;
DEGREE, step, phase; PERIOD, stretch, interval, span; stagecoach, diligence,
omnibus. See SUPPORT, VEHICLE.

stagger, *v.* reel, sway, totter, lurch; waver, hesitate; surprise, stun, jar, shock, startle, take aback; alternate. See AGITATION, OSCILLATION.

stagnant, *adj.* static, inert; foul; sluggish, dull, torpid. See INACTIVITY.
Ant., flowing; see ACTIVITY.

staid, *adj.* demure, serious, sedate, settled, INEXCITABLE.

stain, *n.* COLOR, dye, dyestuff; discoloration; blotch, blot, smear, smudge;
BLEMISH, tarnish; stigma, taint, brand. See UNCLEANNESS, DISREPUTE.

stairway, *n.* stairs, steps, staircase, Escalator; companionway, ladder. See
ASCENT, DESCENT.

stake, *n.* post, peg, pile; palisade; burning, execution; wager, bet, ante,
pot; SECURITY, earnest, deposit; interest, claim, holding; prize, REWARD.
See CHANCE, PROPERTY.

stale, *adj.* passé; rancid, dried up, tasteless, INSIPID, flat, vapid; trite, DULL,
banal; overtrained. *Slang*, corny. See DETERIORATION.

stalk, *n.* stem, pedicle, petiole. See SUPPORT.

stalwart, *adj.* strong, brawny, husky; dauntless, steadfast. See POWER.
Ant., WEAK, timid.

stammer, *v.* stutter, hesitate, falter, hem and haw, trip over one's own
tongue, lisp; jabber, gibber; sputter, splutter; swallow one's words; missay.
See SPEECH.

stamp, *n.* impression, symbol, device, SEAL, trademark, brand; authorization, certification, approval, ASSENT; postage; die, rubber stamp; certificate,
wafer, label; kind, sort, quality. See INDICATION.

stanch, staunch, *adj.* loyal, reliable, faithful, constant, steadfast; seaworthy,
strong. See PROBITY.

stand, *v.* abide, tolerate, endure, SUPPORT; last, persist; remain upright;
pause, halt, stop; be, remain; stagnate; be valid; put, place; bear, undergo;
stand by, up, *or* for; represent, mean (with *for*). See DURABILITY, MEANING,
INDICATION.

standard, *n.* emblem, ensign; criterion, measure, grade, exemplar, norm,
canon, prototype, ethics. See INDICATION, MEASUREMENT.

standing, *n.* station, rank, REPUTE; duration, continuance; status, rating.
See DURABILITY.

stanza, *n.* verse, stave, strophe. See POETRY.

staple, *adj.* chief, principal; stable, established, regular; marketable, popular. See STABILITY, SALE.

star, *n.* sun, celestial body; pentagram; asterisk; prima donna, leading man,
chief performer; DESTINY; planet. See INDICATION, DRAMA.

stare, *v.i.* gaze, gape, gawk; stand out, be conspicuous. See VISION, CURI-
OSITY.

starry, *adj.* spangled, stellar, stellate, star-studded; starlit; shiny, glittering.
See LIGHT.

start, *v.* begin, commence, set out; jerk, jump, shy; loosen, crack; originate; set going; loosen, crack; startle, rouse. See BEGINNING, PROPULSION,
IMPULSE, SURPRISE.

startle, *v.t.* start, alarm, frighten, shock, surprise, amaze. See SURPRISE.

starve, *v.* hunger, famish, fast; pine; pinch, scrimp, deny. See ASCETICISM,
PARSIMONY, POVERTY. *Ant.*, see SUFFICIENCY.

state, *n. & v.* —*n.* condition; category; estate; lot; case, mood, disposition,
temper; pickle, contretemps, quandary, dilemma, plight; aspect, APPEAR-
ANCE; constitution, habitude, frame; pomp, great dignity, formality, CIR-
CUMSTANCE; mode, modality; FORM, tone, tenor, turn; FASHION, style,
character, rank, situation, position, status; nation, country, government;
commonwealth. *Colloq.*, make-up; kilter; shape. —*v.* allege, say, assert,
declare, avow, aver, express, make a statement. See CIRCUMSTANCE,
SPEECH.

stated, *adj.* fixed, regular, designated, established. See STABILITY.

stately, *adj.* impressive, imposing, grand; dignified, noble, lofty. See
OSTENTATION, IMPORTANCE. *Ant.*, see PLAINNESS, UNIMPORTANCE.

statement, *n.* assertion, declaration, AFFIRMATION; report; bill, account.
See ACCOUNTING.

statesman, *n.* legislator, diplomat, solon, Draco; politician. See DIREC-
TION.

station, *n. & v.* —*n.* place, position; office, situation; rank, standing; depot, terminal; headquarters, stopping place, post. —*v.t.* set, place, assign, post. See LOCATION, REPUTE.

statue, *n.* SCULPTURE, effigy, image.

status, *n.* position, rank, standing; state, condition. See CIRCUMSTANCE.

statute, *n.* law, ordinance, enactment; rule. See LEGALITY.

stay, *v.* check, stop; detain, delay; defer; SUPPORT, brace; appease; outlast; linger, tarry, remain; endure, last; dwell, sojourn; stick, stay put; continue. See HINDRANCE, END, DURABILITY, PRESENCE.

steadfast, *adj.* firm, unswerving, constant, sta(u)nch. See RESOLUTION, PROBITY. *Ant.,* capricious, unreliable; see DOUBT.

steady, *adj.* firm, secure, stable; constant, unvarying, uniform; regular, habitual; trustworthy. See STABILITY.

STEALING [791]

Nouns—**1,** stealing, theft, thievery, robbery; abduction, kidnaping; abstraction, appropriation; plagiarism; rape, depredation, poaching, raid; spoliation, plunder, pillage, sack, rapine, brigandage, foray; extortion, blackmail; graft; piracy, privateering, buccaneering; burglary; housebreaking; peculation, pilfering, embezzlement; fraud, swindle (see DECEPTION); kleptomania; larceny, grand larceny, petty larceny; pickpocketing, shoplifting, highway robbery; holdup, stickup, mugging; hijacking. *Slang,* make, heist, snatch; haul, score.

2, THIEF, robber, burglar, sneak thief, housebreaker.

Verbs—**1,** steal, thieve; rob, purloin, pilfer, filch, swipe, crib, palm; abstract, appropriate, plagiarize; abduct, kidnap; make, walk, *or* run off *or* away with; seize, TAKE; spirit away; plunder, pillage, rifle, sack, loot, ransack; spoil, spoliate, despoil, strip, sweep, gut, forage; blackmail, pirate, maraud, poach, smuggle, run; hold up, stick up, hijack. *Slang,* heist; snatch.

2, swindle, peculate, embezzle; sponge, mulct, rook, bilk, milk, pluck, fleece, defaud; obtain under false pretenses; live by one's wits; rob Peter to pay Paul; set a thief to catch a thief. *Colloq.,* rook, shake down. *Slang,* wangle.

Adjectives—stealing, thieving, thievish, light-fingered, furtive; piratical, predaceous, predacious, predatory; stolen. *Slang,* hot.

Antonym, see PROBITY.

stealth, *n.* furtiveness, secrecy, slinking action, skulking, stalking. See CONCEALMENT.

steam, *n. & v.* —*n.* VAPOR, water vapor, mist, fog, gas, evaporation. —*v.* cook, boil, simmer; soften, moisten; clean, renovate; progress, speed, travel (propelled by steam). See HEAT, WATER, VELOCITY.

steed, *n.* horse, mount, charger. See CARRIER.

steep, *v. & adj.* —*v.t.* soak, macerate. See WATER. —*adj.* precipitous, abrupt, sheer, declivitous; VERTICAL. *Colloq.,* expensive, costly. See DIRECTION, DESCENT. *Ant.,* see LOWNESS, SMOOTHNESS, CHEAPNESS.

steer, *v.t.* guide, pilot, control; manage, direct; follow (a course). See NAVIGATION, DIRECTION.

steersman, *n.* helmsman, pilot, coxswain. See NAVIGATION.

stem, *n.* tree trunk, stalk, petiole, pedicle; tube, shaft; cutwater, prow; lineage, extraction, derivation. See SUPPORT, OPENING, ANCESTRY.

stench, *n.* fetor, stink, mephitis, fetidness, malodor, (strong) smell. See MALODOROUSNESS. *Ant.,* see FRAGRANCE.

step, *n.* pace, stride; footprint; gait, tread; stair, rung; short distance; interval, gradation; measures, ACTION. See TRAVEL, INDICATION.

sterile, *adj.* barren, UNPRODUCTIVE, unfruitful, unfertile; aseptic, germfree.

sterling, *adj.* genuine, unalloyed, pure; noble, excellent, exemplary; silver. See TRUTH, VIRTUE, MONEY.

stern, *adj. & n.* —*adj.* rigorous, austere; forbidding, grim; strict, harsh, uncompromising. See TRUTH, RESOLUTION, SEVERITY. *Ant.,* see SOFTNESS. —*n.* poop, counter, REAR. *Ant.,* see FRONT.

steward, *n.* AGENT, manager, trustee; provider, caterer; SERVANT, waiter. See DIRECTION, STORE.

stick, *v. & n.* —*v.t.* stab, puncture, prick; put, place, thrust; glue; transfix, impale. See OPENING, COHERENCE. *Slang*, puzzle, stump. —*v.i.* adhere, cling; stay, remain, tarry; stall, freeze, be immobile. See COHERENCE, HINDRANCE. —*n.* piece, branch; cane, staff, cudgel, rod, baton. See SUPPORT.

sticky, *adj.* adhesive, mucilaginous, glutinous, viscous, tenacious. *Colloq.*, humid, muggy; sweaty; tacky. See COHERENCE.

stiff, *adj.* rigid, inflexible, firm, nonfluid; strong, brisk; difficult, hard; severe, excessive; formal, unreserved; awkward, stilted. See HARDNESS, SEVERITY, AFFECTATION. *Ant.*, see SOFTNESS.

stifle, *v.t.* smother, suffocate; extinguish, put down, suppress; repress, check. See KILLING, CONCEALMENT, RESTRAINT.

stigma, *n.* BLEMISH, birthmark; brand, blot, stain, reproach. See DISRE- PUTE, IMPERFECTION. *Ant.*, see REPUTE, PERFECTION.

stigmatize, *v.t.*, denounce, reproach, brand, vilify. See DISREPUTE. *Ant,.* see VINDICATION.

still, *adj.* silent, quiet, hushed; calm, peaceful, tranquil; motionless, at rest, stationary. See SILENCE, MODERATION, REPOSE.

stimulant, *n.* excitant, stimulus, bracer, tonic, spur; liquor. See ENERGY, REMEDY.

stimulate, *v.t.* excite, rouse, animate, stir, spur, invigorate, exhilarate. See EXCITEMENT.

sting, *v. & n.* —*v.* smart, tingle; irritate, trouble, PAIN; wound; nettle, gall. See RESENTMENT. —*n.* wound, prickle, smart, irritation; stimulus, goad; stinger, prickle, nettle. See PAIN, BANE. *Ant.*, see MODERATION.

stingy, *adj.* penurious, miserly, niggardly; scanty, meager. *Colloq.*, near, tight, close. See PARSIMONY. *Ant.*, generous, LIBERAL.

stipend, *n.* compensation, wage, pay, salary. See COMPENSATION.

stipulate, *v.t.* specify, demand, insist upon, negotiate. See AGREEMENT.

stir, *v.t.* move, budge; agitate, incite, arouse; animate, stimulate, provoke. See AGITATION, MOTION, EXCITEMENT. *Ant.*, see REPOSE.

stock, *n.* stem, bole, trunk; race, family; livestock, cattle; gun butt; capital; MERCHANDISE, goods; MATERIALS, raw materials; repertory. *Colloq.*, BELIEF. See ANCESTRY, ANIMAL, STORE, DRAMA.

stocking, *n.* sock, hose, anklet, bobby sox; hosiery. See CLOTHING.

stocky, *adj.* thickset, sturdy, chunky, squat. See SHORTNESS. *Ant.*, see HEIGHT.

stolid, *adj.* inexcitable, impassive, dull, lethargic, sluggish. See MODERATION.

stomach, *n.* appetite, hunger; DESIRE, craving, inclination; maw, craw. *Colloq.*, belly, paunch, corporation. See RECEPTACLE.

stone, *n.* cobblestone, pebble; mineral; gem, jewel; gravestone, tombstone, millstone, whetstone, hearthstone, flagstone, *etc.;* pit, endocarp, pyrene; concretion, calculus. See LAND, INTERMENT.

stool, *n.* cricket, hassock; seat; footrest, footstool; prie-dieu, kneeling stool; piano stool, milking stool, cucking stool. See SUPPORT.

stoop, *v.i.* bend, bow, crouch; condescend, deign; submit. See DEPRESSION, SERVILITY. *Ant.*, see ASCENT.

stop, *v., n. & interj.* —*v.* close; obstruct; sta(u)nch; arrest, halt, impede; inhibit; delay, hold up, detain; discontinue, suspend; END, terminate, conclude; cease, desist. —*n.* halt, standstill, pause; discontinuance, stoppage; stay, sojourn; stopping place, station; period, punctuation mark; brake, catch, skid, detent, curb. —*interj.* halt! belay! avast! stay! cease! See END, CLOSURE, LATENESS.

stopper, *n.* plug, seal, valve, cork, bung, stopcock, stopple, tamp, spike, ramrod, wad, wadding, stuffing, pad, padding; barrier, tourniquet. See CLOSURE. *Ant.*, see OPENING.

STORE [636]

Nouns—**1,** store, accumulation, hoard; mine, vein, lode, quarry; spring, wellspring; treasure, reserve, savings, nest-egg; stock, stock in trade, merchandise; supply, heap (see ASSEMBLAGE); crop, harvest, vintage; supplies, provisions. See PROPERTY.

2, storage, conservation; storehouse, storeroom, depository; depot, warehouse, cache, repository, magazine, arsenal, armory; buttery, larder, granary; bank, vault, safe-deposit box, treasury; museum, gallery, conservatory; menagerie, zoo; reservoir, tank, cistern, pond, millpond.

3, store, department store, shop, mart, market, emporium, commissary, bazaar, fair.

4, storekeeper, clerk, salesclerk, man behind the counter; MERCHANT, purveyor, supplier, caterer, commissary, peddler, sutler; grocer, druggist, *etc.;* quartermaster, batman, steward, purser, supercargo.

Verbs—store; put by, lay by, lay away, set by; stow away; store, lay, heap, put, *or* save up, accumulate, amass, hoard, garner, save; reserve; keep back, hold back; husband, husband one's resources; salt away; deposit; stow, stack, load; harvest; heap, collect, stock up, lay in store, keep file; lay in, provide; preserve. *Slang*, stash.

Adjectives—stored, in store, in reserve; spare, supernumerary; extra.
        Antonyms, SEE WASTE, POVERTY.

---

storehouse, *n.* warehouse, depository, magazine, elevator, granary, arsenal. See STORE.

storm, *n. & v.* —*n.* hurricane, tempest, tornado; spate, flood; cloudburst, blizzard; outburst, commotion; assault, onslaught, ATTACK. —*v.* assault, assail, ATTACK; rage, rant; bluster; blow violently, pour, rain, snow. See RESENTMENT, WIND, WATER, VIOLENCE.

story, *n.* tale, narrative, yarn; report, account, news article; plot; floor, stage, level. See DESCRIPTION, NEWS, RECEPTACLE.

stout, *adj.* stalwart, robust, brawny; doughty bold, dauntless, resolute; determined, stubborn; stocky, thickset, portly. See POWER, COURAGE, SIZE.

straddle, *v.t.* bestride, bestraddle; equivocate; be neutral, sit on the fence. See MIDDLE.

straight, *adj. & adv.* —*adj.* rectilinear, rectilineal; direct; even, right, true, in a line; unbent; undeviating, unturned, undistorted, unswerving; straight as a die *or* an arrow; inflexible; aligned, alined, level, not crooked. See DIRECTION. *Colloq.*, honest, fair, aboveboard, trustworthy. See PROBITY. —*adv.* directly; bluntly; pointblank. *Ant.*, see CURVATURE.

straighten, *v.* render straight, rectify; set straight, put straight; align, aline, true, level; unbend, unfold, uncurl, unravel, unwrap. See DIRECTION. *Ant.*, see DEVIATION, CURVATURE.

straightness, *n.* rectilinearity, directness; inflexibility; verticality, perpendicularity; straight line, beeline, right line, direct line; shortcut; alignment, alinement, truing; honesty, straightforwardness. See DIRECTION, VERTICAL, RIGHT. *Ant.*, see IMPROBITY, DISTORTION.

straightway, *adv.* immediately, forthwith; at once, promptly, speedily, directly. See EARLINESS.

strain, *v.t.* stretch, make taut; strive, exert; sprain; overtax, overstretch; filter, percolate. See EXERTION, CLEANNESS.

strand, *n.* thread, string, fiber, rope, FILAMENT. See LAND.

stranded, *adj.* aground, stuck, left high and dry, grounded; embarrassed, penniless. See STABILITY, DIFFICULTY.

strange, *adj.* unusual, odd, unfamiliar; queer, fantastic; alien, foreign, EXTRANEOUS, outlandish, exotic; eccentric, mysterious. See UNCONFORMITY.

strangle, *v.t.* choke, garrotte, stifle, suffocate; suppress, repress; squeeze, constrict. See KILLING, IMPOTENCE.

stratagem, *n.* trick, subterfuge, artifice, ruse, guile, wile. See DECEPTION.

strategy, *n.* generalship, maneuvering, CONDUCT, warcraft, artifice. See WARFARE.

stray, *v.i.* wander, straggle, roam, rove, ramble; digress; deviate, err. See DEVIATION, ERROR, TRAVEL.

streak, *n.* band, stripe, smear; vein, LAYER; trait, idiosyncrasy. See INDICATION, COLOR.

stream, *n. & v.* —*n.* RIVER, rivulet; rill; gush; trickle; creek, brook, runnel, runlet; current, flow, flux, course, flood, tide, race; shower, outpouring, downpouring. —*v.i.* issue; pour out, forth, *or* down; flow, run, rush; shed; blow, extend, run across *or* along; drift, tend; jet, spurt, gush. See WATER, MOTION, WIND, LIGHT.

street, *n.* thoroughfare, avenue, boulevard, alley; roadway. See PASSAGE.

strength, *n.* POWER, energy; vigor, force; main force, physical force, brute force; tone, tonicity; stoutness, lustiness, robustness, brawn; stamina, nerve, muscle, sinew, thews and sinews, physique; virility, vitality; invigoration, refreshment, stimulation; depth, intensity. *Slang,* beef. *Ant.,* see IMPOTENCE.

strenuous, *adj.* vigorous, energetic, dynamic; arduous, exhausting, straining, laborious. See EXERTION.

stress, *n.* pressure, COMPULSION; emphasis, urgency, IMPORTANCE; accent. See SPEECH.

strict, *adj.* exact, precise; rigid; accurate, meticulous; scrupulous, punctilious; conscientious, nice; stringent, exacting; strait-laced, puritanical. See TRUTH, SEVERITY, PROBITY.

stricture, *n.* censure, criticism, blame, reprehension, RESTRAINT; compression, constriction, CONTRACTION. See DISAPPROBATION, HINDRANCE.

stridency, *n.* stridulation; shrillness, harshness; discord, dissonance, LOUDNESS, ROUGHNESS, SHARPNESS; noise, noisiness, raucousness, cacophony; high note, soprano, treble, tenor, falsetto; creaking, squeaking, twanging, whistling; clangor, clamor. See LOUDNESS, SOUND. *Ant.,* see LOWNESS, SILENCE.

strife, *n.* CONTENTION, emulation, rivalry; altercation; dissension, discord, dispute, quarrel; war, WARFARE; struggle, conflict.

strike, *v.* hit, smite, beat, thump; give, deliver, deal; affect, TOUCH, impress, occur to; blast; lower, take down; collide, bump; conclude, agree upon; attack, smite; hit, collide; walk out, quit, rebel. See IMPULSE, OPPOSITION, EXCITEMENT.

string, *n.* twine, thread, cord; catgut; series, row, line, chain; set, stud; stringed instrument. See FILAMENT, CONTINUITY, MUSICAL INSTRUMENT.

strip, *v. & n.* —*v.* divest, denude, decorticate, peel, pull off; dismantle; plunder, fleece; dispossess, deprive; disrobe, undress; cut in strips. *Slang,* skin. See STEALING, DIVESTMENT. —*n.* hue, stripe, bend, fillet, shred; lath, ribbon. See LENGTH, FILAMENT. *Slang,* comic strip.

strive, *v.i.* endeavor, strain, ESSAY; struggle, contend; quarrel. See CONTENTION. *Ant.,* see INACTIVITY.

stroke, *n.* blow, impact; beat, throb, pulsation; bolt, blast; seizure, apoplexy, shock, feat, exploit, coup; mark, flourish. See IMPULSE, DISEASE, ACTION.

stroll, *n.* ramble, saunter, promenade, walk. See TRAVEL. *Colloq.,* constitutional.

strong, *adj.* vigorous, robust, powerful; brisk, blustering, violent; solid, firm, durable; intense, concentrated; rank, high, gamy, offensive; stable, established, responsible; forceful, convincing; alcoholic, spirituous, hard; energetic, trenchant. See POWER, MALODOROUSNESS, HEALTH. *Ant.,* WEAK.

stronghold, *n.* REFUGE; fort, fortress, citadel; blockhouse; fastness, bulwark. See DEFENSE.

structure, *n.* building, edifice, construction, fabrication; framework, make-up, ARRANGEMENT, composition, anatomy, constitution. See FORM.

struggle, *v. & n.* —*v.i.* strive, strain, endeavor, contend, labor; flounder, writhe, squirm; fight, battle. —*n.* endeavor, effort, CONTENTION, ESSAY; fight, conflict, WARFARE. See EXERTION.

strut, *v.* swagger; stalk, peacock. See VANITY, OSTENTATION.

stubborn, *adj.* perverse, obstinate; dogged, persistent; intractable, unyielding. See RESOLUTION, OBSTINACY. *Ant.,* see ASSENT.

student, *n.* learner; pupil; apprentice; schoolboy, schoolgirl; scholar, schoolman, pedant. See SCHOOL.

studious, *adj.* scholarly, thoughtful, speculative, contemplative, bookish. See KNOWLEDGE, THOUGHT. *Ant.,* see IGNORANCE.

study, *n. & v.* —*n.* meditation, research, examination, investigation; library, atelier, den; sketch, cartoon; étude. —*v.* investigate, weigh, consider, examine; scrutinize; con; memorize; ponder. *Colloq.,* grind. See THOUGHT, INQUIRY.

stuff, *v. & n.* —*v.* cram, pack, jam, fill; pad, wad; plug, block; cast illegal votes; gormandize, gorge, overeat. See COMPLETION, GLUTTONY. —*n.* fabric, cloth, material; nonsense; substance. *Slang,* the goods, the ability.

stumble, *v.t.* trip, stub one's toe; hobble, stagger, lumber; blunder, flounder, stammer; err, slip, backslide. See DESCENT, AGITATION, ERROR. *Ant.*, see CERTAINTY.

stump, *n.* stub, butt, snag, remnant, fag end; rostrum, pulpit; hobble, heavy tread. See REMAINDER, SUPPORT. *Colloq.*, confound, puzzle.

stun, *v.t.* benumb, deaden, daze, stupefy; dizzy; dum(b)found, astound, astonish, bewilder. See INSENSIBILITY, SURPRISE.

stunt, *v. & n.* —*v.* dwarf; cramp, retard, check; perform feats, do tricks, grandstand. See SHORTNESS, CONTRACTION, SKILLFULNESS. —*n.* trick, feat, daredevil(t)ry, tour de force.

stupefy, *v.t.* deaden, dull, numb, narcotize; stun, astound, daze, dum(b)-found. See INSENSIBILITY, SURPRISE.

stupendous, *adj.* prodigious, enormous, astounding, amazing, wonderful, immense, vast, colossal, overwhelming. See GREATNESS, WONDER.

stupid, *adj.* slow-witted, dull, obtuse; benumbed, bemused; absurd, inane; banal, tiresome, tedious, DULL. See IGNORANCE, DENSITY. *Ant.*, see IN-TELLIGENCE, WIT, KNOWLEDGE.

stupor, *n.* lethargy, torpor, apathy, coma, daze. See INSENSIBILITY.

sturdy, *adj.* stalwart, hardy, husky, robust; durable, long-wearing; firm, stubborn, unyielding. See POWER. *Ant.*, WEAK.

stutter, *v.i.* stammer, sputter, hesitate, falter, stumble. See SPEECH.

sty, *n.* pigpen, pigsty; pen; hovel, shed; stable. See INCLOSURE, UNCLEAN-NESS.

style, *n.* FORM, manner, method, way; FASHION; smartness, vogue, mode, chic; craze, fad, rage, last word; practice, habit, (characteristic) behavior, air; diction, phraseology, wording, rhetoric; distinction, elegance. See SPEECH.

stylish, *adj.* fashionable, smart, chic, up-to-date, modish. See FASHION. *Ant.*, see UNCONFORMITY, VULGARITY, OLDNESS.

suave, *adj.* urbane, bland, courteous, gracious; oily, smooth, ingratiating. See COURTESY, SMOOTHNESS. *Ant.*, see ROUGHNESS, DISCOURTESY.

subconscious, *adj. & n.* —*adj.* subliminal, nonconscious, unconscious, auto-matic. See INTELLECT. —*n.* subliminal self, id, unconscious [mental life *or* functioning].

subdue, *v.t.* tame, overcome, master; vanquish, conquer; repress, restrain; soften, tone down. See SUBJECTION, MODERATION.

subject, *n. & v.* —*n.* topic, theme; matter; liege, vassal; citizen. See SERV-ANT, INHABITANT. *Ant.*, see AUTHORITY. —*v.t.* reduce, control, restrain, tame. See SUBJECTION, RESTRAINT.

SUBJECTION [749]

Nouns—subjection, dependence, dependency; subordination; thrall, thral-dom, enthralment, subjugation, oppresssion, bondage, serfdom; feudalism, vassalage, villenage; slavery, enslavement, servitude; constraint, yoke, RESTRAINT; OBEDIENCE.

Verbs—1, be subject, be at the mercy of; depend, lean, *or* hang upon; fall a prey to, fall under, not dare to call one's soul one's own; drag a chain; serve (see SERVANT); obey, comply, submit.

2, subject, subjugate, break in, tame; master; tread down, tread under foot; enthrall, enslave, take captive; take into custody; rule (see AUTHORITY); drive into a corner, hold at sword's point; keep under; hold in bondage; tie to one's apron strings.

Adjectives—subject, dependent, subordinate; feudal, feudatory, in harness; subjected, enslaved, constrained, downtrodden, under the lash, led by the nose; henpecked; the puppet or plaything of; under orders *or* command; under one's thumb; a slave to; in the toils; at the mercy of, in the power, hands *or* clutches of; at the feet of; at one's beck and call (see OBEDIENCE).
Antonym, see FREEDOM.

subjective, *adj.* nonobjective; personal, individual, selfish; introspective, introverted. See THOUGHT.

subjugate, *v.t.* conquer, vanquish, master, subdue; overthrow; enslave. See SUBJECTION.

sublime, *adj.* inspiring, impressive; noble, lofty, exalted, elevated; superb, magnificent, glorious. See HEIGHT, REPUTE, BEAUTY.

submerge, *v.* drown, sink, plunge, dive, submerge, immerse, engulf, inundate; be overshadowed, subordinate to, play second fiddle to. See NAVIGATION, UNIMPORTANCE, WATER.

submission, *n.* submissiveness, nonresistance; OBEDIENCE; surrender, cession; capitulation; resignation; passivity, subjection.

submit, *v.* succumb, yield; bend; resign; defer to, obey; offer, send in (manuscripts, *etc.*); surrender, cede, capitulate, come to terms, give way *or* ground; give in, give up. *Slang,* throw in the towel *or* sponge; knuckle under; say uncle. See OBEDIENCE, CONFORMITY. *Ant.,* see OPPOSITION.

subordinate, *adj.* lower, inferior, secondary; dependent, subservient. See INFERIORITY, UNIMPORTANCE, SUBJECTION. *Ant.,* see SUPERIORITY, IMPORTANCE.

subscribe, *v.* sign, endorse, contribute; ASSENT, AID, abet, back, patronize; undertake, contract. *Ant.,* see DISAPPROBATION, REFUSAL.

subsequent, *adj.* succeeding, following, sequent, later, ensuing, consequent. See SEQUENCE.

subservient, *adj.* servile, submissive, obsequious, cringing, abject; subordinate, contributory, instrumental, subsidiary. See AID, SERVILITY. *Ant.,* see AUTHORITY, SUPERIORITY, IMPORTANCE.

subside, *v.i.* sink, fall, ebb, lower; abate, lessen; settle, precipitate. See DESCENT, DECREASE, GRAVITY. *Ant.,* see ASCENT, INCREASE.

subsist, *v.i.* exist, live, be, continue, survive, abide; eke out a living. See EXISTENCE.

subsistence, *n.* EXISTENCE, being, continuance; maintenance, livelihood, sustenance. See AID.

SUBSTANCE [3]

Nouns—**1,** substance, matter; *corpus,* frame, protoplasm, principle; person, thing, object, article; something, a being, an existence; creature, body, stuff.
2, substantiality, materiality, materialness, reality, corporeality; tangibility; flesh and blood.
3, physics, physical science; somatology, somatics; materialism; materialist, physicist.
Adjectives—substantive, substantial; sound, solid, personal; bodily, tangible, corporeal, real, MATERIAL.
Adverbs—substantially, bodily, essentially, *etc.,* on solid ground; in the flesh. *Antonym,* see INSUBSTANTIALITY.

---

substitute, *n., v. & adj.* —*n.* understudy, replacement, delegate, deputy, agent, factor; scapegoat; whipping boy; proxy; lieutenant, henchman, supplanter; representative; alternate; vicar; stopgap, expedient; SUBSTITUTION; shift, makeshift, apology for. *Colloq.,* sub, stand-in, dummy, ringer, pinchhitter. —*v.* replace, replace with *or* for; exchange, INTERCHANGE; understudy; depute, delegate, act for, play for; supersede; shift, exchange, supplant, alternate, take the place of. *Colloq.,* palm off, ring in, stand in (for), pinch hit (for), go to bat for, take the rap (for). —*adj.* artificial, ersatz; makeshift; imitation, counterfeit, pseudo, tentative, replacing, impermanent; resembling. *Colloq.,* near.

SUBSTITUTION [147]

Nouns—**1,** substitution, commutation; supplanting, supersession, replacement; metonymy (see FIGURATIVE); INTERCHANGE; TRANSFER.
2, substitute, proxy, makeshift, shift, *pis aller,* stopgap, jury-mast, *locum tenens;* dummy, scapegoat; double; changeling; *quid pro quo,* alternative; representative, surrogate, alternate, DEPUTY; viceroy, vicegerent, viceregent; palimpsest; PRICE, purchase money, consideration, equivalent. *Colloq.,* stand-in, pinch-hitter, ghostwriter. *Slang,* ringer, fall guy, goat, patsy.
Verbs—**1,** substitute, put in the place of, change for; deputize, accredit, appoint; make way for, give place to.
2, substitute *or* be deputy for; represent; stand for, appear *or* answer for; fill, step into *or* stand in the shoes of; take the place of, supplant, supersede,

replace, cut out; rob Peter to pay Paul. *Slang*, **cover up** for; be the goat; ghostwrite.

Adjectives—substitutive, substituted, vicarious, temporary; deputy, acting; vice, viceregal.

Adverbs—instead; in the place of, on behalf of, in lieu of, in the stead of; *faute de mieux*, by proxy.

Antonym, see IDENTITY.

subterfuge, *n.* ruse, shift, pretext, artifice, device, stratagem, evasion, CUNNING.

subtle, *adj.* sly, artful, crafty, wily, CUNNING; discerning, acute, penetrating; elusive, unobvious, abstruse, delicate; dainty, fragile, rarefied, ethereal, unsubstantial. See INTELLIGENCE, NARROWNESS. *Ant.*, see EVIDENCE, INFORMATION.

suburbs, *n.* outskirts, environs, purlieus. See NEARNESS.

subvert, *v.i.* overthrow, overturn, upset; ruin, fell, raze. See DESTRUCTION, DEPRESSION.

SUCCESS [731]

Nouns—**1,** success, successfulness; speed; advance, progress; good fortune, luck, run of luck; PROSPERITY; proficiency (see SKILL); profit, ACQUISITION; accomplishment (see COMPLETION).

2, great success, hit, stroke; (lucky) strike; master stroke; *coup de maître;* checkmate; half the battle, prize; trump card. *Colloq.*, smash, smash hit; sleeper, dark horse.

3, victory, triumph, advantage; upper hand, whip hand; ascendance, ascendancy, advantage, SUPERIORITY; mastery (see AUTHORITY); expugnation, conquest, subjugation, SUBJECTION.

4, winner, conqueror, victor; master of the situation.

Verbs—**1,** succeed; be successful, gain one's end *or* ends; crown with success; gain, carry *or* win a point; manage to, contrive to; accomplish, effect (see COMPLETION); do *or* work wonders; score a success.

2, speed, make progress, advance; win, make, *or* find one's way; prosper (see PROSPERITY); make profit (see ACQUISITION); reap the fruits *or* benefit of; reap *or* gather the harvest; make one's fortune, turn to good account. *Colloq.*, do a land-office business. *Slang*, sell like hotcakes; wow them, knock them dead.

3, win, prevail, triumph, be triumphant; gain *or* obtain a victory *or* advantage; master; get *or* have the best *or* better of; get *or* have the upper hand, ascendancy, *or* whip hand; distance, surpass (see SUPERIORITY); come off well, come off with flying colors; make short work of; take *or* carry by storm; win one's spurs; win the battle; win the day, carry the day, win *or* gain the prize *or* palm; have the best of it, have it all one's own way, call the turn, set the pace, have the world at one's feet; carry all before one, remain in possession of the field. *Slang*, win in a walk; romp home; score standing up.

4, defeat, conquer, vanquish, discomfit; overcome, overthrow, overpower, overmaster, overmatch, overset, override, overreach; outwit, outdo, outflank, outmaneuver, outgeneral, outvote; take the wind out of one's sails; beat, beat hollow; rout, lick, drub, floor, best, worst; put down, put to flight, put to rout.

5, surmount *or* overcome a difficulty *or* obstacle; make headway against; stem the torrent, tide, *or* current; weather the storm; turn a corner, keep one's head above water, tide over.

6, silence, quell, checkmate, upset, confound, nonplus, stalemate, trump; baffle (see HINDRANCE); circumvent, elude; trip up, drive into a corner, drive to the wall; run hard, put one's nose out of joint.

7, settle, do for; break the back of; capsize, sink, shipwreck, drown, swamp; subdue, subjugate, subject; victimize, roll in the dust, trample under foot.

8, answer, answer the purpose; avail, take effect, do, turn out well, work well, take, tell, bear fruit; hit the mark, hit the nail on the head; turn up trumps, make a hit; find one's account in.

Adjectives—succeeding, successful, fortunate; prosperous (see PROSPERITY);

triumphant; flushed *or* crowned with success; victorious; set up, in the
ascendant; unbeaten; felicitous, effective.

Adverbs—successfully, with flying colors, in triumph, swimmingly.

Antonym, see FAILURE.

---

succession, *n.* series; SEQUENCE, progression; heirship, inheritance, heritage,
primogeniture, reversion; lineage, family. See DESCENT.

succinct, *adj.* terse, concise, crisp, laconic, meaty, pithy, sententious. See
CONTRACTION, SHORTNESS. *Ant.,* see LOQUACITY.

succor, *v.t.* help, AID, assist, serve, comfort.

sudden, *adj.* abrupt, unexpected; hasty, quick, unpremeditated; instantaneous; precipitate; hot-tempered, rash. See SURPRISE, INSTANTANEITY.

sue, *v.* prosecute, bring suit, petition; beg, petition, solicit, REQUEST; court,
WOO. See LAWSUIT, ENDEARMENT.

suffer, *v.* —*v.t.* endure, encounter, undergo, experience, sustain; allow,
permit, tolerate. See FEELING, PERMISSION. —*v.i.* endure pain, be troubled,
ache; ail, be ill. See PAIN, DISEASE. *Ant.,* see PLEASURE, HEALTH.

SUFFICIENCY [639]

Nouns—**1,** sufficiency, adequacy, enough, satisfaction, competence; MEDIOC-
RITY; fill, fullness, completeness; plenitude, plenty; abundance, copiousness;
amplitude, profusion, prodigality; full measure; luxuriance, affluence,
WEALTH; fat of the land; cornucopia, horn of plenty; mine (see STORE); outpouring; flood. *Colloq.,* lots. *Slang,* scads, oodles, rafts, loads.
2, satiety, satiation, saturation, repletion, glut, excess, surfeit, superfluity;
too much of a good thing, a drug on the market.

Verbs—be sufficient, suffice, do, just do, satisfy, pass muster; sate, be satiated, have enough, eat, drink, *or* have one's fill; roll in, swim in; wallow in;
abound, exuberate, teem, flow, stream, rain, shower down; pour, pour in;
swarm, bristle with, replenish.

Adjectives—**1,** sufficient, enough, adequate, up to the mark, commensurate,
competent, satisfactory, valid, tangible; measured, moderate, temperate,
full, COMPLETE; ample; plenty, plentiful, plenteous; copious, abundant,
abounding, replete, enough and to spare, flush; chock-full, well-stocked,
well-provided; liberal; unstinted, unstinting; stintless; without stint; unsparing, unmeasured, lavish, wholesale; rich; luxuriant; affluent, WEALTHY;
big with, pregnant; unexhausted, unwasted; exhaustless, inexhaustible.
2, satiated, sated, gorged; blasé, jaded; sick (of), fed up.

Adverbs—sufficiently, amply, full, in abundance, in full measure; to one's
heart's content; *ad libitum,* without stint.

Antonym, see INSUFFICIENCY.

---

suffix, *n.* affix, addition, ending. See ADDITION.

suffocate, *v.* smother, stifle, asphyxiate; choke; extinguish; strangle. See
KILLING.

suffrage, *n.* franchise, right to vote; vote, ballot. See CHOICE.

sugar, *n.* sweetening, sucrose, lactose, glucose, dextrose, maltose, fructose,
etc. See SWEETNESS.

suggest, *v.t.* intimate, hint, insinuate; propose, submit; imply, connote;
recommend, advise, advocate. See INFORMATION, MEANING, ADVICE.

suggestive, *adj.* indicative, expressive; thought-provoking, stimulating; re-
mindful, mnemonic; risqué, indecent. See MEANING, SUPPOSITION, MEMORY.

suicide, *n.* self-destruction, self-ruin; *felo-de-se,* self-murder. See KILLING.

suit, *n. & v.* —*n.* petition, appeal, prayer; courtship, wooing; suite, retinue,
train; outfit, set, group, SEQUENCE; LAWSUIT, action, litigation. See RE-
QUEST, ENDEARMENT, ACCOMPANIMENT. —*v.t.* satisfy, please; become, befit;
fit, adapt. See AGREEMENT, BEAUTY.

suitable, *adj.* fitting, appropriate, proper, convenient, apropos, becoming,
fit, fitted, compatible. See AGREEMENT. *Ant.,* see UNCONFORMITY, DIS-
AGREEMENT.

suite, *n.* company, train, retinue, following, escort; set, series, group;
apartment. See ACCOMPANIMENT, CONTINUITY, RECEPTACLE, MUSIC.

suitor, *n.* lover, wooer. *Colloq.,* beau, swain, admirer, boy friend. See LOVE, ENDEARMENT.

sulk, *v.i.* be sullen, pout, mope; grumble, gripe, grouch. See IRASCIBILITY. *Ant.,* see CHEERFULNESS.

sulky, *adj.* sullen, unsocial, surly, morose, glum, moody, moping. See IRASCIBILITY. *Ant.,* see CHEERFULNESS.

sullen, *adj.* sulky; ill-tempered, ill-humored; out of sorts, temper *or* humor; crusty, crabbed; sour, surly, discourteous; moody; spleenish, splenetic; resentful; cross, cross-grained; perverse, wayward, froward; dogged, stubborn; grumpy, glum, grim, morose; scowling, glowering, growling; peevish, irascible. See IRASCIBILITY, DISCOURTESY. *Ant.,* see CHEERFULNESS, COURTESY.

sully, *v.* soil, stain, tarnish, smear; defile, dishonor, blemish, stigmatize. See UNCLEANNESS, DISREPUTE.

sultry, *adj.* hot, oppressive, sweltering, humid, muggy, stifling, close; voluptuous, sensual, sexy. See HEAT.

sum, *n.* QUANTITY, amount; total, aggregate, sum total; substance, gist; problem; summary. See WHOLE, MONEY. *Ant.,* part; see DISJUNCTION.

summary, *n. & adj.* —*n.* compendium, abridgment, abstract, brief, epitome, résumé, digest. —*adj.* prompt, expeditious, speedy, fast, immediate; brief, concise, compact, condensed. See EARLINESS, CONTRACTION. *Ant.,* see WHOLE.

summer, *n.* summertime, summertide; high point, zenith, acme, *etc.* See TIME.

summit, *n.* top, vertex, apex, zenith, pinnacle, acme, peak, culmination; meridian; utmost height; *ne plus ultra*; maximum; climax; culminating, high, crowning *or* turning point; tiptop; crown, point, crest, cap; extremity; mountain top; housetop, rooftop. See HEIGHT. *Ant.,* see LOWNESS, BASE.

summon, *v.t.* call, send for; cite, arraign, subp(o)ena; convoke; rouse, invoke, evoke. See COMMAND, LAWSUIT.

sumptuous, *adj.* lavish, luxurious, splendid, imposing, costly. See OSTENTATION. *Ant.,* see SIMPLENESS, POVERTY.

sun, *n.* daystar, Sol; sunshine, sunlight; prosperity, happiness; star. See UNIVERSE.

sunder, *v.t.* break, separate, sever, dissever, divide. See DISJUNCTION.

sundry, *adj.* various, divers; several, numerous. See MULTITUDE.

sun-god, Ra, Helios, Phoebus, Apollo, Sol, Saturn, Kon-Tiki. See MYTHICAL DEITIES.

sunny, *adj.* warm, bright, sunshiny; cheerful, cheery, blithe; prosperous, palmy, halcyon. See HEAT, CHEERFULNESS, PROSPERITY.

sunrise, *n.* dawn, prime, daybreak, dayspring, aurora, cockcrow, sunup. See MORNING, TIME.

sunset, *n.* twilight, sundown, dusk, nightfall, curfew, eventide. See EVENING, TIME.

superb, *adj.* magnificent, impressive, stately; admirable, excellent; costly, rich; gorgeous, sumptuous. See GOODNESS, BEAUTY.

supercilious, *adj.* disdainful, contemptuous, scornful; arrogant, cavalier. See INSOLENCE.

superficial, *adj.* SHALLOW, cursory, dilettante, slight, slender, trivial, inane; surface, skin-deep. See UNIMPORTANCE. *Ant.,* see DEPTH, GRAVITY.

superfluous, *adj.* unnecessary, needless; excessive, overmuch. See REPETITION.

superintend, *v.t.* oversee, direct, control; boss. See DIRECTION, AUTHORITY.

SUPERIORITY [33]

Nouns—**1,** superiority; greatness, excellence (see GOODNESS); majority, plurality; advantage; preponderance, preponderation; vantage point *or* ground, prevalence, partiality; lead, gain; NOBILITY.
2, supremacy, primacy, preëminence, precedence; victory, triumph; championship; maximum; climax; culmination, SUMMIT, transcendence, transcendency, prepotence, *ne plus ultra;* lion's share, excess, surplus; PERFECTION, sovereignty (see AUTHORITY).
Verbs—be superior, exceed, excel, transcend; outdo, outbalance, outweigh,

outrival; pass, surpass, get ahead of; overtop, override, overpass, over-balance, overweigh, overmatch; top, cap, beat, cut out; beat hollow; outstrip, eclipse, throw into the shade, put one's nose out of joint; have the upper hand, have the whip hand, have the advantage; turn the scale, play first fiddle (see IMPORTANCE); preponderate, predominate, pre-vail; precede, take precedence, come first; come to a head, culminate; beat all others, bear the palm, break the record; become larger, INCREASE, expand.

Adjectives—superior, greater, major, higher; exceeding; great, distinguished, ultra; vaulting; more than a match for; supreme, greatest, utmost, para-mount, preëminent, foremost, crowning; first-rate, important, excellent, unrivaled, peerless, matchless; champion, second to none, nonpareil; un-paralleled, unequaled, unapproached, unsurpassed; superlative, inimitable, incomparable, sovereign, without parallel, *ne plus ultra;* beyond compare, beyond comparison; culminating, topmost; transcendent, transcendental; increased, enlarged. *Slang,* tops.

Adverbs—beyond, more, over; over the mark, above the mark; above par, at the top of the scale, at its height; eminently, preëminently, surpassing, prominently, superlatively, supremely, above all, *par excellence*, principally, especially, particularly, peculiarly, even, yea, still more.

Antonym, see INFERIORITY.

supernatural, *adj.* miraculous, preternatural; abnormal, unearthly, super-human, occult. See UNCONFORMITY, PREDICTION.

supersede, *v.t.* replace, displace, supplant, succeed. See SUBSTITUTION.

supervision, *n.* oversight, surveillance, superintendence. See DIRECTION.

supine, *adj.* recumbent, reclining, prostrate; apathetic, sluggish, torpid; indifferent, passive. See DIRECTION, INACTIVITY, INSENSIBILITY. *Ant.,* prone, erect.

supple, *adj.* limber, lithe, pliant, flexible; yielding, compliant, adaptable; fawning, servile. See SOFTNESS. *Ant.,* see HARDNESS.

supplement, *n.* adjunct, ADDITION, addendum, appendix, complement, con-clusion. See COMPLETION.

supplicate, *v.t.* entreat, petition, pray, beg, beseech. See REQUEST.

supply, *v.t.* PROVIDE, furnish, give, afford, present, contribute, substitute.

SUPPORT [215]

Nouns—**1,** support, maintenance, upkeep, sustenance.

2, ground, foundation, groundwork, substratum, BASE, basis; *terra firma;* purchase, grip, footing, hold, foothold, toehold, handhold; landing, landing stage, landing place; stage, platform; block; rest, resting place; basement, supporter, AID, prop, stand; anvil, bearing; fulcrum, rowlock, oarlock; stay, shore, skid, rib, lap; bar, rod, boom, sprit, outrigger.

3, staff, stick, crutch, alpenstock, baton.

4, post, pillar, shaft, column, pilaster; pediment, pedicle; pedestal; plinth, shank, leg; buttress, jamb, mullion, abutment; baluster, banister, stanchion; balustrade, railing.

5, frame, framework; scaffold, skeleton, beam, rafter, girder, lintel, joist, travis, trave, cornerstone, summer, transom; rung, round, step, sill, tholepin.

6, backbone; keystone; axle, axletree; axis; arch, mainstay.

7, board, ledge, shelf, hob, bracket, trevet, trivet, arbor, rack; mantel, mantelpiece, mantelshelf; slab, console; counter, dresser; flange, corbel; table, trestle; shoulder; perch; stand, sawhorse, horse; easel, desk.

8, seat, throne, dais; divan; chair, bench, form, stool, sofa, settee, stall, armchair, easy chair, rocking chair, Morris chair; love seat, couch, *fauteuil,* ottoman, settle, bench; saddle; pillion; saddle; pommel.

9, bed, berth, bunk, pallet, tester, crib, cot, hammock, shakedown, cradle, litter, stretcher, bedstead; bedding, mattress, paillasse, box spring, spring, pillow, bolster; mat, rug, carpet, linoleum, cushion, four-poster, truckle bed; chair bed, sofa bed, convertible.

10, footstool, hassock; tabo(u)ret; tripod.

11, Atlas, Persides, Atlantes, Caryatides, Hercules.

Verbs—**1,** be supported; lie, sit, recline, lean, loll, rest, stand, step, repose, abut, bear *or* be based on; have at one's back; bestride, straddle, bestraddle.

2, support, bear, carry, hold, sustain, shoulder; hold, back, bolster, shore up; uphold, bear; shore up, prop; underpin; bandage, tape, brace.
3, give *or* support foundations; found, base, ground, imbed, embed.
4, maintain, keep on foot; AID.
Adjectives—supporting, supported, braced, propped, bolstered; founded, based, basic, grounded, built on; fundamental, bottom, undermost.
Adverbs—astride, astraddle.
Antonym, see PENDENCY.

SUPPOSITION [514]

Nouns—supposition, assumption, postulation, condition, presupposition, hypothesis, postulate, theory, data; proposition, position; thesis, theorem; proposal; conceit; conjecture; guess, guesswork; rough guess, shot; surmise, suspicion, inkling, suggestion, association of ideas, hint; presumption (see BELIEF); divination, speculation.
Verbs—**1,** suppose, conjecture, surmise, suspect, guess, divine; theorize; presume, presuppose; assume, fancy, take it; give a guess, speculate, believe, dare say, take it into one's head, take for granted.
2, put forth; propound, propose; start, put *or* give a case, move, make a motion; hazard a suggestion *or* conjecture; put forward a suggestion; submit; allude to, suggest, hint, put it into one's head.
Adjectives—supposing, supposed, given, postulatory; assumed, suppositive, supposititious; gratuitous, speculative, conjectural, hypothetical, theoretical, supposable, presumptive, putative, academic; suggestive, allusive.
Adverbs—supposedly, theoretically, seemingly, if, if so be; on the supposition of, in case of, in the event of; quasi, as if, provided; perhaps; for all one knows; for the sake of argument.
Antonym, see KNOWLEDGE.

suppress, *v.t.* put down, quell, subdue; repress, restrain; conceal; quash; withhold; abolish, ban; stanch, check. See RESTRAINT, CONCEALMENT. *Ant.,* see FREEDOM.
supremacy, *n.* mastery, SUPERIORITY, ascendancy, domination, AUTHORITY.
supreme, *adj.* highest, utmost, paramount, prime, chief, dominant. See SUPERIORITY.
sure, *adj.* certain, positive; dependable, trustworthy; safe, secure; confident, convinced; unfailing, infallible. See CERTAINTY, SAFETY, PROBITY. *Ant.,* see DOUBT, DANGER.
surface, *n.* outside, EXTERIOR, superficies; outward aspect. *Ant.,* see INTERIOR.
surfeit, *n.* excess, glut, superfluity, superabundance, plethora; SATIETY, repletion, engorgement. See SUFFICIENCY. *Ant.,* see INSUFFICIENCY.
surge, *v.i.* rise, swell, billow, seethe, swirl; sweep, rush, stream, gush. See WATER, ASSEMBLAGE.
surly, *adj.* sullen, morose, churlish, gruff, uncivil. See DISCOURTESY, IRASCIBILITY. *Ant.,* urbane, affable; see COURTESY.
surmise, *v.t.* guess, conjecture, suppose, suspect, presume. See BELIEF, SUPPOSITION.
surmount, *v.t.* overtop, rise above; master, surpass, transcend; crown, cap, top; scale, climb over; overcome, conquer. See HEIGHT, ASCENT, SUCCESS. *Ant.,* see FAILURE.
surpass, *v.t.* exceed, excel, overtop, outshine, outdo, outclass, eclipse, outstrip. See SUPERIORITY.
surplus, *n.* surplusage; excess, oversupply, glut; REMAINDER, overage; profit, balance. See SUFFICIENCY, REPETITION. *Ant.,* see INSUFFICIENCY.

SURPRISE [508]

Nouns—nonexpectation, unexpectedness, the unforeseen, unforeseen contingency, miscalculation, astonishment, wonder, surprise, thunderclap, blow, shock, bolt out of the blue.
Verbs—**1,** not expect, be taken by surprise, miscalculate, not bargain for.
2, be unexpected, come unawares, turn up, pop up, drop from the clouds, burst, steal, creep upon one, take by surprise, take unawares, catch napping.

Slang, come from left field.

3, surprise, astonish, amaze, astound; dumfound, startle, dazzle; strike with wonder *or* awe; electrify; stun, stagger, strike dumb, stupefy, petrify, confound, bewilder, flabbergast, fascinate, turn the head, take away one's breath; make one's hair stand on end, make one's eyes pop, take by surprise. *Colloq.*, bowl over, knock for a loop.

Adjectives—**1,** surprised, nonexpectant, unsuspecting, unwarned, off one's guard, inattentive. See WONDER.

2, surprising, unexpected, unlooked for, unforeseen, unhoped for, beyond expectation, unheard of, startling, sudden.

Adverbs—surprisingly, unexpectedly, abruptly, plump, pop, unawares, without warning, like a bolt from the blue, suddenly. *Colloq.*, smack.

Antonym, see EXPECTATION.

surrender, *n. & v.* —*n.* capitulation, cession; RELINQUISHMENT, abandonment, SUBMISSION. —*v.* capitulate, yield, give up; cede, renounce, relinquish. *Ant.*, see OPPOSITION.

surround, *v.t.* encompass, enclose, hem in, encircle; ring; circumscribe; environ; invest, besiege; embrace. See NEARNESS, RESTRAINT, ATTACK.

surrounding, *v.t.* circumjacent, circumambient, encircling, circumferential; suburban, neighboring, environmental. See NEARNESS.

survey, *v.t.* view, examine, inspect, appraise; measure, lay out, plot. See VISION, MEASUREMENT.

survive, *v.* outlive, outlast; live; escape (with one's life); continue, persist, remain, endure, abide, last. See DURABILITY, LIFE. *Ant.*, see DEATH, END.

susceptibility, *n.* liability; allergy; propensity; vulnerability; impressionableness, sensitivity, SENSIBILITY. See TENDENCY. *Ant.*, see HARDNESS, RESOLUTION.

suspect, *v.t.* surmise, infer, conjecture, imagine, suppose, believe; mistrust, DOUBT. See SUPPOSITION. *Ant.*, see BELIEF.

suspend, *v.t.* hang, dangle; defer, postpone, stave off; adjourn, recess, intermit, prorogue, interrupt; debar, exclude. See SUPPORT, LATENESS, END.

suspense, *n.* anxiety, apprehension; uncertainty, indecision, hesitation; discontinuance, interruption, pause, cessation; inaction, abeyance. See EXPECTATION, DOUBT.

suspicion, *n.* mistrust, distrust, apprehension; DOUBT, misgiving, jealousy; SUPPOSITION, inkling, intimation, hint; trace, touch, shade, modicum. See LITTLENESS. *Ant.*, see BELIEF.

sustain, *v.t.* bear up, SUPPORT; maintain, prolong, protract; nourish, provide for; suffer, undergo, experience; uphold, encourage, comfort; corroborate, confirm, ratify, substantiate; maintain without a sponsor (*Radio & TV*). See AID, CONTINUITY, FOOD.

sustenance, *n.* FOOD, nourishment; SUPPORT, maintenance, subsistence; AID.

swagger, *v. & n.* —*v.i.* strut, stalk, BLUSTER, boast, bully. —*n.* arrogance, braggadocio, pomposity. *Colloq.*, swank, side. See VANITY, OSTENTATION. *Ant.*, see MODESTY, SIMPLENESS.

swallow, *v.t.* ingest, gulp, devour, consume; absorb, engulf, assimilate, envelop; retract; bear, endure, submit to; believe, accept. See FOOD, SUBJECTION, CREDULITY.

swarm, *n.* group, crowd, MULTITUDE, horde, colony, hive. See ASSEMBLAGE.

swarthy, *adj.* dark, swart, dusky; dark-complexioned. See COLOR, DARKNESS. *Ant.*; see COLORLESSNESS.

sway, *v. & n.* —*v.* swing, rock; influence, direct, control, rule, bias, prejudice, warp; lurch, rock, roll, reel, dangle, swing. —*n.* domination, rule; influence; OSCILLATION. See CAUSE, AUTHORITY, AGITATION.

swear, *v.i.* affirm, depose, depone, vow; testify, witness; blaspheme, curse. See AFFIRMATION, EVIDENCE, IMPRECATION.

sweep, *v.* brush, clean, vacuum; push, drive, blow, impel; scan; strum; bend, curve; stream, glide, skim. See CLEANNESS, CURVATURE, MOTION.

sweetheart, *n.* lover, love, suitor, beloved, truelove, ladylove. *Colloq.*, beau, swain, boy friend, girl, best girl. *Slang*, gal, sweetie, flame, steady. See LOVE, ENDEARMENT.

SWEETNESS [396]

Nouns—**1**, sweetness, sugariness, saccharinity; sweetening, sugar, molasses, honey, sirup, syrup; saccharine; nectar.

2, sweets, confection, confectionery, confectionary; conserve, preserve, confiture, jam, julep; sugarplum; licorice, marmalade, caramel, candy, candy bar, lollipop, lemon drops, chewing gum, bonbon, jujube, comfit, sweetmeat; taffy, butterscotch, peppermint, chocolate, fudge, *etc.;* manna, nectar, mead, liqueur, cordial, sweet wine, punch; soda, soda water *or* pop, lemonade, carbonated drink; pastry, pie, tart, cream puff, pudding; ice cream, custard; dessert.

3, amiability, gentleness, kindness, good disposition or humor, COURTESY; dearness, lovableness; sentimentality, stickiness.

Verbs—be sweet; sweeten; sugar-coat; candy; mull.

Adjectives—**1**, sweet, saccharine; dulcet, candied, honeyed; luscious, lush; sweetened; sweet as sugar, honey, *or* candy; sugar-coated, sirupy.

2, amiable, gentle, courteous, *etc.;* dear, lovable, affectionate.

Antonym, see SOUR, DISCOURTESY.

---

swell, *v. & n.* —*v.i.* expand, dilate, bulge, protrude; billow; INCREASE, grow, surge. —*n.* swelling, INCREASE; billow, wave, groundswell, sea, roller; rise, slope, knoll. See CONVEXITY. *Slang,* aristocrat, toff. *Ant.,* see DECREASE, CONTRACTION.

swelter, *v.i.* perspire, sweat; be hot. See HEAT.

swerve, *v.i.* turn aside, deviate, shift, sheer, veer, yaw; dodge. See DEVIATION, AVOIDANCE.

swift, *adj.* quick, rapid, fast, fleet, speedy; expeditious. See VELOCITY. *Ant.,* see SLOWNESS.

swindle, *v.t.* defraud, hoax, cheat, fleece, victimize, trick. *Slang,* gyp. See STEALING, DECEPTION.

swine, *n.* pig, hog, porker, sow, boar; scoundrel; sloven, wretch. See ANIMAL, POPULACE.

swing, *v. & n.* —*v.i.* oscillate, sway, wag; depend, dangle; pivot, turn. See OSCILLATION, SUPPORT. —*n.* sweep, sway; rhythm, lilt; scope, range, latitude, FREEDOM; REGULARITY.

switch, *n. & v.* —*n.* twig, sprig, spray; rod, cane, birch; shunt. *Slang,* paraphrase; CHANGE, new version. —*v.t.* cane, whip, lash; shunt, deflect, turn, shift; paraphrase, modify *or* change; transpose. See PUNISHMENT, DEVIATION.

sword, *n.* blade, broadsword, falchion, glaive; rapier, foil, épée, saber, cutlass, *etc.;* war, vengeance, destruction. See ARMS, WARFARE.

sycophant, *n.* parasite, toady, bootlicker, lickspittle, flatterer, fawner, truckler. See SERVILITY.

syllable, *n.* sonant, phone; (*pl.*) tone, accent, inflection. See SPEECH.

symbol, *n.* token, emblem, mark, badge, device, character, letter. See INDICATION, WRITING.

symbolize, *v.t.* represent, indicate, signify, typify, mean, betoken, express, imply. See MEANING, INDICATION.

symmetry, *n.* shapeliness, finish; BEAUTY; proportion, harmony, eurhythm; FORM, uniformity; balance, parallelism; congruity, order. See ARRANGEMENT. *Ant.,* see DISTORTION.

sympathize, *v.i.* feel for, sorrow for; condole; understand; feel sorry for, commiserate. See FEELING.

sympathizer, *n.* upholder, supporter, advocate, champion, well-wisher; commiserator, condoler, FRIEND. See AID. *Ant.,* ENEMY.

sympathy, *n.* AGREEMENT, understanding, accord; compassion, PITY, condolence, commiseration, fellow-feeling; empathy. See FRIEND, ASSENT.

symptom, *n.* sign, INDICATION, token, mark.

synchronism, *n.* synchronization; coexistence; coincidence; simultaneousness; concurrence, concomitance; isochronism; contemporaneousness; interim, meantime. See TIME.

syndicate, *n.* cartel, combine, pool, monopoly, trust; directorate. See PARTY.

synonym, *n.* equivalent, word; see MEANING, WORD. *Ant.*, antonym.

synonymous, *adj.* similar, equivalent, analogous. See MEANING.

system, *n.* coördination, organization, routine, ARRANGEMENT, METHOD, PLAN; classification; complex. *Ant.*, see DISORDER.

T

table, *n.* board; slab; desk, counter; FOOD, diet, fare; cuisine, menu; index, compendium, catalog(ue); chart, tabulation, LIST, schedule; tableland, plateau, mesa. See SMOOTHNESS.

taboo, tabu, *n., v. & adj.* —*n.* prohibition, interdiction, forbiddance. —*v.t.* forbid, prohibit, keep inviolate. —*adj.* forbidden; untouchable, unprofanable, inviolate. See RESTRAINT.

tacit, *adj.* unspoken, unexpressed; silent, mute; implied, understood. See SILENCE. *Ant.*, see INFORMATION.

taciturn, *adj.* reserved, reticent, close, close-mouthed, secretive; curt, laconic. See CONCEALMENT, SILENCE. *Ant.*, see LOQUACITY, DISCLOSURE.

tack, *n. & v.* —*n.* thumbtack, carpet tack, *etc.;* nail; change of course, yaw, veer; route, course, path. —*v.* change course *or* direction; yaw; zigzag (while sailing). See DEVIATION.

tackle, *n. & v.* —*n.* pulley; gear, equipment, apparatus, instruments; luggage. —*v.t.* grapple with; seize; address, attack; attempt, try, undertake. See UNDERTAKING.

tact, *n.* diplomacy; finesse; discretion, consideration. See SKILL, COURTESY. *Ant.*, see DISCOURTESY.

tactics, *n.* strategy, generalship; CONDUCT; maneuvering; policy, diplomacy; mode, METHOD.

tag, *n.* stub, tab, flap; tail, tassel, pendant; slogan, phrase, name, catchword; tatter, shred, rag. See ADDITION, END, INDICATION.

tail, *n.* appendage, END; cauda; tip, extremity; REAR, rudder, queue, pigtail, train. *Slang,* shadow. *Ant.*, see FRONT.

taint, *v. & n.* —*v.* corrupt, spoil, poison; be corrupted; tarnish, stain, sully; pollute, infect, contaminate. —*n.* corruption; spoilage; stigma, dishonor, defilement; fault, flaw, blemish. See IMPROBITY, DISEASE, DISREPUTE, IMPERFECTION. *Ant.*, see PROBITY, HEALTH, PERFECTION.

take, *v. & n.* —*v.* catch, nab, bag, pocket; capture, seize; take away, deduct; receive; accept; reap, crop, gather; get, draw; acquire, appropriate, assume, confiscate, take possession of; lay hands on; commandeer, help oneself to; snatch, grab; pre-empt, usurp; expropriate; deprive of; take *or* carry off; abstract; plagiarize, shoplift, pirate; steal, filch; take by storm; snap up, pick up; do; work; be effective; snap a picture. *Slang,* latch onto, hook, snag. —*n.* taking. *Colloq.*, receipts, gate, haul, swag; shooting of a scene (*photography*). See ACQUISITION, STEALING. *Ant.*, see GIVING, RELINQUISHMENT, LOSS.

taking, *n. & adj.* —*n.* reception; RECEIVING; appropriation, expropriation, confiscation; apprehension; seizure; abduction; subtraction, deduction; abstraction; extortion, theft, STEALING, kidnap(p)ing; dispossession; deprivation, bereavement, DIVESTMENT; distraint, distress; commandeering; attachment; haul, catch. —*adj.* fetching, winning, endearing. See ACQUISITION.

tale, *n.* story, account, recital; count, counting, tally; report; fable, yarn, legend. See DESCRIPTION, NUMERATION, FALSEHOOD.

talent, *n.* gift, faculty, ability, POWER; turn, knack, aptitude; genius. See SKILL. *Ant.*, see UNSKILLFULNESS.

talented, *adj.* gifted; brilliant, artistic. See SKILL. *Ant.*, see UNSKILLFULNESS.

talisman, *n.* lucky piece; charm, amulet, fetish. See SORCERY.

talk, *n. & v.* —*n.* CONVERSATION; chatter, chat, gossip; SPEECH; lecture, discourse; rumor, hearsay. —*v.* say, speak, chat, converse. See INFORMATION, LOQUACITY, COMMUNICATION.

talkative, *adj.* talky, verbose; gossipy; garrulous, prattling, prolix, loquacious, glib, fluent. *Slang,* windy. See LOQUACITY. *Ant.,* TACITURN.

tall, *adj.* high, lofty, towering; long, long-limbed; exaggerated. See HEIGHT. *Ant.,* see LOWNESS.

tally, *n. & v.* —*n.* count, tale, counting; score, check; match, matching; roll call. —*v.* count, tell; suit, correspond, agree, harmonize; check. See LIST, NUMERATION, INDICATION, AGREEMENT.

tame, *adj. & v.* —*adj.* tamed, domestic, domesticated; broken, subdued; meek, gentle; flat; spiritless, feeble. —*v.t.* subdue, cow, break; harness; domesticate. See DOMESTICATION, SUBJECTION. *Ant.,* see VIOLENCE.

tamper, *v.i.* meddle, intermeddle, interfere; bribe, seduce, corrupt, taint; CHANGE, alter. *Colloq.,* doctor, monkey (with). See ACTIVITY, DETERIORATION.

tang, *n.* savor, flavor, TASTE, zest; sharpness, PUNGENCY, tanginess; bite, nip, snappiness.

tangible, *adj.* material, real; touchable, palpable; concrete, perceptible. See FEELING, SUBSTANCE. *Ant.,* see INSUBSTANTIALITY.

tangle, *n. & v.* —*n.* snarl, mixup, jumble, mattedness; complication, involvement. —*v.* mat, snarl; knot, mix inextricably; snare, trap, enmesh; embroil, complicate. See MIXTURE, DISORDER, DIFFICULTY. *Ant.,* see ARRANGEMENT.

tank, *n.* reservoir, cistern; boiler; (*pl.*) armor; panzer; pond, swimming pool. See WATER, RECEPTACLE, STORE, ARMS.

tantalize, *v.* tease, tempt, excite, provoke (with false hopes); balk. See DESIRE. *Ant.,* see EXPECTATION, SUCCESS.

tantrum, *n.* fit, outburst; display (of ill temper); rage, passion, frenzy, paroxysm. See RESENTMENT, IRASCIBILITY. *Ant.,* MODERATION.

tap, *n. & v.* —*n.* spigot, faucet, valve; plug, bung, stopper; knock, rap; tapping, tap dance, soft shoe; shoe tap; taproom, bar, saloon. —*v.* knock, rap, strike, TOUCH; tapdance; broach, draw off (liquor, *etc.*); wiretap; draw upon, nominate. See IMPULSE, OPENING.

taper, *v. & n.* —*v.* narrow; come to a point; lessen, slacken, slack off. —*n.* candle, LIGHT; pyramidal *or* cone shape. See NARROWNESS.

tardy, *adj.* overdue, late, behindtime; slow, slack, dilatory. See LATENESS. *Ant.,* see EARLINESS.

target, *n.* aim, mark; goal; bull's-eye; quarry, object; butt. See PURSUIT.

tariff, *n.* duty, customs, impost. See TAX. *Colloq.,* price, cost.

tarnish, *v.* smirch, taint; dishonor; stain, sully, besmirch; defame; dull, smudge, dim, spot, blemish. See IMPERFECTION, DISREPUTE, UNCLEANNESS. *Ant.,* see REPUTE, CLEANNESS.

tarry, *v.i.* linger, stay, wait; idle, dawdle; visit (with); bide a while, sojourn; procrastinate, delay, dally. See LATENESS, CONTINUITY. *Ant.,* see TRANSIENTNESS.

tart, *adj. & n.* —*adj.* acid, SOUR; sarcastic, acerbic; snappy, sharp; astringent. —*n.* small pie. *Slang,* strumpet. See TASTE, DISCOURTESY.

task, *n. & v.* —*n.* work, stint, job, labor; lesson, assignment, charge, DUTY, chore; drudgery, burden. —*v.t.* strain, tax, overburden, overwork; impose, assign, charge. See BUSINESS, TEACHING, USE, WEARINESS.

taskmaster, *n.* overseer, martinet; slavedriver. See DIRECTION, SEVERITY.

TASTE [390, 850]

Nouns—**1,** taste, tastefulness; good taste, cultivated taste; delicacy, refinement, tact, finesse; nicety, DISCRIMINATION; polish, ELEGANCE; grace; virtû; connoisseurship, dilettantism; fine art; culture, cultivation, fastidiousness; aesthetics.

2, taste, flavor, gusto, savor; sapor, sapidity, aftertaste, tang; sample; tinge, bit, trace, scarp, soupçon; tasting, gustation, degustation; palate, tongue, tooth, stomach.

3, savoriness, tastiness, palatability; unsavoriness, unpalatability, austerity; sweetness, sourness, acidity, acerbity; PUNGENCY.

4, seasoning, CONDIMENT; spice, relish; tidbit, dainty, delicacy, morsel, appetizer, *hors d'oeuvres,* antipasto, delicatessen; ambrosia; nectar; rue, hemlock, myrrh, aloes, gall and wormwood.

5, man of taste, connoisseur; epicure, gourmet; judge, critic, virtuoso; amateur, dilettante.

Verbs—**1,** have good taste, appreciate; judge, criticize, discriminate, distinguish, particularize; single out, draw the line, sift, estimate, weigh, consider, diagnose; pick and choose, split hairs, know which is which.

2, savor, taste, sample; relish, like, enjoy, smack the lips; tickle the palate; turn the stomach, disgust; pall, stale, spoil; sour, curdle, ferment, turn.

Adjectives—**1,** in good taste; tasteful, unaffected, pure, chaste, classical, cultivated, refined; dainty, nice, delicate, aesthetic, artistic; elegant; euphemistic; fastidious, discriminating, discriminative, discerning, perceptive; to one's taste, after one's fancy; *comme il faut.*

2, tasty, flavorful, sapid, saporific; palatable, gustable, gustatory, tastable; PUNGENT, strong; flavored, spicy, hot; sweet, sour, salt, bitter; SAVORY, UNSAVORY.

Adverbs—tastefully, elegantly; purely, aesthetically, *etc.*

Antonym, see VULGARITY.

tasteless, *adj.* insipid, flat; inelegant; inept, clumsy, vulgar, savorless, unappetizing. See INSIPIDITY, VULGARITY, TASTE.

tattle, *v.* prattle, prate; chat, chatter; jabber, talk; reveal (a secret), inform. *Colloq.,* peach, tell on, tell tales. *Slang,* blab; spill the beans. See LOQUACITY, DISCLOSURE. *Ant.,* see SECRET.

taunt, *v.* RIDICULE, scoff, jeer, twit; mock, flout, deride. See ACCUSATION.

taut, *adj.* tight, stretched, tense, strained; keyed up, on edge; snug, tidy, shipshape. See HARDNESS, ARRANGEMENT. *Ant.,* see SOFTNESS, DISORDER.

tautology, *n.* REPETITION, reiteration; redundance; verbosity.

tawdry, *adj.* cheap, showy, flashy; loud, garish; tinsel, gimcrack. See VULGARITY, OSTENTATION. *Ant.,* see ELEGANCE.

tax, *n. & v.* —*n.* assessment, levy, duty, tariff, excise, toll, tithe; impost, custom; rate, income tax, internal revenue. *Slang,* charge. —*v.* assess, rate, COMMAND; charge, accuse; take to task; strain, overwork, burden, fatigue. See ACCUSATION, PAYMENT, EXERTION.

TEACHING [537]

Nouns—**1,** teaching, instruction, edification, education, tuition; tutorship, tutelage; direction, guidance; preparation, training, schooling; discipline; exercise, drill, practice; indoctrination, inculcation, inoculation; explanation, INTERPRETATION. See SCHOOL.

2, lesson, lecture, sermon; apologue, parable; discourse, prelection, preachment; exercise, task.

3, teacher, educator, trainer, instructor, master, tutor, director, coach, disciplinarian; professor, lecturer, reader, prelector, prolocutor; preacher; pastor (see CLERGY); schoolmaster, dominie, pedagogue, abecedarian; schoolmistress, governess; monitor; expositor, interpreter; preceptor, guide, mentor, adviser (see ADVICE); pioneer, apostle, missionary, propagandist.

Verbs—**1,** teach, instruct, edify, school, tutor; cram, prime, coach; enlighten, inform; inculcate, indoctrinate, inoculate, infuse, instil, infiltrate; imbue, impregnate, implant; graft, sow the seeds of, disseminate; give an idea of; put up to, set right, sharpen the wits, broaden one's horizon, open the eyes, bring forward, improve; direct, guide; direct attention to, impress upon the mind *or* memory; beat into, beat into the head; convince (see BELIEF).

2, expound, interpret, lecture, hold forth, preach; sermonize, moralize.

3, train, discipline; bring up, educate, form, ground, prepare, qualify, drill, exercise, practice; nurture, breed, rear, take in hand; break, break in; tame; preinstruct; initiate, inure, habituate. *Collop.,* show the ropes.

Adjectives—teaching, taught, educational; scholastic, academic, doctrinal; disciplinal, disciplinary; instructive, didactic, homiletic; professorial, pedagogic.

Antonym, see LEARNING.

team, *n.* crew, side, aggregation; nine, five, eleven (baseball, basketball *and* football teams); rig, span (of horses); combat team, group; brace, pair, foursome, *etc.* See ASSEMBLAGE, COÖPERATION.

tear, *v. & n.* —*v.* rip, rend, tatter, shred; split, burst, break, part, separate; give; snatch, race; speed, dash, fly. —*n.* break, rent, split; wound; crack, fissure, gap; teardrop (see TEARS). *Slang,* binge, toot, spree, bender, jag. See DISJUNCTION. *Ant.,* mend; see JUNCTION, RESTORATION.

tears, *n.* teardrops; weeping, crying, LAMENTATION.

tease, *v.* plague, annoy, vex, harass; taunt, mock; beg; tantalize; titillate, excite. See PAIN, REQUEST, EXPECTATION.

technique, *n.* technic, execution, style, METHOD. See SKILL.

tedious, *adj.* wearisome, wearing, dry, dry-as-dust, boring, tiresome; irksome; DULL, monotonous, prosy, uninteresting. See WEARINESS, DRYNESS. *Ant.,* see AMUSEMENT.

teem, *v.i.* swarm, abound; multiply, pullulate; rain heavily, pour; bear, generate, produce. See PRODUCTION, SUFFICIENCY.

teeming, *adj.* swarming, abounding, abundant, plentiful; crowded, chockfull, jam-packed; replete, fraught, full, pullulating; raining. See MULTITUDE, SUFFICIENCY. *Ant.,* see RARITY.

teeter, *v.i.* seesaw, rock, sway, totter, tremble; hesitate, vacillate. See OSCILLATION, DOUBT.

teetotal, *adj.* *Colloq.,* all, entire, WHOLE; abstinent; dry, prohibitionist. *Ant.,* see DRUNKENNESS.

telegram, *n.* message; wire, cable. See COMMUNICATION.

telepathy, *n.* psychic communication, thought transference, extrasensory perception; psi.

telephone, *v.* call [up], phone, dial, get through to. See COMMUNICATION.

telescope, *n. & v.* —*n.* glass, spyglass, fieldglass. —*v.* collapse, fold; foreshorten, condense, abridge. See OPTICAL INSTRUMENTS.

tell, *v.* recount, relate, narrate; inform, apprise, acquaint; explain; weigh, matter, influence; reveal, disclose, own, confess, acknowledge, discern, distinguish, make out, see; count, number, reckon, tally; speak, state, declare. See INFORMATION, DESCRIPTION, IMPORTANCE, SPEECH, NUMBER.

temerity, *n.* RASHNESS, boldness, audacity, recklessness, daring. *Slang,* nerve, gall, brass, cheek. *Ant.,* CAUTION, COWARDICE.

temper, *n. & v.* —*n.* temperament, nature, disposition; mood, humor, tone; tantrum, passion, rage; mettle, quality; calmness, composure, equanimity. See IRASCIBILITY, WILL. —*v.t.* moderate, soften; harden, anneal, toughen. See HARDNESS, SOFTNESS.

temperament, *n.* constitution; disposition; nature; humor. See WILL.

temperance, *n.* MODERATION; forbearance; abnegation, renunciation, self-denial, self-restraint, self-control, continence, asceticism; vegetarianism, abstinence; sobriety, soberness, teetotalism, abstemiousness; prohibitionism, dryness. *Ant.,* see DRUNKENNESS.

temperate, *adj.* moderate; ascetic; cautious; mild; SOBER, abstemious, abstinent; continent; Pythagorean; vegetarian. See MODERATION.

tempest, *n.* storm, gale, hurricane, squall, blizzard; EXCITEMENT, tumult, disturbance; maelstrom. See AGITATION, WIND.

tempestuous, *adj.* stormy, raging, furious; gusty, blowy, squally; violent, tumultuous, turbulent. See ROUGHNESS, WIND, AGITATION, *Ant.,* see SMOOTHNESS, INACTIVITY.

TEMPLE [1000]

Nouns—**1,** temple, place of worship; house of God, house of prayer; cathedral, minster, church, kirk, chapel, meetinghouse, tabernacle, basilica, holy place, chantry, oratory; synagogue; mosque; marabout; pantheon; pagoda. **2,** altar, shrine, sanctuary, Holy of Holies, *sanctum sanctorum,* communion table; pyx; baptistery, font; sedilia; reredos; rood-loft, rood-screen; chancel, nave, aisle, transept, vestry, sacristy, crypt, cloisters, churchyard, golgotha, calvary; stall, pew; pulpit, ambo, lectern, reading-desk, confessional; apse, oriel, belfry. **3,** parsonage, rectory, vicarage, manse, deanery, presbytery, Vatican, bishop's palace. **4,** monastery, priory, abbey, friary, convent, nunnery, cloister; sanctuary. *Adjectives*—churchly, claustral, cloistral, cloistered; monastic, conventual.

tempo, *n.* TIME, beat, rate; pace; rhythm. See MUSIC.

temporal, *adj.* worldly, mundane, secular; civil, political, profane, unsacred; temporary, ephemeral, impermanent. See IRRELIGION, TRANSIENTNESS.

tempt, *v.t.* entice, cajole, fascinate, lure, decoy, seduce; provoke, incite, instigate, appeal, attract. See DESIRE.

temptation, *n.* ATTRACTION, enticement, allurement; bait; siren song; provocativeness. See DESIRE.

tenacity, *n.* retention, holding, cohesiveness, cohesion, toughness, STRENGTH; adhesiveness, adhesion, stickiness; resistance, stubbornness, OBSTINACY. See COHERENCE.

tenant, *n.* occupant, occupier, resident, INHABITANT, renter; inmate.

tend, *v.* mind, watch, care for, guard, keep; attend, serve, wait on, incline, bend, bear toward, lean, gravitate. See AID, SERVANT, TENDENCY.

TENDENCY [176]

Nouns—tendency; aptness, aptitude; proneness, proclivity, predilection, bent, turn, tone, bias, set, leaning to, penchant, predisposition, inclination, propensity, susceptibility; likelihood, LIABILITY; quality, nature, temperament; idiosyncrasy; cast, vein, grain; humor, mood; trend, drift; conduciveness, conducement; applicability.

Verbs—tend, contribute, conduce, lead, dispose, incline, verge, bend to, trend, affect, carry, redound to, bid fair to, gravitate toward; be liable; promote, AID.

Adjectives—tending, conducive, working toward, in a fair way to, calculated to; liable; subservient; useful, subsidiary.

Antonym, see OPPOSITION.

---

tender, *v., adj. & n.* —*v.t.* present, OFFER, proffer, hold out; propose, suggest; volunteer. —*adj.* gentle, kind; loving, amorous; sympathetic, soft; humane, merciful; young; fragile, delicate; pathetic, touching; painful, sore. See BENEVOLENCE, LOVE, SOFTNESS, YOUTH, PAIN. *Ant.*, see ROUGHNESS, HARDNESS, SEVERITY. —*n.* MONEY; supply ship; supply car, coal car. See SHIP, VEHICLE.

tenement, *n.* apartment house; flat, dwelling, ABODE; slum.

tenet, *n.* dogma, BELIEF, opinion, creed, doctrine.

tenor, *n.* drift, TENDENCY, import, MEANING, significance; gist, sense; course, manner, mood, nature; DIRECTION. See MUSICIAN, MUSICAL INSTRUMENTS.

tense, *adj. & n.* —*adj.* taut, rigid; intent; excited; high-strung, nervous, strained. See EXCITEMENT, HARDNESS. *Ant.*, see SOFTNESS, MODERATION. —*n.* time, verb, form, inflection. See GRAMMAR.

tension, *n.* strain; tensity; tenseness; stretching; anxiety, nervousness. See HARDNESS, EXCITEMENT.

tent, *n.* canvas; wigwam, tepee; pavilion; shelter. See COVERING, ABODE.

tentative, *adj.* experimental, provisional, conditional, temporary, makeshift. See DOUBT.

tenuous, *adj.* unsubstantial, flimsy; thin, slender; rarefied. See NARROWNESS, RARITY. *Ant.*, see BREADTH, DENSITY.

tenure, *n.* holding; tenancy, occupancy; occupation; habitation, POSSESSION.

tepid, *adj.* lukewarm, mild; indifferent. See HEAT.

term, *n.* word, expression, locution; LIMIT, bound; period, TIME, tenure, duration; semester.

termination, *n.* END, ending, conclusion; LIMIT, bound; result, outcome, consequence, COMPLETION; suffix. *Ant.*, see BEGINNING.

terms, *n.* provisions, limitations, stipulations, conditions; AGREEMENT; relationship, footing.

terrestrial, *adj.* earthly; worldly, mundane, secular, temporal. See LAND.

terrible, *adj.* terrifying, dreadful; awesome, appalling, frightful, horrible, shocking, fearful, alarming. *Colloq.*, excessive. See FEAR. *Ant.*, see CHEERFULNESS.

terrify, *v.t.* terrorize, frighten, alarm; appall, dismay; cow, intimidate; panic, stampede. See FEAR. *Ant.*, see COURAGE.

territory, *n.* REGION, district; POSSESSION; kingdom, state, realm, province. See PROPERTY, LAND.

terror, *n.* FEAR, dread; fright, alarm; dismay, horror; panic. *Ant.,* see COURAGE.

terse, *adj.* concise, brief, curt; pithy, laconic, succinct; short, compact. See CONTRACTION. *Ant.,* see LOQUACITY.

test, *n.* examination; trial, ESSAY; criterion; EXPERIMENT.

testify, *v.* affirm, declare, state, depose, swear, avow, witness. See EVIDENCE.

testimony, *n.* declaration, affirmation; profession; attestation, witness; EVIDENCE; Scriptures. See SACRED WRITINGS.

tether, *v.t.* picket, stake, tie, fasten. See RESTRAINT. *Ant.,* see FREEDOM.

text, *n.* COMPOSITION; matter; textbook; topic, subject, theme. See BOOK, WRITING.

texture, *n.* contexture, intertexture; fiber, nap, tissue, grain, surface; warp and woof; weave; quality. See FORM, ROUGHNESS.

thankful, *adj.* grateful, appreciative; much obliged. See GRATITUDE. *Ant.,* see INGRATITUDE.

thankless, *adj.* ungrateful, unthankful, unappreciative, ingrate; ungracious; unrewarding; unpleasant. See INGRATITUDE.

thanks, *n.* GRATITUDE; acknowledgment, appreciation; thank you; grace. See GRATITUDE. *Ant.,* see INGRATITUDE.

thanksgiving, *n.* grace, PRAYER, praise. See GRATITUDE. *Ant.,* see INGRATITUDE.

thaw, *v.* melt, dissolve, liquefy; soften, unbend. See HEAT, SOFTNESS. *Ant.,* freeze; see COLD, HARDNESS.

theater, theatre, *n.* stage; ARENA; field [of action]; playhouse; DRAMA; motion-picture house; studio.

theatrical, *adj.* dramatic, melodramatic; histrionic; scenic; showy, stagy, affected; vivid, moving. See AFFECTATION, DRAMA, OSTENTATION.

theft, *n.* STEALING, larceny; pilfering, thievery; fraud, embezzlement. *Ant.,* see RESTORATION.

theme, *n.* subject, TOPIC, text; essay, thesis, treatise, dissertation; omposition; melody, motif. See MUSIC, WRITING.

then, *adv.* soon, next, immediately; consequently, therefore, evidently, again; afterwards. See TIME, REASONING.

theology, *n.* RELIGION; creed, BELIEF; doctrine, dogma.

theoretical, *adj.* speculative, hypthetical, conjectural; unapplied, pure, abstract. See NONEXISTENCE, SUPPOSITION. *Ant.,* see SUBSTANCE, EXISTENCE.

theory, *n.* speculation, surmise, conjecture; contemplation; principle, philosophy, doctrine; hypothesis; guess, idea, plan. See SUPPOSITION. *Ant.,* see EXISTENCE.

therefore, *adv.* consequently, hence, wherefore, so, accordingly. See REASONING.

thermometer, *n.* thermostat, pyrometer, calorimeter; clinical thermometer. *Colloq.,* mercury, glass. See MEASUREMENT.

thesis, *n.* proposition, TOPIC, argument; AFFIRMATION; postulate; statement; composition, treatise, dissertation. See WRITING, REASONING.

thicket, *n.* brush, underbrush; grove, coppice, covert. See VEGETABLE.

thief, *n.* robber, crook; sneak thief; pilferer; swindler, confidence man; shoplifter, kleptomaniac; stealer, pirate, purloiner, filcher; burglar, second-story man, *etc.* See STEALING, IMPROBITY.

thin, *adj.* slender, lean, narrow, slim, skinny, underweight, slight, frail; puny; scrawny, bony; lank, lanky; thinned out; watery, weak, diluted; attenuated; faint, dim, threadlike; fine, delicate; gaunt, haggard, drawn, emaciated; spare, meager, spindly, spindling; poor, lame (as an excuse); flimsy, sheer, filmy, gossamerlike. See RARITY, NARROWNESS. *Ant.,* see BREADTH, SIZE.

thing, *n.* affair, matter, CIRCUMSTANCE; deed, act, occurrence; entity, person; POSSESSION, belonging, chattel; item, object, detail, article. See SUBSTANCE. *Ant.,* see NONEXISTENCE.

think, *v.* conceive, imagine; believe, opine, surmise; reflect, meditate, reason, cogitate, contemplate, deliberate, muse; understand, realize. See BELIEF, THOUGHT.

thirst, *n.* dryness; craving, DESIRE; dipsomania, thirstiness, parchedness.
thirsty, *adj.* dry, parched, unslaked, unquenched; arid, craving water; greedy, avid. See DESIRE.
thorn, *n.* spine, briar, bramble; annoyance, irritation. See SHARPNESS.
thorough, *adj.* thoroughgoing; painstaking, exact, careful; complete, absolute, unqualified, arrant, out-and-out; exhaustive, deep, sweeping. See COMPLETION, WHOLE. *Ant.,* see NEGLECT.
thoroughfare, *n.* avenue, highway, street; PASSAGE, way; thruway, stop street, boulevard, turnpike.

THOUGHT [451]

Nouns—**1,** thought, thoughtfulness; reflection, cogitation, consideration, meditation, study, lucubration, speculation, deliberation, pondering; headwork, brainwork; cerebration; deep reflection, rumination, close study, application, ATTENTION; abstract thought, abstraction; contemplation, musing, preoccupation, brown study, reverie, Platonism; self-counsel, self-communing, self-consultation; association of ideas, succession of ideas, flow of ideas; train *or* current of thought.
2, afterthought, mature thought, reconsideration, second thought; retrospection; MEMORY; excogitation; examination (see INQUIRY); invention (see IMAGINATION).
3, IDEA; topic, subject of thought, material for thought; food for thought; subject, subject matter; matter, theme, thesis, text, business, affair, matter in hand, argument; motion, resolution; head, chapter; case, point; proposition, theorem; field of inquiry; moot point, problem.
Verbs—**1,** think, reflect, cogitate, cerebrate, excogitate, consider, deliberate, lucubrate rationalize, speculate, contemplate, meditate, ponder, muse, dream, ruminate; brood upon; animadvert, study; bend *or* apply the mind; digest, discuss, weigh; realize, appreciate; fancy.
2, take into consideration; take counsel, commune with oneself, bethink oneself; collect one's thoughts; revolve, turn over *or* run over in the mind; sleep on; rack one's brains; set one's wits to work; puzzle over; take into one's head; bear in mind; reconsider. *Colloq.,* sweat over, chew the cud, mull over. *Slang,* kick around.
3, occur, present itself, suggest itself; come into one's head; strike one, cross the mind, occupy the mind; have on one's mind; make an impression; sink in, penetrate the mind; engross the thoughts.
Adjectives—thinking, thoughtful, pensive, meditative, reflective, musing, wistful, contemplative, speculative, deliberative, studious, sedate, introspective, Platonic, philosophical; rational; lost in thought, engrossed, absorbed, rapt, preoccupied; in the mind, under consideration.
Adverbs—thoughtfully, reflectively; all things considered.
Antonyms, see RASHNESS.

---

thoughtful, *adj.* considerate, kind, tactful; meditative. See THOUGHT, BENEVOLENCE.
thoughtless, *adj.* rash, reckless, heedless; casual; inconsiderate, unthinking, mindless; unreasoning; careless, indifferent. See RASHNESS. *Ant.,* see CARE.
thrash, *v.t.* beat, spank, whip; flog; strike; defeat, overcome, conquer. See PUNISHMENT, SUCCESS.
thread, *n.* FILAMENT, fiber, hair; string; yarn; linen, cotton, silk, lisle, nylon, *etc.;* course, drift, train (of thought). See DIRECTION, MEANING.
threat, *n.* threatening, menace, defiance, intimidation, denunciation, commination; foreboding, WARNING, OMEN. See OPPOSITION, PREDICTION.
threshold, *n.* sill, doorsill, entrance; outset, BEGINNING; limen, threshold of pain, *etc.* See EDGE. *Ant.,* see END.
thrift, *n.* thriftiness, ECONOMY, frugality, saving; providence, husbandry; vigor, growth, thriving. *Ant.,* see WASTE.
thrifty, *adj.* frugal, saving; sparing; economical; foresighted; provident. See ECONOMY. *Ant.,* see WASTE.
thrill, *n. & v.* —*n.* EXCITEMENT; tremor, vibration; sensation; tingle. *Slang,* kick, charge. —*v.* throb, tingle, shiver; stir, excite, move deeply; vibrate, tremble. See FEELING.

thrive, *v.i.* prosper; batten; succeed; grow, flourish, bloom, flower. See PROSPERITY. *Ant.*, see ADVERSITY, POVERTY.

throat, *n.* neck; gullet; gorge, maw; windpipe, throttle. See OPENING.

throb, *v.i.* beat, pulsate, vibrate, palpitate; quiver, shudder, tremble; ache, hurt. See AGITATION, PAIN.

throne, *n.* royal seat; chair; sovereignty, scepter. See AUTHORITY.

throng, *n.* MULTITUDE, crowd, mob, horde; army, host. See ASSEMBLAGE. *Ant.*, see RARITY.

throttle, *v.* choke, strangle, suffocate; silence, stifle; close. See CLOSURE, KILLING.

through, *prep. & adv.* among, via, by way of; during, throughout; by; with. See PASSAGE, TIME.

throw, *v.* pitch, toss, cast, fling, hurl, sling; propel, project, unhorse, unseat. *Slang,* stop; disconcert; confound. See PROPULSION.

thrust, *v. & n.* —*v.* push, drive, shove, propel; lunge, plunge, ram; stab, pierce; interpose, interject. —*n.* blow, jab, poke; ATTACK, sortie; dig; repartee; POWER. See IMPULSE. *Ant.*, see DEFENSE, RECOIL.

thunder, *v.* shout, bellow; resound, peal, boom, roar, roll, crash. See LOUDNESS.

thus, *adv.* so; consequently, hence. See CIRCUMSTANCE.

thwart, *v.t.* oppose, baffle, foil, frustrate, defeat, block, contravene. See HINDRANCE. *Ant.*, see AID.

ticket, *n.* notice, memorandum, RECORD; label; list, slate, ballot; admission ticket. *Slang,* ducat. See INDICATION.

tickle, *v.t.* excite; gladden, delight, overjoy; please; titillate; amuse, divert. See PLEASURE.

ticklish, *adj.* tickly, excitable; sensitive; unstable, touchy; delicate; critical; risky, dangerous. See EXCITEMENT, DANGER, SENSIBILITY.

tide, *n.* flow, current, flood. See WATER.

tidings, *n.* news, message, intelligence, INFORMATION. See COMMUNICATION.

tidy, *adj. & v.* —*adj.* neat, orderly, trim; prim. *Colloq.,* sizable, considerable. —*v.* arrange, put in order, straighten. See CLEANNESS, ARRANGEMENT. *Ant.*, see UNCLEANNESS, DISORDER.

tie, *n. & v.* —*n.* bond, obligation; shoelace; necktie, cravat; fastening, ligature; draw, tied score, dead heat; beam, post; sleeper. —*v.t.* fasten, attach, join; bind, restrict, confine; knot; equal. See CLOTHING, DUTY, JUNCTION, CONNECTION, EQUALITY. *Ant.*, see DISJUNCTION.

till, *prep. & v.* —*prep.* until, up to, down to. See TIME. —*v.* cultivate, plow, farm. See AGRICULTURE.

tilt, *n. & v.* —*v.* tip, slant, incline, slope; joust. —*n.* joust, tournament; altercation, dispute; speed; slant, slope. See CONTENTION, VELOCITY, OBLIQUITY.

timber, *n.* wood, lumber; log, beam; forest, woodland, stand of timber, timberland. See MATERIALS.

timbre, *n.* resonance; tonal quality; SOUND; tone color; ring, clang. See MUSIC.

TIME [106]

Nouns—**1,** time, duration; period, term, stage, space, span, spell, season, fourth dimension; the whole time; era, epoch, AGE; time of life; moment, instant; INSTANTANEITY, SYNCHRONISM; course, progress, flow, march, stream, *or* lapse of time; Time, Father Time, ravages of time.

2, intermediate time, while, interim, interval, pendency; intervention, intermission, intermittence, interregnum, interlude; LEISURE, spare time; respite.

3, REGULARITY, periodicity, recurrence; anniversary, jubilee; diamond, golden, silver, wooden, paper, *etc.* anniversary; holiday, Christmas, Easter, Thanksgiving, New Year's Day, Independence Day, Memorial Day, Labor Day, Dominion Day, Bastille Day, Boxing Day, *etc.*

4, CHRONOMETRY; calendar, date, millenium, century, decade, year, month (January, February, *etc.*), week, fortnight; day (Sunday, Monday, *etc.*); timepiece, clock, watch; second, minute, hour; MORNING, EVENING, noon, midday, afternoon, twilight, night, midnight; season, spring, summer, fall, autumn, winter; term, semester, quarter.

Verbs—**1,** continue, last, endure, go on, remain, persist; intervene, elapse, lapse, pass, flow, advance, roll on, go by, go on; flit, fly, slip, slide, *or* glide by; take time, take up time, fill time, occupy time; pass, spend, waste, while away, *or* consume time; talk against time; tide over; seize an opportunity, take time by the forelock.
2, synchronize, coexist, coincide, keep pace with, concur.
3, recur, return; alternate, intermit.
Adjectives—**1,** continuing; permanent, perpetual, eternal; REGULAR, steady, periodic, intermittent; synchronous, simultaneous, coeval, contemporary, contemporaneous, coincident(al), concomitant, concurrent; elapsing, passing, aoristic; timely, untimely, punctual, fast, slow, leisurely, unhurried, early, late. See EARLINESS, LATENESS, SLOWNESS.
2, hourly, diurnal, daily, weekly, fortnightly, monthly, menstrual, yearly, annual, biennial, centennial; morning, matutinal, antemeridian; evening, vesper, crepuscular; nocturnal, nightly; vernal, estival, autumnal, wintry, brumal.
Adverbs—**1,** during, pending; during the time, during the interval; in the course of time; for the time being, day by day; in the time of; when; since times immemorial; meantime, meanwhile; in the meantime, in the interim, from day to day, from hour to hour; hourly, always; for a time, for a season; till, until, up to, yet; the while time, all the time; all along; throughout, for good; hereupon, thereupon, whereupon; then; *anno Domini*, A.D., before Christ, B.C., once upon a time; in time, in due time, in season, in the fullness of time, some fine day.
2, regularly, periodically, punctually, synchronously, *etc.;* off and on, now and then *or* again; semi-, bi- (weekly, annual or annually, *etc.*); at dawn, daybreak, sunrise, sun-up, twilight, sunset, *etc.;* together, at the same time, just as, as soon as.

---

timepiece, *n.* clock, watch, chronometer; water glass, hourglass; sundial; stopwatch. See CHRONOMETRY.
timid, *adj.* fearful, cowardly, afraid, fainthearted, timorous; shrinking, bashful, shy, retiring, diffident; irresolute, hesitant; weak. See FEAR, MODESTY. *Ant.,* see COURAGE, RESOLUTION.
tincture, *n.* trace, vestige, touch, dash; tinge, tint, shade; soupçon. See COLOR, MIXTURE.
tinge, *n.* tint, shade, COLOR, dye, stain; flavor, cast. See MIXTURE.
tingle, *v.i.* sting, prickle; thrill. See PAIN, EXCITEMENT.
tinsel, *n.* tawdriness, gaudiness, frippery, show; baubles, gewgaws. See ORNAMENT.
tint, *n.* COLOR, tinge, hue, dye, shade; tone, cast, nuance.
tiny, *adj.* minute, miniature, small, diminutive, wee; microscopic. *Slang,* halfpint. See LITTLENESS. *Ant.,* see SIZE, GREATNESS.
tip, *v. & n.* —*v.* overturn, capsize, upset; incline, slant, tilt; reward. See INVERSION, PAYMENT. —*n.* point, END; apex, summit; clue, hint, WARNING, pointer; gratuity, gift, fee, perquisite, *pourboire.* See HEIGHT, GIVING, INFORMATION. *Ant.,* BASE; see DIRECTION.
tire, *v.* weary, FATIGUE, bore, exhaust, jade, fag. See WEARINESS. *Ant.,* see RESTORATION.
tissue, *n.* gauze, fabric; web, net, mesh; membrane, cartilage, muscle; tissue paper; structure. See LAYER, FORM.
title, *n. & v.* —*n.* name; form of address (sir, madam, Doctor, *etc.*); subheading, subtitle; appellation, designation, caption; legend; epithet; honorific, title of nobility, peerage; status, degree; cognomen, surname. *Colloq.,* handle. —*v.* name, call. See NOMENCLATURE, BOOK, NOBILITY.
toady, *n.* fawner, sycophant, truckler. *Colloq.,* bootlicker. See SERVILITY.
toast, *v.t. & n.* —*v.t.* brown; heat, warm; drink to, pledge, honor. —*n.* toasted bread, zwieback, rusk; health, pledge. See HEAT, CELEBRATION.
tobacco, *n.* smoking; leaf, Burley, latakia, Turkish, Havana, Virginia; cigar, cigarette; snuff, plug, chew. *Colloq.,* weed, Lady Nicotine.
together, *adv.* mutually, reciprocally, unitedly; coincidently, concurrently, simultaneously. See ACCOMPANIMENT, TIME. *Ant.,* see DISJUNCTION.
toil, *n. & v.* —*n.* labor, drudgery; task, work; effort, exhaustion. —*v.* work,

drudge, moil, labor; strive. See EXERTION. *Ant.*, see REPOSE, INACTIVITY.

toils, *n.pl.* snare, net, trap, mesh, web; grip, clutches. See RESTRAINT.

token, *n.* sign, symbol, emblem; feature, trait; souvenir, memento, keepsake; badge, EVIDENCE; slug, substitute coin; earnest, INDICATION.

tolerance, *n.* toleration, allowance; MODERATION, temperance, endurance, forbearance, sufferance, laxity; clemency, leniency. See PERMISSION, FORGIVENESS. *Ant.*, see SEVERITY.

toll, *n.* TAX, impost, charge, fee. See PAYMENT.

tomb, *n.* grave, sepulcher, mausoleum, vault, catacombs. See INTERMENT.

tone, *n.* SOUND; quality; accent, pitch, inflection, modulation, intonation; strain, key, spirit; elasticity, resilience; tension, firmness, tonus; condition; frame of mind, mood; tint, shade, hue. See COLOR.

tongue, *n.* organ of taste *and* speech; communication, SPEECH, LANGUAGE, dialect; pole; flap, projection. See SUPPORT.

tonic, *adj. & n.* —*adj.* invigorating, bracing, refreshing; voiced, sonant; stressed, accented. See HEALTH, SOUND. —*n.* medicine, stimulant; key, keynote. See MUSIC.

too, *adv.* also, likewise; over; additionally, excessively. See ADDITION, REPETITION.

tool, *n.* INSTRUMENT, implement, utensil, device, machine; cat's-paw, dupe; henchman; intermediary. See AID.

tooth, *n.* fang, tusk; canine, incisor, molar, cuspid, bicuspid; eyetooth; tine; cog; TASTE, fondness. *Colloq.*, grinder, chopper. See SHARPNESS.

toothsome, *adj.* toothy, palatable, appetizing; delicious, luscious, dainty, delectable. See TASTE.

top, *n. & v.* —*n.* crown, head; acme, summit, pinnacle; pick, élite; lid, cover. —*v.* crown, cap; prune, excel, dominate. See HEIGHT, SUPERIORITY, CLOSURE, COVERING. *Ant.*, see SUPPORT, LOWNESS, INFERIORITY.

topic, *n.* subject, theme, text, thesis, subject-matter; item, question; BUSINESS, point, point of argument; proposition, statement. See INQUIRY.

torch, *n.* LIGHT, torchlight, brand; flambeau; flashlight. *Slang*, firebug, arsonist. See HEAT, LIGHT.

torment, *n. & v.* —*n.* languish, distress; torture, agony, PAIN. —*v.t.* torture, distress, agonize, rack, afflict. *Ant.*, see PLEASURE.

torpid, *adj.* dormant, sleepy; numb; inert, unmoving, still, stagnant; dull, stupid, apathetic, slothful, sluggish, lethargic; listless. See INACTIVITY. *Ant.*, see ACTIVITY, EXERTION.

torpor, *n.* dormancy, sleep, sleepiness, INACTIVITY, sluggishness, stagnation, apathy, lethargy. *Ant.*, see ACTIVITY.

torrid, *adj.* hot, burning, arid, parched, sizzling, scorching; equatorial, tropical. See HEAT. *Ant.*, see COLD.

torture, *n. & v.* —*n.* PAIN, excruciation, agony, torment; martyrdom, crucifixion; anguish; cruelty. —*v.t.* punish; torment, rack, agonize, martyr; garble, distort, twist, misrepresent. See PUNISHMENT, DISTORTION.

toss, *v.* fling, buffet; agitate, stir; throw, cast; tumble, sway; pitch, roll. See AGITATION, PROPULSION, MOTION.

total, *adj., n. & v.* —*adj.* complete, entire, utter, absolute, WHOLE. —*n.* sum, amount, aggregate, quantity, WHOLE. —*v.t.* add, reckon, tot up; amount to; constitute. See NUMBER, ADDITION.

totter, *v.* shake, tremble, rock, reel, waver; falter, stumble, stagger. See OSCILLATION.

touch, *n. & v.* —*n.* tangibility, taction, tactility; contact; FEELING; palpation, palpability. *Slang*, soft touch. —*v.* feel; palpate; handle, finger, thumb, paw; fumble, grope; brush, glance; border on, abut; move, stir, arouse pity. *Slang*, beg from; panhandle, put the arm *or* bite on.

tough, *adj.* strong, firm; stiff, resilient; vigorous, robust, hardy; stubborn, intractable. *Colloq.*, vicious, rowdy, unruly; difficult, troublesome. See HARDNESS.

tour, *n.* trip, journey, expedition, excursion, junket, jaunt; turn, shift (tour of duty). See TRAVEL.

tournament, *n.* tourney, jousting, contest; match. See CONTENTION.

tow, *v.t.* draw, pull, drag, haul; take in tow. See ATTRACTION.

tower, *n. & v.* —*n.* fortress, castle; skyscraper; campanile, belfry, spire.

—v.i. rise, soar; loom, transcend. See DEFENSE, ASCENT, HEIGHT. *Ant.,* see LOWNESS.

town, *n.* hamlet, burgh, village, city. See ABODE.

toy, *n. & v.* *—n.* plaything, trinket, trifle; doll, puppet. *—v.* trifle *or* play (with); fiddle, dally. See AMUSEMENT, UNIMPORTANCE.

trace, *v. & n.* *—v.* draw, sketch, delineate, copy; track, trail, follow, scent, detect; deduce. See INQUIRY, REPRESENTATION. *—n.* course, path; track, footprint, trail; hint, shade, vestige. See INDICATION, RECORD, LITTLENESS.

track, *v. & n.* *—v.t.* TRAIL, follow, scent; traverse. *—n.* TRACE, trail, wake; vestige; footprints, spoor, scent; path, course; succession; rails; race track, course, turf, cinders; footracing. See INDICATION, CONTENTION.

tract, *n.* expanse, area, REGION; composition, dissertation, treatise. See WRITING.

tractable, *adj.* docile, well-behaved, manageable, adaptable, yielding; malleable, plastic. See FACILITY, SOFTNESS. *Ant.,* see DIFFICULTY, HARDNESS.

traction, *n.* drawing, towage, haulage; draught, draft, pull, haul; rake; suction (as of tire treads), gripping ability, skidproof quality.

trade, *n. & v.* *—n.* BUSINESS; profession, occupation; livelihood; craft; merchandising; commerce, traffic, barter; clientele; purchase and sale, deal. *—v.t.* barter, buy and sell, bargain. See SALE.

tradition, *n.* belief, practice, usage, custom, culture, folklore. See OLDNESS.

traduce, *v.* slander, calumniate, vilify, defame, asperse, malign, disparage. See DETRACTION.

traffic, *n. & v.* *—n.* trade, barter, commerce, BUSINESS; vehicular movement, transportation; dealings, familiarity, intercourse, fraternization. *—v.* trade, deal.

tragedy, *n.* DRAMA; disaster, calamity, castastrophe; crushing blow; DEATH.

tragic, *adj.* dramatic, melodramatic; fatal, dire, disastrous. See DRAMA, DEATH.

trail, *n. & v.* *—n.* track, spoor, footprints; tire, *etc.,* tracks; vestige; scent; path, wake; train. *—v.* TRACK, scent; hang; lag, dawdle, crawl, straggle. See INDICATION. *Ant.,* see PRIORITY.

train, *n. & v.* *—n.* retinue, suite, entourage, procession, cortège; order, SEQUENCE, sequel, succession; railroad cars. *—v.t.* instruct, discipline, drill; educate. See VEHICLE, TEACHING.

trait, *n.* quality, characteristic, peculiarity, idiosyncrasy; custom; feature. See INDICATION, UNCONFORMITY.

traitor, *n.* betrayer; turncoat, renegade; deserter, conspirator; informer; Judas, fifth columnist, quisling. See EVILDOER.

tramp, *n. & v.* *—n.* traveler, vagabond, hobo, vagrant, bum, panhandler; jaunt, journey, hike, freighter; tread, walk, stroll. *—v.i.* walk, tread, step, plod, trudge, travel, hike; trample, stamp. See TRAVEL.

trample, *v.t.* crush, tread, grind, squash, stamp on. See DESTRUCTION.

trance, *n.* daze, stupor; abstraction, ecstasy; somnambulism, sleep-walking; coma, catalepsy; hypnosis. See INSENSIBILITY.

tranquil, *adj.* calm, quiet, undisturbed, composed, serene, placid, peaceful. See MODERATION, REPOSE. *Ant.,* see EXCITEMENT, AGITATION.

tranquilize, *v.* pacify, soothe, appease; calm, still. See PACIFICATION.

transact, *v.* negotiate, deal; CONDUCT, bring about; do; perform, execute.

transaction, *n.* deal, proceeding, ACTION, affair; CONDUCT, act, deed. See BUSINESS.

transcend, *v.* exceed, overpass, surpass, excel, outstrip, outdo. See SUPERIORITY. *Ant.,* see INFERIORITY.

transcribe, *v.* COPY, write, reproduce, engross; decode, decipher.

transfer, *n. & v.* *—n.* transference; transmission, translocation; displacement; removal; relegation; deportation, extradition; conveyance, draft; carrying, carriage; conduction; contagion, infection; transportation, transit, transition; PASSAGE; transplantation, translation; assignment, bargain, sale; exchange, SUBSTITUTION; succession, reversion. *—v.* transmit, transport, transplace, transplant; convey, carry, bear, conduct, bring, fetch, reach; send, dispatch, delegate, consign, deed, relegate, turn over to, deliver, post, mail; ship, embark; shunt; transpose, displace, assign, consign, exchange; substitute. See INTERCHANGE, SALE, GIVING. *Ant.,* see POSSESSION.

transformation, *n.* CHANGE, alteration, transmutation; conversion, transfiguration; metamorphosis; wig, switch.

transgression, *n.* trespass, sin, DISOBEDIENCE, violation, fault, offense, crime, misdeed, slip, misdemeanor; infraction, infringement. See DEVIATION, IMPROBITY, ILLEGALITY. *Ant.,* see VIRTUE.

TRANSIENTNESS [111]

Nouns—transientness, transience, evanescence, impermanence, fugacity, mortality, span; nine days' wonder, bubble, ephemerality; spurt; temporary arrangement, interregnum; brevity, SHORTNESS; VELOCITY, suddenness (see INSTANTANEITY); CHANGEABLENESS.
Verbs—be transient, flit, pass away, fly, gallop, vanish, evanesce, fade, evaporate; blow over.
Adjectives—transient, transitory, transitive; passing, evanescent, volatile, fleeting; flying; fugacious, fugitive; shifting, slippery; spasmodic; temporal, temporary; provisional, provisory; cursory, short-lived, meteoric, ephemeral, deciduous; perishable, mortal, precarious; impermanent; brief, quick, extemporaneous, summary; sudden, momentary, short and sweet.
Adverbs—temporarily, *pro tempore;* for the moment, for a time; awhile, *en passant,* briefly.

Antonym, see DURABILITY.

transit, *n.* PASSAGE; CHANGE, transition; conveyance, transportation.

transition, *n.* PASSAGE, passing; CHANGE, development, flux, modulation; break, graduation, rise, fall; metastasis, metabasis.

translate, *n.* transfer, decipher, decode, render; construe, interpret; transform, transmute, CHANGE.

transmission, *n.* conveyance, transference, sending, communication, conductance; gearshift, gears, torque converter. See PASSAGE, COMMUNICATION.

transmit, *v.* send, TRANSFER, convey, forward, post, mail, wire, telegraph; impart, hand down; admit, conduct; broadcast, COMMUNICATE. See INFORMATION.

transparent, *adj.* lucid, pellucid, crystalline, glassy, clear, limpid, diaphanous, sheer, gauzy, gossamer; translucent; guileless; understandable, clear, evident. See SIMPLENESS, VISION.

transport, *n. & v.* —*n.* transformation, conveyance; movement; (pl.) emotion, ecstasy, rapture; troopship; airplane, CARRIER. —*v.* convey, carry, move, ship; transfer; delight, overjoy. See PASSAGE, PLEASURE.

transportation, *n.* transfer, PASSAGE, conveyance; carriage, freightage, *etc.;* transmission; transport, transporting; shipping, railroading, AVIATION, trucking, motoring, *etc.;* shipment, sending, dispatching; transference; transit. See TRAVEL, VEHICLE, COMMUNICATION.

transpose, *v.* exchange, interchange, reverse, rearrange, invert; substitute, transliterate; CHANGE. See INVERSION, MUSIC.

transverse, *adj.* crossing, cross, athwart, oblique. See OBLIQUITY.

trap, *n. & v.* —*n.* pitfall, snare, net, deadfall; AMBUSH; carriage; trapdoor; (*pl.*) equipment, luggage. —*v.* catch, entrap, snare, net, enmesh, fool, AMBUSH. See DECEPTION, CONCEALMENT, VEHICLE.

trash, *n.* rubbish, garbage, refuse, offal, litter, debris; junk, scrap, WASTE.

travail, *n.* labor, work, drudgery, toil; agony, PAIN. See EXERTION.

TRAVEL [266]

Nouns—**1,** travel; traveling, wayfaring, itineracy, tourism; journey, excursion, expedition, tour, trip, crossing, cruise, grand tour, circuit; procession, caravan; discursion; pilgrimage; ambulation; sleepwalking, somnambulism. *Colloq.,* globe-trotting. See NAVIGATION, PASSAGE.
2, walk, promenade, stroll, saunter, tramp, ramble, jog-trot, turn, perambulation, pedestrianism; driving, riding, posting, motoring, touring; outing, ride, drive, airing, jaunt. See VEHICLE. *Colloq.,* constitutional, hike, spin.
3, roving, vagrancy, nomadism; vagabondism, vagabondage; gadding; flitting; migration, emigration, immigration, intermigration.
4, itinerary, course, route, road, path; bypass, detour, loop; handbook, road map; Baedeker, guidebook.

5, traveler, wayfarer, voyager, itinerant, passenger, tourist, excursionist; explorer, adventurer, mountaineer, peregrinator, wanderer, rover, straggler, rambler; bird of passage; gadabout, vagrant, tramp, vagabond, nomad, Bohemian, gypsy, Arab, Wandering Jew, Hadji, pilgrim, palmer; peripatetic; somnambulist; emigrant, fugitive, refugee; runner, courier; pedestrian, walker, cyclist, passenger; rider, horseman, equestrian, jockey; driver, coachman, whip, charioteer, postilion, postboy; cabdriver; engineer; chauffeur.

Verbs—**1,** travel, journey, course; take a journey; take a walk, go for a walk, have a run; take the air; flit, take wing; migrate, emigrate, immigrate; rove, prowl, roam, range, patrol, pace up and down, traverse; perambulate, circumambulate; nomadize, wander, ramble, stroll, saunter, go one's rounds, gad, gad about.

2, walk, march, step, tread, pace, plod, wend; promenade, trudge, tramp; stalk, stride, strut, foot it, bowl along, toddle; paddle; tread a path; jog on, shuffle on; bend one's steps; make one's way, find one's way, wend one's way, pick *or* thread one's way, plow one's way; slide, glide, skim, skate; march in procession; go to, repair to, hie oneself to, betake oneself to. *Colloq.*, hike, hitchhike, hotfoot, stump. *Slang*, stir one's stumps.

3, ride, take horse, drive, trot, amble, canter, prance, gallop; ride, drive, fly; go by car, train, rail, *or* air. *Colloq.*, joyride. *Slang*, burn up the road.

Adjectives—traveling, ambulatory, itinerant, peripatetic, roving, rambling, gadding, discursive, vagrant, migratory, nomadic; footloose; locomotive, automotive; wayfaring; travel-stained.

Adverbs—on foot, on horseback, on shanks' mare; aboard; en route.

Antonym, see STABILITY.

---

traverse, *v.* cross, ford, range, patrol. See TRAVEL.

treacherous, *adj.* traitorous, treasonable, perfidious, faithless, disloyal, false; untrustworthy, unreliable. See IMPROBITY. *Ant.*, see PROBITY.

treachery, *n.* treason, perfidy, faithlessness, disloyalty, infidelity, falsity, falseness. See IMPROBITY. *Ant.*, see PROBITY.

tread, *v.* walk, step, pace; trample, crush; stamp, tramp; DANCE. See TRAVEL.

treason, *n.* betrayal, disloyalty, faithlessness, sedition, treachery. See IMPROBITY.

treasure, *n. & v.* —*n.* hoard, STORE; wealth, riches. —*v.* value, prize, cherish, appreciate; remember. See MONEY, MEMORY, LOVE. *Ant.*, see HATE.

treasurer, *n.* bursar, purser; financier, banker, cashier, teller; receiver; steward, trustee; paymaster.

treasury, *n.* bank, exchequer; depository, vault, safe, safe-deposit box; till, strongbox, cash register; coffer, chest; purse, wallet, handbag, pocketbook. See RECEPTACLE, STORE, MONEY.

treat, *v.* negotiate, bargain, deal, parley; entertain, pay for; deal with, discuss, teach; dose, attend, doctor. See AGREEMENT, REMEDY, PLEASURE.

treatise, *n.* BOOK, textbook; exposition, discussion, composition, commentary, tract, monograph, dissertation.

treaty, *n.* COMPACT, pact, covenant, concordat, entent, AGREEMENT.

tree, *n.* plant, sapling, scrub, shrub, bush; timber; whiffletree; stake; gibbet, gallows; family tree, pedigree, lineage. See VEGETABLE, PUNISHMENT, ANCESTRY.

tremble, *v.* shake, shiver; vibrate, totter, quake, quaver; shudder, pulsate. See FEAR, OSCILLATION. *Ant.*, see STABILITY.

tremendous, *adj.* stupendous, colossal, huge; extraordinary. See SIZE. *Ant.*, see LITTLENESS.

tremor, *n.* trembling, shivering, shaking, quivering, vibration. See FEAR, OSCILLATION, AGITATION.

trench, *n.* ditch, fosse, dugout; FURROW. See DEFENSE.

trenchant, *adj.* cutting, incisive, penetrating; clearcut, keen, sharp, biting, crisp; energetic. See POWER. *Ant.*, FEEBLE.

trend, *n.* DIRECTION, course, TENDENCY, inclination, drift, tide.

trepidation, *n.* quaking, trembling; alarm, FEAR, AGITATION, perturbation, dread, dismay. *Ant.*, see COURAGE.

trespass, *v.* sin, offend, transgress; encroach, infringe, intrude, invade. See IMPROBITY. *Ant.,* see VIRTUE.

trial, *n.* test, EXPERIMENT; hearing, ordeal; cross, tribulation, affliction; effort, attempt. See ADVERSITY, INQUIRY, LAWSUIT.

tribe, *n.* race, people, sect, group; clan, nation, society; lineage, family stock. See RELATION, ASSEMBLAGE.

tribunal, *n.* court; board, forum; bench, judicatory; court of justice *or* law; court of arbitration; inquisition; seat of judgment *or* justice; bar, bar of justice; drumhead, court-martial. *Slang,* kangaroo court. See JUDGE, JUSTICE.

tributary, *n. & adj.* —*n.* stream, source, affluent; prayer of tribute. —*adj.* subject, subordinate; contributory. See WATER, SUBJECTION.

tribute, *n.* PAYMENT, tax, contribution; gift, offering, service; praise, encomium, compliment. See GIVING.

trick, *n.* artifice, stratagem, craft; illusion, wile, ruse, subterfuge, fraud, imposture, DECEPTION; tour, shift, turn; trait, idiosyncrasy, peculiarity. See DECEPTION, SKILL, UNCONFORMITY.

trickle, *v.i.* drip, dribble, seep. See WATER.

tricky, *adj.* ticklish, intricate; deceitful, evasive, artful, shifty. See DECEPTION, DIFFICULTY. *Ant.,* see INNOCENCE, FACILITY.

trifle, *n. & v.* —*n.* bagatelle, nothing, triviality; gewgaw, trinket, knickknack, gimcrack; particle, bit, morsel, trace. See LITTLENESS, UNIMPORTANCE. —*v.i.* toy, play, dally, fool. See NEGLECT.

trill, *n. & v.* —*n.* vibration, tremor, quaver, tremolo, vibrato. —*v.* sing; quaver; warble. See MUSIC.

trim, *adj. & v.* —*adj.* neat, well-ordered, compact, tidy. —*v.* order, tidy, adjust, dress, arrange; decorate, ORNAMENT, adorn; defeat; cheat; balance, equalize; cut, lop, shear, prune, barber. See ARRANGEMENT, CLEANNESS, SHORTNESS.

trinket, *n.* TOY, plaything, bauble, gewgaw. See ORNAMENT.

trip, *n. & v.* —*n.* journey, excursion, voyage. —*v.* skip; stumble; offend, err; obstruct, halt. See ERROR, LEAP, HINDRANCE.

trite, *adj.* commonplace, ordinary; hackneyed, stale, old; boring, DULL; banal. *Slang,* corny. See WEARINESS.

triumph, *n. & v.* —*n.* joy, exultation, celebration; victory, conquest; accomplishment. —*v.i.* win, conquer, succeed; celebrate, rejoice. See REJOICING, SUCCESS. *Ant.,* see LAMENTATION, FAILURE.

trivial, *adj.* insignificant, unimportant, trifling, picayune, paltry; mean, piddling, small, petty. See UNIMPORTANCE. *Ant.,* see IMPORTANCE.

troop, *n. & v.* —*n.* group, number, party, company, crowd, ASSEMBLAGE. —*v.i.* march, tramp, go. See PROGRESSION.

trophy, *n.* medal, prize, award, cup, loving cup; statuette; palm, laurel, garland of bays; crown, wreath, insignia, feather in one's cap, honor, decoration, garland. *Colloq.,* Oscar, Emmy, Edgar. See PAYMENT, REPUTE, APPROBATION.

tropical, *adj.* torrid, hot, fiery; equatorial. See HEAT.

trot, *v.i.* run, jog, lope; hasten. See MOTION.

trouble, *n. & v.* —*n.* affliction, distress, misfortune, ADVERSITY, calamity; disorder, unrest; DIFFICULTY; pains, exertion, effort; anxiety, perturbation, sorrow, worry. —*v.* disturb, disquiet, perturb; annoy, molest, harass, agitate; worry, distress, grieve; afflict, ail, plague; inconvenience. See AGITATION, PAIN.

troublesome, *adj.* disturbing, annoying, distressing; vexatious, burdensome, grievous, worrisome; DIFFICULT. See PAIN. *Ant.,* see PLEASURE, FACILITY.

trounce, *v.* thrash, beat, flog. See PUNISHMENT.

trousers, *n.* breeches, pantaloons, pants; jeans, slacks, Levis. See CLOTHING.

truant, *n.* shirker, absentee, deserter. See ABSENCE. *Ant.,* see PRESENCE.

truce, *n.* armistice, peace; respite; delay; cessation, lull. See PACIFICATION.

truck, *n.* VEHICLE; lorry, van, pick-up, dump, panel, rack; six-wheeler, half-track; cart, wagon, dray; barrow, dolly.

trudge, *v.* march, slog, tramp, walk, plod. See SLOWNESS. *Ant.,* see VELOCITY.

true, *adj.* faithful, loyal, constant, sincere; certain, correct, accurate; truthful; actual, genuine; legitimate, rightful; real, straight, undeviating. See PROBITY, TRUTH. *Ant.*, see FALSEHOOD, DEVIATION, ERROR.

trumpet, *n. & v.* —*n.* cornet, bugle, horn; ear trumpet. See MUSICAL INSTRUMENT. —*v.* bellow, roar; blow, toot, blare; proclaim. See PUBLICATION, LOUDNESS.

trundle, *v.* roll; wheel; revolve, rotate. See ROTATION.

trunk, *n.* stem, bole; body, torso; proboscis, snout; chest, box; circuit. See RECEPTACLE, SUPPORT.

trust, *n. & v.* —*n.* faith, reliance, confidence, credence, BELIEF; hope, expectation, anticipation; office, charge, task, duty, custody, keeping; CREDIT; cartel, monopoly, association. —*v.* rely, depend, count; commit, entrust, consign; believe, hope, expect; commission; give credit to. See SAFETY. *Ant.*, see DOUBT.

trustworthy, *adj.* reliable, dependable, faithful, trusty, responsible, credible, believable; constant, true, loyal. See PROBITY, BELIEF. *Ant.*, see IMPROBITY, DISBELIEF.

TRUTH [494]

Nouns—**1,** truth, fact, reality; verity, gospel, authenticity; plain, unvarnished, sober *or* naked truth; the Gospel truth; the truth, the whole truth and nothing but the truth. *Slang*, the [real] McCoy, the gooas.

2, truthfulness, VERACITY; accuracy, exactitude; exactness, preciseness, precision.

Verbs—**1,** be true, be the case; stand the test; hold good, hold true, have the true ring; render true, prove true, substantiate (see EVIDENCE); get at the truth (see DISCOVERY). *Colloq.*, hold water.

3, be truthful; speak *or* tell the truth; not lie; speak one's mind; make a clean breast (see DISCLOSURE); cross one's heart.

Adjectives—**1,** true, factual, real, actual, existing; veritable, certain (see CERTAINTY); unimpeachable; unrefuted, unconfuted; genuine, authentic, legitimate; orthodox; pure, sound, sterling, unadulterated, unvarnished, uncolored; well-grounded, well-founded; solid, substantial, tangible, valid; undistorted, undisguised; unaffected, unexaggerated, unromantic, unflattering. *Colloq.*, all wool and a yard wide.

2, exact, accurate, definite, precise, well-defined, just, right, correct, strict; literal; undisguised; faithful, constant, unerring.

3, truthful, veracious; sincere, candid, frank, open, straightforward, aboveboard; honest, trustworthy, reliable, dependable; pure, guileless, bona fide, true blue; scrupulous, conscientious (see PROBITY).

Adverbs—**1,** truly, verily, indeed, really, in reality; with truth, certainly, actually; exactly, verbatim, word for word, literally, *sic*, to the letter, chapter and verse, to an inch; to a nicety, to a hair, to a turn, to a T; neither more nor less; in every respect, in all respects; at any rate, at all events; strictly speaking.

2, truthfully, *etc.*; from the bottom of one's heart; honor bright.

Antonym, see ERROR, FALSEHOOD.

---

try, *v.* ESSAY, endeavor, attempt; test, examine, assay, EXPERIMENT; refine, purify; afflict, beset; strain, tax; judge, hear. See CLEANNESS, PAIN, LAWSUIT.

trying, *adj.* DULL, wearisome, boring; annoying, bothersome, galling, irritating. See WEARINESS.

tryout, *n.* trial; audition, hearing; test, dry run; EXPERIMENT.

tub, *n.* pot, vat, cauldron; washtub, bathtub. See RECEPTACLE. *Slang*, (old *or* slow) ship; tramp, freighter.

tube, *n.* pipe, hose, conduit; tunnel, subway. See PASSAGE.

tuck, *n.* FOLD, pleat, lap.

tuft, *n.* cluster, clump, wisp, bunch, brush; tussock; fetlock, topknot, crest. See ROUGHNESS.

tug, *v.* pull, strain, drag, haul; toil, labor, strive, drudge; tow. See EXERTION. *Ant.*, see PROPULSION.

tumble, *v.* fall, roll; LEAP, spring; throw, overturn, disarrange, dishevel, tousle. See DESCENT, PROPULSION, DISORDER.

tumid, *adj.* swollen, distended, enlarged; protuberant, bulging; bombastic, pompous, inflated; teeming, bursting. See INCREASE, CONVEXITY.

tumult, *n.* commotion, AGITATION, turbulence, DISORDER. *Ant.*, see INACTIVITY.

tune, *n. & v.* —*n.* melody, air; harmony, concord. —*v.* modulate, adjust, attune; harmonize. See MUSIC.

tunnel, *n.* passageway; burrow; crosscut; subway, tube. See OPENING, PASSAGE.

turbid, *adj.* roiled, muddy, cloudy, clouded; muddled. See DISORDER, CLOUDINESS.

turbulence, *n.* DISORDER, VIOLENCE, unrest, disturbance, EXCITEMENT. *Ant.*, see INACTIVITY, MODERATION.

turf, *n.* sod, sward; peat; racetrack. See ARENA, LAND.

turgid, *adj.* distended, swollen, tumid, inflated, bloated; diffuse, pompous, ostentatious, high-flown, bombastic. See INCREASE, LOQUACITY, ORNAMENT. *Ant.*, see CONTRACTION.

turmoil, *n.* confusion, tumult, turbulence, disturbance, AGITATION, commotion; DISORDER. *Ant.*, see INACTIVITY.

turn, *n. & v.* —*n.* ROTATION, REVOLUTION; twirl, twist; deflection, diversion; coil, CONVOLUTION; CHANGE; crisis; aptitude, ability, SKILL; act, skit; spell, shift, tour, trick. —*v.* revolve, rotate, pivot; reel; rebel, retaliate; shape, round, finish; CHANGE, move; invert, reverse; upset, derange; deflect, divert, veer, shift; pervert, prejudice, repel; avert; curdle, ferment, SOUR. See INVERSION, ROTATION.

turncoat, *n.* renegade, deserter, traitor; apostate, recreant. See EVILDOER.

turpitude, *n.* depravity, baseness, wickedness, IMPROBITY. *Ant.*, see PROBITY.

turret, *n.* tower, gazebo, belvedere, cupola. See HEIGHT.

tutor, *n.* teacher, instructor, coach; guardian. See TEACHING.

tuxedo, *n.* dinner jacket, dress suit, smoking jacket. *Colloq.*, black tie. *Slang*, tux, tuck, monkey suit, soup-and-fish. See CLOTHING.

twaddle, *n.* gabble, nonsense, fustian. See ABSURDITY. *Ant.*, see MEANING.

twice, *adv.* doubly, twofold. See NUMBER.

twig, *n.* shoot, branch, tendril, slip, scion. See VEGETABLE.

twilight, *n.* dusk, gloaming, nightfall; shade, shadow. See TIME.

twin, *adj.* double, twofold; fraternal, identical; like. See SIMILARITY, RELATION.

twine, *n.* cord, string, line. See FILAMENT, CONNECTION.

twinkle, *v.* blink, wink; scintillate, sparkle, shine. See LIGHT.

twirl, *v.* twist, spin, rotate, turn, whirl. See CONVOLUTION, ROTATION.

twist, *v.* wind, wreathe, twine, interlace; coil; wrench, contort; wring, screw; pervert. See CONVOLUTION, DEVIATION, DISTORTION.

twitch, *v.i.* jerk, writhe, shake, pull; tug, vellicate. See AGITATION.

tycoon, *n.* shogun. *Colloq.*, magnate, millionaire. See IMPORTANCE.

type, *n.* sign, emblem; kind, CLASS, sort, nature; standard, model, example, ideal; group; letter, figure, character. See INDICATION, PRINTING, SIMILARITY.

typhoon, *n.* hurricane, tornado, storm. See WIND.

typical, *adj.* emblematic, symbolic; characteristic, representative, model, ideal, conforming. See CONFORMITY, INDICATION. *Ant.*, see UNCONFORMITY.

typify, *v.* symbolize, exemplify, embody, represent; prefigure. See INDICATION, REPRESENTATION.

tyranny, *n.* despotism, autocracy, totalitarianism; SEVERITY, rigor, harshness, oppression. See AUTHORITY, ILLEGALITY. *Ant.*, see MODERATION, FREEDOM.

tyrant, *n.* despot, autocrat, oppressor. See AUTHORITY, SEVERITY.

tyro, *n.* beginner, novice, amateur, LEARNER.

U

UGLINESS [846]

Nouns—**1,** ugliness, deformity, disfigurement, blemish; inelegance; want of symmetry, DISTORTION; squalor (see UNCLEANNESS); IMPERFECTION; homeliness, plainness, unloveliness; grotesqueness; unsightliness; gruesomeness, loathsomeness, hideousness; sordidness, squalor.
2, eyesore, sight, fright, specter, scarecrow, hag, harridan, satyr, witch, toad, baboon, monster; Quasimodo, Caliban; gargoyle.
Verbs—be ugly, look unprepossessing; make faces; render ugly, uglify; deface; disfigure; distort, BLEMISH; make sordid *or* squalid.
Adjectives—**1,** ugly, ugly as sin; plain, homely, ordinary, unornamental, inartistic; squalid, unsightly, unseemly, uncomely, unshapely, unlovely; not fit to be seen; unbeautiful; beautiless; foul, dingy.
2, gruesome, misshapen, repulsive, hideous, loathsome, disgusting, nauseating, misproportioned, deformed, disfigured, monstrous; gaunt, thin; dumpy, ill-made, ill-shaped, ill-favored, ill-proportioned; crooked, distorted, hard-featured; ill-looking, haggard, unprepossessing.
3, graceless, inelegant; ungraceful, ungainly, uncouth; stiff; rugged, rough, gross, rude, awkward, inept, clumsy, slouching, rickety; gawky; lumpish; lumbering; hulking, unwieldy; ludicrous.
4, grim, grim-faced, grim-visaged; grisly, ghastly; ghostlike, deathlike; cadaverous, frightful, odious, uncanny, forbidding, repellent, grotesque, horrid, horrible; shocking.

Antonym, see BEAUTY.

---

ulcer, *n.* abscess, infection, sore, fistula. See DISEASE.
ulterior, *adj.* beyond, farther; further, remote; hidden, unavowed. See DISTANCE, FUTURITY. *Ant.*, see NEARNESS, DISCLOSURE.
ultimate, *adj.* farthest, most remote; extreme, last; maximum; terminal, final, conclusive; elemental; eventual. See DISTANCE, END, SIMPLENESS. *Ant.*, see BEGINNING.
ultimatum, *n.* demand, requirement, exaction. See COMMAND.
ultra, *adj.* radical, extreme. See SUPERIORITY. *Ant.*, see INFERIORITY.
ululate, *v.i.* howl, wail, CRY, hoot, bark, mewl, mew, meow, bellow, moo, roar, caterwaul.
ululation, *n.* howling, wailing, snarling, crying, whining, hooting, lowing, mooing, bellowing, roaring, barking; caterwauling, mewling, mewing; screeching, screaming; sirening; moaning. See CRY.
umbrage, *n.* RESENTMENT, offense, dudgeon, pique, huff.
umbrella, *n.* shade, screen; parasol, sunshade, bumbershoot; canopy, COVERING.
umpire, *n.* referee, arbitrator; linesman. See JUDGE, MODERATION. *Ant.*, see VIOLENCE.
unabashed, *adj.* shameless, brazen, unblushing, unashamed. See INSOLENCE.
unaccompanied, *adj.* alone, unattended, solitary, lone. *Ant.*, see ACCOMPANIMENT.
unaccountable, *adj.* inexplicable, mysterious, strange; not responsible, unanswerable. See WONDER, FREEDOM. *Ant.*, see MEANING, RESTRAINT.
unacquainted, *adj.* ignorant, unknowing, uninformed; never introduced, strange. See IGNORANCE.
unadorned, *adj.* bare, severe, austere, unornamented, plain, simple; naked, blank; terse, trenchant. See SEVERITY, SIMPLENESS. *Ant.*, see ORNAMENT, EXAGGERATION.
unadulterated, *adj.* clear, simple; pure, undiluted; genuine, true. See PURITY, TRUTH. *Ant.*, see MIXTURE, EXAGGERATION.
unaffected, *adj.* natural, simple, plain; genuine, sincere; ingenuous, artless;

untouched, uninfluenced, unmoved. See INSENSIBILITY. *Ant.*, see AFFEC-
TATION, FEELING.
unaided, *adj.* unsupported (see AID); single, single-handed.
unanimity, *n.* AGREEMENT, consent, accord. See ASSENT, COÖPERATION.
unanticipated, *adj.* unexpected, unforeseen; surprising, startling. See SUR-
PRISE. *Ant.*, see EXPECTATION.
unarmed, *adj.* weaponless, unprepared, defenseless. See IMPOTENCE.
unasked, *adj.* voluntary, spontaneous; gratis, free; uninvited. See WILL.
unassuming, *adj.* modest, retiring, reserved. See MODESTY. *Ant.*, see
VANITY.
unauthorized, *adj.* unwarranted, unsanctioned; illegal, illegitimate, unconstitutional. See ILLEGALITY, DISOBEDIENCE. *Ant.*, see PERMISSION.
unavoidable, *adj.* inevitable, certain, unpreventable, necessary. See CER-
TAINTY, NECESSITY.
unaware, *adj.* unwary, unwarned; oblivious, ignorant. See IGNORANCE.
unbearable, *adj.* unendurable, intolerable, insufferable, odious. See PAIN.
unbecoming, *adj.* indecorous, unseemly, inappropriate (to), unfitting; ugly,
unattractive, ill-suited, inharmonious. See UGLINESS.
unbelievable, *adj.* incredible; unthinkable, unimaginable, far-fetched, implausible, impossible. See DOUBT. *Ant.*, see BELIEF.
unbeliever, *n.* skeptic, doubter, infidel, agnostic, heretic. See DOUBT,
IRRELIGION. *Ant.*, see CREDULITY, BELIEF.
unbiased, *adj.* impartial, unprejudiced, objective, dispassionate; fair, just,
equitable. See JUSTICE. *Ant.*, see CERTAINTY.
unbound, *adj.* freed, released, untied, loosed; uncommitted, free agent,
plenipotentiary. See FREEDOM, POWER.
unbounded, *adj.* boundless, limitless, unlimited, INFINITE. See SPACE,
FREEDOM.
unbreakable, *adj.* indestructible; shatterproof, tough, durable. See DURA-
BILITY. *Ant.*, see BRITTLENESS.
unbridled, *adj.* unrestrained; violent, licentious; unruly, intractable. See
VIOLENCE. *Ant.*, see MODERATION.
unbroken, *adj.* intact, WHOLE; continuous, constant, uninterrupted, even;
untamed, unsubdued. See CONTINUITY, WHOLE. *Ant.*, see DISJUNCTION.
uncanny, *adj.* mysterious, eery, ghostly, weird, unnatural. See DEMON.
unceasing, *adj.* continuous, uninterrupted; perpetual, eternal, endless. See
CONTINUITY.
uncertainty, *n.* uncertainness, incertitude, DOUBT; hesitation; suspense;
perplexity, embarrassment, dilemma, quandary, bewilderment; timidity;
indecision, vacillation, irresolution, vagueness, obscurity; riskiness, precariousness, insecurity. *Ant.*, see STABILITY, CERTAINTY, RESOLUTION.
unchanged, *adj.* unaltered, *etc.*; (see CHANGE); pristine, erstwhile, undiminished, good as new, the same, as of old; continuous, maintained,
restored.
unchaste, *adj.* lewd, incontinent, wanton, lascivious, lecherous, dissolute,
immoral; unfaithful, adulterous. See IMPURITY. *Ant.*, see PURITY.
uncivilized, *adj.* primitive, simple; barbarous, savage, barbaric. See
SIMPLENESS, UNCONFORMITY, VIOLENCE.

UNCLEANNESS [653]

Nouns—**1**, uncleanness, IMPURITY; filth, defilement, contamination, soilure;
abomination; taint, tainture; MALODOROUSNESS; decay, putrescence, putrefaction; corruption, mold, must, mildew, dry rot; slovenliness, slovenry,
squalor, sordidness.
2, offal, garbage, carrion; EXCRETION; feces, excrement, ordure, dung;
slough; pus, matter, gangrene, suppuration; sewage, sewerage; muck,
guano, manure, compost.
3, dregs, grounds, lees; sediment; dross, precipitate, scoria; ashes, cinders,
clinkers, slag; scum, froth; swill, hogwash; ditchwater, dishwater, bilge-
water; rinsings, parings, offscourings, sweepings; scurvy, scurviness, scurf,
scurfiness; dandruff, tartar.
4, dirt, filth, soil, slop; dust, cobweb, smoke, soot, smudge, smut, grime;
muck, mud, mire, quagmire, alluvium, silt, sludge, slime, slush.

5, drab, slut, slattern, sloven, riffraff; vermin, louse, flea, cockroach.
6, dunghill, dungheap, midden, bog, sink, latrine, outhouse, head, privy, cesspool; sump, slough, dump, dumpheap, cloaca, scrapheap. junkyard, boneyard; drain, sewer; sty, pigsty, lair, den, Augean stables, sink of corruption; slum, rookery.
7, foul-mindedness, obscenity, foulmouthedness; evil-mindedness, dirtiness; foul, evil *or* dirty mind, filthiness; foul play. *Slang*, dirty fighting, dirty deal.
Verbs—**1,** be unclean, become unclean; rot, putrefy, fester, rankle, reek, stink (see MALODOROUSNESS); mold, go bad, spoil, become tainted.
2, render unclean, dirty, soil, smoke, tarnish, spot, smear, daub, blot, blur, smudge, smirch; drabble, draggle; spatter, besmear, bemire, beslime, begrime, befoul; splash, stain, sully, pollute, defile, debase, contaminate, taint, corrupt (see DETERIORATION).
Adjectives—**1,** unclean, dirty, filthy, grimy; soiled; dusty, smutty, sooty, smoky; thick, turbid, draggy; slimy; uncleanly, slovenly, untidy, slatternly, sluttish, draggletailed; uncombed, unkempt; unscoured, unswept, unwiped, unwashed, unpurified; squalid, nasty, coarse, foul, impure, offensive, abominable, piggish, beastly, reeky, sweaty, fetid, obscene; disgusting, nauseating, stomach-turning, revolting, sordid.
2, moldy, musty, mildewed, rusty, motheaten, rancid, bad, gone bad, fusty; scabrous, scrofulous, leprous; rotten, corrupt, tainted; gamy, high, flyblown, verminous, maggoty; putrid, putrescent, putrefied; purulent, carious, infected, infested, peccant, fecal, scurfy, impetiginous; gory, bloody; rotting, crapulous.

Antonym, see CLEANNESS.

---

uncomfortable, *adj.* uneasy; cramped; disturbed, restless; embarrassing, DIFFICULT; unpleasant, distressing. See PAIN.
uncommon, *adj.* unusual, rare, infrequent, sporadic; scarce; remarkable, extraordinary, strange; exceptional, original, unconventional. See RARITY, UNCONFORMITY. *Ant.,* see CONFORMITY.
uncompromising, *adj.* inflexible, unyielding; rigid, strict. See SEVERITY.
unconcerned, *adj.* indifferent, uninterested; disinterested; detached, aloof; unmoved, uncurious. See INSENSIBILITY. *Ant.,* see DESIRE, FEELING.
unconditional, *adj.* absolute, unreserved, unqualified; full, plenary; free. See COMPLETION, FREEDOM. *Ant.,* see LIMIT, RESTRAINT.
unconfined, *adj.* unrestrained, free, unhampered. See FREEDOM.

UNCONFORMITY [83]

Nouns—**1,** unconformity, nonconformity, unconventionality, informality, abnormality; anomaly, anomalousness; exception, peculiarity, irregularity; infraction, breach, violation *or* infringement of law, custom *or* usage; recusance; eccentricity, oddity, DISAGREEMENT.
2, individuality, speciality, idiosyncrasy, originality, mannerism; unusualness, strangeness; aberration; variety, singularity; exemption; mannishness, eonism.
3, nonconformist, nondescript, original; nonesuch, monster, prodigy, wonder, miracle, curiosity, *rara avis;* mongrel, hybrid (see MIXTURE); hermaphrodite; homosexual, bisexual, Lesbian; invert, pervert; monstrosity, rarity, freak; fish out of water; freak of nature; neither one thing nor another; neither fish, flesh nor fowl; one in a million; outcast, pariah, outlaw. *Colloq.*, character, card. *Slang*, crank, crackpot, screwball, fluke, queer fish, wack; homo, fairy, nance, pansy, fag, queer, ladylover, dike.
4, phoenix, chimera, hydra, sphinx, minotaur; griffin, centaur; hippogriff; cockatrice, roc, dragon, sea-serpent; mermaid; unicorn; Cyclops, Medusa, Hydra.
Verbs—be unconformable, leave the beaten track *or* path; baffle *or* beggar description. *Slang*, beat the Dutch.
Adjectives—**1,** unconformable, exceptional, abnormal, anomalous, out of place *or* keeping; irregular, arbitrary; lawless, aberrant, peculiar, unnatural, eccentric, uncommon, extraordinary, outside the pale.
2, unusual, uncommon; rare, singular, unique, curious, odd, extraordinary,

out of the ordinary, strange, monstrous; wonderful, unaccountable; outré, out of the way, remarkable, noteworthy; queer, quaint, *sui generis;* original, unconventional, unfashionable; unprecedented, unparalleled, unexampled, unheard of; fantastic, grotesque, bizarre; outlandish, exotic, weird, out of this world; preternatural; unsymmetric. *Colloq.,* offbeat, offtrail, wacky. *Adverbs*—unconformably; except, unless, save, barring, beside, without, let alone; however, yet, but.
Antonym, see CONFORMITY.

unconquerable, *adj.* indomitable, invincible; irresistible; impregnable. See POWER. *Ant.,* see IMPOTENCE.

unconscious, *adj.* unaware, insensible; stupefied, asleep, out; uninformed, ignorant; submerged, subconscious, suppressed, repressed. See IGNORANCE, INSENSIBILITY.

uncouth, *adj.* boorish, rude, crude, common, vulgar, UNCULTIVATED; awkward, gauche, ungraceful. See VULGARITY. *Ant.,* see TASTE.

uncover, *v.t.* open, unclose, unseal; disclose, discover; reveal, lay bare, expose; undress, denude, bare. See DISCLOSURE, OPENING, DIVESTMENT.

unction, *n.* anointing; unguent, ointment; unctuousness, gushing; fervor. See FEELING.

unctuous, *adj.* bland, fervid; ingratiating, gushing; glib; fatty, oily, greasy; oleaginous, adipose, sebaceous, saponaceous; slippery. See SERVILITY, SMOOTHNESS.

uncultivated, *adj.* unrefined, uncultured, UNCOUTH, rough; illiterate; wild, untilled, primeval. See WASTE, VULGARITY.

undaunted, *adj.* courageous, undismayed; bold, intrepid, dauntless, cool, reckless. See COURAGE. *Ant.,* see COWARDICE.

undeceive, *v.t.* disabuse, disillusion, correct. See INFORMATION.

undecided, *adj.* undetermined, unresolved, unsettled, problematical, uncertain, irresolute, doubtful, hesitant. See DOUBT. *Ant.,* see CERTAINTY.

undemonstrative, *adj.* restrained, reserved; impassive, inexpressive, stolid, apathetic, calm. See MODERATION. *Ant.,* see EXCITEMENT, ENDEARMENT.

undeniable, *adj.* indisputable, incontestable, unquestionable, incontrovertible, irrefutable. See CERTAINTY. *Ant.,* see DOUBT.

under, *prep. & adj.* below, beneath, underneath; subject to, controlled by; inferior, subordinate. See LOWNESS, SUBJECTION. *Ant.,* OVER.

underestimate, *v.* underrate, undervalue, underreckon; depreciate, disparage, detract from; not do justice to; misprize, disprize; RIDICULE; slight, NEGLECT; slur over; make light of, play down, underplay, understate, take no account of; minimize, belittle. See DETRACTION.

underestimation, *n.* understatement, depreciation, DETRACTION; pessimism, pessimist; underestimate, undervaluation, undervaluing; MODESTY, belittlement. *Ant.,* see EXAGGERATION, OVERESTIMATION.

undergo, *v.t.* suffer, experience, endure, sustain, bear, stand, withstand, put up with. See OCCASION, CIRCUMSTANCE, PAIN.

underground, *n. & adi.* —*n.* subway, tube, Metro; (the) resistance, partisans, guerrillas, Maquis. —*adj.* subterranean, buried, interred. See INTERMENT.

underhand, underhanded, *adj.* hidden, secret; deceitful, fraudulent, unfair, tricky; stealthy, sly, clandestine, furtive, devious. See DECEPTION.

underline, *v.t.* underscore; accent, emphasize, urge. See REQUEST.

undermine, *v.t.* excavate, mine, sap; honeycomb; subvert, weaken, demoralize, thwart, frustrate. See CONCAVITY, HINDRANCE, IMPOTENCE.

underneath, *prep. & adv.* beneath, below, lower, nether. See LOWNESS.

underrate, *v.t.* undervalue, UNDERESTIMATE, depreciate; disparage, belittle.

undersigned, *n.* signer, subscriber, endorser, petitioner. See WRITING.

understand, *v.t.* know, comprehend, grasp, catch; perceive, discern, realize, penetrate, apprehend; interpret, construe, fathom; gather, infer, assume. See MEANING, INTELLIGENCE.

understanding, *n.* discernment, comprehension, INTELLIGENCE, KNOWLEDGE, insight, perception; AGREEMENT. See INTELLECT.

undertaker, *n.* funeral director, mortician; sexton; embalmer. See INTERMENT.

UNDERTAKING [676]

Nouns—undertaking; compact, engagement, promise; enterprise, emprise, project; endeavor, venture, pilgrimage; matter in hand, BUSINESS; move, first move, beginning. *Colloq.*, tall order. *Slang*, caper.

Verbs—undertake; engage in, embark on; launch into, plunge into; volunteer; apprentice oneself to; engage, promise, contract, compact; take upon oneself, take on, devote oneself to, take up, take in hand; set about, go about; set to, fall to, fall to work; take the plunge, launch forth; set up shop; put in hand, put in execution; set forward; put one's hand to, turn one's hand to, throw oneself into; begin; broach, institute, originate; put one's hand to the plow, put one's shoulder to the wheel; have in hand, have many irons in the fire. *Colloq.*, tackle, bite off more than one can chew, go in for, go off the deep end, give it a whirl.

Adjectives—venturesome, adventurous.

Adverbs—on the fire. *Colloq.*, in the works.

Antonym, see REFUSAL.

---

undertow, *n.* riptide, undercurrent, backlash; eddy, vortex. See WATER.

underwear, *n.* underclothes, undergarments, lingerie, drawers, union suit, B.V.D.'s®, briefs, panties; foundation [garment], girdle, brassiere, bra, corset. *Colloq.*, unmentionables. See CLOTHING.

undesirable, *adj.* disagreeable, distasteful, objectionable, disliked; inadvisable, INEXPEDIENT. See DISLIKE.

undignified, *adj.* discreditable, inelegant, ludicrous, awkward, *gauche;* mean, degrading; indecorous, ill-bred. See VULGARITY.

undisguised, *adj.* true, genuine; evident, obvious; candid, frank, open. See EVIDENCE.

undivided, *adj.* concentrated, exclusive, WHOLE, intact, entire; single, united.

undo, *v.t.* loose, unlock, unfasten, untie, release; reverse, cancel, neutralize; destroy, ruin. See DISJUNCTION, DESTRUCTION.

undoing, *n.* downfall, defeat, ruin, reversal. See DESTRUCTION.

undone, *adj.* destroyed, lost, ruined; discovered. See FAILURE.

undoubted, *adj.* undisputed, *etc.* (see DOUBT); accepted, sure, assured, certain. See CERTAINTY.

undress, *v.* strip, disrobe, unclothe, dismantle, expose. *Slang*, peel. See DIVESTMENT.

undue, *adj.* unjust, inequitable; improper, inappropriate; extreme, excessive, immoderate, inordinate, exorbitant, unwarranted. See GREATNESS.

undueness, *n.* impropriety; ILLEGALITY; falseness; emptiness; imposition; usurpation, encroachment; presumption, presumptuousness; unnecessariness, excessiveness. See WRONG, INSOLENCE, USELESSNESS. *Ant.*, see RIGHT, USE, COURTESY.

undulate, *v.* surge, fluctuate, ripple, pulsate, wave. See AGITATION.

unearth, *v.t.* exhume, disinter; expose, disclose, discover, uncover; eradicate, uproot. See EJECTION, DISCLOSURE. *Ant.*, see INTERMENT.

unearthly, *adj.* supernatural, uncanny, ghostly, spectral, eerie; appalling, hair-raising. *Colloq.*, exceptional, unusual. See WONDER.

uneasy, *adj.* restless, restive; disturbed, perturbed, disquieted, uncomfortable; anxious, apprehensive, fearful; fidgety, jittery, on edge, jumpy; uncertain, unstable, touch-and-go. See DISCONTENT, FEAR.

uneducated, *adj.* ignorant, untaught, untutored, illiterate. See IGNORANCE.

unemotional, *adj.* apathetic, calm, cool, impassive, unfeeling. See INSENSIBILITY.

unemployed, *adj.* idle, jobless, out of work; loafing, at leisure, at liberty, free, available; looking [around]. See INACTIVITY.

unequal, *adj.* disparate, disproportionate; inadequate; uneven, mismatched, one-sided; inequitable, UNFAIR. See DIFFERENCE. *Ant.*, see EQUALITY.

unequaled, *adj.* unparalleled, unrivaled, unique, matchless, inimitable, peerless, nonpareil, incomparable. See SUPERIORITY. *Ant.*, see EQUALITY, INFERIORITY.

uneven, *adj.* variable; odd; UNEQUAL, disparate; rough, lumpy, broken, rugged. See DIFFERENCE, ROUGHNESS.

unfair, *adj.* unjust, unreasonable, UNEQUAL, inequitable; unsporting; disingenuous; partial, biased, prejudiced, discriminatory. See BADNESS.

unfaithful, *adj.* disloyal, faithless; adulterous, philandering, cheating, untrue, fickle; inaccurate, untrustworthy. See IMPROBITY, FALSEHOOD. *Ant.*, see PROBITY.

unfamiliar, *adj.* unknown; uncommon, strange, novel, new; unacquainted. See UNCONFORMITY.

unfashionable, *adj.* dowdy, old-fashioned, out-of-date; passé, antiquated. *Slang*, corny, old hat. See OLDNESS. *Ant.*, see NEWNESS.

unfasten, *v.t.* loose, loosen; liberate; disconnect, unbind, unfix, unpin. See DISJUNCTION, FREEDOM. *Ant.*, see JUNCTION.

unfathomable, *adj.* fathomless, bottomless, unplumbed, unsounded; unintelligible, inexplicable, incomprehensible. See DEPTH, SECRET.

unfavorable, *adj.* adverse, disadvantageous, inauspicious, unpropitious, unlucky; unfriendly, antagonistic; negative, contrary; inclement; inopportune, untimely. See ADVERSITY.

unfeeling, *adj.* hard, hard-hearted, cold, cold-blooded, cruel; heartless, inhuman, callous, dispassionate; merciless, pitiless, unmerciful, relentless, adamant. See INSENSIBILITY. *Ant.*, see SENSIBILITY, PITY.

unfinished, *adj.* crude, raw, sketchy, rough; incomplete; amateurish, inept; unpainted, *etc.* See IMPERFECTION, UNSKILLFULNESS.

unfit, *adj.* incapable, unqualified, *etc.* (see SKILL); incapacitated, unhealthy, in poor condition; unsuitable, inappropriate, *etc.* (see RIGHTNESS).

unfold, *v.* open, unroll, smooth out (see FOLD); disclose, expose, announce; develop, progress. See INFORMATION.

unforgiving, *adj.* relentless, unrelenting, implacable, unappeasable, inexorable; merciless, pitiless; vengeful. See MALEVOLENCE. *Ant.*, see FORGIVENESS.

unfortunate, *adj.* unlucky, hapless, ill-fated, ill-starred, star-crossed, luckless; unsuccessful, abortive, disastrous, ruinous. *Slang*, out of luck, S.O.L., behind the eight-ball, jinxed, hexed. See ADVERSITY.

unfounded, *adj.* baseless, vain, groundless, ungrounded. See ERROR.

unfriendly, *adj.* hostile, inimical, antagonistic; unfavorable. See HATE.

unfruitful, *adj.* barren, unproductive, infertile, sterile; fruitless. See FAILURE.

ungainly, *adj.* awkward, clumsy; gawky, ungraceful, lumbering; grotesque. See UGLINESS.

ungenerous, *adj.* illiberal; mean, harsh, exacting. See SELFISHNESS.

ungovernable, *adj.* unbridled, irrepressible, unruly, headstrong, uncontrollable, unmanageable, incorrigible; licentious. See DISOBEDIENCE. *Ant.*, see OBEDIENCE.

ungrateful, *adj.* unthankful, ingrate, unappreciative, thankless, forgetful (of favors); unwanted, unpleasing, unwelcome. *Ant.*, see GRATITUDE.

unguarded, *adj.* inadvertent, thoughtless, incautious; with one's guard down; not guarded (see DEFENSE).

unhappy, *adj.* unlucky, UNFORTUNATE; sad, sorrowful, wretched, miserable, dolorous, despondent, disconsolate, inconsolable, gloomy, joyless; inappropriate, dismal; calamitous, disastrous, catastrophic. See DISCONTENT, DEJECTION, ADVERSITY.

unhealthy, *adj.* sickly, infirm, ailing, invalided; delicate, frail; undesirable, inauspicious, ominous. See DISEASE.

unheard-of, *adj.* UNPRECEDENTED, unexampled; unbelievable, inconceivable. See WONDER.

unhinge, *v.t.* unsettle, derange, unbalance. See INSANITY.

unholy, *adj.* unhallowed, unconsecrated, unsanctified; wicked, profane; ungodly, impious, irreligious. *Colloq.*, frightful. See IRRELIGION, IMPIETY.

uniform, *adj.* homogeneous, homologous; of a piece, consistent; monotonous, even, invariable, changeless; stable. See CONFORMITY, AGREEMENT. *Ant.*, see DIFFERENCE, DISAGREEMENT, UNCONFORMITY.

unify, *v.t.* consolidate, combine, amalgamate, join. See JUNCTION.

UNIMPORTANCE [643]

Nouns—**1**, unimportance, insignificance, nothingness, immateriality, inconsequentiality, inconsequence; triviality, levity, frivolity; paltriness, LITTLENESS, USELESSNESS; matter of indifference; no object.

2, trivia, trifle, minutiae, details, minor details; drop in the ocean *or* bucket, pinprick, fleabite, molehill; nothing, nothing worth speaking of, nothing particular, nothing to boast of *or* speak of; bosh; small matter, no great matter, trifling matter; mere joke, mere nothing; hardly *or* scarcely anything; nonentity, cipher; no great shakes; child's play; small beer, small potatoes.

3, toy, plaything, gimcrack, gewgaw, bauble, trinket, bagatelle, kickshaw, knickknack, trifle; trumpery, trash, rubbish, stuff, frippery; chaff, froth, bubble, smoke, cobweb; weed; refuse, scum; joke, jest, snap of the fingers; fudge, fiddlesticks; pack of nonsense, straw, pin, fig, button, feather, two cents, halfpenny, penny, farthing, brass farthing; peppercorn, jot, rap, pinch of snuff, old song. *Colloq.,* red cent, row of pins, hill of beans.

4, nobody, nonentity, cipher, mediocrity, small fry, nine days' wonder, flash in the pan, dummy, straw man. *Colloq.,* lightweight, no great shakes.

Verbs—be unimportant, not matter; signify nothing; not matter a straw; make light of; dispense with; underestimate, belittle, set no store by, not care a straw about; catch at straws, overestimate. *Colloq.,* not give a damn, continental, rap, *or* hang.

Adjectives—**1,** unimportant; of little, small *or* no account *or* importance; immaterial; unessential, nonessential; indifferent; subordinate, inferior, mediocre, average; passable, fair; respectable, tolerable, commonplace; uneventful, mere, common; ordinary, habitual, inconsiderable, so-so, insignificant.

2, trifling, trivial; slight, slender, light, flimsy, frothy, idle; puerile; airy, shallow; weak, powerless (see IMPOTENCE); frivolous, petty, niggling, picayune, piddling; inane, ridiculous, ludicrous, farcical; finical, namby-pamby, wishy-washy, milk and water; inappreciable.

3, poor, paltry, pitiful; contemptible, sorry, mean, meager, shabby, miserable, wretched, vile, scrubby, niggardly, scurvy, beggarly, worthless, cheap, trashy, gimcrack, trumpery; not worth the pains, not worth while, not worth mentioning, not worth speaking of, not worth a thought, damn, *or* straw; beneath notice *or* consideration; futile, vain. *Slang,* measly, punk.

Adverbs—slightly, rather, somewhat, pretty well, tolerably.

Interjections—no matter! tut-tut! pshaw! pooh! pooh-pooh! bosh! humbug! fiddlesticks! fiddlededee! never mind! what of it! what's the odds! stuff and nonsense! *Slang,* nuts! baloney! bunk!

Antonym, see IMPORTANCE.

unintelligibility, *n.* incomprehensibility; inscrutability; inconceivableness; vagueness, obscurity; ambiguity; unrecognizability, illegibility; doubtful meaning; uncertainty; perplexity, confusion; mystification, LATENCY; riddle. *Ant.,* see MEANING.

unintentional, *adj.* accidental, involuntary, inadvertent, unpremeditated, spontaneous. See CHANCE. *Ant.,* see WILL.

union, *n.* unity, concord, uniting, joining, connection; COMBINATION, fusion, coalescence; marriage; confederation, association, alliance. See AGREEMENT, JUNCTION.

unique, *adj.* sole, single; singular, only, *sui generis;* UNEQUALED, matchless, unparalleled, unprecedented. See UNCONFORMITY. *Ant.,* see CONFORMITY.

unison, *n.* harmony, CONCORD; AGREEMENT; union; unanimity.

unite, *v.* join, combine, ally; marry, wed. See JUNCTION, CONNECTION.

unity, *n.* singleness, oneness, individuality; harmony, concurrence; unit; solitude, isolation; entity; individual; homogeneity, IDENTITY, completeness; unification, solidarity. See AGREEMENT, SECLUSION.

UNIVERSE [318]

Nouns—**1,** universe, cosmos, celestial sphere, macrocosm; infinity, span, [all] creation, earth and heaven, [all the] world, ether.

2, HEAVEN, the heavens, sky, empyrean, firmament, vault *or* canopy of heaven, celestial spaces, ceiling.

3, heavenly bodies, luminaries, starry host; nebula, galaxy, Milky Way, constellation, Zodiac; Aries, Aquarius, Cancer, Capricornus, Gemini, Leo, Libra, Pisces, Sagittarius, Scorpius, Taurus, Virgo; Great Bear, Little Bear, Ursa Major, Ursa Minor, Big Dipper, Little Dipper; Andromeda, Auriga, Boötes, Canis Major, Canis Minor, Cassiopeia, Centaurus, Cepheus, Cygnus, Draco, Hercules, Lyra, Orion, Perseus, Pleiades; star, Achenar, Arcturus, Aldebaran, Altair, Antares, Betelgeuse, Canopus, Capella, Centauri, Pollux, Procyon, Rigel, Sirius, Vega; falling star, shooting star, nova, double star, cluster.

4, solar system, sun, orb; planet, Mercury, Venus, Earth, Mars, Jupiter, Saturn, Uranus, Neptune, Pluto; planetoid, asteroid, satellite, moon, Luna, man in the moon, new moon, half moon, crescent, first, *etc.*, quarter; comet, meteor, meteorite; Earth, Terra, [terrestrial] globe, sphere, oblate spheroid, WORLD; cosmic rays, sunspots, aurora borealis *or* australis, northern *or* southern lights; artificial satellite, bird.

5, astronomy, astrometry, astrophysics, spectroscopy, cosmography, cosmogony, cosmology, geography, geodesy, geology, geognosy, geophysics; almagest, ephemeris, star atlas, star map, nautical almanac; observatory, planetarium.

Adjectives—**1,** universal, cosmic, empyrean, ethereal, celestial, heavenly; stellar, astral, sidereal, starry; solar, lunar, planetary, nebular; earthly, terrestrial, mundane.

2, astronomical, astrometrical, astrophysical, spectroscopic, *etc.;* geocentric, heliocentric, Copernican, Ptolemaic; 1st, 2nd, *etc.* magnitude.

3, general, common, natural; worldwide; widespread, broad, wide; catholic, entire, total, unlimited, encyclopedic, all-embracing, complete; prevalent, comprehensive.

---

unjust, *adj.* unfair, inequitable, undue, biased. See WRONG.

unkempt, *adj.* uncombed, disordered, ill-kept; slovenly, untidy, bedraggled. See DISORDER. *Ant.*, see ARRANGEMENT, CLEANNESS.

unkind, *adj.* pitiless, merciless, hard-hearted, cruel, brutal, harsh, inhuman. See MALEVOLENCE. *Ant.*, see PITY, BENEVOLENCE.

unknown, *adj.* incognito; unrecognized; unperceived. See IGNORANCE.

unlawful, *adj.* see ILLEGALITY.

unlike, *adj.* dissimilar, diverse, different, disparate; distinct, separate. See DIFFERENCE. *Ant.*, see SIMILARITY.

unlimited, *adj.* undefined; indefinite; boundless, limitless, uncounted, infinite, full, absolute, unconfined, unconstricted, unrestrained. See FREEDOM, GREATNESS.

unload, *v.* empty, disgorge, discharge, unpack. See DIVESTMENT.

unlock, *v.* unfasten, unbolt, disengage, undo; open; release, uncover, solve (mystery, *etc.*). See OPENING, DISCLOSURE.

unlucky, *adj.* UNFORTUNATE, ill-starred, ill-omened, hopeless, disastrous.

unman, *v.t.* emasculate, devitalize, unnerve, enervate, weaken; effeminize. See IMPOTENCE.

unmanly, *adj.* cowardly; ignoble; effeminate. See COWARDICE.

unmannerly, *adj.* rude, uncivil, ill-mannered; caddish, discourteous. See DISCOURTESY.

unmarried, *adj.* single; bachelor, spinster, maiden, virgin; widowed, divorced; celibate; unwed. See CELIBACY. *Ant.*, see MARRIAGE.

unmeaningness, *n.* meaninglessness, senselessness, ABSURDITY; vagueness, unintelligibility; nonsense, stuff and nonsense; jargon, gibberish, jabber, Jabberwocky; hocus-pocus, mumbo-jumbo; fustian, bombast; balderdash, babble; platitude, inanity; rigmarole, twaddle, trash, rubbish, moonshine, fiddle-faddle, bosh. *Colloq.*, poppycock, tommyrot, applesauce, baloney, doubletalk, hogwash, hooey, bunk, gobbledygook. *Ant.*, see MEANING.

unmerciful, *adj.* merciless, pitiless, inhuman, cruel; unfeeling, relentless, unrelenting; stern, hard-hearted, cold-blooded, callous. See SEVERITY, MALEVOLENCE.

unmistakable, *adj.* obvious, evident, MANIFEST, patent, clear, apparent, plain, open; downright, overt, certain. See EVIDENCE.

unmoved, *adj.* unaffected, impassive, unsympathetic, *etc.* (see FEELING); unconvinced, firm, unwavering, unshaken, steadfast. See INSENSIBILITY, RESOLUTION, STABILITY.

unnatural, *adj.* artificial, factitious; affected, stagy, insincere; strange, abnormal, foreign; monstrous, freakish, misshapen; merciless, cold. See AFFECTATION, MALEVOLENCE, UNCONFORMITY.

unnecessary, *adj.* useless, needless, inessential, superfluous, dispensable. See USELESSNESS.

unoccupied, *adj.* empty, vacant, tenantless; unemployed. See ABSENCE. INACTIVITY.

unpaid, *adj.* owing, due, unsatisfied; unsalaried, volunteer. See DEBT, WILL.

unpalatable, *adj.* distasteful, unsavory, unappetizing; INSIPID; inedible, uneatable, tasteless. See TASTE.

unparalleled, *adj.* UNEQUALED, peerless, unmatched, inimitable.

unpleasant, *adj.* disagreeable, offensive, displeasing, bad, nasty, sickening; noisome; unattractive, unsatisfactory; surly, UNFRIENDLY.

unpopular, *adj.* disliked, unloved, distasteful; out of favor.

unprecedented, *adj.* new, novel, unheard-of, original. See NEWNESS.

unprejudiced, impartial, dispassionate, UNBIASED, uninfluenced.

unpremeditated, *adj.* extempore, impromptu, extemporary, impulsive, spontaneous. See IMPULSE.

unprepared, *adj.* without preparation, unready; incomplete, rudimentary, abortive; immature, unripe, raw, green, crude; coarse; rough, unformed, uncooked, unpolished, unhatched, untaught, uneducated, untrained; premature; undigested; unseasoned, unqualified; unfitted, unorganized, unprovided, unequipped, in dishabille; shiftless, improvident, unthrifty, thoughtless, unguarded; happy-go-lucky; caught napping. See NEGLECT, IMPERFECTION, IMPULSE. *Ant.*, see PREPARATION.

unprincipled, *adj.* unscrupulous, thievish, rascally; lawless, perfidious, dishonest, fraudulent; wicked, evil. See IMPROBITY.

unproductive, *adj.* inoperative; barren, unfertile, unprolific; arid, dry, sterile, unfruitful; fruitless, bootless; fallow; impotent, issueless; unprofitable, useless; null and void, of no effect. See USELESSNESS, IMPOTENCE. *Ant.*, see PRODUCTION, USE.

unprofitable, *adj.* profitless, unbeneficial, unproductive; useless, futile, bootless, fruitless; costly, expensive; unwise, inexpedient. See USELESSNESS.

unqualified, *adj.* unfit, unsuited, ineligible; straight, thoroughgoing; certain, out-and-out, 'outright, unconditional, consummate, complete. See CERTAINTY, UNSKILLFULNESS.

unquestionable, *adj.* indubitable, indisputable, certain, sure, undeniable, irrefutable, incontrovertible. See CERTAINTY.

unquiet, *adj.* disturbed, agitated; restless, unpeaceful. See AGITATION.

unravel, *v.t.* ravel, untwine, disentangle, untangle; develop, explain, unfold. See ARRANGEMENT, INTERPRETATION. *Ant.*, see MISINTERPRETATION.

unreal, *adj.* imaginary, illusionary, illusory, shadowy; imponderable, unsubstantial, fanciful, fictitious; ideal. See IMAGINATION, NONEXISTENCE.

unreasonable, *adj.* irrational, illogical, absurd, senseless, preposterous, ridiculous; immoderate, excessive, extravagant, exorbitant; stubborn, obstinate. See ABSURDITY, RESOLUTION, GREATNESS.

unrefined, *adj.* unpurified, crude, raw, natural, native; unfastidious, uncultivated, rude, coarse, inelegant, vulgar, common. See ROUGHNESS, VULGARITY.

unrelenting, *adj.* relentless, inexorable, unyielding, rigorous, obdurate, remorseless, stern. See MALEVOLENCE, VULGARITY. *Ant.*, see FORGIVENESS.

unreliable, *adj.* untrustworthy, irresponsible, unstable, treacherous, inconstant; unsure, uncertain, fallible. See IMPROBITY, DOUBT.

unreserved, *adj.* frank, outspoken; demonstrative, cordial; unrestricted, absolute. See TRUTH, FREEDOM.

unresisting, *adj.* nonresistant, yielding, acquiescent, submissive, passive. See OBEDIENCE.

unrest, *n.* restlessness, disquiet, uneasiness; AGITATION, insurgence, rebellion. See CHANGEABLENESS.

unrestrained, *adj.* unbridled, unchecked, uncurbed, untrammeled, unbounded, free; inordinate, uninhibited, wanton, lax, loose, rampant. See FREEDOM. *Ant.,* see SUBJECTION, RESTRAINT.

unrestricted, *adj.* unlimited, unconfined, unqualified. See FREEDOM.

unripe, *adj.* premature, immature; precocious, crude. See YOUTH, ROUGHNESS.

unruffled, *adj.* serene, calm, placid, poised, undisturbed. See SMOOTHNESS, CHEERFULNESS.

unruly, *adj.* unmanageable, insubordinate, obstreperous, fractious, refractory, ungovernable, turbulent, boisterous. See DISOBEDIENCE, VIOLENCE.

unsafe, *adj.* insecure precarious, dangerous, risky; perilous; untrustworthy. See DANGER.

unsavoriness, *n.* unpalatability, tastelessness, insipidity; acridness, acridity; acidity, sourness; bitterness, acerbity; bad reputation *or* character; disreputableness. See TASTE, DISREPUTE.

unsavory, *adj.* unpalatable, ill-flavored; bitter, acrid, acerb; offensive, repulsive, nasty; sickening, nauseous, nauseating, loathsome; unpleasant, disagreeable; disreputable, unprepossessing. See TASTE, DISREPUTE.

unscrupulous, *adj.* unprincipled, conscienceless, dishonest. See IMPROBITY.

unseemly, *adj.* unbecoming, unsuitable, unfitting, improper, indecent, indecorous, tasteless. See UNCONFORMITY, VULGARITY. *Ant.,* see TASTE.

unseen, *adj.* imperceptible, INVISIBLE. *Ant.,* see VISION.

unselfish, *adj.* selfless, benevolent, altruistic; charitable, liberal, generous, magnanimous; disinterested, objective; self-sacrificing. See BENEVOLENT.

unselfishness, *n.* selflessness, devotion (to others); self-abnegation, self-sacrifice, self-denial, forgetfulness (of self); Good Samaritanism, good works; renunciation; loftiness, altruism, BENEVOLENCE, philanthropy, charity; highmindedness, NOBILITY, generosity, helpfulness; liberality, bountifulness, magnanimousness, magnanimity; openhandedness, largeness, largeheartedness; impartiality, fairness, lack of prejudice; disinterestedness; considerateness, consideration, tactfulness, thoughtfulness. See AID, GIVING. *Ant.,* see SELFISHNESS.

unsettle, *v.t.* upset, disturb, disarrange, displace, DISORDER; unhinge, derange, unbalance. *Ant.,* see ARRANGEMENT.

unsettled, *adj.* outstanding, unpaid; disturbed, troubled; unfixed, indeterminate. See DEBT, DOUBT. *Ant.,* see ARRANGEMENT, PAYMENT.

UNSKILLFULNESS [699]

Nouns—**1,** unskillfulness, incompetence; inability, inexperience; unproficiency; quackery, maladroitness, ineptness, clumsiness, awkwardness, two left feet.

2, mismanagement, misconduct; maladministration; misrule, misgovernment, misapplication, misdirection, misfeasance.

3, bungling, FAILURE; too many cooks, BLUNDER, mistake, ERROR; gaucherie, act of folly, botch, botchery; bad job; much ado about nothing, confusion, wild-goose chase, boy on a man's errand. *Slang,* snafu.

4, blunderer, bumbler, botcher, butcher, bungler, fumbler, duffer; bull in a china shop; butterfingers; greenhorn, palooka; Mrs. Malaprop.

Verbs—**1,** blunder, bungle, boggle, fumble, botch, flounder, stumble, trip, hobble; make a mess of, make a hash of; make a fool of oneself; play the fool; lose one's head. *Colloq.,* put one's foot in it; foul up. *Slang,* snafu.

2, err, make a mistake (see ERROR); mismanage, misconduct, misdirect, misapply; do things by halves; work at cross purposes; put the cart before the horse; not know what one is about; not know a hawk from a handsaw; kill the goose that lays the golden eggs; cut one's own throat, burn one's fingers; run one's head against a stone wall; fall into a trap, catch a Tartar, bring down the house about one's ears; too many irons in the fire.

Adjectives—**1,** unskillful, inexpert, bungling, awkward, ungainly, clumsy, unhandy, lubberly, gauche, maladroit; left-handed, heavy-handed; inapt, unapt, inept; neglectful; stupid, incompetent; unqualified, ill-qualified; unfit; quackish; raw, green, inexperienced. *Colloq.,* half-baked, all thumbs.

2, unaccustomed, rusty, out of practice, unused, untrained, uninitiated, unconversant, ignorant (see IGNORANCE); shiftless; unadvised, ill-advised, illcontrived; misguided; foolish, wild; infelicitous; penny wise and pound foolish, inconsistent.

Antonym, see SKILL.

unsociable, *adj.* reserved, aloof, distant, shy, solitary, retiring. See SECLUSION.

unsophisticated, *adj.* ingenuous, innocent, simple, guileless, ARTLESS, genuine. See INNOCENCE, SIMPLENESS.

unsound, *adj.* unhealthy, diseased, sickly; deranged, unbalanced, unsettled; untrue, incorrect, faulty, imperfect, illogical; decayed. See DISEASE, ERROR, IMPERFECTION.

unspeakable, *adj.* shocking, dreadful, horrible, execrable, enormous; unutterable, inexpressible, unimaginable. See EVIL, FEAR.

unspoken, *adj.* tacit, implied; unsaid. See SILENCE, MEANING.

unstable, *adj.* irregular, fluctuating, unsteady; inconstant, vacillating, fickle, changeable, variable. See CHANGEABLENESS.

unsteady, *adj.* fluctuating, waving, shifting, vacillating, irresolute, shaky, tottery, wabbly, infirm. See CHANGEABLENESS, DOUBT.

unsuccessful, *adj.* unprosperous, unfortunate, disastrous, unavailing, UNPRODUCTIVE. See FAILURE. *Ant.,* see SUCCESS, PRODUCTION.

unsullied, *adj.* immaculate, spotless, unspotted, pure, flawless, untarnished. See CLEANNESS, PURITY.

unsuspicious, *adj.* trusting, trustful, unsuspecting, credulous, unquestioning, ARTLESS. See BELIEF, CREDULITY. *Ant.,* see DOUBT.

untaught, *adj.* illiterate, unlettered, uneducated See IGNORANCE. *Ant.,* see KNOWLEDGE.

untenable, *adj.* indefensible, insupportable, inconsistent, illogical. See ERROR. *Ant.,* see REASONING, TRUTH.

unthinkable, *adj.* inconceivable, unimaginable, IMPOSSIBLE; repugnant, out of the question; beyond belief, UNBELIEVABLE.

untidy, *adj.* slovenly, careless, disorderly; messy, littered; dowdy, frumpy, slipshod; unkempt. See DISORDER, UNCLEANNESS.

untie, *v.t.* loosen, free, unbind, unknot. See FREEDOM. *Ant.,* see RESTRAINT.

until, *prep.* till, to, up to [the time of]. See TIME.

untimeliness, *n.* intempestivity; inopportuneness, inopportunity, unseasonableness; evil hour; contretemps; intrusion; inexpedience, earliness, lateness, anachronism. *Ant.,* see OCCASION.

untiring, *adj.* tireless, indefatigable, unwearied, unremitting, unrelaxing. See RESOLUTION.

untoward, *adj.* inconvenient, perverse; vexatious; ungraceful, awkward. See ADVERSITY.

untrained, *adj.* unbroken, untamed; raw, inexperienced, green. See UNSKILLFULNESS.

untrue, *adj.* false, trumped-up; unfounded; lying, invented, fabulous, fabricated, forged; fictitious, factitious, supposititious, surreptitious; illusory; treacherous, disloyal, faithless, unfaithful. *Colloq.,* fake. *Slang,* phony. See FALSEHOOD, IMPROBITY. *Ant.,* see TRUTH, PROBITY.

untruth, *n.* FALSEHOOD, lie; prevarication, mendacity, fib, forgery, fabrication, invention; misstatement, misrepresentation; perjury, perversion, falsification, EXAGGERATION; fiction; fable; make-believe; pretense, pretext; sham, DECEPTION; half-truth, white lie; hoax. *Colloq.,* whopper, yarn, tall story; fake. *Slang,* sell. *Ant.,* see TRUTH.

unusual, *adj.* uncommon, rare; out-of-the-way, curious, odd, queer, singular; abnormal, anomalous, exceptional, extraordinary; irregular, bizarre, peculiar; unwonted, unaccustomed. *Colloq.,* off-beat. See UNCONFORMITY, DIFFERENCE.

unutterable, *adj.* UNSPEAKABLE; unpronounceable, incommunicable, indescribable; ineffable. See WONDER.

unveil, *v.t.* disclose, reveal, uncover. See DISCLOSURE.

unwary, *adj.* rash, unwise, indiscreet, imprudent, unguarded, injudicious. See NEGLECT. *Ant.,* see CARE.

unwell, *adj.* ailing, sick, indisposed, ill, invalid, diseased. See DISEASE.
unwieldy, *adj.* clumsy, awkward, cumbersome, ungainly, bulky, ponderous. *Colloq.*, hulking. See GRAVITY, SIZE.
unwilling, *adj.* loath, disinclined, indisposed, averse, reluctant; not content; adverse, opposed, laggard, backward, remiss, slack, slow to; indifferent, squeamish, fastidious; refusing to, recalcitrant, restive, demurring, objecting, unconsenting; grudging, involuntary; forced. See REFUSAL, DISSENT.
unwillingness, *n.* indisposition, indisposedness; lack of willingness, *etc.*, disinclination, DISLIKE, averseness, aversion; renitence; reluctance, hesitation; OBSTINACY; DISSENT. *Ant.*, WILLINGNESS.
unwise, *adj.* foolish, injudicious, imprudent, ill-advised; silly, fatuous, idiotic, senseless, impolitic, indiscreet. See IGNORANCE, ERROR.
unworthy, *adj.* undeserving; worthless; unbecoming, disgraceful, shameful; despicable, discreditable, derogatory. See DISREPUTE.
unyielding, *adj.* immovable, unbending, rigid, inflexible, firm; grim, indomitable, obdurate, stubborn, obstinate, relentless, uncompromising; pertinacious, resolute; intractable, perverse. See HARDNESS, OPPOSITION, RESOLUTION, SEVERITY.
up, *adj.* upward, aloft, above. See ASCENT, HEIGHT. *Ant.*, down.
upbraid, *v.t.* reprove, chide, admonish, rebuke, reprimand, scold; accuse, charge, revile. See DISAPPROBATION. *Ant.*, see APPROBATION.
upheaval, *n.* cataclysm, debacle; AGITATION, UNREST, revolution.
uphill, *adj.* ascending, rising; precipitous; laborious, difficult, strenuous. See EXERTION, OBLIQUITY.
uphold, *v.t.* maintain, support, sustain; champion; approve, encourage. See AID, DEFENSE, SUPPORT. *Ant.*, see OPPOSITION.
uplift, *n.* elevation, IMPROVEMENT, refinement, inspiration.
upper, *adj.* higher, superior. See HEIGHT. *Ant.*, see LOWNESS.
upright, *adj.* vertical, perpendicular, erect; honorable, conscientious, upstanding, honest, righteous. *Colloq.*, straight. See DIRECTION, PROBITY. *Ant.*, horizontal; see OBLIQUITY, IMPROBITY.
uproar, *n.* tumult, hubbub, discord, pandemonium, bedlam, ado, bustle, din, clamor. *Colloq.*, hullabaloo. See DISORDER, LOUDNESS.
uproot, *v.t.* extirpate, eradicate, root out, abolish, destroy. See DESTRUCTION, EXTRACTION.
upset, *v. & n.* —*v.t.* overthrow, overturn, capsize; disturb, bother, discompose, disconcert; disarrange, unbalance; demoralize. —*n.* reversal, overturn, disorder. See DESTRUCTION, INVERSION, AGITATION.
upshot, *n.* outcome, conclusion, result, effect, meaning. See SEQUENCE.
upstart, *n.* parvenu. *Colloq.*, pusher. See INSOLENCE.
up–to–date, *adj.* modern, new, fresh, current, timely; fashionable, modish, stylish; restored, renovated, revised, modernized. See NEWNESS, FASHION.
urban, *adj.* city, town, metropolitan, civic. See ABODE. *Ant.*, rural.
urbane, *adj.* suave, sophisticated, debonair; civil, polite, affable. See COURTESY.
urge, *v. & n.* —*v.* solicit, plead, importune, advocate, exhort, egg on, incite, instigate; press, push. —*n.* impulse, desire, ambition. See HASTE, IMPULSE, REQUEST.
urgent, *adj.* important, imperative, exigent, necessary, critical; importunate, pressing. See IMPORTANCE, REQUEST.

USE [677]

Nouns—**1,** use, employ, employment; exercise, application, appliance; adhibition, disposal; consumption; usufruct; recourse, resort, avail; utilization, service, wear; usage, function, practice, method, HABIT; usefulness (see UTILITY).
2, user, employer, applier, consumer, buyer, purchaser, enjoyer of.
Verbs—**1,** use, make use of, utilize, employ, put to use; put in action, operation, *or* practice; set in motion, set to work; ply, work, wield, handle, maneuver, manipulate; play, play off; exert, exercise, practice, avail oneself of, profit by; resort to, have recourse to, betake oneself to; take advantage of; try.

2, render useful, turn to account, utilize; bring into play; press into service; bring to bear upon, devote, dedicate, consecrate; apply, adhibit, dispose of; make a cat's-paw of; fall back upon, make shift with; make the most of, make the best of.

3, use up, consume, absorb, dissipate; exhaust, drain; expend; tax, wear.

Adjectives—in use; used; well-worn, well-trodden; useful (see UTILITY).

Antonyms, see NEGLECT, WASTE.

USELESSNESS [645]

Nouns—**1,** uselessness, inutility; inefficacy, futility; ineptitude, inaptitude; impracticableness, impracticality; inefficiency, incompetence, IMPOTENCE, UNSKILLFULNESS, worthlessness, vanity, inanity, nugacity; triviality, UNIMPORTANCE.

2, unproductiveness, unprofitableness; infertility, infecundity, barrenness, aridity; labor lost, wild-goose chase.

3, waste; desert, Sahara, wilderness, wild, tundra, marsh; litter, rubbish, odds and ends, cast-offs; shoddy, rags, orts, trash, refuse, sweepings, scourings, rubble, debris; stubble, leavings; dregs; weeds, tares; rubbish heap.

Verbs—**1,** be useless; be unproductive, come to nothing; fail; seek or strive after impossibilities; roll the stone of Sisyphus; bay at the moon, preach to the winds; lock the barn door after the horse is stolen; cast pearls before swine; carry coals to Newcastle. *Colloq.,* chase rainbows.

2, render useless; disable, hamper (see HINDRANCE); cripple, lame; spike guns, clip the wings; put out of gear; decommission, dismantle, disassemble, break up, tear down, raze, demolish, destroy; pull the fangs *or* teeth of, tie one's hands, put in a straitjacket.

Adjectives—**1,** useless, inutile, inefficacious, futile, unavailing, bootless; inoperative, unproductive, barren, infertile, sterile, fallow; unprofitable, null and void; inadequate, insufficient; inept, ineffectual, incompetent, unskillful (see UNSKILLFULNESS); superfluous, dispensable; thrown away, wasted; abortive.

2, worthless, valueless, unsaleable; not worth a straw; vain, empty, inane, gainless, profitless, fruitless; unserviceable, unprofitable; ill-spent; obsolete; good for nothing; of no earthly use; not worth having, unnecessary, unneeded.

Adverbs—uselessly, to little purpose, to no purpose, to little or no purpose.

Antonym, see UTILITY, USE.

usher, *v. & n.* —*v.t.* escort, introduce, announce, induct. —*n.* doorman; escort, groomsman, vestryman. See BEGINNING, RECEPTION.

usual, *adj.* customary, accustomed, habitual, ordinary, wonted, normal, regular, everyday; traditional. See HABIT. *Ant.,* see SURPRISE, UNCONFORMITY.

usurp, *v.t.* seize, expropriate, arrogate, appropriate; conquer, annex, snatch, grab. See ILLEGALITY.

UTILITY [644]

Nouns—utility; usefulness, efficacy, efficiency, adequacy; service, stead, avail; help, AID; applicability, function, value; worth, GOODNESS; productiveness; utilization (see USE).

Verbs—be useful, avail, serve; subserve; conduce, tend; answer *or* serve a purpose; bear fruit, produce (see PRODUCTION); profit, remunerate, benefit, do good; perform *or* discharge a function; do *or* render a service; bestead, stand one in good stead; be the making of; help, AID.

Adjectives—useful, of use; serviceable, good for; instrumental, conducive, tending; subsidiary, helping, advantageous, beneficial, profitable, gainful, remunerative, worth one's salt; valuable; prolific, productive; practical, practicable; pragmatic; adequate; efficient, efficacious; effective, effectual; expedient, applicable, available, ready, handy, at hand, tangible; commodious, adaptable.

Adverbs—usefully, efficiently, *etc.; pro bono publico.*

Antonym, see USELESSNESS.

utmost, *adj.* most, greatest, farthest, furthest; last, final; total, unlimited, full, complete. See END, COMPLETION, WHOLE.

utter, *adj. & v.* —*adj.* total, complete, entire; extreme, unusual; unqualified; stark, sheer, downright, absolute. —*v.t.* speak, voice; pronounce, express, enunciate, deliver. See COMPLETION, WHOLE, SOUND, SPEECH.

V

vacancy, *n.* emptiness, void, vacuum, SPACE; inanity, stupidity, idleness. See ABSENCE. *Ant.,* see PRESENCE, DENSITY.

vacant, *adj.* empty; open, free, untenanted, unoccupied, to let; blank, void, hollow; shallow, brainless, inane. See ABSENCE, OPENING. *Ant.,* see PRESENCE.

vacate, *v.* move out; leave, decamp; abandon, relinquish, surrender, quit; evacuate, leave empty; annul, cancel, invalidate, quash. See RELINQUISHMENT.

vacation, *n.* holiday, rest, time off, leave [of absence]; recess, respite; abandonment, DEPARTURE. See INACTIVITY.

vacillation, *n.* uncertainty; fluctuation; hesitation, faltering, shilly-shallying. See DOUBT, OSCILLATION.

vacuum, *n.* void, vacancy, emptiness, nothingness; SPACE.

vagabond, *n.* hobo, tramp; vagrant, wanderer; idler; beggar. *Colloq.,* bum, knight of the road. See TRAVEL, POPULACE.

vagrant, *n. & adj.* —*n.* VAGABOND, *etc.* —*adj.* wandering, aimless, wayward, roving; erratic, capricious. See TRAVEL.

vague, *adj.* unclear, blurred, blurry; amorphous, shapeless; undefined, uncertain; indistinct; inexact, indefinite; obscure. See DIMNESS, DOUBT. *Ant.,* see CERTAINTY, VISION.

vain, *adj.* proud, conceited; futile, fruitless. See VANITY.

valediction, *n.* farewell speech, valedictory; farewell, good-by(e), adieu. See DEPARTURE, SPEECH.

valet, *n.* SERVANT; manservant, gentleman's gentleman, attendant.

valiant, *adj.* valorous, brave, courageous, gallant; daring, intrepid, dauntless, lionhearted. See COURAGE. *Ant.,* see COWARDICE.

valid, *adj.* sound, logical; legal, binding; well-grounded, just. See TRUTH, REASONING, LEGALITY. *Ant.,* see IMPOTENCE, ILLEGALITY.

valley, *n.* vale; river land; dale, dell, glen; canyon, hollow. See CONCAVITY.

valor, *n.* COURAGE, intrepidity, fearlessness; prowess, heroism, gallantry; daring, derring-do. *Ant.,* see COWARDICE.

valuable, *adj.* precious, costly; worthy, meritorious; estimable; useful. See IMPORTANCE, USE. *Ant.,* see USELESSNESS.

value, *n. & v.* —*n.* usefulness; worth; price, cost, rate, rating; estimation, valuation; merit; significance; SHADE, tone, emphasis. —*v.t.* esteem, prize, treasure, regard highly; appraise, evaluate, assess, rate. See IMPORTANCE. *Ant.,* see CHEAPNESS, UNIMPORTANCE.

vampire, *n.* bloodsucker, bat; ghoul; parasite. *Slang,* siren, seducer, vamp, temptress. See EVILDOER, IMPURITY.

van, *n.* truck, lorry, moving van; forefront, vanguard; *avant garde;* FRONT, head. See VEHICLE. *Ant.,* see REAR.

vanish, *v.i.* disappear, fade out; dissolve; become invisible. *Slang,* decamp, vamoose, beat it. See ABSENCE, DEPARTURE. *Ant.,* see APPEARANCE.

VANITY [880]

Nouns—**1,** vanity, conceit, conceitedness; immodesty, self-esteem, self-love, self-praise; complacency, smugness, *amour propre.*

2, PRIDE, airs, pretensions, mannerism; egotism, egoism; priggishness; coxcombery, vainglory, pretense, OSTENTATION; assurance, INSOLENCE.

3, egotist, egoist, prig, pretender, fop, coxcomb, know-it-all.

4, vainness, futility, USELESSNESS.

Verbs—be vain; put oneself forward; fish for compliments; give oneself airs; BOAST; presume, swagger, strut; plume *or* preen oneself. *Colloq.*, get on one's high horse. *Slang*, put on side, the dog, *or* the ritz.

Adjectives—vain, vain as a peacock, conceited, immodest, overweening, pert, forward; haughty, puffed-up (see PROUD); prideful, vainglorious, high-flown, ostentatious; self-satisfied, smug, complacent, opinionated; imperious, arrogant, pretentious, priggish; egotistic; *soi-disant;* unabashed, unblushing. *Colloq.*, swell-headed.

Adverbs—vainly, priggishly, pridefully, proudly, haughtily, *etc.*

Antonym, see MODESTY.

vanquish, *v.t.* conquer, subdue, subjugate, overcome; quell, silence; worst, rout; MASTER. See SUCCESS. *Ant.*, see FAILURE.

vapid, *adj.* flat, tasteless, INSIPID; tame, spiritless, lifeless, DULL.

VAPOR [326]

Nouns—**1,** vapor, vaporousness, vaporization, volatilization; gaseousness, gaseity; evaporation; distillation, aëration, sublimation, exhalation; volatility.

2, gas, elastic fluid; oxygen, ozone, hydrogen, nitrogen, argon, helium, fluorine, neon; natural gas, coal gas, illuminating gas; sewer gas, poison gas; damp, chokedamp; AIR, vapor, ether, steam, fume, reek, effluvium, miasma, flatus; cloud (see CLOUDINESS).

3, vaporizer, atomizer, still, retort; fumigation, steaming; spray, spray gun, airbrush, sprayer.

4, pneumatics, pneumostatics; aerostatics, aerodynamics.

Verbs—vaporize, volatilize, render gaseous, distill, sublime; evaporate, exhale, smoke, transpire, emit vapor, fume, reek, steam, fumigate.

Adjectives—vaporous, volatile, volatilized, gaseous, gassy, reeking; aëriform, evaporable, vaporizable

Antonym, see DENSITY

variance, *n.* CHANGE, alteration; difference, DISAGREEMENT, DISCORD; jarring; dissension; variation, UNCONFORMITY.

variation, *n.* variance, alteration, CHANGE, modification; diversification; DIVERGENCE, DEVIATION, aberration; innovation. *Ant.*, see IDENTITY, STABILITY.

variegated, *adj.* many-colored, particolored; dichromatic, polychromatic; kaleidoscopic; rainbow-hued, iridescent; opaline, opalescent; prismatic; nacreous, pearly; shot; pied, paint, pinto, piebald; motley; mottled, marbled; pepper-and-salt; dappled, brindle; mosaic, tessellated; plaid; spotted, spotty; speckled, freckled; flecked, striated, barred, streaky, veined; tiger-striped, tabby. See COLOR.

variegation, *n.* dichromism, trichromism; particolor; iridescence, play of colors, polychromy; maculation; spottiness, colorfulness. See COLOR.

variety, *n.* variation, diversity, DIFFERENCE; assortment; kind, CLASS; brand; multifariousness; VAUDEVILLE.

various, *adj.* diversified, multiform, diverse; different; many, several; manifold, numerous, sundry; changeable, unfixed. See DIFFERENCE, MULTITUDE. *Ant.*, see SIMILARITY.

varnish, *n. & v.* —*n.* shellac, lac, lacquer; spar; gloss, mitigation, whitewash, excuse. —*v.t.* paint with shellac, *etc.;* palliate, gloze, gloss, excuse, whitewash; finish.

vary, *v.* CHANGE, alter; fluctuate; differ, disagree. See DIFFERENCE. *Ant.*, see UNIFORMITY.

vase, *n.* urn, cup, chalice, jug, amphora, ampulla. See RECEPTACLE.

vassal, *n.* liege, liegeman, (feudal) tenant; serf; thrall, bondman; subject. See SERVANT.

vast, *adj.* huge, immense; infinite, boundless; immeasurable; tremendous, enormous. See SIZE, SPACE. *Ant.*, see LITTLENESS.

vaudeville, *n.* turns, acts, variety; burlesque, music hall. See DRAMA.

vault, *n. & v.* —*n.* arch, dome, cupola; bank vault, safe; tomb, sepulcher, catacomb; dungeon, cell, cellar; LEAP, jump, pole-vault. —*v.* arch; leap over, jump; pole-vault. See CONVEXITY, INTERMENT.

vaunt, *v.* boast, brag, vapor, talk big. See BOASTING. *Ant.*, see MODESTY.
veer, *v.i.* swerve, shift; jibe, come about, yaw, deviate. See CHANGE, DEVIATION. *Ant.*, see DIRECTION.

VEGETABLE [365, 367]

Nouns—**1,** vegetable kingdom, vegetation, vegetable life; plants, flora, verdure.
2, vegetable, plant; tree, shrub, bush; vine, creeper; herb, herbage; grass; annual, perennial, biennial, triennial.
3, timber, timberland, forest; wood, woodlands; park, chase, greenwood, brake, grove, copse, coppice, thicket, spinney; underbrush, brushwood; tree, shade tree, *etc.*
4, bush, jungle, prairie; heath, heather; fern, bracken; furze, gorse, grass, sod, turf; pasture, pasturage; sedge, rush, weed; fungus, mushroom, toadstool; lichen, moss; growth.
5, foliage, foliation, branch, bough, ramage, leaf; flower, bloom, blossom, bine; pulse, legume, bean, root, bulb.
6, BOTANY, AGRICULTURE, agronomy, horticulture, silviculture; botanist, plant physiologist, horticulturist, etc.; botanical gardens, herbarium, arboretum.
Adjectives—vegetable, herbaceous, botanic; sylvan, arboreous, arborescent, dendritic, woody, grassy, verdant, verdurous; floral; mossy; lignous, ligneous; wooden; woodsy, leguminous; endogenous, exogenous.

vegetation, *n.* vegetable life; flora, verdure, greenery. See VEGETABLE, INACTIVITY.
vehemence, *n.* VIOLENCE, VIGOR; impetuosity; force; ardor, fervor, warmth, zeal. See EXERTION. *Ant.*, see MODERATION.
vehement, *adj.* violent, furious, hot; forcible; impetuous, excited, passionate; fervent, earnest. See EXCITEMENT.

VEHICLE [272]

Nouns—**1,** vehicle, conveyance, equipage, turnout, cart, rig, car, wagon, railroad train. See PASSAGE, TRAVEL.
2, carriage, coach, chariot, chaise, phaeton, landau, barouche, victoria, brougham, sulky; two-wheeler, dogcart, trap, buggy.
3, stage, stagecoach, diligence, mailcoach; hackney; omnibus, bus, cab, taxi, taxicab, hansom. *Colloq.*, jitney, hack.
4, sled, sledge, sleigh, bobsled, toboggan, travois.
5, handcart, pushcart, barrow, wheelbarrow, handbarrow; sedan chair; gocart, baby carriage, perambulator, stroller; wheelchair, litter, stretcher. *Colloq.*, pram.
6, cycle, bicycle, wheel, two-wheeler, tricycle, velocipede, three-wheeler; motorcycle, motor scooter, scooter. *Slang*, bike, trike.
7, automobile, car, motorcar; sedan, coupé, limousine, cabriolet, phaeton, convertible, roadster, touring car; stock car; trailer, caravan; racing car; patrol car, squad *or* police car, patrol wagon, Black Maria; ambulance, hearse; station wagon, beach wagon, suburban; truck, lorry, tractor, van, moving van, semitrailer; wrecker. *Colloq.*, auto. *Slang*, bus, flivver, hotrod, rod, heap, jalopy; prowl car.
8, train, locomotive, passenger train, streamliner; express, local, limited, freight train; subway, subway train, underground, tube, Metro; trolley, streetcar, cable car, interurban, tram, trackless trolley; freight car, boxcar, Pullman, sleeper, refrigerator car, tender, tank car, caboose, dining car, smoking car, day coach.

veil, *n. & v.* —*n.* net, mesh; curtain, screen, cloak, cover; film, haze, CLOUDINESS. —*v.t.* conceal; becloud; disguise; shield, cover, shroud. See CONCEALMENT, COVERING, CLOTHING. *Ant.*, see DISCLOSURE.
vein, *n.* blood vessel; streak, stripe, marbling; rib (of a leaf); [ore] deposit, lode, seam, ledge, leader; thread; bent, humor, disposition, temper. See PASSAGE, COLOR.

VELOCITY [274]

Nouns—**1,** velocity, speed, celerity, swiftness, rapidity, expedition (see AC-TIVITY); acceleration; HASTE; hurry, spurt, rush, dash; smart, lively, swift, *or* spanking pace; flying, flight; gallop, canter, trot, run, scamper; race, horserace, steeplechase; sweepstakes, Derby; handicap; foot race, marathon, relay race.

2, lightning, light, electricity, wind; cannonball, rocket, arrow, dart, quick-silver; telegraph, express train; torrent; hustler; eagle, antelope, courser, racehorse, gazelle, cheetah, greyhound, hare, deer, doe, jackrabbit, squirrel.

Verbs—**1,** speed, hasten, post, scuttle; scud, scour, scamper; run, fly, race, cut away, shoot, tear, whisk, sweep, whiz, skim, brush; bowl along; rush, dash, bolt; trot, gallop, bound, flit, spring, charge, dart; march in double time; ride hard, cover the ground. *Colloq.,* cut along, step along, step lively, zip, cut and run, make it snappy. *Slang,* go all out, go hell-bent for election, go like a bat out of hell; skedaddle; go hell-for-leather, burn up the road; make tracks.

2, hurry, hasten (see HASTE); accelerate, quicken; wing one's way; spur on; crowd on sail; gain ground; show a clean pair of heels; overtake, overhaul, outstrip. *Slang,* stir one's stumps, step on the gas, give her the gun, boot home.

Adjectives—fast, speedy, swift, rapid, quick, fleet; nimble, agile, expeditious, express; flying, galloping, light-footed, nimble-footed; winged, mercurial, electric, telegraphic; light of heel; swift as an arrow; quick as lightning, quick as thought.

Adverbs—swiftly, apace; at a great rate, at full speed, full tilt, posthaste; all sails crowding, heeling over, full steam ahead; trippingly; instantaneously; in seven league boots; with whip and spur; as fast as one's legs will carry one; at top speed; by leaps and bounds. *Colloq.,* on the double, at a fast clip, like mad, like sixty, like all possessed, like greased lightning, like a streak, like a blue streak. *Slang,* P.D.Q., lickety-split, like a bat out of hell; jet-propelled.

Antonym, see SLOWNESS.

---

velvet, *n. & adj.* —*n.* silk, plush, velour, velveteen; mossiness; SMOOTHNESS, SOFTNESS. *Slang,* surplus, winnings, profit; gravy, graft. —*adj.* velvety, mossy; smooth, soft, mild, soothing, bland; light, caressing.

venal, *adj.* money-loving, mercenary, sordid; corrupt, bribable; purchasable (of persons). See IMPROBITY, PARSIMONY. *Ant.,* see PROBITY.

veneer, *n. & v.* —*n.* facing; overlay; coating; shell; superficial polish. See LAYER, COVERING, AFFECTATION.

venerable, *adj.* aged, hoary; respected, revered; patriarchal. See AGE.

veneration, *n.* esteem, RESPECT; admiration, WORSHIP; awe. *Ant.,* see DISRESPECT.

vengeance, *n.* RETALIATION, revenge; vengefulness; reprisal, retribution, nemesis. *Ant.,* see FORGIVENESS.

venial, *adj.* excusable, pardonable, slight, trivial. See MODERATION.

venomous, *adj.* poisonous; spiteful, malicious, malignant; envenomed, noxious, toxic; virulent, deadly. See MALEVOLENCE, DISEASE.

vent, *v. & n.* —*v.t.* utter, express; let out, let off, emit, expel. —*n.* ventilator, OPENING, airhole, air pipe, outlet, funnel; emission; blowhole; utterance, expression. See SPEECH, WIND, AIR.

ventilate, *v.t.* AIR; freshen; disclose, publish. See PUBLICATION.

venture, *v. & n.* —*v.* dare, risk; speculate; undertake; presume, hazard, take a chance. —*n.* enterprise, UNDERTAKING; adventure; speculation, hazard, risk. See RASHNESS, CHANCE.

veracity, *n.* veraciousness, truthfulness, frankness, TRUTH; sincerity, candor, honesty, fidelity; plain dealing, *bona fides;* PROBITY; ingenuousness. *Ant.,* see FALSEHOOD, IMPROBITY.

verbal, *adj.* spoken, oral; unwritten; literal, verbatim, word-for-word. See SPEECH. *Ant.,* see WRITING.

verbose, *adj.* wordy, prolix, repetitive, talkative. See LOQUACITY.

verdant, *adj.* green, grassy; fresh, springlike; inexperienced, naïve, artless.

verdict, *n.* JUDGMENT, ruling, finding, decision, opinion, decree; determination, conclusion; award, sentence. See JUSTICE, LAWSUIT, CHOICE.

verdure, *n.* grass, growth, greenness, greenery. See VEGETABLE.

verge, *n. & v.* —*n.* EDGE, brink, marge, margin; point, eve; LIMIT. —*v.i.* be on the point (of); border, skirt, approach, touch; tend, incline. See TENDENCY, NEARNESS.

verify, *v.t.* corroborate, substantiate; confirm, prove, make certain; establish; identify. See EVIDENCE, SUPPORT. *Ant.,* see NEGATION.

vermin, *n.* pests, insects, rats, mice; scum, riffraff. See ANIMAL, POPULACE.

vernacular, *n.* tongue, dialect; argot, SLANG. See SPEECH.

versatile, *adj.* many-sided; adaptable; skilled. See SKILL.

verse, *n.* versification; POETRY, prosody, poesy; line; stanza; meter, measure; poem, doggerel; (scriptural) passage.

versed, *adj.* skilled, skillful; knowledgeable; accomplished, trained, conversant. See SKILL, KNOWLEDGE. *Ant.,* see UNSKILLFULNESS, IGNORANCE.

version, *n.* rendition; account; translation. See INTERPRETATION.

vertical, *n. & adj.* —*n.* verticality, verticalness, erectness; perpendicularity; straightness. —*adj.* upright, erect, perpendicular; normal; straight, bolt upright, up-and-down, rampant; standing up; rectangular, orthogonal. *Ant.,* see HORIZONTAL, CURVATURE.

vertigo, *n.* dizziness, giddiness, vertiginousness. See INSANITY.

very, *adv.* exceedingly, highly; emphatically, decidedly, notably; unusually, remarkably, uncommonly; extremely, surpassingly. See GREATNESS. *Ant.,* see MODERATION.

vessel, *n.* container; vase, urn, jug; boat, SHIP. See RECEPTACLE.

vest, *v. & n.* —*v.t.* furnish, endow, invest; clothe; give the power *or* right, enfranchise; authorize. —*n.* waistcoat; bodice. *Colloq.,* weskit. See LEGALITY, CLOTHING, PROVISION.

vestige, *n.* trace, REMAINDER, EVIDENCE, relic.

vestments, *n.* canonicals; cloth; habit; robe, gown, frock, surplice, cassock, scapular, scapulary, cope, scarf, amice, chasuble, alb, stole; fanon; tonsure, cowl, coif, hood; calotte; bands; pontificals, pall; mitre, miter, tiara, triple crown; cardinal's hat, red hat, biretta; crozier, pastoral staff; thurible. See CLOTHING.

veteran, *n.* old man, elder, patriarch, graybeard; grandfather, grandmother; old campaigner, seasoned *or* old soldier, ex-soldier; octogenarian, nonagenarian, centenarian. *Colloq.,* oldster, old-timer, codger, gaffer. See COMBATANT, AGE. *Ant.,* see YOUTH.

veto, *n. & v.* —*n.* NULLIFICATION; "no," nyet; pocket veto; disapproval, prohibition. —*v.t.* turn thumbs down; forbid; disallow, prevent, disapprove, prohibit, negate; kill, quash. See DISAPPROBATION, NEGATION, REFUSAL.

vex, *v.* tease, plague, harass, torment; roil, pique; fret, chafe, irritate, annoy, provoke, nettle. *Colloq.,* peeve, rile, upset. See RESENTMENT.

vibration, *n.* vibrating; shaking, shimmying; thrill, quiver, throb, pulsation; AGITATION, trembling; rattling. See OSCILLATION.

vice, *n.* viciousness, evildoing, wrongdoing, wickedness, iniquity, sin, sinfulness; crime, criminality; immorality, IMPURITY, looseness of morals; demoralization, turpitude, moral turpitude, depravity, degradation; weakness, weakness of the flesh, fault, frailty, ERROR; besetting sin; delinquency; sink of iniquity. See EVIL, IMPROBITY. *Ant.,* see GOOD, VIRTUE, PROBITY.

vice versa, oppositely, contrariwise, conversely, turnabout. See OPPOSITION.

vicinity, *n.* neighborhood, locality, vicinage; NEARNESS, proximity; environs, ENVIRONMENT.

vicious, *adj.* sinful, wicked, iniquitous, immoral, WRONG; criminal, disorderly; vile; felonious, nefarious, infamous, heinous; demoralized, corrupt, depraved, perverted; evil-minded, shameless; abandoned, debauched, degenerate, dissolute; reprobate, beyond redemption. See EVIL, IMPROBITY.

vicissitude, *n.* CHANGE; change of fortunes; fluctuation.

victim, *n.* prey; sufferer; DUPE, gull, cat's-paw; sacrifice, martyr. See PAIN.

victimize, *v.t.* cheat, dupe, swindle; hoax, fool, gull; deceive, hoodwink. *Colloq.,* sell, bamboozle. See DECEPTION.

victor, *n.* champion, winner; conqueror, vanquisher. See SUCCESS. *Ant.*, see FAILURE.

victory, *n.* conquest, triumph, SUCCESS; winning, mastery; the palm, laurel, wreath, award, trophy, prize, pennant. *Ant.*, see FAILURE.

victuals, *n.pl.* see FOOD.

vie, *v.i.* rival, emulate; contend, strive, compete. See CONTENTION.

view, *n. & v.* —*n.* sight; panorama, vista, prospect, scene; viewpoint, angle; opinion, BELIEF, notion; APPEARANCE, aspect. —*v.t.* see; survey, scan; watch, witness; consider, regard, study. See VISION, THOUGHT.

vigilance, *n.* CARE; guardedness, watchfulness, alertness; wide-awakeness; caution. *Ant.*, see NEGLECT.

vigilant, *adj.* alert, wary, watchful; wakeful, unsleeping; careful, cautious, circumspect; on the lookout, on the *qui vive.* See CARE. *Ant.*, see NEGLECT.

vigor, *n.* force, POWER, STRENGTH, energy, vehemence; spirit, verve, warmth; vitality; eloquence; grandeur. *Slang*, pep. *Ant.*, see IMPOTENCE.

vile, *adj.* base, debased, low, lowly, mean; repulsive, odious; foul, nasty; EVIL, corrupt, wicked, depraved. See BADNESS, IMPURITY. *Ant.*, see GOODNESS, VIRTUE.

vilify, *v.t.* revile, calumniate; traduce, slander, libel; defame; decry, belittle, slur. See DETRACTION. *Ant.*, see APPROBATION.

village, *n.* town, hamlet, small town. See ABODE.

villain, *n.* blackguard, scoundrel; knave, rascal, rogue; badman; EVILDOER. *Slang*, heavy (see DRAMA). See EVIL. *Ant.*, see GOODNESS.

villainy, *n.* roguery, rascality; criminality, depravity, wickedness, wrong-doing. See EVIL. *Ant.*, see GOODNESS.

vim, *n.* zest, ENERGY, VIGOR; *Colloq.*, pep, zip, ginger.

VINDICATION [937]

Nouns—**1,** vindication, justification, warrant; exoneration, exculpation; ACQUITTAL; whitewashing; extenuation; palliation; softening, mitigation.
2, reply, DEFENSE, objection, demurrer, exception; apology, plea, pleading; excuse, extenuating circumstances; allowance, argument. *Colloq.*, alibi.
3, vindicator, apologist, justifier, defender, defendant (see ACCUSATION).
Verbs—**1,** vindicate, justify, warrant; exculpate, ACQUIT; clear, set right, exonerate, whitewash; extenuate, palliate, excuse, soften; apologize, put a good face upon; mince; gloss over, bolster up. *Colloq.*, whitewash, give a clean bill of health.
2, defend; advocate; stand, stick, *or* speak up for; bear out, support; plead, say in defense; propugn, put in a good word for. *Slang*, go to bat for.
3, make allowance for, take the will for the deed, do justice to; give one his due, give the devil his due; make good; prove one's case.
Adjectives—vindicated, vindicating, vindicatory, vindicative; palliative; exculpatory; apologetic, vindicable; excusable, defensible, pardonable; venial, specious, plausible, justifiable.
Antonym, see ACCUSATION, GUILT.

vindictive, *adj.* vengeful, spiteful; resentful; implacable, rancorous; bearing a grudge. See RETALIATION, RESENTMENT. *Ant.*, see FORGIVENESS.

violate, *v.* break, breach; outrage, profane, desecrate; disrespect; transgress, infringe; usurp, encroach; rape, ravish. See ILLEGALITY, IMPURITY, IMPIETY. *Ant.*, see OBEDIENCE, RESPECT.

VIOLENCE [173]

Nouns—**1,** violence, vehemence, intensity, might, impetuosity; boisterousness; effervescence, ebullition, ebullience; turbulence, bluster; uproar, riot, row, rumpus, devil to pay, the fat in the fire; turmoil, DISORDER; ferment, AGITATION; storm, tempest, rough weather; squall, earthquake, volcano, thunderstorm, cyclone, tornado, hurricane; maelstrom, whirlpool.
2, SEVERITY, ferocity, ferociousness, fierceness, rage, fury; exacerbation, exasperation, malignity; fit, frenzy, paroxysm, orgasm; force, brute force; outrage, strain, shock, spasm, convulsion, throe; hysterics, passion, EXCITEMENT.
3, outbreak, outburst; burst, discharge, volley, explosion, blast, detonation,

rush, eruption, displosion, implosion; torrent; storm center.

4, fury, fiend, dragon, demon, tiger; wild beast; fire-eater, hellion, hellcat, virago, termagant, beldame; madcap; rabble rouser, lynch mob, terrorist, agitator, *agent provocateur;* thug, tough, strongarm man, gunman.

Verbs—**1,** be violent, run high; ferment, effervesce; rampage; run wild, run riot; break the peace; rush, tear; rush headlong, run amuck, raise a riot; lash out, make the fur fly; bluster, rage, roar, riot, storm; seethe, boil, boil over; fume, foam, come in like a lion, wreak, wreck, spread havoc, ride roughshod, out-Herod Herod; spread like wildfire. *Colloq.,* make *or* kick up a row, raise the devil, raise Cain, raise the roof; roughhouse; fly off the handle; blow one's top, let off steam.

2, break out, fly out, burst out; explode, implode, go off, displode, fly, detonate, thunder, blow up, flash, flare, burst; shock, strain.

3, render violent, stir up, excite, incite, urge, lash, stimulate; irritate, inflame, kindle, foment, touch off; aggravate, exasperate, exacerbate, convulse, infuriate, madden, lash into *or* goad to fury; fan the flames, add fuel to the flames.

Adjectives—**1,** violent, vehement; ungentle, boisterous, wild; impetuous; rampant.

2, turbulent; disorderly, blustering, raging, troublous, riotous, tumultuous, obstreperous, uproarious; extravagant, unmitigated; ravening, frenzied, desperate (see RASHNESS); infuriated, furious, outrageous, frantic, hysterical; fiery, flaming, scorching, hot, red-hot; seething; savage, fierce, ferocious, barbarous; headstrong, ungovernable, uncontrollable; convulsive, explosive; volcanic, meteoric; stormy.

Adverbs—violently, *etc.;* amain; by storm, by force, by main force; with might and main; tooth and nail; with a vengeance; headlong.

Antonym, see MODERATION.

---

violin, *n.* fiddle; string; Amati, Stradivarius, Strad, Guarnerius; violinist (see MUSICIAN); (*pl.*) string section. See MUSICAL INSTRUMENTS.

virgin, *n. & adj.* —*n.* maiden; celibate; vestal; spinster. —*adj.* chaste, untouched; maidenly, fresh, virginal, pure; new, uncut, unexplored, primeval. See CELIBACY, NEWNESS, PURITY. *Ant.,* see MARRIAGE.

virile, *adj.* manly, MALE, masculine; vigorous, potent; fully-sexed. *Ant.,* see IMPOTENCE.

virtual, *adj.* practical; implied, implicit; substantial; true, veritable; potential. See SUBSTANCE, NEARNESS.

VIRTUE [944]

Nouns—virtue; virtuousness, GOODNESS; morality; moral rectitude; integrity, PROBITY; nobleness (see REPUTE); prudence; morals, ethics, DUTY; cardinal virtues; merit, worth, excellence, CREDIT; self-control (see RESOLUTION); fortitude, self-denial (see MODERATION); JUSTICE, PURITY; good deeds, good behavior; discharge, fulfillment *or* performance of duty; INNOCENCE.

Verbs—be virtuous, practice virtue; do, fulfill, perform *or* discharge one's duty; redeem one's pledge; behave; command *or* master one's passions; keep on the straight and narrow path; set an example, be on one's good *or* best behavior.

Adjectives—virtuous, good, innocent; meritorious, deserving, worthy, correct; dutiful, duteous, moral, right, righteous, right-minded; well-intentioned, creditable, laudable, commendable, praiseworthy; above *or* beyond praise; excellent, admirable; sterling, pure, noble, exemplary, matchless, peerless; saintly, saintlike; heaven-born, angelic, seraphic.

Adverbs—virtuously, *etc.*

Antonym, see EVIL, IMPROBITY.

---

virulent, *adj.* poisonous, venomous; deadly; toxic, noxious; malignant, malevolent; caustic, acrimonious. See BADNESS, DISEASE, RESENTMENT.

visage, *n.* face, countenance, physiognomy; semblance, look, aspect, guise. *Slang,* puss, phiz, map. See APPEARANCE, FRONT.

viscous, *adj.* viscid; ropy, glutinous, slimy; mucid; sticky, mucilaginous; oleaginous, greasy. See COHERENCE.

visibility, *n.* perceptibility; conspicuousness, conspicuity; distinctness; AP-
PEARANCE; exposure; manifestation; ocular proof, evidence, *or* demonstration; field of view, VISION. *Ant.*, see DARKNESS, BLINDNESS.

visible, *adj.* visual, perceptible, perceivable, discernible, apparent; in view,
in full view, in sight; unclouded; obvious, manifest, plain, clear, distinct,
definite; well-defined, in focus; recognizable; palpable, conspicuous; standing out, prominent, plain as the nose on one's face, as large as life. See
VISION. *Ant.*, INVISIBLE; see BLINDNESS.

VISION [441]

Nouns—**1,** vision, sight, optics, eyesight, seeing; view, look, espial, glance,
ken; glimpse, peep; gaze, stare, leer; perception, contemplation; regard,
survey; observance, observation, examination; inspection, introspection;
reconnaissance, watch, espionage, autopsy; ocular inspection; sightseeing;
perspicacity, discernment. *Slang*, looksee; once over; eyeful.
2, 20-20 vision, *etc.;* farsightedness, eagle eye; nearsightedness, myopia;
myosis, astigmatism, presbyopia; double vision, colorblindness, Daltonism,
night blindness, nyctalopia, hemeralopia; strabismus, cross-eyes, cock-eyes;
squint, cast, cataract, ophthalamania; goggle eyes, wall-eyes.
3, point of view, viewpoint; vantage point; observatory; gazebo, loophole,
crow's nest; belvedere, watchtower; peephole, lookout post; field of view;
theater, amphitheater, arena, vista, horizon; visibility; prospect, perspective; commanding view, bird's-eye view; periscope.
4, visual organ, organ of vision; eye; eyeball; naked eye; retina, pupil,
iris, cornea, white. *Colloq.*, optics, orbs, peeper, peeled *or* weather eye.
5, refraction, distortion; illusion, optical illusion, mirage, phantasm,
specter, apparition; reflection, mirror, image.
Verbs—**1,** see, behold, discern, perceive, have in sight, descry, sight, make
out, discover, distinguish, recognize, spy, espy, get *or* catch a glimpse of;
command a view of; watch, witness, look on; cast the eyes on; see at a
glance. *Colloq.*, spot.
2, look, view, eye; lift up the eyes, open one's eyes, look around, survey,
scan, inspect; run the eye over, reconnoiter, glance around, direct the eyes
to, observe, peep, peer, pry, take a peep; stare (down); strain one's eyes;
fix *or* rivet the eyes on; gaze; pore over; leer, ogle, glare; goggle, stare,
gape, gawk, gawp; cock the eye. *Slang*, get a load of, give the eye, take a
gander at, give the once-over.
3, dazzle, blind; wink, blink, squint; screw up the eyes; have a mote in the
eye; see through a glass darkly.
Adjectives—visual, ocular, seeing; optic, optical; ophthalmic; clear-sighted;
eagle-eyed, hawk-eyed, lynx-eyed, keen-eyed, Argus-eyed; visible; misty,
dim. See DIMSIGHTED.
Adverbs—visibly; in sight of, with one's eyes open; at sight, at first sight, at
a glance; at first blush; *prima facie*.
Antonyms, see BLIND, DIMSIGHTED.

---

visionary, *adj. & n.* —*adj.* idealistic, unpractical, quixotic, utopian; imaginary, delusory, chimerical. —*n.* dreamer, idealist, theorist. See IM-
AGINATION. *Ant.*, realist; see EXISTENCE.
visit, *n. & v.* —*n.* call; interview, appointment; stopover, sojourn. —*v.*
call on, drop in; stop, stay, tarry; sojourn. See ARRIVAL, SOCIALITY.
visitation, *n.* visit; calamity, misfortune; seizure, stroke, blow; disaster;
bad luck, hardship. See ADVERSITY, DISEASE. *Ant.*, see PROSPERITY.
visualize, *v.t.* picture, envision; imagine, project. See IMAGINATION.
vital, *adj.* essential, indispensable, necessary; life-supporting; vivifying, invigorating; alive, live, vibrant, animate. See NECESSITY, LIFE. *Ant.*, see
USELESSNESS.
vitality, *n.* LIFE; vigor, virility; viability. *Ant.*, see DEATH.
vitiate, *v.t.* adulterate, weaken; impair, spoil; destroy, void, invalidate;
corrupt, pollute; deteriorate. See DESTRUCTION, DETERIORATION. *Ant.*, see
IMPROVEMENT.
vituperate, *v.t.* vilify, abuse, revile; reproach, inveigh (against), rebuke,

scold, upbraid; objurgate, tongue-lash. See DETRACTION. *Ant.*, see AP-
PROBATION.

vituperation, *n.* scurrility, invective, abuse; censure, reproach, blame;
scolding. See DISAPPROBATION, DETRACTION. *Ant.*, see APPROBATION.

vivacious, *adj.* lively, animated, sprightly; gay, breezy, spirited; frolicsome,
sportive, cheerful. See VIGOR; LIFE, CHEERFULNESS. *Ant.*, see DEJECTION.

vivacity, *n.* vivaciousness, *etc.* See LIFE, CHEERFULNESS, VIGOR.

vivid, *adj.* striking; telling; picturesque; lifelike, realistic; lively, vital;
vibrant, glowing; fresh, intense, unfaded, brilliant. See MEANING, COLOR,
LIFE, LIGHT. *Ant.*, DULL.

vixen, *n.* female fox; harridan, shrew, witch, scold, virago, harpy. See
FEMALE, EVILDOER.

vocabulary, *n.* words, glossary, word-list; dictionary, lexicon; LANGUAGE.

vocal, *adj.* articulate; spoken, [to be] sung; choral, lyric; VERBAL, oral.
See SPEECH, MUSIC.

vocalist, *n.* singer; tenor, alto, *etc.* *Slang*, crooner, warbler, songstress,
thrush, nightingale. See MUSICIAN.

vocation, *n.* profession; work, trade; calling, occupation. See BUSINESS,
PURSUIT.

vociferous, *adj.* loud, noisy, clamorous; blatant, obstreperous; loudmouthed. See LOUDNESS. *Ant.*, see SILENCE.

vogue, *n.* mode, STYLE, FASHION; practice, custom, usage; favor; HABIT.

voice, *n. & v.* vocality; speaking *or* singing voice; inflection, intonation; tone of voice; ventriloquism, ventriloquy; lung power; vocal cords,
vocalization; CRY, expression, utterance, vociferation, enunciation, articulation; articulate sound, SPEECH; accent, accentuation; emphasis, stress;
singer; tenor, baritone, barytone, bass, basso, soprano, contralto, alto, *etc.;*
representation, vote, participation. —*v.t.* speak, utter; give voice, utterance, *or* tongue to; shout, cry, exclaim, ejaculate; express; vocalize, articulate, enunciate, pronounce, enounce, announce; accentuate; deliver, mouth.
Ant., see SILENCE.

void, *adj., v. & n.* —*adj.* empty, vacuous, blank; unoccupied, untenanted;
devoid, lacking, unfilled; null, invalid; not binding; vain, unreal, unsubstantial. —*v.t.* vacate; abrogate, nullify, negate; evacuate, eject, cast off.
—*n.* emptiness, SPACE, nothingness; vacuum; abyss, chasm. See ABSENCE,
NULLIFICATION, INSUBSTANTIALITY. *Ant.*, see SUBSTANCE, LEGALITY.

volatile, *adj.* gaseous, vaporizable; fickle, changeable, mercurial; light,
giddy; lively; capricious; buoyant, airy. See VAPOR, CHANGEABLENESS.

volition, *n.* WILL, CHOICE, voluntariness; option, preference, willingness.
Ant., see COMPULSION, NECESSITY.

voluble, *adj.* talkative, verbose; fluent, glib. See LOQUACITY.

volume, *n.* BOOK, tome; contents, capacity; bulk, mass, dimensions, SIZE,
quantity. See GREATNESS, MEASUREMENT.

voluminous, *adj.* capacious, big, bulky, copious; ample. See SIZE, GREAT-
NESS. *Ant.*, see LITTLENESS.

voluntary, *adj.* fresh, free-will; volunteered; willing; spontaneous; willed;
unasked; deliberate, intentional; unforced. See WILL. *Ant.*, see COMPUL-
SION.

volunteer, *n. & v.* —*n.* enlister; offerer. —*v.* enlist; offer, proffer; give,
donate. See WILL.

voluptuous, *adj.* sensual, carnal, fleshy, meretricious; epicurean, worldly.
Slang, sexy. See PLEASURE, DESIRE. *Ant.*, see MODERATION.

vomit, *v.* throw up, disgorge, puke; belch, spew, eject. See EJECTION.

voracious, *adj.* ravenous, omnivorous; rapacious; starving, famished, hungry; gluttonous, edacious. See GLUTTONY. *Ant.*, see MODERATION.

vortex, *n.* eddy, whirlpool; maelstrom; whirl; storm center. See ROTATION,
WIND, WATER.

votary, *n. & adj.* —*n.* votarist, devotee, disciple, follower, enthusiast, adherent, zealot. *Colloq.*, fan. —*adj.* votive, dedicated; consecrated; pledged;
devoted. See DESIRE, AFFIRMATION, PIETY.

vote, *n. & v.* —*n.* poll, ballot; franchise, suffrage; CHOICE, voice, option,
election; referendum, plebiscite. —*v.* cast a ballot; choose, select, elect,
establish, enact, ratify, veto, nullify. See AFFIRMATION, REFUSAL.

vouch, *v.t.* guarantee, warrant; affirm, declare; answer for, attest; certify; SUPPORT, back, bear witness. See AFFIRMATION, EVIDENCE. *Ant.,* see NEGATION.

vow, *v. & n.* —*v.* swear, take oath; vouch, affirm; pledge, promise; dedicate, devote; take vows. —*n.* dedication, devotion; oath, swearing; pledge, promise; consecration. See AFFIRMATION.

voyage, *n.* cruise, sea trip, crossing, sail, excursion. See TRAVEL.

VULGARITY [851]

Nouns—**1,** vulgarity, vulgarism; barbarism; bad taste; inelegance, indelicacy; gaucherie, ill-breeding, DISCOURTESY; incivility; coarseness, indecorum, boorishness; rowdyism, blackguardism; ribaldry, obscenity. *Slang,* risqué story, double entendre.

2, gaudiness, tawdriness, finery, frippery, brummagem, tinsel, gewgaws, knickknacks, OSTENTATION.

3, vulgarian, rough diamond; tomboy, hoyden, cub, unlicked cub; lout, churl, knave, clown; barbarian; snob, parvenu, frump, slattern, slut. *Colloq.,* cad, bounder, roughneck.

Verbs—be vulgar, offend, misbehave, roughhouse.

Adjectives—**1,** vulgar, in bad taste, unrefined, coarse, indecorous, ribald, gross; unseemly, unpresentable; common, boisterous, loud; tasteless, obnoxious.

2, dowdy, slovenly, shabby, low, plebeian, uncourtly; uncivil, discourteous, ill-bred, bad-mannered, ill-mannered; ungentlemanly, unladylike, unfeminine; unkempt, uncombed, unpolished, uncouth, rude, awkward; homespun, provincial, countrified, rustic; boorish, clownish; savage, blackguard, rowdy, snobbish; barbarous, barbaric; low, vile, ignoble, monstrous, shocking; obscene.

3, bizarre, outré, outlandish; affected, meretricious, ostentatious, extravagant; gaudy, tawdry, flashy; cheap; obtrusive.

Antonym, see TASTE.

---

vulnerable, *adj.* open (to attack); weak, defenseless; assailable; susceptible. See DANGER, IMPOTENCE. *Ant.,* see SAFETY, POWER.

vulpine, *adj.* foxlike; foxy, crafty, wily, CUNNING.

W

wad, *n.* lump, plug; stuffing, filling, batting. See CLOSURE.

wag, *v. & n.* —*v.* wave, shake, sway, jerk, waggle; wigwag; nod. See OSCILLATION, AGITATION. —*n.* WIT, humorist.

wage, *v.t.* wager; conduct, make, carry on, undertake (as war). See UNDERTAKING, WARFARE.

wager, *n. & v.* bet, stake, gamble, risk, hazard; gage. See CHANCE.

wages, *n.pl.* pay, PAYMENT, hire, COMPENSATION, remuneration; earnings, salary; income.

wagon, *n.* cart, dray, wain; truck, lorry, car; van. See VEHICLE.

waif, *n.* stray, foundling; [street] Arab; homeless child. See LOSS.

wail, *v. & n.* lament, CRY, moan, bewail; howl, ululate, caterwaul; complain. See LAMENTATION.

waist, *n.* girth, MIDDLE, midriff, loin, waistline; bodice, blouse, shirt, tunic. See CLOTHING.

wait, *v.* stay, linger, tarry, abide, remain, bide [one's time]; dally, procrastinate, delay; serve, attend; await, expect, look for. *Slang,* sit tight; cool one's heels; sweat it out. See EXPECTATION.

waiter, *n.* SERVANT, garçon, attendant, steward, servitor, waitress; tray, salver (see RECEPTACLE).

waive, *v.* relinquish, renounce, give up, forgo, disclaim, surrender (a right *or* claim). See RELINQUISHMENT.

wake, *n. & v.* —*n.* path, track, trail, swath; vigil, watch. See REAR, SE-

QUENCE, INTERMENT. —*v.* rouse, arouse, awake, awaken; stir, excite, animate. See ACTIVITY, CARE. *Ant.*, see REPOSE.

wakeful, *adj.* alert, watchful, on guard, on the *qui vive,* vigilant; restless, sleepless, insomniac. See ACTIVITY, CARE. *Ant.*, see INACTIVITY, REPOSE.

walk, *n. & v.* ramble, stroll, promenade, saunter, TRAVEL (on foot), march, parade, tramp, hike; tread, pace, step. *Colloq.* (*n.*) constitutional.

walk, *n.* calling, occupation; sphere, province, department; BUSINESS.

wall, *n.* SIDE, partition, bulkhead, flange, splashboard; rampart, DEFENSE; barrier; fence; cliff, precipice; levee, dike, seawall; (*pl.*) PRISON. See INCLOSURE, HINDRANCE.

wallet, *n.* purse, pocketbook, billfold; bag, pouch, sack, moneybag; pack, knapsack. See RECEPTACLE, MONEY.

wallop, *v.* thrash, beat, strike, punch, hit, clout. See IMPULSE.

wallow, *v.i.* tumble, grovel, ROLL, flounder, welter, toss; revel, delight in, luxuriate in. See LOWNESS, PLEASURE.

wan, *adj.* pale, pallid, waxen, waxy, ashen, ashy, bloodless. See COLORLESSNESS. *Ant.*, see COLOR, HEALTH.

wand, *n.* rod, caduceus, mace, SCEPTER; staff, stick, baton; divining rod, dowsing stick; withe. See SORCERY.

wander, *v.i.* rove, ramble, stroll, walk, range; digress, swerve, deviate, stray; rave, maunder, be delirious; moon; straggle, forage See TRAVEL, DEVIATION, INSANITY. *Ant.*, see STABILITY.

wane, *v. & n.* —*v.i.* DECREASE, lessen, ebb, fade, diminish, peter out, dwindle; abate, subside; decline, sink, fail, slacken. —*n.* FAILURE, ebb, decline, decay, DECREASE. *Ant.*, see INCREASE.

want, *n. & v.* —*n.* need; POVERTY, indigence; lack, dearth, deficiency, ABSENCE; shortage, inadequacy, scarcity; NECESSITY, requirement. —*v.* lack, need; DESIRE, wish, crave; fall short of, be deficient, miss, omit, NEGLECT, fail. See FAILURE, INSUFFICIENCY. *Ant.*, see SUFFICIENCY, WEALTH, INDIFFERENCE.

wanton, *adj. & n.* —*adj.* lewd, licentious, lustful, loose, dissolute, immoral; frolicsome; abandoned; capricious, willful; heedless, reckless; wayward, perverse; luxuriant, rampant, exuberant. See DESIRE, IMPURITY. —*n.* LIBERTINE; flirt, baggage, hussy, trollop. See EVILDOER.

warble, *v.* trill, sing. See MUSIC.

ward, *v. & n.* —*v.t.* watch, guard, defend, protect; fend, parry, stave (off). —*n.* watch, guard, DEFENSE, protector; CARE, charge, custody; protégé(e), dependent, minor; precinct, district; hospital room. See REGION.

warden, *n.* KEEPER; game warden, church warden; custodian, curator; ranger; jailer, turnkey; superintendent. See SAFETY, CLERGY.

warder, *n.* KEEPER; gatekeeper; warden; guard; mace, staff.

warehouse, *n.* STORE, depot, supply dump; storehouse. See RECEPTACLE.

WARFARE [722]

Nouns—**1,** warfare, state of war, fighting, hostilities; war, combat, ARMS, force of arms, the sword; appeal to arms; baptism of fire, ordeal of battle; war to the death, open war, internecine war, civil war; world war, global war; war to end war; revolutionary war, revolution, religious war, crusade; underground warfare; guerrilla warfare; chemical, germ, *or* bacteriological warfare; trench warfare, war of position, war of attrition; aerial, naval, *or* atomic warfare; Mars, Ares, Odin, Bellona; cold war, hot war.

2, campaign, campaigning, crusade, expedition, invasion; investment, siege.

3, battlefield, battleground, field; theater, front; camp, encampment, bivouac, billet; flank, center, salient, line.

4, art of war, tactics, strategy, generalship, soldiership; ballistics, ordnance, gunnery; chivalry; weapons (see ARMS); logistics.

5, battle, fighting (see CONTENTION); service, active service. See COMBATANT.

6, call to arms, mobilization; trumpet, clarion, bugle, pibroch; slogan; war cry, warwhoop; Rebel yell, battle cry; beat of drum; tom-tom; password, watchword; muster, rally.

7, warlikeness, belligerence, bellicosity, combativeness, contentiousness; militarism; chauvinism, jingoism.

Verbs—**1,** go to war, declare war, carry on *or* wage war, let slip the dogs of war; cry havoc; take the field, give battle, join battle; set to, fall to, engage, measure swords with, cross swords; come to blows, come to close quarters; fight, combat; contend (see CONTENTION); battle with; fight it out, fight hand to hand; sell one's life dearly. *Colloq.*, flex one's muscles.

2, arm; raise troops, mobilize; enroll, enlist, sign up; draft, conscript, call to the colors, recruit; serve, be on active service; campaign; wield the sword, bear arms; live by the sword, die by the sword; shoulder a musket, smell powder, be under fire; spill blood. *Colloq.*, join up.

Adjectives—**1,** warring, battling, contending, contentious; armed, armed to the teeth, sword in hand; in arms, under arms, up in arms; at war with; in battle array, in open arms, in the field; embattled, beleaguered, besieged; at swords' points.

2, warlike, belligerent, combative, bellicose, martial; military, militant; soldierlike, soldierly; chivalrous; strategic, tactical.

Adverbs—at war, in the thick of the fray, in the cannon's mouth; at sword's point; on the warpath.

Antonyms, see PACIFICATION, PEACE.

---

warm, *adj.* hot; tepid, lukewarm; sunny, mild, summery; close, muggy; ardent, fervid, fervent; passionate; responsive; glowing, enthusiastic, hearty, affectionate, cordial; lively, excitable; feverish; hasty, quick; alive, living. See HEAT, FEELING, EXCITEMENT. *Ant.*, see COLD.

WARNING [668]

Nouns—**1,** warning, forewarning, caution, *caveat;* notice (see INFORMATION); premonition, foreboding, PREDICTION; lesson, dehortation; admonition, monition; ALARM.

2, warning sign, handwriting on the wall; *mene, mene, tekel, upharsin;* red flag; foghorn; monitor, warning voice, Cassandra, signs of the times, Mother Carey's chickens, stormy petrel, bird of ill omen; gathering clouds, clouds on the horizon; symptom; watchtower, beacon, lighthouse; a cloud no bigger than a man's hand.

3, sentinel, sentry, lookout; watch, watchman; patrol, picket, scout, spy, advance guard, rear guard; watchdog, housedog; Cerberus.

Verbs—**1,** warn, caution; forewarn, prewarn; admonish, premonish; forebode; give notice, give warning; dehort; menace, threaten; put on one's guard; sound the alarm; ring the tocsin.

2, beware, take warning, take heed; keep watch; stop, look and listen.

Adjectives—warning, premonitory, monitory, cautionary; admonitory, admonitive; symptomatic; ominous, foreboding; warned, on one's guard, careful, cautious.

Interjections—beware! take care! look out! watch out!

Antonym, see RASHNESS.

---

warp, *v. & n.* —*v.* twist, bend, swerve, distort; bias, prejudice; pervert; deviate; incline. —*n.* bias, DISTORTION; deflection, TENDENCY; torsion, twist, malformation. See CHANGE, CAUSE.

warrant, *n. & v.* —*n.* warranty, guaranty; pledge, security, surety; authority; summons, writ, permit, pass. —*v.t.* guarantee; vouch for, answer for, certify, secure; affirm; state, maintain; assure, SUPPORT, sanction, authorize, justify. See COMMAND, PERMISSION, AUTHORITY, VINDICATION.

warrior, *n.* see COMBATANT.

warship, *n.* see COMBATANT, SHIP, ARMS.

wary, *adj.* guarded, watchful; alert, cautious; suspicious; discreet, prudent; chary; scrupulous. See CARE. *Ant.*, see RASHNESS, NEGLECT.

wash, *v.* clean, cleanse, deterge, bathe, lave; wet, soak, rinse, drench; purify; irrigate, inundate, flood; scrub, swab; launder; paint, tint, COLOR; lap, lick; brim over, overflow. See CLEANNESS, PAINTING, WATER.

WASTE [638]

Nouns—**1,** waste, wastage; exhaustion, depletion, dissipation; dispersion; ebb; leakage, LOSS; wear and tear; extravagance, wastefulness, PRODIGALITY; MISUSE; wasting, DETERIORATION.

2, waster, wastrel, spendthrift, spender, prodigal, squanderer, profligate. *Colloq.,* sport.

Verbs—waste, spend, misspend, expend, use, misuse, use up, consume, swallow up, overtax, exhaust; impoverish; spill, drain, empty; disperse; cast, throw, fling, *or* fritter away; burn the candle at both ends; go through, squander; waste powder and shot, labor in vain; pour water into a sieve; leak, run out; ebb, melt away, run dry, dry up; deteriorate; throw to the winds.

Adjectives—wasted, thrown away; wasteful, penny-wise and pound-foolish; prodigal, improvident, thriftless, unthrifty, extravagant, lavish.

Antonym, see STORE, PARSIMONY.

watch, *v. & n.* —*v.* look (at), scrutinize, examine; view, stare, ogle; regard, follow, survey; be alert, guard; chaperone, tend, babysit; oversee, superintend; patrol. —*n.* vigil, surveillance, sentry duty; guardianship, CARE; guard, watchman, sentinel, lookout; timepiece, pocket watch, wristwatch. See SAFETY, VISION, CHRONOMETRY. *Ant.,* see REPOSE, NEGLECT.

watchtower, *n.* beacon, lighthouse; lookout *or* observation post. See VISION.

watchword, *n.* countersign, shibboleth; password, catchword; slogan. See INDICATION.

WATER [337]

Nouns—**1,** water, moisture, wetness; drinking water, spring water, mineral water; sea water, salt water, fresh water; serum, serosity; lymph; rheum; diluent; dilution, maceration, lotion; washing, immersion, infiltration, infusion, irrigation; douche, bath; baptism, RAIN, deluge, spate, flood, high water, flood tide. See FLUIDITY.

2, RIVER, waterway, stream; GULF, bay, cove, harbor; OCEAN, sea, LAKE, pond; MARSH, swamp.

3, wave, billow, surge, swell, ripple, rollers, surf, breakers, heavy sea; undercurrent, eddy, vortex, whirlpool, maelstrom; waterspout; jet, spurt, squirt, spout; splash, plash; rush, gush, sluice.

4, waterfall, cascade, linn, cataract, Niagara.

5, hydraulics, hydrodynamics, hydrokinetics, hydrostatics.

Verbs—**1,** be watery; be awash *or* afloat; swim, swim in, brim.

2, water, wet; moisten; dilute; dip, immerse, submerge, plunge, souse, duck, drown; drench, soak, steep, macerate, pickle; wash, sprinkle, lave, bathe, splash; slop; irrigate, inundate, deluge; syringe, douche, inject, gargle.

3, flow, run; issue, gush, pour, spout, roll, stream; drop, drip, dribble, drain, trickle, percolate; bubble, gurgle, spurt, ooze; spill, overflow.

Adjectives—**1,** watery, liquid, aqueous, aquatic, lymphatic; balneal, diluent; brimming, drenching, diluted; weak; wet, moist, soppy, sopping, soaked, wet to the skin.

2, oceanic, marine, maritime, briny; tidal, fluent, flowing, streaming, meandering; riparian, alluvial; lacustrine; marshy, swampy, boggy, paludal, miry, sloppy; showery, rainy, pluvial.

Adverbs—awash, afloat, adrift, asea, under water.

Antonyms, see LAND, DRYNESS.

watercourse, *n.* RIVER, stream, channel, canal; riverbed, wadi, arroyo; waterway.

waterfall, *n.* cascade, falls, drop, rapids; cataract, Niagara. See WATER.

wave, *v. & n.* —*v.* wag, shake, sway, flutter, stream (in the wind); signal, motion, gesture, INDICATION; ROLL, undulate; ripple, swell, billow, flood, surge; flaunt, flourish. —*n.* sea, tide, WATER, ripple, billow, *etc.,* wavelet, undulation; signal, gesture, flourish; CONVOLUTION, curl; marcel, permanent, finger wave.

waver, *v.i.* vacillate, fluctuate, hesitate; sway, tremble, totter; undulate; teeter. See DOUBT. *Ant.,* see RESOLUTION.

wax, *v. & n.* —*v.* cere; grease, coat; smooth; polish; grow, INCREASE, strengthen. See SMOOTHNESS. —*n.* tallow, paraffin(e), beeswax.

way, *n.* PASSAGE, road, route, path, roadway, highway, channel, street, avenue; journey, PROGRESSION, transit; trend, TENDENCY; approach, access, gateway; METHOD, manner, mode, style, fashion; SPACE, interval, stretch, DISTANCE; usage, custom, HABIT, practice, wont; course, routine; PLAN; CONDUCT, FORM; behavior; scheme, device; knack; charm, winsomeness.

wayfarer, *n.* traveler; walker, hiker, rambler, wanderer, pilgrim, journeyer. See TRAVEL.

wayward, *adj.* perverse, willful, froward; capricious; delinquent; changeable; wanton. See OPPOSITION, DISOBEDIENCE.

weak, *adj.* feeble, debilitated, impotent; relaxed, unnerved, strengthless, powerless; weakly, weakened, enfeebled; unstrung; flaccid, anemic; soft, effeminate, feminine, effete, exhausted; womanish; frail, fragile, flimsy, unsubstantial; broken-down, run-down, rickety; tottering, doddering; broken, lame, halt, withered, maimed, shattered, shaken; crazy, shaky; palsied, decrepit; languid, poor, infirm; faint, sickly; vapid, flat, insipid, watery; dull, dry; loose, lax, nerveless; slack, spent, weatherbeaten; decayed, rotten, worn, seedy, languishing, wasted, unsupported, helpless, defenseless. See IMPOTENCE, IMPERFECTION. *Ant.,* STRONG; see POWER.

weak-minded, *adj.* moronic, idiotic, imbecilic, feebleminded; brainless, foolish, witless, empty-headed, vacuous; vacillating; irresolute; fickle. See INSANITY, DOUBT, CHANGEABLENESS. *Ant.,* see RESOLUTION, SANITY.

weakness, *n.* feebleness, debility, decrepitude; atony; languor, enervation; IMPOTENCE; infirmity; effeminacy; fragility, flaccidity; vapidity; INACTIVITY; weakening, enervation; loss *or* failure of strength; delicacy, invalidism, anemia; faintness. See WEAK. *Ant.,* see STRENGTH, RESOLUTION, POWER.

wealth, *n.* riches, fortune, opulence, affluence; PROSPERITY; MEANS, resources, PROPERTY, MONEY; plenty, plenitude, luxuriance, excess, plethora, sufficiency. *Ant.,* see POVERTY, INSUFFICIENCY.

wealthy, *adj.* rich, affluent, opulent, moneyed; worth a fortune; well-to-do, well-off; rich as Croesus. *Colloq.,* made of money, rolling in money; flush, in funds. *Slang,* in the chips, in the money, loaded, filthy rich; in the big time; rolling high. See MONEY. *Ant.,* see POVERTY.

weapon, *n.* see ARMS.

wear, *v. & n.* —*v.* last, endure; USE, show, display; tire, fatigue, weary; bear, don, put on; carry, have on; WASTE, consume, spend; rub, chafe, fray, abrade; jibe, tack, veer, yaw. —*n.* CLOTHING, garb; USE, usage, hard usage; impairment, wear and tear. See DURABILITY, DETERIORATION.

WEARINESS [841]

Nouns—**1,** weariness, tiredness, exhaustion, lethargy, lassitude, FATIGUE; drowsiness, languor, languidness; weakness, faintness.

2, bore, proser, nuisance. *Colloq.,* wet blanket. *Slang,* drip, creep, pain in the neck.

3, wearisomeness, tedium, tediousness, dull work, boredom, ennui, sameness, monotony, twice-told tale; satiety; heavy hours, time on one's hands.

Verbs—**1,** weary; tire, fatigue; bore; weary, *or* tire to death; send *or* put to sleep; pall, sicken, nauseate, disgust; harp on, dwell on. *Slang,* bore stiff.

2, be weary of, never hear the last of; be tired of; yawn.

Adjectives—**1,** wearying, wearing, fatiguing, tiring; wearisome, tiresome, irksome; uninteresting, stupid, bald, devoid of interest, dry, monotonous, dull, arid, tedious, trying, humdrum, flat; prosy, slow, soporific, somniferous; disgusting.

2, weary, tired, spent, fatigued; toilworn, footsore; winded, out of breath; drowsy, sleepy; uninterested, flagging, used up, worn out, blasé; dog-tired, ready to drop, more dead than alive, played out; exhausted, prostrate, on one's last legs, *hors de combat. Slang,* done up, pooped, bushed, fagged, beat.

Adverbs—wearily, boringly, tiresomely, *etc.*

---

weather, *n.* atmospheric conditions; clime, climate. See AIR.

weave, *v.* interlace, intertwine, twine, entwine; loom, spin, fabricate; plait, pleat, pleach, braid, mat. See COMPOSITION.

web, *n.* cobweb, spiderweb; weaving, woven material, TEXTURE, mesh, net; network, hookup; trap, snare, scheme, PLAN; tissue, gossamer.

wed, *v.* marry, espouse; couple, blend, join. See MARRIAGE.

wedge, *n.* tapering block; triangular slab; quoin, chock, sprag, block, shim.

wee, *adj.* tiny, little, minute, small; infinitesimal, microscopic; diminutive, petite. *Colloq.,* teen-weeny. See LITTLENESS. *Ant.,* see GREATNESS, SIZE.

weed, *v. & n.* —*v.t.* root out, extirpate, clear (of weeds); cull; remove, eliminate. See EJECTION. —*n.* unwanted plant; pest, nuisance. *Colloq.,* tobacco, smoking. See VEGETABLE.

weeds, *n.pl.* mourning, black, widow's weeds. See CLOTHING, LAMENTATION.

week, *n.* seven-night; see TIME.

weep, *v.* shed tears, CRY, lament, wail, sob, blubber; mourn, grieve; rain, flow, drip. See LAMENTATION.

weigh, *v.* measure (weight); lift, heft; balance, scale, counterbalance; examine, ponder, consider, mull over, estimate; tell, count; weigh down, be heavy, drag, load, press; oppress, burden, depress; overbalance, bear down. See GRAVITY, IMPORTANCE, MEASUREMENT.

weight, *n. & v.* —*n.* heaviness; heft; overweight, avoirdupois, tonnage, poundage; GRAVITY; ballast; MEASUREMENT; IMPORTANCE, INFLUENCE; significance; pressure, load, burden. —*v.* ballast, load, burden; favor; adjust, compensate.

weird, *adj.* uncanny, eldritch, eerie; ghostly, spectral, unearthly; SUPERNATURAL. *Colloq.,* spooky. See UNCONFORMITY.

welcome, *n., v. & adj.* —*n.* greeting, salutation, cordial reception. *Slang,* glad hand. —*v.t.* greet, salute; embrace, receive (gladly), hail. —*adj.* pleasing, agreeable, acceptable, wanted, gratifying. See COURTESY, RECEIVING, SOCIALITY. *Ant.,* see DISCOURTESY, REFUSAL.

weld, *v.t.* fuse, unite, join, fasten; blend. See JUNCTION.

welfare, *n.* well-being; PROSPERITY, advancement, profit, sake, benefit; social work; happiness, SUCCESS. *Ant.,* see ADVERSITY.

well, *n. & v.* —*n.* fount, font, wellspring; wellhead; reservoir, spring; source, origin; hole, pit, shaft. —*v.i.* issue, gush, brim, flow, jet, rise. See BEGINNING, WATER.

well, *adj. & adv.* —*adj.* healthy, robust, strong, hale, hearty, in good health. —*adv.* rightly, properly; thoroughly, skillfully, accurately; amply, sufficiently, fully, adequately; favorably, worthily; very much; quite, considerably; easily, handily. See HEALTH, SKILL, SUFFICIENCY. *Ant.,* see DISEASE, UNSKILLFULNESS, INSUFFICIENCY.

well–bred, *n.* well-behaved *or* brought up; noble, well-born, gentle; courteous, polished, suave, polite. See COURTESY, NOBILITY. *Ant.,* see DISCOURTESY, POPULACE.

well–known, *adj.* familiar, recognized, famous, renowned; notorious. See REPUTE, KNOWLEDGE. *Ant.,* see NEGLECT, DISREPUTE.

well–to–do, *adj.* comfortable, well off; prosperous, affluent; wealthy, rich. See MONEY, PROSPERITY. *Ant.,* see POVERTY.

welter, *n. & v.* —*n.* confusion, turmoil; jumble, hodgepodge, mishmash; ruck, masses. —*v.i.* WALLOW. See AGITATION, POPULACE, DISORDER.

werewolf, *n.* wolf-man, lycanthrope, *loup-garou* (*Fr.*); changeling. See SORCERY.

west, *n.* Occident; Europe; wild west. See DIRECTION.

wet, *adj., v. & n.* —*adj.* damp, moist, dewy; clammy, dank, humid, dripping; rainy, showery, foggy, misty; soaked, drenched, saturated; watery, waterlogged. —*v.t.* soak, moisten, dampen, drench, saturate; immerse, dip, sprinkle; rain upon. —*n.* wetness, WATER; rain, fog, dew, mist; dampness, MOISTURE, clamminess, *etc.;* antiprohibition. *Ant.,* see DRYNESS.

whale, *n.* cetacean; finback; blue, humpback, killer, sperm, sulphurbottom *or* right whale; orca, rorquel, narwhal, blackfish, dolphin, porpoise, grampus; Moby Dick. *Colloq.,* whopper. See GREATNESS, SIZE.

wharf, *n.* dock, pier, quay, landing; waterfront. See EDGE.

what, *pron.* that which; sort of, kind of; which; how; how great, many, *or* remarkable; whatever, whatsoever, whichever.

wheedle, *v.t.* coax, cajole, persuade; court, humor, flatter. See SERVILITY.

wheel, *n. & v.* —*n.* disk, circle, roller; roulette *or* fortune's wheel; bike, bicycle. *Slang,* VIP, big wheel, bigwig. See CIRCULARITY, VEHICLE. —*v.* roll; trundle, cycle; rotate, revolve, spin, twirl; pivot, about-face, turn, gyrate, whirl, wind.

wheeze, *v. & n.* —*v.* breathe hard, gasp, puff, choke. —*n. Slang,* old joke, gag, chestnut. See WIND, WIT.

when, *adv.* at what time? at the same time; whereupon, just then, whenever. See TIME.

where, *adv.* in what place; whereabouts, whither; in what direction, from what source, place, *etc.* See TIME, PLACE.

whet, *v.t.* sharpen, hone, whetstone, grind; excite, stimulate, provoke, stir up, kindle, quicken, inspire. See SHARPNESS, EXCITEMENT.

whether, *conj.* if, in case; if it is so; in either case. See SUPPOSITION.

while, *conj. & v.* —*conj.* during, as long as, whilst, whereas; although. —*v.* pass the time, kill time. See TIME.

whim, *n.* caprice, fancy, DESIRE, vagary; notion, quirk, crotchet, whimsy; freak; IMPULSE. See CHANGEABLENESS.

whimper, *v. & n.* CRY, whine.

whimsical, *adj.* curious, odd, peculiar, freakish; humorous, waggish, droll; crotchety, capricious, queer, quaint. See CHANGEABLENESS, WIT.

whine, *v.i.* CRY, whimper, complain, moan, snivel. *Slang,* gripe, bellyache. See LAMENTATION.

whip, *n. & v.* —*n.* lash, SCOURGE; quick motion, SNAP. —*v.t.* lash, beat, flog; thrash; conquer, subdue; defeat. See PUNISHMENT, SUCCESS.

whirl, *n. & v.* —*n.* spin, spinning, gyration, turn; flutter, tizzy, confusion; pirouette. —*v.* spin, twirl, turn, rotate, revolve, gyre, gyrate; dance, pirouette. See ROTATION.

whirlpool, *n.* eddy, swirl; vortex, malestrom. See WATER, ROTATION.

whirlwind, *n. & adj.* —*n.* tornado, twister, cyclone, typhoon, hurricane, windstorm. See WIND. —*adj.* fast, speedy, headlong, breakneck, dizzying. See VELOCITY.

whiskers, *n.pl.* beard, hair, stubble; hirsuteness; mustache, sideburns, goatee, Vandyke, muttonchops, *etc.;* bristles; feelers, antennae. See ROUGHNESS.

whisper, *n. & v.* —*n.* murmur, whispering, sigh, breath; hint, intimation, rumor; aside, stage whisper. —*v.* murmur, breathe, divulge, reveal, hint, intimate. See DISCLOSURE, WIND. *Ant.,* see LOUDNESS.

whistle, *n. & v.* pipe, piping, flute. See SOUND.

white, *adj.* snow-white, snowy, milky, chalky; albino; pale, bloodless, colorless; whitewashed, kalsomined, bleached; silver, gray, hoar, frosty; cleansed, purified; Caucasian, Caucasoid. See COLOR, COLORLESSNESS.

whiteness, *n.* whitish color, white, COLORLESSNESS, paleness; milkiness, chalkiness, snowiness; PURITY; hoariness, grayness (of age); lime, paper, milk, ivory, snow, sheet, alabaster; albinoism, blondness, fairness; pallor, ashiness, waxiness, bloodlessness; bleach, etiolation; silveriness; glare, LIGHT, lightness; INNOCENCE, stainlessness. *Ant.,* blackness (see COLOR), DARKNESS.

whitewash, *v.t.* calcimine, kalsomine; whiten; vindicate, exonerate. *Slang,* shut out, blank, skunk. See COVERING, VINDICATION.

who, *pron.* which one, that. See IDENTITY.

WHOLE [50]

Nouns—**1,** whole, totality, totalness, integrity; entirety, ensemble, collectiveness; UNITY, completeness, indivisibility, integration, embodiment; integer. **2,** the whole, all, everything, total, aggregate, one and all, gross amount, sum, sum total, *tout ensemble,* length and breadth of, alpha and omega, be-all and end-all; bulk, mass, lump, tissue, staple, body, trunk, bole, hull, hulk, skeleton. *Slang,* whole kit and caboodle, whole show, whole shebang, whole shooting match; the works.

Verbs—form *or* constitute a whole; integrate, embody, amass; aggregate, assemble; amount to, come to, add up to.

Adjectives—**1,** whole, total, integral, entire, complete; one, individual, wholesale, sweeping.

2, unbroken, uncut, undivided, unsevered, unclipped, uncropped, unshorn;
seamless; undiminished; undemolished, undissolved, undestroyed; indivisible, indissoluble, indissolvable.
Adverbs—wholly, altogether; totally, completely, entirely, all, all in all,
wholesale, in a body, collectively, all put together; in the aggregate, in the
mass, in the main, in the long run; *en masse*, on the whole, bodily, throughout, every inch, substantially, by and large.
Antonym, see PART.

---

wholesale, *adj.* bulk, job-lot, jobbing; at a discount, cheaper; mass, sweeping, general, widespread. See WHOLE, BUSINESS. *Ant.*, retail.
wholesome, *adj.* healthy, beneficial. See HEALTH, PURITY. *Ant.*, see DIS-
EASE, IMPURITY.
whore, *n.* prostitute, harlot, baud, strumpet, streetwalker, call girl, B-girl,
daughter of joy. See EVILDOER.
why, *adv.* wherefore, what for?, for what cause. *Slang*, how come. See
CAUSE.
wicked, *adj.* EVIL, bad; criminal, depraved, iniquitous; cruel, heartless,
sinful, vicious, immoral. See IMPROBITY, IMPURITY. *Ant.*, see GOODNESS,
PURITY, VIRTUE.
wide, *adj.* spacious, widespreading, comprehensive; generous, ample, all-
embracing; broad, large, roomy, extensive; general. See BREADTH, SPACE.
Ant., see NARROWNESS.
wide-awake, *adj.* alert, quick; keen, knowing; informed, astute, watchful,
on guard, unsleeping, vigilant. See CARE, KNOWLEDGE. *Ant.*, see IGNOR-
ANCE, REPOSE.
widow, *n.* survivor (of a husband); relict, dowager; divorcée, grass widow.
See CELIBACY, DIVORCE.
width, *n.* BREADTH, broadness; wideness, span, beam; extent, expanse.
wield, *v.t.* handle, manipulate, ply; brandish, flourish, wave, shake; employ, control, manage. See USE.
wife, *n.* married woman; mate, spouse; *Frau;* housewife, helpmeet, helpmate. *Slang*, the Mrs., madam, little woman, old lady, ball and chain,
better half. See MARRIAGE. *Ant.*, see CELIBACY.
wig, *n.* toupée, toupet; peruke, periwig, switch, transformation; fall; headdress. *Slang*, doily, divot, rug. See ORNAMENT.
wiggle, *v.i.* squirm, shake, wriggle, wag, shimmy. See OSCILLATION.
wild, *adj.* savage, untamed; uncivilized; feral, bloodthirsty, fierce; uncontrolled; amuck, frenzied; inaccurate, intemperate, unwise, foolish; eager,
impetuous, unrestrainable, desert, uninhibited; rank, thick, junglelike, luxuriant; untended, uncultivated; shy, skittish; daring, reckless, rash, breakneck; freak. See VIOLENCE, VULGARITY. *Ant.*, see DOMESTICATION.
wildcat, *n. & adj.* —*n.* lynx, puma, mountain lion, panther, ocelot. —*adj.*,
colloq., risky, venturesome, shoestring; unauthorized, splinter, spontaneous.
wilderness, *n.* wasteland, waste(s), wilds, badlands; desert, sands, Sahara.
See LAND. *Ant.*, see HEAVEN.
wile, *n.* stratagem, subterfuge; CUNNING; trick, dodge.

WILL [600]

Nouns—will, free will, volition, conation, velleity; pleasure; FREEDOM,
discretion; option, CHOICE; voluntariness, spontaneity, spontaneousness;
originality; pleasure, wish, mind; frame of mind, inclination, WILLINGNESS;
intention, predetermination; self-control, determination, RESOLUTION.
Verbs—will, see fit, think fit; determine, resolve, settle, choose, volunteer;
have a will of one's own; have one's own way; exercise one's discretion;
take responsibility; take upon oneself; do of one's own accord.
Adjectives—voluntary, volitional, wilful; WILLING; free, optional; discretionary; minded; prepense; intended; autocratic; unbidden, spontaneous;
original (see CAUSE).
Adverbs—voluntarily, at will, at pleasure; *ad libitum*, as one thinks proper;
according to one's lights; of one's own accord *or* free will; by choice, pur-
posely, intentionally, deliberately.
Antonym, see NECESSITY.

willful, wilful, *adj.* self-willed, arbitrary; headstrong, wayward, obstinate, stubborn, unruly; intentional, deliberate, premeditated. See WILL. *Ant.,* see OBEDIENCE.

willing, *adj.* minded, disposed, inclined, favorable; favorably inclined *or* disposed to; nothing loath; in the mood *or* humor; ready, forward, earnest, eager; bent upon, desirous, predisposed; docile, agreeable, easy-going, tractable, pliant; cordial, hearty; content, assenting, voluntary, gratuitous, spontaneous, unasked, unforced. See WILL, ASSENT. *Ant.,* see REFUSAL.

willingness, *n.* voluntariness; readiness; willing mind *or* heart; disposition, inclination, tendency, leaning; bent, turn of mind, propensity, predisposition, proclivity, penchant, DESIRE; docility, pliability; good will; alacrity, eagerness (see WILLING); ASSENT, compliance, CONSENT; PLEASURE. See WILL. *Ant.,* see REFUSAL, UNWILLINGNESS.

wilt, *v.i.* droop, sag; weaken, languish; wither; collapse. See SOFTNESS.

wily, *adj.* designing, tricky, crafty, foxy; deceitful, crooked, Machiavellian; clever, subtle, CUNNING. *Ant.,* see INNOCENCE, SIMPLENESS.

win, *v.* beat, conquer, MASTER; gain, obtain; get; achieve, accomplish, reach; persuade, sway, convince, influence; succeed, triumph, surpass. See ACQUISITION, SUCCESS, BELIEF.

wince, *v.i.* flinch, RECOIL; shy, quail, shrink. See FEAR, PAIN.

wind, *v.* twist, twine, entwine; coil, curl, spiral; bandage, loop; enfold, infold; wreathe, roll; crank, reel; sinuate, meander, wander. See CONVOLUTION, DEVIATION. *Ant.,* see DIRECTION.

WIND [349]

Nouns, **1,** wind, windiness, draught, draft, flatus, afflatus, AIR; breath, breath of air; puff, whiff, blow, drift; aura; stream, current, undercurrent; sufflation, insufflation, inflation; blowing, fanning, ventilation.

2, gust, blast, breeze, zephyr, squall, gale, half a gale, storm, tempest, hurricane, whirlwind, tornado, samiel, cyclone, twister, typhoon; simoom; harmattan, khamsin, chinook, monsoon, trade wind, sirocco, mistral, bise, tramontane, foehn, levanter; capful of wind; fresh breeze, stiff breeze; blizzard; rough, foul, *or* dirty weather; dirty sky, mare's tail.

3, anemography, aerodynamics; wind gauge, anemometer, pneumatics; weathercock, weathervane; Beaufort scale.

4, breathing, respiration, sneezing, sternutation; hiccough, hiccup; catching of the breath.

5, Aeolus, Boreas, Eurus, Zephyr, Notus, cave of the winds.

6, airpump, lungs, bellows, blowpipe, fan, ventilator, vacuum cleaner, wind tunnel; air pipe; funnel.

*Verbs—***1,** blow, waft; stream, issue; freshen, gather; blow up, bluster; sigh, moan, scream, howl, whistle; breeze.

2, breathe, respire, inhale, exhale, puff; whiffle, gasp, wheeze; snuff, snuffle, sniff, sniffle; sneeze, cough.

3, fan, ventilate; inflate; blow up, pump up.

*Adjectives—*windy, blowing, breezy, gusty, squally; stormy, tempestuous, blustering; boisterous; pulmonic, pulmonary, pneumatic.

Antonym, see CALM

---

window, *n.* casement, dormer, OPENING; pane; bay window, oriel; port, porthole; skylight; embrasure, loophole.

windpipe, *n.* airpipe, trachea; throat, throttle; weasand.

wine, *n.* the grape; drink, liquor; DRUNKENNESS, intoxication; stimulant, alcohol; nectar.

wing, *n. & v.* —*n.* pinion, (feathered) limb, pennon, ala; arm, sail; flank; ell, annex, extension; airfoil; flight, flying. —*v.* fly; disable, wound. See ADDITION, AVIATION, COMBATANT, DRAMA.

wink, *v.* blink, nictitate, nictate; squint; twinkle; overlook, ignore, condone. See VISION, FORGIVENESS, NEGLECT.

winning, *adj.* conquering, victorious, triumphant; winsome, captivating, charming, engaging, entrancing, prepossessing, comely, attractive; persuasive, convincing. See SUCCESS, ATTRACTION, CAUSE.

winnow, *v.t.* select, cull, sift, separate, glean, pick; ventilate, fan, remove chaff. See CHOICE.

winsome, *adj.* gay, merry, lively, sportive; charming, winning, captivating; lovable, adorable, pleasant, attractive. See CHEERFULNESS, LOVE.

winter, *n.* COLD; hibernation; AGE; ADVERSITY.

wipe, *v.t.* clean, rub, brush, dust, mop; dry, towel. See CLEANNESS, DRYNESS.

wire, *n.* (metal) thread, FILAMENT; flex, cord, line; telephone, telegraph, cable; cablegram, telegram. See JUNCTION, COMMUNICATION.

wireless, *n.* radio; radiogram, Marconigram. See COMMUNICATION.

wiry, *adj.* filamentous, filar, threadlike; STRONG, muscular, sinewy; tough; flexible. See FILAMENT. *Ant.,* see SOFTNESS.

wise, *adj.* SAGE, sagacious; learned, profound, deep; judicious, well-advised. See KNOWLEDGE.

wish, *n. & v.* —*n.* DESIRE, WILL; PLEASURE; craving, yearning, want, hankering; INTENTION. —*v.* want, long for, dream of, hope for, ask (for), yearn, crave, hanker. See HOPE, EXPECTATION.

wistful, *adj.* musing, pensive, thoughtful; desirous, wishful, hopeful; eager; craving, yearning. See DESIRE, HOPE, EXPECTATION.

WIT [842]

Nouns—**1,** wit, wittiness; Atticism; salt; esprit, point, fancy, whim, humor, drollery, pleasantry; jocularity; jocosity, jocoseness; levity, facetiousness; waggery, waggishness; comicality.

2, farce, buffoonery, clowning, fooling, tomfoolery; harlequinade; broad farce, broad humor; fun; slapstick; smartness, banter, badinage, retort, repartee, riposte; RIDICULE; horseplay.

3, witticism, jest, joke, conceit, quip, quirk, quiddity, pleasantry; sally; flash of wit, scintillation; *mot, bon mot,* smart saying, epigram; dry wit, cream of the jest. *Slang,* comeback, gag, wisecrack, gag, running gag.

4, wordplay, play upon words, pun, punning, double entendre, EQUIVOCATION; quibble; conundrum, riddle (see SECRET); trifling. *Slang,* chestnut.

5, wit, wag, joker, jester, comedian, comic, humorist, punster.

Verbs—be witty, joke, jest; crack a joke; pun; make fun of, make sport of; retort; banter. *Slang,* wisecrack, come back at.

Adjectives—witty, Attic, quick-witted, nimble-witted; smart, jocular, jocose, droll, waggish, facetious, whimsical, humorous; playful, merry, pleasant, sprightly, sparkling, epigrammatic, pointed, comic.

Adverbs—jokingly, jestingly, *etc.;* in jest, in sport, in play; in fun; not seriously.

Antonym, see DULL.

---

witch, *n.* hag, beldam(e), crone; shrew, scold, dragon; sorceress, enchantress; charmer. See UGLINESS, BEAUTY, SORCERY.

with, *prep.* by, by means of, through; accompanying, alongside, among(st), amid(st), beside, plus; upon, at, thereupon, *etc.* See ACCOMPANIMENT, MIXTURE, ADDITION. *Ant.,* without; see ABSENCE.

withdraw, *v.* remove, separate, subduct; retire, retreat, disengage, draw off; abstract, subtract; recall, rescind, recant; resign, relinquish; abdicate, decamp, depart; shrink, RECOIL, drop out, back out. See DISJUNCTION, DEPARTURE, NULLIFICATION.

wither, *v.* waste, decline, droop, wilt, fade; decay; contract, shrivel, pine, decline, languish; blast, destroy, burn, scorch; cut, scathe. See DETERIORATION, DESTRUCTION, DRYNESS, DISAPPROBATION, CONTEMPT.

withhold, *v.t.* keep back, restrain, detain; check, hold back; hinder; suppress; repress; reserve. See CONCEALMENT, RESTRAINT.

within, *adj. & prep.* in, inside; inward(s), indoor(s). See INTERIOR.

without, *adv. & prep.* outside, outdoor(s), outward, beyond; minus. See EXTERIOR, ABSENCE.

withstand, *v.t.* face, confront; fight off, oppose, defy. See OPPOSITION.

witless, *adj.* senseless, brainless; silly, foolish, pointless, idiotic, moronic, imbecilic; half-witted, DULL, thick, stupid, scatterbrained, muddle-headed. *Slang,* dumb, dopy. See DENSITY, INSANITY. *Ant.,* see WIT, INTELLIGENCE.

witness, *n. & v.* —*n.* testimony, proof, EVIDENCE, corroboration; deponent, eyewitness; testifier, attestor; beholder, observer. —*v.t.* see, observe; attest, sign, subscrıbe to, bear witness to. See EVIDENCE.

wizard, *n.* wonder-worker, conjuror; Merlin; magician, sorcerer. *Colloq.,* master, expert. See SORCERY, SKILL.

woe, *n.* trouble, tribulation; sorrow, grief; unhappiness, misery. See PAIN. *Ant.,* see PLEASURE, CHEERFULNESS.

woman, *n.* see FEMALE, MANKIND. *Ant.,* see MALE.

womanish, *adj.* effeminate, emasculated; unmanly, cowardly (of men); shrill, vixenish; soft, weak. See FEMALE. *Ant.,* see MALE, COURAGE.

WONDER [870]

Nouns—wonder, wonderment, marvel, miracle, mıraculousness, astonishment, amazement, bewilderment; amazedness, admiration, awe; stupor, stupefaction; fascination; sensation; SURPRISE.

Verbs—**1,** wonder, marvel, admire; be surprised, start; stare, open *or* rub one's eyes; gape, hold one's breath; look aghast, stand aghast; not believe one's eyes, ears *or* senses.

2, SURPRISE, astonish, startle, shock, take aback, electrify, stun, stagger.

3, be wonderful, beggar *or* baffle description; stagger belief.

Adjectives—**1,** wonderful, wondrous; miraculous; surprising, unexpected, unheard of; mysterious, indescribable, inexpressible, ineffable; unutterable, unspeakable; monstrous, prodigious, stupendous, marvelous, inconceivable, incredible; unimaginable, strange, uncommon, passing strange, striking, overwhelming.

2, surprised, aghast, agog, breathless, agape; open-mouthed; awestruck, thunderstruck; spellbound; lost in amazement, wonder, *or* astonishment; unable to believe one's senses.

Adverbs—wonderfully, fearfully; for a wonder; strange to say, *mirabile dictu,* to one's great surprise; with wonder.

Interjections—lo! lo and behold! O! what! wonder of wonders! will wonders never cease!

Antonym, see EXPECTATION.

---

wonderful, *adj.* miraculous, marvelous, amazing, astounding. *Colloq.,* great, swell, dandy; colossal, terrific. See WONDER.

wont, *n.* custom, USE, HABIT, routine, practice, usage.

woo, *v.* court, make love to; seek, pursue, solicit; importune. See LOVE, PURSUIT, ENDEARMENT.

wood, *n.* forest, grove, timber, copse, coppice, thicket, spinny, bosque, *bois* (*Fr.*); woods, woodland; board, plank, log, lumber. See TREE, MATERIALS.

wooden, *adj.* wood, woody, ligneous, xyloid; oaken, mahogany, ash, pine, teak, walnut, *etc.;* frame, clapboard, shingle(d); stiff, rigid, expressionless; lifeless. See MATERIALS. *Ant.,* see ANIMATE.

woodwork, *n.* molding, paneling, baseboard, didoes, frames, jambs, sashes; doors. See ORNAMENT.

wool, *n. & adj.* —*n.* fleece; down, hair, worsted, yarn. —*adj.* woolen; knitted; wooly, hairy, fleecy, downy. See SOFTNESS, ROUGHNESS.

wooly, woolly, *adj.* fleecy, fluffy, flocculent, downy. See SOFTNESS, FILAMENT. *Ant.,* see ROUGHNESS.

word, *n.* expression, utterance; syllable, phone, ideophone, phoneme; stem, root, derivative, inflected form; inflection, declension, conjugation; name, noun, pronoun, adjective, adverb, verb, preposition, postposition, conjunction, interjection; particle, article; prefix, suffix, combining form, element; compound, phrase (see SPEECH); neologism, coinage, nonce word; barbarism, corruption; PROMISE; password, watchword; news, INFORMATION.

word game, *n.* acrostic, palindrome, anagram, crossword puzzle, ghosts, riddles, word square, double acrostic; spelling bee; rebus, charades; Scrabble (*T.N.*), Jotto (*T.N.*); Guggenheim, categories, wordplay.

wordy, *adj.* verbose, talkative, loquacious, prolix, garrulous; rambling, circumlocutory, windy, longwinded. See LOQUACITY. *Ant.,* see SHORTNESS.

work, *n. & v.* —*n.* job, occupation, calling, trade, profession; task, stint, employment; drudgery, toil, moil, grind, routine; function; craftsmanship, workmanship; arts and crafts, craft, handicraft; opus, PRODUCTION, WRITING, BOOK, PUBLICATION; office; management; manufacture. —*v.* toil, moil, labor, plod, plug, drudge; run, act, operate, function; leaven, ferment, yeast; USE, employ; succeed, perform, do; effect, exert, strain; embroider, embellish, decorate. *Colloq.*, use elbow grease. See ACTION, SUCCESS, EXERTION. *Ant.*, see INACTIVITY, FAILURE.

workman, *n.* worker, laborer; artisan, craftsman; operator, doer, performer; journeyman, yeoman; Trojan; drudge; mechanic; toiler, moiler. See ACTIVITY, EXERTION. *Ant.*, see INACTIVITY.

works, *n.pl.* factory, plant, mill, workshop, shop; mechanism, machine; fort, rampart, breastworks, earthworks, barricade. *Slang*, everything; abuse. See AGENCY, DEFENSE.

workshop, *n.* workhouse, sweatshop; laboratory, factory, manufactory, mill, rolling mill, sawmill; works, steelworks, ironworks, foundry, furnace; mint; forge, loom; cabinet, atelier, studio, bureau, office, STORE, shop, plant. See BUSINESS.

world, *n.* creation, nature, universe; earth, globe, wide world; cosmos; macrocosm, megacosm; microcosm; sphere, hemisphere; heavens, sky, firmament (see HEAVEN); celestial space, outer space, interstellar space; the void; heavenly bodies, stars, nebulae; galaxy, Milky Way, solar system; constellation, planet, planetoid, satellite, comet, meteor; sun, moon.

worldly, *adj.* experienced, sophisticated; earthly, mundane; terrestrial; profane, secular, carnal; sordid, mercenary; proud, selfish, material, materialistic, unspiritual, irreligious. See SELFISHNESS, IRRELIGION.

worldwide, *adj.* universal, widespread; general, all-embracing, unlimited. See GREATNESS.

worm, *n. & v.* —*n.* earthworm, angleworm; maggot, larva, grub, caterpillar; insect; crawler, nightcrawler; flatworm, platyhelminth, tapeworm, cestode, nematode, roundworm, ascarid, pinworm, annelid; wretch; screw, spiral. See COWARDICE. —*v.* crawl, creep, belly; insinuate (oneself), bore; writhe, wriggle. See PROGRESSION, INSERTION.

worn, *adj.* used, secondhand; frayed, shabby, threadbare; shopworn. See DETERIORATION.

worry, *n. & v.* —*n.* CARE, anxiety, mental anguish, uneasiness, FEAR, apprehension; concern, misgiving. —*v.t.* tease, plague, vex; disturb, fret, upset; torment, torture, trouble, bait, badger; maul, chew, mangle. See PAIN, DISCONTENT.

worship, *n. & v.* —*n.* adoration, devotion, aspiration, homage, service; kneeling, genuflection; religious rites *or* observance; PRAYER, invocation; praise, glorification; psalm, HYMN; divine services, Mass, matins, evensong, vespers; sacrifice, oblation, incense, libation; burnt offering, votive offering; offertory. —*v.* revere, adore, attend services, pay homage; kneel; bow down and worship; pray, supplicate; offer up *or* say one's prayers, tell one's beads; return *or* give thanks; say grace; bless, praise, laud, glorify; give benediction; go to church, attend Mass; communicate; offer sacrifice; fast, deny oneself; vow, offer vows, give alms, be devout, religious *or* orthodox. See RELIGION, RITE. *Ant.*, see DISRESPECT.

worst, *adj. & v.* —*adj.* ultimate, greatest, most extreme, *or* utmost (in a bad sense). See BADNESS, EVIL, ADVERSITY. —*v.t.* best; defeat, conquer. See SUCCESS, SUPERIORITY. *Ant.*, see PROSPERITY, LOSS.

worth, *n.* merit, USE; value; price, cost, estimation; worthiness, IMPORTANCE, VIRTUE, CREDIT; character. See MONEY. *Ant.*, see USELESSNESS.

worthless, *adj.* useless, no good, good-for-nothing; base, vile; valueless; poor, miserable, trashy, unserviceable; trifling; characterless. *Colloq.*, no-account. *Slang*, lousy. See USELESSNESS, WASTE. *Ant.*, see VIRTUE, IMPORTANCE, USE.

worthy, *adj.* deserving, meritorious; virtuous, good; estimable, honest, upright, reputable. See REPUTE, VIRTUE. *Ant.*, see DISREPUTE, IMPROBITY.

wound, *n. & v.* —*n.* injury, hurt; PAIN, painfulness. —*v.t.* injure, hurt, lame, cripple; PAIN; shoot, stab, cut, lacerate, tear, wing; insult, offend, gall, mortify. *Ant.*, see REMEDY.

wrangle, *v.i.* quarrel, bicker, squabble, dispute, altercate, argue, brawl.

wrap, *n. & v.* —*n.* robe, shawl, serape, cloak, coat, cape, cover, wrapper, blanket. —*v.t.* swathe, swaddle, clothe, cover, envelop, inclose; hide, muffle, conceal; fold, lap, wind; pack, package. See CLOTHING, COVERING, CONCEALMENT. *Ant.,* see DISCLOSURE, DIVESTMENT.

wrath, *n.* choler, anger, ire, indignation; fury, rage. See RESENTMENT.

wreath, *n.* garland, lei, chaplet, festoon; laurel wreath, garland of bays; floral ring, decoration. See ORNAMENT.

wreck, *n. & v.* —*n.* DESTRUCTION, ruin, undoing; accident, collision, crack-up, smash-up, crash; shipwreck; derelict; ruined person; human wreckage; break-up; ruins, demolition, wreckage; junk. —*v.t.* smash, crash, crack up; ruin, tear down, demolish, raze, destroy; shipwreck, strand, cast away; shatter, blight, blast. *Slang,* bust up. See FAILURE, REMAINDER. *Ant.,* see SUCCESS, PROSPERITY.

wrench, *v. & n.* —*v.t.* twist, wring; yank, pull; extort, wrest, snatch; sprain, strain, dislocate. —*n.* monkey wrench, spanner; twist, yank, *etc.* See DISTORTION, EXTRACTION.

wrestle, *v.* grapple; strive; struggle with; contend. See CONTENTION.

wretch, *n.* sufferer; beggar, outcast, pariah; knave, villain; rogue, rascal. See PAIN, EVILDOER.

wretched, *adj.* beggarly, worthless, miserable; paltry; mean; pitiful; unhappy, unfortunate; woebegone, tormented, afflicted; shabby, disreputable, deplorable. See BADNESS, DISCONTENT, PAIN, UNIMPORTANCE. *Ant.,* see GOODNESS, CHEERFULNESS, IMPORTANCE.

wriggle, *v.* wiggle; shake, squirm, writhe; shimmy. See OSCILLATION.

wring, *v.t.* wrench, twist; rack, PAIN; squeeze, compress. See DISTORTION.

wrinkle, *n. & v.* —*n.* FURROW, crease, pucker, corrugation, rumple; crinkle, crow's-foot. *Slang,* angle, development, gimmick. —*v.t.* crease, rumple, FOLD. *Ant.,* see SMOOTHNESS.

writ, *n.* process, summons, warrant. See LAWSUIT.

writhe, *v.i.* wriggle, squirm, twist, contort. See DISTORTION, PAIN.

WRITING [590]

Nouns—**1,** writing, chirography, calligraphy, pencraft, penmanship, handwriting, uncial writing, cuneiform, rune, hieroglyph(ic), LETTER; alphabet; stroke of the pen, pen and ink; shorthand, stenography, typewriting; cryptography, code, steganography.

2, cacography, bad hand, illegible hand, scribble, scrawl. *Slang,* hen tracks.

3, WORD, syllable, PHRASE, sentence, paragraph; authorship, composition; pose, poetry. See SPEECH, BOOK, PUBLICATION.

4, manuscript, Ms., Mss., COPY, transcript, rescript, typescript, rough copy *or* draft; fair copy; autograph, monograph, holograph.

5, writer, scribe, amanuensis, scrivener, secretary, clerk, penman, copyist, transcriber; typewriter, typist; calligrapher; author, novelist, poet.

Verbs—write, pen, COPY, engross; write out, transcribe; scribble, scrawl, scratch; interline; write down, record, sign; compose, indite, draw up, dictate; inscribe, dash off, draft, formulate; take pen in hand; typewrite, type; write shorthand.

Adjectives—writing, written, holographic, manuscript; shorthand, stenographic; in writing, in black and white; uncial, runic, cuneiform, hieroglyphic, hieratic; handwritten, cursive, printed, lettered; legible; Spencerian, backhand.

Antonyms, see SPEECH, PRINTING.

---

wrong, *n., v. & adj.* —*n.* erroneousness; grievance; shame, disgrace; EVIL, abomination; injustice, unfairness; vice, iniquity, foul play; undueness, unlawfulness, ILLEGALITY; ERROR, BADNESS, IMPROBITY. —*v.* do an injustice; sin against, maltreat, mistreat. —*adj.* wrongful, EVIL, bad, too bad; incorrect, erroneous, mistaken; unjust, unfair, inequitable; objectionable, unreasonable, unjustifiable; improper, unfit; unjustified, illegal. *Ant.,* see RIGHTNESS, PROBITY, GOODNESS, LEGALITY.

wry, *adj.* crooked, twisted; askew, awry; distorted, contorted; warped. See DISTORTION, OBLIQUITY. *Ant.,* see DIRECTION.

X

xanthic, *adj.* yellow, yellowish; fulvous, tawny.
xanthous, *adj.* blond(e), fair, light-skinned; fair-haired, yellow-haired, golden-haired; yellowish; Mongolian. See COLORLESSNESS.
x–ray, *n.* Roentgen ray; radiation; radiograph. See LIGHT.
xylograph, *n.* woodcut, wood engraving. See ENGRAVING.
xyloid, *adj.* wood, woody, ligneous. See VEGETABLE.
xylophone, *n.* marimba, gamelan(g), vibraphone, vibraharp, Glockenspiel, orchestra bells, sticcado, gigelira, straw fiddle.

Y

yacht, *n.* sailboat, pleasure boat; houseboat; sloop, yawl, ketch; cruiser. See SHIP.
yank, *n. & v., colloq.,* pull, jerk, twist.
yard, *n.* INCLOSURE, court, courtyard, patio. See MEASUREMENT.
yardstick, *n.* ruler; standard, criterion, rule, test, measure. See MEASUREMENT, RELATION.
yarn, *n.* thread, worsted, spun wool; tale, fib, tall story. See FILAMENT, DESCRIPTION, EXAGGERATION.
yawn, *v.i.* gape, open wide; split, part. See OPENING.
yea, *adv.* yes; indeed, truly. See AFFIRMATION, ASSENT.
year, *n.* twelvemonth; fiscal year, calendar year. See TIME.
yearn, *v.i.* pine, long, hanker; grieve, mourn. See DESIRE.
yeast, *n.* leaven, ferment, barm; spume, froth, foam. See AGITATION.
yell, *v. & n.* shout, CRY, scream, shriek, bawl, call; yelp, bark; bellow, roar, hoot. *Colloq.,* squawk, holler. See LOUDNESS.
yellow, *adj. & n.* —*adj.* fair, blond(e), flaxen, light-haired; golden, gold, saffron, ivory, creamy, lemon, xanthic; xanthous; buttery, yolky, ocherous; Mongolian, Mongoloid; jaundiced; jealous, envious; cowardly, craven, fearful, lily- *or* white-livered, afraid, unmanly, pusillanimous; lurid, sensational, melodramatic, scandal-mongering. —*n.* gold, saffron, yellow color; yolk. See COLOR, COWARDICE.
yelp, *n. & v.* bark, squawk, CRY, yap, yip.
yeoman, *n.* freeholder, commoner, farmer; guardsman, beefeater; attendant, retainer; petty officer. See POSSESSION, POPULACE, SERVANT.
yes, *adv. & n.* —*adv.* yea, aye; indeed, true, verily; agreed, surely, certainly, of course, that's right. —*n.* AFFIRMATION; ASSENT. *Ant.,* see NEGATION, DISSENT.
yesterday, *n.* day before; the past. See TIME.
yet, *conj. & adv.* —*conj.* nevertheless, notwithstanding, still, however. —*adv.* still, besides, thus far, hitherto, till now, up to now *or* this time.
yield, *n. & v.* —*n.* crop, harvest, product. —*v.* surrender, cede, abandon, give up; give in, succumb; produce, bear, bring; furnish, supply, afford; soften, relax, give (way); ASSENT, comply, obey. See PRODUCTION, RELINQUISHMENT, OBEDIENCE.
yielding, *adj.* soft, pliant, tractable, docile; submissive, compliant, acquiescent; supple, plastic, flexible; productive, fertile. See SOFTNESS, OBEDIENCE. *Ant.,* see HARDNESS, OPPOSITION.
yoke, *n. & v.* —*n.* union, bond, chain, link, tie; bondage, slavery, oppression, servitude, enslavement, thralldom, vassalage; couple, pair, team. —*v.t.* couple, join, pair, wed; bind, tie, link; bracket, connect, associate. See MARRIAGE, JUNCTION, SUBJECTION.
yokel, *n.* rustic, peasant, countryman. *Colloq.,* hick, hayseed, rube; bumpkin; yahoo. See POPULACE.

young, *adj. & n.* —*adj.* youthful; puerile; ageless; green; adolescent, juvenile, teen-age; fresh, new; inexperienced, immature. See YOUTH. *Ant.,* see AGE, OLDNESS. —*n.* offspring, children.

YOUTH [127]

Nouns—**1,** youth, juvenility, juvenescence, immaturity, juniority; childhood, boyhood, maidenhood, girlhood, youthhood; minority, nonage, teen-age, teens, tender age, bloom; prime of life, flower of life; heyday of youth; school days; ADOLESCENCE, puberty; greenness, callowness, inexperience, puerility.
2, babyhood, infancy, cradle, nursery, apron strings.
3, child, infant, boy, girl, lad, maid, youth, hobbledehoy, stripling, teenager, adolescent. *Colloq.,* kid; bobby soxer, juvenile.
Adjectives—young, youthful, juvenile, immature, green, callow, budding, sappy, unfledged, under age, teen-age, in one's teens; hebetic, adolescent, pubescent; immature; younger, junior; boyish, beardless; maidenly, girlish; infant, infantile, newborn, babyish, childish, puerile.
Antonym, see AGE.

Z

zany, *n.* clown, madcap, buffoon, comic, FOOL, comedian, jester, merryandrew, Punch, pickle-herring; nitwit, dunce. See ABSURDITY.
zeal, *n.* earnestness, devotion, dedication; passion; soul, spirit, ardor, fervor, verve, enthusiasm, eagerness, warmth, energy; zealotry, fanaticism. See ACTIVITY, WILL. *Ant.,* indifference; see COLD.
zealot, *n.* fanatic; visionary, dreamer, enthusiast; bigot; devotee, partisan. *Colloq.,* addict, fan. See CERTAINTY, RESOLUTION,
zenith, *n.* summit, top, acme, apex, pinnacle, apogee; climax, culmination; prime, heyday. See HEIGHT. *Ant.,* nadir; see LOWNESS.
zephyr, *n.* breeze, gentle wind, west wind. See WIND.
zero, *n.* nothing; naught, nought; cipher, none; (in games) love, blank; nobody, not a soul. *Slang,* goose-egg. See ABSENCE, INSUBSTANTIALITY.
zest, *n.* relish, gusto, appetite, enthusiasm, enjoyment, thrill, titillation, exhilaration; tang, twang, pungency, piquance; savor, sauce; edge. *Colloq.,* kick, zip. See TASTE, FEELING.
zigzag, *adj.* back-and-forth, tacking, serrated, jagged; crooked, tortuous. See DEVIATION. *Ant.,* straight, direct; see DIRECTION.
zip, *n. & v.* —*n., Colloq.,* pep, vigor, zest, ginger, ENERGY; whiz, ping, swish. —*v.* move speedily; flash; swish, whiz; close (a zipper). See SOUND, CLOSURE.
zipper, *n.* slide fastener. See CLOSURE.
zone, *n.* region, clime, climate; district, ward, area; belt, girdle, band, girth, cincture. See CIRCULARITY, LOCATION.
zoölogy, *n.* science of animals, study of animal life; natural history, zoögraphy. See ANIMAL.

FOREIGN PHRASES

Translated, with reference to the applicable English categories

ab initio, *Lat.*, from the beginning; see BEGINNING.

ad nauseam, *Lat.*, to the point of nausea; boringly; see WEARINESS.

affaire d'amour, *Fr.*, love affair; see LOVE.

agent provocateur, *Fr.*, professional agitator; see AGITATION, DEMONSTRATION.

Agnus Dei, *Lat.*, Lamb of God; see DEITY.

al fresco, *It.*, in the open air; outdoors; see AIR.

alter ego, *Lat.*, another I; intimate friend; see FRIEND.

amour propre, *Fr.*, self-esteem; see VANITY.

ancien regime, *Fr.*, the old order; see OLDNESS.

ante bellum, *Lat.*, before the war; see OLDNESS.

au contraire, *Fr.*, on the contrary; see DISAGREEMENT; OPPOSITION.

au courant, *Fr.*, up-to-date; informed; see INFORMATION.

au fait, *Fr.*, well informed; see INFORMATION.

au naturel, *Fr.*, nude; see DIVESTMENT.

ave atque vale, *Lat.*, hail and FAREWELL; see DEPARTURE.

Ave Maria, *Lat.*, Hail Mary!; see PRAYER, RELIGION.

beau geste, *Fr.*, a fine deed; see COURAGE.

beau monde, *Fr.*, fashionable society; see FASHION.

belles-lettres, *Fr.*, fine LITERATURE.

bête noire, *Fr.*, object of dislike; see HATE.

billet-doux, *Fr.*, love letter; see LOVE.

bon mot, *Fr.*, witty saying; see WIT.

bon vivant, *Fr.*, epicure; good companion. See SOCIALITY, GLUTTONY.

carpe diem, *Lat.*, make use of the day; see ACTIVITY.

carte blanche, *Fr.*, unlimited authority; see AUTHORITY, FREEDOM.

caveat emptor, *Lat.*, let the buyer beware; see CARE, WARNING.

cave canem, *Lat.*, beware the dog; see WARNING.

chacun à son gout, *Fr.*, each to his own taste; see FREEDOM.

chef d'oeuvre, *Fr.*, masterpiece; see SKILL.

cherchez la femme, *Fr.*, look for the woman; see DISCLOSURE.

comme il faut, *Fr.*, as it should be; see TASTE.

corpus delicti, *Lat.*, the facts connected with a crime; see GUILT.

coup de grâce, *Fr.*, a merciful finishing blow; see KILLING, COMPLETION.

coup d'état, *Fr.*, a political stroke; see REVOLUTION.

cum laude *and* **summa cum laude**, *Lat.*, with [the highest] praise; see SUPERIORITY, APPROBATION.

de facto, *Lat.*, in fact; actual; realistically; see TRUTH

Dei gratia, *Lat.*, by the grace of God; see POWER, RIGHTNESS.

de jure, *Lat.*, by right, lawfully; see RIGHTNESS.

de novo, *Lat.*, from the beginning; see BEGINNING.

Deo gratias, *Lat.*, thank God!; see GRATITUDE.

de profundis, *Lat.*, out of the depths; see PENITENCE.

de rigueur, *Fr.*, obligatory; see TASTE.

dernier cri, *Fr.*, the last word; MODERN; see NEWNESS.

de trop, *Fr.*, too much; see SUFFICIENCY.

deus ex machina, *Lat.*, a contrived instrumentality; see AGENCY.

dolce far niente, *It.*, sweet to do nothing; see REPOSE.

en deshabille, *Fr.*, not dressed for receiving company; see DIVESTMENT.

en famille, *Fr.*, at home; informally; see REPOSE, UNCONFORMITY.

enfant terrible, *Fr.*, an unruly child; see DISOBEDIENCE.

en masse, *Fr.*, all together; in a group; see ASSEMBLAGE.

en rapport, *Fr.*, in harmony; see AGREEMENT.

entre nous, *Fr.*, [just] between us; see DISCLOSURE.

ex cathedra, *Lat.*, from the seat of authority; see AUTHORITY.

exempli gratia, *Lat.*, for example; see INTERPRETATION, TEACHING.

ex officio, *Lat.*, by right of office; see AUTHORITY.

ex post facto, *Lat.*, after the deed [is done]; see COMPLETION.

fait accompli, *Fr.*, an accomplished fact; see COMPLETION.

faux pas, *Fr.*, a false step; ERROR.

fin de siècle, *Fr.*, end of the century; see TIME.

flagrante delicto, *Lat.*, during the commission of the crime; see GUILT.

haut monde, *Fr.*, upper classes; see FASHION.

hic jacet, *Lat.*, here lies; see INTERMENT.

hors de combat, *Fr.*, out of the fight; see DESTRUCTION, KILLING.

ibidem, *Lat.*, in the same place; see IDENTITY.

idée fixe, *Fr.*, a fixed idea; obsession; see BELIEF.

in extremis, *Lat.*, near death; see DEATH.

infra dignitatem, *Lat.*, beneath one's dignity; see DISREPUTE.

in loco parentis, *Lat.*, in the place of a parent; see AGENCY, AUTHORITY.

in statu quo, *Lat.*, in the same condition; see STABILITY.

inter nos, *Lat.*, [just] between us; see DISCLOSURE.

in toto, *Lat.*, in full; wholly; see COMPLETION.
ipse dixit, *Lat.*, he himself has said it; see AUTHORITY.
ipso facto, *Lat.*, [by virtue of] the same fact; see MEANING.

je ne sais quoi, *Fr.*, I don't know what; see SKILL, ELEGANCY.
jeunesse dorée, *Fr.*, gilded youth; see MONEY, WASTE.

laissez faire, *Fr.*, noninterference; TOLERANCE.
lapsus linguae, *Lat.*, a slip of the tongue; see ERROR.
loco citato, *Lat.*, in the place cited; see RELATION.
locum tenens, *Lat.*, a substitute; see SUBSTITUTION.

magnum opus, *Lat.*, masterpiece; see SKILL.
mañana, *Sp.*, tomorrow; see LATENESS.
Man sagt, *Ger.*, they say; see INFORMATION.
mirabile dictu, *Lat.*, marvelous to relate; see WONDER.
mise en scène, *Fr.*, stage setting; see DRAMA.
modus operandi, *Lat.*, method of working; see PRODUCTION.
modus vivendi, *Lat.*, way of living or getting along; see AGREEMENT, COÖPERATION.

ne plus ultra, *Lat.*, that which is peerless; see COMPLETION.
n'est-ce pas?, *Fr.*, isn't it [true]?; see DOUBT.
nicht wahr?, *Ger.*, [is it] not true?; see DOUBT.
nil desperandum, *Lat.*, despair of nothing; see COURAGE.
noblesse oblige, *Fr.*, nobility obligates; see DUTY.
nom de plume, *Fr.*, pen name; see NOMENCLATURE.
non compos mentis, *Lat.*, not of sound mind; see INSANITY.
non sequitur, *Lat.*, it does not follow; see ABSURDITY.
nouveau riche, *Fr.*, newly rich; SNOB.

obiter dictum, *Lat.*, a passing remark; COMMENT.
on dit, *Fr.*, they say; see INFORMATION.

par excellence, *Fr.*, above all others; see SUPERIORITY.
particeps criminis, *Lat.*, ACCOMPLICE.
passim, *Lat.*, here and there; see DISJUNCTION.
peccavi, *Lat.*, I have sinned; see PENITENCE.
per annum, *Lat.*, by the year; see TIME.
per capita, *Lat.*, by the head; EACH.
per diem, *Lat.*, by the day; see COMPENSATION.
per se, *Lat.*, by itself; INTRINSIC.

persona non grata, *Lat.*, an unacceptable person; see HATE.
pièce de résistance, *Fr.*, the main dish, event, etc.; see IMPORTANCE.
prima facie, *Lat.*, at first sight; see EVIDENCE.
pro tempore, *Lat.*, for the time being; see TIME, SUBSTITUTION.

quid pro quo, *Lat.*, something in return; see COMPENSATION, RETALIATION, SUBSTITUTION.
¿quien sabe?, *Sp.*, who knows?; see DOUBT.
qui vive, *Fr.*, alertness; see CARE.
quod erat demonstrandum, *Lat.*, which was to be proved; see EVIDENCE.

rara avis, *Lat.*, rare bird; unusual thing; see RARITY, UNCOMFORMITY.
reductio ad absurdum, *Lat.*, reduction to an absurdity; see PROOF.
requiescat in pace, *Lat.*, rest in peace; see INTERMENT.
res gestae, *Lat.*, things done; see COMPLETION.
rigor mortis, *Lat.*, the stiffness of death; see DEATH.

sanctum sanctorum, *Lat.*, holy of holies; see TEMPLE.
sang-froid, *Fr.*, calmness; see INDIFFERENCE.
savoir-faire, *Fr.*, knowledge of what to do; POISE.
semper fidelis, *Lat.*, always faithful; see PROBITY.
sholom aleichim, *Semitic*, peace be with you; see BENEVOLENCE.
s'il vous plait, *Fr.*, PLEASE.
sine die, *Lat.*, without [setting] a day [to meet again]; see TIME.
sotto voce, *It.*, under the breath; see SPEECH.
status quo, *Lat.*, existing condition; see STABILITY.
sub rosa, *Lat.*, secretly; see CONCEALMENT.
sui generis, *Lat.*, of its own kind; unique; see UNCONFORMITY.

tempus fugit, *Lat.*, time flies; see TIME.
terra firma, *Lat.*, solid ground; LAND.
tour de force, *Fr.*, a feat of skill or strength; see SKILL.
tout à fait, *Fr.*, entirely; see COMPLETION.
tout de suite, *Fr.*, at once; immediately; see EARLINESS.

vade mecum, *Lat.*, go with me; summons; see LAWSUIT.
vae victis, *Lat.*, woe to the vanquished; see RETALIATION.
verbum sapienti, *Lat.*, a word to the wise; see ADVICE.
vis-à-vis, *Fr.*, face to face; see OPPOSITION.
viva voce, *Lat.*, aloud; orally; see SPEECH.

wie geht's?, *Ger.*, how goes it?; how are you?; see CARE.

HOW TO USE THE CATEGORY NUMBERS

In his original Thesaurus, Roget divided all English words into exactly 1,000 groups or categories, depending on the ideas they convey. The Introduction that Roget wrote to his original work (which Introduction is reprinted on the following pages) explains his basis for his groupings.

Each of Roget's original categories bore a number, from 1 to 1,000. When these categories are used in this book, they show the original Roget numbers.

Our purpose in giving the original Roget numbers is as follows: The nearer two category numbers are, the more nearly related are the ideas they represent. For example, you look up the subject DETERIORATION. Suppose it does not precisely serve your needs, but you observe that its number is 659. You can be sure of finding related ideas in categories 658 and 660, to a somewhat lesser extent in categories 657 and 661, and so on. In the index of categories that follows these pages you find the names of these related categories, you look them up in their alphabetical order, and you will usually soon encounter the precise word or phrase you seek.

One must suspect that Roget was so intent on making his total number of categories come out to an even thousand that he added an unnecessary one here and there. The unnecessary ones have not been retained in this edition. Also, Roget often had two categories with the same name, for example CHANCE, which was both 156 and 621, and EXCLUSION, which was both 55 and 77. For the sake of simplicity, all such dual listings have been combined in this book.

The Roget system of grouping word-lists numerically made it necessary for him to include an index almost as long as the effective text of his book, simply so that a user could find the word or idea he was looking for. Since our book lists all words alphabetically, no such index is necessary and it has been possible to give much more space to the useful contents, where the actual words and phrases that are sought may be found. Also, Roget had to expend some categories on simple lists of synonyms. Since this edition is a book of synonyms as well as a Thesaurus, the editors did not find it necessary to make separate categories of these lists of synonyms, but the reader will find them in their appropriate place in the full list of categories.

The reader will find it both interesting and rewarding to read the essential paragraphs of Roget's Introduction, which may be found on the following pages. Though some of the words and locutions may appear archaic or quaint to the modern taste, the eloquence and originality of this great pioneer could hardly be surpassed.

ALBERT MOREHEAD
General Editor

ROGET'S PLAN OF CLASSIFICATION

I. ABSTRACT RELATIONS

Categories Numbered

II. SPACE

III. MATTER

IV. INTELLECT

V. VOLITION

VI. AFFECTIONS

THE CATEGORIES IN NUMERICAL ORDER

When Roget's original name for a category is not the same as the entry in this book, the name or names used in this book follow, in (SMALL CAPITALS).

CLASS I. ABSTRACT RELATIONS

1. Existence

1. Existence
2. Inexistence (NONEXISTENCE)
3. Substantiality (SUBSTANCE)
4. Unsubstantiality
5. Intrinsicality (INTRINSIC)
6. Extrinsicality (EXTRINSIC)
7. State
8. Circumstance

2. Relation

9. Relation
10. Irrelation (DIFFERENCE)
11. Consanguinity (KINDRED)
12. Correlation (RELATION)
13. Identity
14. Contrariety (OPPOSITION)
15. Difference
16. Uniformity (CONFORMITY)
17. Similarity
18. Dissimilarity (DIFFERENCE)
19. Imitation
20. Nonimitation (UNCONFORMITY)
21. Copy
22. Prototype
23. Agreement
24. Disagreement

3. Quantity

25. Quantity
26. Degree
27. Equality
28. Inequality
29. Mean
30. Compensation
31. Greatness
32. Smallness (LITTLENESS)
33. Superiority
34. Inferiority
35. Increase
36. Decrease
37. Addition
38. Nonaddition (DEDUCTION)
39. Adjunct (ADDITION)
40. Remainder
41. Mixture
42. Simpleness
43. Junction
44. Disjunction
45. Vinculum (CONNECTION)
46. Coherence
47. Incoherence
48. Combination
49. Decomposition
50. Whole
51. Part
52. Completeness (COMPLETION)
53. Incompleteness
54. Composition
55. Exclusion
56. Component
57. Extraneousness (EXTRANEOUS)

4. Order

58. Order
59. Disorder
60. Arrangement
61. Derangement

62. Precedence
64. Precursor (FORERUNNER)
66. Beginning
68. Middle
69. Continuity
71. Term
72. Assemblage
74. Focus
75. Class
76. Inclusion
78. Generality
80. Rule
82. Conformity

63. Sequence
65. Sequel
67. End

70. Discontinuity (DISCONTINUANCE)

73. Nonassemblage (DISPERSION)

77. Exclusion
79. Speciality
81. Multiformity
83. Unconformity

5. Number

84. Number
85. Numeration
86. List
87. Unity

88. Accompaniment
89. Duality (NUMERATION)
90. Duplication (NUMERATION)
91. Bisection (NUMERATION)
92. Triality (NUMERATION)
93. Triplication (NUMERATION)
94. Trisection (NUMERATION)
95. Quaternity (NUMERATION)
96. Quadruplication (NUMERATION)
97. Quadrisection (NUMERATION)
98. Five, etc. (NUMERATION)
99. Quinquesection, etc. (NUMERATION)

100. Plurality (NUMBER)
101. Zero
102. Multitude
103. Fewness (FEW, RARITY)
104. Repetition
105. Infinity

6. Time

106. Time
107. Neverness (NONEXISTENCE)
108. Period
109. Course
110. Diuturnity (DURABILITY)
111. Transientness
112. Perpetuity
113. Instantaneity
114. Chronometry
115. Anachronism
116. Priority
117. Posteriority (SEQUENCE)
118. Present [time]
119. Different time (TIME)
120. Synchronism
121. Futurity
122. Preterition (PAST)
123. Newness
124. Oldness
125. Morning
126. Evening
127. Youth
128. Age
129. Infant
130. Veteran
131. Adolescence
132. Earliness
133. Lateness
134. Occasion
135. Intempestivity (UNTIMELINESS)
136. Frequency
137. Infrequency
138. Regularity
139. Irregularity

7. Change

8. Causation

CLASS II. SPACE

1. Space in General

2. Dimensions

3. Form

4. Motion

278. Direction
280. Precession
282. Progression
284. Propulsion
286. Approach
288. Attraction
290. Convergence
292. Arrival
294. Ingress
296. Reception
298. Food
300. Insertion
302. Passage
303. Transcursion (OVERRUNNING)
305. Ascent
307. Elevation
309. Leap
310. Plunge
311. Circuition (CIRCUITY)
312. Rotation
313. Evolution
314. Oscillation
315. Agitation

279. Deviation
281. Sequence
283. Regression
285. Traction
287. Recession
289. Repulsion
291. Divergence
293. Departure
295. Egress
297. Ejection
299. Excretion
301. Extraction

304. Shortcoming
306. Descent
308. Depression

CLASS III. MATTER

1. Matter in General

316. Materiality (SUBSTANCE)

318. World (UNIVERSE)
319. Gravity

317. Immateriality (INSUBSTANTIAL-ITY)

320. Levity

2. Inorganic

321. Density
323. Hardness
325. Elasticity
327. Tenacity
329. Texture
330. Pulverulence (POWDERINESS)
331. Friction
333. Fluidity
334. Gaseity (GAS, GASEOUS, VAPOR)
335. Liquefaction
336. Vaporization (VAPOR)
337. Water
338. Air
339. Moisture
341. Ocean
343. Gulf, Lake
344. Plain
345. Marsh
346. Island
347. Stream
348. River

322. Rarity
324. Softness
326. Inelasticity
328. Brittleness

332. Lubrication

340. Dryness
342. Land

423. Luminary (LIGHT)
425. Transparency (TRANSPARENT)

424. Shade
426. Opacity
427. Semitransparency (DIMNESS)
429. Achromatism (COLORLESSNESS)
431. Blackness (COLOR)

428. Color
430. Whiteness (COLOR)
432. Gray (COLOR)
433. Brown (COLOR)
434. Redness (COLOR)
435. Greenness (COLOR)
436. Yellowness (COLOR)
437. Purple (COLOR)
438. Blueness (COLOR)
439. Orange (COLOR)
440. Variegation
441. Vision

442. Blindness
443. Dimsightedness (DIMSIGHTED)

444. Spectator
445. Optical Instruments
446. Visibility
448. Appearance

447. Invisibility (INVISIBLE)
449. Disappearance

CLASS IV. INTELLECT

1. Formation of Ideas

450. Intellect
451. Thought
453. Idea
454. Topic
455. Curiosity
457. Attention
459. Care
461. Inquiry
463. Experiment
464. Comparison
465. Discrimination
466. Measurement
467. Evidence

452. Incogitancy (IGNORANCE)

456. Incuriosity (INDIFFERENCE)
458. Inattention
460. Neglect
462. Answer

468. Counterevidence
469. Qualification
471. Impossibility (IMPOSSIBLE, CHANCE)
473. Improbability (IMPROBABLE, CHANCE)
475. Uncertainty
477. Intuition
479. Confutation (ANSWER, CONFUTE)

470. Possibility

472. Probability (PROBABLE, CHANCE)

474. Certainty
476. Reasoning
478. Demonstration

480. Judgment
482. Overestimation
484. Belief
486. Credulity
488. Assent
490. Knowledge
492. Scholar

481. Misjudgment
483. Underestimation
485. Unbelief (DOUBT)
487. Incredulity
489. Dissent
491. Ignorance
493. Ignoramus

569. Style
570. Perspicuity
572. Conciseness (CONCISE, SHORT-
NESS)

571. Obscurity
573. Diffuseness

574. Vigor
576. Plainness (SIMPLENESS)
578. Elegance
580. Voice
582. Speech
584. Loquacity
586. Allocution (SPEECH)
588. Interlocution (CONVERSATION)

575. Feebleness (IMPOTENCE)
577. Ornament
579. Inelegance (INELEGANT)
581. Aphony (MUTE, SILENCE)
583. Stammering
585. Taciturnity
587. Response
589. Soliloquy

590. Writing
591. Printing
592. Correspondence
593. Book
594. Description
595. Dissertation
597. Poetry
599. Drama

596. Compendium
598. Prose (WRITING)

CLASS V. VOLITION

1. Individual

600. Will
602. Willingness
604. Resolution
606. Obstinacy

601. Necessity
603. Unwillingness
605. Irresolution (IRRESOLUTE)
607. Tergiversation (CHANGEABLE-
NESS)
608. Caprice (CHANGEABLENESS)

609. Choice
610. Rejection
611. Predetermination (PREDICTION)
613. Habit
615. Motive
617. Plea
618. Good
620. Intention
622. Pursuit

612. Impulse
614. Desuetude (DISUSE)
616. Dissuasion

619. Evil
621. Chance
623. Avoidance
624. Relinquishment

625. Business
626. Plan
627. Method
628. Midcourse (MIDDLE)
630. Requirement
631. Instrumentality
632. Means
633. Instrument
635. Materials
636. Store
637. Provision
639. Sufficiency
641. Redundance (REPETITION)

629. Circuit

634. Substitute

638. Waste
640. Insufficiency

726. Combatant
727. Arms
728. Arena
729. Completion
731. Success
733. Trophy
734. Prosperity

730. Noncompletion (NEGLECT)
732. Failure

735. Adversity
736. Mediocrity (MEDIOCRE, MIDDLE, UNIMPORTANCE)

2. Intersocial

737. Authority
739. Severity
741. Command

738. Laxity
740. Lenity
742. Disobedience
743. Obedience

744. Compulsion
745. Master
747. Scepter (AUTHORITY)

746. Servant
748. Freedom
749. Subjection
750. Liberation

751. Restraint
752. Prison
753. Keeper
755. Commission

754. Prisoner
756. Abrogation (NULLIFICATION)
757. Resignation
758. Consignee (TRANSFER)
759. Deputy
761. Prohibition

760. Permission
762. Consent
763. Offer
765. Request
767. Petitioner

764. Refusal
766. Deprecation (DEPRECATE)
768. Promise
769. Compact
770. Conditions

771. Security
772. Observance
774. Compromise
775. Acquisition
777. Possession
779. Possessor (POSSESSION)
780. Property
781. Retention
783. Transfer
784. Giving
786. Apportionment
787. Lending (DEBT)
789. Taking
791. Stealing
792. Thief
794. Barter
795. Purchase
797. Merchant

773. Nonobservance (NEGLECT)

776. Loss
778. Participation

782. Relinquishment

785. Receiving

788. Borrowing (DEBT)
790. Restitution

793. Booty

796. Sale
798. Merchandise
799. Mart (MARKET, BUSINESS)

800. Money

801. Treasurer
802. Treasury
803. Wealth
805. Credit
807. Payment
809. Expenditure
811. Accounts (ACCOUNTING)
812. Price
814. Dearness (DEAR, PAYMENT)
816. Liberality
818. Prodigality

804. Poverty
806. Debt
808. Nonpayment
810. Receipt

813. Discount
815. Cheapness
817. Economy
819. Parsimony

CLASS VI. AFFECTIONS

1. Affections in General

820. Affections (FEELING, LOVE)
821. Feeling
822. Sensibility
824. Excitation (EXCITEMENT)
825. Excitability

823. Insensibility

826. Inexcitability (INEXCITABLE)

2. Personal

827. Pleasure
829. Pleasurableness (PLEASURE)
831. Content

828. Pain
830. Painfulness (PAIN)
832. Discontent
833. Regret

834. Relief
836. Cheerfulness
838. Rejoicing
840. Amusement
842. Wit
844. Humorist
845. Beauty
847. Ornament

835. Aggravation
837. Dejection
839. Lamentation
841. Weariness
843. Dullness (DULL, SLOWNESS)

846. Ugliness
848. Blemish (IMPERFECTION)
849. Simplicity (SIMPLENESS)

850. Taste
852. Fashion

851. Vulgarity
853. Ridiculousness (ABSURDITY, RID-
        ICULE)
854. Fop
855. Affectation
856. Ridicule
857. Laughingstock

858. Hope
860. Fear
862. Cowardice
864. Caution
865. Desire

859. Hopelessness
861. Courage
863. Rashness

866. Indifference
867. Dislike

868. Fastidiousness (CLEANNESS)
869. Satiety (SUFFICIENCY)
870. Wonder

871. Expectance (EXPECTATION)

872. Prodigy
873. Repute
874. Disrepute
875. Nobility
876. Commonalty (POPULACE)
877. Title
878. Pride
879. Humility
880. Vanity
881. Modesty
882. Ostentation
883. Celebration
884. Boasting
885. Insolence
886. Servility
887. Blusterer

3. Sympathetic

888. Friendship (FRIEND)
889. Enmity (HATE)
890. Friend
891. Enemy (OPPOSITION, HATE)
892. Sociality
893. Seclusion
894. Courtesy
895. Discourtesy
896. Congratulation
897. Love
898. Hate
899. Favorite
900. Resentment
901. Irascibility

902. Endearment
903. Marriage
904. Celibacy
905. Divorce
906. Benevolence
907. Malevolence
908. Malediction (IMPRECATION)
909. Threat
910. Philanthropy
911. Misanthropy (MALEVOLENCE)
912. Benefactor
913. Evildoer
914. Pity
915. Condolence
916. Gratitude
917. Ingratitude
918. Forgiveness
919. Revenge
920. Jealousy
921. Envy

4. Moral

922. Right
923. Wrong
924. Dueness (JUSTICE)
925. Undueness (INJUSTICE)
926. Duty
927. Exemption
928. Respect
929. Disrespect
930. Contempt

931. Approbation
932. Disapprobation
933. Flattery
934. Detraction
935. Flatterer (FLATTERY)
936. Detractor (DETRACTION)
937. Vindication
938. Accusation
939. Probity
940. Improbity
941. Knave
942. Disinterestedness
943. Selfishness
944. Virtue
945. Vice
946. Innocence
947. Guilt
948. Good man (GOODNESS)
949. Bad man (EVILDOER)
950. Penitence
951. Impenitent
952. Atonement

953. Temperance
955. Asceticism
956. Fasting (FAST)
958. Sobriety (MODERATION)
960. Purity

954. Intemperance

957. Gluttony
959. Drunkenness
961. Impurity
962. Libertine
964. Illegality

963. Legality
965. Jurisdiction (JUSTICE, LEGALITY)
966. Tribunal
967. Judge
969. Lawsuit
970. Acquittal

968. Lawyer (LAWSUIT)

971. Condemnation
972. Punishment
973. Reward
974. Penalty
975. Scourge

5. Religious

976. Deity
977. Angel
979. Jupiter (MYTHICAL DEITIES)
981. Heaven
983. Theology
985. Revelation (SACRED WRITINGS)

978. Satan
980. Demon
982. Hell
984. Heterodoxy
986. Pseudorevelation (SACRED WRITINGS)

987. Piety

988. Impiety
989. Irreligion

990. Worship
991. Idolatry
992. Sorcery
993. Spell
994. Sorcerer (SORCERY)
995. Churchdom (RELIGION)
996. Clergy
998. Rite
999. Canonicals (VESTMENTS)
1000. Temple

997. Laity

From ROGET'S ORIGINAL INTRODUCTION

The present work is intended to supply, with respect to the English language, a desideratum hitherto unsupplied in any language; namely, a collection of the words it contains and of the idiomatic combinations peculiar to it, arranged, not in alphabetical order, as they are in a dictionary, but according to the *ideas* which they express. The purpose of an ordinary dictionary is simply to explain the meaning of words; and the problem of which it professes to furnish the solution may be stated thus:—The word being given, to find its signification, or the idea it is intended to convey. The object aimed at in the present undertaking is exactly the converse of this; namely, —the idea being given, to find the word, or words, by which that idea may be most fitly and aptly expressed. For this purpose, the words and phrases of the language are here classed, not according to their sound or their orthography, but strictly according to their signification.

* * *

The assistance it gives is that of furnishing on every topic a copious store of words and phrases, adapted to express all the recognisable shades and modifications of the general idea under which those words and phrases are arranged. The inquirer can readily select, out of the ample collection spread out before his eyes in the following pages, those expressions which are best suited to his purpose, and which might not have occurred to him without such assistance. In order to make this selection, he scarcely ever need engage in any elaborate or critical study of the subtle distinctions existing between synonymous terms; for if the materials set before him be sufficiently abundant, an instinctive tact will rarely fail to lead him to the proper choice. Even while glancing over the columns of this work, his eye may chance to light upon a particular term, which may save the cost of a clumsy paraphrase, or spare the labour of a tortuous circumlocution. Some felicitous turn of expression thus introduced will frequently open to the mind of the reader a whole vista of collateral ideas, which could not, without an extended and obtrusive episode, have been unfolded to his view; and often will the judicious insertion of a happy epithet, like a beam of sunshine in a landscape, illumine and adorn the subject which touches it, imparting new grace, and giving life and spirit to the picture.

*　　*　　*

In constructing the following system of classification of the ideas which are expressible by language, my chief aim has been to obtain the greatest amount of practical utility. I have accordingly adopted such principles of arrangement as appeared to me to be the simplest and most natural, and which would not require, either for their comprehension or application, any disciplined acumen, or depth of metaphysical or antiquarian lore. Eschewing all needless refinements and subtleties, I have taken as my guide the more obvious characters of the ideas for which expressions were to be tabulated, arranging them under such classes and categories as reflection and experience had taught me would conduct the inquirer most readily and quickly to the object of his search. Commencing with the ideas expressing mere abstract relations, I proceed to those which relate to the phenomena of the material world, and lastly to those in which the mind is concerned, and which comprehend intellect, volition, and feeling; thus establishing six primary Classes of Categories.

1. The first of these classes comprehends ideas derived from the more general and ABSTRACT RELATIONS among things, such as *Existence, Resemblance, Quantity, Order, Number, Time, Power.*

2. The second class refers to SPACE and its various relations, including *Motion,* or change of place.

3. The third class includes all ideas that relate to the MATERIAL WORLD; namely, the *Properties of Matter,* such as *Solidity, Fluidity, Heat, Sound, Light,* and the *Phenomena* they present, as well as the simple *Perceptions* to which they give rise.

4. The fourth class embraces all ideas of phenomena relating to the INTELLECT and its operations; comprising the *Acquisition,* the *Retention,* and the *Communication of Ideas.*

5. The fifth class includes the ideas derived from the exercise of VOLITION; embracing the phenomena and results of our *Voluntary and Active Powers;* such as *Choice, Intention, Utility, Action, Antagonism, Authority, Compact, Property,* etc.

6. The sixth, and last class, comprehends all ideas derived from the operation of our SENTIENT AND MORAL POWERS; including our *Feelings, Emotions, Passions,* and *Moral and Religious Sentiments.*

The further subdivisions and minuter details will be best understood from an inspection of the Tabular Synopsis of Categories prefixed to the work, in which are specified the several *topics* or *heads of signification,* under which the words have been arranged. By the aid of this table, the reader will, with a little practice, readily discover the place which the particular topic he is in search of occupies in the series; and on turning to the page in the body of the work which contains it, he will find the group of expressions he requires, out of which he may cull those that are most appropriate to his purpose. For the convenience of reference, I have designated each separate group or heading by a particular number; so that if, during the search, any doubt or difficulty should occur, recourse may be had to the copious alphabetical index of words in the second volume, which will at once indicate the number of the required group.

The object I have proposed to myself in this work would have been but imperfectly attained if I had confined myself to a mere catalogue of words, and had omitted the numerous phrases and forms of expression, composed of several words, which are of such frequent use as to entitle them to rank among the constituent parts of the language.* Very few of these verbal combinations, so essential to the knowledge of our native tongue, and so profusely abounding in its daily use, are to be met with in ordinary dictionaries. These phrases and forms of expression I have endeavoured diligently to collect and to insert in their proper places, under the general ideas they are designed to convey. Some of these conventional forms, indeed, partake of the nature of proverbial expressions; but actual proverbs, as such, being wholly of a didactic character, do not come within the scope of the present work; and the reader must therefore not expect to find them here inserted.

*   *   *

In many cases, two ideas, which are completely opposed to each other, admit of an intermediate or neutral idea, equidistant from both: all these being expressible by corresponding definite terms. Thus, in the following examples, the words in the first and third columns, which express opposite ideas, admit of the intermediate terms contained in the middle column having a neutral sense with reference to the former.

Identity,	*Difference,*	*Contrariety.*
Beginning,	*Middle,*	*End.*
Past,	*Present,*	*Future.*

* FOR EXAMPLE:—To take time by the forelock,—to turn over a new leaf,—to show the white feather,—to have a finger in the pie,—to let the cat out of the bag,—to take care of number one,—to kill two birds with one stone, etc., etc.

In other cases, the intermediate word is simply the negative of each of two opposite positions; as, for example—

Convexity,	*Flatness,*	*Concavity.*
Desire,	*Indifference,*	*Aversion.*

Sometimes the intermediate word is properly the standard with which each of the extremes is compared; as in the case of

Insufficiency,	*Sufficiency,*	*Redundance;*

for here the middle term, *Sufficiency,* is equally opposed, on the one hand to *Insufficiency,* and on the other hand to *Redundance.*

These forms of correlative expressions would suggest the use of triple, instead of double, columns, for tabulating this threefold order of words; but the practical inconvenience attending such an arrangement would probably overbalance its advantages.

It often happens that the same word has several correlative terms, according to the different relations in which it is considered. Thus, to the word *Giving* are opposed both *Receiving* and *Taking;* the former correlation having reference to the *persons* concerned in the transfer, while the latter relates to the *mode* of transfer. *Old* has for opposite both *New* and *Young,* according as it is applied to *things* or to *living beings. Attack* and *Defence* are correlative terms; as are also *Attack* and *Resistance. Resistance,* again, has for its other correlative *Submission. Truth in the abstract* is opposed to *Error;* but the opposite of *Truth communicated* is *Falsehood. Acquisition* is contrasted both with *Deprivation* and with *Loss. Refusal* is the counterpart both of *Offer* and of *Consent. Disuse* and *Misuse* may either of them be considered as the correlative of *Use. Teaching,* with reference to what is taught, is opposed to *Misteaching;* but with reference to the act itself, its proper reciprocal is *Learning.*

Words contrasted in form do not always bear the same contrast in their meaning. The word *Malefactor,* for example, would, from its derivation, appear to be exactly the opposite of *Benefactor;* but the ideas attached to these two words are far from being directly opposed; for while the latter expresses one who confers a benefit, the former denotes one who has violated the laws.

. . . It will be found, on strict examination, that there seldom exists an exact opposition between two words which may at first sight appear to be the counterparts of one another; for, in general, the one will be found to possess in reality more force or extent of meaning than the other with which it is contrasted. The correlative term sometimes assumes the form of a mere negative, although it is really endowed with a considerable positive force. Thus *Disrespect* is not merely the absence of *Respect;* its signification trenches on the opposite idea, namely, *Contempt.* In like manner, *Untruth* is not merely the negative of *Truth;* it involves a degree of *Falsehood. Irreligion,* which is properly *the want of Religion,* is understood as being nearly synonymous with *Impiety.* For these reasons, the reader must not expect that all the words which stand side by side in the two columns shall be the precise correlatives of each other; for the nature of the subject, as well as the imperfections of language, renders it impossible always to preserve such an exactness of correlation.

There exist comparatively few words of a general character to which no correlative term, either of negation or of opposition, can be assigned, and which therefore require no corresponding second column. The correlative idea, especially that which constitutes a sense negative to the primary one, may, indeed, be formed or conceived; but, from its occurring rarely, no word has been framed to represent it; for in language, as in other matters, the supply fails when there is no probability of a demand. Occasionally we find this deficiency provided for by the contrivance of prefixing the syllable *non;* as, for instance, the negatives of *existence, performance, payment,* etc., are expressed by the compound words, *non-existence, non-performance, non-payment,* etc. Functions of a similar kind are performed by the prefixes *dis-, anti-, contra-, mis-, in-,* and *un-.* With respect to all these, and especially the last, great latitude is allowed according to the necessities of the case; a latitude which is limited only by the taste and discretion of the author.

On the other hand, it is hardly possible to find two words having in all respects the same meaning, and being therefore interchangeable; that is, admitted of being employed indiscriminately, the one or the other, in all their applications. The investigation of the distinctions to be drawn between words apparently synonymous, forms a separate branch of inquiry, which I have not presumed here to enter upon; for the subject has already occupied the attention of much abler critics than myself, and its complete exhaustion would require the devotion of a whole life. The purpose of this work, it must be borne in mind, is not to explain the signification of words, but simply to classify and arrange them according to the sense in which they are now used, and which I presume to be already known to the reader. I enter into no inquiry into the changes of meaning they may have undergone in the course of time. I am content to accept them at the value of their present currency, and have no concern with their etymologies, or with the history of their transformations; far less do I venture to thrid the mazes of the vast labyrinth into which I should be led by any attempt at a general discrimination of synonyms. The difficulties I have had to contend with have already been sufficiently great without this addition to my labours.

The most cursory glance over the pages of a dictionary will show that a great number of words are used in various senses, sometimes distinguished by slight shades of difference, but often diverging widely from their primary signification, and even, in some cases, bearing to it no perceptible relation. It may even happen that the very same word has two significations quite opposite to one another. This is the case with the verb *to cleave,* which means *to adhere tenaciously,* and also *to separate by a blow. To propugn* sometimes expresses *to attack;* at other times, *to defend. To ravel* means both *to entangle* and *to disentangle.* The alphabetical index at the end of this work sufficiently shows the multiplicity of uses to which, by the elasticity of language, the meaning of words has been stretched, so as to adapt them to a great variety of modified significations in subservience to the nicer shades of thought, which, under peculiarity of circumstances, require corresponding expression. Words thus admitting of different meanings have therefore to be arranged under each of the respective heads corresponding to these various acceptations. There are many words, again, which express ideas compounded of two elementary ideas belonging to different classes. It is therefore necessary to place these words respectively under each of the generic heads to which they relate. The necessity of these repetitions is increased by the circumstance, that ideas included under one class are often connected by relations of the same kind as the ideas which belong to another class. Thus we find the same relations of *order* and of *quantity* existing among the ideas of *Time* as well as those of *Space.* Sequence in the one is denoted by the same terms as sequence in the other; and the measures of time also express the measures of space. The cause and the effect are often designated by the same word. The word *Sound,* for instance, denotes both the impression made upon the ear by sonorous vibrations, and also the vibrations themselves, which are the cause or source of that impression. *Mixture* is used for the act of mixing, as well as for the product of that operation. *Taste* and *Smell* express both the sensations and the qualities of material bodies giving rise to them. *Thought* is the act of thinking; but the same word denotes also the idea resulting from that act. *Judgment* is the act of deciding, and also the decision to come. *Purchase* is the acquisition of a thing by payment, as well as the thing itself so acquired. *Speech* is both the act of speaking and the words spoken; and so on with regard to an endless multiplicity of words. Mind is essentially distinct from Matter; and yet, in all languages, the attributes of one are metaphorically transferred to those of the other. Matter, in all its forms, is endowed by the figurative genius of every language with the functions which pertain to intellect; and we perpetually talk of its phenomena and of its powers as if they resulted from the voluntary influence of one body on another, acting and reacting, impelling and being impelled, controlling and being controlled, as if animated by spontaneous energies and guided by specific intentions. On the other hand, expressions, of which the primary signification refers exclusively to the properties and actions of matter, are metaphorically applied to the phenomena of thought and volition, and even to the feelings and passions of the soul; and in speaking of a *ray of hope,* a *shade of doubt,* a *flight of fancy,* a *flash of wit,* the *warmth of emotion,* or the *ebullitions of anger,* we are scarcely conscious that we are employing metaphors which have this material origin.

*   *   *

With regard to the admission of many words and expressions, which the classical reader might be disposed to condemn as vulgarisms, or which he, perhaps, might stigmatise as pertaining rather to the slang than to the legitimate language of the day, I would beg to observe that, having due regard to the uses to which this work was to be adapted, I did not feel myself justified in excluding them solely on that ground, if they possessed an acknowledged currency in general intercourse. It is obvious that, with respect to degrees of conventionality, I could not have attempted to draw any strict lines of demarcation; and far less could I have presumed to erect any absolute standard of purity. My object, be it remembered, is not to regulate the use of words, but simply to supply and to suggest such as may be wanted on occasion, leaving the proper selection entirely to the discretion and taste of the employer. If a novelist or a dramatist, for example, proposed to delineate some vulgar personage, he would wish to have the power of putting into the mouth of the speaker expressions that would accord with his character; just as the actor, to revert to a former comparison, who had to personate a peasant, would choose for his attire the most homely garb, and would have just reason to complain if the theatrical wardrobe furnished him with no suitable costume.

Words which have, in process of time, become obsolete, are of course rejected from this collection. On the other hand, I have admitted a considerable number of words and phrases borrowed from other languages, chiefly the French and Latin, some of which may be considered as already naturalised; while others, though avowedly foreign, are frequently introduced in English composition, particularly in familiar style, on account of their being peculiarly expressive, and because we have no corresponding words of equal force in our own language. The rapid advances which are being made in scientific knowledge, and consequent improvement in all the arts of life, and the extension of those arts and sciences to so many new purposes and objects, create a continual demand for the formation of new terms to express new agencies, new wants, and new combinations. Such terms, from being at first merely technical, are rendered, by more general use, familiar to the multitude, and having a well-defined acceptation, are eventually incorporated into the language, which they contribute to enlarge and to enrich. *Neologies* of this kind are perfectly legitimate, and highly advantageous; and they necessarily introduce those gradual and progressive changes which every language is destined to undergo. Some modern writers, however, have indulged in a habit of arbitrarily fabricating new words and a new-fangled phraseology, without any necessity, and with manifest injury to the purity of the language. This vicious practice, the offspring of indolence or conceit, implies an ignorance or neglect of the riches in which the English language already abounds, and which would have supplied them with words of recognised legitimacy, conveying precisely the same meaning as those they so recklessly coin in the illegal mint of their own fancy.